The SAGE Handbook of
Organizational Wellbeing

The SAGE Handbook of Organizational Wellbeing

The SAGE Handbook of Organizational Wellbeing is a comprehensive and cutting-edge work providing the latest insights into a range of perspectives on organizational wellbeing, as well as highlighting global wellbeing issues and exploring new contexts. A multi- and inter-disciplinary work, this handbook embraces ideas and empirical work from a range of fields including psychology, business and management, economics, and science. This handbook draws together current knowledge whilst also outlining emerging issues and directions, making this an invaluable resource for students and researchers spanning a wide array of disciplines.

Part 1: Theoretical Perspectives

Part 2: International Issues and Contexts

Part 3: Developing Organizational Wellbeing

Part 4: Emerging Issues and Directions

The SAGE Handbook of
Organizational Wellbeing

Edited by
Tony Wall
Cary L. Cooper
and Paula Brough

Los Angeles | London | New Delhi | Singapore | Washington DC | Melbourne

Los Angeles | London | New Delhi
Singapore | Washington DC | Melbourne

SAGE Publications Ltd
1 Oliver's Yard
55 City Road
London EC1Y 1SP

SAGE Publications Inc.
2455 Teller Road
Thousand Oaks, California 91320

SAGE Publications India Pvt Ltd
B 1/I 1 Mohan Cooperative Industrial Area
Mathura Road
New Delhi 110 044

SAGE Publications Asia-Pacific Pte Ltd
3 Church Street
#10-04 Samsung Hub
Singapore 049483

Editor: Susannah Trefgarne
Editorial Assistant: Ruth Lilly
Production Editor: Jessica Masih
Copyeditor: Sunrise Settings Ltd.
Proofreader: Sunrise Settings Ltd.
Indexer: KnowledgeWorks Global Ltd.
Marketing Manager: Lucia Sweet
Cover Design: Naomi Robinson
Typeset by KnowledgeWorks Global Ltd.
Printed in the UK

Contents

List of Figures and Tables

FIGURES

TABLES

Notes on the Editors and Contributors

THE EDITORS

Tony Wall is Founder and Head of the International Centre for Thriving, a global-scale collaboration between business, arts, health, and education to deliver sustainable transformation. He has published more than 200 works, including articles in quartile-1 journals, such as the *International Journal of Human Resource Management*, *Journal of Cleaner Production*, and *Vocations & Learning*, as well as global policy reports for the European Mentoring and Coaching Council in Brussels and Lapidus International, which have been translated into 20 languages. His academic leadership and impact has attracted prestigious recognition through the Advance-HE National Teaching Fellowship (awarded to less than 0.2% of the sector) and multiple Santander International Research Excellence Awards. He actively collaborates and consults with large organizations and is developing licenses to enable wider global impact of this work.

Paula Brough is a Professor of Organisational Psychology in the School of Applied Psychology at Griffith University in Brisbane, and Leader of the Occupational Health Psychology Research Lab. Paula's primary research and teaching areas are occupational stress and coping, employee mental health and wellbeing, work engagement, work–life balance, workplace conflict (bullying, harassment, toxic leadership), and the psychosocial work environment. Paula assesses how work environments can be improved via job redesign, supportive leadership practices, and enhanced equity to improve employee health, work commitment, and productivity. Paula works with a variety of organizations to reduce their employees' experiences of stress and burnout. This work includes group and individual training to improve both long-term leadership skills and the follow-on wellbeing and performance of their workers. Paula has authored over 60 industry reports, over 120 journal articles and book chapters, and has produced nine scholarly books based on her research. Paula is an Associate Editor of *Work & Stress*, and is a board member of *Journal of Organizational Behaviour*, *International Journal of Stress Management*, and the *BPS Work–Life Balance Bulletin*.

Cary L. Cooper is the 50th Anniversary Professor of Organizational Psychology and Health at Manchester Business School, University of Manchester. He is a founding President of the British Academy of Management, President of the Chartered Institute of Personnel and Development (CIPD), former President of RELATE, and President of the Institute of Welfare. He is the Founding Editor of the *Journal of Organizational Behavior*, former editor of the scholarly journal *Stress and Health* and Editor-in-Chief of the *Wiley-Blackwell Encyclopaedia of Management*, now in its third edition. He has been an advisor to the World Health

Organization, ILO, and EU in the field of occupational health and wellbeing, was Chair of the Global Agenda Council on Chronic Disease of the World Economic Forum (2009–10; he then served for five years on the Global Agenda Council for mental health of the WEF) and Chair of the Academy of Social Sciences (2009–15). Professor Cooper is the Chair of the National Forum for Health & Wellbeing at Work (comprised of 40 global companies, including BP, Microsoft, the NHS Executive, the UK government, Rolls Royce, and the John Lewis Partnership). He is the author/editor of over 250 books in the field of occupational health psychology, workplace wellbeing, women at work, and occupational stress. He was awarded the CBE in for his contributions to occupational health; and in 2014 he was awarded a knighthood for his contribution to the social sciences.

THE CONTRIBUTORS

Carolyn Axtell is a Senior Lecturer of Work Psychology at the Institute of Work Psychology in Sheffield University Management School. She has more than 20 years' worth of experience leading and conducting research on new ways of working and employee wellbeing within both the public and private sectors. Carolyn's core interest is in designing work to promote employee wellbeing, and she has been involved in conducting several work-design interventions within different organizations. She has published several papers and chapters in her areas of research and was awarded the best-paper prize at the *Journal of Occupational Health Psychology* for her research on a work-design intervention with co-author David Holman. Carolyn is on the editorial boards of the *Journal of Occupational and Organizational Psychology* as well as the *Journal of Business and Psychology*.

Richard Axtell is a creative-writing-for-wellbeing practitioner and works with Lapidus International, the words-for-wellbeing association. He was a researcher for the International Creative Practices for Wellbeing Framework project funded by the T.S. Eliot Foundation and the Old Possum's Trust from 2017 to 2019.

Caroline Biron is a Professor of Occupational Health and Safety in the Management Department at the Faculty of Business and Administration, Université Laval, Quebec. She is also the Director of the Center of Expertise for Occupational Health and Safety, which supports research development and provides practical prevention tools for managers and organizations. Her work focuses mainly on presenteeism at work and the implementation of organizational interventions to reduce exposure to psychosocial risks. She is also a member of the editorial advisory board of the *International Journal of Workplace Health Management* and a researcher at the VITAM Sustainable Health Research Center.

Holly Blake is a Chartered Health Psychologist (CPsychol) and Associate Professor of Behavioural Science at the University of Nottingham. She has expertise in workplace health and wellbeing in the public and private sector. She leads on national workforce evaluations and has significant expertise in the design, delivery, and evaluation of workplace health interventions to promote both the physical and mental health of employees. She sits on numerous strategic boards for wellbeing with major employers, and she is currently engaged in multiple COVID-19 response studies looking at the impacts of the pandemic on employee mental health in the NHS and the private sector.

Helen Brewis has worked as a psychologist for over 15 years, across the private, public, and not-for-profit sectors – both in-house and as a consultant. Helen is a Chartered Occupational Psychologist with the British Psychological Society and a Registered Psychologist with the Health Care and Professions Council. Helen is a Senior Business Psychologist at Robertson Cooper. She works in the delivery team, managing and delivering training, measurement, and strategy projects.

David Brougham is a Senior Lecturer within Massey Business School, specialising in the future of work and future business changes. His research looks at how smart technology, artificial intelligence, automation, robotics, and algorithms are changing the workplace. This includes how employees and business leaders plan to adapt to these technological disruptions. David has written over 20 published refereed journal articles and over 50 refereed conference papers/presentations. He is the Co-Editor of the *New Zealand Journal of Human Resources Management*, has researched on Marsden-funded projects and is an Associate Investigator on a Ngā Pae o te Māramatanga grant. David has won best-conference-paper awards for his work on automation at the Australian and New Zealand Academy of Management. His research has been published in A-ranked and FT50 journals.

Huijun Chen is a current PhD student at Nottingham Trent University (NTU), and her research interests focus on the decision-making process of presenteeism, as well as how to manage presenteeism. Huijun graduated from NTU in 2016 with a Master's degree in Management and Finance and started working for an international bank in China as a financial crime analyst. After working in a fast-paced environment for more than two years, the interesting phenomena Huijun observed at her workplace led her to decide to pursue her PhD in human resource management, focusing specifically on the management of presenteeism.

Sara Connolly is Professor of Personnel Economics at the University of East Anglia. Her research interests are in the areas of gender and wellbeing economics. She is Co-Investigator on the Economic Social Research Council-funded Productivity Outcomes of Workplace Practice, Engagement and Learning hub and Practices and Combinations of Practices for Health and Wellbeing at Work research program. She has published in the *Economic Journal*, the *Journal of European Public Policy*, *Public Administration*, and *Work, Employment and Society*.

Teresa A. Daniel serves as Dean and Professor of the Human Resource Leadership (HRL) Program at Sullivan University (www.sullivan.edu), based in Louisville, Kentucky. She is also the Chair for the HRL concentration in the university's PhD in Management program. An active scholar-practitioner, her growing body of research on the problem of workplace bullying, toxic leadership, and sexual harassment has been actively supported by the national Society for Human Resource Management (SHRM) through numerous articles and interviews, as well as by the publication of her most recent book, titled *Stop Bullying at Work: Strategies and Tools for HR, Legal and Risk Management Professionals* (2016). She is also the author of *Organizational Toxin Handlers: The Critical Role of HR, OD, & Coaching Practitioners in Managing Toxic Workplace Situations* (2020) and *The Management of People in Mergers and Acquisitions* (2001), plus numerous articles and book chapters about contemporary issues at the intersection of HR, leadership, employment law, and ethics, with a focus on counterproductive work behaviors. Dr Daniel was honored as an Initial Fellow of the International Academy on Workplace Bullying, Mobbing, and Abuse in 2014 and as Distinguished Alumnus at Centre College, Danville, Kentucky, in 2002. She is also the 2019 Grand Prize Winner of the national SHRM HR Haiku poetry contest.

Kevin Daniels is Professor of Organizational Behaviour at the University of East Anglia. His research interests relate to workplace wellbeing, health, and safety. He currently holds Associate Editor roles at the *British Journal of Management* and the *European Journal of Work and Organizational Psychology*, and he was previously editor of the latter and associate editor at the *Journal of Occupational and Organizational Psychology* and at *Human Relations*. He is Series Co-editor of Springer Nature's Handbooks in Occupational Health Sciences. He has published work in journals including the *Journal of Organizational Behaviour*, *Journal of Applied Psychology*, *Journal of Management*, *Journal of Management Studies*, *Journal of Occupational and Organizational Psychology*, and *Organization Studies*.

Jonas Debrulle is an Associate Professor at IESEG School of Management, where he has been a faculty member since 2012. He is IESEG's Director of Programs and heads the Bachelor's, Master's, post-graduate, and apprenticeship programs. He is also a Guest Professor at the Faculty of Economics and Business at KU Leuven. He teaches courses in business consultancy, strategic management, and (technology) entrepreneurship. Prior to his academic career, Jonas was a business consultant and project management officer at Delaware Consulting, an ERP service provider. His research interests include business-owner characteristics, entrepreneurial motivations, start-up performance, and new-venture knowledge management. He has published in, among others, the *International Small Business Journal*, *Labour*, *Small Business Economics*, and the *Journal of Small Business Management*.

Alys Bethan Einion-Waller is an Associate Professor at Swansea University, Departmental Research Lead and College Inclusivity Lead. Her background is in women's health and she is Co-Chair of the LGBT+ Staff Network. Her research interests include narratives, identity, hypnobirthing, women's rights and inclusive childbirth care, inclusive feminism, inclusive pedagogies, and qualitative methods. She is a prolific writer and a novelist.

Cihat Erbil is a currently Research Assistant in the Department of Business Administration at Ankara HBV University in Ankara. His research centers on social innovation, social entrepreneurship, and critical management studies. In his studies, he aims to give voice to 'others' and make them visible.

Jack Evans is the Lead Business Psychologist at Robertson Cooper Ltd. He leads consulting projects which aim to measure, understand, and improve employee mental health and wellbeing, working with a range of corporates and public-sector organizations, including Nestle, Rolls Royce, Publicis Groupe, and multiple NHS trusts and government departments. He ensures that Robertson Cooper's services and produces are at the cutting edge of wellbeing, based on the latest science and research.

Victoria Field is a writer and poetry therapist. She was named in *Poetry Review* as a pioneer in the therapeutic use of poetry and writing in the UK. She has co-edited three books as well as numerous articles and chapters on therapeutic writing. She qualified as a Certified Poetry Therapist and Mentor-Supervisor with the International Federation for Biblio-Poetry Therapy. As well as working in health, community, and education settings, she is a Visiting Tutor on the Metanoia Institute MSc in Creative Writing for Therapeutic Purposes and a Researcher at Canterbury Christ Church University. She has published poetry, fiction, and memoir and had three plays professionally produced. Together with Anne Taylor, she delivers successful online courses for the Professional Writing Academy which have been completed by over 200 students from 30 countries.

Cheryl Y. S. Foo is a doctoral candidate in Clinical Psychology at Teachers College, Columbia University. She graduated from the University of Cambridge with a double first-class BA in Psychological and Behavioural Sciences. Cheryl has been a Research Assistant at the Global Mental Health Lab since 2015, focusing on interpersonal psychotherapy (IPT) capacity-building projects for displaced populations. She currently coordinates the Global Challenges Research Fund Research for Health in Conflict (GCRF R4HC-MENA, United Kingdom) grant to scale up IPT delivery and research capacity in Lebanon for persons affected by the Syrian crisis, in collaboration with the Lebanese Ministry of Public Health. She also assists on a pilot study on the effectiveness of IPT for Rohingya refugees in Cox's Bazar, Bangladesh, funded by the United Nations High Commisioner for Refugees. Cheryl is currently developing her research program to address burnout, help-seeking, and resilience among humanitarian aid workers, in order to systematically implement 'care for the carers' for sustainable global mental-health capacity-building efforts.

Anna Foster is Regional Subject Lead and Lecturer in English Education on the PGDE Programme at the University of Manchester. She has worked closely with schools across the north west since joining the university in 2014, working primarily within secondary schools but also with some experience of governance within primary. As an early-career researcher, she developed a focus upon action research before developing interests in organizational spirituality and support and development of employee creativity to support wellbeing. She has published on the impacts of limiting language within the workplace and the use of creative pedagogies to support pupils' progress within secondary English.

Scott Foster joined Liverpool John Moores University in May 2013 after successfully completing two Master's degrees, having previously spent several years working within the retail sector. He also spent several years at Mercedes Benz as a financial controller, mainly in the UK but with some experience of working in Europe. He has published articles on the topic of spirituality in the workplace, with the prime focus on organizational commitment to spirituality in the workplace and the ways in which organizations' policies and procedures cater for employees to express it.

Elliroma Gardiner is an Organizational Psychologist and a Lecturer at the School of Management, QUT Business School. Prior to joining QUT, Elli was a fellow at the Department of Management, London School of Economics and Political Science and a lecturer at the School of Applied Psychology, Griffith University. Her broad research interests are in investigating the interplay between individual differences and contextual features in influencing employee, team, and organizational outcomes. She has published her research findings in several high-quality outlets, including *Psychological Bulletin*, *Human Resource Management Journal*, and the *Journal of Personality*.

Azka Ghafoor is a recent PhD graduate at the Auckland University of Technology. She looks at the influence of psychological, organizational, and work factors on creativity and innovation behaviors as outcomes. She has published in the *International Journal of Innovation Management* and *New Zealand Journal of Employment Relations*. Her research focuses on the influence of (1) stressors, (2) work demands, (3) strain, (4) ethical leadership, (5) climate for innovation, (6) meaningfulness of work, and (7) Psychological capital on the individual- and team-level wellbeing, happiness, satisfaction, and creativity. Previously, she was engaged in training-coordinator and management roles in international firms. She is currently a researcher in a lab under the National Science Challenge (Science for Technological Innovation).

Stephanie L. Gilbert is an Assistant Professor of Organizational Management in the Shannon School of Business at Cape Breton University. She earned a PhD in Industrial-Organizational Psychology from Saint Mary's University, a Master's of Science in Health and Rehabilitation Sciences from Western University, and a BA (Honours) in Psychology and Business Administration from Wilfrid Laurier University. Dr Gilbert has worked with a variety of non-profit and public organizations as well as start-ups. She has applied her psychological and health-sciences backgrounds to implement evidence-based business solutions and to develop and validate organizational assessment tools. Her research activities focus on occupational and personal stress in the workplace, organizational leadership, entrepreneurship, and motivation at work. She teaches in the areas of leadership and organizational behaviour.

Jarrod Haar has tribal affiliations with Ngati Maniapoto and Ngati Mahuta. He is a Professor of Human Resource Management (HRM) at Auckland University of Technology. His research focuses on (1) work–family and work–life balance, (2) Māori employees and Mātauranga Māori, (3) leadership, (4) wellbeing, and (5) R&D and innovation. Professor Haar is a world-class-ranked researcher under the New Zealand research system, has won industry and best-paper awards; and multiple prestigious research grants (Marsden, FRST). He is currently a researcher on a 10-year National Science Challenge (Science for Technological Innovation), on a 3-year Marsden grant (Living Wage), and a 1-year Ngā Pae o te Māramatanga grant exploring Māori employee experiences of HRM. He has over 390 refereed outputs (including 105 journal articles) and serves on the Marsden Fund Council at the Royal Society of New Zealand and convenes the Economics and Human Behaviour Marsden panel.

Juliet Hassard is an Associate Professor of Occupational Health Psychology in the Centre for Organisational Health and Development at the University of Nottingham. Prior to joining the University of Nottingham, she was the Deputy Director of the Centre for Sustainable Working Lives, Birkbeck University of London. Her research examines the human, social, and economic impact of the psychosocial work environment on the health and wellbeing of workers, organizations, and communities. She has consulted on such issues for the European Parliamentary Assembly, the United Nations, the World Health Organization, and the European Work Council. Her research has been published in key journals in her field (*Journal of Occupational Health Psychology* and *Work & Stress*) and used to support the European Agency for Safety and Health at Work's Healthy Workplace Campaign: 'Healthy Workplaces Manage Stress' (2014–15).

Tracy Hatton is Joint Managing Director at Resilient Organisations Ltd. Resilient Organisations Ltd (resorgs.org.nz) is a niche research and consulting group based in Christchurch, New Zealand. Tracy and the Resilient Organisations team are experts in risk and resilience, helping organizations prepare for and get through times of crisis, which includes building high-performing teams able to adapt and innovate. Tracy helps public- and private-sector organizations build their continuity- and crisis-management capabilities and co-created the content for a free disaster-resilience app for small and medium enterprises internationally. Tracy has an MBA and PhD in Disaster Recovery and teaches Organisational Resilience on the University of Canterbury, New Zealand, Executive Development Programme.

Valerie Hervieux is a PhD candidate at Laval University in Quebec. In 2018, she graduated with a Master's degree in Kinesiology, during which she developed and tested an intervention to reduce sedentary behaviour among employees. As part of her PhD, Valerie is interested in the relationship between employee lifestyle habits and presenteeism. She is also researching the effect of psychosocial risks on employees' health behaviours. She is a member of the VITAM Sustainable Health Research Centre and a student member of the Center of Expertise for Occupational Health and Safety.

Ian Hesketh is the Wellbeing Lead at the UK College of Policing and the Senior Responsible Owner (SRO) for the National Police Wellbeing Service in the UK. Ian also supports the National Forum for Health and Wellbeing at Manchester University Alliance Business School. He holds a PhD in Management and Social Psychology and an MBA from Lancaster University. Ian's research interests are centered on wellbeing, leadership, and personal resilience. Notably, he conceived and introduced the concept and phenomena of *Leaveism* to explain human behaviors associated with workplace workload and stress. He is the author of numerous academic papers on workplace wellbeing, personal resilience, change, leadership, and public value; including books and book chapters on these subjects.

Raya A. Jones is a Reader at the School of Social Sciences, Cardiff University, where she teaches psychological perspectives on personality, self and identity, and social development. Her long-term research interests include Jungian and postmodern perspectives, especially dialogical and narrative. A more recent area of inquiry is the discourse of social robotics, in which context she has published articles on social representations of childcare robots, robot-related ethics, and human–robot relationships. Her latest authored book is *Personhood and Social Robotics* (2016). Earlier books include *Jung, Psychology, Postmodernity* (2007), *The Child–School Interface* (1995), and several edited and co-edited volumes, of which the latest is *Narratives of Individuation* (2019).

Rachael Jones-Chick is currently a PhD student in Industrial/Organizational Psychology at Saint Mary's University. Rachael earned an MSc in Applied Psychology (Industrial/Organizational Psychology) from Saint Mary's University and an Honours BA in Psychology from the University of Guelph. Rachael is an active member in the Canadian Society for Industrial and Organizational Psychology and is currently serving as the Student Representative and Co-Newsletter Editor on the committee. Rachael's research interests focus on occupational health psychology, with a special interest in creativity and innovation in the workplace, leadership, and training and development.

Peter J. Jordan is a Professor of Organizational Behavior and the Deputy Director of the Work Organization and Wellbeing Research Centre at the Griffith Business School, Griffith University Brisbane. Peter's current research interests include emotional intelligence, and discrete emotions and employee entitlement in organizations. Prior to working at Griffith he worked for the Federal Government on strategic and operational planning. Peter has published his research in the *Academy of Management Journal*, *Academy of Management Review*, and the *Journal of Organizational Behavior*.

Maria Karanika-Murray is an Associate Professor in Occupational Health Psychology at the Department of Psychology, Nottingham Trent University (NTU). She has a PhD in Applied Psychology and an MSc in Occupational Health Psychology from the University of Nottingham. She is currently Director of the Centre for Public and Psychosocial Health at NTU. She has delivered research for a range of funders, including the European Commission, European Agency for Safety and Health at Work, Social Sciences and Health Research Council of

Canada, Economic and Social Research Council, charities, and industry. She has published widely for academic researchers, policy-makers, and practitioners.

E. Kevin Kelloway is the Canada Research Chair in Occupational Health Psychology and Professor of Organizational Psychology at Saint Mary's University, Halifax. The author/editor of 15 books and over 200 articles and chapters, he is a Fellow of the Association for Psychological Science, the Canadian Psychological Association, the International Association for Applied Psychology, and the Society of Industrial/Organizational Psychology. His research interests include leadership, safety in the workplace, occupational stress, and the psychology of unionization. Active in several professional associations in 2016, he served as President of the Canadian Psychological Association, and he maintains an active consultancy advising both private- and public-sector organizations on issues related to leadership and human resource management.

Justin James Kennedy is a Professor of Applied Neuroscience and Organizational Behavior at UGSM-Monarch Business School, College and University, in Hagendorn, Zug. He is a PhD-supervision professor with Canterbury Christ Church and several other UK universities as part of their academic relationship with the Professional Development Foundation. He is the author of the book *Brain Re-Boot* (2019), an overview of applied neuroscience that proposes various protocols by employing both behavioral and health neuroscience. The book offers brain-based tools and behavioral habits that have been shown to build resilience to stress-related pathology and to improve organizational life in general as part of an executive coaching process or consulting to organizations.

Anne-Kathrin Kleine is a PhD student at the Department of Psychology at the University of Groningen. She received her Master's degree at Leipzig University. Her research interests include positive organizational psychology, proactive work behavior, and entrepreneurship.

The Kintsugi Collective is a collective of people working in business schools in the UK and Denmark: Tony Wall, Chester Business School; Sarah Robinson, Adam Smith Business School; Jamie Callahan, Newcastle Business School; Carole Elliott, University of Sheffield Management School; Tali Padan, Copenhagen Business School; Annemette Kjærgaard, Copenhagen Business School; Maribel Blasco, Copenhagen Business School; and Rasmus Bergmann, University College Copenhagen. As a collective, we want to embrace the spirit of kintsugi in work – 'ultimately to guide shadows to beauty's ends'.

Kairi Kõlves is Associate Professor at the Australian Institute for Suicide Research and Prevention (AISRAP), and Co-director of the WHO Collaborating Centre for Research and Training in Suicide Prevention, School of Applied Psychology, Griffith University. She is also the course convenor of Master's courses. She has been working in suicide research and prevention since 1998. Prior to joining the AISRAP team in 2008, she worked at the Estonian–Swedish Mental Health and Suicidology Institute. Dr Kõlves has been involved in several Australian, Estonian, and international projects and has published over 100 peer-reviewed papers, numerous reports, and book chapters on suicide research and prevention. She is a member of different advisory committees.

Yi-Ling Lai is the the Programme Director of the MSc Organizational Psychology at Birkbeck, University of London. Yi-Ling's research mainly concentrates on the working alliance in the coaching process, in particular factors related to identity. Recently, Yi-Ling extended her research focus by drawing social psychological theory such as identity into organization studies – for instance, social identity and resilience and workplace wellbeing. Yi-Ling also takes active roles in several sub-committees of the British Psychological Society (BPS), including the former Research Officer (Lead) at the Special Group in Coaching Psychology and the Editor of International Coaching Psychology Review.

Lisa Leit, Founder of the International Coach Federation-accredited Happy Whole Human (HWH) Institute of Holistic Wellness, is an expert in the field of developmental psychology. For over 20 years, she has worked with individuals, couples, families, and leadership teams of organizations to help them overcome obstacles and live happy, whole lives. In customized group initiatives, including high-impact coaching and management consulting, her unique, scientifically validated holistic wellness assessment program identifies and addresses hidden risk factors to health and fosters meaningful, measurable, and lasting improvements. The HWH program is based on Lisa's research at the University of Texas at Austin. Her approach is informed by self-directed learning, family systems theory, eco-psychology, change-management principles, negotiation strategies, and applied neuroscience.

Sanna Malinen is an Associate Professor of Organisational Behaviour and HRM at the University of Canterbury. Her background is in organizational psychology, and she researches in the areas of workplace resilience, employee wellbeing, and disaster management. Sanna was part of a research team investigating organizational and employee recovery and wellbeing in the aftermath of the Christchurch, New Zealand earthquakes. She has also conducted research on inter-organizational collaboration in disasters in a mega-flooding context, and on small-business disaster planning and recovery. Sanna has published widely on disaster-related topics and was a co-editor of a book on business and post-disaster management.

Sharna L. Mathieu is a Postdoctoral Research Officer at the Australian Institute for Suicide Research and Prevention (AISRAP), School of Applied Psychology, Griffith University. She has contributed to a number of reports on workplace suicide prevention in the Australian construction industry. Currently, she is working alongside her AISRAP colleagues and a global consortium of experts on the MENTUPP evaluation of workplace suicide-prevention interventions in the healthcare, information-communication-technology, and construction industries across Europe and Australia. Prior to her work in suicide prevention, Sharna worked across several projects and RCTs focused on promoting wellbeing in youth (and their families) with severe mental health conditions.

Thomas D. McIlroy is a psychologist with a Master's degree in organizational psychology, and is in the final year of his PhD at the University of Queensland. His PhD examines unanswered supervisor support in the workplace – that is, when employees actively ask their supervisor for support but do not receive the requested support – and the implications for wellbeing, performance, and employees' connection with others. Another area of his research focuses on the antecedents of work design by examining how power may negatively affect people's propensity to design motivating and enriched work. Mr McIlroy is also a tutor for undergraduate social and organizational psychology courses.

Blake M. McKimmie is a Social Psychologist in the School of Psychology at the University of Queensland. His research focuses on legal decision-making, including the influence of gender-based stereotypes and the influence of different modes of evidence presentation. He is also interested in stress, attitude–behaviour relations, and how group membership influences thinking about the self. He has won a number of teaching awards, including the edX Prize in 2018, and the Australian Award for University Teaching Teacher of the Year in 2019. He is a Senior Fellow of the Higher Education Academy (UK).

Haziq Mehmood works as Assistant Professor School of Professional Psychology – SPP University of Management & Technology Lahore. He received his PhD in Industrial Organizational Psychology from Lingnan University. His areas of interest are industrial-organizational psychology, social psychology, human–computer interaction, and psychometrics. His PhD dissertation focused on the role of social-network sites and their impact on employees' job performance and psychological wellbeing. As a tutor, he taught Psychology Applied to Occupational Safety and Health, Introduction to Psychology, Industrial and Organizational Psychology, and Stress Management, Health, and Life Balance' courses. He has worked in the development sector, where he focused on counseling and intervention plans for suicidal cases, served as a testing and assessment associate, and developed questionnaires for employees' screening.

Kevin Moore is Associate Professor in Psychology at Lincoln University. In 1982 he gained a BSc (Hons) in zoology, and in 1990 was awarded a PhD in psychology, both from the University of Canterbury. He is interested in the social psychology of wellbeing, leisure behavior, and theoretical issues in psychology, and he has published widely in these areas for over 30 years. He is currently exploring how a person-based perspective might affect understandings and theories of human wellbeing, including the ways in which personhood and wellbeing are constituted by social and cultural processes. In 2019, his book *Wellbeing and Aspirational Culture* was published.

Emike Nasamu is a Researcher at the University of East Anglia and a Lecturer in Economics at the University of Chester. Her interests lie in wellbeing economics, political economics, and institutional economics. In addition to her work on workplace wellbeing, she is interested in understanding institutions and the ways in which elements of social capital influence formal and informal institutions. She employs economics laboratory experiments as well as analysis of secondary data sets in her studies. She obtained her PhD from the School of Economics at the University of East Anglia and has undertaken research work for the What Works Centre for Wellbeing.

Katharina Näswall is Professor in Organisational Psychology at the University of Canterbury. Her research focuses on employee wellbeing and factors which lead to psychologically healthy workplaces. She has worked on several projects on psychosocial recovery after disasters, focusing on how businesses can play an important role in individual and community recovery. Katharina currently conducts research on how organizations and managers can make a positive difference and contribute to employee wellbeing. Katharina's vision is to improve mental health and wellbeing for all individuals by making workplaces a positive part of people's lives.

Rachel Nayani is a Lecturer in Organisational Behaviour and Human Resource Management at the University of East Anglia, with expertise in work, behaviour, and sustainable organizational change. Rachel's research primarily involves understanding organizational process and practices for sustainable change and social value including wellbeing, alongside enhanced productivity at work and climate goals. Rachel has undertaken research for the UK's What

Works Centre for Wellbeing at Work, the Institution of Occupational Safety and Health (IOSH), and the Economic Social Research Council (ESRC). She has published in journals such as *Work & Stress* and is a member of the editorial board of the *European Journal of Work and Organizational Psychology*.

Karina Nielsen is Professor of Work Psychology and Director of the Institute of Work Psychology at the University of Sheffield. She has published extensively on the design, implementation, and evaluation of organizational interventions. She is passionate about enhancing our understanding of how we can make such interventions work. Karina has managed large national and international grants on organizational interventions and has won several awards for her work, including best paper in *Work & Stress*, the early-career award from the American Psychological Association and the National Institute for Occupational Safety and Health, and the Eusebio Rial Gonzalez Innovation and Practice Award from the European Academy of Occupational Health Psychology and the European Agency for Occupational Safety and Health at Work. She has published over 100 peer-reviewed book chapters and papers. Her work has been published in *Work & Stress*, *Human Relations*, the *Journal of Occupational Health Psychology* and the *Journal of Organizational Behavior*.

Mustafa F. Özbilgin is Professor of Organisational Behaviour at Brunel Business School, London. He also holds two international positions: Co-Chaire Management et Diversité at Université Paris Dauphine and Visiting Professor of Management at Koç University in Istanbul. His research focuses on equality, diversity, and inclusion at work from comparative and relational perspectives. He has conducted field studies in the UK and internationally, and his work is empirically grounded. His research is supported by international as well as national grants. His work has a focus on changing policy and practice in equality and diversity at work. He is an engaged scholar, driven by values of workplace democracy, equality for all, and humanization of work.

Stephen Palmer is a leading Coaching Psychologist and is President of the International Society for Coaching Psychology (ISCP) and Vice President of the Institute of Health Promotion and Education. He is Professor of Practice at the Wales Academy for Professional Practice and Applied Research, University of Wales Trinity Saint David, and Adjunct Professor of Coaching Psychology at the Coaching Psychology Unit, Aalborg University. He is Coordinating Director of the ISCP International Centre for Coaching Psychology Research and Director of the Centre for Coaching, London. He was the first Chair of the British Psychology Society Special Group in Coaching Psychology and was the first Honorary President of the Association for Coaching. He has authored over 225 articles and written or edited over 50 books including the *Handbook of Coaching Psychology: A Guide for Practitioners* (2nd edition) (with Alison Whybrow, 2019).

Florence Palpacuer is a Professor of Management Studies at the University of Montpellier, where she is co-director of a Chair for Responsible Management and Entrepreneurship (2011–24) funded by the French National Research Agency. She has been studying globalization processes and their social consequences from a management perspective for the last 20 years. Her recent interests include workers' resistance to financialization and the rise of social movements in global value chains. She has published over 50 articles and book contributions on these issues in journals such as *Human Relations*, *World Development*, *Economy & Society*, and the *British Journal of Industrial Relations*. Her two co-authored books, published in French, promote a critical management perspective on the firm-level consequences of neoliberal transformations.

Stacey L. Parker is an Organizational Psychologist and Senior Lecturer in the School of Psychology at the University of Queensland. She researches, teaches, and consults on work and organizational topics. In particular, her research focuses on how to manage stress and improve performance. Through this work, she aims to help organizations and their employees devise new strategies to work healthier while still being productive. She was awarded the Australian Psychological Society's Occupational Health Psychology Doctoral Thesis Award for her PhD research on work motivation and employee wellbeing. She serves on the editorial boards for the *Journal of Occupational Health Psychology* and the *European Journal of Work and Organizational Psychology.*

Jana Patey is a Senior Research Associate at the University of East Anglia specialising in the area of health and wellbeing at work. Prior to joining Norwich Business School, in her HR advisory positions, Jana was responsible for recruitment, remuneration, learning and development, and employee-relations case management across a number of private- and public-sector organizations. Jana also enjoyed teaching undergraduate and postgraduate students at the University of Suffolk, specialising in people management, professional development, and employability skills. Jana's main research and consulting interests are in employee health and wellbeing, organizational psychodynamics, workplace friendship, intersubjectivity, and affect at work.

José Atilano Pena-López holds a PhD in economics and is an Associate Professor of Economic Policy at the University of A Coruña. He has developed the main part of his research within the broad field of socioeconomics, particularly the study of social capital. In this field, he has studied the different approaches of the concept, determinants, and effects. His latest works focus on the studies of individual social capital, personal social networks, and their various effects in terms of wellbeing, status, and social mobility. He has published his research on social capital and wellbeing in the *Economics Bulletin*, the *Handbook of Family Enterprise*, *Social Networks*, the *Journal of Happiness Studies*, the *Journal of Business Ethics*, the *Journal of Mathematical Sociology*, and *Applied Economics.*

Simon Ellis Poole is the Senior Lead in Cultural Education and Research at Storyhouse, Chester's award-winning theater; Programme Leader for the Master's in Creative Practice in Education at the University of Chester; Researcher at the Centre for Research into Education, Creativity and Arts through Practice (RECAP); and with the International Thriving at Work Research Centre. His positions outside of the university include Director of Research for Lapidus International. As a creative producer and entrepreneur, his enterprise and professional activity advances the use and understanding of creativity, creative learning, pedagogy, and creative practice as part of our lives and intrinsic to our wellbeing.

James Campbell Quick is Distinguished University Professor and Professor Emeritus, University of Texas at Arlington, and Professor, Alliance Manchester Business School, University of Manchester. Colonel Quick graduated from Colgate University with Honors and served 27 years in the US Air Force and 3 years on the US Defense Health Board. His signature work is the theory of preventive stress management with his brother Jonathan D. Quick. He is co-author with Debra Nelson of the textbook *Organizational Behavior*, in print for over 25 years. He is a Fellow of the American Psychological Association, where he serves as Chair of the Publications and Communications Board, and the Society of Industrial and Organizational Psychology. He is a member of The Rotary Club of Arlington, Texas, and he is married to the former Sheri Grimes Schember, like Colonel Quick a Paul Harris Fellow.

Alannah E. Rafferty is an Associate Professor in the Department of Employment Relations and Human Resources at Griffith Business School, Griffith University, Brisbane. Her research interests include attitudes to organizational change (e.g. change readiness, commitment to change, resistance to change), leadership (transformational leadership, abusive supervision), and stress and coping during organizational change. Alannah has published her research in the *Journal of Management*, the *Journal of Applied Psychology,* the *Leadership Quarterly*, the *Journal of Occupational and Organizational Psychology*, *Work & Stress*, and the *British Journal of Management*. She has extensive experience in the development, administration, and use of surveys to inform strategic change and leadership development within a range of private- and public-sector organizations in Australia.

Ivan Robertson is co-founder (with Sir Cary Cooper) of Robertson Cooper Ltd – the company provides wellbeing and mental-health solutions to organizations. Ivan was at the University of Manchester (UMIST) for over 20 years, where he was Professor of Work and Organizational Psychology. He is now Emeritus Professor at the university. He is in the top 2% of most influential psychologists in his field. His latest (co-authored) books are *Well-Being: Happiness and Productivity at Work* (2nd edition, 2017), *Work Psychology* (2016), and *Management and Happiness* (2013).

Victoria Ross is a Senior Research Fellow at the Australian Institute for Suicide Research and Prevention, School of Applied Psychology, Griffith University. She has research expertise across workplace suicide prevention, suicide prevention in schools, suicide bereavement and postvention support, preventing suicides at hot spots, and suicide-prevention-program evaluation. She provides expert advice to suicide-prevention advisory committees at regional, state, and national levels. Her research interests span all aspects of evidence-based suicide prevention, policy, and practice. She is currently the Australian Chief Investigator on the international research collaboration Mental Health Promotion and Intervention in Occupational Settings: MENTUPP, which will trial a workplace mental-health intervention in eight sites across Europe and Australia.

Paolo Rungo holds a PhD in economics and is an Associate Professor of Economics at the University of A Coruña, and Director of the Occupational Observatory at the same institution. He is a researcher in the area of socioeconomics and is interested in particular in the interrelation between social capital, education, social mobility, wellbeing, and economic outputs. He has published his research in economics and sociology journals, including the *Journal of Mathematical Sociology*, the *Economics of Education Review*, and the *Bulletin of Economic Research*. He is the Managing Editor and a member of the editorial board of the *European Journal of Government and Economics*.

José Manuel Sánchez-Santos holds a PhD in economics and is currently an Associate Professor in the Department of Economics at the University of A Coruña. His research focuses on socioeconomics, economic policy, and sports economics. He has published articles on these topics in journals such as *Applied Economics*, the *Journal of Happiness Studies*, *Applied Research in Quality of Life*, the *Journal of Policy Modeling*, *Social Science Quarterly*, *Social Networks*, and the *Journal of Business Ethics*.

Antje Schmitt is an Assistant Professor of Organizational Psychology at the University of Groningen. Her research focuses on self-regulation at work, proactive and adaptive work behavior, work events, and occupational wellbeing.

Alison Clare Scott is a writer, ceramicist, psychotherapist, and specialist educational consultant, using multimedia expressive arts and the natural landscape as essential parts of her praxis. She is a Director of iaPOETRY International Academy of Poetry Therapy, was chair of Lapidus International ('where words and wellness meet') from 2015 to 2020, and was a manager of Disability and Learning Support at the University of Wales Trinity Saint David. She has been involved in the development of policies for health, safety, and wellbeing provision nationally and organizationally. She perceives the use of creativity in thinking and practice as a means of improving functioning that enhances and heals the lives of individuals and communities and engenders innovation.

Oi-ling Siu is Chair Professor of Applied Psychology and Dean of Faculty of Social Sciences, Lingnan University. She attended the University of Strathclyde for her undergraduate degree, the University of Hong Kong for her AdvDipEd and Master's degree, and the University of Liverpool for her PhD. Her research interests include occupational stress, work–life balance, and the psychology of safety. She is one of the Top 25 work–family scholars in the world (Google Scholar, May 2017) and was awarded 'Top 50' overall contributor to work and family research by the Work and Family Researchers Network, Washington, DC in 2018. Siu is the Editor of the *International Journal of Stress Management* and Associate Editor of the *Journal of Occupational Health Psychology*.

Jean-François Stich is an Assistant Professor at ICN Business School and a research fellow at CEREFIGE, a research lab in management at Université de Lorraine. His research interests gravitate around the psychological impacts of technology on employees, covering areas such as technostress, telecommuting, and cyberdeviancy. He has published in the *Information Systems Journal*, the *Journal of the Association for Information Systems*, *Information Technology & People*, and *New Technology, Work and Employment*.

Marco Tagliabue is an associate professor at OsloMet – Oslo Metropolitan University – where he received his PhD in behavior analysis. His teaching and research activities include human choice behavior and cooperation with economic and organizational implications. He is affiliated with OsloMet's Cultural Selection and Behavioral Economics Lab, and he is a licensed psychologist in Italy. Prior to entering academia, he held various positions within the HR management and development departments of multinational manufacturing industries. He is mostly concerned with the applied implications of experimental behavior-based interventions. His research is at the crossroads of behavioral economics, behavior analysis, and organizational behavior management.

Monideepa Tarafdar is Professor of Information Systems and Co-Director of the Centre for Technological Futures at Lancaster University (Management School). She is a Lever Hulme Research Fellow. She serves as Senior Editor at *Information Systems Journal*, Associate Editor at *Information Systems Research*, and as Editorial Review board member at the *Journal of MIS*, *Journal of AIS*, and the *Journal of Strategic Information Systems*. She has published extensively in the area of technostress and associated phenomena.

Alvin Kuowei Tay is a National Health and Medical Research Council Research Fellow, School of Psychiatry, UNSW Medicine. He holds concurrent appointments as the Director and adjunct Associate Professor at the Centre for Global Health and Social Change at Perdana University, Kuala Lumpur. He is currently leading the pioneering work on designing, implementing, and evaluating a global Psychosocial Well-being Strategy for the Integrated Security Workforce of the United Nations in New York. In addition, Dr Tay is a Visiting Scholar at Teachers College, Columbia University. Dr Tay's research projects involve the epidemiology of risk factors as well as adapting and implementing psychotherapies with forcibly displaced populations in Malaysia, Papua New Guinea, Bangladesh, and Myanmar. Trained as a clinical psychologist, Dr Tay completed further training in epidemiology and biostatistics, and has published over 70 papers in world-leading journals across epidemiology, medicine, psychiatry, and psychology.

Anne Taylor is a writer, teacher, coach, and group facilitator specialising in therapeutic writing. A widely published health journalist, she has won awards for her journalism and poetry. After a 12-year career as a university lecturer, she completed an MA in Creative Writing and Personal Development and now mentors and runs groups for personal and professional development both face-to-face and online in a variety of health, community, and academic settings. She has a special interest in the medical humanities and has written about her work using creative writing with medical students. Together with Victoria Field she has devised, written, and delivered two successful online courses for the Professional Writing Academy, completed by students from 30 countries, many of whom are health professionals seeking to add creative writing to their toolkit.

Siobhan Taylor is a PhD student at the Institute of Work Psychology, Sheffield University Management School. Prior to joining the Management School, she worked for clothing retailer Next in learning and development roles.

Kevin Teoh is a Chartered Psychologist and the Programme Director of the MSc Organizational Psychology at Birkbeck, University of London. He is also the incoming Executive Officer for the European Academy of Occupational Health Psychology. His primary research interests are around developing healthier workplaces and the translation of research into practice, policy, and public dissemination. Kevin has collaborated extensively with the European Agency for Safety and Health at Work and the Society of Occupational Medicine, and has a particular interest in the working conditions and wellbeing of healthcare workers. He has published in journals such as *Work & Stress* and the *Journal of Occupational Health Psychology*, and is a regular speaker at academic, professional, and public events.

Louise Thomson is a Chartered Occupational Psychologist (CPsychol) and HCPC-registered Practitioner Psychologist specialising in psychological, social, and organizational issues in occupational health and mental wellbeing. She is an Associate Professor in Occupational Psychology at the University of Nottingham, and Lead Academic for the Institute of Mental Health's Research Support and Consultancy Service. Louise has extensive experience of working with the health and social care sector, as well as other public, private, and third-sector clients. She has been a topic expert member of three National Institute for Health and Care Excellence (NICE) committees developing guidance on return-to-work after long-term sickness absence, mental wellbeing at work, and workplace health quality standards.

Ashlea C. Troth is a Professor in Organizational Behavior in the Department of Employment Relations and Human Resources at Griffith Business School, Brisbane. Her research interests include multilevel and multimethod approaches to examining emotional regulation and emotional intelligence in workplaces, and the impact of these phenomena on wellbeing and performance outcomes. She is also interested in the day-to-day work experiences of frontline managers and the role of their emotional-regulation strategies on wellbeing when performing a range of tasks. She has extensive consulting experience and has published in journals such as the *Journal of Organizational Behavior*, the *Leadership Quarterly*, and the *Human Resource Management Journal*.

Michael Ungar is the Director of the Resilience Research Centre and Canada Research Chair in Child, Family and Community Resilience at Dalhousie University. He has led numerous multisite longitudinal research and evaluation projects in more than a dozen low-, middle-, and high-income countries, with much of that work focused on the resilience of marginalized children and families, adult populations experiencing mental health challenges, and organizations and communities exposed to atypical economic and social stressors. Dr Ungar has published over 200 peer-reviewed articles and book chapters on the subject of resilience and is the author of 16 books for mental-health professionals, researchers, and lay audiences. These include *Change Your World: The Science of Resilience and the True Path to Success*, a book for adults experiencing stress at work and at home, and *Multisystemic Resilience: Adaptation and Transformation in Contexts of Change*, a volume for researchers.

Helen Verdeli is Associate Professor of Clinical Psychology, Director of Clinical Training, and the Founder and Director of the Global Mental Health Lab at Teachers College, Columbia University. Dr Verdeli has received funding from governments (US: NIMH; Canada: Grand Challenges Canada; UK: Medical Research Council, Economic and Social Research Council), intergovernmental agencies (WHO; UNHCR), and foundations (NARSAD, Eleanor Cook Foundation, etc.) to test psychotherapy for prevention and treatment of mood disorders. In the past 15 years, Dr Verdeli has played a key role in landmark studies involving adaptation, training, and testing of psychotherapy protocols used by both specialists and non-specialists around the globe. She collaborated internationally with academic groups, ministries of health, local NGOs, and international agencies to alleviate the suffering of adults locally defined as depressed in southern Uganda; war-affected adolescents in internally displaced people (IDP) camps in northern Uganda; traumatized IDP women in Colombia; distressed patients in primary care in Goa, India; depressed community members in Haiti; war-affected Syrian refugees in Lebanon; and Rohingya refugees in Bangladesh. She is the first author of the manual on group interpersonal psychotherapy which has been disseminated globally online by the WHO.

David Watson is a Lecturer in Organisational Behaviour at the University of East Anglia (UEA). David is an interdisciplinary researcher interested in the concept of wellbeing and its relationship with work and how this can inform policy. Over the past few years, David has been working with colleagues at UEA and other institutions to carry out a number of evidence reviews and data analysis of factors influencing the relationship between work, learning, and wellbeing. With colleagues at UEA and RAND he is currently working on a series of case studies as part of a piece of research looking at how wellbeing is created and maintained in organizations and how this connects to productivity. Other research interests include, but are not limited to, political economy of the food system, alternative organizations and economies, learning in relation to wellbeing, Marx's concept of alienation, and wellbeing theory – in particular Marx and wellbeing, the capabilities approach, and the role of wellbeing in policy.

Katrina Witt is a National Health and Medical Research Council Emerging Leader in self-harm and suicide prevention at the Centre for Youth Mental Health at The University of Melbourne. She is also a Senior Editor for the Suicide and Self-Harm Satellite and the Children and Young Person Satellite of the Cochrane Common Mental Disorders Group (CCMD). Her work focuses on effective interventions for self-harm and suicide, and dynamic health-systems modeling. She has published Cochrane and non-Cochrane meta-analyses. She has numerous accolades, including the 2019 Andrej Marušič Early Career Award from the International Association for Suicide Prevention (IASP).

Jennifer Wong is a Research Fellow at the University of Canterbury. Her background is in industrial-organizational psychology. Her research interest are 1) employee health, safety, and wellbeing, and 2) the role that leadership and organizational interventions play in promoting positive outcomes for employees. Jennifer has an ardent interest in research methodologies, particularly mixed and multi-methods designs and participatory action research.

Zara Whysall is an Associate Professor at Nottingham Business School, Nottingham Trent University. She is also Research and Impact Director at business psychology firm Kiddy & Partners, part of the Gateley Group. Zara is a Chartered Psychologist and Associate Fellow of the British Psychological Society, with over 20 years' experience in applied research, management consultancy, and training. Her interest in presenteeism stems from her experience working in the occupational-health industry, where she managed delivery of multidisciplinary occupational health services, and first began conducting presenteeism research to help clients better understand and manage the issue. Zara has a PhD from Loughborough University, a Master's in Occupational Psychology from Nottingham University, and a BSc (First-class Hons) in Human Psychology from Aston University.

Wilson Wong is Head of Insight and Futures/Head of Research, CIPD. Wilson leads the Institute's research, futures, and foresight capability. He has been involved in futures research since 2000. His most recent publication with the Malaysian government was *The Future of Talent in Malaysia 2035*, and he is co-editor of *Human Capital Management Standards: A Complete Guide*. He represents the UK on human capital metrics at ISO/TC260 (HR Standards) and is Independent Chair of the Human Capital Standards Committee (HCS/1) and Deputy Chair of the Knowledge Management Standards Committee (KMS/1) at the British Standards Institution (BSI). His research interests include futures, the psychological contract, fairness, and human capital development and measurement. His career has spanned academia, corporate finance, and national ICT development policy. Wilson's PhD was on opportunity recognition. He is Visiting Professor at Nottingham Business School (NBS), on the Board of IJHRDPPR, the editorial board of HRDQ, and advisory boards at NBS and the Work and Equality Institute. A member of the International Association of Applied Psychology and an Academic Fellow of the CIPD, he was called to the English Bar in 1990.

Hannes Zacher is a Professor of Work and Organisational Psychology at the Institute of Psychology – Wilhelm Wundt, Leipzig University. He received his PhD from the University of Giessen and subsequently held positions at universities in Australia, the Netherlands, and Germany. In his research program, he investigates aging at work and career development; occupational wellbeing and the work–nonwork interface; proactivity and innovation; and leadership and entrepreneurship. His research is well supported by competitive grants and funding from industry partners. He has published in top-tier international outlets, including *American Psychologist*, *Academy of Management Review*, the *Journal of Applied Psychology*, the *Journal of Organizational Behavior*, and *Psychology and Aging*.

1

Organizational Wellbeing: An Introduction and Future Directions

Paula Brough, Tony Wall, and Cary Cooper

ORGANIZATIONAL WELLBEING: WHY AND WHY NOW?

Workplace wellbeing has a long tradition stemming back to the Industrial Revolution of the 19th century. John Ruskin, the British social reformer, reflected, at the beginning of the Industrial Revolution in 1851, on the necessity of employers looking after their workers: 'in order that people may be happy in their work, these three things are needed: they must be fit for it, they must not do too much of it, and they must have a sense of success in it' (Ruskin, n.d.). The American poet and philosopher Henry David Thoreau wrote in 1865 about American industrialization and our need for mass production and business success: 'how prompt we are to satisfy the hunger and thirst of our bodies, how slow to satisfy the hunger and thirst of our souls' (Thoreau, n.d.). During the Great Depression of the 1930s, President Roosevelt understood the need to protect and sustain those adversely affected by the Depression if they were to have a sustainable and humane economy:

'True individual freedom cannot exist without economic security and independence. People who are hungry and out of a job are the stuff of which dictatorships are made. The hopes of the Republic cannot forever tolerate either undeserved poverty or self-serving wealth' (Roosevelt, n.d.). And in recent contemporary times, Bobby Kennedy on his campaign for the Democratic Presidential nomination gave a moving speech at the University of Kansas in 1968 about the need to develop a measure of a country's success and alluded to the concept of Gross National Wellbeing as a better measure than GNP/GDP. He concluded his speech by saying:

> Yet the gross national product does not allow for the health of our children, the quality of their education or the joy of their play. It does not include the beauty of our poetry or the strength of our marriages…It measures neither our wit nor our courage, neither our wisdom nor our learning, neither our compassion nor our devotion to our country, it measures everything in short, except that which makes life worthwhile. (Roosevelt, n.d.)

We have come a long way since John Ruskin and Bobby Kennedy and today employee wellbeing has received considerable recent interest from workers, managers, and HR professionals across a wide gamut of different industries. This is partly due to the long-overdue recognition that 'healthy productive workers' has as much to do with an employee's *mental* health as their physical health. Mentally unhealthy ('toxic') work environments based, for example, on bullying, harassment, violence, and micromanaging supervisors are being increasingly identified and there is a reduced acceptance that any worker should have to endure such environments. Even long-established organizational 'cultural rituals' such as the 'hazing' of military cadets, the 'flirting' with new female firefighters and police officers, and the 'pranking' of new trade apprentices are now perceived quite differently. These changes may be influenced by recent broader social shifts in perspectives, which have identified sexism (via the *'MeToo'* movement) and racism (via the *'Black Lives Matter'* protests), for example, as experiences which should no longer be practised or tolerated. Recognizing the importance of mentally healthy workplaces has also been influenced by recent reductions in the *negative stigma* commonly associated with experiencing mental ill-health. Thus, admitting to suffering from depression, anxiety, panic attacks, or stress has now become much more widely accepted, compared to several years ago. Even in work environments, where being absent for a 'mental health day' or a 'doona [duvet] day', as the Australians call it, is now widely accepted and even encouraged in some circumstances.

However, a key reason for the recent interest in wellbeing and in establishing mentally healthy workplaces is an *economic* one. The economic costs of managing mentally unwell employees are considerable and, despite all our best efforts, continues to increase. Formal workplace mental health compensation claims are primarily caused by overwork

and toxic work environments. They can result in numerous months of lost work days per employee, and can cost organizations millions and national economies tens of billions per annum (Brough et al., 2020). Instigating workplace wellbeing programmes to demonstrate the required formal duty of care and to keep workers healthy and productive has, therefore, occurred primarily in response to these economic costs. The continued growth in these costs clearly demonstrates that there is still considerable work to be conducted to ensure that workplaces do all they can to ensure the mental health and safety of all their workers.

This *Handbook of Organizational Wellbeing* is, therefore, extremely timely. The chapters, written by experienced researchers from around the world, describe 39 aspects of workplace wellbeing. We begin in the first section by exploring the theoretical explanations of what wellbeing is and its primary antecedents. Chapter 2 extends the economic rationales of wellbeing which we noted above, in more detail. Other chapters in this first section describe the associations between wellbeing and personality characteristics (Chapter 3); how wellbeing changes with age, highly relevant for current discussions about retaining older workers (Chapter 4); the influence of emotions (Chapter 5); supervisor support (Chapter 6); and resilience (Chapter 10). Chapters 7 and 8 discuss the influence of an employee's private (non-work) life events on workplace wellbeing, and the relevance this does have for perceptive organizations. Chapter 9 expands the comment noted above about how the *'Black Lives Matter'* movement has influenced workplace wellbeing, as well as the impact of recent gender intersectional perspectives.

Section Two of the *Handbook* focuses on 12 specific contexts which can impact workers' wellbeing. Chapter 11 focuses on how technology and virtual work influences our mental health – an issue which is extremely timely and which many of us are now highly familiar with after our recent COVID-19 lockdowns. Similarly, the adverse impact on our mental health of social network sites has also received recent attention due to the COVID-19 lockdowns, and Chapter 12 provides a formal review of this evidence. Other chapters in this section describe connections between wellbeing and intrapreneurship (Chapter 13); entrepreneurs (Chapter 14); organizations' mergers and acquisitions (Chapter 15); and workers' presenteeism and work addiction (Chapter 16). This section is thus a mix of new topics (intrapreneurship, entrepreneurs) and more established themes (work addiction, mergers, and acquisitions) which can influence a worker's wellbeing. Section Two also includes topics which are highly relevant but generally receive sparse attention in the wellbeing field. Thus, Chapter 17 focuses on LGBTQIA+ workers, Chapter 18 discusses suicide at work, and Chapter 19 assesses the impact of grief at work. Section Two ends with a discussion of trauma: how workers perform in post-disaster settings (Chapter 20) and a review of the mental health of humanitarian aid workers (Chapter 21).

The third section of this *Handbook* consists of 10 chapters discussing the key issues in developing organizational wellbeing. Chapter 22 describes keys aspects of workplace wellbeing interventions or programmes from the individual, teams, and organizational perspectives. Chapters 23 and 24 review the broad contexts of mental health within workplaces and the impact of national contexts for wellbeing interventions, respectively. Chapters 25 to 27 examine the rarely considered connections between work wellbeing and the national arts, nudge theory, and neuroscience applications, respectively. Chapters 28 and 29 in this section review creative initiatives for wellbeing and the impact of wellbeing interventions which adopt a coaching approach. The final two chapters examine the common issues in the measurement of wellbeing and the evaluation of wellbeing strategies.

The fourth and final section of this *Handbook* discusses the future directions

of workplace wellbeing research and practice. Chapter 32 explores how organizational wellbeing can be influenced by indigenous peoples' perspectives. Chapters 33 and 34 focus on the very unusual impact of how play at work and creative practice are each connected with work wellbeing. We include five chapters describing associations between wellbeing and micro-activism (Chapter 35), workers' resistance (Chapter 36), spirituality (Chapter 37), and post-humanism (Chapter 38). Finally, we also include discussions of how organizational wellbeing is impacted by artificial intelligence, big data, and robots (Chapter 41) and wider movements towards understanding human capital (Chapter 42).

We have succeeded in bringing together extremely diverse discussions about organizational wellbeing within this *Handbook*. We anticipate that these discussions will assist managers, researchers, and policy makers to adopt useful, evidence-based wellbeing programmes and policies within their organizations. Above all, we hope that this *Handbook* encourages informed discussions about workers' mental health, and that the growth in workplace mental ill-health experiences and compensation claims can actually be halted.

A FUTURE GAZE

The future of work, and how this might implicate organizational research and practice, is fraught with forecasting risks and problems. This is particularly germane when the purpose of forecasting is to predict and then engineer solutions to resolve issues that present in such predictions. Another purpose of contemplating or visioning futures can be the attempt to create a more idealized vision of a future which prioritizes certain values (over others) with a view to seeking development of ideas from a normative stance – and as such is pre-figurative. As a pre-figurative enterprise, depicting the future of work is a political act that aspires to provoke reflection rather than accurate prediction. Indeed, this is the function of the 'decent work' agenda of the United Nations' sustainable development goals, where work is, for example, fairly paid and work conditions enable people to earn a reasonable living free from unfair discrimination and emotional or physical harm – as the International Labour Organization (ILO) points out, 'roughly half the world's population still lives on the equivalent of about US$2 a day' (ILO, 2020). This is a frame also endorsed by others such as professional bodies (e.g. the CIPD's Manifesto for Work, see CIPD, 2020). So, through this frame, we can start to gaze into a future of organizational wellbeing research and practice.

Through this frame, we can picture the future of work as rich, diverse, and therefore kaleidoscopic: what (decent) work is, how it is governed, and who it involves across generations, genders, and ethnicities is different across sectors and cultures. We see, in this picture of future work, that some work is now occupied by a much older workforce and artificial intelligence is helping us become much more attuned to sustainable ways of working and living. Indeed, ethics behaviour has become much more important in all aspects of work and life, because most of our behaviour is now captured by systems which analyse and predict our behaviour and mark indicators of sub-optimality. In some work, this big data helps managers (or management systems in some cases) make decisions about the adjustment of working conditions such as workload and holidays. Outside of work, we become more intolerant of those systems which make it difficult (or impossible) for those who do not have access to decent work, and generally aspire for others to access it as a normative stance.

Organizational wellbeing in this future state is, therefore, part of the 'new normal', a term now associated with, and popularized during, the COVID-19 pandemic of 2020. In this future, when we talk about organizational wellbeing, we are researching and practising

in ways which are more inclusive and all-encompassing to reflect the rich dynamics of organizational wellbeing. Driven by the 'anytime' possibilities of synchronous communication technologies, we have embraced the conceptual expansion of organizational wellbeing towards temporality: across life spans, across organizational development spans, and across major events and disasters (such as pandemics). We now examine how such temporalities interact with or generate different individual and collective wellbeing needs and resources over time and this informs the design of organizations or the design of organizational arrangements for adaptivity over time (see these chapters for insights into this discussion: 3, 4, 5, 10, 11, 20, 21, 38, and 39). These considerations of course include the way leaders and managers at all levels interact and support others in the organization (see Chapter 6 for insights into this discussion).

Yet in this future, when we talk about organizational wellbeing, we are also more conscious of *who* are we talking about, who we are *not* talking about, and who is indirectly and systematically *excluded* from our organizational wellbeing research and practice. Our concern for these issues will span the ways in which new artificial-intelligence initiatives are introduced at work, the ways they change work, but also those few areas and forms of work which remain the least touched by technologies. Within these spheres, we are actively aware of the diverse experiences of people attempting to access, or who are currently participating in, work. Here, our organizational wellbeing research and practice recognizes the diverse wellbeing needs and resources (i.e. assets) of the ways in which people identify, for example, in terms of age, ethnicity, gender, sex, sexuality, (dis)ability, neuro-diversity, faith or spirituality, pre–post parental status, or economic status. In this future, the last of these – economic status – has become recognized because of the prevalence of people around the world who may be working multiple jobs to survive (and may be termed 'the working poor') (see these chapters for insights into this discussion: 9, 17, 22, 23, and 32). Yet these statuses can be many and multiple, and implicate wellbeing in diverse ways, including the boundaries that are expected or breached during organizational work; individualized interventions by humans or equivalent are commonplace (see Chapters 7, 28, and 38 for insights into this discussion). Our organizational wellbeing research and practice is now sufficiently sophisticated to account for such diversity in this future.

In this future, because of the economic and social impact of organizational wellbeing alongside a greater appreciation of diversity and commitment to ethical behaviour in organizations, we talk about *enhancing* organizational wellbeing in terms of *governmental, national, organizational, and individual* instruments and action. We recognize that to secure longer-term change in in organizational wellbeing in complex cultural systems of education, employment, and welfare, coordinated action is often needed (see these chapters for insights into this discussion: 10, 22, 24, 25, and 34). Such multi-layered activity tackles, at a greater scale, the systemic disadvantage experienced by groups in relation to income, job security/safety, and self-esteem (see Chapter 32 for insights into this discussion). The capture and interpretation of data around such complexities is driven by artificial intelligence which guides machines, robots, and on occasion leaders and managers to alter the performance of employees through minutiae adjustments (or nudges) to work allocation or social interaction (see these chapters for insights into this discussion: 26, 30, and 31).

At the same time, along with coordinated action in the form of policy, legal, and organizational instruments, we are now aware of the co-existence of *compliance and resistance* around organizational wellbeing. In recognition of the notion that 'where there is power, there is resistance' (Mumby et al., 2017), wellbeing research and practice recognizes the importance of each towards understanding the dynamics of developing and changing wellbeing in organizational life. As such, there are implications for the ways in which we deal with micro or major events which resist the actions of organizations (see these chapters for insights into this discussion: 9, 10, 35, and 36). Our understanding of organizational wellbeing research and practice now includes, in this future, the informal alongside the formal arrangements to enable people to express creatively as a way of generating wellbeing in organizational life (see these chapters for insights into this discussion: 29, 33, and 34).

Although you can read the chapters of *The SAGE Handbook of Organizational Wellbeing* and engage with each chapter for your current organizational wellbeing research and practice, we also invite you to reflect on the chapters in terms of a future we do not yet know. As you read with a pre-figurative commitment, you might be curious about questions like: what is said and what is not said? Who does it include and who does it not include or exclude? What cultures or contexts are assumed, and which are excluded? What factors might combine in new and novel ways under conditions of increasing automation and artificial intelligence? What assumptions are being made about ethical standards and norms, and what signs are there that these are changing in or out of work contexts? Such questions, we hope, might drive developments in organizational wellbeing research and practice, and underpin a journey to a new future. This future is, of course, ours for the making, and we look forward to meeting you there.

REFERENCES

Brough, P., Raper, M., and Spedding, J. (2020). 'She'll be right, mate!' Occupational stress research in Australia. In: K. Sharma, C. Cooper, and D. M. Pestonjee (Eds). *Organizational stress around the world: Research and practice.* (pp. 1–27). London, Routledge.

CIPD (2020). *Manifesto for Work 2020*, London, CIPD.

International Labour Organization (2020). *Goal #8: Decent work and economic growth*, available at https://www.ilo.org/global/topics/sdg-2030/goal-8/lang–en/index.htm, accessed 30th July.

Mumby, D. K., Thomas, R., Martí, I., and Seidl, D. (2017). Resistance redux. *Organization Studies*, 38(9), 1157–1183. doi:10.1177/0170840617717554

Roosevelt, F.D. Quotes. (n.d.). *BrainyQuote.com*. Retrieved November 15, 2020, from BrainyQuote.com Web site: https://www.brainyquote.com/quotes/franklin_d_roosevelt_134721

Ruskin, J. Quotes. (n.d.). *BrainyQuote.com*. Retrieved November 15, 2020, from BrainyQuote.com Web site: https://www.brainyquote.com/quotes/john_ruskin_132387

Thoreau, H.D. (n.d.). *AZQuotes.com*. Retrieved November 16, 2020, from AZQuotes.com Web site: https://www.azquotes.com/quote/1377600

PART I

Theoretical Perspectives

2

Understanding the Cost of Mental Health at Work: An Integrative Framework

Juliet Hassard, Kevin Teoh,
Louise Thomson, and Holly Blake

INTRODUCTION

Work-related stress and mental ill-health are large-scale, global problems. Within Europe, stress is the second most commonly reported work-related health problem, reported by over half of the workforce (Eurofound, 2012). In the UK, recent estimates indicate that one in four people will suffer from a common mental health disorder of anxiety, depression or stress during their adult lives (National Institute for Health and Care Excellence (NICE), 2019). The economic impacts of this are profound, with an estimated 54% of all working days lost as a result of ill-health due to work-related stress, depression or anxiety (Health and Safety Executive (HSE), 2019). Levels of absenteeism, unemployment, and long-term disability claims due to stress and mental health problems are increasing in many high-income countries. Mental ill-health has also now overtaken musculoskeletal problems as the leading cause of absence from work and

withdrawal from the labour market in many countries (Organisation for Economic Co-operation and Development (OECD), 2012). This problem is set to increase since the outbreak of COVID-19, caused by severe acute respiratory syndrome coronavirus-2 (SARS-CoV-2) and declared a pandemic by the World Health Organization (WHO) on March 11, 2020. Preliminary evidence gathered before and during the pandemic clearly shows a significant mental health impact of COVID-19 on working-age adults (Daly et al., 2020; Hassard et al., n.d.). The development and maintenance of psychologically safe and healthy workplaces has never been so important.

Internationally, there is growing recognition of the social and economic impact of work-related stress and mental ill-health; and, in turn, of the relative importance of promoting mental wellbeing and preventing the onset of mental disorders at work and within the community (Black, 2008; Farmer and Stevenson, 2017; NICE, 2019).

This is evidenced by an increasing number of policy-level interventions targeting the protection and promotion of mental health at work (e.g. The National Standard of Canada for Psychological Health and Safety in the Workplace, Mental Health Commission of Canada, 2013; Australian national-level guidance, SafeWork Australia, 2019; and a British code of practice on improving health and wellbeing in an organization, British Standards Institute (BSI), 2018) coupled with an increasing number of toolkits and resources in the public domain that are aimed at supporting workplace-level action and intervention (see Leka and Jain (2010) for a review). However, adherence and implementation of such strategies and practices at the workplace level remains problematic (European Agency for Safety and Health at Work (EU-OSHA), 2019).

There is a vast literature on work-related stress and mental health, together with reports of investigations conducted to examine and understand its associated human (e.g. health outcomes) and organizational costs (e.g. sickness absence rates, turnover, productivity; Cox et al., 2000; Leka and Jain, 2010; Eurofound and EU-OSHA, 2014). Comparatively, much less attention has been paid to understanding the economic burden of this social and occupational phenomenon. This emerging evidence base attests to the substantial financial costs associated with psychosocial risks and work-related stress for individual organizations as well as national economies (Hoel et al., 2001; Sultan-Taïeb et al., 2013; McDaid and Park, 2014). In previous work, Hassard and colleagues sought to identify, understand, and critically evaluate the available economic evidence derived from cost of illness (COI) studies across a range of occupational health issues (EU-OSHA, 2014), including work-related stress (Hassard et al., 2018a), bullying and harassment (Hassard et al., 2018b), and work-related aggression and violence (Hassard et al., 2018b).

The aim of this chapter is to build upon the work by Hassard and colleagues, and in so doing seek to cultivate a better understanding and informed discourse at the interface between the disciplines of psychology and economics. We seek to integrate our empirical understanding of the link between work, mental health, and organizational performance within an economic methodological perspective. In particular, we seek to:

- explore the rationale for understanding economic estimates;
- describe key cost and methodological components that underpin many economic estimates derived from COI studies;
- discuss the link between work, mental health, and productivity;
- explore what costs are (and are not) accounted for in such economic estimates; and
- critically discuss the existing gaps in research.

WHY IS IT IMPORTANT TO UNDERSTAND ECONOMIC ESTIMATES?

Understanding the financial cost of mental ill-health and work-related stress to society and organizations is an important avenue by which to assess the magnitude and significance of an occupational or public health problem (Leigh, 2006; Tarricone, 2006; Jo, 2014). However, it can also act as an important source of information with which to develop the business case for health-centred workplace interventions and public policy. For example, the International Labour Organization (Di Martino and Pujol, 2000), the European Commission (EC, 2002) and the British HSE (Bond et al., 2006) are among the many bodies that quote the financial cost(s) associated with work-related strains and stressors to encourage employers and governments to invest in the prevention and management of work-related stress and the promotion of mental health at work.

COI studies aim to estimate the total economic impact of a disease incurred by all relevant stakeholders within society (Bloom et al., 2001; Tarricone, 2006). These studies typically examine a range of cost components, including *direct* (e.g. healthcare and medical costs), *indirect* (e.g. costs due to sickness absence or turnover), and *intangible* costs (e.g. emotional strain and reduced quality of life; Luppa et al., 2007). Identifying and understanding the costs associated with work-related stress and mental health at work can help to make the case for individual and organizational benefits accrued through increased quality of work, work environments, and working lives (Cooper and Dewe, 2008; McDaid and Park, 2014).

Detailed evaluations of these estimated costs, derived from COI studies, have seldom received attention in the broader literature, with some frequently cited figures being produced without clear specification or transparency in their employed methodology (e.g. American Institute of Stress, n.d.). Therefore, we argue that there is a growing need for all those (e.g. researchers, practitioners, change advocates, policy makers, to name a few) who utilize such sources of evidence to better understand and critically evaluate such estimates. While there are other important sources of economic evidence in building a business case in this field (e.g. cost–benefit analysis), this book chapter focuses specifically on COI studies. Therefore, the aim of the following section is to provide a cursory-level introduction to the key methodological components of COI studies.

BASIC CONCEPTS OF COI STUDIES

The aim of COI studies is to estimate the total economic impact of a disease incurred by all relevant stakeholders within a given society (Drummond et al., 2005), with such estimates (ideally) accounting for the direct, indirect, and intangible costs (Dagenais et al., 2008). The objective of COI studies is primarily to itemize, value, and sum the costs of a particular problem (Koopmanschap, 1998). The

following section aims to provide a short introduction on the key features of COI studies, mainly the typology of cost components, epidemiological approaches, and methodological approaches. For a more comprehensive discussion of the key characteristics of COI studies see Larg and Moss (2011).

Typology of Cost Components

The economic burden of a given disease or health problem is estimated by accounting for the costs typically associated with resource consumption, productivity losses, and other 'intangible' burdens within a specified group (Larg and Moss, 2011). As aforementioned, COI studies typically stratify costs into three categories: direct, indirect, and intangible costs (Luppa et al., 2007; Dagenais et al., 2008). Table 2.1 aims to provide some examples of typically examined cost components as identified in previous reviews in the area of occupational health and management (Hassard et al., 2018a, 2018b, 2019).

Direct costs are incurred by the healthcare system, family, society, and the individual, and typically consist of healthcare and non-healthcare costs (Jo, 2014). The former refers to medical care expenditure related to diagnosis, treatment, and rehabilitation, while the latter relates to the consumption of non-healthcare resources (such as transportation, household expenditures, relocating, property losses, litigation; Luppa et al., 2007; Dagenais et al., 2008). Typically, direct medical costs are the easiest to estimate, and, consequently, the most commonly accounted for in many COI studies (e.g. Hassard et al., 2018a). In contrast, evidence of direct non-medical costs is less well documented, or less readily available, making the estimation of aggregated figures typically quite challenging (Luppa et al., 2007; Dagenais et al., 2008) and, consequently, less examined or accounted for (Hassard et al., 2018a, 2018b, 2019).

Table 2.1   Examples of typically examined cost components observed in systematic reviews (Hassard et al., 2018a, 2018b, 2019) of occupational health and management focused COI studies

Topic	Direct	Indirect	Intangible
Work-related stress	Medical: Medical services, medication, treatment, rehabilitation Non-medical: Travel expenses, legal costs, loss of income, fines and penalties, aids and modifications	Productivity-focused: Sickness absence, presenteeism, early retirement, early death, staff turnover and loss of production Non-productivity: None	Non-financial human cost
Bullying and harassment at work	Medical: Doctor visits, medication Non-medical: Compensation, legal, redundancy and early retirement	Productivity-focused: Presenteeism, sickness absence, turnover Non-productivity: Procedures and policies, workplace support (e.g. Employee Assistance Programmes, HR)	None
Work-related physical violence and psychological aggression	Medical: Medical costs, physician and nursing services, hospital charges, drug costs, rehabilitation services, ambulance fees, payments for medical equipment and supplies Non-medical: Legal, compensation, vocational rehabilitation, partial permanent disability benefits, indemnity (fatal)	Productivity-focused: Early death, loss of earnings, sickness absence Non-productivity: Household production losses (e.g. childcare and housework)	Upset and inconvenience suffered

Indirect costs refer to productivity losses due to mortality or morbidity borne by the individual, family, society, or the employer (Larg and Moss, 2011). Most COI studies tend to focus on productivity losses incurred within the occupational context (Béjean and Sultan-Taïeb, 2005; Deloitte, 2017; McTernan et al., 2013). Considerably fewer studies have accounted for non-work-related productivity losses, such as housework, voluntary work, and other unpaid productivity work (Molinier et al., 2008; Larg and Moss, 2011). This finding is mirrored across all three systematic reviews examining a variety of occupational health and management issues (Hassard et al., 2018a, 2018b, 2019). In general, these reviews predominantly accounted for costs associated with sickness absence, staff turnover, and (to a lesser degree) presenteeism.

Intangible costs, by contrast, reflect the financial value prescribed to the pain and suffering and the reduced quality of life experienced by the afflicted individual or group of individuals (Luppa et al., 2007). Due to the difficulty in quantifying such experiences, intangible costs are seldom included in COI studies. Consequently, the empirical importance in allowing valid and reliable cost estimates is acknowledged within both the economic and public health fields (Larg and Moss, 2011). Once again, across all three of the systematic reviews of COI studies very few studies accounted for such costs. This is despite strong evidence derived from the psychological literature observing a link between work-related stress and poor mental health with reduced quality of (working) life (Leka and Jain, 2010; Eurofound and EU-OSHA, 2014).

Epidemiological Approach

The interpretation of COI studies is directly influenced by the epidemiological perspective adopted and utilized by the study: *incidence-* or *prevalence-based*. The incidence[1]-based approach measures the likely avoided costs if new cases are prevented (Larg and Moss, 2011). Such studies sum the estimated lifetime costs that are attributable to cases that occur during the defined incident period, following which future costs are appropriately adjusted to their present-day value (i.e. discounting; Mauskopf, 1998). The results derived from such studies can: (i) demonstrate how costs vary with disease duration (Larg and Moss, 2011); (ii) inform planning interventions targeted at specific stages (Fiscella et al., 2009); and (iii) be used to inform the calculation of baseline costs for cost-effectiveness studies for interventions (Finkelstein and Corso, 2003).

Prevalence[2]-based approaches, in contrast, measure the actual impact of existing cases compared with a hypothetical alternative case prevalence (Larg and Moss, 2011). Such studies measure disease-attributable costs that occur concurrently with prevalent cases over a specific time period (usually one year; Larg and Moss, 2011). This approach is generally considered the most appropriate for assessing the total current economic burden of a health problem (WHO, 2009) as these studies usually include a cross-section of cases, thus capturing the costs at varying stages of disease (Mauskopf, 1998). However, this cross-section of individuals may also include cases that may not be amenable to intervention. Consequently, estimates derived using such an epidemiological approach are generally viewed as less reliable for measuring the potential savings from preventative interventions (WHO, 2009).

Methodological Approach

COI studies can be broadly grouped around three different approaches: top-down,

bottom-up, and deductive (Drummond et al., 2005; Larg and Moss, 2011). In general, the deductive approach is less commonly used than the top-down or bottom-up approaches (Hassard et al., 2018a, 2018b, 2019).

The *top-down (population aggregated-based) approach* measures the proportion of a problem that is due to exposure to the relevant risk factors (Larg and Moss, 2011). Attributable costs are calculated by using aggregated data along with population-attributable fraction calculations (Morgenstern et al., 1980). The empirical rigour of top-down approaches relies heavily on the quality of the epidemiological/secondary data sources used. Consequently, the ability to meaningfully and accurately monitor and measure working conditions and work-related health aliments and conditions is of direct relevance in regard to the quality of such estimates (Hassard et al., 2018a). There is often difficulty in distinguishing group differences in the consumption and utilization of health and other economic resources (Larg and Moss, 2011). Despite this, such an approach is typically quicker and easier to conduct than the bottom-up approach as the former often relies solely on secondary data (Mogyorosy and Smith, 2005).

The bottom-up (person-based) approach estimates costs by calculating the estimated cost per case and extrapolates it to the national or societal level (Larg and Moss, 2011). In this instance, medical expenditure and/or loss of productivity are costed per person or per case, and then multiplied by the number of cases or persons affected (Larg and Moss, 2011). The strength of this approach lies in the potential to identify all relevant cost components for each specific case or person (Wordsworth et al., 2005). However, the lack of appropriate data sources can make thorough calculations time consuming or even, in some cases, unfeasible (Mogyorosy and Smith, 2005).

Finally, the *deductive approach* examines the proportion of costs associated with the given problem, as obtained from the research literature, and applies this fraction to a total estimate of illness (Giga et al., 2008). For example, if mental health was thought to constitute 10% of the total cost of work-related ill-health (estimated to be a hypothetical £100 billion), the estimated costs of mental health at work would, therefore, be £10 billion. The strength of the deductive approach lies in its simplicity. However, it assumes the breakdown and the average cost of workplace aggression are identical to the average cost of work-related ill-health.

AN INTEGRATED THEORETICAL PERSPECTIVE: THE ECONOMIC COST OF MENTAL HEALTH AT WORK

A key objective of this chapter is to integrate contemporary understanding of the link between work, work-related stress, and mental health as understood by the field of psychology, but to integrate this conceptual framework within a COI methodological approach and economic perspective. It is our hope that, in so doing, this will provide a useful conceptual framework to guide

increased understanding, discussion, and further collaboration between the fields of psychology and economics.

To better understand the impact of work-related stress and mental ill-health at work in human, organizational, and economic terms, we need to examine the empirical understanding of the link between work, stress, and mental health, and, in turn, how this stress-based process relates to the aggregated cost components used to derive economic estimates (derived by COI studies) posed by poor mental health at work. It is important to note that we do not represent work-related stress as a health outcome (in its own right), but rather as a psychological state that, when prolonged, chronic, and excessive, is associated with a myriad of health outcomes, including poor mental health outcomes.

Figure 2.1 aims to provide a visual representation of this integrated conceptual model that seeks to bring together the understanding of causes and performance consequences of poor mental health at work, as understood within the psychological literature. We then seek to integrate this conceptual model within the key economic cost components (i.e. the direct, indirect, and intangible

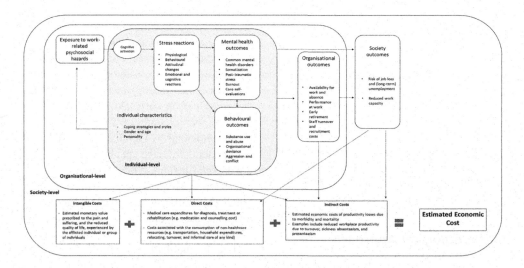

Figure 2.1 A theoretical model on the cost of mental ill-health at work

cost) considered as important when deriving estimates of the financial burden posed by work-related stress and its associated psychological health consequences. Finally, we aim to highlight and recognize that estimating the financial burden posed by work-related stress and poor mental health at work can be represented at various levels: worker, employer, and society. In this section, we seek to examine and discuss this posed theoretical model.

Psychosocial Hazards, Work-Related Stress, and Mental Health

At an individual level, we know that the experience of work can have positive or negative impacts. Work can contribute to the experience of work-related stress and, in the long term, the development of mental ill-health through poor working conditions and work organization issues (Black, 2008; Leka and Jain, 2010; Eurofound and EU-OSHA, 2014; Farmer and Stevenson, 2017; NICE, 2019). Conversely, we know that employment can provide individuals with purpose, financial resources, and a source of identity, which has been shown to promote increased positive mental wellbeing (Bakker et al., 2012). The aim of this section is to provide a cursory introduction to the link between work and workers' mental health; and how this relationship, in turn, is associated with indicators of organizational health and performance. For a more substantive discussion and review of the impact of work and organizational factors on workers' (physical, psychological, and social) health see Leka and Jain (2010).

It is important to note that work-related stress is not an illness or health outcome in its own right; but rather is understood as an adverse (psychological and emotional) reaction people have to excessive pressures or other types of demands placed on them at work (HSE, n.d.). When the experience of work-related stress is excessive, chronic, and prolonged then mental and/or physical illness

may develop (Cox et al., 2000). This includes (but of course is not restricted to) a variety of mental health outcomes, including common mental health disorders or complaints (e.g. depression and anxiety; Stansfeld and Candy, 2006), burnout (Alarcon, 2011), and post-traumatic stress disorders (Cieslak et al., 2011). The empirical literature recognizes several sources, or risk factors, of work-related stress and mental ill-health (often termed 'work-related psychosocial hazards').

Work-related psychosocial hazards concern those aspects of work design and the organization and management of work within their social and environmental contexts which have the potential for causing psychological, social, or physical harm (Cox et al., 2000). These risk factors for work-related stress can broadly include stressors intrinsic to the job, role in the organization, relationships at work, career development, organizational structure and climate, and the home–work interface. Figure 2.1 illustrates the causes of stress, (short-term) stress reactions, long-term health consequences, and individual characteristics, as well as their inter-relationships. It is important to note that such inter-relationships are dynamic in nature and are typically the result of the transaction between the individual and their socio-environmental context.

Stress reactions may result when people are exposed to risk factors at work, particularly when individuals perceive these demands and challenges outweigh their perceived ability or available resources to cope. The role of cognitive appraisal (Folkmand and Lazarus, 1984) is central, therefore, to understanding this transaction between the individual and their work environment. Experienced stress reactions (often viewed as the 'early warning signs' of stress) may be cognitive (e.g. reduced attention and perception, forgetfulness), emotional (e.g. feeling nervous or irritated, low mood, cognitive), behavioural (e.g. aggressive, impulsive behaviour or making mistakes), and/or physiological strain-based reactions (e.g. increase in heart rate, blood pressure, and hyperventilation). A growing body of evidence (Leka and Jain, 2010) indicates that when exposure to work-related psychosocial hazards, and associated short-term stress reactions, persists over a prolonged period of time this can result in long-term health outcomes and impairments and negative attitudinal (e.g. job satisfaction and motivation at work) and behavioural changes (e.g. problem drinking, unhealthy eating patterns, or decreased physical activity). Mental health outcomes (e.g. depression and anxiety) are commonly viewed as a long-term consequence of work-related stress and exposure to a poor psychosocial work environment (Stansfeld and Candy, 2006).

However, there is an increased understanding of the role played by those more positive (health-enhancing/protecting) factors at work in both mitigating the experience of and long-term health impact of work-related stress; but also their direct role in cultivating psychological wellbeing (Bakker et al., 2012; Bauer and Jenny, 2012). These more positive (health enhancing/protecting) factors are typically conceptually understood as job[3] and personal[4] resources. However, a wider set of individual characteristics (such as personality, values, goals, age, gender, level of education, and family situation) can influence one's ability to cope and, therefore, play an important role in mitigating the impact of work-related stress. Broadly speaking, these characteristics can either exacerbate or alleviate the effects of risk factors at work and, in turn, the experience of stress and its long- and short-term health impacts (Cox et al., 2000; Semmer, 2003). Support for these pathways is growing and is evidenced by both meta-analytic reviews and longitudinal studies (e.g. Verkuil et al., 2015).

Linking Work-Related Mental Ill-Health to Economic Costs

As stated previously, the economic estimates of the burden posed by poor mental health at work can be represented at the individual, organizational, and societal level. From an economic perspective, at the individual level, the cost of poor mental health may be related to increased medical/insurance costs related to mental health issues, and reduced income through lost working time and capacity can have monetary implications. The consequences of poor mental health at work are typically represented in the estimated direct and (to a lesser degree) indirect costs in COI studies. However, the costs that go beyond financial measures are termed 'human costs' (Hoel et al., 2001). This refers to the emotional strain, declining health, and reduction in quality of life for the individual. Beyond the associated consequences to the individual's health, there is also evidence that workplace stress is related to poorer relationship quality with spouse, children, and other family members (Dembe, 2001; Amick and Mustard, 2005), marital disharmony and divorce (Sutherland and Cooper, 1996), and negative impacts on the health of the family (Crouter et al., 2001). In economic terms, these associated costs should be captured in 'intangible costs'. Consequently, from a COI perspective, we argue that when considering the cost to individuals associated with work-related stress and poor mental health we should consider (and account for) both direct and 'intangible costs'.

The health impact of psychosocial hazards and work-related stress extends beyond individual health and can also affect the productivity and resiliency of the organization (a concept termed 'organizational healthiness'; see Cox and Thomson, 2000). At the organizational level, poor mental health at work may have significant detrimental implications in relation to productivity; levels of absenteeism; employee turnover; early retirement; and, ultimately, financial performance. These associated consequences of poor mental health at work are, typically, represented in indirect (productivity-related) cost components. Should workers have to take time off work or leave employment due to stress-related illness or poor mental health this could have a direct impact on their level of earnings. Compensation practices differ between countries, with some workers being able to take a finite amount of paid sick leave, while others see a reduction in their wages (Hoel et al., 2001). Even within the EU there are different practices surrounding sick leave (Scheil-Adlung and Sandner, 2010). Alternatively, some workers might have to leave employment completely, losing their salary and possibly their healthcare benefits as well. Therefore, when considering the cost to employers (see next section for a more detailed discussion) estimates should take into account both *direct* and *indirect* cost components. However, we argue later in this chapter that intangible costs associated with human suffering could and do extend to the organizational level; and, therefore, such estimated sub-cost should be considered in economic estimates. While conceptually the psychological literature provides a robust case for their inclusion, the challenges posed in quantifying such intangible aspects of human and organizational suffering in economic terms are challenging, due, in part, to the lack/availability of good quality data on such parameters. However, we argue that inclusion of such intangible costs is important to consider when estimating the cost for employers.

Finally, at a social level, the implications of disease and ill-health associated with chronic work-related stress and prolonged exposure to psychosocial risks at work can increase costs associated with primary and secondary health services and welfare benefits, reduces economic productivity, and can have a significant detrimental impact on a country's Gross Domestic Product (Hoel et al., 2001; Béjean and Sultan-Taïeb, 2005). The long-term impacts of work-related stress and poor mental health at work are, we argue, typically observed in the costs associated with job loss and unemployment, work capacity, and increased early retirement. In this context, all three cost components should be accounted

for to provide an accurate estimate of the 'total' cost of poor mental health at work. However, it is important to note that few COI studies account for all three cost components in their estimates; and, therefore, it is fair to conclude that those available estimates are conservative (at best).

UNDERSTANDING THE COSTS TO EMPLOYERS DUE TO POOR MENTAL HEALTH AT WORK

A psychologically unhealthy workplace has adverse economic consequences for business. Even very minor levels of depression are associated with productivity losses (Beck et al., 2011, 2014) and increases in turnover with the associated costs of additional recruitment and training, with ultimate impacts on the retention of highly skilled workers lost to poor health (McDaid et al., 2008). In general, many estimates tend to focus on the cost for employers by examining the indirect costs (typically, costs associated with sickness absence, presenteeism, and staff turnover) associated with work-related stress and mental ill-health at work. In this section, we aim to look in more detail at the estimated costs for employers of poor mental health due to these three indicators.

There can be substantial immediate productivity losses due to sickness absenteeism. Absence trends in the UK have, by and large, been decreasing; with the exception, however, of periods of leave due to mental health, which have in recent years been observed to be on the rise. For example, the proportion of total days lost due to poor mental health rose from 9.1 to 11.5% between 2009 and 2016 (British Office for National Statistics (ONS), 2017). In the UK, mental ill-health is the fourth most commonly reported reason for spells of sickness absence (ONS, 2019). However, it is commonly agreed that the total days lost due to mental health at work are vastly under-reported (OECD, 2012). The reasons for this vary, but it is well-known that employees can feel reluctant to disclose their mental health condition or experience due to the continued social stigma related to mental illness, and there is also a perceived lack of understanding around mental health conditions by employers, managers, and co-workers (Brohan et al., 2012). The methods used to calculate the cost of sickness absence at work (e.g. human capital method and friction cost approach; see Pike and Grosse, 2018 for further details) are heterogenous, and, consequently, the nature and scale of such figures will and do vary (sometimes quite markedly). A recent review by Pike and Grosse (2018) observed that in COI studies in general there is a lack of standardization of methods used to calculate productivity loss, which makes derived estimates difficult (if not impossible) to compare across studies.

Table 2.2 aims to provide a comparative overview of approaches used by the two studies to provide an exemplar of the different approaches that can be used to derive estimates of the cost of sickness absence due to mental ill-health in the UK. When calculating the cost absence from work due to mental health often immediate costs are calculated (time off work due to that specific spell of absence). However, we know that mental health is also linked with increased risks of developing physical health problems (e.g. coronary heart disease and diabetes) which can lead to risk of further spells of work absenteeism (McDaid and Park, 2014). Therefore, when considering the business case it is important to consider the costs associated with initial spells of absence and the risk of future spells directly or indirectly associated with mental health.

Presenteeism is the loss of productivity that occurs when employers come to work

Table 2.2 Comparative summary of estimates and cost methods for sickness absence, presenteeism, and staff turnover

Source	Cost method	Estimated cost (£billion)
Sickness absence		
Centre for Mental Health (CMH), 2017	Cost of working days lost because of sickness absence x absence days at national level	10.6
Deloitte (2017)	Absence days by industry x industry workforce x absence day costs by industry x mental health proportion by industry	7.9
Presenteeism		
CMH	Applying a cost multiplier of 2.0 (this figure was derived from and informed by the evidence base) to the estimated cost of sickness absenteeism	21.2
Deloitte	Method 1: Presenteeism days by industry x industry workforce x absence day costs by industry x proportion of mental health presenteeism Method 2: Mental health absence cost by industry x presenteeism magnitude by sector	16.8–24.4
Staff turnover		
Deloitte	Method 1 (salaries ≥ 25 k): Staff turnover exit/entry costs x industry workforce x staff turnover exit/entry costs x mental health related staff turnover Method 2 (salaries < 25 k): Salary x exist/entry cost proportion x industry workface x staff turnover exit/entry rate x mental health related staff turnover	7.9
CMH	Proportion of total staff turnover x the average unit cost to employers of staff turnover	3.1

ill and perform below par because of illness (Navarro et al., 2019). However, it is important to note that there exists some level of debate on this definition and its measurement (Navarro et al., 2019), which, in turn, makes it difficult to quantify consistently. In general, presenteeism is hard to measure, many commonly used measures suffer from low levels of validity (Ospina et al., 2015), and few estimates of its costs have been made (McDaid and Park, 2014). Despite these challenges, there is growing evidence to indicate that the economic impact of presenteeism far exceeds that resulting from sickness absence. Some estimates suggest the costs associated with presenteeism are three (Deloitte, 2017) to seven (RAND Europe, 2015) times greater than sickness absence. Such estimates need, however, to be understood within their given national context. For example, in the United States, coverage of occupational sick pay is considerably lower than in many other Western countries and so within this context sickness absence imposes a larger financial penalty for employees, likely resulting in fewer days absence due to stress and mental health problems (Hassard et al., in press).

The higher costs attributable to presenteeism may to some extent be associated with the continued fear of stigma and discrimination by employers and co-workers towards employees. For example, employees may continue to turn up to work even when feeling unwell, rather than taking time off, for which an explicit reason often has to be given (e.g. through a medical certification process for approved sick leave/sick pay). During periods of recession, levels of presenteeism may increase further, in part due to job insecurity and fear of job loss impacting on decisions to take leave when unwell (Galon et al., 2014). For this reason, we speculate that the costs of presenteeism are likely to be considerably higher during and directly following the COVID-19 pandemic since the drastic impacts of COVID-19 on the global economy present a significant challenge to job security for working-age adults globally. Furthermore,

presenteeism is, itself, a strong predictor of future poor mental and physical health (Bergström et al., 2009), which may result in economic costs for employers in both the immediate but also long-term through future sickness absence and presenteeism. From an economic perspective, considering and accounting for such additional costs would yield further insights into the true financial burden to employers of mental ill-health.

The final (indirect) cost component that is typically accounted for in estimates of the cost of mental health to employers is that associated with staff turnover – that is the costs associated with the exit and entry of staff members in a workplace. The estimated proportion of turnover that can be attributed to mental health is estimated to be 7% (Deloitte, 2017).

However, it is important to note that such estimated costs can be impacted by several key factors: type of sector, size of organization, and type of worker. It is common for estimates to use an average cost estimate, which may not accurately represent or account for variability in the 'true' costs associated with staff turnover across sectors, professions, or size of organizations. While a certain level of imprecision in economics exists, many argue that the costs associated with staff turnover are (comparatively) much smaller than sickness absence and presenteeism; and, in the grand scheme of things, this level of imprecision will probably not affect (too dramatically) such cost estimates (Parsonage and Saini, 2017).

MOVING FROM COSTS TO BENEFITS

With the rise in the field of positive occupational health psychology (Bakker et al., 2012; Bauer and Jenny, 2012; Christensen et al., 2017) and, in turn, a growing empirical understanding of the role and impact of those more positive (health-enhancing and protecting) factors in the workplace in relation to individuals' wellbeing and organizations' resiliency and productivity, it is our view that this empirical movement could or should be considered from an economic perspective. A movement from '*what is the economic cost of poor working conditions and mental ill-health at work?*' to (or inclusive of) '*what is the economic benefit for employers of investing in a psychologically safe and healthy work environment through enhanced and varied work and personal resources?*'

Some examples of this conceptual paradigm shift include (but are not limited to):

- from a focus on productivity losses to gains (including enhanced workplace innovation, creativity, and adaptability);
- from impaired/reduced performance to optional human functioning (e.g. achieving the 'flow' at work; Nielsen and Cleal, 2010); and
- from reduced workforce capacity and worker capability (e.g. premature death, early retirement) to sustainable working lives and sustainable employment.

It is our view that achieving a better understanding of both the human and economic benefits (alongside the associated costs) accrued from a psychologically healthy work environment is important to understanding (and quantifying) the total costs of healthcare and lost production due to mental ill-health at work, but also provides a complementary set of arguments to further develop and extend the business case for action. We speculate that this is, or should be, an important future avenue of research and provides an important arena for the inter-disciplinary work between economics and psychology.

CONCLUSION

What is certain is that cost estimates for the cost of mental health at work (from the employer perspective or beyond) should not be taken at face value. Critical understanding of their context and the methodology used is

Table 2.3 Summary of key costs and considerations around cost to employers due to mental health at work (adapted from Deloitte, 2017)

Costs to employers	Costs linked to individual	Absence costs	
		Presenteeism costs	
	Costs linked to teams	Reduction in team productivity resulting in individual absenteeism or presenteeism. A so-called 'ripple effect' in productivity losses, and increased future risks to team members' mental health (e.g. due to increased workload) and further productivity losses (through sickness absence or presenteeism). *Not typically examined in economic costs.*	
	Costs linked to the organization	Staff turnover: exit costs	Staff turnover: entry costs
		Cover all costs with bringing a new employee up to speed in the organization and any productivity losses from this.	Cover all the logistical costs associated with having to attract and recruit new talent (e.g. cost of advertising, temporary workers, interviewing and inducting a new employee).
		Other costs may include medical insurance premiums, occupational health costs, group income protection, sick pay, progression impact, risk of legal and compensation costs. *These are, among others, not typically included in cost estimates.*	

paramount, and we hope that this introductory chapter has helped in better understanding and deciphering such sources of evidence. We would argue that such cost estimates only provide a context-dependent 'snap-shot' of the estimated financial burden posed by mental health at work and are not without their methodological limitation. These estimates do, however, act as an important catalyst in encouraging necessary debate in research, policy, and practice, and can (and often do) act as important 'conversational guesstimates' highlighting the respective burden posed by psychologically unhealthy workplaces and workers (Hassard et al., 2018a). Furthermore, it is also important to further strengthen research that aims to assess the economic value and impact of interventions that seek to enhance and promote wellbeing at work or prevent poor wellbeing. Such sources of evidence are, we believe, vital in communicating the potential economic benefits of such interventions. Despite some of the methodological limitations and conceptual challenges, the (empirical and practical) value of such sources of evidence is clear.

Notes

1 Incidence refers to the number of individuals who develop a specific disease or experience a specific health-related event during a particular time period (such as a month or year).
2 Prevalence refers to the total number of individuals in a population who have a disease or health condition at a specific period of time, usually expressed as a percentage of the population.
3 Job resources are physical, psychological, social, or organizational aspects of the job that function in achieving work goals, reduce job demands and the associated physiological and psychological cost, and stimulate personal growth, learning, and development. Examples are career opportunities, supervisor coaching, role-clarity, and autonomy (Bakker et al., 2012).
4 Personal resources are aspects of the self that are generally linked to resiliency and refer to individuals' sense of their ability to control and

impact upon their environment successfully (Hobfoll et al., 2003).

REFERENCES

Alarcon, G. M. (2011) 'A meta-analysis of burnout with job demands, resources, and attitudes', *Journal of Vocational Behavior*, 79(2), pp. 549–562. doi: https://doi.org/10.1016/j.jvb.2011.03.007

American Institute of Stress (n.d.) *Work Stress: Job Stress is Costly*. Retrieved (December 4, 2020). Available at: http://www.stress.org/workplace-stress/

Amick, B. C. and Mustard, C. A. (2005) 'Labor markets and health: A social epidemiological perspective', In: Bianchi SM, Casper LM, King RB, editors. *Work, Family, Health and Well-being*. Mahwan, NJ: Lawrence Erlbaum; (2005). p. 409–428.

Bakker, A. B., Rodrguez-Munoz, A. and Derks, D. (2012) 'The emergence of positive occupational health psychology', *Psicothema*, 21(1), pp. 66–72.

Bauer, G. F. and Jenny, G. J. (2012) 'Moving towards positive organisational health: Challenges and a proposal for a research model of organisational health development', *Contemporary Occupational Health Psychology (Vol. 2)*, pp. 126–145.

Beck, A., Crain, A. L., Glasgow, R. E., Maciosec, M. V., Solberg, L. I., Unutzer, J. and Whitebird, R. (2011) 'Severity of depression and magnitude of productivity loss', *The Annals of Family Medicine*, 9(4), pp. 305–311.

Beck, A., Crain A. L., Maciosec, M. V., Rossom, R. C., Solberg, L. I., Unutzer, J. and Whitebird, R. (2014) 'The effect of depression treatment on work productivity', *American Journal of Managemet and Care*, 20(8), pp. 294–301.

Béjean, S. and Sultan-Taïeb, H. (2005) 'Modelling the economic burden of diseases imputable to stress at work', *European Journal of Health Economics*, 6(1), pp. 16–23.

Bergström, G., Bodin, L., Hagberg, J., Lindh, T., Aronsson, G. and Josephson, M. (2009) 'Does sickness presenteeism have an impact on future general health?', *International*

Archives of Occupational and Environmental Health, 82(10), pp. 1179–1190.

Black, C. (2008) *Working for a healthier tomorrow: Dame Carol Black's review of the health of Britain's working age*. London: The Stationery Office.

Bloom, D. E., Canning, D. and Sevilla, J. (2001) *The effect of health on economic growth: Theory and evidence*. Cambridge, MA: National Bureau of Economic Research.

Bond, F.W., Flaxman, P.E. and Loivette, S. (2006) A business case for the Management Standards for stress. Technical Report RR431. Health and Safety Executive, Sudbury. Retrieved December 4, 2020. https://www.hse.gov.uk/research/rrhtm/rr431.htm.

Brohan, E., Henderson, E., Wheat, K., Malcolm, E., Clement, S., Barley, E. A., Slade, M. and Thornicroft, G. (2012) 'Systematic review of beliefs, behaviours and influencing factors associated with disclosure of a mental health problem in the workplace', BMC Psychiatry, 12(1), p. 11.

BSI (2018) *PAS 3002: Code of Practice on Improving Health and Wellbeing within an Organization*. British Standards Institute. Retrieved December 4, 2020. Available at: https://shop.bsigroup.com/ProductDetail?pid=000000000030384539

Centre for Mental Health (2017) Mental health at work: The business costs ten years on. https://www.centreformentalhealth.org.uk/publications/mental-health-work-business-costs-ten-years. Retrieved December 4, 2020

Christensen, M., Saksvik, P. Ø. and Karanika-Murray, M. (2017) *The positive side of occupational health psychology*. London: Springer International Publishing.

Cieslak, R., Shoji, K., Douglas, A., Melville, E., Luszczynska, A. and Benight, C. C. (2011) 'A meta-analysis of the relationship between job burnout and secondary traumatic stress among workers with indirect exposure to trauma', *Psychological Services*, pp. 75–86.

Cooper, C. L. and Dewe, P. (2008) 'Wellbeing – absenteeism, presenteeism, costs and challenges', *Occupational Medicine*, 58(8), pp. 522–524.

Cox, T., Griffiths, A. and Rial-Gonzalez, E. (2000) *Research on work-related stress*. Luxembourg: Office for Official Publications of the European Communities.

Cox, T. and Thomson, L. (2000). Organizational healthiness, work-related stress and employee health. In P. Dewe, T. Cox, M.Leiter (eds) *Coping, health, and organizations*. London: Taylor & Francis.

Crouter, A. C., Bumpus, M. F., Head, M. R. and McHale, S. M. (2001) 'Implications of overwork and overload for the quality of men's family relationships', *Journal of Marriage and Family*, 63(2), pp. 404–416.

Dagenais, S., Caro, J. and Haldeman, S. (2008) 'A systematic review of low back pain cost of illness studies in the United States and internationally', *The Spine Journal*, 8(1), pp. 8–20.

Daly, M., Sutin, A. and Robinson, E. (2020) 'Longitudinal changes in mental health and the COVID-19 pandemic: Evidence from the UK Household Longitudinal Study', *PsyArXiv*. doi: https://doi.org/10.31234/osf.io/qd5z7

Deloitte (2017) *Mental health and employers: The case for investment. Supporting study for the independent review*. London: Deloitte MCS Limited.

Dembe, A. E. (2001) 'The social consequences of occupational injuries and illnesses', *American Journal of Industrial Medicine*, 40(4), pp. 403–417.

Drummond, M. F., Sculpher, M. J., Claxton, K., Stoddart, G. L. and Torrance, G. W. (2005) *Methods for the economic evaluation of health care programmes*. New York: Oxford University Press.

EC (2002) *Guidance on work-related stress: Spice of life or kiss of death*. Luxembourg: Publications Office of the European Union.

EU-OSHA (2014) *Calculating the cost of work-related stress and psychosocial risks*. Luxembourg: Publications Office of the European Union.

EU-OSHA (2019) *Third European Survey of Enterprises on New and Emerging Risks (ESENER 3)*. Luxembourg: European Commission. Retrieved December 4, 2020. Available at: https://osha.europa.eu/en/publications/third-european-survey-enterprises-new-and-emerging-risks-esener-3/view

Eurofound (2012) *Fifth European Working Conditions Survey*. Luxembourg. Retrieved December 4, 2020. Available at: https://www.eurofound.europa.eu/publications/report/2012/working-conditions/fifth-european-working-conditions-survey-overview-report

Eurofound and EU-OSHA (2014) *Psychosocial risks in Europe: Prevalence and strategies for prevention*. Luxembourg: Publications Office of the European Union.

Farmer, P. and Stevenson, D. (2017) *Thriving at work: The Stevenson/Farmer Review of Mental Health and Employers*. London: The Stationery Office. Retrieved December 4, 2020. Available at: https://assets.publishing.service.gov.uk/government/uploads/system/uploads/attachment_data/file/658145/thriving-at-work-stevenson-farmer-review.pdf

Finkelstein, E. and Corso, P. (2003) 'Cost-of-illness analyses for policy making: A cautionary tale of use and misuse', *Expert Review of Pharmacoeconomics & Outcomes Research*, 3(4), pp. 367–369.

Fiscella, R. G., Lee, J., Davis, E. J. H. and Walt, J. (2009) 'Cost of illness of glaucoma', *Pharmacoeconomics*, 27(3), pp. 189–198.

Folkmand, S. and Lazarus, R. S. (1984) *Stress, appraisal, and coping*. New York: Springer.

Galon, T., Briones-Vozmediano, E., Agudelo-Suárez, A. A., Felt, E. B., Benavides, F. G. and Ronda, E. (2014) 'Understanding sickness presenteeism through the experience of immigrant workers in a context of economic crisis', *American Journal of Industrial Medicine*, 57, pp. 950–959.

Giga, S., Hoel, H. and Lewis, D. (2008) *The Costs of Workplace Bullying: A Report and Review*. Retrieved December 4, 2020. Available at: http://www.cywu.org.uk/download.php?id=191

Hassard, J., Teoh, K. R. H., Visockaite, G., Dewe, P., and Cox, T.(2018a) 'The cost of work-related stress to society: A systematic review', *Journal of Occupational Health Psychology*, 23(1). doi: 10.1037/ocp0000069, pp. 1–17.

Hassard, J., Teoh, K. R. H., Visockaite, G., Dewe, P., and Cox, T. (2018b) 'The financial burden of psychosocial workplace aggression: A systematic review of cost-of-illness studies', *Work and Stress*, 32(1). doi: 10.1080/02678373.2017.1380726, pp. 6–32.

Hassard, J., Teoh, K. R. H. and Cox, T. (2019) 'Estimating the economic burden posed by work-related violence to society: A systematic review of cost-of-illness studies', *Safety Science*, 119, pp. 208–221.

Hassard, J., Thomson, L., Blake, H., Karanika-Murray, M., Choo, W., Delic, L., Newman, K., Pickford, R. (n.d.) *Wellbeing of the Workforce (WOW) Study: Preliminary Results of Survey during Lockdown*. Retrieved December 4, 2020.Available at: https://institutemh.org.uk/research/projects-and-studies/current-studies/wow-study/wellbeing-of-the-workforce-wow-study

Hassard, J., Jain, A. and Leka, S. (in press) *International comparison of occupational health services and systems: A comparative case study review*. London: Department of Work and Pensions.

Hobfoll, S. E., Johnson, R. J., Ennis, N. and Jackson, A. P. (2003). Resource loss, resource gain, and emotional outcomes among inner city women. *Journal of Personality and Social Psychology*, 84(3), pp. 632–643.

Hoel, H., Sparks, K. and Cooper, C. L. (2001) *The cost of violence/stress at work and the benefits of a violence/stress-free working environment*. Geneva: International Labour Organization.

HSE (2019) *Work-related Stress, Anxiety or Depression Statistics in Great Britain, 2019*. Retrieved December 4, 2020. Available at: https://www.hse.gov.uk/statistics/causdis/stress.pdf

HSE (2020) Work-related stress and how to tackle it. Retrieved December 4, 2020. www.hse.gov.uk/stress/what-to-do.htm

Jo, C. (2014) 'Cost-of-illness studies: Concepts, scopes, and methods', *Clinical and Molecular Hepatology*, 20(4), pp. 327–337.

Koopmanschap, M. A. (1998) 'Cost-of-illness studies', *Pharmacoeconomics*, 23(3), pp. 225–238.

Larg, A. and Moss, J. R. (2011) 'Cost-of-illness studies', *Pharmacoeconomics*, 29(8), pp. 653–671.

Leigh, J. P. (2006) 'Expanding research on the economics of occupational health', *Scandinavian Journal of Work, Environmental and Health*, 32(1), pp. 1–4. doi: 10.5271/sjweh.969

Leka, S. and Jain, A. (2010) *Health impact of pyschosocial hazards*. Geneva: World Health Organisation.

Luppa, M., Heinrich, S., Angermeyer, M. C., König, H. and Riedel-Heller, S. G. (2007) 'Cost-of-illness studies of depression: A systematic review', *Journal of Affective Disorders*, 98(2), pp. 29–43.

Di Martino, V. and Pujol, J. (2000) *The SafeWork training package on drugs and alcohol, violence, stress, tobacco and HIV/AIDS*. Geneva: International Labour Organization.

Mauskopf, J. (1998) 'Prevalence-based economic evaluation', *Value in Health*, 1(4), pp. 251–259. doi: 10.1046/j.1524-4733.1998.140251.x

McDaid, D., Knappe, M. and Medieros, H. (2008) *Employment and mental health: Assessing the economic impact*. London: PSSRU.

McDaid, D. and Park, A.-L. (2014) 'Investing in wellbeing in the workplace', in McDaid, D. and Cooper, C. L. (eds) *The Economics of Wellbeing*. London: John Wiley & Sons, pp. 217–237. doi: 10.1002/9781118539415.wbwell1109

McTernan, W. P., Dollard, M. F., and LaMontagne, A. D. (2013) 'Depression in the workplace: An economic cost analysis of depression-related productivity loss attributable to job strain and bullying', *Work & Stress*, 27(4), pp. 321–333. doi: 10.1080/02678373.2013.846948

Mental Health Commission of Canada (2013) *The National Standard of Canada for Psychological Health and Safety in the Workplace*. Retrieved December 4, 2020. Available at: https://www.mentalhealthcommission.ca/English/what-we-do/workplace/national-standard

Mogyorosy, Z. and Smith, P. (2005) *The main methodological issues in costing health care services: A literature review (No. 007)*. York: Centre for Health Economics, University of York.

Molinier, L., Bauvin, E., Combescure, C., Castelli, C., Rebillard, X., Soulie, M., Daures, J-P. and Grosclaude, P. (2008) 'Methodological considerations in cost of prostate cancer studies: A systematic review', *Value in Health*, 11(5), pp. 878–885.

Morgenstern, H., Kleinbaum, D. G. and Kupper, L. L. (1980) 'Department of Epidemiology and Public Health, School of Medicine, Yale University, New Haven, CT', *International Journal of Epidemiology*, 9(1), pp. 97–104.

Navarro, A., Salas-Nicás, S., Llorens, C., Moncada, S., Molinero-Ruíz, E. and Moriña, D. (2019) 'Sickness presenteeism: Are we sure about what we are studying? A research based on a literature review and an empirical illustration', *American Journal of Industrial Medicine*, 62(7), pp. 580–589.

NICE (2019) *NICEimpact mental health*. Retrieved December 4, 2020. Available at: https://www.nice.org.uk/Media/Default/About/what-we-do/Into-practice/measuring-uptake/NICEimpact-mental-health.pdf

Nielsen, K. and Cleal, B. (2010) 'Predicting flow at work: Investigating the activities and job characteristics that predict flow states at work', *Journal of Occupational Health Psychology*, 15(2), p. 180.

OECD (2012) *Sick on the job?: Myths and realities about mental health and work*. Paris: OECD Publishing. doi: https://doi.org/10.1787/9789264124523-en

ONS (2017) *Number of Days Lost through Sickness Absence by Reason, 2009 to 2016*. London: Office for National Statistics. Retrieved December 4, 2020. Available at: https://www.ons.gov.uk/employmentandlabourmarket/peopleinwork/labourproductivity/adhocs/007211numberofdayslostthroughsicknessabsencebyreason2009to2016uk

ONS (2019) *Sickness Absence in the UK Labour Market: 2018*. London: Office for National Statistics. Retrieved December 4, 2020. Available at: https://www.ons.gov.uk/employmentandlabourmarket/peopleinwork/labourproductivity/articles/sicknessabsenceinthelabourmarket/2018

Ospina, M. B., Dennett, L., Waye, A., Jacobs, P. and Thompson, A. H. (2015) 'A systematic review of measurement properties of instruments assessing presenteeism', *American Journal of Management and Care*, 21(2), pp. e171–185.

Parsonage, M. and Saini, G. (2017) *Mental health at work: The business case ten years on*. London: Centre for Mental Health.

Pike, J. and Grosse, S. D. (2018) 'Friction cost estimates of productivity costs in cost-of-illness studies in comparison with human capital estimates: A review', *Applied Health Economics and Health Policy*, 16(6), pp. 765–778.

RAND Europe (2015) *Health, wellbeing and productivity in the workplace*. Cambridge: RAND Corporation.

Safework Australia (2019) *Work-related psychological health and safety: A systematic approach to meeting your duties. National guidance material.* Safe Work Australia.

Scheil-Adlung, X. and Sandner, L. (2010) *The case for paid sick leave: World health report.* Geneva: World Health Organization.

Semmer, N. (2003) 'Individual differences, work stress and health', in Schabracq, M., Winnubst, J., and Cooper, C. (eds) *Handbook of Work and Health Psychology.* New York: John Wiley & Sons, pp. 83–120.

Stansfeld, S. and Candy, B. (2006) 'Psychosocial work environment and mental health – a meta-analytic review', *Scandinavian Journal of Work, Environment & Health*, 32(6), pp. 443–462.

Sultan-Taïeb, H., Chastang, J., Mansouri, M. and Niedhammer, I. (2013) 'The annual costs of cardiovascular diseases and mental disorders attributable to job strain in France', *BMC Public Health*, 13, p. 748. doi: 10.1186/1471-2458-13-748

Sutherland, V. J. and Cooper, C. L. (1996) 'Stress in the offshore oil and gas exploration and production industries: An organizational approach to stress control', *Stress Medicine*, 12(1), pp. 27–34.

Tarricone, R. (2006) 'Cost-of-illness analysis: What room in health economics?', *Health Policy*, 77, pp. 61–63. doi: 10.1016/j.health pol.2005.07.016

Verkuil, B., Atasay, S. and Molendijk, M. L. (2015) 'Workplace bullying and mental health: A meta-analysis on cross-sectional and longitudinal data', *Plos ONE*, 10(8), pp. 1–16.

WHO (2009) *WHO Guide to Identifying the Economic Consequences of Disease and Injury.* Geneva: World Health Organisation. Retrieved December 4, 2020. Available at: http://www.who.int/choice/publications/d_economic_impact_guide.pdf

Wordsworth, S., Ludbrook, A., Caskey, F. and Macleod, A. (2005) 'Collecting unit cost data in multicentre studies', *The European Journal of Health Economics*, 6(1), pp. 38–44.

3

Personality, Wellbeing and Wellbeing Interventions

Jack Evans, Helen Brewis and Ivan Robertson

INTRODUCTION

Personality is an area of human psychology that has received a considerable amount of attention from scholars. It is also an area that has attracted the interest of practitioners. Scholars have investigated the structure and dynamics of personality and relationships between personality and various other factors, including performance at work, health behaviour and psychological wellbeing. Practitioners have taken and used the results of personality research to develop processes for selection and assessment, behaviour change and other aspects of organizational behaviour.

Many models of the structure of personality have been developed but for the last two decades or so researchers and practitioners have coalesced around the five-factor model (FFM) of personality (Costa & McCrae, 1992). This is the overarching model that will be used in this chapter whenever possible, to explore relationships between personality, wellbeing and wellbeing interventions.

As far as wellbeing is concerned, the focus for this chapter is on the mental health aspects of individual wellbeing, rather than physical health. In particular, the research concerning FFM personality factors, subjective/emotional wellbeing and work-related wellbeing interventions will be explored. There is good reason for researchers and practitioners to take an interest in work-related mental health. Levels of sickness absence due to mental health are significant and mental health-related issues are linked to long-term sickness absence (Åhlin et al., 2018; Strømholm et al., 2015), compromised work performance and are a source of concern for employers and individual employees (Ford et al., 2011; Taris & Schreurs, 2009). Many widely accepted models of the drivers of wellbeing at work concentrate on workplace factors that are related to mental health and psychological wellbeing. The most widely used model of the workplace drivers of mental health has identified key workplace factors: job demands; control; and resources and support (Bakker et al., 2007). Research has also focused on the role of non-work factors, including home life and personal circumstances, commuting, etc. and their interaction with work-related wellbeing (e.g. French et al., 2018). There is no doubt that these situational factors (both work and non-work) are important in determining levels of wellbeing and it is not uncommon for practitioners and researchers alike to limit their interest to these situational factors. In some ways then, this chapter runs counter to conventional views of the drivers of wellbeing by focusing on the role of within-person factors, rather than the situation. As (Bandura, 1986) pointed out with his theory of reciprocal determinism, rather than the situation being a one-way determinant of behaviour there is an *interaction* between the situation, the person and his or her behaviour. In other words, situations and person-factors (such as personality) influence each other and behaviour, which in turn influences the situation and the individual (Figure 3.1).

This approach is more complex but also a more realistic representation of reality. Of course, the situations that we find ourselves in influence how we behave but the kind of person we are makes a difference too – and in turn how we behave may influence the situation. With this more complex model in mind, it makes sense to ask about the role that underlying personality factors might play in determining mental health outcomes and also our view of the situations that we experience.

SITUATIONAL FACTORS, PERSONAL FACTORS AND WELLBEING

The FFM model of personality has identified five main domains of personality: Openness; Conscientiousness; Extraversion; Agreeableness; and Neuroticism (OCEAN). Research has confirmed that the domains provide a reasonably parsimonious and comprehensive representation of the structure of personality (McCrae & Costa, 1987). The domains cover the following aspects of personality: openness (intellectually curious, open to new activities, prefer variety and novelty, fantasy and imagination); conscientiousness (dependable, prudent, methodical, achievement striving); extraversion (gregarious, active, assertive, positive emotions); agreeableness (sympathetic to others, cooperative, trusting); and neuroticism (emotionally unstable, anxious, irritable, depressed).

To provide a finer-grained level of measurement each domain is made up of six facets; for example, the extraversion facets are warmth, gregariousness, assertiveness, activity, excitement-seeking and positive

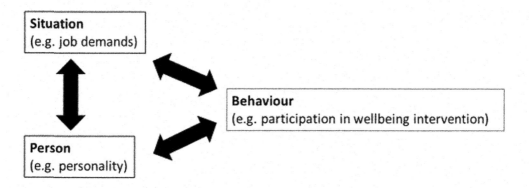

Figure 3.1   Person, situation, behaviour

emotions. At face value, it seems likely that the domains of personality may have links with people's overall levels of subjective wellbeing and mental health. For example, the extraversion facet of positive emotions simply means that individuals are more or less likely to experience positive emotions, depending on their position on this facet. Similarly, the neuroticism facet of depression is associated with how often someone feels unhappy or 'blue'.

As noted above, for most scholars and practitioners the primary influences on workplace wellbeing are seen as the job-related experiences to which individuals are exposed. There is a significant amount of research indicating that job demands are important and, as many studies have shown, excessive demands over a consistent period can lead to psychological health damage (Dalgard et al., 2009; Wood et al., 2011; Kinman et al., 2017). Although excessive job demands are bad, low levels of job demand are also unhealthy. In fact, the healthiest jobs are those where job demands are high, but control, resources and support are also high (Bakker et al., 2003; Podsakoff et al., 2007). In jobs like this the high levels of control, resources and support mitigate the negative impact of high demand, and the demands provide individuals with an opportunity to experience the satisfaction and reward of rising to a challenge and provide a sense of meaning and achievement in work.

Although demands may seem to be an objective feature of any job, a moment's reflection will reveal that different people report different levels of demand, even from exactly the same job; furthermore, there is evidence that these differences in the perception of demand are associated with differences in personality (e.g. Bakker et al., 2003). There is also evidence that personality factors are linked to the extent to which people seek out challenging demands in their jobs; for example, Roczniewska and Bakker (2016) found that extraversion was positively related to seeking structural and social job resources and to seeking challenging job demands. Personality factors have also been linked with the extent to which workers may attempt to craft their job (Plomp et al., 2016).

The picture emerging, then, suggests that although situational factors, such as job demands or control, are linked to mental health, personality may be associated with individuals' experiences of both job factors (e.g. the level of job demand or control) and their levels of psychological wellbeing.

Psychological Wellbeing

So far in this chapter different terms such as mental health, subjective wellbeing or emotional wellbeing have been used more or less interchangeably. Although there are definitions available for these terms it is the case that the boundaries between them and their specific meanings are not always clear. From now on the term psychological wellbeing (PWB) will be used. The following explanation is an attempt to be as clear as possible about what this term covers.

At the most basic level, PWB is quite similar to other terms referring to positive mental states, such as happiness or satisfaction, and in many ways it is not necessary, or helpful, to worry about fine distinctions between such terms. If I say that I'm happy, or very satisfied with my life, you can be pretty sure that my psychological wellbeing is quite high! Although other constructs, such as job satisfaction or motivation, are certainly relevant to overall PWB they are not the same. For example, someone may be satisfied with their specific job but be troubled by relationships with some colleagues, or the quality of management and supervision that they receive, and these troubling factors could influence PWB.

Actually, PWB has two important aspects. The first of those is perhaps the most obvious. It refers to the extent to which people experience positive emotions and feelings of happiness. Sometimes this aspect of PWB is referred to as subjective wellbeing. Subjective wellbeing is a necessary part of overall PWB but on its own it is not enough. Purpose and meaning are also important elements of overall PWB. So the two important ingredients in PWB are the subjective happy feelings brought on by something we enjoy AND the feeling that what we are doing with our lives has some meaning and purpose. 'Hedonic' wellbeing refers to the subjective feelings of happiness and 'Eudaimonic' wellbeing is used to refer to the purposeful aspect of PWB (Ryan & Deci, 2001). Both hedonic and eudaimonic components are essential for overall PWB to be high. Carol Ryff (Keyes & Ryff, 1995) has developed a model that breaks down eudaimonic wellbeing into six key parts: self-acceptance; positive relations with others; autonomy; environmental mastery; purpose in life; and personal growth.

With the above in mind, the use of the term psychological wellbeing in this chapter is a broad term and includes aspects of mental health, subjective wellbeing and emotional wellbeing and meaning and purpose.

PERSONALITY AND PSYCHOLOGICAL WELLBEING

There is a very large body of research examining relationships between personality and health outcomes; Strickhouser et al. (2017) identified over 850 empirical studies. Many of these studies have set out to explore the relationship between personality and psychological wellbeing and, in general, such research has indicated that there are reasonably strong associations between personality and psychological wellbeing. As noted above there are many different terms used for wellbeing indicators and different research studies have focused on various specific indicators. Given the large number of studies available it has been possible for researchers to cumulate the results of individual studies and carry out large-scale meta-analyses to arrive at results based on the integration of earlier individual studies.

Steel et al. (2008) conducted a meta-analysis to explore relationships between personality (including FFM measures) and indicators of subjective wellbeing (SWB). They identified six different categories of SWB: happiness; life satisfaction; positive affect; negative affect; overall affect; and quality of life. Their results showed that neuroticism, extraversion, agreeableness and conscientiousness were all significantly related to all SWB categories. Openness to experience was significantly related to happiness, positive affect and quality of life, but it was not significantly related to life satisfaction, negative affect and overall affect. They note that neuroticism showed the strongest relationship with SWB, particularly for negative affect ($\rho = 0.64$) but relationships for aspects of SWB with extraversion (ρ for positive affect = 0.54) and conscientiousness (ρ for quality of life = 0.51) were also strong.

Strickhouser et al. (2017) carried a meta-synthesis (i.e. a second-order meta-analysis combining the results of 30 existing meta-analyses). They focused their attention on the relationships between FFM personality variables and health outcomes: mental health; physical health; and health behaviour. Taken overall, their results revealed that personality health relationships were strongest for mental health ($\rho = 0.43$), intermediate for health behaviour ($\rho = 0.18$) and relatively weak for physical health outcomes ($\rho = 0.06$). As Strickhouser et al. (2017) note, although the relationship with physical health is relatively weak, the result for this outcome should not be regarded as trivial, since other factors that are considered important in predicting health outcomes (e.g. socio-economic status or IQ) show relationships that are of similar magnitude or smaller.

The strong relationship for mental health supports the earlier findings from Steel et al. (2008) that personality has important and substantial links with mental health. As with the earlier work of Steel et al. (2008), the results from the Strickhouser et al. (2017) study showed neuroticism as the strongest predictor of mental health outcomes. It is, however, important to note that although in their metasynthesis Strickhouser et al. (2017) included a very wide range of indicators in their mental health category (e.g. various clinical disorders, interpersonal deviance, schizophrenia and psychopathy), they were able to include only two studies that used SWB ($\rho = 0.36, 0.17$) as the mental health outcome, one with life satisfaction ($\rho = 0.28$) and one with resilience ($\rho = 0.40$).

It is clear from the large body of research looking at personality and aspects of psychological wellbeing that personality and psychological wellbeing are related but, of course, the existence of correlations between personality and psychological wellbeing, even when based on large-scale meta-analytic research, does not support conclusions about the causal role of personality. In practice, there is debate about the direction of the relationship between personality and wellbeing and the mechanisms that explain the relationships. As far as the direction of the relationship is concerned, there are three main possibilities: personality influences wellbeing; wellbeing influences personality; or personality and wellbeing influence each other reciprocally. The most likely possibility is that these factors influence each other reciprocally (Magee & Biesanz, 2019), although personality has more impact on wellbeing than vice versa (Fetvadjiev & He, 2019).

As far as the mechanism for explaining the correlations between personality and wellbeing is concerned, it could be that underlying differences in personality have a direct influence on psychological wellbeing. For example, one facet of extraversion concerns a person's tendency to experience positive emotions. This stable predisposition could have a direct impact on levels of psychological wellbeing. This is possible but there are also several other potential explanations for the association between personality and psychological wellbeing.

One explanation for the correlations between personality and psychological wellbeing is that there is not really any need to propose a causal chain because the constructs for both factors and the questionnaire items used to measure them are overlapping.

Another possible explanation for the personality–wellbeing relationship is that personality characteristics influence health behaviour, which, in turn, influences wellbeing. The role of personality in health-related behaviour will be discussed more fully in a later section.

WELLBEING INTERVENTIONS

Wellbeing interventions may be conveniently classified into three different levels: primary, secondary and tertiary. Primary-level interventions involve directly addressing the source factor (e.g. the design and core tasks of a job) that is affecting PWB. At the other end of the scale tertiary interventions do not involve any attempt to change things but attempt to provide support to a worker who is experiencing difficulties. The use of Employee Assistance Programmes (EAPs) to provide counselling for employees is an example of a tertiary intervention. At all of these levels a range of different interventions have been used, although primary-level interventions are much less common than secondary or tertiary ones.

At the tertiary level, the most common interventions appear to be EAPs and Mental Health First Aid (MHFA). EAPs provide a service for employees to access, usually by telephone, when they are experiencing difficulties. As with any tertiary intervention, there is little opportunity for EAPs to address any underlying issues that may be creating problems for employees, especially if these require primary-level interventions. EAPs do, nevertheless, provide useful support for employees. For example, in the UK it may take several months before employees can gain access to mental health support through the National Health Service (NHS). Access to an EAP is generally much quicker and recovery rates for EAPs compare well with those of the NHS (Mellor-Clark et al., 2013).

MHFA was originally developed in Australia (Kitchener & Jorm, 2002). The MHFA training (a standardized curriculum, usually over two days) provides participants with training in identifying the signs and symptoms of a range of mental health issues. It also prepares them to provide assistance on an initial response basis and guide people towards professional help. Although not originally developed as a workplace intervention MHFA has become increasingly popular with employers. After initial enthusiasm for the approach and recommendations that it should be used from the Department of Health in 2012 a later evaluation by the UK Health and Safety Executive (HSE, Bell et al., 2018) expressed much more caution about its value. In brief, the HSE review of evidence on the effectiveness of MHFA concluded that, although they found consistent evidence that MHFA training raises employees' awareness of mental health conditions, there was limited evidence that MHFA training leads to sustained improvement in the ability of those trained to help colleagues experiencing mental ill-health. They also found no evidence that the introduction of MHFA training has led to sustained mental health and wellbeing benefits for those supported and as such there is no evidence for MHFA improving the organizational management of mental health in workplaces.

Both EAPs and MHFA focus on employees when they are still in the workplace, at least at the initial point of contact. There are also interventions that are designed to enable employees to return to work after they have taken sick leave for mental health reasons. In general evidence for the effectiveness of these schemes in speeding up the return process once an individual has left work is very limited (e.g. de Vente et al., 2008). It is more effective to identify individuals who are at risk of periods of sickness absence before they leave work and to provide support (e.g. Taimela et al., 2008).

At the secondary level, various types of training for individuals or managers have been developed and implemented in many organizations. Training includes stress management training for individuals and/or mangers, resilience training and mindfulness training. In general, these training interventions have been shown to have a positive impact. For example, a systematic review of resilience training in the workplace (Robertson et al., 2015) revealed a large effect on mental health indicators: mindfulness training improved stress levels, psychological wellbeing and sleep (Bartlett et al., 2019) and stress management training produced overall reductions in psychological strain and emotional exhaustion (Lloyd et al., 2017).

Interventions at the primary level, designed to identify and improve underlying causes of psychological wellbeing problems in the workplace, are much less common than interventions at tertiary or secondary levels. For example, in a meta-analysis of 36 studies Richardson and Rothstein (2008) found only eight had used primary intervention strategies. Demand, control, resources and support are known sources of pressure that can affect psychological wellbeing (e.g. Kinman et al., 2017). Measuring these sources of pressure and redesigning jobs so that the pressures are better balanced can be an effective way of safeguarding or improving psychological wellbeing (e.g. Bond and Bunce, 2001), but because it is a primary-level intervention this type of approach is likely to be time-consuming and disruptive. An alternative to planned job redesign is job crafting. Wrzesniewski and Dutton (2001) describe job crafting as 'what workers do to redefine and reimagine their job to make it more personally meaningful to them'. Several studies have shown that when workers are allowed or encouraged to craft their jobs there are consequential benefits to psychological wellbeing (e.g. Tims et al., 2013; Van Wingerden et al., 2017). Although job crafting can be useful there is also evidence to suggest that its value may be related to individual differences in the approach that managers take and the underlying personality of the worker (Kim & Beehr, 2018; Plomp et al., 2016). These issues will be explored more fully in a later section of this chapter.

Tertiary-level interventions designed to improve physical health also appear to have a beneficial impact on psychological wellbeing. Large-scale meta-analyses have shown that exercise programmes produce significant improvements in both physical and mental health (Emerson et al., 2017; Fibbins et al., 2018). Withdrawal from exercise programmes has a negative impact (Weinstein et al., 2017). There is also some indication that personality differences are related to initial levels of exercise frequency (Kroencke et al., 2019) and this will also be explored further below.

PERSONALITY AND TAKE-UP AND IMPACT OF INTERVENTIONS

Although, as shown above, there is good evidence that various types of intervention can improve psychological wellbeing this can only happen in the workplace if employees engage positively with the intervention. Research into the factors that moderate the take-up and impact of workplace wellbeing interventions is in its infancy. Direct evidence is relatively sparse but evidence from related topics can provide some indication of the key factors that are important. The relevant evidence breaks down into two main areas: health-related behaviour and engagement with wellbeing interventions.

Health-Related Behaviour

As shown earlier in this chapter, there is plentiful evidence of the relationship between personality and wellbeing. There is also evidence that personality is linked to health-related behaviour. Individuals with type-D personality traits (negative affectivity and social inhibition) reported performing significantly fewer health-related behaviours including smoking, poor diet and lack of physical activity than non-type-D individuals. They also report lower levels of social support than non-type-D individuals (Gilmour & Williams, 2012). Personality has also been linked with safety behaviour and speed limit compliance (Griffin & O'Cass, 2010; Ucho & Gbande, 2012). Axelsson et al. (2013, 2014) looked at adherence to medication for people with chronic health conditions. Using an FFM model for personality, Cohen et al. (2004) found that extraversion was a significant negative predictor of compliance with anti depressant medication. This was largely explained by the relation between compliance and the activity facet within extraversion. They also found a negative relation between the feelings facet and compliance, while the modesty facet was a significant positive predictor of compliance with antidepressant medication. Neither severity of depression nor side effects predicted compliance.

At this stage of research into personality and health behaviour, it is difficult to be definitive about which traits are most important, as research has indicated a role for all of the FFM factors. The balance of recent evidence suggests that low extraversion, low conscientiousness and high neuroticism have the strongest links with poorer health-related behaviour but some earlier research has also indicated the importance of agreeableness (Booth-Kewley & Vickers, 1994) and openness to experience (Jerram & Coleman, 1999). Although some studies have indicated the importance of type-D personality as a specific predictor of health-related behaviour, there is evidence that the FFM model provides better prediction of health-related behaviour from personality (Horwood & Anglim, 2017). Interestingly, as well as evidence suggesting that personality influences health-related behaviour, there is also evidence of a reciprocal relationship. In a longitudinal study, Allen et al. (2015) found that physical activity and alcohol intake in particular were associated with mean-level changes in personality scores for several FFM factors.

Engagement with Wellbeing Interventions

There is a significant amount of research focused on the factors that influence engagement with wellbeing interventions. Much of this research has examined online interventions and factors that have been examined include: amount of human contact in delivery (Crutzen et al., 2015); the use of prompts and reminders (Cremers et al., 2014; Göritz & Crutzen, 2012); visual complexity (Crutzen et al., 2012b); peer and counsellor support (Brouwer et al., 2011); and tailored communications and degree of user control (Crutzen et al., 2012a). So far this stream of research does not appear to have explored the extent to which individual differences in personality may interact with the other factors in determining engagement and effectiveness of the interventions. It seems highly likely that some of these factors may have a different impact, depending on underlying personality. For example, peer and counsellor support has been shown to be helpful (Brouwer et al., 2011) and its effectiveness may well be moderated by levels of sociability and anxiety (facets of extraversion and neuroticism).

The available evidence on the role of personality in wellbeing interventions is extremely limited. As noted above there is some evidence that initial levels of exercise frequency are related to personality differences (Kroencke et al., 2019), with extraversion and conscientiousness positively related to initial exercise frequency and neuroticism negatively related. As far as job design and job crafting is concerned there is some limited evidence of the role played by personality. Bakker et al. (2010) found that neuroticism predicted health impairment directly but also

indirectly through its effect on job demands, while extroversion predicted organizational commitment, both directly and indirectly through its effect on job resources. These results suggest that personality plays a role in people's reported levels of job demands and may therefore become important in any job redesign intervention. This possibility is supported by findings that individual differences in personality are associated with job crafting behaviour, with proactive employees benefitting more from job crafting (Plomp et al., 2016; Kim and Beehr, 2018). Although proactive personality is conceptually distinct from the FFM model (Bateman and Crant, 1993; Crant, 1995; Major et al., 2006), it shows strongest relationships with openness and conscientiousness (Travis & Freeman, 2017).

PRACTITIONER PERSPECTIVE

Like other areas of applied psychology, occupational health psychology works with a scientist-practitioner model (Horn et al., 2007), in which the practitioner draws on the scientific research base and uses the available evidence to help design effective interventions. Inevitably, with this approach there are significant gaps in the available research evidence and practitioners deliver interventions that represent their best attempt to interpret available research and use it as best they can to fashion interventions. This short section of the chapter focuses on the implications of the research reviewed from a practitioner perspective and tries to provide some signposts for how practice might eventually benefit from the available research.

Embedding a culture of wellbeing within organizations is an underresearched topic but it is possible that, like embedding a safety culture (Aburumman et al., 2019), it will require positive activity from leaders, managers and employees, supported by organizational processes, including effective monitoring of pressures and levels of wellbeing and mental health. Research reviewed above makes it clear that a unitary approach to work wellbeing interventions is unlikely to yield results – whether the intervention is directed at leadership and management, employees or organizational processes. To have a significant impact on wellbeing and the organizational benefits this can bring, any approach must be tailored to the needs of the organization and its employees. The role that personality might play in this area is a neglected topic and as the research agenda develops there is potential for wellbeing interventions to be tailored more effectively using the new knowledge generated by research into personality and wellbeing.

Common wellbeing interventions such as resilience training (Robertson et al., 2015) or EAPs (Mellor-Clark et al., 2013) are often made available to employees and take-up is then at the discretion of the employees themselves. As research reviewed above illustrates, the take-up of such interventions may be linked to the individual personality of employees.

A potentially underutilized tool, therefore, from a practitioner perspective, is the opportunity (a) for organizations to personalize their approach to wellbeing support, by providing support and offerings that appeal to differences in personality and health identities and (b) to help individuals understand how their personality impacts on their approach to looking after their own wellbeing at work.

The authors have access to personality data gathered over 10 years from 215,000 employees by Robertson Cooper Ltd. The data have already been used to produce various research publications (e.g. Robertson et al., 2012, 2018). These data reveal that there are key differences across the three personality factors that are of demonstrable importance for wellbeing issues: neuroticism, extraversion and conscientiousness. As an illustration of how better understanding of personality may help organizations to tailor interventions more effectively it is instructive to note that within the large sample of employees

mentioned above, scores on neuroticism and extraversion differ for males and females, but levels of conscientiousness do not differ significantly. Research has already established that relationships between key sources of pressure differ in male- or female-dominated work environments (Fila et al., 2017) but the role that personality may play in moderating or mediating gender-related relationships is underexplored and there may be significant benefit to be gained from adapting and personalizing wellbeing interventions based on employee demographic and personal factors.

Leaders and Managers

Much of the focus of this chapter has been on how personality affects an individual's wellbeing – whether directly through their own personality make-up or indirectly via the likelihood that they will undertake healthy behaviours. An alternative angle to consider is how personality affects the wellbeing of other people. Of particular relevance here is the role that manager and leader personality may play in affecting the wellbeing of their team members. Research shows that leaders and managers have an impact on the wellbeing of their teams, and that this impact is influenced by leader and manager personality (Robertson et al., 2014; I. T. Robertson & Flint-Taylor, 2009). For example, employees whose manager is high on the achievement-striving facet of conscientiousness show poorer work–life balance and assertiveness (a facet within extraversion) (Robertson et al., 2014). Perhaps these managers, keen to progress in their organization and with a particularly forceful view, create undue pressure on their team.

A specific illustration of how existing research and personality theory may be used to understand the impact of leaders on their workgroups is provided by Robertson Cooper's Leadership Impact psychometric tool (Robertson Cooper Ltd, 2020). The rule base for the tool is derived from personality research and theory and indicates the extent to which the underlying personality of leaders and managers predisposes them to behave in a challenge-led (likely to lead to high stress and burn-out) or support-led (likely to lead to lack of motivation) fashion. Using challenge or support as the overarching framework, it further classifies leader behaviour into one of four specific approaches: challenge-pace; challenge-results; support-confidence; and support-cooperation. A leader is assigned a Primary and a Secondary style, which could be Balanced (made up of one challenge-led and one support-led style), Burn-out Risk (both challenge-led styles) or Rust-out Risk (both support-led styles).

Data from 64,000 leaders and managers gathered by Robertson Cooper show that 77% of them have a balanced style, 11% have a burn-out risk and 12% rust-out risk. The most common primary style is Support-Cooperation and the most common combination of primary and secondary styles is Support-Cooperation with Challenge-Pace (19% show this combination). As with the raw personality data, differences emerge between groups – women are more likely than males to be balanced (potentially explaining a long-held notion that they are 'better' managers than their male counterparts). The proportion who are balanced is fairly constant across age groups (ranging from 75–78%); however, younger managers are almost three times more likely to have burn-out risk than older counterparts. A slightly higher proportion of leaders and managers in the public sector have a balanced style (78% vs 75%), but the pattern amongst unbalanced leaders and managers is not consistent – burn-out risk is more common amongst private sector leaders (15%) than public sector leaders (10%).

So, organizations putting in place wellbeing interventions that ultimately aim to improve the wellbeing of their workforce may be missing an opportunity, if they do not take personality into account. To some degree, they may risk spending their wellbeing budget on interventions and programmes which will have low take-up, and they may also risk having an organizational culture – set by leaders and managers – which undermines the agenda, potentially influencing the likelihood of burn-out or rust-out for employees. The extent to which the management and leadership population of an organization create a balance, burn-out risk or rust-out risk will depend, to some degree, on the personality make-up of the members of that group. Understanding the underlying personality of managers and leaders provides an opportunity to deliver developmental feedback to help ensure that, as far as possible, they exert a positive influence on the wellbeing of their workgroups.

Practitioner Takeaways

1 Individuals and managers ought to be aware of their personality and what this means for the wellbeing of themselves and of others. Consideration of personality and health identity should be integrated into wellbeing training programmes to allow for a personalized experience.
2 Be aware of the likely success of self-directed wellbeing interventions or programmes, considering the role that personality plays in determining take-up (and/or success).
3 Consider your organization's culture as a sum of the personality of your leaders and managers, and the extent to which they balance challenge and support for their teams.

CONCLUSION

Workplace levels of psychological wellbeing are influenced by a range of exogenous factors, such as the pressures that people work under (e.g. job demands, working conditions, autonomy and control) and the behaviour of managers and leaders. These factors are clearly important but there is also evidence that endogenous, psychological factors, such as underlying personality, also play a role in employees' experiences of psychological wellbeing. Meta-analytic research has established relationships between personality factors (using the FFM), levels of psychological wellbeing and health-related behaviour. A range of different interventions have been used, with varying levels of success, in attempts to improve the psychological wellbeing of employees. Given the links between personality and specific aspects of health-related behaviour it seems likely that personality may help to determine both the take-up and impact of wellbeing interventions. There is very limited research evidence exploring the role of personality in the impact and take-up of interventions, but it is clear that, from both a research perspective and practitioner perspective, the potential role of personality needs to be given more consideration.

REFERENCES

Aburumman, M., Newnam, S., and Fildes, B. (2019). Evaluating the effectiveness of workplace interventions in improving safety culture: A systematic review. *Safety Science*, *115*, 376–392. https://doi.org/10.1016/j.ssci.2019.02.027

Åhlin, J. K., Rajaleid, K., Jansson-Fröjmark, M., Westerlund, H., and Magnusson Hanson, L. L. (2018). Job demands, control and social support as predictors of trajectories of depressive symptoms. *Journal of Affective Disorders*, *235*(April), 535–543. https://doi.org/10.1016/j.jad.2018.04.067

Allen, M. S., Vella, S. A., and Laborde, S. (2015). Health-related behaviour and personality trait development in adulthood. *Journal of Research in Personality*, *59*, 104–110. https://doi.org/10.1016/j.jrp.2015.10.005

Axelsson, M., Brink, E., and Lötvall, J. (2014). A personality and gender perspective on adherence and health-related quality of life in people with asthma and/or allergic rhinitis. *Journal of the American Association of Nurse Practitioners*, *26*, 32–39. https://doi.org/10.1002/2327-6924.12069

Axelsson, M., Cliffordson, C., Lundbäck, B., and Lötvall, J. (2013). The function of

medication beliefs as mediators between personality traits and adherence behavior in people with asthma. *Patient Preference and Adherence*, *7*, 1101–1109. https://doi.org/10.2147/PPA.S49725

Bakker, A. B., Boyd, C. M., Dollard, M., Gillespie, N., Winefield, A. H., and Stough, C. (2010). The role of personality in the job demands-resources model: A study of Australian academic staff. *Career Development International*, *15*, 622–636. https://doi.org/10.1108/13620431011094050

Bakker, A. B., Hakanen, J. J., Demerouti, E., and Xanthopoulou, D. (2007). Job resources boost work engagement, particularly when job demands are high. *Journal of Educational Psychology*, *99*, 274–284. https://doi.org/10.1037/0022-0663.99.2.274

Bakker, A., Demerouti, E., and Schaufeli, W. (2003). Dual processes at work in a call centre: An application of the job demands – resources model. *European Journal of Work and Organizational Psychology*, *12*, 393–417. https://doi.org/10.1080/13594320344000165

Bandura, A. (1986). Social Foundations of Thought and Action: A Social Cognitive Theory. Englewood Cliffs, NJ: Prentice Hall.

Bartlett, L., Martin, A., Neil, A. L., Memish, K., Otahal, P., Kilpatrick, M., and Sanderson, K. (2019). Supplemental material for a systematic review and meta-analysis of workplace mindfulness training randomized controlled trials. *Journal of Occupational Health Psychology*, *24*, 108–126. https://doi.org/10.1037/ocp0000146.supp

Bateman, T. S. and Crant, J. M. (1993). The proactive component of organizational behavior: A measure and correlates. *Journal of Organizational Behavior*, *14*, 103–118. https://doi.org/10.1002/job.4030140202

Bell, N., Evans, G., Beswick, A., and Moore, A. (2018). *Summary of the evidence on the effectiveness of Mental Health First Aid (MHFA) training in the workplace Prepared by the Health and Safety Executive RR1135*.

Bond, F. W. and Bunce, D. (2001). Job control mediates change in a work reorganization intervention for stress reduction. *Journal of Occupational Health Psychology*, *6*, 290–302. https://doi.org/10.1037/1076-8998.6.4.290

Booth-Kewley, S. and Vickers, R. R. (1994). Associations between major domains of personality and health behavior. *Journal of Personality*, *62*, 281–298. https://doi.org/10.1111/j.1467-6494.1994.tb00298.x

Brouwer, W., Kroeze, W., Crutzen, R., De Nooijer, J., De Vries, N. K., Brug, J., and Oenema, A. (2011). Which intervention characteristics are related to more exposure to internet-delivered healthy lifestyle promotion interventions? A systematic review. *Journal of Medical Internet Research*, *13*. https://doi.org/10.2196/jmir.1639

Cohen, N. L., Ross, E. C., Bagby, R. M., Farvolden, P., and Kennedy, S. H. (2004). The 5-factor model of personality and antidepressant medication compliance. *Canadian Journal of Psychiatry*, *49*, 106–113. https://doi.org/10.1177/070674370404900205

Costa, P. T. and McCrae, R. R. (1992). Revised NEO personality inventory (NEO-PI-R) and NEO five-factor inventory (NEO-FFI). In *Odessa FL Psychological Assessment Resources*.

Crant, J. M. (1995). The proactive personality scale and objective job performance among real estate agents. *Journal of Applied Psychology*, *80*, 532–537. https://doi.org/10.1037/0021-9010.80.4.532

Cremers, H. P., Mercken, L., Crutzen, R., Willems, P., De Vries, H., and Oenema, A. (2014). Do email and mobile phone prompts stimulate primary school children to reuse an internet-delivered smoking prevention intervention? *Journal of Medical Internet Research*, *16*. https://doi.org/10.2196/jmir.3069

Crutzen, R., Cyr, D., and De Vries, N. K. (2012). The role of user control in adherence to and knowledge gained from a website: Randomized comparison between a tunneled version and a freedom-of-choice version. *Journal of Medical Internet Research*, *14*. https://doi.org/10.2196/jmir.1922

Crutzen, R., DeKruif, L., and DeVries, N. K. (2012). You never get a second chance to make a first impression: The effect of visual complexity on intention to use websites. *Interaction Studies Interaction Studies Social Behaviour and Communication in Biological and Artificial Systems*, *13*. https://doi.org/10.1075/is.13.3.07cru

Crutzen, R., Viechtbauer, W., Spigt, M., and Kotz, D. (2015). Differential attrition in health behaviour change trials: A systematic review and meta-analysis. *Psychology and Health*, *30*, 122–134. https://doi.org/10.1080/08870446.2014.953526

Dalgard, O. S., Sørensen, T., Sandanger, I., Nygård, J. F., Svensson, E., and Reas, D. L. (2009). Job demands, job control, and mental health in an 11-year follow-up study: Normal and reversed relationships. *Work and Stress*, *23*, 284–296. https://doi.org/10.1080/02678370903250953

de Vente, W., Kamphuis, J. H., Emmelkamp, P. M. G., and Blonk, R. W. B. (2008). Individual and group cognitive-behavioral treatment for work-related stress complaints and sickness absence: A randomized controlled trial. *Journal of Occupational Health Psychology*, *13*, 214–231. https://doi.org/10.1037/1076-8998.13.3.214

Emerson, N. D., Merrill, D. A., Shedd, K., Bilder, R. M., and Siddarth, P. (2017). Effects of an employee exercise programme on mental health. *Occupational Medicine*, *67*, 128–134. https://doi.org/10.1093/occmed/kqw120

Fetvadjiev, V. H. and He, J. (2019). The longitudinal links of personality traits, values, and well-being and self-esteem: A five-wave study of a nationally representative sample. *Journal of Personality and Social Psychology*, *117*, 448–464. https://doi.org/10.1037/pspp0000212

Fibbins, H., Ward, P. B., Watkins, A., Curtis, J., and Rosenbaum, S. (2018). Improving the health of mental health staff through exercise interventions: a systematic review. *Journal of Mental Health*, *27*, 184–191. https://doi.org/10.1080/09638237.2018.1437614

Fila, M. J., Purl, J., and Griffeth, R. W. (2017). Job demands, control and support: Meta-analyzing moderator effects of gender, nationality, and occupation. *Human Resource Management Review*, *27*, 39–60. https://doi.org/10.1016/j.hrmr.2016.09.004

Ford, M. T., Cerasoli, C. P., Higgins, J. a, and Decesare, A. L. (2011). Relationships between psychological, physical, and behavioural health and work performance:

A review and meta-analysis. *Work & Stress*, *25*, 185–241.

French, K. A., Dumani, S., Allen, T. D., and Shockley, K. M. (2018). A meta-analysis of work-family conflict and social support. *Psychological Bulletin*, *144*, 284–314. https://doi.org/10.1037/bul0000120

Gilmour, J. and Williams, L. (2012). Type D personality is associated with maladaptive health-related behaviours. *Journal of Health Psychology*, *17*, 471–478. https://doi.org/10.1177/1359105311423117

Göritz, A. S. and Crutzen, R. (2012). Reminders in web-based data collection: Increasing response at the price of retention? *American Journal of Evaluation*, *33*, 240–250. https://doi.org/10.1177/1098214011421956

Griffin, D. and O'Cass, A. (2010). An exploration of personality and speed limit compliance. *Journal of Nonprofit and Public Sector Marketing*, *22*, 336–353. https://doi.org/10.1080/10495141003718262

Horn, R. A., Troyer, J. A., Hall, E. J., Mellott, R. N., Cotè, L. S., and Marquis, J. D. (2007). The scientist-practitioner model: A rose by any other name is still a rose. *American Behavioral Scientist*, *50*, 808–819. https://doi.org/10.1177/0002764206296459

Horwood, S. and Anglim, J. (2017). A critical analysis of the assumptions of type D personality: Comparing prediction of health-related variables with the five factor model. *Personality and Individual Differences*, *117*, 172–176. https://doi.org/10.1016/j.paid.2017.06.001

Jerram, K. L. and Coleman, P. G. (1999). The big five personality traits and reporting of health problems and health behaviour in old age. *British Journal of Health Psychology*, *4*, 181–192. https://doi.org/10.1348/135910799168560

Keyes, C. and Ryff, C. (1995). The structure of psychological well-being revisited. *Journal of Personality and Social Psychology* 69, 719–727).

Kim, M. and Beehr, T. A. (2018). Can empowering leaders affect subordinates' well-being and careers because they encourage subordinates' job crafting behaviors? *Journal of Leadership and Organizational Studies*, *25*, 184–196. https://doi.org/10.1177/1548051817727702

Kinman, G., Clements, A. J., and Hart, J. (2017). Job demands, resources and mental health in UK prison officers. *Occupational Medicine*, *67*, 456–460. https://doi.org/10.1093/OCCMED/KQX091

Kitchener, B. A. and Jorm, A. F. (2002). Mental health first aid training for the public: Evaluation of effects on knowledge, attitudes and helping behavior. *BMC Psychiatry*, *2*. https://doi.org/10.1186/1471-244X-2-10

Kroencke, L., Harari, G. M., Katana, M., and Gosling, S. D. (2019). Personality trait predictors and mental well-being correlates of exercise frequency across the academic semester. *Social Science and Medicine*, *236*. https://doi.org/10.1016/j.socscimed.2019.112400

Lloyd, J., Bond, W., and Flaxman, P. E. (2017). Work-related self-efficacy as a moderator of the impact of a worksite stress management training intervention: Intrinsic work motivation as a higher order condition of effect. *Journal of Occupational Health Psychology*, *22*, 115–127. https://doi.org/10.1037/ocp0000026

Magee, C. and Biesanz, J. C. (2019). Toward understanding the relationship between personality and well-being states and traits. *Journal of Personality*, *87*, 276–294. https://doi.org/10.1111/jopy.12389

Major, D. A., Turner, J. E., and Fletcher, T. D. (2006). Linking proactive personality and the big five to motivation to learn and development activity. *Journal of Applied Psychology*, *91*, 927–935. https://doi.org/10.1037/0021-9010.91.4.927

McCrae, R. R., and Costa, P. T. (1987). Validation of the five-factor model of personality across instruments and observers. *Journal of Personality and Social Psychology*, *52*, 81–90. https://doi.org/10.1037/0022-3514.52.1.81

Mellor-Clark, J., Twigg, E., Farrell, E., and Kinder, A. (2013). Benchmarking key service quality indicators in UK Employee Assistance Programme Counselling: A CORE system data profile. *Counselling and Psychotherapy Research*, *13*, 14–23. https://doi.org/10.1080/14733145.2012.728235

Plomp, J., Tims, M., Akkermans, J., Khapova, S. N., Jansen, P. G. W., and Bakker, A. B. (2016). Career competencies and job crafting:

How proactive employees influence their well-being. *Career Development International*, *21*, 587–602. https://doi.org/10.1108/CDI-08-2016-0145

Podsakoff, N. P., Lepine, J. A., and Lepine, M. A. (2007). Differential challenge stressor-hindrance stressor relationships with job attitudes, turnover intentions, turnover, and withdrawal behavior: A meta-analysis. *Journal of Applied Psychology*, *92*, 438–454. https://doi.org/10.1037/0021-9010.92.2.438

Richardson, K. M. and Rothstein, H. R. (2008). Effects of occupational stress management intervention programs: A meta-analysis. *Journal of Occupational Health Psychology*, *13*, 69–93. https://doi.org/10.1037/1076-8998.13.1.69

Robertson Cooper Ltd. (2020). *Leadership impact: Validity research and conceptual background*. Manchester: Robertson Cooper.

Robertson, I., Leach, D., and Dawson, J. (2018). Personality and resilience: Domains, facets, and non-linear relationships. *International Journal of Stress Prevention and Well-Being, 2*. http://eprints.whiterose.ac.uk/138377/2.

Robertson, I., Leach, D., Doerner, N., and Smeed, M. (2012). Poor health but not absent: Prevalence, predictors, and outcomes of presenteeism. *Journal of Occupational and Environmental Medicine*, *54*, 1344–1349. https://doi.org/10.1097/JOM.0b013e31825dff4b

Robertson, I., P. Healey, M., P. Hodgkinson, G., Flint-Taylor, J., and Jones, F. (2014). Leader personality and employees' experience of workplace stressors. *Journal of Organizational Effectiveness*, *1*, 281–295. https://doi.org/10.1108/JOEPP-05-2014-0019

Robertson, I., Cooper, C. L., Sarkar, M., and Curran, T. (2015). Resilience training in the workplace from 2003 to 2014: A systematic review. *Journal of Occupational and Organizational Psychology*, *88*, 533–562. https://doi.org/10.1111/joop.12120

Robertson, I., and Flint-Taylor, J. (2009). Leadership, psychological well-being, and organizational outcomes. In Susan Cartwright and Cary Cooper (Eds.), *The Oxford Handbook of Organizational Well Being* (pp. 159–179). Oxford University Press. https://doi.org/10.1093/oxfordhb/9780199211913.003.0008

Roczniewska, M. and Bakker, A. B. (2016). Who seeks job resources, and who avoids job demands? The link between dark personality traits and job crafting. *Journal of Psychology: Interdisciplinary and Applied*, *150*, 1026–1045. https://doi.org/10.1080/00223980.2016.1235537

Ryan, R. M. and Deci, E. L. (2001). On happiness and human potentials: A review of research on hedonic and eudaimonic well-being. *Annual Review of Psychology*, *52*, 141–166. https://doi.org/10.1146/annurev.psych.52.1.141

Steel, P., Schmidt, J., and Shultz, J. (2008). Refining the relationship between personality and subjective well-being. *Psychological Bulletin*, *134*, 138–161. https://doi.org/10.1037/0033-2909.134.1.138

Strickhouser, J. E., Zell, E., and Krizan, Z. (2017). Does personality predict health and well-being? A metasynthesis. *Health Psychology*, *36*, 797–810. https://doi.org/10.1037/hea0000475

Strømholm, T., Pape, K., Ose, S. O., Krokstad, S., and Bjørngaard, J. H. (2015). Psychosocial working conditions and sickness absence in a general population: A cohort study of 21,834 workers in Norway (The HUNT Study). *Journal of Occupational and Environmental Medicine*, *57*, 386–392. https://doi.org/10.1097/JOM.0000000000000362

Taimela, S., Malmivaara, A., Justén, S., Läärä, E., Sintonen, H., Tiekso, J., and Aro, T. (2008). The effectiveness of two occupational health intervention programmes in reducing sickness absence among employees at risk. Two randomised controlled trials. *Occupational and Environmental Medicine*, *65*, 236–241. https://doi.org/10.1136/oem.2007.032706

Taris, T. W. and Schreurs, P. J. G. (2009). Well-being and organizational performance: An organizational-level test of the happy-productive worker hypothesis. *Work & Stress*, *23*, 120–136. https://doi.org/10.1080/02678370903072555

Tims, M., Bakker, A. B., and Derks, D. (2013). The impact of job crafting on job demands, job resources, and well-being. *Journal of Occupational Health Psychology*, *18*, 230–240. https://doi.org/10.1037/a0032141

Travis, J. and Freeman, E. (2017). Predicting entrepreneurial intentions: Incremental validity of proactive personality and entrepreneurial Self-Efficacy as a moderator. *Journal of Entrepreneurship Education*, *20*, 56–68.

Ucho, A. and Gbande, A. (2012). Personality and gender differences in compliance with safety behaviour among factory workers of Dangote Cement Company, Gboko. *IFE PsychologIA: An International Journal*, *20*, 134–141.

Van Wingerden, J., Derks, D., and Bakker, A. B. (2017). The impact of personal resources and job crafting interventions on work engagement and performance. *Human Resource Management*, *56*, 51–67. https://doi.org/10.1002/hrm.21758

Weinstein, A. A., Koehmstedt, C. and Kop, W. J. (2017). Mental health consequences of exercise withdrawal: A systematic review. *General Hospital Psychiatry*, *49*, 11–18. https://doi.org/10.1016/j.genhosppsych.2017.06.001

Wood, S., Stride, C., Threapleton, K., Wearn, E., Nolan, F., Osborn, D., Paul, M., and Johnson, S. (2011). Demands, control, supportive relationships and well-being amongst British mental health workers. *Social Psychiatry and Psychiatric Epidemiology*, *46*, 1055–1068. https://doi.org/10.1007/s00127-010-0263-6

Wrzesniewski, A. and Dutton, J. E. (2001). Crafting a job: Revisioning employees as active crafters of their work. *The Academy of Management Review*, *26*, 179–201. https://doi.org/10.2307/259118

4

Wellbeing and Age in Organizational Life

Hannes Zacher

INTRODUCTION

The goal of this chapter is to review and discuss theory, empirical research, and organizational practice with regard to relationships between individuals' chronological age and different dimensions of occupational wellbeing from a lifespan developmental perspective. In addition, various person-related and contextual mechanisms and boundary conditions of these associations will be elaborated. Consistent with the definition proposed by the World Health Organization (1948), wellbeing encompasses physical, mental, and social dimensions and describes not simply the absence of physical illness. Accordingly, this chapter addresses how different indicators of objective and subjective physical health and wellbeing as well as psychological wellbeing relate to age in the work context and organizational life. Due to demographic changes, the populations and workforces in most developed countries (e.g., Germany, Italy, UK, United States) and many developing countries (e.g., Brazil, China, India) are ageing and becoming more age diverse (Hertel and Zacher, 2018). Due to economic changes, increased healthy life expectancy, and more options for delayed and more flexible retirement entries, it is expected that a growing number of individuals will continue to work in their late 60s, 70s, and even 80s over the coming decades. At the same time, work is increasingly carried out in teams composed of members from several different age groups (Parry and McCarthy, 2017). Accordingly, it is important to understand how, why, and when occupational wellbeing differs between various age groups and changes across the working lifespan.

Whereas *chronological age* refers to the time an individual has lived since birth, *ageing* is a temporal process that goes along with changes (i.e., growth, decline, maintenance) in different physiological and psychological characteristics (Schwall, 2012). The vast majority of studies in work and organizational psychology on age and occupational wellbeing is cross-sectional and, thus, examines age-related differences between groups of younger, middle-aged, and older employees, which cannot simply be interpreted as age-related changes within ageing employees over time (Zacher, 2015). In contrast, due to their time- and cost-intensive nature, there are currently only very few long-term longitudinal studies on age and occupational wellbeing that allow conclusions about the ageing process (e.g., Riza et al., 2018). The lifespan developmental perspective is a meta-theoretical framework that conceives human development and ageing (*ontogenesis*) as a continuous, multidimensional, and multidirectional process driven by both biological and cultural influences, as well as individual action regulation and adaptation to changing environments (Baltes, 1987; Zacher et al., 2019). A complementary approach to the lifespan development perspective is the life course perspective, which focuses on the interplay between structure (e.g., institutions, social context) and individual agency in influencing development but, compared to the lifespan perspective, places a stronger emphasis on the former than the latter (Diewald and Mayer, 2009). The life course perspective originated in the field of sociology and is, therefore, primarily concerned with predicting decisions of groups of individuals in navigating lives and careers. In contrast, the lifespan developmental perspective originated in the field of psychology and is, therefore, generally better suited to examine the role of age for the individual experience of wellbeing, in work and organizational life and beyond. However, an integration of both perspectives can be useful to conceptualize higher-level predictors of occupational wellbeing, such as team, organizational, and institutional factors (Settersten, 2017; Zacher and Froidevaux, 2021).

In the next section, several relevant theories based on the lifespan developmental perspective are introduced, including the model of selection, optimization, and compensation;

socioemotional selectivity theory; the strength and vulnerability integration model; and the motivational theory of lifespan development. These psychological lifespan theories address links between age and especially individual motivation and emotional regulation and are, therefore, useful to understand changes in occupational wellbeing across the lifespan (Rudolph, 2016; Scheibe and Zacher, 2013; Schmitt and Bathen, 2015). Subsequently, results of several meta-analyses and primary empirical studies on age and occupational wellbeing are summarized. It is important to note that the lifespan theories introduced in this chapter were developed in Western countries, particularly the United States and Germany. In addition, most corresponding empirical research on age and wellbeing was, with few exceptions (Fung et al., 1999), carried out in Western countries. Thus, generalizations to other cultural and institutional contexts can only be made with caution (Rudolph et al., 2018a; Tomlinson et al., 2018). The chapter concludes by outlining a number of emerging directions in this area of research as well as suggestions for future theory development and empirical research regarding the role of age for occupational wellbeing. In addition, based on theories and research reviewed in the chapter, practical implications for developing workers' wellbeing across longer periods of time in organizational life are discussed.

THEORETICAL FRAMEWORKS ON AGE AND OCCUPATIONAL WELLBEING

The lifespan developmental perspective superseded traditional stage-based theories of development, which typically proposed several age-based, distinct, and normative stages with corresponding developmental tasks or conflicts that had to be resolved (e.g., generativity vs stagnation; Erikson, 1950; Levinson, 1986). In contrast, the lifespan perspective conceives development as a continuous and more flexible process from conception to death. Baltes (1987) developed a set of seven meta-theoretical propositions about lifespan development. First, the lifespan perspective conceives development as a lifelong process and argues that no age period is superior to others. Second, development is multidirectional within and across domains of functioning and experience, including increases, decreases, and maintenance in physical and psychological wellbeing. Third, development always involves the joint occurrence of gains and losses in functioning and experiences, and losses increasingly outweigh gains with age, and especially in very old age. Fourth, development is modifiable within persons (i.e., intraindividual plasticity), suggesting that person-related and contextual factors can lead to changed trajectories in wellbeing at any point of the lifespan. Fifth, development is historically, culturally, and socially embedded (i.e., principle of contextualism), meaning that interactions between person and context have to be taken into account. Sixth, development depends on the interplay of normative age-graded (e.g., decline in physical strength), normative history-graded (e.g., retirement entry), and non-normative influences (e.g., accidents, lottery wins). Finally, Baltes (1987) proposed that lifespan development should be studied from multiple scientific perspectives, including psychology, medicine, sociology, anthropology, and other fields. The lifespan perspective generally conceives individual development as a process of initiating changes in one's environment and developmental path, as well as the adaptation to changes in the environment and in individual functioning (Baltes, 1997; Baltes et al., 1980).

While there is no specific lifespan developmental theory of age-related changes in physical functioning and objective physical wellbeing, the lifespan perspective generally acknowledges that physical health can decline with age, across the working lifespan (i.e., typically between the late teens and mid

60s), but particularly in old age (i.e., approximately 65 years and older) and very old age (i.e., approximately 85 years and older; Baltes and Smith, 2003). Specifically, the process of ageing involves losses in different physiological and physical abilities, including sensory, muscle, cardiovascular, respiratory, neurological, and immune system functions, which can, in turn, impact on workplace health and safety outcomes such as injuries and accidents (Jex et al., 2007; Maertens et al., 2012). Importantly, however, the lifespan developmental perspective emphasizes that there is a great deal of interindividual and intraindividual variability in physical health-related trajectories with age. For instance, both organizational interventions (e.g., job design, health promotion) and individual compensatory behaviours (e.g., using tools) can weaken the association between age-related changes and occupational health outcomes. In addition, cognitive epidemiology research demonstrates that age-related changes in cognitive functioning (e.g., information processing, problem solving) are associated with changes in health-related outcomes and even mortality (Salthouse, 2012).

Based on the meta-theoretical lifespan perspective, several more specific lifespan theories have been developed that are frequently used in research on work and ageing (Rudolph, 2016) and, in particular, research on age and occupational health and wellbeing (Scheibe and Zacher, 2013). First, the model of selection, optimization, and compensation proposes that individuals adapt to age-related changes in personal or contextual resources and proactively shape their own development by changing their goals either voluntarily or due to losses (i.e., elective and loss-based selection), by increasing or refining their personal investments into goal pursuit (i.e., optimization), and by using alternative goal-relevant means if previous means for goal achievement are no longer available (i.e., compensation; Baltes and Baltes, 1990). According to the model, individuals 'age successfully' and, in particular, are able to maintain or improve their wellbeing with increasing age when they adapt to individual and environmental changes by making use of these action regulation strategies in an 'orchestrated' or combined way (Freund and Baltes, 2000). The model of selection, optimization, and compensation has also been applied in research on emotion regulation, based on the idea that individual select and optimize emotion regulation strategies depend on the availability of resources, including personal capabilities and environmental affordances (Opitz et al., 2012; Urry and Gross, 2010). More specifically, the researchers suggested that the availability of internal and external resources predicts the use of five emotion regulation strategies (i.e., situation selection, situation modification, attentional deployment, cognitive changes, response modulation) which, in turn, may predict wellbeing.

Second, socioemotional selectivity theory attempts to explain age-related differences and changes in social and emotional goals as well as changing goal priorities (Carstensen et al., 1999; Carstensen, 2006). In contrast to the model of selection, optimization, and compensation, the explanatory mechanisms for such age-related differences and changes in goals and goal priorities are not changes in individual or contextual resources, but the perception of remaining time left in life, which has been termed future time perspective (Lang and Carstensen, 2002). Specifically, when people perceive their future time as unlimited (i.e., typically younger adults), they prioritize goals related to knowledge acquisition and expansion of social networks, as these represent activities to maximize future gains. In contrast, when people perceive their future time as limited (i.e., typically older adults), goals related to positive emotions, wellbeing, and meaningfulness are prioritized in order to maximize momentary experiences in the present. Thus, similar to rational choice models, socioemotional selectivity theory suggests that people change their goals with age based on changes

in future time perspective to maximize their returns of investments in their perceived available future time. The idea that time perspective changes with age and, in turn, influences important work outcomes, including occupational wellbeing, has been adapted to the work context (i.e., 'occupational future time perspective'; Zacher and Frese, 2009).

Third, the strength and vulnerability integration model represents an extension of socioemotional selectivity theory (Charles, 2010). The model focuses on age-related strengths and weaknesses in emotion regulation, which in turn impacts on emotional experiences and wellbeing. In addition to future time perspective, the model considers age-related increases in life experience, particularly with regard to emotion regulation and interpersonal skills (Blanchard-Fields, 2007), as well as age-related increases in physiological vulnerabilities (e.g., cardiovascular disease, neurological and hormonal dysfunctions) as explanatory mechanisms. The strength and vulnerability integration model proposes that older people tend to avoid stressors and negative experiences (i.e., situation selection) and generally cope better with low levels of stressors as compared to younger people (Charles and Luong, 2013). In contrast, due to their physiological vulnerabilities and decreased flexibility in biological systems, older people possess lower capacities to deal with high and chronic levels of stressors and corresponding physiological arousal. In other words, their emotion regulation is less effective in these situations as compared to younger people. Thus, older adults should also have more difficulties with regard to intense and chronic, as compared to mild, stressors in organizational life, with respective consequences for their occupational wellbeing.

Finally, the motivational theory of lifespan development (similar to its predecessor, the lifespan theory of control; Heckhausen and Schulz, 1995) proposes that successful ageing requires the optimal use of two complementary action regulation strategies, that is, primary and secondary control strategies (Heckhausen et al., 2010). Whereas primary control strategies involve actions to proactively change the environment to fulfil one's personal needs, secondary control strategies entail adapting the self, including one's ways of thinking and feeling, to changes in the environment in order to maintain, increase, or compensate for existing (low) levels of primary control. The theory assumes that the relationship between age and primary control takes an inverted U-shape pattern, with increases from birth to younger adulthood, a peak in middle age, and a decline during later adulthood. In contrast, secondary control is assumed to increase linearly across the lifespan to support primary control striving.

Based on these lifespan theories, researchers working in the area of work and ageing have developed more specific theorizing on the role of age for occupational health and wellbeing. For example, Scheibe and Zacher (2013) presented a lifespan model of emotion regulation, stress, and occupational wellbeing. According to their model, age is associated with (a) what kinds of affective work events people encounter and how often (i.e., emotional event exposure); (b) the appraisal of and initial emotional response to affective work events (i.e., emotion generation); and (c) the management of emotions and coping with affective work events (i.e., emotion regulation). The researchers proposed that changes in employees' life contexts (e.g., work, family, leisure) mediate the relationships between age and age-related factors on the one hand and the occurrence of affective work events on the other. More specifically, it was assumed that middle-aged (or mid-career) workers, who are approximately between 35 and 50 years old, experience higher levels of strain and lower levels of occupational wellbeing due to increased work–life conflict and increased work responsibilities (Huffman et al., 2013; Zacher et al., 2014b). Furthermore, the model suggests that the relationship between age and the emotional response to affective work events is mediated

by emotion generation via attention and appraisal processes, depending on the nature of the affective work events encountered. The researchers assume that, with increasing age, employees are less strongly affected by interpersonal stressors and more strongly affected by non-interpersonal stressors. Moreover, consistent with the strength and vulnerability integration model, the model suggests that when stressful events have a high emotion-regulatory load (i.e., high intensity, duration, chronicity, or complexity), older workers are equally or more strongly affected than younger workers, independent of event type. Finally, the model proposes that the relationship between age and emotional responses (i.e., occupational strain, wellbeing) is mediated by emotion regulation. In particular, it is assumed that older adults are more motivated than younger adults to avoid or downregulate negative and/or high-arousal affect associated with certain affective work events. Moreover, older employees should be more effective and efficient in avoiding or downregulating negative and/or high-arousal affect resulting from affective work events, especially when the occupational context supports the free choice of regulatory strategies.

Another line of research that is based on the lifespan developmental perspective aims to explain associations between age and occupational wellbeing using the notion of successful ageing at work (Zacher, 2015; Zacher and Schmitt, 2016). Various subjective and objective work outcomes (e.g., job attitudes, performance, occupational wellbeing) can be conceived as indicators of successful ageing at work. With respect to occupational wellbeing, successful ageing entails that workers experience higher than average levels in wellbeing with increasing age. For instance, if the average age-related trend in an occupational wellbeing outcome is decline, then maintenance in wellbeing with age would be considered successful ageing at work. In contrast, if the average trend is positive, higher than average growth in wellbeing would constitute successful ageing. Both individual resources, including personality characteristics and self-regulation skills, and environmental affordances, such as work characteristics and organizational climate, can contribute to successful ageing at work (Kooij et al., 2020; Zacher and Rudolph, 2017).

Finally, also based on the lifespan developmental perspective, researchers have proposed a person–environment fit model of age, occupational strain, and wellbeing (Feldman and Vogel, 2009; Rauvola et al., 2020; Zacher et al., 2014a). The model suggests that age can affect the match between individual abilities and needs on the one hand, and work-related demands and supplies on the other hand. For instance, age-related changes in cognitive abilities and personality may lead to increases or decreases in employees' person–job demands–abilities fit or their needs–supplies fit over time (Zacher et al., 2014a). Moreover, according to the model, age can moderate the relationship between objective person–environment fit and subjective person–environment fit, as well as the relationships between both forms of person–environment fit and occupational strain and wellbeing. For example, the model suggests that the positive relationship between objective and subjective person–job fit is stronger for younger as compared to older employees because, based on socioemotional selectivity theory, older employees have a stronger motivation to perceive their fit as favourable. Similarly, the effects of person–group fit and occupational wellbeing are expected to be stronger for older as compared to younger employees (Zacher et al., 2014a).

In summary, several theories based on the lifespan developmental perspective exist that can be applied to gain a better understanding of relationships between employee age and different indicators of occupational wellbeing. Moreover, several conceptual models on emotion regulation, successful ageing, and person–environment fit in the work context have been proposed that specifically aim to explain age-related differences and changes in occupational wellbeing. In the next section, empirical research on relationships between age and occupational wellbeing based on these theoretical frameworks is reviewed and discussed.

EMPIRICAL RESEARCH ON RELATIONSHIPS BETWEEN AGE AND OCCUPATIONAL WELLBEING

Over the past decades, several primary empirical studies and meta-analyses have examined associations between chronological age and occupational wellbeing. With regard to physical health, it is commonly assumed that older workers have lower levels of health and wellbeing than younger workers (McCarthy et al., 2019; Posthuma and Campion, 2009). However, a meta-analysis by Ng and Feldman (2013) only partially supported such age stereotypes. Based on accumulated results of between four and 59 studies, the researchers showed that age was weakly to moderately related to objective measures of physical ill-health, including blood pressure ($\rho = 0.34$), cholesterol level ($\rho = 0.20$), and body mass index ($\rho = 0.21$), as well as to self-reported measures of insomnia ($\rho = 0.12$), and muscle pain ($\rho = 0.14$). In contrast, age was largely unrelated to overall subjective physical health ($\rho = 0.00$), somatic and psychosomatic complaints (ρs = 0.02 and 0.03, respectively), depression ($\rho = -0.03$), and anxiety ($\rho = -0.01$), and weakly negatively related to poor mental health ($\rho = -0.05$), fatigue ($\rho = -0.10$), negative mood ($\rho = -0.10$), anger ($\rho = -0.15$), and irritation ($\rho = -0.09$). Thus, while age appears to be negatively related to objective physical health and wellbeing, older workers report somewhat higher levels with regard to certain indicators of subjective health and wellbeing than younger workers.

Another meta-analysis examined associations between the use of selection, optimization, and compensation strategies and various work-related outcomes, including job performance and occupational wellbeing (Moghimi et al., 2017). Results showed that strategy use was not only positively related to both self-reported ($\rho = 0.23$) and non-self-reported job performance ($\rho = 0.21$), but also to job satisfaction ($\rho = 0.25$) and job engagement ($\rho = 0.38$) as indicators of occupational wellbeing. However, unexpectedly, strategy use was not significantly related to job strain ($\rho = 0.01$), an indicator of negative occupational wellbeing. In addition, the researchers conducted a systematic review of the literature on the use of selection, optimization, and compensation strategies in the work context and reported that very few studies had examined the use of selection, optimization, and compensation strategies as a mediator or moderator of links between age and occupational wellbeing.

Based on socioemotional selectivity theory (Carstensen et al., 1999), which suggests that older as compared to younger workers prioritize positive emotional experiences and meaningfulness, Ng and Feldman (2010) meta-analytically examined bivariate associations between age and 35 work-related attitudes and occupational wellbeing indicators. They showed that age is generally positively, and weakly to moderately, related to favourable attitudes toward work tasks (e.g., satisfaction with work itself), colleagues and supervisors (e.g., interpersonal trust), and the organization (e.g., commitment). More specifically, and with regard to occupational wellbeing, the researchers found positive relationships between age and overall job satisfaction ($\rho = 0.18$), job involvement ($\rho = 0.25$), affective commitment ($\rho = 0.24$), and organizational identification ($\rho = 0.20$). Furthermore, they found negative relationships between age and perceptions of role ambiguity ($\rho = -0.15$), role conflict ($\rho = -0.14$), and role overload ($\rho = -0.30$), as well as the burnout syndrome dimensions emotional exhaustion ($\rho = -0.08$), depersonalization ($\rho = -0.18$), and reduced personal accomplishment ($\rho = -0.14$). Importantly, most of these associations remained stable when organizational tenure was controlled, and the researchers did not find

much evidence for curvilinear relationships between age and these occupational wellbeing outcomes. Another meta-analysis did not find a significant overall association between age and a more proximal indicator of work-related strain called irritation (Rauschenbach et al., 2013). However, this meta-analysis found a weak positive relationship between age and strain in jobs with high physical demands (e.g., production or construction work), and a reversed U-shaped relationship between age and strain in social jobs (e.g., nurses or teachers), with middle-aged workers reporting the highest levels of strain. Importantly, the findings of these meta-analyses have to be interpreted with some caution, as they are based on mostly cross-sectional data, raising potential concerns regarding the 'healthy worker effect'. That is, workers with low wellbeing may have a higher likelihood of dropping out of the workforce (and out of empirical studies) than workers with higher wellbeing. Moreover, the age ranges included suggest that workers aged 60 years and older are underrepresented in the studies included in these meta-analyses.

While researchers have conceptually addressed person-related (e.g., emotion regulation and coping) and contextual mechanisms (e.g., work events, life context) linking age with occupational health and wellbeing outcomes (Scheibe and Zacher, 2013), no systematic review and very little empirical evidence from primary studies on such mechanisms exists (Doerwald et al., 2016; Zacher and Froidevaux, 2021). For example, research based on the lifespan theory of control showed that older workers use more active problem-focused coping (but not emotion-focused coping) and, thus, experience less strain than younger workers (Hertel et al., 2015). Another study explored contextual work-related mechanisms to explain lower levels in occupational wellbeing (i.e., lower job satisfaction, higher emotional exhaustion) among mid-career workers in the construction industry, as compared to wellbeing at younger and older ages (Zacher et al.,

2014b). The researchers found that time pressure was highest and co-worker social support lowest among middle-aged workers compared to younger and older workers, which explained the decrease in occupational wellbeing in mid-career. The study did not find an association between age and work–family conflict, which may not be surprising given that the sample was predominantly male.

With regard to interactive effects of age with work characteristics on occupational wellbeing, a number of review articles have found mixed evidence (Bal et al., 2008; Mühlenbrock and Hüffmeier, 2020; Ng and Feldman, 2015; Zacher and Schmitt, 2016). A meta-analysis found that age moderated the negative associations of psychological contract breach with trust, job satisfaction, and organizational commitment (Bal et al., 2008). While the relationships of contract breach with trust and organizational commitment were stronger for younger compared to older employees, the relationship between contract breach and job satisfaction was unexpectedly stronger for older compared to younger employees. In their review, Zacher and Schmitt (2016) concluded that 'the patterns of interaction effects of work characteristics and age on occupational well-being are diverse and complex; it appears that the interaction patterns depend not only on the specific work characteristics, but also on the specific occupational well-being indicators under consideration' (2016: 3). This conclusion is mirrored by the findings of a meta-analysis on interactive effects of age and job autonomy on different work outcomes, including job performance and occupational wellbeing (Ng and Feldman, 2015). Based on socioemotional selectivity theory, the researchers argued that older workers would experience job autonomy more positively than younger workers. Consistently, results showed that the negative relationship between job autonomy and emotional exhaustion was stronger for older workers than for younger workers. The authors suggested that older workers might

benefit more from high levels of job autonomy because they may have greater family responsibilities (e.g., eldercare). In contrast, the meta-analysis found that the relationships of job autonomy with job satisfaction, affective commitment, work engagement, job stress, and poor mental health were stronger for younger workers compared to older workers. The authors suggested that, also based on socioemotional selectivity theory, younger workers may react more positively to job autonomy because they place greater priority on knowledge acquisition, attainment of career goals, and impressing others. A recent systematic review on age, job characteristics, and health outcomes by Mühlenbrock and Hüffmeier (2020) suggested that there is some evidence that effects of age on health depend on age-relevant work demands (e.g., information processing vs knowledge), job autonomy, and meaningful work, with high levels of knowledge demands, meaningful work, and job autonomy benefitting older workers. However, the researchers also noted the general lack of studies and a relatively high number of non-significant interactions.

Several recent primary studies examined interactive effects of age and work characteristics on occupational wellbeing (see also Zacher and Froidevaux, 2021). For example, a study found that the association between age and work engagement was positive when task significance, interaction outside of one's organization, or both job characteristics were high, whereas the relationship was non-significant when both characteristics were low (Gostautaite and Buciuniene, 2015). Another study integrated the lifespan perspective with the job demands–resources model to gain a better understanding of the role of age for associations between job demands and job resources with work engagement and burnout (Salmela-Aro and Upadyaya, 2018). Economic problems and information and communication technology demands were positively related to burnout among younger employees, whereas caregiving demands and multicultural work demands were positively related to burnout and negatively related to work engagement among middle-aged and older employees. No age-differential effects were found for personal and job resources. Furthermore, a study examined age as a moderator of effects of job resources (i.e., skill variety, leader–member exchange, procedural fairness) on perceived work-related stress (Yaldiz et al., 2018). When these resources were high, both younger and older workers experienced low levels of stress. In contrast, when resources were low, older workers experienced more stress than younger workers. Finally, based on person–environment fit theory, job design theory, and lifespan theories (i.e., fluid and crystallized intelligence; model of selection, optimization, and compensation; socioemotional selectivity theory), a qualitative study with professional ballet dancers suggested that the interplay between individual factors (i.e., abilities, needs, strategies) and contextual factors (i.e., demands, organizational resources) plays an important role for psychological adjustment and wellbeing with increasing age (Rodrigues et al., 2020).

In summary, a number of meta-analyses on age and various indicators of occupational wellbeing have not supported the stereotype of the generally less healthy older workers. In contrast, and consistent with the lifespan perspective, there appear to be both gains and losses in occupational wellbeing with age. Whereas objective indicators of physical ill-health, such as blood pressure and cholesterol level, increase with age, subjective physical and mental health and wellbeing tend to remain stable or increase with age. Even though relatively few studies on age-related mechanisms and boundary conditions exist, it seems as if both job characteristics and workers' action regulation strategies, as well as their combination, may contribute to higher levels of occupational wellbeing among older as compared to younger workers. In the final section of this chapter, implications of these findings for theory development as well as future research and practice are elaborated.

IMPLICATIONS FOR THEORY DEVELOPMENT, RESEARCH, AND PRACTICE

The present review and discussion of the lifespan developmental perspective and associated lifespan theories and conceptual models suggests several directions for future theory development regarding links between age and occupational wellbeing. First, there is a need for greater integration of specific lifespan theories and related constructs (Haase et al., 2013). The model of selection, optimization, and compensation, socioemotional selectivity theory, and the model of strength and vulnerability integration, as well as the motivational theory of lifespan development, each contribute toward a better understanding of how, why, and when occupational wellbeing may differ across age groups or change with age. However, whereas some of these lifespan theories focus on physiological declines and perceptions of future time left in life, others emphasize people's action regulation, especially goal setting and pursuit, as central mechanisms. An integration of these theoretical frameworks could help to further understand why and under which conditions some dimensions of occupational wellbeing decrease with age, whereas others are maintained or increase with age. It is also necessary to better integrate these motivational lifespan theories (Rudolph, 2016) with theorizing and research on changes in functioning in various physiological and cognitive domains (Ackerman and Kanfer, 2020; Fisher et al., 2017; Salthouse, 2012). Moreover, with few exceptions (Heckhausen et al., 2010), most lifespan theories focus exclusively on intraindividual psychological processes and neglect proximal (e.g., immediate work context) and more distal (e.g., organizational policies, institutional factors) environmental characteristics. Accordingly, it would be important to more strongly integrate insights from lifespan developmental theories with work and organizational psychology theories (e.g., job demands–resources model), but also with life course theories that have been developed in the field of sociology, such as the model of flexible careers across the life course (Moen and Sweet, 2004; Tomlinson et al., 2018; Zacher and Froidevaux, 2021). Based on such a theoretical integration and extension, future theories could adopt a multilevel perspective on age and occupational wellbeing, with predictors residing not only at the intra- and interindividual levels, but also at the job, team, organization, and societal or institutional levels. These models should also incorporate the notion of person–environment fit, which has been suggested to play a key role in successful ageing and occupational wellbeing across the working lifespan (Kooij et al., 2020; Zacher et al., 2014a).

Future empirical research should operationalize and test the person-related and contextual mechanisms and boundary conditions proposed by existing conceptual models on relationships between age and occupational wellbeing (Scheibe and Zacher, 2013; Zacher et al., 2014a). In addition, future research could also focus on updating and extending earlier meta-analytic work in this area, as several meta-analyses have been conducted more than 10 years ago (Zacher and Froidevaux, 2021). Furthermore, consistent with the potential theoretical advancements outlined above, it seems important that future empirical research adopts a multilevel approach to study associations between age and occupational wellbeing, including effects of predictors on multiple levels, as well as cross-level interactions between employee age and higher-level constructs (e.g., Zacher and Yang, 2016). Moreover, researchers have called for increased methodological creativity and rigour in designing studies on age and work (Bohlmann et al., 2018). First, studies should make use of samples with appropriate numbers of participants from different age groups, as older workers have often been underrepresented in previous work. Second, studies on age

and work should operationalize chronological age as a continuous variable instead of splitting it into arbitrary age groups; due to conceptual and methodological problems with the notion of 'generations', researchers should also avoid grouping birth cohorts and examining 'generational differences' (Rauvola et al., 2019; Rudolph and Zacher, 2017). Third, it is further important to consider theoretically appropriate control variables and associated alternative explanations when examining relationships between age and occupational wellbeing, such as job and organizational tenure (Riza et al., 2018). In this regard, researchers have also suggested 'alternatives' to chronological age, such as subjective or perceived age (i.e., how old employees 'feel'), as predictors of work-related outcomes. However, recent studies have suggested that negative associations between subjective age and favourable work outcomes, including occupational wellbeing, become weaker and non-significant when individuals' self-beliefs (i.e., core self-evaluations; Judge, 2009) are statistically accounted for (Zacher and Rudolph, 2019a, 2019b). Fourth, it is advisable to routinely test for potential curvilinear associations between age and work-related variables, especially occupational wellbeing outcomes, as some research has suggested 'peaks' or 'valleys' in wellbeing in midlife or mid-career (Blanchflower and Oswald, 2008; Clark et al., 1996; Zacher et al., 2014b). For instance, a recent meta-analysis found a curvilinear association between age and career commitment (Katz et al., 2019). Finally, scholars interested in age and occupational wellbeing should increasingly adopt alternatives to cross-sectional and single-source survey designs (e.g., experiments, longitudinal studies; Bohlmann et al., 2018). Regarding the latter, several recent studies have demonstrated that controlled experimental manipulations, for instance of age-based discrimination (Armenta et al., 2017), as well as longitudinal studies with multiple waves (Potočnik and Sonnentag, 2013), can significantly advance understanding of changes in occupational wellbeing at higher ages.

Finally, in terms of implications for organizations and policy, it seems advisable that practitioners take into account the existing evidence from meta-analyses and primary studies when designing work and organizational policies, procedures, and jobs, and when motivating and supporting members of different age groups at work (Kooij et al., 2020; Truxillo et al., 2015). For instance, it is important to emphasize that, in contrast to common age stereotypes, research shows only few declines in occupational wellbeing for certain objective indicators of ill-health, whereas many studies show age-related maintenance and increases in subjective physical and mental health and wellbeing. In addition, for many indicators of occupational wellbeing, interindividual variability increases as workers get older, making age a less useful proxy for health and wellbeing in later life (Zacher, 2015). Accordingly, managers should combat negative age-based stereotypes in their organizations, as these can not only lead to age discrimination in employment, but also can be internalized by older workers themselves, with negative consequences for their work motivation and occupational wellbeing (Von Hippel et al., 2012, 2018). With regard to job design, it is important to consider age-related changes in employees' abilities and needs; for instance, there is evidence that older workers report higher occupational wellbeing in jobs that are meaningful and allow them to make use of their skills (Mühlenbrock and Hüffmeier, 2020; Zaniboni et al., 2013). Supervisors and leaders should generally avoid recommendations based on generational stereotypes and instead adopt a lifespan perspective that considers individuals' changing abilities, needs, and work–life circumstances (Rudolph et al., 2018b). Finally, at the organizational level, it seems advisable to create a non-discriminatory as well as ageing- and diversity-friendly climate (i.e., formal policies, practices, and procedures) and culture (i.e., informal values and beliefs; Böhm et al., 2014; Kunze et al., 2011; Zacher and Yang, 2016).

CONCLUSION

The ageing and increasingly age-diverse workforce has resulted in an increased interest among both organizational researchers and practitioners in associations between chronological age and occupational health and wellbeing. The lifespan developmental perspective and its related theories represent useful frameworks to understand how, why, and when occupational health and wellbeing differ between younger and older workers or change with increasing age. Several meta-analyses on bivariate relationships between age and occupational wellbeing have refuted the common stereotype of the generally unhealthy older worker, showing that objective indicators of physical ill-health increase, but also that subjective forms of physical and mental health and wellbeing often increase with age as well. These age-related changes can be explained by both environmental and personal resources, including ageing-supportive job design as well as successful ageing strategies. Future theory development should focus on integrating different lifespan theories, as well as lifespan theories and organizational and sociological life course theories, and applying improved theoretical frameworks to better understand both gains and losses in occupational wellbeing with age. In addition, further empirical research is necessary to better understand the mechanisms and person-related and contextual boundary conditions of associations between age and various dimensions of occupational wellbeing. In their attempts to manage the ageing workforce, organizational practitioners should take into account these research findings when designing work policies, procedures, and jobs, and when motivating and supporting members of different age groups at work.

REFERENCES

Ackerman PL and Kanfer R. (2020) Work in the 21st century: New directions for aging and adult development. *American Psychologist* 75: 486–498.

Armenta BM, Stroebe K, Scheibe S, Postmes, T and Van Yperen NW. (2017) Feeling younger and identifying with older adults: Testing two routes to maintaining well-being in the face of age discrimination. *PLoS ONE* 12: e0187805.

Bal PM, De Lange AH, Jansen PGW and Van Der Velde MEG. (2008) Psychological contract breach and job attitudes: A meta-analysis of age as a moderator. *Journal of Vocational Behavior* 72: 143–158.

Baltes PB. (1987) Theoretical propositions of life-span developmental psychology: On the dynamics between growth and decline. *Developmental Psychology* 23: 611–626.

Baltes PB. (1997) On the incomplete architecture of human ontogeny: Selection, optimization, and compensation as foundation of developmental theory. *American Psychologist* 52: 366–380.

Baltes PB and Baltes MM. (1990) Psychological perspectives on successful aging: The model of selective optimization with compensation. In: Baltes PB and Baltes MM (eds) *Successful aging: Perspectives from the behavioral sciences.* New York: Cambridge University Press, 1–34.

Baltes PB, Reese HW and Lipsitt LP. (1980) Life-span developmental psychology. *Annual Review of Psychology* 31: 65–110.

Baltes PB and Smith J. (2003) New frontiers in the future of aging: From successful aging of the young old to the dilemmas of the fourth age. *Gerontology* 49: 123–135.

Blanchard-Fields F. (2007) Everyday problem solving and emotion: An adult developmental perspective. *Current Directions in Psychological Science* 16: 26–31.

Blanchflower DG and Oswald AJ. (2008) Is well-being U-shaped over the life cycle? *Social Science & Medicine* 66: 1733–1749.

Bohlmann C, Rudolph CW and Zacher H. (2018) Methodological recommendations to move research on work and aging forward. *Work, Aging and Retirement* 4: 225–237.

Böhm SA, Kunze F and Bruch H. (2014) Spotlight on age-diversity climate: The impact of age-inclusive HR practices on firm-level outcomes. *Personnel Psychology* 67: 667–704.

Carstensen LL. (2006) The influence of a sense of time on human development. *Science* 312: 1913–1915.

Carstensen LL, Isaacowitz DM and Charles ST. (1999) Taking time seriously: A theory of socioemotional selectivity. *American Psychologist* 54: 165–181.

Charles ST. (2010) Strength and vulnerability integration: A model of emotional well-being across adulthood. *Psychological Bulletin* 136: 1068–1091.

Charles ST and Luong G. (2013) Emotional experience across adulthood: The theoretical model of strength and vulnerability integration. *Current Directions in Psychological Science* 22: 443–448.

Clark A, Oswald A and Warr P. (1996) Is job satisfaction U-shaped in age? *Journal of Occupational and Organizational Psychology* 69: 57–81.

Diewald M and Mayer KU. (2009) The sociology of the life course and life span psychology: Integrated paradigm or complementing pathways? *Advances in Life Course Research* 14: 5–14.

Doerwald F, Scheibe S, Zacher H and Van Yperen NW. (2016) Emotional competencies across adulthood: State of knowledge and implications for the work context. *Work, Aging and Retirement* 2: 159–216.

Erikson EH. (1950) *Childhood and society,* New York, NY: W. W. Norton.

Feldman DC and Vogel RM. (2009) The aging process and person-environment fit. In: Baugh SG and Sullivan SE (eds) *Research in careers.* Charlotte, NC: Information Age Press, 1–25.

Fisher GG, Chaffee DS, Tetrick LE, Davalos DB and Potter GG. (2017) Cognitive functioning, aging, and work: A review and recommendations for research and practice. *Journal of Occupational Health Psychology* 22: 314–336.

Freund AM and Baltes PB. (2000) The orchestration of selection, optimization, and compensation: An action-theoretical conceptualization of a theory of developmental regulation.

In: Perrig WJ and Grob A (eds) *Control of human behavior, mental processes, and consciousness*. Mahwah, NJ: Lawrence Erlbaum, 35–58.

Fung HH, Carstensen LL and Lutz AM. (1999) Influence of time on social preferences: Implications for life-span development. *Psychology and Aging* 14: 595–604.

Gostautaite B and Buciuniene I. (2015) Work engagement during life-span: The role of interaction outside the organization and task significance. *Journal of Vocational Behavior* 89: 109–119.

Haase CM, Heckhausen J and Wrosch C. (2013) Developmental regulation across the life span: Toward a new synthesis. *Developmental Psychology* 49: 964–972.

Heckhausen J and Schulz R. (1995) A life-span theory of control. *Psychological Review* 102: 284–304.

Heckhausen J, Wrosch C and Schulz R. (2010) A motivational theory of life-span development. *Psychological Review* 117: 32–60.

Hertel G, Rauschenbach C, Thielgen M and Krumm S. (2015) Are older workers more active copers? Longitudinal effects of age-contingent coping on strain at work. *Journal of Organizational Behavior* 36: 514–537.

Hertel G and Zacher H. (2018) Managing the aging workforce. In: Ones DS, Anderson N, Viswesvaran C, et al. (eds) *The Sage handbook of industrial, work and organizational psychology*. 2nd ed. Thousand Oaks, CA: Sage, 396–428.

Huffman A, Culbertson SS, Henning JB and Goh A. (2013) Work-family conflict across the lifespan. *Journal of Managerial Psychology* 28: 761–780.

Jex SM, Wang M and Zarubin A. (2007) Aging and occupational health. In: Shultz KS and Adams GA (eds) *Aging and work in the 21st century*. Mahwah, NJ: Lawrence Erlbaum, 199–223.

Judge TA. (2009) Core self-evaluations and work success. *Current Directions in Psychological Science* 18: 58–62.

Katz IM, Rudolph CW and Zacher H. (2019) Age and career commitment: Meta-analytic tests of competing linear versus curvilinear relationships. *Journal of Vocational Behavior* 112: 396–416.

Kooij DTAM, Zacher H, Wang M and Heckhausen J. (2020) Successful aging at work: A process model to guide future research and practice. *Industrial and Organizational Psychology*. 13: 345–365.

Kunze F, Böhm SA and Bruch H. (2011) Age diversity, age discrimination climate and performance consequences: A cross organizational study. *Journal of Organizational Behavior* 32: 264–290.

Lang FR and Carstensen LL. (2002) Time counts: Future time perspective, goals, and social relationships. *Psychology and Aging* 17: 125–139.

Levinson DJ. (1986) A conception of adult development. *American Psychologist* 41: 3–13.

Maertens JA, Putter SE, Chen PY, Diehl M and Huang YH. (2012) Physical capabilities and occupational health of older workers. In: Hedge JW and Borman WC (eds) *The Oxford Handbook of Work and Aging*. New York: Oxford University Press, 215–235.

McCarthy J, Heraty N and Bamberg A. (2019) Lifespan perspectives on age-related stereotypes, prejudice, and discrimination at work (and beyond). In: Baltes BB, Rudolph CW and Zacher H (eds) *Work across the lifespan*. London, UK: Academic Press, 417–435.

Moen P and Sweet S. (2004) From 'work–family' to 'flexible careers': A life course reframing. *Community, Work & Family* 7: 209–226.

Moghimi D, Zacher H, Scheibe S and Van Yperen NW. (2017) The selection, optimization, and compensation model in the work context: A systematic review and meta-analysis of two decades of research. *Journal of Organizational Behavior* 38: 247–275.

Mühlenbrock I and Hüffmeier J. (2020) Differential work design for different age groups? A systematic literature review of the moderating role of age in the relation between psychosocial work characteristics and health. *Zeitschrift für Arbeits- und Organisationspsychologie* 64: 171–195.

Ng TWH and Feldman DC. (2010) The relationship of age with job attitudes: A meta-analysis. *Personnel Psychology* 63: 667–718.

Ng TWH and Feldman DC. (2013) Employee age and health. *Journal of Vocational Behavior* 83: 336–345.

Ng TWH and Feldman DC. (2015) The moderating effects of age in the relationships of job autonomy to work outcomes. *Work, Aging and Retirement* 1: 64–78.

Opitz P, Gross JJ and Urry HL. (2012) Selection, optimization, and compensation in the domain of emotion regulation: Applications to adolescence, older age, and major depressive disorder. *Social and Personality Psychology Compass* 6: 142–155.

Parry E and McCarthy J. (2017) *The Palgrave handbook of age diversity and work,* London: Palgrave Macmillan.

Posthuma RA and Campion MA. (2009) Age stereotypes in the workplace: Common stereotypes, moderators, and future research directions. *Journal of Management* 35: 158–188.

Potočnik K and Sonnentag S. (2013) A longitudinal study of well-being in older workers and retirees: The role of engaging in different types of activities. *Journal of Occupational and Organizational Psychology*.

Rauschenbach C, Krumm S, Thielgen MM and Hertel G. (2013) Age and work-related stress: A review and meta-analysis. *Journal of Managerial Psychology* 28: 781–804.

Rauvola RS, Rudolph CW, Ebbert L and Zacher H. (2020) Person-environment fit and work satisfaction: Exploring the conditional effects of age. *Work, Aging and Retirement* 6: 101–117.

Rauvola RS, Rudolph CW and Zacher H. (2019) Generationalism: Problems and implications. *Organizational Dynamics* 48: 100664.

Riza SD, Ganzach Y and Liu Y. (2018) Time and job satisfaction: A longitudinal study of the differential roles of age and tenure. *Journal of Management* 44: 2558–2579.

Rodrigues FR, Cunha MP, Castanheira F, Bal PM and Jansen PG. (2020) Person-job fit across the work lifespan – The case of classical ballet dancers. *Journal of Vocational Behavior* 118: 103400.

Rudolph CW. (2016) Lifespan developmental perspectives on working: A literature review of motivational theories. *Work, Aging and Retirement* 2: 130–158.

Rudolph CW, Marcus J and Zacher H. (2018a) Global issues in work and aging. In: Shultz KS and Adams GA (eds) *Aging and work in the 21st century.* New York: Routledge, 292–324.

Rudolph CW, Rauvola RS and Zacher H. (2018b) Leadership and generations at work: A critical review. *The Leadership Quarterly* 29: 44–57.

Rudolph CW and Zacher H. (2017) Considering generations from a lifespan developmental perspective. *Work, Aging and Retirement* 3: 113–129.

Salmela-Aro K and Upadyaya K. (2018) Role of demands-resources in work engagement and burnout in different career stages. *Journal of Vocational Behavior* 108: 190–200.

Salthouse TA. (2012) Consequences of age-related cognitive declines. *Annual Review of Psychology* 63: 201–226.

Scheibe S and Zacher H. (2013) A lifespan perspective on emotion regulation, stress, and well-being in the workplace. In: Perrewé PL, Halbesleben J and Rosen CC (eds) *Research in occupational stress and well-being.* Bingley, UK: Emerald, 167–197.

Schmitt A and Bathen M. (2015) Occupational health, well-being, and aging. In: Pachana NA (ed) *Encyclopedia of geropsychology.* New York: Springer, 1674–1681.

Schwall AR. (2012) Defining age and using age-relevant constructs. In: Hedge JW and Borman WC (eds) *The Oxford handbook of work and aging.* New York: Oxford University Press, 169–186.

Settersten RA. (2017) Some things I have learned about aging by studying the life course. *Innovation in Aging* 1: 1–7.

Tomlinson J, Baird M, Berg P and Cooper R. (2018) Flexible careers across the life course: Advancing theory, research and practice. *Human Relations* 71: 4–22.

Truxillo DM, Cadiz DM and Hammer LB. (2015) Supporting the aging workforce: A research review and recommendations for workplace intervention research. *Annual Review of Organizational Psychology and Organizational Behavior* 2: 351–381.

Urry HL and Gross JJ. (2010) Emotion regulation in older age. *Current Directions in Psychological Science* 19: 352–357.

Von Hippel C, Kalokerinos EK, Haanterä K and Zacher H. (2018) Age-based stereotype threat and work outcomes: Stress appraisals and rumination as mediators. *Psychology and Aging* 34: 68–84.

Von Hippel C, Kalokerinos EK and Henry JD. (2012) Stereotype threat among older employees: Relationships with job attitudes and turnover intentions. *Psychology and Aging* 28: 17–27.

World Health Organization. (1948) *Preamble to the Constitution of the World Health Organization,* Geneva: Author.

Yaldiz LM, Truxillo DM, Bodner T and Hammer LB. (2018) Do resources matter for employee stress? It depends on how old you are. *Journal of Vocational Behavior* 107: 182–194.

Zacher H. (2015) Successful aging at work. *Work, Aging and Retirement* 1: 4–25.

Zacher H, Feldman DC and Schulz H. (2014a) Age, occupational strain, and well-being: A person-environment fit perspective. In: Perrewé PL, Halbesleben J and Rosen CC (eds) *Research in occupational stress and well-being.* Bingley, UK: Emerald, 83–111.

Zacher H and Frese M. (2009) Remaining time and opportunities at work: Relationships between age, work characteristics, and occupational future time perspective. *Psychology and Aging* 24: 487–493.

Zacher H and Froidevaux A. (2021) Life stage, lifespan, and life course perspectives on vocational behavior and development: A theoretical framework, review, and research agenda. *Journal of Vocational Behavior.* DOI: 10.1016/j.jvb.2020.103476

Zacher H, Jimmieson NL and Bordia P. (2014b) Time pressure and coworker support mediate the curvilinear relationship between age and occupational well-being. *Journal of Occupational Health Psychology* 19: 462–475.

Zacher H and Rudolph CW. (2017) Successful aging at work and beyond: A review and critical perspective. In: Profili S, Sammarra A and Innocenti L (eds) *Age diversity in the workplace: An organizational perspective.* Bingley, UK: Emerald, 35–64.

Zacher H and Rudolph CW. (2019a) Just a mirage: On the incremental predictive validity of subjective age. *Work, Aging and Retirement* 5: 141–162.

Zacher H and Rudolph CW. (2019b) Why do we act as old as we feel? The role of occupational future time perspective and core self-evaluations in the relationship between subjective age and job crafting behavior. *European Journal of Work and Organizational Psychology* 28: 831–844.

Zacher H, Rudolph CW and Baltes BB. (2019) An invitation to lifespan thinking. In: Baltes BB, Rudolph CW and Zacher H (eds) *Work across the lifespan.* London, UK: Academic Press, 1–14.

Zacher H and Schmitt A. (2016) Work characteristics and occupational well-being: The role of age. *Frontiers in Psychology* 7: 1411.

Zacher H and Yang J. (2016) Organizational climate for successful aging. *Frontiers in Psychology* 7: 1007.

Zaniboni S, Truxillo DM and Fraccaroli F. (2013) Differential effects of task variety and skill variety on burnout and turnover intentions for older and younger workers. *European Journal of Work and Organizational Psychology* 22: 306–317.

5

Emotions and Wellbeing at Work: A Multilevel Perspective

5

Ashlea C. Troth, Alannah E. Rafferty,
and Peter J. Jordan

INTRODUCTION

> It's business, leave your emotions at the door. *The Wolf of Wall Street*

Interest in how emotions shape organizational attitudes and behaviors has risen over the last couple of decades among scientists and practitioners (Ashforth and Humphrey, 1995; Barsade and Gibson, 2007; Hochschild, 1983). Appreciation of the critical role of workplace emotions emerged during the 1980s. Prior to this, the idea of emotions at work was viewed as ancillary to the more 'rational' concepts of scientific management, which focused on industrial productivity and effectiveness (Ashkanasy et al., 2017). This led to the idea – as evidenced by the opening quote – that emotions were to be ignored as an annoyance at best or, at worst, as something to be eliminated. Unsurprisingly, employee wellbeing was not given much attention at this time either. If it was considered, then the role of emotions – both their experience and

expression – was generally seen as something reflective of poor mental health and low control (i.e., reflective of neuroticism and anxiety; Putnam and Mumby, 1993). In this chapter, we argue that emotions should be seen as an essential component in all workplaces and that the appropriate management of emotions can lead to better employee wellbeing.

Fortunately, it is now widely recognized that emotions are inevitable in the workplace and play a complex role, including a positive one, in relation to wellbeing (Bakker and Oerlemans, 2011). The phrase 'the Affective Revolution' (Barsade et al., 2003) has been coined to describe the transformation of the workplace from an

> 'effective no-go zone' for emotions to one where understanding the role of emotions is now seen to be *de rigueur* for scholars working in the field. (Ashkanasy and Dorris, 2017: 68)

A major research topic of interest has been the role of emotion in workplace wellbeing and its subsequent impact on performance.

Emotion has been largely examined in two main ways in this body of work. First, emotion has been viewed as part of one's daily work and, when considered in this light, is often discussed in terms of emotion work or emotional labor (Hochschild, 1983; Zapf, 2002). Researchers have considered that emotional work or emotional labor has *consequences* for employee wellbeing (Holman et al., 2008). In this vein, it is commonly acknowledged that many employees are not only required to work on tasks that use mental and physical energy, they are also required to manage their emotions as part of the requirement of their job (e.g., nurses are expected to show care and compassion with patients) and that this impacts on their health and wellbeing.

The other major approach that has been adopted is to conceptualize affect as a key dimension or component of wellbeing. This is particularly salient for researchers who take a hedonic approach to wellbeing and conceptualize wellbeing in terms of pleasure attainment and pain avoidance with a focus on happiness (Wright, 2014). This approach contrasts with the eudaimonic approach, which focuses on meaning and self-realization (Ryan and Deci, 2001). For example, Bakker and Oerlemans' (2011) model of subjective wellbeing uses the circumplex model of affect as a theoretical framework to distinguish between specific types of work-related wellbeing, including work engagement, job satisfaction, happiness at work, and workaholism, with links to performance. Likewise, one of the most widely used measures of wellbeing, the Job-Related Affective Wellbeing Scale (JAWS: Van Katwyk et al., 2000) links job stressors to a diverse range of affective states at work. Indeed, researchers examining variables such as burnout (considered the opposite of wellbeing) also use affective terms to describe the phenomenon. Emotional exhaustion is commonly viewed as the key component of the three factors that comprise workplace burnout (Goldberg and Grandey, 2007; Maslach and Jackson, 1981).

The aim of this chapter is to extend consideration of wellbeing through an emotion lens by examining the nexus between emotion and wellbeing at *multiple levels* within the organization (e.g., in the daily work of an employee, between individuals, in workplace relationships, groups, and organization-wide). To achieve this, we employ the five-level model of emotion in organizations (Ashkanasy, 2003; Ashkanasy and Dorris, 2017). Our goal in doing this is to provide a better understanding and recognition of the complex ways emotions and wellbeing are intertwined. We also highlight several relevant affective theories and concepts that guide our thinking at each of these levels, including Affective Events Theory (AET: Weiss and Cropanzano, 1996); the Process Model of Emotional Regulation (Gross, 1998); Emotional Labor (Hochschild, 1983); and Emotional Intelligence (Mayer and Salovey, 1997). A related aim in this chapter is to present a range of practical suggestions or interventions targeted at these different levels that are useful to practitioners, managers, and organizations.

AFFECT, MOOD, AND EMOTION

Given our chapter specifically deals with emotional phenomena, it is important to have clear construct definitions. *Affect* is the overarching term used by scholars to encompass affective dispositions, moods, and emotions (Kelly and Barsade, 2001). Affect is broadly and inclusively defined as a 'subjective feeling state' (Ashforth and Humphrey, 1995). *Dispositional affect* consists of a person's affective predisposition toward perceiving the world around them positively or negatively (Lazarus, 1991). It is an individual difference variable that encapsulates the characteristic way basic emotions are experienced and expressed and permeates all of one's experiences. In contrast, *moods* are low-intensity, diffuse feeling states that usually do not have a clear antecedent (Forgas, 1995) and can be caused by dispositional affect or emotions. *Emotions* are distinct from dispositional affect and moods in that they have a clear cause or target, are shorter in duration, and are more focused and intense (Frijda, 1993). Examples of discrete emotions include fear, anger, happiness, pride, and sadness. The terms dispositional affect, mood, emotion, and affect may all be seen to represent the broader notion of 'affect' in this chapter.

MULTILEVEL MODEL OF EMOTIONS IN ORGANIZATIONS

In our chapter, we argue that it is important to consider the function of emotions in employee wellbeing across multiple levels of the organization. By doing so, we will be able to develop a more comprehensive understanding of the complex and layered nature of the relationship between emotions and wellbeing, which will ultimately lead to more effective and targeted organizational and management practices. We base our discussion on the five-level model of emotion in organizations developed by Ashkanasy (2003; Ashkanasy and Dorris, 2017). This

model outlines five levels at which emotions impact on work experiences for employees (Figure 5.1). The model begins with Level 1, which refers to within-person temporal variability in affect and the influence on attitudes and behavior. Level 2 refers to between-person variability, which refers to more stable individual dispositions, including trait affectivity and emotional intelligence. Level 3 deals with the role of emotions in interpersonal relationships, including the perception and communication of emotion, and emotional labor. Level 4 views affect as a team-level property and includes team affective tone and team leadership. Finally, Level 5 focuses on the organization as a whole and encompasses organization-wide phenomena such as affective culture and climate.

EMOTION AT THE WITHIN-PERSON LEVEL (LEVEL 1) AND WELLBEING

Research at this level recognizes that an employee's experiences at work are far from consistent. Rather, it is typical for employees to experience momentary and daily variations in every aspect of their behavior, thoughts, and feelings (affect). Emotions experienced on a within-person basis in a single day can

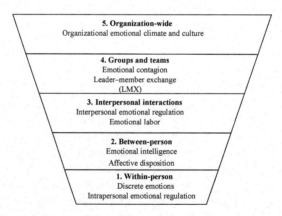

Figure 5.1   Five levels of emotion and relevance to workplace wellbeing (adapted from Ashkanasy, 2003)

be diverse, varying from happy and excited, to surprised, to sad, and to angry and fearful. Affective Events Theory (AET; Weiss and Cropanzano, 1996) is a key theory at this level. AET proposes that a range of daily events at work (e.g., employee and customer interactions, roles, job design) influence employees' emotional responses, which give rise to important attitudinal and behavioral states. Researchers have identified a range of states that emerge from employees' momentary variations in emotional responses including wellbeing-related indicators of psychological safety and job satisfaction as well as learning and goal orientations, and job performance (Alam and Singh, 2019; Ashkanasy and Daus, 2002; Ashton-James and Ashkanasy, 2005; Glasø and Einarsen, 2006). Indeed, there is a burgeoning stream of research that encourages the examination of the dynamic within-person variation of emotion in the workplace (Cropanzano et al., 2017; Fisher and To, 2012).

The focus on examining daily fluctuations in employees' emotional experiences is increasingly captured in occupational stress models linking daily job conditions (stressors: challenge, threat, hindrance) to their reactions (strains) via emotional reactions (Cavanaugh et al., 2000). Drawing on AET, workplace stressors are viewed as affective events (Rodell and Judge, 2009). Challenge stressors (i.e., job demands that are viewed by employees as rewarding work experiences that create an opportunity for personal growth, e.g., job complexity and responsibility) have been shown to lead to positive emotions and wellbeing outcomes. In contrast, hindrance stressors (i.e., job demands that are viewed as obstacles to personal growth or hinder one's ability to achieve valued goals, e.g., role ambiguity and conflict) have been found to lead to negative emotions and wellbeing outcomes (Rodell and Judge, 2009; Searle and Auton, 2015). Importantly, different discrete emotions have been shown to be linked to different appraisals (e.g., anger to appraisals of other responsibility; fear to appraisals of

threat and uncertainty; Smith and Ellsworth, 1985). Understanding that there is within-person variation in employees' emotions at work (in response to workplace events) is important because it reveals that it is these variations in emotional responses that have diverse consequences for wellbeing.

A focus on within-person variations in emotional responses shows that daily fluctuations in employees' wellbeing is partly dependent on the *type* of discrete emotion (e.g., anger or enthusiasm) experienced in relation to an event, and how an individual *regulates* this emotion to respond to different situations. Next, we briefly examine the research linking two discrete negative emotions – anger and fear – to wellbeing. Following this discussion, we discuss the process of emotional regulation as one mechanism by which emotions are managed at the within-person level in daily work life.

Discrete Emotions and Wellbeing

According to Lazarus and Cohen-Charash (2001), discrete emotions provide a more useful source of information to understand employee coping and stress than broader constructs of positive and negative mood or affect. For example, an employee might be angry, frustrated, sad, or ashamed about being reprimanded by their supervisor and this might in part be due to the type of appraisal made about the event. All these emotional responses are negative affective reactions, yet each emotion is linked to varying stressor appraisals and may result in quite different psychological and behavioral consequences impacting wellbeing.

For instance, one of the emotions most frequently researched in relation to workplace stress and wellbeing outcomes for individuals is anger. Gibson and Callister (2010: 68) defined anger as 'an emotion that involves an appraisal of responsibility for wrongdoing by another person or entity and often includes the goal of correcting the perceived wrong'. The experience and expression of anger has usually been regarded as a negatively valenced emotion, with poor consequences for employee wellbeing, especially when of higher intensity and in the context of interpersonal conflict (Andersson and Pearson, 1999). However, it is also important for managers to know that there is a growing recognition that anger can have positive functions (see Geddes et al., 2020; Lazarus and Cohen-Charash, 2001). For example, by being angry, individuals may be able to draw attention to or redress injustice (a common cause of anger). As such, the expression of appropriately expressed anger may contribute to individual wellbeing by drawing attention to stressors in the workplace so they can be resolved and the associated stress reduced.

Another emotion gaining increasing research interest is fear. Although there is a populist view that fear acts to facilitate escape from threats (Frijda, 1986), leading researchers (e.g., see Barrett, 2006; LeDoux, 1998) propose a more fundamental explanation about the role of fear. In particular, these theorists have argued that appraisals of *uncertainty* often drive fear. In general, fear expressions are taboo in the workplace and fear experiences have been negatively associated with wellbeing (Kligyte et al., 2013). However, as with anger, some researchers (e.g., Lerner and Tiedens, 2006) report that fear is not always negative and that it might sometimes be a motivating force to seek help or to help others (Tamir, 2016). Indeed, the rumination process often engaged during a fear experience can result in the effective recognition and management of fear. This process is critical to personal change and growth or as a source of energy to improve productivity and performance (Keegan, 2015). Thus, we argue that discrete emotions are closely tied to wellbeing, but the nature of these ties vary according to the stressor or affective event and appraisal to which they are attached, and how individuals manage those emotions.

The Emotion Regulation Process Model

Another research focus at the within-person level is how individuals manage or modify these discrete emotional experiences and expressions and the subsequent outcomes of this regulation. At this level, we draw on Gross' (1998) emotion regulation (ER) process model, which encapsulates 'the process by which individuals influence which emotions they have, when they have them and how they experience and express these emotions' (1998: 275). Events at work can potentially give rise to a full range of discrete emotions (e.g., happiness, sadness, anger). However, the exact nature of the discrete emotion experienced and expressed partly depends on the use of particular ER strategies (Lawrence et al., 2011) that ultimately impact upon wellbeing.

According to Gross (1998), individuals regulate their emotions using antecedent-focused (prior to the full development of an emotional experience) and response-focused strategies (after the discrete emotion has been experienced). In this regard, Gross identified five broad strategies. The first four comprise antecedent strategies: (1) situation selection, (2) situation modification, (3) attentional deployment, and (4) cognitive change. The fifth is a response-focused response modulation strategy (e.g., expressive suppression) that occurs after a discrete emotion has been experienced. All strategies are intended to increase, to maintain, or to decrease one or more components of the discrete emotion (experiential or expression). Within Gross' process theory, the choice of strategy depends on an individual's emotion-related goals, and the enactment of a strategy can occur consciously, unconsciously, in isolation, or as part of simultaneous regulation attempts (Gross, 2015; Lawrence et al., 2011).

In terms of wellbeing, there is evidence to suggest that individuals who typically regulate their emotions through use of reappraisal report more positive affect, less negative affect, and greater psychological wellbeing than others. On the other hand, individuals who typically use suppression report less positive affect, more negative affect, less social support, and more depression (Gross and John, 2003: John and Gross, 2007). It is also increasingly recognized that the outcomes of ER depend on the intensity and type of emotion being regulated and the context. For example, in terms of anger, there is evidence to suggest that, while the use of re-appraisal regulation should improve employee outcomes, the use of anger expression could result in similar outcomes depending on the intensity and target of the anger (Geddes and Callister, 2007; Geddes et al., 2020). Furthermore, in the face of perceived excessive anger expressed by others, it might be judicious for an employee to engage in suppression of their own expressions of felt anger, at least in the short term. Thus, both the discrete motion and the type of strategy used to regulate a particular emotion in a given context is closely linked to wellbeing outcomes at this level.

EMOTION AT THE BETWEEN-PERSON LEVEL (LEVEL 2) AND WELLBEING

In the previous section we argued that emotions are dynamic and tied to specific events; however, we also know that there are stable differences between persons in affective experiences and attitudes that influence individuals' overall wellbeing. This is captured in Level 2 of the multilevel model of emotions (Ashkanasy, 2003). There are two specific constructs at this level that are important to acknowledge in terms of their relationship to wellbeing: an individual's affective disposition (or trait affect) and emotional intelligence (EI). It is also important to note at this point that both affective disposition and EI ultimately affect an individual's ability to regulate and to manage his or her emotion at work on a daily/event basis (Level 1; see Lawrence et al., 2011).

Affective Dispositions

Trait affectivity, which refers to a personal disposition that influences a person's tendency to experience consistently positive or negative emotions, is related to wellbeing. Negative affectivity (NA) is characterized by an individual's tendency to consistently experience negative emotional moods. Individuals high in NA are 'more likely to report distress, discomfort, and dissatisfaction overtime and regardless of the situation, even in the absence of any overt or objective source of stress' (Watson and Clark, 1984: 483). Individuals high on NA are also more inclined to dwell on their mistakes and shortcomings while focusing on the negative elements of their lives, which can influence their wellbeing (Chang et al., 1997). In contrast, positive affectivity (PA) is the tendency to consistently experience positive emotional states and has been associated with enthusiasm and optimism (Watson and Clark, 1984). There is substantial evidence that job satisfaction relates to PA while this construct is inversely associated with NA (e.g., Brief et al., 1995). There is also evidence to show that the strongest positive relationship between job satisfaction and performance occurs when high value attainment (finding meaning) is coupled with either high positive or low negative affective disposition (Hochwarter et al., 1999). We also know that higher levels of NA are associated with workplace burnout, a counter indicator of wellbeing.

Emotional Intelligence

Another important emotion-related construct that has implications for employee wellbeing at this level is EI. The most broadly accepted definition of EI was provided by Mayer and Salovey (1997), who proposed that the construct consists of four basic abilities: (1) ability to perceive and to recognize emotions in both self and others; (2) ability to incorporate emotional information in decision-making and thinking; (3) ability to understand the effects of emotion in self and others; and (4) ability to use and to manage emotion in self and others.

There is now substantial evidence to show that an individual's level of EI is positively associated with their level of workplace wellbeing (e.g., Brunetto et al., 2012; Carmeli et al., 2009). For example, Fernàndez-Berrocal and Extremera (2016) showed that ability measures of EI were negatively associated with depression and were positively associated with wellbeing, and that these associations were moderated by gender. Further Miao, Humphrey, and Qian's (2017) meta-analysis showed that employees with higher EI have higher job satisfaction, organizational commitment, and lower turnover intentions. They concluded that EI improves job satisfaction by helping employees to reduce negative feelings, by increasing positive feelings, and/or by improving job performance. They also recommended that to produce productive and satisfied workers, organizations should incorporate EI in employee recruitment, training and development programs. Recently, in a group of nurses, Szczygiel and Mikolajczak (2018) showed that EI reduced the impact of negative emotions (anger and sadness) at work on job burnout beyond nurses' demographic characteristics and their dispositional affect. As we discuss in the final section in this chapter, the practical workplace implications for wellbeing of the Level 2 constructs of affective disposition and EI are particularly salient in how they relate to 'fit' in relation to key work-related decisions around selection (Gabriel et al., 2014).

EMOTION IN INTERPERSONAL INTERACTIONS (LEVEL 3) AND WELLBEING

Ashkanasy (2003) explains that Level 3 encompasses interpersonal interactions and associated emotion-related processes. In essence, this part of the model is focused on the perception and communication of emotion in interpersonal exchanges and is consistent with De Dreu et al.'s (2001) idea of emotion as a relational phenomenon. This is a critical level for considering emotionality as organizations, at their core, comprise working relationships between colleagues, between supervisors and subordinates, and between employees and customers. We also know that the quality of these interactions often involves affective elements that are critical to determining important health and wellbeing outcomes.

At this level, we have chosen to focus on emotional labor, its nature, and the role it plays in influencing workplace wellbeing. At the interpersonal level, however, ER is often conceptualized through the lens of emotional labor, especially in regard to wellbeing (see Holman et al., 2008; Zapf, 2002).

Emotional Labor

Hochschild (1983) defined emotional labor as a process by which employees regulate their emotions within interpersonal encounters in order to adhere to organizational emotional display rules. This process of adjusting true feelings 'may involve enhancing, faking, or suppressing emotions' (Grandey, 2000: 95) to produce a prescribed emotional display (e.g., to smile and be pleasant in a service role). Hochschild argued that, when the organization requires employees to display specific emotions in the context of interactions (e.g., be caring and empathetic as a nurse), they enact one of two interpersonal ER strategies: surface acting (suppressing the expression of emotions and faking unfelt emotions) or deep acting (consciously modifying felt emotions to match expressed emotions). Most studies on emotion labor and emotion work also note that emotional labor can result in emotional dissonance. This occurs when an employee is required to express emotions which are not genuinely felt in the particular situation. According to Zapf,

> this may be considered a form of person-role conflict, in which a person's response is in conflict with role expectations regarding the display of emotions… [and thus] a person may feel nothing when an emotion display is required, or the display rule may require the suppression of undesired emotions and the expression of neutrality or a positive emotion instead of a negative one. (Zapf, 2002: 245)

Over time emotional dissonance can be harmful to employee wellbeing.

Emotional labor research has revealed both positive and negative relationships between emotional labor and employee wellbeing. Surface acting (i.e., suppressing the expression of emotions and faking unfelt emotions) is related with low wellbeing, including poor job satisfaction and emotional exhaustion (Bono and Vey, 2005; Grandey, 2003). The connection between deep acting (i.e., modifying the feelings to match the required displays) and wellbeing, however, is less straightforward (Grandey, 2003). For instance, Holman et al.'s (2008) overview of research showed a non-significant association with job satisfaction (Bono and Vey, 2005) and emotional exhaustion (Totterdell and Holman, 2003), but a positive association with personal accomplishment (Brotheridge and Grandey, 2002). In contrast, however, Bono and Vey's (2005) meta-analysis revealed that deep acting is positively linked with emotional exhaustion, but the effect was weaker than for surface acting. One explanation for this pattern of relationships is that the impact of deep acting on exhaustion is mediated by self-authenticity (Brotheridge and Lee, 2002). That is, the negative impact of deep acting on wellbeing that occurs due to the effort required to engage in this type of emotional labor is offset by the positive effect of deep acting on other resources (i.e., more authentic and rewarding relationships).

Researchers also recognize that the consequences of emotion work, when interacting with others, are dependent on personality variables (Level 2) such as positive or negative affective disposition (Zapf, 2002). Evidence also shows that EI moderates the influence of emotional dissonance on general wellbeing and job satisfaction (it reduces the negative effects; Giardini and Frese, 2006). More specifically, EI appears to function as a psychological resource that supports employees' efforts to cope with states of emotional dissonance. In sum, these results underscore the complex and multilevel effects of emotions on wellbeing and show that some employees might be better able to deal with emotion work and emotion labor than others.

EMOTION IN TEAMS AND WORKGROUPS (LEVEL 4) AND WELLBEING

Level 4 of the multilevel model of emotions (Ashkanasy, 2003) incorporates teams and workgroups, acknowledging the increasing use of team structures in organizations. Three important constructs to consider at this level in terms of wellbeing are emotional contagion, affective tone, and the role of Leader–Member Exchange (LMX), the latter assessing the quality of interactions between leaders and followers.

Emotional Contagion and Affective Tone

Two salient and interrelated constructs at this level include the effect of 'emotional contagion in teams' (i.e., when individuals 'catch' or transfer the emotions of others unconsciously and unintentionally to each other; Hatfield et al., 1993) on 'group affective tone' (George, 1990). This latter construct has been defined as occurring when individuals in workgroups tend to experience highly similar levels of affect (e.g., excitement, frustration etc.). Kelly and Barsade (2001) showed that emotional contagion is key to the dissemination of moods in work teams.

There is also evidence to suggest that leaders play a critical role in determining emotional states at a group level, via their disproportionate influence in emotional contagion processes (Sy et al., 2005).

Group-level affective tone is related to wellbeing outcomes. Shared positive moods in teams has been found to be positively related to team satisfaction (Kelly and Spoor, 2007) and team goal commitment (Chi et al., 2011), and has been negatively related to group absenteeism (Mason and Griffin, 2003). It is reasoned that positive group affective tone helps team members build enduring social resources (e.g., cooperation, helping), psychological resources (e.g., optimism, resilience), and physical resources (e.g., more energy) by increasing supportive and encouraging communication during team interactions, which positively impacts on team wellbeing and outcomes (Chi et al., 2011). Conversely, negative group affective states are more likely to be linked to team conflict, absenteeism (George, 1990), exhaustion, and sick days (Knight et al., 2018). In particular, absenteeism, exhaustion, and increased sick days are often proxy measures used to assess employee wellbeing.

Leader–Member Exchange

One way to assess the influence of leadership on followers is through the quality of LMX relationships (Graen and Uhl-Bien, 1995). LMX is another key construct related to emotion at Level 4. LMX focuses on the quality of the relationship between a leader and follower and proposes that leaders develop a range of interpersonal relationships with subordinates. Leaders form low-quality transactional relationships with some employees, while they develop high-quality socioemotional relationships with other followers. The quality of LMX has consequences for the work experiences of both parties and influences the experience of the overall team. A high-quality LMX relationship tends to feature mutual respect, trust, and influence that go beyond the formal employment contract (Graen and Uhl-Bien, 1995; Tse and Troth, 2013). In contrast, low-quality LMX relationships are restricted to the terms derived from the formal employment contact. Compared to peers in high LMX relationships, subordinates in low LMX relationships often receive less supervisory attention, poorer access to resources, and fewer empowerment opportunities, which leads to job dissatisfaction and lower organizational commitment (Gerstner and Day, 1997). All factors that can have a major impact on the experienced wellbeing of employees.

An increasing research focus is on how emotions influence LMX quality (see Tse et al., 2018). Due to the increased proximity and frequency of interactions between subordinates and supervisors within groups, emotions are intrinsically involved in LMX processes in workgroups and teams. Underpinned by AET (Weiss and Cropanzano, 1996), Tse and Troth (2013) showed that the quality of LMX relationships is perceived by subordinates as a source of affective events, which create 'uplifts' (e.g, positive feedback, praise, or inspiration) that produce positive emotional responses or 'hassles' (e.g., unfounded criticism, being overlooked for a development opportunity in favor of another colleague). They also cause negative emotional reactions among workgroup subordinates, with consequences for wellbeing.

EMOTIONS IN ORGANIZATIONS AS A WHOLE (LEVEL 5) AND WELLBEING

Level 5 of the multilevel model (Ashkanasy, 2003) considers the organization-wide role that emotions play. At this level, theorists have considered the emotion phenomena related to organizational culture and climate. Ashkanasy and colleagues (Ashkanasy and

Daus, 2002; Ashkanasy and Härtel, 2014) argued that, at this level, researchers need to consider how organizations can engender a healthy emotional climate. They contend that 'healthy' organizations are broadly characterized by positive emotions, high commitment, and high job satisfaction – leading to high performance and positive outcomes. A positive affective culture and climate is manifested though organizational members' understandings about norms and expectations that exist in the organization (Ashkanasy and Härtel, 2014). These norms and expectations, in turn, are reflected in the affective climate (positive or negative), the norms for emotional expression, and in the organization's emotional history. All of these factors enhance the wellbeing of employees. For example, an organization that has just survived a restructure is likely to have an emotional history that is very different to an organization riding the crest of an economic boom. Knight et al. (2018) argued that an organization develops an overall affective tone, which influences workforce strain such that a positive affective tone reduces strain while a negative affective tone increases strain.

Ashkanasy (2003) contends that the central concept at the organizational level appears to involve the idea of 'emotional climate', defined as 'an objective group phenomenon that can be palpably sensed – as when one enters a party or a city and feels an attitude of gaiety or depression, openness or fear' (de Rivera, 1992: 197). Climate is distinct from culture. The latter construct is more accurately defined as organizational members' espoused beliefs and values that are underpinned by deep-seated assumptions about the organization and its stakeholders (Schein, 2010). Emotional climate, on the other hand, refers to the collective mood of organizational members, including attitudes toward the organization as a whole, their peers, and their leaders. As such, affective climate is a subset of organizational climate (Ashkanasy, 2003).

PRACTICAL IMPLICATIONS OF EMOTIONS FOR WELLBEING

One of the benefits of examining the emotions and wellbeing nexus across multiple levels is that it enables researchers and practitioners, managers and organizations to consider a broader range of more targeted interventions to optimize employee functioning. In this section, being mindful of the framework set out in the five-level model, we discuss seven key practical implications that draw on work by Ashkanasy and Daus (2002) and Ashkanasy and colleagues (2017).

1 *Emotion expressions at work are valuable sources of information.* Level 1 highlighted the range of discrete emotions, beyond a simple dichotomy of positive and negative affect, that result from different appraisals of affective workplace events. These emotions can have both positive and negative consequences for employee wellbeing and performance. The main point made is that these different emotional expressions serve as valuable sources of information about what the individual is thinking and feeling about particular work events and provide early indications of employees' attitudes, health, and wellbeing. It was also highlighted that the research on emotional regulation and labor demonstrates that managers should not assume that all negative emotion expressions are destructive and need to be minimized.

2 *Emotions impact all jobs.* Building on the previous point, it is important that organizations and managers do not expect employees and workplaces to be emotionless. This is counterproductive for wellbeing and performance. Thus, it is important to evaluate the *'emotional impact'* of jobs. As we stressed throughout this chapter, managers need to recognize that all work has an emotional component. This might run counter to more traditional and ingrained beliefs that employees need to be rational and emotionless to be professional. Although we acknowledge that some jobs require more emotion work than others (e.g., care workers, service workers), it is equally clear that emotions impact all jobs.

3 *Emotions in job design.* Just as the tasks, duties, and responsibilities of a job role need to be examined via job analysis, it is also important

to assess the emotional challenges inherent in a job or environment (Ashkanasy and Daus, 2002). There are a range of questions that organizations should consider. Does the job require high emotion management skills of employees? What are the emotionally challenging aspects of the job (e.g., a care worker expected to be tolerant and empathic working with dementia patients prone to anger outbursts)? If the job is emotionally challenging, then how does the manager (Level 3) and organizational structure (Level 5) ensure ways to buffer the emotional impact of more intense affective events (e.g., via scheduling/job rotation to give 'emotion breaks')? This especially applies to providing individual employees with the freedom to use their own initiative with their work.

4   *Emotions and person–job–organization fit.* Overall, the practical workplace implications regarding the Level 2 constructs of affective disposition and EI for wellbeing are particularly salient as they pertain to 'fit' in relation to key work-related decisions. For example, research suggests that there is a need to make comparisons or seek to match the key attributes of job candidates (in this case their affective dispositions) to similar attributes required of jobs, groups, or the organization (Ferris et al., 1985; Judge and Ferris, 1992). There is a need to broaden recruitment and selection processes to consider emotional capability as well as cognitive ability, skills, and experience (Gabriel et al., 2014). For example, it is important when selecting employees and teams to, in part, consider their positive emotional attitude (see Ashkanasy et al., 2017). If organizations are to develop a positive affective climate, then clearly they need to attract employees who are able to demonstrate the personal qualities and skills needed to achieve this outcome. In particular, it is important to consider the EI and affective disposition of leaders, who have disproportionate influence in groups and influence affective climate via emotional contagion. Moreover, recruitment, selection, and socialization of new employees are functions that are inherently emotion-infused and are often the point at which employees begin to learn the emotion norms of an organization regarding emotional expression and the emotional regulation (Liu et al., 2011).

5   *Emotions and organizational training and development processes.* One potential area for focus

relates to the training and development of managers to be aware of, and skilled in, a range of ER strategies to manage emotion-related events with staff appropriately to enhance employee wellbeing. Training employees in EI skills and healthy emotional expression (Jordan et al., 2002) enhances wellbeing. Thus, organizations need to implement training programs across the organization that specifically address emotional skills, including training in emotional intelligence (Slaski and Cartwright, 2003), empathy (Cherniss, 2000), and emotion regulation training (Totterdell and Parkinson, 1999). In essence, training in emotional factors could be applied to enhance organizational wellbeing.

6   *Modeling appropriate emotions by managers.* The emotional labor literature on leadership also has important practical implications and managers need to pay attention to the moods and emotions of their followers (Humphrey et al., 2008) to address wellbeing issues. Humphrey and his colleagues argue that, although managers and other leaders do not have to express emotions continuously, expressing appropriate emotions is a key function that leaders, who should be concerned with both task and relationships, need to perform. This means leaders need training in how to express their emotions effectively and how to use either deep acting or genuine emotional expressions and avoid the harmful psychological effects that accompany surface acting. These scholars also argue that being proficient at the basic skills behind genuine emotional expression and deep acting may make the workplace more productive and pleasant for both leaders and followers, enhancing wellbeing. There is also mounting evidence that leaders need to use considerable judgment about which emotions to display, especially during times of crisis or when confronting other negative workplace events (Ashkanasy et al., 2017). Ashkanasy and his colleagues argue that, at such times, leaders need publicly to display emotions reflective of confidence and hopefulness even if they personally have the same concerns as their subordinates. Although performing surface acting may make leaders more effective, it may also add to leaders' feelings of emotional exhaustion.

7   *Establishing an organization's emotional requirements.* Importantly, and consistent with AET (Level 1; Weiss and Cropanzano, 1996) and organizational affective climate (Level 5),

employees also need to see that there is a match between organizational policies and how they are expected to behave day-to-day, especially in the form of positive organizational support. According to Ashkanasy et al. (2017), engendering positive organizational culture and climate sometimes comes down ultimately to the nature of the work done by individual employees, and including the freedom to use their own initiative within their work.

CONCLUSION

In this chapter, we presented a multilevel perspective on emotions and the interrelationships between some key emotional concepts and processes with wellbeing. This theoretical analysis has resulted in the identification of seven practical implications that should be carefully considered by organizations. Specifically, our review reveals that emotional expressions at work are important sources of information about employees' responses to organizational events, which influence employees' wellbeing and performance. Importantly, emotions may have negative or positive impacts on wellbeing and performance, and this emphasizes the need for organizations to actively manage the emotional impact of all jobs. One aspect of managing the emotional impact of jobs is a recognition that there is a need to assess the emotional impact of jobs via an emotional job diagnosis. A second aspect of managing the emotional impact of jobs involves a recognition that when considering recruiting and selecting staff, the emotional fit of people with jobs and the organization's emotional climate needs to be assessed. A third aspect of managing the emotional impact of jobs is a need to broaden the focus on training and development programs within organizations to recognize the emotional demands of different organizational contexts. A fourth implication of recognizing the role of emotions at work is that workplace leaders need to become skilled at modeling organizationally appropriate emotions. The final implication of recognizing the importance of emotion in the workplace is a need to clarify an organization's emotional requirements. All seven of these implications require organizations to consider emotions as a legitimate business concern, requiring active consideration and management of emotions at multiple organizational levels, in order to maintain individual and organizational wellbeing and performance.

REFERENCES

Alam M and Singh P 2019 Performance feedback interviews as affective events: An exploration of the impact of emotion regulation of negative performance feedback on supervisor–employee dyads. *Human Resource Management Review*. Epub ahead of print. DOI: 10.1016/j.hrmr.2019.100740.

Andersson LM and Pearson CM 1999 Tit for tat? The spiraling effect of incivility in the workplace. *Academy of Management Review* 24(3): 452–471.

Ashforth BE and Humphrey RH 1995 Emotion in the workplace: A reappraisal. *Human Relations* 48(2): 97–125.

Ashkanasy NM 2003 Emotions in organizations: A multilevel perspective. *Research in Multi-Level Issues* 2: 9–54.

Ashkanasy NM and Daus CS 2002 Emotion in the workplace: The new challenge for managers. *Academy of Management Perspectives* 16(1): 76–86.

Ashkanasy NM and Dorris AD 2017 *Emotions in the workplace. Annual Review of Organizational Psychology and Organizational Behavior 4*: 67–90.

Ashkanasy NM and Härtel CEJ 2014 Positive and negative affective climate and culture: The good, the bad, and the ugly. In: Schneider B and Barbera KM (eds) *Oxford Library of Psychology. The Oxford Handbook of Organizational Climate and Culture*. Oxford: Oxford University Press, pp. 136–152.

Ashkanasy NM, Troth AC, Lawrence SA and Jordan PJ 2017 Emotions and emotional regulation in HRM: A multi-level perspective.

Research in Personnel and Human Resources Management 35: 1–52.

Ashton-James CE and Ashkanasy NM 2005. What lies beneath? A deconstructive analysis of affective events theory. In: Ashkanasy NM, Zerbe WJ and Härtel CJ (eds) *Research on Emotion in Organizations* 1. Oxford: Elsevier Science, pp. 23–50.

Bakker AB and Oerlemans W 2011 Subjective well-being in organizations. In: Cameron K and Spreitzer G (eds) *The Oxford Handbook of Positive Organizational Scholarship*. Oxford: Oxford University Press, pp. 178–189.

Barrett LF 2006 Solving the emotion paradox: Categorization and the experience of emotion. *Personality and Social Psychology Review* 10(1): 20–46.

Barsade SG, Brief AP and Spataro SE 2003 The Affective Revolution in Organizational Behavior: The Emergence of a Paradigm. In: Greenberg J (ed) *Organizational Behavior: The State of the Science* 2. Mahwah, NJ: Lawrence Erlbaum, pp. 3–51.

Barsade SG and Gibson DE 2007 Why does affect matter in organizations? *Academy of Management Perspectives* 21(1): 36–59.

Bono JE and Vey MA 2005 Toward understanding emotional management at work: A quantitative review of emotional labor research. In: Härtel CE, Zerbe WJ and Ashkanasy NM (eds) *Emotions in Organizational Behavior*. Cheltenham: Lawrence Erlbaum Associates Publishers, pp. 213–233.

Brief AP, Butcher AH and Roberson L 1995 Cookies, disposition, and job attitudes: The effects of positive mood-inducing events and negative affectivity on job satisfaction in a field experiment. *Organizational Behavior and Human Decision Processes* 62(1): 55–62.

Brotheridge CM and Grandey AA 2002 Emotional labor and burnout: Comparing two perspectives of 'people work'. *Journal of Vocational Behavior* 60: 17–39.

Brotheridge CM and Lee RT 2002 Testing a conservation of resources model of the dynamics of emotional labor. *Journal of Occupational Health Psychology* 7(1): 57–67.

Brunetto Y, Teo ST, Shacklock K and Farr-Wharton R 2012 Emotional intelligence, job satisfaction, well-being and engagement: Explaining organisational commitment and turnover intentions in policing. *Human*

Resource Management Journal 22(4): 428–441.

Carmeli, A, Yitzhak-Halevy M and Weisberg J 2009 The relationship between emotional intelligence and psychological wellbeing. *Journal of Managerial Psychology* 24(1): 66–78.

Cavanaugh MA, Boswell WR, Roehling MV and Boudreau JW 2000 An empirical examination of self-reported work stress among US managers. *Journal of Applied Psychology* 85(1): 65–74.

Chang EC, Maydeu-Olivares A and D'Zurilla TJ 1997 Optimism and pessimism as partially independent constructs: Relationship to positive and negative affectivity and psychological well-being. *Personality and Individual Differences* 23(3): 433–440.

Cherniss C 2000 Social and emotional competence in the workplace. In: Bar-On R and Parker JDA (eds) *The Handbook of Emotional Intelligence: Theory, Development, Assessment, and Application at Home, School, and in the Workplace*. CA: Jossey-Bass, pp. 433–458.

Chi NW, Chung YY and Tsai WC 2011 How do happy leaders enhance team success? The mediating roles of transformational leadership, group affective tone, and team processes. *Journal of Applied Social Psychology* 41(6): 1421–1454.

Cropanzano R, Dasborough MT and Weiss HM 2017 Affective events and the development of leader-member exchange. *Academy of Management Review* 42(2): 233–258.

De Dreu C K, West MA, Fischer AH and Mac-Curtain S 2001 Origins and consequences of emotions in organizational teams. In: Payne RL and Cooper CL (eds) *Emotions at Work: Theory, Research and Applications in Management*. Chichester: Wiley, pp. 199–217.

de Rivera J (1992) *Emotional climate: Social structure and emotional dynamics*. In: Strongman KT (ed) *International Review of Studies on Emotion*, 2. Hoboken, NJ: Wiley, pp. 197–218.

Fernández-Berrocal P and Extremera N 2016 Ability emotional intelligence, depression, and well-being. *Emotion Review* 8(4): 311–315.

Ferris GR, Youngblood SA and Yates VL 1985 Personality, training performance, and withdrawal: A test of the person-group fit hypothesis for organizational newcomers. *Journal of Vocational Behavior* 27(3): 377–388.

Fisher CD and To ML 2012 Using experience sampling methodology in organizational behavior. *Journal of Organizational Behavior* 33(7): 865–877.

Forgas JP 1995 Mood and judgment: The affect infusion model (AIM). *Psychological Bulletin* 117(1): 39–66.

Frijda, NH 1986 *The Emotions*. Cambridge: Cambridge University Press.

Frijda NH 1993 Moods, emotion episodes, and emotions. In: Lewis M and Haviland JM (eds) *Handbook of Emotions*. New York, NY: Guilford Press, pp. 381–403.

Gabriel AS, Diefendorff JM, Chandler MM, Moran CM and Greguras GJ 2014 The dynamic relationships of work affect and job satisfaction with perceptions of fit. *Personnel Psychology* 67(2): 389–420.

Geddes D and Callister RR 2007 Crossing the line(s): A dual threshold model of anger in organizations. *Academy of Management Review* 32(3): 721–746.

Geddes D, Callister RR and Gibson DE 2020 A message in the madness: Functions of workplace anger in organizational life. *Academy of Management Perspectives* 34(1): 28–47.

George JM 1990 Personality, affect, and behavior in groups. *Journal of Applied Psychology* 75: 107–116.

Gerstner CR and Day DV 1997 Meta-analytic review of leader-member exchange theory: Correlates and construct issues. *Journal of Applied Psychology* 82: 827–844.

Giardini A and Frese M 2006 Reducing the negative effects of emotion work in service occupations: Emotional competence as a psychological resource. *Journal of Occupational Health Psychology* 11(1): 63–75.

Gibson DE and Callister RR 2010 Anger in organizations: Review and integration. *Journal of Management* 36(1): 66–93.

Glasø L and Einarsen S 2006 Experienced affects in leader–subordinate relationships. *Scandinavian Journal of Management* 22(1): 49–73.

Goldberg LS and Grandey AA 2007 Display rules versus display autonomy: Emotion regulation, emotional exhaustion, and task performance in a call center simulation. *Journal of Occupational Health Psychology* 12(3): 301–318.

Graen GB and Uhl-Bien M 1995 Relationship-based approach to leadership: Development of leader-member exchange (LMX) theory of leadership over 25 years: Applying a multilevel multi-domain perspective. *The Leadership Quarterly* 6: 219–247.

Grandey AA 2000 Emotional regulation in the workplace: A new way to conceptualize emotional labor. *Journal of Occupational Health Psychology* 5(1): 95–110.

Grandey AA 2003 When 'the show must go on': Surface acting and deep acting as determinants of emotional exhaustion and peer-rated service delivery. *Academy of Management Journal* 46(1): 86–96.

Gross JJ 1998 The emerging field of emotion regulation: An integrative review. *Review of General Psychology* 2: 271–299.

Gross JJ 2015 Emotion regulation: Current status and future prospects. *Psychological Inquiry* 26(1): 1–26.

Gross JJ and John OP 2003 Individual differences in two emotion regulation processes: Implications for affect, relationships, and well-being. *Journal of Personality and Social Psychology* 85(2): 348–362.

Hatfield E, Cacioppo JT and Rapson RL 1993 Emotional contagion. *Current Directions in Psychological Science* 2: 96–100.

Hochschild AR 1983 *The Managed Heart: Commercialization of Human Feeling*. Berkeley, CA: University of California Press.

Hochwarter WA, Perrewe PL, Ferris GR and Brymer RA 1999 Job satisfaction and performance: The moderating effects of value attainment and affective disposition. *Journal of Vocational Behavior* 54(2): 296–313.

Holman D, Martinez-Iñigo D and Totterdell P 2008 Emotional labor, well-being and performance. In: Cartwright S and Cooper C (eds) *The Oxford Handbook of Organizational Wellbeing*. Oxford: Oxford University Press, pp. 331–355.

Humphrey RH, Pollack JM and Hawver T 2008 Leading with emotional labor. *Journal of Managerial Psychology* 23: 151–168.

John OP and Gross JJ 2007 Individual differences in emotion regulation. In: Gross JJ (ed.) *Handbook of Emotion Regulation*. New York: Guilford Press, pp. 351–372.

Jordan PJ, Ashkanasy NM, Härtel CE and Hooper GS 2002 Workgroup emotional intelligence: Scale development and relationship to team process effectiveness and goal focus. *Human Resource Management Review* 12(2): 195–214.

Judge TA and Ferris GR 1992 The elusive criterion of fit in human resources staffing decisions. *Human Resource Planning* 15(4): 47–66.

Keegan S 2015 *The Psychology of Fear in Organizations: How to Transform Anxiety into Well-being, Productivity and Innovation*. London: Kogan Page Publishers.

Kelly JR and Barsade SG 2001 Mood and emotions in small groups and work teams. *Organizational Behavior and Human Decision Processes* 86(1): 99–130.

Kelly JR and Spoor JR 2007 Naïve theories about the effects of mood in groups: A preliminary investigation. *Group Processes & Intergroup Relations* 10(2): 203–222.

Kligyte V, Connelly S, Thiel C and Devenport L 2013 The influence of anger, fear, and emotion regulation on ethical decision making. *Human Performance* 26(4): 297–326.

Knight AP, Menges JI and Bruch H 2018 Organizational affective tone: A meso perspective on the origins and effects of consistent affect in organizations. *Academy of Management Journal* 61(1): 191–219.

Lawrence SA, Troth AC, Jordan PJ and Collins A 2011. A review of emotion regulation and development of a framework for emotion regulation in the workplace. In: Perrewe P and Ganster D (eds) *Research in Occupational Stress and Well-being* 9. Bingley: Emerald Group Publishing, pp. 197–263.

Lazarus RS 1991 Cognition and motivation in emotion. *American Psychologist* 46(4): 352–367.

Lazarus RS and Cohen-Charash Y 2001 Discrete emotions in organizational life. In: Payne RL and Cooper C (eds) *Emotions at Work: Theory, Research and Applications for Management*. London: Wiley, pp. 45–84.

LeDoux J 1998 Fear and the brain: Where have we been, and where are we going? *Biological Psychiatry* 44(12): 1229–1238.

Lerner JS and Tiedens LZ 2006 Portrait of the angry decision maker: How appraisal tendencies shape anger's influence on cognition. *Journal of Behavioral Decision Making* 19(2): 115–137.

Liu Y, Xu J and Weitz BA 2011 The role of emotional expression and mentoring in internship learning. *Academy of Management Learning & Education* 10(1): 94–110.

Maslach C and Jackson SE 1981 The measurement of experienced burnout. *Journal of Organizational Behavior* 2(2): 99–113.

Mason CM and Griffin MA 2003 Group absenteeism and positive affective tone: A longitudinal study. *Journal of Organizational Behavior* 24(6): 667–687.

Mayer JD and Salovey P 1997 What is emotional intelligence? In: Salovey P and Sluyter D (eds) *Emotional Development and Emotional Intelligence: Implications for Educators*. New York: Basic Books, pp. 3–31.

Miao C, Humphrey RH and Qian S 2017 A meta-analysis of emotional intelligence and work attitudes. *Journal of Occupational and Organizational Psychology* 90(2): 177–202.

Putnam LL and Mumby DK 1993 Organizations, emotion and the myth of rationality. In: Fineman S (ed) *Emotion in Organizations*. Thousand Oaks, CA: Sage, pp. 36–57.

Rodell JB and Judge TA 2009 Can 'good' stressors spark 'bad' behaviors? The mediating role of emotions in links of challenge and hindrance stressors with citizenship and counterproductive behaviors. *Journal of Applied Psychology* 94(6): 1438–1451.

Ryan RM and Deci EL 2001 On happiness and human potentials: A review of research on hedonic and eudaimonic well-being. *Annual Review of Psychology* 52(1): 141–166.

Schein EH 2010. *Organizational Culture and Leadership* 2. Chichester: Wiley.

Searle BJ and Auton JC 2015 The merits of measuring challenge and hindrance appraisals. *Anxiety, Stress, & Coping* 28(2): 121–143.

Slaski M and Cartwright S 2003 Emotional intelligence training and its implications for stress, health and performance. *Stress and Health* 19(4): 233–239.

Smith CA and Ellsworth PC 1985 Patterns of cognitive appraisal in emotion. *Journal of Personality and Social Psychology* 48(4): 813–838.

Sy T, Côté S and Saavedra R 2005 The contagious leader: Impact of the leader's mood on the mood of group members, group affective tone, and group processes. *Journal of Applied Psychology* 90(2): 295–305.

Szczygiel DD and Mikolajczak M 2018 Emotional intelligence buffers the effects of negative emotions on job burnout in nursing. *Frontiers in Psychology* 9: 1–10.

Tamir M 2016 Why do people regulate their emotions? A taxonomy of motives in emotion regulation. *Personality and Social Psychology Review* 20(3): 199–222.

Totterdell P and Holman D 2003 Emotion regulation in customer service roles: Testing a model of emotional labor. *Journal of Occupational Health Psychology* 8(1): 55–73.

Totterdell P and Parkinson B 1999 Use and effectiveness of self-regulation strategies for improving mood in a group of trainee teachers. *Journal of Occupational Health Psychology* 4(3): 219–232.

Tse HHM and Troth AC 2013 Perceptions and emotional experiences in differential supervisor-subordinate relationships. *Leadership & Organization Development Journal* 34: 271–283.

Tse HM, Troth AC, Ashkanasy NM and Collins A 2018 Affect and leader-member exchange in the new millennium: A state-of-art review and guiding framework. *The Leadership Quarterly* 29(1): 135–149.

Van Katwyk PT, Fox S, Spector PE and Kelloway EK 2000 Using the Job-Related Affective Well-Being Scale (JAWS) to investigate affective responses to work stressors. *Journal of Occupational Health Psychology* 5(2): 219–230.

Watson D and Clark LA 1984 Negative affectivity: The disposition to experience aversive emotional states. *Psychological Bulletin* 96(3): 465–490.

Weiss HM and Cropanzano R 1996 Affective events theory: A theoretical discussion of the structure, causes and consequences of affective experiences at work. In: Staw BM and Cummings LL (eds) *Research in Organizational Behavior* 18. Westport, CT: JAI Press, pp. 1–74.

Wright TA 2014 Putting your best 'face' forward: The role of emotion-based well-being in organizational research. *Journal of Organizational Behavior* 35(8): 1153–1168.

Zapf D 2002 Emotion work and psychological well-being: A review of the literature and some conceptual considerations. *Human Resource Management Review*, 12(2): 237–268.

6

Requesting and Receiving Supervisor Support and the Implications for Organizational Wellbeing

Thomas D. McIlroy, Stacey L. Parker, and Blake M. McKimmie

INTRODUCTION

Social support from a supervisor is an important job resource that needs to be available to employees for optimal wellbeing. Theoretical frameworks that incorporate supervisor support as a job resource, such as the Job Demand-Control-Support (JDCS) model (Johnson et al., 1989; Johnson and Hall, 1988), Job Demand-Resources (JDR) model (Demerouti et al., 2001), Conservation of Resources (COR) theory (Hobfoll, 1989), and Self-Determination Theory (SDT; Deci and Ryan, 2000; Van den Broeck et al., 2008), propose that having access to supervisor support increases wellbeing and reduces ill-being. Prior reviews provide strong empirical support for this, by demonstrating that greater levels of perceived supervisor support are positively related to beneficial outcomes, such as job satisfaction and commitment, and negatively related to detrimental outcomes, such as stress and burnout (Barak et al., 2009; Luchman and González-Morales,

2013; Mathieu et al., 2019). However, this literature largely focuses on the presence or absence of supervisor support, tending to consider employees as passive recipients of support and neglecting to consider employees' agency. In contrast, literature on proactive employee behaviour, such as job crafting (Rudolph et al., 2017; Tims and Bakker, 2010; Wrzesniewski and Dutton, 2001), feedback seeking (Anseel et al., 2015; Ashford et al., 2016; Ashford and Cummings, 1983), and information seeking (Morrison, 1993), examines the wellbeing-related benefits of employees actively attempting to increase their own social support resources. However, this literature fails to consider whether such attempts come to fruition or not (e.g., a supervisor may not provide the information that is sought).

In this review, we aim to integrate these extant literatures on supervisor support into an overarching framework, and argue for the importance of considering both theoretical perspectives; that is, considering whether or

	Received (+)	Not received (−)
Requested (+)	Answered Support	Unanswered Support
Not requested (−)	Unsolicited Support	Null Support

Figure 6.1   Supervisor support quadrants as a function of when supervisor support is requested and received

not employees actively request support from their supervisor, in addition to whether or not support is subsequently received. In incorporating both perspectives, this chapter extends prior reviews that have examined the effects of supervisor support on wellbeing. As previously noted, prior reviews have focused either on the benefits of receiving supervisor support, or the benefits of having agency in increasing supervisor support, but no reviews have considered both requesting and receiving supervisor support simultaneously. This is an important area to examine, because an employee's level of agency may influence the way the employee interprets the support, differentially affecting their wellbeing.

For example, an employee who requests and receives support (*answered* support) will likely respond favourably because the support is wanted. However, an employee who receives support from their supervisor when it is not wanted (*unsolicited* support) may feel as though they have little control over the situation, or that their supervisor perceives them to be incompetent, and thus respond negatively to the support. Similarly, the detrimental effects of a lack of support will likely be minimized if an employee does not request support (*null* support), perhaps because the employee has no expectation that they will receive support, or the employee feels as though they do not need support. By the same token, an employee who wants and actively requests support but does not receive it (*unanswered* support) may have expected to receive support, so the impact this lack

of support has will likely be more detrimental. We term these different combinations of requesting and receiving support the supervisor support *quadrants* (Figure 6.1). In this chapter, we aim to identify the consequences of these quadrants for wellbeing.

We begin this review with a definition and conceptualization of supervisor support. We then discuss literature that examines the wellbeing-related outcomes of receiving support and requesting support independent of one another, before discussing literature that considers both of these elements simultaneously. In doing so, we consider mismatches between employees' desired and received support, and the subsequent impact on wellbeing. Specifically, we review the literature that examines: support received; support requested; support not requested and received (unsolicited support); and support requested and not received (unanswered support). We conclude by discussing what is currently known and unknown about the impact of supervisor support on wellbeing, and provide directions for future research and theoretical development.

CONCEPTUALIZATION OF SUPERVISOR SUPPORT

Social support is defined as having access to psychological and material resources from interpersonal relationships (Cohen and Wills, 1985). Supervisors can provide different types of social support to employees, including instrumental and emotional support. Instrumental support reflects practical help to solve problems or complete tasks, whereas emotional support reflects empathy, care, and listening to others (Fenlason and Beehr, 1994). Both types of support are highly correlated and have been shown to produce similar outcomes (e.g., Barling et al., 1988; Mathieu et al., 2019), so we aggregate both types of support in our definition of supervisor support.

As previously highlighted, although numerous theories incorporate supervisor support into their frameworks, these theories differ in their conceptualizations and the extent to which they consider particular elements of supervisor support. Typical conceptualizations tend to focus on the benefits of receiving supervisor support and the consequences of not receiving support. For example, resource theories, including the JDCS model, JDR model, and COR theory, view the availability of supervisor support as a crucial resource that needs to be present to reduce stress and increase motivation (Bakker and Demerouti, 2007). Similarly, SDT stipulates that access to job resources, like supervisor support, satisfies the basic psychological needs for competence, autonomy, and relatedness, enhancing motivation and resulting in improved wellbeing (Van den Broeck et al., 2008). Finally, reciprocity theories, such as social exchange theory and organizational support theory, suggest that receiving supervisor support drives employees to reciprocate favourable treatment toward their supervisor and organization, resulting in positive behavioural and affective outcomes (Cropanzano and Mitchell, 2005; Emerson, 1976; Rhoades and Eisenberger, 2002). Although the aforementioned theories consider employees' agency after receiving supervisor support (e.g., employees use the support for their stress reduction or motivation), they do not consider employees' agency in increasing their own social resources a priori; thus, these theories take a relatively passive approach to

the receipt of supervisor support and the subsequent impact on wellbeing.

Rather than passively receiving support from supervisors, employees can also actively seek support to increase their own social resources. Research that focuses on agency in increasing supervisor support, such as the literature on job crafting, feedback seeking, and information seeking, examines the outcomes of support seeking. This support seeking is typically indicated by employees directly requesting support from their supervisor (e.g., Ashford, 1986; Morrison, 1993; Tims et al., 2011). This literature on proactive employee behaviour proposes that actively seeking support improves wellbeing through either reducing uncertainty (Morrison, 2002), or by facilitating a sense of purpose (Wrzesniewski and Dutton, 2001). While acknowledging employees' sense of agency in increasing their own social resources, this literature neglects to consider whether the requested support is acquired.

Overall, the supervisor support literature tends to examine support as being either a passive process, where employees idly receive support (regardless of whether the support is solicited), or as an active process, where employees exhibit agency to increase their own social resources (regardless of whether the desired support is received). In this chapter, we synthesize and expand on these differing conceptualizations by incorporating agency in seeking support and the subsequent receipt of supervisor support. This broader conceptualization considers the perspectives of both the receiver and giver of support, and acknowledges the dynamic interplay between requesting and receiving supervisor support. Although similar conceptualizations have been proposed by research examining social support in specific populations (e.g., cancer patients, employees who have experienced intimate partner violence; Reynolds and Perrin, 2004; Yragui et al., 2012), this broader conceptualization has not been applied to workplace supervisor support. Therefore, in this review, we examine how requesting and receiving supervisor support in the workplace affects employee wellbeing. We conducted a systematic search of the literature in order to identify a broad range of wellbeing-related outcomes.

METHOD

Inclusion Criteria

Given we defined supervisor support as psychological or material resources available from a work supervisor, empirical studies that operationalized supervisor support in a similar way were included. Further, to be included, studies needed to measure general work-related emotional and/or instrumental support, rather than using context-specific measures (e.g., supervisor support for family), and be at the individual level (e.g., 'my supervisor supports me') rather than group level (e.g., 'my supervisor is supportive of all employees'). Consistent with our conceptualization of supervisor support, studies that examined receiving/not receiving supervisor support and studies that focused on employees requesting support from their supervisor were included. All other sources of support (e.g., coworkers, family) were excluded, unless the studies also examined the independent effects of supervisor support. As we were primarily interested in the direct wellbeing-related outcomes of supervisor support, we only included studies that positioned supervisor support as an independent or mediating variable, and studies that examined outcome variables indicative of wellbeing. Finally, studies needed to be applicable to a work setting, and be available in English.

Search Strategy

We consulted with a librarian to refine our search strategy and ensure we used the most effective strategy (Harari et al., 2020; Koffel, 2015). Given the vast literature on supervisor support, we limited our search to the PsycINFO and Business Source Complete databases. We searched the titles and abstracts of articles within these databases for key terms. Search terms included a combination of 'social support', 'supervisor', and 'work', and similar iterations of these terms. Consistent with our conceptualization of supervisor support, search terms related to agency in seeking supervisor support, such as 'information seeking' and 'feedback seeking', were also included. Table 6.1 shows the full list of search terms used. The search returned 3,843 articles. After removing duplicates, the titles and abstracts of 2,864 articles were screened for eligibility.

Table 6.1   Terms used when conducting the literature search

Support-related terms	Supervisor-related terms	Work-related terms
Social support	Supervisor(s)	Work
Supervisor support	Supervisory	Worker(s)
Supervisory support	Manager(s)	Workplace(s)
Manager support	Managerial	Employee(s)
Managerial support		Job(s)
Emotional support		Organization(s)
Instrumental support		Organizational
Social resources		Organization(s)
Support seeking		Organizational
Help seeking		
Feedback seeking		
Information seeking		

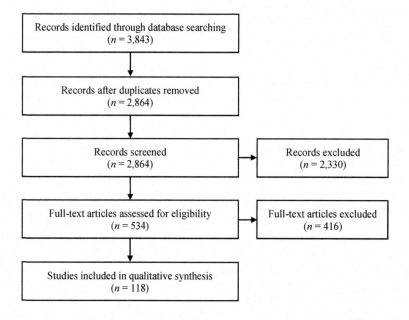

Figure 6.2   Flowchart of the study selection process

We accessed the full text of 534 articles. The final number of articles that met inclusion criteria was 118. Figure 6.2 shows a flowchart of the study selection process.

Data Extraction and Categorization

Data extracted from the studies included sample, sample size, country, study design, supervisor support measure, and outcomes related to wellbeing. We also coded the studies and their outcomes under four categories: received support, requested support, or a combination of these factors – when support is not requested and is received (unsolicited support), or when support is requested and is not received (unanswered support; Figure 6.1).

To organize the broad array of outcomes within each category, we consulted the wellbeing literature and sorted the outcomes accordingly. Across the wellbeing literature, there appears to be a lack of consensus on the dimensions of wellbeing, and

particularly how variables are categorized within the different dimensions. However, it is generally agreed that wellbeing consists of four key dimensions: subjective wellbeing, psychological wellbeing, social wellbeing, and health (Danna and Griffin, 1999; Grant et al., 2007; Ryan and Deci, 2001). There is a degree of overlap between some indicators in these dimensions, so in the next section we describe each dimension and explain how we organized the outcomes within them.

Subjective Wellbeing

Much research has studied subjective wellbeing, which concerns the subjective experiences of employees across all aspects of life. The subjective wellbeing literature has tended to take a *hedonic* approach, equating wellbeing with happiness (Ryan and Deci, 2001). Research within this area often examines emotions and moods (both positive and negative), and satisfaction with life globally and within specific domains, such as work and family

(Diener et al., 1999; Warr, 1990). In the work domain, job-related positive and negative affect are often assessed, in addition to measures of positive work experiences, including job satisfaction, work engagement, and commitment (Bakker and Oerlemans, 2011; Fisher, 2010; Van De Voorde et al., 2012). Subjective wellbeing research also examines satisfaction with the compatibility and balance between work and life (Bakker and Oerlemans, 2011; Danna and Griffin, 1999).

Psychological Wellbeing

In contrast to the hedonic approach adopted by subjective wellbeing research, the psychological wellbeing literature often adopts a *eudaimonic* approach by examining positive psychological functioning, or flourishing (Keyes et al., 2000; Ryan and Deci, 2001). While the hedonic and eudaimonic approaches appear to overlap, it is generally agreed that they are related, yet distinct (Keyes et al., 2002; Linley et al., 2009; Ryan and Deci, 2001). Therefore, we distinguish between these two approaches to capturing wellbeing. From the eudaimonic perspective, Ryff and colleagues (Ryff, 1989; Ryff and Keyes, 1995) theorized six dimensions that capture psychological wellbeing: self-acceptance, positive relations with others, autonomy, environmental mastery, purpose in life, and personal growth. Together, these dimensions are proposed to reflect optimal wellbeing. A complementary eudaimonic approach to wellbeing has also been proposed that is grounded in SDT, and includes the needs for autonomy, competence, and relatedness (Samman, 2007). The fulfilment of these needs is suggested to facilitate wellbeing (Ryan and Deci, 2001; Samman, 2007). In relation to the workplace, organizational psychology research often measures the satisfaction of employees' autonomy, competence, and relatedness needs (Van den Broeck et al., 2016), as well as other motivational constructs, such as empowerment (Spreitzer, 1995).

Social Wellbeing

Social wellbeing refers to individuals' relationship quality with other people in their community (Keyes, 1998). Keyes proposes that social wellbeing consists of five dimensions: social integration, social acceptance, social contribution, social actualization, and social coherence. As social integration and social acceptance are most relevant to the dynamics of requesting and receiving support, we focus on these dimensions. Social integration reflects the extent to which individuals feel as though they belong and are connected to others in their social groups, and social acceptance reflects the extent to which individuals are generally accepting of other people, and includes judgements about kindness and trustworthiness. In the organizational psychology literature, social integration appears to be captured by leader–member exchange, which assesses the quality of the relationship between an employee and their leader (Gerstner and Day, 1997; Grant et al., 2007), and by identification, which measures the extent to which employees feel as though they belong to their organization and its subunits (e.g., work groups; Ashforth and Mael, 1989; Dick et al., 2004). Trust in the organization and its members has also been studied in the organizational psychology literature (Grant et al., 2007; Kramer, 1999), and captures the social acceptance dimension proposed by Keyes (1998). Finally, social support has been suggested as being an indicator of social wellbeing (Grant et al., 2007). Given that social support from a supervisor is the focal predictor in this review, we consider how supervisor support may influence perceived support from other sources, including from coworkers and the organization.

Health

Health is a subcomponent of wellbeing and encompasses mental and physiological indicators (Danna and Griffin, 1999). We categorized outcomes in this dimension of wellbeing if they reflected symptoms of illness or injury (vs wellness). Research in organizational psychology assesses mental and physical health using a number of subjective and objective measures, including depressive and anxious symptoms, stress/strain, burnout, sleep quality, fatigue, psychosomatic symptoms, musculoskeletal pain, general physical health, and biochemical markers using blood and urine samples (Cooper and Cartwright, 1994; Danna and Griffin, 1999; Peterson et al., 2008; Steffy and Jones, 1988; Wilson et al., 2004).

RESULTS

In this section, we describe the wellbeing-related outcomes of the different elements of the supervisor support quadrant model discussed previously (Figure 6.1). We first discuss the breadth of literature related to the receipt of support, before discussing research on requesting supervisor support. We conclude with the scant literature that considers both of these elements together; specifically, support that is not requested and is received

(unsolicited), and support that is requested and is not received (unanswered). For each category, the outcomes are organized into the dimensions of subjective wellbeing, psychological wellbeing, social wellbeing, and health, where possible.

Received Support

The majority of studies ($n = 112$) examined the benefits of receiving supervisor support and the consequences of not receiving support. Popular measures of supervisor support included Eisenberger and colleagues' (2002), Caplan and colleagues' (1980), and Karasek and colleagues' (1998) scales; however, other adapted measures that captured emotional and/or instrumental support were also used. Supervisor support was found to be related to a number of outcomes across a wide variety of countries and industries, supporting the generalizability of the findings. Studies most often examined indicators of subjective wellbeing; however, psychological wellbeing, social wellbeing, and health outcomes were also examined. Table 6.2 shows the list of studies examining each outcome.

Table 6.2 Literature examining the effects of received supervisor support on indicators of subjective wellbeing, psychological wellbeing, social wellbeing, and health

Subjective wellbeing	
Indicator	Studies
Job satisfaction	Aryee and Luk, 1996; Baeriswyl et al., 2016; Caesens et al., 2014; Firth et al., 2004; Fisher, 1985; Fusilier et al., 1986; Hildisch et al., 2015; Korunka et al., 2008; Landsman, 2008; Mansell et al., 2006; Mathieu et al., 2019; Moyle, 1998; Munc et al., 2017; Munn et al., 1996; Lee, 2004; Peterson et al., 2011; Pisanti et al., 2011; Pisarski et al., 2006; Pohl et al., 2016; Rodwell and Munro, 2013; Sawang, 2010; Schirmer and Lopez, 2001; Siu et al., 2015; Sousa–Lima et al., 2013; Stroppa and Spieß, 2011; Tang et al., 2014; Terry et al., 1993; Thompson et al., 2006; Winkler et al., 2015; Yoon et al., 2016
Work-related affect	Cole et al., 2006; Gordon et al., 2019; Munc et al., 2017; Winkler et al., 2015
Work engagement	Bakker et al., 2007; Caesens et al., 2014; Freeney and Fellenz, 2013; Holland et al., 2017; Jose and Mampilly, 2015; Lee and Eissenstat, 2018; Lehner et al., 2013; Munc et al., 2017; Naruse et al., 2013; Nasurdin et al., 2018; Quiñones et al., 2013; Siu et al., 2010
Commitment	Baral and Bhargava, 2010; Casper et al., 2011; Cheng et al., 2015; Fazio et al., 2017; Firth et al., 2004; Fisher, 1985; Frear et al., 2018; Galletta et al., 2016; Kuvaas and Dysvik, 2010; Mathieu et al., 2019; Munc et al., 2017; Nazir et al., 2016; Nichols et al., 2016; Pohl et al., 2016; Rathi and Lee, 2017; Rousseau and Aubé, 2010; Simosi, 2012; Sousa–Lima et al., 2013; Stinglhamber and Vandenberghe, 2003; Vandenberghe et al., 2019
Work-life compatibility	Baeriswyl et al., 2016; Baral and Bhargava, 2010; Bhargava and Baral, 2009; Carlson et al., 2019; Haar et al., 2019; Lo Presti and Mauno, 2016; Nicklin and McNall, 2013; Selvarajan et al., 2013; Siu et al., 2015; Tang et al., 2014; Thompson et al., 2006

Table 6.2 Literature examining the effects of received supervisor support on indicators of subjective wellbeing, psychological wellbeing, social wellbeing, and health (*Continued*)

Indicator	Studies
Psychological wellbeing	
Need satisfaction	Chih Ho, 2017
Intrinsic motivation	Chen et al., 2016; Chih Ho, 2017
Empowerment	Bordin et al., 2007; Jose and Mampilly, 2015; Quiñones et al., 2013
Self-esteem	Dasgupta et al., 2013; Sguera et al., 2018
Social wellbeing	
Leader–member exchange	Gkorezis, 2015
Identification	Horstmeier et al., 2016; Pisarski et al., 2006; van Knippenberg et al., 2007
Trust	Byrne et al., 2012; DeConinck, 2010; Holland et al., 2017; Nifadkar et al., 2019; Sousa–Lima et al., 2013; Stinglhamber et al., 2006; Zhang et al., 2008
Perceived coworker support	Pisarski et al., 2006
Perceived organizational support	Andiyasari et al., 2017; Dai et al., 2018; Dawley et al., 2010; DeConinck and Johnson, 2009; Eisenberger et al., 2002; Frear et al., 2018; Landsman, 2008; Maertz Jr et al., 2007; Melián-González, 2016; Newman et al., 2012; Pazy and Ganzach, 2009; Rhoades et al., 2001; Shanock and Eisenberger, 2006; Yoon and Lim, 1999
Team climate	Pisarski et al., 2006, 2008
Health	
Psychological health	Pisarski et al., 2008
Anxiety and depression	Adriaenssens et al., 2011; Fusilier et al., 1986; Gao et al., 2012; Goldberg and Smith, 2013; Moyle, 1998; Sinokki et al., 2009; Terry et al., 1993
Antidepressant use	Sinokki et al., 2009
Stress/strain	Firth et al., 2004; Park and Jang, 2017; Sawang, 2010; Schirmer and Lopez, 2001; Stroppa and Spieß, 2011; Ulleberg and Rundmo, 1997
Burnout	Baeriswyl et al., 2016; Chen and Chen, 2018; De Lange et al., 2004; Gibson et al., 2009; Ito et al., 1999; Korunka et al., 2008; Lambert et al., 2010; Munc et al., 2017; Pisanti et al., 2011; Russell et al., 1987; Van Doorn et al., 2016; Woodhead et al., 2016; Yürür and Sarikaya, 2012
Fatigue	Parhizi et al., 2013
Sleep	Nakata et al., 2007; Sinokki et al., 2010; Sorensen et al., 2011
Self-rated health	Burr et al., 2017; Marshall and Barnett, 1992
Musculoskeletal pain	Johnston et al., 2007; Krause et al., 1997; Sorensen et al., 2011; Zamri et al., 2017
Inflammatory markers	Nakata et al., 2014
Psychosomatic distress	Adriaenssens et al., 2011

Note: for brevity, the citations in this table are not provided in the reference list. However, a list of all studies included in the review can be accessed on the Open Science Framework (McIlroy et al., 2019)

Subjective wellbeing

Starting with subjective wellbeing, 30 studies found a positive relationship between supervisor support and job satisfaction, making it the most extensively researched indicator of wellbeing. Studies also showed that employees with greater supervisor support had higher positive work-related affect and lower negative work-related affect. Further, supervisor support was found to be associated with other positive work experiences, including greater work engagement, and greater commitment to their supervisor, team, and organization. Supervisor support was also shown to be positively related to work–life balance and work–family enrichment, and negatively related to work–family conflict, suggesting that receiving supervisor support increases employees' perceptions of compatibility between their work and non-work roles.

Psychological wellbeing

In terms of psychological wellbeing, one study found that receiving supervisor support satisfied the psychological needs for autonomy, competence, and relatedness, subsequently increasing self-determined prosocial motivation (i.e., intrinsic motivation to engage in prosocial behaviour). In a similar vein, another study found that supervisor support increased intrinsic motivation more generally. Considered as being a motivational construct, several studies also found that supervisor support was positively associated with psychological empowerment. Together, these findings demonstrate the motivational effects of supervisor support, and reflect the autonomy dimension of psychological wellbeing proposed by Ryff and colleagues (Ryff, 1989; Ryff and Keyes, 1995). Further, related to the self-acceptance dimension of psychological wellbeing, two studies found that supervisor support increased employees' supervisor and organization-based self-esteem, indicating that employees with greater supervisor support felt more valued in the workplace.

Social wellbeing

Employees with greater supervisor support were found to have higher-quality leader–member exchange relationships with their supervisor, and they identified more with their supervisor, team, and organization. As such, receiving supervisor support increased employees' sense of connection with others. Supervisor support was also positively associated with employees' trust in their supervisor and organization. Employees with greater supervisor support also perceived greater levels of support from other sources, including coworkers and the organization. Finally, two studies found that greater supervisor support led to more positive team climates, with team climate reflecting the atmosphere within a team, including elements of trust, cohesiveness, and supportiveness. Together, these findings demonstrate the positive effects of supervisor support on social wellbeing.

Health

Turning to health-related outcomes, several studies found that supervisor support was associated with better mental health, including general psychological health, reduced anxious and depressive symptoms, and lower antidepressant use. Supervisor support was also shown to be negatively associated with indicators of general stress, job-related stress, and burnout. Employees with greater supervisor support also experienced less fatigue and fewer sleeping difficulties. In terms of physical health, supervisor support was found to be positively associated with self-rated general health. Employees with greater supervisor support also reported less musculoskeletal pain, including back, neck, and shoulder pain, and had fewer inflammatory markers identified from blood samples. Finally, supervisor support was found to be associated with lower psychosomatic distress, which incorporates both mental and physical aspects of health.

Requested Support

Several studies examined the direct outcomes of requesting support from a supervisor, for example, by asking for feedback or information. Studies that met inclusion criteria and fell in this category only examined indicators of subjective wellbeing and social wellbeing. With regard to subjective wellbeing, one study found that requesting supervisor support increased employees' organizational commitment (Zou et al., 2015). Several studies also examined indicators of social wellbeing and found that requesting supervisor support increased social integration (Zou et al., 2015), leader–member exchange (Lam et al., 2007; Lapalme et al., 2017; Zheng et al., 2016), and supervisor identification (Young and Steelman, 2014).

Unsolicited Support

None of the studies that met inclusion criteria examined support that was unrequested but received. This is in part because the existing supervisor support literature is largely silent on whether the employees sought the support they received. This demonstrates a need for research examining the receipt of supervisor support to consider employees' sense of agency, which we elaborate on further in the discussion section.

Unanswered Support

Only one study examined requested support and the subsequent receipt (or lack) of supervisor support. Ellis and colleagues (2017) found that newcomers who requested support in the form of asking their supervisor for information were perceived by their supervisor as being more committed, resulting in the supervisor providing information to the employee. Newcomers who received information were also ultimately better socially adjusted, such that they had stronger social connections with others in the organization. In other words, requesting supervisor support appears to indirectly lead to the receipt of support, ultimately improving social wellbeing. While this is an important finding, neither this study, nor any other studies included in the review, considered instances in which supervisor support is requested but not received, and how this affects wellbeing.

DISCUSSION

The aim of this review was to synthesize the literature examining the effects of supervisor support on employee wellbeing, and to provide directions for future research. To achieve this, we expanded typical conceptualizations of supervisor support by incorporating agency and receipt of supervisor support into

an overarching framework. Specifically, we proposed a quadrant model that integrates both the requesting and receiving of supervisor support (Figure 6.1). We developed four categories based on different combinations of the elements within these quadrants: support received; support requested; support not requested and received (unsolicited support); and support requested and not received (unanswered support). We then examined the wellbeing-related outcomes associated with each category. We further distinguished between indicators of psychological wellbeing, social wellbeing, and health within each category, where possible.

What Is Known and What Is Not Known

We first reviewed literature that examined the outcomes of receiving supervisor support. There was substantial evidence demonstrating the benefits of having access to supervisor support across a broad range of outcomes, including indicators of subjective wellbeing, psychological wellbeing, social wellbeing, and mental and physical health. These findings are consistent with previous reviews on the receipt of supervisor support (e.g., Barak et al., 2009; Luchman and González-Morales, 2013; Mathieu et al., 2019), as well as theories that examine supervisor support as a job resource, including the JDCS model (Johnson et al., 1989; Johnson and Hall, 1988), JDR model (Demerouti et al., 2001), COR theory (Hobfoll, 1989), and SDT (Deci and Ryan, 2000; Van den Broeck et al., 2008). There was also evidence for the benefits of exhibiting agency in seeking supervisor support. Requesting supervisor support was positively associated with indicators of psychological and social wellbeing, which is consistent with previous reviews that have examined the benefits of having agency in increasing support (e.g., Ashford et al., 2016; Rudolph et al., 2017), as well as theories on proactive employee behaviour, including job crafting

(Wrzesniewski and Dutton, 2001), feedback seeking (Ashford and Cummings, 1983), and information seeking (Morrison, 1993).

Although the benefits of receiving and requesting supervisor support independent of one another have been well established, much less is known about the dynamic interplay between these factors together. Indeed, the majority of the reviewed supervisor support literature tended to position employees as either passive recipients of support (while being silent on whether the support was requested), or as active agents (while being silent on whether the requested support was received). Only one study that met inclusion criteria examined both the requesting and receiving of supervisor support simultaneously and showed that employees who requested support were generally more likely to receive support, resulting in better social wellbeing (Ellis et al., 2017). This finding is consistent with the most recent update to JDR theory, which proposes that employees who proactively increase their own social resources (e.g., ask a supervisor for help) are likely to have higher levels of social resources, resulting in better wellbeing (Bakker and Demerouti, 2017). However, none of the reviewed studies considered mismatches in supervisor support; that is, situations in which support was not requested but was received (unsolicited support), or situations in which support was requested but was not received (unanswered support), and the implications for wellbeing. As such, we looked to the broader social support literature for further insight.

Research on social support in other contexts that focuses specifically on unsolicited support (e.g., participants receiving unwanted support from a peer in a lab study; older adults receiving unwanted support from friends or family; Deelstra et al., 2003; Smith and Goodnow, 1999) has found that receiving support that is unwanted leads to poorer psychological and physiological wellbeing, such as increased negative affect, lower self-esteem, and increased heart rate. Adopting a more encompassing conceptualization of support, Reynolds and Perrin (2004) used a similar conceptualization to ours, and examined the consequences of wanted support, received support, wanted and received support, and unwanted and received support among female breast cancer patients. The authors found that women who had a higher proportion of support mismatch in the form of receiving support that was unwanted had poorer psychosocial adjustment. Yragui and colleagues (2012) applied the same conceptualization of social support to the study of women who had experienced intimate partner violence and found that only women with a higher proportion of support match, such that they received supervisor support for intimate partner violence when they wanted support, were more satisfied with their job. Together, these findings suggest that receiving unsolicited support (compared to solicited support) negatively affects employee wellbeing, demonstrating that this is a key area of research that needs to be examined in the context of general workplace supervisor support.

Theoretical Implications and Future Research

Although the studies of Reynolds and Perrin (2004) and Yragui and colleagues (2012) incorporated both wanting and receiving in their conceptualization of supervisor support, it is important to note that they did not compare all possible combinations – the authors only included 'wanted and received support' and 'unwanted and received support' in the analyses. Hence, these studies did not examine the relative effects of support that was wanted but not received (unanswered support). This highlights an important aspect that has been neglected in social support research, and indeed supervisor support research in the organizational sciences specifically. Considering both agency and the receipt of support is important, because the degree of agency employees have may influence how they interpret the support (or lack thereof), and ultimately affect their wellbeing. For example, as previously discussed, employees whose requests for support are answered are likely to respond more favourably to the support because it was wanted, compared to employees who receive support that is unwanted. Conversely, employees who do not request or receive support will likely be less affected by the lack of support because there was no expectation that they would receive support, compared to employees who request (and likely expect to receive) support. Therefore, supervisor support may differentially affect wellbeing depending on the extent to which employees have agency, and depending on whether the support is received. As such, future research should examine the proposed quadrants of supervisor support more comprehensively, and, in particular, compare the outcomes of differing combinations of requesting and receiving support: answered support, unanswered support, unsolicited support, and null support (Figure 6.1).

This more comprehensive conceptualization of supervisor support should also be included in future theoretical development. For example, while the JDCS model (Johnson et al., 1989; Johnson and Hall, 1988), JDR model (Demerouti et al., 2001), and SDT (Deci and Ryan, 2000; Van den Broeck et al., 2008) consider how employees use supervisor support as a resource to increase their motivation, these theories should also consider employees' motivation to increase their own social resources from the outset (e.g., an employee with limited supervisor support is likely motivated to increase their own access to supervisor support by requesting it). Conversely, theories and literature that focus on employees' agency in increasing supervisor support, including job crafting (Tims and Bakker, 2010; Wrzesniewski and Dutton, 2001), feedback seeking (Ashford and Cummings, 1983), and information seeking (Morrison, 1993), should consider when active attempts to increase supervisor support are unsuccessful. Although the latest development to JDR theory incorporates both agency and receipt of support (Bakker and Demerouti, 2017), there is an underlying assumption that the act of seeking social resources is successful (i.e., requesting support leads to receiving support). Therefore, this theory does not examine specific instances in which requests for support go unanswered, and the differential implications this may have for wellbeing, which is an important avenue for future theoretical development.

Within the supervisor support literature, there also seems to be a lack of consensus on the mechanisms between supervisor support and wellbeing. While this was beyond the scope of the current review, as we were particularly interested in the direct outcomes of supervisor support, it is interesting to note that several studies incorporated wellbeing indicators as mediators between supervisor support and other wellbeing indicators. The various mediators included job satisfaction, trust in supervisor, work-family enrichment, burnout, and need satisfaction. Future research would benefit from disentangling the nature of the relationships between these highly related variables to uncover the underlying processes between supervisor support and indicators of wellbeing. This would also be important because, as previously discussed, the various combinations of requesting and receiving support may affect wellbeing differently, and these relationships may occur through different intervening mechanisms. Therefore, future research should also aim to uncover why answered support, unanswered support, unsolicited support, and null support might impact wellbeing (Figure 6.1).

We also identified several methodological shortcomings in the literature. Of the articles reviewed, the majority (98 articles out of 118) used self-reported, cross-sectional survey data. The limitations of such methods have been well documented, including self-report bias, common method variance, and causal inference (Donaldson and Grant-Vallone, 2002; Lindell and Whitney, 2001; Podsakoff et al., 2012; Rindfleisch et al., 2008). While a modest number of studies used longitudinal and multi-wave survey designs (20 articles), we encourage more researchers to employ such designs, as they assist with causal inference, by examining how relationships between factors vary over time. For example, we recommend that future research adopt experience sampling methodologies, particularly given that no studies that met inclusion criteria used this type of design. This methodology would allow researchers to track employees' daily experiences and examine the nature of the relationships between supervisor support and indicators of wellbeing more dynamically (Gabriel et al., 2019). This approach would be particularly useful in uncovering the mechanisms of supervisor support, as noted earlier. Similarly, we recommend that research use event-contingent sampling methodologies, which would help researchers track the outcomes when specific instances of the supervisor support quadrants (i.e., answered support, unanswered support, unsolicited support, null support; Figure 6.1) occur (Reis and Gable, 2000). We also identified a need for more experimental research, as only one study manipulated the receipt of supervisor support (Sguera et al., 2018). While literature on social support in other contexts (e.g., receiving support from an experimenter in a lab study; Jimmieson and Terry, 1998; Searle et al., 1999, 2001) has often examined the effects of manipulated social support on wellbeing, our review highlights that more research should manipulate support provided by a supervisor, perhaps by using a work simulation with a virtual or confederate supervisor. Employing experimental designs would allow for stronger inferences of causation by increasing experimental control.

Our review also revealed an abundance of different measures used to study the elements of supervisor support. Regarding the receipt of support, a variety of measures were used to tap into instrumental and emotional support provided by supervisors. Similarly,

several measures captured employees' agency in seeking support, including measures of job crafting, information seeking, and feedback seeking. However, no studies measured requested and received support simultaneously (i.e., considering whether or not support was requested, and whether or not support was received). We argue that examining these elements would provide a more complete understanding of the relationship between supervisor support and wellbeing, and believe a more encompassing measure of supervisor support is needed to capture the different forms of supervisor support. This would allow researchers to compare the unique effects of answered, unanswered, unsolicited, and null support (Figure 6.1).

Practical Implications

Examining the wellbeing-related outcomes of the supervisor support quadrants will also likely have important implications for practice. Identifying the consequences of the dynamics of requesting and receiving supervisor support may help practitioners better understand how supervisors can provide support to employees to enhance wellbeing. For example, if a lack of support is found to be even more detrimental in situations where employees actively request support, it would be important for supervisors and the organization to be aware of how to prevent instances of unanswered support, such as by providing other avenues of support that employees can access if their supervisor is unavailable. Further, organizations could implement policies and procedures, such as redesigning the work of supervisors, to ensure they have the capacity to provide adequate supervision. Given that receiving social support that is unwanted appears to have detrimental effects on wellbeing, it is also important for supervisors to consider whether employees actually want the support that is being offered; otherwise, the support may undermine employees' self-esteem (Deelstra et al., 2003).

CONCLUSION

In this review, we took a more nuanced approach to supervisor support than typical conceptualizations, by proposing a quadrant model that encompasses elements of agency and receipt of supervisor support. We considered how different combinations of these elements affect wellbeing. The findings demonstrate that requesting support and receiving support independent of one another are beneficial for wellbeing. However, no supervisor support research to date, and to the best of our knowledge, has examined mismatches between these elements: when support is not requested but is received (unsolicited), and when support is requested but is not received (unanswered). Insights from the broader social support literature suggest that this avenue of research is well worth exploring in future, as mismatches in support appear to have detrimental effects on wellbeing. Therefore, we encourage researchers to examine the process and the differential effects of unsolicited support and unanswered requests for support, in addition to the general requesting and receipt of support, to better understand the implications for organizational wellbeing. Further, theories that incorporate supervisor support as an available job resource, and theories that examine employees as active agents who can increase their own access to supervisor support, would benefit from incorporating this more encompassing conceptualization of supervisor support into their theoretical frameworks and models.

REFERENCES

References that met inclusion criteria for our review can be accessed on the Open Science Framework (McIlroy et al., 2019).

Anseel F, Beatty AS, Shen W, Lievens F and Sackett PR (2015) How are we doing after 30 years? A meta-analytic review of the antecedents and outcomes of feedback-seeking behavior. *Journal of Management* 41: 318–348.

Ashford SJ (1986) Feedback-seeking in individual adaptation: A resource perspective. *Academy of Management Journal* 29: 465–487.

Ashford SJ and Cummings LL (1983) Feedback as an individual resource: Personal strategies of creating information. *Organizational Behavior and Human Performance* 32: 370–398.

Ashford SJ, De Stobbeleir K and Nujella M (2016) To seek or not to seek: Is that the only question? Recent developments in feedback-seeking literature. *Annual Review of Organizational Psychology and Organizational Behavior* 3: 213–239.

Ashforth BE and Mael FA (1989) Social identity theory and the organization. *Academy of Management Review* 14: 20–39.

Bakker AB and Demerouti E (2017) Job demands–resources theory: Taking stock and looking forward. *Journal of Occupational Health Psychology* 22: 273–285.

Bakker AB and Demerouti E (2007) The Job Demands-Resources model: State of the art. *Journal of Managerial Psychology* 22: 309–328.

Bakker AB and Oerlemans WGM (2012) Subjective well-being in organizations. In: Cameron K and Spreitzer G (eds) *The Oxford Handbook of Positive Organizational Scholarship*. New York: Oxford University Press, pp. 178–187.

Barak MEM, Travis DJ, Pyun H and Xie B (2009) The impact of supervision on worker outcomes: A meta-analysis. *Social Service Review* 83: 3–32.

Barling J, MacEwen KE and Pratt LI (1988) Manipulating the type and source of social support: An experimental investigation. *Canadian Journal of Behavioural Science* 20: 140–153.

Caplan RD, Cobb S, French Jr JRP, Harrison RV and Pinneau SR (1980) *Job demands and worker health: Main effects and occupational differences*. Ann Arbor: Institute for Social Research, University of Michigan.

Cohen S and Wills TA (1985) Stress, social support, and the buffering hypothesis. *Psychological Bulletin* 98: 310–357.

Cooper CL and Cartwright S (1994) Healthy mind; healthy organization – A proactive approach to occupational stress. *Human Relations* 47: 455–471.

Cropanzano R and Mitchell MS (2005) Social exchange theory: An interdisciplinary review. *Journal of Management* 31: 874–900.

Danna K and Griffin RW (1999) Health and well-being in the workplace: A review and synthesis of the literature. *Journal of Management* 25: 357–384.

Deci EL and Ryan RM (2000) The 'what' and 'why' of goal pursuits: Human needs and the self-determination of behavior. *Psychological Inquiry* 11: 227–268.

Deelstra JT, Peeters MCW, Schaufeli WB, Stroebe W, Zijlstra FRH and van Doornen LP (2003) Receiving instrumental support at work: When help is not welcome. *Journal of Applied Psychology* 88: 324–331.

Demerouti E, Bakker AB, Nachreiner F and Schaufeli WB (2001) The job demands-resources model of burnout. *Journal of Applied Psychology* 86: 499–512.

Dick R, Wagner U, Stellmacher J and Christ O (2004) The utility of a broader conceptualization of organizational identification: Which aspects really matter? *Journal of Occupational and Organizational Psychology* 77: 171–191.

Diener E, Suh EM, Lucas RE and Smith HL (1999) Subjective well-being: Three decades of progress. *Psychological Bulletin* 125: 276–302.

Donaldson SI and Grant-Vallone EJ (2002) Understanding self-report bias in organizational behavior research. *Journal of Business and Psychology* 17: 245–260.

Eisenberger R, Stinglhamber F, Vandenberghe C, Sucharski IL and Rhoades L (2002) Perceived supervisor support: Contributions to perceived organizational support and employee retention. *Journal of Applied Psychology* 87: 565–573.

Ellis AM, Nifadkar SS, Bauer TN and Erdogan B (2017) Newcomer adjustment: Examining the role of managers' perception of newcomer proactive behavior during organizational socialization. *Journal of Applied Psychology* 102: 993–1001.

Emerson RM (1976) Social Exchange Theory. *Annual Review of Sociology* 2: 335–362.

Fenlason KJ and Beehr TA (1994) Social support and occupational stress: Effects of talking to others. *Journal of Organizational Behavior* 15: 157–175.

Fisher CD (2010) Happiness at work. *International Journal of Management Reviews* 12: 384–412.

Gabriel AS, Podsakoff NP, Beal DJ, Scott BA, Sonnentag S, Trougakos JP and Butts MM (2019) Experience sampling methods: A discussion of critical trends and considerations for scholarly advancement. *Organizational Research Methods* 22: 969–1006.

Gerstner CR and Day DV (1997) Meta-analytic review of leader-member exchange theory: Correlates and construct issues. *Journal of Applied Psychology* 82: 827–844.

Grant AM, Christianson MK and Price RH (2007) Happiness, health, or relationships? Managerial practices and employee well-being tradeoffs. *Academy of Management Perspectives* 21: 51–63.

Harari MB, Parola HR, Hartwell CJ and Riegelman A (2020) Literature searches in systematic reviews and meta-analyses: A review, evaluation, and recommendations. *Journal of Vocational Behavior* 118: Article 103377.

Hobfoll S (1989) Conservation of resources: A new attempt at conceptualizing stress. *American Psychologist* 44: 513–524.

Jimmieson NL and Terry DJ (1998) An experimental study of the effects of work stress, work control, and task information on adjustment. *Applied Psychology* 47: 343–369.

Johnson JV and Hall EM (1988) Job strain, work place social support, and cardiovascular disease: A cross-sectional study of a random sample of the Swedish working population. *American Journal of Public Health* 78: 1336–1342.

Johnson JV, Hall EM and Theorell T (1989) Combined effects of job strain and social isolation on cardiovascular disease morbidity and mortality in a random sample of the Swedish male working population. *Scandinavian Journal of Work, Environment & Health* 15: 271–279.

Karasek R, Brisson C, Kawakami N, Houtman I, Bongers P and Amick B (1998) The Job Content Questionnaire (JCQ): An instrument for internationally comparative assessments of psychosocial job characteristics. *Journal of Occupational Health Psychology* 3: 322–355.

Keyes CLM (1998) Social well-being. *Social Psychology Quarterly* 61: 121–140.

Keyes CLM, Hysom SJ and Lupo KL (2000) The positive organization: Leadership legitimacy, employee well-being, and the bottom line. *The Psychologist-Manager Journal* 4: 143–153.

Keyes CLM, Shmotkin D and Ryff CD (2002) Optimizing well-being: The empirical encounter of two traditions. *Journal of Personality and Social Psychology* 82: 1007–1022.

Koffel JB (2015) Use of recommended search strategies in systematic reviews and the impact of librarian involvement: A cross-sectional survey of recent authors. *PLoS ONE* 10: e0125931.

Kramer RM (1999) Trust and distrust in organizations: Emerging perspectives, enduring questions. *Annual Review of Psychology* 50: 569–598.

Lam W, Huang X and Snape E (2007) Feedback-seeking behavior and leader-member exchange: Do supervisor-attributed motives matter? *Academy of Management Journal* 50: 348–363.

Lapalme MÈ, Doucet O, Gill A and Simard G (2017) Can 'temps' secure future employment? Investigating the relationship between proactive behaviors and employers' rehiring decision. *Journal of Career Development* 44: 297–310.

Lindell MK and Whitney DJ (2001) Accounting for common method variance in cross-sectional research designs. *Journal of Applied Psychology* 86: 114–121.

Linley PA, Maltby J, Wood AM, Osborne G and Hurling R (2009) Measuring happiness: The higher order factor structure of subjective and psychological well-being measures. *Personality and Individual Differences* 47: 878–884.

Luchman JN and González-Morales MG (2013) Demands, control, and support: A meta-analytic review of work characteristics interrelationships. *Journal of Occupational Health Psychology* 18: 37–52.

McIlroy TD, Parker SL and McKimmie BM (2019) Requesting and receiving supervisor support and the implications for organisational well-being [list of studies included in the review]. *Open Science Framework*. Retrieved from https://osf.io/456me/

Mathieu M, Eschleman KJ and Cheng D (2019) Meta-analytic and multiwave comparison of emotional support and instrumental support in the workplace. *Journal of Occupational Health Psychology* 24: 387–409.

Morrison EW (2002) Information seeking within organizations. *Human Communication Research* 28: 229–242.

Morrison EW (1993) Newcomer information seeking: Exploring types, modes, sources, and outcomes. *Academy of Management Journal* 36: 557–589.

Peterson U, Demerouti E, Bergström G, Samuelsson M, Åsberg M and Nygren Å (2008) Burnout and physical and mental health among Swedish healthcare workers. *Journal of Advanced Nursing* 62: 84–95.

Podsakoff PM, MacKenzie SB and Podsakoff NP (2012) Sources of method bias in social science research and recommendations on how to control it. *Annual Review of Psychology* 63: 539–569.

Reis HT and Gable SL (2000) Event-sampling and other methods for studying everyday experience. In: Reis HT and Judd CM (eds) *Handbook of Research Methods in Social and Personality Psychology*. New York: Cambridge University Press, pp. 190–222.

Reynolds JS and Perrin NA (2004) Mismatches in social support and psychosocial adjustment to breast cancer. *Health Psychology* 23: 425–430.

Rhoades L and Eisenberger R (2002) Perceived organizational support: A review of the literature. *Journal of Applied Psychology* 87: 698–714.

Rindfleisch A, Malter AJ, Ganesan S and Moorman C (2008) Cross-sectional versus longitudinal survey research: Concepts, findings, and guidelines. *Journal of Marketing Research* 45: 261–279.

Rudolph CW, Katz IM, Lavigne KN and Zacher H (2017) Job crafting: A meta-analysis of relationships with individual differences, job characteristics, and work outcomes. *Journal of Vocational Behavior* 102: 112–138.

Ryan RM and Deci EL (2001) On happiness and human potentials: A review of research on hedonic and eudaimonic well-being. *Annual Review of Psychology* 52: 141–166.

Ryff CD (1989) Happiness is everything, or is it? Explorations on the meaning of psychological well-being. *Journal of Personality and Social Psychology* 57: 1069–1081.

Ryff CD and Keyes CLM (1995) The structure of psychological well-being revisited. *Journal of Personality and Social Psychology* 69: 719–727.

Samman E (2007) Psychological and subjective well-being: A proposal for internationally comparable indicators. *Oxford Development Studies* 35: 459–486.

Searle BJ, Bright JEH and Bochner S (2001) Helping people to sort it out: The role of social support in the Job Strain Model. *Work & Stress* 15: 328–346.

Searle BJ, Bright JEH and Bochner S (1999) Testing the 3-factor model of occupational stress: The impact of demands, control and social support on a mail sorting task. *Work & Stress* 13: 268–279.

Sguera F, Bagozzi RP, Huy QN, Boss RW and Boss DS (2018) The more you care, the worthier I feel, the better I behave: How and when supervisor support influences (un)ethical employee behavior. *Journal of Business Ethics* 153: 615–628.

Smith J and Goodnow J (1999) Unasked-for support and unsolicited advice: Age and the quality of social experience. *Psychology and Aging* 14: 108–121.

Spreitzer GM (1995) Psychological empowerment in the workplace: Dimensions, measurement, and validation. *Academy of Management Journal* 38: 1442–1465.

Steffy BD and Jones JW (1988) Workplace stress and indicators of coronary-disease risk. *Academy of Management Journal* 31: 686–698.

Tims M and Bakker AB (2010) Job crafting: Towards a new model of individual job redesign. *SA Journal of Industrial Psychology* 36: 1–9.

Tims M, Bakker AB and Derks D (2011) Development and validation of the job crafting scale. *Journal of Vocational Behavior* 80: 173–186.

Van De Voorde K, Paauwe J and Van Veldhoven M (2012) Employee well-being and the HRM-organizational performance relationship: A review of quantitative studies. *International Journal of Management Reviews* 14: 391–407.

Van den Broeck A, Ferris DL, Chang CH and Rosen CC (2016) A review of self-determination theory's basic psychological needs at work. *Journal of Management* 42: 1195–1229.

Van den Broeck A, Vansteenkiste M, De Witte H and Lens W (2008) Explaining the relationships between job characteristics, burnout, and engagement: The role of basic psychological need satisfaction. *Work & Stress* 22: 277–294.

Warr P (1990) The measurement of well-being and other aspects of mental health. *Journal of Occupational Psychology* 63: 193–210.

Wilson MG, Dejoy DM, Vandenberg RJ, Richardson HA and Mcgrath AL (2004) Work characteristics and employee health and well-being: Test of a model of healthy work organization. *Journal of Occupational and Organizational Psychology* 77: 565–588.

Wrzesniewski A and Dutton JE (2001) Crafting a job: Revisioning employees as active crafters of their work. *The Academy of Management Review* 26: 179–201.

Young SF and Steelman LA (2014) The role of feedback in supervisor and workgroup identification. *Personnel Review* 43: 228–245.

Yragui NL, Mankowski ES, Perrin NA and Glass NE (2012) Dimensions of support among abused women in the workplace. *American Journal of Community Psychology* 49: 31–42.

Zheng D, Wu H, Eisenberger R, Shore LM, Tetrick LE and Buffardi LC (2016) Newcomer leader-member exchange: The contribution of anticipated organizational support. *Journal of Occupational & Organizational Psychology* 89: 834–855.

Zou WC, Tian Q and Liu J (2015) The role of work group context and information seeking in newcomer socialization: An interactionist perspective. *Journal of Management & Organization* 21: 159–175.

Wellbeing and Work–Life Boundaries/Interfaces

James Campbell Quick

INTRODUCTION

Something there is that doesn't love a wall ....
(Frost, 1914: 11)

Good fences make good neighbors. (Frost, 1914: 13)

The point of this chapter is to understand how boundaries and interfaces work to complement each other as organizing devices to regulate work–life systems in order to enhance the wellbeing in organizational life. Robert Frost's (1914) poem 'Mending Wall', from which the opening lines are taken, speaks to the intractability of boundaries and interfaces. There is a paradox here. On the one hand is the instinct to be safe and secure, surrounded by good fences and strong walls. On the other hand is the instinct to be free, go forth into the world, and become the master of one's environment, or one's world, or one's universe. Fences and gates, walls and openings, moats and bridges work in concert to meet these competing instinctual human needs. Boundaries and interfaces work in concert to separate individuals and domains of living while enabling integrated connections and touch points for secure attachments. Boundaries and interfaces are regulatory mechanisms for work–life so as to enhance wellbeing.

Work–life systems need structure and regulation, which boundaries and interfaces provide. Therefore, it is essential to examine the literature on work–life, a literature with the alternative labels work–nonwork, work–family, and work–home. This is a relatively new domain of research dating to the 1990s (Bliese et al., 2017). The authors observe that the 20th century was a period of major political, economic, technological, and societal change that included a dramatic increase in the participation of women in the labor market, from 20% of the female US population employed in 1920 to 60% in 2000. They note that the first two articles on work–family conflict published in the *Journal of Applied Psychology* were in 1994 and 1995, but the societal trend around work boundaries did not really escalate until the era of 1997 to 2017.

How do boundaries and interfaces regulate work–life systems in a way that enhances wellbeing? Positive wellbeing is the desired outcome for employees and employers, for individuals, loved ones, and family members, and ultimately for the social fabric of the community. Wellbeing is a multifaceted construct that is the subject of the first major section of the chapter. Wellbeing is the desired outcome. Hence, begin with the outcome in mind. Sonnentag's (2015) robust review of wellbeing, its structure, and its dynamics provides a key contribution to our understanding of wellbeing. In addition, consideration is given to the moral philosophical tradition of Adam Smith (1759) and more recent life course research by Vaillant (1977, 2012), among others. Picking up Sonnentag's (2015) distinction between a person's hedonic experience of feeling good and her eudaimonic experience of fulfillment and purpose, research on subjective wellbeing (SWB) and psychological wellbeing (PWB) is reviewed.

Therefore, the chapter first examines the construct of wellbeing and then the work–life system before examining the purposes and functions of boundaries and interfaces in regulating work–life in order to enhance wellbeing. Boundaries and interfaces are subjects in some work–life research strands and are background elements in reviewing that research in the second major section of the chapter. The third major section of the chapter examines boundaries and interfaces, barrier and gateways as its primary subject. The section answers questions about the purposes and functions of these organizing devices. Boundaries and interfaces bring order from what otherwise would be chaos, enabling work–life systems to be healthy while enhancing the wellbeing of all members.

THE WELLBEING CONSTRUCT

Sonnentag (2015) characterizes wellbeing as a broad concept that encompasses a person's hedonic experience of feeling good and her eudaimonic experience of fulfillment and purpose. These separable aspects of wellbeing come from different historical roots and focus on different indicators of wellbeing. The hedonic tradition focuses on pleasure and happiness. This tradition gives rise to the line of research on subjective wellbeing. This is a shorter-term approach to wellbeing and is compatible with the study of wellbeing in organizational settings. The major components of SWB include satisfaction, positive affect, happiness, and absence of negative affect. Hence, Diener et al.'s (1999) concept of SWB and happiness enables researchers to study adaptation, goals, coping strategies, and individual dispositional influences.

The second, eudaimonic, tradition gives rise to the line of research on psychological wellbeing. For example, Wright and Cropanzano's (2004) work explores the role of PWB in contributing to job performance. More pointedly, they provide explanatory reasoning and evidence to underpin the validity of the happy/productive worker thesis (the 'Holy Grail' in management) with attention to PWB as the explanatory variable rather than SWB. The major components of PWB include meaning, purpose, growth, and self-actualization (see Hannah et al., 2020: 227, table 1 for comparison of hedonic and eudaimonic traditions). The integrative PWB framework for use in organizations that Hannah et al. (2020) provide has seven components: purpose in life; positive relations with others; self-acceptance; autonomy; environmental mastery; personal growth; and stress tolerance.

More important than her discussion of the wellbeing concept may be Sonnentag's (2015) clear understanding of wellbeing's fluidity, instability, its dynamic fluctuations within a person, and over the course of time. She makes an important distinction between fluctuations due to change and fluctuations due to variability. Fluctuations due to change refer most commonly to enduring developmental changes that are attributable to human growth, development, and maturation. Vaillant's (1977, 2012) life course research of the Harvard Class of 1942 examines fluctuations in wellbeing, both positive and negative, within and among this cohort of men over more than seven decades. Fluctuations due to variability occur within much shorter periods, even hours or days, and are not enduring. Thus, rather than being a trait or even a state construct, wellbeing is a dynamic construct that changes over time and fluctuates within a person (Sonnentag, 2015: 261). Sonnentag identifies job stressors, job resources, interpersonal factors, personal resources, and the work–home interface as five key factors that help explain changes and fluctuations in wellbeing.

The fluctuations in wellbeing may be positive or negative. Quick and Quick (2013) identify positive pathways that can lead to high energy and vitality that characterize positive wellbeing, which is marked by personal integrity, character strength, and virtue. They also identify risk factors for negative wellbeing, which include anxiety and depression (American Psychological Association, 2019a, 2019b). Fredrickson (2009) explores the balance between positive emotions and negative ones, the latter insuring a grounded connection to reality. Sonnentag (2015) notes that experiences at the interface between work and home contribute to some of the fluctuations and variability in wellbeing. This applies to employees as well as those within the home. While the work–family concerns are relatively recent, as Bliese et al. (2017) point out in their 100-year review, there is a much longer moral philosophy tradition in the study and theorizing about wellbeing that dates into the 1700s.

The Moral Philosophy Tradition

This wellbeing tradition is rooted in moral philosophy, and especially in utilitarianism (*Stanford Encyclopedia of Philosophy*, 2008;

Mill, 1910). These roots go back several hundred years to the foundational work of Adam Smith (1759) during the Scottish Enlightenment. Smith (1910) is most associated with the second of his life's work, *The Wealth of Nations*. While health and happiness are the primary aspects of wellbeing of concern here, wealth and prosperity are another set of indicators of wellbeing from an economic and financial perspective (Smith, 1910). However, Smith's (1759) earlier and more important work from his perspective, *The Theory of Moral Sentiments,* is the work for which he was renowned in his lifetime. In this earlier book, he was concerned with health and happiness, which for Smith required the balancing of selfish, social, and unsocial passions within the individual. The social passions are the basis for collective interests while the selfish passions are the basis for individual interests. He set forth the moral sense, the conscience, as the basis for what is right and wrong. For Smith, self-interest, social interest, sympathy, and propriety of action are all quite important.

Wellbeing within this tradition of moral philosophy is concerned with what makes life good for the individual living that life. While Sonnentag (2015) is correct that wellbeing is dynamic and fluctuates over short time periods, especially within the hedonic tradition, moral philosophy looks at the larger, longer-term issue of the person's wellbeing over the course of a lifetime. Hence the value of life course research as done by Vaillant (2012) in particular. This tradition steps back and examines the life in relief, while at the same time being able to observe the twists and turns that are inevitable features of any life over the course of years, decades, even over a century for centenarians.

This dual focus on wellbeing in the moment and over the decades in part may be possible and attributed to a brilliant device achieved by Smith (1759). He argues that a person must divide himself into two persons, one being the person dynamically living the life in the moment and the second being the 'impartial spectator' who is within one's breast but above the fray. He posits this 'impartial spectator' as the one who can render judgment over what is right and good as well as what is wrong and bad. In one sense for Smith (1759), there are two selves in the life well lived, not just one. This becomes relevant in the next section on work–life systems because Quick et al. (2004) propose a work–home framework that includes 'self' in their Venn diagram of the topic: work–home–self. The 'self' is not a simple consideration.

Organizational Leadership

The discussion of wellbeing thus far has focused on the construct as primarily an individual one, with collective implications as demonstrated by Cooper and Quick (2017), especially in the workplace (Bennett et al., 2017). While Smith (1759) might likely suggest that wellbeing is a personal responsibility, wellbeing in organizational life requires consideration of the organizational context. The theory of preventive stress management (TPSM) has long posited in Principle 1 that individual health and organizational health are interdependent (Quick et al., 2013: 104). The wellbeing of the organization hinges on the wellbeing of its members. The extent to which the individuals in the organization experience negative wellbeing is the extent to which the organization is compromised and unwell. Even a very small percentage of employees can cause real systemic harm in an organization (Quick et al., 2014). Therefore, from the assessment of the wellbeing of individual members of the organization we arrive at the wellbeing of the organization. However, that is not the only or final consideration in arriving at wellbeing in organizational life, which is more than the simple sum of individuals. Levinson's (2002) organizational assessment guide takes the organization as the unit of analysis and advances in occupational health have been aimed at reducing the burden of suffering for all concerned (Macik-Frey et al., 2007).

What is important in the organizational context is Principle 2 of the TPSM: Leaders have a responsibility for individual and organizational health (Quick et al., 2013: 104). Hannah et al. (2020) elaborate just how transactional and transformational leadership can serve to bolster PWB in an organization. While transactional leadership hinges on economic exchanges between leaders and followers, transformational leadership hinges on a deeper level of engagement between leader and follower; the relationship is personal. As Hannah and his colleagues point out, transformational leadership behaviors include idealized influence, inspirational motivation, intellectual stimulation, and individualized consideration. Table 3 in their article details the proposed linkages between leadership dimensions and the seven PWB dimensions identified previously, which are purpose, self-acceptance, environmental mastery, personal growth, stress tolerance, positive relationships, and autonomy (Hannah et al., 2020: 227). Transformational leadership scholars have long held that this leadership approach elevates performance above expectations. Like Wright and Cropanzano (2004) in seeking the happy/productive worker 'Holy Grail', Hannah et al. (2020) posit PWB as the key link between leader behaviors and followers' performance. This makes PWB an especially important construct in organizational life.

While the point of this chapter is to consider the wellbeing construct as the desired outcome in organizational life, PWB can also be a mediating or moderating variable within organizational research. For Sonnentag (2015), as for Hannah et al. (2020) as well as Wright and Cropanzano (2004), the outcome construct is performance. Sonnentag (2015) very much treats wellbeing, especially changes and fluctuations in wellbeing, as the mediating variable in her framework (Sonnentag, 2015: 263, figure 1). In addition, within her framework she treats work–home interface as an independent variable, with a feedback loop from wellbeing included. The next major section of this chapter focuses on the work–life system.

WORK–LIFE SYSTEM

This section of the chapter discusses the work–life system and its structure. In addition, there are subsections discussing the alternative constructs used after the dash (work–), the meaning and measurement of work–nonwork balance, spillover/crossover effects, supervisor and leader behavior, international research, two strategies for work–family conflict, and effects of COVID-19. Research findings do not always apply well to specific cases. For example, the late Cokie Roberts did not believe there was any such thing as 'work–life balance' (Gavin et al., 2013); rather, she believed in enacting each and all of the roles (wife, reporter, mother, journalist) life offered. Or Ebby Halliday, the first lady of Dallas real estate for over half a century, who lived a full and enriched life for over 100 years (Poss, 2009). However, her professional and work persona far outsized her comparatively modest but happy personal life (Gavin et al., 2013).

The study of work–life is a relatively new domain of research, dating back just a few decades and likely attributable to the major societal changes in employment and women's participation in the labor force over the past century (Bliese et al., 2017). These scholars foresaw a growth in work–life cycle models and longitudinal databases. The work–life system refers to a person's work engagement and her multiple life engagements beyond work, which may include home, family, social networks, and other interpersonal structures. The work–life system can be analyzed using role theory and in particular the role-set (Merton, 1957). From Merton's sociological framework, a social role and a focal person within a role-set is associated with a set of rights, obligations, and expectations. Social roles serve key functions in individual lives and in society. Frone (2003: 144, figure 7.1) illustrates this in a figure that sets forth examples of four work roles, three family roles, and four other nonwork roles. Specifically, these are:

- Work roles – manager, employee, occupation, union representative;
- Family roles – spouse, parent, offspring; and
- Other nonwork roles – religious roles, community roles, leisure roles, student roles.

Quick et al. (2004) identify a 'self' component into the work–life system, or in their case the work–home system. However, the 'self' is not a well-defined construct theoretically. Heinz Kohut (1971), originator of self psychology, suggests that the 'self' does not exist apart from its manifestations. This would mean that there is no 'self' to be found or discovered. At the same time, 'self' refers to an autonomous and independent person. Kohut's attention to the manifestations of the 'self' refers to the actions, words, behaviors, and impact that a person makes in the world. This has similarities to and is rather consistent with Merton's (1957) role theory in which the person enacts a role, with the enactments being the manifestations coming from the person within a specific social role.

However, the distinction between the self and others is a critical distinction to Adam Smith (1759) and for our purposes here. For Freud, the *Ich* (Germanic 'I') component of the personality may be a close approximation to the 'self'. The *Ich* is essentially the person's executive routine that engages the person with external reality, both physical and interpersonal. Hence, while Kohut's 'self' and Freud's *Ich* are not exactly the same concepts, both constructs refer to the autonomous, independent person essential to consider in the work–life system.

For this chapter, the use of Merton's (1957) role-set, the focal person, and the social structure that surrounds that focal person, both in the work space and the life space, is the primary framework for understanding the work–life system. The 'work' label within the framework is rather universal throughout the academic literature. However, there is significant variance under the 'work' rubric in venues, types of work, ways of working, and so on. Bliese et al. (2017) identified several macro societal trends that influenced 'work' throughout the 20th century. These included technological innovations, information and communication advances, and transformation of jobs within the primary, secondary, and tertiary sectors of the economy. Broadly taken, the 'work' label within work–life is understandable. However, that is not quite the case for what comes after the dash.

What's in a Name?

Work–life system is the framework for this chapter yet the earliest applied research identified by Bliese et al. (2017) in the *Journal of Applied Psychology* used the label work–family conflict in the mid 1990s. This spawned a line of research focused on the work–family system with attention to the focal person's (or in some cases persons' in dual career families), dual social roles as employee and as family member. Because each of these social roles carries rights, obligations, and expectations that may at times conflict between the roles, the central concern became interrole conflict for the focal person.

Iacocca (1985: 289) reported seeing a lot of executives neglect their families, which made him sad. In one case at Ford Motor Company, a young man dropped dead at his desk. Robert McNamara was Ford's president at the time and, when learning of the death, sent out a memo that said 'I want everybody to be out of the office by 9:00 PM'. The fact that he had to issue such a memo clearly suggested to Iacocca that something was not right. Work environments should not become labor camps. Organizations are full of human beings who need leadership that is compassionate, empathetic, and considerate rather than management that treats them like production units and automated machines (Hannah et al., 2020). The family plays a vital role and counterbalance for work.

Sonnentag (2015) and Quick et al. (2004) use the convention of work–home rather than work–family. Home and family may

be overlapping constructs but they are not equivalents. Within a Venn diagram, the two constructs would have overlapping structure as well as independent components. One specific example would be nonfamily members who might well be members of a specific home. The home is likely then a broader term for a focal person's place of abode. Both constructs, family and home, leave aside potentially significant components of a focal person's life space, such as civic and community life. This may be consequential, especially for companies that provide structured opportunities for employees and executives to devote time and effort to community projects with potential long-term benefit to the organization, such as mentoring children to stay engaged in education.

A third label that has been used with work is nonwork; hence, work–nonwork system. This may be the broadest label of the three mentioned so far: family, home, and nonwork. While 'nonwork' does describe the alternative to a focal person's 'work' space, it casts the alternative to work in the negative: nonwork, or one might even say not-work. While negative, the label is inclusive of all elements in a person's life with the exception of work. The 'life' label in work–life is also very broad and inclusive, to conceivably include even the 'work' component of a person's life. The point is that there is not a universally agreed-upon label to pair with work and the different labels have different consequences when it comes to the discussion of boundaries and interfaces.

Meaning and Measurement of Work–Nonwork Balance

The work–life domain has meaning and measurement issues beyond what comes after the dash. Wayne et al. (2017) explore four alternative approaches to work–family balance. Subsequently, Casper et al. (2018) completed a comprehensive and meta-analytic review of the work–nonwork balance literature.

In particular, they were interested in discovering if the jingle fallacy or the jangle fallacy were present. The jingle fallacy is attributing different meaning to a single construct label while the jangle fallacy is using different labels for a single construct. Both fallacies introduce conceptual and operational confusion into the scientific database. They found evidence for the jingle fallacy after reviewing 290 papers and finding 233 conceptual definitions. These 233 conceptual definitions clustered into five distinct, interpretable types. Further, they found highly divergent definitions across time and publication outlet. However, they found one exception related to the use of the three key terms within the work–life domain of study, these three terms being 'conflict', 'enrichment', and 'balance'. The exception they found was an emerging agreement more recently in what they characterize as the better journals in which 'balance' is understood as unidimensional and psychological, as well as being a distinct construct from 'conflict' and 'enrichment'.

Casper and her colleagues (2018) in addition found support for the jangle fallacy with many researchers in the work–life domain using 'balance' as their construct label when in fact what these researchers were referring to was 'conflict' and/or 'enrichment'. Bliese et al. (2017) were explicit in identifying the earlier 1990s *Journal of Applied Psychology* articles as focusing on the construct of work–family conflict. In a separate 22-year review and critique of work and family research across industrial and organizational psychology and organizational behavior, Eby and colleagues (2005) identified work–family conflict as the first of nine topical areas within the literature. They suggest that a more diverse conceptualization of the 'family' construct, to include racial and ethnic variance, is one way of moving this field forward. This reflects the continuing lack of agreement within the field concerning what should follow the dash. The 'home' and 'life' constructs after the dash as well as the 'nonwork' construct are ways in which

the field has broadened the early focus on work–family.

Using Merton's (1957) role-set framework, the early focus on work–family conflict made perfect sense because the focal person in the work–family system was subject to two independent, and at times conflicting, obligations and expectations. This was especially true for women, resulting from the dramatic increase in their participation in the workforce throughout the 20th century. Just as Sonnentag (2015) points out that wellbeing is a dynamic construct, so too are there dynamics within the work–life system to consider. Changes in one component of the system have an impact on other components of the system. The critical resources to consider within the work–life system include time, energy, information, and stress. Managing work–family conflict involves managing the unexpected, tracking small failures, and maintaining resilience (Weick and Sutcliffe, 2015). Beyond the role conflict(s) stress within the work–family system is the psychophysiological stress of the members, which is not always self-contained (Quick et al., 2013) but can crossover to or spillover onto others at work or at home.

Frone (2003: 146) was an early proponent of work–family balance, proposing in his influence-effects model that work-to-family and family-to-work conflict could be mitigated by work-to-family and family-to-work facilitation. He explores both early and contemporary, circa very early 2000s, conceptions of the work–family interface, suggesting that a more integrative and dynamic view of the work–family interface is valuable. Greenhaus and Powell (2006) go beyond balance and the facilitation process to a theory of work–family enrichment, theorizing that experiences in one role may improve the quality of life in the other role. Their proposal is to cast work and family as allies, versus opponents or competitors. Their theory includes two paths to enrichment, one path being instrumental and the second path being affective.

Crossover and Spillover Effects

Westman (2001) explored stress and strain crossover as the process whereby partners transmit the stress and strain of the workplace to their close partners in the family and home, thus impacting the wellbeing of the partner. This is originally conceived from the negative spillover of stress and strain from one component of the work–family system to another; that is, the work-to-home spillover. The close family partner is then, in a sense, infected with a negative impact on their wellbeing. Bakker et al. (2009) focused on the theory and research of crossover of work-related wellbeing from an employee to partners at home. However, they also discussed research that examined the crossover of wellbeing from one employee to another in the workplace. In addition, they found evidence in the literature of positive crossover and spillover effects whereby an employee's enthusiasm for her work may cross over to the partner in a positive way. In the workplace, frequency of interaction, empathy, an employee's susceptibility to contagion, and employee similarities are among the factors that influence the degree of crossover. Hence, the transmission process might be a negative or might be a positive one.

The dynamics of and effects of crossover and spillover are keys to managing the work–life system in a way to mitigate negative impacts on individual wellbeing while maximizing the positive impacts on individual wellbeing. Understanding the processes is a key to enhancing the vitality of the system. For example, in a spousal partnership where the at-home spouse serves a primary role of support for the spouse working outside the home, the negative spillover from work to home may serve a cathartic value for the one working outside the home. While there is value for the one spouse in that spillover and crossover, the risk is that the at-home spouse's wellbeing is negatively affected. However, if that spouse has a discipline or practice that prevents the accumulation of that spillover and crossover, then the system can maintain balance or homeostasis.

Supervisor and Leader Behavior

While the relationship with one's spouse or significant other is often the most consequential interpersonal attachment in the home and family domain of life, the relationship with one's supervisor and/or leader is likely the most consequential one in the work environment. In a quasi-experimental field study of 239 employees and 39 supervisors at six work sites, Hammer et al. (2011) evaluated the impact of work–family interventions on job satisfaction, turnover intent, and physical health. Hammer and colleagues have pioneered Family Supportive Supervisory Behaviors (FSSB) as mediators in their applied research model and treated work–family conflict as a moderator. Work–family conflict did play a moderating role in their results but they recommended additional research on this specific issue. They did find positive FSSB training effects for employees who were in high work–family conflict situations, while there were negative training effects for employees who were in low work–family conflict situations. FSSB had positive effects on job satisfaction and turnover intent, while not having an effect on physical health.

In a separate meta-analytic study, Kossek et al. (2011) drew on 115 samples from 85 studies that included 72,507 employees. They were focusing on the effects of four types of workplace social support on work–family conflict. These four types were general organizational support, family-specific organizational support, general supervisory support, and family-specific supervisory support. The more family-specific forms of social support, both organizational and supervisory, had stronger relationships to work–family conflict than the general forms of social support, either supervisory or organizational. Further analysis suggested a mediating role for organizational work–family-specific support. The key conclusion drawn by Kossek and her colleagues from the results is that work–family-specific support plays a central role in employees' work–family conflict experiences. The supervisor's FSSB can be instrumental in enhancing employee wellbeing while mitigating negative effects of work-to-family negative spillover. The extent to which supervisors and leaders are able to help employees metabolize workplace psychosocial toxins prior to leaving the workplace is the extent to which they enable those employees to leave work unencumbered.

Hannah et al. (2020) are rather specific in theorizing how transactional and transformational leadership can be enacted to bolster the workplace PWB of followers. For example, transformational leaders who inspirationally motivate followers and/or focus individualized consideration directed at a specific follower can enhance a follower's self-acceptance, a key dimension of PWB. Leaders have central roles in influencing follower stress tolerance, especially in times of crisis and emergency. As a, even the, key attachment figure for the follower in the work environment, leaders model and offer individualized attention to enhance followers' transformational coping behaviors. Leaders also help mitigate against regressive coping and negative behaviors because stress tolerance is a key dimension of PWB. Finally, leaders can influence follower autonomy, a third key dimension of PWB, through idealized influence and intellectual stimulation, thus enabling the follower to exercise appropriate self-determination in the workplace and achieve full potential. The alternative to autonomy is external control, which is of course appropriate for a machine but inappropriate for an adult human being.

International Research

Prior to 2010, comparative international studies in the area of work–family were often limited in theoretical scope, with a primary focus on individualism versus collectivism aimed at explaining cross-cultural differences (Greenhaus and Allen, 2011). While limited in scope, the cultural value differences are consequential. For example, in a 1988 scientific exchange to the People's Republic of China by 25 psychologists, social workers, psychiatrists, and biofeedback experts, it became clear that in China the work unit of a person had essentially co-equal authority to the family of origin in either allowing for or blocking educational and career opportunities for an individual. Contrast that with the Swedish approach circa 2007 that followed family supportive policies on the part of work organizations, such as very generous maternity leaves. In a within-country study of Brazilian professionals that was designed to draw from the cultural values of Brazil, Casper et al. (2011) examined the two directions of work–family conflict. They found work interference with family related to higher continuance commitment and perceived supervisor support related to affective commitment. Increasingly, international scholars from Israel, Australia, Germany, and Brazil are influencing the field.

Two Strategies for Work–Family Conflict

Nippert-Eng's (1996) book addresses two alternative strategies for managing work–family conflict and foreshadows the discussion in the next section on boundaries and interfaces. In particular, Nippert-Eng's two strategies are segmentation and integration. Individuals who pursue a strategy of segmentation strive to keep the work and the family domains very separate, allowing rare overlaps between the two domains. Individuals who pursue this strategy keep a clear distinction between their role as employee and their multiple roles within the family, such as wife, mother, daughter, and sibling. Her segmentation strategy emphasizes the importance of boundaries and uses time and/or place to create the separation; hence, when in the workplace during working hours, the clear focus is on the demands associated with the employee role. On the other side, when in the home and family environment, the clear focus is on the demands associated with any one or more of the family roles. While the segmentation strategy reduces conflict between the two domains in the moment, it may have negative unintended consequences if it fails to account for emergencies within one domain or the other when the individual is in the alternate domain.

The second strategy for managing work–family conflict is integration. Using this strategy, an individual does not make clear time and place distinctions for engaging work and family roles. The emphasis is on interfaces versus on boundaries. A person employing this strategy will take calls from work at home as well as accepting calls in, or even family member visits to, the workplace. This strategy comingles the demands and pressures of work and family in a way that the most pressing demands are the ones addressed. The integration strategy hinges on the agreement of other actors in the workplace and family that allows the person the discretionary latitude to in fact reprioritize overall life demands, sometimes prioritizing the work environment before the family while at other times prioritizing the family before the workplace. This is not always possible. One university president forced a star full professor, who was also a wife and a mother, to choose between her career and her family. The president chose to ignore a highly appropriate accommodation that she had arranged that would allow her to accept a plum professional opportunity while living with her family. The dysfunctional consequence of the false forced-choice was the university's loss of a star full professor. As an accomplished, high-impact professional, she became a stellar community leader while engaging her family roles as wife and mother in an equally accomplished manner.

This example illustrates the fact that the focal person alone cannot choose one of the two strategies for managing work–family conflict. Rather, the focal person must negotiate within a work structure and within a family system that enables the latitude to choose either segmentation or integration, or even shades in between. The key to Nippert-Eng's approach is the negotiating dimension of working out the strategy that best suits the focal person and the work–family system with the best interests of all concerned in mind.

Effects of COVID-19

The onset of the global pandemic COVID-19 throws a curve ball into the entire discussion of work–life systems, boundaries, and interfaces. Social distancing and/or shelter-in-place orders were imposed on major sectors of the European and US populations early in the crisis, thus distorting the notion of time and space separation between work and non-work activities. This varied significantly across industrial sectors as well as across sub-population groups. For example, automobiles cannot be mass-produced at home any more than meat processing can be. Alternatively, those engaged in high-technology functions might well work remotely with a computer terminal and internet connections. A relatively high proportion of Asian and White workers fall into this latter category, allowing an appreciable percentage to continue to work. A much lower percentage of Black and Hispanic workers were able to do so.

Fast-tracking research on COVID-19 in the *Journal of Applied Psychology*, *Journal of Occupational Health Psychology*, and *American Psychologist* as this chapter went to press allows for evidence-based findings from this global pandemic as soon as possible. Emerging evidence during the pandemic clearly suggests that the work–family boundary is fraught with fear and danger for frontline caregivers such as physicians and nurses as well as police and emergency medical technicians. The world is still in a steep learning curve concerning this virus and learning implications for organizational life will take time and focused consideration to identify.

The global emphasis needs to be on developing preventive and public health strategies so that more than one in three nations have the capacity for surviving future pandemics (Quick, 2018). Closing national and regional borders may be of epidemiological benefit for infectious diseases but has unintended negative economic consequences in what is a very globally connected world (Nelson and Quick, 2019).

BOUNDARIES AND INTERFACES, BARRIERS AND GATEWAYS

The opening lines of the chapter come from the first and last verses of Frost's (1914) poem 'Mending Wall'. What Frost hits upon is the intractable human needs to explore the world and, simultaneously, feel safe, secure. Boundaries and interfaces, barriers and gateways, moats and bridges, fences and openings are all regulatory mechanisms that enable individuals to fulfill the need to feel safe and secure while at the same time going forth into the world and connecting with others in healthy ways to enhance wellbeing for all concerned (Nelson and Quick, 2019). Partway through 'Mending Wall' the speaker says

Before I built a wall I'd ask to know

What I was walling in or walling out,

And to whom I was like to give offense. (Frost, 1914: 12)

A case illustration of how redrawing one boundary can have a dramatically positive impact on an entire cluster of work–family systems occurred at Fort Hood, Texas, under the command of Major General Rick Lynch, US Army (Lynch, 2013: 15–16). On his third day as the commander, an Army wife in tears confronted him with the words 'You generals are lying to us!' This occurred after the United States had been at war for nearly a decade in the late 2000s and she was upset that her children never saw their father even though he was on station at Fort Hood, not deployed to Iraq or Afghanistan. After reflecting on her feedback, Major General Lynch realized how out of balance things had become between duty and family. Therefore, he issued a sweeping order for all 63,000 soldiers at Fort Hood, the largest army base in the free world. The order directed all soldiers end the duty day in time to be home with family for dinner by 6:00 pm, enforced five days a week. In addition, every soldier and officer was to leave duty at 3:00 pm every Thursday for mandatory family time. Those are two strong boundaries between duty and family, creating breathing room for family life. One more demand – no soldier work on the weekend without the commanding general's personal approval. No request ever received.

One year later the results in wellbeing and productivity indicators provided evidence of the wisdom of that sweeping order. There were significant drops in incidences of domestic violence, divorce, and failed relationships. Hence, morale went up with the redress in work–life balance. More consequentially, the suicide rate dropped precipitously, taking Fort Hood from the top of the Army list with most suicides to the bottom of the list with the lowest suicide rate. In addition, productivity went up. Soldiers and officers became more efficient and more effective along with more productive. The plus component of the work–life balance program was an emphasis on personal safety, for everyone. Traffic accidents on this massive installation nearly disappeared. Before Lynch took command, there was a traffic fatality every 15 or 20 days. At one point, Fort Hood went 245 days without a fatality. Clear boundaries can create work–life balance and improve wellbeing of the whole work–life system for everyone concerned.

The Functions of Boundaries, Barriers, and Fences

Just as Frost (1914) does not come to a clear position as to whether walls are good things or bad things, so too we should be cautious, even circumspect, in the use of boundaries. Boundaries, barriers, and fences have value and at least four functions within the work–life system, which are to (1) provide structure, (2) insure identity, (3) underpin integrity, and (4) provide security. Rights, obligations, and expectations bound roles and roles enable the social structure in which work, family, home, and individuals are situated. The identity as well as integrity of the individual, the family, and workplace proceed from what is within bounds as well as what is out of bounds. Physical barriers, official policies, and/or rules that establish limits for the incumbents within the system may define those internal boundaries. Observation and experience are often the basis for learning about nonphysical boundaries.

Sometimes single adults are out of bounds when it comes to work–family research. In an interview study, Casper et al. (2016) challenged this perception. In fact, they found single adults did have a number of important family roles and that their engagement in these family roles was highly valued. Therefore, single adults did experience meaningful interrole conflict between the work and the family domains.

Another way to consider boundaries in the work–life system is through the research process itself. Kelly et al. (2008) come to a number of conclusions concerning the effect of work–family initiatives. In particular, they call for interdisciplinary research that bridges disciplinary boundaries. While those boundaries are valuable in emphasizing and strengthening disciplinary expertise, the interdisciplinary approach enables a melding that enriches the science base. In addition, they call for greater research-to-practice translation that spans the boundary between academia and the world beyond academic. The call is not to erase the boundary but rather to bridge it. At the same time, practice can inform the research, bridging the boundary in the opposite direction.

The Functions of Interfaces, Bridges, and Gateways

Interfaces, bridges, and gateways have at least three functions within the work–life system, which are to (1) provide support, (2) enable psychological exchanges, and (3) enable material exchanges. Interfaces are the essential elements of social support, which is one of the most robust positive forces in insuring positive wellbeing, provided the relationships are positive. One negative relationship has the potential to cancel out the benefits of as many as five positive relationships, hence the value of boundaries in risky relationships. The support function of interfaces may be the most robust of the functions and has a variety of dimensions: information support, emotional support, instrumental support, evaluative support, and feedback support (Nelson and Quick, 2019). In their study of 5,505 US Army officers, Huffman et al. (2014) found that spouse career support contributed to lower turnover four years later. In addition, their research found that work interfering with family and job satisfaction were mediators of this spousal support-to-turnover relationship.

The critical dyadic interfaces within the work–life system are those between spouses, then between family members and those between leaders and followers, then between coworkers. Compromising any one dyadic interface within the work–life system can cause harm to the wellbeing not only of the individuals involved but of the entire system. The role-set is a sociological web that rests on its boundaries and interfaces for the wellbeing of all concerned.

CONCLUSION

This chapter began with a discussion of wellbeing, a broad concept that encompasses a person's hedonic experience of happiness and her eudaimonic experience of a meaningful, fulfilling, purposeful life. In addition, the chapter considered the moral philosophy tradition in wellbeing. The heart of the chapter reviewed the breadth and depth of research on work–life systems, to include work–family, work–home, work–nonwork, and work–home–self. The boundaries and interfaces within and between sectors of work–life systems are the organizing devices that enable structure and function for healthy work–life systems. The chapter examined the constructs of conflict, balance, and enrichment in the context of work–life systems. In addition, a review of crossover effects, spillover effects, family supportive supervisory behaviors (FSSB), international research, and the strategies of segmentation and integration for work–family conflict was included. The COVID-19 pandemic was included because of its emerging impact on work–life systems, not only from economic and epidemiologic (public health) perspectives, but because of the ethical and moral considerations of this pandemic.

REFERENCES

American Psychological Association (2019a) *The Trait-State Anxiety Inventory*. https://www.apa.org/pi/about/publications/caregivers/practice-settings/assessment/tools/trait-state (downloaded 30 September).

American Psychological Association (2019b) *Beck Depression Inventory (BDI)*. https://www.apa.org/depression-guideline/assessment/ (downloaded 30 September).

Bakker AB, Westman M and van Emmerik IJH (2009) Advancements in crossover theory. *Journal of Managerial Psychology* 24(3): 206–219.

Bennett JB, Weaver J, Senft M and Neeper M (2017) Creating workplace well-being. In: Cooper CL and Quick JC (eds) *The Handbook of Stress and Health: A Guide to Research and Practice*. Chichester, UK: Wiley-Blackwell, pp. 570–604.

Bliese PD, Edwards JR and Sonnentag S (2017) Stress and well-being: A century of empirical trends reflecting theoretical and societal influences. *Journal of Applied Psychology* 102(3): 389–402.

Casper WJ, Harris C, Taylor-Bianco A and Wayne JH (2011) Work–family conflict, perceived supervisor support and organizational commitment among Brazilian professionals. *Journal of Vocational Behavior* 79(3): 640–652.

Casper WJ, Marquardt DJ, Roberto KJ and Buss C (2016) The hidden family lives of single adults without dependent children. In: Allen TD and Eby LT (eds) *The Oxford Handbook of Work and Family*. New York: Oxford University Press, pp. 182–195.

Casper WJ, Vaziri H, Wayne JH, DeHauw S and Greenhaus J (2018) The jingle-jangle of work–nonwork balance: A comprehensive and meta-analytic review of its meaning and measurement. *Journal of Applied Psychology* 103(2): 182–214.

Cooper CL and Quick JC (2017) *The Handbook of Stress and Health: A Guide to Research and Practice*. Chichester, UK: Wiley-Blackwell.

Diener E, Suh EM, Lucas ER and Smith HL (1999) Subjective well-being: Three decades of progress. *Psychological Bulletin* 125: 276–302.

Eby LT, Casper WJ, Lockwood A, Bordeaux C and Brinley A (2005) Work and family research in IO/OB: Content analysis and review of the literature (1980–2002). *Journal of Vocational Behavior* 66(1): 124–197.

Fredrickson B (2009) *Positivity: Groundbreaking Research Reveals How to Embrace the Hidden Strength of Positive Emotions, Overcome Negativity, and Thrive*. New York: Crown Publishers.

Frone MR (2003) Work–family balance. In: Quick JC and Tetrick LE (eds) *Handbook of Occupational Health Psychology*. Washington, DC: American Psychological Association, pp. 143–162.

Frost R (1914) Mending Wall. *North of Boston*. New York: Henry Holt and Company.

Gavin JH, Quick JC and Gavin DJ (2013) *Live Your Dreams, Change the World: The Psychology of Personal Fulfillment for Women*. Riverdale, NY: American Mental Health Foundation Books.

Greenhaus JH and Allen TD (2011) Work–family balance: A review and extension of the literature. In: Quick JC and Tetrick LE (eds) *Handbook of Occupational Health Psychology, Second Edition*. Washington, DC: American Psychological Association, pp. 165–183.

Greenhaus JH and Powell GN (2006) When work and family are allies: A theory of work–family enrichment. *Academy of Management Review* 31(1): 72–92.

Hammer LB, Kossek EE, Anger WK, Bodner T and Zimmerman KL (2011) Clarifying work–family intervention processes: The roles of work–family conflict and family-supportive supervisor behaviors. *Journal of Applied Psychology* 96(1): 134–150.

Hannah ST, Perez AL, Lester P and Quick JC (2020) Bolstering workplace psychological well-being through transactional and transformational leadership. *Journal of Leadership and Organizational Studies* 27(3): 222–240.

Huffman AH, Casper WJ and Payne SC (2014) How does spouse career support relate to employee turnover? Work interfering with family and job satisfaction as mediators. *Journal of Organizational Behavior* 35(2): 194–212.

Iacocca, L with Novak W (1985) *Iacocca: An Autobiography*. New York: Bantam Books.

Kelly EL, Kossek EE, Hammer LB, Durham M, Bray J, Chermack K, Murphy LA and Kaskubar D (2008) Getting there from here: Research on the effect of work–family initiatives on work–family conflict and business outcomes. *Academy of Management Annals* 2(1): 305–349.

Kohut, H. (1971). *The Analysis of the Self*. New York: International Universities Press.

Kossek EE, Pichler S, Bodner T and Hammer LB (2011) Workplace social support and work–family conflict: A meta-analysis clarifying the influence of general and work–family-specific supervisor and organizational support. *Personnel Psychology* 64(2): 289–313.

Levinson H (2002) *Organizational Assessment*. Washington, DC: American Psychological Association.

Lynch R (2013) *Adapt or Die: Leadership Principles from an American General*. Grand Rapids, MI: BakerBooks.

Macik-Frey M, Quick JC and Nelson DL (2007) Advances in occupational health: From a stressful beginning to a positive future. *Journal of Management* 33(6): 809–840.

Merton RK (1957) The role-set: Problems in sociological theory. *The British Journal of Sociology* 8(2): 106–120.

Mill JS (1910) *Utilitarianism, Liberty, and Representative Government*. London: Dent.

Nippert-Eng C (1996) *Home and Work: Negotiating Boundaries through Everyday Life*. Chicago, IL: University of Chicago Press.

Nelson DL and Quick JC (2019) *ORGB6: Organizational Behavior*. Mason, OH: Cengage/South-Western.

Poss M (2009) *Ebby Halliday: The First Lady of Real Estate*. Dallas, TX: Brown Books.

Quick JC, McFadyen MA and Nelson DL (2014) No accident: Health, well-being, performance…and danger. *Journal of Organizational Effectiveness* 1(1): 98–119.

Quick JC and Quick JD (2013) Executive well-being. In: Caza A and Cameron KS (eds) *Happiness and Organizations*, Section VII in David SA, Bonjwell I and Conley Ayers A (eds) *The Oxford Handbook of Happiness*. Oxford, UK: Oxford University Press, pp. 798–813.

Quick JC, Wright TA, Adkins JA, Nelson DL and Quick JD (2013) *Preventive Stress Management in Organizations, second edition*. Washington, DC: American Psychological Association.

Quick JD (2018) *The End of Epidemics: The Looming Threat to Humanity and How to Stop It*. New York: St. Martin's Press.

Quick JD, Henley AB and Quick JC (2004) The balancing act – at work and at home. *Organizational Dynamics* 33(4): 426–438.

Sonnentag S (2015) Dynamics of well-being. *Annual Review of Organizational Psychology and Organizational Behavior* 2: 261–293.

Stanford Encyclopedia of Philosophy (2008) Palo Alto, CA: Stanford University.

Smith A (1759) *The Theory of Moral Sentiments*. Edinburgh, UK: A. Kincaid and J. Bell.

Smith A (1910) *An Inquiry into the Nature and Causes of the Wealth of Nations. Harvard Classics*, Volume 10, C. J. Bullock (ed.). New York: P.F. Collier & Son.

Vaillant GE (2012) *Triumphs of Experience: The Men of the Harvard Grant Study*. Boston,

MA: Belknap Press of Harvard University Press.

Vaillant GE (1977) *Adaptation to Life*. Boston, MA: Little, Brown.

Wayne JH, Butts MM, Casper WJ and Allen TD (2017) In search of balance: A conceptual and empirical integration of multiple meanings of work–family balance. *Personnel Psychology* 70(1): 167–210.

Weick KE and Sutcliffe KM (2015) *Managing the Unexpected, Third Edition*. Hoboken, NJ: John Wiley & Sons, Inc.

Westman M (2001) Stress and strain crossover. *Human Relations* 54(6): 717–751.

Wright TA and Cropanzano R (2004) The role of psychological well-being in job performance. *Organizational Dynamics* 33(4): 338–351.

8

Social Capital and Wellbeing: The Role of Work and Family Relations across Cultures

José Atilano Pena-López, Paolo Rungo and
José Manuel Sánchez-Santos

INTRODUCTION

Wellbeing and happiness, as the subjective appreciation of individual wellbeing (Veenhoven, 1984), have always been associated with social relations. Several studies have emphasized the importance of close relationships with other people for the pursuit of happiness and life satisfaction (see, for example, Argyle, 2002; Veenhoven, 1999). The organizational literature has initially approached the topic of happiness by investigating the construct of job satisfaction (see, for instance, Brief, 1998; Cranny et al., 1992), to later broaden the research agenda and include constructs referring to pleasant judgments or experiences at work (see Fisher, 2010, for a review). In general, most of this literature has focused on the determinants of happiness at work and its consequences on organizational outcomes. In line with this research program, for example, team camaraderie, social support and contact with others have been shown to improve the work environment and, therefore, job satisfaction (Sirota et al. 2005; Warr, 2007). Consequences range from creativity and proactivity (Fritz and Sonnentag, 2009) to motivation (Ilies and Judge, 2005), among many others. However, work relationships or, at least, close personal relationships developed at work, may have consequences well beyond the organizational sphere. Indeed, they may be a significant source of positive emotions and individual wellbeing.

Social capital has been proposed as a conceptual framework that encompasses the interrelations in the individual social sphere, especially social networks, and one's own actions. In its most naive expression, studies that deal with social capital claim that the existence of social networks improves socioeconomic performance, welfare and income (Adler and Kwon, 2002; Dasgupta and Serageldin, 2001; see Fine, 2001, for notable criticisms). Within this research program, several contributions have established a direct link between social capital and subjective wellbeing (Bartolini et al., 2013; Helliwell and Putnam, 2004; Putnam, 2000, among others). This influence is exerted through two main channels: first, social capital improves objective socioeconomic conditions, that is, the extrinsic rewards; second, it provides intrinsic rewards. Surprisingly, the study of the latter is not the mainstream. Furthermore, the boundaries between the two spheres are somewhat blurry. Regarding interpersonal ties, the reality is that 'their instrumental character does not eliminate the fact that the relationship is (or could be) a good in itself, and not simply a means to achieving other objectives' (Gui, 2005). Indeed, sociability, which can be expressed in all kinds of relations, is a significant component of happiness (Argyle, 2002).

Subjective wellbeing is linked to social networks in which individuals express their identity, that is, relational goods. The family environment is a natural framework for the development of such networks. However, any social setting that facilitates the expansion of expressive social ties, including work, could facilitate the development of this relational dimension of happiness (Sacco and Vanin, 2000). Consequently, the necessary question in the analysis of subjective wellbeing at work is whether this is an enabling environment for the generation of relational goods or whether individuals actually generate such goods in the workplace. Furthermore, the development of extrinsic and intrinsic relations within the family or the workplace may be alternative or conflictual (Lavassani and Movahedi, 2014).

This approach has important derivations from the point of view of the organization in the work–life balance. This can also be analyzed through global satisfaction derived from the multiple vital roles (family, work or leisure, for example). Thus, Kirchmeyer (2000) defines this balance as the possibility of achieving fulfilling experiences in all domains of life so that individuals can maximize their satisfaction in this process of redistribution of time between dimensions. That is, get as much satisfaction in the workplace as in the family without role conflicts (Clark, 2000; Kalliath and Brough, 2008).

The present study attempts to analyze the influence that different expressions of social capital, particularly family and work relations, exert on individual subjective wellbeing. With this in mind, we will consider the effect of family and work relationships and, indirectly, the work–family balance issue and its relation to happiness from the point of view of relational goods. This study contributes to the existing literature by introducing relational goods to the subjective wellbeing analysis and the potential conflict between family and work. At the same time, we will study the mediating role of culture in this link. As a case of study, we will also revise the results of an extensive survey conducted on representative samples of people living in Colombia, Costa Rica, Mexico and the United States. The diversity of these societies in terms of wellbeing and social relations requires consideration of the cultural context.

The rest of the chapter is structured in the following sections. First, we review the concept of social capital and the issues involved in the analysis of the role of personal networks on happiness. Particular relevance is given to the concept of relational goods. In the third section, we focus on the relation between the family and work domains. In light of the boundary and border theories, we discuss the possible development of relational goods at the workplace. The fourth summarizes the results of an ample empirical analysis confronting these relations in two different cultural and labor contexts (United States and Latin America). Finally, the last part of the chapter draws conclusions.

SOCIAL CAPITAL, WORK AND FAMILY RELATIONS

The concept of social capital points at the very nature of human beings. We have to distinguish at least two perspectives on this broad and loose concept. The 'mainstream' social capital theory highlights the macro or cultural dimensions, that is, the endowment of associative networks of a society as a whole, traits or characteristics of social organizations, norms, networks and trust that facilitate cooperation and coordination for mutual benefit (Putnam, 1993; Winter, 2001). This macro perspective focuses on formal associations and general trust and their links with social and economic functioning (Knack and Keefer, 1997; Putnam, 1993). However, the study of the individual networks that generate this form of capital is beyond its scope (Bourdieu; 2001; Coleman, 1988; Yang, 2007).

The micro perspective focuses the analysis on the endowment of social relations that an individual has and the resources attached to them (Lin, 1999a, 1999b, 2008). Within this literature, the division between strong and weak ties is especially relevant. First, it is possible to identify a social capital of strong ties, with family members or fellows ('bonding social capital'). Relations with members of other groups, or 'bridging social capital' (like work relations), constitute a second group (Paldam, 2000). From this perspective, social capital is a form of personal investment, a stock, an individual endowment of social networks. This investment is limited by the social structure (inheritance of networks) and context factors (social class, working time, cultural environment...) and its value lies in the resources, material or not, that can be drawn from them. For example, the set of personal networks may be useful in the achievement of personal goals, both instrumental (income or status, for example) and expressive (recognition or mutual aid, for example) (Lin, 1999a, 2008; Van der Gaag and Snijders, 2004). Therefore, we can distinguish between instrumental and expressive networks. While the first are related more so to weak ties, status objectives and bridging social capital, the latter are linked with personal identity, bonding social capital and strong links. In this way, expressive networks have a preferential role on happiness,

but these kinds of links are not necessarily related with the family environment; work relations, clubs, associations etc. can have an expressive dimension (Lin, 2001) where the other is not an object but a subject.

Expressive Relations: Relational Goods in Family and Work

Since Aristotle, human beings have been defined as social beings and, obviously, happiness has a relational dimension. In this sense, not all man's needs are acquisitive, that is, they are not met by the consumption of market goods and, therefore, linked to income. The social dimension is particularly related to expressive needs and to the recognition of our identity in a relationship with a third party (Gui and Stanca, 2010; Iglesias Vázquez et al., 2013; Zamagni, 2004). It is at this point that we have to situate the concept of relational goods. As Becchetti et al. (2008) remark, these goods are a consequence of the need to meet; a set of encounters that generates emotional support, social approval, belonging, acceptance by others, etc. This implies that they are a product of social interaction but with certain personalization (Pena-López and Sánchez-Santos, 2017). The ability of this notion, first introduced by Uhlaner (1989), is to capture the richness of interpersonal relations or encounters where non-contractability prevails.

Following Nussbaum (1995), the main character of these goods is their non-instrumentality, because the relationship is a good in itself and, consequently, their production process is peculiar. These goods are also a byproduct of non-randomized concrete social relationships in which identity is determinant and where the agents are at the same time producing and consuming.

Under this definition, a relational good is clearly a family reunion but, at the same time, it can also be a reunion with colleagues after work or even, under particular conditions, a work meeting. We can include a wide variety of social situations that would not necessarily have the denomination of a family meeting or even a friendship. For these reasons, Bruni (2008) points out that friendship cannot be defined as a relational good, but as a repeated interaction, as a series of encounters and affective states. However, statistically, relational goods are more common in close relations where the identity is preserved in a kind of 'non-contractual' belonging with the absence of instrumentality (Gui, 2000) and, consequently, are more commonly produced and consumed at home. Notwithstanding, the workplace (work environment), associations and organizations, the meetings of friends, the community etc. can produce these kinds of goods under certain conditions (Bruni, 2008; Pena-López et al., 2017; Sacco and Vanin, 2000).

These characteristics are hard to define and even harder to measure, making them non-contractible. Relational goods even surpass the notion of social network and social capital. We are referring to the unaccounted component of an encounter, for example, in a consultation meeting. This encounter paradigm implies a different perspective on employee relations and employer–employee relations (Donati, 2013).

This particular vision of personal exchanges surpasses the perspective of the social exchange or the interpersonal exchange of material and intangible resources (Homans, 1958) for two reasons. The exchange paradigm does not exhaust the meaning of personal interaction because either it has omitted or does not consider the public good characteristic of the social transaction, nor does it convey the idea of a quid pro quo transaction. As Donati (2019) remarks, bilateral satisfaction depends on the encounters both sides supply with satisfactory relational goods, not only with social exchange. With respect to the public good, relations are not only a particular transaction but are also complex situations where individual acts are combined in such a way that outcomes also depend on perceived dispositions and intentions; it is

a personalized link. At the same time, these relations that overcome the simple transaction create a local public good, the consciousness of the 'we' (Gui, 2000).

In short, relational goods are the affective, expressive and non-instrumental side of interpersonal relationships. These particular kinds of 'goods' are (potentially) produced through interaction in any sphere of social life, such as family, friends, peer groups, associations, sports activities, the workplace and other events, but under certain restrictions. They imply a non-instrumental recognition of individuals, which is a 'personalized' relationship (Gui, 2005; Gui and Sugden, 2005). These particular ties, where relational goods emerge, have a direct effect on subjective wellbeing and show a trade-off relation with instrumental social capital expressions (Bruni and Stanca, 2008; Pena-López and Sánchez-Santos, 2017). There is a strong relation between sociability and individual wellbeing. Relational activities have an impact on self-reported life satisfaction, even when reverse causality is taken into account (Becchetti et al., 2008). As a result, this vital goal (happiness) cannot be achieved only through instrumental relations, but it emerges as an indirect result of actions that deviate from strict necessity, in personalizing relations. Although the essential goal of being happy pertains to the individual, its achievement is not a result of purpose-oriented actions.

Social Capital and Relational Goods at Work

Obviously, work influences individual happiness through financial and non-financial factors. Focusing on the latter, aspects such as the work environment, confidence, creativity, independence, etc. have a direct impact. Other variables like the geographical situation of employment, social consideration or social pressures exert an influence which researchers have come to calculate with a compensatory monetary equivalence (Easterlin, 2001; Stutzer and Lalive, 2004). However, there is very little reference to the problem of social capital at work, although it constitutes a part of the so-called hygiene needs linked to the environment in the classical Herzberg two factors theory. The claim derived from the theory is notoriously straightforward and simple: employees tend to be happier and more productive when they are in a better relational environment (Fisher, 2010; Hodson, 2001).

Following mainstream social capital theory, the analyzed effects are related particularly with efficiency. The presence of high intragroup social capital in a company, which is reflected in its shared goals and values, an adequate work environment and high confidence and interpersonal interaction favors the 'group human capital' and global productivity, and thus achieves the final result that the firm seeks. This intragroup social capital in the workplace can also be associated with the term group cohesion. This is identified by the presence of three perceptions and preferences among the members. First, the members identify themselves as members of the group. Second, the members choose to remain in the group in case of a real possibility of integrating into another group and, third, the members perceive the group as better than other groups, especially in the way in which the relationships are established. This sense of belonging, pride and intragroup solidarity has a clear inverse relationship with absenteeism and helps employees solve work-related problems (Tanenbaum et al., 2013).

Despite the evident consequences of social capital in work, there is little consensus on the causal link between social relations and happiness. For example, in Fisher's broad review of happiness at work (2010), he concluded that: 'It appears that happiness is a function of environmental events and circumstances, stable tendencies in the person and the fit between the two, with the possibility of limited modification'. Simultaneously, Fisher recognizes the importance of pleasant relationships at work for happiness, and remarks that 'workplace social connections have not undergone enough scrutiny by researchers' (Haar et al., 2019). The general trend of this research focuses on the study of organizational structures, leadership styles and models of communication with happiness and not the intrinsic nature of the relationships themselves (Agneessens and Wittek, 2008).

Notwithstanding, the influence on happiness is related with expressive dimensions and relational goods. Obviously, in the same sense as general social capital, an interpersonal climate that is nourished on the production and consumption of relational goods in the workspace favors the productivity of workers (Gui, 2005; Sacco and Vanin, 2000). It improves the exchange of information and knowledge, increases cooperation and altruism and results in an overall increase in efficiency. Relational goods operate as compensations that motivate workers 'non-monetarily'. Therefore, at the same time, they are expressive but carry an instrumental value because they affect the economic performance of the group (Sacco and Vanin, 2000). Therefore, the workspace constitutes an appropriate environment for producing these goods. That is, the role of the employees in the workplace permits the development of these encounters.

THE MEDIATING ROLE OF CULTURE AND WORK–FAMILY CONFLICT

In the literature on happiness and social relations, we can find two main issues related with this new concept of relational goods. On the one hand, the mediating role of culture in the generation of these kinds of goods, particularly the distinction between collectivistic and individualistic cultural contexts. On the other hand, the potential effect of the work–family conflict in this singular production function.

Cultural Dimensions and Relational Goods

When addressing the issue of relational goods, one of the most commonly mentioned topics is their cultural constraints, the classical Tönnies (1999) distinction between community and society, and even cold and warm societies. This distinction is based on the kind of relations between members. Community relations are affective and personal, creating a *ligament* between subjects, while associative relationships are instrumental, rational and even tactical. In the first, men treat each other as ends in themselves, in the second as a means to achieving certain ends. In a pure schematic perspective, the family is a community while the workplace is an association. This does not mean that there are two trends coexisting in permanent conflict generating social realities. Thus, a work organization can appeal to the community's feelings and we can find communities in the workplace, but the logic behind both social institutions is clearly different and both reflect a kind of dialectic between an organic will and an affective will. In society, relations are established based on individual interests and indifference to each other, while in the community, relations are imbued with affectivity.

We can transpose this general vision of the problem to the study of the dimensions of culture. The different cultural contexts have a direct impact on the extent of these types of networks and their effects on subjective wellbeing. Culture influences every aspect of life and, although it is not deterministic, it is a kind of system of thought built on a consensus of values, norms and symbols, which influences the interactions and choices of individuals. Hofstede's approach (1984, 2001) considers the existence of six dimensions that would allow a basic differentiation of these various consensuses of values to be established: individualism vs. collectivism, power–distance, masculinity vs. femininity, uncertainty avoidance, long-term orientation vs. short-term orientation and indulgence vs. restraint. From this set, one particular dimension can potentially affect the generation of relational goods: individualism vs. collectivism (Pena-López and Sánchez-Santos, 2014).

This scale reflects the predominance of the individual against all forms of collectivism. Thus, it collects the extent to which individuals are integrated into cohesive groups and follow their guidelines or, on the contrary, adopt their own choices. In individualistic cultures, individuals make their own decisions, whereas in collectivist societies they prioritize collective interests and expect loyalty and reciprocity from the group. Those cultures, such as the Latin American ones, clearly marked by collectivism, are more likely to develop networks of strong support relationships. Thus, the dominance of family institutions is key. In sharp contrast, more individualistic societies such as those of the Anglo-Saxon tradition are more likely to extend weak relations and have a lesser link with the family institution or the close community. Thus, collectivistic societies will supply more social support that can mitigate the potential conflict between family and work (Drummond et al., 2016)

Considering the logic of this dimension, it could be assumed that cultures that are more collectivistic or less individualistic have a greater propensity for developing networks of relationships in the workplace. In this sense, we can find two conflicting forces in our binomial case of analysis: Latin America and the United States. In sum, production of relational goods is contextually and culturally conditioned: collectivist societies will present a greater endowment of relational goods; but in the workplace, culture dimensions can exert a contradictory influence on this production process of relational goods.

Family–Work Conflict

Considering the objective of our revision, there is a classic object of study necessarily involved: the work–family balance. The production of relational goods is natural in the family context; however, although possible in the context of work, not all theoretical perspectives on the functioning of relations at work accept this form of link as proper of this social framework.

The family–work conflict appears as a consequence of the fragmentation of identities, roles and belonging. Conflict arises when there are competing demands between work and family roles; pressures of family and work domains are incompatible in some respect (Drummond et al, 2016; O'Driscoll and Brough, 2004). People need affiliation and belonging, but subject identity is fragmented and built by multiple interactions in their various social roles. Any individual can identify with a diverse set of roles that integrate their various domains of life: family, social environment, religious grouping, work etc. Such identification involves an alignment of interests and values and the natural conflict of identities can affect not only productivity but also personal relations and subjective wellbeing. This interference can occur in both directions: work–family interference (WFI) and family-to-work interference (FWI).

In the case of the workspace, to work in an organization is a source of personal identity as part of a collective, and so the individual incorporates the norms, values and interest of the organization. As with any other form of social capital, the network of relationships established with other employees and with family members affects this process of role alignment and conflict. Particularly, the lack of social support from colleagues and family members can exacerbate the experience of work–family conflict (Blanch and Aluja, 2012). This way, support from the workmates alleviates the WFI in terms of subjective wellbeing and, in the other direction, support from family members alleviates FMI (O'Driscoll and Brough, 2004).

The analytical approaches to this conflict can be articulated according to two theoretical perspectives: the boundary and border theories. The boundary theory establishes the existence of two interdependent sections in

personal life: work and family. Both sections are differentiated by roles and responsibilities. However, since both are interdependent, each section exerts an influence over the other, but an individual cannot simultaneously exercise roles in both. Thus, individuals constantly experience a transformation of executed roles and expectations in both sections, and so they have to leave a role and play another (Ashforth et al., 2000; Chen et al., 2005). Within this perspective, the individual cannot have family roles and workplace roles at the same time. In this sense, expressive relations that are the base of relational goods are not common roles in the workplace. Consequently, social relations can constitute relational goods inside the family or group of friends and not in a workplace environment.

The border theory does not contradict what the previous theory expresses, but remarks on the increasing blurring boundaries between work and family. This approach goes on to analyze the nature of the influence that each section exerts on the other with the objective of proposing ways to channel conflicts between the two. This perspective is rooted in contemporary societies and the general need for integration between both social spaces. Therefore, the object of this proposal is to integrate or balance roles and expectations typical of both sections (Lavassani and Movahedi, 2014). In this way, the border theory proposes the management of these fuzzier lines between work and family (Clark, 2000). In this sense, both spaces can generate relational goods and the influence on subjective wellbeing can be based on relational goods produced in a family context or in a work context. Consequently, both can alleviate WFI and FWI. Both perspectives can be considered an evolution in the ways of understanding personal roles in the workplace and in the family. This evolution can be categorized in three stages.

The boundary theory responds to the earliest structuralist-segmentation theoretical views, and proposes a separation between family and work because of the supposed negative effect of the interferences (Blood and Wolfe, 1960 from Michela and Hargis, 2008). The next step, the compensation view of the 1970s and 1980s, remarked on the necessity of a kind of family relief or the family as an environment of satisfaction that the employee cannot find in the workplace. This approach opened the possibility of a balance between the two (Zedek and Mosier, 1990). Since the 1990s, the border theory considers both the positive and the negative influences, namely, one role may strengthen the other, or one role may overload the other. In this later approach, spillovers and enrichment between social environments may occur. In a spillover, the experience in one space affects the other positively. Furthermore, from the enrichment view, the experience in one role may favor the development of the other. Thus, there is a positive link and synergies in both directions WFI and FWI (Kirchmeyer, 1993). This new consensus can only be understood in the context of a certain developed labor market that supports family enrichment within the new family–work context. For example, changes in gender perspective, changes in family model, new forms of compatibility and of course new forms of work organization (Byron, 2005; Lavassani and Movahedi, 2014).

Thus, there is a set of contextual and organizational variables that can affect the differentiation of roles creating boundaries. For example, gender is an additional constraint; social norms, roles and the different constructions of the concept of the ideal worker mean that men and women face the problem of balance differently, particularly when we are talking about mothers (Cuddy et al., 2004; Drummond et al., 2016; Ford et al., 2007; Reynolds, 2005). These different perceptions influence, for example, a diverse response when at the birth of a child a partner chooses to reduce their working hours. Age, family situation, profession, level of income and perceived stress also influence the conflict. The pressure of professional careers can lead to forsaking family life and the loss of relational goods (Williams and Boushey, 2010). Recent trends, particularly in developed countries,

recognizing the role of women as mothers and giving them a preferential character has led to a certain change in trends, reducing the existing boundaries. Similarly, the rise of women as providers of the family reinforces this tendency to displace men as the dominant role in the family (Zuo and Tang, 2000). These role changes also take place among men. There is a growing tendency to recognize that work is not a sufficient source of satisfaction and rebalancing work and personal relationships is sought (Thorne, 2011).

Similarly, the characteristics and composition of the family can also exert an influence. We can find a variability of situations: single people, de facto couples, married couples with and without children. Couples and parents who are working may experience less family satisfaction. The amount of time spent on work may reduce the satisfaction derived from family relationships, by limiting the possibility of covering the responsibilities, roles and tasks that come with that identity. Family members simply do not have the favorable conditions for the production of relational goods. In a relevant percentage of the cases, they will be forced to contract care or resort to instrumental relationships to cover family roles. This means normalizing or accepting a structural lack of time and partially abandoning a personal role (Williams and Boushey, 2010). Recent tendencies to reorganize the equilibrium between family and work result in role compatibility in favor of the border theory. Therefore, the changing roles that are more typical of developed societies are closer to the border theory. These changes can foster a new perspective on work and family roles where social support and family and workplace ease WFI and FWI.

In short, relational goods occur both in family and in workplace environments; however, there are limits between both. For the boundary theory, both social environments are differentiated since roles and standards are diverse. The border theory considers that relational goods can be produced in both environments because they are interrelated.

In our case of analysis, we will try to contrast these perspectives in two culturally different labor markets; that is, which expression of social relations can have an effect on subjective wellbeing and if this is compatible with one particular approach.

RELATIONS WITH FAMILY AND COLLEAGUES, AND WELLBEING: THE CASE OF LATIN AMERICAN COUNTRIES VERSUS THE UNITED STATES

The Understanding High Happiness in Latin America Project (Rojas et al., 2018) offers an opportunity to study family and work relationships, and their association with wellbeing, in different cultural contexts empirically. A telephone survey was conducted with representative samples of the populations of three Latin American countries (Colombia, Costa Rica and Mexico) and the United States by way of comparison. The sample includes 3,741 complete observations, 2,687 for the group of Latin American countries, and the rest for the United States. Respondents were asked about their wellbeing, personal relations and other personal characteristics.

As is well documented in the literature, Latin Americans tend to report higher self-reported happiness. Happiness is measured in this survey by the usual self-assessment question, 'taking into account the whole life', on a scale of 1 ('extremely unhappy') to 7 ('extremely happy'). Figure 8.1 presents the distribution of this variable by group of countries. The skewness of the distribution for the Latin American countries is, as expected, higher; the mean level of happiness in Latin American countries ($M = 5.670$, $SD = 0.920$) is significantly higher than in the United States ($M = 5.112$, $SD = 1.301$), $t(4224) = 16.043$, $p < 0.001$ (OECD, 2013).

In light of our discussion on the nature of social relations and the role of culture, it is worth observing some differential traits of Latin American countries vis-à-vis the United States. Social relations are generally perceived as 'warmer' in Latin American countries. For example, respondents in the survey were directly asked whether they agreed with the following sentence: 'In our society, interpersonal relations are warm and close'. Responses ranged from 1 ('completely agree') to 5 ('completely disagree'). The percentage of Latin Americans who agreed with this sentence (responses 4 or 5 combined) was about 65%, compared to 43% in the United States; the mean response value

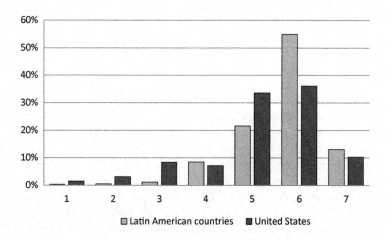

Figure 8.1   Distribution of the level of happiness by group of countries

was significantly higher for Latin American respondents ($M = 3.573$, $SD = 1.023$) than respondents in the United States ($M = 3.281$, $SD = 1.037$); $t(3697) = 7.811$, $p < 0.001$. Latin American countries appear to constitute a more fertile context for the development of relational goods.

Also, as we observed earlier, a less individualistic society may favor the development of relational goods. Figure 8.2 depicts the distributions of responses expressing the degree of agreement with the sentence 'When making important decisions, I think about my family's wellbeing before mine' (on a scale of 1 to 5, where 1 means 'completely agree' and 5 means 'completely disagree'). Of the Latin American respondents, 43.61% declared that they 'completely agree' with the sentence, compared to 29.98% of respondents in the United States. The mean response value of Latin Americans ($M = 1.728$, $SD = 0.801$) is significantly lower than that of respondents in the United States ($M = 2.075$, $SD = 0.939$), $t(3735)$, $p < 0.001$.

This result hints at a greater degree of collectivism in Latin American countries compared to the United States. Note, however, that collectivism takes the form of familism here, where the family is regarded as the only collective that matters. In this social context, the improved development of relational goods is mostly confined within the boundaries of the family. Hence, satisfaction with family relations must be one of the main drivers of happiness. Relational goods may still be developed throughout work relationships, but the workplace is not the first place to look in the pursuit of wellbeing. Familism reinforces the boundaries of the family, where people nurture their identities and pursue their wellbeing.

Indeed, in Latin American countries, the family emerges as the context where positive emotions can be naturally shared. On a scale of 1 to 6 expressing the frequency of sharing positive emotions with close family members, Latin Americans ($M = 4.784$, $SD = 1.461$) scored significantly higher than residents of the United States ($M = 4.468$, $SD = 1.226$), $t(3707)$, $p < 0.001$.

Thus, results of the Understanding High Happiness in Latin America Project show that, on average, people from these Latin American countries, compared to the United States, perceive themselves as happier and enjoy warmer social relations, especially with the family. Besides, familism emerges as a dominant trait in those cultures.

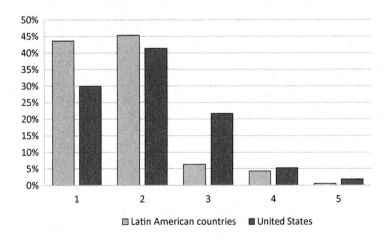

Figure 8.2   **Distribution of the degree of agreement with the sentence 'When making important decisions, I think about my family's wellbeing before mine' (1: 'completely agree'; 5: 'completely disagree')**

As discussed above, however, the workplace may enhance the development of relational goods and improve wellbeing, too. Two survey questions may serve as examples to clarify this issue. First, respondents were asked about the frequency with which they talked about 'personal feelings, interests and aspirations' with their colleagues. On a 1 ('never') to 5 ('several days a week') scale, we observed an almost flat but U-shaped distribution, with no significant differences between countries. In addition, respondents were asked about the frequency of sharing positive emotions, like happiness or enthusiasm, with colleagues. Of the complete sample, 21.5% declared that they 'always' do it. In this case, the mean response of Latin Americans ($M = 3.903$, $SD = 1.730$) was higher than that of residents of the United States ($M = 3.635$, $SD = 1.323$), $t(1868) = 3.332$, $p < 0.001$; a result in line with the improved development of relational goods in Latin American countries.

Hence, the family emerges as a privileged field for personal relations, but relational goods are also developed in the workplace and may enhance happiness. However, the association of work relationships with happiness may depend, among other factors, on culture, which affects the boundaries between the family and the work contexts. The Understanding High Happiness in Latin America Project shows that the association between happiness and deep work relations is stronger in the United States than in Latin American countries. For example, it is possible to measure the association between happiness and the frequency of talking with colleagues about personal matters. These variables appear to be positively associated in all countries, but the strength of the association is higher in the United States (Pearson χ^2 (24) = 80.854, p < 0.001, Cramér's V = 0.181) than in Latin America (Pearson χ^2 (24) = 48.431, p = 0.002, Cramér's V = 0.092).[1] Similarly, sharing positive emotions with colleagues is more strongly associated with happiness for United States respondents (Pearson χ^2 (30) = 124.793, p < 0.001, Cramér's

V = 0.206) than Latin Americans (Pearson χ^2 (30) = 58.777, p = 0.001, Cramér's V = 0.096).[2]

These results highlight the relational-good nature of work relationships in the United States, where the boundaries between family and work tend to be less defined. In other words, in the United States, both family and work relationships are likely to produce relational goods and, thus, increase happiness. In Latin American countries, however, which are characterized by higher degrees of collectivism/familism, work relationships seem to contribute less to improved happiness. Good work relationships are not directly linked to enhanced happiness, and the family maintains its privileged role as provider of relational goods. Notwithstanding, this statement has to be controlled by another potential influence: changes in organizational culture. The development of more horizontal management strategies can also foster this new perspective on work relationships in more advanced labor markets.

CONCLUSION

The study of revealed subjective wellbeing prioritizes a unidimensional perspective of the social capital concept focused on formal associationism and subjective wellbeing, even when this is theoretically questionable. This results in neglecting strong ties, family, friends and work relationships, which is remarkable when considering the weight of the family in life, and the traditional family and work conflict, especially for happiness. The concept of relational goods links social relationships with subjective wellbeing. These are the affective, expressive and noninstrumental side of interpersonal relationships and are (potentially) produced through interactions in any sphere of social life, such as family, friends, peer groups, associations and the workplace.

The interpersonal relationships climate that is nourished by the production and consumption of relational goods favors the productivity of workers, improves the exchange of information and knowledge, increases cooperation and altruism and results in an overall increase in efficiency. At the same time, relational goods operate as compensations that motivate workers 'non-monetarily' and in the form of subjective wellbeing. Analyzing this link, we also have to consider two contextual variables that can mediate: culture and work–family conflict. Culture can exert an influence through the collectivism–individualism dimension. Collectivist societies tend to show a greater endowment of relational goods; but in the workplace, culture dimensions can exert a contradictory influence on this production process of relational goods.

In the analysis of family–work conflict, we can find two general perspectives that are stages in an evolution of work organization. For the boundary theory, both social environments are differentiated since roles and standards are diverse. The border theory considers that relational goods can be produced in both environments because they are interrelated. In our case of analysis, we review these perspectives in two cultural contexts: the United States and Latin America. A simple descriptive analysis of our international sample highlights the existence of two different societies. Comparatively, the Latin American case shows a higher level of subjective wellbeing and different individual social capital profiles. In the United States, associationism is dominant, whereas in our Latin American case, the strong links between family, friends and neighbors are the dominant dimensions.

Family relationships are relevant for wellbeing in all of their manifestations, both for the United States and for Latin America, while work relationships are only significant regarding the United States. These results imply a cultural contextualization of the two theoretical proposals mentioned, the boundary and border theories. It could be stated from these results that the border perspective would have some explanatory capacity for

the United States, but not for the case of Latin America. For the latter, differentiation of work and family roles is stricter. This result may be explained by cultural differences, differences in labor market functioning or even differences in generalized human resources management. Future studies can examine the determinants of these perceived differences of effect on subjective wellbeing of workplace relationships.

Notes

1 Cramér's V is a measure of association between two discrete variables, designed to be $0 \le V \le 1$.
2 Although beyond this chapter's scope, these conclusions hold when controlling for other relevant characteristics: level of education, economic situation, sex, age, civil status and having children. These associations have been checked by ordered logistic regressions, with the level of happiness as the dependent variable, and the mentioned characteristics as controls. Results are available upon request.

REFERENCES

Adler, P. A. and Kwon, S. W. (2002) Social capital: prospects for a new concept, *Academy of Management Review*, 27 (1): 17–40.

Agneessens, F. and Wittek, R. (2008) Social capital and employee wellbeing: disentangling intrapersonal and interpersonal selection and influence mechanisms, *Revue Francaise de Sociologie*, 49 (3): 613–637.

Stutzer, A. and Lalive, R. (2004) The role of social work norms in job searching and subjective wellbeing, *Journal of the European Economic Association*, 2 (4): 696–719.

Argyle, M. (2002) *The psychology of happiness*, London, Routledge.

Ashforth, B., Kreiner, G. and Fugate, M. (2000) All in a day's work: boundaries and micro role transitions, *Academy of Management Review*, 25 (3): 472–491.

Bartolini, S., Bilancini, E. and Pugno, M. (2013) Did the decline in social connections depress Americans' happiness? *Social Indicators Research*, 110 (3): 1033–1059.

Becchetti, L., Pelloni, A. and Rossetti, F. (2008) *Relational goods, sociability, and happiness*, Department of Communication, University of Teramo, Working Paper, 39.

Blanch, A. and Aluja, A. (2014) Social support (family and supervisors), work–family conflict, and burnout, *Human Relations*, 65 (7): 811–833.

Bourdieu, P. (2001) The forms of capital. In Granovetter, M. and Swedberg, R. (eds) *The sociology of economic life*, Oxford, Westview Press, 2nd ed., 97–111.

Brief, A. P. (1998) *Attitudes in and around organizations*, Thousand Oaks, CA, Sage.

Bruni, L. (2008) *El precio de la gratuidad*, Madrid, Editorial Ciudad Nueva.

Bruni, L. and Stanca, L. (2008) Watching alone: relational goods, television and happiness, *Journal of Economic Behaviour and Organization*, 65 (3): 506–528.

Byron, K. (2005) A meta-analytic review of work–family conflict and its antecedents, *Journal of Vocational Behavior*, 67 (2): 169–198.

Chen, I., Lai, I., Lin, Y. and Cheng, Y. (2005) *Blurring boundaries: the working-at-home employees*. Proceeding of EURAM conference, Germany.

Clark, S. (2000) Work/family border theory: a new theory of work/family balance, *Human Relations*, 53 (6): 747–770.

Coleman, J. (1988) Social capital in the creation of human capital, *American Journal of Sociology*, 94: 95–120.

Cranny, C. J., Smith, P. C. and Stones, E. F. (eds.) (1992) *Job satisfaction: advances in research and applications*, New York, The Free Press.

Cuddy, A., Fiske, S. and Glick, P. (2004) When professionals become mothers, warmth doesn't cut the ice, *Journal of Social Issues*, 60 (4): 701–718.

Dasgupta, P. and Serageldin, I. (2001) *Social capital, a multifaceted approach*, Washington, World Bank.

Donati, P. (2013) The added value of social relations, *Italian Journal of Sociology of Education*, 5 (1): 19–35.

Donati, P. (2019) Social life and the enigma of the relationship: the paradox of relational goods, *Società Mutamento Política*, 10 (20): 11–21.

Drummond, S., O'Driscoll, M., Brough, P., Siu, O., Tims, C. and Riley, D. (2016) The relationship of social support with well-being outcomes via work-family conflict: moderating effects of gender, dependents and nationality, *Human Relations*, 70 (5): 1–22.

Easterlin, R. A. (2001) Income and happiness: towards a unified theory, *The Economic Journal*, 111 (473): 465–484.

Fine, B. (2001) *Social capital versus social theory*, New York, Routledge.

Fisher, C (2010) Happiness at work, *International Journal of Management Reviews*, 12: 384–412.

Ford, M. T., Heinen, B. A. and Langkamer K. L. (2007) Work and family satisfaction and conflict: a meta-analysis of cross-domain relations, *Journal of Applied Psychology*, 92 (1): 57–80.

Fritz, C. and Sonnentag, S. (2009) Antecedents of day-level proactive behavior: a look at job stressors and positive affect during the workday, *Journal of Management,* 35: 94–111.

Gui, B. (2000) Beyond transactions: on the interpersonal relations of the economic reality, *Annals of Public and Cooperative Economics*, 7 (2): 139–169.

Gui, B. (2005) From transactions to encounters: the joint generation of relational goods and conventional values. In Gui, B. and Sugden, R. (eds) *Economics and social interaction*, Cambridge, Cambridge University Press, 23–51.

Gui, B. and Stanca, L. (2010) Happiness and relational goods: well-being and interpersonal relations in the economic sphere, *International Review of Economics*, 57: 105–118.

Gui, B. and Sugden, R. (2005) Why interpersonal relations matter for economics. In Gui, B. and Sugden, R. (eds) *Economics and social interactions, Accounting for Interpersonal Relations*, Cambridge, Cambridge University Press, 1–22.

Haar, J., Schmitz, A., Di Fabio, A. and Daellenbach, U. (2019) The role of relationships at work and happiness, *Sustainability*, 11: 3443–3448.

Helliwell J. and Putnam R. D. (2004) The social context of wellbeing, *Philosophical Transactions of the Royal Society*, London, Series B: 1435–1446.

Hodson, R. (2001) *Dignity at work*, Cambridge, Cambridge University Press.

Homans, C. (1958) Social behaviour as exchange, *American Journal of Sociology*, 62: 597–606.

Iglesias Vázquez, E., Pena López, A. and Sánchez Santos, J. M. (2013) Bienestar subjetivo, renta y bienes relacionales: los determinantes de la felicidad en España, *Revista Internacional de Sociología*, 71 (3): 567–592.

Ilies, R. and Judge, T. A. (2005) Goal regulation across time: the effects of feedback and affect, *Journal of Applied Psychology*, 90, 453–467.

Hofstede, G. (1984) *Culture's consequences, international differences: Work–related values: 5 (Cross cultural researcher and methodology)*, London, Sage.

Hofstede, G. (2001) *Cultural consequences: Comparing values, behaviors, institutions and organizations across nations*, 2nd ed., Thousand Oaks, CA, Sage.

Kalliath, T. and Brough, P. (2008) Work-life balance: a review of the meaning of the balance construct, *Journal of Management and Organization*, 14: 323–327.

Kirchmeyer, C. (1993) Nonwork-to-work spillover: a more balanced view of the experiences and coping of professional women and men, *Sex Roles*, 28 (9–10): 531–552.

Kirchmeyer, C. (2000) Work-life initiatives: greed or benevolence regarding workers' time. In Cooper, C. and Rousseau, D. (eds) *Trends in organizational behavior*, Chichester, Wiley, 7: 79–93.

Knack, S. and Keefer, P. (1997) Does social capital have an economic pay off? A cross country investigation, *Quarterly Journal of Economics*, 112: 1251–1288.

Lavassani, K. and Movahedi, B. (2014) Developments in theories and measures of work-family relationships: from conflict to balance, *Contemporary Research on Organization Management and Administration*, 2 (1): 6–19.

Lin, N. (1999a) Social networks and status attainment, *American Review of Sociology*, 25: 467–487.

Lin, N. (1999b) Building a network theory of social capital, *Connections*, 22 (1): 28–51.

Lin, N. (2001) *Social capital. A theory of social structure and action*, Cambridge, Cambridge University Press.

Lin, N. (2008) A network theory of social capital. In Castiglione, D. et al. (eds) *The handbook of social capital*, New York, Oxford University Press, 50–70.

Michela, J. and Hargis, M. (2008) Linking mechanisms of work–family conflict and segmentation, *Journal of Vocational Behavior*, 73 (3): 509–522.

Nussbaum, M. (1995 [1986]) *La fragilidad del bien: fortuna y ética en la tragedia y la filosofía griega*, Madrid, Visor.

O'Driscoll, M. and Brough, P. (2004) Work–family conflict, psychological and social support, *Equal Opportunities International*, 23 (1): 36–56.

OECD (2013) *Guidelines on measuring subjective wellbeing*, Paris, OECD Publishing.

Paldam, M. (2000) Social capital: one or many? Definition and measurement, *Journal of Economic Surveys*, 14 (5): 629–653.

Pena López, J. A. and Sánchez Santos, J. M. (2017) Individual social capital: accessibility and mobilization of resources embedded in social networks, *Social Networks*, 49: 1–11.

Pena-López, J. A., Sánchez- Santos, J. M. and Membiela-Pollan, M. (2017) Individual social capital and subjective wellbeing: the relational goods, *Journal of Happiness Studies*, 18: 881–901.

Pena-López, J. A. and Sánchez-Santos, J. M. (2014) Does corruption have social roots? The role of culture and social capital, *Journal of Business Ethics*, 122 (4): 697–708.

Putnam, R. (1993) *Making democracy work: civic traditions in modern Italy*, Princeton, NJ, Princeton University Press.

Putnam, R. (2000) *Bowling alone, the collapse and revival of American community*, New York, Simon and Schuster.

Reynolds, J. (2005) In the face of conflict: work–life conflict and desired work hour adjustments, *Journal of Marriage and Family*, 67 (5): 1313–1331.

Rojas, M., Willis, E., Hansberg, O., Millán, R. and Abdallah, S. (2018) *Understanding high happiness in Latin America: human relations and spirituality in a life well lived*. Available at http://www.happinessandwellbeing.org/rojas (accessed 5 April 2020).

Sacco, P. L. and Vanin, P. (2000) Network interaction with material and relational goods: an exploratory simulation, *Annals of Public and Cooperative Economics*, 71 (2): 229–259.

Sirota, D., Mischkind, L. A. and Meltzer, M. I. (2005) *The enthusiastic employee,* Upper Saddle River, NJ, Wharton School Publishing.

Tannenbaum, R., Weschler, I. and Massarik, F. (2013) *Leadership and organization*, Oxford, Routledge.

Thorne, B. (2011) The crisis of care. In Garey, A. I. and Hansen, K. V. (eds) *At the heart of work and family*, New Brunswick, Rutgers University Press, 149–160.

Tönnies, F. (1999) *Community and society*, New York, Routledge.

Uhlaner, C. (1989) Relational goods and participation: incorporating sociability into a theory of rational action, *Public Choice*, 62, 253–285.

Van der Gaag, M. and Snijders, T. (2004) Proposals for the measurement of individual social capital. In Flap, H. D. and Volker, B. (eds) *Creation and returns of social capital*, London, Routledge, 199–218.

Veenhoven, R. (1984) *Conditions of happiness*, Dordrecht, Reidel Publishing Company.

Veenhoven. R. (1999) Quality-of-life in individualistic society, *Social Indicators Research,* 48, 159–188.

Warr, P. (2007) *Work, happiness and unhappiness,* Mahwah, NJ, Lawrence Erlbaum.

Williams, J. and Boushey, H. (2010) *The three faces of work–family conflict: the poor, the professionals, and the missing middle center*, Center for American Progress, Hastings College of the Law.

Winter, I. (2001) *Toward a theorized understanding of family life and social capital*, Working paper no. 1, Melbourne University, Melbourne.

Yang, K. (2007) Individual social capital and its measurement in social surveys, *Survey Research Methods*, 1 (1): 19–27.

Zamagni, S. (2004) Towards an economics of human relations: on the role of psychology in economics, *The Group-Analytic Society (London), Group Analysis*, 37 (1): 17–32.

Zedeck, S. and Mosier, K. (1990) Work in the family and employing organization, *American Psychologist*, 45 (2): 240–251.

Zuo, J. and Tang, S. (2000) Breadwinner status and gender ideologies of men and women regarding family roles, *Sociological Perspectives*, 43 (1): 29–43.

9

Social Movements and Wellbeing in Organizations from Multilevel and Intersectional Perspectives: The Case of the #blacklivesmatter Movement

Mustafa F. Özbilgin and Cihat Erbil

INTRODUCTION

Wellbeing is often defined as a state of equilibrium and thriving in the context of other constructs such as health, happiness, prosperity, satisfaction, ability to cope with stress, to retain meaning, purpose and dignity in life (Cartwright and Cooper, 2009; Dodge et al., 2012; Rath and Harter, 2010). In the context of work, wellbeing is studied among workers, managerial cohorts, leadership and other stakeholder communities. Cartwright and Cooper (2011) frame wellbeing as a vantage point from which to strengthen organizations by building healthy interpersonal relationships among workers and other stakeholder communities. When studied in the field of organization studies, wellbeing is often studied as an individual phenomenon, an organizational construct (Cartwright and Cooper, 2011) or a macro-structural concern (Mitra, 2018) that could be managed through wellbeing interventions. In this paper, we explore the widely neglected extra-organizational

forces that impact on wellbeing at work, i.e. the social movements that have wellbeing concerns as their core struggles.

Wellbeing emerges as a multifaceted construct and a responsibility that is shared by multiple actors (Diener et al., 2003). For example, individuals have responsibility for their own wellbeing and self-care (Narasimhan et al., 2019; Shanafelt et al., 2005), families have responsibility for the wellbeing of their children and other members (Umberson et al., 2010), educational establishments have responsibility for the wellbeing of students (Aldridge et al., 2016) and work organizations have responsibility for the wellbeing of their workers (Cooper and Leiter, 2017) and the consumers and communities with which they interface (Rosenbaum, 2015). Nation states have responsibility for the wellbeing of their citizens, residents and visitors (Alcock and Glennerster, 2001). In such a broadening circle of responsibility, we see that international agencies, nation states and global organizations have far-reaching roles and significant resources and regulatory power for ensuring better quality of wellbeing of individuals in a global context. Despite widespread responsibilization of institutions for wellbeing of individuals in the global context, there remains widespread imbalances in the quality of wellbeing of individuals nationally and internationally. In addressing the imbalances in wellbeing among individuals, social movements play a role in identifying wellbeing concerns of disadvantaged communities, bringing these to public attention and mobilizing broad-based support for changes in regulatory systems, resource allocation methods and symbolic and social treatment of a particular group.

A social movement is a group of individuals getting together in order to achieve one or more goals (Tilly and Wood, 2020). Social movements are emergent, loosely organized and decentralized entities, which do not have strong formal structures at the point of their inception and often through their life course (Castells, 2015). Contemporary social movements are often driven by demands for behavioral, social or political changes such as democratization, humanization, elimination of discrimination and disadvantage and protection of the environment (Tilly and Wood, 2020). Social movements expose the suppression of wellbeing and human rights concerns by revealing false political rhetorics (Holmes, 2019) and play important roles in inspiring and shaping social mores, political beliefs, economic behaviors, political agendas and rights and responsibilities among actors in their societies. Benford (1997) explains that social movements are defined and framed in a wide range of ways, and yet the empirical evidence to support some of the claims around social movements remains limited. One of the earlier, yet oft-cited classifications of social movements is offered by David Friend Aberle (1966), who framed social movements in four types: alternative, redemptive, reformative and revolutionary (transformational). Aberle classifies social movements according to what they want to

change (do they target individual beliefs and behaviors or whole society) and to what extent they want to make changes (in certain points as limited or in radical manner). Alternative social movements aim at partial changes in the behaviors of individuals. One prominent example is the #madd (Mothers Against Drunk Driving) movement, which urges people to quit the behavior of driving and drinking (Christiansen, 2009). On the other hand, redemptive social movements aim at a fundamental change in individuals' thought and belief systems. Such movements have mostly been initiated by religious organizations. Prominent examples are #weightwatchers and #AA (Alcoholics Anonymous), which seek to change the behavior of individual members of the social movement. In contrast to the two former movements, reformative and revolutionary movements focus on a change in society, not individuals. Reformative social movements address the operation of institutions supporting social structure and norms, not the social structure itself, and attempt to make reforms of the problematic aspects. For example, the #metoo and #blacklivesmatter movements seek to combat sexual harassment and racism respectively in social and institutional settings. Revolutionary social movements aim to change social structure radically and expect a dramatic change in the whole society. The communist revolutions in China and Russia, Islamic revolution in Iran and the republican revolution in France could be considered examples of ideologically and religiously inspired revolutions that changed the social, political and economic life where they took place. Although Aberle's classification of social movements is widely accepted, the boundary conditions of these categories are often blurred. For example, most social movements have claims of revolution but often they settle for reformation or even small stepwise changes. In this chapter, we focus on reformative social movements that seek to transform adverse institutional arrangements that suppress the wellbeing of certain segments of a population. As a caveat, we do not consider social movements as monolithic or fixed. Instead, we focus on their intersectional character and the dynamically changing nature of their discourses and practices. We focus on the interplay between social movements and wellbeing from an intersectional lens, problematizing the individualization of wellbeing and demonstrating the utility of institutional and intersectional perspectives to wellbeing as supported by reformative social movements.

In this chapter, we focus on reformative social movements which are progressive and have emancipatory potential, such as feminist, human rights, civil liberties, LGBTI+, disability, age and class-related social movements which have the wellbeing of large segments of society at their core. Further, we study a relationship which remains underexplored in the extant literature, the interplay between wellbeing and reformative social movements, revealing how wellbeing features as an important agenda item in social movements, and serves three roles: first, an antecedent, i.e. poor wellbeing among a social group due to discrimination, disadvantage, exclusion, or underrepresentation. Second, a key agenda item which shapes campaigns of reformative social movements, such as demands of social movements to improve wellbeing for disadvantaged communities; and third, an outcome, improvements in social and legal regulations that improve the wellbeing of individuals at work. In this chapter, we explore this virtuous spiral, where social movements, which are formed in order to address common problems of wellbeing, work to improve wellbeing for their members and wider communities. In order to achieve this we explore the intersectional character of social movements and their agendas for change across salient identity struggles such as gender, ethnicity, age, disability, sexual orientation and social class.

Intersectionality is a philosophical perspective to studies of diversity and equality. It was introduced by Kimberlé Crenshaw (1990), a law scholar who argued that studying gender and ethnicity in isolation is not sufficient to understand African American women's experience in the United States. Instead, Crenshaw advocated the study of categories of difference together. In contemporary studies of intersectionality, scholars have identified both cumulative and surprising outcomes of studying gender, ethnicity, race, class, sexual orientation, disability and other categories together. Kamasak et al. (2019a) suggest that intersectionality is not only an individual phenomenon, but that institutions also have intersectional character. For example, some institutions are dominated by white, male, upper-class, heterosexual and able-bodied individuals and resultantly their structures and decision-making mechanisms privilege the conditions of this group better. As a result, institutions are imbued with intersectional character as much as individuals; and institutions have mechanisms that produce and normalize inequalities (Acker, 1989, 2006a, 2006b, 2012; Healy et al., 2011; Nkomo and Rodriguez, 2019). This approach has implications for how intersectionality could be treated and managed in workplaces. An institutional approach would stipulate changing workplaces, institutional arrangements, routines, structures and use of time and places in order to make it more inclusive for all identity categories of difference. In this chapter, we take an institutional view of intersectionality, exploring it in the context of social movements, and show how intersectional solidarity, tensions, challenges and hostilities among and across categories of social diversity manifest in the context of extra- and intra-organizational politics.

SOCIAL MOVEMENTS AND INTERSECTIONALITY: SOLIDARITY, DIVISIONS, TENSIONS AND SEPARATISM

Some scholars argue that the expansion of global capitalism has engendered new forms of exploitation, discrimination and violation of human rights and wellbeing of individuals. Remarkably, Stiglitz (2012) explains that neoliberal expansion of capitalist interests exploits vulnerabilities and creates inequality among communities. Bağlama (2018: 161) argues that, despite the structural transformation of capitalism, the fundamental operation of the money-oriented world has not changed because the dichotomy between the exploiter and the exploited has not essentially changed and the exploitation of human labor has been increasingly perpetuated in new forms, leading to inequalities and injustices all around the world. In the absence of effective coercive regulatory mechanisms in the field of international business, global organizations could on the one hand profess a commitment to equality, diversity and inclusion for all, and on the other, pursue cheap labor and resources and weak regulation on human rights, health and safety among some groups and in some countries in order to generate commercial value (Özbilgin et al., 2016). Untamed expansion of capitalism with its interest exploitation of untapped resources internationally creates uneven distribution of wellbeing across different groups, communities and regions, causing deterioration of equality and human rights, leading to political, social, environmental and economic crisis globally. Progressive and reformative social movements emerge in response to such crises and imbalances. For example, the feminist movement seeks to address historical disadvantages associated with social and economic organization of gender roles and gender inequalities. Similarly, the anti-racist and postcolonial social movement seeks to redress historical disadvantages.

The inequalities created in the free-market order, legitimized by competitiveness, are made non-objectionable by competitive logics where the winner gets all (Frank and Cook, 2010; Walter, 2010). The competitive economic games diffuse any objections and resistance by asserting their own rules of the competitive game, causing marginalization of the groups which do not have any access

to shaping rules of the economic game. Social movements can emerge in such critical moments where the rules of the economic, social or political games unfairly disadvantage a group of people. For example, women's right to vote was such a struggle (Nentwich et al., 2015), where women who would like to have political participation had to organize in order to challenge the established order. The result of the international women's suffrage movement was the legitimation of the right to vote for women, improving women's wellbeing through legitimating their political, social and economic participation.

Women's rights and feminist movements have gained an intersectional character more recently. For example, the #metoo movement, which mobilized to combat sexual harassment and violence against women, has received broad-based support from other social movements. #metoo has snowballed into a social movement which exposes a systematic problem in treatment of women. Tarana Burke, who is the initiator of the movement, has devised the #metoo hashtag on Twitter to voice the rights of African American young women like herself in order to make visible the sexual abuse and violence they are subjected to in cities (Gill and Orgad, 2018). She has initiated a civil society movement, with the hashtag #metoo. However, the #metoo movement was made visible and popular by a white American actress, Alyssa Milano, who confessed in a tweet that she has been sexually abused and urged others who have been sexually abused like herself, to come out and fight against sexual harassment. What is really interesting in this case is how politics of gender and race played out and how we witness the emergence of a morally suspicious pecking order between these two dimensions in interplay: when the movement was initiated by a woman of color to address intersectional issues of gender and race, the movement became popular and white women's interests were better represented as race issues became almost invisible.

The #metoo movement, which has an intersectional architecture from its foundation, and was able to retain it in the course of its development, highlighted that work environments remain highly male-dominated and women who are trying to work in such places are facing sexual and other forms of abuse, harassment and hostilities as a result. Such adverse conditions of work for women from different walks of life triggered the #metoo movement and the solidarity demonstrated towards the movement retained an intersectional character. The movement has garnered solidarity by exposing other blind spots in preventing gender discrimination, resilience of gender inequalities in paid work and sexist norms in the working environments, in the home and within households. However, the fact that sexual abuse is both anachronistic and an ever-present condition has become crystallized with the #metoo movement (Hemmings, 2018).

With its central focus on sexual harassment and abuse, the #metoo movement was able to reach out to a wide international audience. The #metoo hashtag generated millions of tweets from 85 different countries and this international campaign has made it possible for a silenced group of women, who suffered widespread sexism and harassment, to make their voices heard (Constance et al., 2018). Women's historical silence has been a sign of the strength of the male-dominated gender order that prevented women's voices being heard. In its recent manifestations, the #metoo movement has been adopted, albeit with some tensions with other movements, as an umbrella term to fight against violence, harassment and abuse against children, LGBTI+ (e.g. #iamlgbt, #iamrefugee), migrants and minorities, rights of animals and environmental concerns. The solidarity afforded by the #metoo movement to other movements and the solidarity that is offered to the #metoo movement by other social movements is remarkable. Social movements could gain legitimacy and power through drawing solidarity from other progressive social movements through intersectional solidarity, if they are able to overcome or limit their internal divisions and external hostility from other groups. Similarly, social movements could inform values and norms, changing social beliefs about social order such as gender relations. For example, Moor and Kanji (2019) illustrate the change of norms in women's domestic negotiations through their connectivity with extra-familial ties with other women in social networks. In the same vein, Soytemel (2013) argues that women's informal networks have a major impact, not only on making ends meet for their household, but also on the wellbeing of their neighborhood communities, through the solidarity that they show.

Heeding the appeals by social movements, more enlightened employers may commit to taking appropriate progressive actions. For example, in response to the #metoo movement, there were some legal changes, e.g. the Fair Wages and Healthy Families Act was passed through in response to the #metoo movement in Arizona in 2016 and organizations have generated policies and practices in order to respond to this law (Curry, 2018), and some organizations, such as Microsoft, have amended their working policies and transformed their working environments into safe spaces for everyone in response to the #metoo movement (Leopold et al., 2019). The #metoo movement has also challenged sexual abusers and cases of misconduct. For example, the *New York Times* (Carlsen et al., 2018) reports that the #metoo movement has brought down 201 powerful men in the United States and half of their replacements were women. Ashwin and Kabeer (2018) summarize the International Labour Organization report which shows that the national and organizational context for tackling sexual harassment leaves much room for progress:

International Labour Organization (ILO) research on violence and harassment at work published in 2017 found that 23 per cent of the 80 countries studied did not have a legal definition of sexual harassment at work, while a further 12 per cent only allowed for 'vertical' harassment (that is, harassment by superiors, not co-workers). Meanwhile, 25 per cent of countries in the study had no protections against reprisals for complainants. Where legal protection is weak or absent, a code of conduct will clearly be harder to enforce. But even in the presence of a suitable legal framework, a code of conduct is not a very effective tool for redressing a power imbalance. (2018: 1)

Like all social movements, the #metoo movement was also subject to resistance and backlash due to its potential to shake the status quo and force through significant changes to power relations. In particular, the #metoo movement was exposed to men's resistance which gathered under the #himtoo hashtag. Male resistance to female emancipation is not new. However, this time the male resistance appeared weak, fragmented and limited when compared to the #metoo movement (Boyle and Rathnayake, 2019). In some countries, such as India and Turkey, the #metoo movement was well received in some feminist circles but received limited legal or organizational support in practice (BBC Türkçe, 2018; Pegu, 2019). As Rowe (1990) explained, resistance to equality may transform into subtle forms and become underground and difficult to spot. Therefore, we are likely to see the true outcome of the #metoo movement and the backlash against it in the future.

While some reformative social movements such as #metoo have wide focus and targets from their inception in terms of wellbeing improvements that they seek, others may start with a narrow focus and widen as they gain intersectional solidarity from other social movements. One pertinent example of such a movement is the #gezipark movement, which was triggered by protest against a specific incident, i.e. plans to cut trees in a public city park in Taksim Square (the modern center of the city) in Istanbul, in order to develop a multiplex building site. After the initial protests by environmentalists, #gezipark galvanized support from across all social movements that opposed various

draconian measures in Turkey, including the feminist movement, workers' movements, youth movements, disability rights movements, collectives of artists and intellectuals, spiritual and religious movements and many other groups. In fact, #gezipark has become the largest social movement in the history of Turkey and the Ottoman Empire, mobilizing millions of people across the country and internationally to defend not only the trees in #gezipark but also much wider issues of environmental concerns, democracy, human rights and civil liberties in Turkey.

The #gezipark protests were nation-wide civil protests, which brought together millions from all segments of society and across the largest cities in the country. The #gezipark movement is often cited as a democratic protest to demand social, environmental and economic transformation and progress in the country (Mert, 2019) The movement included youth groups, secularists, Kemalists, leftists, environmentalists, feminists, LGBTI+, Kurds, Alevis, anti-capitalist Muslims, soccer fans, professionals and workers (Arat, 2013). Commentators on #gezipark often consider it as the first critical historical moment in which solidarity and togetherness were experienced by the masses in Turkey (Acar and Uluğ, 2016). To its participants, it has provided the possibility of accepting their identities as a protest movement, and their own individual identities as women, youth, minority ethnic, LGBTI+, minority religious and spiritual human beings, enabling them to gain visibility in public, with their own identities (Kamasak et al., 2019a). The movement was also a very exciting moment for the boundaries between identity groups to be lifted in favor of solidarity. For example, there were images of Kurds with Kemalists, religious groups with LGBTI+ fighting together against police brutality. The #gezipark movement used artistic and humoristic expressions in order to counteract the brutality and violence with which they are handled. The peaceful nature of the protests has enabled the movement to retain widespread support even from conservative segments of Turkish society (Taştan, 2013).

The interplay between the #gezipark movement and Turkish businesses received considerable coverage in the media. Public naming of non-supportive businesses has caused considerable decline in the customer base of such businesses. Businesses which supported protests gained recognition and customer support but faced challenges from the police and the state. Turkmenoglu (2016) notes that the business reactions to the #gezipark social movement have encouraged business leaders to consider the wellbeing of their staff, and that of the protestors, alongside issues of environment and democracy in the country. The awareness that the #gezipark movement fostered was invaluable in drawing attention of the state to its role as a regulator and businesses to the demands and sensitivities of the public.

Increasingly, social movements coordinate efforts with and show solidarity to other social movements with similar causes and create spaces to develop shared narratives in order to reach a global audience and a wider social base for support (Vassilopoulou et al., 2019). A remarkable example of this is the women's marches, which have not only garnered support from women's rights networks and feminist movements, but also achieved intersectional solidarity from other human rights movements such as anti-racist and LGBTI+ movements (Özbilgin, 2018). Yet, for social movements that seek to promote the wellbeing of certain groups, some commentators argue that such broad-based intersectional solidarity may dilute the key priorities of the social movement. Resultantly, the social movement may sustain divisions and divergent interests. For example, social movements that supported women in leadership positions, such as the feminist movement in Scandinavian countries, have benefited mainly white upper-class heterosexual women. Lack of recognition from dominant groups and poor levels of intersectional solidarity have sustained divisions within this social movement

and served well the interests of a narrow band of women to secure leadership and board-level appointments (Forstenlechner et al., 2012; Kakabadse et al., 2015; Samdanis and Özbilgin, 2020; Sayce and Özbilgin, 2014).

Sometimes, within the wide-based intersectional solidarity framework, those who are the most marginalized may be sidelined after they show solidarity with the mainstream social movement. In fact, it would be possible to notice this trend in the case of the #metoo and #gezipark movements in their aftermath. In the case of the #metoo movement, the movement has benefited mainly white heterosexual women, although the movement was intersectional from its inception. In the same way, the #gezipark movement benefited most the Kemalist supporters as feminist and LGBTI+ agendas were later sidelined. Divisions arise in all social movements. For example, the Dyke March, the Trans March and the Drag March are performed on dates which are very close to the LGBTI+ March in New York, dividing the already weak movement (Drucker, 2015). Similarly, some social movements involve certain tensions because exclusionary tendencies may occur as groups within social movements feel marginalized or wish to retain their priorities in competition with other supporters in the social movement. One of these is the TERF (Trans Exclusionary Radical Feminist) label, originating from the belief of radical feminists that the problems of women can only be experienced by those who are born biologically as women. Thus, prominent figures such as J. K. Rowling and Germaine Greer have argued for exclusion of trans women from women's movements and networks (Brown, 2018; Ennis, 2019). The SWERF (Sex Worker Exclusionary Radical Feminist) label is also produced by radical feminists to claim that sex workers do not have a place in the feminist movement as they blame sex workers for reproducing gender inequality. It is no surprise that such exclusionary movements in fact are imbued with white privilege (i.e. J. K. Rowling made her comments on exclusion of trans women at the height of the #blacklivesmatter movement), cis privilege and economic class privilege of some women (Fischer, 2017). It is important to look at the consequences of such trans exclusionary movements on the upsurge in the murder of and violence against trans women in Britain and other countries (Dearden, 2019).

Some social movements show separatist character along religious, ethnic, nationalist and sexist lines and therefore their agendas for wellbeing are limited by their ingroup supporters. Such separatist movements seek to foster wellbeing of a narrow category of individuals. For example, nationalist LGBTI+ movements could seek to exclude migrants, refugees and non-nationals from their activities and support mechanisms. For example, 'White Power, White Pride!'. It is dubious how groups who subscribe to one progressive agenda alone, while retaining discriminatory and exclusionary views on other social causes, could promote wellbeing for all. In fact, such single-agenda social movements could render many forms of injustice, inequality and exploitation invisible in societies and workplaces. In particular, if a social movement has a single agenda and fails to recognize other social movements, struggles for equality and justice, and demands for wellbeing, they are likely to remain marginal and anemic in terms of the support and legitimacy that they could foster. While it is important for social movements to retain their core values and priorities, as separatists would argue, it is evident that intersectional solidarity does not necessarily dilute the priorities and impact of social movements. Reflecting on a number of social movements that target improving the wellbeing of individuals, we show that intersectional solidarity in social movement improves the reach and impact on wellbeing.

In the next section, we turn to the debate on wellbeing and welfare, warning against individualizing tendencies of wellbeing and standardizing tendencies of welfare approaches in relation to social movements.

SOCIAL MOVEMENTS AS RESISTANCE TO INDIVIDUALIZATION OF WELLBEING: FROM WELFARE TO WELLBEING

Social movements emerge when the social contract is not sufficient to deliver the desired welfare outcomes for groups of individuals. Social movements negotiate both wellbeing of individuals and welfare for states. At this juncture, we need to explore the distinctions between welfare and wellbeing. Welfare is often used as a way of framing collective wellbeing of individuals, often at the level of nation states. Welfare states cover aspects of health, education, transportation and unemployment, and provide safety nets for individuals against discrimination, unemployment, poor health and educational outcomes. Some scholars explain that there has been both a scholarly and a policy turn from a social and solidaristic notion of welfare to a psychological and individualized notion of wellbeing in the last four decades (Jonsen et al., 2013). This semantic turn in exploring individual motivation, satisfaction and happiness at work instead of social standards of such qualities has meant that the responsibility for effective management of wellbeing has shifted from social and collective responsibility to an individual responsibility, where each individual's wellbeing is considered an outcome of their life project (Özbilgin and Slutskaya, 2017), whereas, in the previous discourse of welfare, the responsibility for individual wellbeing was shared among industrial relations actors. Often, the micro and macro perspectives on wellbeing represent two different traditions of approaching wellbeing with limited cross-fertilization of ideas. In order to bridge this gap in the literature, we examine an extra-organizational force, i.e. social movements, and explore its individual, organizational and structural consequences for wellbeing, offering to transcend levels by building a bridge of understanding about how constructs such as wellbeing and welfare at each level are intricately connected to the others.

In fact, the distinction between this wellbeing and welfare is inherent in social movements. The #occupy movement, for example, has risen as an objection to individuals losing their wellbeing as a result of deepening inequalities in the neoliberal context which puts profits before people. The #occupy movement is a social movement that had a tremendous impact with thousands of people in Wall Street, New York City, going out on the streets to protest the financialization of social and political life with dire consequences for humanity (Gibson, 2013). After this movement, #occupy became an umbrella term for all movements in major cities (i.e. #indignados in Spain, #nuitdebout in France, #occupycentral in Hong Kong, #occupylondon in England), based on the strategy of 'occupying' public spaces by camping out (Pérez Navarro, 2018) in order to re-humanize public spaces.

With #occupy, there was a tension between natural and legal rights of ownership, between public good and private property rights. The movement sought to challenge the status quo and demanded a different future (Pickerill and Krinsky, 2012). Economic inequalities, unequal citizenship rights, ecological concerns, militarism and draconian politics were targeted in these movements with the participation of different social groups (Butler, 2015). With #occupy, ritualizing and institutionalizing of protest became visible, as different groups brought their own agendas of change and this added to the strength of the movement to stand in solidarity.

It would be misleading to think that the inequalities that set #occupy in motion could be viewed only at one level of analysis. Neoliberalism and the decline of the social consequently led to the emergence of new frames to regulate wellbeing at work, pushing the responsibility away from the welfare state and the employers to the individual workers. Naturally, wellbeing is indexed on the individual level of analysis. Responsibilization,

based on individuals taking responsibility for their choices within the economic system in which they are partners with their free will (Gray, 2009), has become a significant marker of the neoliberal ideology.

Some social movements have a collective interest rather than the individual wellbeing of their members at heart. For example, the #fairtrade movement, which can be traced back to the development of a co-operative movement in the 19th century and gained its contemporary form and started spreading in the 1960s and 1970s (Moore, 2004), is based on an ideology of encouraging community development in some of the most deprived areas of the world (Doherty et al., 2013). It is a trading partnership that aims at the sustainable development and improvement of the living conditions and protection of marginalized workers and producers, especially in the Global South (Reed, 2009). It has brought forward the possibility of disadvantaged producers reaching wider markets without exploitation. It also seeks to stop the exploitation of fragile workers (e.g. children, women), in the supply chain. The #fairtrade movement has contributed to the establishment of organizational norms around gender equity (Lyon et al., 2010), focused attention on social and economic effects created by consumption preferences and voiced appeals to consumers to have a responsible attitude (Castaldo et al., 2009). It has emphasized the importance of noting the social rights in commercial relationships and, thus, fostering human rights and social welfare and individual wellbeing.

Social movements today offer us possibilities to reconnect wellbeing with a social and economic contract among key actors, i.e. workers, employers and the welfare system of the state. One of the criticisms that could be leveled at social welfare discourses has been their lack of refinement in capturing social diversity and failing to meet intersectional needs of individuals, offering broadbrush safety nets. In this context, wellbeing discourse has emerged to refocus attention on individual needs for balance, thriving beyond what social safety nets could provide as basic possibilities of life. Yet wellbeing discourses are also critiqued for their lack of attention to social welfare and wider community issues beyond the wellbeing of an often privileged group of insiders in societies and organizations. In this context, social movements play a pivotal role in negotiating not only better welfare systems but also better wellbeing for their members and society at large.

PROMOTING WELLBEING VIA SOCIAL MOVEMENTS: WELLBEING AS AN INDIVIDUAL AND AN INSTITUTIONAL CONSTRUCT

In this paper we propose two significant shifts in thinking about wellbeing and intersectionality in the context of social movements. First, wellbeing could be framed as an institutional responsibility. Organizations rather than individuals alone could be responsibilized in order to promote wellbeing of individuals. For example, during the Covid-19 epidemic there has been widespread support for the National Health Service staff and workers through the #SaveNHS campaign and movement, fought against UK government plans to privatize and individualize the healthcare system. The #SaveNHS movement sought to fight against Americanization of the healthcare system in the UK, which could render healthcare a predominantly individual burden, instead of a shared responsibility. At the same time, the movement was raising awareness of declining terms and conditions of work for NHS staff and their vulnerability in the course of the epidemic.

Second, the notion of intersectionality could be framed as an institutional rather than an individual construct. We demonstrated that this is happening partly in the case of social movements which draw on support from other social movements. The #SaveNHS movement highlighted, for example, issues

with ethnic and racial disadvantage in the NHS as black and minority-ethnic staff and communities were more adversely affected by the pandemic. Similarly, transsexuals, HIV patients, older people and people with multiple illnesses and disabilities were also highlighted as vulnerable communities. Another international example is from Israel: after a transgender youth was stabbed to death in the northern city of Israel, Tamra, where the Arabs mostly live, feminist and LGBTI+ groups gathered both to defend queer rights in Israel and Palestine and to protest invasion (Ziv, 2019). Such intersectional solidarity brings greater power behind a social movement and may potentially have a stronger impact on the common agendas such as welfare of women or LGBTI+ in this particular case.

The fact that different social movements offer support to each other, or that different groups unite and act around a common wellbeing issue, can be decisive in the recovery of human rights and civil liberties. But the gains from social movements need to be translated into social and legal regulation for societies and institutions to comply. The #tiananmensquare protests and subsequent movement provided such changes in the legal and social regulation of life in China. #tiananmensquare is a social movement that broke out with the impact of the economic bottleneck and the oppressive policies of the government in China in the 1980s. It represents the reactions of the workers, students, public officers and intellectuals expressing the expectations of cross-class dissident collation in Tiananmen Square in April 1989 (Mason and Clements, 2002). The #tiananmensquare movement was considered a milestone for communist China (Zhao, 2004). China was forced to transform its closed economy into commercial relations via bilateral agreements and constructed 'market-economy socialism', which is its own brand (Barron, 2019). The legal and economic reforms, infrastructure and educational necessities which were required by the market economy transformed to have significant importance (Earle, 1991). Even though it has created the expectation of an expanding middle class, it can be observed today that this was not yet the case. Therefore, social movements may start reforms in the direction of better wellbeing but the journey involves multiple stakeholders such as the employers, the state and other significant institutions, which collectively shape the wellbeing and welfare arrangements in the aftermath of a social movement.

Legal protection of rights acquired through social movements helps organizations to regulate their wellbeing and welfare systems without relying on voluntarism alone. Coercive social and legal measures could present strong encouragement for organizations to improve their wellbeing provision at work for all (Özbilgin, 2018). Moreover, social movements give visibility to demands for better regulation of social, economic and political regimes for wellbeing. In this respect, #marriageequality is a striking example, representing how a social movement has led to sweeping changes in legal and social regulation and recognition of same-sex marriages. Same-sex marriage is a human rights demand that emerged in the United States in the 1990s. The central demand of the #marriageequality or #mariagepourtous (in French) was that the LGBTI+ partnerships and relationships should have the same status as legal marriages. The #marriageequality movement that supported equality of marriage rights for LGBTI+ individuals has galvanized into an international movement and achieved marriage equality in law and social norms across many countries, under adverse conditions and severe resistance from religious and conservative segments of society. With the United States legally accepting same-sex marriage in the year of 2015, it has become a global movement represented by the hashtag #marriageequality, which has diversified later into a broad social change agenda, emphasizing legitimating and cultural acceptance of LGBTI+ relationships through the #lovewins hashtag.

Social movements not only engage with individual aspects of wellbeing but also focus on negotiations with nation states and other actors for development of welfare regimes. In the next section we study the case of the #blacklivesmatter movement and how it seeks to improve wellbeing through intersectional and institutional perspectives.

THE BLM (#BLACKLIVESMATTER) MOVEMENT AND WELLBEING: INTERSECTIONS AND INSTITUTIONAL PERSPECTIVES

The #blacklivesmatter movement is a social movement that focuses on racism against African Americans and minority ethnic groups. In 2012, when an African American teenager, Trayvon Martin, was killed by the police, this murder was protested with the #blacklivesmatter hashtag; and this hashtag has turned into an umbrella term that brings together different groups that fight against racism, xenophobia and discrimination. It has been used to highlight incidents and systemic and institutional mechanisms of racism against African Americans. Along with African Americans, #blacklivesmatter has also lifted the veil of invisibility on 'others' who are subjected to violence and discrimination by the state, the institutions of employment, healthcare, the police and prison services. A wide range of social movements including the feminist, LGBTI+ and trade union movements, among others, have declared their support for #blacklivesmatter. In this respect, #blacklivesmatter has gained an intersectional character in terms of its support base. In 2020, #blacklivesmatter has turned to be a movement re-energized by the masses who are on the street with the publication of images about the killing of an African American man, George Floyd, by the police in Minneapolis, Minnesota. The public outrage at this racist murder has reignited the

#blacklivesmatter movement in the United States and also internationally.

The Covid-19 pandemic also has an interesting relationship with the re-emergence of the #blacklivesmatter movement. Measures that are taken to combat the Covid-19 pandemic in the United States, such as stay-at-home orders, interruption in non-essential businesses and social isolation, has increased unemployment to an unprecedented level in the history of the country, and many people have fallen into financial difficulties. Black African and minority ethnic communities in the United States were severely and more adversely affected than white Americans by these regulatory measures. The fact that the country lacks social welfare mechanisms and that the accessibility of health services is determined by the financial capacities of individuals has opened the gap between social classes and fueled ethnic divisions. Workers of color are typically employed in front-line work and chronically locked in lowly paid work. In their working lives, they experience institutionalized racial disparities in wages and benefits, and employment discrimination. The pandemic has deepened the rift in working rights for the disadvantaged such as African Americans, Hispanics, Latina and other minorities. The OECD (2020) reports that low-paid workers and young people are more exposed to unemployment in the pandemic process. As seen in healthcare statistics, one-third of those hospitalized because of Covid-19 are African Americans, despite representing only 18% of the population (Millett et al., 2020). Due to poor living conditions and difficulties in accessing the health system compared to whites, for example, African Americans are 1.5 times more likely to be without health insurance (Artiga et al., 2020), and they have more chronic diseases such as diabetes, hypertension and obesity. This made African Americans more vulnerable and more susceptible to death (Poteat et al., 2020) in the Covid-19 pandemic. Thus, the #blacklivesmatter movement is considerably tied to economic, social and political welfare and individual wellbeing agendas in the United States and internationally.

With the effects of Covid-19, #blacklivesmatter has made racial divisions more obvious and turned into an era for racial justice as well as economic inclusiveness (Foroohar, 2020). With its polyphonic nature, which receives support from a wide range of social movements, it has expanded its scope by creating its own sub-slogans and resonating in different geographies. The intersectionality of solidarity that the movement received, as well as the intersectional character of its demands (Bowleg, 2012), has been strengthened with international-level support. Voices are rising with the slogans #decoloniseUK and #decoloniseacademia in the UK against exploitation and discrimination and the symbols that represent them appear to turn into demands for change. In response, universities have declared that they will make their curricula more diverse, inclusive and international (Batty, 2020). Objections against racism have increased with #blmberlin in Berlin and all over the country. The Chancellor of Germany, Angela Merkel, has expressed explicitly that racism still exists and needs to be fought in Germany as in all societies. Likewise, the Prime Minister of the Netherlands, Mark Rutte, has made statements that his country will promote and protect the rights of minorities (Van Brunnersum, 2020). Speaking of the existence of 'systematic discrimination' in the Netherlands underlines the symbolic acknowledgment that the #blacklivesmatter movement is a worldwide issue, which concerns modern-day racism internationally.

Institutional racism in the context of public sector work organizations such as the police force, the national health service and others in the UK is not a new debate. It was coined by the Stephen Lawrence Inquiry Report (Macpherson, 1999), which revealed racism in the police and other public sector organizations, and which led to reforms and public duty for these institutions to reform their racialized structures (Kamasak et al., 2019b).

The Stephen Lawrence Inquiry and responses to it by subsequent governments have generated significant legal changes, bringing about race duty and monitoring of transformation of public sector organizations in terms of their race relations and equality efforts. The most important aspect of these changes was the recognition that racism is not an interpersonal issue alone, but is institutional, and that institutions with their procedures, policies and practices may generate racist outcomes. This recognition has inculcated an understanding that training alone will not address racism in the UK. There should be organizational change and development activities to challenge racist institutional practices. However, the impetus for race equality reforms to combat institutional racism has lost some impetus over time. More recently, the hostile environment policy (HEP) of the Conservative government and the resultant Windrush generation scandal have revealed that the UK has not been very effective in rooting out racism (Vassilopoulou et al., 2019). As the race agenda was ignored by consecutive governments the #blacklivesmatter movement has been well received in the UK, as it touched an open sore in race relations in the country and in organizations which suffered from institutional racism. In fact, #blacklivesmatter has received its second largest support in the UK, showing how entrenched, relevant and silent the race equality issues still are in the country. There are multifaceted and multilevel efforts to consider race equality once again as the Covid-19 crisis has also highlighted the disparate impacts on black and minority communities in the country, a pattern similar to that in the United States.

The first comprehensive social movement that occurred in the 21st century was the #arabspring, which started with a young street vendor from Tehran setting himself ablaze as a reaction to the police brutality that he had been exposed to, at the end of 2010, and is characterized as a fundamental challenge to the postcolonial political order of the Arab world (Ismael and Ismael, 2013).

It has set populations in motion in Egypt, Saudi Arabia, Iran, Iraq, Kuwait, Bahrain, Yemen, Lebanon, Syria, Tunisia, Morocco and Jordan. The demands of the #arabspring movement, which has been fueled by deep inequalities, were to secure humane living conditions, for people to be their authentic selves without fear of oppression and to have freedom for their thoughts and beliefs (Ansani and Daniele, 2012; Malik and Awadallah, 2013). Authoritarianism and masculine militarism, which created privilege for the social hierarchy and positioned women as second-class citizens, were also in the scope of this movement (Al-Ali, 2012; Mhajne and Whetstone, 2018). Together with the coalition of political elites which were empowered by the movement and non-governmental organizations (NGOs) taking active part in the movement, legal and political reforms which provided achievements concerning women's rights and some fragile forms of civil liberties have been enacted (Moghadam, 2018). Like the #blacklivesmatter movement, the #arabspring movement was intersectional and multifaceted in its character, bridging the demands of state welfare and individual wellbeing.

Wellbeing, indexed to individuals' own efforts, also nourishes interest-based scrutiny of systems and structures. With social movements, certain agenda items can also turn into sites of conflict or solidarity. As a matter of fact, the oppositional slogans produced against #blacklivesmatter are also manifold. For example, the #whitelivesmatter and #bluelivesmatters hashtags, which are strong displays of white fragility (DiAngelo, 2018), support the police and public powers, and #alllivesmatter as a generic call denies systematic oppression of African Americans and tacitly condones institutional racism. Despite some opposition as outlined here, the #blacklivesmatter movement has received widespread support from an international and intersectional base.

While the movement develops solidarity and resistance, at the macro level, there are some policy and legal changes. For example, Donald Trump signed an executive order to limit police powers in prosecutions in the United States. Declarations from heads of nation states have in general been supportive of the causes that the movement has supported. Groutsis et al. (2019) state that human rights violations and deterioration of economic, social and political institutions at the level of nation states could undermine national efforts to compete for and attract talent, causing migration of talented individuals to other countries in search of better expression of their civil liberties. Social movements such as #blacklivesmatter could highlight and warn nation states about such violations of human rights. Yet, in order for nation states to heed the call for progress offered by social movements, there is need for competent political leadership, which could partner with social movements for social change.

At the meso level, institutions and organizations are alleging their support for the #blacklivesmatter movement. For example, the H&M brand (2020), which has been criticized for humiliating African Americans with its visuals and slogans in past advertising campaigns, has announced that it has provided financial aid to NGOs operating to protect the education, health and legal rights of African Americans in support of the movement. It also stated that it would take concrete steps against racism. Two global firms, Adidas and Nike, which dominate the clothing industry, also condemned the violence against African Americans and declared that they would transform the policies in their companies to support minorities. Beyond the rhetoric, some commentators within the #blacklivesmatter movement scrutinize organizations which supposedly support the movement asking them about the composition of their boards of directors (Ritson, 2020), their methods of recruitment of employees and the prevention of discrimination based on race and gender in pay (Lipman, 2020). We can expect organizational responses to scrutiny

and public questioning by the #blacklivesmatter movement in due course.

At the micro individual level, the #blacklivesmatter movement has raised awareness about contemporary and entrenched forms of racism. The movement has brought together a global audience and drawn attention to the relevance of the fight against racism internationally and across intersections of social movements. Responsibilization of the individual in the fight against racism has also witnessed emergence of divergent local interventions that are inspired by the message of the #blacklivesmatter movement.

The #blacklivesmatter movement presents an interesting example of a social movement which has far-reaching effects across macro-, meso- and micro-level actors, inculcating both short-term responses and long-term demands for change. We are yet to see the long-term changes in the world of work, as the avalanche of demands for racial equality soar with the intersectional solidarity that other progressive social movements show to the #blacklivesmatter movement.

CONCLUSION

In this chapter, we examined how social movements support wellbeing at work and how framing of the concepts of wellbeing and intersectionality not only from micro individual but also from meso institutional and macro transnational perspectives could help to responsibilize individuals, organizations and macro-level actors such as employers (Amin, 2020), trade unions (Uniglobalunion.org, 2020) and the welfare states for better wellbeing for all. Social movements are significant actors in voicing wellbeing concerns and pursuing agendas for improving wellbeing for individuals in institutional settings. In fact, if we examine all gains in human rights and civil liberties, equality, diversity, inclusion and overall wellbeing at work, social movements have given the impetus for those legal and social gains and progress, rather than voluntary organizational measures. Although social movements may inform institutional changes at meso level (Van Wijk et al., 2013), organizational discourses in the field of management and organization studies nevertheless continue to ignore the role of social actors such as social movements and interest groups in understanding the impetus for promoting wellbeing for all, across all diversity categories in fair and equal measure. In this chapter we addressed this problematic treatment of wellbeing by exploring contemporary social movements, focusing on #blacklivesmatter as a central case study and other movements to illustrate our arguments from an intersectional perspective.

In particular, we focus on the problematic of whose responsibility should wellbeing be. With the neoliberal turn, the responsibility for caring for the wellbeing of workers has shifted from macro-level actors such as trade unions, international social movements and welfare states towards responsibilization of the individual in terms of their self care at work, focusing on their identity differences at the individual level. We caution against this turn, and explain how social movements are significant partners in improving wellbeing for all, if organizations listen to their intersectional and diverse demands and build effective ties with social movements. Individualization of wellbeing, without social movements, could limit the scope and effectiveness of wellbeing interventions and improvements at work.

Drawing on examples from a wide range of social movements, we outlined in this chapter how social movements are pivotal for wellbeing at work and in society. In particular we noted that wellbeing concerns often propel the emergence of social movements and inform their agendas, and often wellbeing features as an outcome of the efforts of progressive social movements. Yet we also identified that, in order for reformative social movements to be

successful and effective, they need to gain intersectional solidarity from other progressive social movements, overcome hostilities among their ranks and build alliances with other progressive and reformative social and institutional partners. We also identified that short-term gains are not particularly significant achievements of social movements, and instead long-term institutional changes should be targeted, even when these are harder to achieve. Yet for sustainable improvements to wellbeing of all individuals, long-term and institutional visions are necessary for change.

In particular, global organizations today have excessive power to shape wellbeing for their workers and communities in which they operate. Yet their practices continue to deliver imbalanced outcomes, often moving resources from some regions such as developing countries where labor laws are weak and inequalities are unattended. While they bank their businesses on such morally questionable exploitative contexts, they may provide higher standards of wellbeing in other regions such as developed countries with sophisticated legal protections for certain aspects of equality (Özbilgin, 2019). For example, a global organization may offer gender equality in the boardroom in one country, which serves the needs of white upper-class women well, and fail to consider issues of race equality in the same boardroom context (Özbilgin et al., 2016). In the absence of global regulatory mechanisms that can control how global organizations operate, social movements emerge as significant actors in regulating global organizations in terms of how they move resources and manipulate rules across their global value chains and distribute wellbeing in uneven ways. Therefore, we conclude that social movements emerge as significant future players that can negotiate normative and ethical principles by which wellbeing should be redistributed in an increasingly changing world order in which the divide between the haves and the have-nots continues to widen.

REFERENCES

Aberle D (1966) *The Peyote Religion Among the Navajo.* Aldine, Chicago, IL.

Acar Y and Uluğ ÖM (2016) Examining prejudice reduction through solidarity and togetherness experiences among Gezi Park activists in Turkey. *Journal of Social and Political Psychology*, 4(1), 166–179.

Acker J (1989) *Doing Comparable Worth: Gender, Class and Pay Equity.* Temple University Press, Philadelphia, PA.

Acker J (2006a) *Class Questions: Feminist Answers.* Rowman & Littlefield, Lanham, MD.

Acker J (2006b) Inequality regimes: Gender, class and race in organizations. *Gender & Society*, 20(4), 441–464.

Acker J (2012) Gendered organizations and intersectionality: Problems and possibilities. *Equality, Diversity and Inclusion: An International Journal*, 31(3), 214–224.

Al-Ali N (2012) Gendering the Arab spring. *Middle East Journal of Culture and Communication*, 5(1), 26–31.

Alcock P and Glennerster H (Eds.) (2001) *Welfare and Wellbeing: Richard Titmuss's Contribution to Social Policy.* Policy Press, Chicago, IL.

Aldridge JM, Fraser BJ, Fozdar F, Ala'i K, Earnest J and Afari E (2016) Students' perceptions of school climate as determinants of wellbeing, resilience and identity. *Improving Schools*, 19(1), 5–26.

Amin S (2020) *Black Lives Matter*, Available at: https://www.farrer.co.uk/news-and-insights/blogs/black-lives-matter/# (accessed 24 June 2020).

Ansani A and Daniele V (2012) About a revolution: The economic motivations of the Arab Spring. *International Journal of Development and Conflict*, 2(3), 1250013.

Arat Y (2013) Violence, resistance, and Gezi Park. *International Journal of Middle East Studies*, 45(4), 807–809.

Artiga S, Orgera K and Damico A (2020) *Changes in health coverage by race and ethnicity since the ACA, 2010–2018.* Available at: https://www.kff.org/racial-equity-and-health-policy/issue-brief/changes-in-health-coverage-by-race-and-ethnicity-since-the-aca-2010-2018/ (accessed 14 June 2020).

Ashwin S and Kabeer N (2018) *Taking #MeToo into global supply chains.* Available at: https://blogs.lse.ac.uk/businessreview/2018/02/05/taking-metoo-into-global-supply-chains/ (accessed 23 June 2020).

Bağlama SH (2018) *The Resurrection of the Spectre: A Marxist Analysis of Race, Class and Alienation in the Post-war British Novel.* Peter Lang, Berlin.

Barron L (2019) *How the Tiananmen Square massacre changed China forever.* Available at: https://time.com/5600363/china-tiananmen-30-years-later/ (accessed 14 June 2020).

Batty D (2020) *Only a fifth of UK universities say they are 'decolonising' curriculum.* Available at: https://www.theguardian.com/us-news/2020/jun/11/only-fifth-of-uk-universities-have-said-they-will-decolonise-curriculum (accessed 18 June 2020).

BBC Türkçe (2018) *Türkiye'de kadınlar 'Sen de anlat' (#MeToo) diyebiliyor mu?* Available at: https://www.bbc.com/turkce/haberler-turkiye-42666440 (accessed 28 June 2020).

Benford RD (1997) An insider's critique of the social movement framing perspective. *Sociological Inquiry*, 67(4), 409–430.

Bowleg L (2012) The problem with the phrase women and minorities: Intersectionality – an important theoretical framework for public health. *American Journal of Public Health*, 102(7), 1267–1273.

Boyle K and Rathnayake C (2019) #HimToo and the networking of misogyny in the age of# MeToo. *Feminist Media Studies*, 1–19, DOI: 10.1080/14680777.2019.1661868

Brown M (2018) *Women avoid transgender debate for fear of reaction, says Jo Brand.* Available at: https://www.theguardian.com/world/2018/oct/10/women-avoid-transgender-debate-fear-reaction-jo-brand-germaine-greer-feminism (accessed 23 June 2020).

Butler J (2015) *Notes toward a Performative Theory of Assembly.* Harvard University Press., Cambridge, MA.

Carlsen A, Salam M, Miller CC, Lu D, Ngu A, Patel JK and Wichter Z (2018) *#MeToo brought down 201 powerful men.* Available at: https://www.nytimes.com/interactive/2018/10/23/us/metoo-replacements.html?mtrref=www.google.comandgwh=CFE95C419013CBDD0BB17D96A21E8F5E

andgwt=payandassetType=PAYWALL (accessed 23 June 2020).

Cartwright, S and Cooper CL (Eds.). (2009). *The Oxford handbook of organizational wellbeing*. Oxford University Press, New York, NY.

Cartwright S and Cooper CL (2011) The role of organizations in promoting health and wellbeing. In: Cartwright S and Cooper CL (eds) *Innovations in stress and health* (pp. 153–172). Palgrave Macmillan, London.

Castaldo S, Perrini F, Misani N and Tencati A (2009) The missing link between corporate social responsibility and consumer trust: The case of fair trade products. *Journal of Business Ethics*, *84*(1), 1–15.

Castells M (2015) *Networks of Outrage and Hope: Social Movements in the Internet Age*. John Wiley and Sons, Cambridge, UK.

Christiansen J (2009) Four stages of social movements. *EBSCO Research Starters*, 14–45.

Constance R, Annette G and Hilary W (2018) Gender and environmental education in the time of #MeToo. *The Journal of Environmental Education*, *49*(4), 273–275.

Cooper CL and Leiter MP (Eds.) (2017) *The Routledge Companion to Wellbeing at Work*. Taylor and Francis, New York, NY.

Crenshaw K (1990) Mapping the margins: Intersectionality, identity politics, and violence against women of color. *Stanford Law Review*, *43*, 1241–1299.

Curry MK (2018) Sexual assault leave in the# metoo era: Companies should know an employee's legal right to time off. *Employment Relations Today*, *44*(4), 27–31.

Dearden L (2019) *Hate crimes rise 10 per cent amid surge in anti-gay and transgender attacks*. Available at: https://www.independent.co.uk/news/uk/crime/hate-crimes-england-wales-lgbt-rise-anti-gay-transgender-attacks-a9156291.html (accessed 23 June 2020).

DiAngelo R (2018) *White Fragility: Why It's So Hard for White People to Talk about Racism*. Beacon Press, Boston, MA.

Diani M (1992) The concept of social movement. *The Sociological Review*, *40*(1), 1–25.

Diener E, Scollon CN and Lucas RE (2003) The evolving concept of subjective well-being: the multifaceted nature of happiness. *Advances in Cell Aging & Gerontology*, 15, 187–219.

Dodge R, Daly A, Huyton J and Sanders L (2012) The challenge of defining wellbeing. *International Journal of Wellbeing*, *2*(3), 222–235. doi:10.5502/ijw.v2i3.4

Doherty B, Davies IA and Tranchell S (2013) Where now for fair trade? *Business History*, *55*(2), 161–189.

Drucker P (2015) *Warped: Gay Normality and Queer Anti-Capitalism*. Brill, Leiden, Netherlands.

Earle BH (1991) China after Tiananmen Square: An assessment of its business environment. *Case Western Reserve Journal of International Law*, *23*, 421.

Ennis D (2019) *J.K. Rowling comes out as a TERF.* Available at: https://www.forbes.com/sites/dawnstaceyennis/2019/12/19/jk-rowling-comes-out-as-a-terf/#39ba31dc5d70 (accessed 23 June 2020).

Fischer M (2017) Trans responses to Adichie: Challenging cis privilege in popular feminism. *Feminist Media Studies*, *17*(5), 896–899.

Foroohar R (2020) *Black Lives Matters is about race and class*. Available at: https://www.ft.com/content/28dc48f8-b36b-4848-8e73-774999a8e502 (accessed 17 June 2020).

Forstenlechner I, Lettice F and Özbilgin MF (2012) Questioning quotas: Applying a relational framework for diversity management practices in the United Arab Emirates. *Human Resource Management Journal*, *22*(3), 299–315.

Frank RH and Cook PJ (2010) *The Winner-Take-All Society: Why the Few at the Top Get So Much More than the Rest of Us*. Random House, New York, NY

Garg S (2020) Hospitalization rates and characteristics of patients hospitalized with laboratory-confirmed coronavirus disease 2019 – COVID-NET, 14 States, March 1–30, 2020. *MMWR. Morbidity and Mortality Weekly Report*, 69, 458–464.

Gibson MR (2013) The anarchism of the Occupy movement. *Australian Journal of Political Science*, *48*(3), 335–348.

Gibson R (2018) *Same-Sex Marriage and Social Media: How Online Networks Accelerated the Marriage Equality Movement*. Routledge, London, UK.

Gill R and Orgad S (2018) The shifting terrain of sex and power: From the 'sexualization of culture' to #MeToo. *Sexualities, 21*(8), 1313–1324.

Gray GC (2009) The responsibilization strategy of health and safety: Neo-liberalism and the reconfiguration of individual responsibility for risk. *The British Journal of Criminology, 49*(3), 326–342.

Groutsis D, Vassilopoulou J, Kyriakidou O and Özbilgin MF (2019) The 'new' migration for work phenomenon: The pursuit of emancipation and recognition in the context of work. *Work, Employment and Society,* DOI: https://doi.org/10.1177/0950017019872651

Guest D and Conway N (2004) *Employee Wellbeing and the Psychological Contract: A Research Report.* CIPD, London.

Healy G, Bradley H and Forson C (2011) Intersectional sensibilities in analysing inequality regimes in public sector organizations. *Gender, Work & Organization, 18*(5), 467–487.

Hemmings C (2018) Resisting popular feminisms: Gender, sexuality and the lure of the modern. *Gender, Place and Culture, 25*(7), 963–977.

Holmes IV O (2019) For diversity scholars who have considered activism when scholarship isn't enough!. *Equality, Diversity and Inclusion: An International Journal, 38*(6), 668–675.

H&M (2020) *A message from Helena Helmersson.* Available at: https://www2.hm.com/en_us/home/selected/information.html (accessed 20 June 2020).

Ismael JS and Ismael ST (2013) The Arab Spring and the uncivil state. *Arab Studies Quarterly, 35*(3), 229–240.

Jonsen K, Tatli A, Özbilgin MF and Bell MP (2013) The tragedy of the uncommons: Reframing workforce diversity. *Human Relations, 66*(2), 271–294.

Kakabadse NK, Figueira C, Nicolopoulou K, Hong Yang J, Kakabadse AP and Özbilgin MF (2015) Gender diversity and board performance: Women's experiences and perspectives. *Human Resource Management, 54*(2), 265–281.

Kamasak R, Özbilgin M, Baykut S and Yavuz M (2019a) Moving from intersectional hostility to intersectional solidarity. *Journal of Organizational Change Management, 33*(3), 456–476.

Kamasak R, Özbilgin MF, Yavuz M and Akalin C (2019b) Race discrimination at work in the United Kingdom. In: Vassilopoulou J, Brabet J and Showunmi V (eds) *Race Discrimination and Management of Ethnic Diversity and Migration at Work.* Emerald Publishing Limited, Bingley, UK.

Leopold J, Lambert JR, Ogunyomi IO and Bell MP (2019) The hashtag heard round the world: How #MeToo did what laws did not. *Equality, Diversity and Inclusion: An International Journal, DOI: https://doi.org/10.1108/EDI-04-2019-0129*

Lipman J. (2020) *Op-ed: How the Black Lives Matter movement can avoid #MeToo's missteps to create lasting change.* Available at: https://www.cnbc.com/2020/06/11/how-black-lives-matter-movement-can-avoid-metoos-missteps.html (accessed 21 June 2020).

Lyon S, Bezaury JA and Mutersbaugh T (2010) Gender equity in fairtrade–organic coffee producer organizations: Cases from Mesoamerica. *Geoforum, 41*(1), 93–103.

Macpherson SW (1999) *The Stephen Lawrence Inquiry – Report of an Inquiry by Sir William Macpherson of Cluny. Cm 4262-I.* London: HMSO.

Malik A and Awadallah B (2013) The economics of the Arab Spring. *World Development, 45,* 296–313.

Mason TD and Clements J (2002) Tiananmen Square thirteen years after: The prospects for civil unrest in China. *Asian Affairs: An American Review, 29*(3), 159–188.

Mert A (2019) The trees in Gezi Park: Environmental policy as the focus of democratic protests. *Journal of Environmental Policy and Planning, 21*(5), 593–607.

Mhajne A and Whetstone C (2018) The use of political motherhood in Egypt's Arab Spring uprising and aftermath. *International Feminist Journal of Politics, 20*(1), 54–68.

Michelon G, Rodrigue M and Trevisan E (2020) The marketization of a social movement: Activists, shareholders and CSR disclosure. *Accounting, Organizations and Society, 80,* 101074.

Millett GA, Jones AT, Benkeser D, Baral S, Mercer L, Beyrer C, et al. (2020). Assessing differential impacts of COVID-19 on Black communities. *Annals of Epidemiology, 47,* 37–40.

Mitra S (2018) *Disability, Health and Human Development*. Palgrave Macmillan, London.

Moghadam VM (2018) Explaining divergent outcomes of the Arab Spring: The significance of gender and women's mobilizations. *Politics, Groups, and Identities*, 6(4), 666–681.

Moor L and Kanji S (2019) Money and relationships online: Communication and norm formation in women's discussions of couple resource allocation. *The British Journal of Sociology*, 70(3), 948–968.

Moore G (2004) The fair trade movement: Parameters, issues and future research. *Journal of Business Ethics*, 53(1–2), 73–86.

Narasimhan M, Allotey P and Hardon A (2019) Self care interventions to advance health and wellbeing: A conceptual framework to inform normative guidance. *BMJ*, DOI: http://dx.doi.org/10.1136/bmj.l668

Nentwich JC, Özbilgin MF and Tatli A (2015) Change agency as performance and embeddedness: Exploring the possibilities and limits of Butler and Bourdieu. *Culture and Organization*, 21(3), 235–250.

Nkomo SM and Rodriguez JK (2019) Joan Acker's influence on management and organization studies: Review, analysis and directions for the future. *Gender, Work & Organization*, 26(12), 1730–1748.

OECD (2020) *The world economy on a tightrope*. Available at: http://www.oecd.org/economic-outlook/june-2020/ (accessed 15 June 2020).

Özbilgin M (2018) *What the racial equality movement can learn from the global fight for women's rights*. Available at: https://theconversation.com/what-the-racial-equality-movement-can-learn-from-the-global-fight-for-womens-rights-105616 (accessed 12 June 2020).

Özbilgin M (2019) Managing Diversity and Inclusion in the Global Value Chain. *Strategies in Accounting and Management*, 1(2), 1–3.

Özbilgin M and Slutskaya N (2017) Consequences of neo-liberal politics on equality and diversity at work in Britain: Is resistance futile? In: Chanlat JF and Özbilgin M (eds) *Management and Diversity*. Emerald Publishing Limited, Bingley, UK.

Özbilgin M, Tatli A, Ipek G and Sameer M (2016) Four approaches to accounting for diversity in global organisations. *Critical Perspectives on Accounting*, 35, 88–99.

Pegu S (2019) MeToo in India: Building revolutions from solidarities. *Decision*, 46(2), 151–168.

Pérez Navarro P (2018) 'Where is my tribe?' Queer activism in the Occupy movements. *InterAlia: A Journal of Queer Studies*, 13(13), 90–101.

Pickerill J and Krinsky J (2012) Why does Occupy matter? *Social Movement Studies*, 11(3–4), 279–287.

Poteat T, Millett G, Nelson LE and Beyrer C (2020) Understanding COVID-19 risks and vulnerabilities among Black communities in America: The lethal force of syndemics. *Annals of Epidemiology*, 1–3.DOI: https://doi.org/10.1016/j.annepidem.2020.05.004

Rath T and Harter J (2010) *Wellbeing: The Five Essential Elements*. Gallup Press, New York, NY.

Reed D (2009) What do corporations have to do with fair trade? Positive and normative analysis from a value chain perspective. *Journal of Business Ethics*, 86(1), 3–26.

Ritson M (2020) *If 'Black Lives Matter' to brands, where are your black board members?* In: Marketing Week. Available at: https://www.marketingweek.com/mark-ritson-black-lives-matter-brands/ (accessed 20 June 2020).

Rosenbaum MS (2015) Transformative service research: Focus on well-being. *The Service Industries Journal*, 35(7–8), 363–367.

Rowe MP (1990) Barriers to equality: The power of subtle discrimination to maintain unequal opportunity. *Employee Responsibilities and Rights Journal*, 3(2), 153–163.

Samdanis M and Özbilgin M (2020) The duality of an atypical leader in diversity management: The legitimization and delegitimization of diversity beliefs in organizations. *International Journal of Management Reviews*, 22(2), 101–119.

Sayce S and Özbilgin MF (2014) Pension trusteeship and diversity in the UK: A new boardroom recipe for change or continuity? *Economic and Industrial Democracy*, 35(1), 49–69.

Shanafelt TD, West C, Zhao X, Novotny P, Kolars J, Habermann T and Sloan J (2005) Relationship between increased personal well-being and enhanced empathy among internal medicine residents. *Journal of General Internal Medicine*, *20*(7), 559–564.

Soytemel E (2013) The power of the powerless: Neighbourhood based self-help networks of the poor in Istanbul. *Women's Studies International Forum*, *41*, 76–87.

Stiglitz JE (2012) Macroeconomic fluctuations, inequality, and human development. *Journal of Human Development and Capabilities*, *13*(1), 31–58.

Taştan C (2013) The Gezi Park protests in Turkey: A qualitative field research. *Insight Turkey*, 15(3), 27–38.

Tilly C and Wood LJ (2020) *Social Movements, 1768–2008*. Routledge, New York, NY. Uniglobalunion.org (2020) Global trade union movement: Unified in support of Black Lives Matter. Available at: https://uniglobal-union.org/news/global-trade-union-movement-unified-support-black-lives-matter (accessed 24 June 2020).

Turkmenoglu M (2016) *Examining the responses and coping mechanisms of food leaders in the face of challenges: A case from Turkey*, PhD Thesis, Brunel University, UK.

Umberson D, Pudrovska T and Reczek C (2010) Parenthood, childlessness, and well-being: A life course perspective. *Journal of Marriage and Family*, *72*(3), 612–629.

Van Brunnersum MS (2020) *Dutch PM deems 'Black Pete' tradition racist.* Available at: https://www.dw.com/en/dutch-pm-deems-black-pete-tradition-racist/a-53700075 (accessed 18 June 2020).

Van Wijk J, Stam W, Elfring T, Zietsma C and Den Hond F (2013) Activists and incumbents structuring change: The interplay of agency, culture, and networks in field evolution. *Academy of Management Journal*, *56*(2), 358–386.

Vassilopoulou J, Brabet J and Showunmi V (Eds.) (2019) *Race Discrimination and Management of Ethnic Diversity and Migration at Work: European Countries' Perspectives*. Emerald Group Publishing, Bingley, UK.

Vassilopoulou J, Kyriakidou O, Da Rocha JP, Georgiadou A and Mor Barak M (2019) International perspectives on securing human and social rights and diversity gains at work in the aftermath of the global economic crisis and in times of austerity. *European Management Review*, *16*(4), 837–845.

Walter M (2010) Market forces and indigenous resistance paradigms. *Social Movement Studies*, *9*(2), 121–137.

Zhao D (2004) *The Power of Tiananmen: State–Society Relations and the 1989 Beijing Student Movement*. University of Chicago Press, Chicago, IL.

Ziv O (2019) *Queer Palestinian community holds 'historic' protest against LGBT violence* Available at: https://www.972mag.com/queer-palestinian-protest-lgbt-violence/ (accessed 15 June 2020).

10

Organizational Resilience: Complex, Multisystemic Processes during Periods of Stress

Michael Ungar

INTRODUCTION

There are multiple (and competing) ways to describe resilience, with scholars from different disciplines still largely siloed from one another. A recent network citation analysis by Xu and Kajikawa (2017), for example, identified 10 clusters of research that refer to resilience, among them business systems and engineering, telecommunication systems, psychology and social science and ecological and environmental science. There was, however, very little overlap in the patterns of citations. An emerging interest in multisystemic resilience is challenging this disciplinary pattern of research, showing instead that there are a set of principles common to biological, social, institutional, built and natural systems when experiencing adversity (Biggs et al., 2012; Ungar, 2018). Arguably, a transdisciplinary, multisystemic understanding of resilience provides a better means for modeling the complex processes that explain why organizations can endure challenges, whether

internal or external, continuing to function optimally and even grow through the experience. To explain these patterns of development under stress, one has to account for multiple systems and multiple scales of each system. With regard to organizations, that means understanding how the resilience of a workforce depends on the quality of their social relations in the workplace, leadership, the physical environment in which they work and external stressors in the community and wider economy, as well as the built and natural environment in which an organization conducts its affairs. A multisystemic conceptualization of resilience highlights the reciprocal interactions between each system.

Resilience is, therefore, not a trait of an individual or an organization, but is better described as the process of systems interacting in ways that support positive functioning and preferred outcomes. Though these processes vary, in general they can be grouped under two broad categories: those that help individuals or groups (e.g., an organization) *navigate* to the resources required for sustainable recovery, adaptation or transformation, and those that reflect an individual or group's ability to *negotiate* for the resources that are provided to match the needs of individuals and groups that need them (Ungar, 2011). In this sense, resilience is a dynamic model of complex relationships that shows both equifinality (many means to a single end) and multifinality (many means to many different ends, all of which are seen as successful). These processes can be found occurring at the level of individuals inside organizations, as well as at the level of the organizations themselves, their communities, and more broadly at the level of the surrounding communities, governments and natural environments. The more that one nested system achieves resilience, the more likely co-occurring systems will as well.

This, then, is the focus of this chapter, to explore a multisystemic understanding of resilience in the context of organizations, whether that is a government service or institution providing health care, a for-profit business, a community of individuals who interact face-to-face or online, or a social ecological system where humans and the natural environment are mutually dependent. Each organization (i.e., system) is bounded by a set of relationships, though, as the research shows, these boundaries are highly permeable, creating the opportunity both to experience external threats that challenge an organization's sustainability while providing access to the resources required for optimal functioning under stress (i.e., resilience). The chapter begins with a discussion of the seven principles common to systems that show resilience, applying each principle to organizations at the level of the people in the organization, the organization itself and the external environments that shape the organization's functioning. The chapter then applies these principles to a rural community (a complex set of interdependent organizations) that depends on oil and gas extraction and the problems that dependency is causing

individuals, families, businesses and governments when the price of oil remains low.

PRINCIPLES FOR ORGANIZATIONAL RESILIENCE

There have been many efforts to compile a list of principles that explain the functioning of systems that show resilience. For example, Biggs et al. (2012) identified a set of seven principles that govern the functioning of social ecological systems (those in which human social systems and the natural environment interact, such as the management of a natural resource like a fishery; recovery from a natural disaster; the preservation of a spiritually meaningful natural feature of the landscape; etc.). These policy-relevant principles to enhance resilience of ecosystem services include processes such as: maintaining diversity and redundancy; managing connectivity; managing feedbacks; fostering an understanding of social ecological systems as complex adaptive systems; encouraging learning and experimentation; broadening participation; and promoting polycentric governance systems. A very different approach to organizational resilience is reflected in the development of the Flourishing at Work Scale (FAWS), which assesses 10 factors that relate to emotional wellbeing and functioning on the job (Rothmann et al., 2019). These include positive affect, low negative affect, job satisfaction, autonomy, competence, relatedness, engagement, meaningful work, learning and social wellbeing.

Though concerned with very different systems, assessments of systemic wellbeing are typically composed of a shortlist of factors associated with coping under stress. What is less clear is how stressors like workload, economic conditions and family demands (e.g., an ill child) can change the amount of positive influence any single factor will have on outcomes. This notion of differential impact (Ungar, 2017) as it relates to resilience suggests the need for a list of guiding principles that explain resilience in ways that remain responsive to changing environments and the risks and advantages they bring organizations. A comprehensive list of principles which are an amalgamation of concepts from diverse disciplines, including biology, psychology, economics, sociology, management, computer science and ecology, has been recently suggested by Ungar (2018). Each of these resilience-related principles is discussed below with reference to organizational processes.

Principle #1. Resilience occurs in contexts of adversity. The study of resilience is distinguished by the presence of stressors. Positive psychology, for example, has focused on character traits and other aspects of optimal function that are generic across populations. The study of resilience, however, focuses on what happens when systems are under stress and the specific processes employed to sustain or grow systems in suboptimal conditions. In this sense, the study of resilience is the study of how resources are matched to stressors, in much the same way that Jonge and Dormann (2006) propose a matching hypothesis which moderates the impact of specific stressors like job demands or physical strain with resources tailored to those problems (e.g., flexible work hours; occupational health and safety rules). While all employees benefit from similar interventions by a responsible employer, it is the employees in organizations who are exposed to the most risk and adversity who benefit a disproportionate amount. There are, however, at least two problems with the matching hypothesis. First, the factors that predict successful coping with on-the-job stress are seldom as one-dimensional as the matching hypothesis suggests. In a complex system like an organization, strain in one area can also be influenced by indirect support from other parts of the organization. For example, Boyer and Bond (1999) compared the rates of burnout and employee dissatisfaction among case managers providing two different kinds of services in the community to patients discharged from hospital with severe mental illnesses. Employees who provided traditional case management (TCM) reported far higher rates of negative emotions than those who were part of work teams delivering assertive community treatment (ACT). TCM is structured in ways that gives individual workers responsibility for a large number of clients whom they then have to surround with networks of support. The work is isolating and frequently frustrating as patients tend to exhibit many problem behaviors and experience high rates of readmission to hospital. ACT, meanwhile, is organizationally very different. It is delivered by a multidisciplinary team that usually includes a nurse, a psychiatrist, two case managers and other allied health professionals like an occupational therapist. The ACT model emphasizes low client–staff ratios, flexibility in where services are delivered (in the patient's home, or at the manager's office), a team approach with shared caseloads, and plenty of flexibility for workers to decide how long they will offer services to their patients. In this case, the factors making staff more resilient to the stress of working with a difficult-to-engage population are more organizational (and multisystemic) than individual. These include support from team members, collective efficacy, and the ability to sustain long-term relationships with patients.

The second problem with the matching hypothesis is that, while the intensity or chronicity of a stressor may be quantifiable, stressors are experienced in qualitatively different ways depending on the meaning that individuals and organizations attach to their experience of the stress. For example, increasing workload demands may be experienced positively or negatively depending on whether they are the result of a business flourishing (and an employee feeling part of a team that is valued for its contribution) or the result of layoffs and resulting work redistribution. Both increases in workload are quantitatively the same, but only the first instance provides a meaning system which makes employees more resilient during a period of increased workload. The distinction between positive and negative experiences of stress requires that research on organizational resilience distinguishes between stressors that are harmful and those that are positive, what Selye (1975) referred to as 'eustress'.

All of this means that organizations and their constituent parts will be triggered by the adversity. At the level of individuals, these triggers produce protective strategies ranging from hyperarousal to hypoarousal, depending on genetic predispositions and experiences of past trauma which shape the body's stress response system (Ellis and Del Giudice, 2014). Metaphorically, organizations (as examples of complex systems) can also experience stress as positive or negative, spurring innovation through reorganization and expansion, or becoming overwhelmed and functioning poorly during a crisis. Clearly, the context in which the stressors occur and what they mean to the organization will shape the organization's ability to respond. For example, large corporations may not be able to adapt as nimbly as smaller businesses when confronted by a paradigm-shifting change in technology, as the photographic products giant Kodak discovered in the early 2000s when over a period of just a few years the industry went digital. Ironically, Kodak actually invented digital photography in 1975 but held it back from being marketed for fear of hurting its lucrative film business. Under the stress of digitalization by its competitors, Kodak was unable to display the resilience required to restructure. As always, resilience is the process of overcoming a non-normative stress, but that stress and the resources required are contextually sensitive to both the opportunities present in the environment (like a technological development) and the meaning attached to these changes which label them as helpful or unhelpful.

Principle #2. Resilience is a process. While systems have characteristics that make them more likely to experience resilience, the presence of these characteristics is, in itself, not resilience. Resilience is always a process whereby a system interacts with other systems to optimize its functioning (Masten, 2014; Ungar, 2018). In practice, this means that a business with an excellent human resources department, funding for innovation, health and safety procedures and a culture of safety is positioned better than its competitors to withstand external stressors (like a change in market). The concept of resilience, however, does not describe the company in its static state of readiness. We could say the company is well-resourced, well-prepared, or organizationally agile but its resilience is only evident when these resources are used to deal with an atypical threat. The result is typically a change to how the system functions, demonstrating the capacity of the system under stress to achieve a new level of behavior (e.g., increased production of goods or services), return to a previous state (e.g., profitability), or transform itself and another system to achieve a new equilibrium (e.g., a merger occurs between two competitors to reduce conflict and improve capacity for innovation) (see Gunderson and Holling, 2002). Resilience is, therefore, not a trait of the company, but a description of the company as it takes action to overcome adversity. When engaged in processes that promote the organization's sustainability or protect the company from external threats, we say the company shows resilience. Without the presence of adversity (see Principle #1), the company is simply well-functioning, well-managed or equipped to be responsive, but it is not in and of itself resilient. This semantic distinction is critical to understanding resilience, as without it resilience becomes another ambiguous synonym for successful, or capable, traits that can apply to any system under any condition (good or bad). Resilience, by contrast, is only found when systems engage in processes that help them deal with unusual stressors. These processes can look very different depending on the resources available and the context in which organizations function. Five processes are found in the resilience literature:

Persistence. The least dynamic process related to resilience is persistence. A system remains in a state of apparent calm despite serious threats to its survival, but that calm is only possible because other co-existing systems protect it from having to change. One can think of well-subsidized industries that are protected by governments through tariffs as one example of resilience as persistence. Towns that are no longer economically viable, but whose infrastructure is maintained, are another example of the process of persistence in a context where failure should be the result. To persist, a system must receive the support it needs to continue to function, though the nexus of control resides with the surrounding structures and their willingness to engage in protective processes.

Resistance. A system that shows resistance when under threat is actively maintaining its functioning. Organizations that resist change respond to external threats but are not seeking substantive changes in what they do or how they do it. Instead, their strategy is to employ their resources to resist disruption. For decades, tobacco companies resisted the science that showed their product caused cancer, with remarkable success. Even when many high-income countries restricted access to tobacco products, they resisted the threat by diversifying their markets, expanding into low- and middle-income countries with less restrictive public health legislation. These strategies are typical of a system that maintains its equilibrium by exerting just enough influence over its environment to sustain a previous regime of behavior. The strategy may bring temporary relief. When rural communities lose their main industry (e.g., a fishery closes due to the collapse of the fish stock), these communities often will resist government-mandated closures of local infrastructure like schools and hospitals. The strategy of resistance keeps the community viable until new economic activity can be found. Resistance, however, need not involve all levels of an organization or system. Resistance by a single level may protect the entire system from threat. For

example, maintaining a community school has the potential to keep the population and tax base stable until new industries can be found to replace those that closed.

Recovery. An organization's ability to recover, or bounce back (Zolli, 2012), implies a return to normative functioning prior to exposure to an atypical stressor. The notion of recovery, however, is ontologically flawed as systems that are disrupted are changed by that disruption and never return to the same previous state. Recovery is, instead, a process of finding a new regime of behavior that integrates lessons learned during the period of disruption. For example, a power company that experiences a major disruption in service may correct the problem and recover to a previous level of functioning, but its resilience is most likely to be reflected in new procedures or changes in equipment to prevent the same problem from occurring in the future (Kruk et al., 2015). The experience of stress improves the system's functioning even though the system looks, at least superficially, to be doing the same things it did at the same level of efficiency.

Adaptation. An organization that adapts to non-normative stress shows the capacity to learn in order to maintain its sustainability. Adapted systems will look different, or behave differently, but they do not necessarily remove the threat which caused them to change in the first place. These changes often occur at multiple scales within a system. For example, health care organizations are always responding to changing population health trends including accessibility. Health care reform, however, has typically resulted in adaptation of systems to meet people's needs. For example, changes to the law in the United States required every citizen to purchase health care by adapting the rules to suit a private health insurance model. The fundamental conditions which continue to provide unequal care to all US citizens, or bankrupt families with large deductibles and poor-quality insurance plans, have not been fundamentally changed. Adaptation means accommodation to the stressor but may not result in the stressor (i.e., the need for equitable access to health care) being removed.

Transformation. Transformation results when a system (or organization) changes the conditions that put it at risk and, as a consequence, improves its capacity to cope under stress (its resilience). Transformations typically occur at one or more scales, or across multiple systems, simultaneously. For example, technological breakthroughs, changes in licensing, and emergence of the 'gig economy' have threatened the viability of the taxi industry. While the system that imposed strict controls over taxi licenses is coming to an end, a potentially more sustainable model of urban transportation is being created by ride-sharing services like Uber and Lyft. The taxi system as it was had reified into an antiquated system highly resistant to change despite the potential to have self-disrupted before Uber made taxis obsolete. This same process of transformation leading to resilience appears at other systemic levels too. For example, a business unit with exploitive management may be a catalyst for workers to protect themselves by threatening to unionize, which in turn forces a business to address the concerns of its employees, making the organization more resilient through a process of transformation. The workers, in this case, did not persist, resist, recover or adapt (though they may have tried each of these resilience strategies previously). The basis for their resilience is the transformation of their workplace and the conditions in which they carry out their employment.

Principle #3. There are tradeoffs between systems when a system experiences resilience. When organizations engage in processes associated with resilience, not all parts benefit equally even if the organization as a whole becomes sustainable. In this sense, where one part of a system experiences the 'steeling effect' that results from dealing with manageable amounts of risk and innovating new solutions (e.g., that part of the system grows), other parts of the system

may find new regimes of behavior threaten their viability. Returning to the example of a health care system, whereas a publicly funded health care system tends to be associated with national health outcomes and costs less per capita, those with the most money and the private health care providers lose in the transformation to a single-payer system. This pattern of winners and losers is typical of strategies that produce resilience as change necessarily disrupts established regimes that privileged some systems or individual parts of systems over others.

Principle #4. A resilient system is open, dynamic and complex. A system that shows resilience tends to be open to new information that informs functioning. Concepts like balance and equilibrium are only temporary states, snapshots of dynamic processes that make organizations more complex, and therefore give them more options for transformation. Systems that show more heterogeneity (e.g., a diverse workforce, interdisciplinarity in work teams, or vertical integration of the means of production) are likely to be better able to withstand unpredictable sources of stress like a product failure or natural disaster. These changes help organizations modify their practices for the better when resilience is the goal. For example, large manufacturers of personal care products have been accustomed to selling their goods by the pallet, large volumes distributed to warehouses where they are then broken into smaller batches and sent to individual stores. Every phase of production and distribution relied on large-volume shipping and sales. This model, however, has been challenged by online marketers and on-demand delivery of product to warehouses that charge the supplier for storage. In this context, traditionally profitable businesses are having to rethink the way they produce and ship product, selling smaller-sized lots more frequently while maintaining their traditional business model for other retailers. In this sense, these businesses are becoming more complex and dynamic, integrating new technology and opportunities as they become available.

Principle #5. A resilient system promotes connectivity. Whether it is interactivity through social media or the forming of industry associations, resilient systems tend to promote connectivity as a means for solving intransigent problems. Within systems, across scales, and between systems, connectivity gives systems the benefit of better access to resources when needed. Immigrant communities, for example, often create for themselves tight-knit diaspora with cultural and religious institutions as places for networking. These networks serve many functions, from being a source of information about government programs and policies, to offering the social networks required to find employment or engage in the informal economy.

Connectivity can, however, also threaten resilience if it leads to exploitation. After all, ecosystems can be destroyed by an invasive species released into the environment through human activity like shipping. Patent infringement can occur when researchers move from one employer to the next, unintentionally, or intentionally, sharing proprietary information. Like all aspects of resilience, any principle may be beneficial or a threat to functioning depending on the value proposition that shapes its application. If, for example, we think of a disease like Ebola which has thus far infected mostly people in some extremely poor nations, the availability of treatments from western pharmaceutical companies is too disconnected to have a positive impact on the spread of the disease. This changes, however, if government or international organizations step in, increasing the connections between the developers of a drug and those who need it, while monetizing that connection in a way that ensures the patent holder still benefits (i.e., maintains its ability to conduct research and future product development). When connectivity increases exploitation, or makes one or more systems less viable, then the resilience of a single system may not be sustainable even if it appears to benefit temporarily.

Principle #6. A resilient system demonstrates experimentation and learning. Organizations that show resilience learn from experience and integrate learning into future efforts to resist, recover, adapt and transform (for organizations showing persistence, the learning takes place in the systems that protect it from disturbance rather than the focal system itself). These characteristics of systems, however, depend on the quality of the supports available to the system. In the case of businesses or government agencies, for example, a culture that encourages innovation and leadership that supports experimentation is likely to keep an organization functioning during economic and social upheaval. This has been the catalyst for the technology sector, which has created incubators for innovation, though many other industries are seeing similar efforts to place researchers side-by-side, and to integrate disciplinarily diverse teams under one roof in order to ensure one system learns from the other. For example, the Howard Hughes Medical Institute (HHMI) in Ashburn, Virginia, is an endowed research facility that brings together leading-edge researchers with computer technicians and developers of innovative research equipment, grouped into small working groups that are co-located and encouraged to share ideas through informal lunchtime chats and seminars. Such innovation has led to a number of critical break throughs (intended and unintended), including Eric Betzig's Nobel-prize-winning development of super-resolved fluorescence microscopy which has made it possible to study the nanodimension of substances. Even much smaller-scale organizations like a restaurant may find itself more resilient by adapting menus or changing hours as the demographic characteristics of the surrounding community changes. In every case, including HHMI, experimentation leads to many failures, but each failure informs better decisions for the future (Pahl-Wostl, 2009).

Principle #7. A resilient system includes diversity, redundancy and participation.

The more parts of a system available to support a system maintain its functioning, the more likely the system is to remain sustainable. Resilience is, therefore, about diversity (many different parts of a system bringing many different resources to solve problems), redundancy (more than one part of a system can fulfill the same functions) and participation (as many parts of a system as possible engaged in making the system successful; Crane, 2017). These principles are routinely applied to complex engineered systems like airplanes where multiple systems are designed to take over when one system fails. They also characterize resilient nations, with processes like immigration producing net long-term economic and social benefits (Hiebert, 2017). Organizations that resist diversifying, overly specialize roles, or discourage participation (e.g., misunderstand the value of whistleblower legislation and the need to keep the names of those who come forward confidential) will in the long run disadvantage their organizations by discouraging innovation or dampening the motivation of organizational stakeholders to correct the course of the organization when it is threatened. The willingness to engage in an organization and maintain its resilience has much to do with the value placed on participation by stakeholders (Usdin, 2014; Wessells, 2015). Employees, for example, will likely assess what is in it for them personally if they take the risk of naming a problem. The individual may feel that their personal resilience is better served by a change of job rather than risking angering management in an organization that is unpredictable in how it handles conflict. Governance structures and the checks and balances on how systems operate are another set of systems that make participation of potential benefit to an organization under stress.

All three traits of organizations, however, must be matched to the context in which they appear. For example, the nuclear disaster that occurred in northern Japan following the 2011 tsunami was the result of the back-up generators meant to power the plants after a power outage being on the ground rather than on the roof of the facilities. While the positioning of the back-up power made sense during an earthquake, it failed during a tsunami, becoming flooded and malfunctioning. How diversity, redundancy and participation occur will influence the resilience of the systems involved. Riccardo Patriarca (in press), for example, reviewed aspects of organization that produce safety, concluding that safety of a socio-technical system (one in which people and machines operate together) is not a resident quality of either the people or the machines, but instead a constantly changing quality of how those elements interact and the demands placed on both by the environment. In general, a system is more resilient to disturbance when more elements are engaged in keeping that system functioning.

INDIVIDUALS AND ORGANIZATIONS: THE MULTIPLE SYSTEMS THAT PREDICT RESILIENCE

Each of the seven principles implicates both the individuals inside an organization as well as the technical, policy and leadership resources of the organization that are available to maintain an organization's resilience. These internal resources, in turn, depend on the vast networks of external factors that either support an organization's longevity or threaten it with obsolescence or dysfunction. Despite the need to consider all these intersecting dimensions of an organization, the most common focus for studies of resilience remains individuals and the interventions intended to help them adapt better to a demanding workplace. This section reviews what individuals do to maintain their personal resilience or accommodate themselves to excessive on-the-job demands. It then focuses on the resources individuals need to succeed, and finally shows that individuals are only one of many systems interacting in ways that make organizations more resilient under stress. Throughout this discussion, concepts related to the seven principles are discussed.

Rugged individuals. Approaches to worker resilience in organizations have mostly focused on individual factors that make workers better adapted to stressful situations. For example, soldier fitness programs are designed to make armed forces personnel capable of withstanding operational stressors (Reivich et al., 2011) without necessarily challenging the systems that create stress in the first place. For example, much of what is known about post-traumatic stress suggests a relationship between exposure to an external stressor and access to future supports to debrief that stress and support a traumatized individual's reintegration back into social networks that can be supportive. For soldiers, the network of Legions and other meeting spaces once served the role of providing structured environments that promised routine and security, along with access to people with shared histories (many of these have been closed in recent years as the number of veterans declines). Online meeting spaces have helped fill the void. Leadership, too, is implicated in the ability of a soldier (or any employee) to function well in a context of unusual stress (Sinek, 2018). The need for both individual hardiness and the sources of support to sustain resilience requires a more complex model to explain the resilience of individuals in organizations. Ungar (2019) has shown through a review of resilience

science that being both rugged and resourced is more likely to produce individuals with the capacity to withstand stress than when attention is focused exclusively on promoting personal change through self-help or other individualized interventions. Organizational resilience means changing individuals and changing their environments at the same time. The myth of the rugged individual and the subsequent psychologizing of human experience has, however, over-emphasized individual responsibility for coping. This neo-liberal perspective has meant that organizations developing programs for workplace wellness have placed too much responsibility for worker health on workers themselves. This is especially noticeable in the recent emphasis on mindfulness-based stress reduction training and other third-generation cognitive therapies that promote self-regulation. As Ronald Purser (2019) explains, the approach to these practices has turned spiritually grounded practices into consumable mind games with little chance of them sustaining long-term change without diligent practice regimes and a community of support. A more progressive workplace assesses the sources of stress and available supports that exist across multiple systems within an organization and external to it and their potential positive impact on worker and organizational success. These factors can be grouped broadly under the categories of rugged and resourced. This R2 model of resilience includes the factors listed in Table 10.1.

Table 10.1   R2: Rugged qualities and supportive resources associated with organizational resilience

Rugged qualities	Resources
Gratitude	Structure
Self-confidence	Accountability
Optimism	Supportive relationships
Problem-solving	A powerful identity
Mindfulness	Experiences of control
Sleep	Fair treatment
Nutrition	Culture
Physical activity	Basic needs

The eight rugged characteristics reflect much of the writing on self-improvement which is common in the human resources and career development literature (e.g., Diener and Biswas-Diener, 2008). Studies of gratitude, for example, have shown many positive individual and relational benefits. For example, in an experiment which asked couples to make random expressions of gratitude to their partners, there was an overall benefit for the relationship, though the impact was greater when the partner receiving the expression of gratitude was more responsive (Algoe and Zhaoyang, 2016). Likewise, individual workers that demonstrate self-confidence, optimism and good problem-solving skills tend to outperform their colleagues (Salanova and Ortega-Maldonado, 2019). Mindfulness and other strategies to deal with anxiety or workplace stress have shown moderate effect sizes on outcomes (Goldberg et al., 2018), though it is unclear at what level of risk exposure these interventions work best or for which people from which contexts and cultures. The final three aspects of rugged individualism are related to physical health, with sleep, nutrition and physical activity well-validated factors that contribute to employees functioning better psychologically and physically (Dowlati et al., 2017; Felder et al., 2017; O'Brien et al., 2018). While all eight factors have an evidence base that shows they are effective at increasing the resilience of individuals inside organizations, they all reflect a highly individual paradigm for success. Each is a trait of the individual and interventions, whether referral to a therapist or enrolment at a gym, position the locus of change within the individual. This notion of individual motivation and sole responsibility has been critiqued as excessively narrow and therefore unable to account for the many complex systems which interact in people's lives (Ehrenreich, 2009; Purser, 2019). It is these other systems and the processes whereby they interact that improve the odds that individuals and organizations both succeed in mutually dependent ways.

Resourced individuals and their organizations. In contrast, a complementary set of resources are also likely to influence the wellbeing of workers, though in this case it is organizations themselves which share responsibility with employees to ensure that interventions to increase accessibility to each resource are successfully implemented. Among the most common factors that improve resilience is structure, which implies reasonable expectations of employees to perform their duties, as well as systems of accountability which make workplaces predictable environments in which to operate and be rewarded for one's efforts. Leadership plays a large part in making these and other resources available. And yet the discourse regarding employee wellbeing tends to emphasize what employees can do to better their situation rather than the minimum standards of supervision and care that organizations need to provide to make their employees, and their organization as a whole, resilient (Sinek, 2018). For example, flexible work hours can help parents of young children establish a better work–life balance, with women who have responsibilities for children reporting the greatest increases in organizational commitment and job satisfaction when they are given the ability to adapt their work hours to their families' needs (Siegel et al., 1997). When employers build in sufficient safeguards for redundancy, or encourage more women in senior management (the principle of diversification), their businesses are likely to experience improved workplace communication and employee engagement in decision-making processes (Melero, 2011).

The remaining six resources in the R2 model continue these same trends, with supportive relationships being facilitated by organizations to create opportunities for employees to maintain continuity in their attachments with colleagues and build a sense of belonging within the organization. Likewise, an organization that creates opportunities for employees to use their skills provides the means for individuals to develop powerful identities and experience control, or self-efficacy, in regard to the decisions that affect their work. These qualities of a workplace facilitate experiences for employees which promote individual resilience and organizational growth and sustainability, encouraging people to be both selfish and selfless at the same time (Sober and Wilson, 1998). In each case, it is the environment and the many systems which interact within and between organizations which create the opportunities for these aspects of resilience to be realized. For example, sense of self-efficacy is not an individual set of cognitions, but the result of experiences in which individuals are provided the opportunities to make a difference in the world around them, whether that is planning their workday or shutting down a car assembly line when an irregularity is detected.

Fair treatment, the sixth resource in the R2 model, occurs in contexts where there is respect for human rights. This includes a harassment-free environment in which to function, as well as the procedural safeguards needed to address concerns when they arise. It is ironic that resilience has for so long been discussed with rarely a mention of social justice, even as human rights legislation has expanded and popular movements, whether the fight to close the gender gap in pay scales or the #metoo movement, have shown that a more sustainable workforce is one that has access to fair treatment. While there will always be a few individuals who survive abusive treatment inside organizations, far better to create the conditions for all organizational stakeholders to succeed when there are potential threats.

Culture, too, is reinforced by organizations, for example, by helping individuals maintain their heritage culture, or promoting an organizational culture which provides the building blocks and accommodations necessary for resilience (e.g., a culture of respect that becomes institutionalized – for example, maternity and paternity leaves are sufficiently long to help new parents adapt to their role and return to work with the supports they need in place). Facilitating continuity of culture may also mean that organizational leadership ensures tolerance for different dress or flexibility in scheduling and holiday time.

Finally, workplaces that pay sufficient wages and governments that emphasize occupational health and safety practices are, together, likely to contribute to meeting the basic needs of employees while maintaining the profitability of the the business and avoiding unintended harm in the workplace. (Levine et al., 2012).

This list of factors demonstrates that organizations which are complex need to address concurrently the requirements of their employees/residents/participants at multiple systemic levels. Individual change is seldom enough if people are to navigate and negotiate effectively for the internal and external resources they and their organization need for success, especially when exposed to a non-normative stressor like an economic recession, an act of violence in the workplace, or more chronic exposure to stress through excessive demands on employee time or a lack of personal boundaries as a result of round-the-clock electronic communication that obligates employees to respond.

This list is not unique in the field of organizational resilience, though the distinction made in the R2 model between helping individuals and organizations become both rugged and resourced brings clarity to an otherwise complicated body of research and practice. Among the models which support this view of organizations as a setting for complex processes of navigation and negotiation is Crane's (in press) Resilient Work Systems Framework (Figure 10.1). Though slightly less of an integration of individually focused initiatives to make employees more resilient, Crane's model focuses on eight dimensions of work that promote or inhibit worker resilience scored from low to high. All eight dimensions can be influenced by an organization or the other systems with which

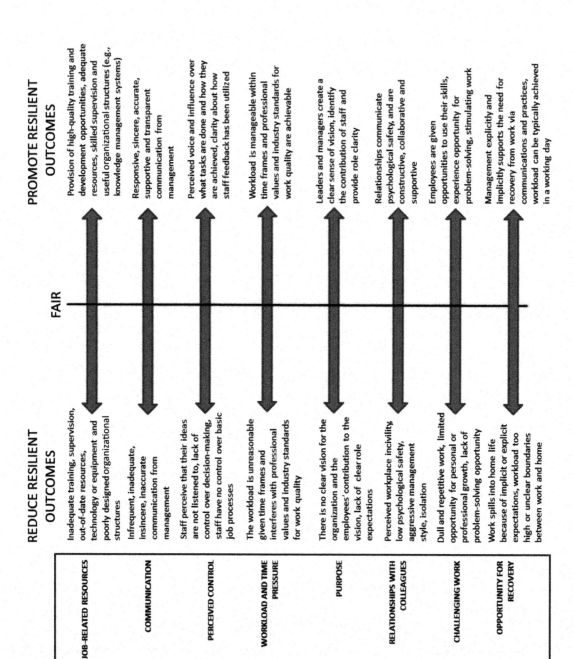

Figure 10.1   The Resilient Work Systems Framework for assessing organizational contributors to resilience (Crane, in press)

an organization interacts, with the expectation that a change at the organizational, team or individual level will directly or indirectly result in changes in other dimensions of the Framework as well. In this sense, the model is complex, with many combinations of factors producing contextually specific results that ensure the sustainability of the organization. For example, there is attention to the culture of the organization and its provision of opportunities for training, supervision and structure, as well as team communication, efficacy, workload, shared mission (also a function of good leadership), relationships with colleagues, opportunities for skill development (and the powerful identities that follow) and the time away from work to adequately recover and prepare for future demands.

The following case example reflects both the seven principles discussed earlier and the list of rugged and resourced factors associated with resilience as they apply to a community as a whole (the organization).

Example: Maple Ridge. Maple Ridge[1] is a community (in this instance, the organization which is the focus of this case study) of 7,000 that is highly dependent upon the extraction of oil and gas for its economy. A review of the world price for crude oil shows a direct link over time to the economic boom-and-bust cycles of the community, with boom times bringing a rapid expansion in new housing, decreases in undeveloped land such as wetlands used by migratory birds, and large increases in household income, along with serious pressures on families as primary earners (usually adult males) work long hours to meet the demand for labor. As a consequence of the town's attraction as a place to find work, it also has struggled to deal with large numbers of transient workers, the availability of alcohol and drugs and a lack of other economic choices beyond employment in the oil and gas industry.

While these pressures put the population under continuous stress during both economic boom-and-bust periods, the town

has developed plans to cope. Prior to 2014, amid a stronger economy, the town implemented a number of strategies to attract and retain families, including building an award-winning daycare, a small number of subsidized housing units to make rents more affordable for young families, improving the schools, improving the recreational paths outside the town and encouraging investment in its downtown core of services for young workers like a gym and coffee shops. These efforts had a positive impact on the wellbeing of individuals and the community's sense of social cohesion until the price of oil tumbled in 2014 and a declining tax base put pressure on the municipality to stop funding anything but core services. Those initial adaptations to make the town more resilient to boom-and-bust economic changes were replaced with resistance strategies that mobilized support for the building of pipelines and insisted that government support the oil industry through legislative and taxation means.

More recently, a small but growing number of people are pushing for a transformation of the local economy, exploiting new opportunities in the production of hemp and legalized marijuana, revisiting its agricultural and forestry industries, encouraging small businesses and focusing on the production of 'clean' energy solutions for the use of oil and gas. They have also worked at addressing the alcohol and drug problems in the community and keeping the schools and other infrastructure functioning well to ensure the community remains an attractive place to settle.

At the level of individuals, however, mounting stress related to the economic downturn continues to put economic pressure on households, with employment shortages and pressure to be on-call around the clock for available shifts. This pressure is dealt with through the use of substances (a negative solution) or by building stronger connections with family and community (a positive solution). In the community, there are also opportunities for self-improvement, including access to outdoor recreation, sports centers and a private gym. Equally important, the town through its Department of Family and Community Services has initiated a series of monthly dinners to create a sense of community cohesion, built a skateboard park to give youth in the community a place to be, and offered a number of supports to parents of young children, seniors and those with mental and physical health challenges. All of these strategies have supplemented the efforts by individuals to find the resources they need for wellbeing through the town's municipal programs and by addressing problems in the broader economy through labor mobility and economic diversification.

IMPLICATIONS FOR INTERVENTIONS TO IMPROVE ORGANIZATIONAL RESILIENCE

Given the complexity of organizations and the multiple intersecting systems that they interact with, interventions that are intended to improve resilience need to address multiple systems simultaneously. As Russell Ackoff (1999) observed, it is often better to achieve partial solutions to many different parts of a complex problem than to seek complete resolution of a single problem affecting one part of a system (leaving the rest of the system vulnerable). More commonly, however, resilience is addressed at the level of individuals (Robertson et al., 2015), providing personal training in problem-solving or emotional regulation through interventions like mindfulness-based stress reduction or workplace wellness programs. When it comes to building psychological capital, there is a common argument that, as employees acquire more, they will be able to be more productive and engaged. This psychological capital includes qualities like self-confidence and efficacy, optimism and a positive attitude towards success in the future (Luthans et al., 2015). While the list is

intuitively obvious, the research to support such claims has avoided the issues raised by the study of resilience: at what level of risk exposure do these individual attributes produce the required change? Remarkably, studies of these psychological constructs have often been done with the highly selective sample of university students under laboratory conditions, making the application of such findings to contexts like boom-and-bust economies difficult to know.

For these reasons, strategies for organizational resilience that put responsibility for change on individuals within an organization rather than on the organization as a whole are largely untested, especially in contexts where employees are experiencing atypical amounts of stress. By contrast, more holistic approaches (in many cases also untested) consider the changes systems need to make to help employees and other organizational subsystems (e.g., computer networks, human resources, production lines) perform optimally. For example, human burnout in the workplace should not be described as a failure of the individual, but as the dysfunction of systems that put individuals at risk. Future research needs to examine both individual and organization-wide resilience and the factors and processes associated with positive outcomes at different levels of stress.

This emerging multisystemic focus is evident in some approaches to worker wellbeing such as Cusack et al.'s (2016) Health Services Workplace Environmental Resilience (HSWER) model, which promotes nurses' resilience by addressing the multiple environmental factors that influence performance on the job including both nursing staff support (such as workplace climate, respectful communication and access to timely consultation) and nursing staff development (such as good leadership, opportunities to advance skills and mentorship). Though Cusack et al.'s work is specific to nurses in clinical settings, such efforts reflect systemic responses to organizational stress by addressing the needs of multiple systems all at once, from the personal to the professional. This means understanding both the capacity of organizations to facilitate employee resilience and the broader social constructions of the meanings people hold that decide which sources of support they value most. As Curt Coffman and Kathie Sorensen write (based on a comment by management consultant Peter Drucker), 'culture eats strategy for lunch' (2013). Efforts to improve resilience that are not properly negotiated and culturally relevant in a specific organizational setting are likely to experience resistance during implementation.

CONCLUSION

A focus on organizational resilience and the processes that promote and sustain wellbeing shifts attention from the study of breakdown and disorder to the conditions that make success possible under stress. This shift in perspective creates a learning environment in which organizations (from the smallest workplace team to entire governments) can be studied to better understand the mechanisms that promote and protect systems when they are exposed to non-normative stress. Organizational resilience, however, is much more complicated than assisting employees to develop their capacity to 'think positively' or 'feel motivated'. Beyond these individual qualities associated with ruggedness, an organization that shows resilience needs to resource the many systems upon which it depends. Adaptation to stress is only one way that organizations and their employees/residents/participants/citizens accommodate to stress. Depending on the quality of the threat experienced by an organization, and the resources that are available and accessible, organizations will employ a number of different strategies to cope, from resisting change altogether to transforming the environment surrounding the organization to make the organization and the people who are part of it more resilient.

Note

1 The name of the community has been changed to protect the identity of study participants.

REFERENCES

Ackoff R (1999) *Recreating the Corporation: A Design of Organizations for the 21st Century*. Oxford, UK: Oxford University Press.

Algoe SB and Zhaoyang R (2016) *Positive psychology in context: Effects of expressing gratitude in ongoing relationships depend on perceptions of enactor responsiveness*. The Journal of Positive Psychology 11(4): 399–415. DOI: 10.1080/17439760.2015.1117131

Biggs R, Schlüter M, Biggs D, Bohensky EL, BurnSilver S, Cundill G, Dakos V, Daw TM, Evans LS, Kotschy K, Leitch AM, Meek C, Quinlan A, Raudsepp-Hearne C, Robards MD, Schoon ML, Schultz L and West PC (2012) Toward principles for enhancing the resilience of ecosystem services. *Annual Review of Environment and Resources* 37: 421–448. DOI: 10.1146/annurev-environ-051211-123836

Boyer SL and Bond GR (1999) Does assertive community treatment reduce burnout? A comparison with traditional case management. *Mental Health Services Research* 1: 31–45. DOI: 10.1023/A:1021931201738

Coffman C and Sorensen K (2013) *Culture Eats Strategy for Lunch: The Secret of Extraordinary Results, Igniting the Passion Within*. Denver, CO: Laing Addison Press.

Crane MF (ed)(2017) *Managing for Resilience: A Practical Guide for Employee Wellbeing And Organizational Performance*. London, UK: Routledge.

Crane MF (in press) The resilient work systems framework for assessing organizational contributors to resilience. In: Ungar M (ed) *Multisystemic Resilience: Adaptation and Transformation in Changing Contexts*. New York, NY: Oxford University Press.

Cusack L, Smith M, Hegney D, Rees CS, Breen LJ, Witt RR, Rogers C, Williams A, Cross W and Cheung K (2016) Exploring environmental factors in nursing workplaces that promote psychological resilience: Constructing a unified theoretical model. *Frontiers in Psychology* 7: 600. DOI: 10.3389/fpsyg.2016.00600

Diener E and Biswas-Diener R (2008) *Happiness: Unlocking the Mysteries of Psychological Wealth*. Oxford, UK: Blackwell.

Dowlati Y, Ravindrana AV, Segald ZV, Stewart DE, Steiner M and Meyera JH (2017) Selective dietary supplementation in early postpartum is associated with high resilience against depressed mood. *PNAS* 114(13): 3509–3514. DOI: 10.1073/pnas.1611965114

Ehrenreich B (2009) *Bright-sided: How the Relentless Promotion of Positive Thinking Has Undermined America*. New York, NY: Metropolitan.

Ellis BJ and Del Giudice M (2014) Beyond allostatic load: Rethinking the role of stress in regulating human development. *Development and Psychopathology* 26(1): 1–20. DOI: 10.1017/S0954579413000849Publ

Felder JN, Laraia B, Coleman-Phox K, Bush N, Suresh M, Thomas M, Adler N, Epel E and Prather AA (2017) Poor sleep quality, psychological distress, and the buffering effect of mindfulness training during pregnancy. *Behavioral Sleep Medicine* 16(6): 611–624. DOI: 10.1080/15402002.2016.1266488

Goldberg SB, Tucker RP, Greene PA, Davidson RJ, Wampold BE, Kearney DJ and Simpson TL (2018) Mindfulness-based interventions for psychiatric disorders: A systematic review and meta-analysis. *Clinical Psychology Review* 59: 52–60. DOI: 10.1016/j.cpr.2017.10.011

Gunderson LH and Holling CS (eds)(2002) *Panarchy: Understanding Transformations in Human and Natural Systems*. Washington, DC: Island Press.

Hiebert D (2017) Immigrants and refugees in the housing markets of Montreal, Toronto and Vancouver, 2011. *Canadian Journal of Urban Research* 26(2): 52–78.

Jonge J and Dormann C (2006) Stressors, resources, and strain at work: A longitudinal test of the triple-match principle. *The Journal of Applied Psychology* 91: 1359–1374. DOI: 10.1037/0021-9010.91.5.1359.

Kruk ME, Myers M, Varpilah ST and Dahn BT (2015) What is a resilient health system? Lessons from Ebola. *The Lancet* 385(9980): 1910–1912. DOI: 10.1016/S0140-6736(15)60755-3

Levine D, Toffel M and Johnson M (2012) Randomized government safety inspections reduce worker injuries with no detectable job loss. *Science* 336(6083): 907–911.

Luthans F, Youssef-Morgan CM and Avolio BJ (2015) *Psychological Capital and Beyond*. New York, NY: Oxford University Press.

Masten AS (2014) *Ordinary Magic. Resilience in Development*. New York, NY: Guilford Press.

Melero E (2011) Are workplaces with many women in management run differently? *Journal of Business Research* 64(4): 385–393.

O'Brien MS, Robinson R, Frayne S, Mekary JR, Fowles DD and Kimmerly DS (2018) Achieving Canadian physical activity guidelines is associated with better vascular function independent of aerobic fitness and sedentary time in older adults. *Applied Physiology, Nutrition, and Metabolism* 43(10): 1003–1009. DOI: 10.1139/apnm-2018-0033

Pahl-Wostl C (2009) A conceptual framework for analysing adaptive capacity and multi-level learning processes in resource governance regimes. *Global Environmental Change* 19(3): 354–365. DOI: 10.1016/j.gloenvcha.2009.06.001

Patriarca R (in press) Resilience engineering for socio-technical safety management. In: Ungar M (ed) *Multisystemic resilience: Adaptation and Transformation in Changing Contexts*. New York: Oxford University Press.

Purser R (2019) *McMindfulness: How Mindfulness Became the New Capitalist Spirituality*. London, UK: Repeater.

Reivich KJ, Seligman EP and McBride S (2011) Master resilience training in the U. S. Army. *American Psychologist* 66(1): 25–34.

Robertson IT, Cooper CL, Sarkar M and Curran M (2015) Resilience training in the workplace from 2003 to 2014: A systematic review. *Journal of Occupational and Organizational Psychology* 88(3): 533–562. DOI:10.1111/joop.12120

Rothmann S, Van Zul LE and Rautenbach C (2019) Measuring flourishing @ work interventions: The development and validation of the flourishing-at-work scale. In: Van Zyl LE and Rothmann S (eds) *Positive Psychological Intervention Design and Protocols for Multi-Cultural Contexts*. Cham, Switzerland: Springer, pp. 241–276.

Salanova M and Ortega-Maldonado A (2019) Psychological capital development in organizations: An integrative review of evidence-based intervention programs. In: Van Zyl LE and Rothmann S (eds) *Positive Psychological Intervention Design and Protocols for Multi-Cultural Contexts*. Cham, Switzerland: Springer, pp. 81–102.

Selye H (1975) Stress and distress. *Comprehensive Therapy* 1(8): 9–13.

Siegel P, Mosca J and Karim K (1997) Impact of flexible work hours on organizational commitment and job satisfaction in small business organizations. *Journal of Business and Entrepreneurship* 9(1): 81–98.

Sinek S (2018) *Leaders Eat Last*. London, UK: Penguin.

Sober E and Wilson DS (1998) *Unto Others: The Evolution and Psychology of Unselfish Behavior*. Cambridge, MA: Harvard University Press.

Ungar M (2011) The social ecology of resilience: Addressing contextual and cultural ambiguity of a nascent construct. *American Journal of Orthopsychiatry* 81(1): 1–17. DOI: 10.1111/j.1939-0025.2010.01067.x

Ungar M (2017) Which counts more? The differential impact of the environment or the differential susceptibility of the individual? *British Journal of Social Work* 47(5): 1279–1289. DOI: 10.1093/bjsw/bcw109

Ungar M (2018) Systemic resilience: Principles and processes for a science of change in contexts of adversity. *Ecology and Society* 23(4): 34. DOI: 10.5751/ES-10385-230434

Ungar M (2019) *Change Your World: The Science of Resilience and the True Path to Success*. Toronto, ON: Sutherland House.

Usdin L (2014) Building resiliency and supporting distributive leadership post-disaster: Lessons from New Orleans a decade (almost) after hurricane Katrina. *The International Journal of Leadership in Public Services* 10(3): 157. DOI: 10.1108/IJLPS-07-2014-0010

Wessells MG (2015) Bottom-up approaches to strengthening child protection systems: Placing children, families, and communities at the center. *Child Abuse & Neglect* 43: 8–21. DOI: 10.1016/j.chiabu.2015.04.006

Xu L and Kajikawa Y (2017) An integrated framework for resilience research: A systematic review based on citation network analysis. *Sustainability Science* 13(1): 235–254. DOI: 10.1007/s11625-017-0487-4

Zolli A (2012) *Resilience: Why Things Bounce Back*. Toronto, ON: Simon & Schuster.

PART II

International Issues and Contexts

Virtual Work, Technology and Wellbeing

Monideepa Tarafdar and Jean-François Stich

INTRODUCTION

Information technology (IT) has enabled work to be conducted beyond the physical confines of the physical office and beyond the temporal confines of the nine-to-five office hours. *Virtual work* refers to work that, through the use of IT, enables employees to work and interact across geographical and temporal boundaries (Raghuram et al., 2019). In this chapter, we define virtual work as the commonly understood work arrangements that are not accomplished in the physical office (e.g., remote work, telecommuting) and that are made possible through a range of IT such as computers, smartphones, email, video-conferencing tools and intranets. While virtual work has been around for a long time, every single citizen of the world has been jolted into noticing it since the onset of the Covid-19 pandemic. An article in the *Financial Times* recently noted, 'In six weeks we've taken almost the entirety of the back offices of corporate America [indeed in all

countries][1] and moved them to kitchens and living rooms and it's been pretty seamless, (Morris et al., 2020). Furthermore, a number of surveys have reported that once the pandemic winds down, it is unlikely that the nature of office work will go back to what it was before (Dombey and Hall, 2020). It is expected that the new ways of working will involve more people working virtually without going into a physical office. A key distinction between virtual and non-virtual work is the indispensable and vital role of IT. Every single work task executed by the individual that does not require the actual manipulation of physical objects – ranging across interacting with colleagues, analysing problems, conducting meetings, communicating with customers and suppliers – is mediated through an IT application. Indeed, as we have discovered since countries started locking down one by one starting in March 2020, 'working' means getting tasks done by looking into a screen to make sense of text, voices, faces and people. Put plainly – such

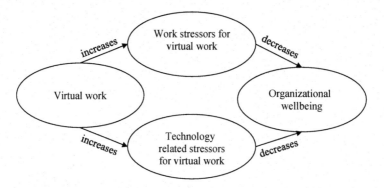

Figure 11.1   The impact of virtual work on organizational wellbeing

relentless dependence on IT causes stress. 'Zoom fatigue' is now an expression familiar to almost every office (non!)going employee (Fosslien and Duffy, 2020).

The goal of this chapter is to shine a light on the stress caused by virtual work and its effects on organizational wellbeing. We suggest that virtual work creates stress in two ways (Figure 11.1). In the first, through the top path, it increases work-related stressors by adversely affecting work relationships and work–life balance, and by increasing workload. Through the bottom path, it increases technostress, that is, the stress from the use of technology, by intensifying technostress-creating conditions. Through each of these paths, virtual work can have non-beneficial impacts on organizational wellbeing. In the rest of the chapter we examine how these effects come about, thereby highlighting the importance of the virtual work context for understanding and researching organizational wellbeing.

VIRTUAL WORK AND WORK STRESS

Virtual work changes the way work is conducted and, through that, influences the way work creates stress. Traditionally, work has been perceived to be stressful when work relationships are dysfunctional, when work–life balance and job security are compromised or when workloads are too intense (Faragher et al., 2004). Virtual work has opened up new risks by transforming these traditional work stressors (Stich, 2020), such as when bullying becomes cyberbullying (Baruch, 2005), or when 24/7 information overload worsens feelings of work overload (Barley et al., 2011). In this section, we review how the impact of virtual work affects three traditional work stressors, namely, work relationships, workload and work–life balance.

Work Relationships

Organizations are places of social relationships and interactions. Yet 'having to live and work with others can be one of the most stressful aspects of life' (Sutherland and Cooper, 2000: 98). The exposure to perpetual and demanding social interactions can be difficult to bear. At first, virtual work may seem to be a way to reduce the stress from demanding social interactions at work because it enables people to work in places away from the office/colleagues, such as from home, trains, planes, co-working spaces, cafes or public parks. For employees who wanted such 'escape', bringing work away from the office can reduce the emotional exhaustion induced by social interaction (Windeler et al., 2017). Virtual work can also offer respite from office politics (Mann and Holdsworth, 2003), background noise (e.g., background hum of conversations) and interruptions (e.g., unexpected/unwanted hallway encounters) that can make social interactions mentally exhausting (Fonner and Roloff, 2010).

However, all changes are not for the better. Virtual work can be an isolating experience (Cooper and Kurland, 2002), where employees become 'out of sight and out of mind' and are left out of important email threads or important information (Hemp, 2009). Furthermore, employees are often ill-equipped and under-trained to communicate through asynchronous means such as email (Soucek and Moser, 2010). Such communication can be difficult to interpret, especially in the absence of visual cues (Byron, 2008). For example, email messages can be erroneously interpreted as hostile, lead to aggressive responses and, thus, conflict escalation (Friedman and Currall, 2003). For instance, messages that contain capital letters or exclamation points for emphasis tend to be (mis)perceived as hostile (Turnage, 2007), although that may not have been the sender's intent. Lacking the real-time feedback necessary to self-regulate, individuals may shoot off a response based on their (mis)interpretation of an email, and not realizing their mistake until they receive a response. They may also not be aware of lack of clarity in their communication. Research shows that people tend to overestimate the clarity of their own email (e.g., in nuances such as humour) even when the recipient does not think so (Kruger et al., 2005)! Such lack of agreement is stressful to both senders and recipients (Brown et al., 2014) and can inadvertently damage work relationships (Friedman and Currall, 2003), thereby creating stress.

More alarmingly, electronic communication makes it easier to diminish and damage the social dimension of work because individuals can 'hide' behind virtual communication (or non-communication). Virtual work has created the risk for 'electronic' incivility

and bullying (Baruch, 2005; Lim and Teo, 2009). Studies have found that over 80% of their participants experienced negative virtual encounters in the previous six months (Coyne et al., 2017). Intimidations and insults are common forms of 'cyber incivility' conducted through email (Baruch, 2005). Indeed, a new form of incivility related to virtual work is to 'say nothing' – it is easy to ignore specific colleagues by not replying to email from them if one does not want to acknowledge their views and contributions or show interest in them (Lim and Teo, 2009). Over time, when such negative experiences become repeated against the victim, they may transform into 'cyberbullying' (Farley et al., 2016), the virtual extension of work bullying (Baruch, 2005). Cyberbullying has even been found to be more damaging and stressful than traditional bullying, because bullied employees have more difficulty in detaching psychologically from it, given that it occurs anytime and anywhere and does not need a face-to-face encounter (Coyne et al., 2017).

Even for those employees who do not actually do virtual work but work with colleagues who do, there is trouble. They tend to be more frequently interrupted than before, as the burden of having to deal with people who stop by the office is now solely on them (Yap and Tng, 1990). They tend to handle more tasks by themselves, perhaps because they feel the remote colleagues may be difficult to reach or may not respond in a timely manner (Golden, 2007). They find themselves between a rock and a hard place – on the one hand their work relationships are damaged by their colleagues' doing virtual work, and on the other they feel denied the benefits of virtual work (Rockmann and Pratt, 2015).

Work–Life Balance

Stress stemming from conflict between work and home roles is transformed due to virtual work (Cooper et al., 2001). In traditional work settings, the interface between work and home gets blurred when emotions transfer from one role to the other or when work hours are extended in order to meet deadlines. Virtual work has provided employees with the means to bring work away from their offices and beyond their office hours. Generally, this is perceived as a work benefit. Employees ask for and negotiate 'flexible work hours' to be able to work from home (Bayazit and Bayazit, 2017). Such flexibility reduces commuting time and provides autonomy as to when and where to work, so that work and personal demands can be better balanced (e.g., doing sport, running errands, taking care of children) (Wheatley and Bickerton, 2016). This sort of flexibility, however, comes with constant connectivity (Stich et al., 2015).

Indeed, the autonomy employees believe they will find in virtual work is often counterbalanced by work pressures that constrain such autonomy (ter Hoeven et al., 2016). The capacity to work anytime, anywhere, often 'leashes' employees, and creates difficulties for them to disengage from work (Boswell and Olson-Buchanan, 2007). Constant connectivity has even been presented as a form of addiction (Mazmanian et al., 2013), as inboxes and devices are compulsively monitored. Employees are becoming aware of this trade-off between autonomy and work–life conflict; some have even sued their employers, who they hold as liable, for their addiction to virtual work (Kakabadse et al., 2007)! In France, for example, a company was asked to compensate a former employee for all the time he had to spend monitoring his corporate smartphone and responding to emails outside office hours (Samuel, 2018). The logic was that the employee had been 'on call', for which compensation was due. As can be seen in these examples, work demands pile up even outside office and office hours, thereby threatening the balance between work and home.

Employees engaged in virtual work may try to use evening hours to catch up with the work emails they did not find the time to handle during their office hours. The time spent for family or personal matters is thus reduced, and so is employees' energy. When working from home, conducting even small work tasks in downtime bears the risk of interfering with personal and family time (Derks et al., 2015). Personal activities may have to be interrupted in order to respond to an urgent work demand, thereby creating work–life conflict (Delanoeije et al., 2019). Conversely, personal and family demands may push virtual workers to interrupt work tasks (Delanoeije et al., 2019). Either ways, it takes time and cognitive effort to get back into what one was doing before the interruption, which is stressful. Such interruptions are, however, less stressful for employees who prefer to integrate work and home roles (Gadeyne et al., 2018) or who are highly engaged (Derks et al., 2015).

Workload

Workload is an important source of stress, both when it is in excess (i.e., overload) and in deficit (e.g., boredom) (Cooper et al., 2001). Virtual work is often presented as a way to facilitate the quick sharing of business-critical information, and thus as a way to increase productivity (Sumecki et al., 2011). In practice, however, virtual work has also created new work demands for employees, leading to increased perceptions of workload stress.

Virtual work allows information to flow freely, and with less constraints than in a traditional work setting. For instance, prior to electronic communication and photocopies, employees who desired to transmit typed documents to multiple recipients had to reproduce them using carbon papers. Such 'carbon copying' was very time-consuming, as each iteration could only copy the original document approximately five times. In virtual work, 'carbon copies' – CCs – are done instantaneously and effortlessly using email, with unlimited numbers of recipients. This feature tends to be misused by employees, who often lack the necessary training, understanding or empathy to judge who really needs to receive their messages (Soucek and Moser, 2010; Stich et al., 2017). This results in large volumes of emails being exchanged. Furthermore, emails arrive continuously and continue to pile up even in the employee's absence. Dealing with such amount of information is time-consuming, which is one reason why virtual work tends to increase work overload stress (Barley et al., 2011; Stich et al., 2019a). It has been estimated that employees spend, on average, 29 minutes per day reading email (Jackson et al., 2006). Even more time is thus lost to write and answer emails, or to manage, sort and clean email inboxes (Kalman and Ravid, 2015). The increase in workload stress because of virtual work is not specific to email, and has been found across a range of IT such as enterprise social networking or video-conferencing (Stich et al., 2017).

An additional way through which virtual work may increase perceptions of workload stress is through interruptions. Although employees are also interrupted in traditional workplaces, virtual work has extended the reach of interruptions and allowed them to be 'tapped on the shoulder virtually' (Stich et al., 2017). Virtual interruptions (e.g., incoming emails) are difficult to resist and insidiously disrupt employees' workflows. Employees believe they only react to incoming emails every hour (Renaud et al., 2006), but the reality shows that the majority of incoming emails are reacted to within five minutes (Renaud et al., 2006) and sometimes even within six seconds (Jackson et al., 2001). Although email software can be set up so that emails are only retrieved on a certain interval, the default setup is to retrieve emails every five minutes, and most employees leave their inboxes open all day and handle emails as they arrive (Barley et al., 2011). Additionally, there may be interruptions by family members and home demands (Delanoeije et al., 2019). The amount and frequency of interruptions has thus been shown to be higher in

virtual work (e.g., emails, phone calls) (Van Solingen et al., 1998). It then takes from one to 15 minutes to reengage in the task at hand (Jackson et al., 2001; Van Solingen et al., 1998), unless the interruption brought information that was needed for the task. Handling these interruptions thus consumes a significant amount of time, estimated at 29 minutes per day (Gupta and Sharda, 2008). This loss thus increases employees' workloads, and the associated stress (Stich et al., 2019a).

In this section we have explained how virtual work can exacerbate the work stressors associated with work relationships, work overload and work–life conflict. In the next section we examine how virtual work can aggravate conditions that create technostress, that is, the stress emanating from the use of IT.

VIRTUAL WORK AND TECHNOSTRESS

The inexorable relationship between virtual work and IT has been poignantly revealed by the current pandemic, which has necessitated the sustained and relentless use of all kinds of applications to execute organizational work. IT applications for virtual work include aids for asynchronous (e.g., email tools and data-repository tools such as OneDrive) and synchronous (e.g., virtual meeting and file-sharing tools such as Teams and Zoom, and chat tools such as Slack) communication. They also include enterprise workflow applications through which tasks and business processes such as order processing, invoicing, and customer relationship management are executed.

Technostress-Creating Conditions from Virtual Work

We have known for quite some time now that use of IT can be a source of stress in the workplace, referred to in the literature as *technostress*. IT users experience technostress because they perceive the demands made by IT as threatening to their organizational well-being (Tarafdar et al., 2019). Such demands can come from the very characteristics of IT that are perceived as beneficial, such as any-where–anytime connectivity, availability, device and application reliability, anonymity of interaction, and constant novelty and new-ness of features and functionalities (Ayyagari et al., 2011). Envisaged and intended to be useful, and to a large extent they are indeed, these technology characteristics, when taken to the extreme, can cause conditions that IT users perceive as stressful.

The literature has revealed different tech-nostress-creating conditions (see Tarafdar et al., 2019). Many of these conditions are particularly relevant for virtual work. For example, techno-invasion embodies the invasive effect of IT in situations where employees can be reached anytime and any-where. Particularly in the case of virtual work, because there are no physical interac-tions during the usual nine-to-five workday, employees may feel the need to be constantly 'online', either checking email or reporting their presence on applications such as Teams. While the upside of this may be that manag-ers perceive them as active and responsive, the downside is constant tethering to work. Indeed, the overwhelming feeling associ-ated with techno-invasion is that IT pervades every aspect of work life, and since work life is constantly accessible through IT, it is easy to get to a situation where the workday never ends (Eurofound and the International Labour Office, 2017). The individual faces the demand from IT use of always being con-nected to work, and feels invaded.

A second salient technostress-creating con-dition for virtual work is techno-overload. Simply put, IT forces the pace of work. In virtual work, given the lack of a physical cut-off of meetings and interactions, work-related information is electronically generated and keeps coming at employees almost non-stop. In contrast to face-to-face interactions that are bound by the physical limitations of speech

and eye contact, information generated elec-tronically can be done at a much greater pace because one does not have to react to such cues, especially for asynchronous interac-tions. Co-workers can engage in quick virtual interactions and response, such as answering emails and text messages quickly and in real time, leading to relentless and rapid back and forth of work-related communication and a corresponding increase in the pace of work. Further, analysing social cues is difficult in video-conferencing and places additional cog-nitive burden on the individual, who has to do more work just to understand what the other person is actually saying or thinking. A recent article (Jacobs, 2020) sums it up well: 'You are trying to see how everyone's reacting … You dart your eyes across the screen to see how engaged they are. When people are joining calls they are probably still emailing. I leave a call and think, "Oh gosh, did I get my point across, did I lose that person?"' Worse, even with all the synchronous video-conferencing, asynchronous demands do not reduce; there is always the next file to read and the next email to answer before calling it a day. Email over-load (Dabbish and Kraut, 2006), information overload and communication overload (Hemp 2009) are fallouts of techno-overload.

Another IT-related stress creator for vir-tual work is techno-complexity. It is simply a fact of virtual work that IT users have to understand and learn about the features of the applications. Not doing so adversely impacts their ability to get the job done. They are forced to spend time and effort in figur-ing out how to use various functions, espe-cially if their colleagues are using them. For example, while most people use applications such as Teams for virtual meetings, not many use them for file sharing, where use of email is more prevalent. If one is in a committee where other members prefer to share files using Teams, one may feel compelled to do the same, and feel inadequate if they did not. This sort of hidden work is never accounted for in the employee's regular work tasks. It places the demand on the employee to learn complex things that are not directly part of their actual work and which they do not get credit for in their performance evaluations. After all, a salesperson, for example, gets their raise based on the extent to which they fulfil their sales quota, and not on how well they can use customer relationship management applications for tracking customers. And yet they have to learn the features of such applications in order to do their work. Such activities place a demand on employees to deal with complexity borne out of the use of IT which adversely affects their performance (Tarafdar et al., 2015).

To make matters even worse, enterprise applications keep changing as organizations buy new software and upgrade existing versions. Therefore, just using the technology itself can be unsettling because users have to be on the alert for installing and updating applications, especially security-related patches and upgrades. As a result, they experience what is known as techno-uncertainty. Timely response and support from the IT help desk (which is also IT-mediated as one has to fill out online forms!) is not always a given. Indeed, one of the most stressful aspects of IT use in virtual work is the threat that comes from not ensuring that the software one is using is up-to-date; not doing so can lead to lack of compliance and policy violation.

Who Is More Prone to Technostress from Virtual Work?

While there is not much empirical research on who may be more susceptible to technostress, we do know that certain personality and individual characteristics can influence the extent to which employees experience technostress. One important factor here is personality (Srivastava et al., 2015). Individuals with obsessive compulsive personalities or neurotic dispositions have a tendency to perceive difficult situations as threatening (Spector et al., 2000). Such individuals may perceive the reliability and constant availability of technology as presenting requirements to be available for work round the clock, feel insecure about missing out on important matters if they are not, and be disturbed by the blurring of boundaries between work and home. Another important factor to be considered is the individual's technology self-efficacy (Compeau and Higgins, 1995), that is, the extent to which the individual thinks he or she is capable of using IT. Those with a high technology self-efficacy can have a negative influence on the extent to which the individual experiences negative effects from the presence of technostress-creating conditions (Tarafdar et al., 2015). Indeed, people with low self-efficacy are more likely to feel threatened when faced with greater job demands in terms of higher workload and need for responsiveness (Schaubroeck and Merritt, 1997). Low technology self-efficacy can reduce the individual's confidence in dealing with IT. Is it possible to find a sweet spot where the individual can harness the capabilities of technology and at the same time not be stressed by them? One way to reduce the extent to which the individual experiences technology-related stress is to bring about a fit between their own needs and their environment. Research shows that in the case of use of email applications, for example, individuals who perceive a greater fit between the extent of email use they want to engage in and are actually engaged in experience a lower extent of work-related stress (Stich et al., 2019b).

Can Organizations Make It Better or Worse?

Technostress can lead to a plethora of negative outcomes detrimental to both the individual and the organization (Tarafdar et al., 2019). Job-related negative outcomes include low job satisfaction, task performance, innovation and organizational commitment, and high turnover intentions, role overload, role conflict and job-related anxiety

(Ragu-Nathan et al., 2008; Sprigg and Jackson, 2006; Tarafdar et al., 2007). Negative wellbeing-related outcomes include exhaustion, burnout and strain (Ayyagari et al., 2011; Barber and Santuzzi, 2015; Barley et al., 2011; Reinke and Chamorro-Premuzic, 2014). Moreover, individuals who experience technostress are frustrated with many aspects of IT use, and are often unwilling or reluctant to comply with security requirements (D'Arcy et al., 2014).

What can organizations do to help? Employees working virtually find it easy to be available outside of work hours and/or respond immediately to work communication coming through email, chat messages on applications such as Slack, or postings coming through on social networking applications (Barber and Santuzzi, 2015). Very often, and in the absence of clear organizational expectations and guidelines, they *do* make themselves available and *do* respond immediately, even if they experience, for example, techno-invasion. It is necessary that organizations frame explicit guidelines for technology use. Such guidelines should have a dual objective – to help employees take advantage of the capabilities of IT and at the same time to avoid technostress. For example, recognizing the flexibility that is possible from virtual work, such policies can encourage employees to shape their own work patterns and at the same time adjust to their colleagues' work patterns. In our experience, this is not always the case and organizations are not proactive enough about developing such guidelines. Increasingly, users are taking matters into their own hands and shaping their own responses. The first author cites an example from a colleague's email signature – 'Please note that whilst I may choose to correspond by email during evenings and weekends as it fits best with my preferred working pattern, I do not expect responses during these times'. Here, this individual is sending a clear message about their expectations to co-workers. Similarly, individuals can also frame strategies for answering emails, for example, stating that they will not answer emails during specific times, as a work practice. Research also shows that organizational conditions that inhibit the negative effects of technostress creators include the presence of remote IT helpdesk support and technology manuals for employees to access (Ragu-Nathan et al., 2008). Ironically enough, IT itself can help employees cope. For example, email filters can route emails to specific folders automatically, thereby helping users manage the flow of incoming email (Soucek and Moser, 2010). Smartphones have apps (e.g., Google's Digital Wellbeing app[2]) that provide users with information about which apps they use and how frequently, with the aim of helping them develop habits for 'unplugging'. Individuals can thus leverage certain IT to make virtual work a less stressful experience.

Organizations can also do things to make it worse! For example, with virtual work exists the possibility of digital monitoring and surveillance, which can come in many forms – email and Internet use monitoring, application use monitoring and client interaction monitoring (Miller and Weckert, 2000; Stanton and Weiss, 2000). Indeed, many office communication application suites now provide dashboards of the employees' use of various applications such as email. Such monitoring can generate fears of job insecurity, loss of privacy and infringement of personal space (Zuboff, 2015), further aggravating the negative impacts of technostress. Coping with technostress is a matter of individual action and one size does not fit all (Tarafdar et al., forthcoming). Therefore, the other thing that organizations can do to make it worse is to mandate how IT 'should' be used, completely disregarding both the flexibility offered by IT and the individual's productive appropriation of its features. In this context, organizational policies that, for example, prohibit or limit the use of email during certain times of the day are less helpful than those that suggest to employees various ways of reducing email overload, leaving them to decide what works best for them.

CONCLUSION

So, where do we stand with regard to the effect of virtual work on organizational wellbeing? By changing the ways work is conducted, virtual work changes the experience of organizational wellbeing. Traditional work stressors such as relationships, work–life balance and workload are affected in adverse ways. The dependence on IT makes work relationships more difficult to maintain and work itself more difficult to contain, especially for employees who are less able to manage the interruptions, ambiguity and pervasiveness of computer-mediated communication. Employees may clearly appraise IT as the culprit of their work overload or work–life invasion, thereby making IT a stressor of its own. Having to use IT and cope with its complexity can also be a stressful experience by itself. Individual characteristics and organizational interventions can, however, help to cope with such work stressors. There are a number of ways of doing so, for instance by training users to help them gain confidence in using IT, or by developing organizational guidelines for IT use.

This book chapter has attempted to develop links between the literature on work stress and technostress, in the context of virtual work. To date, these two streams have been researched separately – in occupational psychology for the former and in information systems for the latter (Tarafdar et al., 2019). Our interdisciplinary approach suggests that they may be investigated together by distinguishing the impacts of technology-related stressors and work stressors on organizational wellbeing (Figure 11.1). Investigating them together opens up new avenues for future research and for enriched understanding of virtual work stress. On the one hand, the information systems discipline brings theoretical frameworks to bear on IT design, IT implementation, IT use and end user perceptions characteristics. On the other hand, occupational psychology brings theoretical frameworks on stress (e.g., transactional stress, person–environment fit) to interpret the effect of IT on organizational phenomena. Future research may try to combine these complementary literature strands to better explain the process of virtual work stress. Furthermore, we note that some aspects of virtual work stress remain currently understudied. Coping mechanisms have rarely been examined in the context of virtual work. Although technostress has been researched in various contexts such as social networks (Tarafdar et al., 2020) or corporate IT (Tarafdar et al., 2007), it has not been researched in the contexts of virtual teams and telecommuting, which are important virtual work arrangements. Finally, research is only starting to investigate the positive challenges and outcomes that can be associated with virtual work in the form of techno eustress (Tarafdar et al., 2019) and its associated effects on organizational wellbeing.

Virtual work brings much to organizations and individuals in terms of productivity (Stich et al., 2015) and worldwide connectivity (Raghuram et al., 2019). It is largely desired and well-received among organizations and individuals alike. It is therefore important to understand and tackle its negative influence on organizational wellbeing to leverage the benefits. We suggest that it is necessary to take stock of its limitations and research ways to address and mitigate its stressful aspects.

Notes

1 Added by authors.
2 https://wellbeing.google/

REFERENCES

Ayyagari, R., Grover, V. and Purvis, R. (2011), 'Technostress: Technological antecedents and implications', *MIS Quarterly*, Vol. 35 No. 4, pp. 831–858.

Barber, L.K. and Santuzzi, A.M. (2015), 'Please respond ASAP: Workplace telepressure and employee recovery', *Journal of Occupational Health Psychology*, Vol. 20 No. 2, pp. 172–189.

Barley, S.R., Meyerson, D.E. and Grodal, S. (2011), 'E-mail as a source and symbol of stress', *Organization Science*, Vol. 22 No. 4, pp. 887–906.

Baruch, Y. (2005), 'Bullying on the net: Adverse behavior on e-mail and its impact', *Information & Management*, Vol. 42 No. 2, pp. 361–371.

Bayazit, Z. E. and Bayazit, M. (2017). How do flexible work arrangements alleviate work-family-conflict? The roles of flexibility i-deals and family-supportive cultures. *The International Journal of Human Resource Management*, Vol. 30 No. 3, pp. 400–435. https://doi.org/10.1080/09585192.2017.1278615

Boswell, W.R. and Olson-Buchanan, J.B. (2007), 'The use of communication technologies after hours: The role of work attitudes and work-life conflict', *Journal of Management*, Vol. 33 No. 4, pp. 592–610.

Brown, R., Duck, J. and Jimmieson, N. (2014), 'E-mail in the workplace: The role of stress appraisals and normative response pressure in the relationship between e-mail stressors and employee strain', *International Journal of Stress Management*, Vol. 21 No. 4, pp. 325–347.

Byron, K. (2008), 'Carrying too heavy a load? The communication and miscommunication of emotion by email', *Academy of Management Review*, Vol. 33 No. 2, pp. 309–327.

Compeau, D.R. and Higgins, C.A. (1995), 'Computer self-efficacy: Development of a measure and initial test', *MIS Quarterly*, Vol. 19 No. 2, pp. 189–211.

Cooper, C.D. and Kurland, N.B. (2002), 'Telecommuting, professional isolation, and employee development in public and private organizations', *Journal of Organizational Behavior*, Vol. 23 No. 4, pp. 511–532.

Cooper, C.L., Dewe, P.J. and O'Driscoll, M.P. (2001), *Organizational Stress: A Review and Critique of Theory, Research, and Applications*, Sage, Thousand Oaks, CA.

Coyne, I., Farley, S., Axtell, C., Sprigg, C., Best, L. and Kwok, O. (2017), 'Understanding the relationship between experiencing workplace cyberbullying, employee mental strain and job satisfaction: A dysempowerment approach', *The International Journal of Human Resource Management*, Vol. 28 No. 7, pp. 945–972.

Dabbish, L.A. and Kraut, R.E. (2006), 'Email overload at work: An analysis of factors associated with email strain', *Proceedings of the 2006 20th Anniversary Conference on Computer Supported Cooperative Work*, ACM, Banff, Alberta, Canada, pp. 431–440.

D'Arcy, J., Herath, T. and Shoss, M.K. (2014), 'Understanding employee responses to stressful information security requirements: A coping perspective', *Journal of Management Information Systems*, Vol. 31 No. 2, pp. 285–318.

Delanoeije, J., Verbruggen, M. and Germeys, L. (2019). Boundary role transitions: A day-to-day approach to explain the effects of home-based telework on work-to-home conflict and home-to-work conflict. *Human Relations*, Vol. 72 No. 12, pp. 1843–1868. https://doi.org/10.1177/0018726718823071

Derks, D., van Duin, D., Tims, M. and Bakker, A.B. (2015), 'Smartphone use and work–home interference: The moderating role of social norms and employee work engagement', *Journal of Occupational and Organizational Psychology*, Vol. 88 No. 1, pp. 155–177.

Dombey, D. and Hall, B. (2020), 'Life after lockdown: Welcome to the empty-chair economy', *Financial Times*, 1 May, available at: https://www.ft.com/content/0d86289a-8b96-11ea-a01c-a28a3e3fbd33 (accessed 13 June 2020).

Eurofound and the International Labour Office. (2017), *Working Anytime, Anywhere: The Effects on the World of Work*, Publications Office of the European Union, Luxembourg, and the International Labour Office, Geneva.

Faragher, E.B., Cooper, C.L. and Cartwright, S. (2004), 'A shortened stress evaluation tool (ASSET)', *Stress and Health*, Vol. 20 No. 4, pp. 189–201.

Farley, S., Coyne, I., Axtell, C. and Sprigg, C. (2016), 'Design, development and validation of a workplace cyberbullying measure, the WCM', *Work & Stress*, Vol. 30 No. 4, pp. 293–317.

Fonner, K.L. and Roloff, M.E. (2010), 'Why teleworkers are more satisfied with their jobs than are office-based workers: When less contact is beneficial', *Journal of Applied Communication Research*, Vol. 38 No. 4, pp. 336–361.

Fosslien, L. and Duffy, M.W. (2020), 'How to combat Zoom fatigue', *Harvard Business Review*, 29 April, available at: https://hbr.org/2020/04/how-to-combat-zoom-fatigue (accessed 13 June 2020).

Friedman, R.A. and Currall, S.C. (2003), 'Conflict escalation: Dispute exacerbating elements of e-mail communication', *Human Relations*, Vol. 56 No. 11, pp. 1325–1347.

Gadeyne, N., Verbruggen, M., Delanoeije, J. and De Cooman, R. (2018), 'All wired, all tired? Work-related ICT-use outside work hours and work-to-home conflict: The role of integration preference, integration norms and work demands', *Journal of Vocational Behavior*, Vol. 107, pp. 86–99.

Golden, T.D. (2007), 'Co-workers who telework and the impact on those in the office: Understanding the implications of virtual work for co-worker satisfaction and turnover intentions', *Human Relations*, Vol. 60 No. 11, pp. 1641–1667.

Gupta, A. and Sharda, R. (2008), 'SIMONE: A Simulator for Interruptions and Message Overload in Network Environments', *International Journal of Simulation and Process Modelling*, Vol. 4 No. 3–4, pp. 237–247.

Hemp, P. (2009), 'Death by information overload', *Harvard Business Review*, Vol. 87 No. 9, pp. 83–89.

ter Hoeven, C.L., Zoonen, W. van and Fonner, K.L. (2016), 'The practical paradox of technology: The influence of communication technology use on employee burnout and engagement', *Communication Monographs*, Vol. 83 No. 2, pp. 239–263.

Jackson, T.W., Burgess, A. and Edwards, J. (2006), 'A simple approach to improving email communication', *Communications of the ACM*, Vol. 49 No. 6, pp. 107–109.

Jackson, T.W., Dawson, R. and Wilson, D. (2001), 'The cost of email interruption', *Journal of Systems and Information Technology*, Vol. 5 No. 1, pp. 81–92.

Jacobs, E. (2020), *'Paranoia creeps into home-working | Free to read'*, 18 June, available at: https://www.ft.com/content/e50ce245-09fd-4831-a90b-953ef51a2281 (accessed 19 June 2020).

Kakabadse, N., Porter, G. and Vance, D. (2007), 'Addicted to technology', *Business Strategy Review*, Vol. 18 No. 4, pp. 81–85.

Kalman, Y.M. and Ravid, G. (2015), 'Filing, piling, and everything in between: The dynamics of E-mail inbox management', *Journal of the Association for Information Science and Technology*, Vol. 66 No. 12, pp. 2540–2552.

Kruger, J., Epley, N., Parker, J. and Ng, Z.-W. (2005), 'Egocentrism over e-mail: Can we communicate as well as we think?', *Journal of Personality and Social Psychology*, Vol. 89 No. 6, pp. 925–936.

Lim, V.K.G. and Teo, T.S.H. (2009), 'Mind your e-manners: Impact of cyber incivility on employees' work attitude and behavior', *Information & Management*, Vol. 46 No. 8, pp. 419–425.

Mann, S. and Holdsworth, L. (2003), 'The psychological impact of teleworking: Stress, emotions and health', *New Technology, Work & Employment*, Vol. 18 No. 3, p. 196.

Mazmanian, M., Orlikowski, W.J. and Yates, J. (2013), 'The autonomy paradox: The implications of mobile email devices for knowledge professionals', *Organization Science*, Vol. 24 No. 5, pp. 1337–1357.

Miller, S. and Weckert, J. (2000), 'Privacy, the workplace and the internet', *Journal of Business Ethics*, Vol. 28 No. 3, pp. 255–265.

Morris, S., Thomas, D. and Edgecliffe-Johnson, A. (2020), 'The end of the office? Coronavirus may change work forever', *Financial Times*, 1 May, available at: https://www.ft.com/content/1b304300-0756-4774-9263-c97958e0054d (accessed 13 June 2020).

Raghuram, S., Hill, N.S., Gibbs, J.L. and Maruping, L.M. (2019), 'Virtual work: Bridging research clusters', *Academy of Management Annals*, Vol. 13 No. 1, available at: https://doi.org/10.5465/annals.2017.0020.

Ragu-Nathan, T.S., Tarafdar, M., Ragu-Nathan, B.S. and Qiang Tu. (2008), 'The consequences of technostress for end users in organizations: Conceptual development and empirical validation', *Information Systems Research*, Vol. 19 No. 4, pp. 417–433.

Reinke, K. and Chamorro-Premuzic, T. (2014), 'When email use gets out of control: Understanding the relationship between personality and email overload and their impact on burnout and work engagement', *Computers in Human Behavior*, Vol. 36, pp. 502–509.

Renaud, K., Ramsay, J. and Hair, M. (2006), '"You've got e-mail!" … Shall I deal with it now? Electronic mail from the recipient's perspective', *International Journal of Human-Computer Interaction*, Vol. 21 No. 3, pp. 313–332.

Rockmann, K.W. and Pratt, M.G. (2015), 'Contagious offsite work and the lonely office: The unintended consequences of distributed work', *Academy of Management Discoveries*, Vol. 1 No. 2, pp. 150–164.

Samuel, H. (2018), 'British firm ordered to pay €60,000 by French court for breaching employee's "right to disconnect' from work"', *The Telegraph*, 1 August, available at: https://www.telegraph.co.uk/news/2018/08/01/british-firm-ordered-pay-60000-french-court-breaching-employees/ (accessed 29 January 2019).

Schaubroeck, J. and Merritt, D.E. (1997), 'Divergent effects of job control on coping with work stressors: The key role of self-efficacy', *Academy of Management Journal*, Vol. 40 No. 3, pp. 738–754.

Soucek, R. and Moser, K. (2010), 'Coping with information overload in email communication: Evaluation of a training intervention', *Computers in Human Behavior*, Vol. 26 No. 6, pp. 1458–1466.

Spector, P.E., Zapf, D., Chen, P.Y., Frese, M. and others. (2000), 'Why negative affectivity should not be controlled in job stress research: Don't throw out the baby with the bath water', *Journal of Organizational Behavior*, Vol. 21 No. 1, pp. 79–95.

Sprigg, C.A. and Jackson, P.R. (2006), 'Call centers as lean service environments: Job-related strain and the mediating role of work design', *Journal of Occupational Health Psychology*, Vol. 11 No. 2, pp. 197–212.

Srivastava, S.C., Chandra, S. and Shirish, A. (2015), 'Technostress creators and job outcomes: Theorising the moderating influence of personality traits', *Information Systems Journal*, Vol. 25 No. 4, pp. 355–401.

Stanton, J.M. and Weiss, E.M. (2000), 'Electronic monitoring in their own words: An exploratory study of employees' experiences with new types of surveillance', *Computers in Human Behavior*, Vol. 16 No. 4, pp. 423–440.

This is an academic article. Please change the reference to:

Stich, J.-F. (2020). A Review of Workplace Stress in the Virtual Office. *Intelligent Buildings International*, Vol. 12 No. 3, pp. 208–2020.

Stich, J.-F., Farley, S., Cooper, C.L. and Tarafdar, M. (2015), 'Information and communication technology demands: Outcomes and interventions', *Journal of Organizational Effectiveness: People and Performance*, Vol. 2 No. 4, pp. 327–345.

Stich, J.-F., Tarafdar, M., Cooper, C.L. and Stacey, P. (2017), 'Workplace stress from actual and desired computer-*mediated* communication use: A multi-method study', *New Technology, Work and Employment*, Vol. 32 No. 1, pp. 84–100.

Stich, J.-F., Tarafdar, M., Stacey, P. and Cooper, C.L. (2019a), 'E-mail load, workload stress and desired e-mail load: A cybernetic approach', *Information Technology & People*, Vol. 32 No. 2, pp. 430–452.

Stich, J.-F., Tarafdar, M., Stacey, P.K. and Cooper, C.L. (2019b), 'Appraisal of email use as a source of workplace stress: A person-environment fit approach', *Journal of the Association for Information Systems*, Vol. 20 No. 2, pp. 132–160.

Sumecki, D., Chipulu, M. and Ojiako, U. (2011), 'Email overload: Exploring the moderating role of the perception of email as a "business critical" tool', *International Journal of Information Management*, Vol. 31 No. 5, pp. 407–414.

Sutherland, V. J. and Cooper, C. L. (2000). *Strategic stress management: An organizational approach*. UK: Palgrave Macmillan.

Tarafdar, M., Cooper, C.L. and Stich, J.-F. (2019), 'The technostress trifecta – techno eustress, techno distress and design: An agenda for research', *Information Systems Journal*, Vol. 29 No. 1, pp. 6–42.

Tarafdar, M., Maier, C., Laumer, S. and Weitzel, T. (2020), 'Explaining the link between technostress and technology addiction for social networking sites: A study of distraction as a coping behavior', *Information Systems Journal*, Vol. 30 No. 1, pp. 96–124.

Tarafdar, M., Pirkkalainen, H., Salo, M. and Makkonen, M. (2020). Taking on the Dark Side – Coping with Technostress. *IT Professional*, Vol. 22, pp. 82–89.

Tarafdar, M., Pullins, E. B. and Ragu-Nathan, T. S. (2015). Technostress: negative effect on performance and possible mitigations. *Information Systems Journal*, Vol. 25 No. 2, pp.103–132.

Tarafdar, M., Qiang T., Ragu-Nathan, B.S. and Ragu-Nathan, T.S. (2007), 'The impact of technostress on role stress and productivity', *Journal of Management Information Systems*, Vol. 24 No. 1, pp. 301–328.

Turnage, A.K. (2007), 'Email flaming behaviors and organizational conflict', *Journal of Computer-Mediated Communication*, Vol. 13 No. 1, pp. 43–59.

Van Solingen, R., Berghout, E. and Van Latum, F. (1998), 'Interrupts: Just a minute never is', *IEEE Software*, Vol. 15 No. 5, pp. 97–103.

Wheatley, D. and Bickerton, C. (2016), 'Time-use and well-being impacts of travel-to-work and travel-for-work', *New Technology, Work and Employment*, Vol. 31 No. 3, pp. 238–254.

Windeler, J.B., Chudoba, K.M. and Sundrup, R.Z. (2017), 'Getting away from them all: Managing exhaustion from social interaction with telework', *Journal of Organizational Behavior*, Vol. 38 No. 7, pp. 977–995.

Yap, C.S. and Tng, H. (1990), 'Factors associated with attitudes towards telecommuting', *Information & Management*, Vol. 19 No. 4, pp. 227–235.

Zuboff, S. (2015), 'Big other: Surveillance capitalism and the prospects of an information civilization', *Journal of Information Technology*, Vol. 30 No. 1, pp. 75–89.

Intentions behind the Use of Social Network Sites and their Association with Employees' Job Performance and Wellbeing

Haziq Mehmood and Oi-ling Siu

INTRODUCTION

Social networking is a prevalent and vital feature of the present era. The use of social network sites (SNSs) is increasing with every passing day and has become an essential and salient feature in our societies. Modern-day people use SNSs as a mode of communication. People have many reasons to use SNSs, including communication, entertainment, and emotional support. This trend is more common among youth and emerging adults because new technologies are convenient and trendy. SNSs have proved to be beneficial; however, they have been showing many unhealthy impacts on human lives. In this regard, many researchers have described the positive and negative consequences of SNSs that might affect individuals' work (i.e., work performance) or health (i.e., addiction).

Many researchers have studied individuals' time spent on SNSs per day. Participants responded that they spend 10 to 60 minutes

daily on Facebook. Similarly, according to a study by Pempek et al. (2009), participants use SNSs for an average of 27.93 minutes per day on weekdays and 28.44 minutes per day on holidays. Likewise, a study reported that students use SNSs for 175.4 minutes daily (Olufadi, 2016). The use of SNSs has increased with the passage of time to become an essential part of everyone's life. The number of social media users has been increasing in recent years, and it has become part of routine life. SNSs change patterns of using the internet and disseminating information, expression, and socialization. In comparison to the different types of social media, SNSs have gained particular attention due to the way they change modes of interpersonal relationships.

According to Boyd and Ellison (2007), SNS is 'a web-based facility in which a user develops a public or semi-public profile within the system, communicates with the other users and shares a common connection to view others in the same system'. In recent studies, social media has been defined as an 'internet-based form of interaction and communication channel, and arising from user-generated content'. This means that social media is any form of computer-mediated communication in which users not only set their profile but also have the chance to see others' content and interact with users. Ellison and Boyd (2013) define social media as

> A networked communication platform in which participants have uniquely identifiable profiles that consist of user-supplied content, content provided by other users, and system-provided data, users can publicly articulate connections that can be viewed and traversed by others and can consume, produce, and interact with streams of user-generated content provided by their connections on the site. (Ellison and Boyd, 2013)

SNSs generally entail the creation and maintenance of online relationships, both personal and professional, via various platforms.

Researchers use the term social *network* sites rather than social *networking* sites. The term *networking* suggests that it is for initiation of the relationship between strangers, as if that is the primary practice on SNSs. SNSs are unique in this case. Users not only initiate new relationships but, frequently, they focus more on latent ties with individuals already known offline (Haythornthwaite, 2005). Their visibility on SNSs depends on the platform and the user's instructions of how much information to show. Default profiles on some sites are visible to everyone, whereas, on some sites, users choose settings according to their choice and use.

SNSs are not merely a trend but have become a habit of every person's life. Long-term internet use affects people's behaviour. There are some factors that are identified as relevant to using SNSs, such as social consciousness, getting attention and avoiding loneliness, feelings of connectedness by acquiring entertainment, freedom of opinion, and extending social relationships. Most studies in this context have measured intensity of use, privacy factors, personality traits, gender, age, and self-presentation (Waheed et al., 2017).

In addition, the repetition of visits, and time spent, of SNSs are similar determinants of users. The frequency of SNS use depends on the company and interest related to sharing information. Moreover, it can also depend on attention-seeking behaviours. SNSs take much time and attention from an individual. They make one lose track of time. They help in bonding and staying connected with others (e.g., companions, family, and friends), creating and keeping up new ties. Moreover, they help a person to be part of a group of friends and to feel an essential piece of a community (Waheed et al., 2017).

Employees use SNSs to maintain relationships; pass time; seek information, convenience, and entertainment; carry out social investigation; and update their status (Joinson, 2008). SNSs also help users to keep in touch with old friends and make new friends. There are some additional uses, such as knowing about events, organizing social events, sharing personal information, and feeling connectedness (Raacke and Bonds-Raacke, 2008).

Many professionals focus more on utilitarian values as compared to hedonic values. The information present on SNSs is the same for all users, but it depends on the user's perception of how they are taking benefit from that information. In an employee's case, it might be different, and they may focus less on pleasure-related activities like entertainment (Lin et al., 2014).

Studies have investigated how different cultures' users of SNSs differ in their behaviours. A culture influences an individual's level of comfort concerning how perfectly they fit into specific organizations. Additionally, cultural differences in the use of SNSs have also been determined by age and gender (Blomfield et al., 2014). Researchers demonstrated that males tend to use SNSs for entertainment. In contrast, females tend to use SNSs to engage them, impress others with pictures and posts, and also remain in connection with others (McAndrew and Jeong, 2012; Wang et al., 2014).

MOTIVATION TO USE SNSs

Previous literature has outlined various motivations for individuals to use Facebook. Alhabash et al. (2014) conducted a study on the motivation behind the use of Facebook among Taiwanese users. They figured out seven reasons: socialization, entertainment, information sharing, escapism, self-documentation, medium appeal, and self-expression. Another study identified the motivation among university students for using other prominent SNSs like Facebook, Twitter, and Instagram. They found that students use SNSs for social interaction, entertainment, passing time, self-documentation, and because they are convenient to use (Alhabash and Ma, 2017).

Researchers Lampe et al. (2006) demonstrated that people use SNSs to get information about others. People maintain relationships with others by connecting with them, and it also fulfils their need to belong.

Joinson's (2008) study with college students identified seven motivations for using Facebook. Participants reported that they use SNSs for social connections, photographs to share their identities, content, social networking surfing, social investigation, and to share their feelings in the form of status updates. The author also identified that younger users are more attracted to the entertainment feature and passing the time on SNSs in comparison to older users.

Similarly, Whiting and Williams' (2013) qualitative study explored users' intentions in using social media and identified 10 factors. A total of 25 in-depth interviews with people aged between 18 and 56 years were conducted. The researchers found that users most often use social media for social information and information seeking (88% of users). The second highest factor was passing the time (76% of users). Participants reported using social media for entertainment (64%), relaxation (60%), and for communicating and expressing their opinions (56%; Whiting and Williams, 2013). Whiting and Williams' (2013) study found that social media is also used for convenience (52%), information sharing (40%), and surveillance/watching others (20%).

Motivation is divided into two forms: extrinsic and intrinsic. Extrinsic motivation is perceived as helpfulness in achieving some reward external to oneself such as increasing performance, while intrinsic motivation is related to implicitly rewarding tasks. Researchers found that these motivations are present in information technology systems as usefulness and enjoyment (Davis et al., 1992). These motivations affect the individual's perception of using information technology. Individuals were willing to use SNSs because they offer interactions with friends and peers. They provided a pleasure-oriented platform by enhancing fun factors for individuals like posting photos and watching films (Sledgianowski and Kulviwat, 2009). SNS users get constant attention from other users. Compliments and feedback from friends and relatives are a source of reinforcement for users, which increases their participation in SNSs.

Employees' intention to use SNSs plays a vital role in determining the job performance of the employees and this relationship is mediated by wellbeing. Adding to this, being social animals, humans naturally strive for affiliation and association with other beings and lack of association affects them socially.

Pai and Arnott (2013) have examined users' adoption of SNSs in the context of Facebook, focusing on a means-end approach. They have explained the consequences and values by drawing a hierarchical value map and argued that a need for belonging is fulfilled by using SNSs. The best feature of SNSs is that they provide instant responses on uploading pictures and playing interactive games, which provide an opportunity to meet with friends and remain in contact. When a user is browsing Facebook pages or visiting groups already created on SNSs, these features help users to gain new thoughts and get feedback from others. It is an excellent way to learn and to brainstorm about various issues. People use these platforms to find discussion groups or pages according to their interests, or become involved in gossip. People use SNSs mostly for interaction and communication. They can also be used for business and learning. SNSs like Facebook and Instagram are used for marketing, event planning, and making strong connections with friends.

Researchers have identified the factors that are involved in the motivation and continuance of using SNSs for information. The primary and basic features of SNSs are that their integrity has increased over the years as a reliable source of information and they have opened up space where users can interact with audiences (Ku et al., 2013). People can obtain useful information from SNSs, which may help them to learn innovative information inexpensively. The second factor is 'entertainment', as SNSs are in reality contending to give the most captivating conversation and quality pleasure to their users and provide an opportunity to relax after a busy day (Ku et al., 2013). The third is 'fashion', as people get innovative ideas about style and trends by staying in touch with others (Ku et al., 2013). The fourth factor is 'sociability', in the sense that SNSs utilize distinctive ways to generate friendliness among their users. Ku et al.'s (2013) last factor is 'relationship maintenance', in which the user maintains relationships with people (e.g., family, friends), including those who live long distances apart. This facilitates regular and ongoing contact with others, makes interactions easy, and can improve relationships. Relationship maintenance and entertainment are primary factors, and fashion is a less critical factor (Ku et al., 2013).

In sum, SNSs provide a variety of features to the users, who, according to their needs and interests, individually choose the sites. There are some SNSs platform-specific to the young generation which mainly provide entertainment. In the case of employees, some sites are particularly for professionals, who use them for knowledge, professional help, and information about future prospects. These characteristics of SNSs motivate employees to continue to use SNSs.

WORK PERFORMANCE AND SNSs

Humans need to interact socially with people either in virtual reality or in reality. It has been observed as a human psychological phenomenon that interaction makes one feel fulfilled. Nowadays, the leading source of human contact is social media. SNSs are easily accessible sources of human contact but are associated with several problems (i.e., excessive usage of SNSs in the workplace, resulting in de-productivity of performance; Kelleher and Sweetser, 2012).

While some researchers argue that the use of SNSs wastes time, others consider SNS use as a principal component to productivity/ improvement in job performance. Concerns mainly centre around the struggle to maintain equilibrium between workload demands (Bradley et al., 2013). Furthermore, research trends have been moving toward increasing exploration of workers' job performance, while the use of SNSs has increased in offices. A study of Lee and Lee (2018) examined the impact of an SNS (i.e., Facebook) on job performance among office workers in South Korea. It also aimed to explore the moderating effects of the task's characteristics. However, the results demonstrated that SNS use (i.e., Facebook) had a significant positive effect on job performance for work purposes. In addition, task interdependence had non-significant positive effects on work performance and exhibited a negative moderation between the impact of SNSs and work performance.

Another study was conducted based on media synchronicity (Wang et al., 2016) which explored social capital theories and the influence of SNSs on employees' work performance. Data were collected from 379 Chinese professionals. The study results revealed that if SNSs could be used to facilitate knowledge transfer, then they could promote work performance (Wang et al., 2016).

Furthermore, a study conducted by Charoensukmongkol (2014) explored employees' ways of perceiving work-related tasks, supervisors' and coworkers' support, and workload/job-related demands, to ultimately examine their associations with SNS use in the workplace. Likewise, it also included analyses of the relationship between job performance and job satisfaction, followed by several significant impacts of SNSs at work. Snowball sampling was used to collect data with 170 employees in Thailand to investigate the study's variables and their relationship with SNS use during office hours. Statistical analyses revealed that colleagues' support and workload or job-related demands had significant positive associations with intensity of SNS use. Moreover, it was also identified that there was a positive relationship between job performance and SNS use in the workplace.

Several empirical studies have identified that SNS use negatively impacts employees' performance. Brooks (2015) found in his study that the excessive use of SNSs during work hours affected attention and performance and led toward negative consequences.

A web-based cross-sectional survey comprising 11,018 employees investigated the significance of the link between the use of SNSs during working hours and self-reported work performance on personal purposes The result of the study concluded that the use of SNSs had a negative effect on work performance, although this effect was minor. The researchers suggested that this minor effect was possible due to the self-report performance measure (Andreassen et al., 2014).

Syrek et al. (2018) conducted a study to examine non-work social media use during office hours in the context of work engagement. A total of 334 white-collar employees participated in the study, with an average age of 33.8 years. The results of the study suggested that using social media for non-work use is very common among white-collar employees, and they spend an average of 39 minutes per day on non-work related social media. Employees who used social media excessively throughout the day had lower work engagement. The researchers

concluded that employees who use social media more have lower work motivation and performance.

The relationship between job performance and use of SNSs has two dimensions: in some contexts, SNS use affects the employees' performance and causes distractions. However, the literature also supports the positive side of SNSs in that they can facilitate the employee's performance and their effect depends on the type of use. The employee's perception toward SNSs, their motivation, and the basis on which they are using them are important factors in explaining this relationship.

PSYCHOLOGICAL WELLBEING AND SNSs

Wellbeing is not just avoidance from getting sick physically, but also includes the health of an employee at social, physical, biological, and mental levels. An employee who has good wellbeing performs duties more efficiently and productively than employees with poor wellbeing. The ubiquitous way in which people interact in routine life with one another on SNSs is actually a pillar of wellbeing. A person's feelings, moment-to-moment experiences, and the satisfaction they feel with their lives are unique to each individual.

A study conducted by Choi and Lim (2016) observed the impact of social and information technology excesses on psychological wellbeing, followed by the excessive use of SNSs as a mediator. They conducted a study with a sample size of 419 employees aged between 20 and 40 years. The results revealed that excessive social and information technology use did not have a direct effect on psychological wellbeing, despite the excessive use of SNSs as a mediator among these variables.

Koch et al. (2012) conducted a study to find out the positivity effects of internal social networking systems in US financial organizations. They used boundary theory and the theory of positive emotions. The results of the study revealed blurred boundaries between work life and social life. This boundary increases positive emotions among employees who use their organizations' internal social networking systems. In comparison, employee non-users working at the level of middle management experience isolation, anger, and frustration. The study also concluded that the use of a social networking system decreases turnover but improves employee morale.

Different types of internet use influence relationships between the user and social and psychological outcomes. Solitary forms of internet use (e.g., surfing) appear to have no positive effect on social connectedness and wellbeing, while communication with existing friends may have a positive effect on social connectedness and wellbeing (Valkenburg and Peter, 2009).

The relationship between SNS use and its outcomes may also depend on the type of SNS use. There are at least two broad types of SNSs in terms of their primary function for users. The social communication type includes wall postings and exchanging comments, while the entertainment function includes solitary games and listening to music. Valkenburg and Peter (2009) concluded that internet use, in general, has a positive effect on wellbeing when it is used for interaction with existing friends.

Huang et al. (2010) reported that internet use is a positive predictor of psychological wellbeing when it is used for social communication, but is unrelated to psychological wellbeing when it is used for entertainment functions. Overall, previous research has indicated that it is essential to take account of the different functions of SNS use when making predictions about its effects on users' social and psychological wellbeing.

One study of Bonds-Raacke and Raacke (2010) focused on motivation for using Facebook, such as making new friends or connecting with old friends, in relation to psychological wellbeing. The results revealed a positive relationship between Facebook use and psychological wellbeing for users who aim to remain connected with family and friends. In contrast, Facebook use and psychological wellbeing were negatively related for users whose focus was to make new friends. The intensity of Facebook use was also negatively related with psychological wellbeing.

Verduyn et al. (2017) studied active and passive use of SNSs and found that participants who are actively engaged on SNSs exhibit a stronger positive link with subjective wellbeing in comparison to passive users. Passively using SNSs gives rise to social comparison and envy.

Some organizations such as Adidas have introduced policies related to SNS use. The primary purpose of these policies is to instruct employees on how to use social media during work hours. More specifically, they instruct employees to try to avoid excessive SNS use, be respectful when commenting on SNSs, and do not disclose private information on SNSs (Adidas, 2011). SNS use has both positive and negative links with employees' psychological wellbeing, but it also depends on users' perspectives and purposes.

To summarize, psychological wellbeing is dependent on many factors in connection with the use of SNSs. It depends on a person's attitude (i.e., whether SNSs are being used to stay in contact with old friends). Moreover, the intensity of using SNSs, frequency, and many similar factors need to be given importance in understanding the relationship.

THEORETICAL BACKGROUND

Many theoretical frameworks have been identified in the literature to explain individuals' use of SNSs. Ngai et al. (2015) divided the theories into three groups: personal behaviour theories, social behaviour theories, and mass communication theories.

An individual has a limited attention span which only grasps several messages at a time, in a constellation-type pattern. Moreover, only a few messages are selected, so only a few messages will impact an individual (Knobloch-Westerwick and Sarge, 2015). Over the previous six decades, it has been found by researchers that individuals do not pay attention randomly; rather, they attend to specific media and messages that meet their particular psychosocial needs and beliefs (Katz and Lazarsfeld, 1955).

In the 1940s, a paradigm emerged that aimed to explore 'what people do with the media' or 'what media do to people' (Katz, 1959: 2). Under this new paradigm, many early studies showed that media use is an outcome, meaning that exposure processes were only given scant attention. In contrast, the selectivity paradigm gained importance in the early 1950s and became a vital element of media effects theories. In 1940, a selectivity paradigm was found, which had two theoretical perspectives: uses and gratifications theory (Katz et al., 1973;) and selective exposure theory (Knobloch-Westerwick and Sarge, 2015).

According to uses and gratifications theory (Katz et al., 1974), people are active users of social media. They use social media according to their needs. The media gratifies the individual's needs differently. Katz et al. (1973) identified different needs from the social and psychological viewpoint and then classified these needs into five categories: emotional, cognitive, habitual, personal integrative and social integrative needs. Emotional needs are "needs related to strengthening aesthetic, pleasurable, and emotional experience" (Katz et al., 1973, p. 166). Cognitive needs are "related to strengthening information, knowledge, and understanding. Habitual needs can be thought of as ritualized media use driven by needs such as background noise. Personal integrative needs are needs in which people update their status or possibly post an image using social media to advertise their lifestyles. SNSs provide opportunities for people to manage these

needs. Social integrative needs are those in which people remain in contact with their family members.

Zillmann (2000) observed that media use is actually the originator of consequences, and that selective exposure theory is also affected by media. There is a significant distinction between the two perspectives. The uses and gratifications theory claims that media users act as individuals with rational and enlightened minds and the ability to choose; however, selective exposure theory suggests that media users are unaware of their selection intentions. The uses and gratifications theory used self-reports to observe media use behaviours and the selective exposure theory used discrete observational methods (Knobloch-Westerwick and Sarge, 2015).

The aforementioned theories explained that media use is an arbitrator between the precursors and consequences of media effects. The implication of this indicated that those who can choose their media can partially shape the effects of media upon them. Later, in research, it was found that three factors were essential influencers of selective media use: dispositional, developmental, and social context (Valkenburg et al., 2016).

The users' temperament, personality, gender, motivation, and mood are included in the dispositional factors. People typically avoid information on social media that causes discomfort and is incompatible with their existing knowledge. This idea is derived from the cognitive dissonance theory by Festinger (1962) and explains why users focus on those platforms of social media which give them information related to their beliefs and do not cause any discomfort and dissonance. There are many types of evidence showing that users focus on pleasant information. Selecting specific media to use is not only caused by cognitive dissonance; there are many other factors responsible (Donsbach, 2009).

In developmental factors, people prefer specific media according to their age. In this case, if viewers come across irrelevant media content, then they would pay less attention to it or avoid it altogether. In this context, researchers have found that toddlers are most fascinated by media shows with slow motion and relatable frameworks, and do not appear concerned about character details. Preschool children tend to prefer a faster pace, adventurous themes, and well-defined characters. Adolescents, keen users of social media, always like entertainment which has humour, mocking, or unexpected events (Valkenburg and Peter, 2013). Age-related factors are more significant between younger, middle-aged, and older adults. Younger people are more inclined to choose arousing, uplifting, frightening, and violent content as compared to adults who prefer meaningful media content (Mares et al., 2008; Mares and Sun, 2010).

Social contextual aspects have different boundaries to using media on different levels (i.e., micro-, meso-, and macro-level approaches). This occurs in situations where parents, educational institutions, and organizations limit or restrict media use (Nathanson, 2001).

There are many theories and models to explain the intentions behind the use of technology. These frameworks are related to explaining the individual's intentions in using social media. They also explain the different types of social media based on several factors; namely, perceived ease of use, perceived usefulness, subjective norms, and facilitating conditions.

The technology acceptance model (TAM) (Davis, 1985) is relevant to explain people's use of SNSs. This model has two versions: the theory of reasoned action (TRA) and the theory of planned behaviour (TPB). The TRA is based on explaining the individual's behaviour by intention and focusing on one's attitudes toward the behaviour and subjective norms. The TAM breaks the concept of attitude into two factors specifically in the context of technology use: perceived usefulness and perceived ease of use. Perceived usefulness is defined as the use of technology to improve job performance, which will help in financial and non-financial matters. Perceived ease of use is defined as one's assessment of whether the system or technology will be easy to use, and no effort will be required. TAM's primary focus is to measure the intention of an individual to use the technology or not.

Since the late 1990s, many social media sites have been developed with different features. Many of those sites faltered and closed down because they were not able to fulfill individuals' needs. The most widely used SNS is Facebook, which has 2 billion monthly users. Facebook has implemented many useful features and remains popular all over the world. SNSs such as Facebook fulfill audience needs, and individuals continue their intentions to use these sites.

All SNSs specifically give benefits to individuals. For example, LinkedIn is useful for both employees and employers, as students who are near graduation maintain their LinkedIn profile, so employers can easily find them for hiring. There are some features in common across all the SNSs, for instance, communication, socialization, seeking help, and making plans.

The TAM is basically established for technology use in organizational settings. This model is already used by researchers to study social media and SNSs (e.g., Facebook). The researchers found that 88% of users of Facebook and LinkedIn are in the age range of 50–64 (Madden and Smith, 2010). These researchers showed that it is easy to use SNSs and make an account. It is already a feature of these SNS platforms that users do not need any training to use them. As described in the TAM model, perceived usefulness plays an essential part in explaining the individual's intention to use social media or technology systems. Usefulness is defined as 'the degree to which a person believes that using a particular system would enhance his or her job performance'. When the individual feels a system is useful, he or she thinks positively about it (Davis, 1989 p.321).

Many scholars (Pontiggia and Virili, 2010; Sledgianowski and Kulviwat, 2009) have found that users' thinking as to the usefulness of a system has significant influence and is positively related to the adoption of information technology. SNS users care about whether SNSs allow them to effectively build and maintain relationships, provide a way for them to create profiles, and enable people to reach out to one another. Some scholars have discovered that users' perceived usefulness of SNSs affects their positive intentions to use them (Sledgianowski and Kulviwat, 2009).

CONCLUSION

Social media influences individuals' daily lives. It has become a need of everyone to remain connected through SNSs. The use of SNSs is not only common among all ages, but is also influenced by the individuals' aims and attitudes toward using SNSs. Most studies that have explored the relationship between users and SNSs have focused on university student populations and their academic performance. This chapter mainly focuses on employees' perspectives toward the use of SNSs during office hours. Employees' perceptions are different toward SNSs, and their use also varies in many aspects. SNSs offer a variety of functions, considering users' age, individual needs, personality, and country (Duggan et al., 2015). Research on use of SNSs tends to focus on youth, due to the perception that only youth indulge in misuse of SNSs.

The basic concept is how people perceive social sites and how their perceptions influence their social media choices. In the modern era, the use of technology is compulsory in every profession, so no employee can deny using technology systems. SNSs are very easy to use, and most people prefer to use them on their cell phones. SNSs have different features for employees to improve performance, and those factors are also valuable for organizations. Through SNSs, employees are able to gain knowledge, learn new skills,

and feel motivated and productive in their jobs (Moqbel and Kock, 2018). SNSs offer the potential for employees to improve their skills by supporting multi-tasking, knowledge acquisition, motivation, and productivity. However, these positive benefits are gained only when employees use SNSs intelligently, which depends on users' intentions toward and perception of SNSs. To facilitate this intelligent use of SNSs, organizations should develop correct attitudes in their employees for using social networks. In addition, SNSs should be taken as positive and ethical mediums of social communication. Ultimately, it depends on the employees to use the SNSs in constructive ways for learning, getting information, and seeking help from other professionals.

Employers' primary concerns regarding SNS use are psychological wellbeing and job performance. Organizations are typically concerned about these two factors because they closely relate to organization profit, quality, and stability. To address these issues, comprehensive studies are needed. Previous studies tended to measure users' behaviour by calculating the time that participants spend on specific social media platforms. This approach is problematic given the rapid pace of technological development, including development of SNSs, as new features are continually developed while old features mature. In this era of development, it is difficult to interpret the users' attitudes by only focusing on usage time.

During work, employees have to face many distractions, which can be external or internal. On some tasks, employees need more concentration. Organizations typically focus on the quality and quantity of work. To reduce external distractions, many employers provide peaceful environments, and personal space in offices. Although external distractions can be moderated, internal distractions are always present. Cell phones are often a source of external and internal distractions, and most people feel the need to remain in constant contact with others using their cell phones. Previous studies have demonstrated that cell phones are significant interruptions during work hours; importantly, these devices negatively affect employees' work quality and wellbeing. In addition, organizations need to consider strategies for their employees' wellbeing and performance in their workplaces. Mindfulness-related interventions can positively affect employees' mental and physical health. Employers can increase work performance and productivity of their employees by mitigating the interruption effect. Some organizations have developed policies for employees to use SNSs in the office, but in most cases, these are not workable. Employees perceive the restrictions on using SNSs as negative and they become involved in cyber loafing.

SNSs can be beneficial for employees, as there are many features that support collaboration and professional development. A more positive attitude toward the use of SNSs can also decrease employees' wellbeing: a person can get benefits from the use of SNSs but at the same time this is a risk factor for behavioural addiction. Supervisors can consider these factors to help employees and for their own benefits. Ultimately, employees' psychological wellbeing and job performance are the main concerns of many organizations, and so it can be helpful to develop policies and rules related to the use of SNSs for employees.

REFERENCES

Adidas. (2011). *Social media guidelines for Adidas group employees*. Retrieved from https://s3-us-west-2.amazonaws.com/articleresources/adidas-Group-Social-Media-Guidelines1.pdf. Accessed: 23.01.2019

Alhabash, S. and Ma, M., 2017. A tale of four platforms: Motivations and uses of Facebook, Twitter, Instagram, and Snapchat among college students? *Social Media+ Society*, 3(1), 2056305117691544.

Alhabash, S., Chiang, Y.H. and Huang, K., 2014. MAM & U&G in Taiwan: Differences in the uses and gratifications of Facebook as a function of motivational reactivity. *Computers in Human Behavior*, 35, pp. 423–430.

Andreassen, C.S., Torsheim, T. and Pallesen, S., 2014. Predictors of use of social network sites at work: A specific type of cyberloafing. *Journal of Computer-Mediated Communication*, 19(4), pp. 906–921.

Bonds-Raacke, J. and Raacke, J. (2010). MySpace and Facebook: Identifying dimensions of uses and gratifications for friend networking sites. *Individual differences research*, 8(1), pp. 27–33.

Blomfield Neira, C.J. and Barber, B.L., 2014. Social networking site use: Linked to adolescents' social self-concept, self-esteem, and depressed mood. *Australian Journal of Psychology*, 66(1), pp. 56–64.

Bradley, B.H., Klotz, A.C., Postlethwaite, B.E. and Brown, K.G., 2013. Ready to rumble: How team personality composition and task conflict interact to improve performance. *Journal of Applied Psychology*, 98(2), p. 385.

Brooks, S., 2015. Does personal social media usage affect efficiency and well-being? *Computers in Human Behavior*, 46, pp. 26–37.

Carr, C.T. and Hayes, R.A., 2015. Social media: Defining, developing, and divining. *Atlantic Journal of Communication*, 23(1), pp. 46–65.

Charoensukmongkol, P., 2014. Effects of support and job demands on social media use and work outcomes. *Computers in Human Behavior*, 36, pp. 340–349.

Choi, S.B. and Lim, M.S., 2016. Effects of social and technology overload on psychological well-being in young South Korean adults: The mediatory role of social network service addiction. *Computers in Human Behavior*, 61, pp. 245–254.

Davis, F. D. (1985). *A technology acceptance model for empirically testing new end-user information systems: Theory and results* (Doctoral dissertation, Massachusetts Institute of Technology).

Davis, F. D. (1989). Perceived usefulness, perceived ease of use, and user acceptance of information technology. *MIS quarterly*, pp. 319–340.

Davis, F.D., Bagozzi, R.P. and Warshaw, P.R., 1992. Extrinsic and intrinsic motivation to use computers in the workplace 1. *Journal of Applied Social Psychology*, *22*(14), pp. 1111–1132.

Donsbach, W., 2009. Cognitive dissonance theory – A roller coaster career: How communication research adapted the theory of cognitive dissonance. In H. Tilo (pp. 128–149) *Media choice*. Routledge.

Duggan, M., Ellison, N.B., Lampe, C., Lenhart, A. and Madden, M., 2015. *Demographics of key social networking platforms*. Retrieved from, https://www.pewresearch.org/internet/2015/01/09/demographics-of-key-social-networking-platforms-2/. Accessed: 05.02.2019

Ellison, N.B. and Boyd, D.M., 2013. Sociality through social network sites. In Dutton W. H. (pp. 152–172) *The Oxford handbook of internet studies*. Oxford University Press.

Festinger, L., 1962. *A theory of cognitive dissonance* (Vol. 2). Stanford University Press.

Haythornthwaite, C., 2005. Social networks and Internet connectivity effects. *Information, Community & Society*, *8*(2), pp. 125–147.

Huang, C.L., Fallah, Y.P., Sengupta, R. and Krishnan, H., 2010. Adaptive intervehicle communication control for cooperative safety systems. *IEEE Network*, *24*(1), pp. 6–13.

Joinson, A.N., 2008, April. Looking at, looking up or keeping up with people? Motives and use of Facebook. In *Proceedings of the SIGCHI conference on Human Factors in Computing Systems* (pp. 1027–1036). ACM.

Katz, E., 1959. Mass communications research and the study of popular culture: An editorial note on a possible future for this journal. *Departmental Papers (ASC)*, p.165.

Katz, E. and Lazarsfeld, P.F., 1955. *Personal influence: The part played by people in the flow of mass communications*. Free Press.

Katz, E., Blumler, J.G. and Gurevitch, M., 1973. Uses and gratifications research. *The Public Opinion Quarterly*, *37*(4), pp. 509–523.

Katz, E., Blumler, J.G. and Gurevitch, M., 1974. *The uses of mass communications: Current perspectives on gratifications research* (p. 19). Sage.

Kelleher, T. and Sweetser, K., 2012. Social media adoption among university communicators. *Journal of Public Relations Research*, *24*(2), pp. 105–122.

Knobloch-Westerwick, S. and Sarge, M.A., 2015. Impacts of exemplification and efficacy as characteristics of an online weight-loss message on selective exposure and subsequent weight-loss behavior. *Communication Research*, *42*(4), pp. 547–568.

Koch, H., Gonzalez, E. and Leidner, D., 2012. Bridging the work/social divide: The emotional response to organizational social networking sites. *European Journal of Information Systems*, *21*(6), pp. 699–717.

Ku, Y.C., Chen, R. and Zhang, H., 2013. Why do users continue using social networking sites? An exploratory study of members in the United States and Taiwan. *Information & Management*, *50*(7), pp. 571–581.

Lee, S. Y. and Lee, S. W. (2018). The effect of Facebook use on office workers' job performance and the moderating effects of task equivocality and interdependence. *Behaviour & Information Technology*, *37*(8), pp. 828–841.

Lampe, C., Ellison, N. and Steinfield, C., 2006, November. A Face (book) in the crowd: Social searching vs. social browsing. In *Proceedings of the 2006 20th anniversary conference on Computer Supported Cooperative Work* (pp. 167–170). ACM.

Lin, H., Fan, W. and Chau, P.Y., 2014. Determinants of users' continuance of social networking sites: A self-regulation perspective. *Information & Management*, *51*(5), pp. 595–603.

Madden, M. and Smith, A., 2010 'Reputation management and social media', *Pew Internet & American Life Project*, Washington, DC. [online] Available at: https://www.pewresearch.org/internet/2015/01/09/demographics-of-key-social-networking-platforms-2/. Accessed: 23.03.2019

Mares, M.L. and Sun, Y., 2010. The multiple meanings of age for television content preferences. *Human Communication Research*, *36*(3), pp. 372–396.

Mares, M.L., Oliver, M.B. and Cantor, J., 2008. Age differences in adults' emotional motivations for exposure to films. *Media Psychology*, *11*(4), pp. 488–511.

McAndrew, F.T. and Jeong, H.S., 2012. Who does what on Facebook? Age, sex, and relationship status as predictors of Facebook use. *Computers in Human Behavior*, *28*(6), pp. 2359–2365.

Moqbel, M. and Kock, N., 2018. Unveiling the dark side of social networking sites: Personal and work-related consequences of social networking site addiction. *Information & Management*, *55*(1), pp. 109–119.

Nathanson, A.I., 2001. Parents versus peers: Exploring the significance of peer mediation of antisocial television. *Communication Research*, *28*(3), pp. 251–274.

Ngai, E.W., Moon, K.L.K., Lam, S.S., Chin, E.S. and Tao, S.S., 2015. Social media models, technologies, and applications: An academic review and case study. *Industrial Management & Data Systems*, *115*(5), pp. 769–802.

Olufadi, Y., 2016. Social networking time use scale (SONTUS): A new instrument for measuring the time spent on the social networking sites. *Telematics and Informatics*, *33*(2), pp. 452–471.

Pai, P. and Arnott, D. C. (2013). User adoption of social networking sites: Eliciting uses and gratifications through a means–end approach. *Computers in Human Behavior*, *29*(3), pp. 1039–1053.

Pempek, T.A., Yermolayeva, Y.A. and Calvert, S.L., 2009. College students' social networking experiences on Facebook. *Journal of Applied Developmental Psychology*, *30*(3), pp. 227–238.

Pontiggia, A. and Virili, F., 2010. Network effects in technology acceptance: Laboratory experimental evidence. *International Journal of Information Management*, *30*(1), pp. 68–77.

Raacke, J. and Bonds-Raacke, J., 2008. MySpace and Facebook: Applying the uses and gratifications theory to exploring friend-networking sites. *Cyberpsychology & behavior*, *11*(2), pp. 169–174.

Sigerson, L. and Cheng, C., 2018. Scales for measuring user engagement with social network sites: A systematic review of psychometric properties. *Computers in Human Behavior*, *83*, pp. 87–105.

Sledgianowski, D. and Kulviwat, S., 2009. Using social network sites: The effects of playfulness, critical mass and trust in a hedonic context. *Journal of Computer Information Systems*, *49*(4), pp. 74–83.

Syrek, C.J., Kühnel, J., Vahle-Hinz, T. and De Bloom, J., 2018. Share, like, twitter, and connect: Ecological momentary assessment to examine the relationship between non-work social media use at work and work engagement. *Work & Stress*, *32*(3), pp. 209–227.

Valkenburg, P.M. and Peter, J., 2009. Social consequences of the Internet for adolescents: A decade of research. *Current Directions in Psychological Science*, *18*(1), pp. 1–5.

Valkenburg, P.M. and Peter, J., 2013. Five challenges for the future of media-effects research. *International Journal of Communication*, *7*, p. 19.

Valkenburg, P.M., Peter, J. and Walther, J.B., 2016. Media effects: Theory and research. *Annual Review of Psychology*, *67*, pp. 315–338.

Verduyn, P., Ybarra, O., Résibois, M., Jonides, J. and Kross, E., 2017. Do social network sites enhance or undermine subjective well-being? A critical review. *Social Issues and Policy Review*, *11*(1), pp. 274–302.

Waheed, H., Anjum, M., Rehman, M. and Khawaja, A., 2017. Investigation of user behavior on social networking sites. *PloS One*, *12*(2), p. e0169693.

Wang, P., Chaudhry, S., Li, L., Cao, X., Guo, X., Vogel, D. and Zhang, X., 2016. Exploring the influence of social media on employee work performance. *Internet Research*, *26* (2), pp. 529–545.

Whiting, A. and Williams, D., 2013. Why people use social media: A uses and gratifications approach. *Qualitative Market Research: An International Journal*, *16*(4), pp. 362–369.

Zillmann, D. (2000). Mood management in the context of selective exposure theory. *Annals of the International Communication Association*, *23*(1), pp. 103–123.

Intrapreneurship and Wellbeing in Organizations

Elliroma Gardiner and Jonas Debrulle

INTRODUCTION

Organizations internationally have recognized the potential that employee contributions to innovation and opportunity recognition can have on firm growth (Antoncic and Antoncic, 2011) as well as on the community (Portales, 2019). The dedicated efforts of global companies, such as Apple, Amazon and Google, to stimulate and support entrepreneurship from within are well known, so much so that even small- to medium-sized enterprises see the merits of investing in employees to think like an 'entrepreneur' (Hughes and Mustafa, 2017). Employee efforts to initiate and manage changing requirements in response to shifts in the global economy are seen as a source of strategic competitive advantage (Kuratko and Audretsch, 2013).

Known by many names, including corporate entrepreneurship (Dess et al., 2003) and corporate venturing (Antoncic and Hisrich, 2003), intrapreneurship (Pinchot, 1985), that is, acting like an entrepreneur in an organization, seems to have universal application. With employees at every level of the organization recognized as potential intrapreneurs (Amo, 2010), and with research showing that intrapreneurial employees outperform other employees (Bosma et al., 2010), intrapreneurship is no longer just the domain of managers (Floyd and Lane, 2000). A diverse range of workforce, including nursing (Ekiyor and şenel, 2017), engineering (Ronen, 2010), white collar (Di Fabio and Gori, 2016) and the public service (Preenen et al., 2019) – including the US Department of Defence (Wood et al., 2008) – have been identified as benefiting from intrapreneurship. Indeed, research on intrapreneurship knows no geographical limit, with work conducted across the globe in Europe (Valsania et al., 2016), North America (Bolton and Lane, 2012) and Asia (Woo, 2018). Intrapreneurship, therefore, seems to be a phenomenon which can be engaged in by any worker regardless of status, industry or location.

It is true that having the opportunity to be creative and autonomous, and to demonstrate skill and high performance, is likely to be motivating and empowering for employees (Blanka, 2019). The chance to action an idea and implement changes is one that would be cherished by engaged employees. At the same time, however, employees are also likely to be concerned about the uncertainty and risk inherent in intrapreneurship. For instance, large organizations which emphasize intrapreneurship may create ambiguity about role expectations (Floyd and Lane, 2000). Middle managers may be particularly vulnerable to role conflict, finding it difficult to decide what proportion of their efforts should be spent on intrapreneurial experimentation and what proportion should remain within their traditional operational duties (Wakkee et al., 2010). And, of course, not every project is going to be successful. Intrapreneurial employees who are committed to a project are likely to experience the negative emotion of grief as a result of project failure (Shepherd et al., 2009).

We know that poor employee health is expensive for firms and nations. The latest figures from the United States show that workplace stress costs the US economy upwards of US$500 billion per year (American Psychological Association, 2015). High figures have also been reported in the UK (£15 billion, Health and Safety Executive, 2019) and Europe (€20 billion per year, European Agency for Safety and Health at Work, 2014), with workers who are passion-driven or in caring professions most at risk (Gardner et al., 2019). Of the limited research which has been conducted exploring intrapreneurship and wellbeing, a picture is emerging of intrapreneurship as a two-edged sword, capable of both supporting and suppressing psychological and physical health (Gawke et al., 2018). Whilst this early research echoes similar paradoxical findings from research on entrepreneurs (see Wiklund et al. (2019) for a review), the marked differences between the antecedents of intrapreneurship and

entrepreneurship (Douglas and Fitzsimmons, 2013) mean that research on the latter is only partially informative on the former. The lack of research investigating the positive and negative consequences that intrapreneurship may have on employee health and wellbeing is of concern because the strategic gains enjoyed by companies with intrapreneurial employees are likely to be undermined if the costs of intrapreneurship on the wellbeing of employees are too great.

The aim of the current chapter is to evaluate and synthesize the extant research which intersects the two largely unrelated domains of intrapreneurship (and its related facets such as proactivity) and health and wellbeing, with the view to exploring the practice and research implications of this research. The chapter is structured as follows. The next section provides an overview of the key features and definitions of intrapreneurship. This is followed by a section detailing the theoretical approaches for research on the association between intrapreneurship and wellbeing. Then, an examination of the extant literature on intrapreneurship and wellbeing is presented. Following this, implications for practice and research are drawn, and an outlook is provided on future research in the field of intrapreneurship and wellbeing.

DEFINITIONS AND KEY THEORIES

What is intrapreneurship? Intrapreneurship, a subfield of entrepreneurship, was first coined by Pinchot (1985) and reflects the idea that even individuals working within organizations can act like entrepreneurs. There is currently no single accepted definition of intrapreneurship (Blanka, 2019; Neessen et al., 2019), perhaps due to existing debates as to whether intrapreneurship is distinct from other related concepts such as corporate entrepreneurship, entrepreneurial orientation and employee venturing. Common across this cluster of terms, however, is the inherent value in the human capital of entrepreneurial employees (Amo, 2010).

Debates withstanding, intrapreneurship can be broadly defined as voluntary proactive behaviour of an employee towards the recognition of opportunities, generation of new ideas and creation of new products, services or business lines to benefit the organization (Edú Valsania et al., 2016). Intrapreneurship is as an extra-role behaviour, something supported by rather than dictated by firms (Rigtering and Weitzel, 2013). Behaviourally, intrapreneurship is seen as generating creative ideas, favouring experimentation in problem solving, acting in anticipation of future problems or needs, taking bold action, being proactive or competitive and working autonomously (Wakkee et al., 2010).

Intrapreneurship has been conceptualized as both an organizational- and individual-level construct (Wakkee et al., 2010), where the pursuit of opportunities is fundamental at both levels (Stevenson and Jarillo, 1990). Where conceptualizations of intrapreneurship are akin to corporate entrepreneurship or entrepreneurial orientation, the research conceives intrapreneurship as an organizational-level variable that is manufactured and monitored using a 'top-down' process by the organization (Sharma and Chrisman, 1999). Most of what we know about intrapreneurship is the result of organizational-level research (Covin and Slevin, 1991). Keys features of intrapreneurial organizations include creating new ventures and businesses, product/service and process innovations, self-renewal, risk-taking, proactiveness and competitive aggressiveness (Antoncic and Antoncic, 2011).

Although there is substantially less research conducted on intrapreneurship at the individual level, the body of evidence is growing. Studies which focus on the 'bottom-up' process, modelling individual intrapreneurial characteristics and behaviours of employees, adopt the individual level of conceptualization (Rigtering and Weitzel, 2013). Generally, research focusing on the individual views

intrapreneurship as a form of individual difference, where a combination of specific traits reflects a propensity to engage in intrapreneurship. For instance, Di Fabio's (2014; Di Fabio and Kenny, 2018) 'Intrapreneurial Self-Capital' identifies core self-evaluation, hardiness, creative self-efficacy, resilience, goal mastery, decisiveness and vigilance as essential characteristics needed to overcome the challenges when engaging in intrapreneurship. Intrapreneurial self-capital is thought to be improved through training as well as being an inherent trait (Alessio et al., 2019; Di Fabio et al., 2017). A recent systematic review which analysed 32 papers focusing on individual-level intrapreneurship from 2015 to 2016 identified that perspectives on this form of intrapreneurship tended to focus on personality characteristics, human capital, social capital and the characteristics of managers and supervisors.

KEY THEORIES

An influential theory which tries to incorporate both organizational and individual characteristics is Kuratko and colleagues' (Hornsby et al., 1993) Intrapreneurship Model. Unlike other views of intrapreneurship as an individual difference (i.e., Intrapreneurial Self-Capital, Di Fabio and Gori, 2016; Di Fabio and Kenny, 2018), Kuratko's model views intrapreneurship as a process not dissimilar to entrepreneurship. The intrapreneurship process starts with considering organizational antecedents (e.g., work discretion, management support, rewards, time availability, organizational boundaries) and individual antecedents (e.g., risk-taking personality, desire for autonomy, goal orientation, internal locus of control, need for achievement). Interaction of these antecedents with a 'precipitating event', that is, an environmental or organizational change, triggers a decision in the employee to act intrapreneurially. The next step in the model involves assessing the feasibility of the idea, followed by actions with respect to consuming available resources and overcoming barriers. The result of this multi-step and multi-level nexus is the implementation of the intrapreneurial idea.

A more current model, which coincidently incorporates Kuratko's (Hornsby et al., 1993) model, was put forward by Neessen and colleagues (2019). Informed by their systematic analysis of 106 articles on intrapreneurship from 1989 to 2017, the authors created a new integrative framework that models how individual and organizational factors interact to predict intrapreneurial outcomes, which in turn predict the ultimate outcome, namely, organizational performance. Organizational factors in the model include management support, organizational structure, rewards/reinforcements, work discretion and resources. The model proposes that organizational factors moderate the relationship between individual intrapreneurship and organizational intrapreneurial outcomes.

Intrapreneurship is undoubtedly a burgeoning area of research. However, the results of the two aforementioned reviews (i.e., Blanka, 2019; Neessen et al., 2019) indicate that, despite interest and value in the topic, the lack of a universal definition of intrapreneurship coupled with inconsistencies as to whether intrapreneurship is an individual- and/or an organizational-level variable has resulted in a rather fragmented field. Indeed, even the results of these two systematic reviews are somewhat in conflict, with one advocating that intrapreneurship is a multi-dimensional construct (Neessen et al., 2019) in line with Kuratko and colleagues' (Hornsby et al., 1993) model and the other conceptualizing intrapreneurship as an individual-level concept (Blanka, 2019). Despite this promising work, there is a dearth of intrapreneurship-specific theories which explain the impact of intrapreneurship on employee wellbeing. Neither Kuratko et al. (Hornsby et al., 1993) nor Neessen et al. (2019) have included individual outcomes other than enactment of

intrapreneurial behaviour in their models. Both models indicate that once an individual makes their 'input', the only important 'output' is organizational-level performance. Neither model includes a feedback loop to capture employee learning through the intrapreneurial process. There is also no mechanism which explains how individuals are supposed to sustain their intrapreneurial characteristics throughout the intrapreneurship process. Both models make important contributions to the field, redefining intrapreneurship as multi-level and setting a more holistic, theoretically sound research agenda. However, they both fall short of providing insights into how individuals experience intrapreneurship past the initiation phase.

THEORETICAL APPROACHES TO WELLBEING

In terms of understanding the association between intrapreneurship and wellbeing, the specialized and well-validated socio-cognitive models of Job Demands–Resources Theory (JD-R, Bakker and Demerouti, 2014), Approach–Avoidance Motivation (Eysenck, 1997; Gray and McNaughton, 2000) and Self-Determination Theory (Deci et al., 2017) are considerably more informative than the specific intrapreneurship models discussed in the previous section.

JOB DEMANDS–RESOURCES THEORY

One theory that has been employed by researchers to explain the relationship between intrapreneurship and wellbeing is the JD-R theory (Bakker and Demerouti, 2014), which is an evolution of the Job Demands–Resources model (Demerouti et al., 2001). Arguably the most well-known theoretical framework to model occupational stress, the theory has been shown to predict a range of important individual work outcomes such as burnout, work engagement and performance (Bakker and Demerouti, 2017). The first key component of this model, job demands, refers to 'physical, social, or organizational aspects of the job that require sustained physical or mental effort and are therefore associated with certain physiological and psychological costs' (Demerouti et al., 2001: 501). The second key construct, job resources, include 'physical, psychological, social, or organizational aspects of the job that may […] be functional in achieving work goals, reduce job demands and its related costs, or stimulate personal growth and development' (Demerouti et al., 2001: 501).

JD-R theory explains how job demands and resources have unique and multiplicative effects on employee stress and motivation (Bakker and Demerouti, 2014). More specifically, JD-R theory proposes that job demands and resources are predictive of two causal (and largely independent) processes, namely a health impairment process and a motivational process. The health impairment process models the detrimental impact that high job demands can have on employee health, including exhaustion at work, psychosomatic health complaints and repetitive strain. In contrast, the motivational process demonstrates the positive impact that employees can experience, in the form of work enjoyment, engagement and motivation, as a result of having enough job resources to manage demands. Together, these two pathways explain how insufficient job resources can negatively impact health and how job resources can buffer the impact of job demands and poor health outcomes (Bakker and Demerouti, 2017).

Whilst over two decades of research has seen the JD-R model and (more recently) theory applied to a range of different settings, including entrepreneurship (Dijkhuizen et al., 2016), its application to intrapreneurship is only quite recent. Gawke and colleagues (2018) published the first study enlisting JD-R theory to predict wellbeing and performance

outcomes for employee intrapreneurship. Testing and extending both the motivational and health impairment pathways, the authors hypothesized that work engagement and work exhaustion, respectively, would mediate the relationship between employee intrapreneurship and in-role performance, innovativeness and work avoidance. Results with a Dutch sample of 241 employee dyads revealed full support for the motivational pathway hypothesis and partial support for the health impairment hypothesis. Employee intrapreneurship was positively related to work engagement, which in turn was related to higher levels of innovativeness and in-role performance and lower levels of work avoidance. The authors took this finding to suggest that employee intrapreneurship can increase work engagement through increasing the employee's capacity for goal attainment and job crafting. Employee intrapreneurship was also positively associated with exhaustion, resulting in lower in-role performance and higher levels of work avoidance. Work exhaustion and innovativeness were found to be unrelated to employee intrapreneurship. These results provide insights into the potential wellbeing and performance costs of employee intrapreneurship and extend JD-R theory by demonstrating that employee intrapreneurship can be simultaneously motivating and depleting for employees.

Kattenbach and Fietze's (2018) research with almost 600 German media and IT industry professionals also demonstrates the utility of using JD-R theory as a lens by which to view the intrapreneurship–wellbeing relationship. The focus of their work was on employee entrepreneurial orientation, which reflects the tendency of an individual to engage in entrepreneurial activity (Bolton and Lane, 2012). However, the traits underlying entrepreneurial orientation are almost identical to those which underlie individual-level intrapreneurship, namely, innovation, proactiveness and risk-taking (Bolton and Lane, 2012). Conceptualizing entrepreneurial orientation as a form of personal resource,

Kattenbach and Fietze (2018) tested the health impairment process, hypothesizing that entrepreneurial orientation would partially mediate the link between job demands and resources as well as job resources and burnout. Results showed that entrepreneurial orientation mediated the relationship between emotional demands, workload, cognitive workload and exhaustion. Specifically, their findings revealed that lower workloads and emotional demands and higher levels of cognitive workload positively predicted entrepreneurial orientation, which then triggered lower levels of burnout. They also found that high levels of decision latitude (a job resource) were associated with higher levels of entrepreneurial orientation, which in turn led to lower exhaustion. These results suggest that employees who are entrepreneurially orientated and who perceive their work environment favourably are less likely to experience exhaustion. In this way, individual intrapreneurship can have a positive impact on wellbeing.

APPROACH–AVOIDANCE MOTIVATION

Other concepts that offer insights into the wellbeing of intrapreneurs are the constructs of approach and avoidance motivation. There are a number of different ways to conceptualize self-regulation via approach and avoidance, including biosocially (i.e., Eysenck, 1997), as neurobiological motivations (i.e., Gray, 1970; Gray and McNaughton, 2000) and as neurocortical activity (i.e., Harmon-Jones et al., 2006). Very generally, however, approach tendencies involve the action of behaviour towards (usually rewarding) stimuli whilst avoidance involves the action of behaviour away from (usually punishing) stimuli (Patterson and Newman, 1993). The interaction of these self-regulation tendencies is thought to underlie the manifestation of most human behaviour (Collins et al., 2017).

One of the most popular conceptualizations of approach and avoidance motivations is via the revised Reinforcement Sensitivity Theory (r-RST, Gray and McNaughton, 2000), which offers not only a descriptive account but also a causal basis for personality traits related to approach and avoidance (e.g., Gray, 1970). This model consists of three interactive systems, namely the Fight/Flight/Freeze system (FFFS), the Behavioural Activation System (BAS) and the Behavioural Inhibition System (BIS) (Gray and McNaughton, 2000). The FFFS mediates response to both conditioned and unconditioned aversive stimuli and is sensitive to threat and danger (Gray and McNaughton, 2000). BAS, on the other hand, is the physiological mechanism that is believed to regulate appetitive motivation and is sensitive to signals of reward, nonpunishment and escape from punishment. Activation of BAS promotes and motivates an individual towards a goal. In contrast, BIS is an aversive motivational system which controls the experience of anxiety in response to anxiety-relevant cues (Gray, 1970). According to the original RST theory, BIS is sensitive to signals of punishment, nonreward and novelty and works to inhibit behaviour that may lead to negative outcomes.

Although all three components are implicated in human behaviour, purposeful motivated behaviour is thought to be primarily mediated by the BAS and BIS. Certainly, this was the view taken by Gawke and colleagues (2018) in their study with Dutch workers. As mentioned previously, interested in understanding the personal wellbeing costs and benefits of intrapreneurship for employees, the researchers uncovered links between intrapreneurship and engagement as well as exhaustion. Supplementing JD-R theory, the authors included BAS and BIS in their model to test whether BAS would moderate the mediated relationship between employee intrapreneurship and job performance via work engagement, and whether BIS would moderate the mediated relationship between employee intrapreneurship and job performance via exhaustion. Moderated mediated regression analysis revealed that BAS enhanced the indirect relationship between employee intrapreneurship and in-role performance and innovativeness via engagement. Similarly, support was found for the indirect relationship between employee intrapreneurship and work avoidance via exhaustion. These findings highlight the role which individual differences can play in differentially impacting the wellbeing experiences of employees who engage in intrapreneurship.

A quantitative diary study conducted by Cangiano et al. (2019) also examined, albeit indirectly, the association between avoidance and wellbeing outcomes using a sample of 94 Australian employees. Relevant to this current chapter, the authors tested the existence of a 'strain pathway' whereby the uncertainty and risky nature of proactive work behaviours (an important facet of intrapreneurship) would engender anxiety (a biosocial operationalization of avoidance motivation) in employees, which would in turn make it difficult for employees to psychologically detach at the end of a workday. They hypothesized that only the ill effects of proactivity would be experienced if the employee's supervisor was perceived as punitive. Multilevel analysis supported the hypothesis, finding evidence that proactive behaviour, whilst beneficial to the organization, has the potential to be damaging to the individual.

SELF-DETERMINATION THEORY

One other theorical approach which has been employed to investigate the wellbeing of intrapreneurs is Self-Determination Theory (SDT, Deci et al., 2017). Being a macro theory of motivation, SDT posits that individuals thrive, grow and experience wellbeing when their basic psychological needs for competence, autonomy and relatedness are met. Competence refers to the capability of

individuals to achieve and demonstrate their full abilities. Autonomy refers to the flexibility of an individual to make their own decisions and to work and think independently. Relatedness is concerned with being able to create and sustain high-quality relationships with others. Thirty years of research has shown that employee wellbeing is highest when the socio-contextual conditions satisfy these basic needs (Deci et al., 2017).

Enlisting SDT, Cangiano and colleagues (2019) proposed that competence would mediate the relationship between proactive work behaviour and vitality. The researchers put forward three arguments for why they thought proactivity would be linked to competence. First, they argued that individuals would experience a sense of mastery as they tried to overcome the challenges in being proactive. Second, positive outcomes associated with initial proactivity would likely fuel further self-impressions of competence. Third, the self-initiated aspect of proactivity would mean any felt benefits would be entirely attributable to the individual's own ability and competence. Cangiano et al.'s (2019) research with dyads of managers and subordinates found support for their proposition. Proactivity was positively associated with competence, and competence mediated the relationship between proactivity and vitality. This study provides evidence that being proactive provides an opportunity for individuals to meet their fundamental need for competence and achievement, and that fulfilment of this need results in employees who are energized and high in vitality.

Also using SDT as a theoretical lens, Strauss et al. (2017) conducted some interesting research investigating the effects of proactive behaviours on employee wellbeing. Specifically, it was hypothesized that for employees experiencing high levels of controlled motivation (characterized by coercion and pressure) and low levels of autonomous motivation (characterized by low intrinsic interest in the work), engagement in proactive behaviour would reduce an employee's resources, ultimately resulting in high levels of job strain. The authors adopted a time-lagged study with 127 full-time employee–supervisor dyads across a variety of Canadian and US businesses. The results showed that supervisor-rated proactive behaviour was positively associated with job strain when controlled motivation was high whilst autonomous motivation was low. Yet under all other conditions such as high controlled and high autonomous motivation, proactivity had no impact on strain. These findings indicate that autonomous motivation may have a powerful buffering effect, reducing the negative impact of proactivity on worker wellbeing.

The only published study that directly contrasts entrepreneurs and intrapreneurs with respect to wellbeing was conducted by Shir et al. (2019). The study was based on the 2011 Swedish Global Entrepreneurship Monitor survey and used interview data from 1,837 workers, of whom 251 were early-stage entrepreneurs. The aim of the study was to test a two-stage multi-path mediation model. Specifically, it was hypothesized that the relationship between active engagement in entrepreneurship and wellbeing would be mediated by autonomy and that relatedness and competence would moderate this mediated relationship. Analysis revealed partial support for the model, that is, autonomy mediated the association between active engagement in entrepreneurship and wellbeing via the positive influence of relatedness and competence. Interestingly, when comparing intrapreneurs and entrepreneurs, entrepreneurs reported higher levels of wellbeing than intrapreneurs since both direct and indirect effects of active engagement in entrepreneurship emerged for entrepreneurs whilst only a direct effect was found for intrapreneurs. Specifically, next to higher levels of life satisfaction and evaluative wellbeing (direct effect), entrepreneurship was also shown to indirectly stimulate feelings of competence and relatedness through increasing levels of psychological autonomy, whilst intrapreneurs' ability to self-organize

is largely restricted by organizational constraints and procedures. Linking back to SDT, the findings of this study demonstrate that entrepreneurship can lead to wellbeing when these innate psychological needs for autonomy, relatedness and competence are met. An important implication, as noted by the authors, is that wellbeing is likely to be differentially affected depending on the type of entrepreneurial work and the psychological mechanisms underpinning it.

SUMMARY

J-DR, approach–avoidance motivation and SDT are useful theoretical lenses through which to understand how intrapreneurship influences employee wellbeing. These theories, either individually or in combination, assist in explaining how intrapreneurship can both support and hinder the psychological and physical health of workers. It is interesting to note, however, that whilst the number of empirical studies enlisting these theoretical approaches is very small, the studies are all relatively recent – within the last four years or so. Together, the contemporary empirical evidence, which is well grounded in established theory, highlights the individual costs and benefits experienced by intrapreneurial workers.

INTRAPRENEURSHIP AND WELLBEING

Moving on now to studies which investigate intrapreneurship and wellbeing outside of the theoretical lenses mentioned previously, the work of Ekiyor and şenel (2017) provides evidence from Turkey which corroborates the findings of Gawke and colleagues (2018). The focus of their research was on understanding whether individuals experiencing burnout would be less likely to engage in intrapreneurship. After surveying a sample of nurses, an occupational group with a traditionally high prevalence of burnout (Vargas et al., 2014), the authors found a positive relationship between the two variables. The cross-sectional nature of the research, unfortunately, makes it difficult to determine whether intrapreneurship leads to burnout or whether burnout renders employees unable to engage in intrapreneurship. Nevertheless, the significant association between intrapreneurship and burnout does highlight that individuals engaging in intrapreneurship may be vulnerable.

Contrasting evidence is provided by Ronen (2010). The aim of this study was to determine the relative importance of various individual traits in the prediction of intrapreneurial tendencies and to identify what impact (if any) intrapreneurial tendencies would have on various individual outcomes. Using a study of high-tech Israeli engineers, the study enlisted a longitudinal design, where self-reported data on personality, intrapreneurial tendencies and health and work outcomes were collected at Time 1 and again 15 months later (at Time 2). Supervisor ratings of employee job performance were also collected at Time 2. Intrapreneurial tendencies were found to be significantly negatively related to burnout, meaning that engineers with high intrapreneurial tendencies tended to report lower levels of burnout. Intrapreneurial engineers seemed to also enjoy high levels of work engagement and role autonomy. They were more absorbed in and dedicated to their work and also felt freer to make autonomous decisions. This result is in stark contrast to that of Ekiyor and şenel's study (2017), which found burnout to be associated with lower levels of intrapreneurship. The longitudinal design of Ronen (2010) is advantageous, tentatively suggesting that it is more likely that intrapreneurship impacts wellbeing (for good or bad), rather than wellbeing impacting intrapreneurship.

It is worth mentioning that in addition to these mixed findings with respect to negative and positive associations between intrapreneurship and wellbeing, there has been some research indicating that there may not be a relationship between the two variables at all. For example, a Dutch study aimed at understanding the longitudinal effects of task challenge on skill utilization, affective wellbeing (i.e., positive affect) and intrapreneurial behaviour found that task challenge positively predicted skill utilization and intrapreneurship but not affective wellbeing (Preenen et al., 2019). In other words, whilst challenging work might be a useful way to enhance skill utilization and intrapreneurship behaviour, it does not necessarily mean that employees are going to be happier.

Broadening the evidence base to include studies investigating links between wellbeing and more specific intrapreneurial traits such as self-efficacy and proactivity (see de Jong et al., 2015) is likely to yield some useful insights into how aspects of intrapreneurship differentially impact employee wellness. For example, Di Fabio and colleagues' research with Italian samples from various occupations have shown consistently positive moderate-to-high correlations between intrapreneurial self-efficacy and life satisfaction (Di Fabio and Kenny, 2018) and flourishing (Di Fabio and Gori, 2016). These studies demonstrate that engagement in intrapreneurship can have profound positive benefits on individuals, helping them to feel fulfilled, accomplished and living the 'good life'.

Interested in examining the strength and nature of the relationship between self-efficacy and job burnout, Shoji and colleagues (2016) conducted a comprehensive meta-analysis of 57 original studies (N = 22,773) published between 1998 and 2011. Amongst other findings, they reported –0.33 as the average effect-size estimate for the association between self-efficacy and burnout, indicating a small but significant relationship. Interestingly, and relevant when thinking about the high potential for intrapreneurship endeavours to fail, the largest average effect size between self-efficacy and burnout was with the 'lack of accomplishment' facet (–0.49). These associations were quite robust regardless of how self-efficacy or burnout was measured.

Turning now to proactivity, another key facet of intrapreneurship, a study by Cunningham and De La Rosa (2008) looked at the relationship between proactive personality and wellbeing. Proactive personality is an individual difference variable which captures the propensity of an individual to be 'minimally hindered by situational constraints and maximally empowered to take personal initiative to ensure a positive outcome' regardless of environmental constraints (Cunningham and De La Rosa, 2008: 272). It was hypothesized that proactive personality would moderate the relationship between controllable work and nonwork stressors (such as work–life interference) and job as well as life satisfaction. The authors reasoned that whilst high levels of perceived control are positively linked with psychological health and positive work attitudes, trying to exercise control over workplace stressors which are outside of an employees' control is likely to exacerbate experiences of stress. Enlisting a cross-sectional design, the researchers surveyed 133 university academics from a variety of universities across the United States. However, moderated multiple regression revealed that proactive personality only moderated the relationship between nonwork stressors and life satisfaction, indicating that whilst proactive personality may ameliorate experiences of work stress, its effects are likely to be contingent on the nature of the stressor. This body of work is both limited (in terms of quantity) and disparate (in terms of sample and measurement). However, what work has been conducted is relatively recent, highlighting the evolving interest in intrapreneurship-like traits and worker wellbeing.

IMPLICATIONS FOR PRACTICE

There are important practical implications for senior executives and human-resources professionals to understand with respect to how intrapreneurship differentially impacts employee wellbeing. Like any strategic decision, organizations should at the outset do a thorough analysis of their goals, business processes, infrastructure and accumulated human and social capital. Central determinants of successful intrapreneurial task behaviour appear to be the employees' intrinsic drive for entrepreneurship together with a well-balanced supportive organizational climate. Organizations that provide their entrepreneurship-minded workers with the skills, networks and other resources that workers often lack and require to engage in independent entrepreneurial tasks are likely to indirectly stimulate the corporate ability for new product and/or process innovations (Sörensen and Fassiotto, 2011). Yet to reap such benefits in a sustainable way, organizations not only have to clarify what they offer intrapreneurial employees in terms of skills acquisition and network building, but they also need to carefully consider the longer-term human and psychological impact of such organizational demands on their constituents' wellbeing and health. One implication of the body of evidence thus far is that not all organizations profit from the entrepreneurship-development process their employees go through as much as they can, and that whilst there are many benefits, there are also substantial costs.

Like entrepreneurship, intrapreneurship is an emotionally demanding process characterized by high levels of uncertainty. This study has explored the diverse mix of emotions that can be linked to intrapreneurship, including positive states such as increased levels of autonomy, job and life satisfaction (Shir et al., 2019) but also higher levels of work-related strain (Gawke et al., 2018). Considering the research discussed in this chapter, organizations would be wise to adapt their organizational climate to ensure that employees are motivated and capable to undertake intrapreneurial task behaviour sustainably. Applying J-DR theory, reducing organizational demands and increasing available resources are crucial first steps (Gawke et al., 2018). For instance, reducing the number of formal procedures in the implementation of tasks would be useful (Antoncic and Antoncic, 2011). The provision of managerial support and encouragement as well as rewards in the form of employee discretion, job autonomy and work design are all likely to have a positive impact on intrapreneurship (Neessen et al., 2019) and wellbeing (Huo et al., 2019). Initiatives aimed at improving entrepreneurial self-efficacy, growth and development as well as the provision of coaching are additional practices which could be implemented to support intrapreneurship and wellbeing by ensuring that employees receive guidance and encouragement along the way (Antoncic and Antoncic, 2011; Shepherd et al., 2009).

The importance of leadership is a recurring theme in both the intrapreneurship and wellbeing literatures, with the findings largely complementary. For instance, punitive leadership has been found to moderate the relationship between proactivity and wellbeing, such that it reduces the wellbeing experienced by proactive employees (Cangiano et al., 2019). Similarly, authentic leadership, which has been shown to increase employee wellbeing through positively impacting work climate (Nielsen and Daniels, 2016), has also been identified as a key antecedent to intrapreneurship (Valsania et al., 2016). Transformational leadership, too, has been found to positively influence psychological wellbeing (Arnold, 2017) and intrapreneurship (Valsania et al., 2016). Interestingly, however, both the intrapreneurship and wellbeing literatures warn that even 'positive' leadership styles such as transformational leadership may negatively impact intrapreneurship and wellbeing in certain contexts (Djourova et al., 2019). Organizations interested in encouraging intrapreneurship should be cognizant of the impact that leaders and managers may have on intrapreneurship and wellbeing. Those leading should create environments which reward creativity and involve participation of followers at every step of the intrapreneurial process.

FUTURE RESEARCH

Future research efforts should be directed towards formulating or perhaps even reconciling existing theories of intrapreneurship with specialized theories of wellbeing and strain. The current chapter demonstrates that exciting new work aimed at addressing this gap is underway. Yet, despite two recent high-quality systematic reviews (Blanka, 2019; Neessen et al., 2019) and targeted original empirical research (i.e., Gawke et al., 2018), the field is disjointed with inconsistencies in how intrapreneurship is defined, conceptualized and measured. Until these fundamental issues are worked out, ensuing studies on entrepreneurship (including those investigating wellbeing outcomes) are formulated and conducted on precarious footing. The critical importance of theory to practice and practice to theory is well known (Ployhart and Bartunek, 2019). Hence, delays in developing a valid theory of intrapreneurship stunt the growth of empirical research, which in turn limits the refinement of theory and hinders the growth of knowledge of how the health and wellbeing of intrapreneurs can best be supported.

Relatedly, an obvious area for future attention by researchers is with respect to disentangling how individual- and organizational-level intrapreneurship impacts the health of individual employees. Individuals, rather than organizations, innovate, so it is crucial that further exploration of the wellbeing costs and benefits to workers is undertaken. Multi-level and longitudinal designs are likely to be particularly revealing, facilitating comprehensive investigation of how various types of intrapreneurship impact wellbeing as well as modelling how wellbeing may fluctuate depending on the stage of intrapreneurship. Given the generally wide acceptance that intrapreneurship is a multi-level construct, it is surprising that so few multi-level studies have been conducted. Like entrepreneurship, intrapreneurship is not static; there are emotional highs and lows in pitching ideas and hitting roadblocks (Wiklund et al., 2019). Failure to consider these temporal shifts is likely to yield an artificially narrow view of the impacts of intrapreneurship on workers.

Another area worthy of future research is investigating whether the impacts of intrapreneurship on wellbeing are experienced differently by males and females. There are known gender differences in experiences of wellbeing (Batz and Tay, 2018). We know from a study using a large nationally representative sample of US workers that females (particularly those who have children) are less likely than males with similar characteristics to engage in intrapreneurship (Adachi and Hisada, 2017). This may be because females typically receive fewer job resources than males (Magee, 2013). We also know that female workers tend to report lower levels of job satisfaction and higher levels of job stress than their male colleagues (Wilks and Neto, 2013). Longitudinal research from Canada provides some relevant convergent evidence, showing that female entrepreneurs appraised high financial needs and low social support as more stressful than male entrepreneurs, which in turn led to higher psychological distress lasting several months after launching their business (Chadwick and Raver, 2019). Therefore, given that gender differences exist with respect to becoming an intrapreneur and experiencing distress, it is important to more fully understand if and how gender differentially impacts the wellbeing of male and female intrapreneurs.

CONCLUSION

'The true value of entrepreneurship as a corporate concept lies in the extent to which it helps organisations create *sustainable competitive advantage*' (Kuratko, 2012: 239). Studies from around the globe show that intrapreneurship can provide a competitive advantage (e.g., Paek and Lee, 2018). An organizational climate strongly supportive of entrepreneurship yet neglecting personnel wellbeing may, irrespective of its stimulus to intrapreneurial task engagement, turn out to be detrimental to the organization's long-term competitiveness. Therefore, understanding the health and wellbeing implications of intrapreneurship on employees is at the heart of establishing whether such competitive advantage is sustainable.

REFERENCES

Adachi T and Hisada T (2017) Gender differences in entrepreneurship and intrapreneurship: An empirical analysis. *Small Business Economics* 48(3): 447–486.

Alessio F, Finstad GL, Giorgi G, et al. (2019) Intrapreneurial self-capital. An overview of an emergent construct in organizational behaviour. *Quality-Access to Success* 20(173): 156–162.

American Psychological Association (2015) *Stress in America – Paying with our health*. Available at: https://www.apa.org/news/press/releases/stress/2014/stress-report.pdf

Amo BW (2010) Corporate entrepreneurship and intrapreneurship related to innovation behaviour among employees. *International Journal of Entrepreneurial Venturing* 2(2): 144–158.

Antoncic B and Hisrich RD (2003) Clarifying the intrapreneurship concept. *Journal of Small Business and Enterprise Development* 10: 7–24.

Antoncic JA and Antoncic B (2011) Employee satisfaction, intrapreneurship and firm growth: A model. *Industrial Management & Data Systems* 111(4): 589–607.

Arnold KA (2017) Transformational leadership and employee psychological well-being: A review and directions for future research. *Journal of Occupational Health Psychology* 22(3): 381.

Bakker AB and Demerouti E (2014) Job demands–resources theory. In C Cooper and P Chen (Eds.), *Wellbeing: A complete reference guide*. Chichester: Wiley-Blackwell, pp. 1–28.

Bakker AB and Demerouti E (2017) Job demands–resources theory: Taking stock and looking forward. *Journal of Occupational Health Psychology* 22(3): 273.

Batz C and Tay L (2018) Gender differences in subjective well-being. In: Diener E, Oishi S and Tay L (eds) *Handbook of well-being*. Salt Lake City, UT: DEF Publishers.

Blanka C (2019) An individual-level perspective on intrapreneurship: A review and ways forward. *Review of Managerial Science* 13(5): 919–961.

Bolton DL and Lane MD (2012) Individual entrepreneurial orientation: Development of a measurement instrument. *Education+Training* 54(2/3): 219–233.

Bosma N, Stam FC and Wennekers A (2010) *Intrapreneurship: An international study EIM Research Report H201005*. Zoetermeer: EIM.

Cangiano F, Parker SK and Yeo GB (2019) Does daily proactivity affect well-being? The moderating role of punitive supervision. *Journal of Organizational Behavior* 40(1): 59–72.

Chadwick IC and Raver JL (2019) Not for the faint of heart? A gendered perspective on psychological distress in entrepreneurship. *Journal of Occupational Health Psychology* 24(6): 662.

Collins MD, Jackson CJ, Walker BR, et al. (2017) Integrating the context-appropriate balanced attention model and reinforcement sensitivity theory: Towards a domain-general personality process model. *Psychological Bulletin* 143(1): 91.

Covin JG and Slevin DP (1991) A conceptual model of entrepreneurship as firm behavior. *Entrepreneurship Theory and Practice* 16(1): 7–26.

Cunningham CJ and De La Rosa GM (2008) The interactive effects of proactive personality and work-family interference on well-being. *Journal of Occupational Health Psychology* 13(3): 271.

de Jong JP, Parker SK, Wennekers S, et al. (2015) Entrepreneurial behavior in organizations: Does job design matter? *Entrepreneurship Theory and Practice* 39(4): 981–95.

Deci EL, Olafsen AH and Ryan RM (2017) Self-determination theory in work organizations: The state of a science. *Annual Review of Organizational Psychology and Organizational Behavior* 4: 19–43.

Demerouti E, Bakker AB, Nachreiner F, et al. (2001) The job demands-resources model of burnout. *Journal of Applied Psychology* 86(3): 499–512.

Dess GG, Ireland RD, Zahra SA, et al. (2003) Emerging issues in corporate entrepreneurship. *Journal of Management* 29(3): 351–378.

Di Fabio A (2014) Intrapreneurial self-capital: A new construct for the 21st century. *Journal of Employment Counseling* 51(3): 98–111.

Di Fabio A and Gori A (2016) Neuroticism and flourishing in white collar workers: From self-esteem to intrapreneurial self-capital for adaptive outcomes. In A Di Fabio (ed) *Neuroticism: Characteristics, Impact on Job Performance and Health Outcomes*. New York, NY: Nova Science Publishers, pp. 129–146.

Di Fabio A and Kenny ME (2018) Intrapreneurial self-capital: A key resource for promoting well-being in a shifting work landscape. *Sustainability* 10(9): 3035.

Di Fabio A, Palazzeschi L and Bucci O (2017) In an unpredictable and changing environment: Intrapreneurial self-capital as a key resource for life satisfaction and flourishing. *Frontiers in Psychology* 8: 1819.

Dijkhuizen J, Gorgievski M, van Veldhoven M, et al. (2016) Feeling successful as an entrepreneur: A job demands–resources approach. *International Entrepreneurship and Management Journal* 12(2): 555–573.

Djourova NP, Rodríguez Molina I, Tordera Santamatilde N, et al. (2019) Self-efficacy and resilience: Mediating mechanisms in the relationship between the transformational leadership dimensions and well-being. *Journal of Leadership & Organizational Studies* 27(3): 256-270. 1548051819849002.

Douglas EJ and Fitzsimmons JR (2013) Intrapreneurial intentions versus entrepreneurial intentions: Distinct constructs with different antecedents. *Small Business Economics* 41(1): 115–132.

Edú Valsania S, Moriano JA and Molero F (2016) Authentic leadership and intrapreneurial behaviour: cross-level analysis of the mediator effect of organizational identification and empowerment. *International Entrepreneurship Management Journal* 12: 131–152.

Ekiyor A and Şenel G (2017) Effect of the burn-out syndrome on intrapreneurship: A practice in province Ankara. *Asian Journal of Economics, Business and Accounting* 3(2): 1–11.

European Agency for Safety and Health at Work (2014) *Calculating the cost of work-related stress and psychological risks*. Available at: https://osha.europa.eu/en/publications/calculating-cost-work-related-stress-and-psychosocial-risks (Accessed 23 November 2020)

Eysenck H (1997) Personality and experimental psychology: The unification of psychology and the possibility of a paradigm. *Journal of Personality and Social Psychology* 73(6): 1224–1237.

Floyd SW and Lane PJ (2000) Strategizing throughout the organization: Managing role conflict in strategic renewal. *Academy of Management Review* 25(1): 154–177.

Gardner RL, Cooper E, Haskell J, et al. (2019) Physician stress and burnout: The impact of health information technology. *Journal of the American Medical Informatics Association* 26(2): 106–114.

Gawke JC, Gorgievski MJ and Bakker AB (2018) Personal costs and benefits of employee intrapreneurship: Disentangling the employee intrapreneurship, well-being, and job performance relationship. *Journal of Occupational Health Psychology* 23(4): 508–519.

Gray J (1970) The psychophysiological basis of introversion-extraversion. *Behaviour Research and Therapy* 8(3): 249–266.

Gray J and McNaughton N (2000) *The Neuropsychology of Anxiety: An Enquiry into the Functions of the Septo-Hippocampal System*. Oxford: Oxford University Press.

Harmon-Jones E, Lueck L, Fearn M, et al. (2006) The effect of personal relevance and approach-related action expectation on relative left frontal cortical activity. *Psychological Science* 17(5): 434–440.

Health and Safety Executive (2019) *Health and Safety at Work: Summary Statistics for Great Britain 2019*. Available at: https://www.hse.gov.uk/statistics/overall/hssh1819.pdf (accessed 1 July 2020).

Hornsby JS, Naffziger DW, Kuratko DF, et al. (1993) An interactive model of the corporate entrepreneurship process. *Entrepreneurship Theory and Practice* 17(2): 29–37.

Hughes M and Mustafa M (2017) Antecedents of corporate entrepreneurship in SMEs: Evidence from an emerging economy. *Journal of Small Business Management* 55(sup1): 115–140.

Huo M-L, Boxall P and Cheung GW (2019) Lean production, work intensification and employee wellbeing: Can line-manager support make a difference? *Economic and Industrial Democracy*. 0143831X19890678.

Kattenbach R and Fietze S (2018) Entrepreneurial orientation and the job demands-resources model. *Personnel Review* 47(3): 745–764.

Kuratko DF (2012) Corporate entrepreneurship. In D Hjorth (ed) *Handbook on organisational entrepreneurship*. Northampton, MA: Edward Elgar Publishing Ltd, pp. 226–241.

Kuratko DF and Audretsch DB (2013) Clarifying the domains of corporate entrepreneurship. *International Entrepreneurship and Management Journal* 9(3): 323–335.

Magee W (2013) Anxiety, demoralization, and the gender difference in job satisfaction. *Sex Roles* 69(5–6): 308–322.

Nielsen K and Daniels K (2016) The relationship between transformational leadership and follower sickness absence: The role of presenteeism. *Work & Stress*, 30(2), 193–208.

Neessen PC, Caniëls MC, Vos B, et al. (2019) The intrapreneurial employee: Toward an integrated model of intrapreneurship and research agenda. *International Entrepreneurship and Management Journal* 15(2): 545–571.

Paek B and Lee H (2018) Strategic entrepreneurship and competitive advantage of established firms: Evidence from the digital TV industry. *International Entrepreneurship and Management Journal* 14(4): 883–925.

Patterson CM and Newman JP (1993) Reflectivity and learning from aversive events: Toward a psychological mechanism for the syndromes of disinhibition. *Psychological Review* 100(4): 716–736.

Pinchot III G (1985) Intrapreneuring: Why you don't have to leave the corporation to become an entrepreneur. *University of Illinois at Urbana-Champaign's Academy for

Entrepreneurial Leadership Historical Research Reference in Entrepreneurship.

Ployhart RE and Bartunek JM (2019) Editors' comments: There is nothing so theoretical as good practice – A call for phenomenal theory. *Academy of Management Review* 44(3): 493–497.

Portales L (2019) Social intrapreneurship, the main factor of social innovations within traditional Companies. In *Social innovation and social entrepreneurship*. Cham: Palgrave Macmillian, pp. 147–160.

Preenen PT, Dorenbosch L, Plantinga E, et al. (2019) The influence of task challenge on skill utilization, affective wellbeing and intrapreneurial behaviour. *Economic and Industrial Democracy* 40(4): 954–975.

Rigtering J and Weitzel U (2013) Work context and employee behaviour as antecedents for intrapreneurship. *International Entrepreneurship and Management Journal* 9(3): 337–360.

Ronen S (2010) Chapter 13 Determinants of intrapreneurship among high-tech engineers. In A Malach-Pines and MF Öxzbilgin (eds) *Handbook of research on high-technology entrepreneurs*. Cheltenham: Edward Elgar Publishing, pp. 233–251.

Sharma P and Chrisman JJ (1999) Toward a reconciliation of the definitional issues in the field of corporate entrepreneurship. *Entrepreneurship Theory and Practice* 23(3): 11–28.

Shepherd DA, Covin JG and Kuratko DF (2009) Project failure from corporate entrepreneurship: Managing the grief process. *Journal of Business Venturing* 24(6): 588–600.

Shir N, Nikolaev BN and Wincent J (2019) Entrepreneurship and well-being: The role of psychological autonomy, competence, and relatedness. *Journal of Business Venturing* 34(5): 105875.

Shoji K, Cieslak R, Smoktunowicz E, et al. (2016) Associations between job burnout and self-efficacy: A meta-analysis. *Anxiety, Stress, & Coping* 29(4): 367–386.

Sørensen J and Fassiotto M (2011) Organizations as fonts of entrepreneurship. *Organization Science* 22(5): 1322–1331.

Stevenson H and Jarillo J (1990) A paradigm of entrepreneurship: Entrepreneurial management. *Strategic Management Journal* 11: 17–27.

Strauss K, Parker SK and O'Shea D (2017) When does proactivity have a cost? Motivation at work moderates the effects of proactive work behavior on employee job strain. *Journal of Vocational Behavior* 100: 15–26.

Valsania SE, Moriano J and Molero F (2016) Authentic leadership and intrapreneurial behavior: Cross-level analysis of the mediator effect of organizational identification and empowerment. *International Entrepreneurship and Management Journal* 12(1): 131–152.

Vargas C, Cañadas GA, Aguayo R, et al. (2014) Which occupational risk factors are associated with burnout in nursing? A meta-analytic study. *International Journal of Clinical and Health Psychology* 14(1): 28–38.

Wakkee I, Elfring T and Monaghan S (2010) Creating entrepreneurial employees in traditional service sectors. *International Entrepreneurship and Management Journal* 6(1): 1–21.

Wiklund J, Nikolaev B, Shir N, et al. (2019) Entrepreneurship and well-being: Past, present, and future. *Journal of Business Venturing* 34(4): 579–588.

Wilks D and Neto F (2013) Workplace well-being, gender and age: Examining the 'double jeopardy' effect. *Social Indicators Research* 114(3): 875–890.

Woo HR (2018) Personality traits and intrapreneurship: the mediating effect of career adaptability. *Career Development International* 23(2): 145–162.

Wood CC, Holt DT, Reed TS, et al. (2008) Perceptions of corporate entrepreneurship in air force organizations: Antecedents and outcomes. *Journal of Small Business & Entrepreneurship* 21(1): 117–131.

14

Entrepreneurs' Psychological Wellbeing

Anne-Kathrin Kleine and Antje Schmitt

INTRODUCTION

Entrepreneurship may be understood as the creation of a new venture (e.g., Gartner, 1988) and the occupational choice of working self-employed for that business (e.g., Gorgievski and Stephan, 2016). By exploring and exploiting innovative products and services and creating new jobs, entrepreneurs contribute to both economic growth and the breakthrough of services and goods that fulfill social needs (e.g., Wiklund et al., 2019). In light of the crucial role entrepreneurs play in a country's economic and societal development, supporting entrepreneurial activities by fostering positive and limiting negative impacting factors of entrepreneurial wellbeing should be of high general interest.

Entrepreneurial wellbeing has been defined as 'the experience of satisfaction, positive affect, infrequent negative affect, and psychological functioning in relation to developing, starting, growing, and running an entrepreneurial venture' (Wiklund et al., 2019: 582). Psychological

wellbeing (PWB) is an integral part of a fulfilling life and the basis of human functioning (Diener, 2000; Ryan and Deci, 2000a).

Researchers have argued repeatedly for the relevance of considering wellbeing as an indicator of entrepreneurial success (e.g., Shepherd and Haynie, 2009; Wiklund et al., 2019). Entrepreneurs with high PWB possess the mental resources needed to pursue their goals and persist in the face of adversity (Wiklund et al., 2019).

Interestingly, being an entrepreneur may be associated with opposite effects on wellbeing. On one side, it is seen that individuals often choose an entrepreneurial career because of non-material benefits associated with it, such as the engagement in purposeful activities that let them derive meaning from their work and sharpen their talents and skills; this, in turn, affects their wellbeing positively (Wiklund et al., 2019). However, next to the benefits that are associated with an entrepreneurial career, entrepreneurs have to cope with several potential stressors, such as uncertainty, high responsibility, workload, and time pressure (Stephan, 2018), which, in turn, might threaten their wellbeing.

While overviews of contextual, behavioral, and personal factors that influence the entrepreneur's PWB exist (e.g., Stephan, 2018), integrating health and wellbeing theories into a literature overview helps in understanding the underlying mechanisms and interrelated effects of those variables on entrepreneurial wellbeing. For example, while resource-and-demands theories (e.g., Demerouti et al., 2001) enhance our understanding of how personal and contextual resources buffer the negative effects of stress-enhancing job demands, self-determination theory (Ryan and Deci, 2000a) explains the positive effects of autonomy-enhancing job characteristics on entrepreneurial PWB. This chapter provides an overview as well as a critical reflection of current research findings on the entrepreneurs' PWB, based on their theoretical underpinnings. We do not provide a conclusive summary of research findings, but present exemplary studies, aiming to enhance the reader's understanding of the connection between theoretical perspectives and empirical studies. Based on our literature review, we reveal gaps both in current theorizing and empirical studies on the entrepreneurs' PWB, and we provide recommendations for future research.

PSYCHOLOGICAL WELLBEING AMONG ENTREPRENEURS

Researchers commonly distinguish between hedonic and eudaimonic forms of wellbeing (e.g., Ryan and Deci, 2001). Hedonic wellbeing refers to the presence of positive affect and the absence of negative affect (e.g., subjective wellbeing; Diener, 1984), while eudaimonic wellbeing entails experiences of meaningfulness associated with the engagement in intrinsically motivating tasks, self-development, and human functioning

(e.g., Ryan and Deci, 2001). Moreover, wellbeing may be understood as a continuum ranging from ill-being (e.g., depression, burnout) to wellbeing (e.g., positive affect, job satisfaction) (Warr, 1990). In this chapter, we conceptualize wellbeing in terms of both hedonic and eudaimonic views and take account of indicators at both ends of the ill-being–wellbeing continuum.

Bottom-up theories of life satisfaction argue that multiple life domains such as health, family, and work contribute to a person's overall experience of satisfaction (e.g., Hart, 1999). The strength of the relationship between a person's life-domain satisfaction and overall life satisfaction is assumed to be influenced by the relevance a person ascribes to a specific life domain (Oishi et al., 1999). Entrepreneurs commonly perceive their occupation as a central part of their lives. Accordingly, the relationship between work and general life satisfaction is shown to be stronger for entrepreneurs than for salaried workers (Loewe et al., 2015). In the chapter, we thus consider wellbeing concepts at different levels of abstraction (e.g., job satisfaction and general life satisfaction).

Long-term studies showed that individuals' wellbeing fluctuates over time (Fujita and Diener, 2005) and there is also substantial variability in weekly (e.g., Totterdell et al., 2006) as well as daily (e.g., Uy et al., 2017) wellbeing indicators in entrepreneurial samples. Whenever possible, we take account of the fluctuating nature of PWB constructs (e.g., by differentiating between cross-sectional and longitudinal assessments of PWB).

ENTREPRENEURSHIP: PERSON, BEHAVIOR, AND CONTEXT VIEWS

Entrepreneurship may be studied from different perspectives. First, entrepreneurship can be understood in terms of the individual characteristics of the entrepreneur (Bird, 1988; Rauch and Frese, 2007). This conceptualization stems from the claim that how a person becomes an entrepreneur and how this person acts within the role of an entrepreneur is influenced by that person's needs, beliefs, and values (Bird, 1988). Indeed, it was found that entrepreneurs differ from managers in some personality characteristics. In two meta-analytic summaries, entrepreneurs were shown to be more conscientious and open to experiences, less neurotic and less agreeable, more extraverted and risk-prone, and had a higher need for achievement than managers (Brandstätter, 2011; Zhao and Seibert, 2006).

Second, from a behavioral perspective, entrepreneurship is defined in terms of the actions the entrepreneur performs (e.g., Gatewood et al., 1995). Specifically, entrepreneurial behaviors may be understood as the (sequential) set of actions that have to be performed when founding and leading a business, such as hiring and training employees, and producing, distributing, and marketing products or services (Gatewood et al., 1995), or in terms of general behavioral tendencies, such as competitive, proactive, and innovative behaviors, as well as risk-taking (Covin and Slevin, 1989).

Finally, entrepreneurship may be defined in terms of the firm characteristics and the wider (social) context in which the entrepreneur operates (e.g., Ács and Audretsch, 2006; Audretsch, 2012). Ács and Audretsch (2006) argue that all phases of the entrepreneurial process are embedded within a system of social interactions. That is, to establish, run, and develop a business, entrepreneurs have to interact with their environment by communicating with stakeholders, for example. This tenet fits research findings showing that a country's monetary policy, social climate, or unemployment rate may influence innovation and entrepreneurship activities (e.g., Marcotte, 2013).

Distinguishing between person, context, and behavior perspectives on entrepreneurship helps in understanding the antecedents of entrepreneurial wellbeing (Figure 14.1).

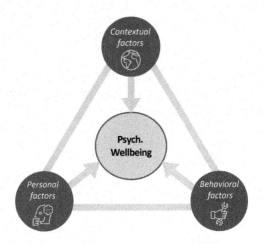

Figure 14.1 The entrepreneur's psychological wellbeing is subject to contextual, behavioral, and personal factors

Drawing from a person-centered perspective, individual characteristics, such as needs and values, may affect entrepreneurs' wellbeing directly (e.g., Berglund et al., 2016). Next, entrepreneurs' PWB may benefit from the actions they perform. For example, holding promising negotiations may feel rewarding and enhance their level of satisfaction. Finally, the entrepreneurs' context confronts them with demands (e.g., high uncertainty) and provides them with resources (e.g., social support) that affect their PWB (e.g., Leung et al., 2020). In the following, we explain from multiple theoretical perspectives how person, behavior, and context factors enhance or diminish the entrepreneur's PWB. Table 14.1 provides an overview.

PREDICTING ENTREPRENEURS' WELLBEING: THEORY AND RESEARCH FINDINGS

Resource-and-Demands Theories

On a general level, job demands are those aspects of a job that require sustained mental

Table 14.1   Example study findings

Theory	Findings	Authors
Conservation of resources theory (Hobfoll, 1989)	Role stress mediated the effect of organizational, environmental, and personal demands and resources on satisfaction and exhaustion	Wincent et al., 2009
	Job stress mediated the effect of work–family conflict on job satisfaction	Schjoedt, 2020
Job-demands-control model (Karasek, 1979)	Lower levels of stress among self-employed compared to employees were partly explained by the difference in perceived job control	Hessels et al., 2017
	Independent effects of work demands, control, and support on strain and depression; the highest level of strain was found among pessimistic entrepreneurs who experience high demands and low control	Totterdell et al., 2006
Job-demands-resources model (Demerouti et al., 2001)	Work–family conflict was the strongest predictor of strain and engagement; synergy between work and family was related to lower strain and higher engagement; strain and engagement predicted growth and exit intentions	Beutell et al., 2019
	Strongest association between neuroticism and burnout was found among low-conscientious entrepreneurs	Perry et al., 2008
Self-determination theory (Ryan and Deci, 2000b)	Higher wellbeing was reported among opportunity as compared to necessity entrepreneurs	Block and Koellinger, 2009
	The positive effect of entrepreneurship on wellbeing was mediated by autonomy	Shir et al., 2019
Goal orientation theory (Dweck,1986)	Learning goal orientation increased the negative effect of affect spin on wellbeing and venture goal progress; high affect spin together with high performance goal orientation was associated with better wellbeing and venture progress	Uy et al., 2017
Social-cognitive theory (Bandura,1977)	Self-efficacy partially explained the positive associations between self-employment and wellbeing	Bradley and Roberts, 2004
	Self-efficacy predicted both short- and longer-term enthusiasm and work engagement	Laguna et al., 2017
	Self-efficacy negatively moderated the effect of improvisation on job satisfaction	Hmieleski and Corbett, 2008
Transactional stress theory (Folkman, 1984)	Active coping strategies predicted immediate and long-term wellbeing positively; avoidance coping improved immediate wellbeing among experienced entrepreneurs	Uy et al., 2013
	Employees reported more negative emotions than entrepreneurs when using problem- and emotion-focused coping	Patzelt and Shepherd, 2011

Table 14.1 Example study findings (Continued)

Theory	Findings	Authors
Affective events theory (Weiss and Cropanzano, 1996)	Stressful events are more strongly related to both mental and physical health than satisfaction-related events; overwork as the most commonly experienced event; bankruptcy as the most intense stressor; satisfaction of clients was the most experienced and the most intense satisfaction-related category	Lechat and Torrès, 2017
Person–environment fit theory (Edwards et al., 1998)	Analytic entrepreneurs reported higher satisfaction in more structured work contexts than intuitive entrepreneurs; the reverse effect was found in less structured environments	Brigham et al., 2007
	The effect of positive expectancy violation on wellbeing was mediated via person–environment fit	Hmieleski and Sheppard, 2019
Hedonic treadmill model (Brickman and Campbell, 1971)	Job satisfaction improved shortly after people became self-employed; after approximately three years, they returned to their previous level of satisfaction	Hanglberger and Merz, 2015

or physical effort and are therefore associated with physiological and psychological costs, such as exhaustion. Personal and job resources act as health-protecting factors that help individuals reduce the negative effects of job demands (e.g., Demerouti et al., 2001). Demands-resources theories describe how individuals seek to acquire or protect their resources and how stress emerges in an environment in which there is a loss, threat of a loss, or lack of an expected gain of resources (Conservation of Resources Theory, COR, Hobfoll, 1989). Demands-resources theories further explain how the effects of job demands, as potential sources of stress, may be alleviated by (a) job control (i.e., autonomy and decision latitude) (Job-Demand-Control (JDC) model, Karasek, 1979) and (b) job and personal resources in general (Job-Demands-Resources (JDR) model, Demerouti et al., 2001; Xanthopoulou et al., 2007).

Due to their high job demands and tendency to identify with their jobs, entrepreneurs are particularly prone to experiencing work–family conflicts. For example, entrepreneurs can experience pressure and inner conflicts as a result of the perception that the two roles (entrepreneur vs family member) are incompatible (e.g., Shelton, 2006). Drawing from COR, Schjoedt (2020) interprets work-and-family conflicts as threats of resource loss when the entrepreneur is requested to engage in behavior in two incompatible domains. Indeed, work-and-family conflicts were found to enhance stress, which consequently led to diminished job satisfaction.

COR theory predicts that a lack of resources may beget further loss, resulting in a loss spiral, while a resource gain may result in gain spirals (Hobfoll, 2001). For example, imagine an entrepreneur who just founded her company. At a certain point, she might realize that she needs to hire specialists for taking over certain tasks she cannot completely do alone. If she finds the support she needs quickly, she might be able to deliver the high-quality products she promised her customers in time. If, on the other hand, she runs into problems finding suitable employees, the products will be of lower quality or the delivery is delayed. In the first scenario, she would have time to put extra effort into building a good relationship with the main customers, consequently resulting in a further gain in resources, while in the second scenario, she would have to get involved in compensating for the damage done, likely leading to a further loss in resources. Leung et al. (2020) proposed that instrumental and emotional social support would contribute to the entrepreneur's maintenance of a resource reservoir, consequently initiating a gain spiral. Using a cross-sectional study design, the authors found the effect of emotional and social support on work satisfaction, family satisfaction, and work stress to be mediated via work–family balance. However, contrary to their assumption, instrumental support affected work–family balance negatively.

According to JDR theory, job demands and resources affect health and wellbeing directly, as well as interactively (i.e., resources buffer the negative effects of demands on health and wellbeing, and high demands paired with high resources result in higher engagement; Bakker and Demerouti, 2007). For example, Beutell et al. (2019) found that, among several demands, work–family conflict was the strongest negative predictor of both strain and engagement. Perry et al. (2008) examined the interactive effects of contextual demands and personality characteristics; the strongest association between neuroticism and burnout was found among low-conscientious entrepreneurs, which supports the notion that conscientiousness may act as personal resources that buffer the negative effects of neuroticism on burnout when being faced with constraints (Perry et al., 2008).

Per JDC theory, it has been argued that the decision authority associated with the freedom to decide when and how to complete one's tasks may alleviate the stress-enhancing effects of high demands (Hessels et al., 2017). Hessels et al. (2017) showed that the low level of stress among self-employed

individuals – as compared to that of employed workers – was explained by the difference in job control between the self-employed and wage workers. Relatedly, in a daily diary study, Totterdell et al. (2006) found evidence of a more complex relationship between entrepreneurs' perceived daily work control and strain: high levels of daily control were associated with less strain during weeks of high demands for pessimistic entrepreneurs, but not for optimistic entrepreneurs. The highest level of strain was found among pessimistic entrepreneurs who experienced high demands and low control.

Self-Determination Theory

The satisfaction individuals derive from the autonomy of leading their own business is a central motive for becoming self-employed (e.g., Benz and Frey, 2008; Shir et al., 2019). According to self-determination theory (SDT), the fulfillment of the three psychological needs – autonomy, competence, and relatedness – is key for optimal human functioning and individual wellbeing (Ryan and Deci, 2000b). Work activities that satisfy these needs are increased intrinsic motivation, internalization of one's work tasks and goals, and higher wellbeing (Ryan and Deci, 2000a, 2000b).

Shir et al. (2019) examined the roles of autonomy, competence, and relatedness as mediators of the effect of entrepreneurship on wellbeing. As predicted, autonomy mediated the positive effect of being an entrepreneur on psychological wellbeing. However, being an entrepreneur did not affect individuals' sense of relatedness or competence when controlling for the effects of autonomy. That is, the positive effect of entrepreneurship seems to work entirely through the channel of autonomy.

Entrepreneurs may experience different levels of autonomy depending on their reason for becoming an entrepreneur (e.g., Binder and Coad, 2016). Opportunity entrepreneurs (i.e., those who founded their business because they came across a business opportunity) commonly report higher levels of wellbeing than necessity entrepreneurs (i.e., those who founded their business out of necessity, e.g., to escape unemployment) – an effect that has been explained by differences in perceived autonomy (Binder and Coad, 2016). The positive effects of opportunity entrepreneurship on individual wellbeing were found to be robust across studies and held for different indicators of wellbeing, such as job satisfaction, distress, mortality, and subjective wellbeing (Stephan, 2018).

Self-Regulation Theories

According to a self-regulation perspective, individuals maintain or enhance their level of functioning through setting, striving towards, attaining, revising, and disengaging from goals (e.g., Locke and Latham, 2002). Over the past decades, scholars have proposed a number of self-regulation theories, such as goal orientation theory (e.g., Dweck, 1986; Vandewalle, 1997) or social-cognitive theory (Bandura and Cervone, 1986).

Goal orientation theory proposes that self-regulatory processes depend on individual goals (e.g., DeShon and Gillespie, 2005; Elliot, 1999). Uy et al. (2017) investigated how entrepreneurs' regulatory focus mitigates the negative effects of affect spin (i.e., fluctuations of positive and negative affect in response to affective events). The authors argue that performance-approach-oriented individuals (i.e., those who self-regulate towards attaining competence- and performance-related goals; Elliot, 1999) adopt proven strategies in response to affect-laden events rather than engaging in exploratory forms of behavior, thus saving resources required for affect regulation. In contrast, learning-goal-oriented entrepreneurs (i.e., those who self-regulate towards the development of intrinsically derived competence and personal development; Elliot, 1999) would

try to make sense of affect fluctuations and thus engage in exploratory behavior, which, in turn, increases their processing demands and consequently consumes necessary resources. As predicted, it was found that learning goal orientation increased the negative effect of affect spin on wellbeing and venture goal progress. Moreover, high affect spin together with high performance goal orientation was positively associated with psychological wellbeing and venture progress.

Social-cognitive theory (Bandura and Cervone, 1986) explains how self-efficacy – the individual's belief in his or her capacity to execute behaviors necessary to accomplish goals (Bandura, 1977) – influences a person's behavior. For example, individuals with high self-efficacy persist in the face of adversity and recover quickly from failure (Bandura, 1977). It has been proposed that higher job satisfaction among entrepreneurs as compared to wage workers may be explained by higher levels of perceived self-efficacy (Bradley and Roberts, 2004). In line with their assumption, Bradley and Roberts (2004) found that the positive relationship between self-employment and job satisfaction diminished when self-efficacy was taken into account. However, self-efficacy may not be beneficial for the entrepreneur's PWB under all circumstances.

Based on social-cognitive theory, Hmieleski and Corbett (2008) proposed that the entrepreneur's self-efficacy would mitigate the stress-enhancing effects of improvisational behavior (i.e., the execution of novel and untrained behaviors) on work satisfaction. Contrary to their assumptions, the authors found a negative moderating effect of self-efficacy. That is, work satisfaction was lower for entrepreneurs who engaged in improvised forms of behavior and reported high self-efficacy than for those who reported low self-efficacy. One explanation might be that entrepreneurs who improvise and report high self-efficacy over-engage in their work, leading to a loss of resources and increased stress (Hmieleski and Corbett, 2008).

Transactional Stress Theory

According to transactional stress theory, individuals appraise potential stressors as either challenging, threatening, or harmful (Folkman, 1984). Depending on the appraisal of the situation, individuals engage in coping behaviors to resolve the situation and reach favorable outcomes (Folkman, 1984). In the case of a favorable resolution, positive emotions are elicited, while distress arises from unresolved or unfavorable coping outcomes (Folkman, 1984; Folkman and Lazarus, 1980). Folkman and Lazarus (1980) proposed two main categories of coping reactions, namely problem- vs emotion-focused coping. While problem-focused coping refers to dealing with stressful events by developing action plans and focusing on the next steps, emotion-focused coping refers to the regulation of negative events by psychological withdrawal or seeking support from others (Folkman and Lazarus, 1980). For example, an entrepreneur who expects a product delivery delay might engage in problem-focused coping by setting up a plan on how to respond to the expected delivery delay and communicating his ideas to the stakeholder. An emotion-focused coping response, on the other hand, might entail distracting himself from the negative consequences of the expected delivery delay by focusing on tasks he experiences as more rewarding.

Patzelt and Shepherd (2011) suggested that, due to their high decision latitude, self-employed individuals might have more options to change their work environment and should thus be more effective in coping with stressful situations than employees. They found that both problem- and emotion-focused coping moderated the effect of being employed vs self-employed on negative emotions. That is, employees reported more negative emotions than entrepreneurs in both high problem- and emotion-focused coping.

Uy et al. (2013) found that while active (i.e., problem-focused) coping strategies predicted both immediate and long-term wellbeing positively, avoidance (i.e., emotion-focused) coping improved immediate wellbeing only among experienced entrepreneurs. The authors conclude that prior start-up experience increases entrepreneurs' knowledge of effective coping strategies, thus facilitating the effective use of avoidance coping as indicated by higher immediate wellbeing. Their findings point at the important role of entrepreneurs' individual resources, such as experience, when investigating the effects of coping on PWB.

Affective Events Theory

Affective events theory (AET, Weiss and Cropanzano, 1996) proposes that workers' emotional reactions to events that occur while doing their job affects their work attitudes, as well as their affect- and judgment-driven behaviors. A response to a certain event is assumed to depend on personal attributes, appraisal, and coping styles. That is, AET proposes a direct link between affective events and job satisfaction. It also indicates an indirect effect on wellbeing via affect-based behaviors, like organizational citizenship or problem-solving behavior. Drawing from AET, Lechat and Torrès (2017) analyzed the effects of business-relevant biographic events (e.g., conflict with a supplier, professional travel) on entrepreneurs' mental and physical health. They found that stress-related events were more strongly related to both mental and physical health than satisfaction-related events. Overwork was the stressor most commonly experienced and bankruptcy was the least experienced and most intense of all stressors. Clients' satisfaction was both the most experienced and the most intense satisfaction-related category.

Person–Environment Fit Theory

Person–environment (P–E) fit theory entails the presumption that perceived congruence between personal and environmental factors enhances performance and wellbeing (e.g., Edwards et al., 1998; Edwards and Shipp, 2007). P–E fit may be distinguished into two branches: supplementary fit (i.e., the perception of similarity between person and environment characteristics), and complementary fit (i.e., the degree to which a person and the environment complement each other). Moreover, fit may be examined on multiple levels (i.e., fit between the person and their job, work unit/group, organization, or vocation) (Edwards and Shipp, 2007).

Drawing from P–E fit theory, Brigham et al. (2007) examined the association between a fit in decision-making style and the level of organizational formalization on job satisfaction among entrepreneurs. While analytic entrepreneurs reported higher satisfaction in more structured work contexts than did intuitive entrepreneurs, the reverse effect was seen in less structured environments. Moreover, in less structured environments, intuitive owner-managers expressed a weaker intention to exit than analytic entrepreneurs; conversely, for more structured work environments, they reported a stronger intention to exit.

Hmieleski and Sheppard (2019) investigated whether the effect of a positive violation of stereotypical gender roles on work satisfaction, firm performance, and work–family conflict would be mitigated via person–job fit. The authors propose that creativity, as an agentic person characteristic, is more commonly ascribed to male than to female entrepreneurs. Thus, women who score high on creativity are suggested to perceive this as a positive expectancy violation. In the same vein, male founders' level of teamwork (as a communal person characteristic ascribed to female entrepreneurs) was proposed to be perceived as a positive expectancy violation, consequently enhancing the perception of person–work fit for men. Positive expectancy violation, in turn, was proposed to enhance the perception of being well-suited for an entrepreneurial career, thus increasing person–job fit.

Drawing from P–E fit theory, person–job fit was predicted to positively affect work satisfaction and firm performance and to diminish work–family conflict. As hypothesized, it was found that the effect of creativity was mediated via person–job fit for women, but not for men. Conversely, the effect of teamwork on work–family conflict and new-venture performance was mediated via person–job fit for men, but not for women.

Hedonic Treadmill Model

According to Brickman and Campbell's (1971) hedonic treadmill model, the experience of new incentives that come along with performing novel tasks is associated with a positive short-term shift in subjective wellbeing. After some time, however, individuals would return to their baseline level of wellbeing. Hanglberger and Merz (2015) assessed the temporal dynamics of the resource gain associated with self-employment. In line with the hedonic treadmill model, the authors found that job satisfaction improved shortly after people became self-employed. This effect lasted for only three years. After that period, individuals returned to the previous level of satisfaction. The authors conclude that the resources gained by becoming self-employed (e.g., higher autonomy) are subject to adaptation effects, thus explaining the transient nature of wellbeing gains among entrepreneurs.

SUMMARY AND CRITICAL REFLECTION OF RESEARCH FINDINGS

In Figure 14.2, we provide a model of entrepreneurial wellbeing that integrates those different theoretical perspectives. Resource-and-demands theories (e.g., COR theory, JDC model, JDR model) explain how person and context factors exhibit additive as well as interactive effects on entrepreneurs'

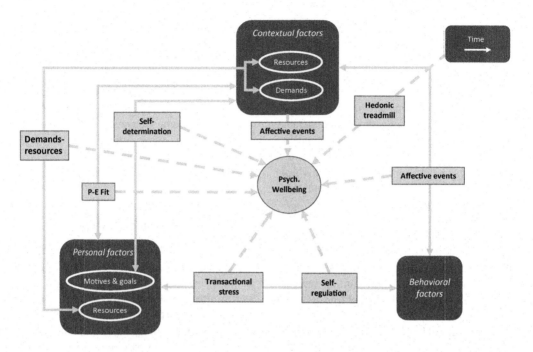

Figure 14.2   An integrative model of the antecedents of entrepreneurs' psychological wellbeing

wellbeing. The same demands and resources have been studied from different theoretical perspectives. For example, work-and-family conflict has been interpreted as both a threat of a loss of resources (Schjoedt, 2020) and as a demand (Beutell et al., 2019). Moreover, while we gained some understanding of the effects of demands and resources, we lack understanding of how resource gain-and-loss spirals affect the entrepreneur's PWB over time.

Self-determination theory explains how the individual need for autonomy may be satisfied by following an entrepreneurial career (e.g., high decision latitude), thus contributing to individual wellbeing. However, in the entrepreneurship context, no similar evidence was found regarding the need for competence and relatedness (Shir et al., 2019).

Self-regulation theories propose that individuals' actions are informed by personal goals and beliefs. Some evidence was found for the positive effects of cognitive processes,

such as goal orientation (Uy et al., 2017) and self-efficacy (Laguna et al., 2017) on entrepreneurial wellbeing. Behavioral processes have mainly been omitted, although they are relevant across self-regulation theories, for example, behavioral strategies are based on salient goals (Elliot, 1999), and individuals act if they believe they are able to attain certain outcomes (Bandura, 1977).

Transactional stress theory integrates personal and behavioral components by proposing that cognitive appraisal of potential stressors elicits behavioral responses (i.e., coping), which, in turn, affect wellbeing. Research on entrepreneurs' PWB that draws from transactional stress theory mainly focuses on the effects of (active vs passive) coping on PWB outcomes (e.g., Patzelt and Shepherd, 2011; Uy et al., 2013). Thus, the tenet that PWB and stress are the results of a process entailing cognitive appraisal and coping responses has been neglected in the entrepreneurship literature (see Li et al., 2018 for an example in the occupational health literature).

Investigations of the effects of affective events on entrepreneurs' PWB outcomes are scarce. While Lechat and Torrès (2017) found some evidence for the direct relationship between certain affective events and mental and physical health, the role of affect-based behavior for entrepreneurial wellbeing remains unexplored.

P–E fit theory proposes that fit between personal and environmental characteristics has positive consequences for individual PWB. For example, a fit between preferences for a certain decision-making style (i.e., intuitives vs analysts) and the level of organizational formalization (i.e., low vs high level of formalization of work procedures) were shown to enhance job satisfaction among entrepreneurs (Brigham et al., 2007). Researchers investigating the effects of P–E fit on entrepreneurs' PWB have neglected the proposed distinction between supplementary and complementary fit, as well as considerations regarding the alignment of outcome variables and the level of the environment under investigation (i.e., vocation, organization, group, or job; see Edwards and Shipp, 2007).

Finally, according to the hedonic treadmill model, although new incentives and stimuli may elicit short-term benefits, individuals eventually return to their initial level of wellbeing. In the entrepreneurship context, support for the model has been found in only one study so far (Hanglberger and Merz, 2015).

RECOMMENDATIONS FOR FUTURE RESEARCH

First, based on the research gaps identified above, we recommend focusing on processes that have been suggested by theory but remain under-explored, such as the role of cognitive appraisal in the coping process or the role of the need for connectedness and

competence in autonomous self-regulation. Below, we outline how research may benefit from a stronger integration of behavioral processes and an examination of processes over time, as well as the investigation of eudaimonic wellbeing outcomes.

Incorporating Behavior

Most research on entrepreneurial wellbeing concentrates on the effects of contextual and personal characteristics. Integrating a behavioral perspective may foster a deeper understanding of the processes that affect entrepreneurs' PWB. For example, Uy et al. (2017) argue that individuals with a performance orientation adopt success-proven behavioral strategies to reach their goals, thus saving resources in the long run. In contrast, those with a learning goal focus rather engage in exploratory behaviors that consume resources. However, the question of whether exploratory behavior mitigates the negative effects of learning-goal orientation on wellbeing remains unresolved in their research.

In contrast to owner-managers of established firms, entrepreneurs are often exposed to situations demanding they engage in risky and unpracticed forms of behavior (e.g., Das and Teng, 1998). Counterintuitive findings, such as a negative interaction effect of self-efficacy with improvisational behavior on work satisfaction (Hmieleski and Corbett, 2008) are in line with the controversial effects of proactive behavior for individual wellbeing and functioning addressed by occupational health researchers (e.g., Bolino et al., 2010; Crant, 2000) and warrant further investigation.

Until today, researchers have only explored the direct effects of affective events on the entrepreneur's mental and physical health (e.g., Lechat and Torrès, 2017). A stronger focus on the entrepreneurs' cognitive and behavioral reactions to affective events, such as appraisal and coping, may help to explain the occurrence of daily ups and downs and their relationship with entrepreneurs' overall wellbeing.

Accounting for Variability over Time

Levels of antecedents of entrepreneurial wellbeing and wellbeing itself may change over time (e.g., Fujita and Diener, 2005). However, most research on entrepreneurial wellbeing still relies on cross-sectional designs (see Stephan, 2018). Longitudinal designs offer the possibility to explore entrepreneurs' day-to-day behaviors, cognitions, and affective states (Lévesque and Stephan, 2020). For example, by investigating fluctuations of PWB over time, researchers may investigate adaptation processes proposed by theories on adaptation over time, such as the hedonic treadmill model (Hanglberger and Merz, 2015). The role of time is also important in another regard: Researchers have proposed the division of an entrepreneurial career into distinct phases, such as (1) potential entrepreneurs, (2) nascent entrepreneurs who are involved in setting up their business, (3) owner-managers of a new business, and (4) owner-managers of an established business (Bosma and Kelley, 2019). Future research may uncover differences in the effects of person–behavior–context dynamics on PWB across entrepreneurial career stages.

Finally, research investigating reversed causal processes is scarce. For example, entrepreneurial wellbeing might affect the way stressors are perceived (see Nohe et al., 2015). Longitudinal designs offer the possibility to examine these reciprocal relationships. Moreover, behavior does not only result from cognitive and emotional processes but may follow from the engagement in certain forms of behavior (Gielnik et al., 2015). Accordingly, future research should focus more strongly on disentangling the complex relationships between entrepreneurial cognition, emotions, behavior,

and PWB. Both longitudinal designs and experiments may help clarify the relationship between the appraisal of external stimuli, acting upon them, and indicators of entrepreneurial PWB.

Focusing on Eudaimonic Wellbeing

Although wellbeing theories, such as SDT, posit that the fulfillment of psychological needs is essential not only for health and wellbeing but also for psychological growth (Ryan and Deci, 2000a), most research on entrepreneurial wellbeing concentrates on hedonic forms of wellbeing, like job satisfaction or positive affect. Entrepreneurs often have to adopt a completely new skill set and learn from the errors they make to secure and foster business success (e.g., Cope, 2005). Research on the entrepreneur's PWB may benefit from finer-grained analyses of the processes that affect eudaimonic and hedonic wellbeing differently. For example, while the experience of positive work events likely leads to entrepreneurial satisfaction, learning from errors and exploration may be more strongly related to eudaimonic wellbeing outcomes, such as self-development and learning (Minniti and Bygrave, 2001). Moreover, reasons for becoming self-employed often go beyond motives like financial benefits or enhanced wellbeing. Exploring the processes that foster eudaimonic forms of wellbeing would allow us to better guide the entrepreneur towards realizing their full potential and being intrinsically motivated to pursue their entrepreneurial goals (Ryan and Deci, 2000a).

RECOMMENDATIONS FOR PRACTICE

Regarding practical implications, study findings based on resource-and-demands theories indicate that one of the most severe stressors related to lower PWB is work–family conflict. To alleviate the experienced conflict between work and family roles, entrepreneurs might make use of the advantage of being able to work flexibly and schedule time with their family consciously (e.g., Bayazit and Bayazit, 2019).

As an entrepreneurial career fulfills the need for individual autonomy, individuals should be mindful of the reasons for becoming an entrepreneur. That is, people with a high need for autonomy might benefit more from an entrepreneurial career than those with a low need for autonomy.

Research on goal orientation revealed that entrepreneurs who are high in affect spin – that is, those who experience high frequencies of fluctuations of positive and negative affect, might benefit from focusing on performance goals rather than learning goals. Specific goal orientations are trainable (e.g., Stevens and Gist, 1997). Accordingly, entrepreneurs high in affect spin might integrate goal orientation into their skill training plan.

Finally, regarding the effects of coping on wellbeing, findings by Uy et al. (2013) suggest that while experienced entrepreneurs might benefit from both active and avoidance coping, novice entrepreneurs benefit only from active coping. These findings suggest that, before entrepreneurs have acquired considerable experience and know which coping strategies work for them, they are well-advised to engage in active (i.e., problem-focused) coping. Problem-focused coping skills can be acquired in training programs that focus on dealing with context-dependent obstacles, such as stakeholder management training (see Drnovsek et al., 2010).

REFERENCES

Ács ZJ and Audretsch D (2006) *Handbook of entrepreneurship research: An interdisciplinary survey and introduction*. Boston, MA: Springer.

Audretsch D (2012) Entrepreneurship research. *Management Decision* 50(5): 755–764.

Bakker AB and Demerouti E (2007) The job demands-resources model: State of the art. *Journal of Managerial Psychology* 22(3): 309–328.

Bandura A (1977) Self-efficacy: Toward a unifying theory of behavioral change. *Psychological Review* 82(2): 191–203.

Bandura A and Cervone D (1986) Differential engagement of self-reactive influences in cognitive motivation. *Organizational Behavior and Human Decision Processes* 38(1): 92–113.

Bayazit ZE and Bayazit M (2019) How do flexible work arrangements alleviate work-family-conflict? The roles of flexibility i-deals and family-supportive cultures. *The International Journal of Human Resource Management* 30(3): 405–435.

Benz M and Frey BS (2008) Being independent is a great thing: Subjective evaluations of self-employment and hierarchy. *Economica* 75(298): 362–383.

Berglund V, Johansson Sevä I and Strandh M (2016) Subjective well-being and job satisfaction among self-employed and regular employees: Does personality matter differently? *Journal of Small Business and Entrepreneurship* 28(1): 55–73.

Beutell NJ, Alstete JW, Schneer JA and Hutt C (2019) A look at the dynamics of personal growth and self-employment exit. *International Journal of Entrepreneurial Behavior and Research* 25(7): 1452–1470.

Binder M and Coad A (2016) How satisfied are the self-employed? A life domain view. *Journal of Happiness Studies* 17(4): 1409–1433.

Bird B (1988) Implementing entrepreneurial ideas: The case for intention. *Academy of Management Review* 13(3): 442–453.

Block J and Koellinger P (2009) I can't get no satisfaction – necessity entrepreneurship and procedural utility. *Kyklos* 62(2): 191–209.

Bolino M, Valcea S and Harvey J (2010) Employee, manage thyself: The potentially negative implications of expecting employees to behave proactively. *Journal of Occupational and Organizational Psychology* 83(2): 325–345.

Bosma N and Kelley D (2019) Global Entrepreneurship Monitor 2018/2019 Global Report. Gráfica Andes, Chile: *Global Entrepreneurship Research Association (GERA)*.

Bradley DE and Roberts JA (2004) Self-employ-ment and job satisfaction: Investigating the role of self-efficacy, depression, and senior-ity. *Journal of Small Business Management* 42(1): 37–58.

Brandstätter H (2011) Personality aspects of entrepreneurship: A look at five meta-analyses. *Personality and Individual Differences* 51(3): 222–230.

Brickman P and Campbell DT (1971) Hedonic relativism and planning the good society. In: Appley MH (ed) *Adaptation-level theory.* New York, NY: Academic Press, pp. 287–305.

Brigham KH, De Castro JO and Shepherd DA (2007) A person-organization fit model of owner-managers' cognitive style and organi-zational demands. *Entrepreneurship Theory and Practice* 31(1): 29–51.

Cope J (2005) Toward a dynamic learning per-spective of entrepreneurship. *Entrepreneur-ship Theory and Practice* 29(4): 373–397.

Covin JG and Slevin DP (1989) Strategic man-agement of small firms in hostile and benign environments. *Strategic Management Jour-nal* 10(1): 75–87.

Crant JM (2000) Proactive behavior in organi-zations. *Journal of Management* 26(3): 435–462.

Das TK and Teng BS (1998) Time and entrepre-neurial risk behavior. *Entrepreneurship Theory and Practice* 22(2): 69–88.

Demerouti E, Bakker AB, Nachreiner F and Schaufeli WB (2001) The job demands-resources model of burnout. *Journal of Applied Psychology* 86(3): 499–512.

DeShon RP and Gillespie JZ (2005) A motivated action theory account of goal orientation. *Journal of Applied Psychology* 90(6): 1096–1127.

Diener E (1984) Subjective well-being. *Psycho-logical Bulletin* 95(3): 542.

Diener E (2000) Subjective well-being: The sci-ence of happiness and a proposal for a national index. *American Psychologist* 55(1): 34–43.

Drnovsek M, Örtqvist D and Wincent J (2010) The effectiveness of coping strategies used by entrepreneurs and their impact on per-sonal well-being and venture performance. *Journal of Economics and Business* 28(2): 193–220.

Dweck CS (1986) Motivational processes affecting learning. *American Psychologist* 41(10): 1040–1048.

Edwards JR, Caplan RD and Harrison RV (1998) Person-environment fit theory: Conceptual foundations, empirical evidence, and direc-tions for future research. In: Cooper CL (ed) *Theories of organizational stress.* Oxford: Oxford University Press, pp. 28–67.

Edwards JR and Shipp AJ (2007) The relation-ship between person-environment fit and outcomes: An integrative framework. In: Ostroff C and Judge TA (eds) *Perspectives on organizational fit.* San Francisco, CA: Jossey-Bass, pp. 209–258.

Elliot AJ (1999) Approach and avoidance moti-vation and achievement goals. *Educational Psychologist* 34(3): 169–189.

Folkman S (1984) Personal control and stress and coping processes: A theoretical analysis. *Journal of Personality and Social Psychology* 46(4): 839–852.

Folkman S and Lazarus RS (1980) An analysis of coping in a middle-aged community sample. *Journal of Health and Social Behavior* 21(3): 219.

Fujita F and Diener E (2005) Life satisfaction set point: Stability and change. *Journal of Per-sonality and Social Psychology* 88(1): 158–164.

Gartner WB (1988) 'Who is an entrepreneur?' is the wrong question. *American Journal of Small Business* 12(4): 11–32.

Gatewood EJ, Shaver KG and Gartner WB (1995) A longitudinal study of cognitive fac-tors influencing start-up behaviors and suc-cess at venture creation. *Journal of Business Venturing* 10(5): 371–391.

Gielnik MM, Spitzmuller M, Schmitt A, Kle-mann DK and Frese M (2015) 'I put in effort, therefore I am passionate': Investigating the path from effort to passion in entrepreneur-ship. *Academy of Management Journal* 58(4): 1012–1031.

Gorgievski MJ and Stephan U (2016) Advanc-ing the psychology of entrepreneurship: A review of the psychological literature and an introduction. *Applied Psychology* 65(3): 437–468.

Hanglberger D and Merz J (2015) Does self-employment really raise job satisfaction?

Adaptation and anticipation effects on self-employment and general job changes. *Journal for Labour Market Research* 48(4): 287–303.

Hart PM (1999) Predicting employee life satisfaction: A coherent model of personality, work, and nonwork experiences, and domain satisfactions. *Journal of Applied Psychology* 84: 564–584.

Hessels J, Rietveld CA and van der Zwan P (2017) Self-employment and work-related stress: The mediating role of job control and job demand. *Journal of Business Venturing* 32(2): 178–196.

Hmieleski KM and Corbett AC (2008) The contrasting interaction effects of improvisational behavior with entrepreneurial self-efficacy on new venture performance and entrepreneur work satisfaction. *Journal of Business Venturing* 23(4): 482–496.

Hmieleski KM and Sheppard LD (2019) The Yin and Yang of entrepreneurship: Gender differences in the importance of communal and agentic characteristics for entrepreneurs' subjective well-being and performance. *Journal of Business Venturing* 34(4): 709–730.

Hobfoll SE (1989) Conservation of resources: A new attempt at conceptualizing stress. *American Psychologist* 44(3): 513–524.

Hobfoll SE (2001) The influence of culture, community, and the nested self in the stress process: Advancing conservation of resources theory. *Applied Psychology* 50(3): 337–421.

Karasek RA (1979) Job demands, job decision latitude, and mental strain: Implications for job redesign. *Administrative Science Quarterly* 24(2): 285.

Laguna M, Razmus W, Żaliński A and Zalinski A (2017) Dynamic relationships between personal resources and work engagement in entrepreneurs. *Journal of Occupational and Organizational Psychology* 90(2): 248–269.

Lechat T and Torrès O (2017) Stressors and satisfactors in entrepreneurial activity: An event-based, mixed methods study predicting small business owners' health. *International Journal of Entrepreneurship and Small Business* 32: 537–569.

Leung YK, Mukerjee J and Thurik R (2020) The role of family support in work-family balance and subjective well-being of SME owners.

Journal of Small Business Management 58(1): 130–163.

Lévesque M and Stephan U (2020) It's time we talk about time in entrepreneurship. *Entrepreneurship Theory and Practice* 44(2): 163–184.

Li F, Chen T and Lai X (2018) How does a reward for creativity program benefit or frustrate employee creative performance? The perspective of transactional model of stress and coping. *Group and Organization Management* 43(1): 138–175.

Locke EA and Latham GP (2002) Building a practically useful theory of goal setting and task motivation: A 35-year odyssey. *American Psychologist* 57(9): 705–717.

Loewe N, Araya-Castillo L, Thieme C and Batista-Foguet JM (2015) Self-employment as a moderator between work and life satisfaction. *Academia Revista Latinoamericana de Administración* 28(2): 213–226.

Marcotte C (2013) Measuring entrepreneurship at the country level: A review and research agenda. *Entrepreneurship and Regional Development* 25(3-4): 174–194.

Minniti M and Bygrave W (2001) A dynamic model of entrepreneurial learning. *Entrepreneurship Theory and Practice* 25(3): 5–16.

Nohe C, Meier LL, Sonntag K and Michel A (2015) The chicken or the egg? A meta-analysis of panel studies of the relationship between work–family conflict and strain. *Journal of Applied Psychology* 100(2): 522–536.

Oishi S, Diener E, Suh E and Lucas RE (1999) Value as a moderator in subjective well-being. *Journal of Personality* 67(1): 157–184.

Patzelt H and Shepherd DA (2011) Negative emotions of an entrepreneurial career: Self-employment and regulatory coping behaviors. *Journal of Business Venturing* 26(2): 226–238.

Perry SJ, Penney LM and Witt LA (2008) Coping with the constraints of self-employment: A person-situation model of entrepreneurial burnout. *Academy of Management Proceedings* 2008(1): 1–6.

Rauch A and Frese M (2007) Born to be an entrepreneur? Revisiting the personality approach to entrepreneurship. In: Baum R,

Frese M and Baron RA (eds) *The psychology of entrepreneurship*. New York, NY: Lawrence Erlbaum Associates Publisher, pp. 41–65.

Ryan RM and Deci EL (2000a) Intrinsic and extrinsic motivations: Classic definitions and new directions. *Contemporary Educational Psychology* 25(1): 54–67.

Ryan RM and Deci EL (2000b) Self-determination theory and the facilitation of intrinsic motivation, social development and well-being. *American Psychologist* 55(1): 68–78.

Ryan RM and Deci EL (2001) On happiness and human potentials: A review of research on hedonic and eudaimonic well-being. *Annual Review of Psychology* 52(1): 141–166.

Schjoedt L (2020) Exploring differences between novice and repeat entrepreneurs: Does stress mediate the effects of work-and-family conflict on entrepreneurs' satisfaction? *Small Business Economics*, DOI: https://doi.org/10.1007/s11187-019-00289-9

Shelton LM (2006) Female entrepreneurs, work-family conflict, and venture performance: New insights into the work-family interface. *Journal of Small Business Management* 44(2): 285–297.

Shepherd D and Haynie JM (2009) Birds of a feather don't always flock together: Identity management in entrepreneurship. *Journal of Business Venturing* 24(4): 316–337.

Shir N, Nikolaev B and Wincent J (2019) Entrepreneurship and well-being: The role of psychological autonomy, competence, and relatedness. *Journal of Business Venturing* 34(5): 1–17.

Stephan U (2018) Entrepreneurs' mental health and well-being: A review and research agenda. *Academy of Management Perspectives* 32(3): 290–322.

Stevens CK and Gist ME (1997) Effects of self-efficacy and goal-orientation training on negotiation skill maintenance: What are the mechanisms? *Personnel Psychology* 50(4): 955–978.

Totterdell P, Wood S and Wall T (2006) An intra-individual test of the demands-control model: A weekly diary study of psychological strain in portfolio workers. *Journal of Occupational and Organizational Psychology* 79(1): 63–84.

Uy MA, Foo MD and Song Z (2013) Joint effects of prior start-up experience and coping strategies on entrepreneurs' psychological well-being. *Journal of Business Venturing* 28(5): 583–597.

Uy MA, Sun S and Foo MD (2017) Affect spin, entrepreneurs' well-being, and venture goal progress: The moderating role of goal orientation. *Journal of Business Venturing* 32(4): 443–460.

Vandewalle D (1997) Development and validation of a work domain goal orientation instrument. *Educational and Psychological Measurement* 57(6): 995–1015.

Warr P (1990) The measurement of well-being and other aspects of mental health. *Journal of Occupational Psychology* 63(3): 193–210.

Weiss HM and Cropanzano R (1996) Affective events theory: A theoretical discussion of the structure, causes and consequences of affective experiences at work. In: Staw BM and Cummings LL (eds) *Research in organizational behavior: An annual series of analytical essays and critical reviews*. Greenwich, CT: JAI Press: Elsevier, pp. 1–74.

Wiklund J, Nikolaev B, Shir N, Foo MD and Bradley S (2019) Entrepreneurship and well-being: Past, present, and future. *Journal of Business Venturing* 34(4): 579–588.

Wincent J, Örtqvist D and Ortqvist D (2009) A comprehensive model of entrepreneur role stress antecedents and consequences. *Journal of Business and Psychology* 24(2): 225–243.

Xanthopoulou D, Bakker AB, Demerouti E and Schaufeli WB (2007) The role of personal resources in the job demands-resources model. *International Journal of Stress Management* 14(2): 121–141.

Zhao H and Seibert SE (2006) The Big Five personality dimensions and entrepreneurial status: A meta-analytical review. *Journal of Applied Psychology* 91(2): 259–27.

15

Mergers, Acquisitions and Wellbeing in Organizational Life: The Critical Role of Human Resources

Teresa A. Daniel

INTRODUCTION

When companies pay close attention to the people aspects of a merger or an acquisition, they greatly increase the chances that the deal will fulfill its promise. That's why, in the final analysis, HR can make or break an M and A. (Giffin and Schmidt, 2002: 9)

Mergers and acquisitions (herein referred to as 'M and A', 'combinations', 'deals', or 'transactions') are tools companies use to improve organizational performance and increase competitive advantage by maximizing synergy and efficiencies. They are often described as creating a situation wherein '2 + 2 = 5' (Cartwright and Cooper, 1993b: 57) or referred to as the '1 + 1 = 3' effect (Marks and Mirvis, 2010: 3). These deals are generally designed to achieve rapid growth, expand market share, improve brand strength, diversify risk, or achieve competitive advantage through innovation, among other goals (e.g. Lupina-Wegener, 2013; Schuler and

Jackson, 2001; Porter, 1987, 1985; Chatterjee, 1986; Hovers, 1971).

In addition to the achievement of these organization synergies, some researchers have suggested that there is an element of CEO hubris that serves as a driving force for many of these transactions (Hayward and Hambrick, 1997; Roll, 1986). Regardless of the reason, it appears that it has become all but impossible in our global environment for companies to compete without growing and expanding through M and A transactions (Christensen et al., 2011).

These deals frequently have a profound impact on the employees of both companies as the two organizations attempt to integrate their operations and their cultures into a single entity – often over the course of many years. Even where there is a high degree of cultural compatibility between the two companies, M and A still create a great deal of anxiety and stress for the people involved (Marks et al., 2017; Cartwright and Cooper, 2000, 1993a). The early involvement of the company's human resources (HR) team can help to mitigate this anxiety and stress for employees and help the new organization begin to more quickly realize the intended benefits of the transaction. This chapter will examine HR's role during M and A transactions and how their involvement impacts both employee wellbeing and organizational effectiveness – and ultimately the success or failure of the transaction.

For purposes of this chapter, a merger will be defined as integrating two relatively equal entities into a new organization. An acquisition will be defined as the purchase of a target organization by a lead entity. The word 'combination' or 'transaction' will be used interchangeably to reference either a merger or acquisition (Marks and Mirvis, 2011).

THE BUSINESS CASE FOR HR'S INVOLVEMENT

Although generally undertaken for good reasons, the research shows that mergers and acquisitions create disruption, anxiety, anger, and fear among employees that can seriously impact their health and wellbeing (Schweiger et al., 1987). Power struggles among senior leaders jockeying for positions, titles, pay, and incentives can set up conditions that are ripe for ethical lapses that can wreak havoc on both the organization and its employees (Daniel, 2013a).

This combined set of unsettled conditions and stressful emotions experienced by both employees and senior leaders in the early days leading up to and following a combination is commonly referred to as 'merger syndrome' (Marks and Mirvis, 1986: 50–1; see also Marks, 1980). The situation is described like this:

> For executive leaders, the merger syndrome is a combination of uncertainty and the likelihood of change, both favorable and unfavorable, that produces stress and, ultimately, affects perceptions and judgments, interpersonal relationships, and

the dynamics of the combination itself. In companies, the syndrome is manifested by increased centralization and lessened communication that leave people in the dark about the combination such that they produce 'worst case' scenarios that distract employees from regular duties and cause them to be obsessed with the impact of the combination upon themselves and their work areas. (Marks and Mirvis, 1986: 50–1)

This syndrome can poison an organization by undermining employee morale and by eroding any sense of loyalty, trust, commitment, or teamwork. The climate of fear and uncertainty impacts employees in *both* organizations, resulting in a loss of productivity, as well as increased absences, distraction and disengagement, lower employee morale, and higher turnover, among other things (McCann and Gilkey, 1988; Schweiger et al., 1987: 130).

In addition to the impact on people, research suggests that these transactions generally have a negative impact on the economic performance of the newly combined entity (Marks, 1999; Cartwright and Cooper, 1993b; Kitching, 1967). Although estimates of M and A failure vary, there is a fair amount of consensus among both scholars and practitioners that most of them do not end in success. Some studies have estimated that 70 to 90% of all transactions fail to achieve their anticipated strategic and financial objectives (e.g. Schoenberg, 2006; Charman, 1999; Nahavandi and Malekzadeh, 1993; Walsh, 1989). Other studies are slightly more generous, suggesting that between 20 to 60% of all deals fail (Weber, 1996; Marks, 1988). Still other studies report that failed transactions hover around 50% (e.g. Lin et al., 2006; Ashkenas and Francis, 2000).

Regardless of the statistic that you choose to reference, it is clear that these types of transactions do not reliably result in their intended benefits. The stark reality is that the prospects of a failed combination are quite high (Akroli, 2016; Bruner, 2002). This is often due to the fact that the average acquirer materially overestimates the synergies the transaction will yield – which is why so many deals are ironically referred to as 'the winner's curse' (Christofferson et al., 2004; Thaler, 1992).

This high rate of failure is most frequently attributed to incompatible cultures, drastically different management styles, poor motivation, loss of key talent, poor communication, an absence of emotionally intelligent leadership, diminished trust, and uncertainty of long-term goals (Hrala, 2019; Schuler and Jackson, 2001; Cartwright and Cooper, 2000; Sirower, 1997).

Other factors include: 'an inadequate road map, *senior HR professionals brought in too little, too late*; senior HR professionals lacking in either/both business/global experience; and inadequate skills base overall; and ultimately, failed organizational change' (Charman, 1999). Similarly, Schweiger and Weber (1989) determined that while HR issues were deemed to be very important to the success of a transaction by executives, human-factor issues did not get a lot of attention. Not surprisingly, no more than 50% of these transactions achieve the levels of success initially anticipated (Cartwright and Cooper, 2000: 3, 1996).

Schmidt (2001), reporting on a Society for Human Resource Management (SHRM) study, suggested that M and A failure was the result of an inability to overcome key obstacles in the following areas: the new organization's inability to sustain financial performance, loss of productivity, incompatible cultures, loss of key talent, and clash of personalities and management styles. Sadly, the real winners are often exclusively the lawyers, bankers, and accountants who arrange, advise, and consult executives about the execution of these combinations (McManus and Hergert, 1988).

There is apparent consensus among both scholars and practitioners that the active involvement of HR throughout the M and A process is critical to the ultimate success of any combination (e.g. Brooks, 2019; Antila and Kakkonen, 2008; Antila, 2006; Hunt and Downing, 2006; Aguilera and Dencker, 2004; Schmidt, 2001; Giles, 2000, among

many others); however, it has been reported that only 35% of senior HR executives were actually involved in M and A activities (Giles, 2000; Liberatore, 2000). A later SHRM study determined an upward trend in HR involvement, finding that HR was substantially involved in 72% of the successful deals but in only 39% of those that failed (Schmidt, 2001).

That HR would not *always* be involved in the due diligence and post-merger integration efforts given their knowledge and expertise in the domain of people-related issues is both surprising and disappointing. There is, perhaps, no other organizational role that has more importance to the success or failure of the transaction's ultimate outcome (e.g. Bhaskar, 2012; Calipha et al., 2010; Marks and Mirvis, 2011; Brown, 2005; Schmidt, 2001; Love, 2000; Zukis and McGregor, 1999; Mirvis and Marks, 1992, among others).

As noted by Giffin and Schmidt (2002: 7):

In short, success depends on aligning the people, organizational and cultural assets of the new entity. Once a deal is sealed, nothing is more important to a successful outcome than effectively managing these 'soft issues'.

Many of the obstacles most responsible for M and A failure fall directly within the domain and expertise of HR. If these issues are handled poorly (or, worse yet, ignored entirely), the result is a significant impact on the wellbeing of both employees and the organization (Cartwright and Cooper, 1996, 1993a). This chapter will examine the critical role of HR professionals in M and A and the complexities they face in managing these responsibilities during times of great disruption and change.

KEY ORGANIZATIONAL ROLES OF HR PROFESSIONALS DURING M AND A

Based on a review of relevant management studies and practitioner literature, along with the author's first-hand knowledge of these issues while practicing as both an employment lawyer and HR practitioner, this chapter will utilize a conceptual framework that suggests HR professionals have at least five uniquely significant organizational roles when it comes to their involvement in mergers and acquisitions. These include: chief communicator, integration leader, employee advocate, counselor to and protector of management interests, and organizational toxin handler. Each of these roles will be examined next.

ROLE AS CHIEF COMMUNICATOR

Having a well-planned communication strategy is mission-critical to the success of any transaction (Zagelmeyer et al., 2018; Angwin et al., 2014; Siegenthaler, 2011). Some researchers have suggested that it is the single most important factor throughout the M and A process. Why? Because 'its effect on employees through this trying time is pervasive and significantly influences the adoption of a new culture, the change process itself, and the level of stress employees can experience' (Appelbaum et al., 2000: 649). HR has a pivotal role in communicating information to employees both before, during, and after the transaction has closed (Adomako et al., 2013).

Effective communication involves providing clear, truthful, continuous, and up-to-date information to the entire workforce about the shared vision for the new company, the nature and progress of the integration, the anticipated benefits of the transaction, and the expected outcomes along with rough timelines for future decisions (e.g. Kusstatscher and Cooper, 2004; Stieler, 2003; Cartwright and Cooper, 2000, 1992). Communication can impact both motivation and commitment, and it can also promote a sense of inclusion and belonging among employees (Welch and Jackson, 2007).

Communicating clearly (and often) about the reasons for the transaction and its desired outcomes helps to create stability for employees by decreasing levels of uncertainty, stress, and anxiety (Daniel and Metcalf, 2001; Daniel, 1999; Marks and Mirvis, 1992; Bridges, 1991) and by helping to increase trust and influence employee attitudes, behavior, and performance, all of which work together to positively impact the chances of M and A success (Zagelmeyer et al., 2018; Angwin et al., 2014). It can also help employees begin to develop expectations for what life may be like after the combination (Marks and Mirvis, 2011; Chatman and Cha, 2003).

Active and frequent two-way communication can also help to assure employees that the new leadership team has the ability to move the organization in the right direction (Angwin et al., 2014). As aptly noted by Richardson and Denton (1996) as quoted in Appelbaum et al. (2000: 658).

[T]here is no such thing as information overload throughout a merger process. The best strategy to employ at this time is to divulge constantly what is known, so that employees will always be on the receiving end of information.

Davy et al. (1989: 650) further offered these practical guidelines designed to increase the effectiveness of M and A communication:

- Information should be timely;
- Information should be as comprehensive as possible;
- Information should be repeated in many media;
- Information must be perceived as credible by employees;
- The rationale for organizational changes should be communicated; and the communication program needs to be well planned and should continue throughout the period of organizational transition which can take place over a period of several years.

Be Honest and Truthful

Critical to successful integration is the manner in which the decisions are implemented. The highest priority is that the acquiring company needs to be straightforward about what is happening and what is planned. Even when the news is bad, the one thing employees of newly acquired companies appreciate most is the truth (Stieler, 2003). That includes being able to say 'we don't know' about certain areas or 'we have not yet decided' about others (Whalen, 2002). Being honest also includes sharing information about when and by what process (and according to what timeline) a decision is expected to be reached.

The truth also means acknowledging some of the stress and other emotions that are undeniably present. Early on, employees will likely experience 'shock, disbelief, and grief followed by resentment, anger or depression' (Hunsaker and Coombs, 1988: 57). Organizations must be vigilant not to succumb to the default strategy of telling employees things will be 'business as usual' when the reality is that significant change is occurring all around them.

A better option is to openly and honestly acknowledge the changes and continuously explain to employees what is changing and, most importantly, *why.* Moreover, organizations should also be careful not to 'talk merger and act acquisition'. This sends a confusing message to employees when the actual reality is that one company is clearly the majority stakeholder and can (and probably will) end up making most of the important decisions (Marks and Mirvis, 2001: 86).

Deal with the Critical Issue of 'Me'

It is human nature to consider one's personal circumstances in the midst of the uncertainty caused by these types of transactions. The 'me' issues, which include decisions about title, salary, bonus opportunity, job location, position, reporting relationships, authority, scope of decision-making, office space, key procedures, and other 'perks' of the job, need to be given high priority by the integration

team (Siehl, 1990; Davy et al., 1988). Unless these issues are quickly addressed, employees will remain anxious and distracted; as a result, progress on the company's key strategic and integration objectives will be slow at best (Marks and Mirvis, 1985; Greenhalgh, 1983).

In addition to rapidly addressing the 'me' issues, Kusstatscher and Cooper also highlight the importance of recognizing the accomplishments of employees and treating people as valued persons throughout the integration process and beyond:

> It might sound simple, but the key factor for successful people management in the post-merger integration process seems to be appreciation. (Kusstatscher and Cooper, 2004: 172)

It is how employees are handled in the first three to six months that will set the tone for future relations between employees of the two companies (Angwin, 2004; McCann and Gilkey, 1988: 65). Interestingly, 53% of all deals fail in their integration phase and not during the earlier phases of negotiations or due diligence (Habeck et al., 2000, 1999).

Communicate about Big Decisions Early

It is fair to say that M and A transactions involve significant change – in management structure and reporting relationships, leadership roles, job eliminations, operating philosophy, systems, processes, policies, procedures, strategy, and/or office location. Given that change is inevitable, these important career and life-impacting decisions should be made and announced to employees as soon as possible after the deal is signed (e.g. Kusstatscher and Cooper, 2004; Marks and Mirvis, 1992; Appelbaum et al., 2000) – ideally within the first few days or weeks (Nahavandi and Malekzadeh, 1993; Hunsaker and Coombs, 1988).

The driving goal of the post-merger integration focus should be to make important people-related decisions as fast as is humanly possible in order to quickly reduce fear, anxiety, and uncertainty and begin to provide a sense of stability for employees (e.g. Kusstatscher and Cooper, 2004; Staw et al., 1981; Greenhalgh and Jick, 1979). In addition, as suggested by Schmidt (2001): 'most changes should be spaced out evenly, but take-aways should be done at once, if possible'.

Communicate Decisions about Role Changes and/or Job Eliminations Humanely

Once decisions about roles and job elimina- tions have been made, it is important to treat those employees who will be negatively impacted by the transaction with dignity, respect, and support (Daniel, 2017b, 1999; Kusstatscher and Cooper, 2004). The *ways* in which these decisions are both made and communicated will – in the long run – be as important as the actual decisions themselves (Rodriguez-Sanchez et al., 2014; Daniel and Metcalf, 2001; Appelbaum et al., 2000; Daniel, 1999).

Treating people who will not remain with the organization fairly and with respect is not only the right thing to do, it is also a power- ful way of showing those who remain what kind of company they are now working for, and to help them begin to develop some posi- tive feelings toward the new organization (Angwin, 2004; Daniel and Metcalf, 2001; Daniel, 1999; Schweiger and Weber, 1989; Schweiger et al., 1987; Golembiewski, 1979).

Help Employees Navigate 'the Neutral Zone'

Just after the merger, employees often feel threatened by all of the changes and new expectations which, all too often, seem to be 'forced down their throats'. People who are learning to adjust to new ways of doing things will naturally be more hesitant as they test how familiar skills work in unfamiliar settings or attempt to operate in a new culture among people with whom they do not yet have established relationships.

This period is what William Bridges has characterized as 'the neutral zone' (Bridges, 1991). It is the time when people are caught between the old ways and the new – and nei- ther provide satisfactory answers – yet. He memorably describes this stage of change as: 'the nowhere between two somewheres' (Bridges, 1991: 35). Marilyn Ferguson, an American futurist, elaborates further on this 'in-between' phase experienced by employees during periods of significant change like this:

> It's not so much that we're afraid of change or so in love with the old ways, but it's that place in between that we fear. It's like being between tra- pezes. It's Linus when his blanket is in the dryer. There's nothing to hold on to. (Ferguson, quoted in Bridges, 1991: 34)

In the context of M and A, navigating this period is a journey from one identity to the other – and like it or not, that journey takes time (Marks and Mirvis, 2011, 1992). Some researchers have compared the intense emo- tions commonly felt by employees as an expe- rience that is much like the loss of a loved one (Sherer, 1994). Some people will actually experience the stages of grief and mourn the passing of their former organization (Cartwright and Cooper, 2000: 46–50). They can and will work through these natural emo- tions if their feelings of loss are acknowledged and they sense anyone actually cares. If empa- thy is not demonstrated during this period, though, the process of adapting to the 'new normal' will take even longer (Bridges, 1991).

Promote Openness to New and Creative Solutions to Old Problems

Although the neutral zone can be a time of confusion and fear, it is important to recog- nize that it can also be a time of great innovation. It is during the gap between the old and the new that the organization is most likely to be receptive to truly creative solutions. As noted by Marks et al. (2017):

> The change brought on by M and A often opens the door to all kinds of innovation. Teams and individuals who might ordinarily have no chance to present ideas to senior leadership suddenly find themselves with access to a receptive audience, and those who are willing to speak up get noticed.

Treat the past with respect

When the past way of operating is ridiculed or attacked, people may feel a need to defend the old practices. This situation may inadvertently consolidate the resistance against the transition and the leaders seeking to make changes. Instead, managers may have a better chance of actually being heard if they make a strong case about why the 'new way' may work better than what has been done in the past. The challenge is to make the distinction non-judgmentally (Bridges, 1991: 30), while emphasizing that the challenges created by the new company now call for different responses and approaches (Daniel and Metcalf, 2001; Appelbaum et al., 2000; Daniel, 1999). Managers must explain how the company intends to move from the past to achieve the organization's new future – over and over and over (Marks and Mirvis, 2011; Bramson, 2000).

Throughout this transition, it is important to honor the past for what it has accomplished and show respect to the people who were part of it. As noted by Appelbaum et al. (2000: 653):

> [P]eople crave to be treated with respect, to be identified with the new organization, to be accepted as members of the new team and to keep this status and prestige within the new organization (Lake 1997).

Listening, empathizing, and communicating continuously with employees throughout the M and A process appears to be a '*key ingredient*' in the success or failure of a transaction (Appelbaum et al., 2000). In addition, a positive perception among employees about the new management team's fairness, integrity, and objectivity is important in order to keep people engaged enough to do the hard work required to make the transaction successful (O'Malley and Baker, 2020; Daniel and Metcalf, 2001).

ROLE AS INTEGRATION LEADER

HR professionals are widely viewed as the organizational insiders best suited to take a leading role in M and A integration efforts given the importance of the management of people issues to the ultimate success or failure of a transaction (e.g. Brooks, 2019; Marks and Mirvis, 2011; Steynberg and Veldsman, 2011; Antila and Kakkonen, 2008; Antila, 2006; Aguilera and Dencker, 2004; Cartwright and Cooper, 2000, 1996; Hunt and Downing, 1990, among many others). HR's role in both the pre-merger due-diligence stage as well as the post-merger integration phase of the transaction will be examined next.

Pre-Merger Due Diligence

The inclusion of a broad array of disciplines enhances pre-merger due diligence (Christofferson et al., 2004). HR professionals typically play pivotal roles in this early phase of the deal-making (Marks and Mirvis, 2001). It is during this time that information about talent and culture – along with assessments of employee and retiree health-care plans and costs; defined-benefit and defined-contribution plans, costs, and liabilities; compensation programs; employment contracts and policies; legal exposure; and more – can provide insights into the valuation of a company and a better understanding of its workforce (SHRM, 2016b; Price and Walker, 2000).

Companies can inadvertently overpay or assume significant and unexpected liabilities if they do not conduct careful due diligence before finalizing the transaction. As a result, HR's involvement in the earliest stages of the transaction is critical to ensuring that these undesirable outcomes do not occur (Calipha et al., 2010; Mirvis and Marks, 1992).

Post-Merger Integration Efforts

Once the deal is consummated, areas of early focus for the HR integration team most typically include:

People integration (e.g. decisions about employees in terms of who stays – and in which roles – and who will be terminated);
Procedural integration (e.g. standardizing work policies, procedures, and processes in an effort to improve efficiencies and productivity);
Sociocultural integration (e.g. merging the two organizational cultures); and
Physical integration (e.g. combining assets and operations, determining the location of the corporate headquarters).

Throughout the integration process, HR must be adept at quickly recognizing potential problems, identifying solutions, and, most importantly, persuading management to adopt their recommendations. Each of these areas of integration focus will be discussed separately below.

People Integration

Communication

Active communication is a key role for HR practitioners both before, during, and after the transaction has been closed. See the previous section about HR's role as Chief Communicator for more information about this critical function.

Retention of key employees

The retention of key employees is a primary focus of this post-merger phase (Galpin and Herndon, 2000; Price and Walker, 2000). Because rapid decision-making is critical, confidential interviews with 'star performers' should occur in advance of the actual closing date to make the organization's intentions about their future opportunities with the new company crystal clear (Pritchett, 1987, 1985). It is generally the organization's 'best and brightest' managers who are immediately targeted by headhunters in an attempt to lure them away to other organizations (Marks and Mirvis, 1985).

Uncertainty and chaos are typical in the early days post-merger; as a result, it is no surprise that it is top performers with the most opportunities who often leave first (Brahma and Srivastava, 2007; Walsh and Ellwood, 1991: 215). In fact, it has been estimated that 47% of all senior managers in an acquired firm leave within the first year after the deal is closed. But the exodus doesn't stop there; within the first three years, 75% of those in senior positions are typically gone, and within five years 58% of all managers have left (Walsh, 1989: 313).

The loss of key employees can seriously erode the value of a transaction for the acquiring firm; as a result, many companies utilize 'retention agreements' that include incentives to encourage executives and other key employees to stay with the new company for a specified period of time (Miller, 2014). In addition to a loss of talent, perhaps equally damaging and just as costly, though, are those people who stay on the payroll but who emotionally 'check out' and fail to perform at their previous levels of productivity. If not handled with care, a company may inadvertently end up with a group of second-rate employees on its payroll – those who simply had the fewest alternatives (Daniel and Metcalf, 2001; Daniel, 1999).

Employee selection and downsizing

Most deals are premised on assumptions about synergies and efficiencies that will result in a reduction in the number of employees needed to run the new organization. This means that HR will spend a great deal of time assessing employee knowledge, skills, and abilities to decide who will stay (and in which roles) and whose jobs will be terminated. The strategy may include terminations, early retirements, and/or a longer-term plan simply not to fill certain positions as they become vacant in the future.

These early decisions about people and roles (referred to previously as the 'me' issues) are critical to begin to stabilize the new organization but are clearly a significant challenge for most deals (PWC, 2017). Importantly, these job-related decisions need to be made rapidly (Hunsaker and Coombs, 1988; Nahavandi and Malekzadeh, 1993). If the process is handled quickly, transparently, and fairly, it is much more likely that employees will view senior leaders as credible and capable of leading the new organization forward. Conversely, if the decisions occur in a haphazard manner or if they are strung out over a long period of time, employee commitment to the new organization and its leadership will suffer and may not be regained for some time (if ever).

Procedural Integration

According to SHRM (2016a), some of the key post-merger issues that must be addressed by the HR integration team include the following.

Creation of new policies and procedures to guide the new organization

In conjunction with senior leaders, HR must develop and communicate to employees a cogent people-related strategy that includes key policies, procedures, rules, and guidelines to govern employee behavior, and related workplace expectations (e.g. attendance, time off, vacations, harassment, drug testing, privacy).

Development of compensation and incentive strategies

HR will likely be involved in the review of both organizations' compensation systems

and have a mandate to design a new one that better fits the goals of the new organization. Employees will be acutely concerned about how the new system will affect them; as a result, decisions should be announced as soon as reasonably possible. Researchers have suggested that this is one of the most contentious issues for HR managers to handle during any M and A situation because of the personal impact on both executives and employees alike (Pande and Krishnan, 2007). The difficulty is often due to significant pay differentials between the two merging companies which makes the design of an equitable system even more complex.

Development of employment contracts and executive pay strategies

Senior leaders of the new organization will be anxious to see what types of special arrangements (e.g. employment contracts, stock options, special retirement provisions, severance agreements) will be offered to them. The development of a comprehensive executive compensation strategy is complex and will require active involvement from outside consultants and company lawyers. It will also require the approval of the new organization's board of directors.

Creation of a comprehensive employee benefits program

Just as with compensation programs, HR will be required to link disparate employee benefits into a new program that fits the new circumstances. This is a complex undertaking. Employees are sure to be anxious about how their benefits will be changing so information about 'the new package' needs to be widely shared as soon as it is available.

Socio-Cultural Integration

Socio-cultural integration is defined as the combination of groups of people possessing established norms, beliefs, and values (Lund and Whitt, 2017). This stage of integration can involve sharp conflicts as different organizational cultures, managerial viewpoints, HR management systems, and other aspects of organizational life come into contact (Stahl and Mendenhall, 2005: 6; Schweiger, 2002).

Because culture encompasses the beliefs and assumptions shared by members of an organization and influences all areas of group life, there is always a degree of misalignment, regardless of the perceived similarity between the two firms. Although all aspects of a successful integration share complexities, it is the merger of two different cultures which is most often the source of contentious conflict and the most difficult to achieve (Lund and Whitt, 2017; Love, 2000; Deal and Kennedy, 1982).

PHYSICAL INTEGRATION

HR is also sometimes involved in issues related to physical integration. This includes decisions about combining assets and operations and determining the headquarters location; however, these are most typically operationally driven decisions in which HR generally has only a supporting role.

ROLE AS EMPLOYEE ADVOCATE

Another key role for HR professionals is to serve as an employee advocate for employees who feel that they have been treated unfairly by a manager or colleague (Daniel, 2018, 2013b, 2012; SHRM 2016a; Grillo, 2014; Bakuwa, 2013; Ulrich and Brockbank, 2005; Ulrich, 1997). Emotionally charged problems that commonly arise include their perceptions that employment or termination decisions have been made unfairly, complaints about harassment or discrimination, substance abuse, and personality or work conflicts (Kulik et al., 2009).

In this role, HR is required to take action to protect employees from abusive and/or unfair managers, while at the same time safeguarding the prerogative of managers to push employees to meet (or exceed) company performance goals even though they may be perceived as a 'tough' boss (Daniel, 2018, 2009; Daniel and Metcalf, 2016) Striking that balance, though, is not an easy task.

ROLE AS ADVISOR TO AND PROTECTOR OF MANAGEMENT/ ORGANIZATIONAL INTERESTS

In terms of advising and protecting management interests, HR practitioners possess considerable strength in four key areas (Daniel, 2013b):

Education and training of the workforce;
Mitigation of risk to the organization (e.g. minimizing the potential for lawsuits or regulatory violations);
Providing reliable basic HR services (e.g. policy development, strategies about human capital deployment, hiring, benefits, and communication); and
Protecting the interests of both employees and management (e.g. investigating and resolving workplace conflicts, coaching and challenging senior leaders about important people-related decisions).

HR is generally the first point of contact for the reporting and investigation of employee complaints. If the allegations are confirmed, HR generally first confers with legal counsel and then with senior leaders to determine the appropriate consequences and to provide support for the complainant (Daniel, 2018, 2013b, 2012; Daniel and Metcalf, 2016). The investigative aspect of the role has often caused HR to be perceived as the 'internal police' of the organization, a characterization to which most practitioners object and a role which they generally find to be uncomfortable (Fox and Cowan, 2015; Daniel, 2013b, 2012).

Ulrich (1997) acknowledges the paradox inherent in the multiple roles that HR must navigate, especially when it comes to representing the interests of both employee and the organization. He argues that HR professionals 'can both represent employee needs *and* implement management agendas, be the voice of the employee *and* the voice of management, act as partner to both employees *and* managers' (1997: 45) – but it clearly is not easy to navigate these often-competing roles. It is not surprising, then, that more than half of the HR leaders surveyed by a global talent management firm reported feeling 'overwhelmed' and 52% reported that they 'did not have the ability to fully cope' with the complexity of the role (SHRM, 2013).

ROLE AS 'ORGANIZATIONAL TOXIN HANDLER'

M and A generate intense emotions for employees – feelings like anger, frustration, stress, disappointment, anxiety, and even fear. While fairly predictable, it is the way organizations handle them – or do not – that can create a serious problem for both employees and, ultimately, the organizations that they serve.

If the situation is managed poorly or employee feelings are avoided altogether, the chronic anger or prolonged stress creates results in an undesirable by-product known as *organizational toxicity*. The word 'toxic' comes from the Greek 'toxikon' which means 'arrow poison'. In a literal sense, the term in its original form means to kill (poison) in a targeted way (arrow). Over time, the buildup of these toxic emotions will create a workplace culture where employees feel devalued, demoralized, and often hopeless – and most assuredly not productive or actively engaged.

Peter Frost (2003, 2004) first identified and coined the term for the special role some employees take on in an effort to alleviate this toxicity for employees – he referred to these individuals as *toxin handlers*. He described toxin handlers as people within an organization who 'voluntarily shoulder the sadness, frustration, bitterness, and the anger that are endemic to organizational life'. In a nutshell, toxin handlers act much like a kidney or the immune system in a human body – by neutralizing, dissipating, and dispersing organizational toxins that build up over time as a result of difficult decisions made by the organization – like M and A – which impact employees (Frost and Robinson, 1999: 185).

HR practitioners are regularly confronted by distressed employees who bring emotionally charged problems to them during a transaction with the expectation that they will receive help to resolve the issue (Daniel, 2017a). A recent empirical study determined that a central aspect of the HR professional's role is to act as an organizational toxin handler (Daniel, 2020, 2019a, 2019b, 2019c). In fact, 58% of the participants reported helping employees deal with toxic emotions on a *daily* basis, a finding that exceeded the 25% previously reported in a study by Kulik et al. (2009: 707). That practitioners assume this role is not actually unexpected given that 'caring about people' has historically been a hallmark contribution of the HR profession (Meisinger, 2005; Falcone, 2002).

When engaged in this work, Daniel (2019a, 2017a) found that HR engages in six core activities: empathetic listening, suggesting solutions and providing resources, working behind the scenes and providing a safe space, confidential counseling, strategizing communications and reframing difficult messages, and coaching and advising managers. By doing this work, HR toxin handlers enable other employees to stay focused and do their own jobs (Daniel, 2020, 2019c; Metz et al., 2014). Without them, the organizational toxicity would continue to build, resulting in higher levels of turnover, increased health costs, more litigation, and reduced levels of employee morale and productivity (Daniel, 2020, 2019a, 2017a).

Although HR routinely assists employees, they also feel a strong responsibility to support senior leaders and to drive positive organizational outcomes (Daniel, 2013b). Navigating these competing role demands is not easy; as a result, HR's organizational role is inherently complex and somewhat paradoxical. This constant tension poses a real risk to their own personal physical and emotional wellbeing over time. The personal impact on them ranges from significant physical and emotional exhaustion, feelings of sadness and anger, high stress, lack of sleep, and burnout, to a deterioration of their personal relationships, overall health, and home life (Daniel, 2020, 2019b, 2017a).

CONCLUSION

The role of human capital in the ultimate success of any transaction is perhaps best stated by Cartwright and Cooper (1992: 142):

> The role of people in determining merger and acquisition outcomes is in reality not a soft but a hard issue. Without the commitment of those who produce the goods and services, make decisions, and conceive strategies, mergers and acquisitions will fail to achieve their synergizing potential as a wealth-creating strategy.

Active interventions by HR to reduce the emotional fallout from M and A activity can help to ease the transition for employees and improve their sense of wellbeing and confidence about the new organization and where it is headed. The sooner this occurs, the earlier the organization can begin to realize some of the intended benefits of the transaction and employees can turn their attention back to their work and stop feeling so stressed about their future.

For most companies, a merger or acquisition is a major gamble – and the viability of the company's future is often at stake. To improve the odds of success, organizations must proactively include HR so that people issues can be considered along with other strategic, operational, and financial issues – both

before, during, and after the transaction. HR's active involvement every step of the way is by no means a guarantee that the combination will be successful; without them, though, the prognosis for a positive outcome is dismal at best.

REFERENCES

Adomako S, Gasor GK and A Danso (2013) Examining human resource managers' involvement in mergers and acquisitions process in Ghana *Journal of Management Policy and Practice*, *14*(6), 25–36.

Aguilera R and Dencker J (2004) The role of human resource management in cross-border mergers and acquisitions *The International Journal of Human Resource Management*, *15*, 1355–1370.

Akroli GK (2016) Mergers and acquisitions failure rates and perspectives on why they fail *International Journal of Innovation and Applied Studies*, *17*(1), 150–158.

Angwin DN, Mellahi K, Gomes E and E Peter (2014) How communication approaches impact mergers and acquisitions outcomes *The International Journal of Human Resource Management*, *27*(20), 2370–2397.

Angwin DN (2004) Speed in M and A integration: The first 100 days *European Management Journal*, *22*, 418–430.

Antila EM and Kakkonen A (2008) Factors affecting the role of HR managers in international mergers and acquisitions: A multiple case study *Personnel Review*, *37*(3), 280–299.

Antila EM (2006) The role of HR managers in international mergers and acquisitions: A multiple case study *The International Journal of Human Resource Management*, *17*(6), 999–1020.

Appelbaum SH, Gandell J, Yortis H, Proper S, and F Jobin (2000) Anatomy of a merger: Behavior of organizational factors and processes throughout the pre-during-post-stages (part 1) *Management Decision*, *38*(9), 649–661.

Ashkenas RN and Francis SC (2000, November/ December) Integration managers: Special leaders for special times *Harvard Business Review,* 78(6):108–114.

Bakuwa RC (2013) Exploring the HR professional's employee advocate role in a developing country: The case of Malawi *Australian Journal of Business and Management Research, 2,* 39–48.

Bhaskar AU (2012) HR as business partner during mergers and acquisitions: The key to success is to get involved early *Human Resource Management International Digest, 20*(2), 22–23.

Brahma SS and Srivastava KB (2007) Communication, executive retention, and employee stress as predictors of acquisition performance: An empirical evidence *Journal of Mergers and Acquisitions, 4*(4), 7–26.

Bramson RN (2002) HR's role in mergers and acquisitions *Training and Development, 54*(10): 69–66.

Bridges WM (1991) *Managing transitions: Making the most of change* Reading, PA: Addison-Wesley.

Brooks G (2019, March 15) *How HR is key to successful mergers and acquisitions* Forbes https://www.forbes.com/sites/forbeshumanresourcescouncil/2019/03/15/how-hr-is-key-to-successful-mergers-and-acquisitions/?sh=7c3e82eb4a2d4 (Accessed November 19, 2019)

Brown D (2005) More HR input leads to more merger success: Study *Canadian HR Reporter, 18,* 1–4.

Bruner RF (2002) Does M and A pay? A survey of evidence for the decision-maker *Journal of Applied Finance, 12*(1), 48–69.

Calipha R, Tarba S and DM Brock (2010) Mergers and acquisitions: A review of phases, motives, and success factors *Advances in Mergers and Acquisitions, 9,* 1–24.

Cartwright S and Cooper CL (2000) *HR know-how in mergers and acquisitions* London: Chartered Institute of Personnel and Development.

Cartwright S and Cooper CL (1996) *Managing mergers, acquisitions, and strategic alliances: Integrating people and cultures* Oxford: Butterworth-Heinemann.

Cartwright S and Cooper CL (1993b) The role of culture compatibility in successful organizational marriage *Academy of Management Executive, 7*(2), 57–70.

Cartwright S and Cooper CL (1993a) The psychological impact of merger and acquisition on the individual: A study of building society managers *Human Relations, 46,* 327–347.

Cartwright S and Cooper CL (1992) *Mergers and acquisitions: The human factor* Oxford: Butterworth-Heinemann.

Charman A (1999) *Global mergers and acquisitions: The human resource challenge* Alexandria, VA: Institute for International Human Resources/Society for Human Resource Management.

Chatman JA and Cha SE (2003) Leading by leveraging culture *California Management Review, 45*(4), 20–34.

Chatterjee S (1986) Types of synergy and economic value: The impact of acquisitions on merging and rival firms *Strategic Management Journal, 7*(2), 119–139.

Christensen CM, Alton R, Rising C and A Waldeck (2011, March) *The big idea: The new M & A playbook.* https://hbr.org/2011/03/the-big-idea-the-new-ma-playbook. (Accessed November 5, 2019)

Christofferson SA, McNish RS and DL Sias (2004, May) *Where mergers go wrong* McKinsey and Company Retrieved from https://www.mckinsey.com/business-functions/strategy-and-corporate-finance/our-insights/where-mergers-go-wrong (Accessed October 10, 2019)

Daniel TA and Metcalf GS (2016) *Stop bullying at work: Strategies and tools for HR, legal and risk management professionals* (2nd edition) Alexandria, VA: SHRM Books.

Daniel TA and Metcalf GS (2001) *The management of people in mergers and acquisitions* Westport, CT: Quorum Books.

Daniel, TA (2020) *Managing toxic emotions at work: The critical role of HR, OD & coaching practitioners on employee well-being and organizational effectiveness* New York, NY: Palgrave Macmillan.

Daniel TA (2019c, March 25) *Viewpoint: How toxin handlers reduce organizational pain* SHRM's HR Daily Newsletter Retrieved from https://www.shrm.org/resourcesandtools/hr-topics/employee-relations/pages/viewpoint-how-toxin-handlers-reduce-organizational-pain.aspx (Accessed November 11, 2019)

Daniel TA (2019b, March 13) *Viewpoint: How HR can protect itself from toxic emotions*

SHRM's HR Daily Newsletter Retrieved from https://www.shrm.org/ResourcesAndTools/hr-topics/employee-relations/Pages/Viewpoint-How-HR-Can-Protect-Itself-from-Toxic-Emotions.aspx (Accessed November 3, 2019)

Daniel TA (2019a, March 6) *Viewpoint: HR as toxin handlers* SHRM's HR Daily Newsletter Retrieved from https://www.shrm.org/resourcesandtools/hr-topics/employee-relations/pages/are-you-a-toxin-handler.aspx (Accessed November 3, 2019)

Daniel TA (2018) The role of human resources in the prevention of workplace bullying and mobbing In Duffy M and Yamada DC (Eds), *Workplace bullying and mobbing in the United States* (pp. 235–284) Santa Barbara, CA: ABC=CLIO.

Daniel TA (2017b, August 27) *Your employees are not criminals, so why treat them that way? Kentucky SHRM Magazine* Retrieved from https://kyshrmmecgnvcom/archives/item/225-your-employees-are-not-criminals-so-why-treat-them-that-way (Accessed October 7, 2019)

Daniel TA (2017a) Managing toxic emotions at work: HR's unique role as the 'organizational shock absorber' *Employment Relations Today*, *43*(4), 13–19.

Daniel TA (2013b) Executive perceptions about the effectiveness of human resources *Employment Relations Today*, *40*(2), 1–11 Retrieved from https://doi.org/10.1002/ert.21405 (Accessed October 15, 2019)

Daniel TA (2013a, July) *Executive success and the increased potential for ethical failure* SHRM's Quarterly Legal Report Retrieved from https://www.academia.edu/11728733/Executive_Success_and_the_Increased_Risk_of_Ethical_Failure (Accessed October 15, 2019)

Daniel TA (2012) Caught in the crossfire: When HR practitioners become targets of bullying *Employment Relations Today*, *39*(1), 9–16.

Daniel TA (2009). *'Tough boss' or workplace bully: A grounded theory study of insights from human resource professionals* Doctoral Dissertation, Fielding Graduate University Retrieved from https://www.proquest.com/docview/305169091 (Accessed August 5, 2019)

Daniel TA (1999) Between trapezes: The human side of making mergers and acquisitions work *Compensation and Benefits Management*, *15*(1), 19–37.

Davy JA, Kinicki A, Scheck C and J Kilroy (1989) Acquisitions make employees worry: Companies ease the pain through effective communication *Personnel Administrator*, 84–90.

Davy JA, Kinicki A, Kilroy J and C Scheck (1988) After the merger: Dealing with people's uncertainty *Training and Development Journal*, *42*(11), 57–61.

Deal TE and Kennedy AA (1982) *Corporate cultures: The rites and rituals of corporate life* Reading, MA: Perseus Books.

Falcone P (2002) Understanding the HR mindset *HR Magazine*, *47*(10), 117–122.

Fox S and Cowan RL (2015) Being pushed and pulled: A model of US HR professionals' roles in bullying situations *Personnel Review*, *44*(1), 119–139.

Frost PJ and Robinson S (1999, July/August) The toxic handler: Organizational hero – and casualty *Harvard Business Review* Retrieved from https://hbr.org/1999/07/the-toxic-handler-organizational-hero-and-casualty (Accessed March 18, 2018)

Frost PJ (2004) Handling toxic emotions: New challenges for leaders and their organization *Organizational Dynamics*, *33*(2), 111–127.

Frost PJ (2003) *Toxic emotions at work: How compassionate managers handle pain and conflict* Boston, MA: Harvard Business School Publishing.

Galpin TJ and Herndon M (2000) *The complete guide to mergers and acquisitions* San Francisco, CA: Jossey-Bass Publishers.

Giffin AF and Schmidt JA (2002) *Why HR can make or break your M and A* Institute for Mergers and Acquisitions Retrieved from https://imaa-institute.org/docs/m&a/towersperrin_04_why_hr_can_make_or_break_your_M-and-A.pdf (Accessed October 3, 2019)

Giles P (2000) The importance of HR in making your merger work *Workspan*, 16–20.

Golembiewski R (1979) *Approaches to planned change: Part two* New York, NY: Marcel Dekker.

Greenhalgh L (1983) Managing the job insecurity crisis *Human Resource Management*, *22*(4), 431–445.

Grillo MC (2014, October 8) *Straddling the line or embracing the dichotomy: HR's role as an employee advocate as necessary to remain (or become) a business partner* Cornell HR Review Retrieved from https://ecommons.

cornell.edu/handle/1813/72944 (Accessed October 3, 2019)

Habeck MH, Kroger F and MR Tram (2000) *After the mergers: Seven rules for successful post-merger integration* London/New York, NY: Financial Times/Prentice Hall.

Habeck MH, Kroger F and MR Tram (1999) *After the merger* London/New York, NY: Financial Times/Prentice Hall.

Hayward M and Hambrick D (1997) Explaining the premiums paid for large acquisitions: Evidence of CEO hubris *Administrative Science Quarterly, 42*(1), 103–127.

Hovers J (1971) *Expansion through acquisitions* London: Business Books.

Hrala J (2019, June 22) *Mergers and acquisitions: Everything HR needs to know* Career Minds Retrieved from https://blog.career-minds.com/mergers-and-acquisitions (Accessed November 1, 2019)

Hunsaker PL and Coombs MW (1988) Mergers and acquisitions: Managing the emotional issues *Personnel, 67,* 56–63.

Hunt W and Downing S (1990) Mergers, acquisitions and human resource management *The International Journal of Human Resource Management, 1*(2), 195–210.

Kitching J (1967, November/December) Why do mergers miscarry? *Harvard Business Review, 45*(6), 84–101.

Kulik CT, Creegan C, Metz I and M Brown (2009, September/October) HR managers as toxic handlers: The buffering effect of formalizing toxic handling *Human Resource Management, 48*(5), 695–716.

Kusstatscher V and Cooper C (2004) *Managing emotions in mergers and acquisitions* Retrieved from https://www.amazon.com/Managing-Emotions-Acquisitions-Horizons-Management/dp/1845420810 (Accessed September 29, 2019)

Lake, D.J (1997) Frameworks for human resource. professionals participating in business relationships. Human resource mangement, 36(1), 129–134.

Liberatore MD (2000) HR's relative importance in mergers and acquisitions *Human Resource Executive,* March 2, 48.

Lin BW, Shih-Chang H and PC Li (2006) Mergers and acquisitions as a human resource strategy: Evidence from US banking firms *International Journal of Manpower, 27,* 126–142.

Love CK (2000) *Mergers and acquisitions: The role of HRM in success* Kingston, ON: IRC Press.

Lund MH and Whitt CF (2017) *Change management in mergers and acquisitions* Proacteur Retrieved from https://pdf4pro.com/amp/view/change-management-in-mergers-amp-acquisitions-a46d3.html (Accessed March 7, 2019)

Lupina-Wegner AA (2013) Human resource integration in subsidiary mergers and acquisitions: Evidence from Poland *Journal of Organizational Change Management, 28,* 872–894.

Marks ML, Mirvis P and R Ashkenas (2017, March/April) Surviving M and A *Harvard Business Review* Retrieved from https://hbr.org/2017/03/surviving-ma (Accessed September 22, 2019)

Marks ML and Mirvis PH (2011) A framework for the human resources role in managing culture in mergers and acquisitions *Human Resource Management, 50*(6), 859–887.

Marks ML and Mirvis PH (2010) *Joining forces: Making one plus one equal three in mergers, acquisitions, and alliances* San Francisco, CA: Jossey-Bass.

Marks ML and Mirvis PH (2001) Making mergers and acquisitions work: Strategic and psychological preparation *Academy of Management Executive, 15*(2), 80–92.

Marks ML and Mirvis PH (1992) Rebuilding after the merger: Dealing with 'survivor sickness' *Organizational Dynamics, 21*(1), 18–23.

Marks ML and Mirvis PH (1992) *Managing the merger: Making it work* Paramus, NJ: Prentice Hall.

Marks ML and Mirvis PH (1986) The merger syndrome *Psychology Today, 20*(10), 36–42.

Marks ML and Mirvis PH (1985, Summer) Merger syndrome: Stress and uncertainty *Mergers and Acquisitions,* 50–55.

Marks ML (1999) Surviving a merger *Electric Perspective, 24*(6), 26–35.

Marks ML (1988, January/February) The merger syndrome: The human side of corporate combinations *Journal of Buyouts and Acquisitions,* 18–23.

Marks ML (1980) How to treat the merger syndrome *Journal of Management Consulting, 4*(3), 42–51.

McCann J and Gilkey R (1988) *Joining forces* Englewood Cliffs, NJ: Prentice-Hall.

McManus ML and Hergert ML (1988) *Surviving merger and acquisition* Glenview, IL: Scott, Foresman and Co.

Meisinger SR (2005) The four Cs of the HR profession: Being competent, curious, courageous, and caring about people *Human Resource Management, 44*(2), 189–194.

Metz I, Brown M, Cregan C and CT Kulik (2014) 'Toxin handling' and well-being: The case of the human resource manager *European Journal of Work and Organizational Psychology, 23*(2), 248–262.

Miller S (2014, October 10) *In M and As, financial awards target key talent* SHRM Retrieved from https://www.shrm.org/resourcesand-tools/hr-topics/compensation/pages/mergers-retention-bonuses.aspx (Accessed October 10, 2019)

Mirvis PH and Marks ML (1992) The human side of merger planning: Assessing and analyzing *Human Resource Planning, 15,* 69–93.

Nahavandi A and Malekzadeh A (1993) *Organizational culture in the management of mergers* Westport, CT: Quorum Books.

O'Malley M and Baker WF (2020) *Organizations for people: Caring cultures, basic needs, and better lives* Stanford, CA: Stanford University Press.

Pande A and Krishnan KS (2007) Knotted forever *Harvard Business Review, 76*(1), 165–170.

Porter ME (1987) From competitive advantage to corporate strategy *Harvard Business Review, 65*(3), 43–59.

Porter ME (1985) *Competitive analysis* New York, NY: Free Press.

Price KF and Walker JW (2000) Perspectives: Why do mergers go right? *Human Resource Planning,* 6–8.

Pritchett P (1987) *After the merger: The authoritative guide for integration success* New York, NY: McGraw Hill.

Pritchett P (1985) *After the merger: Managing the shock waves* New York, NY: Dow Jones-Irwin.

PWC (2017, March) *2017 M and A Integration Survey Report* Retrieved from https://www.pwc.com/us/en/services/deals/library/ma-integration-survey/people-change-management.html (Accessed August 9, 2019)

Richardson P and Denton DK (1996) Communicating change *Human Resource Management, 35*(2), 203–216.

Rodriguez-Sanchez JL, Ortiz-de-Urbina-Criado M and EM Mora-Valentin (2014) Human resources management and mergers and acquisitions: Perspectives and challenges In Nelson WD (Ed), *Advances in business and management* (pp. 67–87) New York, NY: Nova Science Publishers.

Roll R (1986) The hubris hypothesis of corporate takeovers *Journal of Business, 59*(2), 197–216.

Schmidt JA (2001, June 1) *The correct spelling of M and A begins with HR* SHRM Retrieved from https://www.shrm.org/hr-today/news/hr-magazine/pages/0601schmidt.aspx (Accessed July 20, 2019)

Schoenberg R (2006) Measuring the performance of corporate acquisitions: An empirical comparison of alternative metrics *British Journal of Management, 17,* 361–370.

Schuler R and Jackson S (2001) HR issues and activities in mergers and acquisitions *European Management Journal, 19*(3), 239–253.

Schweiger DJ and Weber Y (1989) Strategies for managing human resources during mergers and acquisitions: An empirical investigation *Human Resource Planning, 12,* 69–86.

Schweiger DJ, Ivancevich J and F Power (1987) Executive actions for managing human resources before and after acquisition *Academy of Management Executive, 1,* 127–138.

Schweiger DM (2002) *M and A integration: A framework for executives and managers* New York, NY: McGraw Hill.

Sherer J (1994) Corporate cultures: Turning 'us versus them' into 'we' *Hospitals and Health Networks, 68*(9), 20–22.

Siegenthaler PJ (2011) What role for HR during mergers and acquisitions? *Human Resource Management International Digest, 19*(1), 4–6.

Siehl C (1990) After the merger: Should executives stay or go? *Academy of Management Executive, 4*(1), 50–59.

Sirower ML (1997) *The synergy trap: How companies lose the acquisition game* New York, NY: The Free Press.

Society for Human Resource Management Foundation (SHRM) (2016b) *Creating a more human workplace where employees and businesses thrive* Retrieved from https://www.shrm.org/hr-today/trends-and-forecasting/special-reports-and-expert-views/

Documents/Human-Workplace.pdf (Accessed October 4, 2019)

Society for Human Resource Management (SHRM) (2016a) *Managing human resources in mergers and acquisitions* Retrieved from https://www.shrm.org/resourcesandtools/tools-and-samples/toolkits/pages/merger-sandacquisitions.aspx (Accessed October 4, 2019)

Society for Human Resource Management (SHRM) (2013, August 2) *Organizational complexity overwhelms many HR leaders* Retrieved from https://blog.shrm.org/workforce/organizational-complexity-overwhelms-many-hr-leaders (Accessed October 4, 2019)

Stahl GK and Mendenhall ME (2005) *Mergers and acquisitions: Managing culture and human resources* Stanford, CA: Stanford Business Books.

Staw BM, Sandelands LE and JE Dutton (1981) Threat-rigidity effects in organizational behavior: A multilevel analysis *Administrative Science Quarterly*, *26*(4), 201–524.

Steynberg RP and Veldsman TH (2011) A comprehensive, holistic people integration process for mergers and acquisitions *Journal of Human Resources Management*, *9*(1), 16.

Stieler F (2003) Die acht Erfolgsfaktoren eines Mergers (Eight success factors of a merger) *Magazine for Organisation*, *5*, 280–284.

Thaler RH (1992) *The winner's curse: Paradoxes and anomalies in economic life* Princeton, NJ: Princeton University Press.

Ulrich D and Brockbank W (2005) *The HR value proposition* Boston, MA: Harvard Business Press.

Ulrich D (1997) *HR champions: The next agenda for adding value and delivering results* Cambridge, MA: HBR Press.

Walsh JP and Ellwood JW (1991) Mergers, acquisitions, and the pruning of managerial deadwood *Strategic Management*, *12*(3), 201–217.

Walsh JP (1989) Top management turnover following mergers and acquisitions *Strategic Management Journal*, *9*, 173–183.

Weber Y (1996) Corporate culture fit and performance in mergers and acquisitions *Human Relations*, *49*(9), 1181–1202.

Welch M and Jackson PR (2007) Rethinking internal communication: A stakeholder approach *Corporate Communication*, *12*(2), 177–198.

Whalen PT (2002, April/May) Correcting common misconceptions about communicating during mergers and acquisitions *Communication World*, 6–9.

Zagelmeyer S, Sinkovics RR, Sinkovics N and V Kusstatscher (2018) Exploring the link between management communication and emotions in mergers and acquisitions *Canadian Journal of Administrative Sciences*, *35*(1), 93–106.

Zukis B and McGregor C (1999, November/December) *Human resources: A critical component to your M and A success in Japan Success Stories*, Japan PwC Unifi Network.

16

Managing Presenteeism to Optimize Health and Performance

Maria Karanika-Murray, Caroline Biron, Valerie Hervieux, Zara Whysall, and Huijun Chen

INTRODUCTION

Presenteeism, defined as attending work whilst sick, represents an increasing concern for occupational health practitioners, human resource management practitioners, managers and business leaders for occupational health practitioners, human resource management practitioners, managers, and business leaders, as it sits firmly at the intersection of health and performance (Ipsen et al., 2020). The phenomenon of presenteeism has received increasing attention in the last two decades, as its costs and prevalence compare highly unfavourably with absenteeism. Although an invisible illness, presenteeism has been estimated to cost the UK economy £15.1 billion annually, whereas the cost for absenteeism is £8.4 billion annually (Centre for Mental Health, 2011). Presenteeism is highly prevalent in all occupations, industries, sectors, and countries (Kinman, 2019; Soloviev, et al., 2018). This combination of high prevalence and high cost places

presenteeism at the forefront of concerns for work psychology, occupational health, and management science and practice. In this chapter we define presenteeism, outline some of the current debates in the field, and present practical solutions on how it can be best managed.

Presenteeism has been viewed as a choice for the presentee, with sickness absenteeism as the alternative (Macgregor and Cunningham, 2018; Miraglia and Johns, 2016). A range of personal characteristics (e.g., boundarylessness: Aronsson and Gustafsson, 2005; being a woman, a younger worker, a manager, or self-employed: Johansen et al., 2014), work characteristics (e.g., not wanting to burden colleagues, work overload, pressure from supervisors: Ferreira et al., 2019; Johansen et al., 2014), and organizational characteristics (e.g., legitimacy of absence/presence: Ruhle and Süß, 2019; absence policy: Ferreira et al., 2019) influence this choice, often making the decision more complex, highly prone to error, and potentially leading to dysfunctional presenteeism, a concept that we will describe later. However, evidence indicates the existence of a positive relationship between absenteeism and presenteeism (Leineweber et al., 2012), highlighting that the balance between the two depends on the health condition itself (Whysall et al., 2018).

This chapter is not a comprehensive review of the literature of presenteeism — not only because the field has grown geometrically in the last few years and therefore a comprehensive review would require equivalent substantial space, but also because such invaluable contributions can be found elsewhere (e.g., Garrow, 2016; Johns, 2010; Knani et al., 2015; Lack, 2011; Lohaus and Habermann, 2019; Miraglia and Johns, 2016; Schultz and Edington, 2007; Skagen and Collins, 2016).

DEFINING PRESENTEEISM

Two definitions and corresponding research streams have branched out since Cary Cooper first coined the term 'presenteeism' (Cooper, 1996; Ishimaru et al., 2020). The first focused on the phenomenon of attending work whilst sick and the associated health impairment (Aronsson et al., 2000) and the second on the resulting loss of productivity due to ill-health (e.g., Stewart et al., 2003). Each has attracted researchers from a range of disciplines, but with much overlap. Since the consequences of a behaviour are not tautological with the behaviour itself, definitional conflation should be studiously avoided (Karanika-Murray and Cooper, 2018). Clear definitions are the foundation for accurate measurement, reliable research, actionable practice, and effective intervention. Therefore, we retain the definition of presenteeism as attending work whilst sick (Ruhle et al., 2020).

Presenteeism is a highly idiosyncratic behaviour since it depends on a range of subjective work and health factors (Johns, 2010) – these can include the specific health condition (e.g., chronicity, mental or physical health), the nature of the work (e.g., manual/non-manual, teamwork requirements), orientation to work (e.g., work engagement, job insecurity), and orientation to health (e.g., personal values, individual differences). Since it is a function of health and performance (Karanika-Murray and Biron, 2020), presenteeism is also a highly dynamic behaviour (Cooper and Lu, 2016), as opposed to a fixed state, that can change as the presentee's evaluation of his/her health condition or work demands and priorities change. There is reliable evidence that presenteeism can lead to a cycle of poor attendance behaviour (future sickness absenteeism) (Bergström et al., 2009) and therefore moving towards understanding how it can be managed is an important next step.

For an interdisciplinary field, presenteeism has relatively weak conceptual foundations, for a range of reasons. The behaviour itself is has been typically viewed as an endpoint rather than part of a chain of work behaviours (Karanika-Murray et al., 2015). In addition, little is known about the mechanisms that drive presenteeism (but see emerging research on decision-making: Halbesleben et al., 2014; and new research on the role of organizational context and resources: Bergström et al., 2020; Liu et al., 2020). However, the fact that presenteeism sits at the intersection of two well-established disciplines, occupational health and organizational behaviour, also brings opportunities to integrate these fields and expand its conceptual foundations. The emerging nascent theorizing in the field of presenteeism is promising (Lohaus and Habermann, 2019) as it delineates a move from the more descriptive 'what' questions to understanding explanatory mechanisms, with insights from more established research areas. This will also help to address concerns that the field is a-theoretical (Johns, 2010; Liu et al., 2020).

Recent insights place the individual at the centre of presenteeism behaviour (Ruhle et al., 2020). Presenteeism is not something that happens to the presentee; rather, the presentee enacts the behaviour on the basis of their health status and performance goals. A fundamental psychological principle is that behaviour is a function of the individual and their environment (Lewin, 1997). Environment here takes the form of a range of individual, job, and organizational resources that describe the antecedents of presenteeism (e.g., Roelen and Groothoff, 2010). The presentee's evaluations serve as the glue between the range of antecedents and expected outcomes of that behaviour (Whysall et al.,; Halbesleben et al., 2014; Johns, 2010).

Consequently, this shift of focus to the person invites questions around what purpose presenteeism behaviour may serve. Describing presenteeism as purposeful behaviour implies that for different presentees, presenteeism will fulfil different goals (Karanika-Murray and Biron, 2020; Ruhle et al., 2020) or have different benefits (Johansen et al., 2014; Whysall et al., 2018). This is something of a paradox considering the negative outcomes of presenteeism on health and performance/productivity and of monetary cost to organizations. However, by separating potential benefits from potential costs in the short and the long term, it offers a more comprehensive understanding and the potential to develop better ways to manage presenteeism.

PRESENTEEISM IS A FUNCTION OF HEALTH AND PERFORMANCE

The approach to presenteeism as a purposeful behaviour can allow us to apply principles of organizational behaviour and behaviour change to inform evidence-based interventions. Presenteeism is a type of attendance behaviour that is purposeful, adaptive, and intentional: 'an adaptive behaviour aimed at meeting work and performance demands

during impaired capacity owing to ill-health' (Karanika-Murray and Biron, 2020: 6). It is behavioural engagement with work despite a health-related impairment that would otherwise imply disengagement and temporary withdrawal from work in the form of sickness absence. Enacting presenteeism is aimed at balancing a weakened health capacity, on the one hand, with job demands and expectations to perform at work, on the other (Whysall et al., 2018) and this encapsulates the potential for conflict between health and performance and the permutations that this balancing act can lead to. The interaction or tension between (ill-)health and performance demands is important: what does presenteeism 'achieve' for health and for performance that renders it a 'useful' behaviour and in what context?

The degree of conflict between performance demands and health impairment is important also because it can help to define different points of (im)balance. The Health–Performance Framework of Presenteeism (HPFP, Karanika-Murray and Biron, 2020) was developed to decipher how gradations in health and in performance – the health-performance interaction – can give rise to different enacted presenteeism behaviours and types of presentees. The HPFP approaches presenteeism as an adaptive behaviour that serves the function of balancing performance demands vis-a-vis an impaired health capacity and defines four quadrants or configurations of health and performance (high–high, low–low, low–high, and high–low).

Next, we outline these types of presenteeism and outline the targets and priorities for supporting each type, but discuss specific interventions in a subsequent section. We separate intervention targets/foci from intervention content/activities because some solutions may be beneficial to more than one type of presenteeism. Figure 16.1 illustrates the four types of presenteeism and lists possible interventions.

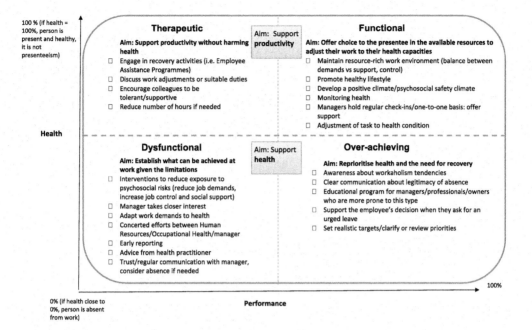

Figure 16.1   Interventions aimed to support health and productivity for each type of presenteeism (adapted from Karanika-Murray and Biron, 2020)

FUNCTIONAL PRESENTEEISM

Functional presenteeism is the high-health–high-performance quadrant that describes being able to maintain a usual level of productivity with no further deterioration to health and perhaps even with the possibility to facilitate recovery from the health condition. Functional presenteeism is the ideal balance between the demands placed by ill-health and the demands to be productive.

Research supports this, including evidence from the return-to-work literature (Mikkelsen and Rosholm, 2018; Nielsen et al., 2018) and the value of work for health and wellbeing. A supportive work environment that can provide the necessary resources to the individual presentees is crucial (Sanderson et al., 2008; Whysall et al., 2018). Under a supportive work environment, functional presenteeism can be a sustainable behaviour in the longer term (Miraglia and Johns, 2016) if it is able to support both health/recovery and also performance/work commitments. Although presenteeism is associated with poorer health in the long term, a resource-rich psychosocial work environment can buffer its negative effects on health (Bergström et al., 2020). Specifically, presentees with higher social support and job control and lower job demands reported a lower decline in future general health compared to presentees working in an environment with fewer resources (Bergström et al., 2020). However, functional presenteeism may become dysfunctional if not managed appropriately, or may slip into overachieving presenteeism. For example, employees who had more than five self-reported sickness presenteeism episodes within one year had poorer subsequent wellbeing (Gustafsson and Marklund, 2011). Similarly, there is an increased risk of developing depression for non-depressed individuals who have worked eight or more days as presentees (Conway et al., 2014).

Priorities for Supporting Functional Presentees

The aim of managing functional presenteeism is to offer choice to the presentee in terms of the available resources to adjust the given work tasks according to the given health limitations or capacities, as highlighted in Table 16.1. This adjustment can be temporary or permanent, depending on the chronicity of the health condition. The priority is (1) to ensure that the presentee (and his/her manager) knows his/her limits, in terms of health capacities and tasks that can be performed, and (2) to not slip into other types of presenteeism, so that the health condition and usual productivity are not further impaired.

Functional presenteeism is achieved when individuals are able to maintain their usual level of productivity despite ill-health. This is conditional on the health condition not

Table 16.1   Illustrative fictional examples of each type of presenteeism

Sam: functional presenteeism with musculoskeletal disorder → stays functional
Sam is a university lecturer who has been suffering from musculoskeletal disorders for several years. Despite a carpal tunnel syndrome that fluctuates with the amount of screen/keyboard work and of sedentary time spent daily, she hardly ever takes any time off work in relation to this issue. With a highly flexible schedule, she can prepare her online teaching using a voice-recognition application, thus giving her wrists a break from typing tasks. Her immediate supervisor is highly supportive and encourages her to take regular breaks and time off when needed. Feeling supported, she knows she can count on her organization to help her fully carry on with her work, such as a small ad-hoc budget to hire help with her marking and other tasks that are more demanding for her wrists. Following her doctor's advice, she uses anti-inflammatory medicine when her symptoms become more acute and arranges to rotate certain tasks with colleagues in order to do less computer work during those days.

Drew: dysfunctional presenteeism with seasonal flu → becomes absent
Drew is affected by a virus. At first he feels minor symptoms and continues to work. After several days of pushing himself and avoiding taking time off work, the majority of his employees test positive. However, as the owner of a small company, he does not want to let his employees down or see his workload accumulate by taking any time off. Whilst his situation worsens, he works from home to avoid contamination, which allows him some flexibility to rearrange his work depending on how he felt during the day. In the end though, his condition worsens, and he has to be hospitalized with respiratory problems, and, of course, has to take sick leave.

Morgan: overachieving presenteeism with high psychological distress → becomes dysfunctional
During the Covid-19 pandemic, Morgan, a middle-manager in a high-tech firm, feels greatly under pressure. Having to manage a team of 16 technicians, he is receiving conflicting mandates from top management. On the one hand, productivity levels need to remain as usual despite the fact that the whole team are now fully teleworking, yet at the same time he is constantly hearing complaints from his team about their difficulties in balancing home and work demands, taking care of children/home schooling whilst working. Trapped between these conflicting demands, he is increasingly aware that his mental health is deteriorating as he is experiencing symptoms of high psychological distress. Not wanting to let his employees down or disappoint his bosses, Morgan persists in working and in achieving performance targets, against all odds. After a few months, he starts feeling depressed, having panic attacks, and is unable to concentrate. Instead of reaching out to his manager, he tries to hide the growing client backlog for fear of coming under fire from top management.

Charlie: therapeutic presenteeism with anxiety problems → becomes functional
Charlie works as a welder in a small business with fewer than 20 employees. The workplace feels like a family and her boss and colleagues are highly supportive. Recently, her ageing mother became ill and had to move in with her, her husband, and their three children. Caring for her mother requires considerable time daily, which is taking a toll on her marriage. At work, she is increasingly distracted and feels she's unable to concentrate. Despite her reduced performance, her colleagues have been very understanding and supportive. Using medication to manage her anxiety, she decides to continue working as her workplace feels a good place to be and it gives her the opportunity to take a break from the difficult situation she is confronted with at home. Charlie's manager notices a change in her demeanour at work, and asks how Charlie is during one of their regular catch-ups. Charlie feels comfortable to share how she feels because of the good relationship they have, and as a result her manager offers to change the rota for Charlie to move to a less intricate welding task until she feels better. Eventually, with the medication, help from her family, and support from her workplace, her work performance improves and she returns to her full range of duties.

interfering with the type of work or tasks, the work environment being adaptable, and resources for effective completion of work duties being available. This requires active monitoring of work tasks against health capacities to detect any imbalance that can move the presentee towards dysfunctional or overachieving presenteeism. The degree of contagiousness of the health condition is a consideration: adjustments such as remote working may be needed even if the presentee's productivity and health can be sustained if the health condition impacts on colleagues. Regular manager–employee communication and consultation is an essential ingredient for identifying specific adjustments.

DYSFUNCTIONAL PRESENTEEISM

Dysfunctional presenteeism is the low–low configuration that describes a negative impact on both health and performance. This is an unsustainable type of presenteeism because it neither supports recovery from ill-health nor helps to maintain the usual level of productivity. It can lead to a loss spiral in health or performance as illustrated by evidence on the long-term impact of presenteeism on sickness absenteeism, emotional exhaustion, and depleted resources (Demerouti et al., 2009b).

Dysfunctional presentees are at high risk of both health impairment and productivity loss. Dysfunctional presenteeism's deleterious effects on both health and performance arise where no attempts are made to adjust work demands or the work environment in light of the health impairment, thereby overstretching work capacity. This can impede recovery and triggers a downward spiral of impaired future health (Aronsson et al., 2011; Bergström et al., 2009). Dysfunctional presenteeism is an unsustainable choice that can lead to reduced productivity, further impaired health, and a longer period of sickness absenteeism than might have been necessary in the first place.

Priorities for Supporting Dysfunctional Presentees

Managing dysfunctional presenteeism should prioritize re-establishing what can be achieved at work whilst also being aware of how such adjustments impact on cognitive, mental, or physical health. A balance between the two priorities is essential but, if this is not possible, sickness absenteeism should be encouraged to support speedier recovery. Dysfunctional presenteeism requires a reconsideration of what resources are needed or how work tasks can be adjusted to the specific health impairment, in order to gradually move the presentee to functional presenteeism.

Of primary importance is line managers' ability to understand health and performance, alertness to red flags, and concerted efforts to support presentees at the first signs of ill-health or impaired performance. Early reporting of ill-health and regular communication can help to build trust between managers and employees. A key decision, in discussion with the employee and with advice from qualified health practitioners, is whether sickness absence is the best option or whether work adjustments are possible. Appropriate adjustments to work tasks and the working environment can move the presentee towards functional presenteeism, in order to allow the presentee to sustain productive work and recovery, or towards therapeutic presenteeism, if performance expectations are lowered. At the organizational level, consideration should be given to whether broader factors, such as strict sickness absence policies or practices (e.g., rigid trigger point systems, punitive return-to-work interviews) that deter employees from taking warranted sickness absence (Bergström et al., 2009) encourage dysfunctional presenteeism.

THERAPEUTIC PRESENTEEISM

Therapeutic presenteeism is the high-health–low-performance quadrant that describes a situation in which a greater emphasis is placed on health and a lesser focus on performance — work is a 'refuge' (Dew et al., 2005; Knani et al., forthcoming), whilst productivity is reduced. For example, employees describing their workplace as a sanctuary (Dew et al., 2005) or their co-workers as family and engaging in presenteeism because they feel that the camaraderie offered is supporting their health (Knani et al., forthcoming).

Although therapeutic presentees' productivity is compromised, the positive impact of work on health can be beneficial. Often it is possible to manage or adjust an individual's work tasks in such a way that the individual can not only remain at work whilst experiencing ill-health, but doing so also supports their recovery. Indeed, encouraging and supporting individuals to remain in work during ill-health or to return to work as soon as possible after is the cornerstone of vocational rehabilitation (Waddell and Burton, 2006). Work itself can be restorative; it offers purpose and identity and a sense of accomplishment (Johns, 2010). Even a small degree of 'exposure' to employment (as low as between one and eight hours per week) can yield positive benefits (Kamerāde et al., 2019). Consequently, a degree of therapeutic presenteeism may not only be inevitable, but is actually a desirable component of effective vocational rehabilitation following illness (Whysall et al., 2018). In the short term or as a transitional stage only, therapeutic presenteeism can support recovery, but, in the longer term, it is unsustainable as productivity remains impaired.

Priorities for Supporting Therapeutic Presentees

The priority when supporting therapeutic presentees is to support productivity without impairing health further. Aligning work tasks to the limited health capacities can help to maximize the therapeutic value of work. Timing is important when targeting action for therapeutic presenteeism. This type is more likely after or at the recovery stage of an acute health event, so close monitoring and responsiveness are important. Working in a psychosocially healthy environment with adjustable demands can provide better recovery than staying at home for an extended period of time (Aronsson and Gustafsson, 2005). In addition, since therapeutic presenteeism is more likely for employees who suffer from chronic health conditions (when long-term absence may not be an option), providing manager and colleague support and identifying red flags can help the presentee refocus on work without additional pressure and with no health detriment – together, these targets can help to design interventions to support functional presenteeism.

OVERACHIEVING PRESENTEEISM

Overachieving presenteeism describes the low-health–high-performance configuration of presentees who are able to remain at their usual productivity level but at the expense of their recovery. In the short term, one can adjust, recover, and maintain a good performance. However, in the long term, a lack of respite can be damaging for both mental and physical health (Kivimäki et al., 2005) and can lead to exhaustion (Demerouti et al., 2009b) and future absenteeism (Bergström et al., 2009; Skagen and Collins, 2016). The work environment is important here: group norms can augment overachieving presenteeism behaviour by moderating absence behaviour, especially for individuals with liberal attitudes towards attendance (Väänänen et al., 2008). For example, a two-year longitudinal study showed that leaders' presenteeism increased both presenteeism and absenteeism of the employees (Dietz et al., 2020).

Priorities for Supporting Overachieving Presentees

The target when supporting overachieving presentees is to re-prioritize health and the need for recovery whilst discouraging unrealistic performance targets, thus guiding the presentee towards functional presenteeism. Overachieving presenteeism can further debilitate health in the short and long term. To manage overachieving presenteeism is to garner, review, and apply the appropriate resources to reduce the presentee's focus and priorities to complete work whilst reviewing what is feasible in view of the specific health impairment.

In overachieving presenteeism, it is important to explore the drivers to overwork at the expense of health, including individual characteristics such as attitude to work, perfectionism, or workaholism (Karanika-Murray et al., 2015). The line manager role is crucial here for instigating work adjustments that can support recovery, understanding the given health limitations, and moderating performance expectations until health recovers. At the organizational level, workplace culture, climate, and practices that promote unhealthy work behaviours should also be targeted. For example, a presenteeism culture where an uncaring work environment offers limited options and encourages presenteeism through fear of job loss (Dew et al., 2005). A review of shared attitudes and behaviours and of performance management and reward systems that sustain overachieving presenteeism can help to identify targets for interventions.

PRINCIPLES FOR DEVELOPING INTERVENTIONS

The priorities for supporting presentees that we outlined earlier can inform more tailored interventions in presenteeism. Next, we outline key principles for developing interventions to manage presenteeism, before we present examples from the intervention literature.

Important for developing interventions is the observation that these four types of presenteeism are dynamic states as well as individual tendencies (Karanika-Murray and Biron, 2020). Presentees may move from one type of behaviour to another as their health status changes or as work tasks and performance expectations are adjusted. Once the presenteeism decision has been made (Whysall et al., the aim is to move the presentee to a state of optimal balance between their health and performance, i.e., functional presenteeism. If either or both health or performance are severely impaired, sickness absenteeism should be encouraged. Thus, any intervention should start with an assessment of the presentees' idiosyncratic needs combined with an assessment of the available resources to support them. Since the manager is the 'match-maker' or broker between performance requirements and work resources, including both personal and organizational resources, management training would be beneficial.

In addition, since behaviour is a function of the person and the environment (Lewin, 1997), taking a multilevel approach to understanding the presenteeism behaviour and understanding the presentee's experience within his/her job and organizational context are essential. Indeed, context, in the form of workplace policies and practices, organizational climate and team climate (Schulz et al., 2017), and shared norms and expectations (Ruhle and Süß, 2019), is a key influence for presenteeism. This has profound implications for developing interventions as it puts organizational resources in the spotlight.

Not all types of presentees require the same types of support and not all approaches to intervention will be appropriate for all types of presenteeism. However, examples from cognate literatures are good starting points for presenteeism interventions. Systematic reviews show that workplace health promotion can promote a healthy lifestyle (Maes et al., 2012; Mhurchu et al., 2010), increase work productivity (Proper et al., 2002), and decrease presenteeism (Ammendolia et al., 2016; Cancelliere et al., 2011). However, not every programme will be effective for all participants and there is no 'one size fits all' approach (Formanoy et al., 2016).

INTERVENTIONS TO MANAGE PRESENTEEISM

The presenteeism intervention literature is not well developed, but there is good indication of what may work in practice, which we can extrapolate from nascent intervention research and evidence from other fields. Health and performance are inseparable and many of the interventions listed below have the potential to address both. For clarity, we distinguish those with a *primarily health* focus from those with a *primarily performance* focus. Since productivity is not possible in the absence of health, presenteeism interventions can start by improving health.

Promoting Health and Performance through Better Mental and Physical Health

A focus on encouraging a healthy lifestyle can foster functional presenteeism. Compared to employees with healthy lifestyles, those with unhealthy lifestyles are less productive, and have higher absenteeism (Pelletier et al., 2004). This can be achieved, for example, by providing incentives to engage in physical activity, providing safe spaces, or modifying the physical work environment to encourage physical activity (Carnethon et al., 2009). Improving health by improving modifiable risk factors (e.g., physical activity, blood pressure, or cholesterol), which are nearly five times more costly than chronic conditions, can also lead to gains in productivity (Lenneman et al., 2011).

Two mechanisms influence the relationship between physical activity and presenteeism:

prevention and *control of* chronic diseases (Burton et al., 2014; Walker et al., 2017a). People who are more physically active develop fewer chronic diseases (prevention) and have better control of their condition (control). Improvements in productivity are due to improvements in physical health indicators (e.g., body mass index, fitness, musculoskeletal function) (Christensen et al., 2015; Walker et al., 2017b) and mental health (e.g., wellbeing, stress, mood) (Brown et al., 2011; Burton et al., 2005).

Social support can be appropriate as a presenteeism intervention target, especially for therapeutic presenteeism, as it can buffer the negative effects of presenteeism (Knani et al., 2018). In addition, physical activity with co-workers combines activity with social support and can improve interpersonal relationships as well as communication and can contribute to a positive work climate (Eime et al., 2013; Kanamori et al., 2015). Interventions could also focus on improving healthy eating habits. A programme developed to increase levels of physical activity, increase fruit/vegetable consumption, and decrease intake of fats and sugars was effective in achieving all these targets (Sternfeld et al., 2009). Finally, to maximize the effectiveness of opportunities in organizations to support a healthy lifestyle, through policy and work environment approaches, a multilevel approach is important. Indeed, 'lifestyle change can be facilitated through a combination of learning experiences that enhance awareness, increase motivation, and build skills and, most important, through the creation of opportunities that open access to environments that make positive health practices the easiest choice' (O'Donnell, 2009: iv).

There is also evidence for the dual value of recovery for health and performance. A higher need for recovery or insufficient recovery can be a precursor of work-related health problems (Sluiter et al., 2003). For overachieving presentees it might be appropriate to encourage recovery when needed, because it is the ability to recover (Demerouti et al.,

2009b) that may protect health. Recovery during non-work time (Demerouti et al., 2009a) should be encouraged. Daily recuperation is more crucial to employee health and well-being than recuperation during vacations (Sonnentag, 2001, 2003) to maintain well-being and work performance (Demerouti et al., 2009a). Although different presentees may value different means to recovery, certain activities are more conducive to recovery than others. Unsurprisingly, work-related activities performed in non-work time inhibit recovery, since recovery can only occur when work demands are absent (Sonnentag, 2001). However, taking part in recreational activities does not guarantee recovery (Demerouti et al., 2009a). Respite happens when the activity is pleasurable: it is not a specific activity per se but rather the motivational and psychological attributes associated with the activity that determine the potential for recovery (Sonnentag et al., 2017). Furthermore, organizations should 'pay attention to the work process when working overtime is structural' (Formanoy et al., 2016) by diminishing job strain, effort–reward imbalance and long work hours to improve performance and minimize health consequences (Carnethon et al., 2009).

Promoting Health and Performance through Better Management and Organization of Work

Because organizations tend to pay more attention to productivity than to individual health (Schultz and Edington, 2007) for obvious reasons and reasons related to access to information, there may be a temptation to encourage employees who are unwell to return to work before they are ready. This should be done cautiously and following medical advice in order to discourage dysfunctional presenteeism and a cycle of ill-health and impaired productivity. A discussion between manager and employee can help to identify which and how work demands and tasks can be adjusted

to the individual's health condition and capacities to achieve a certain level of productivity. Being guided by the health condition itself is essential: vocational counselling, work redesign, adjustment of hours or tasks gradually depending on the presentee's stage of recovery (Lerner et al., 2010).

Good and open communication with managers and colleagues is essential for bolstering practical and emotional social support (Fay, 2011; Mellor et al., 2020). This can be achieved in a number of ways. On-site occupational health (OH) clinics can offer advice and support before the health condition deteriorates (Lerner et al., 2010) and during sick leave. On-site OH clinics would be convenient for employees, saving travel time to a healthcare provider, and for employers, since on-site care would result in less absenteeism and fewer unattended health problems (Engberg et al., 2018). Social-networking opportunities such as intranet forums, workshops, and focus groups, can be useful for employees with mental health conditions (Ammendolia et al., 2016).

Consideration should also be given to whether the organization's culture, policies, and practices promote attendance at the expense of health and/or performance. In contrast to an organizational culture that reflects a 'sanctuary' (Dew et al., 2005), the 'battleground' culture reflects a work environment that is challenging, where management is distant, and presenteeism occurs 'because of loyalty to the professional image, colleagues, and the institution' (Dew et al., 2005: 2279). More flexibility and flexible resources – for instance, providing cover for employees to take sickness absence, temporarily adjusting workload, or modifying work duties (Aronsson et al., 2000) – would help to discourage presenteeism for employees who may not want to let colleagues down.

Furthermore, good leadership is as essential for managing presenteeism as it is for any work behaviour. Leaders' behaviours and attitudes towards presenteeism can have a direct impact upon employee behaviours (e.g., social learning theory: Bandura and Walters, 1977) and changing leaders' behaviour can impact employee psychological wellbeing (Maurya and Agarwal, 2015). Thus, awareness-raising and training/educational programmes for managers and supervisors (Mazzetti et al., 2019) on managing presenteeism and being a role model would be useful to help create a positive workplace climate to enhance job morale (Schaefer and Moos, 1996) and strengthen resilience (Woolley et al., 2011). An annual health risk appraisal 'can help forecast health-related human capital risks and establish the relative appropriateness for a variety of individual and workplace interventions' (Schultz and Edington, 2007: 548).

Preventing ill-health from deteriorating is essential for shifting dysfunctional towards therapeutic presenteeism. A supportive and friendly working environment and high adjustment latitude are key for maintaining productivity of employees who have mental health conditions without adding psychological burden (Whysall et al., 2018). High adjustment latitude means that employees can adapt the work demand to the needs of their current health condition (Hansson et al., 2006).

To ensure that work remains restorative for health, good communication is necessary to understand an employee's work abilities and discuss work adjustments or suitable duties (Roelen and Groothoff, 2010), especially with changing work demands or health status. Particularly in relation to chronic ailments, this may require input from a qualified health professional. 'Keep-in-touch' mechanisms can help employees to maintain social connections whilst on long-term sick leave, so long as these do not inhibit rest and recovery. With severe and chronic health conditions, it may be necessary to consider a role change or even ill-health retirement. This should be done after efforts have been made to identify adaptations to enable individuals to remain at work or when is not feasible to maintain those adjustments, in close consultation with the employee, and under the advice of an occupational health physician.

A forward-looking approach to managing presenteeism with a focus on turning non-functional presenteeism into more functional behaviour would benefit the presentee's work team and organization as a whole. Actions that concern changes in work organization or policy/practices, as opposed to individual-focused solutions, are more preventative (Lamontagne et al., 2007). As such, by supporting a positive workplace culture, presenteeism management can yield sustainable long-term gains for the organization, supporting organizational learning, and building intervention leadership (Ipsen et al., 2018) and healthy workplaces. For example, manager training (Mazzetti et al., 2019), leading by example (Dietz et al., 2020), reviewing policies and practices, or developing a positive climate/psychosocial safety climate (Liu and Lu, 2020; Liu et al., 2020). In this way, successful management of presenteeism can be embedded in the structure and fabric of the organization.

CONCLUSION

A focus on promoting functional presenteeism has several implications for research and practice. First, it allows the health and productivity concerns to be disentangled. The HFPR allows presenteeism behaviour to be disentangled from the severity of the health problem and performance impairment (Biron et al., under review) and to shift focus and resources for supporting the individual presentee with appropriate action.

Second, a focus on understanding the adaptive function of presenteeism emphasizes the need to develop better measures. Most presenteeism research has so far used a single-item measure of the frequency of working whilst ill (Aronsson et al., 2000; Ruhle et al., 2020). This may also underestimate the prevalence of presenteeism related to mental health, because some presentees may not consider mental ill-health as a legitimate reason for absence (Miraglia and Johns, 2016). It does not take into consideration the severity of the health ailment, nor the extent to which performance or different aspects of performance are affected during that period, nor how the presentee may prioritize health and performance concerns.

Third, presenteeism is a dynamic process and not a fixed state, since health and performance covary (Karanika-Murray and Biron, 2020). This calls for more longitudinal research and for methodologies such as diary studies that allow researchers to capture the mechanisms that can help presentees to move towards functional presenteeism. A minute focus on underlying mechanisms of change can also help us to develop better theory of when and how presenteeism happens.

Fourth, supporting presentees and developing interventions for presenteeism should start by understanding the individuals' considerations that make up the decision-making process underlying presenteeism behaviour (Whysall et al.,). This decision-making process is highly dependent on the type and severity of the health ailment, the individual's work capacity at that time, personal characteristics, the resources provided for sick employees, the workplace and organizational context, and the broader socio-political and economic context. Indeed, presenteeism increases in a fragile economic situation because the choice to be absent from work is constrained when job insecurity is high (Karanika-Murray and Cooper, 2018).

Although an imperative, especially in the current uncertain economic context and the Covid-19 pandemic, prioritizing employee mental and physical health has also been an elusive target. We are still a long way from understanding how to support health and performance at the same time (Ipsen et al., 2020), but we can define this as the ultimate aim of functional presenteeism: to support health and productivity in tandem.

REFERENCES

Ammendolia C, Côté P, Cancelliere C, Cassidy JD, Hartvigsen J, Boyle E, Soklaridis S, Stern P and Amick B (2016) Healthy and productive workers: Using intervention mapping to design a workplace health promotion and wellness program to improve presenteeism. *BMC Public Health,* 16(1): 1190.

Aronsson G and Gustafsson K (2005) Sickness presenteeism: Prevalence, attendance-pressure factors, and an outline of a model for research. *Journal of Occupational & Environmental Medicine,* 47(9): 958–966.

Aronsson G, Gustafsson K and Dallner M (2000) Sick but yet at work. An empirical study of sickness presenteeism. *Journal of Epidemiology and Community Health,* 54: 502–509.

Aronsson G, Gustafsson K and Mellner C (2011) Sickness presence, sickness absence, and self-reported health and symptoms. *International Journal of Workplace Health Management,* 4(3): 228–243.

Bandura A and Walters RH (1977). *Social learning theory.* Prentice Hall, Englewood Cliffs, NJ.

Bergström G, Bodin L, Hagberg J, Aronsson G and Josephson M (2009) Sickness presenteeism today, sickness absenteeism tomorrow? A prospective study on sickness presenteeism and future sickness absenteeism. *Journal of Occupational & Environmental Medicine,* 51(6): 1–10.

Bergström G, Gustafsson K, Aboagye E, Marklund S, Aronsson G, Björklund C and Leineweber C (2020) A resourceful work environment moderates the relationship between presenteeism and health. A study using repeated measures in the Swedish working population. *International Journal of Environmental Research and Public Health,* 17(13): 4711.

Biron C, Karanika-Murray M and Ivers H (under review) *Toward the validation of a presenteeism typology – a proof-of-concept study.*

Brown HE, Gilson ND, Burton NW and Brown WJ (2011) Does physical activity impact on presenteeism and other indicators of workplace well-being? *Sports Medicine,* 41(3): 249–262.

Burton WN, Chen C-Y, Li X, Schultz AB and Abrahamsson H (2014) The association of self-reported employee physical activity with metabolic syndrome, health care costs, absenteeism, and presenteeism. *Journal of Occupational and Environmental Medicine,* 56(9): 919–926.

Burton WN, McCalister KT, Chen C-Y and Edington DW (2005) The association of health status, worksite fitness center participation, and two measures of productivity. *Journal of Occupational and Environmental Medicine,* 47(4): 343–351.

Cancelliere C, Cassidy JD, Ammendolia C and Côté P (2011) Are workplace health promotion programs effective at improving presenteeism in workers? A systematic review and best evidence synthesis of the literature. *BMC Public Health,* 395 (2011). https://doi.org/10.1186/1471-2458-11-395

Carnethon M, Whitsel LP, Franklin BA, Kris-Etherton P, Milani R, Pratt CA and Wagner GR (2009) Worksite wellness programs for cardiovascular disease prevention: A policy statement from the American Heart Association. *Circulation,* 120(17): 1725–1741.

Centre for Mental Health (2011). *Managing Presenteeism: A Discussion Paper.* Available at: http://www.centreformentalhealth.org.uk/managing-presenteeism (Accessed July 22th 2020).

Christensen JR, Kongstad MB, Sjøgaard G and Søgaard K (2015) Sickness presenteeism among health care workers and the effect of BMI, cardiorespiratory fitness, and muscle strength. *Journal of Occupational and Environmental Medicine,* 57(12): e146–e152.

Conway PM, Hogh A, Rugulies R and Hansen ÅM (2014) Is sickness presenteeism a risk factor for depression? A Danish 2-year follow-up study. *Journal of Occupational and Environmental Medicine,* 56(6): 595–603.

Cooper CL (1996) Hot under the collar. *Times Higher Education Supplement,* 21 June, 12–16.

Cooper CL and Lu L (2016) Presenteeism as a global phenomenon: Unraveling the psychosocial mechanisms from the perspective of social cognitive theory. *Cross Cultural & Strategic Management,* 23(2): 216–231.

Demerouti E, Bakker AB, Geurts SAE and Taris TW (2009). Daily recovery from work-related effort during non-work time. In: Sonnentag, S., Perrewé, P.L. and Ganster, D.C. (Ed.) *Current Perspectives on Job-Stress Recovery (Research in Occupational Stress and Well Being,* Vol. 7). Emerald Group Publishing Limited, Bingley, pp. 85–123.

Demerouti E, Le Blanc PM, Bakker AB, Schaufeli WB and Hox J (2009) Present but sick: A three-wave study on job demands, presenteeism and burnout. *Career Development International,* 14(1): 50–68.

Dew K, Keefe V and Small K (2005) 'Choosing' to work when sick: Workplace presenteeism. *Social Science Medicine,* 60: 2273–2282.

Dietz C, Zacher H, Scheel T, Otto K and Rigotti T (2020) Leaders as role models: Effects of leader presenteeism on employee presenteeism and sick leave. *Work & Stress,* 34(3): 300–322.

Eime RM, Young JA, Harvey JT, Charity MJ and Payne WR (2013) A systematic review of the psychological and social benefits of participation in sport for children and adolescents: Informing development of a conceptual model of health through sport. *International Journal of Behavioral Nutrition and Physical Activity,* 10(1): 98.

Engberg JB, Harris-Shapiro J, Hines D, McCarver P and Liu HH (2018) The impact of worksite clinics on teacher health care utilization and cost, self-reported health status, and student academic achievement growth in a public school district. *Journal of Occupational and Environmental Medicine,* 60(8): e397–e405.

Fay MJ (2011) Informal communication of coworkers: A thematic analysis of messages. *Qualitative Research in Organizations and Management,* 6(3): 212–229.

Ferreira AI, Mach M, Martinez LF, Brewster C, Dagher G, Perez-Nebra A and Lisovskaya A (2019) Working sick and out of sorts: A cross-cultural approach on presenteeism climate, organizational justice and work–family conflict. *The International Journal of Human Resource Management,* 30(19): 2754–2776.

Formanoy MA, Dusseldorp E, Coffeng JK, Van Mechelen I, Boot CR, Hendriksen IJ and Tak EC (2016) Physical activity and relaxation in the work setting to reduce the need for recovery: What works for whom? *BMC Public Health,* 16(1): 866.

Garrow V (2016). Presenteeism: A review of current thinking. *Institute for Employment Studies*, May, Report no. 507.

Gustafsson K and Marklund S (2011) Consequences of sickness presence and sickness absence on health and work ability: A Swedish prospective cohort study. *International Journal of Occupational Medicine and Environmental Health*, 24(2): 153–165.

Halbesleben JRB, Whitman MV and Crawford WS (2014) A dialectical theory of the decision to go to work: Bringing together absenteeism and presenteeism. *Human Resource Management Review*, 24(2): 177–192.

Hansson M, Boström C and Harms-Ringdahl K (2006) Sickness absence and sickness attendance – what people with neck or back pain think. *Social Science & Medicine*, 62(9): 2183–2195.

Ipsen C, Karanika-Murray M and Hasson H (2018) Intervention leadership: A dynamic role that evolves in tandem with the intervention. *International Journal of Workplace Health Management*, 11(4): 190–192.

Ipsen C, Karanika-Murray M and Nardelli G (2020) Guest editorial: Addressing mental health and organisational performance in tandem: A challenge and an opportunity for bringing together what belongs together. *Work & Stress*, 34(1): 1–4.

Ishimaru T, Mine Y and Fujino Y (2020) Two definitions of presenteeism: Sickness presenteeism and impaired work function. *Occupational Medicine*, 70(2): 95–100.

Johansen V, Aronsson G and Marklund S (2014) Positive and negative reasons for sickness presenteeism in Norway and Sweden: A cross-sectional survey. *BMJ Open*, 4(2): e004123.

Johns G (2010) Presenteeism in the workplace: A review and research agenda. *Journal of Organizational Behavior*, 31(4): 519–542.

Kamerāde D, Wang S, Burchell B, Balderson SU and Coutts A (2019) A shorter working week for everyone: How much paid work is needed for mental health and well-being? *Social Science & Medicine*, 241: 112353.

Kanamori S, Takamiya T and Inoue S (2015) Group exercise for adults and elderly: Determinants of participation in group exercise and its associations with health outcome. *The Journal of Physical Fitness and Sports Medicine*, 4(4): 315–320.

Karanika-Murray M and Biron C (2020) The health-performance framework of presenteeism: Towards understanding an adaptive behaviour. *Human Relations*, 73(2): 242–261.

Karanika-Murray M and Cooper CL (2018). Presenteeism: An introduction to a prevailing global phenomenon. In: Lu, L and Cooper, CL (eds.) *Presenteeism at work*. Cambridge University Press, Cambridge, pp. 9–34.

Karanika-Murray M, Pontes HM, Griffiths MD and Biron C (2015) Sickness presenteeism determines job satisfaction via affective-motivational states. *Social Science & Medicine*, 139: 100–106.

Kinman G (2019) Sickness presenteeism at work: Prevalence, costs and management. *British Medical Bulletin*, 129(1): 69–78.

Kivimäki M, Head J, Ferrie JE, Hemingway H, Shipley MJ, Vahtera J and Marmot MG (2005) Working while ill as a risk factor for serious coronary events: The Whitehall II study. *American Journal of Public Health*, 95(1): 98–102.

Knani M, Biron C and Fournier PS (2018). Presenteeism revisited: A critical review of existing definitions and measures In: Lu, L and Cooper, CL (eds.) *The Cambridge Companion to Presenteeism at Work*. Cambridge University Press, Cambridge, pp. 35–68.

Knani M, Fournier PS and Biron C (2015) Sickness presenteeism in SMEs: A critical review. *The Business & Management Review*, 6(4): 271.

Knani, M., Fournier, P.-S and Biron, C. (accepted). Revisiting presenteeism to broaden its conceptualization: A qualitative study in SME's WORK: *A Journal of Prevention, Assessment, and Rehabilitation*.

Lack DM (2011) Presenteeism revisited: A comprehensive review. *Aaohn Journal*, 59(2): 77–91.

Lamontagne AD, Keegel T, Louie AM, Ostry A and Landsbergis PA (2007) A systematic review of the job-stress intervention evaluation literature, 1990–2005. *International Journal of Occupational and Environmental Health*, 13: 268–280.

Leineweber C, Westerlund H, Hagberg J, Svedberg P and Alexanderson K (2012) Sickness presenteeism is more than an alternative to sickness absence: Results from the population-based SLOSH study. *International Archives of Occupational and Environmental Health,* 85(8): 905–914.

Lenneman J, Schwartz S, Giuseffi D and Wang C (2011) Productivity and health: An application of three perspectives to measuring productivity. *Journal of Occupational & Environmental Medicine,* 53(1): 55–61.

Lerner D, Adler DA, Rogers WH, Chang H, Lapitsky L, McLaughlin T and Reed J (2010) Work performance of employees with depression: The impact of work stressors. *American Journal of Health Promotion,* 24(3): 205–213.

Lewin K (1997). *Resolving social conflicts and field theory in social science.* American Psychological Association, Washington, DC.

Liu B and Lu Q (2020) Creating a sustainable workplace environment: Influence of workplace safety climate on Chinese healthcare employees' presenteeism from the perspective of affect and cognition. *Sustainability,* 12(6): 2414.

Liu B, Lu Q, Zhao Y and Zhan J (2020) Can the psychosocial safety climate reduce ill-health presenteeism? Evidence from Chinese healthcare staff under a dual information processing path lens. *International Journal of Environmental Research and Public Health,* 17(8): 2969.

Lohaus D and Habermann W (2019) Presenteeism: A review and research directions. *Human Resource Management Review,* 29(1): 43–58.

Macgregor J and Cunningham JB (2018) To be or not to be...at work while ill: A choice between sickness presenteeism and sickness absenteeism in the workplace. *Journal of Organizational Effectiveness: People and Performance,* 5(4): 314–327.

Maes L, Van Cauwenberghe E, Van Lippevelde W, Spittaels H, De Pauw E, Oppert J-M, Van Lenthe FJ, Brug J and De Bourdeaudhuij I (2012) Effectiveness of workplace interventions in Europe promoting healthy eating: A systematic review. *European Journal of Public Health,* 22(5): 677–683.

Maurya MK and Agarwal M (2015) Relationship between supportive leadership, mental health status and job satisfaction of civil police constables. *Journal of the Indian Academy of Applied Psychology,* 41(3): 103.

Mazzetti G, Vignoli M, Schaufeli WB and Guglielmi D (2019) Work addiction and

presenteeism: The buffering role of managerial support. *International Journal of Psychology,* 54(2): 174–179.

Mellor NJ, Michaelides G, Karanika-Murray M, Vailland D and Saunder L (2020) Social support as protective factor of the effects of part-time work on psychological health: A moderated mediation model. *International Journal of Workplace Health Management* (Vol. and No. ahead-of-print).

Mhurchu CN, Aston LM and Jebb SA (2010) Effects of worksite health promotion interventions on employee diets: A systematic review. *BMC Public Health,* 10(1): 62.

Mikkelsen MB and Rosholm M (2018) Systematic review and meta-analysis of interventions aimed at enhancing return to work for sick-listed workers with common mental disorders, stress-related disorders, somatoform disorders and personality disorders. *Occupational and Environmental Medicine,* 75(9): 675.

Miraglia M and Johns G (2016) Going to work ill: A meta-analysis of the correlates of presenteeism and a dual-path model. *Journal of Occupational Health Psychology,* 21(3): 261–283.

Nielsen K, Yarker J, Munir F and Bültmann U (2018) Igloo: An integrated framework for sustainable return to work in workers with common mental disorders. *Work & Stress,* 32(4): 400–417.

O'Donnell MP (2009) *Definition of health promotion 2.0: Embracing passion, enhancing motivation, recognizing dynamic balance, and creating opportunities.* Sage, Los Angeles, CA.

Pelletier B, Boles M and Lynch W (2004) Change in health risks and work productivity over time. *Journal of Occupational & Environmental Medicine,* 46(7): 746–754.

Proper KI, Staal BJ, Hildebrandt VH, Van der Beek AJ and Van Mechelen W (2002) Effectiveness of physical activity programs at worksites with respect to work-related outcomes. *Scandinavian Journal of Work, Environment & Health,* 28(2): 75–84.

Roelen CAM and Groothoff JW (2010) Rigorous management of sickness absence provokes sickness presenteeism. *Occupational Medicine,* 60(4): 244–246.

Ruhle SA, Breitsohl H, Aboagye E, Baba V, Biron C, Correia Leal C, Dietz C, Ferreira AI, Gerich J, Johns G, Karanika-Murray M, Lohaus D, Løkke A, Lopes SL, Martinez LF, Miraglia M,

Muschalla B, Poethke U, Sarwat N, Schade H, Steidelmülle C, Vinberg S, Whysall Z and Yang T (2020) 'To work, or not to work, that is the question' – recent trends and avenues for research on presenteeism. *European Journal of Work and Organizational Psychology,* 29(3): 344–363.

Ruhle SA and Süß S (2019) Presenteeism and absenteeism at work – an analysis of archetypes of sickness attendance cultures. *Journal of Business and Psychology,* 35(2): 241–255.

Sanderson K, Hobart J, Graves N, Cocker F and Hobart BO (2008) Presenteeism and mental health: Can the problem be part of the solution? *Occupational Psychology,* 7(1): 17–34.

Schaefer JA and Moos RH (1996) Effects of work stressors and work climate on long-term care staff's job morale and functioning. *Research in Nursing & Health,* 19(1): 63–73.

Schultz AB and Edington DW (2007) Employee health and presenteeism: A systematic review. *Journal of Occupational Rehabilitation,* 17(3): 547–579.

Schulz H, Zacher H and Lippke S (2017) The importance of team health climate for health-related outcomes of white-collar workers. *Frontiers in Psychology,* 8: article 74.

Skagen K and Collins AM (2016) The consequences of sickness presenteeism on health and wellbeing over time: A systematic review. *Social Science & Medicine,* 161: 169–177.

Sluiter J, De Croon E, Meijman T and Frings-Dresen MHW (2003) Need for recovery from work related fatigue and its role in the development and prediction of subjective health complaints. *Occupational and Environmental Medicine,* 60(suppl 1): i62–i70.

Solovieva S, Leinonen T, Husgafvel-Pursiainen K, Heliövaara M and Viikari-Juntura E (2018) Occupational differences in sickness presenteeism trend. *European Journal of Public Health,* 28(suppl_4): cky213. 391.

Sonnentag S (2001) Work, recovery activities, and individual well-being: A diary study. *Journal of Occupational Health Psychology,* 6(3): 196–210.

Sonnentag S (2003) Recovery, work engagement, and proactive behavior: A new look at the interface between nonwork and work. *Journal of Applied Psychology,* 88(3): 518.

Sonnentag S, Venz L and Casper A (2017) Advances in recovery research: What have we learned? What should be done next? *Journal of Occupational Health Psychology,* 22(3): 365.

Sternfeld B, Block C, Quesenberry Jr CP, Block TJ, Husson G, Norris JC, Nelson M and Block G (2009) Improving diet and physical activity with ALIVE: A worksite randomized trial. *American Journal of Preventive Medicine,* 36(6): 475–483.

Stewart WF, Ricci JA, Chee E, Hahn SR and Morganstein D (2003) Cost of lost productive work time among US workers with depression. *Journal of American Medical Association,* 289(23): 3135–3144.

Väänänen A, Tordera N, Kivimäki M, Kouvonen A, Pentti J, Linna A and Vahtera J (2008) The role of work group in individual sickness absence behavior. *Journal of Health and Social Behavior,* 49(4): 452–467.

Waddell G and Burton AK (2006). *Is work good for your health and well-being?* The Stationery Office, London.

Walker TJ, Tullar JM, Diamond PM, Kohl III HW and Amick III BC (2017a) The association of self-reported aerobic physical activity, muscle strengthening physical activity, and stretching behavior with presenteeism. *Journal of Occupational and Environmental Medicine,* 59(5): 474.

Walker TJ, Tullar JM, Diamond PM, Kohl III HW and Amick III BC (2017b) The relation of combined aerobic and muscle-strengthening physical activities with presenteeism. *Journal of Physical Activity and Health,* 14(11): 893–898.

Whysall Z, Bowden J and Hewitt M (2018) Sickness presenteeism: Measurement and management challenges. *Ergonomics,* 61(3): 341–354.

Whysall, Z., Karanika-Murray, M., and Chen, H. (2021). Understanding the process of decision-making for presenteeism behavior: An integration and conceptual model. In: L. Lapierre and C. Cooper (Eds.), *Cambridge Companion to organizational stress and well-being.* Cambridge University Press.

Woolley L, Caza A and Levy L (2011) Authentic leadership and follower development: Psychological capital, positive work climate, and gender. *Journal of Leadership & Organizational Studies,* 18(4): 438–448.

17

LGBTQIA Identities and Organizational Wellbeing

Alys Bethan Einion-Waller

INTRODUCTION

It could be argued that one of the most important issues in equality of access to all of life's resources is employment. The focus of business models and organizational studies on the organization tends to view dominant models of understanding as those towards which employees must be aligned. However, in the emergence of queer theory as an understanding of the intellectual and applied facets of the complexities of queer life and experience, there is a growing awareness of the limitations of dominant ideologies when addressing the complexities of occupational life (Rumens, 2018) and organizational wellbeing.

In particular, with a growing understanding of the ways in which heteronormativity and cisnormativity have affected the ways in which LGBTQIA (lesbian, gay, bisexual, trans, queer, intersex, asexual) people experience employment (Rumens, 2018), organizational studies have been found lacking in the

way they address the specifics of an inclusive workplace and its contribution to the wellbeing of its employees. Yet any scholarship on organizational wellbeing must be characterized by an inherent commitment to inclusive practices and an inclusive culture which supports all members to thrive within the organizational space (physical, psychological and virtual). Just as feminist activism has moved far beyond simply focusing on establishing and securing the rights and wellbeing of women in all walks of life to encompass equality for all genders and a commitment to freedom from oppression (Bell et al., 2020), so should organizational studies focus on removing any sources of oppression, inequality or negative impact on the self.

I write this chapter from an insider perspective, as a member of the LGBTQIA community, and as a leader in equalities within my organization. For five years, I have led the LGBT+ Staff Network at a higher education institution, and have worked on a variety of projects to embed inclusivity into the working environment. However, as an academic within a health discipline, and as an LGBTQIA role model and ally, I have also become more aware of the impact of organizational factors on the wellbeing of any organization's members. These factors include legacies of systemic sexism; systemic heteronormativity and cisnormativity; systemic racism; systemic classism and ageism; lack of embedded awareness of inequalities of access to enrichment activities; and issues with cultures of valorization of socially defined 'norms' of body size, shape and appearance. Whilst I am lucky enough to work within an environment with clearly defined policies and publicly disseminated values of no-tolerance for discrimination, the fact is that any organization based in historical organizational structures is carrying a legacy of culture and identity which can be experienced as exclusive or unsupportive by people with identities of difference, as well as any individual who has commitments outside of the organization such as family and care responsibilities.

The term I use here, identities of difference, is not one which sets LGBTQIA people apart from some defined 'mainstream', but rather one which shows that identities of difference are a form of empowerment. In this I follow in a powerful legacy of reclaiming the form and function of oppression, 'flipping' it to reframe difference as power. For many LGBTQIA people, differentiation from what they might perceive as repressive social norms is a form of self-empowerment. Yet, at the same time, all human beings need to feel a sense of belonging to the social groupings into which they place themselves, either through personal choice or through necessity. For wellbeing, people of diverse gender, sex and sexuality (DGSS) need to feel safe, secure, comfortable and valued in their workplace. It is not enough to require that people simply learn to fit in with organizational culture and function within an organization's systems. *The organization itself must create the conditions in which all people can thrive.*

Almost two decades prior to writing this chapter, I was subjected to direct discrimination in a workplace. In this workplace, I was unfairly treated, in many ways, and eventually accused of lying about something. Despite my protestations, I was not believed, and was told, by a senior manager, that 'We all know you people can't be trusted'. In doing this, the manager excluded me not only from belonging in and with my work colleagues (using 'We all know' to signify her membership of the dominant group and my exclusion from it) but also from the professional values, morals and identity that were associated with my role and to which I fervently ascribed. In essence, this discrimination alienated me from my own profession and resulted in my inability to stay within that organization and nearly resulted in me leaving the profession I love. In the time before and after that incident, I was subject to systematic and sustained bullying which resulted in a demonstrable impact on my mental, emotional and social health, and ultimately excluded me from that workplace. Since the Equality Act (2010), there is less overt discrimination against people of DGSS, but inequalities in the perception of such people, and challenges in deeply gendered and heteronormative or gender-polarized workplaces, roles and cultures continue to impact on the wellbeing of employees and the organizations which employ them. These inequalities stem from deep-seated perceptions, beliefs and assumptions about certain types of people, some overt, some apparently innate, all of which can negatively impact on the wellbeing of organizational members.

In this chapter, the focus is on the means by which organization wellbeing can be promoted through creating inclusive environments for LGBTQIA people as part of its wider diversity practice. However, it must be acknowledged that everyone is intersectional, and everyone's experience derives from that intersectionality. The intersections of specific identities and socially defined characteristics (in itself a problematic area) remains very poorly researched and therefore less well understood, as in the case of the intersections of DGSS and race/ethnicity, for example. Therefore, wellbeing for individuals must be seen as stemming from the uniqueness of their being, not from categorization into a defined identity, and, similarly, people should not be reduced to their identity labels when those labels themselves limit how the individual might be seen.

Having said this, society works with and through labels, identities and constructs, and personal experience is mediated through public identity. The history of the LGBTQIA movement is one of first fighting for legal protection and acceptance of identities, and then for better understanding of people with such identities, and then for legal protection for people in employment, and in access to all aspects of what is defined as social life by a heteropatriarchal capitalist system, in many cases. It can be recognized that not all cultures are capitalist and heteropatriarchal, but the so-called 'Global Economy' is largely dependent on this system with its embedded inequalities, innate assumptions and limited vision of the person. It is also built on the lack of recognition of the value of gendered work, where women's work, or home care, parenting, care of the sick and dependent, and management of family life are not recognized as work, and those providing such care, largely women, are not remunerated or recognized for their role or contribution to the economy.

There are two ways in which organizations can consider wellbeing of individuals. The first is through contributing to eliminating inequalities in experience through anti-discriminatory practices and policies, and the second is through celebrating diversity in a way that promotes others to follow suit, creating a culture of inclusion or a workplace that is 'culturally safe' (Butler-Henderson et al., 2018). This latter is perhaps the hardest to achieve, because it involves a requirement not for people to follow policies, laws or guidelines, but to address in themselves their potential for bias, stereotyping or discrimination. It requires individuals to confront themselves and their own cognitive dissonance which allows them to hold perceptions, opinions and beliefs that run counter to those espoused in diversity policies. In a recent inclusivity event, I was confronted with a colleague who, after a lengthy description of an inclusivity toolkit for educators, responded with the comment that inclusivity was not relevant to him and his discipline. How does one address that issue without conflict? How can organizational cultures address the wellbeing of LGBTQIA members through a whole-staff approach? How can organizations manage both the wellbeing of their LGBTQIA members and those whose ways of knowing, thinking and being are challenged by the very notion of diversity? These are the questions this chapter hopes to answer.

INSIDE, OUTSIDE, OTHER

Let us begin by considering the concept of the 'other'. Much has been written on this issue of 'othering'. Staszak (2009 43), defines otherness as 'the result of a discursive process by which a dominant in-group (the Self) constructs one or many out-groups (Other) by stigmatizing a difference – real or imagined – presented as a negation of identity and thus a motive for potential discrimination'. Thus, othering is a process of division, valorizing the identity and norms of a majority group, whilst the identity and norms of a 'minority' group are associated with less desirable attributes and qualities. It is the human condition to categorize discrete objects in the observed world and to assign labels to them. However, it is a social world which provides the categories, labels, and the associated symbolic value of those labels. To understand then the nature of discrimination and prejudice is to understand how stereotypes derive from the human desire to label, and to simplify engagement with a complex social world through widespread generalization of that label.

This makes huge assumptions, particularly that *any* label applies universally to objects of that type. When I lead gender-awareness sessions for staff, my starting point is that stereotypes negatively impact everyone, either by limiting their vision or limiting their experience and opportunities. So the first step that we can consider, when addressing wellbeing of LGBTQIA people within occupational and organizational life, is to address people's assumptions about each other. We are remarkably unaware, for the most part, of all of the factors impacting upon an individual. But the ability to be oneself at work is a core aspect of the wellbeing of an employee, and directly relates to productivity, attrition and, ultimately, business outcomes. It has long been established that effective diversity management improves organizational outcomes (Qin et al., 2014, Williams and Mavin, 2014). The very nature of diversity management is that it is focused on difference. But in our culture, difference has, for too long, been considered negative. Celebrating diversity is challenging when there exists a dominant, accepted 'norm' which marks itself as a 'norm' and therefore defines all else as different and, somehow, 'less than'. Thus, there is a case for adopting a 'norm-critical' approach to managing diversity within organizations (Christensen, 2018: 103).

It is this kind of approach, which criticizes the norms which most members of the organization are invested in and are comfortable with, which makes it the most challenging in terms of wellbeing, because by challenging norms, we actually destabilize the concept of self for many organizational members, and this could in fact lead to mental disequilibrium and personal or psychological distress. However, it is also vital to recognize that norms are defined by dominant social groups. Those who are most challenged by a norm-critical approach to organizational wellbeing are those who perhaps have most enjoyed the privilege that is associated with belonging to that dominant group.

Thus, the first issue which must be confronted in developing an organizational environment in which individuals from 'minority identities', or rather, whose identities are resistant to gendered and heteronormative assumptions, can thrive, is that of power relations. Diversity itself is 'a social construct reflecting existing power relations' (Christensen, 2018: 104). Yet the global workplace, whether it itself functions locally, nationally or globally, is addressing radically growing diversity within its employees and its clients/service users (Chavez and Weisinger, 2008). This kind of heterogeneity challenges norms and assumptions, and requires more knowledge and understanding of how to respond to this (Jansen et al, 2015; Jang and Ko, 2017). The inherent power dynamics within organizational systems speak to not only how diversity practices are manifested, but how diversity itself is conceptualized and communicated. Therefore, there is a need for a form of radical self-awareness within organizations, in which the roots of institutional assumptions (and inequalities) are exposed, noted and addressed proactively.

DEFINING ORGANIZATIONAL WELLBEING FOR PEOPLE OF DIVERSE GENDER, SEX AND SEXUALITY

Organizational wellbeing is defined as the ability of a company or employing organization to generate a workplace culture and working environment within which its members, at whatever level, can reach their full potential, achieve personal and occupational goals, and support the organization's strategic success. This includes supporting the wellbeing of individuals and their potential to maintain their wellbeing within the workplace.

Although extant policy and governmental support exists in the UK that directly addresses wellbeing, with the creation of the What Works Centre for Wellbeing in 2015

(Bache, 2019), the manifestations of organizational wellbeing are as diverse as the organizations themselves (and their members). Indeed, Bache (2019) suggests that this is perhaps an area of policy and practice which is particularly open to multiple understandings and discourses. Griggs and Howarth (2011) show that it is hard to achieve consensus around what constitutes wellbeing, as people have different definitions depending on their backgrounds and identities. There is also the fact that, in general, discourses tend to problematize wellbeing (Griggs and Howarth, 2011). It is viewed as particularly challenging because of the lack of agreement on what constitutes wellbeing and what might be good solutions for wellbeing (Bache et al., 2016). Bache (2019) gives an example of this: in the UK, many believe that it is an individual state under control of the individual and therefore an issue of personal accountability. This in itself must be problematic because an individual, particularly an employee, does not have control over many of the conditions and factors which affect them. Bache (2019) further identifies as problematic the conflation of wellbeing with happiness. However, defining wellbeing based on policy is also problematic, and Bache (2019) rather argues that wellbeing approaches should be based on evidence derived from experiential knowledge rather than on large-scale objective statistics. This goes against the grain of organizational cultures in many parts of the developed world. It would seem, however, that when it comes to the wellbeing of employees of DGSS, addressing experiential approaches would be a positive way forward.

Other aspects of wellbeing relate to a wider concept of the self which is perhaps less well addressed in the corporate literature and the discourses of organizational behaviour and management, and that is the spiritual dimension of the self (Foster and Wall, 2019). Ways in which individuals experience and make sense of the world, either in relation to an organized and defined religion or spiritual

practice, or in a more personal sense, should be accounted for. A key element of spiritual wellbeing is connectedness, particularly with others (Foster and Wall, 2019). Yet, as we will see in this chapter, connectedness with others may be a significant challenge for people of DGSS.

It is clear, therefore, that there is work to be done on enhancing wellbeing for employees of DGSS, and that that work must come from both the bottom up and the top down. But it is vital that organizations understand the factors which impact on employees of DGSS, and can, in response, start considering real solutions, co-created, to generate a working environment which supports true inclusion of all.

THE EXPERIENCE OF INEQUALITY IN THE WORKPLACE FOR PEOPLE OF DGSS

The literature has long established the fact that people of DGSS experience challenges, barriers and discrimination in occupational life, and although the situation has improved since the introduction of Equalities Legislation in many countries, the underlying conditions, attitudes, beliefs and cultures that brought about these inequalities remain persistent in many contexts. Such issues can include biases in the recruitment process due to sexual orientation; dismissal; lack of success in gaining promotion or advancement; a sexual orientation pay gap; and a lack of career and employment opportunities (Arabsheibani et al., 2005; Ahmed et al., 2013). Informally, sexual-orientation discrimination may take the form of unwelcome/bizarre/awkward jokes, verbal abuse/harassment, loss of credibility or harm to professional reputation, homophobia, lack of inclusivity and acceptance, and being excluded from work-related events, often without the awareness of the LGBTQIA individual (Badgett et al., 2007). Some research has also identified that indices of intersectionality in identity compound the experience of inequality. Discrimination and abuse against LGBTQIA staff were also found to be higher among trans, disabled and LGBTQIA persons from black, Asian or minority ethnic backgrounds (Bachmann and Gooch, 2018).

Salaries or wage differences between heterosexuals and LGBTQIA employees have been found, especially among gay men compared to heterosexual men (Badgett, 1995; Clain and Leppel, 2001; Berg and Lien, 2002; Black et al., 2003). Lesbian women, on the other hand, in some contexts, received higher wages compared to heterosexual women but studies revealed additional domestic responsibilities for traditional heterosexual women make them prefer part-time jobs or employment, and other underlying factors (Clain and Leppel, 2001; Black et al., 2003; Plug and Berkhout, 2004; Arabsheibani et al., 2005). It must not be forgotten that women who are LBTQIA experience all of the challenges of being a woman in the employment context, alongside the additional challenges of their sexuality. Mental health and wellbeing is particularly affected by economic and employment-related issues (WHO/ILO, 2000). The literature demonstrates that factors such as stereotyping and discrimination impact on job performance and interact with mental health and wellbeing (Schmader et al., 2008; Borrel et al., 2010). These factors also interact with the experience of job satisfaction, and affect employee organizational commitment, which also affects performance (Hicks-Clarke and Iles, 2000; Cohen-Charash and Spector, 2001).

Yet the literature suggests also that when people are able to 'come out' in terms of gender and sexuality, their job satisfaction improves (Day and Schoenrade, 1997). Keeping one's sexual/personal identity secret has a significant impact on mental and physical health, particularly as this requires a degree of hard work in keeping quiet about core aspects of personal life. This can directly affect work output and effectiveness (Madera, 2010). This adds to a burden of increased mental health challenges that are experienced by LGBTQIA people in general. There is evidence to suggest that people of different DGSS will experience different forms of discrimination. In one study, Aksoy et al. (2019) discovered sexual minorities, especially gay men, are less likely to attain managerial and leadership positions compared to heterosexuals. It is therefore evident that discrimination on the basis of sexual orientation continues. Social and economic engagement are key to personal wellbeing, and to fail to challenge enduring inequalities in workplaces adds to a culture in which people of DGSS remain aware of threats of a more extreme nature in their personal and public lives. The Home Office (2019) cites a rise in hate crimes in the UK, and shows that these have increased since the EU referendum in 2016. Another study has identified an increase in hate crimes related to sexual orientation (Bachmann and Gooch, 2017). These crimes may not occur in the workplace, but other threats can exist, including persistent micro-aggressions that undermine a person's sense of satisfaction, their confidence in being themselves at work or their relationships with their co-workers. This negatively affects employees' psychological well being, thus affecting work performance, and increasing employment inequalities (Byers, 1999).

THE PRACTICE OF DIVERSITY AND INCLUSION

The literature shows that the regulatory frameworks which require organizations to provide inclusive working environments can help to support equality, diversity and inclusion (EDI), but, for example, Ozeren and Aydin (2016) show that even when these regulations are in place, such as in the case of the UK, their principles are not always necessarily reflected in organizational practices that properly support inclusion. However, the literature also shows that effective diversity approaches are based within a climate of inclusion, and a culture in which a diverse workforce is supported to collaborate and work with and for each other for a better working environment (Downey et al., 2015). As stated above, a key starting point is the conversation about EDI, which should take place on every level of the organization, and should be both formally introduced in specific activities, and also a part of less formal opportunities to raise related issues. The challenge here, as Downey et al. (2015) cite, is that by focusing on some minorities within the institution, others can feel discriminated against, as can be seen in current arguments about trans rights and the emergence of what has been described as gender-critical feminism, which, contrary to the history of feminism, is insisting on the reality of biological determinism. Downey et al. (2015; and James et al., 2001) suggest that focusing too much on minority members can alienate those who belong to the 'majority group'. Yet this is perhaps a necessary consequence of pushing the boundaries of inclusion for people of DGSS. There is in organizational and other social contexts a tendency for people to form 'in-groups' and leave others as 'out-groups' depending on certain demographics (Chen et al., 2016) which can then, as suggested by theories of social identity and self-categorization (Reynolds et al., 2003; Tajfel and Turner, 2004), result in those in the 'in-group' defining the 'out-group' employees by their difference, which can result in stereotyping, bias and prejudice. There is also well-documented evidence of resistance to diversity values and activities, resulting in accusations of minorities receiving special treatment, or some powerful criticism of diversity practices (Hill, 2009; Cocchiara et al., 2010).

Thus, in order to secure greater acceptance and 'buy-in' for diversity policies and practices, those who do *not* belong to the minority group must be included in the dialogues about EDI and how principles can be embedded in organizational practices (Jansen et al., 2015). The main target of messages about EDI practices should be the majority population (Jansen et al, 2015), ensuring that the company does not simply keep 'preaching to the choir'. This can be a real challenge. In running LGBTQIA and gender diversity-focused events over the last five years, both internally and externally, I tend to see the same people representing the same diverse identities, and it seems almost impossible to engage those who do not see the relevance of diversity to them in activities that support diversity. What is needed is a culture in which everyone is talking about diversity as part of their role and activities, at some level, and views this not as a personal issue but as a professional or occupational one. It is clear that an inclusive culture within an organization is established by not just the existence and dissemination of policies, but by there being an attitude of inclusion, embracing everyone regardless of and because of their diversities (Holladay et al., 2003).

In my work, I have become very aware of the ways in which persistent social structures are maintained through mutual storytelling. We repeat the same scripts and the same narratives without becoming conscious of their impact or of their very nature as the means by which we construct our reality. Thus, if we are to achieve organizational wellbeing for people of DGSS and for all organizational members, the starting point must be to change that narrative in such a way that people of DGSS are not stereotyped, not subjected to prejudice, and are protected, actively and constantly, from prejudice and discrimination. Diversity must become everyone's business, as a matter of course, and this must happen through changing the organizational climate to one in which people can be supported through their own personal-professional growth, especially through the process of adapting to a newly complex version of 'normal'. The organization itself must tell and retell a narrative of positive inclusion which recognizes the forces and factors impacting on its employees, including both internal and external factors, and provides them with the means by which to develop responses to these.

ORGANIZATIONAL PRACTICES THAT PROMOTE AN INCLUSIVE CLIMATE

One way of achieving this narrative change, and through it drive a culture change, would be through developing leaders within the organization who are either LGBTQIA themselves or who actively demonstrate dynamic managerial capabilities (Fainshmidt et al., 2017; Helfat and Martin, 2015) alongside diversity awareness, which will support the ability of the organization to adapt to the vast complexity of changing social understandings and proactively support an environment which fosters the wellbeing of people of DGSS. According to Adner and Helfat (2003: 1012), dynamic managerial capabilities are 'capabilities with which managers build, integrate, and reconfigure organisational resources and competences'. However, Kamasak et al. (2020: 20) argue that in recent years the discourse around this idea 'has shifted away from external forces to firms' behavioural, cognitive and social processes as the underpinnings of internal competencies to refine understanding of how firms sense (and shape) opportunities and threats, seize opportunities and reconfigure resources and structures to maintain evolutionary and economic fitness'. This involves diversity in leadership and leaders who are diversity competent. Yet much of the research on dynamic managerial capabilities demonstrates an adherence to outmoded concepts of gender. Kamasak et al. (2020: 22) in particular argue that, in their research,

misappropriation of gender as sex differences leads to essentialisation, reduction of gender to biological determinism, of women and men's dynamic managerial capabilities. In these pieces of

research, gender is treated as a binary category without further elaboration of gender categories … reducing the complexity of gender differences to sex differences.

The literature shows that leadership itself is defined in gendered terms (Ford, 2006; Leicht et al., 2014; Zoller and Fairhurst, 2007 in Ashcraft and Murh, 2018), which can negatively impact on a person's wellbeing through the association of certain attributes and behaviours with gendered stereotypes (Ashcraft and Muhr, 2018), which in turn perpetuate gender inequalities and impact on people of DGSS through entrenched expectations of conformity. This may be particularly challenging for people of diverse genders, non-binary gender identities and trans gender identities.

Therefore, it is not enough for managers to develop skills in inclusion and diversity support. It might be that a core component of dynamic managerial capability is to see people as people and to actively remove the inherent gendered and heteronormative biases that people have acquired throughout the course of their lives. Kamasak et al. (2020: 29) describe this as 'gender proofing', which can help to identify the causes of inequalities, but focusing on 'the essence rather than the form or appearance of dynamic capabilities'. For this, it would seem, organizations need to rewrite the very scripts that operate to define and determine understanding of individuals via a gendered lens, changing the narrative to one in which individuals are both de-gendered and gender-celebrated, and within which certain capabilities which are associated negatively with gendered stereotypes are reframed, challenged or resisted (e.g. Leicht et al., 2014) in terms of their value and benefit to organizations.

However, at the same time, the organization must support the change leaders and role models who will lead on changing that script. At another recent diversity event I was working specifically with a group of colleagues who had asked for support on managing difficult topics in a learning environment – specifically those relating to trans people and the current media discourses. My focus was on strategies to manage what can become a very charged debate in any context, with a polarization of opinions. As I introduced the various strategies that could be used, one of the colleagues began behaving in the exact manner that required the discussion of these strategies in the first place. Whilst apposite, in retrospect, the behaviour demonstrated both the need for the strategies and the issues that organizations face. You cannot change people's minds or require that they change them. Morally and ethically that is not allowable. But you can require that people behave in a certain way, and when objections are raised (I was accused of being prejudiced because I had described my experience of some content in a well-known online group as transphobic) you can recognize that they come from an individual's deeply held perceptions and values, and address that conflict proactively.

What promotes organizational wellbeing is creating a culture and climate in which people feel able to state that they are uncomfortable with someone's opinion, but that it does not result in a breakdown of communications or relationships. It also requires a valorizing of the individual experience, to avoid those testimonies which challenge the dominant group's knowledge and power being minimized or rejected as unfounded (Dotson, 2014). This requires creating a culture in which people can learn to challenge behaviours with questions framed as simple enquiries, rather than oppositional viewpoints. For example, had the colleague simply asked, 'why do you perceive that as transphobic?', we could have debated the issue neutrally, each explored and shared our viewpoints, and agreed to disagree. But framing the objection as an attack on someone espousing inclusive practices does not promote discussion, it places both speakers as oppositional opponents required to defend their position, instead of simply explaining it. Management of organizations set the tone and culture as much as anyone else might, and

the starting point is to create a narrative that frames this less confrontational approach, and others like it, as standard. It means using inclusive language, linguistic structures and modes of communication which foster collaboration, rather than conflict. The issue was resolved when the discussion was channelled in such a way that the colleague effectively argued my point for me, and I was able to smile and agree with them, which left them with no opposition and, therefore, no conflict. Yet most organizations appear to be built on competition, and not on true collaboration. Perhaps it may seem impossible to create a shared vision, a new story of who and what you are within the organization, and what the organization is to you, yet this is vital for true change and for the wellbeing of the workforce.

SUPPORTING A DIVERSE WORKFORCE

There is no doubt that proactive diversity management has positive outcomes for organizations (Barak, 2015; Brimhall et al., 2014; Downey et al., 2015). One of the ways in which companies can enhance their organizational outcomes and improve the psychological and social wellbeing of their staff is to recruit and retain employees who represent the social demographics of those who use or access the organization (Sabharwal, 2014) and to ensure that they keep those staff by reducing attrition (Dirks and Ferrin, 2002), to generate and maintain a positive environment. However, this is not necessarily the case within many organizations, and it does little to address the needs of DGSS employees who may not be strongly represented in the consumer demographic of their organization. Positive diversity practices can enhance employee retention and, in particular, increase job satisfaction (Acquavita et al., 2009; Cramwinckel et al., 2018), which will add to employee wellbeing. But what exactly do these positive practices look like?

A CLEAR MESSAGE

How EDI is communicated, and when, and through what means and media, are fundamental questions and speak strongly to creating a culturally safe workplace for all in which diversity is celebrated as a matter of course. Whilst it is clear that EDI itself is performative (Cabantous et al., 2016), it is vital to work with the understanding that if the focus is only on diversity management as a means to better productivity and business success, the messages and practices used can act as another means over exercising power, and can 'marginalise employees by reinforcing stereotypes and prejudices that provoke and widen gaps between people' (Christensen, 2018: 105). It is also important to avoid the trap of making accreditation or awarding of 'badges of honour' such as a place in the Stonewall Workplace Equality Index (WEI) the focus of LGBTQIA inclusion practices, as this is simply not sufficient for creating a culture in which people of DGSS can thrive and experience the same optimal wellbeing as everyone else.

Whilst such charter marks as the WEI have great benefits in targeting EDI work towards standards set by advocates for inclusion and equality and the celebration of diversity, they are merely a symbol of what should be an underlying culture change and should reflect true organizational behaviour, not simply the targeting of specific policies and practices, such as Pride events, as a means of enhancing the organization's identity. Thus, it is vital that not only is the message clear about LGBTQIA inclusion, but that community members contribute to that message themselves through dialogue with the institution and its non-LGBTQIA members. It must be remembered that for organizations, the practice of diversity is associated with strategic power and with the associated organizational benefits, but these benefits are not limited to performance and productivity, but other aspects of organizational behaviour such as innovation and creativity

(Jackson and Joshi, 2011). Being engaged in and rewarded for innovation, creativity and other personal-professional crossover experiences can only add to employee wellbeing overall. At the same time, organizations must create a culture in which 'dangerous knowledge' becomes 'situated knowledge' (Bell et al., 2020), so that there is the scope for all employees to present diverse experiences and have their needs acknowledged and addressed, and where conflict occurs, to have this properly mediated.

It is vital also that organizations avoid the trap of addressing only one aspect of identity at a time when promoting an inclusive workplace. Intersectionality must be the foundation of all practices, policies and communications. There is a need for the organization itself to understand and work with 'multiple intersecting process of identification' (Christensen, 2018: 108) and to ensure that these processes are reflected in the messages that are given about the workplace environment. This could contribute to creating the culturally safe workspace that is needed for people of DGSS, and research seems to suggest that organizational practices which address inclusivity and equality can be the catalyst that does bring about changes in employee behaviour (Brief and Barsky, 2005). A culturally safe and inclusive organization nurtures a culture of valuing everyone, and this can result in members of different identity groups working together to establish and maintain a climate of celebrating diversity (Downey et al., 2015).

Returning to the issue of power dynamics, there is some evidence to suggest that a more flattened power structure and shared responsibility for creating and fostering a positive workplace culture might result in greater commitment by all employees to diversity practices and values (Ashikali and Groeneveld, 2015). Ahmed (2007, 2012) has identified that policies – for example, in higher education – which support diversity do not bring about sufficient change. Brewis (2019) discusses diversity training, which is recognized as a means by which organizations can implement the requirements of equality legislation (Tatli and Özbilgin, 2007 in Brewis, 2019). But this requires a considerable investment of resources if it is to have any effect.

'TEACHING' DIVERSITY AND INCLUSION?

Crucial to fostering an inclusive environment is the organization's commitment to supporting all members to develop a better awareness and understanding of EDI and of institutional challenges to this. This hinges on both embedding a culture where EDI is seen as the norm, through communication, training and information sharing, and developing individual appreciation of EDI as relevant to the self. However, this must be something that is developed in line with the principles of the location and culture in which the organization is located, which can present specific problems for multi-national or inter-national organizations, or even organizations operating across different locations within the same nation. As diversity can be viewed in itself as a social construct (Holck et al., 2016), then attention must be paid first to how identity is constructed locally, and how diversity is constructed within the context in which it is being addressed. People's perceptions of difference and sameness are both subjective and relational (Ghorashi and Sabelis, 2013).

As I have discussed earlier, presenting people with information that suggests that they are acting/thinking against a particular moral stance tends to result in resistance and backlash. It must be remembered that people's ways of knowing, their sources of knowledge and their innate assumptions are deeply embedded and, depending on their social and personal networks, often regularly reinforced. To challenge people's perception of norms and stereotypes is to challenge their sense of self, which then involves a process

of challenge to the perception of the self as an inherently good person (Brewis, 2019). Thus, it is not simply enough to present a one-off training event or online course. For LGBTQIA inclusivity practices addressing complex ideas of identity, fluidity and sex and gender, there is a requirement for something more, something which embeds this learning as part of professional development practices and works alongside the process of 'becoming' that is inherent in any occupational role. This then positively supports employee and organizational wellbeing.

This could perhaps be addressed through a process of voicing (Bizjak, 2018) in which the transformative power of personal narratives is used to raise awareness and increase understanding. Bizjak (2018: 6) suggests that 'stories give the possibility of inclusion because they represent an expression of voice in organizations. Writing stories about their own account portray an individual point of view that allow the readers to dialogue with otherness'. However, this could be viewed as making employees vulnerable through that visibility, and increasing the threat to them and to their careers. Bizjak (2018) is speaking specifically about trans people and the value of their unique knowledge about gender binarism and heteronormativity, but visibility can be both empowering and disempowering depending on the context. It demands choices of people of DGSS that are not required of those who are not of DGSS. It is therefore something which could both add to employee wellbeing and challenge it, depending on the context. In a supportive environment, self-disclosure can be a positive experience (Lloren et al., 2017). Yet in an environment where anyone perceives a risk to themselves of sharing their voices, this becomes a negative influence on health and wellbeing.

Another approach is to see the organization not as an island, an entity in itself, but as part of society and as part of interlinking networks of organizations with whom there is the potential to share activities, practices and relationships that help foster a positive climate. Within higher education, a large number of UK institutions who have staff networks to support LGBTQIA employees have formed 'The Network of Networks in Higher Education', which, as a body, constantly maintain contact with each other, share good and best practice, offer opportunities for shared exploration of key issues and generate regular meetings for sharing of activities and mutual support. This in itself is a form of empowerment and shared responsibility, but it is notable that for many of these networks, it is the staff of DGSS themselves who lead and run them, attend events and share the practice. Could there not be a similar vision in which organizations network both with staff of DGSS and with all other staff to explore effective practices, both within the organization and across organizations? The way forward is not clear in this respect. Employee networks such as this are a vital component of a supportive workplace, offering peer support and a safe place for self-disclosure. They offer a space for people to explore who they are and to seek support during times of destabilization and realization of the self in context. But they are also a source of activism and organizational change. Yet for many they are deemed the province of queer activists; employees may not want to join them as they do not wish to be known by their sexuality at work. Yet the contribution of a supportive peer network to employee wellbeing is evident.

POLICY

Policy is used by organizations and by governments to adapt to the challenges of the vast complexity that is our social world. Policy exists at the personal level, organizational level and public level (Devon Dodd and Hébert-Boyd, 2000). It consists of administrative policy which deals with administrative procedures, and substantive policy which focuses on the legislation, programmes and practices that concern a sizable and substantial part of the works in a community (Smith, 2003: 11–12). Policies both respond to and create social conditions and inequalities. A report by an expert group on gender and employment from the European Commission on the Trends for Women report by the International Labour Organization indicated some key factors such as roles within the household, differences in human capital investment, comparative biological advantages, socialization and stereotypes, preferences and prejudices, entry barriers and organizational practices as leading to gender segregation in the workplace (ILO, 2017). If we take forward that the foundation for much of the inequalities, stereotypes and prejudices that negatively impact people of DGSS is based on gender stereotyping, then policies which address gender disparities become policies which also support LGBTQIA inclusion and the erosion of those prejudices. National and international policies such as the labour laws of the EU have had significant impact on ensuring the rights of workers are protected (Turner, 2013).

In the UK, policies which directly affect LGBTQIA employees and organizations include the Equality Opportunities Policy, the Employment Rights Act 1996, and health and safety and equality and diversity policies. Furthermore, the UK Equality Act 2010 seeks to protect minority characteristics including age, disability, gender reassignment, race, sex, sexual orientation, religion or belief, pregnancy and maternity, and marriage and civil partnership (Gov.UK, 2019). In the devolved UK governments, there have been further developments, such as the Scotland Act 2016 on areas of equal opportunities policy, and the Welsh Government's Equality and Inclusion Funding Programme 2017–2020 and Strategic Equality Objectives 2020–2024. These policies are aimed at addressing the persistent inequalities and discrimination in employment that undermine true economic and social growth (ILO, 2019; Gov.UK, 2020).

However, policies such as these cannot and will not be enough, as they do not address the underlying culture of a society which is founded on principles which valorize certain gendered traits (as defined by that culture) over others, and within which neo-liberal approaches fail to make safe the lives of diverse people. It is not enough to simply gender-proof policies, where gender-proofing is described as 'the check carried out on any policy proposal to ensure that any potential gender discriminatory effects arising from that policy have been avoided and that gender equality is promoted' (European Institute for Gender Equality, 2019). Policies must be diversity-proofed taking into account intersectional identities relating to gender and sexuality, identity, ethnicity and social class. Furthermore, the gendered and constructed nature of inequality must consider multiple impacts, such as those on parents, carers or people whose circumstances require them to work a second or even a third job (though ideally this would not be necessary as any organization would ensure its employees have a living wage).

The challenge of using organizational policy to support the wellbeing of people of DGSS in the workplace is complex, and the evidence relating to their benefits is mixed. The literature shows that policies can have significant effects, limited effects or no effects in relation to improving equality or enhancing business success (Badgett et al., 2013; McFadden, 2015). Workplace policies have, however, been shown to contribute to better mental health and wellbeing in some research, particularly in relation to the ability to be 'out' at work for some people of DGSS (Lloren et al., 2017). However, this is not always the case, and managing one's identity at work can come with costs, particularly for specific groups. For example, Zurbrügg and Miner (2016) identified that, for women of DGSS, sexuality disclosure could result in negative colleague behaviours more than for men of DGSS. Williamson et al. (2017: 7), however, suggest that 'hiding one's sexual

orientation at work may lead to depletion of resources in the form of personal characteristics (i.e. self-esteem, identity) and energy', which results in stress and impacts on their personal relationships. Concealment of aspects of the self is definitely associated with increased emotional distress (Malterud and Bjorkman, 2016) so policies that unequivocally support diversity and celebrate diverse identities are a foundation stone for better wellbeing for people of DGSS. It would also seem that in order to promote wellbeing, organizational policy must take into account intersecting characteristics, such as ethnicity, gender, age and relationship status, and also consider that people of DGSS may already be carrying an increased burden of stress in the workplace.

CONCLUSION

Activities for promoting organizational wellbeing must recognize that whilst not all employees have equal needs or equal experiences, there are many potential issues for the organization to recognize as contributing to wellbeing for people with specific identities. This includes a fundamental culture of recognition and understanding of identity and diversity and the ways in which these intersect, within people, within organizations, between people within organizations and between the organization and external entities and individuals. Ultimately, promoting wellbeing is everyone's business; it is not just the province of human resources, or management, to create policies for promoting inclusion and preventing discrimination, although this is fundamental to promoting an inclusive culture. Nor is it the province of LGBTQIA people themselves to drive the equalities agenda within an organization, although their experience, skills, knowledge and perspective should be viewed as resources which could contribute to that agenda. Staff networks can provide a safe and supportive space to empower individuals within the organization, but these should be developed by staff with specific characteristics and focus on the needs of members, not on external quality marks and awards, although these can be useful in providing a driver and business case for equalities work.

Policies must be diversity-proofed, and this is where the experiences of people of DGSS can have a similar double-sided benefit. Engaging people of DGSS with people from the non-DGSS community in developing, monitoring and implementing policies can both improve the respect for people of DGSS and improve their sense of their diversity being something that is valued, celebrated and considered of worth to the organization and to their colleagues. Fostering co-creation activities and networks among people of varying identities across all characteristics (and not limiting this to those covered by the Equality Act 2010) would also foster a sense of belonging, and could work towards dissolving the boundaries between 'in-groups' and 'out-groups', enabling individuals to develop relationships that would otherwise perhaps not develop. This could also support people to 'voice' their experiences or important issues relating to their identities in a more supportive environment. Shared knowledge, co-creation of knowledge and diverse representation in all spaces and company outputs must be supported by organizational commitment to ensure all members have the skills to challenge inequality and recognize individual identities as contributing to the overall success of the organization.

Ultimately, however, for people of DGSS to maximize their wellbeing in the workplace, they need to know that they are in a safe working environment and that their safety is promoted. We all need to feel comfortable being ourselves in the workplace and to feel that there will be no inherent cost or risk associated with that. Thus, policies on diversity awareness, training and standards must be compulsory, as must proper training which engages people in dialogues and

addresses people's assumptions and preconceptions in an effective way. These must be supported and reinforced by organizational practices which enforce these policies proactively and visibly. This requires ensuring buy-in from all organizational members, and sharing the message that difference is valued, and that we can agree to disagree but continue to work in a culture of mutual respect and unconditional positive regard. This will pay dividends in wellbeing for all staff; in particular, it will mean that people of DGSS will not be facing barriers, challenges and experiences in the workplace that negatively impact on their wellbeing, and which support their ability to achieve personal and professional goals by enjoying true organizational membership.

REFERENCES

Acquavita, S. P., Pittman, J., Gibbons, M., and Castellanos-Brown, K. (2009) Personal and organizational diversity factors' impact on social workers' job satisfaction: Results from a national internet-based survey. *Administration in Social Work*, 33(2), 151–166. doi:10.1080/03643100902768824

Adner, R., and Helfat, C. E. (2003) Corporate effects and dynamic managerial capabilities. *Strategic Management Journal*, 24(10), 1011–1025.

Ahmed, S. (2007) You end up doing the document rather than doing the doing: Diversity, race equality and the politics of documentation. *Ethnic and Racial Studies*, 30, 590–609.

Ahmed, S. (2012) *On being included: Racism and diversity in institutional life*. Durham, NC: Duke University Press.

Ahmed, A. M., Andersson, L., and Hammarstedt, M. (2013) Are gay men and lesbians discriminated against in the hiring process? *Southern Economic Journal*, 79(3), 565–585.

Aksoy, G. C., Carpenter, S. C., Frank, J., and Huffman, L. M. (2019) Gay glass ceilings: Sexual orientation and workplace authority in the UK. *Journal of Economic Behaviour and Organization* 159, 167–80. https://doi.org/10.1016/j.jebo.2019.01.013

Arabsheibani, R. G., Marin, A., and Wadsworth, J. (2005) Gay pay in the UK. *Economica*, 72(286), 333–347.

Ashcraft, K. L., and Muhr, S. L. (2018) Coding military command as a promiscuous practice? Unsettling the gender binaries of leadership metaphors. *Human Relations*, 71(2), 206–228.

Ashikali, T., and Groeneveld, S. (2015). Diversity management in public organizations and its effect on employees' affective commitment. *Review of Public Personnel Administration*, 35(2), 146–168. doi:10.1177/0734371x13511088

Bachmann, C., and Gooch, B. (2017). *Stonewall. LGBT In Britain. Hate Crime And Discrimination*. https://www.stonewall.org.uk/system/files/lgbt_in_britain_hate_crime.pdf Accessed 10-11-20.

Bachmann, L. C., and Gooch, B. (2018). *Stonewall. LGBT In Britain*. Work Report. https://www.stonewallcymru.org.uk/resources/lgbt-wales-work Accessed 10-11-20.

Bache, I., Reardon, L., and Anand, P. (2016) Wellbeing as a wicked problem: Negotiating the arguments for the role of government. *Journal of Happiness Studies*, 17(3), 893–912.

Bache, I. (2019) How does evidence matter? Understanding 'what works' for wellbeing. *Social Indicators Research*, 142. 1153–1173 doi:10.1007/s11205-018-1941-0

Badgett, M. V. L., Durso, L. E., Mallory, C., and Kastanis, A. (2013) *The business impact of LGBT-supportive workplace policies*. Los Angeles, CA: The Williams Institute.

Badgett, L. M. V., Lau, H., Sears, B., and Ho, D. (2007) *Bias in the workplace: Consistent evidence of sexual orientation and gender identity discrimination*. The Williams Institute, CA: UCLA School of Law.

Badgett, M. L. (1995) The wage effects of sexual orientation discrimination. *Industrial and Labor Relations Review*, 48, 726–739.

Barak, M. E. (2015). Inclusion is the key to diversity management, but what is inclusion? *Human Service Organizations Management, Leadership & Governance*, 39(2), 83–88. doi:10.1080/23303131.2015.1035599

Bell, E., Merilainen, S., Taylor, S., and Tienari, J. (2020) Dangerous knowledge: The political, personal, and epistemological promise of feminist research in management and organization studies. *International Journal of Management Reviews*, 22, 177–192.

Berg, N., and Lien, D. (2002) Measuring the effect of sexual orientation on income: Evidence of discrimination. *Contemporary Economic Policy*, 20, 394–414.

Bizjak, D. (2018) Silencing/voicing transgender people at work: An organizational perspective. *PIJ* 3, (1/2), 5–13.

Black, D., Makar, H., Sanders, S., and Taylor, L. (2003) The earnings effects of sexual orientation. *Industrial and Labor Relations Review*, 56(3), 449–469.

Borrell, C., Artazcoz, L., Gil-González, D., Pérez, G., Rohlfs, I., and Pérez, K. (2010) Perceived sexism as a health determinant in Spain. *Journal of Women's Health*, 19(4), 741–750.

Brewis, D. N. (2019) Duality and fallibility in practices of the self: The 'inclusive subject' in diversity training. *Organization Studies*, 40(1), 93–113.

Brief, A. P., and Barsky, A. (2005) Establishing a climate for diversity: The inhibition of prejudiced reactions in the workplace. *Research in Personnel and Human Resources Management*, 19, 91–129. doi:10.1016/s0742-7301(00)19004-8

Brimhall, K. C., Lizano, E. L., and Barak, M. E. (2014) The mediating role of inclusion: A longitudinal study of the effects of leader–member exchange and diversity climate on job satisfaction and intention to leave among child welfare workers. *Children and Youth Services Review*, 40, 79–88. doi:10.1016/j.childyouth.2014.03.003

Butler-Henderson, K., Kemp, T., McLeod, K., and Harris, L. (2018) Diverse gender, sex and sexuality: Managing culturally safe workplaces. *HIM-Interchange*, 8, 10–14.

Byers, B. (1999) Hate crimes in the workplace: Worker-to-worker victimisation and policy responses. *Securities Journal*, 12, 47–58. https://doi.org/10.1057/palgrave.sj.8340040

Cabantous, L., Gond, J.-P., Harding, N., and Learmouth, M. (2016) Critical essay: Reconsidering critical performativity. *Human Relations*, 69(2), 197–213.

Chavez, C. I., and Weisinger, J. Y. (2008) Beyond diversity training: A social infusion for cultural inclusion. *Human Resource*

Management, 47(2), 331–350. doi:10.1002/hrm.20215

Chen, G., Crossland, C., and Huang, S. (2016) Female board representation and corporate acquisition intensity. *Strategic Management Journal*, 37(2), 303–313. doi:10.1002/smj.2323

Christensen, J. F. (2018) Queer organising and performativity: Towards a norm-critical conceptualisation of organisational intersectionality. *Ephemera: Theory & Politics In Organization*, 18(1), 103–130.

Clain, S. H., and Leppel, K. (2001) An investigation into sexual orientation discrimination as an explanation for wage differences. *Applied Economics*, 33, 37–47.

Cocchiara, F. K., Connerley, M. L., and Bell, M. P. (2010) 'A GEM' for increasing the effectiveness of diversity training. *Human Resource Management*, 49, 1089–1106.

Cohen-Charash, Y., and Spector, P. E. (2001) The role of justice in organizations: A meta-analysis. *Organizational Behavior and Human Decision Processes*, 86, 278–321. doi:10.1006/obhd.2001.2958

Cramwinckel, F. M., Scheepers, D. T., and Toorn, J. V. (2018) Interventions to reduce blatant and subtle sexual orientation- and gender identity prejudice (SOGIP): Current knowledge and future directions. *Social Issues and Policy Review*, 12(1), 183–217. doi:10.1111/sipr.12044

Day, N. E., and Schoenrade, P. (1997) Staying in the closet versus coming out: Relationships between communication about sexual orientation and work attitudes. *Personnel Psychology*, 50(1), 147–163.

Devon Dodd J., and Hébert Boyd, M. (2000) *Capacity building: Linking community experience to public policy. Population and public health branch*. Ottawa: Health Canada.

Dirks, K. T., and Ferrin, D. L. (2002) Trust in leadership: Meta-analytic findings and implications for research and practice. *Journal of Applied Psychology*, 87(4), 611–628. doi:10.1037//0021-9010.87.4.611

Dotson, K. (2014) Conceptualizing epistemic oppression. *Social Epistemology*, 28, 115–138.

Downey, S. N., Werff, L. V., Thomas, K. M., and Plaut, V. C. (2015) The role of diversity practices and inclusion in promoting trust and employee engagement. *Journal of Applied Social Psychology*, 45(1), 35–44. doi:10.1111/jasp.12273

European Institute for Gender Equality (2020) *Gender Proofing: Definition* https://eige.europa.eu/thesaurus/terms/1202 Accessed 27-11-20.

Fainshmidt, S., Nair, A., and Mallon, M.R. (2017) MNE performance during a crisis: An evolutionary perspective on the role of dynamic managerial capabilities and industry context. *International Business Review*, 26(6), 1088–1099.

Ford, J. (2006) Discourses of leadership: Gender, identity and contradiction in a UK public sector organization. *Leadership*, 2(1), 77–99.

Foster, S., and Wall, T. (2019) Organizational initiatives for spiritual wellbeing in the workplace, in Leal Filho, W. (Ed.), *Encyclopedia of the United Nations Sustainability Goals: Good Health and Wellbeing*. Springer. https://www.springer.com/series/ Accessed 10-11-20.

Ghorashi, H., and Sabelis, I. (2013) Juggling difference and sameness: Rethinking strategies for diversity in organizations. *Scandinavian Journal of Management*, 29(1), 78–86.

Gov.UK (2019) *Unemployment. Ethnicity Facts and Figures.* https://www.ethnicity-facts-figures.service.gov.uk/work-pay-and-benefits/unemployment-and-economic-inactivity/unemployment/latest Accessed 13-06-20..

Griggs, S., and Howarth, D. (2011) Discourse and practice: Using the power of wellbeing. *Evidence and Policy*, 7(2), 213–226.

Helfat, C. E., and Martin, J. A. (2015) Dynamic managerial capabilities: Review and assessment of managerial impact on strategic change. *Journal of Management*, 41(5), 1281–1312.

Hicks-Clarke, D., and Iles, P. (2000) Climate for diversity and its effects on career and organisational attitudes and perceptions. *Personnel Review*, 29, 324–345. 10.1108/00483480010324689

Hill, S. (2009) Directions in health communication. *Bulletin of the World Health Organization*, 87(9), 648. doi:10.2471/blt.09.070680

Holck, L., Muhr, S. L., and Villesèche, F. (2016) Identity, diversity and diversity management: On theoretical connections, assumptions and implications for practice. *Equality, Diversity and Inclusion*, 35(1), 48–64.

Holladay, C. L., Knight, J. L., Paige, D. L., and Quiñones, M. A. (2003) The influence of framing on attitudes toward diversity training. *Human Resource Development Quarterly*, 14(3), 245–263. doi:10.1002/hrdq.1065

Home Office (2019) *Hate Crime, England and Wales, 2018/19*. https://www.gov.uk/government/statistics/hate-crime-england-and-wales-2018-to-2019 Accessed 13-09-20.

International Labour Organization (2017) *World Employment and Social Outlook 2017: Trends for Women 2017*. Geneva.

International Labour Organization (2019) *World Employment and Social Outlook 2019: Trends*. Geneva.

Jackson, S. E., and Joshi, A. (2011) Work team diversity, in Zedeck, S. (Ed.), *Handbook of Industrial and Organizational Psychology*, Vol. I, pp. 651–686. Washington, DC: American Psychological Association.

James, E. H., Brief, A. P., Dietz, J., and Cohen, R. R. (2001) Prejudice matters: Understanding the reactions of Whites to affirmative action programs targeted to benefit Blacks. *Journal of Applied Psychology*, 86(6), 1120–1128. doi:10.1037/00219010.86.6.1120.

Jang, Y., and Ko, Y. (2017) Sources of scientific creativity: Participant observation of a public research institute in Korea. *Journal of Open Innovation: Technology, Market, and Complexity*, 3(1). doi:10.1186/s40852-017-0052-5 https://www.mdpi.com/2199-8531/3/1/1 Accessed 01-11-20

Jansen, W. S., Otten, S., and Zee, K. I. (2015) Being part of diversity: The effects of an all inclusive multicultural diversity approach on majority members' perceived inclusion and support for organizational diversity efforts. *Group Processes & Intergroup Relations*, 18(6), 817–832. doi:10.1177/1368430214566892

Kamasak, R., Ozbilgin, M., Kucukaltan, B., and Yavuz, M. (2020) Regendering of dynamic managerial capabilities in the context of binary perspectives on gender diversity. *Gender in Management: An International Journal*, 35(1), 19–36.

Leicht, C., de Moura, G. R., and Crisp, R. J. (2014) Contesting gender stereotypes stimulates generalized fairness in the selection of leaders. *The Leadership Quarterly*, 25(5), 1025–1039.

Lloren, A., and Parini, L. (2018) How LGBT-supportive workplace policies shape the experience of lesbian, gay men, and bisexual employees. *Sexuality Research and Social Policy*. 14, 289–299. doi:10.1007/s13178-016-0253-x

McFadden, C. (2015) Lesbian, gay, bisexual, and transgender careers and human resource development: A systematic literature review. *Human Resource Development Review*, 14, 125–162.

Madera, J. M. (2010) The cognitive effects of hiding one's homosexuality in the workplace. *Industrial and Organizational Psychology*, 3, 86–89.

Malterud, K., and Bjorkman, M. (2016) The invisible work of closeting: A qualitative study about strategies used by lesbian and gay persons to conceal their sexual orientation. *Journal of Homosexuality*, 63, 1339–1354.

Ozeren, E., and Aydin, E. (2016) What does being LGBT mean in the workplace? A comparison of LGBT equality in Turkey and the UK, in Klarsfeld, A., Ng, E. S., Booysen, L. A. E., Christiansen, L. C., and Kuvaas, B. (Eds), *Research Handbook of International and Comparative Perspectives on Diversity Management*, pp. 199–226. Cheltenham: Edward Elgar.

Plug, E., and Berkhout, A. (2004) Effects of sexual preference on earnings in the Netherlands. *Journal of Population Economics*, 17(1), 117–131.

Qin, J., Muenjohn, N., and Chhetri, P. (2014) A review of diversity conceptualizations: Variety, trends, and a framework, *Human Resource Development Review*, 13(2), 133–157.

Reynolds, K. J., Turner, J. C., and Haslam, S. (2003). Social identity and self-categorization theories' contribution to understanding identification, salience and diversity in teams and organizations, in Polzer, J. (Ed.) *Identity Issues in Groups (Research on Managing Groups and Teams, Vol. 5)*, pp. 279–304. Bingley: Emerald Group Publishing Limited. doi:10.1016/s1534-0856(02)05011-9

Rumens, N. (2018) *Queer business: Queering organization sexualities*. London: Routledge.

Sabharwal, M. (2014) Is diversity management sufficient? Organizational inclusion to further performance. *Public Personnel*

Management, 43(2), 197–217. doi:10.1177/ 0091026014522202

Schmader, T., Johns, M., and Forbes, C. (2008) An integrated process model of stereotype threat effects on performance. *Psychological Review*, 115(2), 336–356.

Smith, L. B. (2003) *Public Policy and Public Participation. Engaging Citizens and Community in the Development Of Public Policy*, pp. 11–12. Ottawa: Health Canada. https:// atrium.lib.uoguelph.ca/xmlui/bitstream/ handle/10214/3139/Smith_Public_Policy_ and_Public_Participation_Engaging_Citizens_ and_Community_in_the_Development_of_ Public_Policy_complete.pdf?sequence=24& isAllowed=y Accessed 4-11-20.

Staszak, J.-F. (2009) Other/otherness, in Kitchin, R. and Thrift, N. (Eds), *International Encyclopedia in Human Geography*, Vol. 8, pp. 43–47. Amsterdam: Elsevier. https://doi. org/10.1016/B978-008044910-4.00980-9

Tajfel, H., and Turner, J. C. (2004) The social identity theory of intergroup behavior, in Jost, J. T. and Sidanius, J. (Eds.), *Key Readings in Social Psychology. Political Psychology: Key Readings*, pp. 276–293. Hove: Psychology Press. https:// doi.org/10.4324/9780203505984-16

Tatli, A., and Özbilgin, M. (2007) Diversity management as calling: Sorry, it's the wrong number, in Koall, I., Bruchhagen, V., and Höher, F. (Eds), *Diversity Outlooks*, pp. 457–473.

Munster: LIT-Verlag. https://www.academia. edu/345482/Diversity_Management_as_Calling_Sorry_it_s_the_wrong_number_ Accessed 22-7-17.

Turner, C. (2013). *Unlocking employment law*. London: Routledge.

Williams, J., and Mavin, S. (2014) Guest editorial: Progressing diversity in HRD theory and practice. *Human Resource Development Review*, 13(2), 127–132.

Williamson, R. A., Beiler-Maya, A., Locklear, L. R., and Clark, M. A. (2017) Bringing home what I'm hiding at work: The impact of sexual orientation disclosure at work for same-sex couples. *Journal of Vocational Behavior*, 103(A), 7–22. https://doi.org/ 10.1016/j.jvb.2017.08.005

World Health Organisation/International Labour Organisation (2000) *Mental Health and Work: Impact, Issues and Good Practices* Geneva: WHO/ILO https://www.who.int/mental_ health/media/en/712.pdf accessed 11-11-20.

Zoller, H., and Fairhurst, G. (2007) Resistance leadership: The overlooked potential in critical organization and leadership studies. *Human Relations*, 60(9): 1331–1360.

Zurbrügg, L., and Miner, K. N. (2016) Gender, sexual orientation, and workplace incivility: Who is most targeted and who is most harmed? *Frontiers in Psychology*, 7, 1–12. http://dx.doi.org/10.3389/fpsyg.2016.00565

18

Preventing Suicide in the Workplace

Victoria Ross, Sharna L. Mathieu,
Katrina Witt and Kairi Kõlves

INTRODUCTION

Suicide is a complex public health concern that has devastating and far-reaching implications for individuals, families and the workplace. Globally, suicide claims the lives of over 800,000 people each year and it is estimated that for every suicide death, there are over 20 other individuals attempting suicide (World Health Organization, 2014). Although active employment is typically considered a protective factor against suicide, the majority of working-age people who die by suicide are employed at the time of death (Milner et al., 2014; Yip and Caine, 2011). In addition, there is increasing evidence that those employed in certain occupational sectors are at elevated risk of suicide compared with the general employed population (Andersen et al., 2010; Milner et al., 2013). From a public health perspective, there is a clear motivation to implement effective workplace suicide prevention initiatives, particularly for those occupational

groups at high risk of suicide (Milner et al., 2014; Milner and LaMontagne, 2018). This chapter will provide an overview of evidence for high-risk occupational groups and their associated risk factors, and then outline existing workplace suicide prevention interventions and the available evidence for the effectiveness of these programmes.

Milner et al. (2013) were the first to apply a rigorous methodology to summarize existing literature on occupation and suicide. Their systematic review and meta-analysis of suicide mortality across occupational skill-level groups analysed 34 studies from a wide range of countries (including the United States, Canada, Europe, the UK, Japan, Korea, New Zealand and Australia). Results showed that the highest risk of suicide was seen in 'elementary' occupations such as laborers and cleaners, plant and machine operators and ship's deck crew. Workers in service occupations such as police, and skilled agricultural, forestry and fishery workers were also at high risk (Milner et al., 2013). The lowest risk of suicide was seen in the highest skill-level group of managers and moderately skilled group of clerical support workers. Overall, the results of the meta-analysis indicated that suicide was highest in male-dominated and lower-skilled jobs, and lowest in higher-skilled jobs.

Since Milner and colleagues' (2013) review, there has been a growing body of international research which not only supports the premise that poor working conditions are related to risk of suicidal behaviours (Milner et al., 2018), but has also identified specific occupational sectors associated with a consistently higher risk of suicide, including police and armed services (Grassi et al., 2019; Milner et al., 2017b); medical professionals such as doctors (Fink-Miller and Nestler, 2018; Milner et al., 2016), nurses (Davidson et al., 2019, 2020b; Kõlves and De Leo, 2013) and veterinarians (Milner et al., 2015; Tomasi et al., 2019); agricultural workers (Klingelschmidt et al., 2018; Milner et al., 2013); and construction workers (Andersen et al., 2010; Heller et al., 2007).

The relationship between occupation and suicide may be influenced by a wide range of factors. Exposure to poor working conditions or psychosocial job stressors such as low job control, high job demands, effort–reward imbalance and high levels of job insecurity have been associated with poor mental health (Bonde, 2008; Madsen et al., 2017). However, while psychosocial job stressors and mental health issues are important risk factors, these are unlikely to completely explain the higher rates of suicide for some occupations compared to others (Milner and LaMontagne, 2018). For the purpose of this chapter, we will focus on the occupational groups for which there is the strongest evidence in relation to risk of suicide (i.e., police/correctional/defence force, healthcare professionals and veterinarians, agriculture and construction).

Before we delve more deeply into how specific risk factors impact the relationship between occupational groups and suicide, we will provide a brief overview of the interpersonal theory of suicide (ITS; Joiner, 2005; Van Orden et al., 2010), which is a useful perspective for understanding how these risk factors impact on suicidal behaviours. The theory proposes that suicidal desire is caused by the simultaneous presence of the constructs of thwarted belongingness and perceived burdensomeness (and subsequent feelings of hopelessness). However, while these feelings may instil a desire for suicide, they are not sufficient to lead to a suicide attempt. For this to occur, it is hypothesized that one must acquire the ability for lethal self-injury. According to the theory, the capability to actually engage in suicidal behaviour emerges via habituation in response to repeated exposure to physically painful and/or fear-inducing experiences (Van Orden et al., 2010). As outlined below, those in occupations with routine exposure to trauma and death (and with access to lethal means) are at increased risk of developing an acquired capability for suicide.

OCCUPATIONAL RISK FACTORS

Job Stress and Burnout

Across sectors, a number of psychosocial job stressors such as high job insecurity, high job demands, low job control and job stress (i.e., the combination of high job demands coupled with low job control) have been associated with adverse mental health outcomes, including suicidal ideation and behaviour (Law et al., 2020; Milner et al., 2018). Those employed in the police, correctional and defence force sectors experience unique job stressors in addition to these. In particular, adverse chronobiologic working conditions, such as night-shift work and physically demanding and dangerous working conditions (Baumert et al., 2014) have all been associated with increased psychological distress and suicide risk for those working in these sectors (Duxbury and Halinski, 2017).

Heightened levels of job stress, and particularly stemming from routine occupational rather than operational sources, may therefore play a key role in increasing stress (Finney et al., 2013; Webster, 2013), mental ill-health (Garbarino et al., 2013) and suicidal behaviour (Singh et al., 2013) in these occupations.

Job stress and particularly burnout have also been highly documented within the healthcare profession and are similarly linked to poor mental health and wellbeing, including suicide in veterinarians (Andela, 2020), doctors (Stehman et al., 2019) and nurses (Accardi et al., 2020). Healthcare professions are also characterized by overwork and long hours; however, they additionally carry the responsibility for life and death decisions in patient care, and staff typically work within complex, hierarchical hospital systems (Rothenberger, 2017). Such workplace factors overlap with individual, home and social factors to contribute to the high levels of stress and burnout reported by workers (Accardi et al., 2020). With recent increases in pandemic events such as Severe Acute Respiratory Syndrome (SARS), Middle Eastern Respiratory Syndrome (MERS) and most notably the current global COVID-19 pandemic, healthcare workers have experienced huge increases in patient volumes, decreases in their sense of control, inadequate resources and access to personal protective equipment, and are increasingly cut off from social support networks (e.g., when required to self-isolate for quarantine purposes), which further serve to increase workplace stress (Galbraith et al., 2020). Unfortunately, workplace stress and burnout are associated with anxiety and depressive symptoms, substance misuse and suicide in these professionals, with nurses and physicians more likely to experience job problems preceding suicide than the general working population (Davidson et al., 2020b).

For other health professionals such as veterinarians (Hanrahan et al., 2018) and paramedics (Stanley et al., 2016), secondary traumatic stress and compassion fatigue appear important in considering the mental health and safety of these workers, and may be especially compounded in situations of low job control and perceived futility of care, such as constant exposure to many unwanted and sick animals in the case of veterinarians (Hanrahan et al., 2018). More research is needed to determine whether job stress and burnout contribute to suicide in these workers.

Access to Means of Suicide

Certain occupations provide workers with easy access to, and familiarity with, weapons and potentially lethal substances (Milner et al., 2017a). Occupational-related access to highly lethal suicide methods, such as firearms, may play a key role in increasing the risk of suicide in those employed in the protective services and defence force. Persons with occupational access to firearms are significantly more likely to use these means to end their lives as compared to those employed in occupations without access to this method, and this may be particularly so for females employed in these professions (Milner et al., 2017a). Where studies have investigated the source of these firearms, research suggests that individuals employed in these sectors are most likely to use their service-issue firearm (Costa et al., 2019; Grassi et al., 2019).

In the healthcare sector, doctors, nurses and veterinarians have knowledge of lethal medications/dosages and access to such substances for their work. In this profession, female doctors and nurses who die by suicide are significantly more likely to die from medication self-poisoning than males, and females who take their own life in the general working population (Milner et al., 2017a). In one prevalence study of suicide in Australian veterinarians and veterinarian nurses, self-poisoning using animal euthanasia medications was the most common method of suicide for these workers. This was directly tied to their occupational knowledge and skillsets (Milner et al., 2015). One interesting exception appears to be paramedic personnel. In the suicide prevention literature, paramedic personnel tend to be categorized alongside other emergency-service workers (e.g., police, fire-fighters), and while more paramedics have been shown to use self-poisoning than other emergency professions, overall they are more likely to use non-work-related means for suicide (Milner et al., 2017b). More research is required to understand the unique factors that contribute to suicide in this population (Stanley et al., 2016).

Workers in the agricultural industry also have easy access to lethal means (e.g., firearms, poisons) and are also more likely to use these methods to end their lives than those without access to means. Studies have shown that suicide by firearm is the leading method of suicide in farmers (Milner et al., 2017a), particularly in high-income countries (Klingelschmidt et al., 2018). In contrast, in low- and middle-income countries, those working in the agriculture and farming sector have ready access to highly lethal pesticides (Gunnell et al., 2017; Mew et al., 2017).

Exposure to Death and Acquired Capability for Suicide

Consistent with the ITS described earlier, people working in certain high-risk occupations may have the propensity to develop an acquired capacity for suicide as part of their work roles, including knowledge and familiarity with ways of dying. Some occupations also place workers in situations where they may be regularly exposed to death and suffering. Those working in the police/correctional/defence services and healthcare are routinely exposed to death and dying in others (Carleton et al., 2019), including deaths by suicide (Aldrich and Cerel, 2020). This has been widely implicated in the theoretical underpinnings of suicidal behaviours

whereby a desensitization to human death may result in lower inhibition, and thereby contribute to an acquired capacity for suicidality in these workers (e.g., combat exposure; Van Orden et al., 2010).

Other high-risk occupations are routinely exposed to the repeated death and suffering of animals. For example, Milner and colleagues (2015) linked veterinary workers' familiarity and routine exposure to companion-animal euthanasia/death to the ITS. Through their work, agricultural workers may be involved in ending the lives of animals. Additionally, exposure to death and suffering of farm animals may be linked to suicidality in Australian farmers (Perceval et al., 2019). During times of drought, the need to euthanize starving livestock has been traditionally the role of males, who have attempted to protect their families from the emotionally distressing experience (Perceval et al., 2019).

Workplace Culture

A positive workplace culture and strong social ties within the workplace may enhance feelings of belonging in workers (Waller, 2020). However, workplaces that are socially isolating or undervalue the wellbeing of workers through workplace cultures that stigmatize help-seeking or mental health/suicide can foster feelings of loneliness, worthlessness and a perceived sense of burden upon those they work with and those they seek to provide for. Both concepts are central to the ITS, where shame/self-hate are linked to perceived burdensomeness and loneliness is linked to a thwarted belonging (Van Orden et al., 2010).

Suicide Stigma and Shame

In military and service personnel, mental health stigma and shame is far-reaching and can be self-directed or perceived in the workplace or community and can manifest in an avoidance of disclosure and/or resistance to self-labelling (Ben-Zeev et al., 2012). Unfortunately, while mental health problems such as depression and Post-Traumatic Stress Disorder (PTSD) are relatively common and have been linked to suicide in this workforce, shame itself is also related to suicidal thinking in defence force veterans (Bryan et al., 2013). A similar picture emerges for first responders (e.g., police). First responders are often required to assist with suicidal clients or attend the scene where someone has died by suicide (Aldrich and Cerel, 2020). For police officers, these experiences can have ongoing implications for the mental health and wellbeing of workers and yet officers still report perceptions of workplace stigma and difficulties in seeking help (e.g., Ross et al., 2020). A recent meta-analysis investigated mental health stigma and reported common stigma-based fears of help-seeking in first responders (Haugen et al., 2017). These were related to fears around confidentiality of services, adverse career implications and perceived judgement within the workplace. Stigma was related to PTSD and depression, and maladaptive coping strategies such as alcohol use (Haugen et al., 2017). In another systematic review of suicidality in first responders, stigma was identified as a barrier to engaging with help services that may make workers more vulnerable to suicidal thoughts and behaviours (Stanley et al., 2016).

The healthcare sector is also not immune to the stigma and damaging perceptions of mental health and suicide. While this has been largely researched in relation to the experiences and outcomes of suicidal patients (Pompili et al., 2005; Ross and Goldner, 2009), health professionals are just as likely to fail to identify depression or anxiety in themselves or colleagues and report substantial self-stigma against suicide (McCleary-Gaddy and Scales, 2019; Watson et al., 2020). Such perceptions begin or are present early in their careers. Veterinary students,

for example, report they would be unlikely to personally seek help or disclose suicidal concerns despite high co-occurring levels of self-reported suicidal ideation (Cardwell et al., 2013). Medical students too report high stigma of suicide (McCleary-Gaddy and Scales, 2019). Unfortunately, stigma of mental health issues and suicide is cited as a key systemic barrier preventing help-seeking for doctors (Kalmoe et al., 2019). Workplaces have an imperative to support the de-stigmatization of help-seeking/offering within the profession (Beautrais, 2020) by moving away from a culture that places significant pressure on workers to be stoic and fault-free (Accardi et al., 2020; Rothenberger, 2017).

Masculine Norms

Dominant Western masculine norms which value characteristics such as self-reliance, stoicism and ability to provide for one's family, are associated with suicidal thoughts and behaviours, as help-seeking behaviours are often framed as 'weak' (Coleman, 2015; Granato et al., 2015; King et al., 2020). For example, an Australian longitudinal study of over 13,000 males found that the characteristic of self-reliance, in particular, was linked to increased risk of suicidal thinking (Pirkis et al., 2017).

The defence force is a traditionally male-dominated sector, and the instilling of masculine ideals such as self-reliance and stoicism during military training and deployment has adverse implications for suicide and help-seeking (Burns and Mahalik, 2011). Masculinity also impacts the transition back to civilian life (Bulmer and Eichler, 2017), where additional complications such as post-traumatic stress (Jakupcak et al., 2006) and/ or disruption to self-identity following taking another life during combat (Maguen et al., 2011), may further interact with a loss of 'male' identity. This may enhance feelings of loneliness, shame, guilt weakness/worthlessness and ultimately anxiety, depression and suicide. When combined with 'male' self-reliance and an inability to communicate and process emotions, help-seeking is reduced, and these complex psychological processes are often left untreated, self-medicated or prone to treatment attrition (Lorber and Garcia, 2010).

Dominant socio-cultural attitudes and adherence to norms of masculinity characterized by self-reliance, stoicism and a strong work ethic are also common in farmers and rural communities, which impacts help-seeking (Kaukiainen and Kõlves, 2020; Perceval et al., 2017). Furthermore, they have been reported to utilize maladaptive masculine coping strategies to deal with increasing psychological distress and physical illness through avoidance and/or isolation – working longer hours, increasing consumption of alcohol or illicit drugs, withdrawing from social interactions and a reluctance to seek help (Kunde et al., 2017). A Canadian study suggested that agrarian values linked with traditional masculinity are associated with poorer mental health outcomes in males working in the agriculture industry (Roy et al., 2017). Traditional masculinity was also considered a central element in the suicide of farmers, as described by their close family and rural community members in Australia (Kunde et al., 2018; Perceval et al., 2017, 2018).

An important example of masculine norms as a potential risk factor for suicide can also be seen within the male-dominated sector of the construction industry. In addition to the stress and physical demands of construction work, the industry is characterized by a culture dominated by traditional masculine beliefs (Broadbent and Papadopoulos, 2014; Powell et al., 2018). In a study examining the impact of a construction-industry workplace suicide prevention programme, clients who had received assistance through the programme identified the issue of traditional male attitudes such as stoicism and the importance workers place on being the 'provider', as key obstacles to help-seeking within the construction industry (Ross et al., 2019).

Factors Unique to Agricultural Workers

Climatic and economic conditions

Strong dependence on climatic conditions is a unique stressor in the agriculture sector, making those working in the sector particularly vulnerable to exposure of extreme climatic events such as hurricanes, floods and drought (Hirsch and Cukrowicz, 2014; Perceval et al., 2019). For Australian farmers, drought has been an important contributor to increasing psychological stress, exacerbating feelings of uncertainty and lack of control over farming. Extreme climatic conditions threaten the quality and value of the land and livestock, thereby affecting financial security (Kunde et al., 2017; Perceval et al., 2019). In addition, other environmental factors such as government and regulatory changes, as well as other external changes including economic downturns (particularly the global financial crisis) are additional stressors that perpetuate feelings of lack of control and uncertainty within the agriculture sector (Hirsch and Cukrowicz, 2014; Merriott, 2016; Perceval et al., 2019).

Geographic and social isolation

Work in agriculture can also be socially isolating due to high workload and decreased social involvement (Hirsch and Cukrowicz, 2014; Klingelschmidt et al., 2018; Perceval et al., 2018). A decline of social integration due to demographic changes in rural communities has been considered as an influencing risk on suicide. Globally, rural populations are in decline, and so is the workforce employed in the sector. Over the past two decades, employment in agriculture has dropped from 48.2% to 32.1% in low- to middle-income countries and from 5.6% to 3.1% in high-income countries (World Bank, 2020). Consequently, farmers and people living in rural communities are experiencing increased feelings of social isolation. In addition to the declining agricultural populations, geographical isolation also contributes to the reduction or lack of mental health and other services as reported in a number of countries, which hinders suicide prevention (Hirsch and Cukrowicz, 2014; Ringgenberg et al., 2018). Travelling long distances for physical and/or mental health concerns has been reported, as well as the transient nature and frequent turnover of GPs and psychiatric doctors in public health (Perceval et al., 2019).

WORKPLACE SUICIDE PREVENTION INTERVENTIONS

Suicide prevention interventions can be classified as primary, secondary or tertiary. Primary prevention acts to increase awareness of suicide and suicide risks well before the onset of suicidal behaviour. Examples are suicide awareness education, life skills training and restriction of access to lethal means. Secondary suicide prevention aims to decrease the likelihood of a suicide attempt through reducing or eliminating suicidal risk factors through early identification and provision of help. Finally, tertiary prevention aims to reduce the consequences for those who have already suffered from suicide ideation and attempts (Wasserman and Durkee, 2009).

In their guidelines for workplace suicide prevention the World Health Organization (2006) recommends that effective prevention activities should include a combination of:

- organizational change aimed at preventing and reducing job stress;
- the de-stigmatization of mental health problems and help-seeking (including awareness raising);
- recognition and early detection of mental health and emotional difficulties; and
- appropriate intervention and treatment through employee mental health resources.

Unfortunately, there is a lack of information on effective workplace suicide prevention initiatives, as very few have been evaluated, either among those that have been developed for specific organizational contexts or those developed as general training packages (Milner et al., 2014). Below we outline what is known about workplace suicide prevention programmes for high-risk occupations and the available evidence for their effectiveness.

Police, Correctional and Defence Force

Despite the increased risk of suicide in this sector, most prevention work has focused on improving recognition of suicide risk in others given the role of those working in these sectors as first responders. A comprehensive systematic review of suicide prevention activities in this sector revealed that, of those programmes that have been developed specifically for the prevention of suicide for those working in these sectors, most studies were of programmes developed for defence force personnel and for police (Witt et al., 2017).

The majority of these programmes have focused on prevention activities such as psychoeducation and awareness-training suicide surveillance procedures to establish the prevalence of suicidal behaviour; gatekeeper training; crisis-response and intervention-teams employee-wellbeing programmes; better integration of existing alcohol- and drug-use treatment programmes; and peer-support programmes (Witt et al., 2017). A number of these programmes also provide additional prevention activities such as a 24-hour crisis telephone hotline and mandating attendance at annual mental health 'check-ups'. Tertiary-level support was also provided through postvention services for those exposed to the suicide death of a colleague (Witt et al., 2017).

While these programmes have collectively been found to be effective in reducing suicide rates post-intervention by as much as half (Witt et al., 2017), few have provided primary-level suicide prevention activities, particularly activities aimed at minimizing the impact of routine organizational-level stressors. This is important given that organizational stressors, rather than operational stressors, may play a larger role in increasing stress (Finney et al., 2013; Webster, 2013), mental ill-health (Garbarino et al., 2013) and suicidal behaviour (Singh et al., 2013). There were three notable exceptions: two aimed at police (LaMontagne et al., 2017; Mehlum, 1998) and one at defence force personnel (Knox et al., 2003), that directly addressed common sources of organizational-level stress by providing leadership training to all senior ranks. Leadership style can significantly impact on employee mental health and may even help to counteract the association between job stress and mental ill-health in these occupational sectors (Russell, 2014). These programmes therefore initiated activities to improve leadership style, such as through the implementation of 360-degree leadership evaluations and personalized leadership coaching for senior ranks (LaMontagne et al., 2017).

However, in most cases where primary-level activities have been implemented, the focus has been on improving the psychological resiliency of the individuals; for example, implementing changes to personnel selection procedures or deployment screening procedures (Warner et al., 2011), or providing resiliency training (e.g., Warner et al., 2011). While there has been increasing interest in the role of individual-level resiliency training on reducing stress in these occupational sectors (McCraty and Atkinson, 2012), there is currently little evidence of the effectiveness of resiliency training on suicidal behaviour (Zamorski, 2011). Additionally, placing the onus for prevention at the individual level is stigmatizing and potentially dangerous, as this implies that the individual who died by suicide lacked resilience. A thorough assessment of barriers to implementation of these programmes is warranted to identify which approaches are feasible and effective for these occupational sectors which are characterized by exposure to unique psychosocial job stressors, high levels of staff turnover and hierarchical management structures which can impede effective implementation (LaMontagne et al., 2017).

Healthcare and Veterinary Sectors

Consistent with the previous sector, many suicide prevention interventions developed for the healthcare and veterinary sector have focused on providing the necessary education for healthcare workers in identifying and supporting suicidal clients/patients (Haas et al., 2005). However, given the elevated risk for suicide in this workforce it is important that organizations ensure modifiable workplace changes are made to improve the occupational health and wellbeing of these workers, including addressing workplace cultures and stigma (World Health Organization, 2006). Organizations and academic institutions are increasingly encouraging self-care practices in healthcare for students and staff to counter the impacts of job stress and burnout on mental health and suicide. However, there is a need for more evaluation to determine the acceptability, effectiveness and sustainability of such practices (Accardi et al., 2020; Beautrais, 2020; Kalmoe et al., 2019; Witt et al., 2019). Furthermore, while there are differences in thresholds for individual coping and resilience, there are also systemic barriers that may impede the uptake of these practices in healthcare workers (Kalmoe et al., 2019). These include being time-poor and overworked, and a competitive, highly driven, perfectionist workplace culture (Kalmoe et al., 2019). In one study, for example, nurses who were routinely encouraged and supported by their supervisors to take meal breaks were more likely to do so (as one may expect), and this was found to have positive implications for their mental wellbeing and fatigue recovery (Hurtado et al., 2015). Other health professionals benefitted from increases in protected work time for emotional debriefing or peer supervision (Davidson et al., 2020a; Dunn et al., 2008).

Additional concerns regarding confidentiality, fear of legal recourse or loss of professional licencing/promotion present another complex barrier to help-seeking in this industry (Kalmoe et al., 2019); however, this is not easily reconciled. Organizations and those in leadership positions have the opportunity and responsibility to implement modifiable workplace factors to facilitate safer work practices (LaMontagne et al., 2007, 2014). Such structural changes may support mental health and reduce suicidality in workers without simply relying on individuals to engage in their own practices that may not be feasible and further contribute to pressure, stress, alienation and stigma experienced by burnt out and vulnerable workers (Whitehead, 2006).

In veterinarians, primary, secondary and tertiary interventions at an individual and organizational level have been proposed (e.g., more reliable monitoring of mental health and suicidality in staff, reduction in stigmatizing or unsafe work practices, postvention support) (Bartram et al., 2010). For medical staff and students, mindfulness training (Zeller and Levin, 2013) and the development of tailored mobile applications/web-based programmes (Pospos et al., 2018) have also been suggested. However, there is limited implementation and evaluation of workplace suicide prevention interventions generally, and less so in the healthcare (Milner et al., 2014) or veterinary industries (Bartram et al., 2010).

More recently, the Healer Education Assessment and Referral (HEAR) suicide prevention programme was developed and adapted for medical and nursing professionals (Accardi et al., 2020; Davidson et al., 2018b). The programme provides suicide prevention education and is combined with an assertive screening of workers to identify those experiencing mental health problems or suicidality and providing those identified with referrals to receive confidential supports. An evaluation of the HEAR programme with nurses in the United States found that nurses were highly stressed/burnt out and reported intense loneliness, with a portion (5–14% from 2016–2019) reporting recent suicidal ideation (Accardi et al., 2020). The HEAR

programme was sustainable and acceptable to nursing staff and, importantly, appears highly transferrable between healthcare organizations (Accardi et al., 2020).

Agriculture and Farming Sectors

Given that the stressors and risk factors affecting the lives of agricultural workers and leading to higher risk of suicide are multifactorial, suicide prevention has to be considered at multiple levels. However, to date, only a limited number of activities have been reported (Hagen et al., 2019; Reed and Claunch, 2020). Limiting access to means has shown to be the most effective suicide prevention activity (Mann et al., 2005; Zalsman et al., 2016). Limiting access to pesticides at a local community level has been evaluated in a small number of studies with limited sample sizes, providing limited evidence (Reifels et al., 2019). However, restricting access to pesticides through national bans on highly lethal pesticides appears to be effective in reducing suicides, while evidence in restricting sales was found to be less consistent (Gunnell et al., 2017). Nevertheless, wider interventions at the government level might be necessary considering reports from India that farming and agriculture suicides are related to the wider agrarian crisis, which needs to be addressed through regulations in agriculture rather than improving mental health care (Merriott, 2016; Sathyanarayana Rao et al., 2017).

There is some evidence of effectiveness of gatekeeper training in workplaces and community organizations. A gatekeeper training programme of frontline agricultural workers and farmers in Australia, using a before, after and three-month follow-up design, showed an increase in suicide literacy and confidence to help others, which remained at the follow-up. In addition, a notable improvement in wellbeing was reported by participants at the three-month follow-up (Perceval et al., 2020).

Given those working in agriculture and farming often live in rural and remote areas, digital platforms have been utilized to provide suicide stigma training directly to these workers (Kennedy et al., 2020). In a recent Australian study, the Ripple Effect digital intervention was evaluated in a sample of male farmers with a lived experience of suicide (Kennedy et al., 2020). While there were minimal significant reductions in suicide stigma and literacy as measured by self-report surveys, qualitative findings demonstrated positive effects with regard to aspirations and intentions for help-seeking and offering in this high-risk occupational group (Kennedy et al., 2020). Further research into the use of technology in providing primary-, secondary- and tertiary-level interventions to these workers is crucial.

Construction Industry

Within the Australian construction industry, Mates in Construction (MATES) was developed as a workplace suicide prevention and early intervention programme. Gatekeeper training is provided to workers as part of a suite of training and support programmes (including a suicide prevention hotline, field officers and case-management support to workers and their families). General Awareness Training (GAT) is designed to reduce suicide stigma and encourage help-offering and help-seeking. Connector training is provided to workers who wish to become site volunteer gatekeepers who can identify and safely engage with people at risk and connect them to professional help. Finally, ASIST (suicide first aid), is where key workers are trained to make a safe plan for a person at risk of suicide and connect them to external resources (Ross et al., 2020). Evaluation studies have demonstrated the social validity and general impact of the MATES programme (Gullestrup et al., 2011). Significant increases in suicide prevention awareness in GAT participants (Gullestrup

et al., 2011; Ross et al., 2019, 2020) and shifting attitudes towards suicide and mental health (King et al., 2018) have also been demonstrated. In addition, analysis of the Australian National Coroners' Information System (NCIS) data showed some decrease in male suicides in the Queensland construction industry in the first five years after the introduction of the programme compared to the five years before (Martin et al., 2016). The MATES programme has also been implemented in the mining industry, where it has been found to increase help-seeking behaviours and reduce stigma around mental health issues (Sayers et al., 2019).

CONCLUSION

This chapter aimed to present a general overview of workplace suicide prevention, including the high-risk occupational groups and their work-related risk factors, existing workplace suicide prevention interventions and evidence of their effectiveness. Although a range of intervention programmes have been developed for various sectors, unfortunately there remains a lack of robust evidence for workplace suicide prevention interventions. There is a strong need to further develop, implement and rigorously evaluate workplace interventions. Effective suicide prevention in these occupational sectors requires a multi-level approach, combining primary-, secondary- and tertiary-level prevention activities aimed at both the individual and organization (Witt et al., 2017). Further exploration of how both routine organizational as well as operational stressors influence suicidal thoughts and behaviours among these personnel is also required, as well as elucidation of the influences between these stressors. In many cases suicide prevention activities have the potential to be integrated into existing workplace mental health activities (Milner et al., 2014). While a negative environment characterized by poor leadership and high job stress may have direct impacts on mental ill-health and suicide risk (e.g., through bullying and emotional burnout), there may also be more insidious effects, such as inhibiting positive help-seeking behaviours. Clearer reporting of suicide mortality rates, as well as proxy indications such as self-harm presentations to emergency departments, will also be necessary to help establish those at greatest risk of suicide and at what point in their careers (Witt et al., 2017).

REFERENCES

Accardi R, Sanchez C, Zisook S, et al. (2020) Sustainability and outcomes of a suicide prevention program for nurses. *World Views on Evidence-Based Nursing* 17: 24–31.

Aldrich R and Cerel J. (2020) Occupational suicide exposure and impact on mental health: Examining differences across helping professions. *Journal of Death and Dying* 1–15.

Andela M. (2020) Burnout, somatic complaints, and suicidal ideations among veterinarians: Development and validation of the Veterinarians Stressors Inventory. *Journal of Veterinary Behavior* 37: 48–55.

Andersen K, Hawgood J, Klieve H, et al. (2010) Suicide in selected occupations in Queensland: Evidence from the State suicide register. *Australian and New Zealand Journal of Psychiatry* 44: 243–249.

Bartram DJ, Sinclair JM and Baldwin DS. (2010) Interventions with potential to improve the mental health and wellbeing of UK veterinary surgeons. *Veterinary Record* 166: 518–523.

Baumert J, Schneider B, Lukaschek K, et al. (2014) Adverse conditions at the workplace are associated with increased suicide risk. *Journal of Psychiatric Research* 57: 90–95.

Beautrais A. (2020) Stress and suicide in medical students and physicians. *The New Zealand Medical Student Journal* 30: 11–14.

Ben-Zeev D, Corrigan PW, Britt TW and Langford L. (2012) Stigma of mental illness and service use in the military. *Journal of Mental Health* 21(3): 264–273.

Bonde JPE. (2008) Psychosocial factors at work and risk of depression: A systematic review of the epidemiological evidence. *Occupational and Environmental Medicine* 65(7): 438–445.

Broadbent R and Papadopoulos T. (2014) Improving mental health and wellbeing for young men in the building and construction industry. *Journal of Child & Adolescent Mental Health* 26(3): 217–227.

Bryan CJ, Ray-Sannerud B, Morrow CE and Etienne N. (2013) Shame, pride, and suicidal ideation in a military clinical sample. *Journal of Affective Disorders* 147(1–3): 212–216.

Bulmer S and Eichler M. (2017) Unmaking militarized masculinity: Veterans and the project of military-to-civilian transition. *Critical Military Studies* 3(2): 161–181.

Burns SM and Mahalik JR. (2011) Suicide and dominant masculinity norms among current and former United States military servicemen. *Professional Psychology: Research and Practice* 42(5): 347–353.

Cardwell JM, Lewis EG, Smith KC, et al. (2013) A cross-sectional study of mental health in UK veterinary undergraduates. *Veterinary Record* 173: 266–272.

Carleton R, Afifi T, Taillieu T, et al. (2019) Exposures to potentially traumatic events among public safety personnel in Canada. *Canadian Journal of Behavioural Science* 51: 37–52.

Coleman D. (2015) Traditional masculinity as a risk factor for suicidal ideation: Cross-sectional and prospective evidence from a study of young adults. *Archives of Suicide Research* 19(3): 366–384.

Costa T, Passos F and Queiros C. (2019) Suicides of male Portuguese police officers – 10 years of national data. *Crisis* 40: 360–364.

Davidson JE, Accardi R, Sanchez C, et al. (2020a) Nurse suicide: Prevention and grief management. *American Nurse Journal* 15: 14–17.

Davidson JE, Proudfoot J, Lee K, et al. (2019) Nurse suicide in the United States: Analysis of the Center for Disease Control 2014 National Violent Death Reporting System dataset. *Archives of Psychiatric Nursing* 33: 16–21.

Davidson JE, Proudfoot J, Lee K, et al. (2020b) A longitudinal analysis of nurse suicide in the United States (2005–2016) with recommendations for action. *World Views on Evidence-Based Nursing* 16: 6–15.

Davidson JE, Zisook S, Kirby B, et al. (2018b) Suicide prevention: A healer education and referral program for nurses. *The Journal of Nursing Administration* 48: 85–92.

Dunn LB, Iglewicz A and Moutier C. (2008) A conceptual model of medical student well-being: Promoting resilience and preventing burnout. *Academic Psychiatry* 32: 44–53.

Duxbury L and Halinski M. (2017) It's not all about guns and gangs: Role overload as a source of stress for male and female police officers. *Policing and Society* 28: 930–946.

Fink-Miller EL and Nestler LM. (2018) Suicide in physicians and veterinarians: Risk factors and theories. *Current Opinion in Psychology* 22: 23–26.

Finney C, Stergiopoulos E, Hensel J, et al. (2013) Organizational stressors associated with job stress and burnout in correctional officers: A systematic review. *BMC Public Health* 13(82): 1–13.

Galbraith N, Boyda D, McFeeters D, et al. (2020) The mental health of doctors during the COVID-19 pandemic. *BJPsych Bulletin* 1–4.

Garbarino S, Cuomo G, Chiorri C, et al. (2013) Association of work-related stress with mental health problems in a special police force unit. *BMJ Open* 3(7): 1–13.

Granato S, Smith P and Selwyn C (2015) Acquired capability and masculine gender norm adherence: Potential pathways to higher rates of male suicide. *Psychology of Men & Masculinities* 16(3): 246–253.

Grassi C, Del Casale A, Cucè P, et al. (2019) Suicidio nella Polizia di Stato italiana nel periodo 1995–2017 [Suicide among Italian police officers from 1995 to 2017]. *Rivista di Psichiatria* 54(1): 18–23.

Gullestrup J, Lequertier B and Martin G. (2011) MATES in construction: Impact of a multimodal, community-based program for suicide prevention in the construction industry. *International Journal of Environmental Research and Public Health* 8(11): 4180–4196.

Gunnell D, Knipe D, Chang S-S, et al. (2017) Prevention of suicide with regulations aimed at restricting access to highly hazardous pesticides: A systematic review of the international evidence. *The Lancet Global Health* 5(10): e1026–e1037.

Haas A, Hegerl U, Lonnqvist J, et al. (2005) Suicide prevention strategies: A systematic review. *Journal of the American Medical Association* 294: 2064–2074.

Hagen BNM, Albright A, Sargeant J, et al. (2019) Research trends in farmers' mental health: A scoping review of mental health outcomes and interventions among farming populations worldwide. *PLoS ONE* 14(12): 1–20.

Hanrahan C, Sabo BM and Robb P. (2018) Secondary traumatic stress and veterinarians: Human–animal bonds as psychosocial determinants of health. *Traumatology* 24: 73–82.

Haugen PT, McCrillis AM, Smid GE and Nijdam MJ. (2017) Mental health stigma and barriers to mental health care for first responders: A systematic review and meta-analysis. *Journal of Psychiatric Research* 94: 218–229.

Heller TS, Hawgood JL and De Leo D. (2007) Correlates of suicide in building industry workers. *Archives of Suicide Research* 11: 105–117.

Hirsch JK and Cukrowicz KC. (2014) Suicide in rural areas: An updated review of the literature. *Journal of Rural Mental Health* 38: 65–78.

Hurtado DA, Nelson CC, Hashimoto D, et al. (2015) Supervisors' support for nurses' meal breaks and mental health. *Workplace Health & Safety* 63(3): 107–115.

Jakupcak, M, Osborne TL, Michael S, Cook JW and McFall M. (2006) Implications of masculine gender role stress in male veterans with posttraumatic stress disorder. *Psychology of Men & Masculinity* 7(4): 203–211.

Joiner TE. (2005). *Why people die by suicide*. Cambridge, MA: Harvard University Press.

Kalmoe MC, Chapman MB, Gold JA, et al. (2019) Physician suicide: A call to action. *Missouri Medicine* 116: 211–216.

Kaukiainen A and Kõlves K. (2020) Too tough to ask for help? Stoicism and attitudes to mental health professionals in rural Australia. *Rural and Remote Health* 20: 5399.

Kennedy AJ, Brumby SA, Versace VL, et al. (2020) The ripple effect: A digital intervention to reduce suicide stigma among farming men. *BMC Public Health* 20: 1–12.

King TL, Gullestrup J, Batterham PJ, et al. (2018) Shifting beliefs about suicide: Pre-post evaluation of the effectiveness of a program for Workers in the Construction Industry. *International Journal of Environmental Research and Public Health* 15(10): 1–13.

King TL, Shields M, Sojo V, et al. (2020) Expressions of masculinity and associations with suicidal ideation among young males. *BMC Psychiatry* 20: 1–10.

Klingelschmidt J, Milner A, Khireddine-Medouni I, et al. (2018) Suicide among agricultural, forestry, and fishery workers: A systematic literature review and meta-analysis. *Scandinavian Journal of Work, Environment and Health* 44: 3–15.

Knox K, Litts D, Talcott G, et al. (2003) Risk of suicide and related adverse outcomes after exposure to a suicide prevention programme in the US Air Force: Cohort study. *British Medical Journal* 327: 1376.

Kõlves K and De Leo D. (2013) Suicide in medical doctors and nurses: An analysis of the Queensland Suicide Register. *The Journal of Nervous and Mental Disease* 201(11): 987–990.

Kunde L, Kõlves K, Kelly B, et al. (2017) Pathways to suicide in Australian farmers: A life chart analysis. *International Journal of Environmental Research and Public Health* 14: 352.

Kunde L, Kõlves K, Kelly B, et al. (2018) 'The masks we wear': A qualitative study of suicide in Australian farmers. *The Journal of Rural Health* 34: 254–262.

LaMontagne AD, Keegel T and Vallance D. (2007) Protecting and promoting mental health in the workplace: Developing a systems approach to job stress. *Health Promotion Journal of Australia* 18: 221–228.

LaMontagne AD, Martin A, Page K, et al. (2014) Workplace mental health: Developing an integrated intervention approach. *BMC Psychiatry* 14: 1–11.

LaMontagne AD, Martin A, Page K, et al. (2017) *An integrated workplace mental health intervention in Victoria Police: Results of a cluster-randomised trial.* Accessed 13 July 2020, from: research.iscrr.com.au/__data/assets/pdf_file/0020/1024715/an-integrated-workplace-mental-health-intervention-in-Victoria-Police.pdf

Law P, Too L, Butterworth P, et al. (2020) A systematic review on the effect of work-related stressors on mental health of young workers. *International Archives of Occupational and Environmental Health* 93: 1–12.

Lorber W and Garcia HA. (2010) Not supposed to feel this: Traditional masculinity in psychotherapy with male veterans returning from Afghanistan and Iraq. *Psychotherapy: Theory, Research, Practice, Training* 47(3): 296.

Madsen IE, Nyberg ST, Hanson LM, et al. (2017) Job strain as a risk factor for clinical depression: Systematic review and meta-analysis with additional individual participant data. *Psychological Medicine* 47(8): 1342–1356.

Maguen S, Luxton DD, Skopp NA, et al. (2011) Killing in combat, mental health symptoms, and suicidal ideation in Iraq war veterans. *Journal of Anxiety Disorders* 25(4): 563–567.

Mann JJ, Apter A, Bertolote J, et al. (2005) Suicide prevention strategies: A systematic review. *The Journal of the American Medical Association* 294: 2064–2074.

Martin G, Swannell S, Milner A and Gullestrup J. (2016) Mates in construction suicide prevention program: A five year review. *Journal of Community Medicine & Health Education* 6(465): 1–8.

McCleary-Gaddy AT and Scales R. (2019) Addressing mental illness stigma, implicit bias, and stereotypes in medical school. *Academic Psychiatry* 43: 512–515.

McCraty R and Atkinson M. (2012) Resilience training program reduces physiological and psychological stress in police officers. *Global Advances in Health Medicine* 1: 44–66.

Mehlum L. (1998) Forebygging av selvmord blant unge – Nyere erfaringer fra Forsvaret [Prevention of suicide in young people – Recent experiences from the armed forces]. *Tidsskr Nor Loegeforen* 118: 1724–1726.

Merriott D. (2016) Factors associated with the farmer suicide crisis in India. *Journal of Epidemiology and Global Health* 6: 217–227.

Mew EJ, Padmanathan P, Konradsen F, et al. (2017) The global burden of fatal self-poisoning with pesticides 2006–15: Systematic review. *Journal of Affective Disorders* 219: 93–104.

Milner A and LaMontagne, AD. (2018) Suicide prevalence and suicide prevention in the workplace. In Burke RJ and Cooper CL (Eds.), *Violence and Abuse In and Around Organisations*. Routledge, London. pp. 59–76. Available from: https://books.google.com.au/books?id=cipKDwAAQBAJ&pg=PT132&dq=suicide+in+agriculture+milner+witt&hl=en&sa=X&ved=2ahUKEwja5PqPzv3qAhWoxjgGHfXrD5EQ6AEwAHoECAYQAg#v=onepage&q=suicide%20in%20agriculture%20milner%20witt&f=false (accessed 20 July 2020).

Milner AJ, Maheen H, Bismark MM, et al. (2016) Suicide by health professionals: A retrospective mortality study in Australia, 2001–2012. *Medical Journal of Australia* 205: 260–265.

Milner AJ, Niven H, Page K, et al. (2015) Suicide in veterinarians and veterinary nurses in Australia: 2001–2012. *Australian Veterinary Journal* 93: 308–310.

Milner AJ, Page K, Spencer-Thomas S, et al. (2014) Workplace suicide prevention: A systematic review of published and unpublished activities. *Health Promotion International* 30: 29–37.

Milner AJ, Spittal MJ, Pirkis J, et al. (2013) Suicide by occupation: Systematic review and meta-analysis. *British Journal of Psychiatry* 203: 409–416.

Milner AJ, Witt K, LaMontagne AD, et al. (2018) Psychosocial job stressors and suicidality: A meta-analysis and systematic review. *Occupational and Environmental Medicine* 75(4): 245–253.

Milner AJ, Witt K, Maheen H, et al. (2017a) Access to means of suicide, occupation and the risk of suicide: A national study over 12 years of coronial data. *BMC Psychiatry* 17: 125.

Milner AJ, Witt K, Maheen H, et al. (2017b) Suicide among emergency and protective service workers: A retrospective mortality study in Australia, 2001 to 2012. *Work* 57: 281–287.

Perceval M, Kõlves K, Reddy P, et al. (2017) Farmer suicides: A qualitative study from Australia. *Occupational Medicine* 67: 383–388.

Perceval M, Kõlves K, Ross V, et al. (2019) Environmental factors and suicide in Australian farmers: A qualitative study. *Archives of Environmental & Occupational Health* 74: 279–286.

Perceval M, Reddy P, Ross V, et al. (2020) Evaluation of the SCARF Well-Being and Suicide Prevention Program for Rural Australian Communities. *The Journal of Rural Health* 36: 247–254.

Perceval M, Ross V, Kõlves K, et al. (2018) Social factors and Australian farmer suicide: A qualitative study. *BMC Public Health* 18: 1367.

Pirkis J, Spittal MJ, Keogh L, et al. (2017) Masculinity and suicidal thinking. *Social Psychiatry and Psychiatric Epidemiology* 52(3): 319–327.

Pompili M, Girardi P, Ruberto A, et al. (2005) Emergency staff reactions to suicidal and self-harming patients. *European Journal of Emergency Medicine* 12(4): 169–178.

Pospos S, Young IT, Downs N, et al. (2018) Web-based tools and mobile applications to mitigate burnout, depression, and suicidality among healthcare students and professionals: A systematic review. *Academic Psychiatry* 42: 109–120.

Powell A, Galea N, Salignac F, et al. (2018) Masculinity and workplace wellbeing in the Australian construction industry. In *Proceeding of the 34th Annual ARCOM Conference*. Belfast, UK. pp. 321–330.

Reed DB and Claunch DT. (2020) Risk for depressive symptoms and suicide among US primary farmers and family members: A systematic literature review. *Workplace Health & Safety* 68: 236–248.

Reifels L, Mishara BL, Dargis L, et al. (2019) Outcomes of community-based suicide prevention approaches that involve reducing access to pesticides: A systematic literature review. *Suicide and Life-Threatening Behavior* 49: 1019–1031.

Ringgenberg W, Peek-Asa C, Donham K, et al. (2018) Trends and characteristics of occupational suicide and homicide in farmers and agriculture workers, 1992–2010. *The Journal of Rural Health* 34: 246–253.

Ross CA and Goldner EM. (2009) Stigma, negative attitudes and discrimination towards mental illness within the nursing profession: A review of the literature. *Journal of Psychiatric and Mental Health Nursing* 16: 558–567.

Ross V, Caton N, Gullestrup J and Kõlves K. (2019) Understanding the barriers and pathways to male help-seeking and help-offering: A mixed methods study of the impact of the Mates in Construction Program. *International Journal of Environmental Research and Public Health*, 16(16): 2979.

Ross V, Caton N, Gullestrup J and Kõlves K. (2020) A longitudinal assessment of two suicide prevention training programs for the construction industry. *International Journal of Environmental Research and Public Health* 17(3): 803.

Ross V, Koo YW and Kõlves K. (2020) A suicide prevention initiative at a jumping site: A mixed-methods evaluation. *EClinicalMedicine* 19: 100265.

Rothenberger DA. (2017) Physician burnout and well-being: A systematic review and framework for action. *Diseases of the Colon and Rectum* 60: 567–576.

Russell L. (2014) An empirical investigation of high-risk occupations: Leader influence on employee stress and burnout among police. *Management Research Review* 37: 367–384.

Sathyanarayana Rao TS, Gowda MR, Ramachandran K, et al. (2017) Prevention of farmer suicides: Greater need for state role than for a mental health professional's role. *Indian Journal of Psychiatry* 59: 3–5.

Sayers E, Rich J, Rahman MM, et al. (2019) Does help seeking behavior change over time following a workplace mental health intervention in the coal mining industry? *Journal of Occupational and Environmental Medicine* 61(6): e282–e290.

Singh R, Ram M and Sharma MS. (2013) Predictors of suicidal ideation among police personnel. *Journal of Organisation and Human Behaviour* 2(1): 45–52.

Stanley IH, Hom MA and Joiner TE. (2016) A systematic review of suicidal thoughts and behaviors among police officers, firefighters, EMTs, and paramedics. *Clinical Psychology Review* 44: 25–44.

Stehman CR, Testo Z, Gershaw RS, et al. (2019) Burnout, drop out, suicide: Physician loss in emergency medicine, Part I. *The Western Journal of Emergency Medicine* 20: 485–494.

Tomasi SE, Fechter-Leggett ED, Edwards NT, et al. (2019) Suicide among veterinarians in the United States from 1979 through 2015.

Journal of the American Veterinary Medical Association 254: 104–112.

Van Orden K, Cukrowicz K, Witte T, et al. (2010) The interpersonal theory of suicide. *Psychological Review* 117(2): 575–600.

Waller L. (2020) Fostering a sense of belonging in the workplace: Enhancing well-being and a positive and coherent sense of self. In Dhiman S (Ed), *The Palgrave Handbook of Workplace Well-Being*. Palgrave Macmillan, Cham. pp. 1–27.

Warner C, Appenzeller G, Parker J, et al. (2011) Suicide prevention in a deployed military unit. *Psychiatry* 74: 127–141.

Wasserman D and Durkee T. (2009) Strategies in suicide prevention. In Wasserman D and Wasserman C. (Eds.), *Oxford Textbook of Suicidology and Suicide Prevention. A Global Perspective*. Oxford University Press, New York.

Watson C, Ventriglio A and Bhugra D. (2020) A narrative review of suicide and suicidal behavior in medical students. *Indian Journal of Psychiatry* 62: 250–256.

Webster J. (2013) Police officer perceptions of occupational stress: The state of the art. *Policing: An International Journal of Police Strategies & Management* 36: 636–652.

Whitehead D. (2006) Workplace health promotion: The role and responsibility of health care managers. *Journal of Nursing Management* 14: 59–68.

Witt K, Boland A, Lamblin M, et al. (2019) Effectiveness of universal programmes for the prevention of suicidal ideation, behaviour and mental ill health in medical students: A systematic review and meta-analysis. *Evidence-based Mental Health*, 22(2): 84–90.

Witt K, Milner AJ, Allisey A, et al. (2017) Effectiveness of suicide prevention programs for emergency and protective services employees: A systematic review and meta-analysis. *American Journal of Industrial Medicine* 60: 394–407.

World Bank. (2020) *Employment in agriculture*. Available from: https://data.worldbank.org/indicator/SL.AGR.EMPL.ZS (accessed 1 July 2020).

World Health Organization. (2006) *Preventing suicide: A resource at work*. WHO, Geneva.

World Health Organization. (2014) *Preventing suicide: A global imperative*. WHO, Geneva.

Yip PSF and Caine ED. (2011) Employment status and suicide: The complex relationships between changing unemployment rates and death rates. *Journal of Epidemiology and Community Health* 65: 733.

Zalsman G, Hawton K, Wasserman D, et al. (2016) Suicide prevention strategies revisited: 10-year systematic review. *The Lancet Psychiatry* 3: 646–659.

Zamorski M. (2011) Suicide prevention in military organizations. *International Review of Psychiatry* 23: 173–180.

Zeller JM and Levin PF. (2013) Mindfulness interventions to reduce stress among nursing personnel: An occupational health perspective. *Workplace Health Safety* 61: 85–89.

19

Grief in the Workplace

Stephanie L. Gilbert and E. Kevin Kelloway

INTRODUCTION

'In this world', Benjamin Franklin is reputed to have written, 'nothing is certain, except death and taxes'. Although Franklin may not have been the originator, we all recognize the inherent truth of the sentiment. Both individuals and organizations employ advisors (e.g., accountants or financial specialists) to help them to minimize the negative impact of their annual tax assessments. When it comes to death, however, there is little or no guidance available despite the costs to organizations and employees of ignoring the issue. Organizations are left to deal with death, grief, and bereavement relying on whatever resources they have developed by trial and error, borrowed from other organizations, or inherited from previous administrations. Bereaved employees are forced to navigate organizational policies and manage workplace issues and stress at a time in their lives when they are at their most vulnerable. Moreover, as Franklin noted, all employees are likely to experience the death of a loved one during their working career – an observation that an aging population and the current Covid-19 pandemic has made even more salient. In 2003, The Grief Recovery Institute estimated that bereavement in the workforce due to multiple types of losses cost the United States economy \$75 billion annually, with grief due to loss of a loved one specifically costing \$37.5 billion (James and Friedman, 2003). These costs may grow if the prevalence of bereavement increases.

Although rarely considered in the organizational or human resource (HR) management literature, bereavement can lead to significant emotional, physical, and cognitive changes that can make the adjustment back to work after a loss incredibly difficult for grieving employees (Gibson et al., 2010). These effects can both manifest in the workplace, and be magnified by work stress (Bhagat, 1983; Gates, 2001). In this chapter, we focus on these effects. Specifically, we review the small body of literature in organizational behavior/organizational psychology on grief in the workplace (e.g., Eyetsemitan, 1998; Hazen, 2003, 2009; Wilson et al., 2019), draw upon literature in related fields, discuss implications of the research for practitioners, and highlight areas which could benefit from future research. There have been several calls by management researchers for more studies on the subject of grief in the workplace (Charles-Edwards, 2009; Hazen, 2009; Kinder and Cooper, 2009; Stein and Winokuer, 1989; Vickers, 2005; Wilson et al., 2019). We echo those calls and hope, in this chapter, to lay the groundwork for more research focused on grief in the workplace. Although we recognize that grief may result from many types of losses, most of the literature we review here focuses on grief due to the loss of a loved one.

GRIEF AND WORK

Grief and bereavement support for employees is unlikely to be a priority for many organizations (Charles-Edwards, 2009). However, organizations that neglect issues of death and grief do so at their own risk and at great costs to their employees and the organization as a whole (Tehan and Thompson, 2013). We suggest that organizations have both a practical and a moral imperative to pay more attention to issues around bereavement. The practical argument emerges from the costs of bereavement and the likelihood of grief manifesting in the workplace and affecting work-related behaviors and outcomes, which are discussed below. The moral argument proceeds from the observation that organizations have a duty of care to offer reasonable accommodation to their employees with respect to occupational health legislation for both physical and psychological health (Kinder and Cooper, 2009). A balanced approach to supporting grieving employees must consider their individual needs as well as the performance demands of

the organization (Lattanzi-Licht, 1999). When employees return to work on average three days following a loss, they are still actively grieving and the workplace will play a role in their ability to recover and return to normal levels of functioning. Facilitating this process by offering resources to help grieving employees cope will benefit both the employee and the organization. We begin with a review of the literature on prevalence of bereavement in the workplace followed by an examination of the experience of the nature of grief and its consequences.

PREVALENCE OF BEREAVEMENT

An aging population and the worldwide Covid-19 pandemic (an unprecedented and novel cause of global fatalities) have undoubtedly contributed to the number of employees who are experiencing bereavement at the current time. Bereavement refers to the process of going through and assimilating to a loss (Cutcliffe, 2002), while grief is the emotional experience of recovering from and coping with a loss (Stroebe et al., 1993). The prevalence of bereavement in the workforce is largely unknown and there have been few attempts to quantify prevalence of bereavement. Complicating estimates, 'hidden' bereavement leave may be taken informally and may go unreported or is reported as sick leave, vacation, or unpaid leave, while others may not take any form of leave when bereaved (Gilbert et al., 2021; Stephen et al., 2015). As a result, formal reports of bereavement leave are likely to be underestimates of total bereavement in the workforce. Point estimates of bereavement-related leave (i.e., the number of employees taking bereavement leave at any given time) range from 3.2% to 5% of the working population (Wilson et al., 2019). Lifetime prevalence, however, must be close to 100% of employees as it is almost inconceivable that an individual could go through an entire career without experiencing at least one bereavement. As Steve Jobs noted, 'Death is the destination we all share. No one has ever escaped it'.

Bereavement may result from death within or outside of the work environment. Loss of a loved one in one's personal life is a type of personal stressor that can lead to significant amounts of strain, and lead to negative outcomes at work, including employee burnout (Hakanen and Bakker, 2017; Mather et al., 2014; Moos et al., 2006). Loss may also happen within the workplace context. Prevalence rates of death in the workplace will vary based on level of risk in the industry or work context. In some work domains, such as the military and healthcare, death is a predictable aspect of work, and as such it is addressed more openly and proactively in these settings (Charles-Edwards, 2009). Thompson (2009) generated a typology of work contexts in terms of the degree of focus on death, comprised of (1) primary focus on death (e.g., funeral homes, hospices); (2) central focus on death (e.g., emergency services, military); (3) continuous focus on death (e.g., healthcare, social services); and (4) periodic focus on death (e.g., most other workplaces). The typology emphasizes that no workplace will escape the inevitability of death arising eventually, but that it will be more salient in some workplaces over others. Tehan and Thompson (2013) argued that the negative implications of ignoring issues around death or loss will be greater in workplaces where the risk of contending with death is higher. Below, we elaborate further on the nature of loss that occurs in the workplace context.

THE NATURE OF GRIEF

Although enshrined in popular literature and even medical and nursing textbooks (Corr, 2020; Downe-Wamboldt and Tamlyn, 1997), the early suggestion that individuals proceed through a set series of 'stages' of grief (e.g., Bowlby, 1980; Jacob, 1993; Kübler-Ross,

1969; Kübler-Ross and Kessler, 2005; Parkes and Weiss, 1983) has been subject to considerable criticism (e.g., Bonanno and Boerner, 2007; Stroebe et al., 2017) and has not been empirically supported (Holland and Neimeyer, 2010). In fact, Kübler-Ross's (1969) work on the stages of grief was initially developed based on anticipatory grief experiences by dying people awaiting their own death, rather than experiences of bereaved people who had lost a loved one. The attractiveness of stage theories may come from the sort of order and predictability they can bring to a complex process (Hall, 2014). However, these theories fail to recognize complex and individual trajectories of grief that may be influenced by the unique needs and circumstances of the griever (Hall, 2014). Newer theories of bereavement are more flexible and acknowledge the idiosyncratic nature of grief.

The period of time a person grieves for will depend on many factors, but some estimate that the process of recovery to baseline levels of functioning for most people may take many months and up to several years following the loss (Bonanno and Kaltman, 2001; Hall, 2014; Zhang et al., 2006). Normal, acute mourning will last for weeks or months and by about six months post-loss, grief will no longer interfere as much with daily life, although grievers may miss their loved one for years or even a lifetime afterwards (Bonnano et al., 2002; Hall, 2014).

A wide body of evidence has examined common manifestations of acute grief as well as more complicated manifestations, and these include physical, psychological, and social aspects. Alwdin (1990) described bereavement as one of the most stressful life events that impacts physical health. Physically, grief can manifest as sleep disruption, weight loss, increased doctor's visits (Bonanno and Kaltman, 2001), increased illness and medication use, and reduced perceived health (Thompson et al., 1984). A large body of evidence suggests that, especially in the early months following a significant loss, mortality risk increases (Kaprio et al., 1987; Stroebe and Stroebe, 1993). Psychologically, grief can manifest as cognitive disorganization and difficulty concentrating and making decisions (Bonnano and Kaltman, 2001; Tehan and Thompson, 2013). Socially, grief can lead to withdrawal from others, usually in the short term following loss, and irritability (Horowitz et al., 1997; Tehan and Thompson, 2013; Parkes and Weiss, 1983). Bereaved people have greater difficulty starting new relationships after a loss (Horowitz et al., 1997; Schneider et al., 1996) and those who express their pain to others are more likely to be avoided by others (Bonanno and Keltner, 1997; Capps and Bonanno, 2000). Complicated grief is defined by distress over separation from a deceased loved one as well as behavioral, cognitive, and emotional symptoms that impair social, occupational, and other functioning, and that last for at least six months following the loss (Hall, 2014; Ott, 2003). Complicated grief often requires treatment in order to resolve and can be assessed at least six months following the loss (Shear et al., 2005). More severe and long-lasting grief such as complicated grief have been linked to the development of mental illness, such as depression, as well as to more severe physical illness, and premature death (e.g., Alwdin, 1990; Byrne and Raphael, 1994; Carr et al., 2000, 2001; Prigerson et al., 2009; Wilcox et al., 2015).

Several individual-level factors may influence the experience of grief including the presence of pre-existing mental illness, socioeconomic status, and gender (Schulz et al., 2006; Stroebe et al., 2006). The nature of the relationship to the deceased person and to what extent it was problematic can play a role (Schwarzer and Leppin, 1989), as well as the degree of closeness to the person (Stroebe et al., 2006). The nature of the loss itself, including to what degree it was unexpected, involved trauma, violence, or was perceived as preventable (Bugen, 1977; Burke and Neimeyer, 2013; Field and Filanosky, 2009; Wijngaards-de Meij et al., 2005), can influence grief. Complicated grief is more likely for people with avoidant coping styles

(Morina, 2011; Nazali and Yildrim, 2017), high neuroticism, lack of preparedness for the death, and high dependency on the lost loved one prior to the death (Burke and Neimeyer, 2013; Lobb et al., 2010). Cognitions related to bereavement may also increase the risk of developing complicated grief, depression, and anxiety and such cognitions include negative beliefs about the self, the world, life, future, and threatening interpretations of grief (Boelen et al., 2003, 2006). Resilience has also been shown to influence grief experiences and the ability to find meaning in the loss, and maintain psychological and cognitive function in the face of difficulty (Bonanno, 2004; Bonanno et al., 2001). These and other factors will be significant influences on the nature of employees' grief.

Grief in the Work Setting

Although bereavement can result in individuals taking short-term leave from the workplace, we must also recognize that grief is not confined to these periods. Rather, grief experienced in one's personal life can spill over into the workplace to affect work behaviors and outcomes, suggesting that grief may have far-reaching effects for both the individual and the organizations. Moreover, work stress may worsen these effects (Bhagat, 1983; Gates, 2001), resulting in an escalating cycle of work stress and impaired wellbeing. Thus, an individual may return to work following bereavement but, as a result of a continued grieving process, be unable to concentrate or focus on tasks. The inability to concentrate or focus would comprise 'hidden' characteristics of grief (as opposed to open characteristics such as crying or behaving differently at work) and these difficulties may not be appreciated by others at work as being caused by the loss (Tehan and Thompson, 2013). This lack of understanding by others in addition to the resulting decrements in performance may lead to increased pressure to perform or 'snap out of it', leading to even more personal distress.

Some studies have linked certain work outcomes to loss. Bereaved employees are more likely to experience greater physical and psychiatric sickness absence in the year following their loss (Wilcox et al., 2015) and are more likely to quit their jobs or change careers following loss (Gilmer et al., 2012; Hazen, 2003) or to overwork as a way to escape their grief (Gilmer et al., 2012). In some cases, people may engage in compensatory behaviors such as overperforming at work as a way to cope with personal stress, but more often, life stress would lead to reduced performance (Bhagat, 1983; Dennis et al., 1956; Tunstall, 1962). In other cases, loss may require surviving family members to leave the workforce. Alam et al. (2012) examined the bereavement experiences of parents over 18 months after losing a child to cancer. Of these parents, 67% of fathers kept working full time whereas the majority of mothers either reduced their work schedule or took time off, and mothers were still hesitant to return to work 18 months after their loss. Some of the fathers reported having lost interest and motivation with their work, sometimes seeking more meaningful job opportunities instead. Another study found that bereaved people are less likely to be employed in the first two years following their loss compared to matched non-bereaved controls (Stephen et al., 2015).

Most grief manifestations would be incompatible with productive work. Grief causes changes in emotional, physical, and cognitive health, as well as attitudes towards both work and life, which can make the adjustment back to work after a loss incredibly difficult for grieving employees (Gibson et al., 2010). Bereavement can require significant social readjustment that may be greater for intimate and co-dependent relationships, such as the loss of a spouse (Holmes and Rahe, 1967). Many problems may result from grief that may influence employees' ability to engage in productive work and positive social interactions at work. Readjustment back to the work environment can be extremely difficult while grieving due to changes in physical, mental, and emotional health and to changes

in perspective on work and life as a whole (Gilmer et al., 2012; van der Klink et al., 2010; Wilcox et al., 2015). Below, we discuss workplace factors that can either facilitate, or hinder, employees' recovery following loss.

FACTORS THAT HINDER GRIEF RECOVERY AT WORK

Bereaved employees bring their grief to work with them and it influences their ability to work effectively. However, individual employees may not be willing or able to express their grief in the workplace. Disenfranchised and stifled grief both refer to an inability to openly acknowledge or express one's grief (Doka, 1989; Eyetsemitan, 1998). Grief is more likely to be stifled or disenfranchised (Doka, 1989; Hazen, 2003) in the workplace, where emotional-display norms preclude employees from expressing grief in that environment and because managers may not understand the needs of grieving employees. Workplaces in which there is a lack of organizational support or understanding of the bereavement process, or where employees are expected to return to work before they are ready, may stifle grief (Eyetsemitan, 1998). The field of work–life conflict addresses what Kanter (1977: 8) referred to as 'the myth of separate worlds', where the world of work and the world of the family are incompatible (Greenhaus and Beutell, 1985). Compartmentalization of one's loss and work responsibilities is often a required coping mechanism in order for grieving people to be able to work productively (Lattanzi-Licht, 1999). But such compartmentalization is not always possible, especially during intense personal loss, which can affect every domain of an employee's life. An inability to compartmentalize may lead to significant role conflict where, as Bento (1994) noted, the role of work and the role of the griever are incompatible. Further, although grief is pervasive, others at work often do not know what to say or how to help grieving employees (Sandberg and Grant, 2017).

As with broader society, death and dying are taboo subjects in the workplace, where professional norms predominate and sometimes preclude grieving people from expressing their pain. Bereaved employees may commonly experience insensitivity, embarrassment, or an unwillingness by others to acknowledge their loss (Charles-Edwards, 2009). Due to the professional nature of work relationships, there may be an inability to convey the intense feelings of personal loss to others at work who are not familiar with the relationship, leading to a lack of understanding and empathy. Bereaved individuals make up a vulnerable population that may be especially sensitive to the reactions of others (Charles-Edwards, 2009; Tehan and Thompson, 2013) and more vulnerable to stress due to their depleted resources (Ennis et al., 2000; Holohan et al., 1999; Wells et al., 1999). Further, bereaved employees may face work repercussions such as poor performance evaluations or slower advancement in their careers as a result of lower work productivity, taking leave, or other difficulties they face at work due to their grief (Gibson et al., 2010; Gilbert et al., 2021). Tehan and Thompson (2013) argued that bereaved employees are often in need of protection from stigma and discrimination that may arise from their grief and grief symptoms. Further, issues of disclosure and confidentiality can reduce employees' sense of safety and trust in others (Thompson and Thompson, 2013). When employers, managers, and co-workers handle bereaved employees' grief poorly or unsympathetically, organizational effectiveness and efficiency may be negatively impacted (Tehan and Thompson, 2013). However, if job stress is minimal and the workplace is healthy, then these factors may buffer the effects of personal stress on work (Bhagat, 1983). Next, we turn to workplace factors that may help grieving employees.

FACTORS THAT PROMOTE GRIEF RECOVERY AT WORK

Work itself can also provide benefits in the way of stability, structure, familiarity, social contact, and 'normalcy' that can be helpful for some grieving employees (Fitzpatrick, 2007; Harnois and Gabriel, 2000; Hazen, 2009). For some, home may be a lonely place or one where the grieving employee must support other family members, whereas work can provide both distraction and sources of support (Charles-Edwards, 2009). The workplace, as a social context where employees spend much of their time, may play a significant role in a bereaved employee's amount of distress and ability to readjust following loss and may be able to offer a number of resources to reduce distress and promote employee wellbeing (Charles-Edwards, 2009; Sunoo and Sunoo, 2002). Social support can be an important resource to help grieving people cope with anxiety, depression, and feelings of separation (Reed, 1998).

Work may also enhance employees' lives by providing an opportunity to detach from personal stressors. A weekly diary study based on the work–home resources model examined the effects of personal stress from a major life event, like loss, on work outcomes. Bakker et al. (2019) found that self-efficacy promoted engagement at work, especially for those who engaged in psychological detachment from their major life event. Psychological detachment occurs when an individual stops thinking about, and paying attention to, a particular event, allowing them to recover from a stressful circumstance, replenish resources, and improve their wellbeing (Bakker et al., 2019; Sonnentag et al., 2017). Work may offer grievers an opportunity to think about something other than their loss, which may be restorative for some employees and allow them to channel resources into productive work that feels meaningful rather than to ruminate over the event. Opportunities to temporarily detach from preoccupation with a loss may help to reduce symptoms of anxiety, depression, and anger while still maintaining a healthy bond with, rather than 'letting go' of, their lost loved one (Hall, 2014).

Other benefits of work for grief are shown in research highlighting the role of meaning at work in healing. A central issue in grieving is often a crisis of meaning, whereby the value and importance of one's usual goals, tasks, and even work are now called into question (Lattanzi-Licht, 1999; Neimeyer and Sands, 2011). Failure to find meaning following a loss, such as 'making sense' of the loss itself or finding benefits from the loss, is related to the development of complicated grief (Hall, 2014). Work may offer opportunities to engage in meaningful endeavors that can help employees cope with loss. Hazen (2003) found that women who had experienced perinatal loss experienced greater healing when they were able to connect their lost child to their workplace in some way. In Bakker et al.'s (2019) study, for those with high work-role centrality (identifying with and finding meaning in one's work role), the effect of detachment on the self-efficacy–work-engagement relationship was even stronger, suggesting that meaning in one's work can facilitate the benefits of detachment for work engagement. Compassionate leaders, through facilitating meaning-making, may also be helpful resources to grieving employees (Dutton et al., 2002), which is discussed further below.

LOSS AT WORK

Work-related loss may result from death of a colleague, patient, or patron in the workplace. Loss of a colleague may result in feelings of grief across whole teams of employees. The International Labour Organization (ILO, 2020) estimates that 2.3 million people worldwide die of accidents and diseases each year – a rate corresponding to 6,000 deaths per day (ILO, 2020). Although most of these deaths are related to disease (and presumably do not occur at the workplace), a substantial number of deaths result from the 340 million accidents that occur each year (ILO, 2020). Workplace deaths may also result from suicide – the majority of suicides occur among those who are of working age (World Health Organization, 2006) and the majority of those who commit suicide are employed at the time of their death (Yip and Caine, 2011).

The suicide of a colleague and sudden death in the workplace can be distressing for the surviving employees and can sometimes present unique stressors related to publicity of the loss, possible impacts on the organization's reputation, and issues related to the organization having to interface with the family of the deceased employee (Kinder and Cooper, 2009). Workplace accidents and suicides are often unexpected, due to traumatic incidents, and may be followed by long investigations into the cause (Aitken, 2007). The nature of workplace death can lead to unique bereavement issues characterized by blame, anger, feelings of vulnerability in surviving employees, and trauma from witnessing such incidents. These individual reactions may be heightened by publicity about the incident, or the tarnished reputation of the organization resulting from media accounts. Although media attention may feel intrusive, it may also serve to validate the severity of the loss for some employees, serving as a form of acknowledgment and recognition (Charles-Edwards, 2009). Many forms of work-related loss will also bring about workplace change, which may involve new staff, changing duties, or new safety systems that may add stress for employees. Kinder and Cooper (2009) argue that it is important for organizations to have in place clear crisis-management systems in order to deal effectively with unexpected events such as sudden death or suicide. Moreover, there is a need for, and evidence supporting the effectiveness of, workplace-based suicide-prevention programs (Milner et al., 2014).

SUPPORTING THE GRIEVING EMPLOYEE

Drawing upon relevant literature on grief at work, we have identified some critical factors that are most likely to support grieving employees. First are the nature and implementation of the bereavement leave policy(ies) as well as bereavement support resources available through the organization, but also important is the nature of leadership in supporting employees. Below, we discuss each of these factors in turn and then present an evidence-based model of support for grieving based on interviews with bereaved employees (Gilbert et al., 2021).

Bereavement and Compassionate Leave Policies

At the organizational level, bereavement leave policies and procedures will influence employees' experiences with working while grieving. Organizational responses to bereavement are often limited to a set period of bereavement leave depending on the relationship to the deceased person. For example, leave provisions typically average four days for loss of a spouse or child, and one to three days for other relationships such as a parent or extended family (SHRM, 2016). Typically, no leave is provided for a friend or colleague, although individuals may be able to take personal days (i.e., not formally classed as bereavement leave) in such situations. The average bereavement leave in Canada is short (on average 2.5 days plus 1.7 days for travel; Wilson et al., 2019).

Societal 'grieving rules' are embedded into these policies, which suggest how long it is acceptable for someone to grieve the loss of a loved one and how much distress should be experienced based on the relationship to the deceased person (Doka, 1989; Harris, 2010). Most employees will be expected to resume work duties while still experiencing

significant grief, and perhaps also shock and disbelief about their loss (Melhem et al., 2013).

Many organizations lack policies that consider the various experiences and complexities of grief and existing policies are often perceived as poor (Moss, 2017). Bereavement leave policies are sometimes unclear (McGuiness, 2009), which may lead employees to take even less leave than they may be entitled to (Bauer and Murray, 2018; Moss, 2017; Wilson et al., 2019) and lead to inconsistency in policy implementation (McGuiness, 2009). When policies and bereavement procedures are unclear, bereavement may be treated very differently across managers and this may lead to perceptions of procedural injustice across employees. Having no bereavement leave policy at all can present more problems. Wilson et al. (2019) found that 34.4% of surveyed Canadian organizations had no bereavement leave policy at all and that smaller organizations were least likely to have one (only 41% of small organizations had a policy). In organizations with no policy, 2.2% of bereaved employees took a bereavement leave which averaged 1.6 days in length compared to 3.2% in organizations that had a policy, where the average leave was 3.45 days in length (Wilson et al., 2019).

McGuinness (2009) presents a helpful example of a high-quality bereavement leave policy that incorporates leave entitlement (paid, unpaid, and annual leave options are presented), the process of returning to work, employee bereavement support, health and safety, cultural diversity, and the organizational values. He notes that leave entitlement options in such a policy should be considered a minimum standard that offers flexibility that not all employees will necessarily need. Including bereavement support in the policy may be important because bereaved employees are not always aware if they have access to bereavement support counseling or other resources through their employee assistance program (EAP) or benefits plan coverage (Gilbert et al., 2021). Such resources may be critical in supporting the mental health of grieving employees over time and their capacity to engage in productive work. In times of crisis, such as a sudden death at work or traumatic loss, organizations may consider providing additional counseling. Hughes and Kinder (2007) describe best practices for making counseling services available to employees.

Leadership

Palmer (2004) argued that managers may play an even more important role than bereavement-related policies and procedures, in supporting grieving employees. The direct supervisor of the grieving employee plays an important intermediary role between the employee and the organization, and sometimes playing the role of front-line first responder to an employee who has experienced a loss (Kinder and Cooper, 2009; Purcell and Hutchinson, 2007). Once the supervisor is made aware of the loss, they can then take action to report the loss to the organization and implement the organization's bereavement leave policy. Managers may also be instrumental in promoting a healthy workplace culture in advance of a death that will be more supportive for employees coping with grief or other challenges.

Leaders can offer critical support and resources that help the employee cope with demands (Hammer et al., 2009) and have the power to divert certain resources towards employees who need them (Dutton et al., 2002). Managers may offer both formal and informal resources, flexible forms of accommodation, and encourage resource utilization, such as EAP programs (Dimoff and Kelloway, 2016). In Gilbert et al.'s (2021) study, much of the accommodation, if offered, was provided informally by the manager. In many cases, especially when HR policies are unclear or non-existent, bereavement leave and other support may be up to the discretion of managers, who rarely receive guidance on how to implement bereavement leave policies (Hall et al., 2013; McGuinness, 2009).

The manager themselves may need support in dealing with highly sensitive situations like death (Kinder and Cooper, 2009), as they are unlikely to have training in the area. Social support from their own manager or counseling as well as a clear knowledge of policies and procedures in advance of a loss occurring may be key supports for leaders. Managers may also need basic education about the grief process and possibly also in recognizing symptoms of complicated grief (e.g., long-term symptoms of depression, anxiety, anger, withdrawal) and to know where to refer their employee for help (Charles-Edwards, 2009). Similar training has been helpful for promoting managers' mental health awareness and confidence in recognizing and helping employees who are dealing with mental illness (Dimoff and Kelloway, 2016).

Leaders can play an important role in developing a healthy and supportive workplace which may promote better recovery for grieving people and may encourage employees to take full advantage of bereavement supports at work. Support is critical for wellbeing in the workplace (Yarker et al., 2010), but may be especially important for employees dealing with loss. Managers and others at work can be a source of compassion, support, and socialization that can help with adjustment after loss (Aber, 1992; Gilbert et al., 2021; Lin et al., 1986; Pavalko and Smith, 1999). On the other hand, the effects of bereavement on one's ability to work may be exacerbated by insensitive or inconsiderate responses by managers, which are felt significantly by the employee (Charles-Edwards, 2009). Leaders can also play an important role in building a healthy and supportive work climate, generally (for a review, see Nielsen, 2014), and can directly encourage wellbeing in non-work domains (e.g., family and personal life). Family-supportive supervisor behaviors involve talking with employees about non-work issues, role modeling effective work and non-work balance, working with employees to develop plans that address work and non-work conflict, and developing work solutions that maximize employees' work and non-work wellbeing (Hammer et al., 2013). These behaviors may encourage employees to take full advantage of policies (Hammer et al., 2007) such as bereavement/compassionate leave and workplace accommodation, whereas in unsupportive environments, employees may be less likely to benefit from such policies due to fear of negative repercussions.

Leaders can also support grieving employees through compassion. Compassion refers to 'an interpersonal process involving the noticing, feeling, sense making, and acting that alleviates the suffering of another person' (Dutton et al., 2014: 277). Leaders can influence the extent to which the workplace is characterized by compassion by creating a culture that emphasizes and recognizes compassionate behavior and through modeling appropriate responses to pain and suffering (Dutton et al., 2002). Compassionate leaders promote a work context characterized by meaning-making, where employees can express their feelings and make sense of pain, and by action where people can find ways to alleviate their pain (Dutton et al., 2002). Receiving compassion from others can help people who are grieving to recover psychologically from their loss, reduce anxiety, increase positive emotions, and increase the individual's attachment and commitment to the organization and their sense that their organization really cares about and values them (Dutton et al., 2014; Frost and Robinson, 1999; Lilius et al., 2008; Lin et al., 1986; Pavalko and Smith, 1999). There can be a contagious effect of compassion, such that others in the work environment may emulate compassionate leaders, leading to upward spirals of compassion that promote healing (Dutton et al., 2002).

THE CARE MODEL

Gilbert et al. (2021) conducted an interview study of 14 employees who had lost a close family member in the preceding five years and who subsequently returned to work. Four key themes that each characterized more positive employee experiences of grieving at work emerged from the data. Gilbert et al. (2021) used the acronym CARE to describe these themes, which involved: (1) communicating clearly and promptly about bereavement leave options and support resources; (2) accommodating the employee's unique needs; (3) recognizing and acknowledging the loss both soon after the loss as well as over time; and (4) empathetic responses towards the employee about the loss. Inherent in all themes were instrumental, informational, and emotional support from the supervisor, co-workers, the organization, and sometimes also other parties such as customers, clients, or students.

Communication: the first theme was characterized by effective two-way communication soon after the loss about the loss itself, the employees' needs, and bereavement leave policies and available bereavement supports. Such communication often involved the bereaved employee and either a manager or an HR representative. Ineffective communication sometimes led to stress and ambiguity related to navigating policy and administrative issues, such as difficulty getting timely approval for leave, or confusion about leave options. For example, after a perinatal loss, one participant did not take any bereavement leave because she was not aware that she was eligible to take leave. Two-way communication about the employees' needs also helped to develop effective individualized accommodation plans. For example, when a participant's sister was terminally ill, he worked with his boss to be able to take bereavement leave in advance of her death so he could visit her and say his goodbyes. Effective communication will help the employee to communicate their needs, to get the support they need, and to explain their circumstances that may require individualized accommodation (Nilsson et al., 2013).

Accommodation: accommodation plans maximized benefits to employees when their unique needs were considered. Accommodation options that were offered to participants included scheduling additional staff to assist the bereaved employee, reassigning work, offering flexible deadlines, flexible hours, and shorter work days, or the option to work from home. Many participants' co-workers went out of their way to accommodate them as well by assisting them with their workloads. Accommodation was necessary for some participants in order for them to keep up with their workload, or to avoid emotional triggers in their work environment. For example, some participants noted that after their loss they had difficulty maintaining professionalism at work and worried about experiencing unexpected distress that may lead to crying in front of others. Importantly, effective communication with the employee about their needs should inform accommodation plans, given that providing the wrong type of support may be counterintuitive or even cause stress in grieving employees (Flux et al., 2019). For example, although work from home options were welcomed by some participants, others wanted to work at work so that they could get out of the house and feel some 'normalcy'.

Recognition: recognition and acknowledgment of the loss both early on and over time emerged as a prevalent theme that served to validate the employee's grief experience. Other studies have also supported the importance of acknowledgment of loss in the workplace for recovery (Fitzpatrick, 2007; Hazen, 2003, 2006, 2009). Due to professional norms and emotional-display requirements, loss may be more likely to go unacknowledged at work because people may not know what to say, may be trying to avoid upsetting the person, or may try to give them 'space'.

But a lack of recognition that the employee is going through a painful time can make them feel unsupported, and may result in the belief that they are not valued or appreciated at work (Charles-Edwards, 2001). Simple acts of recognition, such as conveying sympathies, sending food, sympathy cards or flowers, or checking in on how employees are coping with the loss both early on and in the following months, were important to participants. Some of them remembered the people who failed to acknowledge their loss in any way even years following the experience.

Emotional Support: emotionally supportive responses involved understanding the emotions and the pain experienced by grieving employees. Emotional support, characterized by compassion and empathy, was often inherent in all the above themes of communication, accommodation, and recognition for employees who had positive experiences. At times, participants received unsupportive responses to their loss from others characterized by awkward interactions, avoidance by others, pushy advice about 'getting over' the death, and stigma associated with their grief. A lack of emotional support may lead to greater stifling of grief at work and sometimes to negative repercussions for grieving employees. For example, one study participant received a bad performance evaluation due to lower productivity following the loss of his mother in which grief was not mentioned in the report as a possible contributing factor. Other studies have also found that lack of emotional support related to negative outcomes like poor performance evaluations and lack of work adjustments or performance concessions are seen as unfair by employees (Gibson et al., 2010; Moss, 2017; Russell, 1998).

Gilbert et al. (2021) highlighted the role of the workplace in offering resources such as emotional, instrumental, and informational support that may improve employees' experiences. The CARE model may be applied to any level in the organization to describe how co-workers, managers, or HR professionals respond to bereavement and loss. These practices may reduce additional work-related stressors that further deplete grieving employees' resources at a time when they are already coping with great pain.

Implications

Bereavement support should take place at the primary, secondary, and tertiary levels. At the primary level, before a loss takes place, organizations should develop clear bereavement leave policies, as evidence suggests that a lack of policy, or unclear policies, can create stress for grieving people and may lead to shorter bereavement leave (Wilson et al., 2019). Organizations should also ensure that managers and HR professionals are familiar with the bereavement-related policies (e.g., bereavement leave, flexible and personal days) and support resources that are available through the organization, as well as the possible accommodation options for grieving employees. Basic proactive training on grief may also help managers and HR professionals to understand the effects of grief and potential range of limitations and needs of grieving employees. Such training, as well as clear bereavement leave policies and procedures, may convey to employees that mental health and wellbeing through grief are generally valued at the organization (McGuinness, 2009).

At the secondary level, intervention would address a particular loss once it has occurred and may involve formal and informal communication between managers and/or HR professionals and the grieving employee, conveying sympathies, and communicating the necessary information about leave options and bereavement support resources. The CARE model (Gilbert et al., 2021) may be utilized to ensure that co-workers, managers, and HR professionals are supporting employees' needs for clear communication, accommodation, recognition of their loss, and empathetic responses.

At the tertiary level, support may address any longer-term consequences of the loss itself and may involve recognizing signs that an employee is experiencing complicated grief symptoms and may benefit from a referral to a doctor or to any available bereavement support resources. Evidence suggests that intervention in the way of outreach and referral may be more effective for people who have developed complicated grief symptoms than for newly bereaved employees, who may benefit most from simply undergoing the natural grieving process (Schut and Stroebe, 2005). Programs that educate managers to recognize signs of complicated grief and familiarize them with the available bereavement support resources through the organization or community may be part of tertiary grief intervention. Evidence-based programs have been successfully developed to train managers in recognizing signs of mental illness and to refer employees to an appropriate resource for help (Dimoff and Kelloway, 2016).

IMPLICATIONS FOR POLICY MAKERS

Clear bereavement leave policies that incorporate some flexibility can help employees to integrate their loss with dignity and to avoid pressure to return to work before they are ready (Thompson and Thompson, 2009). Bereavement leave legislation varies by country, with three days of paid bereavement leave offered in Canada, China, and Luxembourg, up to eight days in Chile and Taiwan, and two days in Australia and Spain (Blackburn and Bulsara, 2018). Just a few days of bereavement leave may not allow for enough time to handle practical matters such as dealing with financial and legal issues, settling the estate of the dead loved one, memorial/funeral planning, visiting with family members, and also to attend to the work of grief itself (Blackburn and Bulsara, 2018). To acknowledge the strain that bereaved parents face, in 2020 Jack's Law came into effect in the UK, which provides two weeks of paid leave to parents who have lost a child under age 18 (Parveen and Murray, 2020). Some organizations are also offering longer bereavement leave. Facebook now offers 20 days of bereavement leave for an immediate family member and up to 10 days for an extended family member (Sandberg and Grant, 2017). Zillow Group, SurveyMonkey, Adobe, and Mastercard have followed suit, and also now offer extended paid leave to bereaved employees. Offering extended bereavement leave options may have significant impacts on the employees' wellbeing and ability to recover from grief, and may have implications for their long-term work attitudes.

A Call for Research

There is a need for additional research on the role of grief in the workplace and the factors that influence the employee experience. Research is needed to examine the prevalence of bereavement in the workforce (recognizing that not all bereaved employees may take formal bereavement leave), and the predictors and outcomes of bereavement leave policy implementation. How frequently is leave handled through formal bereavement leave policies and through informal mechanisms, and what are the outcomes of each method? Anecdotal evidence as well as findings from Gilbert et al. (2021) suggest that, in many cases, bereavement leave may be handled informally by managers and may not be reported as formal bereavement leave. Additional research is needed on bereavement leave policy implementation and to develop evidence-based recommendations for bereavement leave policies and procedures.

Research on employees' grief experiences in the workplace may inform the development of assessment tools to measure the quality of these experiences, to study predictors

and outcomes of those experiences, and to evaluate the efficacy of bereavement support policies and practices. Research should also examine the challenges and/or resources available to managers who support bereaved employees (Gibson et al., 2010) and how managers may be better equipped to support grieving employees. Specifically, managers may benefit from evidence-based proactive bereavement support training for managers aimed at helping employees cope with loss. More research is needed to understand how organizations can prepare for bereavement leave and assist bereaved employees with return to work (Gibson et al., 2010; Wilson et al., 2019). To serve that aim, researchers may develop tools to assess employees' readiness to return to work to determine if additional time off work is needed (Andersen et al., 2012).

Employees who have experienced a loss will bring their grief to work with them. This chapter explored the issue of grief and death in the workplace and the impact that grief may play on employee and organizational outcomes as well as the impact that workplaces may have on employees' grief experiences. Much research is needed to understand the predictors and outcomes of employees' grief experiences at work.

REFERENCES

Aber CS (1992) Spousal death, a threat to women's health: Paid work as a 'resistance resource'. *Image: The Journal of Nursing Scholarship* 24(2): 95–100.

Aitken A (2007) Work-related bereavement. *Bereavement Care* 26(3): 57.

Alam R, Barrera M, D'Agostino N, Nicholas DB and Schneiderman G (2012) Bereavement experiences of mothers and fathers over time after the death of a child due to cancer. *Death Studies* 36(1): 1–22.

Aldwin CM (1990) The Elders Life Stress Inventory: Egocentric and nonegocentric stress. In: Stephens MAP; Crowther JH, Hobfoll SE,

Tennenbaum DL (eds) *Stress and coping in later-life families*. New York, NY: Hemisphere, pp. 49–69.

Andersen MF, Nielsen KM and Brinkmann S (2012) Meta-synthesis of qualitative research on return to work among employees with common mental disorders. *Scandinavian Journal of Work, Environment and Health* 38(2): 93–104.

Bakker AB, Du D and Derks D (2019) Major life events in family life, work engagement, and performance: A test of the work-home resources model. *International Journal of Stress Management* 26(3): 238.

Bauer JC and Murray MA (2018) 'Leave your emotions at home': Bereavement, organizational space, and professional identity. *Women's Studies in Communication* 41(1): 60–81.

Bento RF (1994) When the show must go on. *Journal of Managerial Psychology* 9(6): 35–44.

Bhagat RS (1983) Effects of stressful life events on individual performance effectiveness and work adjustment processes within organizational settings: A research model. *Academy of Management Review* 8(4): 660–671.

Blackburn P and Bulsara C (2018) 'I am tired of having to prove that my husband was dead'. Dealing with practical matters in bereavement and the impact on the bereaved. *Death Studies* 42(10): 627–635.

Boelen PA, Den Bout Jv, De Keijser Jo and Hoijtink H (2003) Reliability and validity of the Dutch version of the Inventory of Traumatic Grief (ITG). *Death Studies* 27(3): 227–247.

Boelen PA, Van Den Hout MA and Van Den Bout J (2006) A cognitive-behavioral conceptualization of complicated grief. *Clinical Psychology: Science and Practice* 13(2): 109–128.

Bonanno GA (2004) Loss, trauma, and human resilience: Have we underestimated the human capacity to thrive after extremely aversive events? *American Psychologist* 59(1): 20.

Bonanno GA and Boerner K (2007) The stage theory of grief. *Journal of the American Medical Association* 297(24): 2692–2694.

Bonanno GA and Kaltman S (2001) The varieties of grief experience. *Clinical Psychology Review* 21(5): 705–734.

Bonanno GA and Keltner D (1997) Facial expressions of emotion and the course of conjugal bereavement. *Journal of Abnormal Psychology* 106(1): 126.

Bonanno GA, Papa A and O'Neill K (2001) Loss and human resilience. *Applied and Preventive Psychology* 10(3): 193–206.

Bonanno GA, Wortman CB, Lehman DR, Tweed RG, Haring M, Sonnega J, Carr D and Nesse RM (2002) Resilience to loss and chronic grief: A prospective study from preloss to 18-months postloss. *Journal of Personality and Social Psychology* 83(5): 1150.

Bowlby J (1980) *Attachment and Loss: Vol. 3: Loss*. London: Hogarth Press and the Institute of Psycho-Analysis.

Bugen LA (1977) Human grief: A model for prediction and intervention. *American Journal of Orthopsychiatry* 47(2): 196.

Burke LA and Neimeyer RA (2013) *11 Prospective Risk Factors for Complicated Grief*. New York, NY: Routledge.

Byrne GJA and Raphael B (1994) A longitudinal study of bereavement phenomena in recently widowed elderly men. *Psychological Medicine* 24(2): 411–421.

Capps L and Bonanno GA (2000) Narrating bereavement: Thematic and grammatical predictors of adjustment to loss. *Discourse Processes* 30(1): 1–25.

Carr D, House JS, Kessler RC, Nesse RM, Sonnega J and Wortman C (2000) Marital quality and psychological adjustment to widowhood among older adults: A longitudinal analysis. *The Journals of Gerontology Series B: Psychological Sciences and Social Sciences* 55(4): 197–207.

Carr D, House JS, Wortman C, Nesse R and Kessler RC (2001) Psychological adjustment to sudden and anticipated spousal loss among older widowed persons. *The Journals of Gerontology Series B: Psychological Sciences and Social Sciences* 56(4): 237–248.

Charles-Edwards D (2001) Responding to bereavement at work. *Bereavement Care* 20(3): 41–42.

Charles-Edwards D (2009) Empowering people at work in the face of death and bereavement. *Death Studies* 33(5): 420–436.

Corr CA (2020) Elisabeth Kübler-Ross and the 'five stages' model in a sampling of recent

American textbooks. *OMEGA – Journal of Death and Dying* 82(2): 294–322.

Cutcliffe JR (2002) Understanding and working with bereavement. *Mental Health Practice* 6(2): 29–36.

Dimoff JK and Kelloway EK (2016) Resource utilization model: Organizational leaders as resource facilitators. *The Role of Leadership in Occupational Stress* Vol 14, 141–160.

Doka K (1989) *Disenfranchised Grief: Recognizing Hidden Sorrow*. Lexington, MA: DC Health and Company.

Downe-Wamboldt B and Tamlyn D (1997) An international survey of death education trends in faculties of nursing and medicine. *Death Studies* 21: 177–188.

Dutton JE, Frost PJ, Worline MC, Lilius JM and Kanov JM (2002) Leading in times of trauma. *Harvard Business Review* 80(1): 54–61.

Dutton JE, Workman KM and Hardin AE (2014) Compassion at work. *Annual Review of Organizational Psychology and Organizational Behaviour* 1(1): 277–304.

Ennis NE, Hobfoll SE and Schröder KE (2000) Money doesn't talk, it swears: How economic stress and resistance resources impact inner-city women's depressive mood. *American Journal of Community Psychology* 28(2): 149–173.

Eyetsemitan F (1998) Stifled grief in the workplace. *Death Studies* 22(5): 469–479.

Field NP and Filanosky C (2009) Continuing bonds, risk factors for complicated grief, and adjustment to bereavement. *Death Studies* 34(1): 1–29.

Fitzpatrick TR (2007) Bereavement among faculty members in a university setting. *Social Work in Health Care* 45(4): 83–109.

Fitzpatrick TR, Spiro III A, Kressin NR, Greene E and Bossé R (2001) Leisure activities, stress, and health among bereaved and non-bereaved elderly men: The normative aging study. *OMEGA – Journal of Death and Dying* 43(3): 217–245.

Flux L, Hassett A and Callanan M (2019) How do employers respond to employees who return to the workplace after experiencing the death of a loved one? A review of the literature. *Policy and Practice in Health and Safety* 17(2): 98–111.

Frost P and Robinson S (1999) The toxic handler: Organizational hero – and casualty. *Harvard Business Review* 77(4): 97–97.

Gates DM (2001) Stress and coping: A model for the workplace. *AAOHN Journal* 49(8): 390–398.

Gibson J, Gallagher M and Jenkins M (2010) The experiences of parents readjusting to the workplace following the death of a child by suicide. *Death Studies* 34(6): 500–528.

Gilbert SL, Mullen J, Kelloway EK, Dimoff J, Teed M, and McPhee T. (2021) *The C.A.R.E. Model of Employee Bereavement Support.* Under review.

Gilmer MJ, Foster TL, Vannatta K, Barrera M, Davies B, Dietrich MS, Fairclough DL, Grollman J and Gerhardt CA (2012) Changes in parents after the death of a child from cancer. *Journal of Pain and Symptom Management* 44(4): 572–582.

Greenhaus JH and Beutell NJ (1985) Sources of conflict between work and family roles. *Academy of Management Review* 10(1): 76–88.

Hakanen JJ and Bakker AB (2017) Born and bred to burn out: A life-course view and reflections on job burnout. *Journal of Occupational Health Psychology* 22(3): 354.

Hall C (2014) Bereavement theory: Recent developments in our understanding of grief and bereavement. *Bereavement Care* 33(1): 7–12.

Hall D, Shucksmith J and Russell S (2013) Building a compassionate community: Developing an informed and caring workplace in response to employee bereavement. *Bereavement Care* 32(1): 4–10.

Hammer LB, Ernst Kossek E, Bodner T and Crain T (2013) Measurement development and validation of the Family Supportive Supervisor Behavior Short-Form (FSSB-SF). *Journal of Occupational Health Psychology* 18(3): 285.

Hammer LB, Kossek EE, Yragui NL, Bodner TE and Hanson GC (2009) Development and validation of a multidimensional measure of family supportive supervisor behaviors (FSSB). *Journal of Management* 35(4): 837–856.

Hammer LB, Kossek EE, Zimmerman K and Daniels R (2007) Clarifying the construct of family-supportive supervisory behaviors (FSSB): A multilevel perspective. In Perrewé PL and Ganster DC (eds) *Research in Occupational Stress and Well-being: Vol. 6.*

Exploring the Work and Non-work Interface. Bingley, UK: Emerald Group, pp. 165–204.

Harnois G and Gabriel P (2000) *Mental Health and Work: Impact, Issues and Good Practices*. World Health Organization: Geneva.

Harris D (2010) Oppression of the bereaved: A critical analysis of grief in western society. *OMEGA – Journal of Death and Dying* 60(3): 241–253.

Hazen MA (2003) Societal and workplace responses to perinatal loss: Disenfranchised grief or healing connection. *Human Relations* 56(2): 147–166.

Hazen MA (2006) Silences, perinatal loss, and polyphony. *Journal of Organizational Change Management* 19(2): 237–249.

Hazen MA (2009) Recognizing and responding to workplace grief. *Organizational Dynamics* 4(38): 290–296.

Holahan CJ, Moos RH, Holahan CK and Cronkite RC (1999) Resource loss, resource gain, and depressive symptoms: A 10-year model. *Journal of Personality and Social Psychology* 77(3): 620.

Holland JM and Neimeyer RA (2010) An examination of stage theory of grief among individuals bereaved by natural and violent causes: A meaning-oriented contribution. *OMEGA – Journal of Death and Dying* 61(2): 103–120.

Holmes TH and Rahe RH (1967) The social readjustment rating scale. *Journal of Psychosomatic Research* 11(2): 213–218.

Horowitz MJ, Siegel B, Holen A, Bonanno GA, Milbrath C and Stinson CH (1997) Diagnostic criteria for complicated grief disorder. *American Journal of Psychiatry* 154: 904–910.

Hughes R and Kinder A (2007) *Guidelines for Counselling in the Workplace*. Lutterworth: British Association for Counselling and Psychotherapy.

International Labour Organization (ILO) 2020 *World statistics: The enormous burden of poor working conditions*, viewed 4 July 2020, https://www.ilo.org/moscow/areas-of-work/occupational-safety-and-health/WCMS_249278/lang–en/index.htm

Jacob SR (1993) An analysis of the concept of grief. *Journal of Advanced Nursing* 18(11): 1787–1794.

James JW and Friedman R (2003) *Grief Index: The 'Hidden' Annual Costs of Grief in America's Workplace*. Sherman Oaks, CA: The Grief Recovery Institute Educational Foundation Inc.

Kanter RM (1977) Some effects of proportions on group life. In Reiker PP and Carmen E (eds) *The Gender Gap in Psychotherapy*. Boston, MA: Springer, pp. 53–78.

Kaprio J, Koskenvuo M and Rita H (1987) Mortality after bereavement: A prospective study of 95,647 widowed persons. *American Journal of Public Health* 77(3): 283–287.

Kinder A and Cooper CL (2009) The costs of suicide and sudden death within an organization. *Death Studies* 33(5): 411–419.

Kübler-Ross E (1969) *On Death and Dying*. New York, NY: Scribner.

Kübler-Ross E and Kessler D (2005) *On Grief and Grieving: Finding the Meaning of Grief through the Five Stages of Loss*. New York, NY: Simon and Schuster.

Lattanzi-Licht M (1999) When dreams don't work: Professional caregivers and burnout. *Journal of Palliative Care* 15(2): 62.

Lilius JM, Worline MC, Maitlis S, Kanov J, Dutton JE and Frost P (2008) The contours and consequences of compassion at work. *Journal of Organizational Behavior: The International Journal of Industrial, Occupational and Organizational Psychology and Behavior* 29(2): 193–218.

Lin N, Ensel WM and Dean A (1986) The age structure and the stress process. In Lin N, Dean A and Ensel WM (eds) *Social Support, Life Events and Depression*. Orlando, FL: Academic Press, pp. 213–230.

Lobb EA, Kristjanson LJ, Aoun SM, Monterosso L, Halkett GK and Davies A (2010) Predictors of complicated grief: A systematic review of empirical studies. *Death Studies* 34(8): 673–698.

Mather L, Blom V and Svedberg P (2014) Stressful and traumatic life events are associated with burnout – A cross-sectional twin study. *International Journal of Behavioral Medicine* 21(6): 899–907.

McGuinness B (2009) Grief in the workplace: Developing a bereavement policy. *Bereavement Care* 28(1): 2–8.

Melhem NM, Porta G, Payne MW and Brent DA (2013) Identifying prolonged grief reactions in children: Dimensional and diagnostic approaches. *Journal of the American Academy of Child and Adolescent Psychiatry* 52(6): 599–607.

Milner A, Page K, Spencer-Thomas S and Lamontagne AD (2014) Workplace suicide prevention: A systematic review of published and unpublished activities. *Health Promotion International* 30(1): 29–37.

Moos RH, Brennan PL, Schutte KK and Moos BS (2006) Older adults' coping with negative life events: Common processes of managing health, interpersonal, and financial/work stressors. *The International Journal of Aging and Human Development* 62(1): 39–59.

Morina N (2011) Rumination and avoidance as predictors of prolonged grief, depression, and posttraumatic stress in female widowed survivors of war. *The Journal of Nervous and Mental Disease* 199(12): 921–927.

Moss J (2017) Making your workplace safe for grief. *Harvard Business Review Online*. Available at: https://hbr.org/2017/06/making-your-workplace-safe-for-grief (accessed 27 November 2020).

Nazali HC and Yildirim EA (2017) The relationship between grief process and attachment styles in the cases with the treatment of complicated grief: A prospective study. *European Psychiatry* 41(1): 354.

Neimeyer RA and Sands DC (2011) Meaning reconstruction in bereavement: From principles to practice. In Neimeyer RA, Harris DL, Winokuer HR and Thornton GF (eds) *Grief and Bereavement in Contemporary Society: Bridging Research and Practice*. New York, NY: Routledge, pp. 9–22.

Nielsen KJ (2014) Improving safety culture through the health and safety organization: A case study. *Journal of Safety Research* 48: 7–17.

Nilsson MI (2013) Psychosocial situation and work after breast cancer surgery – women's experiences. *Inst för klinisk neurovetenskap/Dept of Clinical Neuroscience*. Solna: Karolinska Institute, pp. 1–49.

Dennis N, Henriques F and Slaughter C (1956) *Coal Is Our Life: An Analysis of a Yorkshire Mining Community*. London: Eyre and Spottiswoode.

Ott CH (2003) The impact of complicated grief on mental and physical health at various points in the bereavement process. *Death Studies* 27(3): 249–272.

Palmer FA (2004) *Grief in the workplace: A case study of how grief associated with the death of a child affects the organization* (Doctoral dissertation). Regent University, Virginia Beach, VA.

Parkes CM and Weiss RS (1983) *Recovery from Bereavement*. New York, NY: Basic Books.

Parveen N and Murray J (2020) Bereaved parents to be entitled to two weeks' paid leave from work. *The Guardian*, 23 Jan 2020.

Pavalko EK and Smith B (1999) The rhythm of work: Health effects of women's work dynamics. *Social Forces* 77(3): 1141–1162.

Prigerson HG, Horowitz MJ, Jacobs SC, Parkes CM, Aslan M, Goodkin K, Raphael B, Marwit SJ, Wortman C, Neimeyer RA and Bonanno G (2009) Prolonged grief disorder: Psychometric validation of criteria proposed for DSM-V and ICD-11. *PLoS Med* 6(8) p.e1000121.

Purcell J and Hutchinson S (2007) Front-line managers as agents in the HRM-performance causal chain: Theory, analysis and evidence. *Human Resource Management Journal* 17(1): 3–20.

Reed MD (1998) Predicting grief symptomatology among the suddenly bereaved. *Suicide and Life-Threatening Behavior* 28(3): 285–301.

Russell K (1998) Returning to employment after bereavement. *Bereavement Care* 17(1): 11–13.

Sandberg S and Grant A (2017) *Option B: Facing Adversities, Building Resilience and Finding Joy*. New York, NY: Alfred A. Knopf.

Schneider, D.S., Sledge, P.A., Shuchter, S.R. and Zisook, S., 1996. Dating and remarriage over the first two years of widowhood. *Annals of Clinical Psychiatry*, 8(2), pp. 51–57.

Schulz R, Boerner K, Shear K, Zhang S and Gitlin LN (2006) Predictors of complicated grief among dementia caregivers: A prospective study of bereavement. *The American Journal of Geriatric Psychiatry* 14(8): 650–658.

Schut H and Stroebe M (2005) Interventions to enhance adaptation to bereavement. *Journal of Palliative Medicine* 8(3): 1–8.

Schwarzer R and Leppin A (1989) Social support and health: A meta-analysis. *Psychology and Health* 3(1): 1–15.

Shear K, Frank E, Houck PR and Reynolds CF (2005) Treatment of complicated grief: A randomized controlled trial. *Journal of the American Medical Association* 293(21): 2601–2608.

Society for Human Resource Management (SHRM; 2016) *SHRM survey findings: Paid* leave in the workplace. Available at: https://www.shrm.org/hr-today/trends-and-forecasting/research-and-surveys/pages/2016-paid-leave-in-the-workplace.aspx (accessed 27 November 2020).

Sonnentag S, Venz L and Casper A (2017) Advances in recovery research: What have we learned? What should be done next? *Journal of Occupational Health Psychology* 22(3): 365.

Stein AJ and Winokuer HR (1989) Monday mourning: Managing employee grief. In Doka, K. (ed) *Disenfranchised Grief: Recognizing Hidden Sorrow*, Lexington, MA: Research Press, pp. 91–102.

Stephen AI, Macduff C, Petrie DJ, Tseng FM, Schut H, Skår S, Corden A, Birrell J, Wang S, Newsom C and Wilson S (2015) The economic cost of bereavement in Scotland. *Death Studies* 39(3): 151–157.

Stroebe M, Schut H and Boerner K (2017) Cautioning health-care professionals: Bereaved persons are misguided through the stages of grief. *OMEGA – Journal of Death and Dying* 74(4): 455–473.

Stroebe M, Stroebe W and Hansson RO (1993) *Handbook of Bereavement*. Cambridge: Cambridge University Press.

Stroebe MS, Folkman S, Hansson RO and Schut H (2006) The prediction of bereavement outcome: Development of an integrative risk factor framework. *Social Science and Medicine* 63(9): 2440–2451.

Stroebe W and Stroebe MS (1993) Determinants of adjustment to bereavement in younger widows and widowers. In Stroebe MS, Stroebe W and Hansson RO (eds) *Handbook of Bereavement: Theory, Research, and Intervention*. Cambridge: Cambridge University Press, pp. 208–226.

Sunoo JJM and Sunoo BP (2002) Managing workplace grief – Vision and necessity. *Pepperdine Dispute Resolution Law Journal* 2(3): 391.

Tehan M and Thompson N (2013) Loss and grief in the workplace: The challenge of leadership. *OMEGA – Journal of Death and Dying* 66(3): 265–280.

Thompson LW, Breckenridge JN, Gallagher D and Peterson J (1984) Effects of bereavement on self-perceptions of physical health in elderly widows and widowers. *Journal of Gerontology* 39(3): 309–314.

Thompson N (2009) *Loss, Grief and Trauma in the Workplace*. Amityville NY: Baywood.

Thompson N and Thompson S (2009) Loss, grief and trauma. In Thompson N and Bates J (eds) *Promoting Workplace Well-being*. Basingstoke and New York, NY: Palgrave Macmillan, pp. 71–82.

Tunstall J (1962) *The Fishermen*. London: MacGibbon and Kee.

van der Klink MA, Heijboer L, Hofhuis JG, Hovingh A, Rommes JH, Westerman MJ and Spronk PE (2010) Survey into bereavement of family members of patients who died in the intensive care unit. *Intensive and Critical Care Nursing* 26(4): 215–225.

Vickers MH (2005) Bounded grief at work: Working and caring for children with chronic illness. *Illness, Crisis and Loss* 13(3): 201–218.

Wells, JD, Hobfoll SE and Lavin J (1999) When it rains, it pours: The greater impact of resource loss compared to gain on psychological distress. *Personality and Social Psychology Bulletin* 25(9): 1172–1182.

Wijngaards-de Meij L, Stroebe M, Schut H, Stroebe W, van den Bout J, van der Heijden P and Dijkstra I (2005) Couples at risk following the death of their child: Predictors of grief versus depression. *Journal of Consulting and Clinical Psychology* 73(4): 617.

Wilcox HC, Mittendorfer-Rutz E, Kjeldgård L, Alexanderson K and Runeson B (2015) Functional impairment due to bereavement after the death of adolescent or young adult offspring in a national population study of 1,051,515 parents. *Social Psychiatry and Psychiatric Epidemiology* 50(8): 1249–1256.

Wilson DM, Punjani S, Song Q and Low G (2019) A study to understand the impact of bereavement grief on the workplace. *OMEGA – Journal of Death and Dying*. doi: 10.1177/0030222819846419 (accessed 27 November 2020).

World Health Organization (2006) *Preventing Suicide, a Resource at Work*. Department of Mental Health and Substance Abuse. Geneva: WHO, pp. 1–31.

Yarker J, Munir F, Bains M, Kalawsky K and Haslam C (2010) The role of communication and support in return to work following cancer-related absence. *Psycho-Oncology* 19(10): 1078–1085.

Yip PS and Caine ED (2011) Employment status and suicide: The complex relationships between changing unemployment rates and death rates. *Journal of Epidemiology and Community Health* 65(8): 733–736.

Zhang B, El-Jawahri A and Prigerson HG (2006) Update on bereavement research: Evidence-based guidelines for the diagnosis and treatment of complicated bereavement. *Journal of Palliative Medicine* 9(5): 1188–1203.

Employee Wellbeing in Post-Disaster Settings

Sanna Malinen, Katharina Näswall, and
Tracy Hatton

INTRODUCTION

Workplaces are increasingly seen as important contributors to employee health and
wellbeing (Deloitte, 2017; Inceoglu et al.,
2018; Kossek et al., 2012). Past research in
the post-disaster space suggests that workplaces can also represent a significant stabi-
lizing force in individuals' lives following a
disaster, and therefore aid the recovery of
employees, and ultimately, their communities (Mooney et al., 2011; Hobfoll et al.,
2007). However, despite the prevalence of
disasters and their vast impact on people
and societies, little is known about individual needs, attitudes, and wellbeing in a
workplace context, and what role workplaces can play in supporting the recovery
and wellbeing of their employees (Nilakant
et al., 2013b, 2016). Furthermore, much of
the scholarly knowledge stems from
research in the initial phases of disasters,
i.e., the response and short-term recovery
phases, even though the impacts of disasters

last for years or even decades post disaster
(Rubin, 2009).

This chapter sets out to discuss how
workplaces can support wellbeing for the
benefit of their employees and the organization. This chapter is particularly relevant
for those interested in how workplaces can
facilitate post-disaster recovery. Not only are
disasters increasingly common, at the time
of writing, many organizations all over the
world are struggling to cope with the ongoing impacts of the COVID-19 pandemic,
including how to manage employee needs
and concerns (Worley and Jules, 2020).
Considering the wide-reaching impacts of
disasters (Cheatham et al., 2015), it is surprising that research is relatively scarce on
the impacts of disasters on employees and
on how organizational resources can help
or hinder employee wellbeing and recovery. One plausible reason for the lack of
research is the challenging nature of conducting research during or after disasters (Hall
et al., 2016a), an area we will also address

in this chapter. We argue that understanding employee wellbeing in a post-disaster context warrants significant attention as such events are not only consequential for employees, but for organizational recovery, and ultimately, for our communities. Business and organizational survival and functioning are important drivers of community recovery (MacDonald et al., 2015), and employees' roles within this are central: organizational recovery is reliant on employee contributions (McClain, 2007; Walker and Hatton, 2020). Therefore, organizational plans and initiatives to support employee wellbeing are not only beneficial for the employees, but organizations themselves will gain from such efforts.

Furthermore, organizations have a social responsibility to care for their employees, beyond just their health and safety responsibilities. While many OECD countries' health and safety legislation recognizes employee fatigue and stress as potential hazards to be managed (e.g., New Zealand's Health and Safety at Work Act, 2015), scholars suggest that employers also have a moral responsibility to care for their staff (Williams, 2018). Indeed, a vast body of work shows that employment has great implications for people's life satisfaction and that workplaces can either support or hinder people's sense of good life (Dockery, 2003; Heller et al., 2002; Unanue et al., 2017). In a disaster setting, the role of the workplace in people's life satisfaction is likely to be further heightened, as workplaces can significantly support (or hinder) employee wellbeing, when their out-of-work life may be in turmoil.

In this chapter, we discuss the impact of disasters on employee wellbeing and what organizations have done, and can and should do, to aid and support their staff wellbeing and recovery. This chapter begins with an overview of existing research on employee wellbeing in post-disaster contexts. We then discuss the challenges related to conducting research on employee wellbeing in a post-disaster context and provide some reflections for future research to take into consideration.

We end the chapter by providing practical recommendations based on scholarly evidence for organizations to care for their staff, thereby contributing to community post-disaster recovery.

OVERVIEW OF PAST RESEARCH IN THE AREA

We begin our review of the literature on employee wellbeing and post-disaster recovery by briefly outlining gaps in disaster research related to employee wellbeing. We then discuss the importance of employee wellbeing on organizational and community recovery and the impact of disasters on employees, as well as organizational responses to support employees and the impact of these.

Disasters and Disaster Management

For the purpose of this chapter, we use Mayner and Arbon's (2015: 24) definition of a disaster as 'the widespread disruption and damage to a community that exceeds its ability to cope and overwhelms its resources'. Examples of such events include the US terrorist attack of September 11, 2001, the COVID-19 pandemic, extreme weather-related events often related to climate change, such as hurricanes, floods, and bush fires, as well as earthquakes, such as the Kobe, Japan (1995) and Canterbury, New Zealand (NZ; 2010–2011) earthquakes (where the authors reside), and tsunamis, such as the Indian Ocean tsunami of 2004. The societal and economic impacts of disasters such as these are enormous and wide-reaching, and the costs have been increasing in the past few decades (Botzen et al., 2019; O'Keefe et al., 1976). Hoeppe (2016), for example, suggests that, since the 1980s, the frequency of disasters that cause significant loss has increased by a factor of three, due in part to the increased exposure of an urbanizing world. In 2018 alone, over 300 disasters affected 68 million people and resulted in economic losses of U$131.7 billion (Centre for Research on the Epidemiology of Disasters, 2019). Indeed, most individuals are likely to face a disaster at some stage in their lifetime (Norris, 1992).

A vast disaster management literature exists examining preparation for, and recovery from, disasters. Disaster management is usually described as having four phases: mitigation/risk reduction, preparedness, response, and recovery, both short and long term. Most research on the wellbeing of employees in disaster settings focuses on the response and recovery phases, but the mitigation and preparedness phases are largely absent in the literature. Further, research on the recovery phase has often focused on short-term recovery, while much less is known on the long-term impacts of disaster recovery on employee wellbeing. This is an issue we will address in this chapter.

In addition, business organizations have rarely been the focus of disaster research (Webb et al., 2000). Where organizations have been of interest, focus has been on community organizations and their role in recovery (e.g., Gibbs et al., 2016; Poulton et al., 2020). Furthermore, research has largely been directed at an organizational level of analysis, where the attention has been on the entire organization's ability to cope, manage, and recover from a disaster (see e.g., Kay, 2019; Khan and Sayem, 2013; Tierney, 2004; see also www.resorgs.co.nz), rather than on employee disaster experiences.

Employee Wellbeing Contributes to Community Recovery

Employees are an integral part of organizational recovery (McClain, 2007; Hatton et al., 2016), since staff must be able to successfully contribute for organizations to recover, or even thrive, in an uncertain environment. Resuming business operations is an essential part of community disaster recovery (MacDonald et al., 2015; Webb et al., 2000), but to do this, employees must be able to contribute to organizational goals, and they will be much more able to do so if their wellbeing (i.e., the combination of feeling good and doing well, cf. Huppert, 2009) is supported. When employees are not feeling well, their performance and contribution to an organization are likely to suffer (MacDonald, 2005). Organizations also have a clear social responsibility for the wellbeing of their staff (Williams, 2018). Thus, a key aspect of organizational, and therefore community, recovery is the wellbeing of the workforce. This was recently recognized in June 2018, when new International Standard (ISO 22330) guidelines for people aspects of business continuity were published (ISO, 2018). The guidelines set out recommendations for how organizations can plan to support both the psychological and practical needs of employees. Other research is also emerging that makes recommendations for organizational responses to support employee wellbeing and recovery post disaster (Malinen et al., 2020; McClain, 2007), showing that the awareness and interest in this area is growing.

It is noteworthy that a significant literature exists on the health and wellbeing of first responders and emergency-service staff in disaster settings and how they are affected when involved in the immediate response. This research is essential to understand the impacts of extreme work environments on employee health and wellbeing. However, while acknowledging the importance of this research, in this chapter we focus on non-emergency service staff to enhance our understanding of the workplaces' role in supporting employee wellbeing, in a hope to encourage further research in this area.

The Impacts of Disaster on Employees

A notable characteristic of most disasters is that employees are affected not only in their workplaces, but also in their lives outside of work. The impacts of disasters on employees are many and varied, from loss of property or of family members, to significant changes to employment situations and livelihoods. Importantly, disaster impacts are not equated with losses. Communities with high insurance cover for disasters still experience significant issues that may impact employee wellbeing. For example, the Canterbury, NZ earthquake sequence of 2010–2011, combined with unique insurance policies, created significant impacts on focus and productivity for businesses with many managers and staff needing to spend considerable time and energy on resolving their own residential issues (Hatton et al., 2020).

Negative emotional responses to disaster-related events outside of work are common, and can spill over to work-life (Mainiero and Gibson, 2003), affecting how employees are able to function at work (Malinen et al., 2019; Näswall et al., 2017). The reverse may also be true when disaster-related organizational coping strategies contribute to negative employee reactions, which can spill over to life outside work (Sinclair et al., 2020). The interplay between work and life outside work is often overlooked in disaster contexts, resulting in a risk that employees have to manage their emotional reactions without any support from their employer.

At the time of writing, the evolving COVID-19 pandemic is a fitting example of a disaster context, where anxiety over health concerns and the global financial implications, among other concerns, are taking a toll on the wellbeing of many. Employees under quarantine and/or physical-distancing restrictions have been put under tremendous pressure to deliver on work goals, while many are also required to home-school children and/or care for dependents, not to mention the many people who have lost their jobs due to layoffs (Pfeffer, 2020). Looming unemployment is a serious concern for many, including those whose employment traditionally has been secure (Poulton et al., 2020). The perceived threat of job loss can be detrimental for mental health (Jiang and Lavaysse, 2018), and both job loss (Strully, 2009) and unemployment (Cygan-Rehm et al., 2017; McKee-Ryan et al., 2005) are well-known risk factors for poor mental health. Indeed, a recent report suggests that while the full mental health impacts from the COVID-19 pandemic are yet to be seen, increasing unemployment is likely to contribute to the negative mental health impacts of the pandemic (Poulton et al., 2020).

Other negative emotional responses to disasters include fear and anxiety (Ashkanasy and Daus, 2002) and these emotional reactions can affect employees' ability to do their work. For example, Mainiero and Gibson's (2003) survey of employees three months after the events of September 11 in the United States showed that many had trouble sleeping and concentrating at work. In the context of Hurricane Katrina, Goodman and Mann (2008) found that many employees were, for example, behaving out of character, implying

---

Case example: the post-disaster realities – 2010–2011 Canterbury, NZ earthquakes

John is a senior manager in an IT company. Following the 2011 Canterbury, NZ earthquake, his home was badly damaged and judged uninhabitable, and his company's premises were cordoned off and inaccessible. John's wife worked long hours as a nurse while his two high-school-age children were displaced from their damaged school premises and site-shared with another school. Over the two years that followed, John dealt with complicated insurance and compensation schemes for his residential house, supported his company to set up temporary premises, endured 10,000 aftershocks, and slept with his children in his room as they needed comfort throughout the aftershocks. It is very likely that these events outside of work affected how he was able to carry out his job, and John was not alone. Many employees were going through similar procedures, giving them a shared experience.

the need for managers to show concern for their employees' wellbeing. Malinen and colleagues (2019) reported significant increased emotional labour by managers who were dealing with highly stressed team members and customers in the aftermath of the Canterbury, NZ earthquakes. Similar sentiments have been expressed in the COVID-19 situation, where employees and leaders themselves are dealing with increased demands influencing their work behaviour (Hammer and Lindsey, 2020).

Further post-disaster research suggests severe mental health challenges in the aftermath of a disaster. Employees (beyond first responders and emergency personnel) can present with symptoms of post-traumatic stress disorder, affecting employee performance (Williams, 2018). For example, DeSalvo et al. (2007) found that over 20% of employees in a large organization showed symptoms of post-traumatic stress disorder following Hurricane Katrina. The negative mental health effects after the 2009 Australian bushfires were significant and long-lasting (Gibbs et al., 2016), and impacts of the 2010–2011 NZ earthquakes on mental health were, and continue to be, significant (Humphrey and Renison, 2015; Spittlehouse et al., 2014). Four years after the most significant tremor in the Canterbury, NZ earthquake sequence, there had been over a 40% increase in adult, and close to a 70% increase in child and youth, mental health service needs (Humphrey and Renison, 2015). Organizations, and leaders in particular, therefore cannot simply consider employee needs and concerns in the context of the workplace but should be encouraged to also consider the broader situation in which employees live and how they are affected by their work environment. Research outside of the disaster context is clear on the beneficial impact of a positive work environment on employee mental health and wellbeing (Mind, 2017/18), and in turn, employee wellbeing contributes to the increased employee efforts (MacDonald, 2005). Next, we review some examples of organizational responses directed at supporting their employees post disaster.

Organizational Responses to Support Employee Recovery and Wellbeing

The literature on the impact of disasters on human-resource-related practices and processes is largely absent (Goodman and Mann, 2008; but see Nilakant et al., 2013a; MacDonald, 2005 for exceptions), but the research that does exist clearly illustrates the value of focusing on employees, and their emotions and needs, in the aftermath of a disaster.

Organizational responses to support employees vary from tangible support, such as housing and financial assistance, to support for employees' everyday job tasks and duties, to support for employees' psychological wellbeing. Regardless of the type of support, research suggests that offering support for employee wellbeing pays dividends for organizations (see Riggle et al., 2009 for review outside of the disaster context). For example, research conducted in the Canterbury, NZ earthquake context indicates that organizations with faster recovery had uniquely people-oriented organizational cultures (Nilakant et al., 2016; Walker et al., 2020). Clear differences were found between organizations that prioritized the wellbeing of their employees above the bottom line. In these organizations, leaders displayed high levels of empathy, actively listened to their staff's concerns, responded to them appropriately, and acknowledged the individual differences in the recovery process.

Being supported by a workplace also clearly impacts employees' job-relevant attitudes (Byron and Peterson, 2002; Nilakant et al., 2016). Organizational provisions of tangible support to their employees, such as housing and financial assistance, result in more positive work-related attitudes, as well as less strain (Sanchez et al., 1995). How resources are distributed is important, and positive justice perceptions have been found to influence both job satisfaction and organizational commitment in a post-disaster context (Harvey and Haines III, 2005). Perceptions of organizational support can buffer links between fears of future crises and job attitudes (e.g., in context of terrorism; Malik et al., 2017), as well as cushion the impact of work-related stress or external demands on job attitudes (Hochwarter et al., 2008; Reade and Lee, 2012). Research from outside of the disaster context further supports the importance of work-related resources and how they can buffer the negative impacts of various work-related demands (Bakker and Demerouti, 2007; Demerouti et al., 2017).

An important resource supporting people's wellbeing, both in and external to a disaster context, is people's social networks. It is clear that social connectedness has a strong positive influence on employee mental health (Chiaburu and Harrison, 2008; Meyers et al., 2013). Further, a number of studies have highlighted the importance of social capital (Aldrich, 2012) and social support (Abramson et al., 2010; Mooney et al., 2011) in overall disaster-recovery outcomes. In the context of the Australian bushfires, social networks were found to be central to recovery (Gibbs et al., 2016), a finding supported by other disaster-related research (Paton et al., 2013). Importantly, a workplace can be a key source of informal social support, forming an important part of many individuals' networks and social connections. Workplaces offer employees a space to talk and share their experiences (Hatton et al., 2016), although importantly, a positive workplace culture needs to be in place to facilitate such discussions and for employees to feel safe to do so (Mainiero and Gibson, 2003). This presents an opportunity for workplaces to deliberately create a supportive environment, thereby helping their employees cope with the disaster, with potential positive effects for employees' life outside work.

Workplaces can influence their employees' day-to-day tasks to support their recovery and wellbeing in general. For example, some workplaces relaxed performance targets and implemented a flexible working hours policy following the Canterbury, NZ earthquakes (Hatton et al., 2016; see also Malinen et al., 2019; McClain, 2007). Increased role demands may also occur during some disasters, such as during the COVID-19 pandemic (Sinclair et al., 2020), where employees may have faced greater work demands due to increased virtual work. A recent study on job resources provided by workplaces during the COVID-19 pandemic found that employees found flexibility and control over how and when one completed work duties were helpful, and also showed that job control was related to employee wellbeing (Malinen et al., 2020). Employees were appreciative of employers who understood their pressures of balancing home life with job duties given that many employees were working from home at the time of the research while looking after their children or other dependents. North et al. (2010) similarly found that employees found it challenging to try to balance their own emotional needs and workplace demands following the September 11 terrorist attacks in the United States, making it important for employers to be aware that work–life balance will likely be a challenge after disasters.

A strong theme coming through the literature on disaster impacts on employees is individual differences in how employees are affected and respond to disasters. In the aftermath of the September 11 terrorist attack in the United States, Mainiero and Gibson (2003) found that females, those living with children, and those closer to the event were more affected by the event, and of course, within these groups, there would have been vast differences as well. As noted above, working remotely in a NZ-wide lockdown during the COVID-19 pandemic also demonstrated how employees desired flexibility in completing their work duties to fit them with their non-work situation, and that the need for flexibility differed between employees (Malinen et al., 2020). Consideration of individual employee needs and concerns is therefore paramount to ensure appropriate resources and to avoid 'one size fits all' initiatives that may be counterproductive. Research suggests that human resource and organizational policies, and leadership, need to be flexible enough to cope with changing employee needs in the aftermath of disasters (Nilakant et al., 2013b), as employees may react differently and at different times following a disaster. For example, in disasters where employees' property have been affected, while time off from work to deal with insurance challenges is useful to many in the early recovery phase, these needs may continue for years for some individuals. Workplace policies should therefore have the flexibility to adapt to such long-term needs.

A further recurring finding in the literature on employee wellbeing in the post-disaster context is the role that leaders play in supporting their employees. This theme resonates well with the general organizational literature, which clearly shows the impact that leaders have on employee wellbeing (Inceoglu et al., 2018). However, this also raises questions about who is supporting the leaders. Malinen et al. (2019) discuss the impacts on middle-level managers in the aftermath of the Christchurch, NZ earthquakes. These leaders showed strong commitment to ensure business recovery and their team wellbeing, but their own wellbeing suffered greatly. Leader wellbeing is an important area which we return to in our recommendations below.

Evidence also suggests that while some workplaces are excellent at providing support in the initial few months following a disaster (Malinen et al., 2019), the long-term impacts of disasters on employees are not often considered by employers. The time frame of post-disaster research is often limited to the first few months following the event, while the impacts of many disasters are evident long after the event. That is, recovery is often a long-term process, often lasting years after the initial event. This was clearly evident in the Canterbury, NZ earthquake sequence. Aftershocks continued for numerous years, with over 8,000 aftershocks experienced in the first year following the initial earthquake (Hall et al., 2016b), representing recurring stressors continuously reminding people of the trauma. Organizational plans for supporting their employees therefore had to be revised, often continuously, to consider the post-disaster impacts for numerous years.

ORGANIZATIONAL PLANNING AND OPPORTUNITIES

Unfortunately, organizations are often poorly prepared for disasters (Orlitzky, 2000). When plans do exist, they frequently focus on impacts such as premises or IT rather than on the impacts on employees. Hatton et al. (2016)

Case example: supporting employees through the COVID-19 pandemic

Sharon works four days a week for a medium-sized research company. When a four-week stay at home order was imposed, her workload remained largely unchanged, with large projects continuing. Her work was able to be completed remotely and her organization was set up for this. Sharon's partner was also required to work remotely; however, the day-care centre for her two-year-old child was closed. Recognizing the strain this placed upon Sharon (and other employees like her), Sharon's employer extended their flexible hours policy to incorporate work being spread across all seven days of the week and all hours of the day. Her employer made it clear that deadlines could be relaxed, where needed, and instituted team meetings three times a week scheduled for her son's nap time. Over half of the team meeting conversation was about the stay-at-home experience. Additionally, they instituted an honesty-based flexible leave system where Sharon could retrospectively notify the organization that she took the equivalent of a day's leave spread over a two-week period. While this time of working at home was still challenging for Sharon, these flexible policies enabled her to balance her commitments and improved the loyalty and engagement she felt for her organization.

conducted research on business continuity plans following the Canterbury, NZ earthquakes and found that existing business continuity plans were often not helpful in responding to personal and community disruption; a significant oversight in planning was acknowledged by the participating organizations. Furthermore, the long-term nature of disaster recovery further complicates effective organizational planning, particularly when the future is highly volatile and uncertain, such as in the current COVID-19 pandemic. Battisti and Deakins' (2012) research suggests that business continuity plans for small businesses rarely exist (also Bethany, 2019). Planning is central to recovery, but plans need to be flexible enough to account for unforeseen circumstances and plans should be considered living documents, to be adjusted as the event and recovery situation evolves.

Employee redundancies are a common response to crises. While the rationale for layoffs may be justified, layoffs often result in unintended, detrimental consequences, including erosion of trust, poorer interpersonal relationships, and increased employee turnover, to name a few (Cameron, 1994, 1998; Cameron et al., 1991; Gittell et al., 2006), and expected improvements in organizational performance generally are not realized (Datta et al., 2010). Gittell and colleagues (2006) found that redundancies actually hindered recovery of airlines after the September 11 terrorist attacks, and non-disaster studies indicate that layoffs often incur higher costs, rather than the cost savings they were designed to result in (Pfeffer and Veiga, 1999). Organizational layoffs and furloughs disconnect individuals from their key social connections, which, as noted above, are important for recovery and wellbeing.

Disasters, while devastating to individuals, organizations, and communities, may also offer unexpected opportunities to improve organizational systems and functioning, including their

systems for supporting employee wellbeing. Crises may prompt organizations to rethink their operations (Worley and Jules, 2020), and offer opportunities for learning and innovation (Nilakant et al., 2016; Walker et al., 2020). A Business Continuity Institute Survey published in May 2020 indicated that 54% of organizations would not go back to their pre-COVID business model (Business Continuity Institute, 2020). At a time when employees are dealing with significant uncertainties in their personal lives, upheaval and change within their workplace elevates the level of resilience and innovative thinking needed to maintain effective function. For example, the COVID-19 crisis has contributed to a large proportion of the workforce working from home, resulting in organizations having to alter their way of engaging with their staff and clients. It has been suggested that this may be the start of a permanent shift in how work is viewed in relation to the rest of employees' lives (cf. Sinclair et al., 2020). Perhaps a more flexible approach to when and where work is done is possible, resulting in better work–life balance, less stress, and better wellbeing for staff, and potentially higher productivity and better work outcomes for the organization. Previous disaster research has also shown that when organizations are forced to review and revise their way of doing business, or change their priorities, employee experiences and wellbeing are often improved (Näswall et al., 2017; Walker et al., 2020). Thus, when organizations can pause and reflect on how they can best navigate the post-disaster environment and learn from others and previous research (cf. Worley and Jules, 2020), there are opportunities to create meaningful and permanent change for the better.

Disasters may therefore offer a chance to consider incorporating employee-related matters into planning activities, including short- and long-term planning for employee wellbeing post-disaster. We will discuss this further below under recommendations.

CHALLENGES TO CONDUCTING POST-DISASTER RESEARCH

In reviewing the literature on employee wellbeing in post-disaster settings, it has become apparent that there are a number of areas where more research would be valuable. For example, there is a need for longitudinal research on employee recovery and organizations' role in this recovery over time, and for research that increases our understanding of the role of organizations in community recovery and societal post-disaster change. The lack of research in the area of employee wellbeing in post-disaster settings may be related to the challenges that researchers face when conducting such research. These challenges may be especially prevalent in research on employee wellbeing, which requires access to participants and organizations that have been impacted by the disaster themselves, whereas many other disciplines focusing on more physical impacts (e.g., engineering) may find it easier to conduct their research in a disaster context. The challenges organizational researchers often face include impacts of the subject matter on participant and researcher wellbeing, ethics of conducting post-disaster research, and a need for coordinated efforts by researchers.

While social science research often has strict procedures in place for ensuring the wellbeing of their participants, researcher wellbeing has not traditionally been explicitly considered. When conducting research in a post-disaster setting, local researchers may have been impacted themselves by the disaster (Hall et al., 2016a). In addition, researchers are often exposed to traumatic stories as part of their data collection, resulting in emotional reactions and potentially impacting researcher wellbeing. Researchers need to be aware of this potential risk and have appropriate self-care strategies in place to avoid secondary traumatization.

A challenge raised by Hall et al. (2016a) was related to the need for considering the ethics of conducting research in a post-disaster setting, where the researchers can be seen as benefiting from the negative experiences of others (see also Carrie et al., 2009). While researchers often feel it is their duty to document and interpret events, those living through the disaster may feel researchers take advantage of their misfortune. Asking participants to recall traumatic events has the potential to further exacerbate the trauma, raising important questions about whether research is the right thing to do. While the knowledge gained from the effects of disasters on individuals, and the research, is valuable for planning, there needs to be a balance between the need to document and risk of interfering with the recovery. Being sensitive to participants' reactions and ensuring they are in a frame of mind to give informed consent to participate will be an important part of counteracting the potential ethical dilemma of conducting research involving humans post disaster.

Disaster contexts may also attract numerous researchers to investigate similar issues (Beaven et al., 2016). There are often multiple research teams from other cities and countries arriving at a disaster site, with the aim of documenting the disaster from their angle. This abundance of researchers can create research fatigue among those living through the disaster, and result in a reluctance to participate. There is a need for coordinated efforts by researchers in disaster research, to avoid alienating the potential participants.

All in all, the process and challenges of doing post-disaster research have been greatly understudied (Hall et al., 2016a). Research methods may need to be adjusted, and gold-standard research designs are often not possible (Wordsworth et al., forthcoming). For example, pre-measures are not often possible given the sudden onset of event(s) (for an exception, see Birkeland et al., 2017); rather, research methods need to be adaptive to the context (Walker et al., 2020). Furthermore, many researchers lack experience in conducting research in such challenging settings, and furthermore, each disaster situation has its unique challenges, requiring approaches that may not have been documented previously. The unique aspects of each disaster setting also raise issues around generalizability (Stallings, 2007).

However, disasters do offer a unique context where research can discover phenomena otherwise left unexplored (Hall et al., 2016a), including the study of how the workplace can impact on individual and community recovery and wellbeing. Further knowledge is essential for organizations to better prepare for and respond to future disasters. This would be facilitated by a closer collaborative relationship between organizations and researchers prior to the disaster context. Such collaborative relationships would be mutually beneficial in non-disaster situations as well; since disasters are often unpredictable, having a pre-established relationship enables researchers to quickly respond and document disaster reactions among staff. Researchers may also be able to provide information for organizations on what is considered best practice so far, which could improve organizational responses to support employee wellbeing.

RECOMMENDATIONS: PROMOTING WELLBEING IN A POST-DISASTER CONTEXT

In this final section, we outline some practical recommendations to organizational leaders on how they can work to support employee wellbeing in a post-disaster environment. We structure this section based on the phases of disaster, including mitigation and preparation, response, and recovery.

Mitigation and Preparation Phases

Planning for disasters is an essential organizational function (Hochwarter et al., 2008), particularly as it is highly likely that some type of crisis will impact all organizations at some stage in their existence (Mainiero and Gibson, 2003). One of the key planning tools for organizations to ensure post-disaster functioning of operations is a business continuity plan. Paton and Johnston (2015) also suggest including household preparedness as part of business continuity planning, acknowledging the inter-relationship between business and community recovery (MacDonald et al., 2015). Specific principles, initiatives, and co-ordinating structures for supporting employees to perform in a crisis should be a part of any organization's business continuity planning process, drawing upon and extending existing organizational policies where possible. Planning the necessary support mechanisms in advance is likely to quicken the ability to enact these, with adaptation as necessary.

Response Phase

The response phase largely focuses on the immediate and short-term needs of communities (United Nations Office for Disaster Risk Reduction, n.d.), and usually includes the time period of a few days to a few weeks following an event (MacDonald et al., 2015). During this phase, organizations should focus on offering tangible support for the acute needs of employees (Hobfoll et al., 2007), which is likely to also lead to enhanced attitudes towards organizations (Malinen et al., 2019; Sanchez et al., 1995). Walker et al. (2020) describe an example of a leader who hired a mobile coffee shop for his workers who were working long hours to repair a city's infrastructure following an earthquake. This gesture signalled that the leader cared about employees' needs and significantly helped boost staff morale.

The role of communication is critical in both the response and recovery phases. However, even the simple act of contacting employees may be challenging during the disaster response and recovery phases. For example, Goodman and Mann (2008) found that some employers were unable to reach their staff for around a month after Hurricane Katrina due to power outages and employees moving locations for safety. However, making contact and providing information from organizations about how the disaster is affecting the business and how the organization will handle these effects is important for reducing uncertainty and helping employees feel connected and supported. Even if communication does not reach everyone, it is important that a communication plan is part of the immediate, and ongoing, organizational response. It is also important to provide information to counteract rumours and misinformation (Mainiero and Gibson, 2003). One simple way of providing information could be to add a new section to the company's website where information can be accessed when employees need it.

Another key issue in the initial response phase is that employees and leaders leading the initial response are at a significant risk of experiencing burnout (Goodman and Mann, 2008). Many leaders are committed to their employer and team members, and therefore put in significant effort and hours to ensure the survival of the business and the wellbeing of their employees. However, while the short-term effects to others are often beneficial, the long-term impacts of these efforts may lead to employee exhaustion and burnout (Malinen et al., 2019), which in turn may result in leaders not being able to engage in supportive behaviours to the same extent (Byrne et al., 2014). Planning appropriate cover and support for 'essential' employees to ensure they can engage in adequate recovery is necessary to ensure the long-term availability of these key people.

Our recommendation is to ensure that initial employee needs are supported, which often means providing non-work-related support, such as financial assistance, facilities, or even emergency repairs. Within the workplace, flexible work practices should be promoted where possible, including control over where and when work is completed (Malinen et al., 2020). Special leave arrangements have been used in the response and recovery phases and can provide employees with much needed relief in balancing work and non-work commitments.

Recovery Phase

Recovery can be defined as 'short-term activities that restore vital life-support systems to minimum operating standards and long-term activities that return life to normal' (McLoughlin, 1985: 166). It can be useful to divide the recovery phase into short (weeks to months following the disaster) and long term (months to years following the disaster) recovery (MacDonald et al., 2015). In both short- and long-term recovery phases, employee needs are likely to change, vast individual differences in needs may be observed, and therefore the support offered by organizations should change as well (Orlitzky, 2000).

In the short term, functionalist solutions, provided by the organization to all employees have been recommended (Orlitzky, 2000), such as providing opportunities for flexible work, including allowing working from home (Mainiero and Gibson, 2003) and accommodating temporary rearrangement of tasks – for example, staff may not have to travel if they are experiencing a fear of flying or are reluctant to leave their family.

Line managers are often given the responsibility of dealing with their employees' emotional concerns, while few are actually trained in such skills (Mainiero and Gibson, 2003). Skills such as leader empathy have been identified as essential for providing support to staff in a post-disaster context (Nilakant et al., 2013b). Emotional labour has been found to be evident with line managers, who not only attempt to support their team, but are also dealing with their own disaster-related challenges (Malinen et al., 2019). We therefore strongly advocate for training of leaders in order to equip them with the skills to support staff wellbeing and recognize the signs that staff are struggling (cf. Dimoff and Kelloway, 2019; Mainiero and Gibson, 2003). Caring for leaders themselves should also be planned for in both short- and long-term recovery phases.

Long-Term Recovery

As suggested earlier, guidance for organizations on how to manage short-term effects of disasters is emerging, but the literature on long-term recovery efforts in supporting employee wellbeing is scarce.

Orlitzky (2000) proposes organizations develop a culture that integrates functionalist and radical-humanist paradigmatic aspects over the different phases. The radical-humanist approach would be more useful in the long-term recovery, focusing on each individual's own recovery trajectory and those needs that arise as the recovery phase continues. Orlitzky (2000) suggests that the long-term phase is aided by external providers who are not part of the organization, who can focus on an individual's needs and stories without taking the organization into account. We would argue, however, that the organization would have a role in facilitating and making available such external supports – for example, through employee assistance programmes (Paul and Thompson, 2006).

The initial needs for tangible support are likely to shift towards needs for social support, and social gatherings and counselling services may become more important resources later in the recovery phase (Hatton et al., 2016; Sanchez et al., 1995). The few studies that exist on long-term recovery suggest that there are vast individual differences in the ways that employees cope and recover from disasters (Sanchez et al., 1995) and therefore managers and organizational responses should be adaptive and flexible to respond to such differences (Mainiero and Gibson, 2003; Nilakant et al., 2016; Walker

et al., 2020). One way of ensuring such flexibility could be to train managers in how to detect trauma reactions and how to support employees through such reactions (Mainiero and Gibson, 2003). Post-traumatic stress reactions (and symptoms of post-traumatic stress disorder) develop over time and it is important for managers to be open to detecting such symptoms well beyond the initial disaster response (Williams, 2018).

In the case of the Canterbury, NZ post-disaster recovery, one of the fundamental findings was that the organizations that demonstrated a faster and more successful recovery had clearly employee-centric cultures (Nilakant et al., 2016; Walker et al., 2020). These findings also resonate with Kendra and Wachtendorf (2003), where the culture of the organization was a key driver of resilient organizations in the context of the September 11 terrorist attacks. Walker and colleagues (2020; Nilakant et al., 2016) describe more adaptive organizations as those that prioritized their employee needs and wellbeing and viewed their employees' wellbeing and ability to contribute as a prerequisite for organizational recovery. They had leaders who were empathetic, open to employee concerns and suggestions, and were attuned to individual differences in response to the evolving situation. Importantly, these organizations had foundations for such a culture before the onset of the disaster (Nilakant et al., 2016; Walker et al., 2020). Our key recommendation for organizational leaders is therefore to begin now, so that the organization is better prepared for future challenges.

CONCLUSION

The benefits of investing into employee wellbeing in a post-disaster environment are unmistakable. Not only will organizations be stronger by having a workforce that is likely to be better able to contribute and show loyalty to caring organizations, but organizational efforts will also contribute towards community wellbeing and recovery. However, a lack of understanding of the different phases of employee recovery makes it challenging for organizations to be able to support their staff in an appropriate way. Building an employee-centric culture (Walker et al., 2020) will enhance employee and community recovery from disasters, as well as benefiting organizations during more stable times. However, building such a culture is near impossible during a crisis, when efforts are often directed at business survival, making it imperative that employee wellbeing is at the forefront of leaders' minds before a disaster strikes. In addition to building a culture where employees are valued, we strongly advocate for greater planning and preparedness for organizations, including planning for employee responses and needs in a disaster context.

REFERENCES

Abramson DM, Stehling-Ariza T, Park YS, et al. (2010) Measuring individual disaster recovery: A socioecological framework. *Disaster Medicine and Public Health Preparedness* 4: S46–S54.

Aldrich DP. (2012) *Building resilience: Social capital in post-disaster recovery*. Chicago, IL: University of Chicago Press.

Ashkanasy NM and Daus CS. (2002) Emotion in the workplace: The new challenge for managers. *The Academy of Management Executive (1993–2005)* 16: 76–86.

Bakker AB and Demerouti E. (2007) The Job Demands-Resources model: State of the art. *Journal of Managerial Psychology* 22: 309–328.

Battisti M and Deakins D. (2012) Business measure perspectives from New Zealand small firms: Crisis management and the impact of the Canterbury earthquakes. *Report from BusinesSMEasure 2011*. Hamilton, New Zealand: Massey University.

Beaven S, Wilson T, Johnston L, et al. (2016) Research engagement after disasters: Research coordination before, during, and after the 2011–2012 Canterbury earthquake sequence, New Zealand. *Earthquake Spectra* 32: 713–735.

Bethany MP. (2019) The role of social capital in small business disaster recovery: A multiple case study of Christchurch and Kaikoura businesses PhD thesis, *Management, Marketing and Entrepreneurship*. Christchurch, New Zealand: University of Canterbury.

Birkeland MS, Nielsen MB, Hansen MB, et al. (2017) The impact of a workplace terrorist attack on employees' perceptions of leadership: A longitudinal study from pre-to postdisaster. *The Leadership Quarterly* 28: 659–671.

Botzen WJW, Deschenes O and Sanders M. (2019) The economic impacts of natural disasters: A review of models and empirical studies. *Review of Environmental Economics and Policy* 13: 167–188.

Business Continuity Institute. (2020) *Coronavirus: A pandemic response*. Available at https://www.thebci.org/resource/bci-coronavirus—a-pandemic-response-2020.html (accessed June 2020).

Byrne A, Dionisi AM, Barling J, et al. (2014) The depleted leader: The influence of leaders' diminished psychological resources on leadership behaviors. *The Leadership Quarterly* 25: 344–357.

Byron K and Peterson S. (2002) The impact of a large-scale traumatic event on individual and organizational outcomes: Exploring employee and company reactions to September 11, 2001. *Journal of Organizational Behavior* 23: 895–910.

Cameron KS. (1994) Strategies for successful organizational downsizing. *Human Resource Management* 33: 189–211.

Cameron KS. (1998) Strategic organizational downsizing: An extreme case. In: Cooper CL and Rousseau D (eds) *Trends in organizational behavior*. New York: John Wiley, 185–229.

Cameron KS, Freeman SJ and Mishra AK. (1991) Best practices in white-collar downsizing: Managing contradictions. *The Executive* 5: 57–73.

Carrie YBA, Barrett EJ and Martinez-Cosio M. (2009) Ethical issues in disaster research: Lessons from Hurricane Katrina. *Population Research and Policy Review* 28: 93–106.

Centre for Research on the Epidemiology of Disasters. (2019) *Natural disasters 2018*. Brussels: CRED.

Cheatham B, Healy A and O'Brien Kuusinen B. (2015) *Improving disaster recovery: Lessons learned in the United States*. McKinsey & Company. New Media, Australia. Available at https://www.mckinsey.com/~/media/mckinsey/business%20functions/risk/our%20insights/improving%20disaster%20recovery/improving_disaster_recovery_280615_final.ashx (accessed June 2020)

Chiaburu DS and Harrison DA. (2008) Do peers make the place? Conceptual synthesis and meta-analysis of coworker effects on perceptions, attitudes, OCBs, and performance. *Journal of Applied Psychology* 93: 1082–1103.

Cygan-Rehm K, Kuehnle D and Oberfichtner M. (2017) Bounding the causal effect of unemployment on mental health: Nonparametric evidence from four countries. *Health Economics* 26: 1844–1861.

Datta DK, Guthrie JP, Basuil D, et al. (2010) Causes and effects of employee downsizing: A review and synthesis. *Journal of Management* 36: 281–348.

Deloitte. (2017) At a tipping point? Workplace mental health and wellbeing. *The Deloitte Centre for Health Solutions*, March 2017, London Available at www2.deloitte.com/content/dam/Deloitte/uk/Documents/public-sector/deloitte-uk-workplace-mental-health-n-wellbeing.pdf (accessed June 2020)

Demerouti E, Van den Heuvel M, Xanthopoulou D, et al. (2017) Job resources as contributors to wellbeing. In: Cooper CL and Leiter MP (eds) *The Routledge companion to wellbeing at work* (1st ed.). Abingdon: Routledge Taylor & Francis Group, 269–283.

DeSalvo KB, Hyre AD, Ompad DC, et al. (2007) Symptoms of posttraumatic stress disorder in a New Orleans workforce following Hurricane Katrina. *Journal of Urban Health* 84: 142–152.

Dimoff JK and Kelloway EK. (2019) Signs of struggle (SOS): The development and validation of a behavioural mental health checklist for the workplace. *Work & Stress* 33: 295–313.

Dockery AM. (2003) *Happiness, life satisfaction and the role of work: Evidence from two Australian surveys* Available at Available at https://melbourneinstitute.unimelb.edu.au/assets/documents/hilda-bibliography/working-discussion-research-papers/2001-2004/Dockery_happiness_life_satisfaction.pdf (accessed June 2020)

Gibbs L, Bryant R, Harms L, et al. *Beyond Bushfires: Community Resilience and Recovery Final Report*. November 2016, University of Melbourne, Victoria, Australia.

Gittell JH, Cameron K, Lim S, et al. (2006) Relationships, layoffs, and organizational resilience: Airline industry responses to September 11. *The Journal of Applied Behavioral Science* 42: 300–329.

Goodman D and Mann S. (2008) Managing public human resources following catastrophic events: Mississippi's local governments' experiences post-Hurricane Katrina. *Review of Public Personnel Administration* 28: 3–19.

Hall CM, Malinen S, Nilakant V, et al. (2016a) Undertaking business, consumer and organisational research in a post-disaster setting. In: Hall CM, Malinen S, Vosslamber R, et al. (eds) *Business and post-disaster management: Business, organisational and consumer resilience and the Christchurch earthquakes*. Abingdon: Routledge, 251–268.

Hall CM, Malinen S, Vosslamber R, et al. (2016b) Introduction: The business, organisational and destination impacts of natural disasters – the Christchurch earthquakes 2010–2011. In: Hall C, Malinen S, Vosslamber R, et al. (eds) *Business and post-disaster management: Business, organisational and consumer resilience and the Christchurch earthquakes*. Abingdon: Routledge, 3–20.

Hammer L and Lindsey A. (2020) Lead with empathy during the COVID-19 crisis. *The Conversation*.

Harvey S and Haines III VY. (2005) Employer treatment of employees during a community crisis: The role of procedural and distributive justice. *Journal of Business and Psychology* 20: 53–68.

Hatton T, Grimshaw E, Vargo J, et al. (2016) Lessons from disaster: Creating a business continuity plan that really works. *Journal of Business Continuity & Emergency Planning* 10: 84–92.

Hatton T, Vargo JJ and Seville E. (2020) Business recovery from disaster: Creating an enabling environment for surviving and thriving. In: Slick JAKJ (ed) *Disaster and emergency management: Case studies in adaptation and innovation series*. Oxford: Butterworth-Heinemann.

New Zealand Health and Safety at Work Act. (2015). Wellington, New Zealand: New Zealand Government.

Heller D, Judge TA and Watson D. (2002) The confounding role of personality and trait affectivity in the relationship between job and life satisfaction. *Journal of Organizational Behavior* 23: 815–835.

Hobfoll SE, Watson P, Bell CC, et al. (2007) Five essential elements of immediate and mid-term mass trauma intervention: Empirical evidence. *Psychiatry* 70: 283–315.

Hochwarter WA, Laird MD and Brouer RL. (2008) Board up the windows: The interactive effects of hurricane-induced job stress and perceived resources on work outcomes. *Journal of Management* 34: 263–289.

Hoeppe P. (2016) Trends in weather related disasters – Consequences for insurers and society. *Weather and Climate Extremes* 11: 70–79.

Humphrey A and Renison P. (2015) *Earthquake stress triggers mental health issues*. Christchurch, New Zealand: The Press.

Huppert FA. (2009) A new approach to reducing disorder and improving well-being. *Perspectives on Psychological Science* 4: 108–111.

Inceoglu I, Thomas G, Chu C, et al. (2018) Leadership behavior and employee well-being: An integrated review and a future research agenda. *The Leadership Quarterly* 29: 179–202.

ISO. (2018) *Security and resilience – Business continuity management systems – Guidelines for people aspects of business continuity*; SO/TS 22330:2018.

Jiang L and Lavaysse LM. (2018) Cognitive and affective job insecurity: A meta-analysis and a primary study. *Journal of Management* 44: 2307–2342.

Kay E. (2019) Business recovery from disaster: A research update for practitioners. *Australasian Journal of Disaster and Trauma Studies* 23: 83–89.

Kendra JM and Wachtendorf T. (2003) Elements of resilience after the World Trade Center disaster: Reconstituting New York City's emergency operations centre. *Disasters* 27: 37–53.

Khan MAU and Sayem MA. (2013) Understanding recovery of small enterprises from natural disaster. *Environmental Hazards* 12: 218–239.

Kossek EE, Kalliath T and Kalliath P. (2012) Achieving employee wellbeing in a changing work environment: An expert commentary on current scholarship. *International Journal of Manpower* 33: 738–753.

MacDonald C, Davies B, Johnston DM, et al. (2015) *A framework for exploring the role of business in community recovery following disasters*. Lower Hutt, New Zealand: GNS Science, Te Pū Ao.

MacDonald LAC. (2005) *Wellness at work: Protecting and promoting employee wellbeing*. London: CIPD Publishing.

Mainiero LA and Gibson DE. (2003) Managing employee trauma: Dealing with the emotional fallout from 9–11. *Academy of Management Perspectives* 17: 130–143.

Malik OF, Shahzad A and Kiyani TM. (2017) The impact of terrorism-induced fear on job attitudes and absenteeism following a national traumatic event: Evidence from Pakistan. *International Journal of Conflict and Violence (IJCV)* 11: 1–18.

Malinen S, Hatton T, Naswall K, et al. (2019) Strategies to enhance employee well-being and organisational performance in a postcrisis environment: A case study. *Journal of Contingencies and Crisis Management* 27: 79–86.

Malinen S, Wong J and Näswall K. Effective workplace strategies to support employee wellbeing during and post a pandemic. *New Zealand Journal of Employment Relations* 45(2): 17–32.

Mayner L and Arbon P. (2015) Defining disaster: The need for harmonisation of terminology. *Australasian Journal of Disaster and Trauma Studies* 19: 21–25.

McClain M. (2007) Employee crisis communication and disaster assistance planning: Providing disaster assistance to employees and their families. *Journal of Business Continuity & Emergency Planning* 1: 213–220.

McKee-Ryan FM, Song Z, Wanberg CR, et al. (2005) Psychological and physical well-being during unemployment: A meta-analytic study. *Journal of Applied Psychology* 90: 53–76.

McLoughlin D. (1985) A framework for integrated emergency management. *Public Administration Review* 45: 165–172.

Meyers MC, van Woerkom M and Bakker AB. (2013) The added value of the positive: A literature review of positive psychology interventions in organizations. *European Journal of Work and Organizational Psychology* 22: 618–632.

Mind. (2017/2018) *Workplace Wellbeing Index: Key Insights.* mind.org.uk/work (accessed June 2020).

Mooney MF, Paton D, de Terte I, et al. (2011) Psychosocial recovery from disasters: A framework informed by evidence. *New Zealand Journal of Psychology* 40: 26–38.

Näswall K, Malinen S and Kuntz J. (2017) Resilience development through an organisation-led well-being initiative. In: Chmiel N, Fraccaroli F and Sverke M (eds) *An introduction to work and organizational psychology: An international perspective* (3rd ed.). London: Wiley, 506–513.

Nilakant V, Walker B, Kuntz J, et al. (2016) Dynamics of organisational response to a disaster: A study of organisations impacted by earthquakes. In: Hall CM, Malinen S, R. V, et al. (eds) *Business and post-disaster management.* London and New York: Routledge, 35–47.

Nilakant V, Walker B and Rochford K. (2013a) *Post-disaster management of human resources: Learning from an extended crisis.* Christchurch, New Zealand: Resilient Organisations/University of Canterbury.

Nilakant V, Walker B, Rochford K, et al. (2013b) Leading in a post-disaster setting: Guidance for human resource practitioners. *New Zealand Journal of Employment Relations* 38: 1–13.

Norris FH. (1992) Epidemiology of trauma: Frequency and impact of different potentially traumatic events on different demographic groups. *Journal of Consulting and Clinical Psychology* 60: 409–418.

North CS, Pfefferbaum B, Hong BA, et al. (2010) The business of healing: Focus group discussions of readjustment to the post-9/11 work environment among employees of affected agencies. *Journal of Occupational and Environmental Medicine* 52: 713–718.

O'Keefe P, Westgate K and Wisner B. (1976) Taking the naturalness out of natural disasters. *Nature* 260: 566–567.

Orlitzky M. (2000) Survivors' needs and stories after organizational disasters: How organizations can facilitate the coping process. *Journal of Personal and Interpersonal Loss* 5: 227–245.

Paton D and Johnston D. (2015) The Christchurch earthquake: Integrating perspectives from diverse disciplines. *International Journal of Disaster Risk Reduction* 14: 1–5.

Paton D, Mamula-Seadon L and Selway KL. (2013) Community resilience in Christchurch: Adaptive responses and capacities during earthquake recovery. *GNS Science Report* 2013/37.

Paul R and Thompson C. (2006) Employee assistance program responses to large scale traumatic events: Lessons learned and future opportunities. *Journal of Workplace Behavioral Health* 21: 1–19.

Paton D, Mamula-Seadon L and Selway KL. (2013) Community resilience in Christchurch: Adaptive responses and capacities during earthquake recovery. *GNS Science Report* 2013/37.

Pfeffer J and Veiga JF. (1999) Putting people first for organizational success. *The Academy of Management Executive (1993–2005)* 13: 37–48.

Poulton R, Gluckman P, Menzies R, et al. (2020) *Protecting and promoting mental wellbeing: Beyond COVID-19.* Koi Tū: The Centre for Informed Futures fifth paper in 'The Future is Now' Conversation Series. https://informedfutures.org/wp-content/uploads/Protecting-and-Promoting-Mental-Wellbeing.pdf (accessed June 2020).

Reade C and Lee H-J. (2012) Organizational commitment in time of war: Assessing the impact and attenuation of employee sensitivity to ethnopolitical conflict. *Journal of International Management* 18: 85–101.

Riggle RJ, Edmondson DR and Hansen JD. (2009) A meta-analysis of the relationship between perceived organizational support and job outcomes: 20 years of research.

Journal of Business Research 62: 1027–1030.

Rubin CB. (2009) Long term recovery from disasters – The neglected component of emergency management. *Journal of Homeland Security and Emergency Management* 6: 1–17.

Sanchez JI, Korbin WP and Viscarra DM. (1995) Corporate support in the aftermath of a natural disaster: Effects on employee strains. *Academy of Management Journal* 38: 504–521.

Sinclair RR, Allen T, Barber L et al. (2020). Occupational health science in the time of COVID-19: Now more than ever. *Occupational health science*, 1–22. Advance online publication. https://doi.org/10.1007/s41542-020-00064-3.

Spittlehouse JK, Joyce PR, Vierck E, et al. (2014) Ongoing adverse mental health impact of the earthquake sequence in Christchurch, New Zealand. *Australian & New Zealand Journal of Psychiatry* 48: 756–763.

Stallings RA. (2007) Methodological issues. In: Rodriguez H, Quarantelli EL and Dynes RR (eds) *Handbook of disaster research.* New York: Springer, 55–82.

Strully KW. (2009) Job loss and health in the U.S. Labor Market. *Demography* 46: 221–246.

Tierney KJ. (2004) Businesses and disasters: Vulnerability, impacts, and recovery. In: Rodriguez H, Quarantelli EL and Dynes RR (eds) *Handbook of disaster research.* New York: Springer, 275–296.

Unanue W, Gómez ME, Cortez D, et al. (2017) Revisiting the link between job satisfaction and life satisfaction: The role of basic psychological needs. *Frontiers in Psychology* 8: 680.

United Nations Office for Disaster Risk Reduction. (n.d.) *Terminology: Response.* https://www.undrr.org/terminology/response (accessed June 2020).

Walker B and Hatton T. (2020) Five principles to follow if your job is to lead your staff through the coronavirus crisis. *The Conversation.* https://theconversation.com/five-principles-to-follow-if-your-job-is-to-lead-your-staff-through-the-coronavirus-crisis-134642 (accessed June 2020).

Walker B, Malinen S, Nilakant V, et al. (2020) Organizational Resilience in Action: A Study of a Large Scale, Extended-Disaster Setting. In Powley E, Caza B, Caza A (eds) *The research handbook of organisational resilience.* Cheltenham: Edward Elgar Publishing, 320-337

Webb GR, Tierney KJ and Dahlhamer JM. (2000) Businesses and disasters: Empirical patterns and unanswered questions. *Natural Hazards Review* 1: 83–90.

Williams SD. (2018) Social responsibility and potential management interventions to address employees' post traumatic stress. *Review of General Management* 28: 22–29.

Wordsworth R, Hall CM, Prayag G, et al. (forthcoming). *Critical perspectives on disaster and crisis research: Revealing and responding to vulnerability.* Research Methodology in Strategy and Management, Emerald.

Worley CG and Jules C. (2020) COVID-19's uncomfortable revelations about agile and sustainable organizations in a VUCA world. *The Journal of Applied Behavioral Science.* https://journals.sagepub.com/doi/full/10.1177/0021886320936263

21

Humanizing Work: Occupational Mental Health of Humanitarian Aid Workers

Cheryl Y. S. Foo, Helen Verdeli, and
Alvin Kuowei Tay

INTRODUCTION

Since the turn of the 21st century, the increasingly frequent, complex, and protracted humanitarian emergencies, have substantially increased both the demand for humanitarian aid work and the emotional burden on the workers who carry out the operations on the ground. Between 2015 and 2018, the number of humanitarian aid workers (HAWs) in the field grew by 27% to an estimated 569,700 personnel (ALNAP, 2018). Despite its significant expansion, in 2018, this workforce was still dismally deficient in adequately serving the estimated 206 million people in 81 countries who needed humanitarian assistance (Development Initiatives, 2019). HAWs consist of both national and international personnel, and volunteers of supranational agencies (e.g., United Nations (UN) humanitarian agencies, International Red Cross and Red Crescent Movement (ICRC) societies), and local and international non-governmental organizations (NGOs) that provide assistance to support the basic needs of the affected populations in humanitarian crisis contexts (see Figure 21.1 for humanitarian response clusters). HAWs provide service under conditions of political insecurity, civil conflicts, poverty, famine, infectious diseases, and/or natural disasters. They are at an increased risk of experiencing threats and incidents of violence, as well as exposure to trauma and chronic stress (Jachens, 2019). Facing these extraordinary stressors, HAWs have been found to be at a high risk of adverse mental health outcomes, sometimes comparable to or even more than that of the local population in the same humanitarian setting (Ager et al., 2012; Lopes Cardozo et al., 2013; Thormar et al., 2013), The poor mental health of HAWs will have consequences on the functioning and productivity of humanitarian aid organizations (UN, 2018; Welton-Mitchell, 2013).

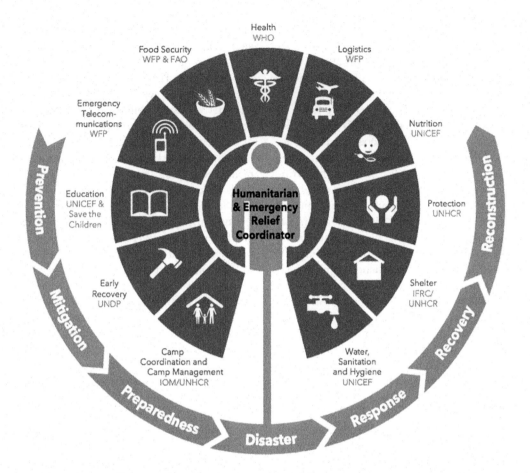

Figure 21.1. Humanitarian response clusters and corresponding lead agencies. From 'Reference Module for Cluster Coordination at Country Level', by Inter-Agency Standing Committee Sub-Working Group on the Cluster Approach and the Global Cluster Coordinators' Group, © 2015 United Nations. Reprinted with the permission of the United Nations.

Most of the occupational stress research on HAWs has primarily been conducted within the traumatic stress response paradigm (Connorton et al., 2012). Working in humanitarian aid exposes staff directly to potentially traumatic events (PTEs) such as experiencing or witnessing threats and incidents of violence (e.g., attacks, kidnappings, and accidents), which may even result in injury and death (Stoddard et al., 2019). HAWs are also at increased risk of indirect exposure to the trauma of the communities they serve, resulting in secondary traumatic stress (Figley,

2002). Post-traumatic stress disorder (PTSD), and its common comorbid conditions (e.g., depression, anxiety, and hazardous alcohol consumption) have been highly prevalent among this occupation group (Strohmeier and Scholte, 2015; United Nations High Commissioner for Refugees (UNHCR), 2016). In a review of trauma-related mental health problems in national staff from various disaster and conflict-affected countries, Strohmeier and Scholte (2015) reported that many studies found that national staff experienced a large number of traumatic events, with a study in Northern Uganda reporting that more than 50% of national workers had experienced five or more PTEs (Ager et al., 2012). International and Kosovar Albanian national HAWs who were exposed to a higher number of traumatic events were also more likely to be at an increased risk of PTSD and depression at post-deployment (Lopes Cardozo et al., 2005, 2012). However, these research findings from the trauma exposure paradigm face critical methodological issues that limit our ability to draw strong conclusions. In these studies, prevalence rates were based on self-report rather than structured clinical interviews; assessment tools were also not specifically validated for the HAW population coming from heterogeneous socio-cultural backgrounds. Furthermore, studies also varied in timing of assessment (i.e., different times during or after deployment and trauma exposure), which may lead to elevated rates of pathology.

Investigations on the mental health of HAWs have now moved away from focusing solely on trauma exposure and psychopathological outcomes, and are complemented with a multi-dimensional and multi-level occupational health approach (Jachens, 2019). This follows from a parallel line of research on the psychosocial and organizational factors determining employee wellbeing, which started 15 years ago and recently gained more visibility because of its empirical support (Schütte et al., 2014; Stansfeld and Candy, 2006). Research has found that organizational aspects of humanitarian aid work, rather than incidence of trauma, are perceived as the main sources of stress and are more strongly associated with negative mental health outcomes among HAWs (Jachens, 2019; Jachens et al., 2018, 2019).

From a psychosocial hazards perspective, HAWs face not only emergency-related environmental stressors on the ground but also chronic and unique work-related stressors that may contribute to burnout, an occupational syndrome recognized in the 11th Revision of the International Classification of Diseases (ICD-11) (World Health Organization (WHO), 2019) Burnout, burnout dimensions

of emotional exhaustion, depersonalization, and diminished personal accomplishment (Maslach et al., 1996) have been increasingly assessed among HAWs. If unaddressed, burnout and common mental disorders among aid workers can lead to higher accident and illness rates, absenteeism (UN, 2018: 7), loss of efficiency and productivity, lower performance, lower work commitment and engagement, and leaving the field of humanitarian work entirely (Curling and Simmons, 2010; Welton-Mitchell, 2013).

Given the organizational implications of provider mental health on the sustainability of local and global humanitarian assistance, as well as humanitarian aid organizations ethical and legal 'duty of care' towards employees (Jachens, 2019; Nobert and Williamson, 2017), the World Humanitarian Summit (WHS) expressed their commitment to systematically address and invest in the physical, psychological, and psychosocial care of humanitarian staff (WHS Secretariat, 2015). While humanitarian aid organizations are beginning to prioritize the mental health and psychosocial needs of the aid workforce in their staff welfare policies and guidelines (e.g., Antares Foundation, 2012; Core Humanitarian Standard Alliance on Quality and Accountability, 2014: 31; Inter-Agency Standing Committee (IASC), 2007; Pitotti and Clements, 2020; UN, 2018; UNHCR, 2016), the breadth of suggestions takes different approaches and is inconsistently implemented in practice (Welton-Mitchell, 2013). As such, a comprehensive, multi-domain (i.e., personal, interpersonal, psychosocial, contextual), and multi-level (i.e., individual, team, managerial, organizational) psychosocial risk research and assessment is necessary to develop appropriate, evidence-based policies, and intervention strategies for the mental health and psychosocial support of HAWs.

In line with this recommendation, this chapter will provide a review and synthesis of the contemporary scientific knowledge on the organizational and psychosocial factors influencing mental health and wellbeing of national and international HAWs.

The last section will summarize recommendations for intervention strategies for the pre-, during-, and post-deployment phases of humanitarian operations, informed by existing guidelines and the current evidence base. Throughout, there will be a distinction made between national and international staff, discussing how each group may have different risk and protective factors. National and international staff's different needs and priorities for organizational support will also be considered.

COMPOSITION OF HUMANITARIAN AID ORGANIZATIONS

The landscape of humanitarian organizations is varied. There are thousands of aid organizations that differ in size; geographic scope of work (local, national, regional, or international); scope of practice (single sector or multi-sectoral); service focus; mission (secular, interventionist, or faith-based); target beneficiaries (entire population, vulnerable populations, ages and/or genders); and timing of activities (acute, recovery, rehabilitation, and/or development phase) (Shahpar and Kirsch, 2018). The UN is recognized as the lead coordinating body for humanitarian strategy and response through the Inter-Agency Standing Committee (IASC) and the Office for the Coordination of Humanitarian Affairs (OCHA). To improve coordination among the humanitarian sector, the UN implemented the Cluster Approach in 2005 (WHO, 2007), where each of the 11 service clusters is assigned a UN agency as a cluster lead. The lead agency partners with the host government and other national and international organizations to build response capacity. The clusters and their corresponding lead agencies are shown in Figure 21.1.

The humanitarian aid sector is oligopolistic in structure, where a small number of the largest international organizations command the majority of staff, funding, and expenditure (ALNAP, 2018: 103–104). Due to the uncertain renewal of short-term contracts that are determined by external funding, and the short duration of projects granted by larger agencies (ALNAP, 2018: 106), staff from smaller NGOs often experience long-term employment insecurity (Young et al., 2018). Two studies independently showed that working for an international NGO compared to a UN-related agency was associated with higher levels of depression symptoms (Lopes Cardozo et al., 2013), and co-morbid anxiety symptoms (Ager et al., 2012). Ager et al. (2012) suggested that the institutionalized structures of UN and partner organizations may be better able to provide and implement formal and in-house staff support strategies and services, which may protect employees from mental health problems. Given the pyramid structure of the humanitarian sector and the disparities between organizations, organization type may therefore be an important determinant of aid workers' psychosocial wellbeing.

Humanitarian personnel comprise professional national staff (employees from the local population), international staff (expatriates), and volunteers. While the vast majority of the humanitarian workforce are volunteers, there is a scarce amount of literature on this group. This chapter will therefore focus on research with national and international staff. National staff make up over 90% of the total field personnel and have increased over the last years (ALNAP, 2018) due to the localization agenda set during the 2016 World Humanitarian Summit (Barbelet, 2018), which called for for humanitarian action to shift to local actors. Consequently, more risk is transferred to national staff as international aid groups limit their operational presence in more politically unstable and dangerous conflict-affected zones (Stoddard, 2020). The following section will describe the risks and stressors associated with humanitarian work, and how it differs between national and international staff.

PSYCHOSOCIAL STRESSORS IN HUMANITARIAN AID

Humanitarian aid work is intrinsically demanding, as HAWs operate in high-risk humanitarian settings, with a poverty of resources, while usually being away from family and friends for extended periods of time (Welton-Mitchell, 2013; UN, 2018). Although the bulk of research has focused on environmental stressors and critical incidents of trauma inherent in the nature of humanitarian work, organizations guided by recent research have also been paying more attention to the chronic work-related psychosocial hazards. Psychosocial hazards can be understood as the interactions between job content, work organization and management, and other environmental organizational contexts (Cox and Griffiths, 2005). In cross-sectional studies with local HAWs from Sri Lanka and Northern Uganda, chronic stressors cited such as financial pressures, lack of recognition for work by management, difficult relationship with management and colleagues, and tensions in the disparity of treatment between international and national staff, were related to higher levels of anxiety symptoms (Lopes Cardozo et al., 2013), and higher levels of emotional exhaustion (Ager et al., 2012). Similarly, the most frequently endorsed stressors by UNHCR staff (Welton-Mitchell, 2013) and UNICEF staff (Curling & Simmons, 2010; MacDonald & Curling, 2004) were also work-related stressors, including: high workload, inability to achieve work goals and objectives, status of employment contract, and feeling undervalued or unable to contribute to decision making.

Psychosocial hazards can be categorized into six psychosocial domains and their relevant dimensions as listed in Table 21.1, following the typology of the Copenhagen Psychosocial Questionnaire (COPSOQ) (Burr et al., 2019). The COPSOQ is a widely applied, internationally validated, and comprehensive occupational risk assessment and research tool (Nolle, 2018) which was also

used to inform the UN Risk Assessment Framework for the psychosocial wellbeing of all security personnel around the world. Assessment Framework (Tay, 2020, personal communication). Table 21.1 summarizes the contextual, traumatic, and psychosocial stressors commonly reported by HAWs, and how they may be experienced differently among national and international staff.

National and International Aid Workers

National staff face the dual challenge of working to support their communities while also being subjected to the same extreme stressors and traumatic experiences related to the humanitarian emergencies in their countries (Eriksson et al., 2013; Lopes Cardozo et al., 2005). Especially in post-conflict settings and diverse international organizations, national staff survivors may work alongside colleagues whose nationality, ethnicity, tribe, or religion is that of the perpetrator group, thus putting national staff at risk for PTSD symptoms and distress (Strohmeier et al., 2018; Tay, 2020, personal communication). National staff also face more security risks due to the increasing localization of aid (Stoddard, 2020). It has been consistently found that national staff are around five times more likely than international workers to be victims of violence, with sometimes fatal consequences (Stoddard et al., 2011, 2019). In multiple studies, national staff also reported financial concerns as the top priority chronic stressor (Ager et al., 2012; Eriksson et al., 2013: 669). This is unsurprising given that national staff are often paid less than their expatriate counterparts (Ajieth Bunny, 2017), which can contribute to feelings of injustice and demotivation (McWha-Hermann and Mullins, 2018). Indeed, Ager et al. (2012) reported that 59% of the national staff in Uganda endorsed 'tensions in disparity of treatment between national and international staff' as the most frequent stressor.

Table 21.1 Stressors experienced by humanitarian aid workers, and differences between national and international staff.

Domains and dimensions		Stressors	Differences between national and international staff
CONTEXTUAL		• Uncertainty about political stability • Hardship conditions related to food, housing, transportation, healthcare, and finances • Inadequate safety and protection equipment • Inadequate amenities • Isolation or inadequate communication with family and friends	• National staff may not be provided with paid accommodation • International staff may struggle more with adjusting to new living and working environments, and experience cultural and language barriers • International staff may be separated from family and may not have their usual social support network • National staff may have more available social support as a protective factor
CRITICAL INCIDENTS AND POTENTIALLY TRAUMATIC EVENTS		• Direct threats to life • Moral injury • Lack of emergency planning • Sexual harassment and gender-based violence	• National staff may face more security risks due to increasing localization of aid • National staff may be less protected by limited evacuation plans, health insurance, training, and adequate psychological support
PSYCHOSOCIAL			
Demands at work	*Workload and work pace*	• Work overload • High pace and high levels of time pressure	
	Emotional demands	• Secondary exposure to traumatic experiences of aid recipients • Criticism of work by media or beneficiary community	
Work organization and job contents	*Influence at work*	• Low participation in decision-making • Lack of control over workload and pacing	
	Control over working time	• 'Emergency culture' where there may be pressure to respond immediately to crises and tasks • Inflexible work schedules • Unpredictable and/or long hours	
Interpersonal relations and leadership	*Role in organization*	• Role ambiguity and role conflict due to multiple and competing responsibilities that may be out of job scope	• More national staff may be in lower-grade service provision jobs, while more international staff may be in management and leadership positions
	Quality of leadership	• Lack of recognition for work accomplishment • Poor and inconsistent quality of supervision and management	

(Continued)

Table 21.1   Stressors experienced by humanitarian aid workers, and differences between national and international staff. (*Continued*)

Domains and dimensions		Stressors	Differences between national and international staff
	Social support from colleagues and supervisors	• Poor relationship with superiors • Interpersonal conflict with colleagues and supervisors	• International staff had cited more conflicts with team members and management
	Sense of community at work	• Weaker organizational identity and cohesion among smaller NGOs, compared to lead UN agencies and large international NGOs	
Work-individual interface	*Job insecurity and insecurity over working conditions*	• Job insecurity due to short-term contracts	• National staff may be paid less compared to international staff • National staff had cited more job insecurity worries • National staff had perceived fewer career progression opportunities
	Work–life conflict	• Difficult maintaining work–life balance • Conflicts between work and home demands	• International staff had perceived more difficulties with work–life balance
Social capital	*Horizontal, vertical, and organizational trust*	• Lack of trust in leadership • Lack of accountability, justice, and fairness in organization in handling of critical incidents, conflicts, and feedback from employees	• National staff had cited inequality in treatment between international and national staff
Conflicts and offensive behaviour	*Workplace violence*	• Real and perceived gossip and slander, bullying, cyber bullying, threats of violence, and sexual harassment	

Even though national staff far outnumber international staff in many humanitarian aid organizations, national staff are often provided with less comprehensive entitlements of benefits and services (e.g., paid accommodation, health insurance, training, psychological support, and evacuation plans), compared to international staff (Ehrenreich and Elliot, 2004; Eriksson et al., 2013). Finally, national staff also reported more job insecurity due to their short-term contracts and the difficulty of renewing contracts (Strohmeier et al., 2019). A related concern among national staff is also the lack of career progression from lower grade service provisions, and the difficulty they face in proving their professionalism in the absence of additional training and certification, compared to international staff (Stoddard et al., 2011).

On the other hand, international staff may struggle more with living away from their usual social support network of family and friends. They therefore reported more concerns with maladjustment, and reported more difficulties coping with cultural and language barriers (Antares Foundation, 2012). Without a strong social support network to balance out intensive work demands, international staff reported poorer work–life balance and more conflicts with team members and management (Antares Foundation, 2012; Strohmeier et al., 2019).

Taken together, the different priority psychosocial stressors experienced by national and international staff point to different and multiple pathways of risk and resilience, as well as the need for appropriate interventions specific to each group's needs.

PREVALENCE AND DEMOGRAPHICS OF BURNOUT IN HUMANITARIAN AID WORKERS

Burnout has been identified as a significant consequence of psychosocial stress and predictor of other common mental disorders and job satisfaction among HAWs (UNHCR, 2016). As defined in the ICD-11, burnout is a 'syndrome resulting from chronic workplace stress that has not been successfully managed' (WHO, 2019: QD85) and is characterized by three dimensions: emotional exhaustion (EE), depersonalization (DP), and reduced personal accomplishment (PA) (Maslach et al., 1996, 2001). EE refers to feelings of being emotionally and physically depleted. DP touches upon the interpersonal context of burnout and is characterized by excessively distant and cynical attitudes towards recipients of service. Reduced PA is described by feelings of inefficacy and lack of achievement in one's work. In all the studies with HAWs reviewed in this section, self-reported burnout is assessed by the Maslach Burnout Inventory for Human Social Services (MBI-HSS) (Maslach et al., 1996). Burnout is measured both as a continuous variable on each dimension, as well as a dichotomous variable based on the cut-offs proposed by Maslach et al. (1996: 6) (i.e., 27 or more for EE, 13 or more for DP, and 31 or less for PA). These cut-offs indicate the upper-third percentile of the normative population used to develop the scale (Maslach et al., 1996) and are acknowledged by the authors as non-diagnostic guidelines (Maslach et al., 2018).

Overall, the prevalence of burnout among HAWs is high, with approximately 40% of HAWs experiencing high risk of burnout in at least one dimension (Eriksson et al., 2009).

This rate is comparable to that reported by US physicians (Medscape, 2020), including emergency medicine physicians (Stehman et al., 2019). Altogether, cross-sectional studies found point prevalence rates of 24–45% for EE, 9–24% for DP, and 10–43% for PA (Ager et al., 2012; Eriksson et al., 2009; Jachens et al., 2019; Strohmeier et al., 2018; UNHCR, 2001 (unpublished study cited in Welton-Mitchell, 2013: 31), 2016). In the only longitudinal study so far, international staff from NGOs were found to have a higher prevalence of depression and emotional exhaustion at post-deployment compared to pre-deployment, with symptoms persisting at three to six months follow-up (Lopes Cardozo et al., 2012). HAWs also had an increased prevalence rate of anxiety and DP at post-deployment compared to pre-deployment, but no longer at follow-up (Lopes Cardozo et al., 2012). Consistently across all studies, the number of cases of burnout (i.e., caseness defined as the score above cut-offs on all three subscales) is surprisingly low, with rates of 1–5% (Ager et al., 2012; Eriksson et al., 2009; Lopes Cardozo et al., 2013; UNHCR, 2016). This suggests that despite the unique challenges of humanitarian work and the work environment, the majority of aid workers can still mobilize protective factors and utilize coping resources to stay resilient (Eriksson et al., 2009; McKay, 2011).

Gender and Age

Female HAWs showed higher risk for EE (Ager et al., 2012) and diminished PA (Jachens et al., 2019; UNHCR, 2016) compared to their male colleagues. In addition to their multiple roles and greater involvement in care-related activities in the household, female HAWs also experience a high incidence of gender-based violence in the workplace (Stoddard et al., 2019). In 64% of the reported cases of sexual violence in an aid worker sample, the perpetrator was a colleague of the survivor (Nobert and

Williamson, 2017). These factors may contribute to more burnout and psychological distress among female HAWs.

Younger HAWs were also found to be at a higher risk of experiencing EE (Eriksson et al., 2009) and DP (Jachens et al., 2019) compared to their older colleagues. Relatedly, Lopes Cardozo's team (2012) found that aid workers who were on their first assignment were at a higher risk for developing mental health problems compared to those who had already been deployed several times. As Eriksson et al. (2009: 681) suggested, older workers may exhibit more job engagement as they represent those who have committed to aid work as a career, and may also have developed more successful coping skills for the stressors experienced at work over time.

Region of Work

Unique to this occupation group, predictors of burnout include the region of work, contract type (national or international staff), and direct work with beneficiaries. In an organization-wide survey with UNHCR staff working in all regions, it was found that employees in the Europe region and Middle East and North Africa (MENA) region were more likely to be classified as at risk for EE and DP respectively, while employees at Headquarters (HQ, Switzerland) were most likely to be at risk for both these burnout dimensions (UNHCR, 2016). Among HQ-based employees, high pressure, limited resources, low control over work, and decision-making were among reasons cited for psychological distress (UNHCR, 2015). Thus, while it has been suggested that institutionalized structures of UN and related organizations may have more resources and formalized staff support services that serve a protective function for staff (Ager et al., 2012: 719), there may also be within-organization differences based on the specific region's organizational culture that contribute as stressors. As such, socio-cultural

understandings of work culture must also be taken into account as they may influence bureaucratic processes, as well as norms of working hours, pace, and work–life balance.

Contract Type

Contract type had a weaker relationship with the burnout dimensions: international staff working in UNHCR were slightly more likely to be classified as at risk for diminished PA and EE than national staff (UNHCR, 2016). Similarly, in organizations in South Sudan, a higher although not statistically significant proportion of international staff compared to national staff reported EE (29% vs. 19%) and DP (23% vs. 18) (Strohmeier et al., 2018). These findings together point to the possibility that despite the higher number of psychosocial stressors faced (Table 21.1), national staff may be better able to mitigate these risks with more available social support, which has been consistently found to be a strong protective factor against burnout and other mental health outcomes in this group (Ager et al., 2012; Eriksson et al., 2009; Lopes Cardozo et al., 2005).

Direct Work with Beneficiaries

Working as a predictor of burnout directly with people of concern has inconsistent findings in the UNHCR (2016) study, 23 out of 26 of the respondents who were at risk for burnout on all dimensions worked directly with people of concern. However, when burnout dimensions were assessed separately, UNHCR staff who worked with people of concern were, in fact, less likely to be at risk for DP and diminished PA compared to staff who did not work directly with beneficiaries (UNHCR, 2016). It was also found among aid workers in South Sudan that working with beneficiaries was associated with lower, not higher, levels of EE (Strohmeier et al., 2018). As observational data from Staff Counselling in the HQ revealed, working far away from people of concern was in fact a reason cited for psychological distress among HQ-based employees (UNHCR, 2015).

Summary and Limitations

In sum, HAWs experience higher rates of EE and DP, similar to rates found among emergency personnel and first responders (UNHCR, 2016). Staff who are female, younger, working at the UN HQ, or international have been found to be more vulnerable to burnout. Targeted strategies and interventions can be tailored to these specific groups. Working directly with beneficiaries, contrary to expectations, did not conclusively influence higher risk of burnout among HAWs. In fact, as several qualitative studies have shown, working with beneficiaries can provide HAWs a sense of reward and reinforce a strong sense of altruistic purpose and 'giving back' (Brooks et al., 2015). This may improve HAWs self-esteem and protect them from being disengaged with their work (Jachens et al., 2018; McCormack and Bamforth, 2019). These findings together may indicate the greater importance of alleviating organizational stressors associated with managerial and coordination functions, over an emphasis on the emotional demands of working with vulnerable and distressed populations (Strohmeier et al., 2018: 14).

These figures should be interpreted with caution. Due to the low response rates (10–35%) typically received by these online surveys, these results may not adequately represent the scope of the problem. It may be that individuals with burnout would have already left the organization, or chose not to complete the survey. These studies also did not control for self-selection bias for the point of their career HAWs might decide to work at HQ, or for individual differences that may lead to the choice of working directly with beneficiaries. In addition, some groups

of HAWs may also not have been represented. For example, field-based staff with limited internet access and staff who do not read English may not have participated in these online English-language surveys. Finally, further research is required to confirm inconsistent and discrepant findings, and will benefit from being supplemented with more in-depth qualitative understandings to better explain risk and protective factors.

UTILITY OF OCCUPATIONAL HEALTH MODELS: ORGANIZATIONAL RISK AND PROTECTIVE FACTORS

Occupational health models can help conceptualize the relationship between organizational stressors and mental health and psychosocial outcomes, in order to identify appropriate risk-targeted interventions for stress-related working conditions. To understand risk and protective factors, the Effort–Reward Imbalance (ERI) model (Siegrist, 1996) and Organizational Support Theory (OST) (Eisenberger et al., 1986) are the most commonly tested occupational health models among HAWs.

Effort–Reward Imbalance Model

The ERI model has been tested with national and international HAWs in an international organization based in Geneva (Jachens et al., 2016, 2019) and with UNHCR staff (UNHCR, 2016). The ERI model posits that a lack of reciprocity between effort (i.e., working under pressure, heavy workload, and job demands) and potential rewards (i.e., financial compensation, esteem reward, promotion aspects, and job security) will lead to emotional distress, burnout, and other negative health effects (Siegrist, 1996). The model further explains individual variation by positing the moderating effect of overcommitment. Overcommitted individuals will exert disproportionate effort under low reward conditions, intensifying the negative effects of ERI (Siegrist, 1996).

There is strong evidence for the utility of ERI to explain the relationship between organizational stressors and mental health outcomes for aid workers. Studies assessing ERI found it to be a better predictor of mental health outcomes and burnout than trauma exposure. In the UNHCR (2016) study, the rates of ERI, at a global prevalence of 72%, was found to be much higher than the rates for any mental health or behavioural outcome. For UNHCR staff, each unit of increase in ERI score showed them as 4.62 times more likely to be at risk for EE; ERI also predicted risk of DP (2.32 times more) and diminished PA (1.45 times more) (UNHCR, 2016). The strong relationship between ERI and EE was also found by Jachens' team (Jachens et al., 2019), even after adjusting for secondary traumatic stress and PTSD. Indicating important gender-based differences, Jachens et al. (2019) found the associations between DP and high effort, and DP and high overcommitment were significant for females only in the fully adjusted model with covariates. In another study, Jachens et al. (2016) also found that ERI in female HAWs was associated with three times the risk for heavy alcohol consumption compared to that found with male HAWs.

Organizational Support Theory and Perceived Organizational Support

From the Organizational Support Theory (OST) perspective (Eisenberger et al., 1986), Perceived Organizational Support (POS) plays an important role in mitigating the risks of adverse psychosocial and psychological outcomes (Kurtessis et al., 2017). POS represents the level at which staff believe their organization cares about their wellbeing and values their contributions. POS was associated with lower perceived stress and greater mental wellbeing among humanitarian volunteers from the Sudanese Red Crescent Society (Aldamann et al., 2019), middle-managers in a faith-based agency (Eriksson et al., 2009), and aid workers in South Sudan (Strohmeier et al., 2018). In addition, Aldamann et al. (2019) also found that perceived helplessness and perceived self-efficacy fully mediated the relationship between POS and the mental health of humanitarian volunteers, suggesting the impact of POS on socio-emotional needs such as affiliation and self-esteem. Furthermore, evidence that low POS was related to greater psychopathology among Indonesian Red Cross community volunteers at 18 months after being deployed for the 2006 Yogyakarta earthquake response (Thormar et al., 2013), suggests that the importance of POS extends beyond the deployment period.

Team Cohesion and Manager Support

Interpersonal relationships in the workplace can be both a stressor and a protective factor. Among HAWs in South Sudan (Strohmeier et al., 2018) and national staff in Northern Uganda (Ager et al., 2012), higher levels of team cohesion with co-workers was associated with better mental health outcomes. More specifically, strong team cohesion was associated with lower levels of DP (Strohmeier et al., 2018), reinforcing the fact that effective team working can help employees to be more engaged and find meaning in their work.

Interestingly, qualitative and quantitative studies reveal different relationships between strong supervisory ties and higher team cohesion with management. Thematic analysis of interviews with aid workers employed by a UN-aligned organization showed that managers were seen to be an 'incredible source of support' in helping staff deal with work stress and overload (Jachens et al., 2018: 627). In quantitative studies, however, it was found that the presence of supervision was associated negatively with mental wellbeing (Aldamann et al., 2019). Higher levels of team cohesion with management were also associated with higher, rather than lower, levels of DP (Strohmeier et al., 2018). This unexpected finding was explained by the possibility that supervisors could be seen as agents of the organization (Eisenberger et al., 2002), and thus, more engagement with supervision may have resulted in additional stress and exhaustion (Inceoglu et al., 2018). Negative attitudes towards beneficiaries (DP) could also be prevalent among managers, which could have spillover effects on team members (De Beer et al., 2017). It may also be important to assess the aim (e.g., compliance monitoring, or mentorship and consultation) and quality of supervision, as poor supervision has been often identified in qualitative studies to contribute to more stress among aid workers (Jachens et al., 2018; Young et al., 2018).

Limitations and Recommendations for a Broad-based Psychosocial Risk Assessment

One major critique of using a single occupational stress model is that it does not capture all psychosocial stressors that HAWs are likely to be exposed to in the workplace. The effect of these combinations of stressors is likely to be additive and can explain more variance in the outcome measures than independent variables in isolation (Jachens and Houdmont, 2019). Following promising research of studying the effects of psychosocial models in combination (Calnan et al., 2004), Jachens and Houdmont (2019) tested the efficacy of the ERI model and the Job Demand-Control (JDC) model (Karasek and Theorell, 1990) separately and in combination with HAWs from a large international organization in Geneva. The JDC model posits that exposure to working conditions of high work demands and low control leads to

stress reactions. When tested in combination by developing a composite index, the two models together provided a superior estimation of the likelihood of psychological distress than what was achieved by either model independently (Jachens and Houdmont, 2019).

Furthermore, psychosocial risk assessment can also benefit from looking at organizational-level aspects rather than different aspects of job design. A qualitative study found that employees perceived an 'emergency culture' in a UN-aligned organization, where the 'constant feeling of crisis within the organization' and urgency to meet deadlines and humanitarian needs was a source of stress and also an accepted cultural norm in the organization (Jachens et al., 2018: 624). Especially given the potential of managerial support to be both a stressor and protective factor, a promising framework to assess in combination is the psychosocial climate (PSC) theory (Dollard and Bakker, 2010; Dollard et al., 2019), which evaluates senior management values and attitudes towards care and practices in relation to employee psychosocial wellbeing.

PROMOTING MENTAL HEALTH AND WELLBEING AND ADDRESSING RISK IN HUMANITARIAN AID WORKERS: EVIDENCE-BASED INTERVENTIONS AND STRATEGIES

Organizational psychosocial factors predicting HAWs' mental health and wellbeing are modifiable and changes can be implemented by aid organizations. Indeed, many aid agencies and organizations are responding to this need by developing key guidelines and actions for aid-worker wellbeing. The UN System, for example, recently developed a five-year strategy from 2018 to 2023 to optimize the mental health and wellbeing of their staff (UN, 2018), with priority actions cutting across four levels of support and intervention (IASC, 2007: 11–13), impacting individuals, colleagues and their families, the workplace environment, and organizational context (UN, 2018: 13–16). Another example guideline set out by the Antares Foundation (2012) addresses eight key principles that span the phases of humanitarian response. This section will bring together the multi-level and multi-phasic approach of these two guidelines and make recommendations for strategies based on the evidence base and implications of the results from the ERI and OST models (Table 21.2). Recommendations will also take into account the distinct needs of different groups (e.g., national and international staff, female aid workers, managers and leadership, type of aid work).

Table 21.2 Summary of prevention and intervention strategies across staff, team, and organizational levels, and various phases of deployment.

Areas of prevention and intervention		Staff level	Team and organizational level
Policy and human resource management		• Enhance reward measures • Regulate workplace demands	• Manager training for good management practices and leadership skills • Manager team-building • Continued funding and lobbying with donors for staff mental health and psychosocial support (MHPSS) • Ongoing monitoring, evaluation, and accountability for implementation of staff MHPSS policies
Security risk management		• Equitable and available security training and resources • Better amenities and basic supplies	• Invest in staff with expertise in security risk management • Improve negotiation skills and outreach capacities • Stricter internal harassment policies, especially on sexual harassment
Pre-deployment	Screening and assessment	• Screen for risk factors (e.g., previous psychiatric history, trauma history) and resilience factors (e.g., social support)	
	Training and preparation	• Provide psychosocial wellbeing, psychological first aid (PFA), critical incident response, and stress management training to all personnel	• Provide training for peer helpers and external MHPSS professionals
During humanitarian operations	Monitoring	• Ongoing monitoring for risk of burnout and psychological distress, and job-related outcomes	

Table 21.2 Summary of prevention and intervention strategies across staff, team, and organizational levels, and various phases of deployment. (*Continued*)

Areas of prevention and intervention		Staff level	Team and organizational level
	Ongoing support	• Ongoing supervision • Readily available and confidential supportive counselling, PFA, and external MHPSS referrals (including telecounselling) • Continuing education on mental health issues • Readily available needs-based training	• Implement formal peer support programmes • Supervision and support for managers, field counsellors, peer helpers, security personnel, and external MHPSS professionals • Organize work-sponsored social activities • Recreational activities in work environments (e.g., nets, balls, board games) • Ensure equitable access to staff support services for national and international staff
	Crisis intervention and support	• Readily available and confidential supportive counselling, PFA, and external MHPSS referrals (including telecounselling)	• Manager training to recognize and manage burnout symptoms in team members, to encourage help-seeking, and to build resilience in team
Post-deployment	Rehabilitation and reintegration	• Continued access to confidential psychosocial support services	• Non-stigmatizing reintegration policies after rehabilitation from mental illness or leave of absence

Protection of Safety and Risk Management

At a basic level, humanitarian aid organizations must ensure adequate and equitable security and risk management policies, as well as optimal working conditions for both national and international staff. More needs to be done to narrow disparities in the level of security training and resources (e.g., off-hours transportation, communications equipment, site security at home) that are offered to international as opposed to national staff (Stoddard, 2020). In addition, since most aid-worker attacks are committed by national-level non-state armed groups (NSAGs), Stoddard (2020) recommends that agencies invest in negotiation skills and outreach capacities with NSAGs. Furthermore, working conditions and quality of life for all staff, especially field staff, should be improved by

providing better amenities and basic supplies. These include: clean drinking water, essential medicines, protective personal equipment, reliable transportation, accommodation and workspace, and liberal internet and phone service use policies.

Pre-deployment Training

A significant pre-deployment protective factor is preparedness and training (Brooks et al., 2015), although systematic reviews of pre-deployment advice guidelines have found a lack of evidence-based literature (Costa et al., 2015; Opie et al., 2020). In an intervention study, the group of participants from disaster volunteer dispatch organizations in Japan who received pre-departure psychoeducation intervention on managing critical incident stress were less likely to be at risk for PTSD, compared to the non-intervention group at post-deployment (Okanoya et al., 2015). Pre-deployment training can also emphasize individual coping mechanisms and stress management, especially since an avoidant coping style has been significantly positively associated with PTSD, anxiety, and depression among HAWs (Eriksson et al., 2001; Lopes Cardozo et al., 2013). A one-session stress management group, which provided psychoeducation on stress reactions and coping skills (e.g., deep breathing, monitoring sleep and eating patterns, self-care, seeking social support, establishing a safe place) was found to decrease anxiety, depression, and PTSD symptoms at pre- and post-test for national humanitarian workers in the Central African Republic (De Fouchier and Kedia, 2018). As De Fouchier and Kedia (2018) illustrated in their discussion of integrating participants' conceptual model of mental health that was associated with spirit and witchcraft beliefs with neurobiological explanations of stress reactions, training has to be culturally adapted and contextually sensitive to the staff population and humanitarian context. Pre-deployment training can also anticipate the potential risks experienced differently by national and international staff, or different types of aid work (e.g., WHO and International Labour Organization, 2018), such that different support strategies and resources can be prepared and mobilized ahead of time as well.

Balancing Effort and Reward

Ongoing throughout deployment, occupational risk and protective factors can be addressed following recommendations from ERI and OST perspectives, respectively. ERI interventions can be managerial and organizational strategies that reduce the imbalance between perceived effort and reward. Examples of reward measures that have emerged as themes from two separate qualitative studies with aid workers in South Sudan (Ajieth Bunny, 2017; Strohmeier et al., 2019) include providing competitive benefit and salary packages, health insurance, recognition

for achievements, skill enhancement and professional development, and career progression opportunities. As discussed earlier, and corroborated by Strohmeier et al.'s (2019) findings, these improvements of rewards are more important to national aid staff than international aid staff.

At the same time, according to the ERI model, the simultaneous reduction of workplace demands will also help reduce adverse effects. Job demands can be regulated such as by effective distribution of workload among team members, providing sufficient paid vacation days, and allowing adaptable and flexible working schedules to achieve work–life balance.

Improving Organizational Support

From an OST perspective, POS can be improved by strengthening team cohesion with colleagues and supervisors, and building trust in leadership (Jachens et al., 2018; Young et al., 2018). Once again, it is important to consider the nuanced differences between national and international staff in what they regard as priority in terms of organizational support. As Strohmeier et al. (2019) found among aid workers in South Sudan, national staff emphasized improvements related to greater equality between employees, while international staff emphasized improvements to team cohesion. For international staff in field environments away from their families, colleagues may take on a more important role to fulfil needs for social support and companionship (Strohmeier et al., 2019). Organizations can therefore implement formal peer support programmes (e.g., UNHCR's Peer Support Personnel Network) and work-sponsored social activities, which have been found to be more utilized and perceived as more useful than formal sources of support such as in-house staff counsellors (Curling and Simmons, 2010). At the same time, equity of treatment of staff needs to be ensured, in order for national staff to feel better supported by their organizations (Strohmeier et al., 2019).

Psychosocial Safety Climate

As indicated by PSC theory, manager support determines the organizational psychosocial safety climate and can influence employees' mental health positively (Dollard et al., 2019). To improve perceived manager support and quality of management, specialized training for managers can be provided on how to improve psychosocial safety climate (e.g., recognizing and managing burnout symptoms in their team members, encouraging help-seeking), and on good management principles and skills (e.g., project planning, time management, staff motivation, assessing and providing feedback).

In addition, improved access to quality and confidential psychosocial support services was the most frequent proposal to improve organizational support and address mental health issues during deployment (Strohmeier et al., 2019). This can refer to systematically implementing wellbeing promotion programmes, universal promotion of health and wellbeing in the workplace, destigmatizing mental illness and improving levels of help-seeking, and immediate and continued access to counselling and mental health referral services that protect employee confidentiality. Othman et al. (2018) provide a promising example of an integrated staff psychosocial support programme for health staff working with internally displaced Syrians in a conflict zone in Syria in the primary health centres. Their pilot study implemented a six-month programme of group sessions addressing individual, team, organizational, and contextual challenges to resilience in the workplace. The programme reduced occupational stressors such as role ambiguity, and enhanced personal relationships with colleagues and superiors (Othman et al., 2018).

Furthermore, mental health and psychosocial interventions that have been effective for vulnerable persons in humanitarian contexts can also be adapted for HAWs as they experience similar contextual stressors. This can potentially be delivered in a stepped-care model. For example, the Adaptation and Development after Persecution and Trauma (ADAPT) model (Tay and Silove, 2016) and its domains addressing safety and security, losses and separation from loved ones, access to justice, and existential meaning, may be appropriate as a universal intervention for humanitarian staff working in post-conflict settings. Interpersonal Psychotherapy (IPT), in addition, can be adapted for treatment of more severe cases of psychological distress among HAWs who are experiencing grief, role transitions, interpersonal conflicts, and social isolation (Verdeli et al., 2003; WHO and Columbia University, 2016).

Psychosocial support also needs to extend to post-deployment, which is a time when psychological distress and post-traumatic stress symptoms often appear (Lopes Cardozo et al., 2012). A non-stigmatizing rehabilitation and reintegration into the organization and humanitarian role thus needs to be facilitated at post-deployment.

Sustainability: Funding and Accountability

Finally, an important consideration and caveat is the limited funding and financial resources dedicated to staff welfare and psychosocial support in humanitarian organizations (Strohmeier, 2018). Some recommendations to this end include ensuring that staff support funding mechanisms are sustainable (e.g., factoring staff support into overhead costs of projects), and strengthening the role of donors with evidence-based lobbying (Strohmeier et al., 2019; WHS Secretariat, 2015). It is thus important to improve monitoring and accountability by tracking the wellbeing of aid workers across all employment types through comprehensive screening and assessment, at all phases of deployment. Monitoring and evaluation should also occur at the organizational level to ensure that organizations implement and meet the indicators of evidence-based recommendations and guidelines of staff support (WHS Secretariat, 2015).

HUMANIZING WORK: CONCLUSIONS AND FUTURE DIRECTIONS

As Joan Halifax (2018) described, for personnel in the caring professions, including HAWs, what is needed to the job well may act as a double-edged sword: empathy can result in empathic distress and over-engagement in work can lead to burnout. As this chapter reviewed, in addition to high rates of critical incident exposure and secondary traumatic stress, chronic organizational psychosocial stressors also have a significant impact on the mental health, wellbeing, and job-related outcomes for HAWs. As humanitarian aid organizations begin to prioritize the protection and promotion of aid workers' wellbeing, future research should target organizational stress-related outcomes, while also taking into consideration the diverse needs of different groups of aid workers. While there are distinct challenges faced by national and international staff requiring different priority interventions, future research can also look more closely at gender-based differences, job-position level differences, and individual differences in coping styles among this occupation group to further delineate tailored interventions. More research can also be done on resilience and post-traumatic growth among HAWs, so that organizations can help staff capitalize on resilience and motivational factors, and foster greater psychosocial and psychological safety in organizational cultures.

Methodologically, research in this field will benefit from more mixed methods studies. Supplementing quantitative research with qualitative understandings will provide a more in-depth elaboration and explanation of the relationship between psychosocial stressors and psychological states that is more contextually relevant to the demographic group, humanitarian setting, and/or organization. Exploratory sequential mixed methods design can also be utilized, where qualitative studies first tease out potential mechanisms that are then tested statistically. Qualitative studies can also follow up intervention studies, to provide more nuanced understanding of attitudes towards interventions and possible mechanisms of change. In addition, more longitudinal analyses will be necessary to give more insights on the mental health sequelae, various pathways to risk and resilience across stages of deployment, and bi-directional effects that can illuminate mechanisms of change underlying stressor-health relations.

It is necessary and possible to humanize the critical work of helping others in the most vulnerable and challenging humanitarian settings. It will require a broad-based, multi-domain (i.e., personal, interpersonal, psychosocial, contextual), and multi-level (i.e., individual, team, managerial, organizational) risk assessment approach, which can inform comprehensive mental health and psychosocial support intervention guidelines and strategies in humanitarian aid organizations. An effective and accountable implementation of strategies which protect, prevent, and manage acute and chronic exposures to stress inherent in humanitarian aid work, will be worthwhile for aid workers, their families, their aid organization, and, by extension, the communities of beneficiaries they serve.

REFERENCES

Ager A, Pasha E, Yu G, Duke T, Eriksson C and Lopes Cardozo, B (2012) Stress, mental health, and burnout in national humanitarian aid workers in Gulu, Northern Uganda. *Journal of Traumatic Stress* 25(6): 713–720.

Ajieth Bunny A (2017) *Retaining skilled workers in a conflict setting: a study of human resource management approaches in international non-governmental development organizations in South Sudan.* Available here: https://researchrepository.rmit.edu.au/discovery/delivery?vid=61RMIT_INST:Researc hRepository&repId=12248298100001341# 13248381630001341 (accessed 28 June, 2020).

Aldamann K, Tamrakar T, Dinesen C, Wiede-mann N, Murphy J, Hansen M, Elsheikh Elsiddig B, Reid T and Vallière F (2019) Caring for the mental health of humanitar-ian volunteers in traumatic contexts: the importance of organisational support. *European Journal of Psychotraumatology* 10(1): 1694811.

ALNAP (2018) *The State of the Humanitarian System. ALNAP Study.* London: ALNAP/ODI. Available here: https://sohs.alnap.org/system/files/content/resource/files/main/SOHS%20Online%20Book%201%20 updated.pdf (accessed 28 June, 2020).

Antares Foundation (2012) *Managing Stress In Humanitarian Workers: Guidelines For Good Practice.* Amsterdam: Antares Foundation.

Barbelet V (2018) *As local as possible, as inter-national as necessary: Understanding capac-ity and complementarity in humanitarian action.* Overseas Development Institute.

Brooks SK, Dunn R, Sage CA, Amlôt R, Green-berg N and Rubin GJ (2015) Risk and resil-ience factors affecting the psychological wellbeing of individuals deployed in humani-tarian relief roles after a disaster. *Journal of Mental Health* 24(6): 385–413.

Burr H, Berthelsen H, Moncada S, Nübling M, Dupret E, Demiral Y, Oudyk J, Kristensen TS, Llorens C, Navarro A, Lincke H, Bocéréan C, Sahan C, Smith P, Pohrt A and International COPSOQ Network (2019) The third version of the Copenhagen Psychosocial Questionnaire. *Safety and Health at Work* 10: 482–503.

Calnan M, Wadsworth E, May M and Smit AP (2004) Job strain, effort-reward imbalance, and stress at work: competing or comple-mentary models? *Scandinavian Journal of Public Health* 32(2): 84–93.

Connorton E, Perry MJ, Hemenway D and Miller M (2012) Humanitarian relief workers and trauma-related mental illness. *Epidemio-logic reviews* 34(1): 145–155.

Core Humanitarian Standard on Quality and Accountability (2014) *CHS Alliance, Group URD and the Sphere Project*, 1–24. Available

here: https://www.mhinnovation.net/sites/default/files/downloads/resource/Core%20 Humanitarian%20Standard%20%28 CHS%29%20on%20Quality%20and%20 Accountability.pdf (accessed 28 June, 2020).

Costa M, Oberholzer-Riss M, Hatz C, Steffen R, Puhan M and Schlagenhauf P (2015) Pre-travel health advice guidelines for humani-tarian workers: A systematic review. *Travel Medicine and Infectious Disease* 13(6): 449–465.

Cox T and Griffiths A (2005) The nature and measurement of work-related stress: theory and practice. In: Wilson JR and Corlett N (eds) *Evaluation of Human Work*, 3rd edi-tion. Abingdon: Routledge.

Curling P and Simmons KB (2010) Stress and staff support strategies for international aid work. *Intervention* 8(2): 93–105.

De Beer J, Scherrer R and Rothmann I (2017) Stress, burnout and derailment and resilience in leadership. In: Johnson AJ and Veldsman TV (eds) Leadership dynamics and wellbeing: Perspectives from the front line. Randburg: KR Publishing.

De Fouchier C and Kedia M (2018) Trauma-related mental health problems and effec-tiveness of a stress management group in national humanitarian workers in the Central African Republic. *Intervention* 16: 103–109.

Development Initiatives (2019) *Global Humani-tarian Assistance Report 2019.* UK: Develop-ment Initiatives Ltd. Available here: https://reliefweb.int/sites/reliefweb.int/files/resources/GHA%20report%202019_0.pdf (accessed 28 June, 2020).

Dollard MF and Bakker AB (2010) Psychosocial safety climate as a precursor to conducive work environments, psychological health problems, and employee engagement. *Jour-nal of Occupational and Organizational Psy-chology* 83(3): 579–599.

Dollard MF, Dormann C and Idris MA (2019). *Psychosocial Safety Climate: A New Work Stress Theory.* Switzerland: Springer Nature.

Ehrenreich JH and Elliot TL (2004) Managing stress in humanitarian aid workers: a survey of humanitarian aid agencies' psychosocial training and support of staff. *Peace and Con-flict* 10(1): 53–66.

Eisenberger R, Huntington R, Hutchison S and Sowa D (1986) Perceived organizational support. *Journal of Applied Psychology* 71(3): 500–507.

Eisenberger R, Stinglhamber F, Vandenberghe C, Sucharski IL and Rhoades L (2002) Perceived supervisor support: contributions to perceived organizational support and employee retention. *Journal of Applied Psychology* 87(3): 565–573.

Eriksson CB, Bjorck JP, Larson LC, Walling SM, Trice GA, Fawcett J, Abernethy AD and Foy DW (2009) Social support, organisational support, and religious support in relation to burnout in expatriate humanitarian aid workers. *Mental Health, Religion and Culture* 12(7): 671–686.

Eriksson CB, Lopes Cardozo B, Ghitis F, Sabin M, Gotway Crawford C, Zhu J, Rijnen B and Kaiser R (2013) Factors associated with adverse mental health outcomes in locally recruited aid workers assisting Iraqi refugees in Jordan. *Journal of Aggression, Maltreatment and Trauma* 22: 660–680.

Eriksson CB, Vande Kemp H, Gorsuch R, Hoke S and Foy DW (2001) Trauma exposure and PTSD symptoms in international relief and development personnel. *Journal of Traumatic Stress* 14: 205–212.

Figley CR (2002) *Treating compassion fatigue*. New York: Brunner-Routledge.

Halifax J (2018) *Standing at the edge: finding freedom where fear and courage meet*. New York: Flatiron Books.

Inceoglu I, Thomas G, Chu C, Plans D and Gerbasi A (2018) Leadership behavior and employee well-being: an integrated review and a future research agenda. *The Leadership Quarterly* 29(1): 179–202.

Inter-Agency Standing Committee (IASC) (2007) *IASC Guidelines on Mental Health and Psychosocial Support in Emergency Settings*. Geneva: IASC. Available here: https://interagencystandingcommittee.org/system/files/legacy_files/guidelines_iasc_mental_health_psychosocial_june_2007.pdf (accessed 28 June, 2020).

Jachens L (2019) humanitarian aid workers' mental health and duty of care. *Europe's Journal of Psychology* 15(4): 650–655.

Jachens L and Houdmont J (2019) Effort-reward imbalance and job strain: a composite indicator approach. *International Journal of Environmental Research and Public Health* 16(4169): 1–9.

Jachens L, Houdmont J and Thomas R (2016) Effort-reward imbalance and heavy alcohol consumption among humanitarian aid workers. *Journal of Studies on Alcohol and Drugs* 77: 904–913.

Jachens L, Houdmont J and Thomas R (2018) Work-related stress in a humanitarian context: a qualitative investigation. *Disasters* 42(4): 619–634.

Jachens L, Houdmont J and Thomas R (2019) Effort–reward imbalance and burnout among humanitarian aid workers. *Disasters* 43(1): 67–87.

Karasek R and Theorell T (1990) *Healthy work: stress, productivity, and the reconstruction of working life*. New York: Basic Books.

Kurtessis JN, Eisenberger R, Ford MT, Buffardi LC, Stewart KA and Adis CS (2017) Perceived organizational support: a meta-analytic evaluation of organizational support theory. *Journal of Management* 43(6): 1854–1884.

Lopes Cardozo B, Crawford CG, Eriksson C, Zhu J, Sabin M, Ager A, Foy DW, Snider L, Scholte W, Kaiser R, Olff M, Rijnen B and Simon W (2012) Psychological distress, depression, anxiety, and burnout among international humanitarian aid workers: a longitudinal study. *PLoS one* 7(9): e44948.

Lopes Cardozo B, Holtz TH, Kaiser R and Gotway CA (2005) The mental health of expatriate and Kosovar Albanian humanitarian aid workers. *Disasters* 29(2): 152–170.

Lopes Cardozo B, Crawford C, Petit P, Ghitis F, Sivilli TI, Scholte WF, Ager A and Eriksson C (2013) Factors affecting mental health of local staff working in the Vanni region, Sri Lanka. *Psychological Trauma: Theory, Research, Practice, and Policy* 5(6): 581–590.

MacDonald LF and Curling P. (2004). *Caring for Us: Stress in Our Workplace*. Geneva: UNICEF.

Maslach C, Jackson SE and Leiter MP (1996) *Maslach burnout inventory manual*, 3rd edition. Palo Alto: Consulting Psychologists Press.

Maslach C, Jackson SE and Leiter MP (2018) *Maslach burnout inventory manual*, 4th Edition. Menlo Park: Mind Garden, Inc.

Maslach C, Schaufeli WB and Leiter MP (2001) Job burnout. *Annual Review of Psychology* 52: 397–422.

McCormack L and Bamforth S (2019) Finding authenticity in an altruistic identity: The 'lived' experience of health care humanitarians deployed to the 2014 Ebola crisis. *Traumatology* 25(4): 289–296.

McKay L (2011) *Resilience: building resilient managers in humanitarian organizations. Strengthening key organizational structures and personal skills that promote resilience in challenging environments. n. p.: People in Aid*. Available here: https://reliefweb.int/sites/reliefweb.int/files/resources/resilience%282%29_0.pdf. (accessed 28 June, 2020).

McWha-Hermann I and Mullins M (2018) Spotlight on humanitarian work psychology: Project FAIR – Fairness in Aid Remuneration. *The Industrial-Organizational Psychologist* 55(4). Available here: http://siop.enoah.com/tip/jan18/editor/ArtMID/13745/ArticleID/331/CategoryID/65/CategoryName/554/Spotlight-on-Humanitarian-Work-Psychology-Project-FAIR-Fairness-in-Aid-Remuneration (accessed 28 June, 2020).

Medscape (2020) *National physician burnout & suicide report 2020: the generational divide*. Chicago: American Medical Association.

Nobert M and Williamson C (2017) Duty of care: protection of humanitarian aid workers from sexual violence. *Report the Abuse*. Available here: https://reliefweb.int/sites/reliefweb.int/files/resources/RTA%20Duty%20of%20Care%20-%20Protection%20of%20Humanitarian%20Aid%20Workers%20from%20Sexual%20Violence.pdf (accessed 28 June, 2020).

Nolle I (2018) *List of publications with COPSOQ published in peer-reviewed indexed journals*. Freiburg: COPSOQ International Network.

Okanoya J, Kimura R, Mori M, Nakamura S, Somemura H, Sasaki N, Ito Y and Tanaka K (2015) Psychoeducational intervention to prevent critical incident stress among disaster volunteers. *Kitasato Medical Journal* 45: 62–68.

Opie E, Brooks S, Greenberg N and James Rubin G (2020) The usefulness of pre-employment and pre-deployment psychological screening for disaster relief workers: a systematic review. *BMC Psychiatry* 20(211): 1–13.

Othman M, Steel Z and Lawsin C (2018) Addressing occupational stress among health staff in non-government controlled Northern Syria: supporting resilience in a dangerous workplace. *Torture Journal* 28: 104–123.

Pitotti M and Clements MA (2020) *Working well? Aid worker wellbeing and how to improve it*. Geneva: CHS Alliance.

Schütte S, Chastang JF, Malard L, Parent-Thirion A, Vermeylen G and Niedhammer I (2014) Psychosocial working conditions and psychological well-being among employees in 34 European countries. *International Archives of Occupational and Environmental Health* 87(8): 897–907.

Shahpar C and Kirsch TD (2018) Who's who in humanitarian emergencies. In: Townes D, Gerber M and Anderson M (eds) *Health in humanitarian emergencies: principles and practice for public health and healthcare practitioners*. Cambridge: Cambridge University Press, pp. 25–34.

Siegrist J (1996) Adverse health effects of high-effort/low-reward conditions. *Journal of Occupational Health Psychology* 1(1): 27–41.

Stansfeld S and Candy B (2006) Psychosocial work environment and mental health: a meta-analytic review. *Scandinavian Journal of Work, Environment & Health* 32(6): 443–462.

Stehman CR, Testo Z, Gershaw RS and Kellogg AR (2019) Burnout, drop out, suicide: physician loss in emergency medicine, part I. *The Western Journal of Emergency Medicine* 20(3): 485–494.

Stoddard A (2020) *Necessary risks: professional humanitarianism and violence against aid workers*. Cham: Springer Nature.

Stoddard A, Harmer A and Haver K (2011) Aid worker security report 2011: spotlight on security for national aid workers – issues and perspectives. *Humanitarian Outcomes 3*. Available here: https://reliefweb.int/sites/reliefweb.int/files/resources/AidWorkerSecurityReport20112.pdf (accessed 28 June, 2020).

Stoddard A, Harvey, P, Czwarno M and Brekenridge M (2019) Aid worker security report 2019: Speakable – addressing sexual violence and gender-based risk in humanitarian aid. *Humanitarian Outcomes*, June. Available here: https://www.humanitarianoutcomes.org/sites/default/files/publications/awsr_2019_0.pdf (accessed 28 June, 2020).

gees (UNHCR) (2016) *Staff well-being and mental health in UNHCR*. Geneva: UNHCR.

Strohmeier H (2018) *Organizational staff support in South Sudan: an overview of current services and recommendations for future initiatives*. Edinburgh: Queen Margaret University.

Strohmeier H and Scholte WF (2015) Trauma-related mental health problems among national humanitarian staff: a systematic review of the literature. *European Journal of Psychotraumatology* 6(1): 28541.

Strohmeier H, Scholte WF and Ager A (2018) Factors associated with common mental health problems of humanitarian workers in South Sudan. *PloS one* 13(10): e0205333.

Strohmeier H, Scholte WF and Ager A (2019) How to improve organisational staff support? Suggestions from humanitarian workers in South Sudan. *Intervention: Journal of Mental Health and Psychosocial Support in Conflict Affected Areas* 17(1): 40–49.

Tay AK and Silove D (2016) The ADAPT model: bridging the gap between psychosocial and individual responses to mass violence and refugee trauma. *Epidemiology and Psychiatric Sciences* 26(2): 1–4.

Thormar SB, Gersons BPR, Juen B, Djakababa MN, Karlsson T and Olff M (2013) Organizational factors and mental health in community volunteers: the role of exposure, preparation, training, tasks assigned, and support. *Anxiety, Stress & Coping* 26(6): 624–642.

United Nations (UN) (2018) *A healthy workforce for a better world: United Nations system of mental health and well-being strategy*. Geneva: UN.

United Nations High Commissioner for Refugees (UNHCR) (2015) *Staff health watch 2015*. Geneva: UNHCR.

United Nations High Commissioner for Refugees (UNHCR) (2016) *Staff well-being and mental health in UNHCR*. Geneva: UNHCR.

Verdeli H, Clougherty KF, Bolton P, Speelman L, Lincoln N, Bass J, Neugebauer R and Weissman MM (2003) Adapting group interpersonal psychotherapy for a developing country: experience in rural Uganda. *World Psychiatry* 2(2): 114–120.

Welton-Mitchell CE (2013) *UNHCR's mental health and psychosocial support*. Geneva: UNHCR.

World Health Organization (WHO) (2007) *World Health Organization: the cluster approach*. Available here: www.who.int/hac/techguidance/tools/manuals/who_field_handbook/annex_7/en/ (accessed 28 June, 2020).

World Health Organization (WHO) (2019) *International classification of diseases for mortality and morbidity statistics*, 11th revision. Available here: https://icd.who.int/browse11/l-m/en (accessed 28 June, 2020).

World Health Organization and Columbia University (2016) *Group Interpersonal Therapy (IPT) for depression: WHO generic field-trial version 1.0*. Geneva: WHO.

World Health Organization and International Labour Organization (2018) *Occupational safety and health in public health emergencies: a manual for protecting health workers and responders*. Geneva: WHO.

World Humanitarian Summit Secretariat (2015) *Restoring humanity: synthesis of the consultation process for the World Humanitarian Summit*. New York: UN.

Young TK, Pakenham KI and Norwood MF (2018) Thematic analysis of aid workers' stressors and coping strategies: work, psychological, lifestyle and social dimensions. *Journal of International Humanitarian Action* 3(19): 1–16.

PART III

Developing Organizational Wellbeing

22

Workplace Interventions:
Individual, Team, Organizational

Ian Hesketh

INTRODUCTION

The recent COVID-19 pandemic has had a profound effect on almost all workplaces throughout the world. What is clear is that some of the traditional approaches to doing business are to be turned on their heads. The content of this chapter includes an in-depth practical exploration of the impact on the workforce, the likely workplace adaptation and the future workplace viewed through the lens of wellbeing in UK policing. Modelling previous research and evidence, this work strives to paint a picture of how wellbeing interventions can successfully be deployed in the workplace. This chapter will then consider the practical implications that provoke further research to hone and improve working life for individuals, teams and the organization. This chapter begins with a look at stress, the underpinning premise that arguably explains many of the behavioural responses experienced in the workplace. Of course, these are considerably heightened due to the impact of COVID-19. Included is a brief look at the origins and development of stress as a field of study. It is generally accepted that, despite some stress, work is generally regarded as good for people. It keeps them busy, challenges them and provides meaning and purpose. This factor has also played out in the COVID-19 pandemic, with the social value of work highlighted in relation to isolating and shielding. Underlining the principle that as well as bad stress, so called *Distress*, some amount of stress is actually good for people, termed *Eustress*.

Commonly attributed to Hans Selye, this chapter will discuss the pertinence of stress and resilience in the workplace, specifically, the signs of stress, personal resilience and the role of leaders, managers and organizations. In this chapter, resilience is viewed through the lens of positive psychology, drawing on the work of Martin Seligman and other key influencers in the positive psychology field. Having discussed the benefits of personal resilience, the extensive research in policing of Ian Hesketh and Cary Cooper is modelled, together with practical interventions to illuminate personal resilience. This chapter will then progress to develop the notion of how organizations generally can deliver meaningful training. This training is having to be done against a backdrop of extreme caution, specifically around physical distancing, unnecessary social gatherings and the general extant business appetite for education in the workplace, including the perceived exposure risks involved. The chapter will also relate practical experiences of transitioning to digital delivery and the likely future of embedding training experiences into a workforce working in parallel with both existing and future potential threats from pandemics. This includes the use of augmented and virtual reality, sometimes referred to collectively as extended reality (XR), and the practical considerations to consider when repurposing existing training practices to a new working paradigm. These practical illustrations are context sensitive, but it is hoped the examples will highlight the varying considerations that such extensive transformation brings to the workplace; even though this 'workplace' may be a 'virtual space'. This chapter concludes with some reflections on current practice and the future direction of research in this fascinating field of study, with a general acknowledgement there is a paucity in research within this academic discipline.

STRESS

Job-related stress is defined as, 'the adverse reaction people have to excessive pressures or other types of demand placed on them. There is a clear distinction between pressure, which can create a "buzz" and be a motivating factor, and stress, which can occur when this pressure becomes excessive' (HSE, 2007: 7). Stress has a profound effect on workforces across all occupations. Indeed,

policing has been described as an occupation high in emotional labour that can cause a great deal of stress (Hesketh and Cooper, 2017). Therefore, the successful recognition and management of it is critical to employee wellbeing. As noted in a quote by Killoran (2013), 'stress is not what happens to us. It's our response to what happens. And response is something we can choose'. The origin of the concept of stress is commonly attributed to the work of Hans Selye (1907–1982). Selye, an endocrinologist, was born in Vienna and grew up in Hungary. He studied for a doctorate in Prague and then later moved to study in Maryland in the United States. Selye subsequently moved to Canada to study stress at McGill University and latterly the Université de Montréal. The roots of stress are to be found in a letter Selye penned to the journal *Nature* (Selye, 1936), in which he detailed the results of his somewhat questionable experiments with rats. During these experiments he observed some seemingly odd results. The nature of the experiments, by today's research standards, are somewhat shocking (if not illegal), but the outcome of his results is that he uncovered what is now commonly accepted as *stress responses*, although Selye did not initially label it as *stress responses*, preferring to call it *general adaptation syndrome* (GAS). However, what is clear from his research is that the animals (rats) exhibited stressors, no matter what the tests involved (e.g., administering virtually any toxic substance, by physical injury, or by environmental stress). In other words, the stress response was present due to the presence of 'something' happening or about to happen [to the rats].

If accounts are to be believed, Selye was a rather clumsy scientist who regularly dropped the lab rats whilst trying to inject them, resulting in him having to chase them around his lab and recapture them. These traumatized (randomized) rats exhibited the same physiological changes as the ones that had been treated (injected), and so his [stress] theory began to emerge (Sapolsky, 2004). In this early work Selye was actually carrying out research with the aim of uncovering new sex hormones by injecting ovarian extracts into rats and witnessing changes. These changes included enlargement of the adrenal glands, thymic and lymphoid structure atrophy and bleeding ulcers in the stomach. His research clearly identified the physiological response. Selye went on to categorize how our [human] physiological reaction to stress can be viewed in three stages:

1 The Alarm Stage, when the stressor triggers the hypothalamic pituitary adrenal axis (HPA), activating the sympathetic nervous system and arousing the body's defences (i.e. fight or flight response)
2 The Resistance Stage (adaption and attempt to regain internal balance)
3 The Exhaustion Stage, which occurs only if the stress continues and the adaptation stage (2) is not successful, leading to depletion of the body's energy reserves due to the persistence of stressful events. This can lead to stress-related disorders.

What is noteworthy is that within this body of research begins the theoretical development and understanding of stress responses. The initial paper by Selye is not perhaps what contemporary academics may be accustomed to. It stretches to a mere few hundred words. However, it paved the way to uncovering the extent to which stress affects all. Particularly, Selye noted that increasing the exposure to stimuli (pain in this case) initially resulted in the deployment of coping mechanisms, 'If the treatment be continued with relatively small doses of the drug or relatively slight injuries, the animals will build up such resistance that in the later part of the second stage the appearance and function of their organs returns practically to normal' (Selye, 1936). However, this was only up to a point, whereby the subject would become exhausted, 'with further continued treatment, after a period of one to three months (depending on the severity of the damaging agent), the animals lose their resistance and succumb with symptoms

similar to those seen in the first stage, this phase of exhaustion being regarded as the third stage of the syndrome' (Selye, 1936). Thus, it appears Selye also somewhat stumbled upon the concepts of burnout and resilience, a further fascinating area of study in the field of wellbeing discussed later in this chapter.

In its very simplest form, a person experiences stress when their ability to cope (what can be classified as their resilience) is exceeded. This is obviously different in all human beings, with varying responses dependent on a whole host of variables. The *fight or flight* response is both well documented and widely cited. Originally coined by Walter Bradford Cannon, a US physiologist, in 1915 to describe an animal's responses to threats in bodily changes in pain, hunger, fear and rage (Cannon, 1915). He showed that when animals (cats in Cannon's experiments) are threatened, they discharge catecholamines, especially norepinephrine and epinephrine to prepare for the fight or the flight. Likewise, when a person (human being) experiences a stressor, this manifests as a stimulus that the brain perceives as stressful and triggers a chemical response.

Clearly, as neuroscience is developing at a burgeoning pace (and, thank goodness, employing more humane experiments), researchers and practitioners are understanding more and more about the chemicals involved and the impact of these gushes of stimuli. These chemical responses prepare the body to fight or flight, though there have been developments of the theory to include further aspects (freeze and appease). As well as activating numerous bodily systems, it also closes down several others. The stress response is predicated on the release of chemicals that mobilize the body to potentially work a lot harder. Muscles will require lots of energy immediately and in a useable form, such as glucose, fats and protein. The heart rate, blood pressure and breathing all increase to facilitate the circulation of these nutrients and oxygen around the body.

During stress, as mentioned, other bodily functions close down. Digestion shuts down, growth and reproductive systems also cease or slow significantly, as does the immune system. Thus, it can be seen that prolonged exposure to stress is undesirable and leads to what Selye describes as the exhaustion stage within the GAS model; what may now be referred to, in terms of work, as burnout.

Selye did eventually expand his thinking to humans, what he called diseases of adaptation (1946). High blood pressure and heart disease being amongst the many stress outcomes he noted. It is now generally accepted that the same occurs with psychological stressors as it does with physiological stressors, which are far more common in modern living environments (for humans that is). What is critical, in response to this knowledge and understanding, is how organizations, managers and individuals can recognize, control and even reduce stress and stressors in the workplace, or stressors attributed to work or the workplace (which now may very well be the home). This is achieved by looking at the antidote to stress, part of which is commonly accepted to be personal resilience. It is acknowledged that it is highly unlikely that a modern working environment can remove stress. What is suggested here is the notion that this can be reduced, recognized and controlled with the introduction of simple workplace interventions. These interventions centre around personal resilience, creating the right working environment and effective leadership (Hesketh and Cooper, 2017). This chapter will major on the personal resilience aspects of this trio.

RESILIENCE

The advantages of having a resilient organization, workforce, teams and individual employees are many. Personal resilience is broadly viewed as the antidote to stress. Zander et al. (2013) argue that strong personal resilience can mitigate the effects of stress. Within this chapter is a focus on personal resilience, whether that comes naturally in that you have the resilience levels you are born with, or if it can actually be learned or trained. Selye suggested the notion that there may be good stress, which he termed Eustress, as opposed to the more commonly described bad stress, or Distress (Selye, 1984). Luthans suggests [personal] resilience is 'the capacity to bounce back from adversity, conflict, failure or even positive events, progress and increased responsibility' (Luthans, 2002: 702). Academics have toyed with the notion of work as a social function, in that it can be viewed in a number of ways. According to Wrzesniewski and Dutton (2001: 184), 'people with jobs focus on financial rewards for working, rather than pleasure or fulfilment; those with careers focus primarily on advancement; and those with callings focus on enjoyment of fulfilling, socially useful work'. This distinction is, for many, really important in how stress and personal resilience are considered in the workplace. Therefore, it seems sensible to view that the way one personally considers work impacts greatly on how they function. Do individuals or teams transact with it (work for financial gain only, for example), or are they submersed in it (a so-called 'calling')? This intersects with the notion of flow, as described by Seligman in his description of positive psychology in the workplace, 'engagement is about flow: being one with the music, time stopping, and the loss of self-consciousness during an absorbing activity' (2011: 11). Here, Seligman suggests that time almost stands still when one is absorbed by a task, engaged in work and being fulfilled by it. This would require little personal resilience as the work is clearly enjoyable, rewarding and worthwhile, as in the idiom, 'time flies whilst you're having fun'. This also connects directly to the key wellbeing tenets of meaning and purpose (Ryff and Keyes, 1995), which it is suggested underpin personal resilience. When work is challenging, the meaning and purpose one gains from it can bring extra satisfaction. 'We must never forget that we may also find meaning in life even when confronted with a hopeless situation' (Frankl, 1963: 6).

Therefore, if work does not do this for the individual, for whatever reason, their ability to cope, their resilience, may be stretched. The analogy of the elasticity of resilience has also been used to describe its precarious state (Lazarus, 1993). This is also supported by Vaillant (2002: 285), who described the elastic properties of resilience as, 'A twig with a fresh, green living core. When twisted out of shape, such a twig bends but it does not break; instead it springs back and continues growing'. Further, Haglund et al. (2007: 899) suggest, 'resilience refers to the ability to successfully adapt to stressors, maintaining psychological wellbeing in the face of adversity'. So, what makes a person resilient? The resilience factors developed by Southwick and Charney (2012) suggests ten areas that impact on personal resilience:

1 Optimism
2 Facing Fears
3 Moral Compass
4 Drawing on Faith
5 Supportive Networks
6 Role Models
7 Regular Training
8 Brain Fitness
9 Cognitive and Emotional Flexibility
10 Meaning, Purpose and Growth.

These ten elements have been developed by various academics and business consultants over the years. The developments have been largely due to the recognition that people may not necessarily all have been a prisoner of war, experienced great trauma or tragedy as in Southwick and Charney's analogies. However, the underpinning philosophy of what can impact on personal resilience appears to have remained sound, even for those with routine day to day challenges of family, commuting, IT, fatigue and so on, all of which impact on work and the workplace of course.

The question now is how do people learn these coping mechanisms and tweaks to lifestyle that can improve personal resilience? This next section examines training and considers the additional difficulties brought about by the pandemic.

TRAINING

The issue of training to support employees in the work they are being asked to perform is significant. It is important to the individual, the team they are being asked to work in and the organization as a whole. This can be in relation to Health and Safety, organizational objectives such as targets, or even part of corporate social responsibility, to name but a few. In terms of policing, it may be considered of even greater significance due to the challenges police officers and police staff members may face. At the crisis end of this spectrum it could lead to their career end 'when people in high-risk occupations sustain psychological injury in the normal course of their work, the sequelae of trauma-related health issues can cause them to become no longer employable in such roles' (Thompson and Dobbins, 2018: 23).

The question of resilience training efficacy has been the subject of much debate over recent years. In 2015, a systematic review identified that there had been no meaningful synthesis of resilience training efficacy from 2003–2014 (Robertson et al., 2015). However, since this date there has been extensive research to provide a strong argument that resilience training, in a policing context at least, is highly effective (Hesketh et al., 2015, 2018, 2019, Hesketh and Cooper, 2020; Smith et al., 2015). This is further supported in a more recent systematic review of resilience training in high-risk occupations (Brassington and Lomas, 2020).

With respect to the consequences of the COVID-19 outbreak, traditional classroom delivery training options are clearly in need of review. However, first this section will focus on the efficacy of training, in this case by providing practical examples from programmes in the UK police service. This will hopefully illuminate the theoretical principles being used in practice, illustrating what works well and what needs to be developed. It is important to point out that notions of wellbeing are context sensitive and here the modelling is conducted in what is a physically and psychologically highly volatile environment, that of policing. It is set in an occupation that works seven days a week and around the clock to, primarily, keep citizens safe from harm and to facilitate a lawful society. On top of this, police are also required to perform a plethora of other roles of which there are far too many to mention.

Firstly, and to set the scene, policing in the UK has undergone radical change in the period 2010–2019. The date purposely stops shorts of the date of the COVID-19 outbreak, which is discussed in more depth in the following sections, as it is not, in all honesty, possible to comprehend the upheaval of the pandemic set against any sensible comparator, it is one in its own. Although what this essentially describes is a period of long and painful austerity and transformation, the nine years cannot be compared to the five months of lockdown the country (UK), at the time of writing, is emerging from. The pre-COVID-19 (2010–2019) period's pressures and volatility have been largely attributable to government-imposed economic cutbacks and the subsequent downsizing in all areas of policing that followed, so-called austerity measures. Although this is now seemingly reversing, to meet those challenges many emergency service organizations in the UK, including the police, had to make drastic cutbacks in support functions in an effort to keep the 'frontline' fully staffed (around 20% is commonly reported, although this changes from police force to police force in the UK). As a direct consequence, there has also been a considerable decrease in overall wellbeing reported across police officers and police staff members. For example, according to MIND, a mental health charity, 70.4% of UK police personnel had personal experience of mental health problems (MIND, 2019a).

Resilience training research (Hesketh et al., 2018, 2019) has centred on the assumption that resilience is based on personal characteristics and skills that can be learned and developed through appropriate and professionally delivered training. The characteristics and skills involved in these interventions included building personal levels of resilience and managing wellbeing in a workplace setting. The objectives were for training attendees to understand resilience and to learn how to build and maintain resilience, both in themselves and others. Input on how to recognize signs of stress, what areas of personality help or hinder resilience and how social support can play a defining role were all contained within the training programmes. These programmes included a mixture of presentations framing the resilience factors mentioned earlier (Southwick and Charney, 2012) and examples from practice to breathe life into the theory. To solidify the thinking on personal resilience and to bring the subject to life in a practical setting, delegates at these training sessions were also asked to consider their own situations, to fill the training with real world examples. The sessions also included a number of case studies and interactive tasks to probe attendees' understanding and encourage critical thinking and inspire them to further share their own experiences for the benefit of others. A later (post-training) survey of police officers and police staff was conducted, using a wellbeing psychometric instrument called A Short Stress Evaluation Tool (ASSET) (Faragher et al., 2004). The survey was carried out by officers and staff who had attended the training programmes, along with a sample who had not for comparison. The questions in the ASSET survey instrument captured attitudes and perceptions that are known to cause stress in the workplace. These are referred to as the six essentials (Cooper et al., 2005) and are:

1   Resources and Communications
2   Control
3   Work Relationships
4   Balanced Workloads
5   Job Security and Change
6   Job Conditions.

The survey findings clearly showed that improvements in relation to measures of Resources and Communications, Control, Work Relationships, Balanced Workload, Work–life Balance, Job Conditions, Engagement, Commitment of Employees to Organization, and Perceived Commitment of Organization Towards Employees are clearly evident for those who had undertaken resilience training compared to those who had not. A further resilience study worthy of note was conducted by Davies et al. (2008). This investigated the profile of resilience in a sample of community first responders who were trained in defibrillation. What stands out is that the study identified a resilience phenomenon accounted for by certain enabling core beliefs about their role, their capacity and about the meaning of negative and positive outcomes for themselves. It seems that, adding to Southwick and Charney's inventory, the ability to act with emotional detachment appears a further resilience mechanism. This mindset seemed to protect the community first responders (essentially, they were volunteers) against the development of adverse reactions to stress or from becoming unduly concerned about negative outcomes. The responders were capable of operating with a high degree of naturally occurring resilience to stress or undermining anxiety.

Further research on resilience and spirituality somewhat supports why this resilience phenomenon may transpire (Smith et al., 2015). Again, this intervention employed ASSET to probe the results and here it was observed Southwick and Charney's element of faith combining with a sense of striving for meaning and purpose in life, or duty to the

public in the police case. On the surface, the survey results may not seem to relate to the aspects of meaning, purpose and faith. However, there was a deeper look into the issues and the factors that underpin them, issues such as feeling part of a community, feeling supported, recognized, important and valued, feeling connected to others and feeling work has meaning and purpose. These aspects begin to highlight the fact that aspects connected to meaning, purpose and faith may underpin many of them. If this is the case, then it would seem prudent to consider the range of other aspects of resilience that assist in coping with the high levels of stress now being regularly encountered in many workplaces, and not just policing, as in this example. Having established an effective classroom delivery mechanism for resilience training that was being socialized up and down the country in numerous UK police forces, the COVID-19 outbreak and associated restrictions forced a rethink of the entire delivery mechanism. The following section provides the science and paints a picture of the practical situations faced by UK policing. Of course, the biggest issue is that policing cannot simply lockdown, isolate and shield en masse.

COVID-19

The global impact of the outbreak, which is unprecedented in its severity and transmissibility, has meant that organizations have had to rapidly and strategically review a whole host of workplace issues, if not ALL workplace issues. As stated by the UN Deputy-Secretary-General Amina J. Mohammed in 2020, 'as the world wrestles with the unprecedented implications of the COVID-19 coronavirus pandemic, we are facing a human crisis unlike any we have experienced, and our social fabric and cohesion is under stress'. Phrases such as social distancing, isolating, shielding, furloughing, flattening the curve, the 2 metre rule, face masks, frequent handwashing, lockdown, social bubbles, antibody and antigen tests are all now common parlance. Amazingly, although all are now common household phrases, these were almost all unknown or little used prior to the turn of 2020. A few months has literally turned the world on its head.

On 11 March 2020, the World Health Organization (WHO) declared the Novel Coronavirus 2019, which came to be known as COVID-19, a global health pandemic (WHO, 2020). The initial epicentre was reported as Wuhan Hubei province, China (Wu et al., 2020).

COVID-19 causes severe acute respiratory syndrome coronavirus 2; SARS-CoV-2 previously known as 2019-nCoV. The severity of the virus is higher in older patients and disproportionately affects people with comorbidities. However, there have been fatalities amongst perfectly healthy young people.

COVID-19 has spread rapidly throughout the world. The first televized scenes in the UK of the devastation caused by COVID-19 came from Northern Italy and were quickly followed by equally traumatic images from other countries, as they frantically searched for strategies to at least suppress the virus. These measures centred on the so-called 'flattening the curve', in which drastic attempts were being made to slow the rates and spread of infection, reducing fatalities and protecting global healthcare systems from being overwhelmed. Indeed, in the UK, in government messaging around the pandemic a strong emphasis was placed on protecting the National Health Service (NHS) from being effectively overwhelmed. This element continued to feature throughout the response and is clearly still a worry. The first occupations to fully experience the severity of the outbreak were accident and emergency intensive care units that immediately flagged the urgent requirements for extra bed resources and ventilators. A global emergency shortage of personal protection equipment (PPE) followed almost immediately, as did an initial

run on supermarkets, citizens worrying about depleting stocks of household commodities and food. The global panic played out through media channels across the globe and still is, to some extent. Some healthcare professionals had previous valuable experience in dealing with previous outbreaks such as SARS and MERS. Although all those called to respond to the public health emergency experienced heightened workload demands, increased exposure and an elevated risk of infection, many paid the ultimate price for their dedication and commitment (see, for example, Waldrop, 2020). During the SARS outbreak, one in five cases globally were healthcare workers (Chan-Yeung, 2004). Although the numbers for the COVID-19 outbreak have yet to be totalled, it is entirely probable the vulnerability of Emergency Services Responders will take a similar path. Like any other member of the public, the police are at risk of being exposed to the virus.

The difference is that police must respond to calls, which, in most cases, means dealing with unknown situations. In a normal state of affairs policing typically involves situations in which physical violence is involved. What is being increasingly seen are occurrences of psychological damage, with perpetrators claiming to be infected with COVID-19 spitting at officers or shouting in their face. As such, there is the emergence a new form of post-traumatic stress developing in the shadows of COVID-19. Research on effective interventions (Hesketh and Tehrani, 2018a, 2018b; Richens et al., 2020) has a new and challenging dynamic to consider in the realm of post-incident trauma interventions. As this develops, there is a need to critically rethink and consider how to socialize it within policing so that the guidance is understood and usable. At the time of writing, the notion of classroom delivery (for any form of training) is not a favourable option. The majority of western countries are in the recovery phase of the pandemic and are looking to reduce gatherings of people when possible, recommending social distancing as a normal way of life and embarking on area shutdowns for outbreaks accompanied by trace, track and isolate measures in response. Therefore, organizations must look to alternate methods of delivering guidance, education and training programmes within their businesses. This is discussed in further detail in the following section.

DIGITAL DELIVERY

One of the options organizations are seriously considering is a wholesale move onto digital delivery platforms. COVID-19 has effectively pushed this agenda to the forefront within most public facing organizations. Research into the use of mobile apps and digital gadgetry use has painted a picture of the state of research within the field in emergency service work in the UK (Marston et al., 2020). To summarize, it is fair to say that this is limited. However, as with most public service organizations within the UK, the police are striving to bridge that space. The use of MS Teams, Zoom, SKYPE and Blackboard have all been quickly adapted to fill the void. However, there are already signs being exhibited that the workforce is becoming tiresome of online meetings and training sessions.

The National Police Wellbeing Service (NPWS), which is discussed in the case study that follows, is looking at the benefits of Virtual and Augmented reality, known collectively as XR. To distinguish, virtual reality is where users wear a headset and are fully immersed in computer-generated environments, commonly seen in gaming. Augmented reality is where computer images are superimposed onto the user's view of the real world, through a screen or headset. Although augmented reality is a more complex challenge, as it requires scenarios simulating within the software. However, the realism this provides offers police officers and staff an immersive experience where they can make mistakes without risk, hone their skills and learn new techniques. This

also fulfils distancing requirements and therefore does not expose them to unnecessary health risks. Pokémon Go is an example of where these are integrated as one (XR), though quite how policing would utilize this is unclear; at this point in time at least! With global spending on XR technology forecast (pre COVID-19) to increase by 78.5% in the forthcoming year (Marr, 2020), these technologies will be key for organizations that are looking for alternatives to digital delivery. As these expand there is likely to be an influx of new solutions offering even greater immersion and realism, as well as innovative use of case-based simulations to further heighten the trainee experience.

As illustrated in the next section, a full programme of work is mapped out to facilitate full digital delivery of service offerings within policing. How this transpires, of course, will depend very much on the direction the virus takes. Two realistic scenarios would be, firstly, in response to a global vaccination programme, where it is effectively eradicated. The second would be one in which the public lives side by side with the virus for many years to come. This second scenario, which may include future outbreaks of a similar nature, would see a substantial urgency placed around digital delivery, or non face-to-face delivery, whatever that may look like. Many organizations are now seeking to, at the very least, have some online digital presence and an alternative to traditional classroom-based learning solutions. The aim of many, including policing, is to look to programmes that are focused on augmented and virtual reality solutions along with self-study and digital online training. To provide insight, the programme of work being undertaken by the NPWS is discussed in the next section.

CASE STUDY

By way of background, the Police in England and Wales employs approximately 211,400 people. In 2019 this was made up of 122,400 police officers, 62,800 police staff, 10,100 police community support officers, 4,400 designated officers and 11,700 special constables. Police Scotland has a further 17,430 police officers and 5,709 police staff. The Police Service of Northern Ireland has 6,855 police officers and 2,392 police staff (Gov. UK, 2020a). The UK government has announced an uplift of a further 20,000 police officers to this number (Gov.UK, 2020b). Wellbeing is a relatively new phenomenon in UK policing, having only been a subject of interest since the early 2010s. The introduction of the National Police Wellbeing Service (NPWS) and its associated digital platform Oscar Kilo (OK) has revolutionized the way police officers or police staff in the UK address many issues related to wellbeing. These are on an individual, team and organizational level. The objective of the NPWS is to strive to enhance working environments in health and wellbeing in police officers and staff throughout the UK. A significant part of this is the responsibility to quickly expedite how to focus on optimizing live service digital delivery to enhance these efficiencies further.

Illustrating the need for wellbeing services in UK police populations, it soon becomes apparent why the continuous development and implementation of wellbeing interventions is so critical for policing. Although, in this chapter the research modelled is from the UK, a broader search will reveal a similar picture globally. There is an important caveat to all of the findings detailed below, in that they were conducted pre COVID-19. At the time of writing there have been no significant peri- or post-COVID-19 survey results. There have been numerous 'snap-shots' conducted but these have not been reported here, largely due to concerns over the reliability of flash surveys.

A 2019 survey (n = 5,081) of emergency service staff and volunteers conducted by the UK mental health charity MIND revealed that 67% of respondents reported they had lived experience of mental health problems, more than double that of the UK workforce in general (MIND, 2019b). A survey (n = 16,857) of serving UK police officers and staff in 2018 conducted by the University of Cambridge and sponsored by Police Care UK found that 90% of respondents reported being exposed to trauma. Of this, 98% was reported as being work-related. The analysis suggested that of the officers/staff who had experienced trauma, about 20% would be diagnosable as suffering from PTSD or complex PTSD (Miller, 2018).

As part of the NPWS, the programme commissioned the first national survey of all police agencies in the UK (n = 34,529). The objective of this survey was to establish nuances in wellbeing between police service departments within policing, as well as rank and grade differentials, tenure, sex and other factors within policing that impacted on wellbeing. Of the 15 police officer occupational job types we considered, those that were involved with safeguarding the public and criminal investigations reported the lowest average levels of wellbeing overall. For the police staff occupational job types, those who worked in custody, prisoner reception and contact management departments, such as those within communications rooms, reported the lowest average levels of wellbeing when compared to that of 18 other police staff occupational roles. It was considered these occurrences of low levels of energy were indicative of individuals facing substantial stressors within the workplace. Police officers reported moderately low average levels of emotional energy, whilst police staff reported moderate average levels of energy. On average, police officers reported lower levels of mental health than police staff. The average scores for the frequency of experiencing post-traumatic stress symptoms suggest that police officers and police staff are exposed to stressful or traumatic experiences in work (Graham et al., 2020). This supports the findings from what MIND (2019b) and Miller (2018) reported.

In response to the findings and an abundance of other information garnered over years, the NPWS has launched eight live service offerings, as below:

1 Leadership for Wellbeing: developing Executive Leaders and Line Managers who can lead and manage their organizations in a way which facilitates wellbeing and improves performance
2 Individual Resilience: building individual resilience of officers and staff by developing their understanding and use of positive psychology, and other techniques, to enhance personal wellbeing and improve their ability to support others
3 Peer Support for Wellbeing: delivering a national peer support model and network in order to provide the best care and support to Officers and Staff
4 Psychological Risk Management: high-risk roles are screened for potential psychological trauma and wellbeing screening is available for all
5 Trauma Management: providing a police-specific post-incident support and disaster management model of care for officers and staff that provides clear strategic and tactical direction specific to wellbeing when dealing with major incidents. Known as Emergency Services Intervention Programme (ESTIP).
6 Wellbeing at Work: Occupational Health support, advice and liaison. Post-inspection peer support
7 Mobile Wellbeing Outreach Service: providing access to Wellbeing Services at the place of work, in order to increase the opportunity to access wellbeing services. These have been particularly useful during the COVID-19 pandemic
8 Physical Wellbeing: Including fitness mentoring and initiatives in terms of contemporary approaches with police charities and collaborations with several UK Universities.

The eight elements all begin by providing workshops, materials, toolkits and an online network to build the skills and abilities of executives, senior, middle and first line managers. Due to COVID-19 this has become increasingly problematic. It is clear that there is an immediate need to move towards digital delivery channels. On top of the above eight live services there has been an ambitious plan of capability development. These new capabilities will allow policing to address such issues as fatigue and shift pattern management, which has been a concern for most emergency services workers over a number of years, with a requirement to work around the clock in response to the demands placed upon the services. There is also an ambition to enhance live service number eight (above), which hinges around physical wellbeing. There is a live piece of work in development looking at numerous options with regard to physical activity within policing. The third piece of capability development involves the strategic health relationships with other emergency service and NHS providers, and how these cohere with our occupational health offerings within the UK. The final two capabilities hinge around developing digital capability, as mentioned throughout this chapter, and is an area that is considered of optimum importance. Finally, a data analytics project is considering how to use data to inform best practice.

PRACTICAL IMPLICATIONS

As policing is a UK public sector organization, there is the need to consider how to eventually deliver these digital services. To this end, there are many considerations. These include, but are not limited to, issues of budget, procurement, stakeholder alignment, diverse user needs, legal, technological, data capture and storage constraints. What has then to be considered, of course, is piloting, testing and refining a final product that is fit for purpose in an extremely volatile and ambiguous working environment. These then have to be evaluated to confirm they are usable in the setting intended and are providing good value for money. To achieve all this, the NPWS forms small teams which include several subject matter experts, service users from all levels of the organization, business planning teams that include experts in procurement, digital delivery, communications and engagement specialists. A small team of programme planners and programme managers is also required, as well as strategic oversight, including financial expertise and senior service users. These, of course, include executives for final sign off. These are all practical requirements when conceiving, creating, developing and delivering any new service to public sector organizations within the UK. When these programme plans go well, the findings from this research support the position that this impacts significantly on the wellbeing of officers, staff and extended service users such as contractors and service partners.

CONCLUSION AND FUTURE DIRECTIONS

To provide some headlines as to the priorities for UK policing, and this is most likely relevant for many organizations, the main points of focus are as follows. Within the NPWS there is an urgency to develop digital, remote, augmented, virtual and essentially distant offerings. As Marston et al. (2020) argue, 'although the NPWS offers a broad approach to supporting the health and wellbeing of policing personnel it tends to rely on reasonably traditional, e.g. face to face, mechanisms of support and does not, at least explicitly, incorporate more contemporary, digital solutions'. Moving forward, NPWS aims to provide clinical governance for Occupational Health standards and a strategic liaison with the NHS. This coheres with the vision of a Police Covenant and responds to the UK government consultation into Front Line Policing carried out earlier in the year (Graham et al., 2019). This consultation recommended, amongst many other things, that a Chief Medical Officer and Health and Safety lead be recruited into the NPWS. The NPWS programme has engaged with the UK Government Home Office to ratify the support of the Department for Health and Social Care (DHSC) and NHS England in order to

formalize NPWS as the delivery channel for the 'Health and Wellbeing' element of the Police Covenant. Although these references are set in the context of policing, the underpinning concepts and workplace challenges are relevant to organizations in all sectors of industry; see for example the work of the National Forum for Health and Wellbeing at Work (Cooper and Litchfield, 2015). All share the desire to meet the challenges both the modern working environment and the COVID-19 pandemic have provided.

Hopefully this chapter has provided some insight into stress and the impact of good levels of personal resilience in the workplace, all set against a working environment coping with the impact of the COVID-19 pandemic. This chapter has strived to emphasize how difficult it is to conduct any meaningful training within organizations when social distancing measures and other virus protection interventions are in place. Quite rightly, organizations prioritize the wellbeing of their employees, volunteers and associates above classroom training requirements. In the horizon-scanning activities conducted for this chapter, this has been recognized and acknowledged. It is hoped that the benefit of transitioning to digital service delivery is clearly illustrated here. The progress made in terms of technical aspects of working life have been accelerated enormously due to the COVID-19 outbreak in all sectors. It is the ambition that NPWS will move quickly to embrace new technologies as an alternative to traditional learning environments, namely augmented and virtual reality, as a method of delivering training within police populations. However, this will take an enormous amount of consideration, planning and testing for suitability and scalability, not to mention the generational impacts we have witnessed in the launch of other tech-dependent initiatives. The challenges are there for all and it is hoped this chapter has provided some practical guidance on the considerations and approaches available together with the underpinning rationale for such transformation.

REFERENCES

Brassington, K. and Lomas, T. (2020). Can resilience training improve wellbeing for people in high-risk occupations? A systematic review through a multidimensional lens. *The Journal of Positive Psychology*, DOI: 10.1080/17439760.2020.1752783.

Cannon, W. B. (1915). *Bodily Changes in Pain, Hunger, Fear and Rage: An Account of Recent Researches into the Function of Emotional Excitement*. New York and London: Appleton.

Chan-Yeung, M. (2004). Severe acute respiratory syndrome (SARS) and healthcare workers. *International Journal of Occupational Environmental Health*, 10, 421–427.

Cooper, C., Cartwright, S. and Robertson, S. (2005). Work environments, stress, and productivity: an examination using asset. *International Journal of Stress Management*, 12, 4, 409–423.

Cooper, C. and Litchfield, P. (2015). *The National Forum for Health and Wellbeing at Work*. Available at: www.alliancembs.manchester.ac.uk/research/health-wellbeing-forum/ Accessed 17/07/2020.

Davies, E., Maybury, B., Colquhoun, M., Whitfield, R., Rossetti, T. and Vetter, N. (2008). Public access defibrillation: psychological consequences in responders. *Resuscitation*, 77, 2, 201–206.

Faragher, E. B., Cooper, C. L. and Cartwright, S. (2004). A shortened stress evaluation tool (ASSET). *Stress and Health*, 20, 189–201.

Frankl, V. (1963). *Man's Search for Meaning: An Introduction to Logotherapy*. Boston MA: Beacon Press.

Gov.UK. (2020a). *Police Workforce England and Wales Statistics*. Available at: www.gov.uk/government/collections/police-workforce-england-and-wales Accessed 24/07/2020.

Gov.UK. (2020b). *Police Officer Uplift Statistics*. Available at: www.gov.uk/government/collections/police-officer-uplift-statistics Accessed 24/07/2020.

Graham, L., Plater, M., Brown, N., Zheng, Y. and Gracey, S. (2019). *Research into Workplace Factors, Wellbeing, Attitudes and Behaviour in Policing: Summary of Evidence and Insights*. Presented for the Front-Line Review of Policing. London: Home Office. Available at: http://library.college.police.uk/docs/Research_into_Workplace_Factors_Well-being_Attitudes_and_Behaviour_in_Policing.pdf Accessed 06/11/2020.

Graham, L., Plater, M., Brown, N., Zheng, Y., Gracey, S., Weinstein, N. and Legate, N. (2020). *National Police Wellbeing Survey 2019*. Available at: https://oscarkilo.org.uk/wp-content/uploads/2020/06/ISSUED-2019-National-Police-Wellbeing-Survey-1.pdf Accessed 17/07/2020.

Haglund, M., Nestadt, P., Cooper, S., Southwick, S. and Charney, D. (2007). Psychobiological mechanisms of resilience: relevance to prevention and treatment of stress-related psychopathology. *Development and Psychopathology*, 19, 3, 889–920.

Health & Safety Executive (HSE). (2007). *Managing the Causes of Work-Related Stress. HSE Management Standards*. Available at: https://safetyresourcesblog.files.wordpress.com/2014/10/managing-the-causes-of-work-related-stress-a-step-by-step-approach-using-management-standards.pdf Accessed 13/07/2020.

Hesketh, I. and Cooper, C. (2017). *Managing Health and Well-Being in the Public Sector: A Guide to Best Practice*. London: Routledge Psychology Press.

Hesketh, I. and Cooper, C. (2019). *Wellbeing at Work: How to Design, Implement and Evaluate an Effective Strategy*. London: Kogan Page.

Hesketh, I. and Cooper, C. (2020). Stress and well-being of police officers. In: Burke, R. J. and Pignata, S. (eds) *Handbook of Research on Stress and Well-being in the Public Sector*. Cheltenham: Edward Elgar Publishing. 260-275

Hesketh, I., Cooper, C. and Ivy, J. (2015). Well-being, austerity and policing: is it worth investing in resilience training? *Police Journal: Theory, Practice and Principles*, 88, 3, 20–30.

Hesketh, I., Cooper, C. and Ivy, J. (2018). Asset rich, peelers poor: measuring and efficacy of resilience training in policing. *Australian Journal of Evidence Based Policing*, 3, 3, 31–38.

Hesketh, I., Cooper, C. and Ivy, J. (2019). Leading the asset: resilience training efficacy in UK policing. *Police Journal: Theory, Practice and Principles*, 92, 1, 56–71.

Hesketh, I. and Tehrani, N. (2018a). *Psychological Trauma Risk Management in the UK Police Service*. Oxford: Oxford University Press.

Hesketh, I. and Tehrani, N. (2018b). The role of psychological screening for emergency service responders. *International Journal of Emergency Services*. https://doi.org/10.1108/IJES-04-2018-0021.

Killoran, M. (2013). in Pestonjee, D. and Pandey, S. (eds) *Stress and Work: Perspectives on Understanding and Managing Stress*. New Delhi: Sage, Chapter 2 The Neuropsychology of Stress. Rajeswaran, J., and Bennett, C. p 15.

Lazarus, R. (1993). From psychological stress to the emotions: a history of changing outlooks. *Annual Review of Psychology*, 44, 1–21.

Luthans, F. (2002). The need for and meaning of positive organizational behavior. *Journal of Organizational Behavior*, 23, 695–706.

Marr, B. (2020). *The 5 Biggest Virtual and Augmented Reality Trends in 2020 Everyone Should Know About*. Available at: www.forbes.com/sites/bernardmarr/2020/01/24/the-5-biggest-virtual-and-augmented-reality-trends-in-2020-everyone-should-know-about/#7bee3f9224a8 Accessed 17/07/2020.

Marston, H., Hadley, R., Pike, G. and Hesketh, I. (2020). Games for health & mental health apps for police & blue light personnel: a scoping review. *Police Journal: Theory, Practice and Principles*, DOI: 10.1177/0032258X20937327.

Miller, J. (2018). *Establishing the Evidence Base: 'Policing: The Job & The Life' Survey*. Available at: www.policingtrauma.sociology.cam.ac.uk/survey Accessed 15/07/2020.

MIND. (2019a). *Wellbeing and Mental Health Support in the Emergency Services: Our Learning and Key Recommendations for the Sector*. Available at: www.mind.org.uk/media-a/4571/bluelight-programme-legacy-report_english-summary.pdf Accessed 15/07/2020.

MIND. (2019b). *Mental Health in the Emergency Services: Our 2019 Survey Results – Police Service*. Available at: www.mind.org.uk/media-a/4849/2019-survey-police-service-summary.pdf Accessed 15/07/2020.

Mohammed, A. (2020). *Digital Meeting of the UN Forum COVID Action Programme 8th April, 2020*. Available at: www.weforum.org/agenda/2020/04/covid-19-action-call-8-apr/ Accessed 17/07/20.

Richens, M., Gauntlett, L., Tehrani, N., Hesketh, I., Weston, D., Carter, J. and Amlot, R. (2020). Early post-trauma interventions in organizations: a scoping review. *Frontiers in Psychology*, DOI: 10.3389/fpsyg.2020.01176.

Robertson, I., Cooper. C., Sarkar, M. and Curran, T. (2015). Resilience training in the workplace from 2003 to 2014: a systematic review. *Journal of Occupational Psychology*, 88, 3, 533–562.

Ryff, C. and Keyes, C. (1995). The structure of psychological well-being revisited. *Journal of Personality and Social Psychology*, 69, 4, 719–727.

Sapolsky, R. M. (2004). *Why Zebras Don't Get Ulcers*, 3rd ed. New York: Melia.

Seligman, M. E. P. (2011). *Flourish: A Visionary New Understanding of Happiness and Well-Being*. Free Press.

Selye, H. (1936). A syndrome produced by diverse nocuous agents. *Nature*, 138, 3479, 32.

Selye, H. (1946). The general adaptation syndrome and the diseases of adaptation. *Journal of Endocrinology*, 17, 4, 231–247.

Selye, H. (1984). *The Stress of Life*. New York: McGraw-Hill.

Smith, J., Hesketh, I. and Charles, G. (2015). Developing understanding of the spiritual aspects to resilience. *International Journal of Public Leadership*, 11, 1, 34–45.

Southwick, S. and Charney, D. (2012). *Resilience: The Science of Mastering Life's Greatest Challenges*. Cambridge: Cambridge University Press.

Thompson, S. R. and Dobbins, S. (2018). The applicability of resilience training to the mitigation of trauma-related mental illness in military personnel. *Journal of the American Psychiatric Nurses Association*, 24, 1, 23–34.

Vaillant, G. (2002). *Aging Well: Surprising Guideposts to a Happier Life from the Landmark Harvard Study of Adult Development*. New York: Little, Brown.

Waldrop, T. (2020). *New York City Police Department Has Lost 29 Members to COVID-19*. Available at: www.cnn.com/2020/04/19/

us/new-york-city-police-covid-19-deaths/ index.html Accessed 17/07/2020.

World Health Organization (WHO). (2020). *WHO Director-General's Opening Remarks at the Media Briefing on COVID-19*. Available at: www.who.int/dg/speeches/detail/who-director-general-sopening-remarks-at-the-media-briefing-oncovid-19 Accessed 17/07/2020.

Wrzesniewski, A. and Dutton, J. E. (2001). Crafting a job: revisioning employees as active crafters of their work. *The Academy of Management Review*, 26, 2, 179–201.

Fan Wu, Su Zhao, Bin Yu, Yan-Mei Chen, Wen Wang, Zhi-Gang Song, Yi Hu, Zhao-Wu Tao, Jun-Hua Tian, Yuan-Yuan Pei, Ming-Li Yuan, Yu-Ling Zhang, Fa-Hui Dai, Yi Liu, Qi-Min, Wang, Jiao-Jiao Zheng, Lin Xu, Edward C.Holmes and Yong-Zhen Zhang. (2020). A new coronavirus associated with human respiratory disease in China. *Nature*, 579, 7798, 265–269.

Zander, M., Hutton, A. and King, L. (2013). Exploring resilience in paediatric oncology nursing staff. *Collegian*, 20, 1, 17–25.

23

The Three Pillars of Mental Health in the Workplace: Prevention, Intervention and Accommodation

Rachael Jones-Chick and E. Kevin Kelloway

Mental health issues are one of the primary causes of disability among the working population (Mental Health Commission of Canada [MHCC], 2012; WHO, 2019a). It is estimated that 1 in 5 people will experience a significant mental health problem (National Alliance on Mental Illness [NAMI], 2019; WHO, 2002, 2004) resulting in an estimate of more than 450 million people being affected worldwide (World Health Organization [WHO], 2004). Until relatively recently, the scope of the problem – and the associated costs – have been well documented to little effect. Organizations have largely ignored issues of mental health, satisfying themselves with establishing Employee Assistance Programs (EAPs) and, perhaps, some allowance within benefit programmes to access mental health services.

This minimalist approach is clearly ineffective. As a result of the stigmatization many people go undiagnosed or misdiagnosed (Corrigan, 2004). Correspondingly, the mental health resources that organizations provide for individuals are typically under-utilized (Linnan et al., 2008; Reynolds and Lehman, 2003). EAPs, for example, are often under-accessed and under-utilized (Canadian Medical Association, 2013) with some estimating that fewer than 5% of employees use these programmes (Attridge et al., 2013). Moreover, the people who could often benefit the most from these resources are also the least likely to use them (Hunt and Eisenberg, 2010; Linnan et al., 2008). In developing their resource utilization model for mental health services, Dimoff and Kelloway (2016) suggested that resources may be under-utilized because (a) individuals do not recognize the need for additional help, (b) individuals may not know what resources were available to them, and (c) they may not know how to access the resources available.

There are signs that this is changing. Indeed, Kelloway (2017) suggested that a confluence of policy and economic issues has led to an unprecedented opportunity to implement mental health programmes in organizations. As he noted 'Organizations, as never before in my memory, are looking for solutions, interventions and programmes focused on mental health issues' (Kelloway, 2017: 2). Moreover, organizational interest in mental health issues has been accompanied by general awareness programmes that highlight the prevalence of mental health issues and destigmatize help-seeking behaviour. As a result, we have a growing demand for mental health services and programmes and a growing list of organizations that are willing to invest in these resources.

Perhaps not surprisingly, and as is the case with more broadly focused workplace health programmes, a plethora of consultants and experts have rushed in to meet this need. Many of these programmes are, at best, weakly supported by empirical data (Dimoff et al., 2014). For example, the Roads to Mental Readiness programme is a workplace mental health programme that has been implemented in the armed forces and for public safety professionals (e.g., police, border services, paramedics, firefighters) in Canada. Although the programme has been widely, and indeed almost universally, implemented across the country, rigorous assessment of the programme suggests that it has little to no effect on individual mental health (Carleton et al., 2018; Fikretoglu et al., 2019). Although there is some evidence that the programme reduces stigma around mental health issues, public safety professionals overwhelmingly see workplace resources as a 'last resort' (Carleton et al., 2020).

The originators of Roads to Mental Readiness are to be credited with their rigorous approach to evaluation. Although the results were perhaps disappointing, it is through the accumulation of such evidence that we are able to address issues of workplace mental health. Without a solid evidence-based foundation, we run the risk of confusing doing 'something' with doing 'something that works'. Our goal in this chapter is to begin to lay the foundations for effective and evidence-based mental health programmes in the workplace.

We suggest that mental health programming in organizations needs to be based on some recognition of both the nature of mental health issues and the nature of organizations. First, we recognize that the workplace itself can be a significant source of stress for individuals and can negatively affect individual mental health. Surveys by the American Psychological Association (APA) have generally found that work is one of the most stressful domains for many people (e.g., APA, 2012) and a large number of people report feeling stressed almost all of the time (Center for Disease Control [CDC], 2014). As Dimoff et al. (in press) note, workplace stressors are not likely to be the sole cause of mental health problems but can certainly exacerbate existing or developing conditions. Moreover, implementing awareness programmes or similar types of mental health programming in the workplace while allowing negative organizational conditions to exist is surely to result in a loss of credibility for the broader programme. Thus, we suggest that as a first priority, organizations need to clean up their own house and focus on primary prevention by assessing and addressing stressful conditions in the workplace.

Second, although a focus on prevention, or primary intervention, is frequently advocated by stress researchers (e.g., Kelloway et al., 2008), we recognize that mental health issues may not originate in the workplace but frequently do manifest in the workplace – affecting work behaviours and outcomes (see for example Dimoff and Kelloway, 2019). Organizations have a mandate to help individuals in crisis, and a focus on intervention – identifying individuals who need help and ensuring that they have access to the resources and supports that they need – is warranted.

Finally, individuals experiencing mental health problems may not be able to stay at work and one resource that is frequently provided by organizations is medical leave. We note that this is frequently mislabelled as 'stress leave' or 'mental health leave' but is, most typically, the same short- and long-term disability programming that is offered for all medically diagnosed conditions. As Kelloway (2017) notes, there are two issues that are of particular interest. First, how do we bring people back to work after being off on either short-term or long-term disability? Second, how do we arrange for people to stay at work while they are experiencing a mental health problem – recognizing that work is a significant source of social support for many people. Both questions are fundamentally questions of accommodation – what changes do we make to the workplace (e.g., structures, routines, tasks) that will allow individuals to successfully return to, or remain in, the workplace?

We follow Kelloway (2017) in suggesting that an effective and comprehensive workplace mental health programme would address each of these points – prevention, intervention and accommodation. In the remainder of this chapter we discuss each form of programming in more detail – building the case for evidence-based programming that addresses prevention, intervention and accommodation around mental health issues in the workplace.

PILLAR 1: PREVENTION

There is not just one cause for mental health disorders, and they can occur due to an interaction of environmental and genetic factors at any point in life, making prevention difficult (WHO, 2002). The multitude of risk factors calls for a diverse prevention strategy. In an organizational setting this focus has frequently been undertaken under the guise of a 'healthy workplace' programme. Healthy workplace programmes are defined as 'employer-sponsored initiatives directed at improving the health and wellbeing of workers' (Goetzel et al., 2008: 4) and are often undertaken with the expectation that employers can mitigate costs by improving

productivity, reducing absenteeism and reducing healthcare costs (Goetzel and Ozminkowski, 2008).

Grawitch et al. (2015) describe the utility of a comprehensive psychologically healthy workplace programme for employee stress management. They highlight the importance of preventing stress-related outcomes that occur from several sources, such as the organizational context, non-work life demands and job requirements, rather than only treating employee stress through wellness programmes and training sessions. Using a broader conceptualization and a strategic approach (i.e., needs assessment, management support, employee involvement, comprehensive strategy, implementation plan and evaluation plan) to identify and remedy sources of stress in the organization is suggested to have more pronounced effects on employee wellbeing through effective stress management (Grawitch et al., 2015).

Kornhauser's (1965) seminal investigations and the influential *Work in America* report (Secretary of Health, Education and Welfare, 1974) focused the attention of researchers on issues related to workplace stress and laid the foundation for prevention-oriented interventions in organizations. Sauter et al. (1990), writing on behalf of the National Institute for Occupational Safety and Health (NIOSH) in the United States, identified workplace stress as one of the ten leading causes of workplace death and a national epidemic in the United States. They identified six major classes of workplace stressors: (a) role stressors (e.g., intra-and inter-role conflict, ambiguity), (b) work load and pace; (c) work scheduling; (d) career concerns; (e) job content and control; and (f) interpersonal stressors (Sauter et al., 1990). A substantial amount of research supports the importance and negative effects of such stressors (for a review see Kelloway and Day, 2005).

Other approaches to a healthy workplace emphasize the provision of organizational resources that either mitigate the impact of stressors or contribute directly to individual wellbeing (Kelloway and Day, 2005). The APA, for example, promotes a psychologically healthy workplace model that incorporates five types of resources: recognition, involvement, growth and development, health and safety, and work–family balance (see, for example, Grawitch et al., 2006). Similarly, the six antecedents of a healthy workplace provided in Kelloway and Day's (2005) model are (a) safety of work environment; (b) work–life balance; (c) culture of support, respect and fairness; (d) employee involvement and development; (e) work content and characteristics; and (f) interpersonal relationships at work. A holistic model such as this would require the participation of the entire organization to achieve a healthy workplace that fosters employee wellbeing. If successful, however, a healthy workplace can not only prevent poor mental health outcomes for employees but can have other individual outcomes such as behavioural and physiological wellbeing, as well as positive societal and organizational outcomes, including improved performance and reputation (Kelloway and Day, 2005).

The enactment of a national standard for psychological health and safety in Canada (Canadian Standards Association, 2013) is also designed to promote a healthy workplace. The standard is voluntary but has been adopted or used as a template by many organizations. As Kelloway (in press) notes, the standard may also provide organizations with a form of due diligence, to the extent that if organizations implement the standard they can claim to be following best practices in the creation of a healthy workplace.

Four general principles underpin the standard. Organizations are required to have a corporate commitment to improving psychological health and safety, to have leadership commitment to the issue, to involve employees in the identification of workplace issues and the design of workplace programmes, and to ensure the confidentiality of individuals. The standard also identifies 13 environmental features or workplace conditions that overlap with previous models, vis: organizational culture, psychological and social support, clear leadership and expectations, civility and respect, psychological demands, growth and development, recognition and reward, involvement and influence, workload management, engagement, balance, psychological protection and protection of physical safety. Others have followed the lead of the standard in proposing measures and models that reflect the standard (Ivey et al., 2018).

As Kelloway and Day (2005) note, most of these models are simple taxonomies with no underlying theory of what might constitute a psychologically healthy workplace. Moreover, there is a remarkable dearth of intervention studies showing that changing the conditions identified in any of the models cited above actually results in improved employee wellbeing. The research in this area continues to be dominated by cross-sectional, self-report surveys (Kelloway, in press; Kelloway and Francis, 2012). Intervention studies with strong designs (e.g., random assignment to conditions, use of control groups, longitudinal measures) are required to justify the claims made in this area. Such interventions are notoriously difficult to conduct (see Karinika-Murray and Biron, 2015). As Kelloway (in press) noted, despite the difficulties, intervention research offers the single greatest source about the conditions that affect wellbeing in organizations. Showing that a change in organizational practice results in a corresponding change in wellbeing that cannot be otherwise attributed is a substantial contribution to our knowledge of how organizational conditions affect wellbeing.

PILLAR 2: INTERVENTION

Going Beyond Prevention: Why is Intervention Necessary?

While changing workplace conditions to positively affect employee wellbeing may be one way to prevent mental health issues from arising in the workplace, not all mental health issues start in the workplace, so prevention alone will not provide a comprehensive workplace mental health programme (Kelloway, 2017). This is why the second pillar of mental health (i.e., intervention) is necessary. As Kelloway (2017) equates, public health programmes for children such as vaccination and dental screening clinics are administered in schools since this is an easy way to reach children, and this may also be an effective model for employee mental health intervention delivery. Since many adults spend their days in a workplace, it may be convenient to deliver mental health interventions in organizations, not only to address mental health problems that arise in the workplace but also to target mental health issues that may arise outside of work.

What Makes a Successful Organizational Mental Health Intervention?

Possibly the most important, yet often overlooked, initial step to ensuring the success of a mental health intervention is ensuring that people who would benefit from the intervention are able to access it. Mental health disorders are very prevalent, with an estimated 264 million people living with depression and, often, symptoms of anxiety globally (WHO, 2019b). Not surprisingly, this prevalence of common mental health disorders occurs in a large percentage of the working population and results in a significant economic impact. In fact, the WHO (2019a) estimates that depression and anxiety disorders generate lost productivity costs adding up to US$1 trillion each year. Encouragingly, mental health interventions are suggested to be worth the cost of implementation, with every US$1 put into scaled-up treatment for common mental health disorders having a return of US$4 in improved health and productivity (WHO, 2019a). Unfortunately, the

employees who need these programmes most often do not access mental health interventions. Additionally, not all mental health interventions are created equal, with some popular programmes providing minimal evidence of improvements for employees. In order to reap the health and productivity benefits that can occur as a result of workplace mental health interventions, we must consider what makes a successful intervention (and how to make it accessible to those who need it).

Awareness versus behaviour change

Mental health awareness interventions are an increasingly popular format for organizations to use to improve employee wellbeing. These programmes typically aim to improve employee mental health related outcomes by improving mental health awareness within the organization (Affinity Work Health & Wellbeing Hub, 2019). Mental health awareness programmes are delivered in many different formats with various content and delivery options; however, most programmes focus on improving general knowledge and awareness around mental health and decreasing stigma, rather than changing behaviours in a way that will impact employees who are actually experiencing challenges with their mental health (Affinity Work Health & Wellbeing Hub, 2019).

Most mental health awareness programmes have little evidence of effectiveness, as many programmes are only evaluated for employee reactions to training or use surveys to evaluate anticipated changes as a result of the training immediately after the intervention (Booth et al., 2017). There is also little to no evidence of the effectiveness of most mental health training programmes of the benefit to people who come into contact with trainees (Booth et al., 2017). Much like the leadership development programmes discussed in pillar 1 as a prevention mechanism, there is little agreement on the characteristics that result in the most effective training outcomes.

In their review of mental health training pro-grammes for non-mental health training pro-fessionals, Booth et al. (2017) found that the length of training in the 19 studies examined ranged from 13 minutes to over 40 hours. Additionally, there was high variation in the types of content delivered in mental health training programmes, with some addressing a broad mental health focus and others adopt-ing a specific focus on one mental health issue (Booth et al., 2017). We know that men-tal health awareness programmes improve employee awareness of mental health and in some cases improve the ability of employees to identify various mental health challenges, but we do not yet know if these programmes lead to behaviour changes that can actually prevent or improve mental health outcomes, highlighting the need for more evaluations of longer-term effects and behavioural changes.

Level of intervention

The level of the intervention may also be an important consideration for the success of organizational mental health training. Interventions may occur at the individual level with employees or at the leader level with management, with potentially different effects from each implementation level. As discussed above, many mental health inter-ventions are run for employees at the indi-vidual level with demonstrated improvements in awareness, knowledge and reduced stigma, and some reports of intention to change behaviour, but little to no evidence of actual behaviour change (Affinity Work Health & Wellbeing Hub, 2019; Booth et al., 2017).

At the leader level of intervention, similar to the individual level, there is evidence that mental health interventions improve man-agers' mental health awareness and stigma (Gayed et al., 2018). There is less evidence demonstrating the impact of leader level train-ing on employee mental health outcomes; however, some studies have started to emerge demonstrating the value of leader mental health training for supporting employee men-tal health (Dimoff et al., 2016; Morgan et al.,

2018). According to Dimoff and Kelloway's (2016) Resource Utilization Model, lead-ers can assist employees who are struggling with recognizing that they need help, iden-tifying available organizational resources and accessing those resources, as long as the leader is able to identify when employees are struggling. Based on the improvements to leader mental health literacy as a result of mental health awareness programmes, lead-ers who have received training may be well-equipped to act as 'resource facilitators' to support employee mental health. Even with trained leaders, there are external factors that may prevent the application of knowl-edge from training to changed behaviours or employee outcomes. Shann et al. (2019) found that the nature of the work environ-ment, the collective readiness and capabil-ity of the organization to address mental health issues, the attitudes of others in the workplace and the broader political context affected leader application of intervention learning. While difficult to achieve, broader organizational culture changes may be nec-essary to ensure greater success in mental health training across intervention levels.

Examples of Organizational Mental Health Interventions

Mental health first aid

Developed by Kitchener and Jorm (2002), Mental Health First Aid is the most widely used and evaluated mental health awareness intervention (Affinity Work Health & Wellbeing Hub, 2019). Mental Health First Aid was developed to teach individuals mental health literacy and to provide initial tools to provide support to others experienc-ing mental health problems (Dimoff et al., 2016; Kitchener and Jorm, 2002). While the Mental Health First Aid programme has been evaluated extensively and has demonstrated effectiveness for improving mental health literacy and self-efficacy to provide support for others, there is a lack of evidence demonstrating changes in behaviour that improve outcomes for employees experiencing mental health challenges within organizations.

MHAT

While research has established that mental health awareness training can improve employee knowledge and awareness around mental health disorders (Booth et al., 2017), Dimoff et al. (2016) point out that based on the work of Bandura (1993), this does not determine whether the training will result in engagement in particular activities or behaviour change. Dimoff et al. (2016) suggest that training leaders may be a more successful way to achieve behaviour change in employees. Working from the observation that leaders may be in a unique position to be able to identify and assist employees with mental health issues due to their frequent contact with employees, Dimoff et al. (2016) developed an intervention for workplace leaders called Mental Health Awareness Training (MHAT).

The three-hour MHAT training is a brief training session to enhance leaders' mental health literacy. Evaluation of the programme revealed promising results, with a longitudinal field experiment design finding improvements in leaders' knowledge, attitudes, self-efficacy and promotion intentions surrounding mental health, with results sustained over an eight-week follow-up period. Taking the evaluation of the programme further than awareness and beginning to evaluate behaviour change, Dimoff et al. (2016) found a significant cost-saving to the organization that received the MHAT training programme. Dimoff et al. (2016) found a 27% (almost 19 days') reduction in the average duration of mental health claims during the first nine months following the intervention in organizations that received the MHAT training. These findings suggest the occurrence of actual behaviour change in employees, in addition to improved mental health literacy in the leaders who received the training.

PILLAR 3: ACCOMMODATION

Work can have many benefits for our mental health, which is one reason why successful return-to-work (RTW) and stay-at-work interventions are important components in the 'Accommodation Pillar' of mental health in the workplace. Furthermore, absenteeism in the form of sick leave and presenteeism in the form of lost productivity due to illness at work are very expensive for organizations. Therefore, bringing workers back successfully and in a timely manner after a mental health leave or helping employees to stay at work with accommodations while dealing with a mental health condition are good strategies both for employees and for the organization.

Return-to-Work Interventions

Returning to work can buffer against mental health problems associated with not working; however, employers must be cautious when considering how to bring people back to work after a period of disability leave resulting from a mental health disorder.

In general, the RTW literature for physical disabilities supports the notion that RTW interventions are successful in reducing the duration and associated costs of work disability leave (Franche et al., 2005). Franche et al. (2005) explored five intervention components and found moderate evidence that they reduced the duration of workplace disability leave. The five intervention components are contact with the worker and with the healthcare provider, work accommodation offers, ergonomic work site visits, supernumerary replacements and return-to-work coordination. Unfortunately, there was minimal evidence for the positive effect of the accommodation interventions on quality-of-life outcomes such as perceived health or general health and symptom severity for the employees (Franche et al., 2005). While this research provides recommendations for several practices that lead to successful RTW programmes in terms of bringing employees back to work, more research is needed to identify practices that will also ensure sustained improved quality of life for the returning employees. Additionally, the existing stigma towards invisible injuries may contribute to failed RTW interventions and chronic disability for employees returning from a mental health-related leave due to workers not asking for, or taking advantage of, RTW arrangements (Eakin, 2005; Francis et al., 2014; Tarasuk and Eakin, 1995). Furthermore, not all established RTW strategies may be transferrable to mental health concerns.

In a recent Institution of Occupational Safety and Health (IOSH) report, Joosen et al. (2017) conducted a study on the RTW process for employees on leave due to mental health issues to identify barriers and facilitators in the process from a multi-stakeholder perspective at various lengths of leave (short-, medium- and long-term absence). Results from a study with stakeholders in the RTW process (mental health and occupational health professionals, general practitioners and managers) found five main themes that lead to successful RTW, with substantial overlap with the themes identified by Franche et al. (2005). Joosen et al. (2017) identified the five themes of: employee motivation to work and emotions, cognitions and coping that do not impede RTW (such as fear and anxiety of not being able to cope); type of work (work should be adapted to ensure the employee's ability to be successful and build confidence, but should also be fulfilling and motivating); a safe, welcoming and stigma-free work environment; a personalized approach to RTW support; and collaboration between healthcare professionals (to align interventions and activities). In a second study involving interviews with employees on the RTW process, nine barrier themes and seven facilitating themes were identified for successful RTW after short-, medium- and long-term leaves (Joosen et al., 2017). There were several

themes that overlapped with the themes identified by stakeholders; however, many notable distinctive themes also emerged from the employee data. For example, some of the unique barriers and facilitators (opposite of the barriers) identified by employees were inadequate management and/or RTW policies, poor interpersonal relationships with managers or colleagues, and issues in private life due to illness (lack of support/ accommodations). Given the gap between what stakeholders and employees perceive as essential in creating a successful RTW process, it is important for stakeholders involved in the development of RTW policies to consult with employees to ensure that the process will be as successful as possible.

Stay-at-Work Interventions

Unemployment in itself is a risk factor for mental health problems, so employers should also consider how they can keep people in the workplace rather than having them go off on disability leave when possible by providing accommodation and support in the workplace. Stay-at-work interventions are also important because many common mental health conditions are recurring, with the possibility for ongoing absences and productivity/performance deficits as a result (Pomaki et al., 2012). Therefore, while there is significant overlap between RTW and stay-at-work interventions, it is important to distinguish between the two to ensure that employees can continue to receive adequate accommodations after returning from a mental health leave or as a preventative measure before requiring a formal leave. In their review, Pomaki et al. (2012) found moderate support for improved work functioning and quality of life from the facilitation of access to clinical treatment and workplace-based high-intensity psychological intervention among employees who were working while experiencing depression (Wang et al., 2007). At a

12-month follow up post-intervention, Wang et al. (2007) found employees had improved job retention and effective hours working, and an increased proportion of employees who had improved symptoms and who had experienced recovery (Pomaki et al., 2012). A key feature to successful stay-at-work interventions may be the ability to tailor the intervention to individual employee needs. The intervention in the Wang et al. (2007) study offered different types of treatment, such as psychoeducational booklets, telephone or in-person CBT, and psychiatric treatment (Pomaki et al., 2012). While this type of intervention may sound intimidating to employers due to the associated financial commitment, the review by Pomaki et al. (2012) found that the economic benefits of facilitating access to clinical treatment exceeded the costs of administering the interventions. More specifically, the Wang et al. (2007) workplace-based psychological intervention resulted in cost savings for the employer and the value of increased hours worked exceeded the cost of the intervention (Pomaki et al., 2012).

Special Considerations

The effect on employers

The importance of leaders in the RTW process is a key component for success identified by employees. Managers can help to facilitate employee self-awareness and control in the return process, help employees to see the value in their work and reduce work pressure through work adjustments and accommodations (Joosen et al., 2017). Therefore, in addition to training managers in the prevention and intervention 'pillars' discussed previously in this chapter, a leader intervention to accommodate employees returning from mental health absences may also be a successful approach. It is important to note, however, that putting the responsibility on leaders to help in the

accommodation process for employees returning to work could place a lot of added pressure on management. It would be essential to also ensure that there are proper supports in place for leaders to prevent mental health issues from developing due to this potential added stress.

Translation for small companies

Small companies or companies that hire many temporary and seasonal workers may uniquely benefit from transformational leadership as an occupational health intervention. Kanste et al. (2007) found that transformational leadership had a stronger negative relationship with reduced emotional exhaustion and de-personalization for temporary workers than for permanent workers. Transformational leadership may function as a substitute for benefits and security that permanent workers receive, that temporary workers do not have. Using this logic, small companies may also benefit from accommodation interventions for leaders, as they may not have formal processes in place to ensure a smooth transition back to work for employees returning from leave. Having good, supportive leaders may buffer the stress that can come with returning to work or with staying at work while experiencing mental health difficulties by creating a positive workplace either during mental health difficulties or upon returning from leave.

CONCLUSION

The prevalence of mental health disorders in the workplace, in addition to the challenging etiology of mental health disorders, calls for a comprehensive approach to workplace mental health programmes. To effectively address employee mental health in the workplace, we suggest a three-pillar approach consisting of prevention, intervention and accommodation.

REFERENCES

Affinity Work Health & Wellbeing Hub (2019) *Mental Health Awareness: Summary of Evidence*. Available at: http://affinityhealthhub.co.uk/d/summarys/mental-health-awareness-summary-of-evidence.pdf (accessed 24 June 2020).

American Psychological Association (APA) (2012) *The Impact of Stress*. Available at: www.apa.org/news/press/releases/stress/2011/impact.aspx (accessed March 2016).

Attridge M, Cahill T, Granberry SW and Herlihy PA (2013) The National Behavioral Consortium industry profile of external EAP vendors. *Journal of Workplace Behavioral Health* 28(4): 251–324.

Bandura A (1993) Perceived self-efficacy in cognitive development and functioning. *Educational Psychologist* 28: 117–148.

Booth A, Scantlebury A, Hughes-Morley A, Mitchell N, Wright K, Scott W and McDaid C (2017) Mental health training programmes for non-mental health trained professionals coming into contact with people with mental ill health: a systematic review of effectiveness. *BMC Psychiatry* 17: 196. DOI 10.1186/s12888-017-1356-5.

Canadian Medical Association (2013) *Mental Health*. Available at: www.cma.ca/En/Pages/mental-health.aspx (accessed 3 August 2015).

Canadian Standards Association (2013) *Psychological health and safety in the workplace: Prevention, promotion, and guidance to staged implementation*. Ottawa: Canadian Standards Association.

Carleton RN, Afifi TO, Turner S, Taillieu T, Vaughan AD, Anderson GS, Ricciardelli R, MacPhee RS, Cramm HA, Czarnuch S and Hozempa K (2020) Mental health training, attitudes toward support, and screening positive for mental disorders. *Cognitive Behaviour Therapy* 49(1): 55–73.

Carleton RN, Korol S, Mason JE, Hozempa K, Anderson GS, Jones NA, Dobson KS, Szeto A and Bailey S (2018) A longitudinal assessment of the road to mental readiness training among municipal police. *Cognitive Behaviour Therapy* 47(6): 508–528.

Center for Disease Control (2014) *Workplace Health Promotion: Depression*. Available at: https://www.cdc.gov/workplacehealthpromotion/health-strategies/depression/index.html (accessed 25 November 2020).

Corrigan P (2004) How stigma interferes with mental health care. *American Psychologist* 59(7): 614–625.

Dimoff JK and Kelloway EK (2016) Resource utilization model: organizational leaders as resource facilitators. In: Gentry WA, Clerkin C, Perrewé PL, Halbesleben JRB and Rosen CC (eds) *Research in Occupational Stress and Wellbeing Volume 14: The Role of Leadership in Occupational Stress*. London: Emerald, pp. 141–160.

Dimoff JK and Kelloway EK (2019) Signs of struggle (SOS): the development and validation of a behavioural mental health checklist for the workplace. *Work & Stress* 33(3): 295–313.

Dimoff JK, Kelloway EK and Bernstein M (2016) Mental Health Awareness Training (MHAT): The development and evaluation of an intervention for workplace leaders. *International Journal of Stress Management* 23(2): 167–189.

Dimoff JK, Kelloway EK and MacLellan AS (2014) Health and performance: science or advocacy? *Journal of Organizational Effectiveness: People and Performance* 1: 316–334.

Dimoff JK, Vogel WES and Yoder O (in press) Mental health in the workplace: Where we've been and where we're going. In Kelloway EK and Cooper CL (eds). *Research Agenda for Work and Wellbeing*. Elgar.

Eakin JM (2005) The discourse of abuse in return to work: a hidden epidemic of suffering. In: Peterson CL and Mayhew C (eds) *Occupational Health and Safety: International Influences and the 'New' Epidemics*. Amityville: Baywood, pp. 159–174.

Fikretoglu D, Liu A, Nazarov A and Blackler K (2019) A group randomized control trial to test the efficacy of the Road to Mental Readiness (R2MR) program among Canadian military recruits. *BMC Psychiatry* 19(1): 326–340.

Franche RL, Cullen K, Clarke J, Irvin E, Sinclair S, Frank J and the Institute for Work & Health (IWH) Workplace-Based RTW Intervention

Literature Review Research Team (2005) Workplace-based return-to-work interventions: a systematic review of the quantitative literature. *Journal of Occupational Rehabilitation* 15: 607–631.

Francis L, Cameron J, Kelloway EK, Catano VM, Day A and Hepburn G (2014) The working wounded: stigma and return to work. In: Chen P and Cooper C (eds) *Wellbeing in the Workplace: From Stress to Happiness.* Oxford: Wiley-Blackwell, pp. 1–18.

Gayed A, Milligan-Saville JS, Nicholas J, Bryan BT, LaMontagne AD, Milner A, Madan I, Calvo RA, Christensen H, Mykletun A, Glozier N and Harvey SB (2018) Effectiveness of training workplace managers to understand and support the mental health needs of employees: a systematic review and meta-analysis. *Occupational and Environmental Medicine* 75: 462–470.

Goetzel RZ and Ozminkowski RJ (2008) The health and cost benefits of work site health-promotion programs. *Annual Review of Public Health* 29(1): 303–323.

Goetzel RZ, Roemer EC, Liss-Levinson RC and Samoly DK (2008) *Workplace Health Promotion: Policy Recommendations that Encourage Employers to Support Health Improvement Programs for Their Workers.* A paper commissioned by Partnership for Prevention, Emory University. Available at: http://citeseerx.ist.psu.edu/viewdoc/download?doi=10.1.1.460.912&rep=rep1&type=pdf (accessed 25 November 2020).

Grawitch MJ, Ballard DW and Erb KR (2015) To be or not to be (stressed): the critical role of a psychologically healthy workplace in effective stress management. *Stress and Health* 31: 264–273.

Grawitch MJ, Gottschalk M, Munz MJ (2006) The path to a healthy workplace: A critical review linking healthy workplace practices, employee well-being, and organizational improvements. *Consulting Psychology Journal: Practice & Research* 58(3): 129–147.

Hunt J and Eisenberg D (2010) Mental health problems and help-seeking behavior among college students. *Journal of Adolescent Health* 46: 3–10.

Ivey GW, Blanc J-RS, Michaud K and Dobreva-Martinova T (2018) A measure and model of psychological health and safety in the workplace that reflects Canada's national standard. *Canadian Journal of Administrative Science*, doi: 10.1002/cjas.1500.

Joosen M, Arends I, Lugtenberg M, van Gestel H, Schaapveld B, van der Klink J, van Weeghel J, Terluin B and Brouwers E (2017) *Barriers to and Facilitators of Return to Work after Sick Leave in Workers with Common Mental Disorders: Perspectives of Workers, Mental Health Professionals, Occupational Health Professionals, General Physicians and Managers.* Report for the IOSH Research Committee. Available at: https://research.tilburguniversity.edu/en/publications/barriers-to-and-facilitators-of-return-to-work-after-sick-leave-i (accessed 25 November 2020).

Kanste O, Kyngäs H, Nikkilä JO (2007) The relationship between multidimensional leadership and burnout among nursing staff. *Journal of Nursing Management* 15(7): 731–739.

Karinika-Murray M and Biron C (eds) (2015) *Derailed Organizational Interventions for Stress and Well-Being: Confessions of Failure and Solutions for Success.* New York: Springer.

Kelloway EK (2017) Mental health in the workplace: towards evidence-based practice. *Canadian Psychology* 58(1): 1–6.

Kelloway EK (in press) Chasing the dream: the healthy and productive workplace. In: Graf P and Dozois D (eds) *Advances in Applied Psychology.* Chichester: Wiley.

Kelloway EK and Day AL (2005) Building healthy organizations: what we know so far. *Canadian Journal of Behavioural Science* 37: 223–235.

Kelloway EK, Day A and Hurrell JJ (2008) Workplace interventions for occupational stress. In: Sverke M, Hellegren J and Naswall K (eds) *The Individual in the Changing Working Life.* Cambridge: Cambridge University Press, pp. 419–441.

Kelloway EK and Francis L (2012) Longitudinal research and data analysis. In: Sinclair R, Wang M and Tetrick L (eds) *Research Methods in Occupational Health Psychology.* New York: Routledge, pp. 374–394.

Kitchener BA and Jorm AF (2002) Mental health first aid training for the public: evaluation of effects on knowledge, attitudes and helping behavior. *BMC Psychiatry* 2: 10–15.

Kornhauser, A (1965) *Mental Health of the Industrial Worker*. New York: Wiley.

Linnan L, Bowling M, Childress J, Lindsay G, Blakey C, Pronk S, ... and Royall P (2008) Results of the 2004 national worksite health promotion survey. *American Journal of Public Health* 98: 1503–1509.

Mental Health Commission of Canada (MHCC) (2012) *Changing Directions, Changing Lives: The Mental Health Strategy for Canada*. Calgary: MHCC.

Morgan AJ, Ross A, Reavley NJ and Doran AJ (2018) Systematic review and meta-analysis of mental health first aid training: effects on knowledge, stigma, and helping behaviour. *PLoS ONE* 13(5), DOI: 10.1371/journal.pone.0197102.

National Alliance on Mental Illness (2019) *Mental Health by the Numbers*. Available at: www.nami.org/learn-more/mental-health-by-the-numbers (accessed 25 November 2020).

Pomaki G, Franche RL, Murray E, Khushrushahi N and Lampinen TM (2012) Workplace-based work disability prevention interventions for workers with common mental health conditions: a review of the literature. *Journal of Occupational Rehabilitation* 22: 182–195.

Reynolds GS and Lehman WE (2003) Levels of substance use and willingness to use the employee assistance program. *The Journal of Behavioral Health Services & Research* 30: 238–248.

Sauter SL, Murphy LR and Hurrell Jr JJ (1990) Prevention of work-related psychological disorders. *American Psychologist* 45: 1146–1153.

Secretary of Health, Education, and Welfare (1974) *Work in America. (A report of a Special Task Force to the Secretary of Health, Education, and Welfare)*. Cambridge, MA: MIT Press.

Shann C, Martin A, Chester A and Ruddock S (2019) Effectiveness and application of an online leadership intervention to promote mental health and reduce depression-related stigma in organizations. *Journal of Occupational Health Psychology* 24(1): 20–35.

Tarasuk V and Eakin J (1995) The problem of legitimacy in the experience of work-related back injury. *Qualitative Health Research* 5: 204–221.

Wang PS, Simon GE, Avorn J, Azocar F, Ludman EJ, McCulloch J, Petukhova MZ and Kessler RC (2007) Telephone screening, outreach, and care management for depressed workers and impact on clinical and job performance outcomes: a randomized controlled trial. *The Journal of the American Medical Association* 298(12): 1401–1411.

World Health Organization (WHO) (2002) *Prevention and Promotion in Mental Health*. Available at: www.who.int/mental_health/media/en/545.pdf (accessed 20 January 2020).

World Health Organization (WHO) (2004) *The Summary Report on Promoting Mental Health: Concepts, Emerging Evidence, and Practice*. Geneva: World Health Organization.

World Health Organization (WHO) (2019a) *Mental health in the workplace: Information sheet*. Available at: www.who.int/mental_health/in_the_workplace/en/ (accessed 24 June 2020).

World Health Organization (WHO) (2019b) *Depression*. Available at: www.who.int/news-room/fact-sheets/detail/depression (accessed 20 January 2020).

24

National Approaches to Wellbeing Interventions: The UK Management Standards as an Example

Karina Nielsen, Carolyn Axtell and Siobhan Taylor

INTRODUCTION

Poor wellbeing is increasingly considered a significant challenge in modern society. In the OECD countries, approximately 15% of the working population suffer from stress, anxiety and depression, resulting in long-term sickness absence for about half of this group (OECD, 2014). In Europe, 25% of workers have experienced work-related stress (Vargas et al., 2014) and in the UK, the National Labour Force Survey showed that stress, anxiety and depression accounted for 44% of work-related ill-health and 57% of working days lost (HSE, 2018). Psychosocial working conditions such as work demands, social relations and autonomy have a high prevalence in the working population (Parker et al., 2017; Vargas et al., 2014) and have been found to be related to health and wellbeing outcomes (Madsen et al., 2017).

Acknowledging the risks of poor psychosocial working conditions, legislative frameworks have been implemented requiring organizations to manage psychosocial risks (EU-OSHA, 2016). In the European Union, the Framework Directive 89/391/EEC on Safety and Health of Workers at Work established employers' general obligations to ensure workers' health and safety, including the management of psychosocial risks (European Council, 1989). Framework agreements on work-related stress have been introduced to emphasize the importance of managing psychosocial risks in particular (European Social Partners, 2004). As a result, the EU member states have developed their own legislation and strategies. Despite the EU Directive and Frameworks, a recent survey (EU-OSHA, 2019) found that 21% of the (at the time 28) EU countries perceived psychosocial risks to be more challenging to manage than other Occupational Health and Safety (OSH) risks. A possible explanation for this challenge is that neither the Framework Directive nor Framework agreements stipulate *how* the countries in the EU should implement psychosocial risk management.

In this chapter, we present the UK Health and Safety Executive's approach to managing the psychosocial work environment, the Management Standards (MS), and based on current work psychology theory and research we suggest why organizations may face challenges and what can be done to overcome these challenges. We focus on the MS as it is one of the most clearly described approaches that has been implemented for some time and has been adopted by other national approaches, i.e. Work Positive in Ireland (Nielsen and Noblet, 2018) and INAIL in Italy (Nielsen and Noblet, 2018; Ronchetti et al., 2015; Toderi et al., 2013).

WHY IS PSYCHOSOCIAL RISK MANAGEMENT SO CHALLENGING?

To obtain a better understanding of the challenges faced by organizations aiming to manage the psychosocial work environment, Schuller (2020) interviewed representatives from 34 organizations who had direct responsibility for managing psychosocial working conditions. The results of the interviews revealed six key barriers. First, psychosocial working conditions are less tangible than other health and safety risks (e.g. ergonomics and chemicals) and going through all phases of the process was time-consuming meaning that the situation had changed by the time actions were being implemented. Second, key players in organizations perceived wellbeing issues to be the responsibility of the individual and not the organization's responsibility. These beliefs resulted in a focus on individual-level activities rather than a focus on changing the way work is organized, designed and managed. Third, a related challenge was that key stakeholders saw poor psychosocial working conditions as part of the job, for example high work pressure in hospital wards. Fourth, a lack of accountability

at all levels within organizations, in particular line managers, were seen as a problem as they often did not assume the necessary responsibility for managing the psychosocial work environment and workers were often not given a realistic opportunity to have their voices heard. Fifth, a challenge was reported that those who had formal responsibility were not necessarily the ones best suited to implement changes and did not always have the sufficient budget to allocate to implementing changes. Finally, often a structured process for the implementation of activities to improve psychosocial working conditions did not exist. Additional challenges have also been identified. The EU Emerging Survey on New and Emerging Risks (ESENER) identified the reluctance to talk openly about issues to be a major challenge (EU-OSHA, 2019). Other challenges identified include fostering readiness for change (Nytrø et al., 2000), lack of awareness of stress and wellbeing, and competing priorities (Langenham et al., 2013).

INTRODUCTION TO THE MANAGEMENT STANDARDS

The MS were launched in 2004 with two peer-reviewed papers published in *Work & Stress* outlining the theoretical underpinnings (MacKay et al., 2004) and the development of the MS (Cousins et al., 2004). These standards define the characteristics of an organization where the risks from work-related stress are effectively managed and controlled. Although the MS are not regulations in themselves, nor an approved code of practice, they do form guidance which helps employers to fulfil their legal obligations to employee health and wellbeing. Under the Management of Health & Safety at Work Regulations 1999, employers in the UK have a legal responsibility to assess the risk of ill-health arising from work activities (including stress related ill-health), and in accordance with the Health & Safety at Work Act 1974, employers also have a duty to take measures to control the risks identified (as far as reasonably practicable). The most recent version of the MS is described on a website www.hse.gov.uk/stress/standards/# and a guide to the legal requirements can also be found at: www.hse.gov.uk/pubns/hsc13.pdf.

The MS outlines a step-by-step approach to managing psychosocial working conditions. Underlying principles include assessment of psychosocial working conditions using surveys and pre-existing data and participation, either directly engaging workers or through worker representatives. The content of the MS is defined as six psychosocial working conditions that are associated with health and wellbeing, productivity and sickness absence. The six conditions are: Demands, which include workload and work patterns; Control, which covers the amount of influence people have over the way they work; Support, which includes encouragement and resources provided by colleagues, management and the wider organization; Relationships, which cover the social relations and acceptable behaviours; Roles, which focus on the extent to which workers know what is expected of them in the organizations and that there are no conflicting expectations; and finally, Change, which covers the extent to which workers are informed about changes and that changes are managed in a way that is not related to poor wellbeing.

The MS process goes through five phases: 1) identify psychosocial risks, 2) identify who can be harmed and why (identifying at-risk groups), 3) evaluate the risks (identifying problems and developing solutions), 4) record your findings, which covers developing and implementing action plans and, finally, 5) monitor and review (review the implementation of action plans and the evaluation of whether they are effective and decide which corrective action to take if not effective). Although not formally defined as a stage, the MS include a preparation phase where it is recommended to set up a

steering group, ensuring commitment from key stakeholders in the organizations at all levels, and to develop a plan the for project and a communication plan. To accompany the MS, a workbook has been made available with top tips and a checklist of what to do. In reviews of national approaches to managing the psychosocial work environment, Nielsen et al. (2010) and Nielsen and Noblet (2018) identified a similar set of five phases across a range of approaches in Spain, Italy, Ireland, Germany, Belgium and Canada. The UK MS were also reviewed. The five phases identified in these reviews were preparation, screening (covering MS phases 2–4), action planning, implementation (covering MS phase 4) and evaluation (covering MS phase 5). In addition to summarizing and comparing these approaches the reviews sought to validate the approaches based on existing research, including research focusing directly on evaluating the national approaches but also wider organizational intervention literature.

In the following, we describe each of the five phases starting with the preparation phase and discuss critical issues at each phase, suggesting solutions and providing recommendations for how the challenges reported by organizations may be overcome.

Step 0: Preparation

Despite not being identified as a specific step, the MS recommends that before beginning the step-wise intervention process, preparation is needed to set up the project (for more information see www.hse.gov.uk/stress/standards/before.htm). The key elements of this preparation are: ensuring commitment, setting up a steering group and developing a communication plan, and in organizations that do not yet have an organizational stress policy, to develop such a policy. The MS state that it is crucial to ensure both senior management and employee commitment. Senior managers also function as role models, and it is suggested that if management does not clearly signal their commitment to the project, workers are unlikely to follow suit. The MS suggests that three arguments can be put forward to create commitment. First, managing the psychosocial work environment is a legal requirement in the UK; second, there is a business case following the 'happy worker-productive worker' thesis that workers high in wellbeing perform better; and third, the moral case – work-related stress can have serious long-term effects such as cardiovascular diseases, gastrointestinal disease and poor lifestyle such as alcohol or drug abuse.

The MS suggests establishing a steering group consisting of key stakeholders in the organizations. These stakeholders include senior management, worker or worker representatives such as health and safety representatives or union representatives, line managers and Human Resource and Occupational Health representatives. The advantage of a steering group is that workload is more evenly distributed, workers' expertise of what changes are needed are exploited, and it does not rely on one person to ensure progress. Two key roles should be fulfilled by members of the steering group: a *project champion* who functions as the face of the process, and a day-to-day champion who has got *project management* skills. Finally, a communication strategy should be developed that includes details of what should be communicated to whom, when and by which means.

The preparation phase is undoubtedly a crucial phase that influences the remainder of the process (Nielsen et al., 2010; Nielsen and Noblet, 2018), but it is not without its challenges. Despite the MS emphasis on getting senior management on board, this is a major challenge (Schuller, 2020). In their interview study of 100 organizations' experiences implementing the MS, Mellor et al. (2011) found that senior managers were reluctant to address stress issues as they perceived stress to be part of the job. This finding suggests that although bringing forward arguments or

cases for managing the psychosocial work environment is important, more work is needed to educate senior management (and for that matter all key stakeholders) in what a good psychosocial work environment could look like and why it is important to create good psychosocial working conditions. We will return to this issue in phase 3.

As pointed out by Schuller (2020), line management often presents a challenge to get on board, as they are not held accountable for managing the project at the group and team levels. This challenge is also an issue in the MS where limited attention is paid to the role of line managers. Although it is recommended that line managers be represented on the steering group, their role is overlooked in the preparation phase. However, line managers are often the ones to communicate the vision and the aims and objectives of changes, and they are also responsible for implementing changes at the team or work group levels; thus ensuring their commitment is crucial. Nielsen (2017) argued that line managers can either make or break an intervention. They play a crucial role in making changes happen and ensuring ongoing commitment; however, they may also obstruct progress either through lack of communication or by not allowing time for changes to be made or for workers to become engaged in the process. Nielsen (2017) argued that line managers may break interventions for good reason. If managing psychosocial working conditions is not integrated into core activities of teams and work groups and the line manager's key performance indicators, then line managers may not fully commit to the MS process as evidenced by Biron et al. (2010). Despite having received training and participated in workshops, only a third of the line managers in the organization even distributed the survey to assess the psychosocial working conditions. Moreover, Mellor et al. (2011) found that line managers were often unavailable. Line managers are often selected on the basis of their professional expertise, but line managers lacked the necessary skills and knowledge for the wellbeing intervention (Mellor et al., 2011). Supplementary to the MS, the UK HSE supported research into the competencies that line managers need to support employee wellbeing (Lewis et al., 2010; Yarker et al., 2008); however, these competencies have not been integrated into the MS.

The preparation phase needs to consider how to ensure line managers' commitment. In addition, as part of the preparation phase, existing policies and practices should be reviewed on how to integrate the MS process. Furthermore, line managers should be trained such that they possess the necessary skills. Nielsen et al. (2013) suggested that line managers should not only be trained in the process but should also develop specific action plans for how the intervention could be aligned with their other responsibilities.

Step 1: Identify the Risk Factors

In the first step of the MS, the focus is on education. It is emphasized that the focus of the MS is to understand how organizational level issues impact specific work groups or large numbers of workers. It is argued that by removing a stressor or an adverse working condition, many affected workers can be helped as opposed to managing individual cases. The MS acknowledges that individual support may be necessary where it has not been possible to remove the stressor. It is recommended that the steering group be familiar with the six standards, how the MS translates into the specific organizational setting and discussions are initiated on adverse working conditions specific to the organization in question.

The MS focus on prevention is aligned with general recommendations to the importance of tackling the causes of stress and poor wellbeing, rather than the symptoms (ETUC, 2004; EU-OSHA, 2010; ILO, 2001). The focus on prevention also tackles the second challenge identified by Schuller (2020),

that psychosocial risk management is often perceived as the individual's responsibility.

Although it is crucial that members of the steering group understand the MS and the processes underlying the MS, research points to the importance of communicating the aims and the process to the entire intervention group. Sensemaking theory (Weick, 1995) suggests external stimuli prompt workers to develop cognitive schemas. Workers are not just passive recipients of interventions (Nielsen, 2013) but actively generate meaning of what matters to them and this sensemaking determines their actions (De Jaegher and Di Paulo, 2008). Stensaker et al. (2008) found that participants need to feel involved to make sense of the changes introduced and thus sensemaking is important to ensure buy-in and ownership over the changes brought about by the intervention. Workers who understand the rationale behind interventions, in this case the MS, are more likely to support the change (Maitlis and Christianson, 2014). As a result, workers may be more motivated to complete questionnaires, participate in ad hoc working groups and develop action plans, thus playing an active role in shaping the MS process.

Step 2: Who Can Be Harmed and How

In this step, focus is on identifying workers at risk and what these risks are by comparing working conditions against the six MS. The MS suggest that existing organizational data such as productivity data, sickness absence records and turnover rates can identify groups at risk or informal data collection such as walk- and talk-throughs, focus groups or team meetings. The primary tool, however, in this phase is the HSE Indicator Tool. The HSE Indicator Tool is a standardized questionnaire which measures the six MS: Demands, Control, Relationships, Support, Roles and Change. The Indicator Tool has been validated in UK samples, in both the private and the public sectors and benchmark figures are available for UK occupations (Edwards et al., 2008; Edwards and Webster, 2012). Once the survey has been completed, it is recommended to feed back the results to workers.

A recent review of the empirical studies that had used the HSE Indicator Tool in their research identified 13 studies which all reported a number of challenges with its use (Brookes et al., 2013). First, the Indicator Tool is often not used in its entirety. Second, benchmarking may not be appropriate for all occupational groups, e.g. high-stress sectors. Third, the Indicator Tool was found not to include all working conditions relevant to all occupations. Finally, none of the studies reported that any action had been taken to improve working conditions as a result of the survey. An additional criticism of the HSE Indicator Tool could be that it does not include any out comes of poor working conditions. No wellbeing or stress measures are included and this makes it impossible to determine the impact of any of the six MS on the surveyed workers' stress and wellbeing. In reviews of the MS, the relevance of the HSE Indicator Tool has been questioned (Cox et al., 2009; Tyers et al., 2009). Globalization, increased competition, significant digital development, austerity and the recent COVID-19 pandemic have reshaped the working conditions of employees and increased the potential for stress in the workplace (Mark and Smith, 2008). Globalization has created a 24/7 working culture affecting home–life balance. Increased competition has raised concerns about job security. Digital development places demands on an ageing workforce to keep pace with technology. Austerity has reduced contract size but increased zero-hour contracts (Dollard et al., 2007). The volatile nature of the economy coupled with precarious working has created an environment in which it is unclear where the responsibility for health and safety lies. Research on the MS has argued that they should reflect the broader organizational

issues as well as the operational issues that are representative of the psychosocial working conditions facing workers in organizations today (Cox et al., 2009; Mellor et al., 2011; Tyers et al., 2009).

These criticisms resonate with wider criticisms of standardized questionnaires in intervention research. Nielsen et al. (2014) developed a tailored questionnaire aimed at identifying the resources and demands experienced by mail carriers in the Danish national postal service. Based on interviews and focus groups, they developed tailored items that were specific to the population and, rather than using Likert type scales, they tapped into workers' appraisals of whether working conditions were perceived to be a resource or a hindering demand (Lazarus and Folkman, 1984; van den Broeck et al., 2010). They also included outcomes of job insecurity, burnout and work engagement. In the feedback of survey results, Nielsen et al. (2014) reported the percentage of workers reporting an aspect of the work environment as either positive or problematic. They also presented risk ratios of whether a working conditions was linked to either burnout, job insecurity and work engagement. Nielsen et al. (2014) also reported the percentages for the number of staff reporting a working condition to be problematic or reporting a positive aspect of work.

In interviews and focus groups, Nielsen and colleagues (2014) explored how this approach had been experienced by managers and workers in the intervention group. They reported that the tailored items in the survey meant that workers felt the survey was relevant to them (Nielsen et al., 2014). They also acknowledged that developing a tailored questionnaire may be time-consuming and resource-intensive, but the results pointed to the importance of including measures relevant to the occupational group in question. In Italy, the authorities have adopted the MS but have also further developed it, for example by supplementing the HSE Indicator Tool with outcome measures and working conditions specific to the population (Di

Tecco et al., 2020). Another example is the KIWEST, which has been developed for use in the university sector in Norway (Innstrand et al., 2015).

Step 3: Evaluate the Risks, Explore Problems and Develop Solutions

The main objective of the third step is to discuss the results of the previous step and develop solutions. Participation is emphasized in this step as well and it is suggested that focus groups should be held with representative samples of workers to develop solutions. The MS suggests that discussing the results in focus groups is important because the screening may not have captured issues most important to staff and new issues may emerge during discussions that have not been covered by the HSE Indicator Tool. This acknowledgement of the limitations of the HSE Indicator Tool calls for a review of the approach and the tailoring of survey instruments as discussed above.

The use of focus groups is argued to reap the benefits of a) making use of workers' expertise of adverse working conditions, b) using workers' knowledge of how solutions will work in practice, and c) involving workers in developing and agreeing solutions means they are more likely to work towards implementing changes. All these benefits are generally recognized as advantages of participatory processes (Nielsen et al., 2010; Nielsen and Noblet, 2018; Nielsen and Randall, 2012). The empirical studies evaluating the MS, however, point to a number of challenges in this step. Broughton et al. (2009) found that most organizations had not progressed past setting up a steering group and gathering data from the Indicator Tool. Mellor et al. (2013) found that many organizations had not used the foucs-group approach. Organizations found the use of focus groups to be challenging, time-consuming and resource-intensive (Cox et al., 2009; Mellor et al., 2013; Tyers et al.,

2009) and outputs were not easily translated into action points, neither were they clearly related to the results from the Indicator Tool (Tyers et al., 2009). Furthermore, Tyers et al. (2009) found that experienced and impartial facilitators achieved better outcomes. In their evaluation of the MS, Broughton et al. (2009) and Mellor et al. (2013) concluded that while organizations were proficiently implementing steps 1 and 2, organizations found it challenging to move beyond these steps.

A common distinction exists between direct (workers being directly involved in participatory processes) and indirect participation (workers being involved through representatives) (Walters et al., 2012). Based on sensemaking theory (Weick, 1995), it could be questioned whether indirect participation when discussing the results of the screening is sufficient. Participation in the discussion of results provides stimuli and cues that workers translate into cognitive schemas and these schemas drive behaviours (Weick, 1995). In support of direct participation, Weber and Manning (2001) found that participants who actively participated in the implementation did revise their cognitive schemas. Discussing the results of data collection is likely to lead to collective sensemaking (Stensaker et al., 2008).

Rather than having focus groups, results could be discussed at the team level in team meetings; this could enable collective sensemaking. It is possible that through discussions of working conditions, members of the work team develop a shared meaning of the problems (Weick, 1995) and this shared meaning enables a joint understanding of what needs to change. It may also help workers to understand each other's perspectives better. Not all workers may be equally affected by adverse working conditions (Abildgaard et al., 2018b) and so discussing results at the team level may facilitate a better understanding of different perspectives within the work group. An additional benefit of having these discussions at the team level would be that the discussions can be integrated into existing team meetings and practices. This integration would eliminate the resources and the time required at the same time as ensuring that those that need to understand the impact of work practices and procedures, go through a sensemaking process and develop an understanding of each other's perspectives. In organizations where tools and methods are already in existence for continuous improvement (such as Kaizen), the discussions could be integrated into these systems (Augustsson et al., 2015). Using pre-existing tools and methods may capitalize on workers' familiarity with the tools and minimize the burden of parallel systems and processes (Smith, 2002).

Where such systems are not in place, templates and guidance for how to discuss results should be made available to enable progress. The ARK process provides one example: individual workers each select three working conditions they would like to preserve and three they feel need to change. These are then discussed in plenary sessions and the working conditions to prioritize are agreed (Christensen et al., 2019).

Step 4: Record Your Findings, Develop and Implement Action Plans

After the consultation with workers, the MS recommend that suggested solutions be collated and an overall action plan developed. Solutions should be reviewed with a view to setting goals that can be evaluated, prioritizing solutions and demonstrating commitment to address workers' concerns. It is suggested this work be done by the steering group. Recommendations for the development of an overall action plan include that actions are given an order of priority, should be deemed capable of tackling issues of concern and include a review (to check that it does successfully address the targeted issue). The necessary resource to implement action should be allocated, clear responsibility for actions allocated and there should be a

realistic timescale for implementation. Furthermore, actions should be aimed at different levels in the organization (i.e. individual, group, leader or wider organization). The action plan should include strategies for how they should be implemented at the lower levels of the organization and how the implementation will be monitored. Research supports the development of multi-level action plans (Day and Nielsen, 2017; LaMontagne et al., 2007; Nielsen and Noblet, 2018) and detailed action plans (Nielsen and Noblet, 2018).

As in the previous step, the development of an overall action plan in the MS implies indirect participation. In support of this, Mellor et al. (2013) found that workers were not directly involved in developing solutions. However, Cornwall (2008) argues that workers only have a voice if they have agency in determining future directions. Sensemaking theory suggests that organizational members come to understand the world by taking action and then observing the outcomes of this action (Weick, 1995); this implies that all workers need to be involved in the action planning process to fully understand and buy into action plans. Stensaker et al. (2008) suggested that workers involved in a participatory process act as both sensemakers and sensegivers. The participatory process ensures shared meanings and collective autonomy (De Jaegher and Di Paulo, 2008) as workers collectively job craft changes in working conditions (Nielsen, 2013).

In her study of the challenges of psychosocial risk management, Schuller (2020) found that one of the solutions to a time-consuming process was to devolve as many activities to the lower levels (teams and work groups) as possible so that changes could be implemented quickly if something did not have the intended effects. This suggests that a move from developing and implementing actions at the steering-group level to the work-team level may be beneficial.

Using existing continuous improvement processes may also be beneficial in this step for the same reasons. Where these do not exist, tools and methods should be developed that enable the development of detailed action plans and plans for follow-up. One example of such a tool is the improvement board (Wåhlin-Jacobsen, 2018). As part of the project in three manufacturing companies, an improvement board was developed, inspired by Kaizen boards (Imai, 1986). The board enabled work teams to work through a phased approach for developing and implementing action plans. Underlying the improvement board, was a set of 'ground rules', e.g. rules of discussion, who would lead meetings and when they would take place. The improvement board went through five phases. In the first phase, workers would note ideas and frustrations on sticky notes. These could be based on the results of the survey. The sticky notes were then moved across the board as the process developed. In the next phase, sticky notes would be prioritized. The tools were used to help prioritize which working conditions to change by focusing discussion on a) which changes would enhance wellbeing, quality of outputs and productivity, thus focusing on a win-win-win situation and enhancing the understanding of the interplay between the three; b) the balance between demands and resources; and c) the action radius, including discussions on the resources required to address an issue and the ability of the work team to implement the change. Based on these discussions, sticky notes would be moved to either a field containing a 'trash can' for sticky notes that would not be considered further, or a 'parking lot' for those sticky notes that should be reconsidered at a later stage. Prioritized sticky notes were moved to a field called 'Who does what when?' and responsibility and deadlines for implementation identified. The final field was named 'Done!' and once the action had been implemented the sticky note would be moved here. Colleagues who had been instrumental in completing the plan would be acknowledged and once a number of actions had been successfully

implemented, the successes would be celebrated. According to the theory of distributed cognition (Hutchins, 1995), visualization is a physical representation that enables shared awareness of the process and the content of actions. The improvement boards may enable collective sensemaking and provide an effective tool for getting an overview of actions planned and implemented.

The Nielsen et al. (2014) study found that the reporting of both resources and hindering demands was well-received (Nielsen et al., 2014). Participants found that the focus on positive aspects of work helped create a positive atmosphere in which to develop action plans. Furthermore, in some cases it may not be feasible to minimize demands, and identifying resources may be important as strengthening resources may buffer the adverse effects of demands that cannot easily be reduced (Vignoli et al., 2017). Focusing on both resources and demands could help overcome the challenge identified by Schuller (2020) that key stakeholders saw adverse psychosocial working conditions as part of the job. Focusing on both resources and demands may also have the benefit of providing a stronger business case: working on developing resources and increased work engagement may build the case for the 'happy-productive' worker (Nielsen et al., 2017).

Involvement in the action planning stage may fulfil basic needs. According to Social Determination Theory (Deci and Ryan, 2000), humans have three basic needs: autonomy, belongingness and competence. Involving workers at the action planning stage may fulfil the need for autonomy as they have a say in determining which actions to take. Jointly discussing and agreeing actions at the team level may also fulfil the need for belonging as workers feel they are part of a team, but also part of the wider organization as they provide input to what must be changed at higher levels within the organization. Through discussions about what the best action may be to address identified issues, workers fulfil their need for competence.

Step 5: Monitor and Review

In the fifth and final step of the MS, the recommendation is to review actions taken in the previous steps. This review involves monitoring whether action plans have been implemented according to plan and evaluating whether these actions have achieved the intended outcomes. It also involves reviewing whether further action or data collection is required. If it is found that actions were ineffective, then a review is required to identify what else can be done. If actions are working, it needs to be reviewed to see if it should be implemented organization-wide.

In the final step of the MS, participation is also recommended. The MS suggests that meetings can be set up to review progress, possibly during existing team meetings, but also informal chats can be instructive. Indirect participation is also encouraged involving union or other staff representatives. The MS suggest repeating the survey will enable the analyses of any changes in the six standards. It is recommended to do this as part of a continuous improvement process, e.g. annually. Finally, reviewing existing data such as turnover, sickness absence and productivity will show any improvements in these outcomes.

The literature recommends monitoring and evaluating effects by following the principles of participation (Nielsen and Noblet, 2018); however, there are issues that perhaps could be elaborated. First, there is little information about how to monitor and implement changes. One of the challenges identified by Schuller (2020) was the lack of accountability at all organizational levels, but in particular the line-management level. In the organizational intervention literature, it is widely recognized that often line managers are responsible for managing the intervention process at the lower levels. Indeed, Nielsen (2017) argued that line managers can either make or break an intervention. She argued that line managers must have the necessary skills to implement actions, but it is equally important they be given the necessary resources and that psychosocial risk management be integrated into their daily responsibilities and key performance indicators (Nielsen, 2017).

Second, participation is mainly seen in the MS as an exercise through which to gather information about workers' perceptions, but emphasis is not put on whether workers have developed a better understanding of psychosocial risk management or how to better manage their working conditions. The fifth challenge identified by Schuller (2020) revolved around the fact that those who had formal responsibility within an organization were not necessarily the best suited to implement changes. This calls for empowerment of workers. Processes should be put in place that allow workers to reflect on their learning. Sustainability in organizational interventions is often understood to be whether an action has had long lasting effects; however, in today's global environment, changes happen quickly and new risks emerge as can be seen in the recent COVID-19 crisis. It could be argued that true sustainability can only be achieved when workers develop the competence and capability to identify and manage emerging psychosocial risks.

DISCUSSION

EU and national legislation puts the emphasis on prevention of stress and poor wellbeing, i.e. addressing adverse working conditions as the source rather than the symptoms. Despite the legislative frameworks, organizations report challenges successfully managing the psychosocial work environment (e.g. Schuller, 2020). In this chapter we have provided a critical review of one country's approach, the UK Management Standards, developed by the Health and Safety Executive, to managing the psychosocial work environment. The MS are laudable as they provide a detailed process of managing psychosocial working conditions and clear guidance on what are considered psychosocial working conditions. The MS overcome the challenges of a lack of overall structured process as identified by Schuller (2020); however, theory and research suggest that they could be improved. Primarily, the appropriateness of the HSE Indicator Tool and the quality of the participatory process can be questioned. Based on research and psychological theory, we have made suggestions for how the MS intervention process may be optimized. These suggestions may translate to other national approaches.

We call for a revision of the HSE Indicator Tool to allow for more flexibility, taking into account sector- and occupation specific psychosocial working conditions and the changed nature of work with precarious employment contracts, self-employment and digitalization. We also call for the inclusion of stress and wellbeing outcomes and innovative ways of feeding back results. There are no objective levels of adverse psychosocial working conditions that have proven effects on workers' stress and wellbeing (Nielsen et al., 2014) because workers' appraisals of working conditions within their organizations play a key role in their reactions, so our methods need to reflect this. Screening needs to capture what is important to the workers in particular organizational contexts. Only then can appropriate actions be developed and implemented.

Organizations employing the MS approach report difficulties in ensuring employee participation; this implies that the MS lack guidance as to how organizations can achieve this process. In this chapter we have argued that the participatory process may be best achieved by moving the focus from indirect representation and time-consuming and resource-intensive supplementary processes to direct participation at the work group and team level, integrating the MS process into existing work practices and procedures. This shift does not mean that management does not have an overall responsibility to review organizational policies and procedures which may be associated with adverse working conditions, stress and poor wellbeing.

Moving as many activities to the team level at steps 2–5 may give workers a voice, thus overcoming the challenge of psychosocial risk management identified by Schuller (2020) that workers are not given a realistic opportunity to have their voices heard. Nielsen and Miraglia (2017) argued that it is not only the content of action plans but also the way the interventions are implemented that brings about improved wellbeing. Participation has been found to be related to social support, which in turn is related to job satisfaction (Nielsen and Randall, 2012). Participation can thus be seen as a means to an end (Abildgaard et al., 2018a) and a sensemaking process. The social aspects of sensemaking are particularly important in organizational settings (Maitlis, 2005), and shared understandings occur through collective sensemaking processes (Maitlis and Christianson, 2014).

Direct participation and integration of the psychosocial risk management process may have benefits in their own right. Von Thiele Schwarz et al. (2017) found that incorporating wellbeing issues into existing continuous performance systems such as Lean was related to improved wellbeing. Integrating these different processes may enhance sensemaking as workers are already familiar with these systems and a win-win situation can be achieved supporting the business case for considering the wellbeing issues at the same time as addressing performance issues. Furthermore, von Thiele Schwarz et al. (2017) found that the integrated process also resulted in workers reporting they had developed the capabilities to identify and manage psychosocial issues. In other words, an added benefit of direct participation is organizational learning and sustainable change.

Critique has been raised that organizations have sought workers' feedback but failed to subsequently address the issues raised (Broughton et al., 2009; Mellor et al., 2013). This is likely to be seen as a breach of the psychological contract and may increase cynicism and commitment (Rosseau 2010). It is therefore crucial that once organizations commit to the MS, they go through all phases; however, organizations need support to do so. We argue that the MS should be developed to include practical tools to support the participatory process. The development of concrete and easy to use tools will help organizations manage the process successfully.

CONCLUSION

In summary, although the MS is to be commended for not only being one of the first policies to provide guidance on psychosocial risk management and stress and wellbeing in relation to both process and content, this chapter suggests that a review of the approach is appropriate, both in light of recent research and psychological theory.

REFERENCES

Abildgaard JS, Hasson H, von Thiele Schwarz U, Løvseth L, Ala-Laurinaho A and Nielsen K (2018a) Forms of participation: the development and application of a conceptual model of participation in work environment interventions. *Economic and Industrial Democracy*, doi.org/10.1177/0143831X17743576.

Abildgaard JS, Nielsen K and Sverke M (2018b) Can job insecurity be managed? Evaluating an organizational-level intervention addressing the negative effects of restructuring. *Work & Stress* 32(2): 105–123.

Augustsson H, von Thiele Schwarz U, Stenfors-Hayes T and Hasson H (2015) Investigating variations in implementation fidelity of an organizational-level occupational health intervention. *International Journal of Behavioral Medicine* 22(3): 345–355.

Biron C, Gatrell C and Cooper CL (2010) Autopsy of a failure: evaluating process and contextual issues in an organizational-level work stress intervention. *International Journal of Stress Management* 17(2): 135-158.

Brookes K, Limber C, Deacy C, O'Reilly A, Scott S and Thirlaway K (2013) Systematic review: work-related stress and the HSE management standards. *Occupational Medicine* 63(7): 463–472.

Broughton A, Tyers C, Denvir A, Wilson S and O'Regan S (2009) *Managing Stress and Sickness Absence: Progress of the Sector Implementation Plan, Phase 2*. Brighton: The Institute for Employment Studies.

Christensen M, Innstrand ST, Saksvik PØ and Nielsen K (2019) The line manager's role in implementing successful organizational interventions. *The Spanish Journal of Psychology* 22: E5.

Cornwall A (2008) Unpacking 'participation': models, meanings and practices. *Community Development Journal* 43(3): 269–283.

Cousins R, Mackay CJ, Clarke SD, Kelly C, Kelly PJ and McCaig RH (2004) 'Management standards' work-related stress in the UK: practical development. *Work & Stress* 18(2): 113–136.

Cox T, Karanika-Murray M, Griffiths A, Wong YYV and Hardy C (2009) *Developing the management standards approach within the context of common health problems in the workplace: a Delphi study (Research Report 687)*. Merseyside: Health and Safety Executive.

Day A and Nielsen K (2017) What does our organization do to help our well-being? Creating healthy workplaces and workers. In N Chmiel, F Fraccaroli and M Sverke (eds) *An Introduction of Work and Organizational Psychology*. Oxford: Wiley Blackwell, pp. 295–314.

Deci E and Ryan R (2000) The 'what' and 'why' of goal pursuits: human needs and the self-determination of behavior. *Psychological Inquiry* 11(4): 227–268.

De Jaegher H and Di Paolo E (2008) Making sense in participation: an enactive approach to social cognition. *Emerging Communication* 10: 33–47.

Di Tecco C, Nielsen K, Ghelli M, Ronchetti M, Marzocchi I, Persechino B and Iavicoli S (2020) Improving working conditions and job satisfaction in healthcare: a study concept design on a participatory organizational level intervention in psychosocial risks management. *International Journal of*

Environmental Research and Public Health 17(10): 3677–3691.

Dollard M, Skinner N, Tuckey MR and Bailey T (2007) National surveillance of psychosocial risk factors in the workplace: an international overview. *Work & Stress* 21(1): 1–29.

Edwards JA and Webster S (2012) Psychosocial risk assessment: measurement invariance of the UK Health and Safety Executive's Management Standards Indicator Tool across public and private sector organizations. *Work & Stress* 26(2): 130–142.

Edwards JA, Webster S, Van Laar D and Easton S (2008) Psychometric analysis of the UK Health and Safety Executive's Management Standards Work-related Stress Indicator Tool. *Work & Stress* 22(2): 96–107.

ETUC (2004) *Framework Agreement on Work-related Stress.* Brussels: European Trade Union Confederation.

EU-OSHA (2010) *European Survey of Enterprises on New and Emerging Risks, 2010.* Available at: www.esener.eu (accessed 25 April 2020).

EU-OSHA (2016) *Second European Survey of Enterprises on New and Emerging Risks (ESENER-2). Overview Report: Managing Safety and Health at Work.* Luxembourg: Publications Office of the European Union.

EU-OSHA (2019) *Third European Survey of Enterprises on New and Emerging Risks (ESENER-3). First Findings.* Luxembourg: Publications Office of the European Union.

European Council (1989) *Council Directive of 12 June 1989 on the Introduction of Measures to Encourage Improvements in the Safety and Health of Workers at Work (89/391/EEC). OJ L* 1989, 183: 1–8.

European Social Partners (2004) *Framework Agreement on Work-related Stress.* Brussels: European Social Partners – ETUC, UNICE (BUSINESSEUROPE), UEAPME and CEEP.

HSE (2018) *Work Related Stress Depression or Anxiety Statistics in Great Britain, 2018.* Available at: www.hse.gov.uk/statistics/causdis/stress.pdf (accessed 5 May 2020).

Hutchins E (1995) *Cognition in the Wild.* Cambridge MA: MIT Press.

ILO (2001) *Guidelines on Occupational Safety and Health Management Systems.* Geneva: International Labour Office.

Imai M (1986) *Kaizen: The Key To Japan's Competitive Success* (First edition). New York: McGraw-Hill/Irwin.

Innstrand ST, Christensen M, Undebakke KG and Svarva K (2015) The presentation and preliminary validation of KIWEST using a large sample of Norwegian university staff. *Scandinavian Journal of Public Health* 43(8): 855–866.

LaMontagne AD, Keegel T, Louie AM, Ostry A and Landsbergis PA (2007) A systematic review of the job-stress intervention evaluation literature, 1990–2005. *International Journal of Occupational and Environmental Health* 13(3): 268–280.

Langenham MK, Leka S and Jain A (2013) Psychosocial risks: is risk management strategic enough in business and policy making? *Safety and Health at Work* 4(2): 87–94.

Lewis R, Yarker J, Donaldson-Feilder E, Flaxman P and Munir F (2010) Using a competency-based approach to identify the management behaviours required to manage workplace stress in nursing: a critical incident study. *International Journal of Nursing Studies* 47(3): 307–313.

Lazarus, RS, and Folkman S (1984) *Stress, appraisal, and coping.* New York: Springer publishing company.

MacKay CJ, Cousins R, Kelly PJ, Lee S and McCaig RH (2004) 'Management standards' and work-related stress in the UK: policy background and science. *Work & Stress* 18(2): 91–112.

Madsen IE, Nyberg ST, Hanson LM, Ferrie JE, Ahola K, Alfredsson, L, Batty GD, Bjorner JB, Borritz M, Burr H, Chastang JF, de Graaf R, Dragano N, Hamer M, Jokela M, Knutsson A, Koskenvo M, Koskinen A, Leineweber C, Niedhammer I, Nielsen ML, Nordin M, Oksanen T, Peitersen JH, Pentti J, Plaisier I, Salo P, Singh-Manoux A, Suominen S, ten Have M, Theorell T, Toppinen-Tanner S, Vahtera J, Väänänen, A, Westerholm PJM, Westerlund H, Fransson EI, Heikkilä K, Virtanen M, Rugulies R, Kivimäki, M and for the IPD-Work Consortium (2017) Job strain as a risk factor for clinical depression: systematic review and meta-analysis with additional individual participant data. *Psychological Methods* 47(8): 1342–1356.

Maitlis S (2005) The social processes of organizational sensemaking. *Academy of Management Journal* 48(1): 21–49.

Maitlis S and Christianson M (2014) Sensemaking in organizations: taking stock and moving forward. *The Academy of Management Annals* 8(1): 57–125.

Mark GM and Smith AP (2008) Stress models: a review and suggested new direction. *Occupational Health Psychology* 3: 111–144.

Mellor N, MacKay C, Packham C, Jones R, Palferman D, Webster S and Kelly P (2011) 'Management standards' and work-related stress in Great Britain: progress on their implementation. *Safety Science* 49(7): 1040–1046.

Mellor N, Smith P, Mackay C and Palferman D (2013) The 'management standards' for stress in large organizations. *International Journal of Workplace Health Management* 6(1): 4–17.

Nielsen K (2013) How can we make organizational interventions work? Employees and line managers as actively crafting interventions. *Human Relations* 66: 1029–1050.

Nielsen K (2017) Leaders can make or break an intervention: but are they the villains of the piece? In K Kelloway, K Nielsen and J Dimoff (eds) *Leading to Occupational Health and Safety: How Leadership Behaviours Impact Organizational Safety and Well-being*. Chichester: Wiley, pp. 197–209.

Nielsen K and Miraglia M (2017) Critical essay: what works for whom in which circumstances? On the need to move beyond the 'what works?' question in organizational intervention. *Human Relations* 70(1): 40–62.

Nielsen K, Abildgaard JS and Daniels K (2014) Putting context into organizational intervention design: using tailored questionnaires to measure initiatives for worker well-being. *Human Relations* 67(12): 1537–1560.

Nielsen K, Nielsen MB, Ogbonnaya C, Känsälä M, Saari E and Isaksson K (2017) Workplace resources to improve both employee well-being and performance: a systematic review and meta-analysis. *Work & Stress* 31(2): 101–120.

Nielsen K and Noblet A (2018) Organizational interventions: where are we, where do we go from here? In K Nielsen and A Noblet (eds) *Organizational Interventions for Health and Well-being: A Handbook for Evidence-based Practice*. Oxford: Routledge, pp. 1–23.

Nielsen K and Randall R (2012) The importance of employee participation and perception of changes in procedures in a teamworking intervention. *Work & Stress* 29(2): 91–111.

Nielsen K, Randall R, Holten AL and Rial-González E (2010) Conducting organizational-level occupational health interventions: what works? *Work & Stress* 24(3): 234–259.

Nielsen K, Stage M, Abildgaard JS and Brauer CV (2013) Participatory intervention from an organizational perspective: employees as active agents in creating a healthy work environment. In G Bauer and G Jenny (eds) *Concepts of Salutogenic Organizations and Change: The Logics Behind Organizational Health Intervention Research*. Dordrecht: Springer, pp. 327–350.

Nytrø K, Saksvik PØ, Mikkelsen A, Bohle P and Quinlan M (2000) An appraisal of key factors in the implementation of occupational stress interventions. *Work & Stress* 14(3): 213–225.

OECD (2014) *Making Mental Health Count: The Social and Economic Costs of Neglecting Mental Health Care*. Paris: OECD Publishing.

Parker SK, Morgeson FP and Johns G (2017) One hundred years of work design research: looking back and looking forward. *Journal of Applied Psychology* 102(3): 403–420.

Ronchetti M, Di Tecco C, Russo S, Ghelli M and Iavicoli S (2015) An integrated approach to the assessment of work-related stress risk: comparison of findings from two tools in an Italian methodology. *Safety Science* 80: 310–316.

Rousseau, DM (2010) The individual–organization relationship: The psychological contract. In S. Zedeck (Ed.), *Apa Handbook of Industrial and Organizational Psychology, Vol. 3. Maintaining, Expanding, and Contracting the Organization*. Washington, DC: American Psychological Association, pp. 191–220.

Schuller K (2020) Interventions as the centrepiece of psychosocial risk assessment: why so difficult? *International Journal of Workplace Health Management* 13(1): 61–80.

Smith D (2002) *IMS: Implementing and Operating*. London: BSI British Standards Institution.

Stensaker I, Falkenberg J and Grønhaug K (2008) Implementation activities and organizational sensemaking. *The Journal of Applied Behavioral Science* 44(2): 162–185.

Toderi S, Balducci C, Edwards JA, Sarchelli G, Broccoli M and Mancini G (2013) Psychometric properties of the UK and Italian versions of the HSE Stress Indicator Tool. *European Journal of Psychological Assessment* 29(1): 72–79.

Tyers C, Broughton A, Denvir A, Wilson S and O'Regan S (2009) *Organisational Responses to the HSE Management Standards for Work-related Stress: Progress of the Sector Implementation Plan Phase 1.* Contract Research Report, 693. Liverpool: Health and Safety Executive.

Van den Broeck A, De Cuyper N, De Witte H and Vansteenkiste M (2010) Not all job demands are equal: differentiating job hindrances and job challenges in the Job Demands–Resources model. *European Journal of Work and Organizational Psychology* 19(6): 735–759.

Vargas O, Flintrop J, Hassard J, Irastorza X, Milczarek M, Miller J, Parent-Thirion A, Van Houten G and Vartia-Väänänen M (2014) *Psychosocial Risks in Europe: Prevalence and Strategies for Prevention* (928971218X). Luxembourg: Eurofound and EU-OSHA.

Vignoli M, Nielsen K, Guglielmi D, Tabanelli TC and Violante FS (2017) The importance of context in screening in occupational health interventions in organizations: a mixed methods study. *Frontiers in Psychology: Organizational Psychology* 8: 1347, doi: 10.3389/fpsyg.2017.01347.

Von Thiele Schwarz U, Nielsen K, Stenfors-Hayes T and Hasson H (2017) Using Kaizen to improve employee wellbeing: results from two organizational intervention studies. *Human Relations* 70(8): 966–993.

Wåhlin-Jacobsen CD (2018) Valid and taken seriously? A new approach to evaluating kaizen-inspired (and other) intervention tools. In K Nielsen and A Noblet (eds) *Organizational Interventions for Health and Wellbeing: A Handbook for Evidence-based Practice.* Oxford: Routledge, pp. 105–128.

Walters D, Wadworth E and March K (2012) *Worker Representation and Consultation on Health and Safety: An Analysis of the Findings of the European Survey of Enterprises on New and Emerging Risks (ESENER).* Brussels: Publications Office of the European Union.

Weber PS and Manning MR (2001) Cause maps, sensemaking, and planned organizational change. *The Journal of Applied Behavioral Science* 37(2): 227–251.

Weick KE (1995) *Sensemaking in Organizations.* Thousand Oaks, CA: Sage.

Yarker J, Lewis R and Donaldson-Feilder E (2008) *Management Competencies for Preventing and Reducing Stress at Work: Identifying the Management Behaviours Necessary to Implement the Management Standards, Phase Two.* Sudbury: HSE Books.

National Arts and Wellbeing Policies and Implications for Wellbeing in Organizational Life

Simon Ellis Poole and Alison Clare Scott

INTRODUCTION

There is general agreement nowadays of the value of the arts to our health and wellbeing, for instance personal experience of music to lift depression, words to express our lived emotions, the aesthetic quality of a work of visual art that can take us to deeper understanding. The arts include a 'broad and diverse landscape of interrelated creative practices and professions, including performance arts (including music, dance, drama, and theatre), literary arts (including literature, story, and poetry), and the visual arts (including painting, design, film) (see UNESCO 2006)'

For many, their relevance to mental and physical health is a given, to sustain, to prevent deterioration, or to improve the healing process. An appreciation of their value to health and wellbeing is often due to specific personal experience. Indeed, as Victoria Hume, Director of Arts Council England's Culture Health and Wellbeing Alliance stated in an interview (July 2020), 'People get it when they've done it', observing that it is a 'slow, iterative process of building

champions' who are conveying the necessary messages that shift attitudes. The events of the COVID-19 pandemic and lockdown in 2020 have caused many to consider again their priorities and how they can better sustain their own situations, as Dr Clive Parkinson, international arts and health advocate, Director of Arts for Health at Manchester Metropolitan University UK, and Visiting Fellow at the University of New South Wales Australia, observed (July 2020): 'The importance of culture and the arts in all their forms, to impact on health, wellbeing and social change, has never felt so relevant' (Wall, 2019: 1).

The benefit of the expressive arts for the work environment, similarly, can be supportive for the employee and employer, with improved attendance, heightened concentration, management of stress or anxiety, enhanced teamwork and augmented output being some of the benefits. However, quantifiable evidence is in short supply and yet is often considered a necessity before agreement is made for funding. How do we ensure that the contribution of the arts to health and wellbeing is understood and implemented by organizations? Once their worth is understood, there is a need for the possibilities of their implementation to be explored and for the activities to be incorporated into the structures of the workplace as an essential resource. This assumes a willingness on the part of the artists to play their part in such an operation and a sharing of ethics, and requires adjustment in the use of their talents and skills towards an outcome that may be different for them.

The World Health Organization (WHO) considered wellbeing as an intrinsic factor for health, building it into their constitution. They placed *wellbeing* in their first principle of health, which is: 'a state of complete physical, mental and social well-being and not merely the absence of disease or infirmity' (WHO, 2020). The benefits of this to the workplace have gradually been better understood, moving forward from considerations solely of health and safety in relation to injury or medical conditions. The societal attitude towards mental health has become more positive and less discriminatory, which is reflected in organizational strategies. The trend is to include a greater emphasis on the improvement of levels of health, and the understanding of wellbeing extends to job satisfaction and happiness at work. Rokho Kim of the WHO (2012) spoke about the reasons for the attachment of value to this aspect of life:

- Why health, safety, and wellbeing at work?
- Workers are half of the whole population.
- Healthy workforce is a prerequisite for sustainable development and social wellbeing.
- Risks at stake:
  ○ Workers: loss of health and wellbeing
  ○ Company: loss of productivity and profit
  ○ Community: loss of solidarity and equity
  ○ Country: loss of 4–5% of GDP.
- Prevention can make 'win-win-win-win'. (Rokho, 2012)

The argument for preventative work in order to avoid crises is a given and events in relation to the COVID-19 pandemic have demonstrated how destructive a crisis can be to the global and national economy, to businesses, to social structure and to individuals.

A shift in emphasis at a national level requires governmental will to view success differently. A recent collaboration in 2018 by the governments of Scotland, Iceland and New Zealand has led to the first 'Wellbeing Economy Governments' policy, which is shifting the perception of success from GDP to that of 'quality of life' of the citizens of their nations and is beginning to place wellbeing at the centre of their focus, i.e. 'driving the wellbeing agenda in economic, social, and environmental policymaking' (Trebeck, 2019). It does not seem insignificant that these countries share female gender leaders; the World Economic Forum recently published findings that indicated that countries with female leaders were also responding in ways that curbed COVID-19's spread more effectively and that one of these ways was evident in policies that focused on protecting people's wellbeing not their country's economies (Garikipati and Kambhampati, 2020). In 2019, Iceland's Prime Minister urged other governments to place wellbeing 'ahead of GDP in budget priorities' and Jacinda Ardern for New Zealand has performed a global first with a wellbeing budget which prioritizes 'mental health, domestic violence and child poverty' (Gregory, 2019). Scotland has placed wellbeing at the heart of its national performance framework (see McColl, 2018) and includes a statement that identifies creative and cultural expression as a significant element. In her TEDTalk about the launch of this tri-governmental collaboration, Sturgeon argued, 'what we choose to measure matters'; for GDP 'measures the output of all of our work', but 'says nothing about the nature of that work', that values need to change for global sustainability and a long-term view, and 'the objective of economic policy should be collective wellbeing; how happy and healthy a population is, not just how wealthy a population is' (Sturgeon, 2019).

A strategic approach to ensuring that well-being is implanted within an organization comes via policies, for example a mental health policy, which can be driven by national examples from government departments and public health. The range of effects pertinent to work are described in detail thus:

> [l]ost production from people being unable to work; reduced productivity from people who are ill at work; lost production from absenteeism, accidents at work; lost production from premature death; loss of the breadwinner of a dependent family; unwanted pregnancy; untreated childhood disorders lead to educational failure, hence to unemployment and to illness in adult life; untreated parental disorders leading to childhood disorders and a cycle of disadvantage. (Friedl et al., 2005: 2)

In recognizing the importance of mental health to society and a nation's economy, action to protect and support the workforce at all levels needs to be built into the workplace structure, ensuring that it becomes an assumption rather than an exception. It is a matter, too, of the implementation of human rights for mental health. In the foreword to Friedl et al.'s 2005 book on developing mental health policy, Levyt describes the worldwide adversity that arises from mental illness:

> This burden is not only from disability and suicide, but also from the loss of economic productivity, family burden, reduced access to and success of health promotion, prevention and treatment programmes, and mortality from the associated vulnerability to physical disease, including infectious diseases. (2005: 10)

The argument, therefore, for utilizing strategic means to insinuate and embed best practice for mental health into business thinking rests on the understanding of the potential losses if preventative and supportive measures are not undertaken. Success depends on the drive for this existing at all levels, from the boardroom and throughout the workforce. The involvement of expressive arts as an automatic part of this process is not yet a common factor.

EFFICIENCY DRIVES, THE ECONOMIC IMPERATIVE AND THE SUPPOSED NEED FOR RESILIENCE IN THE WORKFORCE

The Stevenson-Farmer Independent Review into Mental Health in the workplace (Stevenson and Farmer, 2017) was commissioned by Theresa May in January 2017. Around this time, each person suffering from stress, depression or anxiety was taking 21.2 days off work on average (GOV.UK, 2019). The review aimed to understand how employers could better support all individuals in employment, including those with poor mental health or wellbeing. The independent research organization Monitor Deloitte was asked to support this review by exploring the following questions:

- What was the cost of poor mental health to employers?
- What was the return on investment (ROI) to employers from mental health interventions in the workplace?
- What could employers learn from international examples in terms of good practice?

In response to these questions, Siegel and Hampson (2017) of Monitor Deloitte calculated the cost of poor mental health in the workplace to be a significant number at £33bn–£42bn, the mid-point of which was equivalent to almost 2% of UK GDP in 2016. In accordance with this, the 'Centre for Mental Health' found that in 2016/17, ten years on from 2006 when they had initially collected data (Parsonage, 2007), the cost of poor mental health in the workplace was £39.4bn in that year; an estimate that represents an increase of 35% on the corresponding total for 2006 (Parsonage, 2007; Parsonage and Saini, 2017). This cost is borne by businesses of all sizes and across all industries. Siegel and Hampson's (2017) analysis showed the costs per employee across the UK as ranging from £497 to £2,564, depending on the industry and sector.

Parsonage and Saini's (2017) results were again similar at £1,300 per UK employee. The £39.4bn cost to employers is due to three main factors. These are £21.2bn brought about by presenteeism; £10.6bn due to sickness and absence; and the remaining £3.1bn due to staff turnover (Parsonage and Saini, 2017). Of huge significance to this pilot project is that these costs are disproportionately born in the public sector, particularly in healthcare. The research also found that the return on investment of workplace mental health interventions was overwhelmingly positive, with an average ROI of 4:1 (Siegel and Hampson, 2017).

Of great import are the figures that the likes of Koivumaa-Honkanen et al. (2004) elucidate in their study. They show that an individual's wellbeing predicts subsequent work disability especially amongst the normally healthy. Furthermore, that wellbeing predicts a broad range of general health outcomes including, for example, working days lost through illness five years later (Koivumaa-Honkanen et al., 2004), or the likelihood of stroke six years later and of cardio-vascular disease ten years later (Lyubomirsky et al., 2005, as cited in Mind, 2017). These figures not only show how personally devastating poor mental health can be to individuals but also how resilience-building is an attractive notion for organizations, and why they should safeguard against employee poor mental health, and why therefore it has begun to be built into workforce routines. 'Resilience-building' is a contentious topic that cannot be dealt with in any detail in this work, but needless to say, if left unresolved, issues surrounding wellbeing create amplified issues for employers, and ultimately society, in the long term.

It should be noted, though, that resilience-building as a notion could also seem attractive to employers for more nefarious motives. For example, if poor mental health or wellbeing exists within a workforce, suggesting this is due to a lack of resilience, it sidesteps the employer taking any responsibility, instead maintaining that it is the supposedly lacking employee who is accountable. It assumes they are the flawed aspect of the organization and asks of them to change. In this more cynical, or perhaps just resistant-to-neoliberal-impact-agendas stance, resilience can be seen as synonymous with compliance. There is an assumption that the organizational systems are healthy and the environments non-toxic, and that it is the employee who needs to make adjustments.

The current and potential provision of the creative arts in relation to health and wellbeing was investigated by the UK parliamentary cross-party group (APPG), which reported its findings and found that 'The arts make a significant contribution to improving the lives, health and wellbeing of patients, service users and carers, as well as those who work in health and the arts' (Arts Council England, 2007: 4, cited by APPG, 2017). However, it is acknowledged that there is a paucity of research that provides the required evidence and that which is available is often 'inconclusive'. Engagement in the arts can entail activity on a number of levels, i.e. creative expression through a variety of media, for self-expression or as part of a group, listening to, viewing or reading works by musicians/singers/poets/artists/playwrights/authors. The benefits of the arts to the health agenda are broader than might usually be expected, as they include, 'self-confidence, self-esteem, sense of empowerment, reduction in anxiety and depression, a reduction in risk factors related to long-term care, reduction in medicine, enhanced cognitive skills, sense of achievement, and reduced use of healthcare' (Maughan et al., 2016; Stickley and Eades 2013; Stickley and Hui 2012a; Thomson et al., 2015, all as cited in Wall et al., 2019a: 8).

The US Department for Arts and Culture (USDAC) refers extensively in its report, *Arts and Well-Being: Toward a Culture of Health* (Goldbard, 2018), to the findings of the UK's All-Party Parliamentary Group on Arts, Health and Wellbeing's report (2017), whilst recognizing the difference between the cultures, i.e. 'the sheer number of public sector studies, interventions, and actions … [that] illustrate the advantage that comes from considering social well-being from the perspective of a relatively well-nourished public sector' (Goldbard, 2018: 7). Thus, there was a need to establish a definition of 'health' as a starting point, employing the World Health Organization's constitutional principles (see www.who.int/about/who-we-are/constitution) and a focus on the necessity for social and cultural measures. If the aim transcends and subsumes the wellbeing of individual patients, instead extending to a state in which 'good health flourishes across geographic, demographic, and social sectors' (Hagan, 2016, cited by Goldbard, 2018: 3), then strategies to engage people in promoting their own health along with the larger society's must be multidimensional, flexible, improvizatory and long term.

In order to address this broader aim, three areas of focus are identified by Goldbard, the USDAC chief policy wonk:

- On PREVENTION: including social interventions that can prevent suffering by addressing the conditions that cause it; also on education about risks and remedies both for those not currently experiencing diminished well-being and to those who are.
- On ADVOCACY: groups or projects formed to change public views of health or illness, advocating for the rights of those vulnerable to or coping with health challenges.
- On TREATMENT: interventions designed to serve and support those living with disease or other health impairments, often taking place in healthcare environments. (Goldbard, 2018: 12)

Working to this agenda, the role of the arts is considered to be integral in effecting change at each of these levels. Numerous international examples of good practice that cover all of these are cited in the report (e.g. Malawi; Calgary, Canada; Turin, Italy; Johannesburg and Soweto, South Africa; Los Angeles, United States; Oxford, England; Otago, New Zealand; Bosnia; and Peru),

alongside Parkinson's *Manifesto on Arts for Health* parts one and two (2011; 2012) (which takes the stance that 'creativity goes beyond materialism and is like food and water, art is an expression of imagination and a powerful vehicle for social change') (Parkinson, 2011: 12), and *A Recoverist Manifesto* which specifically regards work in Italy, the UK and Turkey with thinking around 'recovery from substance misuse', and that argues for 'a wider conversation around cultural change' (Parkinson, 2014, cited by Goldbard, 2018: 13).

There is an identification of the qualities that are needed for those artists who work in the field of wellbeing and health, i.e. that they should be skilled in their media and rooted in community, perceiving that it may not be suitable for everyone; with an acknowledgement that capabilities may have to be developed such as:

- Deep listening and creative strategies to unearth the parables, metaphors, and narratives that shape people's relationship to health;
- Approaches that give full value to our ability to respond to threats to health and well-being not only through medical protocols, but through engaging creativity, emotion, and imagination; and
- Artistic skill to return those stories to their creators and to the larger society in ways that engage empathy and spark the desire and social imagination to change what's not working. (Goldbard, 2018: 4)

The Creative Health report from the APPG (2017) had an influential impact internationally since it was comprehensive in its evidence and recommendations. It led to the establishment of the Strategic Alliance for Culture, Health and Wellbeing in the UK, which has demonstrated how developments can be moved forward from such a document. Movement has been careful and deliberate, with the creation of sub-groups focusing on different areas; for instance, following representation with charities, the National Lottery Heritage Fund now has a 'wellbeing' component. Arts Council England has been working with health managers to create a facility for 'social prescription' so that medical professionals will be able to select an activity from a variety of arts amongst other possibilities and prescribe it in addition to, or as an alternative to, allopathic medication. There is movement towards consensus about the requirements for use of the arts and arts practitioners as a joint approach in health delivery, approaching a code of practice and coordination with Higher Education so as to provide a means of ensuring suitable skills training and development; and a code of ethics is underway, working from bio-psycho-social models.

Since the launch of the UK report, the response in Wales which began with legislation in 2015 with the Wellbeing of Future Generations Act, has led to a Memorandum of Understanding (September 2017) between Arts Council Wales and the Welsh NHS Confederation and an increase in dialogues with members of the Cross Party Group on Arts and Health in the Welsh Assembly. There is an expressed desire to find ways to convince others of the relationship between the arts and wellbeing, 'The agreed areas of work will include advancing good practice; promoting collaboration, coordinating and disseminating research and working together to identify how arts can contribute to peoples' health and wellbeing' (The NHS Confederation 2018: 12).

There seems to be a firmer commitment at a national level now to the understanding of the power of the arts in the improvement of health and wellbeing. It is understood that they should be regarded as a necessary addition to pharmaceutical prescriptions and suitable care arrangements. They are also useful for health promotion and prevention, improving health environments and are beneficial for staff/employees. The Welsh NHS Confederation explains their benefits thus:

Arts and creativity are key to mental health because:

- It's a way of self-expression. Unexpressed thoughts and feelings can be very damaging and it's important to let them out in a healthy way. As well as allowing you to express your thoughts and feelings, creativity can help you to make sense of them and it can help put things in perspective.
- It gives you something to focus on. Creativity can help take the focus away from destructive, negative thoughts. It is a healthy way of channelling negative energy into something positive.
- It can be enjoyable. Doing something enjoyable gives you good feelings which help you feel better about yourself.
- It teaches you to focus on the process. Creativity can teach you to be mindful and immersed in the present moment.
- It gives you purpose and meaning. Creativity gives you something meaningful to do.
- You can learn something new. Creativity is an opportunity, for example, learning to draw or play a musical instrument, and can help you to build confidence.
- It can give you a sense of accomplishment. Accomplishment can come from the process of doing or learning and it's not necessarily about the end result. As a bonus, you may feel a sense of achievement when you create something.
- It can be a way of connecting with other people. Doing something that you enjoy is an opportunity to connect and make friends with like-minded people.
- It is therapeutic. The benefits of creativity are recognised. There is widespread use of creativity as therapy, for example, art and music therapy. (The NHS Confederation 2018: 2)

The field of arts therapy is one of professional practice, with an expectation of regulation of standards of clinical service, which differentiates it from artist activity per se.

The benefits of the expressive arts to health and wellbeing are being demonstrated at a variety of projects; for instance, the 'Framework for Woodland Skills Instructors and Psychotherapists' in Monmouth is using photography, ceramics and creative writing alongside woodland skills training with emergency services and forces staff who are affected by complex trauma/PTSD, establishing the benefit of the natural landscape as a third key element. The contribution to resilience is also a factor, whilst in the United States:

> [c]reative activity undertaken outside of work has been seen to hasten recovery from work strain and enhance work-related performance, leading researchers to conclude that organizations 'may benefit from encouraging employees to consider creative activities in their efforts to recover from work'. (Eschleman et al., 2014: 1)

There is no consistency of direction for the inclusion of the arts as part of health and wellbeing policies in organizations, nor at a national level. Australia and Wales seem to lead the way, with collaboration between national agencies providing good examples and allocation of funding to relevant projects. In Australia in 2013, 'the Standing Council on Health and the Meeting of Cultural Ministers endorsed a national arts and health framework' (APPG, 2017: 54). The expressive arts need vocal advocates of the value that they offer, in order to persuade leaders in business to commit to their inclusion in vision and planning for their organizations.

ART FOR ART'S SAKE

The means of ensuring that wellbeing is supported by organizations rests in a cultural adoption of well-written explicit policies and allocation of suitable levels of finance that will provide the incentive for positive change in practice. The creative arts provide an effective medium for that change, although the understanding of their value may not yet be prevalent:

> Expressive writing practices have, for some time, been linked to a strengthened immune system, various medical markers of health such as blood pressure, reduced indicators of stress, longer-term mood changes, and ability to deal with social and work life (Pennebaker 1997). (Wall et al., 2019b: 2)

However, there is a preference for qualitative rather than quantitative research in the arts field, whilst there also seems to be a lack of clarity about its therapeutic role in health and wellbeing. The differentiation between arts therapy, arts participation and arts appreciation is not always specified in investigations as to its advantages. A further difficulty lies in the uncertainty of explanations about the beneficial process. As Pennebaker (2004) wrote on the subject of expressive writing:

> Although the expressive writing paradigm has generally produced positive health outcomes, a recurring puzzle concerns how and why it works. No single theory or theoretical perspective has convincingly explained its effectiveness. This may be attributable to the fact that expressive writing affects people on multiple levels – cognitive, emotional, social and biological – making a single explanatory theory unlikely. (2004: 138)

In an environment where a precision of thought is required and 'value for money' rules financial allocation, there is insufficient flexibility to determine to place the arts at the centre of a wellbeing policy.

Having worked in the field of creative writing for therapeutic purposes, with incorporation of the visual arts, there is direct experience of the benefits for those who engage with these activities, both for practitioners and participants. Creative writing and art therapy unlock pathways to recovery from post-traumatic stress:

> The use of written expression in improving mental and physical health with respect to trauma has received support in numerous studies (e.g. Donnelly and Murray, 1991; Francis and Pennebaker, 1992; Lange, 1994; Murray and Segal, 1994, Pennebaker, 1993; Spera et al, 1994). (Mazza, 2003: 14)

The use of visual arts to connect with non-verbal material and bring it into a form which can then be rendered in verbal language can be beneficial for dealing with emotional material relating to, e.g. depression and anxiety. The process is described in three 'phases' by Bucci: '"referential phase 1" which allows "the breakthrough in thinking", "referential phase 2" where "images (are) put into language in early draft form" and "reformulation" when insight occurs through the "study of images, rewriting and reflection"' (Robinson, 2000: 79–84).

The ways that writing and reading can be used to assist the process of recovery are supportive of any talking therapy, as long as the practitioner is suitably trained and experienced. Thus, a creative writing session must be led with care and due attention to the therapeutic focus. Written texts may provide comfort or insights from descriptions of parallel experience that we can identify with, whilst difference can facilitate insights in a non-challenging way. Correspondingly, self-expression in our own writing of our own lived truths in response to prompts (verbal and visual) can help us to find our voice and give a sense of greater strength. The use of fiction can further assist us in the use of the third person, making it easier to encounter our feelings indirectly, as described by Richo (2008: 32):

> We do not simply remember an event or loss mentally. We feel it, and this feeling is a signal that we have something to address, process, resolve, and then integrate. Instead, we might refer it to, transfer it into someone else who resembles the characters in our story.

The writing process can be therapeutic per se and in a creative writing workshop, there is more than one stage in the activity, which facilitates the participant's work to get in touch with their emotions in a non-damaging way and to begin to make changes to their internal landscape. It is described in more detail by Hynes and Hynes-Berry (2012: 145):

> The act of writing in itself involves the steps of recognition, examination, juxtaposition, and self-application. Then as the written material becomes the material for discussion, the emotions and concepts are processed again.

A practitioner will ensure that participants are encouraged to write without inhibition or fear with an understanding of the vulnerability that needs to be protected and safety ensured in sessions:

> Expressive writing comes from our core. It is personal and emotional writing without regard to form or other writing conventions, like spelling, punctuation, and verb agreement ... [It] is not so much what happened as it is how you feel about what happened or is happening (Evans, 2012).

The sessions are designed to facilitate a sense of empowerment in the writer, with control in their relationship with the language, in the material which they encounter and in the expression of their emotions. It is possible to work individually and with groups, and this type of activity is well suited to this arrangement, as researched and verified by Mazza (1981), who 'found that poetry therapy did advance group cohesion and self-discovery' (Mazza, 2003: 114). The expressive arts are well suited to communication with self, online communication and group work.

However, if those with influence have not encountered the benefits of the arts and are not convinced of it, there will be no detectable shift in cultural and organizational attitudes to advance the provision, and opportunities will be lost. If it is not built into, say, a mental health policy, there will be no safeguards and the human right to wellbeing will be missing an essential dimension. One way of addressing this could be to target the (future) strategy drivers of an organization and give them the experience. For instance, in 2019 a group of trainee GPs undertook a day of 'arts and health' activities as part of a residential event in Sevenoaks, Kent, UK, provided by London Arts in Health Forum. As well as drama, singing and drawing, the doctors experienced writing for wellbeing through an experienced practitioner and member of Lapidus International (an organization for practitioners who are concerned with writing for wellbeing). The aims were that they would leave 'knowing the power such projects can have, for them to be advocates for arts and health activities and also to feel confident when accessing or suggesting arts and health to patients or colleagues' (Field, 2019). Feedback confirmed that the goals of the day had been achieved.

THE NATIONAL CONTEXT AND A CASE IN POINT

The human encounter at the center (sic) of therapy will always be a deeply subjective, nonquantifiable experience. (Yalom and Leszcz, 2005: 34)

Yalom and Leszcz's (2005) comment could be misleading if read with no knowledge of what has happened in the field of wellbeing research since it was written. The concept of 'wellbeing' especially in relation to work has been quantified both quantitively and qualitatively the world over (see Siegel and Hampson, 2017, for detailed case studies of several governmental approaches around the globe). It may still be thought of as deeply subjective in many cases, but that does not mean it remains enigmatic or 'holographic' as Ereaut and Whiting (2008) describe, nor a slippery elision of constructs (Ecclestone and Hayes, 2009: 374). On the contrary, in the 2014 independent report *Wellbeing and Policy*, Lord Gus O'Donnell et al., go a good way to 'legitimate subjective well-being as a principal objective for public policy alongside traditional goals like higher GDP' (Bakhshi, 2014: 304).

It does, however, seem evident that whilst wellbeing has been adopted in UK political and policy discourse more sincerely since the end of the 20th century, there are as many definitions of it as there are governmental departments (Spratt, 2016). Nonetheless, research interest in mental health, wellbeing, wellness and recovery, and the relationship individuals or collectives have with their workplace, has been increasing in the 2010s. Wellbeing's status as a structuring concept, particularly as a policy issue in the UK, can be seen to gather further momentum from 2010 when the 'Prime Minister's speech on wellbeing' made way for the launch of the 'national happiness index' (Cameron, 2010).

Crucially, in more recent years, responsibilities towards wellbeing have become 'taken for granted' in our considerations of employment, and increasingly employers have been called upon to shoulder some responsibility. This tendency is becoming further entrenched in the discourse, especially around means of employers levering change for personnel (Cooper and Mallalieu, 2017; O'Donnell et al., 2014; Robertson and Cooper, 2011). O'Donnell et al. (2014) argue (supported by a dozen pages of references) that a comprehensive and profound evidence base is now in existence to back and sustain the prioritization of wellbeing as an objective across the policy spectrum (Bakhshi, 2014). The growth in methodological developments and organizational structural studies concerning wellbeing and aiding workers to recover and return to work is testament to this (Petriglieri, 2020).

Wellbeing then is invoked in many contexts, in many workplaces, and is a hotly debated academic topic as the previous contextualization demonstrates. The following section offers another example, through the consideration of one particular nationwide research project undertaken by Mind, the mental health charity. The project was assessed several times by independent evaluators and also yielded many academic research papers.

Between 2015 and 2019, Mind delivered the 'Blue Light Programme', an ambitious programme aimed at reducing stigma, promoting wellbeing and improving mental health support for those working or volunteering in the ambulance, fire, police, and search and rescue services. It was chosen as an example of how organizational change was attempted during the period when literature concerned with arts and wellbeing policies began to gain traction, nationally and internationally. It was also chosen because it notably did not engage with the arts in any notable way and instead operated within a more economic-based paradigm, of the kind already described, which, for example, being outcome-driven, would see increased employee resilience as a measure; this was indeed the third strand out of five.

The work had mixed outcomes. For example, the legacy of the programme, as a whole, seemed to have had some positive impact according to Mind itself. In early 2019, Mind's Mental Health in the Emergency Services Survey found that (Mind, 2019):

- Staff and volunteers were far more likely to say their organization:
    - encourages them to talk about mental health (64 per cent compared with 29 per cent)
    - supports people with mental health problems well (53 per cent versus 34 per cent).
- They were also much more likely to be aware of the support available to help them manage their mental health (65 per cent versus 46 per cent).
- Perceptions were more positive among those who had involvement in the Blue Light Programme, compared with those who hadn't.

However, independent evaluations of the project's auxiliary research hypotheses proved to be inconclusive, as no demonstrable positive impact was seen from introducing an online programme that complemented the traditional group activities, for example (Wild, 2016). This should not be seen in a negative light though as this side project was a research and development type investigation to see if an online support facility might enhance or increase participant results. Wild's (2016) evaluation rigorously assessed Mind's resilience intervention for emergency workers in a large-scale randomized controlled trial. She found that the resilience intervention performed similarly to the online control intervention, meaning that there were no specific effects associated with the intervention (Wild, 2016). It does beg the question though as to whether in a post-COVID-19 world online interventions may become more popular, or indeed be perceived more negatively due to the increased screen time employees will now necessarily undertake.

Generally, participants who received both types of intervention enjoyed them and learned something from them. All participants felt that the intervention had a positive impact on them, which interviews with the facilitators also confirmed (Wild, 2016). Participants felt that the inclusion of a face-to-face element in

the mixed intervention was particularly valuable because of the peer support effects. The Economic Foundation (2017) that undertook a similar, yet qualitative piece of research found that, in reality, the quantity of concrete peer support that took place was possibly limited by small group sizes and absences. So this opinion was based on their expectations of the benefit of peer support as much as it was based on their actual experiences of the intervention (Foundation, 2017). The interview sample itself also raised concerns about the intervention's intended audience (Foundation, 2017), as the majority of participants were clerical support workers with an interest in wellbeing rather than the frontline emergency service personnel the project was perhaps more intended to serve. This in many ways highlights a broader problem, that of a systemic issue and failure to go beyond lip-service to the notion of embedding wellbeing strategies, and a move towards a protective or preventative approach rather than managing a reactive one. It demonstrates how even venerable charities such as Mind were at the time still reluctant to champion work which recognized the place of arts in organizations, or as organizations being reflective of society.

Whilst this project and research were clearly demonstrative of an upturn in interest in wellbeing, the central premise had not taken account of the growing movement linking the arts and wellbeing. So instead it was developed in a way that did not privilege the expressive, the individual or the humanistic.

Results from the 2019 Mind survey, despite some positive impact, particularly in terms of awareness-raising amongst employees, shows that poor mental health remains an issue for the emergency services:

- The number of staff and volunteers reporting good or very good mental health has gone down since 2015, from 53 to 45 per cent.
- The number of service personnel reporting poor mental health has increased from 14 to 21 per cent.

- Those with lived experience of mental health problems are less confident than colleagues that the culture in their organization is improving (57 per cent confidence compared with 73 per cent of those without lived experience).

Excessive workload continues to top the list of factors contributing to people feeling mentally unwell or stressed. But trauma is now cited by many as a source of pressure (Mind, 2019).

In summary, the Mind project attempted to improve wellbeing within the organizations of a particular sector, with varied outcomes, and this could be seen as indicative of a wider issue regarding systemic change within organizations. At the 2020 Virtual Trauma summit in Belfast, Maté stated, 'I'm not optimistic that this society will be all that easy to change. I'm not optimistic about that at all'. This gives rise to some broader questions; for example, could a more cohesive marriage between understandings of the arts and wellbeing benefit such programmes or catalyse change without restructuring systems? The Mind project certainly raised awareness of wellbeing, but it is not clear how it managed to do this, nor whether the multitude of options available to practitioners, like engagement with the arts, were methodologically embedded. To be fair, this was not really the intention of the project, but whether arts-based practice as research-type methodologies could have been utilized for greater positive impact is certainly an area that could be further explored. There is writing on this topic, and innovative methods for such work too, all of which are pushing conventional research project boundaries (Mackenzie et al., 2019; Poole et al., 2019; Poole and Solé, 2019). So, perhaps there are possibilities within dissensus?

Questions aside, wellbeing projects like this abound in organizations and they address the dominant political narrative's request to consider wellbeing for economic purposes. But how we understand the arts and their relationship to wellbeing is in itself an inimitable and necessarily indefinable collision of concepts. Even wellbeing on its own is often thought ill-defined, but as Ereaut and Whiting (2008) point out, it is never criticized as an ideal; it is universally accepted as positive. The prevalent and broad acceptance of the concept, alongside the flexibility of its definition, they suggest, makes a theoretically advantageous concept to marry policies and actions across diverse agencies (such as health, the police force, fire service or military) as the concept embraces an array of professional standpoints. The same can be said of the arts. Given the public sector costs that are directly associated with employee wellbeing, for example Siegel and Hampson (2017) attribute estimated costs somewhere between £5.5bn and £7.2bn to 'presenteeism' alone, it makes good economic sense not to just accept but act through considerate restructuring and policy design that recognizes the relationship for what it is, without asking it to fit into or change a system. To echo Maté's points from the Visual Trauma summit in 2020, it is too difficult to change systems even though we may be willing to do so; embracing the arts and wellbeing for how they are understood by professionals and practitioners that work with and within them then would seem a potentially viable possibility.

CONCLUSION: SHIFTING THE PARADIGM

A reader could delve back into the texts of 2017 and before and find a vibrant, high-quality literature engaging in concerns and thinking about wellbeing in organizations. If one were to pull together questions born out of this literature, one may come up with something like the following, which has been largely informed through a synthesis of Monitor Deloitte's (Siegel and Hampson, 2017) research, the Stevenson and Farmer review (2017) and Sir Cary Cooper's work on wellbeing (Cooper and Mallalieu, 2017), particularly the 2017 document *Creating Well Workplaces*. These are questions that organizations might have appositely asked of themselves at that time (and still could):

- What is the opportunity that could make a tangible difference to wellbeing by fundamentally changing the contract between employers and employees about where responsibility for workplace wellbeing lies?
- How can your organization leverage self-management and personal responsibility to respond to the challenges of modern work practices?
- How can a sustainable impact on your workforce wellbeing be achieved?
- What is the cost of poor mental health to you as an employer?
- What is the return on investment (ROI) for you as an employer from your current mental health interventions in the workplace? What could they be, given the evidence?
- What could employers learn from international examples in terms of good practice?

The literature since 2017, though, whilst still perhaps contingent of the themes born out of the literature mentioned, has themes that in some way answer these questions, or rather extend the debate. They call into question how organizations are fundamentally operating, intimating that if they are part of or serve society, then perhaps the way in which their success or prosperity is measured should be more reflective or expressive of that society. This continued debate or next step is emerging because of the perspective of the original questions. One might see the new, developing themes as a '"relational aesthetics" of organizations' to borrow from the art movement of the same name. However these themes or answers might be described, they have, in the following paragraphs, been summarized from international perspectives.

Employee presenteeism and employee sickness are extremely costly in the UK and are likewise evidenced globally, particularly for public sector organizations, and they show no signs of reducing. On the contrary, there is a strong evidence base that suggests that without a change of workplace practices, the problem of poor mental health in workforces, and equally slow mental health recovery, will not improve.

Therefore, coupling the evidence that the ROI of workplace mental health interventions is overwhelmingly positive, with the evidence that arts-based therapies are being used to great success in the organizational life of numerous sectors in the UK (but even more so in other countries), it would suggest high levels of psychological wellbeing amongst employees, and improved mental health recovery would be a highly likely outcome of any project. Not to mention that cost-efficiency itself, especially if implemented in a proactive manner, would be bettered. All in all, as Sir Cary states, this will:

> [t]ranslate into good news for any organization – including lower sickness-absence levels, attraction and retention of talented people and more satisfied customers, clients or service users. People with higher levels of psychological wellbeing work better, live longer and have happier lives. Engagement and well-being can sustain each other and lead to a healthier and more productive organization – a win-win for employees and employer. (Robertson and Cooper, 2011).

This all remains tantalizingly apposite in the current climate and speaks eloquently to the corporate world, with a familiar language. But there remains the difficulty of this compromise, however, because that is what it is from the perspective of many arts-therapy practitioners: a compromise, in order to survive, and whether this actually compromises the intentions of arts and wellbeing policies so as to irrevocably pollute the fidelity of their vision remains to be seen.

Globally speaking, however, we can see that there is increasingly an attempt to address the bigger question, which the UK in certain sectors has been a little slow to implement compared to our international counterparts: 'Where does the responsibility for wellbeing lie in today's new world of work? and, where does it lie in a post-COVID world?'

The evidence base is clear, from cultural and policy change to operations and practice, it is progressively more the employer's responsibility to provide support for the employee; it is also clear that it is in everybody's interest that they do. More contemporary research shows how the more progressive and responsive institutions and organizations have left the age of 'it comes with the territory' mindset far behind. Even Mind's Blue Light programme, despite not embracing arts-based catalysts for change, evidences this for example. It is publicly acknowledged when one of their paramedic campaign champions is quoted as saying: 'We can't take the stress out of this job we choose to do, but we can let people know that they're not alone'. Perhaps then an employee's vulnerability to poor mental health is beginning to be recognized as part of some jobs, but for now, for ethical as well as economic reasons, for wealth and wellbeing, one might say the paradigm is only starting to shift to a place where wellbeing is structured into work patterns or affecting policymakers' trajectories. Perhaps another challenge for employers or wonks, therefore, is to get ahead of the curve and work towards addressing the future landscape of work, rather than simply addressing the current issues. Could new frameworks, such as the aforementioned 'Framework for Woodland Skills Instructors and Psychotherapists', which uses art therapies in a woodland context, be the kind of resource that addresses the much-needed shift in the paradigm? Could they as emerging means support wellbeing in the workforce and engender structured team- or peer-support models as systemic, proactive measures that promote wellbeing in the workforce, for example, and futureproof our services (and businesses)? Could wonks and policymakers begin to steer our societies not by economics but by wellbeing?

This epicureanism or utopianism certainly seems possible, but many deeply entrenched assumptions remain in terms of what keeps an organization healthy, and they would need to evolve if national policy enactment were to grow beyond being reactionary or mealy mouthed. Equally, policy would need to authentically and genuinely engage in debate around whether economic measures of national prosperity are really reflective of society's dominant interests. Any obsession with justifying risks through cost-benefit analyses would need to evolve; the persistent challenge of psychometric measures being more highly valued than other non-economically based measures or approaches would need to be removed. Even the age-old artist's complaint of funders erring towards positivist methodological paradigms and thus not giving the arts and wellbeing policies a real chance to systemically operationalize within organizational cultures, would need to be dealt with. The potential implications of critically and reflexively embedded arts and wellbeing policies upon wellbeing in organizational life could be revolutionary, but if the arts are seen as slaves to wellbeing, neither will prosper. They are intrinsically linked and one cannot serve the other.

REFERENCES

All-Party Parliamentary Group on Arts, Health and Wellbeing (2017) *Creative Health: The Arts for Health and Wellbeing*. Available at: www.artshealthandwellbeing.org.uk/appg-inquiry/ (Accessed 07.08.20).

Arts Council England (2007) *A Prospectus for Arts and Health*. London: Arts Council England.

Bakhshi H (2014) Review of 'Wellbeing and Policy' by O'Donnell G, Deaton A, Durand M, Halpern D and Layard R. *Cultural Trends* 23(4): 304–307. (Accessed 07.08.20).

Cameron D (2010) *PM speech on wellbeing*. Available at: www.gov.uk/government/speeches/pm-speech-on-wellbeing (Accessed 17.06.2020).

Cooper C and Mallalieu J (2017) *Creating Well Workplaces: Helping Employees to Play Their Part*. Available at: www.robertsoncooper.com/creating-well-workplaces/ (Accessed 14.07.2020).

Ecclestone and Hayes (2009) *Changing the subject: the educational implications of developing emotional well-being*, Oxford Review of Education, 35:3, 371-389, DOI: 10.1080/03054980902934662

Ereaut G and Whiting R (2008) *What do We Mean By 'Wellbeing'? And Why Might it Matter?* Available at: https://dera.ioe.ac.uk/8572/1/dcsf-rw073%20v2.pdf (Accessed 13.05.2020).

Eschleman KJ, Madsen J, Alarcon G and Barelka A (2014) Benefiting from creative activity: The positive relationships between creative activity, recovery experiences, and performance-related outcomes. *Journal of Occupational and Organizational Psychology* 87(3): 579–598.

Evans JF (2012) Expressive writing. *Psychology Today*. Available at: www.psychologytoday.com/gb/blog/write-yourself-well/201208/expressive-writing (Accessed 26.01.2020).

Field V (2019) *Arts and Health GP Training for Lapidus*, 16 July.

Foundation N (2017) *An Evaluation of Mind's Resilience Intervention for Emergency Workers: Qualitative Interview Findings*. Available at: www.mind.org.uk/media/24693634/blue-light-programme_resilience-course-report-qualitative-interview-findings.pdf (Accessed 29.06.2020).

Friedl L, Jenkins R, McCulloch A and Parker C (2005) *Developing a National Mental Health Policy*. Hove: Psychology Press Ltd.

Gabor Maté by Clive Corry – Gabor Maté on Coronavirus, Trauma, Addictions and the Future (2020) *Virtual Trauma Summit*, Belfast, 19.06.2020. Available at: https://action-trauma.com/event/virtual-trauma-summit/

Garikipati S and Kambhampati U (2020) *Women Leaders Are Better at Fighting the Pandemic*. Available at: www.weforum.org/agenda/2020/07/women-leaders-policymakers-covid19-coronavirus/ (Accessed 07.08.2020).

Goldbard A (2018) *Art & Well-being: Toward a Culture of Health*. US Department of Arts and Culture (USDAC). Available at: https://usdac.us/cultureofhealth (Accessed 07.08.2020).

GOV.UK (2019) *Working Days Lost in Great Britain*. Available at: www.hse.gov.uk/statistics/dayslost.htm (Accessed 30.05.2020).

Gregory A (2019) Governments should put wellbeing ahead of GDP in budget priorities, Iceland PM urges. *The Independent*. 4 December. Available at: www.independent.co.uk/news/world/europe/iceland-gdp-wellbeing-budget-climate-change-new-zealand-arden-sturgeon-a9232626.html (Accessed 01.08.2020).

Hagan E (2016) Taking note: The impact of art in building a culture of health. In *National Endowment for the Arts*. Available at: www.arts.gov/art-works/2016/taking-note-impact-art-building-culture-health (Accessed 07.08.2020).

Hynes AC and Hynes-Berry M (2012) *Biblio/Poetry Therapy: The Interactive Process, A Handbook*, 2nd edition. Clearwater: North Star Press of St. Cloud.

Koivumaa-Honkanen H, Koskenvuo M, Honkanen R, Viinamäki H, Heikkilä K and Kaprio J (2004) Life dissatisfaction and subsequent work disability in an 11-year follow-up. *Psychological Medicine* 34(2): 221–228.

Levyt J (2005) Foreword. In Friedl L, Jenkins R, McCulloch A and Parker C (eds), (pp. 10) *Developing a National Mental Health Policy*. Hove: Psychology Press Ltd.

Mackenzie A, Wall T and Poole S (2019) Applied fantasy and well-being. In Leal W, Özuyar PG, Pace P, Azeiteiro U and Brandli L (eds) *Encyclopedia of the Sustainable Development Goals: Transforming the World We Want*. New York: Springer.

Mazza, N. (1981) *Poetry and Group Counseling: An Exploratory Study*. Tallahassee, FL.: Florida State University.

Mazza N (2003) *Poetry Therapy: Theory and Practice*. New York: Brunner-Routledge.

McColl P (2018) *Is it a Petal? Is it a Cog? No, it's Scotland's National Performance Framework*. Available at: www.nesta.org.uk/blog/is-it-a-petal-is-it-a-cog-no-its-scotlands-national-performance-framework/ (Accessed 01.08.2020).

Mind. (2017). *Wellbeing and Mental Health Support in the Emergency Services, Legacy Report*. Retrieved from https://www.mind.org.uk/media-a/4524/20046_mind-blue-light-programme-legacy-report-v12_online.pdf (Accessed 18.11.2020).

Mind (2019) *Wellbeing and Mental Health Support in the Emergency Services*. Available at: www.mind.org.uk/media/34557768/blue-light-programme-legacy-report_english-summary.pdf (Accessed 03.06.2020).

The NHS Confederation (2018) *Arts for Health and Wellbeing*. Available at: www.nhsconfed.org/-/media/Confederation/Files/Wales-Confed/Arts-for-Health-and-Well-being.pdf (Accessed 13.05.2020).

O'Donnell G, Deaton A, Durand M, Halpern D and Layard R (2014) *Wellbeing and Policy*. Available at: https://lif.blob.core.windows.net/lif/docs/default-source/commission-on-wellbeing-and-policy/commission-on-wellbeing-and-policy-report—march-2014-pdf.pdf?sfvrsn=0 (Accessed 13.05.2020).

Parkinson C (2011) *Manifesto on Arts for Health: Part One*. Manchester: Arts for Health.

Parkinson C (2012) *Manifesto on Arts for Health: Part Two*. Manchester: Arts for Health.

Parkinson C (2014) *A Recoverist Manifesto*. Manchester: Arts for Health.

Parsonage M (2007) *Mental Health at Work*. Available at: www.centreformentalhealth.org.uk/sites/default/files/2018-09/mental_health_at_work.pdf (Accessed 13.05.2020).

Parsonage M and Saini G (2017) *Mental Health at Work: The Business Costs Ten Years On*. Available at: www.centreformentalhealth.org.uk/sites/default/files/2018-09/CentreforMentalHealth_Mental_health_problems_in_the_workplace.pdf (Accessed 16.05.2020).

Pennebaker JW (1997) Writing about emotional experiences as a therapeutic process. *Psychological Science* 8(3): 162–166.

Pennebaker JW (2004) Theories, therapies, and taxpayers: On the complexities of the expressive writing paradigm. *Clinical Psychology Science and Practice* 11(2): 138–142.

Petriglieri G (2020) F**k science!? An invitation to humanize organization theory. *Organization Theory* 1: 1–18.

Poole S and Solé L (2019) Informal music-making and well-being. In Leal W, Özuyar PG, Pace P, Azeiteiro U and Brandli L (eds) *Encyclopedia of the Sustainable Development Goals: Transforming the World We Want*. New York: Springer, n.p.

Poole S, Marichalar-Friexa E and Scott C (2019) Psychogeography and well-being. In Leal W, Özuyar PG, Pace P, Azeiteiro U and Brandli L (eds) *Encyclopedia of the Sustainable Development Goals: Transforming the World We Want*. New York: Springer, n.p.

Richo D (2008) *When the Past Is Present: Healing the Emotional Wounds That Sabotage Our Relationships*. Boston: Shambala.

Robertson IT and Cooper CL (2011) *Wellbeing: Productivity and Happiness at Work*. Basingstoke: Palgrave Macmillan.

Robinson M (2000) Writing well: Health and the power to make images. *Journal of Medical Ethics* 26: 79–84.

Rokho K (2012) *WHO and Wellbeing at Work*. Available at: www.hsl.gov.uk/media/202146/5_kim_who.pdf. (Accessed 01.06.2020).

Siegel S and Hampson E (2017) *Mental Health and Wellbeing in Employment: A Supporting Study for the Independent Review*. Available at: www2.deloitte.com/uk/en/pages/public-sector/articles/mental-health-employers-review.html (Accessed 11.06.2020).

Spratt J (2016) Childhood wellbeing: What role for education? *British Educational Research Journal* 42(2): 223–239.

Stevenson D and Farmer P (2017) *Thriving at work: The Stevenson / Farmer review of Mental Health and Employers*. Available at: https://assets.publishing.service.gov.uk/government/uploads/system/uploads/attachment_data/file/658145/thriving-at-work-stevenson-farmer-review.pdf (Accessed 19.06.2020).

Sturgeon N (September 2019) *Why Governments Should Prioritize Well-being*. Available at: www.youtube.com/watch?v=gJzSWacrkKo (Accessed 10.07.2020).

Trebeck K (2019) *Here We Go: First Wellbeing Economy Governments Policy Lab Underway*. Available at: https://wellbeingeconomy.org/here-we-go-first-wellbeing-economy-governments-policy-lab-underway-katherine-trebeck (Accessed 08.08.20).

Wall T, Österlind E, and Fries J (2019), Springer Nature Switzerland AG 2019 In W. Leal Filho (ed.), *Encyclopedia of Sustainability in Higher Education*, https://doi.org/10.1007/978-3-319-63951-2_523-1

Wall T, Fries J, Rowe N, Malone N and Österlind E (2019a) Drama and theatre for health and well-being. In Leal Filho W (ed.) *Encyclopedia of Sustainability in Higher Education*. Cham: Springer Nature.

Wall T, Österlind E and Fries J (2019b) Arts-based approaches for sustainability. In Leal Filho W (ed.) *Encyclopedia of Sustainability in Higher Education*. Cham: Springer Nature.

Wild J (2016) *An Evaluation of Mind's Resilience Intervention for Emergency Workers*. Available at: www.mind.org.uk/media/4627959/strand-3.pdf (Accessed 13.06.2020).

World Health Organization (WHO) (2020) *Constitution*, signed on 22 July 1946 by the representatives of 61 States and entered into force on 7 April 1948. New York: World Health Organization. Available at: www.who.int/about/who-we-are/constitution (Accessed 01.06.2020).

Yalom ID and Leszcz M (2005) *The Theory and Practice of Group Psychotherapy*, 5th edition. New York: Basic Books.

26

Nudge Theory Applied to Wellbeing at Work

Marco Tagliabue

INTRODUCTION

Wellbeing is a complex construct that can be approached from several viewpoints. Wellbeing can be affected by interventions at different levels and, overall, it reflects a variety of human experiences (e.g., including inequalities) (Ruggeri, 2019). As highlighted in the previous chapters, organizational wellbeing not only relates to the aspects of the physical environment at work (e.g., determining quality and safety) but also includes the biological, psychological, and social components of the members of an organization. In this chapter, the focus is on a behavioral approach to wellbeing at work that makes use of contextual elements to increase employees' safety, satisfaction, engagement, and the working climate at large (see European Agency for Safety and Health at Work, 2013).

Specifically, the contextual cues described in this chapter are termed *nudges* aimed at affecting wellbeing, specifically at the workplace. Although they represent only one of the several techniques available for altering behavior inside or outside the organization, nudges are able to achieve important results, while retaining relatively low implementation costs. That is, nudges are cheap and easy to avoid, but potentially just as effective or even more effective at changing behavior than 'traditional' approaches that resort to incentives (Benartzi et al., 2017). Thus, nudges represent a useful tool for promoting wellbeing within the typical busy, time-restrained, and expense-attentive contemporary organization. Concurring with the way O'Neill (2018: 2) put it, taken together, this chapter submits to a wellbeing approach. It advocates nudging people to 'maintain and promote healthy decisions and behaviors through policies, programs, work culture, and workspace design'.

Nudge theory refers to a conceptual approach and a collection of tools and techniques aimed at influencing behavior (Thaler and Sunstein, 2008; Marchiori et al., 2017).

The former is typically referred to as *nudging*, whereas *nudges* intend the single interventions targeting a pinpointed behavior. In his general textbook, Ebbinghaus (1908) stated that psychology has a long past but a short history and the same may be affirmed about nudging. In fact, despite the relative novelty of nudge theory, the influence of behavior is a topic that has been studied for a long time and from several fields of inquiry. For example, both psychology and economics researchers have shown how choice and decision-making can be guided by contextual factors without the agent being necessarily aware of their effects (Smith and Decoster, 2000; Kahneman, 2011). Similar to resolving some of the current challenges in healthcare (Vlaev et al., 2016), wellbeing can only be reached by influencing behavior: at work, this means targeting employees' organizational behavior. Specifically, Torri and Toniolo (2010: 363) defined wellbeing at work as 'the organization's ability to promote and maintain the physical, psychological and social workers' wellbeing at all levels and for every job'. In this broad context, nudges may not work unless they are adapted to the specificity of each context and adjusted to the target behavior of which these levels are comprised.

Differently from other techniques of behavior change, nudges possess two fundamental features that are embedded in their definition and are likely to have contributed to their spread among scholars and practitioners. First, they retain freedom of choice, which means that no coercion or penalty is applied if the agent chooses to reject the nudge. For example, the employee who refuses to attend the recommended company yoga class should not be penalized in any way by the leadership, financially or otherwise. Second, nudges are economically advantageous because they are designed to be relatively cheap to implement and they do not program for any monetary incentive for following the nudge. That is, employees may not be paid to sign up for the same yoga class or else it would not be a nudge any more.

Not only has nudging received a noteworthy attention from scholars and practitioners; nudges have also started being embedded in the policymaking efforts of several organizations and agencies. This initiative is included under the umbrella of *behavioral insights*, which refer to the application of evidence-based principles of behavior to inform and design policies that target agents' choices and decision-making (see Ruggeri et al., 2020b). Once a nudge policy is in place, it is the organization's responsibility to translate it into a workspace nudge that exploits the encompassing natural and social features (e.g., signposting, defaults, etc.). Improving the physical work environment can facilitate desired behavior and promote wellbeing (Ruggeri et al., 2019: 162). By modifying the context for the good of the workers, nudges can positively affect the levels of co-creation, collaboration and sharing, community connection, and autonomy, which are critical to performance, satisfaction, and retention.

DEVELOPING NUDGES FOR WELLBEING AND ORGANIZATIONAL LIFE

Because of the ubiquity of behavior that characterizes all aspects of our private and social lives, nudging is an approach that can be effectively applied to virtually any domain, including wellbeing. Some examples of previously implemented nudges for increasing wellbeing beyond organizational behavior include eating healthier (Hanks et al., 2012), increasing physical activity (Lakerveld et al., 2018), attaining education (Damgaard and Nielsen, 2018), and improving long-term savings (Garcia and Vila, 2018).

Notwithstanding, it seems that nudge theory applied to work and organizational settings is not as extensively addressed in the literature as in other domains of application. Supposedly, this may partly be due to a more conservative approach of privately owned companies to share their insights and findings with their peers (who may eventually turn into competitors), or by the yet unbridged gap between academia and the industry or servicing domains (see Gera, 2012). Consideration of the wellbeing of employees should be paramount to any responsible employer, policymaker, and society altogether. As previously stated, nudging represents a freedom-preserving and cost-effective approach to increasing wellbeing at work, which should be resorted to more often than it is currently documented in the literature.

Some of the threats to wellbeing at work include physical, mental, and social factors (Naci and Ioannidis, 2015), which are in effect also while at work. Nevertheless, nudges are not 'silver bullets' and need to be adjusted to the uniqueness of each target behavior (e.g., compliance with personal protective equipment, uptake of company benefits programs, or establishing collaborative goals). Thus, nudges are useful tools for developing wellbeing in and for organizational life, as long as they are grounded on an evidence-based approach and they do not possess the claim of replacing traditional measures of wellbeing (e.g., policies and procedures). Similar to the conclusions of Benartzi et al. (2017) in governmental policymaking, nudges should be rather viewed as their cost-effective complement, wherein 'Well-being is perhaps the most critical outcome measure of policies' (Ruggeri et al., 2020a: 14).

In the remaining sections of this chapter, the reader is first to be presented with a definition and context for nudge theory in organizational settings. A simple model of a functional analysis of nudges is advanced and put in relation to target behaviors and their consequences on wellbeing. Next, ten important types of nudges applied to organizational wellbeing are listed and several examples are provided to illustrate the breadth of applications and provide suggestions for developing further the scope of nudging interventions. In the third section, some

diagnostic models for implementing nudge theory into policymaking and organizational routines are proposed. They are informed by the work of international organizations that have been mapping and consulting on large-scale behavior change. In the fourth section, the scope of nudging is expanded to include boosting and reinforcement, which may be particularly useful at educating about and sustaining behavior for wellbeing. Lastly, there is a discussion of some ethical concerns of nudging and recommendations for practitioners. As with other cases of behavioral influence, the justification for nudges should be limited to means and not ends, even though they preserve freedom (Sunstein, 2014).

WHAT IS A NUDGE AND HOW CAN IT BE OPERATIONALIZED IN RELATION TO WELLBEING?

The term *nudge* was formally operationalized by Thaler and Sunstein (2008) as a simple cue for steering choice in a given direction. In the authors' words, a nudge is 'any aspect of the choice architecture that alters people's behavior in a predictable way without forbidding any options or significantly changing their economic incentives' (2008: 6). Alternative definitions have been advanced in recent years emphasizing either the role of incentives (e.g., Hansen, 2017), the simplifying effects on decision processes (e.g., Benartzi et al., 2017), or the contingent relation with the environment (e.g., Simon and Tagliabue, 2018). In fact, the choice architecture included in the authors' words refers to the environment or the contextual variables in which the behavior takes place. Choice architecture is inevitable (Sunstein, 2015) insofar as the environment needs necessarily to be organized in one way or another. For example, the fruit and vegetable snack section could be placed before or after the sweet and sugary snack section at the company cafeteria and their disposition will likely influence our choice as consumers. Nevertheless, if both sections are present (for removing either of them would limit choice and thus not count as a nudge), one has to come before the other. Thus, choice architecture is not only ubiquitous but also unavoidable, which represents the third argument for nudging in addition to being cost-effective and retaining freedom of choice (Schmidt and Engelen, 2020).

There are typically two ways for producing effective behavioral change: one is to create rules and have people follow them; another is exploiting contingent relations between a behavior and its consequences on the environment (i.e., in most cases, an *if, then* relation, although a temporal relation may suffice). For example, an organization may introduce a new rule in the form of a policy that makes it mandatory to take a short outdoor walk during lunch break. Alternatively, it may invest in an outdoor walking path and encourage the employees to take the same short walk and, thus, experience directly the effects on their physical and mental wellbeing (i.e., a contingency-shaped behavior). However, for a behavioral contingency to be complete, there may be an antecedent term preceding the behavior: both the improved pathway and encouragement, in the previous example. The function of this term is to signal the availability of a certain type of consequence if a specific behavior is displayed. Alternatively, antecedents may alter the value of those consequences depending on the agent's motivation to act (see Michael, 1982) (e.g., increasing employees' motivation to walk, enhancing certain positive benefits and diminishing negative ones).

Next, let us turn to analyzing the cumulative effects of individual behavior that is targeted by a nudging approach. In fact, the scope of the intervention is usually never limited to the level of the single, but includes the achievement of large-scale behavior change, one nudge at a time. Once the target behavior has been identified and

operationalized, the functional analysis can take into account the role of the consequences that reach beyond the agent's experience, such as in the case of prophylactic programs. For example, it is increasingly common that organizations offer the choice of vaccinating against seasonal influenza on the premises or at no charge. Some consequences of taking up the offer and getting the flu shot are immediate and certain, such as taking (paid) time off from work or experiencing some discomfort due to the injection, while other consequences are delayed and uncertain, for example achieving immunization to the current season's virus variation within the whole organization or society (thus avoiding symptoms of influenza). It is clear that some of these consequences are positive and tend to evoke a higher probability that the behavior occurs, whereas others are negative and tend to decrease future occurrences of that behavior. So that is the behavior-consequence relation. Let us now turn to the antecedent-behavior relation. Antecedents of the target behavior comprise the third and last element of the (three-term) contingency analysis. They comprise the events or conditions that may elicit or alter the value of the consequences of taking the vaccine shot (e.g., eliciting the importance of vaccinating on health prevention, reminding of the convenience of signing up, etc.).

Nudges usually operate at the level of the antecedents, providing a signal or guiding behavior. In a scientific study conducted in an academic setting in the United States, the authors addressed prompts to increase the uptake of an organizational vaccination program. Milkman et al. (2011) identified two conditions in addition to the control group, in which the participants received a follow-up prompt to agree on a date (group 2) or on a date and time (group 3) once they agreed to take the flu shot. More technically put, they altered the choice environment (the sign-up form) by providing a cue (the nudge), which allowed participants to experience the positive consequences (potential immunization) of prophylactic behavior (vaccinating). In the end, both nudges were effective on the target behavior and led to higher vaccination rates: group 2 featured a 1.5% increase compared to the control group and group 3 (including both date and time prompt) featured a 4.2% increase compared to the control group. This result was both statistically significant and meaningful (Milkman et al., 2011).

The example above illustrates how a functional analysis of behavior can include and improve our understanding of the effects of a nudge and its relation to the other terms. Figure 26.1 provides a more general representation of this relation, which may serve as the starting point for developing forthcoming applications of nudging to wellbeing at work. More examples and guidance are provided in the continuation of this chapter, but it suffices here to note that: (a) the start of the analysis coincides with the identification of the target behavior, and (b) the relations among the

three terms (depicted by the arrows) are not universal givens, but rather vary depending on subjective and collective past experiences. For example, similar consequences may be perceived as either positive or negative, or different antecedents may elicit the same behavior.

A LIST OF TEN IMPORTANT NUDGES APPLIED TO WELLBEING AT WORK: EXAMPLES AND LESSONS

Because organisms are surrounded by an environment at all times and choice is ubiquitous, nudges are virtually yet deliberately in place all the time, whether the agent is aware of them or not. Table 26.1 provides a summary of some recent nudging interventions to organizational wellbeing, divided by area, for an easier consultation. They are analyzed in detail next, listed in their respective type of nudge. Sunstein (2014: 585–587) compiled a list of ten important nudges that

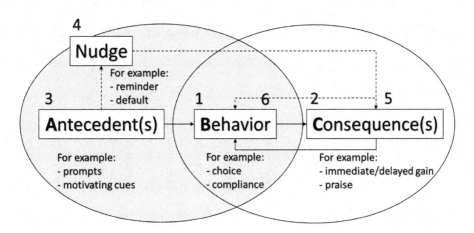

Figure 26.1.   Illustration of a three-term functional analysis of behavior (solid lines) and the effect of nudging (dashed lines) in the model, according to the following procedure (1) pinpoint the target behavior and (2) identify its consequences; (3) list any antecedents that may elicit behavior and (4) develop a nudge that (5) alters the value of its consequences, which (6) drive future occurrences of the target behavior. Whereas nudging operates on antecedent-behavior relations (colored in grey), it may suffice to change behavior as a function of its consequences on the environment (colored in white).

Table 26.1 Example of interventions included in the text that parallel a functional analysis of behavioral contingencies.

Author(s), year	Type of study	Target behavior	Intervention	Main results
Arno and Thomas, 2016	Systematic review and meta-analysis	Healthy food choice	–	15.3% increase of healthier food choice
Birnbach et al., 2013	Applied research	Hand hygiene among medical students	Priming with citrus scent	Increase of hand hygiene compliance from 51% to 80% ($p < .001$)
Capraro et al., 2019	Laboratory experiment	Pro-social behavior	Moral nudges and economic games	44% increase of charity donations
Cioffi et al., 2015	Applied research	Food purchasing in a university cafeteria	Food items labeling with caloric content	7% decrease of calories intake
Cohen et al., 2006	Applied research	Minority students' performance	Timely and targeted socio-psychological interventions	Increase in performance and increasing integrity and self-worth views
Evans et al., 2012	Applied research	Sedentary behavior	Prompts and reminders on computer screens	Positive results, although not in all conditions and with small samples
Franklin et al., 2019	Applied research	Financial decision making	Disclosing information	Disclosure nudges were more effective than social nudges
Holland et al., 2005	Laboratory experiment	Cleaning behavior	Priming with citrus scent	Increase of behavior frequency of cleaning
Inland Revenue service of New Zealand (OECD, 2017)	Applied research	Flu shot uptake	Increasing the ease and convenience of the sign-up procedure	33% vaccination increase
King et al., 2014	Applied research	Drugs prescription	Charts simplification	Reduced prescription errors
Marcano-Olivier et al., 2019	Applied research	Food purchase	Cafeteria layout redesign	Significant consumption increases of fruit, vitamin C, and fiber; no change in vegetable consumption
Milkman et al., 2011	Applied research	Uptake of seasonal influenza shot	Implementation intentions and stating date/ time and date.	1.5% — 4.2% increase of shots uptake
Thaler and Benartzi, 2004	Applied research	Retirement contributions	Default enrollment and incremental contributions	78% uptake

Van Der Meiden et al., 2019	Applied research	Office stair use	Posters and footprints nudges	Effective as long as the nudge is in place
Van Hoecke et al., 2018	Applied research	Stair climbing in company and mall	Footprints and health message nudges	Significant in the company, not in the mall; more effective when footprints were combined with health message
Vanclay et al., 2011	Applied research	Food purchasing	Food items labeling with carbon emissions	Small effect
Western Cape Government of South Africa (OECD, 2017)	Applied research	Walking	Social norms and gamification	Average 2.8 kilograms weight loss
Wilson et al., 2016	Systematic review	Food and beverage choices	-	Combined salience and priming nudges showed healthier choices

Note: interventions comprise the antecedent term of a behavior (target), and main results include aggregate or cumulative consequences.

are especially effective for policy purposes (see Tomer, 2018: 8). With few or no adjustments, they could become workplace nudges that can steer organizational behavior towards 'better' directions for both employers and employees. For each nudge, at least one example or case is provided.

Establishing Default Rules

This is arguably the simplest yet most effective nudge for the reason that the agent needs do nothing to be 'better off', which translates to improving employees' wellbeing. This is also the most 'paternalistic' of all nudges, because it supposes that the choice architect (employer or manager) knows best what optimal decisions or outcomes look like. Conversely, defaults are notably known not to work when they collide with previously ranked preferences. Allegedly, the most famous example of applying default rules for wellbeing at work is the *Save More Tomorrow* retirement plan created by Thaler and Benartzi (2004) that featured automatic enrollment in the company's pension scheme (while increasing proportionally employees' contributions; see also nudge type 'Assist People to Choose Positive Courses of Action Using Precommitment Strategies') and resulted in a 78% uptake. Another example of the power and extensive use of defaults concerns the design of cafeterias and lunchrooms. As previously noted, the order in which food items are presented (i.e., the default choice architecture) exerts an influence on their likelihood of being selected. For example, several layouts have been tested to increase the choice of fruit and vegetables (Marcano-Olivier et al., 2019) or limiting the sale of sugary soft drinks (Wilson et al., 2016). In a recent systematic review and meta-analysis, Arno and Thomas (2016) found that nudging interventions on dietary behavior and food choice resulted in a 15.3% increase of healthier food choice.

Simplifying Existing Programs

Simplification refers to nudges that can improve the participation to currently available programs and initiatives. (Too much) complexity of tasks and information is usually the biggest barrier to uptake behavior, whose effects reach beyond the workplace and may include participating in educational programs, saving and investing behavior, and alleviating poverty and unemployment (see Sunstein, 2014). Achieving wellbeing can also be simplified by implementing this class of nudges in organizational policies: creating new programs or ensuring that they are used to their fullest. For example, King et al. (2014) significantly reduced prescription errors in a London teaching hospital by simplifying the standard prescription charts. Similarly, routines and forms in other organizational departments can be addressed in the same fashion, such as improving safety in production facilities and reducing stress in accounting.

Using Social Norms to Inform People About What Others Typically Do

Informing about other people's choices is likely to exert an influence on the agent's decision-making. Differently from simple nudges that target independent choice behavior, norm nudges exploit the comparison and relationships of interdependent behavior for reducing the tension between individuals' interests and collective interests (Bicchieri and Dimant, 2019). For example, resorting to social norms may have important repercussions on psychological health and stress prevention, informing of colleagues' uptake of flexible working programs, taking breaks at regular intervals, or complying with organizational policies and deadlines. In the 'Walk 4 Health' initiative of the Western Cape Government of South Africa, health behaviors among employees increased by combining social norms with gamification. Specifically, the intervention resulted in 70% of the participants losing on average 2.8 kilograms (= 6.2 pounds) of weight (in OECD, 2017).

Increasing the Ease and Convenience of Activities

Increasing convenience works almost as effectively as default rules do: instead of doing nothing, the agent is required to do very little, which increases the attractiveness of this option. Technically put, these nudges reduce the cost of responding (i.e., effort following choice behavior) of the preferred alternative and moving it to another alternative. For example, providing access to a gym, swimming pool, or other training facilities on the organization's premises or very closely located lowers the 'cost' of working out due to commuting time, membership hassle, and the agents' convenience altogether. For example, the Inland Revenue service of New Zealand increased the uptake of the flu shot among its employees by 33% thanks to increases in ease and convenience of the program (OECD, 2017). Similarly, other health programs offered at various organizations can include a similar design to make it as attractive as possible for the workers to sign up and avoid the health downsides and occupational costs associated with seasonal flu.

Providing Full Disclosure Regarding Market and Government Activities

Nudging in an ethical way presupposes transparency towards the recipients of a policy or the workers in the organization. Simply informing them about the consequences that are likely to occur if a certain course of action is undertaken may suffice to steer choice, which is the essence of disclosure nudges. Disclosure can concern data, costs, consumption (e.g., nudging

energy-efficient behavior), and other information that is relevant for the decision maker at the point of choice, especially pertaining to financial and economic matters. For example, in a recent study Franklin et al. (2019) tested the effectiveness of disclosure nudges on financial decision-making (i.e., making advantageous financial choices that have a higher expected value) and found that these (together with boosts) were more effective than social nudges.

Providing Warnings Regarding the Risks of Private and Public Activities

Warnings are mostly but not exclusively graphic; they can be either positive (e.g., a green leaf as a rewarding symbol associated with environmentally friendly behavior – switching off the lights when leaving the office), or negative, such as the horrendous images printed on cigarette packages. From a functional perspective, warnings are discriminative stimuli that signal the availability of certain types of consequences. They exploit our attentional system, which has a limited capacity, and repeated exposure to warnings, learning from them, could lead to creating rules under similar contingencies (e.g., stop smoking, never touch high voltage electricity cables, take the stairs, etc.). As another example of nudging healthier nutrition behavior, the display of food items can be accompanied by traffic light eco-labels signaling the environmental footprint of a single food item (e.g., as CO_2 emissions) or its caloric contents. In a study by Cioffi et al. (2015), the authors registered a 7% decrease in the mean total calories in a university cafeteria on food purchasing behavior labeled food. Vanclay et al. (2011) found similar small effects when labeling groceries with embodied carbon emissions, and it is possible to relate to the use of warnings across virtually all areas of wellbeing at work: from prevention to corporate responsibility.

Assist People to Choose Positive Courses of Action Using Pre-commitment Strategies

These types of nudges include commitment devices that target the tendency to procrastinate that may arise whenever the point of choice approaches. Smoking cessation, saving behavior, completion of education programs and other goals are more easily achievable when the *present* 'self' is in concert with the *future* 'self', although the consequences to which it entails are yet unavailable (e.g., respectively, decreased cancer risk, purchasing a home, and obtaining a promotion after graduation). For example, Cohen et al. (2006) used timely and targeted socio-psychological interventions similar to nudges to successfully increase minority students' performance while reinforcing positive views of integrity and self-worth (in Ruggeri, 2019). Furthermore, pre-commitment nudges should be as personalized as possible to increase their effectiveness, leveraging on the uniqueness of the recipient instead of one-size-fits-all campaigns: this includes both choice personalization and delivery personalization (see Mills, 2020).

Providing Reminders to People With a Great Deal on Their Minds

Reminders and other timely nudges that prompt to action work by addressing autopilot-steered behavior, whose underlying processing system was called by Kahneman (2003) System 1 (implicit, fast, and effortless), to a more deliberative, resource-demanding, and effortful System 2. This differentiation represents the basis of dual process theory, or a two-system view, and it has been argued that all nudges share the same objective of bringing behavior from the control of System 1 to being steered by System 2. Others distinguished between System 1 nudges (e.g., warnings, reminders, and other nudges that exploit and correct for biases – systematic errors in decision-making) and

System 2 nudges, which aim at educating and include disclosure, pre-commitment strategies, and other 'empowering' nudges. In order to be as effective as possible, reminders should be timed with precision and personalized to the receivers' characteristics in relation to the target behavior. For example, it is not uncommon to receive an SMS or email prior to medical appointments and tax-due dates, or a buzz through smartwatches reminding a sedentary office worker that they should take a break after sitting still for a long time. Technological advancements have greatly impacted how and where reminders are delivered. For example, Evans et al. (2012) embedded prompts and reminders on the work computer screens to reduce sedentary behavior and found encouraging results, although the sample was small and the workers were exposed to an educational session too. Similarly, nudging may take the form of priming, which is also effective at steering behavior, although it exploits a lower threshold of awareness. For example, the smell of citrus alone was able to increase cleaning behavior among experimental participants in relation to their surrounding environment (Holland et al., 2005) and hand hygiene among medical students (Birnbach et al., 2013), with important protective implications for both practitioners and users. Lastly, it is noteworthy that reminders may be perceived as annoying by the workers of an organization if their preferences diverge greatly from the reminded behavior or if they do not have the tools or skills to fulfill it, even though they wanted to (e.g., due to clearance or hardware).

Eliciting People's Implementation Intentions

Implementation intentions comprise prompts to reduce the intention-behavior gap (see also Gollwitzer and Sheeran, 2009). This type of nudge has mostly been adopted in relation to health and voting behavior, such as 'Do you plan to vaccinate? Do you plan to vote?'

(Sunstein, 2014). Implementing intentions serves as a mechanism for reducing any dissonance that characterizes identity, beliefs, and course of action. For example, Milkman et al. (2011) tested the effectiveness of implementation intentions on the uptake of seasonal influenza vaccines among the employees of a US utility firm. In this case, the target behavior was the taking up of the flu shot, whereas the aim of the intervention was to increase the vaccination rate. The increase in uptake ranged between 1.5% and 4.2%, depending on the experimental group compared to the control group.

Informing People of the Nature and Consequences of Their Own Past Choices

This tenth and last important nudge is similar to applying social norms, except that the norm is directed to oneself. This may also be reframed as an issue of consistency (with oneself), especially when large datasets are available to employers and providers about past choices (see 'smart disclosure' in the United States and the 'midata project' in the UK, in Sunstein, 2014). Although applications of this type of nudge are not easy to find in the literature, Capraro et al. (2019) explored the effects of moral nudges in sustaining pro-sociality and found that not only does it help to ask people 'What they think is the morally right thing to do' on a single occurrence of pro-social behavior, but it also increased charity donations by 44%.

FRAMEWORKS FOR BEHAVIOR CHANGE: FROM PINPOINTING TO LONGITUDINAL FOLLOW-UP

Despite the field of nudging being influenced from interdisciplinary efforts, one widely agreed upon requirement is the adoption of an empirical approach to programs of behavior change. In fact, nudges have never been considered 'silver bullets', although there are some patterns of nudges that tend to work better than others, depending on the context of application (see Sunstein, 2017). For example, norm-nudging, which comprises a powerful approach thanks to eliciting social expectations, works best when 'behavior is conditional on both *empirical* and *normative* expectation' (Bicchieri and Dimant, 2019: 25); default nudges are most effective whenever consistent with pre-existing preferences (e.g., Dinner et al., 2011).

This section contains an overview of some of the frameworks and diagnostic tools available that can guide the implementation of nudges according to an empirical approach: from conceptualization, to implementation and measurement. Without going into too much detail, nor pretending to give a comprehensive account of them, the aim herein is to emphasize the methodological approach to nudging. This is even more important when embedding nudges into the policymaking cycle, as the audience may be very large and there may be responsibilities towards the public stakeholders when appraising their effectiveness.

Historically, the first tool developed for implementing behavioral insights into policymaking was MINDSPACE, which rested partially on the foundation of the Behavioral Insights Unit at the UK Prime's Minister Office (Dolan et al., 2012). MINDSPACE is a framework and checklist that includes nine nudges that are effective for behavior change, six of which coincide with the nudges suggested by Thaler and Sunstein (2008: 81–100). The mnemonic MINDSPACE stands for *Messenger, Incentives, Norms, Defaults, Salience, Priming, Affect, Commitments,* and *Ego*. The authors suggest starting with an analysis of the context in which one or more of the suggested nudges are likely to work (e.g., committing to achieving a daily physical activity target, say 10,000 steps a day (Williams et al., 2005)); next, they go on to advocating the need to produce and analyze data that is useful to determine the effectiveness of the behavior change intervention (Dolan et al., 2012).

The Behavioral Insights Team stood behind two subsequent publications that included an introduction to the use of randomized control trials (RCTs) in policy evaluation (Haynes et al., 2012) and a simplified framework for leveraging four important aspects of decision-making called EAST (Algate et al., 2015). The former stresses the importance of an empirical approach to nudging in policymaking, wherein *What Works?* should be dictated by data and a rigorous design (and not left to chance). Whereas RCTs are considered the 'gold standard' in other fields such as medicine or education, they are not as widely resorted to in policymaking, despite being potentially cost-effective in the long run (Haynes et al., 2012). The EAST framework is a simple consultation tool for driving effective behavior change by leveraging on four powerful contextual dimensions: once more, EAST is an acronym that stands for *Easy, Attractive, Simple*, and *Timely*. According to the authors, nudges and any other intervention aimed at modifying behavior are most effective when possessing these characteristics, which relate to the three-term contingency illustrated in the previous sections: providing antecedents that change the value of consequences (e.g., introducing a timely prompt or signaling the attractiveness of positive consequences).

The second framework for implementing behavioral evaluations and interventions applied to the policymaking cycle is termed BASIC (OECD, 2019), which stands for *Behavior, Analysis, Strategy, Intervention*, and *Change*. BASIC was developed specifically for the policymaker and has some specific features of this domain, such as strategy changes that target policy solutions (e.g., increasing pension savings). Nevertheless, it starts with the identification of the target behavior and concludes with a follow-up plan for measurement and upscaling.

Next, the behavioral economics group at the Rotman School of Management in Toronto, Canada, focused on the application of nudges and other behavior-change tools and policies specifically in organizations. The '4As' program, standing for *Assess, Aim, Action*, and *Amend*, are pragmatic steps for implementing behavioral insights in work settings (Feng et al., 2018). What is specific about this model, however, is a continuity of monitoring and intervening thanks to feedback mechanisms (i.e., *Adjust*) which are usually not included in the other diagnostic models introduced earlier.

Lastly, the Mind, Behavior and Development Unit at the World Bank (2015) engaged in the task of mapping and operationalizing the steps to undertake ordinary decision-making processes, focusing specifically on the criticalities represented by 'bottlenecks'. For example, these are cases in which belief- and intention-action gaps are highest and other contextual elements are likely to get in the way and interfere with taking optimal choices (e.g., due to limited time, lack of skills, social reprehension, etc.). The steps for a behavioral insights project include identifying a framework (based on an objective), targeting specific behavior for change, analyzing the context, describing the intervention, and evaluating its effectiveness (with lessons learned). Interestingly, the authors specified that the target does not necessarily need to be a behavior, for it may also comprise an attitude or knowledge to reach the development objective. Similarly, Ideas 42 developed a model that depicts the behavioral design process and includes the following steps: *Define, Diagnose, Design, Test*, and *Scale* (Robertson et al., 2017).

BOOSTING AND REINFORCING AS ALTERNATIVES OR ENHANCEMENTS OF NUDGING

As reported in the introductory section of this chapter, nudge theory is a relatively new, innovative, and cost-effective approach to wellbeing. However, it has also received criticisms mainly due to its paternalistic approach and the yet uncertain effects of nudges in the long term. Let us take them up one at a time and discuss possible ways to overcome these and possibly other shortcomings of nudges that do not work. In fact, Sunstein (2017) identified two principal classes of reasons why nudges may fail: the first reason is tied to the antecedent term and includes a set of preferences that affects behavior more strongly than how the nudge does. The second reason is the development of countermeasures among the 'recipients' of nudging interventions, which are termed *counternudges* and contrast the effect of the nudge.

Nudge theory rests on the heuristics and bias research program developed by Tversky and Kahneman (1974), whose tenets comprise the presence of systematic errors (biases) in judgment and decision-making and their explanation in terms of cognitive approximations of 'good enough' solutions (heuristics; i.e., rules of thumb). Moreover, nudges are forms of expressing a politico-philosophical or ideological approach, labelled *libertarian paternalism* (Kosters and Van Der Heijden, 2015). Similar to the way in which a GPS device helps us reach our destination, nudges show the way to behave (paternalism) without forcing any turn or decision (libertarian) (see also Sunstein, 2018).

Conversely, the simple heuristics program (also referred to as fast and frugal heuristics; see Raab and Gigerenzer, 2015) represents an alternative research program to the heuristics and bias program that rests on the computational ability of the agent and the ecological validity of heuristic strategies (Gigerenzer et al., 2011). Similarly to nudging and nudges, this research program originated a conceptual approach called *boosting* and tools and techniques labelled *boosts*. Electively, boosting interventions target the policymaking cycle and aim at reaching out to the recipients of the policy with an active approach and extending their capacity to take better-informed decisions (Grüne-Yanoff and Hertwig, 2016).

Boosts go beyond considering the agent as a 'passive' receiver of interventions and builds computational capacity and literacy by helping the agent learn how to take better choices and decisions for life (e.g., understanding relative risks of medical prognoses or Bayesian updating when computing probable financial outcomes). Thus, boosts reach beyond the scope of nudges and in a way are preferable to the latter, for they empower the agent and need not be necessarily considered context-dependent.

Boosting provides a repertoire of skills that are learned and retained for use on future occasions, while learning alternative behaviors is slower and more difficult in the case of nudging. In fact, nudging may be ineffective as soon as the cues are withdrawn from the environment and the choice architecture reverts back to the original arrangement that preceded the intervention. However, boosts are generally more expensive to implement and their effects are slower at establishing alternative behavior, for the set of skills needs first to be acquired by the agent (Hertwig and Grüne-Yanoff, 2017). Boosting may represent an effective approach to increase levels of work satisfaction, because it comprises several behaviors that are recurrent and may be learned. For example, in a recent meta-analysis, Huell et al. (2016) found a positive moderate relationship between leader-member exchange (LMX) and job-related employee wellbeing ($r = 0.35$, $p < 0.001$) and a moderate negative relationship between LMX and negative wellbeing ($r = -0.29$, $p < 0.001$). However, LMX is known to comprise a complex and endured pattern of behavior between manager and employee (e.g., providing consequences, delivering feedback, engaging in team activities, etc.), such that a nudge may not suffice to affect repeated occurrences of their exchanges. On the other hand, by applying boosting principles, the parts are empowered by expanding (boosting) their competencies and fulfilling their objectives (Grüne-Yanoff and Hertwig, 2016: 156).

While both nudges and boosts operate by introducing or altering behavioral antecedents, behavior is a function of its consequences on the environment; as such, altering consequences is likely to alter the behavior on which those consequences are contingent. Specifically, theories of reinforcement program the addition of positive consequences (or the removal of negative ones) that increase the likelihood of future instances of the target behavior. For example, increasing the use of stairs while decreasing the use of elevators in office buildings has been targeted by several nudging interventions, and with successful results (e.g., Van Hoecke et al., 2018; Van Der Meiden et al., 2019). Specifically, the authors altered the micro-environment (Hollands et al., 2013) by adding some footprints leading to the stairs, which served as a prompt and led to behavior change. However, as soon as the nudge was withdrawn (i.e., the footprints were removed), stair use decreased again to pre-intervention levels (Van Der Meiden et al., 2019: 323). This result is not surprising because the immediately available (positive) consequences contingent on the behavior (e.g., the release of dopamine at the neuronal level or a sense of satisfaction and accomplishment at the psychological level) may not exert a strong enough control on successive stairs-taking behavior than its delayed consequences do: preventing obesity and other cardiovascular diseases, or maintaining a good health condition. Thus, new consequences could be introduced or modified so as to maintain the behavior that the nudge was effective at eliciting but whose long-term effects are likely to stop when consequences are withdrawn or fade as the agent becomes accustomed to the 'new' choice architecture. Some of these consequences may include praise from supervisors and peers, be it verbal or non-verbal, public or private; or earning points redeemable with non-cash prizes as an attempt to gamify wellbeing, at the end of which all should be winners.

Taken together, nudging, boosting, and nonetheless principles of reinforcement comprise only some of the elements included under the umbrella of *behavioral welfare economics* (e.g., Bleichrodt et al., 2001; Camerer et al., 2003). This is a normative framework that focuses on the direct relation between choice and welfare outcomes, rather than its mediated effects through wellbeing or underlying objectives (Bernheim, 2008). Although the topic reaches beyond the scope of this chapter, the broader field of behavioral economics has informed the domain of public welfare in the latest years. Similarly, nudges and other techniques of altering antecedents and consequences of behavior should also inform wellbeing at work.

FROM THEORY TO PRACTICE: ENGAGING EMPLOYERS AND SUPERVISORS FOR THE WORKERS' GOOD

One of the main tenets that make nudging a permissible approach to influencing choice is maintaining an ethical compass that not only can point to the greater good of the interventions (i.e., achieving wellbeing) but is also agreed upon by the recipients of the nudges (workers agreeing on the ends of nudging). In fact, it was previously affirmed that manipulation of 'means' paternalism and not 'ends' paternalism makes the use of nudging justifiable (Sunstein, 2014; Rachlin, 2015). Since the first formulation of the scope of nudging, Thaler and Sunstein (2008: 5) emphasized how the choices that nudging enables agents to make are '*better* as judged by themselves' (emphasis added). This disclosure helps retain and respect the agent's preferences and lessen the degree of paternalism (i.e., the invasiveness on behavior) (Sunstein, 2018).

Throughout the present chapter, a nudging approach to wellbeing was defined, operationalized, and analyzed. By submitting to an empirical approach, employers and managers should consider implementing nudges in their workplaces to increase the wellbeing of their employees, while retaining low intervention costs and a relatively simple implantation structure. Starting from a functional analysis of organizational behavior, this chapter provides a brief introduction to theory and tools for getting started with experimentation, for the workers' *good* (without necessarily compromising on the shareholders' *good*). Moreover, alternatives and enhancements of nudges were provided: these are able to better meet the complexity of some types of organizational practices and performance, which include boosting, providing consequences, and embedding a behaviorally informed analysis in policies and routines. Although this domain of application is still in its infancy, there is a strong need for enhancing applied research and innovating the field of nudge theory at work with continuous data-driven experimentation, documenting it, and sharing *what works* with the rest of the community. Only this way may a universal approach to nudging organizational wellbeing be achieved.

REFERENCES

Algate F, Gallagher R, Nguyen S, Ruda S, Sanders M, Pelenur M, Gyani A, Harper H, Reinhard J and Kirkman E. (2015) *EAST: Four simple ways to apply behavioural insights*. London: The Behavioural Insights Team.

Arno A and Thomas S. (2016) The efficacy of nudge theory strategies in influencing adult dietary behaviour: A systematic review and meta-analysis. *BMC Public Health* 16: 1–11.

Bank W. (2015) *World development report 2015: Mind, society, and behavior*. Washington, DC: World Bank.

Benartzi S, Beshears J, Milkman KL, Sunstein C, Thaler H.R, Shankar M, Tucker-Ray W, Congdon J.W, and Galing S. (2017) Should governments invest more in nudging? *Psychological Science* 28: 1041–1055.

Bernheim BD. (2008) Behavioral welfare economics. *NBER Working Paper*. Milan: National Bureau of Economic Research.

Bicchieri C and Dimant E. (2019) Nudging with care: The risks and benefits of social information. *CeDEx Discussion Paper Series*. The University of Nottingham: Centre for Decision Research and Experimental Economics (CeDEx).

Birnbach DJ, King D, Vlaev I, Rosen LF and Harvey PD. (2013) Impact of environmental olfactory cues on hand hygiene behaviour in a simulated hospital environment: A randomized study. *Journal of Hospital Infection* 85: 79–81.

Bleichrodt H, Pinto JL and Wakker PP. (2001) Making descriptive use of prospect theory to improve the prescriptive use of expected utility. *Management Science* 47: 1498–1514.

Camerer C, Issacharoff S, Loewenstein G, O'Donoghue T and Rabin M. (2003) Regulation for conservatives: Behavioral economics and the case for 'asymmetric paternalism'. *University of Pennsylvania Law Review* 151(3): 1211–1254.

Capraro V, Jagfeld G, Klein R, Mul M and van de Pol I. (2019) Increasing altruistic and cooperative behaviour with simple moral nudges. *Scientific Reports* 9: 11880–11890.

Cioffi CE, Levitsky DA, Pacanowski CR and Bertz F. (2015) A nudge in a healthy direction: The effect of nutrition labels on food purchasing behaviors in university dining facilities. *Appetite* 92: 7–14.

Cohen G, Garcia J, Apfel N and Master A. (2006) Reducing the racial achievement gap: A social-psychological intervention. *Science* 313(5791): 1307–1310.

Damgaard MT and Nielsen HS. (2018) Nudging in education. *Economics of Education Review* 64: 313–342.

Dinner I, Johnson EJ, Goldstein DG and Liu K. (2011) Partitioning default effects: Why people choose not to choose. *Journal of Experimental Psychology: Applied* 17(4): 332–341.

Dolan P, Hallsworth M, Halpern D, King D, Metcalfe R and Vlaev I. (2012) Influencing behaviour: The mindspace way. *Journal of Economic Psychology* 33: 264–277.

Ebbinghaus H. (1908) *Psychology: An elementary text-book*. Boston, MA: Heath.

European Agency for Safety and Health at Work. (2013) *Well-being at work: Creating a positive work environment. A literature review.* Luxembourg: European Agency for Safety and Health at Work.

Evans RE, Fawole HO, Sheriff SA, Dall PM, Grant PM and Ryan CG. (2012) Point-of-choice prompts to reduce sitting time at work: A randomized trial. *American Journal of Preventive Medicine* 43(3): 293–297.

Feng B, Oyunsuren J, Tymko M, Kim M and Soman D. (2018) *How should organizations best embed and harness behavioural insights? A playbook.* Toronto: Behavioral Economics in Action at Rotman (BEAR).

Franklin M, Folke T and Ruggeri K. (2019) Optimising nudges and boosts for financial decisions under uncertainty. *Palgrave Communications* 5.

Garcıa JM and Vila J. (2018) Nudging long-term saving: The Ahorra+ program. *Journal of Behavioral Economics for Policy* 2: 49–53.

Gera R. (2012) Bridging the gap in knowledge-transfer between academia and practitioners. *International Journal of Educational Management* 26: 252–273.

Gigerenzer G, Hertwig R and Pachur T. (2011) *Heuristics: The foundations of adaptive behavior.* New York: Oxford University Press.

Gollwitzer PM and Sheeran P. (2009) Self-regulation of consumer decision making and behavior: The role of implementation intentions. *Journal of Consumer Psychology* 19: 593–607.

Grüne-Yanoff T and Hertwig R. (2016) Nudge versus boost: How coherent are policy and theory? *Minds and Machines* 26: 149–183.

Hanks AS, Just DR, Smith LE and Wansink B. (2012) Healthy convenience: Nudging students toward healthier choices in the lunchroom. *Journal of Public Health* 34: 370–376.

Hansen PG. (2017) The definition of nudge and libertarian paternalism: Does the hand fit the glove? *European Journal of Risk Regulation* 7: 155–174.

Haynes L, Service O, Goldacre B and Torgerson D. (2012) *Test, learn, adapt: Developing public policy with randomised controlled trials.* London: Cabinet Office Behavioural Insights Team.

Hertwig R and Grüne-Yanoff T. (2017) Nudging and boosting: Steering or empowering good

decisions. *Perspectives on Psychological Science* 12: 973–986.

Holland RW, Hendriks M and Aarts H. (2005) Smells like clean spirit: Nonconscious effects of scent on cognition and behavior. *Psychological Science* 16: 689–693.

Hollands GJ, Shemilt I, Marteau TM, Jebb SA, Kelly MP, Nakamura R, Suhrcke M and Ogilvie D. (2013) Altering micro-environments to change population health behaviour: Towards an evidence base for choice architecture interventions. *BMC Public Health* 13: 1218–1223.

Huell, F, Vincent-Höper, S, Bürkner, PC, Gregersen, S, Holling, H and Nienhaus, A. (2016). *Leader-member exchange and employee well-being: A meta-analysis.* Academy of Management Proceedings, *2016*(1): 13537.

Kahneman D. (2003) A perspective on judgment and choice: Mapping bounded rationality. *American Psychologist* 58: 697–720.

Kahneman D. (2011) *Thinking, fast and slow.* New York: Farrar, Straus and Giroux.

King D, Jabbar A, Charani E, Bicknell C, Wu Z, Miller G, Gilchrist M, Vlaev I, Franklin BD and Darzi A. (2014) Redesigning the 'choice architecture' of hospital prescription charts: A mixed methods study incorporating in situ simulation testing. *BMJ Open* 4: e005473.

Kosters M and Van Der Heijden J. (2015) From mechanism to virtue: Evaluating nudge theory. *Evaluation* 21: 276–291.

Lakerveld J, Mackenbach JD, de Boer F, Brandhorst B, Broerse JEW, de Bruijn G-J, Feunekes G, Gillebaart M, Harbers M, Hoenink J, Klein M, Mensink F, Middel C, de Ridder DTD, Rutters F, Sluijs I, van der Schouw YT, Jan Schuitmaker T, te Velde SJ, Velema E, Waterlander W, Brug J and Beulens JWJ. (2018) Improving cardiometabolic health through nudging dietary behaviours and physical activity in low SES adults: Design of the supreme nudge project. *BMC Public Health* 18: 899-907.

Marcano-Olivier M, Pearson R, Ruparell A, Horne PJ, Viktor S and Erjavec M. (2019) A low-cost behavioural nudge and choice architecture intervention targeting school lunches increases children's consumption of fruit: A cluster randomised trial. *International*

Journal of Behavioral Nutrition and Physical Activity 16: 20-28.

Marchiori D, Adriaanse MA and De Ridder D. (2017) Unresolved questions in nudging research: Putting the psychology back in nudges. *Social Personality Psychology Compass* 11: e12297.

Michael J. (1982) Distinguishing between discriminative and motivational functions of stimuli. *Journal of the Experimental Analysis of Behavior* 37: 149–155.

Milkman KL, Beshears J, Choi JJ, Laibson D and Madrian BC. (2011) Using implementation intentions prompts to enhance influenza vaccination rates. *Proceedings of the National Academy of Sciences* 108: 10415–10420.

Mills S. (2020) Personalized nudging. *Behavioural Public Policy*. Cambridge University Press, 1–10. DOI: 10.1017/bpp.2020.7

Naci H and Ioannidis JPA. (2015) Evaluation of wellness determinants and interventions by citizen scientists. *Journal of the American Medical Association* 314: 121–122.

O'Neill M. (2018) *The workspace nudge for well-being*. Keighley: Haworth.

OECD. (2017) *Behavioural insights and public policy: Lessons from around the world*. Paris: OECD Publishing.

OECD. (2019) *Tools and ethics for applied behavioural insights: The BASIC toolkit*. Paris: OECD Publishing.

Raab M and Gigerenzer G. (2015) The power of simplicity: A fast-and-frugal heuristics approach to performance science. *Frontiers in Psychology* 6: 1672.

Rachlin HC. (2015) Choice architecture: A review of *Why Nudge: The Politics of Libertarian Paternalism*. *Journal of the Experimental Analysis of Behavior* 104: 198–203.

Robertson T, Darling M, Leifer J, Footer O and Grodsky D. (2017) *Behavioral design teams: The next frontier in clinical delivery innovation?* New York: The Commonwealth Fund.

Ruggeri K. (2019) What is impact?. In: Ruggeri K (ed.) *Behavioral insights for public policy: Concepts and cases*. Abingdon: Routledge, 218–236.

Ruggeri K, Berkessel J, Achterberg J, Prinz GM, Luna-Navarro A, Jachimowicz JM and Whillans AV. (2019) Work and workplace. In: Ruggeri K (ed.) *Behavioral insights for public*

policy: Concepts and cases. Abingdon: Routledge, 156–173.

Ruggeri K, Garcia-Garzon E, Maguire Á, Matz S and Huppert FA. (2020a) Well-being is more than happiness and life satisfaction: A multidimensional analysis of 21 countries. *Health and Quality of Life Outcomes* 18: 192-207.

Ruggeri K, Linden SVD, Wang C, Papa F, Riesch J and Green J. (2020b) *Standards for evidence in policy decision-making*. PsyArxiv Preprint: Center for Open Science. DOI: 10.31234/osf.io/fjwvk

Schmidt AT and Engelen B. (2020) The ethics of nudging: An overview. *Philosophy Compass* e12658.

Simon C and Tagliabue M. (2018) Feeding the behavioral revolution: Contributions of behavior analysis to nudging and vice versa. *Journal of Behavioral Economics for Policy* 2: 91–97.

Smith ER and Decoster J. (2000) Dual-process models in social and cognitive psychology: Conceptual integration and links to underlying memory systems. *Personality and Social Psychology Review* 4: 108–131.

Sunstein CR. (2014) *Why nudge? The politics of libertarian paternalism*. New Haven: Yale University Press.

Sunstein CR. (2015) The ethics of nudging. *Yale Journal on Regulation* 32: 413–450.

Sunstein CR. (2017) Nudges that fail. *Behavioural Public Policy* 1: 4–25.

Sunstein CR. (2018) 'Better off, as judged by themselves': A comment on evaluating nudges. *International Review of Economics* 65: 1–8.

Thaler RH and Benartzi S. (2004) Save more tomorrow™: Using behavioral economics to increase employee saving. *Journal of Political Economy* 112: S164–S187.

Thaler RH and Sunstein CR. (2008) *Nudge: Improving decisions about health, wealth, and happiness*. New Haven: Yale University Press.

Tomer JF. (2018) Understanding the value and potential of nudging: Improving well-being and reducing socio-economic dysfunctions. *SSRN Electronic Journal*. DOI: 10.2139/ssrn.3207845

Torri P and Toniolo E. (2010) Organizational wellbeing: Challenge and future foundation.

Giornale Italiano di Medicina del Lavoro ed Ergonomia 32: 363–367.

Tversky A and Kahneman D. (1974) Judgment under uncertainty: Heuristics and biases. *Science* 185: 1124–1131.

Vanclay JK, Shortiss J, Aulsebrook S, Gillespie AM, Howell BC, Johanni R, Maher MJ, Mitchell KM, Stewart MD and Yates J. (2011) Customer response to carbon labelling of groceries. *Journal of Consumer Policy* 34: 153–160.

Van Der Meiden I, Kok H and Van Der Velde G. (2019) Nudging physical activity in offices. *Journal of Facilities Management* 17: 317–330.

Van Hoecke A-S, Seghers J and Boen F. (2018) Promoting stair climbing in a worksite and public setting: Are footprints enough? *American Journal of Health Promotion* 32: 527–535.

Vlaev I, King D, Dolan P and Darzi A. (2016) The theory and practice of 'nudging': Changing health behaviors. *Public Administration Review* 76: 550–561.

Williams B, Bezner J, Chesbro S and Leavitt R. (2005) The relationship between achievement of walking goals and exercise self-efficacy in post-menopausal African American women. *Journal of Geriatric Physical Therapy* 28(3): 123.

Wilson AL, Buckley E, Buckley JD and Bogomolova S. (2016) Nudging healthier food and beverage choices through salience and priming: Evidence from a systematic review. *Food Quality and Preference* 51: 47–64.

27

Applications of Neuroscience to Improve Wellbeing in Organizational Life

Justin James Kennedy and Lisa Leit

INTRODUCTION

The application of neuroscience toward well-being in organizational life has been an emerging field of research over the last few decades and Branchi and Alleva (2006) proposes that these protocols are developing as a specific domain within the fields of management science, organizational behavior, human resource management, and related areas. According to Bandura (1991) the key focus should be understanding the application of brain-based wellbeing systems and offering tools for healthy behavior change within the organizational context. Lupien SJ, Maheu F, Tu M, et al. (2007) suggests that understanding how to effectively apply the findings from neuroscience may lead to positive neurophysiological and psycho-social health benefits. To enhance health and wellbeing in organizations, learning from neuroscience should be applied practically (Parsons, 2019) as this approach has shown to sustain health and improve wellbeing at work. Lupien SJ, Maheu F, Tu M, et al. (2007) also suggests that tangible benefits from brain-based interventions demonstrate direct benefits that improve wellbeing in organizational life. If neuroscience is to remain relevant and respected as an applied science, measurable results that validate healthy behavior change are a prerequisite. As a result, applications of neuroscience should be employed as behavior-based interventions, and to be causally related to the organizational context. For example, work–life imbalance and psychological pressure have been associated with causing chronic stress, increased cortisol (the 'stress hormone'), and lifestyle related disease (Lupien SJ, Maheu F, Tu M, et al. 2007).

If chronic occupational diseases are reduced due to the application of neuroscience, this needs to be empirically measurable by drawing on several case studies from different organizational contexts. This chapter considers how brain-based wellbeing interventions can potentially influence behavioral choice. This is to ensure a direct association between the application of neuroscience protocols and the resulting improvement of wellbeing in organizational life. Here the focus will be on the primary neurological drivers that inform psychological and physiological needs that are related to behavior change, and which result in healthy habit formation (Erickson, et al., 2005). The relevance of social neuroscience, organizational neuroscience, health neuroscience, behavioral neuroscience, and related fields are discussed with regards to improving healthy behavior change. Behaviors that reduce occupational stress, obesity, sleep related disorders, and the other forms of lifestyle and chronic disease will be discussed.

In this chapter the primary focus is not on the neuroanatomical functions of wellbeing as these are mainly relevant to academic neuroscientists and clinicians. Rather, it will address how neurological functions can influence and drive choices and in turn how this informs wellbeing in organizational life. Looking at the neuropsychology of decision making and how choices are influenced not only by neural activity, the chapter will refer to the models of organizational cognitive neuroscience (Erickson, et al., 2005).

Three case studies will illustrate how brain-based interventions can specifically influence building resilience and wellbeing at work. Although the relationship between neuroscience and wellbeing is an emerging area of study, it is strongly suggested that multi-directional theoretical relationships in the organizational context be included. These include health neuroscience, organizational cognitive neuroscience, neuroeconomics, and behavioral neuroscience (Camerer, 2008) as well as associated business disciplines. This is toward ensuring possible research and proposal of a meta-model that integrates organizational wellbeing neuroscience. This chapter is envisioned to be an entry point to understand applied neuroscience research associated with specific practices that enhance wellbeing in organizational life.

HOW TO APPLY NEUROSCIENCE

Research into the application of neuroscience to support organizational wellbeing is at a critical juncture (Gage, 2002). Applied neuroscience has proposed models for understanding how the brain processes information, associated with wellbeing at work (Camerer, 2008). Organizations can now use brain-based protocols to track sleep, heart rate variability, and other health related data to build stress resilience, to control burnout, and to ensure an overall experience of wellbeing. Some applications have made various physiological data points available to explain how emotional, social, psychological, and environmental triggers are driven by unconscious neurological states. These can often be associated with decisions and behavior, and what causes health related choice. Many organizations are looking at brain-scanning technology such as electroencephalography (EEG), skin conduction, and neuro-cardiac monitors to measure them neurophysiologically (Orndorff-Plunkett et al., 2017) and improve wellbeing. With this data, and several interventions that employ tools from health neuroscience, neuroeconomics and other areas can be applied to improve behavioral choice toward resolving some of the primary concerns that reduce wellbeing in organizational life. However, neuroscience often presents more problems than functional solutions and one key challenge is finding scholars who can effectively apply neuroscientific research (Gajewski and Falkenstein, 2016). Due to the lack of published protocols this can often result in practitioners being led by consultants or technology providers, who both have a biased agenda. There are over 5 million people suffering from stress related concerns associated with burn out (De Sio et al., 2016). So here the literature will be scrutinized, technology challenged, and practices evaluated in order to understand what are the validated benefits, to suggest the future for brain-based protocols as part of research in the field of organizational wellbeing (Cortese et al., 2016).

In most complex organizational systems, it has been shown that work consumes a large part of most individuals' time and lives (Johnson and LeBreton, 2004). This confirms that the regular week for employees in the United States has risen to almost 50 hours. Health neuroscience includes understanding the interrelationship between the brain and the physical, emotional, and mental health that define wellbeing. Practical tools presented from health neuroscience can be relevant to the organizational context (ibid.) because these neurological markers can inform how self-directed changes can improve healthy workplace practices that influence organizational wellbeing as a whole. Table 27.1 shows some of the anatomical functional regions associated with neurophysiological wellbeing.

Erickson, et al., (2005) explains the impact that behavioral choice has on neurological health and how organizations that reward healthy choice observe a direct benefit, which is a key marker of overall health and wellbeing. This research can be used to enlighten organization wellbeing practices to have a direct health, psychological, and emotional benefit (Öhman and Mineka, 2001). Adolphs et al. (1994) described that neurological

health is directly associated with emotional regulation of the brain and emotion, which suggests there are core emotions, and these are suggested to influence behavioral choice associated with: anger, disgust, fear, and sadness. Ekman (1994) further suggests that these emotions are associated with specific neurological regions. Disgust is associated with activity in the insula, fear with the amygdala, anger with the OF Cortex and sadness with the AC cortex (Inzlicht et al., 2015) acknowledging the core emotions to include happiness and surprise, associated with activity in regions including the amygdala and hippocampus. Here, emotional wellbeing is achieved by triggering the brain's dopamine reward pathway, activity in regions such as the insula, amygdalae, and hippocampi which can motivate action to take place. This can explain why the brain tends to react and get immediate rewards when a neurological reward occurs by eating sugar (carbohydrates are essentially sugars), which will give a boost of energy and a possible emotional benefit (Plutchik, 1983). Organizational wellbeing initiatives that reward healthy behavior can influence people to make new and healthier choices associated with wellbeing (Davidson et al., 2009).

Table 27.1   Key neuroanatomical areas for the study of wellbeing in organizational life.

amygdalae	Two almond-shaped clusters of nuclei that have a key role in the processing of emotions, initially as fear.
brainstem	Includes midbrain, pons, and medulla oblongata that regulate breathing, heart rate, and blood pressure.
basal ganglia	Subcortical nuclei for motor control, learning, executive function, emotion, reward, and habit formation.
cerebellum	(Latin for 'little brain'.) This is responsible for voluntary movements, balance, and physical coordination.
cingulate cortex	An integral part of emotion formation and processing, associated learning, short- and long-term memory.
hippocampi	Found each side of the brain, each hippocampus is a region associated with memory as well as regulating, motivation, emotion, and learning.
hypothalamus	Links the nervous and the endocrine system. Maintains the homeostasis and hormone production.
insular cortex	In the lateral sulcus involved in pain perception, emotion, and associated with trigger compulsive behavior.
prefrontal cortex	Implicated in complex cognitive behavior, personality decisions, working memory, and social behavior.
thalamus	Relays sensory information. Has roles in motor activity, emotion, memory, attention, and arousal

New healthy behaviors then can also receive a 'feel-good' reward of the neurotransmitter dopamine (Davidson et al., 2009). If a wellbeing program triggers this same emotional reward system, it can be applied to motivate people to become healthier. Healthy choices can be then linked to nutrition, exercise, and other behavior-based choices. For example, by rewarding people to exercise, the brain releases dopamine (Van Van Hoomissen et al., 2004) if the new reward is emotionally attractive. This will result in behaviors that improve overall wellbeing but only if the brain 'buys in' hormonally (Van Hoomissen, 2004). In short, reward behaviors that improve neurological health as part of organizational intervention, and wellbeing will potentially follow.

Health neuroscience in association with behavioral neuroscience, also referred to as biopsychology or psychobiology, offers opportunity toward improving occupational wellbeing levels systemically as behavioral neuroscientists functioning in the organizational context study the neurophysiological processes between behavioral choice and the occupational environment (Butler and Senior, 2007). The goal is to understand how environment-behavior and organizational relationships are represented in the brain in order to improve behavior change (Butler and Senior, 2007). As a result, neuroscience as part of organizational-wellbeing interventions may be useful to understand how the brain automatically responds to change at work. This is because a neurological response to change occurs when the emotional reward and threat systems are activated (Öhman and Mineka, 2001). Behavior can be activated positively or negatively in response to environmental triggers which directly influence neurology and the choices people make. Applying behavioral neuroscience in the organizational-wellbeing context is complex as behaviors are often emotionally loaded unconscious reactions. In evolutionary terms, these neurological responses were intended to increase specific survival behaviors (Kivimäki, 2002). These survival behaviors

include increasing control over the environment, self-direction, and a chance to be recognized for social achievement (Ekman, 1994). When the organization offers self-directed behavior-based wellbeing opportunities that are emotionally reward based, people tend to become more motived to engage. If organizations orient this in certain ways, it can result in reinforcing an 'incorrect' or unhealthy behavior and the brain stops producing dopamine. A wellbeing program, if implemented poorly, may unintentionally cause a threat rather than a neurological reward response as this not only makes it difficult to encourage healthy behavioral change but may also result in low levels of engagement in wellbeing initiatives. Neurophysiologically this results in an increased level of cortisol and is in part an indicator of diminished health and poor immune function (Erickson, 2005).

Neurological methods include measures for heart rate, skin temperature, blood pressure, hormones, and brain activity as these methods have recently been adopted by organizational and leadership wellbeing scholars, and offer some opportunities for extending our understanding of health and resilience at work (Glover et al., 2001). This can be associated with protocols of organizational cognitive neuroscience to outline the neuropsychological impacts within organizational context (Butler and Senior, 2007). This helps us to understand the neurobiological mechanisms that influence decision-making, trust, and the importance of self-determination at work. However, the use of these methods in organizational wellbeing needs additional study. The workplace is largely a social experience (Campbell, 2010) where functional social bonds are associated with increased concentration of oxytocin and vasopressin that are associated with increased trust (Dimoka, 2010). This 'group think' may unconsciously result in people not engaging (Campbell, 2010), as the first part of any wellness program must be to ensure the program is not perceived as socially threatening (Dimoka, 2010). Neuroscience applications for wellbeing in organizational life could identify the behavioral responses associated with optimizing psycho-social safety (Kivimäki, 2002). This usually includes optimizing social health, empathy, trust, and compassion as part of programs to sustain wellbeing in organizational life (Dimoka, 2010).

With regards to the neuropsychology of wellbeing, neuroeconomics is a field that explains how the brain is automatically triggered by emotions and social cues according to Campbell (2010), neuroeconomics seeks to explain irregularities in thinking and can be associated with neurological regions (Camerer, 2008). The amygdala, as outlined earlier, has been shown to trigger automatic affect, especially fear (Öhman and Mineka, 2001), whereas controlled 'logical' cognition occurs in the orbital and prefrontal cortex (pFC). However, automatic neural activity in the amygdala causes an emotional trigger to proceed pFC activity. Emotional choices are made first and about one-eighth of a second before conscious awareness, allowing rational choices to be made only afterwards. Organizations can infuse 'wellbeing biases' to motivate change and cause a dopamine reward by employing behavioral and emotional prompts that improve choices and healthier habits (Dimoka, 2010).

Health neuroscience, behavioral neuroscience, neuroeconomics, and other associated fields (Erickson, 2005) collectively explain how hormonal release unconsciously directs behavioral choice. Campbell (2010) has shown that this informs pFC activity and can be associated with healthy behavior change. If organizations tap into this 'reward system' it may be able to consciously and unconsciously influence choice. This is key to understanding how neuroscience applied in the organizational context can be relevant toward improving wellbeing. It can help organizations motivate change if rewards have social (increasing oxytocin and vasopressin neurotransmitters) and emotional components increasing dopamine reward pathways and reducing cortisol (Schneiderman et al., 2005).

STRESS KILLS BRAINS

There are over 5 million people suffering from stress related concerns associated with stress (De Sio et al., 2018) which are directly related to lifestyle disease and overall health. Such data can be invaluable to ensure measurement and design of relevant wellbeing tools. Neurons, as part of attrition, reduce in their total amount naturally, but chronic stress kills brain cells much more frequently. Brain cells get replaced with new ones, due to the action of a protein called brain-derived neurotrophic factor (BDNF) (Altar et al., 1994). Consistent stress releases cortisol which reduces BDNF and new brain cells are not as frequently produced. This results in the brain size reducing in the hippocampus and the prefrontal cortex. It can cause reduced function of storing new memories, cause poor decision making, and reduce self-control over impulses that impact health and wellbeing. One example is that this can result in the brain craving immediate energy found as sugars, colloquially called 'stress eating' as chronic stress over arousal has a neurophysiological cost being directly associated with demanding work, harassment, and many other stressors which are directly related to 'allostatic loading' as per Porges S. (2007) of the hypothalamus–pituitary–adrenal (HPA) axis (Rivest, 2001). The HPA axis is a neuroendocrine system that includes the hypothalamus, pituitary gland, and adrenal glands, which have critical roles in basal homeostasis and in the neurophysiological response to stress. Reduced HPA control of the immune response, and chronic levels of cortisol, result in dysfunction of neurological systems as inflammatory reactions occur, referred to as allostatic loading. This marks a reduction in the working memory pathways and reduced problem-solving ability (Butler and Senior, 2007).

Chronic stress is associated with increased cortisol levels, and has shown to affect functions of the gut-brain axis (GBA), which plays a direct role resulting in many lifestyle diseases (Mayer et al., 2006). As per obesity statistics from the UK Parliament Health Survey Network where 28.7% of adults in England are obese (body mass index [BMI] of 30+) and a further 35.6% are considered seriously overweight. The insula, dorsolateral prefrontal cortex, anterior cingulate cortex, orbitofrontal cortex, and ventromedial prefrontal cortex are all activated in response to over eating high-calorie food (Mayer et al., 2006). Furthermore, routinely over eating can lead people to confuse intentions and habits and even create false memories about eating unhealthily (Kelley et al., 2009).

Wagner et al, (2005) describes how the brain craves unhealthy food by describing neurological components of response inhibition. Hublin J-J, Richards MP, (2009) suggest the evolution of hominin diets offering an integrated approaches to palaeolithic subsistence and that these previous hominids had lack of access to carbohydrates especially sugar. Eaton SB, Cordain L. (1997) further explais that foods heavy in easily metabolized calories increased prehistoric human survival rates. Carbohydrates and sugars were previously scarce source (Avena NM, Hoebel BG. 2003). The evidence for sugar addiction and behavioral and neurochemical effects of intermittent, excessive sugar intake (Avena NM, Hoebel BG. 2003) details how it alters the emotional relationship to over-eating sugars. The reward, dopamine pathway and the impact of food volume and type has direct implications for obesity due to activation of the amygdala as nutrition reward directs behavior to eat more than is needed as a guard against scarcity as described by Volkow ND. (2008). In brief the brain encourages one to eat excess cardohydrates as way behaviour that protects against seasons when there is limited access to nutrition. Today the situation has reversed. We now have excessive access to sugars of all kinds. The brain still operates as though it is scarce. Excees nutrition has direct impacts on chonic disease and wellbeing (Avena NM, Hoebel BG. 2003). As per Somerville and Casey

(2010), the role of the nasal microbiome and the proximity to the blood brain barrier may result in becoming hungry when smelling food and these odors cause increased interest in eating that food type (Wager et al., 2005). Just by thinking about the smell of any food (like bread baking) can result in the reward pathway triggering a dopamine release and result in wanting to eat bread (a full list of associated food aromas and the influence of fragrances on psychophysiological activity is explained by Angelucci et al., 2014). By linking emotional function with stomach and overall intestinal health, organizational wellbeing programs can attend to both requirements (Herz, 2009). The importance of gut microbiota in relation to health and mood is often associated with lifestyle disease (Wager et al., 2005). Poor sleep hygiene, certain cardiac diseases, stroke, type 2 diabetes, smoking, alcoholism, and others including drug abuse are also considered lifestyle diseases (Mayer et al., 2006).

In the workplace, for stress, depression, and anxiety related issues, technology from neuroscience has been applied, and these neurofeedback tools (Orndorff-Plunkett et al., 2017) have often been part of wellbeing interventions. EEG neurofeedback devices can be applied to detect electrical charges from the activity of brain cells, and EEG neurofeedback products have been shown to help deal with stress, sleep, and anxiety disorders (Orndorff-Plunkett et al., 2017). Application of other technology that measures the brain includes repeated transcranial magnetic stimulation (rTMS), which stimulates the release of neurotransmitters, while neurofeedback trains the brain and can yield changes in brainwaves. Transcranial direct current stimulation (tDCS) is the neuromodulation of a harmless direct current which is also non-invasive to stimulate nerve cells. These are still not readily available directly as part of in-house wellbeing programs, but have been applied externally in wellness clinics to remedy lifestyle disease and depression. Other tools include magnetic resonance imaging (MRI), which scan the anatomical brain structure, and functional magnetic resonance imaging (fMRI), which scan metabolic activity (Rosano, 2010). These can be applied to measure brain activity; however, it remains unclear how relevant these tools will be to the organizational domain due to cost and application requirements. These and other technologies can be used to measure the brain and may show how to reduce symptoms of depression, stress, anxiety, and other pathologies (Vernon et al., 2003). Providers of neurofeedback technologies suggest that their products are most effective (Surmeli, 2012); however, some of these products are not FDA-approved (Cortese et al., 2016) and, as a result, further studies are required, especially for improved wellbeing in organizational life. Many application sessions are often required, which is expensive, whereas tools from behavioral neuroscience appear to offer similar results. There are several technologies launched or under development that could be invaluable, but more research is needed to validate claims in the context of organizational wellbeing, as per Surmeli (2012).

THE CASE STUDIES THAT APPLIED NEUROECONOMICS, HEALTH, AND BEHAVIORAL NEUROSCIENCE

The following three case studies discuss commercial initiatives which were commissioned in relation to wellbeing programs. They have not been previously published and are discussed here to demonstrate the application of neuroscience rather than advice or guidance. This section should be considered in relation to how healthy behavior is influenced, not only by triggering neural activity but also through the application of subtle neurological prompts that result in adoption of new habits associated with wellbeing at work. These could help validate health and behavioral neuroscience interventions as part of organizational wellbeing programs (Priebe S et al., 2011). The studies employed

neurophysiological and neuropsychological markers that may serve as references for further research. These three cases are: 'This is your captain speaking', 'I love you DHEA', and the 'Lean-green-canteen-machine'.

THIS IS YOUR CAPTAIN SPEAKING

Lack of sleep is a global issue and poorly managed brain-arousal at bedtime presents as symptoms of stress, anxiety, and hyperactivity which are particularly prevalent when changing time zones (Akerstedt et al., 2007). Why do we need sleep? Sleep is indispensable for good health and wellbeing throughout life and getting enough quality sleep, at the right time, sustains neurophysiological health, along with improving overall wellbeing, because while asleep the brain is active and moves through a series of stages for repairing the body (Waterhouse et al., 2007). During REM sleep the brain is filing useful information it has learned, and forms new neural pathways to aid learning and memory (Buzsáki, 1989). Sleeping balances hormones, controls blood sugar levels, and the immune system. Cerebrospinal fluid is released during deep sleep in order to clear waste products out of the brain similar to what the lymphatic system does to the rest of the body. So how much sleep is needed is a good question, but the answer is not simple. The average adult sleeps for about eight hours. Einstein slept for over 12 hours and Winston Churchill about four, whereas Da Vinci apparently slept no more than two hours at a time, so there is no hard and fast rule. Yet the lack of a good night's rest can lead to poor concentration, and poor awareness of the environment, weight gain, raised blood pressure, loss of motivation, controlling emotions and behavior (Buzsáki, 1989).

The neurotransmitter, cortisol, is a reliable indicator of the neurophysiological stress load that is associated with lack of sleep (Cajochen et al., 1999). This initiative was conducted in the United States in

2018 and evaluated the stress levels of airline pilots to improve their sleeping habits, which is referred to as 'sleep hygiene' (Buzsáki, 1989). The initiative involved measuring cortisol levels during an eight-week wellbeing and health coaching program designed to measure and improve 25 self-selected pilots that slept poorly for at least three hours less than their individual sleep requirement and also woke up feeling 'groggy'. This initiative measured self-directed sleep hygiene behavior and change associated with the pilots' cortisol saliva samples taken in the morning and afternoon when not flying. Saliva samples were taken over an eight-week period where the student implemented specific behavioral neuroscience coaching protocols to improve sleep hygiene (Kennedy, 2019). The initiative found that there was a reduction in salivary cortisol levels, and better sleep habits were related to stress reduction and improved sleep hygiene in the study group. The cortisol levels of 19 pilots returned to their normal ranges, 10 to 20 micrograms (ug/dl) (Dalmazi et al., 2012), between 06h00 – 08h00, and 3 to 10 ug/dl at 17h00, which were usually less than 5 ug/dl after the usual bedtime. Five pilots found no benefit and three found minimal benefit with sleeping duration increasing by 1 to 1.2 hours but not feeling energized when waking.

The results of the initiative demonstrated that self-directed sleep hygiene can be improved from healthy behavior changes associated with the pilots' new sleeping habits. The pilots who found most benefit showed improved overall sleep hygiene, and quantity increased between 2.7 and 3.6 hours. Most importantly, this group reported feeling less groggy and more energized when waking up. Measurement of concentration, and awareness of the environment and situation along with weight gain and raised blood pressure were not effectively measured. Sleep quality was only measured via the pilot's self-perception. The key findings suggest that brain-based behavioral change coaching helped to bring cortisol

to a normal range for some pilots. By measuring cortisol levels (Vicennati et al., 2000), the benefit of the stress reduction coaching for improved sleep hygiene was validated in part. No control group was included in the study and legitimacy needs to be further scrutinized before further exposure of the coaching protocols to other pilots. The majority of the participants (61%) who found benefit did retain sleep hygiene behaviors six months post the study. However, further organizational research needs to be published in this area.

I LOVE YOU DHEA

As mentioned, DHEA (dehydroepiandrosterone) is a naturally occurring hormone (Arlt et al., 1998) that can be taken orally to enhance wellbeing and performance in various product forms and is often used and abused in professional sports and other arenas referred to inappropriately as a dietary or nutrition ingredient, but it is a hormone (Tummala and Svec, 1999) and replacement products are easily available on retail shelves as a supplement to improve general health, performance, and emotional wellbeing. DHEA has also been credited with the capacity to fight infection, and manage weight by changing how the body metabolizes and stores fat (Tummala and Svec, 1999). DHEA reduction is associated with stress causing hormonal imbalances, and causes adrenal fatigue (Arlt et al., 1998). Furthermore, the lack of DHEA may cause exhaustion (i.e. burnout) and is linked to cognitive stress and depression (Kautz M, et al 2020). DHEA supplements have shown to boost positive mood, temporarily, and is used as part of a wellbeing initiative to reduce anxiety, depression, and psychological stress could be effective (Arlt et al., 1998).

A wellbeing commercial initiative included 52 self-selected employees from a car manufacturing plant, who were aged between 31 and 59. Each had been previously diagnosed with minor depression symptoms. All received DHEA for six weeks. While receiving DHEA, 23 people showed a 38% decrease in depression using the Hamilton Rating Scale for Depression (HAM-D), a standard rating scale for symptoms (Mocking et al., 2001). Eleven responded to the placebo and eight employees receiving DHEA were equally depressed, compared with all receiving the placebo. The rest of the 52 who had reduced depression symptoms self-selected to further apply a smaller dose (25 mg / day) and remained resilient to depression for over six months. One year later, those involved in the initiative had all stopped using DHEA and cited reasons like 'It's too expensive' or 'I don't have the time to buy it' and used these to explain their adverse behavior change. The learning here is that initiatives that are not part of an organizational-wellbeing system that supports new appropriate and effective behaviors are most often not maintained (Santor et al., 2001). Wellbeing programs in general should ensure initiatives have support systems in place to help people maintain their newly found healthy behaviors. Further organizational research needs to be published in this area.

THE LEAN-GREEN-CANTEEN-MACHINE

The processes of decision making and how healthy choices inform wellbeing can be observed in relation to specific forms of applied neuroscience (Weber et al., 2002). This can include neuroeconomics, health neuroscience, and behavioral neuroscience. Eating and self-control are often linked, and people often judge themselves for excessive and unhealthy eating habits. This is sometimes not fair as limited food options influence choice (Bahadoran et al., 2012). As mentioned earlier, the brain desires a high calorie food which improves chances of survival; however, the self-aware mind wants to eat healthily and maintain wellbeing (Thompson, 2003). An illustration of this

dichotomy was shown in this case-study initiative where the application of health neuroscience and neuroeconomic behavior protocols influenced food choice.

This initiative included various organizational-wellbeing interventions as part of health and wellness programs within a Dubai-based retail corporation, and focused on influencing self-selected eating choices. The initiative was designed to reduce high levels of obesity, and the application of neuroeconomic protocols attempted to influence behavioral choice by creating a healthy eating place nicknamed the 'lean-green-canteen'. This was part of an overall wellness initiative to improve employees' levels of health and wellbeing. Previously the 'old' canteen was unattractive in design and had only offered high-calorie deep-fried 'junk-food' options that everyone enjoyed but was agreed by management to be a primary concern related to the obesity problem at hand. As part of the wellbeing program, a new canteen was designed to be very attractive, having fresh and healthy themes throughout. It had plants, sunny landscape photos, healthy vegetable pictures, relaxing enjoyable music softly playing, paintings of happy faces, and even delicious herb smells being infused at the entrance doors' air conditioner. This was all intentional in order to influence the brain's visual, auditory, physical, emotional, and nasal sensory perceptions of food taste and food selection (Blundell et al., 1991).

Pre-portioned colorful and healthy meals, vegetables and salads of 200g each, were laid out in attractive displays and made easily available upon arrival. The previous unhealthy options were only available at a separate less attractive buffet table at the back of the canteen, requiring subjects to walk over 12 meters to find their previous 'junk-food' options. After the new 'green canteen' was opened, behavior was observed to note food choice and eating habits (they were informed of the organizational plans to influence their neurological pre-conscious emotional reward and satiety systems and a legal disclaimer was required for consent). The new canteen context was intentionally designed to trigger food self-selection to observe whether people would make healthy food selection choices or in fact any choice if their brains were unconsciously and consciously prompted and suggested to make healthy choices (Tversky and Kahneman, 1974).

The initiative was conducted over three months and results showed an increased amount of vegetables being eaten. A decrease in calorie intake from 145 kcal $p<0.01$ to 122 kcal $p<0.01$ was observed. This confirmed that the neurological influences due to the environmental refurbishment and food attractiveness directly informed self-selected healthy food selection. With limited access to fMRI technology, the neurological function of five subjects' ventral tegmental areas (VTA) (Bäckman et al., 2006) showed activation associated with food selection. This activation in the VTA caused a release of the neuropeptide hypocretin (hcrt or orexin), which is associated with neural activation from food-related aromas. This was associated with the unconscious and conscious prompts generating behavior change that was useful in the initiativein relation to reward processing regarding eating habits and encoding reward-related signals that drive anticipatory and consummatory behaviors. The fMRI data correlated to dopamine reward sensitivity, which validated that people's eating habits can be influenced by the activation of the referred behavioral triggers (Maldjian, 2003).

These results were only observed in the new canteen and not tested in other contexts, but studies have confirmed similar results (Rosano, 2010). The findings suggest that the application of health neuroscience and neuroeconomic protocols showed them to be effective in influencing food selection in this context. Some 36% of subjects sustained an average 3.6% weight loss per their results, or their healthy food selection was maintained for six months after the study, but further protocols are required to validate findings.

Social behavior that impacts wellbeing and food choice could be invaluable to consider as part of a system that measures eating habits and overall wellbeing in organizational life. The research from social neuroscience was not included in this initiative; however, it would be valuable to evaluate how new social norms around eating habits could be responsible for behavior change. The suggestion is that there are also related external characteristics which include sociological, cultural, and environmental triggers that were not addressed in enough detail from the study (Slavin and Green, 2007). Wellbeing programs could make food choices to be self-selected rather than being limited to only eating certain food groups.

DISCUSSION AND FUTURE DIRECTIONS

Across the cases studies, there is the shared responsibility of individuals and the organization to drive and sustain wellbeing; however, the organization that wants to support wellbeing may often find that it requires them to develop further systems that prompt the brains of people to make healthy choices. If an organization wants to maintain such healthy behavior, it needs to offer consistent support and address concerns to maintain motivated healthy behavioral choices. This is because it takes energy or 'brain power' to build a new healthy habit (Tversky and Kahneman, 1974), which is difficult for many people who feel overstretched at work. Several examples of protocols that direct behavior change were areas associated with neurological function. This chapter has shown several neurological influences over behavior change. For example, the findings from several studies explain that wellbeing must start with a good night's rest as without a healthy sleep routine (sleep hygiene), the brain cannot remember, learn, or be healthy and be ready for the next day if the cerebrospinal fluid has not functioned as it should (Knapska, 2006), resulting in damaging effects with respect to wellbeing. Similarly, there are innumerable diets available and many are useful to enhance wellbeing in organizational life. The most consistent research findings and meta studies (Hoffman and Gerber, 2013) suggest having a Mediterranean diet is very effective for improving health and wellbeing and has shown to improve GBA axis functions, especially by including pickled foods. In parallel excessive aerobic exercise routines may also result in cardiac distress and it is very appropriate to address the relation between aerobic exercise, wellbeing and the heart. it is important to discuss the most suitable dosage of aerobic exercise for adults in the context preventing cardiovascular diseases Araújo CG (2015).

The affiliation between applied neuroscience and organizational wellbeing is an emerging field of study (Pastva et al., 2004). But healthy behavior change is nuanced and there are various wellbeing neuroscience curricula that might be effective but are more appropriately seen as one spoke of a wheel in a dynamic organizational system that improves wellbeing in organizational life. The application of neuroscience does not require a wellbeing program to be branded a 'brain-based' intervention to offer benefit. In fact, applied neuroscience interventions that ensure benefits of behavior change do not need to refer to the brain at all. For this emerging field to add empirical value, wellbeing initiatives associated with applied neuroscience must deliver a clear link to change in behavior that shows sustained wellbeing in organizational life, so, does the application of neuroscience only confirm what is already known within the field of organizational wellbeing? This is often a valid criticism and the term 'neurohype' (Bartoszeck and Bartoszeck, 2012) which has emerged which refers to exaggerated brain-based claims. It was tested as a hypothesis with a group of 21 (uninformed) MBA students doing a short neuroscience course, and three qualified expert neuroscientists attending in a supporting role. It was found that presenting information or explanations using irrelevant neuroscience jargon was perceived as more valid than other explanations that did not reference the brain. Students and neuroscientists alike believed information to be more valuable if the brain was mentioned. So, could referring to neuroscience offer a placebo effect? Instead of answering this, the use of neuroscience to justify wellbeing program design has shown to offer no or very limited practical behavior-based solutions or useful tools. Validation will come from evidence of application, rather than misquoting false statements like 'we only use 10% of our brain's capacity' (Bartoszeck and Bartoszeck, 2012). Organizational wellbeing systems should only consider brain-based initiatives as supportive and not primary. As a result, the application of neuroscience can only have a partial impact on improving organizational wellbeing. For neuroscience to secure its place it must present evidence of enhanced and sustained wellbeing in the organizational context.

The task ahead to validate the relevance of neuroscience is simple but not easy. It is simple in the sense that we know how to measure the brain and improve behavioral wellbeing due to the application of neuroscience. But it is complex in that there is no generic model as to how neuroscience is most effectively contextualized for the needs of the individuals or the organization at large. This is not to discourage the scholar, but rather to ensure research in this domain is held to a higher standard by associating healthy behavior change with measurable neurological markers that can be observed in organizational behavior. Practitioners that want to apply interventions and employ tools from neuroscience to measure and improve the impact on wellbeing in organizational life can have an invaluable impact on the future developments in this context, if they refer to the research before engaging in any so-called 'brain-based wellness' program (Chandola et al., 2006).

The lack of academic research and communication between clinicians and researchers is perhaps the most significant limit to the application of neuroscience as future directions are still emerging although the topic of neuroscience is in vogue in the context of organizational wellbeing, knowledge about the brain in isolation will have little, if any, value. Future research should involve validating protocols that promote sustained meaningful, measurable, and lasting healthy changes, which are influenced by health and behavioral neuroscience stimuli and offer data that supports neurological and overall wellbeing (Giannaki, 2013). And, even then, the application of neuroscience will never be able to provide all the answers on how to promote health and wellbeing. At best, scholars of applied neuroscience can contribute to the existing field of interdisciplinary knowledge and might help us identify the burning questions to support future research and effective applied initiatives.

REFERENCES

Adolphs, R., Tranel, D., Damasio, H., Damasio, A., (1994). Impaired recognition of emotion in facial expressions following bilateral damage to the human amygdala. *Nature*, 372, 69–672.

Akerstedt T., Kecklund G., Axelsson J., (2007). Impaired sleep after bedtime stress and worries. *Biological Psychology* 76: 170–173.

Altar C.A, Boylan C.B, Fritsche M, Jackson C, Hyman C, Lindsay R.M., (1994). The neurotrophins NT-4/5 and BDNF augment serotonin, dopamine, and GABAergic systems during behaviorally effective infusions to the substantia nigra. Journal of Experimental Neurology. 130: 31–40.

Angelucci, F.L., Silva, V.V., Dal Pizzol, C., Spir, L.G., Praes, C.E., Maibach, H., (2014). Physiological effect of olfactory stimuli inhalation in humans: An overview. *International Journal of Cosmetic Science* , 36, 117–123.

Araújo CG. Componentes aeróbico e não-aeróbicos da aptidão física: fatores de risco para mortalidade por todas as causas. Revista Factores Risco. 2015;35(1-3):36–42.

Arlt W. Androgen therapy in women. (2006) *European Journal of Endocrinology.* 2006;154(1):1–11.

Avena NM, Hoebel BG. A diet promoting sugar dependency causes behavioral cross-sensitization to a low dose of amphetamine. Neuroscience. 2003b;122:17–20.

Bäckman, C., Malik, N., Zhang, Y., Shan, L., Grinberg, A., Hoffer, B., Westphal, H., Tomac, A., (2006). Characterization of a mouse strain expressing Cre recombinase from the 3⊠ untranslated region of the dopamine transporter locus. *Genesis*, 44, 383–390.

Bahadoran, Z., Mirmiran, P., Golzarand, M., Hosseini-Esfahani, F., Azizi, F., (2012). Fast food consumption in Iranian adults; dietary intake and cardiovascular risk factors: Tehran lipid and glucose study. *Archives of Iranian Medicine*, 15(6), 346–351.

Bandura A. *Social cognitive theory of self-regulation. Organisation Behavavior Human Decision Process.* Front. Psychol., 21 September 2018. 1991;50: 248–87 doi: https://doi.org/10.3389/fpsyg.2018.01738 https://www.frontiersin.org/articles/10.3389/fpsyg.2018.01738/full.

Bartoszeck, A., Bartoszeck F., (2012). How in-service teachers perceive neuroscience as connected to education: An exploratory study. *European Journal of Educational Research.* 1, 301–319.

Benson H, Dryer T, Hartley LH., (1978). Decreased VO2 consumption during exercise with elicitation of the relaxation response. *J Human Stress* 4: 38–42.

Branchi I. and Alleva E., (2006). Communal nesting, an early social enrichment, increases the adult anxiety-like response and shapes the role of social context in modulating the emotional behavior. *Behavioral Brain Research.* 172, 299-306. 10.1016/j.bbr.2006.05.

Butler M.J.R., Senior C., (2007). Towards an organizational cognitive neuroscience. *Annals of the New York Academy of Sciences.* 1118, 1–17.

Buzsáki, G., (1989). Two-stage model of memory trace formation: A role for 'noisy' brain states. *Neuroscience*, 31, 551–570.

Cajochen C, Khalsa S, Wyatt J, Czeisler C, Dijk D, (1999) EEG and ocular correlates of circadian melatonin phase and human performance decrements during sleep loss. *The Journal of Physiology* 1999 Sep;277(3 Pt 2):R640-9. doi: 10.1152/ajpregu.1999.277.3.r640.

Camerer, C., (2008). The potential of neuroeconomics. *Economics and Philosophy*, 24(3), 369–379.

Campbell, A., (2010). Oxytocin and human social behavior. *Journal of the Society for Personality and Social Psychology, Inc*, 14, 281–295.

Chandola, T., Brunner, E., Marmot, M., (2006). Chronic stress at work and the metabolic syndrome: Prospective study. *BMJ*, 332, 521–525.

Cortese A., (2016)., Multivoxel neurofeedback selectively modulates confidence without changing perceptual performance. *Nature Communications*. 7: 13669.

Davidson J, Kudler H, Smith R, Mahorney SL, Lipper S, Hammett E, et al. Treatment of post-traumatic stress disorder with amitriptyline and placebo. *Arch Gen Psychiatry*. 1990;47:259–266.

De Sio S, Cammalleri V, Pocino RN, Murano S, Perri R, Buomprisco G, De Giusti M, Vitali M. (2019) *A Cross-Sectional Study on Prevalence and Predictors of Burnout among a Sample of Pharmacists Employed in Pharmacies in Central Italy*. Biomed Res Int. 2019 Dec 24;2019:8590430. doi: 10.1155/2019/8590430. eCollection 2019. PMID: 3195005

Dalmazi Di., Vicennati V., Rinaldi E., et al. (2012), Progressively increased patterns of subclinical cortisol hypersecretion in adrenal incidentalomas differently predict major metabolic and cardiovascular outcomes: a large cross-sectional study. *European Journal of Endocrinology*. 2012;166(4):669–677. doi: 10.1530/eje-11-1039

De Sio S., Letizia C., Petramala L., Saracino V., Cedrone F., Sanguigni P., Buomprisco G., Perri R., Trovato Battagliola E., Mannocci A., La Torre G., (2018). Work-related stress and cortisol levels: is there an association? Results of an observational study. *European Review for Medical and Pharmacological Sciences*.; 22(24): 9012-9017. doi: 10.26355/eurrev_201812_16672. PMID: 30575947.

Dimoka, A., (2010). What does the brain tell us about trust and distrust? Evidence from a functional neuroimaging study. *MIS Quarterly*, 34, 2, 373–377.

Eaton SB, Cordain L. Evolutionary aspects of diet: old genes, new fuels. Nutritional changes since agriculture. World Rev Nutr Diet. 1997; 81: 26–37. pmid:9287501

Ekman, P., (1994). Strong evidence for universals in facial expressions: A reply to Russell's mistaken critique. *Psychological Bulletin Journal*, 115, 268–287.

Erickson K.I, Colcombe S.J, Raz N., Korol D.L, Scalf P., Webb A., Cohen N.J, McAuley E., Kramer A.F., (2005). *Neurobiol Aging*.; 26(8): 1205-13.

Fung, C., (2013). The impact of a population-level school food and nutrition policy on dietary intake and body weights of Canadian children. *Preventive Medicine*, 57, 6, 934–940.

Gage, F., (2002). Neurogenesis in the adult brain. *Journal of Neuroscience*. 22, 612–613.

Gajewski, P.D., Falkenstein, M., (2016). Physical activity and neurocognitive functioning in aging: A condensed updated review. *European Review of Aging and Physical Activity*. 13, 1, 10.1186/s11556-016-0161-3.

Giannaki, C., (2013). Effect of exercise training and dopamine agonists in patients with uremic restless legs syndrome: A six-month randomized, partially double-blind, placebo-controlled comparative study. *British Medical Journal, Nephrology*, 14, 194, doi: 10.1186/1471-2369-14-194.

Glover GH, Law CS. Spiral-in/out BOLD fMRI for increased SNR and reduced susceptibility artifacts. Magn Reson Med. 2001;46: 515–522.

Herz, R.S., (2009). Aromatherapy facts and fictions: A scientific analysis of olfactory effects on mood, physiology and behavior. *International Journal of Neuroscience*, 119, 263–290.

Herz, R.S., (2009). Aromatherapy facts and fictions: A scientific analysis of olfactory effects on mood, physiology and behavior. *Int. J. Neurosci*, 119, 263–290.

Hoffman, R., Gerber, M., (2013). Evaluating and adapting the Mediterranean diet for non-Mediterranean populations: A critical appraisal. *Nutrition Reviews*, 71, 573–584.

Hublin J-J, Richards MP, editors (2009) The evolution of hominin diets. Integrating approaches to the study of palaeolithic subsistence. Dordrecht: Springer-Verlag Netherlands; 2009.

Inzlicht, M., Bartholow, B., Hirsh, J., (2015). Emotional foundations of cognitive control. *Trends in Cognitive Science*. 19, 126–132.

Johnson, J.W., LeBreton, J.M., (2004). History and use of relative importance indices in organizational research. *Organizational Research Methods*, 7, 238–257.

Kautz M, Coe CL, McArthur BA, Mac Giollabhui N, Ellman LM, Abramson LY, Alloy LB. (2020) Longitudinal changes of inflammatory biomarkers moderate the relationship between recent stressful life events and prospective symptoms of depression in a diverse sample of urban adolescents. *Brain Behavior Immunisation*. 2020 May;86:43-52. doi: 10.1016/j.bbi.2019.02.029.

Kennedy, J.J., (2019). Brain Reboot: *A Change of Mind Will Change Your Brain*. Amazon Publishing, Kindle Books.

Kivimäki, M., (2002). Work stress and risk of cardiovascular mortality: Prospective cohort study of industrial employees. *British Medical Journal*, 325, 857–860.

Knapska E., Walasek G., Nikolaev E., Neuhäusser-Wespy F., Lipp H.P., Kaczmarek L., Werka T. Differential involvement of the central amygdala in appetitive versus aversive learning. *Learn Mem.* 2006;13: 192–200. doi: 10.1101/lm.54706.

Lupien SJ, Maheu F, Tu M and T E Schramek (2007) The effects of stress and stress hormones on human cognition: implications for the field of brain and cognition. *Brain Cognition.* 65(3): 209–237.

Maldjian, J., (2003). An automated method for neuroanatomic and cytoarchitectonic atlas-based interrogation of fMRI data sets. *Neuroimage*, 19, 1233–1239.

Mayer, E., Tillisch, K., Bradesi, S., (2006). Modulation of the brain-gut axis as a therapeutic approach in gastrointestinal disease. *Aliment Pharmacological Therapy* , 6, 919–933.

Mocking R.J, Assies J, Koeter M.W. (2012). Bimodal distribution of fatty acids in recurrent major depressive disorder. *Biological Psychiatry* 71:e3–5. 10.1016/j.biopsych.2011.09.004

Öhman, A., Mineka, S., (2001). Fears, phobias, and preparedness: Toward an evolved module of fear and fear learning. *Psychological Review*, 108, 483–522.

Orndorff-Plunkett F., Singh F., Aragón O.R, Pineda J.A (2017) assessing the effectiveness of neurofeedback training in the context of clinical and social neuroscience. *Journal of Brain Science. 2017 Aug 7*;7(8):95. doi: 10.3390/brainsci7080095. PMID: 28783134; PMCID: PMC5575615.

Parsons H., Houge Mackenzie S., Filep S., Brymer E. (2019). *Subjective well-being and leisure, in Good Health and Well-Being. Encyclopedia of the UN Sustainable Development Goals*, eds Leal Filho W., Wall T., Azul A., Brandli L., Özuyar P. (Cham: Springer). 10.1007/978-3-319-69627-0_8-1

Priebe S, Reininghaus U. (2011) Fired up, not burnt out – focusing on the rewards of working in psychiatry. Epidemiol Psychiatr Sci. 2011;20:303–5.

Plutchik, R., (1983). Emotions in Early Development: A Psycho-evolutionary Approach – Theory, Research and Experience, Vol 2: *Emotions in Early Development*. New York: Academic Press, pp. 221–257.

Porges S. W. (2007). The polyvagal perspective. *Biol. Psychol.* 74, 116–143. 10.1016/j.biopsycho.2006.06.00

Rivest, S., (2001). How circulating cytokines trigger the neural circuits that control the hypothalamic-pituitary-adrenal axis. *Psychoneuroendocrinology*, 26, 761–788.

Rosano, C., (2010). Psychomotor speed and functional brain MRI 2 years after completing a physical activity treatment. *Journal of Gerontology, Biological sciences and medical sciences.*, 65, 639–647.

Santor DA, Coyne JC. (2001) Examining symptoms expression as a function of symptom severity: item performance on the Hamilton Rating Scale for depression. *Psychological Assessment.* 2001;13:127–139

Slavin, J., Green, H., (2007). Dietary fibre and satiety. *Nutrition. Bulletin*, 32, 32–42.

Somerville, L., Casey, B., (2010). Developmental neurobiology of cognitive control and motivational systems. *Current Opinions in Neurobiology*, 20, 2, 236–241.

Surmeli, D., (2012). Schizophrenia and the efficacy of qEEG-guided neurofeedback treatment: A clinical case series. *Clinical EEG and Neuroscience*, 43, 2, 133–144.

Thompson, O., (2003). Food purchased away from home as a predictor of change in BMI z-score among girls. *International Journal of Obesity*, 28, 2, 282–289.

Tummala, S., Svec, F., (1999). Correlation between the administered dose of DHEA and serum levels of DHEA and DHEA-S in human volunteers: Analysis of published data. *Journal of Clinical Biochemistry* , 32, 355–361.

Tversky, A., Kahneman, D., (1974). Judgment under uncertainty: heuristics and biases. *Science*, 185, 4157, 1124–1131.

Van Hoomissen, J., (2004). Prepro-galanin messenger RNA levels are increased in rat locus coeruleus after treadmill exercise training. *Neuroscience Letters*, 299, 69–72.

Vernon, D., Egner, T., Cooper, N., Compton, T., Neilands, C., Sheri, A., (2003). The effect of training distinct neurofeedback protocols on aspects of cognitive performance. *International Journal of Psychophysiology*, 47, 1, 75–85.

Volkow ND. Overlapping neuronal circuits in addiction and obesity: evidence of systems pathology. *Philos. Trans. R. Soc. Lond. B. Biol. Sci.* 2008;363:3191–3200.

Wagner D. D., Boswell R. G., Kelley W. M., Heatherton T. F. (2012). Inducing negative affect increases the reward value of appetizing foods in dieters. *J. Cogn. Neurosci.* 24, 1625 a-1633 10.1162/jocn_a_00238

Weber E.U, Blais A.R, Betz N.E. ,(2002). A domain-specific risk-attitude scale: Measuring risk perceptions and risk behaviors. *Journal of Behavioral Decision Making* 15(4): 263.

28

Psychologically Informed Coaching Interventions and Workplace Wellbeing

Yi-Ling Lai and Stephen Palmer

INTRODUCTION

This chapter focuses on the application of coaching in workplace life and wellbeing areas since the *Annual Health and Well-being at Work* report by the Chartered Institute of Personnel and Development (CIPD, 2020: 3) indicated 'an unhealthy workforce means an unhealthy business'. Specifically, organizations are encouraged to take a proactive approach to support employees' psychological wellbeing. Coaching, which is a learner-centred reflective process by means of interpersonal interactions between coaches and coachees, can offer employees an opportunity to experience positive behavioral changes and performance growth through the improvement of organizational life (Grant, 2017). Indeed, Dodge and colleagues (2012) pointed out that a good understanding of employees' life satisfaction and work–life challenges facilitates profound organizational and cultural changes. Accordingly, this chapter explains in what way psychologically informed coaching interventions support individuals' workplace relationships, emotional responses and strengths to overcome challenges.

Nearly one in three workers in Europe and the United States reported that they are affected by stress at work. Work-related stress, depression and anxiety can result in reduced work performance and absenteeism, costing an estimated 3% to 4% of gross national product (Carolan et al., 2017). Recent scientific evidence has confirmed that cognitive behavioral grounded interventions facilitated the recovery of employees diagnosed with depression and/or anxiety (Joyce et al., 2016). Meanwhile, there has been increasing literature indicating a proactive and positive approach is preferable to prevent employees from psychological distress. Therefore, psychologically informed coaching can help or facilitate non-clinical populations for sustained behavioral changes drawn on a therapeutic approach and positive psychology through developing a richer picture of the coachee's behaviors, motivations, values and beliefs during the coaching process (Grant and Palmer, 2002).

This chapter includes three suggestions for future practice. First, organizations should take a proactive approach to support individuals' organizational life, including employee relations, stress management and work resilience building, through psychological-based approaches. Second, the development of individuals' workplace life and wellbeing should be considered as part of the organizational learning process, such as identifying employees' strengths to flourish in their work-life or overcome challenges. Third, the bottom-up and learner-centred approach, which facilitates an individual to reflect on their own thoughts objectively and develop a forward-looking mindset, is preferable. Recent research has indicated that the positive psychological state promotes an individual's intrinsic motivation for sustainable changes.

This chapter commences with a brief introduction of workplace coaching and its effectiveness on individual and organizational level outcomes in accordance with existing research evidence. Next, the role psychology plays in the workplace coaching is discussed. Subsequently, issues related to people's organizational life, such as employee and peer relationships, psychological distress and work resilience are addressed. Considering that coaching has been increasingly applied in professional-related learning and development areas, this chapter draws upon contemporary research evidence to articulate these two disciplines.

COACHING AND ORGANIZATIONAL LIFE

Coaching Definitions

Coaching has been described as a cross-disciplinary learning and development intervention (e.g. adult learning, management, social sciences and psychology) due to the various coaches' backgrounds and coaching settings. At the early stage of coaching practice, a coach-centred approach with a directive 'teaching-based element' was promoted: 'coaching is mainly concerned with the immediate improvement of performance and development of skills by a form of tutoring or instruction' (Parsloe, 1999: 52). Coaches provide specific guidelines and instructions to coachees in the coaching process. Alongside the increased application of coaching in organizational development, coaching has evolved into a 'learner-centred' process that engages coachees to develop their own action plans for sustainable behavioral changes and self-development. Whitmore (1996) explained that coaching is unlocking people's potential to maximize their own performance and helping coachees to learn rather than to teach them or impart any skills. Later, Grant (2001) added new features to the coaching definition: 'a collaborative, solution-focused, results orientated and systematic process in which the coach facilitates the enhancement of work performance, life experiences, self-directed learning and personal growth of coachee'. Grant's definition highlights that coaching is a two-way (coach-coachee) interactive process aimed at developing applicable solutions and plans for the coachee's continuous learning and growth at the workplace. Further, the relations between 'organizational objective' and 'coaching' were noted in the coaching definition: 'coaching aims to develop a person's skills and knowledge so that their job performance improves, hopefully leading to the achievement of organizational objectives'. De Haan (2008) also stressed that the aim of coaching is to improve coachees' performance by discussing their relationship to certain experiences and issues such as how to work with others and making sense of organizational life. These definitions indicate the coach, coachee and organization all play a key role in the coachee's learning and development process;

and the essence of relationship in the coaching process is highlighted.

Passmore and Fillery-Travis (2011) offered a broader view of coaching based on the summary of relevant literature: coaching is a Socratic-based future-focused dialogue between a facilitator (coach) and a participant (coachee/client), where the facilitator uses open questions, summaries and reflections which are aimed at stimulating the self-awareness and personal responsibility of the participant. Lai (2015) integrated ten international notable coaching pracademics' (i.e. an academic and practitioner) perspectives and added new characteristics into coaching: coaching is a reflective process between coaches and coachees, which helps or facilitates coachees to experience positive behavioral changes through continuous dialogues and negotiations with coaches to meet coachees' personal or work goals. Lai's new interpretation of the coaching definition aligns with recent coaching literature by distinguishing coaching as a relationship-based learning and development process.

The Difference Between Coaching and Other Helping Interventions

Coaching has been often compared with two similar helping interventions: mentoring and counselling. Overall, the main focus of these three developmental activities is to improve participants' personal wellbeing or professional growth by means of applying psychological or philosophical principles in a one-on-one interaction process. The following sections summarize the main similarities and differences between coaching, counselling and mentoring.

Coaching and mentoring: Whereas coaching and mentoring both offer a one-to-one developmental relationship that is designed to enhance a person's work-related development, mentoring is usually arranged between a more senior mentor conveying knowledge to a junior mentee about how to improve in a specific job or vocation. Precisely, mentors are expected to share similar professional experiences or knowledge with mentees, but coaching much less focuses on technical knowledge applied to a specific job (Joo, 2005). Coaching also differentiates from mentoring in its use of a structured process, involving specific models and assessments, to provide both awareness in the coachee and the development of specific plans for improvement (Joo, 2005). Overall, coaching is a short-term and goal-orientated developmental activity with a formal contracting process with the organization and coachee (Joo, 2005).

Coaching and counselling/therapy: In general, the initial motivation of clients to undertake counselling/therapy is different from coaching. For example, the individual usually expects to eliminate psychological problems and clinical disorders through counselling/therapy sessions, and to improve their personal life wellbeing. In contrast, a coaching participant anticipates an improvement in personal and professional development in the workplace (Bachkirova, 2019). The organization may have a significant influence on the desired outcomes if the coaching engagement is sponsored. Furthermore, the focus of counselling/therapy may involve any matters relevant to the client's personal life, but the coaching process usually only concentrates on the agreed goals set and contracted with the coachee and the sponsoring organization. The expected outcomes and evaluation methods are defined prior to the first session with the involved parties (e.g. coachee, supervisors and other stakeholders). Moreover, the context of the interventions in the counselling/therapy process are not limited as the focus or topic may involve any area of the client's life (e.g. family, work, past or future). However, coaches normally declare the area of their own expertise, for example skill coaching, career coaching or executive coaching (Bachkirova, 2019).

In summary, workplace coaching usually involves a three-way affiliation between the coach, the coachee and organizational stakeholders (Louis and Fatien Diochon, 2014). Besides, the contracting process in a workplace coaching setting is more formal and structured in comparison to that of mentoring, and the coaching relationship is often a shorter-term engagement, as most organizations expect concrete outcomes within a definite time frame (Eby et al., 2010).

The Development and Research Evidence of Coaching

With the increasing popularity of coaching in the workplace, the effectiveness of coaching has become a focus for stakeholders (e.g. HR practitioners and program evaluators), as well as for coaches and scholars promoting evidence-based management (Briner, 2012; Passmore and Fillery-Travis, 2011). Accordingly, several systematic literature reviews have been conducted to respond to the question of whether coaching generates positive outcomes (Briner, 2012). These reviews (Jones et al., 2016; Theeboom et al., 2014) concluded that coaching generally facilitated positive outcomes for individual-level learning and development, such as the coachees' beliefs in their capabilities to mobilize the motivation, cognitive resources and actions to achieve their goals (i.e. self-efficacy; Bandura and Wood, 1989: 408) and self-assessment of specific learning outcomes (i.e. goal-attainment; King, 1968). In addition, Theeboom et al.'s (2014) review revealed that coaching had significant positive effects on organizational level psychological states, such as coping mechanisms (e.g. resilience), wellbeing, work attitudes and goal-related self-regulation.

Whereas recent research evidence discovered that coaching generated positive effects on workplace wellbeing-related issues (Theeboom et al., 2014), Grant (2017) acknowledged that coaching has entered its third generation by shifting the focus from performance management and talent development into psychological wellbeing of individuals to appreciate the complexity of change and to promote sustainable organizational cultural development.

According to Grant (2017), the first generation of coaching occurred in the 1990s with performance management as the key focus. Coaching was often regarded as a controlled mechanism to enhance employees' behavioral changes to better fit 'organizational norms' (Diochon and Lovelace, 2015). For instance, organizations adopted coaching to 'teach' or 'demonstrate to' managers how to carry out performance-related conversations with 'difficult' employees. This 'direct and instructional' style of coaching was criticized for its limitations. With the increase of knowledge economy, coaching can be turned into a space for resistance (Diochon and Lovelace, 2015) when the organizational power surpassed individuals' development needs and interests (Shoukry and Cox, 2018). Therefore, a more participative coaching style emerged which acknowledged individual differences in the change process, such as emotional intelligence (Goleman, 1998).

Considering that organizations shifted their priority from employees' performance to competition for recruiting and retaining talented employees in the early 2000s, a more humanistic, goal-focused version of coaching conversation emerged. This coaching focused on individuals' change and development, and is referred to as 'customized' and 'learner-driven' journey (Grant, 2017). Meanwhile, coaching evaluations were broadened to investigate coachees' self-awareness, self-understanding and commitment to their goals or organizations (Lai and Palmer, 2019). Some adult learning (e.g. transformational learning theory) and psychotherapy-based (e.g. cognitive behavioral coaching (CBC)) constructs were included to correspond to new dimensions in this coaching process. Indeed, there is a considerable growth in terms of experimental trials to examine the effectiveness of commonly used coaching models, such as CBC or the GROW model (Lai and Palmer,

2019). The increase in coaching research studies indicated a stronger awareness of evidence-based practice. However, this type of outcome-based and quantitative focused research which attempts to 'prove' the efficacy of coaching in a specific work context often neglected contextual factors, such as organizational political structures and power dynamics (Shoukry and Cox, 2018). In addition, Grant (2012) suggested that overly focusing on organizational outcomes and results in the coaching process may lead to distress, disengagement and burnout, as the coachee struggles to achieve unrealistic or inappropriate goals.

Accordingly, Grant (2017) recognized the recent development of a new generation of coaching that does more than mere 'performance enhancement' (Jones et al., 2016). For instance, organizations started to explore more sophisticated ways of dealing with complexity and uncertainty and considered coaching as a means of fostering cultural change and creating a culture of quality conversations (Cameron and Green, 2015). Some coaching literature (Spence and Grant, 2005) also revealed that between 25% and 50% of individuals who attend workplace coaching may have underlying mental issues like stress and burnout. Organizations are paying more attention to their employees' workplace wellbeing. The explanation is a good understanding of an individual's work-life satisfaction, such as working relationships, workload and personal life challenges, and has been identified as an important indicator of employees' performance and motivation to change (Dodge et al., 2012). Grant (2017) recognized that both wellbeing and performance should be considered in the organizational life and proposed a Performance/Well-being Matrix® to serve as a pragmatic lens through which to guide the workplace coaching process.

Essentially, there has been a close relationship between coaching interventions and organizational life. The coaching focus has ranged from performance-focused outcomes, individual learning and development, towards work-life satisfaction. Considering that the new generation of coaching has paid much more attention to contextual factors such as individual differences and process, psychology as a theoretically grounded science that deepens our understanding of people's motivations and emotions was also urged to be included within the coaching practice. Therefore, a concise discourse on the role psychology plays in coaching practice and research is discussed in the following section.

Coaching and Psychology

The primary aim of executive or life coaching is to facilitate the coachee's sustained cognitive, emotional and behavioral change (Douglas and McCauley, 1999) and people's international interactions play the key role in this change process (Palmer and McDowall, 2010). Thus psychologists have become considerably involved in the coaching industry since the 1990s. To offer a clearer theoretical association between coaching and psychology, Grant (2001) conducted a narrative review to investigate whether behavior CBT and solution-focused theory (SFT) had positive effects on adult learning and development intervention for non-clinical populations, such as coaching. This review indicated that it is crucial to acknowledge coachees' socio-cognitive factors such as psychological mindedness, self-awareness and self-regulation, to facilitate better coaching outcomes. In order to further the development of psychological approaches in the coaching context, Grant established the first unit of 'Coaching Psychology' at the University of Sydney, Australia. There have been a growing number of professional psychology bodies established, for instance, the British Psychological Society (BPS), and the Special Group in Coaching Psychology (SGCP), led by Stephen Palmer and associates, was launched in 2004. The aim of these professional bodies is to promote evidence-based practice by encouraging the research and study of Coaching Psychology in a variety of personal, organizational and training contexts.

To distinguish the characteristics of Coaching Psychology, several definitions were provided by coaching scholars with a psychology background. According to Grant and Palmer (2002), Coaching Psychology aims to enhance personal and professional performance in normal people within the general population, underpinned by models of coaching grounded in established therapeutic approaches. In addition, Passmore (2010) described Coaching Psychology as the scientific study of behavior, cognition and emotion within coaching practice to deepen our understanding and enhance our practice within coaching. Lai (2015) added new elements by highlighting that Coaching Psychology facilitates sustained behavioral changes with a deeper and richer picture of the coachee's behaviors, motivations, values and beliefs based on scientific evidence.

The amount of psychological-focused coaching research (both qualitative and quantitative) has increased since the beginning of the 21st century. In particular, the relevant publications doubled (k=164) between 2010 and 2018, compared to the first decade of the 2000s (k=67; Lai and Palmer, 2019). This indicates that more coaching scholars have acknowledged the value of drawing upon cognitive and behavioral science in the coaching setting. Some coaching papers (e.g. Bono et al., 2009) have argued that there is little evidence of differences in practice when comparing chartered psychologists with coaches from other professional disciplines. However, Bono et al. (2009) also revealed that psychologist coaches were more likely to use multisource behavioral data as diagnostic and assessment tools as well as to establish behavioral change goals in comparison with non-psychologist coaches.

Generally speaking, there is no rigorous research as yet to examine the levels of effectiveness of those most frequently used psychologically informed frameworks, such as CBC (Lai and Palmer, 2019). Nevertheless, psychotherapy-grounded theory, such as the professional helping relationship (i.e. working alliance) between the coach and coachee, was examined as the important antecedent of desired coaching outcomes like perceived effectiveness and self-efficacy (Graßmann et al., 2020). Meanwhile, the level of people's self-efficacy has been confirmed as an influential indicator of their psychological wellbeing in the organization (Zee and Koomen, 2016). Accordingly, there has been an indication of positive associations between coaching and workplace wellbeing. The following sections summarize the common mental welfare issues in the organization and explain how psychotherapy-grounded coaching constructs such as cognitive behavioral and positive psychology coaching models can be applied to enhance people's organizational life and workplace wellbeing.

ORGANIZATIONAL LIFE AND WORKPLACE WELLBEING

The *Health and Well-being at Work* annual report by CIPD (2020) indicated the top two causes of stress are heavy workloads and management style. Whereas employers and public policy drivers have in general increased their awareness to address employees' mental health and workforce wellbeing, most organizations still adopt a reactive, rather than a proactive, approach. Specifically, more preventive actions are urged to be adopted, for instance to help employees develop their strengths and coping behaviors through training or coaching as part of their organizational learning and development strategy. This report summarizes several important indicators associated with employees' mental welfare in the organization. These are the relationship with management, social relationships with colleagues, stress and anxiety, and work resilience.

Management Style and Employee Relations

Even though most of the workplace wellbeing literature pays attention to heavy workloads and psychological effects (e.g. stress), recent studies indicated a consistent association between the leader–member relation and employees' wellbeing (Skakon et al., 2010). Leader-member exchange (LMX), which was described as an approach to examine the quality of the relationship between a leader and a follower (Martin et al., 2016), has been confirmed as a contributing factor to reduce employees' stress level (Gilbreath and Benson, 2004) and burnout (Yagil, 2006). Meanwhile, employees' job satisfaction and intrinsic motivation were strengthened when leaders offered more communication opportunities or showed empathetic behaviors towards employees' work-life challenges (Gilbreath and Benson, 2004).

In addition, specific leadership style plays a key role in the enhancement of employees' mental welfare. Transformational leadership, where the leader is recognized as an idealized influencer and role model to offer inspirational motivation and encourage subordinates to be creative and approach problems in new ways, has confirmed its positive effects on employees' self-awareness, self-efficacy and meaning of their job (Skakon et al., 2010). Accordingly, the analysis by Skakon and colleagues (2010) concluded that positive leader behaviors (support, empowerment and consideration) are associated with a low degree of employee stress and with high employee affective wellbeing. Conversely, abusive behaviors are found to be associated with negative employee outcomes.

Social Relationships with Peers

Social relationships with colleagues are also commonly linked with stress at work, such as interpersonal conflicts and bullying. Interpersonal conflict was identified as one of the work-related stressors since individuals who are obstructed or irritated by another individual inevitably react to it when they are in conflict (Van de Vliert, 1997). Specifically, conflict is the tension an individual experience due to perceived differences with others (O'Connor et al., 2002). Hence, conflicts usually trigger obstructions, and these obstructions may cause feelings of reduced control and increased uncertainty that have been considered important prerequisites of a stress response (Quick et al., 1997). In addition, conflicts negatively impact on people's self-esteem (O'Connor et al., 2002), especially when it occurs with another group member because people have a generic need to establish positive and enduring relationships with members in the same team (Baumeister and Leary, 1995). Consequently, there is growing evidence showing that interpersonal conflicts may be one of the most important stressors in the workplace (Spector and Jex, 1998). Recent studies that have examined conflict-stress appeared to be positively correlated to the three indicators of wellbeing: emotional exhaustion, absenteeism and turnover intentions.

The other frequently identified workplace relationship issue is bullying, as there has been research evidence to show that workplace bullying has adverse effects on employee performance. Workplace bullying was identified as one of the causes of employees' negative psychological wellbeing, such as stress and emotional strain (Hauge et al., 2010). Furthermore, some studies (e.g. Devonish, 2013) have indicated workplace bullying has significant associations with employees' job satisfaction and depression for both the short and long term.

Stress and Anxiety

Stress is defined as the individual's responses (psychological, physiological and behavioral) towards external environmental demands, threats and challenges (Ganster and Perrewé,

2011). Environmental events that trigger these processes are commonly referred to as stressors, while the individual's responses are sometimes called strains (Griffin and Clarke, 2011). In fact, the right amount of pressure, which can vary from person to person (e.g. job demands, time urgency and workload), can have positive effects on work motivation and performance; conversely, employees may lose their motivation when there is a persistent lack of challenge and competition in the workplace (Lepine et al., 2005). People may develop a 'general adaption syndrome' (GAS) that characterizes stress as an arousal response with three distinct stages: alarm, resistance and finally exhaustion (Selye, 1956). People usually draw on adaption energy through both physical and mental resources to try to restore themselves back to stable and balanced in the 'resistance' stage. Nevertheless, if the process of resistance uses up a person's adaption energy, they will enter an exhaustion stage. According to Ganster and Rosen (2013), perceived heavy workloads and constant stress had negative impacts on individuals' affective outcomes, such as anxiety. Anxiety is the subjective feeling of tension, apprehension, nervousness and worry associated with an arousal of the autonomic nervous system (Spielberger, 1983). Further, these psychological effects may cause stress-related health complaints (e.g. headache, fatigue, gastrointestinal problems).

Resilience is the motivational force within everyone that drives them to pursue wisdom, self-actualization, to be in harmony with a spiritual source of strength and beliefs in one's capabilities to mobilize the motivation, cognitive resources, and courses of action needed to meet given situational demands (Richardson, 2002). The main distinction between resilience building and other psychological effects (such as stress management) is that the former emphasizes the preventive and proactive efforts to promote wellness and competence (Masten, 2007). Whereas resilience-building programs facilitate moderate positive effects on work performance and wellbeing by identifying people's coping strategies and strengths (Vanhove et al., 2016), applying theories of positive psychology (more details are presented in the following sections) in workplace resilience development appears to be advantageous.

Managerial support, social relationships with peers, heavy workloads and resilience are important topics in workplace wellbeing. Meanwhile, psychologically grounded constructs and approaches have been encouraged in recent research evidence, such as self-efficacy, strength-based approaches and positive cognitive states. Accordingly, the following sections intend to discuss in what way two prominent disciplines in psychology – cognitive and positive psychology – enhance contemporary workplace wellbeing issues.

Work Resilience

Work resilience has received more attention from organizations and scholars to prevent absenteeism, counterproductive work behavior and other stress-related issues (Vanhove et al., 2016). Resilience is defined as the process when individuals successfully use their capabilities and resources (i.e. protective factors) to protect themselves against the negative consequences associated with adverse experiences (Masten, 2007).

WORKPLACE WELLBEING AND PSYCHOLOGICALLY INFORMED COACHING FRAMEWORKS

Cognitive Behavioral Approaches

The cognitive behavioral approach is based on the Stoic concept that 'people are not affected by things but by the view they take of them' (Palmer and Williams, 2013: 320). Precisely, people 'determine [themselves] by the meaning [they] give to situations, i.e. cognitions' (Palmer and Williams, 2013: 320). Cognitive behavioral approaches assume that an individual may develop meta-cognitive skills to observe their own thoughts objectively, then think logically to develop their own ways to overcome challenges and behavioral changes. For instance, acceptance and commitment therapy (ACT) focuses on the acceptance of mental events by seeing them non-judgementally, using mindfulness-based thinking and goal-directed actions (Brewin, 2006). Cognitive behavioral approaches have been extensively studied and recognized as one of the most validated psychotherapeutic frameworks (Williams and Palmer 2013), such as anxiety (Hofmann and Smits, 2008) and anger management (Beck and Fernandez, 1998) in the clinical setting. Furthermore, cognitive behavioral-based theories have been increasingly used in the workplace to help employees, for instance stress management for business/executive coaching (Dryden and Gordon, 1993) and resilience building (Robertson et al., 2015).

In the 1990s, coaching practitioners started adapting cognitive behavioral grounded approaches within workplace coaching scenarios (Palmer and Williams, 2013). Cognitive behavioral coaching (CBC) is defined as 'an integrative approach which combines the use of cognitive, behavioral, imaginal and problem solving techniques and strategies within a cognitive behavioral framework to enable clients to achieve their realistic goals' (Palmer and Szymanska, 2019: 108). According to Lai and Palmer (2019), CBC was the most frequent exclusively studied coaching framework in the organizational setting. Overall, these studies revealed positive associations between CBC and coachees' self-efficacy, self-awareness and organizational commitment (e.g. Bozer et al., 2015). In fact, workplace coaching has been applied to a broader perspective, since a good understanding of employees' life satisfaction and both positive and negative effects when dealing with work-life challenges have

been distinguished as a more comprehensive approach to foster profound organizational and cultural changes (Dodge et al., 2012).

To offer a clearer picture of current coaching research in workplace wellbeing, the following section summarizes several empirical coaching studies that adapted CBC to facilitate a better organizational life for employees. Grant and colleagues (2009) took an initial randomized controlled study with 41 executives in a public health agency for a ten-week coaching program. Their coaching program combined the 360-degree feedback assessment, which was designed to raise participants' awareness of their current leadership behaviors, and CBC to facilitate the development of forward thinking, realistic goals and actions. In general, this program enhanced participants' workplace wellbeing through helping their goal attainment, stress levels and resilience, while there was no significant impact on participants' anxiety and depression indicators. In the next year, a similar study was carried out with 50 high school teachers (Grant et al., 2010) and the research results were aligned with the study in the public health agency setting (Grant et al., 2009). Accordingly, this goal-striving developmental coaching itself can improve wellbeing, and this is particularly the case when the goals are personally relevant and aimed at enhancing self-leadership skills. Furthermore, one coaching study (David et al., 2016) embedded the rational emotive behavioral therapy (Ellis, 1962) approach into CBC, to facilitate self-awareness towards particular types of cognitive processes for clients' emotional barriers to goal attainment in the financial banking sector. Their research findings indicated a cognitive-behavioral executive coaching program is effective in improving managerial soft skills, depressive mood and distress. To summarize, CBC, which emphasizes emotional support and forward-looking psychological states of coaches, appears to enhance individuals' workplace wellbeing.

POSITIVE PSYCHOLOGY APPROACHES

Positive psychology is the study of optimal human functioning and considers topics such as happiness, wisdom, creativity and human strengths (Linley and Harrington, 2005). Positive psychology considers the individual as a whole, focusing on strengths, positive behaviors and purpose (Boniwell et al., 2018). With the increase of combining personal life and organizational effectiveness, the application of positive psychology into organizational studies has attracted more practitioners and scholars (Donaldson and Ko, 2010). The effectiveness of positive psychology on wellbeing has been confirmed by several meta-analyses in both clinical and non-clinical settings. For instance, Mazzucchelli et al. (2010) validated behavioral activation interventions, and an approach to facilitate positive reinforcement (Hopko et al., 2003) had positive effects on university students' wellbeing. In addition, Donaldson and Ko (2010) indicated positive psychology has been well studied in the following organizational-related topics: leadership, organizational development and change, coaching, job satisfaction and stress.

Grant and colleagues (2009) have asserted that both positive psychology and coaching psychology are abundance-based and solution-focused, and assume people have a natural tendency to want to grow and develop their potential, and that they thrive within the supporting environment. Positive psychology coaching (PPC) is an evidence-based coaching practice informed by the theories and research of positive psychology for the enhancement of resilience, achievement and wellbeing (Green and Palmer, 2014; Green and Palmer, 2018). Several coaching frameworks grounded on positive psychology were also established. For example, the co-active coaching model developed by Whitworth et al. (2007) encourages both coaches and coachees to actively participate in the coaching process and form an alliance to have a greater understanding of the coachees' needs. One of the pioneering empirical research studies of PPC was conducted by Yu et al. (2008) to facilitate work behaviors and wellbeing of managers in a large Australian teaching hospital. This study revealed PPC generated positive effects on coachees' proactivity (e.g. taking charge, individual innovation), goal-attainment and motivation (e.g. self-efficacy). Furthermore, Jarzebowski et al. (2012) combined theories of positive psychology with a feedback approach to develop coachees' self-awareness, motivation and regulatory fit (i.e. preferred manner during goal pursuit) for learning and performance improvement in a leadership development coaching program. The study results indicated participants who received coaching increased the time they invested on their work tasks. Specifically, the level of motivation increased following feedback that contained promotion goals.

Moreover, Weinberg (2016) studied how a strength-based coaching conversation promotes individuals' lives during the organizational change. Weinberg's study (2016) offered three coaching sessions to senior leaders in a university in the UK, focusing on stress management during their role and responsibility change. The study results indicated that exposure to coaching did prevent an increase in psychological strain, but only when participants volunteered to take part in this development program. Overall, existing research evidence revealed that coaching based on positive psychology theories promoted individuals' organizational performance and psychological wellbeing. This can be a direction for future coaching research and practice by engaging research evidence of positive psychology in the organizational setting.

PRACTICAL SUGGESTIONS

Following the theoretical discussion throughout this chapter, three practical suggestions are made for future practice-related organizational life issues. First, the organization should take a more proactive approach to support individuals' organizational life including psychological wellbeing and employee relations. Whereas most organizations offer mental wellbeing support to their employees, recent research evidence, such as positive psychology emphasizing people's strength, happiness and positive behaviors, has indicated organizations should take a preventive proposition and develop employees' capability to flourish in their workplace life. Second, the development of individuals' workplace life and wellbeing should be part of the organizational learning process. There is an increase in coaching literature highlighting that the quality of organizational life is the foundation of workplace performance and growth as a good understanding of employees' life satisfaction, and work-life challenges facilitate sustainable organizational and cultural changes. Third, interventions used to promote employees' learning and organizational life should be a learner-centred approach, considering that individuals' metacognitive skills to observe their own thoughts objectively and forward-looking psychological states elicit individuals' intrinsic motivation for change. In fact, coaching, which is a bottom-up, cognitive and emotional affected method to facilitate self-awareness and identify customized plans for positive changes, offers a fitting approach to support contemporary organizational life and wellbeing. Accordingly, organizations could apply coaching in a broader way to support and promote employees' work–life balance.

CONCLUSION

With the increased working hours due to globalization and technology, people's lifestyles have been significantly affected by their work environment, relationships with peers, managers and clients, and job content. Whereas employees' workplace wellbeing becomes an important influence as part of organizational strategy, organizations have invested more resources on supporting their employees' mental wellbeing, such as stress or anxiety management. Meanwhile, more and more research evidence and decision drivers suggest a more proactive and preventive approach should be considered since employees' organizational life is an important indicator of sustainable organizational performance. Hence, the bottom-up and more person-focused processes to help employees to identify their strengths and development plans to overcome work-related challenges is urged. We propose that a learner-centred reflective intervention like coaching provides individuals with opportunities to reflect on their motivation, attitudes, behaviors and relationship with their organization through meaningful dialogues with the coach. In addition, psychologically informed coaching frameworks such as CBC and PPC may offer a more in-depth picture of individuals' cognitive and emotional reactions to facilitate sustainable changes. The main purpose of this chapter is to call attention to individual differences when studying issues related to organizational life, such as workplace relationship, psychological wellbeing and resilience. In addition, we encourage the development and application of evidence-based approaches that facilitate longstanding organizational cultural changes.

REFERENCES

Bachkirova T (2019) Role of coaching psychology in defining boundaries between counselling and coaching. In Palmer S and Whybrow A (eds) *Handbook of Coaching Psychology: A Guide for Practitioners* (2nd ed.). Oxford: Routledge, pp. 487–499.

Bandura A and Wood R (1989) Effect of perceived controllability and performance standards on self-regulation of complex decision making. *Journal of Personality and Social Psychology 56*(5): 805–814.

Baumeister RF and Leary MR (1995) The need to belong: desire for interpersonal attachments as a fundamental human motivation. *Psychological Bulletin 117*(3): 497–529.

Beck R and Fernandez E (1998) Cognitive-behavioral therapy in the treatment of anger: a meta-analysis. *Cognitive Therapy and Research 22*(1): 63–74.

Boniwell I, Kauffman C and Silberman J (2018) The positive psychology approach to coaching. In Cox E, Bachkirova T and Clutterbuk D (eds) *The Complete Handbook of Coaching* (2nd ed.). London: Sage, pp. 153–166.

Bono J, Purvanova R, Towler A and Peterson D (2009) A survey of executive coaching practices. *Personnel Psychology 62*(2): 361–404.

Bozer G, Joo BK and Santora JC (2015) Executive coaching: does coach-coachee matching based on similarity really matter? *Consulting Psychology Journal: Practice and Research 67*(3): 218–233.

Brewin CR (2006) Understanding cognitive behaviour therapy: a retrieval competition account. *Behaviour Research and Therapy 44*(6): 765–784.

Briner RB (2012) Does coaching work and does anyone really care? *OP Matters 16*(17): 4–12.

Cameron E and Green M (2015) *Making Sense of Change Management: A Complete Guide to the Models, Tools and Techniques of Organizational Change*. London: Kogan Page.

Carolan S, Harris PR and Cavanagh K (2017) Improving employee well-being and effectiveness: systematic review and meta-analysis of web-based psychological interventions delivered in the workplace. *Journal of Medical Internet Research 19*(7): e271.

Chartered Institute of Personnel Development (CIPD) (2020) *Health and Well-being at Work Annual Survey*. Available at www.cipd.co.uk/knowledge/culture/well-being/health-well-being-work (accessed 22 June 2020).

David OA, Ionicioiu I, Imbăruş AC and Sava FA (2016) Coaching banking managers through the financial crisis: effects on stress, resilience, and performance. *Journal of Rational-Emotive & Cognitive-Behavior Therapy 34*(4): 267–281.

de Haan E (2008) *Relational coaching: Journeys Towards Mastering One-To-One Learning*. Chichester: John Wiley & Sons.

Devonish D (2013) Workplace bullying, employee performance and behaviors. *Employee Relations 35*(6): 630–647.

Diochon PF and Lovelace KJ (2015) The coaching continuum: power dynamics in the change process. *International Journal of Work Innovation 1*(3): 305–322.

Dodge R, Daly AP, Huyton J and Sanders LD (2012) The challenge of defining wellbeing. *International Journal of Wellbeing 2*(3): 222–235.

Donaldson SI and Ko I (2010) Positive organizational psychology, behavior, and scholarship: a review of the emerging literature and evidence base. *The Journal of Positive Psychology 5*(3): 177–191.

Douglas CA and McCauley CD (1999) Formal developmental relationships: a survey of organizational practices. *Human Resource Development Quarterly 10*(3): 203– 220.

Dryden W and Gordon J (1993) *Peak Performance: Become More Effective at Work*. Didcot: Mercury.

Eby LT, Butts MM, Durley J and Ragins BR (2010) Are bad experiences stronger than good ones in mentoring relationships? Evidence from the protégé and mentor perspective. *Journal of Vocational Behavior 77*(1): 81–92.

Ellis A (1962) *Reason and Emotion in Psychotherapy*. Englewood, NJ: Lyle Stuart.

Ganster DC and Perrewé PL (2011) Theories of occupational stress. In Quick JC and Tetrick LE (eds) *Handbook of Occupational Health Psychology*. Washington, DC: American Psychological Association, pp. 37–53.

Ganster DC and Rosen CC (2013) Work stress and employee health: a multidisciplinary review. *Journal of Management 39*(5): 1085–1122.

Gilbreath B and Benson PG (2004) The contribution of supervisor behaviour to employee psychological well-being. *Work & Stress 18*(3): 255–266.

Goleman D (1998) The emotional intelligence of leaders. *Leader to Leader 10*: 20–26.

Grant AM (2001) *Toward a psychology of coaching: The impact of coaching on metacognition, mental health and goal attainment*. PhD Thesis. University of Sydney, Australia.

Grant AM (2012) An integrated model of goal-focused coaching: an evidence-based framework for teaching and practice. *International Coaching Psychology Review 7*(2): 146–165.

Grant AM (2017) The third 'generation' of workplace coaching: creating a culture of quality conversations. *Coaching: An International Journal of Theory, Research and Practice 10*(1): 37–53.

Grant A and Palmer S (2002) *Coaching psychology workshop*. Annual conference of the Division of Counselling Psychology, BPS, Torquay, May.

Grant AM, Curtayne L and Burton G (2009) Executive coaching enhances goal attainment, resilience and workplace well-being: a randomised controlled study. *The Journal of Positive Psychology 4*(5): 396–407.

Grant AM, Green LS and Rynsaardt J (2010) Developmental coaching for high school teachers: executive coaching goes to school. *Consulting Psychology Journal: Practice and Research 62*(3): 151–168.

Graßmann C, Schölmerich F and Schermuly CC (2020) The relationship between working alliance and client outcomes in coaching: a meta-analysis. *Human Relations 73*(1): 35–58.

Green S and Palmer S (2014) *Positive psychology coaching: enhancing resilience, achievement and well-being*. Workshop presented on 15 November 2014, at the 4th International Congress of Coaching Psychology, Melbourne, Australia.

Green S and Palmer S (2018) *Positive Psychology Coaching in Practice*. New York: Routledge.

Griffin MA and Clarke S (2011) Stress and well-being at work. In Zedeck S (ed.) *APA Handbook of Industrial and Organizational Psychology: Maintaining, Expanding, and Contracting the Organization*. Washington, DC: American Psychological Association, pp. 359–397.

Hauge LJ, Skogstad A and Einarsen S (2010) The relative impact of workplace bullying as a social stressor at work. *Scandinavian Journal of Psychology 51*(5): 426–433.

Hofmann SG and Smits JA (2008) Cognitive-behavioral therapy for adult anxiety disorders: a meta-analysis of randomized placebo-controlled trials. *The Journal of Clinical Psychiatry 69*(4): 621–632.

Hopko DR, Lejuez CW, Ruggiero KJ and Eifert GH (2003) Contemporary behavioral activation treatments for depression: procedures, principles, and progress. *Clinical Psychology Review 23*(5): 699–717.

Jarzebowski A, Palermo J and van de Berg R (2012) When feedback is not enough: the impact of regulatory fit on motivation after positive feedback. *International Coaching Psychology Review 7*(1): 14–32.

Jones J, Woods S and Guillaume Y (2016) The effectiveness of workplace coaching: a meta-analysis of learning and performance outcomes from coaching. *Journal of Occupational and Organizational Psychology 89*(2): 249–277.

Joo BKB (2005) Executive coaching: a conceptual framework from an integrative review of practice and research. *Human Resource Development Review 4*(4): 462–488.

Joyce S, Modini M, Christensen H, Mykletun A, Bryant R, Mitchell PB and Harvey SB (2016) Workplace interventions for common mental disorders: a systematic meta-review. *Psychological Medicine 46*(4): 683–697.

King IN (1968) A conceptual framework for nursing. *Nursing Research 17*(7): 27–31.

Lai Y (2015) *Enhancing evidence-based coaching through the development of a coaching psychology competency framework: Focus on the coaching relationship*. PhD Thesis, University of Surrey, UK.

Lai Y and Palmer S (2019) Psychology in executive coaching: an integrated literature review. *Journal of Work-Applied Management 11*(2): 143–164.

Lepine JA, Podsakoff NP and Lepine MA (2005) A meta-analytic test of the challenge stressor–hindrance stressor framework: an explanation for inconsistent relationships among stressors and performance. *Academy of Management Journal 48*(5): 764–775.

Linley PA and Harrington S (2005) Positive psychology and coaching psychology: perspectives on integration. *The Coaching Psychologist 1*(1): 13–14.

Louis D and Fatien Diochon P (2014) Educating coaches to power dynamics: managing multiple agendas within the triangular relationship. *Journal of Psychological Issues in Organizational Culture 5*(2): 31–47.

Martin R, Guillaume Y, Thomas G, Lee A and Epitropaki O (2016) Leader–member exchange (LMX) and performance: a meta-analytic review. *Personnel Psychology 69*(1): 67–121.

Masten AS (2007) Resilience in developing systems: progress and promise as the fourth wave rises. *Development and Psychopathology 19*(3): 921–930.

Mazzucchelli TG, Kane RT and Rees CS (2010) Behavioral activation interventions for well-being: a meta-analysis. *The Journal of Positive Psychology 5*(2): 105–121.

O'Connor KM, De Dreu CK, Schroth H, Barry B, Lituchy TR and Bazerman MH (2002) What we want to do versus what we think we should do: An empirical investigation of intrapersonal conflict. *Journal of Behavioral Decision Making, 15*(5): 403-418.

Palmer S and McDowall A (2010) The coaching relationship: putting people first: an introduction. In Palmer S and McDowall A (eds) *The Coaching Relationship: Putting People First.* London: Routledge, pp. 1–8.

Palmer S and Szymanska K (2019) Cognitive behavioural coaching: an integrative approach. In Palmer S and Whybrow A (eds) *Handbook of Coaching Psychology: A Guide for Practitioners* (2nd ed.). Oxford: Routledge, pp. 108–127.

Palmer S and Williams H (2013) Cognitive behavioral approaches. In Passmore J (ed.) *The Wiley-Blackwell Handbook of the Psychology of Coaching and Mentoring.* Oxford: Wiley & Sons, pp. 319–338.

Parsloe E (1999) *The Manager as Coach and Mentor.* London: CIPD Publishing.

Passmore J (2010) A grounded theory study of the coachee experience: the implications for training and practice in coaching psychology. *International Coaching Psychology Review 5*(1): 48–62.

Passmore J and Fillery-Travis A (2011) A critical review of executive coaching research: a decade of progress and what's to come. *Coaching: An International Journal of Theory, Research and Practice 4*(2): 70–88.

Quick JC, Quick JD, Nelson DL and Hurrell JJ Jr. (1997) *Preventive Stress Management in Organizations.* Washington, DC: American Psychological Association.

Richardson GE (2002) The metatheory of resilience and resiliency. *Journal of Clinical Psychology 58*(3): 307–321.

Robertson IT, Cooper CL, Sarkar M and Curran T (2015) Resilience training in the workplace from 2003 to 2014: a systematic review. *Journal of Occupational and Organizational Psychology 88*(3): 533–562.

Selye H (1956) *The Stress of Life.* London: McGraw-Hill.

Shoukry H and Cox E (2018) Coaching as a social process. *Management Learning 49*(4): 413–428.

Skakon J, Nielsen K, Borg V and Guzman J (2010) Are leaders' well-being, behaviours and style associated with the affective well-being of their employees? A systematic review of three decades of research. *Work & Stress 24*(2): 107–139.

Spector PE and Jex SM (1998) Development of four self-report measures of job stressors and strain: interpersonal conflict at work scale, organizational constraints scale, quantitative workload inventory, and physical symptoms inventory. *Journal of Occupational Health Psychology 3*(4): 356–367.

Spence GB and Grant AM (2005) Individual and group life-coaching: initial findings from a randomised, controlled trial. *Evidence-based Coaching 1*: 143–158.

Spielberger CD (1983) *State-Trait Anxiety Inventory: Bibliography* (2nd ed.). Palo Alto, CA: Consulting Psychologists Press.

Theeboom T, Beersma B and van Vianen A (2014) Does coaching work? A meta-analysis on the effects of coaching on individual level outcomes in an organizational context. *Journal of Positive Psychology 9*(1): 1–18.

Van de Vliert E (1997) *Complex Interpersonal Conflict Behaviour: Theoretical Frontiers.* Hove: Psychology Press.

Vanhove AJ, Herian MN, Perez AL, Harms PD and Lester PB (2016) Can resilience be developed at work? A meta-analytic review of resilience-building program effectiveness. *Journal of Occupational and Organizational Psychology 89*(2): 278–307.

Weinberg A (2016) The preventative impact of management coaching on psychological strain. *International Coaching Psychology Review 11*(1): 93–105.

Whitmore SJ (1996) *Coaching for Performance: The New Edition of the Practical Guide*. London: Nicholas Brealey.

Whitworth L, Kimsey-House K, Kimsey-House H and Sandahl P (2007) *Co-active Coaching: New Skills for Coaching People toward Success in Work and Life* (2nd ed.). California: Davies-Black Publishing.

Williams H and Palmer S (2013) The SPACE model in coaching practice: a case study. *The Coaching Psychologist* 9(1): 1104–1748.

Yagil D (2006) The relationship of abusive and supportive workplace supervision to employee burnout and upward influence tactics. *Journal of Emotional Abuse* 6(1): 49–65.

Yu N, Collins CG, Cavanagh M, White K and Fairbrother G (2008) Positive coaching with frontline managers: enhancing their effectiveness and understanding why. *International Coaching Psychology Review* 3(2): 110–122.

Zee M and Koomen HM (2016) Teacher self-efficacy and its effects on classroom processes, student academic adjustment, and teacher well-being: a synthesis of 40 years of research. *Review of Educational Research* 86(4): 981–1015.

PART IV

Emerging Issues and Directions

29

Creative-reflective Inquiries and Wellbeing in Organizations

Victoria Field and Anne Taylor

INTRODUCTION

We are writing this chapter in April 2020 when the world we live in is very different from a few short weeks ago. We live in small towns at opposite ends of the South of England. Paradoxically, we are physically isolated and yet the level of connection between people all over the world has never been higher. Like most people, we are watching the news of the Covid-19 pandemic unfolding in virtually every country of the world and seeing how different governments and health bodies are developing their own strategies. Organizations and businesses respond to the challenge in different ways, many with a sense of impending collapse and some innovating and thriving in this new reality. Throughout this uncertain, shaky, worrying time, more and more people are turning to the use of words, language and creativity to sustain their personal and organizational wellbeing. By the time you are holding this book in your hand, or reading it

on screen, we have no doubt that the need for healing and the promotion of wellbeing will be a priority and a requirement for organizations of all kinds as they recover.

The structures of our economies, political systems and organizations within them are changing. 'The first become last' and vice versa. People stacking supermarket shelves and caring for bodily needs of the sick are more vital than airline executives and those running the stock exchange. World leaders are not immune from infection. Co-operation is replacing competition. So where does that leave creative and reflective inquiries in this time of flux? In many ways change was already a 'given'. Organizations and individuals have always struggled to become 'Comfortable with Uncertainty', to quote the title of a book by Buddhist thinker Pema Chödrön (Chödrön, 2002). She writes that it is 'necessary to move toward turbulence and doubt however we can. We explore the reality and unpredictability of insecurity and pain' (Chödrön, 2002: 1). Change cannot be avoided but does require adjustment. This position is echoed by James Pennebaker, a pioneer in the use of expressive writing, who has long held that, 'When people write about major upheavals they begin to organise and understand them' (Pennebaker, 1990: 185).

He continues by suggesting that the benefits come from organizing what might seem chaotic material: 'Once people can distil complex experiences into more understandable packages, they can begin to move beyond the trauma' (Pennebaker, 1990: 185).

Even BC (Before-Covid), organizations realized that creative and reflective practices engage people and can augment more utilitarian processes. On an individual level, creative processes have long been used in settings such as one-to-one psychotherapy, in supervision, in occupational therapy groups and in the burgeoning 'Arts for Health' world (Fancourt, 2017). Some managers and consultants bring creativity into the workplace. For example, colleagues may engage in reflective and reflexive practice, visioning, self-supervision and story-making. Creative and reflective inquiry is increasingly foregrounded even if there is a way to go before it is centre stage.

This impulse is highlighted at times of stress. In the UK in April 2020, there was an upsurge in online resources for the arts. Actor Patrick Stewart read a Shakespeare sonnet a day on Twitter and daily poems and bedtime stories were being offered by celebrities on various channels. Artists were painting either to reflect the situation, or to take our minds away from it, such as David Hockney in Normandy (BBC, 2020).

These initiatives are shared by individuals and organizations, perhaps instinctively, but also with an understanding that in times of challenge we need to see our humanity reflected back to us through these creative art forms. Such needs echo the way a starving orchestra premiered a new work by Shostakovich in 1942 during the siege of Leningrad (BBC, 2016). At times of crisis the creative arts speak to our basic humanity.

Writers specifically are drawn to 'giving sorrow words', whether in blogs or think-pieces for public consumption, or personal journals or email correspondence, as a way of processing emotion. Some of this is aimed at an audience, for example the poetry anthology *These are the Hands* edited by poet Deborah Alma and GP Dr Katie Amiel (Alma and Amiel, 2020). Much of it though will remain private.

The dual process of people seeing themselves reflected in the art of others, and creating their own artistic work in response, is encapsulated in a model described by poetry therapy pioneer, Nicholas Mazza. He suggests that biblio-poetry therapy comprises Reflective, Expressive and Symbolic modes, the so-called RES model (Mazza, 2003). People see or hear something outside themselves which reflects their experience. Then they express themselves in response and their own response becomes the subject of their observations. This hall of mirrors is central to the use of reflective and creative inquiry.

For us, the 'Symbolic' mode can have a broader remit than that described by Mazza. As well as what happens in the creative space – for example, whether writing is published or kept private, a painting is destroyed or put on the wall – there is always a wider cultural and social context. The Symbolic includes the macro level of the culture of an organization: a university being different from a big utility company, a small voluntary organization from a high-profile national one. Even when organizations are comparable, the Symbolic operates at a micro level when we consider, for example, the rooms where this work might happen, who facilitates for whom, and how the process is owned. We argue that these three dimensions – Reflective-Expressive-Symbolic – of creative and reflective inquiry offer a powerful way of making sense of the world. The model can be usefully generalized beyond biblio-poetry therapy techniques.

Creative and reflective inquiry necessarily engages the imagination. Throughout this chapter we will be referring to the efficacy of using metaphor and paying attention to intuition and the gifts of dreams and mythology. In this work, we draw on the fruitful tension between letting go and reining in, between freedom and control. Creative and reflective inquiry is exciting and liberating but also, like fire, potentially hazardous, so we ask you to proceed with caution. We will give some guidance on how to approach this work at the beginning of our journey through the territory.

In this chapter, we will describe three examples of ways of approaching creative and reflective inquiry in organizations, namely:

- Reflective and reflexive writing
- journalling
- Biblio-poetry therapy.

For each of these areas, we will outline some of the theoretical underpinnings for their use in organizations, give examples of techniques and their outcomes, and make recommendations for further exploration.

Both of us know from our experience as facilitators, writers and researchers that these processes are iterative. In individual lives and in the lives of organizations, challenges come round again in different forms and people find themselves confronting an issue similar to those encountered previously. This means that creative and reflective inquiry is not something to do once and then forget. Rather, these techniques are analogous to exercise and offer a 'care' model rather than a 'cure'. They can be revisited at different times, with different results and new insights. So rather than seeing what follows as a linear account, we encourage you to go back and dip in as appropriate.

How to Work with These Techniques

First, we would like to outline some of the caveats around this kind of work. No matter how experienced people are, they can

sometimes be surprised at the intensity of their own writing, or how something they read can elicit buried memories or repressed emotion. Of course, this is one of the reasons creative and reflective inquiry can be so powerful and bring benefits and insights. As Robert Frost wrote, 'No surprise in the writer, no surprise in the reader, no tears in the writer, no tears in the reader' (Frost, 1939, Preface, unnumbered page). James Pennebaker is convinced that it is the suppression of emotion that creates disease, whether physical or emotional (Pennebaker, 1997a). In many large organizations, where people feel that they are not heard, unhappiness manifests as absenteeism and long-term sickness, especially with symptoms that doctors find difficult to diagnose definitively. Bringing things into the open has a role to play in promoting health and the arts can facilitate this without pathologizing or medicalizing distress.

Writing and other expressive arts such as drawing, collage, dancing or singing have the advantage that the person working with them is in control of the process. It is important to stress that it is always acceptable and sometimes advisable to stop writing at any point. If someone is home alone, we recommend setting up some structure to act as a safe container. Someone might write for a set period of time. For example, Gillie Bolton recommends six minutes as long enough to move beyond superficial thoughts but not long enough to get carried away and lose connection with outside reality (Bolton, 1999: 37). Julia Cameron in her classic *The Artist's Way* (1994) suggests filling one or two sheets of paper and then stopping.

The techniques we discuss can be usefully adopted by individuals, but there are benefits in having a facilitator who can stand outside the group and encourage participants to reflect on the similarities and differences in the responses. As Chavis (2011) suggests:

[f]acilitators working with a group ... often deliberately juxtapose the differing or similar responses of various participants and invite them to

consider one another's responses, in order to move the therapeutic conversation to a deeper level, while including everyone in the process. (Chavis, 2011: 76)

This interplay and honouring of both common ground and individual difference is fundamental to using creative processes to promote organizational wellbeing.

When working with a group within an organization, there are additional ethical considerations. One which requires open and clear consideration is confidentiality within the group and, especially, its limits. If the session is taking place in the workplace, it is important to clarify to what extent participants in any group process are explicitly invited to share personal and potentially painful information, and what the consequences might be. It is worth spending time thinking about the ground rules for any process in advance and agreeing them with the group.

Whilst reflective and creative inquiry for organizational wellbeing is not therapy, it certainly draws on therapeutic techniques and so the importance of establishing clear boundaries cannot be overstated. Most people are heavily invested in their work and their roles in various organizations form a core part of their identity. If there are dysfunctional processes in an organization and these are explored using creative inquiry, there is likely to be a high level of emotional responding. When offering these techniques, it is important to reflect in advance what kind of outcomes might occur and how these will be worked through.

We will now explore three areas of creative and reflective practice that can promote wellbeing in organizations and individuals. Whilst we focus on writing techniques, as these are easily accessible, the practices can be adapted to work with visual materials (such as drawing or collage in reflective writing and journalling) or performance (such as drama or spoken word in biblio-poetry therapy).

Reflective and Reflexive Writing

If your organization were a pudding, what kind of pudding would it be? What would it need to make it more attractive or palatable? This is perhaps not the question that immediately springs to mind when considering the most effective way to cope with change, or find a structural or managerial solution, or to engender a sense of wellbeing.

It is prompts such as this, however, that are emblematic of the medium of reflective writing for reflective practice. This approach harnesses the physical act of writing with intuition, imagination and creativity and provides an effective vehicle for exploration, the possibility of discovering new perspectives and the potential for transformation.

Reflecting on our behaviour and the meaning of events and experiences is central to our learning and to finding a productive and meaningful path through our lives and careers. For organizations, effective reflective practice is an opportunity to promote collegiate working, good communication and effective team building and for managing uncertainty and change.

Yet as individuals and organizations we take refuge in habitual ways of thinking and working, framed within established cultures and belief and value systems. The same habitual thinking can apply to the way we reflect. In our experience as facilitators, creative reflective writing can help to dislodge fixed patterns of thinking and uncover new perspectives.

Reflective writing, particularly in the form of learning or reflective journals, has become an intrinsic part of the tradition of professional reflective practice that grew out of Kolb's learning cycle (1984) and Schön's 'reflective practitioner' (1983). These models proposed that we learn by applying our experience – our feelings, values, knowledge, skills and theory – to reflect on an event to make sense of it.

Proponents of creative reflective writing for reflective practice and personal development

(Bolton, 2014; Hunt and Sampson, 2006) suggest that it is possible to engender a deeper level of reflection and reflexivity to this process by adding creativity and imagination to the mix.

According to Qualley (1997), reflection involves giving a subject careful consideration and contemplation independently of others, whilst reflexivity is a deeper ongoing process that involves critical engagement with the other, whether that might be 'an other idea, theory, person, culture, text, or even an other part of one's self' (Qualley, 1997: 11).

The act of tapping into thoughts and emotions about an event or experience and writing them out on a page provides an opportunity to extend this reflexive process, 'stand outside' ourselves and reflect back – and to have 'a dialogue with the self' (Bolton and Wright, 2012: 38).

Creative writing, where we draw on parts of ourselves, our imperfect memories and imagination and different points of view is, according to Celia Hunt, a reflexive pursuit (Hunt and Sampson, 2006: 5). In addition, she suggests reflecting on the writing process itself further enhances reflexivity and offers an additional pathway to understanding (Hunt and Sampson, 2006: 6).

Reflective writing of the type we describe is by nature expressive, exploratory, creative and often playful. It can be an individual pursuit or be facilitated in groups within organizations. In a typical session participants are encouraged to write intuitively by hand, writing just for themselves in order to access their authentic thoughts and feelings. This expressive writing, often labelled free-writing or flow-writing (which will reappear in the section below on Journalling) is often done at speed, to produce a sense of freedom, and curtailed within a time limit of a few minutes.

A facilitator will use a series of writing prompts to generate self-exploration. In an organizational setting these might be designed to address a specific remit, for example around team building or decision making, or to introduce participants to some tools for self-care. Often these prompts will involve use of descriptive writing, imagination or writing about an experience or incident from an alternative perspective, or in a particular genre or from a particular point of view.

Entering into the imagined life of another gives insight into the feelings of others and can enhance empathy and communication. This might involve a manager describing an event through the first person eyes of an employee, for example, or a doctor describing themselves through the eyes of a patient.

Writing also encourages participants to move out of their comfort zone and to enter a place of uncertainty either as an individual or organization. Bolton and Wright describe this as a liminal space 'where normal assumptions and stable understandings are questioned and sometimes overturned'. Accepting 'certain uncertainty' (Bolton and Wright, 2012: 29) and entering this space is a necessary part of the reflexive process.

One variety of prompt that can be particularly effective is metaphor. Metaphors afford opportunity for transformation because they correspond to the original experience they are describing through isomorphism. This means that the form of the metaphor is different from the original experience but has a similar organization.

The pudding exercise at the beginning of the section, for example, is a way of challenging assumptions that might be embedded deep within the culture of an organization. The element of surprise and humour promotes a playful approach and allows participants to work in the gap between imagination and reality.

Another oft-used prompt is the 'furniture game'. Here, participants are asked to describe a colleague, client or themselves through a series of metaphors such as a piece of furniture, an animal, a landscape and so on. The same could be applied to a team or broader group or organization. Field and Ansari (2007) describe a workshop using the furniture game in which participants wrote in the first person, second person and then used metaphor to explore an emotion. Poet Angela Stoner described herself as a tree:

> In my hollowed out darkness live tiny creatures. They may seem repulsive to you but I have learned to love their tiny scurryings and see beauty even in dung beetles ....

And then addressed someone significant through the metaphor of a storm:

> You are a jagged flash
>
> scissoring the sky
>
> switching from black to silver .... (in Field and Ansari, 2007: 113)

As is apparent in these examples, metaphor and symbolism enable us to give form to those aspects of life that are most challenging or difficult to communicate such as our relationships, problems, fears and desires. They can become a vehicle for conversations and ideas that might be difficult to challenge head on.

Many organizational coaches are adapting the Clean Language symbolic modelling method of questioning developed by Lawley and Tompkins (2000) to work closely with clients to get them to go deep into their own unique metaphors without leading or influencing them in any way.

The language is described as 'clean' because it is designed as far as possible to be a blank page on which the client paints a metaphorical landscape. Combining this with intuitive writing in which participants respond in as much detail as possible to a series of clean language questions can prompt deep exploration and a map for action. A sample of the type of questions (Sullivan and Rees, 2008: 17) might be:

> When this organisation is working at its best it is like what?
>
> And what kind of ... is that ... (replacing ... with your metaphor)?
>
> Is there anything else about ...?
>
> Where (or whereabouts) is ...?

> What kind of ... is that?
>
> What will you see or hear?
>
> Is there anything else about ...?

Participants might then be encouraged to reflect in writing on what needs to happen next and what resources and conditions are required to initiate change. These questions and techniques can be used to write through personal challenges and ambitions.

Another prompt that can be effective for those facing challenges in their professional lives, and drawn from the journal writing toolbox, is the scribing of an unsent letter to someone or something. Writing a letter to a wise imaginary mentor, for example, can be a powerful device for finding clarity, accessing our internal coach and for reminding us of what we know already.

Sharing results of writing that emerges from prompts using metaphors, or otherwise, in the safety of a group provides an opportunity for voices to be heard, assumptions around organizational hierarchies or cultures to be challenged and fresh perspectives to be considered and discussed. Outcomes can be taken back into practice.

Reflective practice within organizations is a way of engaging colleagues and preventing mistrust and fragmentation and is essential for ethical practice. Expressive and explorative writing which develops 'confidence, cooperation and collaboration' (Bolton, 2014: 130) can be an enjoyable and dynamic part of this.

Journalling

People have been recording their personal experiences in diaries and journals for centuries. Whilst diary writing tends to focus on the external world and a record of daily experiences, journalling takes the writer on an internal exploration of feelings and responses. The journal is a private and personal place for reflective and creative inquiry.

Keeping a journal is a popular pursuit. A cursory internet search of the term journalling throws up a plethora of courses, blogs and prompts offering tips and guidance on how to pursue this practice. The success of *MIND Journal* for men (2020) is one example, as is the establishment of the Journalversity online community (2020) which has come out of the US-based Center for Journal Therapy (2018). There are numerous apps available to help build up a journal writing practice featuring gratitude or motivation or self-reflection.

A journal is a place for expressive and reflective writing, where people can put their innermost thoughts and feelings into words in order to make sense of themselves and to navigate their way through events and experiences. It is no surprise, perhaps, that more people are realizing the therapeutic value of writing and opening their journals in a world that is, as we write, filled with uncertainty and stress brought to us by the Covid-19 pandemic:

> For those working within organisations, keeping a personal journal can be a powerful resource for finding emotional and mental clarity, mapping and managing, working through change, for validating experience and for sitting with ambiguity or indecision. (Thompson, 2011: 31)

The value of expressive writing – writing with the intention of putting our innermost thoughts and feelings into words – is backed by scientific research. It has been shown to improve our emotional and also physical wellbeing and our ability to cope with challenging situations.

James Pennebaker's research in the 1980s showed that expressive writing about a traumatic event in short bursts over a number of days can make people feel better physically and emotionally (Pennebaker and Beall, 1986). Further studies conducted in various contexts and with varied populations have demonstrated objectively measurable benefits for conditions such as asthma (Jones et al., 2008), irritable bowel syndrome (Halpert et al., 2010), blood pressure (McGuire et al.,

2005), depression and anxiety (Sloan et al., 2008), arthritis (Lumley et al., 2011) and cancer (Rosenberg et al., 2002).

The way in which expressive writing brings benefits is unclear. It is thought to be a mixture of catharsis, a way of helping us to 'get things off our chest' (Pennebaker, 1997a) and a means of finding coherent narratives and meaning in our lives (Smyth et al., 2001). Pennebaker and Chung believe expressive writing is effective because it allows us to stand back and examine our lives and find new perspective, serving as a 'life course correction' (Pennebaker and Chung, 2007: 37).

Whilst Pennebaker acknowledges that writing is not a 'cure all' for everyone and can sometimes be a painful process, he recommends it as 'preventative maintenance' for health:

> The value of writing or talking about our thoughts and feelings lies in reducing the work of inhibition and in organising our complicated mental and emotional lives. Writing helps to keep our psychological compass oriented. (Pennebaker, 1997b: 197)

Expressive writing, sometimes labelled free-intuitive writing, free writing or flow-writing, has also been used and promoted by writers and teachers as a means of overcoming blocks and prompting creativity. These are techniques which share common ground. They focus on writing privately, without consideration of audience or style, on writing to free up thinking, and as a means of accessing the unconscious process.

The potential therapeutic value of keeping a journal came to the fore in the 1960s and 1970s when US psychologist and psychotherapist Ira Progoff developed the Intensive Journal process after realizing that clients who wrote in a journal were able to work through their issues more rapidly. His method, adapted in the United States by a network of thousands of journal consultants, is an instrument for 'self-guidance' helping participants to 'crystalise decisions', identify goals and to find meaning in life (Progoff, 1975: 3). Rather than therapy, Progoff described his series of journalling prompts as providing 'active techniques that enable an individual to draw upon his inherent resources for becoming a whole person' (Progoff, 1975: 9).

Over the years journal writing has grown in popularity and is increasingly used by practitioners when working with individuals and groups in a range of organizational settings such as health and social care and in educational organizations. Writing, particularly in the form of learning and reflective journals, became a natural and intrinsic part of reflective practice, which expanded in popularity alongside journal writing for personal growth.

Expressive writing, when practised without time limits in particular, can prompt uncomfortable and unwelcome feelings. For this reason people working in the field of journal therapy often use a series of timed, structured exercises and prompts, all carefully designed to inspire but within appropriate boundaries which afford control over potentially difficult emotions or material.

Outlined here are two classic prompts, Dialogue and Steppingstones, both of which can be adapted for further exploration of organizational relationships, politics and influences.

Dialogue is a classic journal writing technique devised by Progoff and developed and used by others including Kathleen Adams in *Journal to the Self* (Adams, 1990: 102). The prompt elicits a conversational exchange between the writer and someone or something else, where the writer plays both parts, on the premise that this encourages a conversation between their conscious and unconscious selves and throws up opportunities for integration and new perspectives.

The Steppingstones technique is also at the heart of Progoff's Intensive Journal process. The prompt invites journal writers to compile a list of 12 events that come to mind when they spontaneously reflect on the course of their life as a moving stream, starting with

the first stone 'I was born'. The list should be completed quickly and without 'self-conscious analysis', each stone described in a single word or phrase. The process 'gives us a direct experience of the wholeness of our life as it has been in motion over the years', and 'enables us to recognise the large implications and possibilities that lie implicit, and often hidden in individual events' (Progoff, 1975: 119).

Significant life markers can be chronological or in random order and are likely to change if you repeat the exercise at a later date. Each stepping stone then becomes a potential springboard for a further piece of writing that follows from the phrase 'It was a time when...':

> As you recall the time, you will often find that lessons left incomplete are offered back up for learning, old wounds that never quite healed are offered back up for healing. (Adams, 1990: 153)

An important part of the journal writing process is the re-reading of expressive or reflective writing and writing a short reflection on what has been observed. Adams and Thompson describe this as the feedback loop (Thompson, 2011: 34). Using this is not obligatory. Some might feel that writing as a cathartic process is enough and re-reading is unnecessary and unproductive. Whether digital or handwritten, pursued as a daily practice, with prompt or without, there are no set rules for keeping a journal.

As with reflective writing and biblio-poetry therapy, journal writing is also often practised in group settings, during which a skilled facilitator will select appropriate prompts to inspire participants to write together, and then to share and bear witness to one another's words.

Biblio-Poetry Therapy

A poem is literally 'a thing made of words'. Many people claim to be baffled by contemporary poetry and yet, at times of collective grief (such as a school shooting in the United States or the death of Princess Diana in the UK), or personal importance (such as a wedding or funeral), it is common for poems to be read, written and shared.

As we have described, the act of putting something in writing can be healing, whether it is a journal entry or experimenting with metaphor in reflective practice. We will begin by considering what it is about poetry that might be uniquely healing.

The approach to literature in creative and reflective inquiry is different from that in conventional English classes in an educational setting. Here, in creative and reflective inquiry, a poem is a tool for personal and organizational development rather than a literary artefact or an object of discussion (Hynes and Hynes-Berry, 2012: 32). Geri Chavis (2011) describes the poem as 'a *vehicle* for insight' (Chavis, 2011: 20), that is, a mechanism by which new ways of thinking can be encouraged. Vehicle is, of course, a metaphor and suggests a sense of movement from one perspective to another. The word metaphor comes from the Greek to 'carry across'.

The kinds of poems chosen in this context are typically concrete and easy to understand but with a metaphorical hinterland that allows the reader to uncover deeper meanings. Poetry therapists talk about the 'rich ambiguity' of poems, which means they can be discussed again and again and still yield new insights. The poems used in reflective and creative inquiry are those that elicit a 'feeling' response first rather than a cognitive one. Welsh poet, R.S. Thomas described poetry as that 'which arrives at the intellect by way of the heart' (Thomas, 2004: 355). Such poems are not didactic or heavy-handed but allow the reader to 'find themselves' in the experiences and impressions described.

Sherry Reiter (2009) argues that poetry and dreams both use the same three psychological mechanisms, namely imagery, condensation and displacement (Reiter, 2009: 12). Imagery relates to the imagination and

poems stimulate us to imagine scenarios. The language in a poem is precise and condensed, conveying a whole world in a few lines. Poetry, like all literature, can take us to another time or place. This 'displacement' enables us to have some distance from the material so that we can look at it objectively and our reactions can also surprise us. This is where creative and reflective inquiry differs from psychotherapy. Psychotherapy encourages people to become immersed in an emotional state and to re-experience it in a safe space whereas therapeutic writing and biblio-poetry therapy aim to come at experiences from a fresh angle and create a sense of perspective. Participants are encouraged to acknowledge their emotional reactions and they may have a sense of catharsis, but because the poem remains an outside element, there is always a distance. Some practitioners refer to the poem as the co-facilitator in the room.

Hynes and Hynes-Berry (2012) describe the poem as a *catalyst* for new insights. Rather than focusing immediately on a problem or difficulty, participants respond to a piece of literature in a way that allows for a sense of competence, worth and autonomy (Hynes-Berry, 2012: 32–48). A facilitator using the poem in an organizational setting would typically ask some questions to enable participants to engage with the poem and to locate themselves and their own experience within the poet's words.

The poem may evoke a sense of recognition that the poet has captured something authentic about human experience. There will be personal emotional responses to the material, and typically in a group, differences. Someone might see the poem as being sad; another, that it has elements of optimism. These differences of opinion about a poem are helpful in an organizational setting as they demonstrate how there is no inherent truth about a situation. Someone's loss might be another's opportunity and that it is possible, for example, to be both frightened and excited at the same time. A poem also gives permission to feel certain emotions and for participants to compare and contrast their own feelings with those expressed in the text.

The biblio-poetry therapy model developed by the International Federation for Biblio-Poetry Therapy, based in the United States, typically has five stages. The opening of a session comprises a warm-up writing exercise such as those described above in the sections on journalling and reflective writing. The warm-up acts as a transition between the outside world and the business of the group. It enables people in the room to move from their daily concerns, to connect with their own feelings and to become present and acknowledge how they are in the moment.

The second stage is the sharing of a text, reading it aloud and discussing responses. A text is typically a poem, but it might be a prose extract, a song, or a film clip. The intention is to open an imaginative space where participants in a session can access feelings alongside cognitive responses. There are literally thousands of poems which are suitable for this work. To give just one example, there is a short poem by African-American poet, Langston Hughes (1901–1967) called *Island* in which in eight short rhyming lines, the speaker of the poem implores a 'wave of sorrow' not to drown them but to carry them to an island where the 'sands are fair' (Hughes, 1994: 376). The poem uses simple, rhythmic language and there is often a sigh of recognition when it is read in a group.

The poem is clearly about sorrow and reflects the common experience that sad emotions come in waves. Someone who is grieving may at times feel at risk of being drowned or overwhelmed by these waves. A sense of overwhelm can also be a common complaint amongst colleagues in organizations under pressure and the poem speaks to that. The poem is also 'richly ambiguous' in that the 'wave of sorrow' can refer to any number of life events, including, but not limited to, bereavement, relationship breakdown, professional or personal disappointment, regrets or feelings of guilt.

However, the poem is not one of despair. A wave of sorrow might drown someone but it may also carry them to an island where the 'sands are fair'. The word 'island' is open to interpretation. For an organization undergoing changes and challenges, it might be useful to explore the idea of waves, what the island might look like and what it would mean not to drown. It may be helpful to draw on the clean language techniques outlined earlier. Again there will be differences of perception. One person's island might feel lonely and remote; another's, a source of sanctuary.

Poems typically combine imagery and metaphor with a sense of a narrative in progress. The concise and compressed nature of many poems makes them more accessible than, say, short stories or plays. They can be read aloud, even learned by heart, in a relatively short time. The structure can be aesthetically satisfying and often people find reciting favourite poems a source of solace and pleasure. Poetry though is full of paradox. Something that seems superficially simple, once discussed in a group, can reveal surprising depths. This, we believe, is to do with the power of metaphor and imagery. Just as with dreams, a single image can be explored over and over again and yield new insights. A poem typically combines images and this makes them particularly useful as a tool to promote health and wellbeing.

The third stage of a biblio-poetry session is the 'expressive' mode, where participants write their own poem in response to what they have read and the subsequent discussion. There might be a specific prompt from the facilitator or they may be invited to write from a line or image in the poem under discussion, or whatever comes. Having everyone write to the same prompt is helpful when an organization may be working with a particular question or issue, and an open prompt preferable when the focus may be more on personal development. The writing can take any form and need not be 'poetic' although often, the pieces produced will naturally take on some of the poetic qualities of the original.

Again, as described above, a limited time of say six to ten minutes encourages spontaneous and authentic responses.

Participants are then invited to share their pieces in a non-judgemental and enquiring way. There is no literary criticism as these are first drafts and often the writer is still unsure what they might 'mean'. This can be a very powerful experience and often both reader and listener might be moved to tears by giving voice to important and maybe never previously expressed thoughts and ideas.

The fifth and final stage of a biblio-poetry therapy session is some kind of closing ritual to set an intention for the group and act as a bridge to the outside world. Sometimes the facilitator might create a group poem from the lines of poems by individual participants.

The International Federation for Biblio-Poetry Therapy has codified this practice and acts as a professional organization accrediting qualifications in biblio-poetry therapy. However, the use of poems and literature for individual and organizational wellbeing is widespread outside this specific professional niche. Some practitioners use poetry therapy techniques under other professional umbrellas such as teaching, coaching, counselling, medicine, mindfulness training or occupational therapy and biblio-therapy techniques are also employed informally. This might be in book clubs, yoga sessions, religious and spiritual gatherings, or simply as a way to focus at the beginning of team meetings in business or other institutions. To put it metaphorically, a poem can act as a mirror, a door, a map, a window and for many, a key poem can become a friend.

CONCLUSION AND FUTURE DIRECTIONS

This has been a necessarily brief excursion into the use of creative and reflective inquiry to promote wellbeing in organizations and we hope you may be inspired to try some of these exercises and explore further. As ethical practitioners, we firmly advise trying these techniques personally first before considering how and where they might be used with others.

Different organizational contexts, such as the workplace, hospices, hospitals and libraries, all require close attention both to the content of the session and the wider symbolic aspects. It is important to establish the ethos of the practice, the credentials of the practitioner and philosophy informing them, whether recreational, therapeutic, or for personal or professional development. Practical considerations such as the length of session and how the writing is introduced will vary considerably. For example, in a hospice setting, practitioners may work at the bedside and 'scribe' for a patient. A community group in a public library is likely to be quite unboundaried, requiring careful considerations of ground rules. We encourage you to seek out appropriate professional support and sources of guidance, through courses, reading and attending workshops as a participant wherever possible.

The UK's All-Party Parliamentary Group on Arts and Health (APPG, 2017) collected evidence on the impact of a broad range of arts activities including some characterized as 'sedentary leisure pursuits, such as television viewing and playing computer games' (APPG, 2017: 93), but Wall et al. (2019) argue that frames of reference, which include a conscious intention to encourage sense-making and reconfiguring of one's own self-understanding, offer a more purposeful and focused harnessing of benefits.

Wall et al. (2019) have observed, 'Creative writing for health and well-being has emerged from a constellation of arts-based practices which have been explicitly linked to health and well-being'. In times of challenge and stress, it is helpful to focus on the specific and manageable. It may be impossible for an individual to change the world, but everyone has the potential to change some aspect of their immediate environment, or their perspective on it, and writing is a potent tool for this. The processes we have described, according to Wall et al. (2019) have a role in 'resolving the social and cultural challenges facing today's world' (UNESCO, 2010: 8). There is still much work to be done in clarifying and amplifying that role.

We have highlighted the flexibility and cross-disciplinary nature of the use of creative and reflective inquiry and this remains both a strength and a challenge for research into its benefits. The practice is only partly codified – for example in the training programmes offered by the International Federation for Biblio-Poetry Therapy or the Center for Journal Therapy, or the MA courses in Creative Writing for Therapeutic Purposes and Creative Writing and Wellbeing taught by the Metanoia Institute and Teesside University, respectively. All of these have related but distinct philosophies and practices in terms of goals, intentions and intended outcomes.

There is a need for further research into the use of creative and reflective writing for wellbeing as articulated by Williamson and Wright (2018). One of the challenges for practitioners and commissioners of this work is to find ways of evaluating the impact of these techniques on wellbeing and to disseminate findings in a way that acknowledges the complex and holistic mechanisms at work. Reductionist and positivist studies in quasi-laboratory conditions such as those by Pennebaker described above have provided some evidence but at the expense of the rich and imaginative possibilities offered by creative approaches (Williamson and Wright, 2018). A systematic review on the effects of therapeutic writing on long-term conditions was inconclusive, not because of the lack of demonstrable benefits, but because it was impossible to compare studies in a meaningful way (Nyssen et al., 2016).

Williamson and Wright (2018) make a plea for a central repository for research in this area. Relevant journal articles are spread across many disciplines and are sometimes difficult to locate. They also call for 'practice

models' that can be replicated and the creation of a research mindset in practitioners so that both experience-far (the positivist approach) and experience-near (autoethnographic) can inform and develop the other. Lapidus International is spearheading this with the creation of a new journal, LIRIC (Lapidus International Research and Innovation Community), launched in December 2020 (LIRIC Journal, 2020).

We would like to finish with the image of Indra's Net, which originates in Hindu and Buddhist traditions. According to legend, Indra created the world as a giant interconnected net with a pearl tied at every knot. Every idea, person, organization and concept imaginable exists as one of these pearls and reflects every other pearl. When one moves, everything moves. For us, reflective and creative inquiry works in a similar way. When one person gains an insight or feels empowered, the increase in wellbeing is felt throughout the whole net. As Daisy Fancourt describes it, 'the arts have been shown to affect intergroup behaviour and reduce social unrest, including reducing conflict in communities, promoting prosocial behaviour, furthering social change, and promoting collective action' (Fancourt, 2017: 40). In these unprecedented times, we need such interventions more than ever.

REFERENCES

Adams, K (1990) *Journal to the Self*. New York: Grand Central Publishing.

All-Party Parliamentary Group on Arts, Health and Wellbeing (APPG) (2017) *Creative Health: The Arts for Health and Wellbeing*. Available at: www.artshealthandwellbeing. org.uk/appg-inquiry (accessed 30 June 2020).

Alma, D and Amiel, K (2020) *These Are the Hands: Poems from the Heart of the NHS*. Oswestry: Fairacre Press.

BBC (2016) *Shostakovich's symphony played by a starving orchestra*. Available at: www.

bbc.co.uk/news/magazine-34292312 (accessed 5 April 2020).

BBC (2020) *David Hockney shares exclusive art from Normandy, as 'a respite from the news'*. Available at: www.bbc.co.uk/news/entertainment-arts-52109901 (accessed 5 April 2020).

Bolton, G (1999) *The Therapeutic Potential of Creative Writing: Writing Myself*. London: Jessica Kingsley Publishers.

Bolton, G (2014) *Reflective Practice, Writing and Professional Development*. London: Sage.

Bolton, G and Wright, J (2012) *Reflective Writing in Counselling and Psychotherapy*. London: Sage.

Cameron, J (1994) *The Artist's Way*. London: Macmillan.

Center for Journal Therapy (2018) Website available at: www.journaltherapy.com (accessed 10 June 2020).

Chavis, G (2011) *Poetry and Story Therapy*. London: Jessica Kingsley Publishers.

Chödrön, P (2002) *Comfortable with Uncertainty*. Boston, MA: Shambhala.

Fancourt, D (2017) *Arts in Health: Designing and Researching Interventions*. Oxford: Oxford University Press.

Field, V and Ansari, Z (2007) *Prompted to Write*. Truro: Fal Publications.

Frost, R (1939) *Collected Poems of Robert Frost*. New York: Holt and Company.

Halpert, A, Rybin, D and Doros, G (2010) Expressive writing is a promising therapeutic modality for the management of IBS: a pilot study. *American Journal of Gastroenterology* 105(11): 2440–2448.

Hughes, L (1994) *The Collected Poems of Langston Hughes*. New York: Knopf.

Hunt, C and Sampson, F (2006) *Writing, Self and Reflexivity*. Basingstoke: Palgrave Macmillan.

Hynes, A and Hynes-Berry, M (2012) *Biblio/Poetry Therapy*. St Cloud, MN: North Star Press.

Jones, C, Theadom, A, Smith, H, Hankins, M, Bowskill, R, Horne, R, Frew, A (2008) Writing about emotional experiences to improve lung function and quality of life in patients with asthma: a 3-month follow up of a randomised controlled trial. *Thorax* 63: A18–A20.

Journalversity (2020) Website available at: www.myjournalversity.com (accessed 11 June 2020).

Kolb, D (1984) *Experiential Learning: Experience as the Source of Learning and Development*. Englewood Cliffs, NJ: Prentice-Hall.

Lawley, J and Tompkins, P (2000) *Metaphors in Mind: Transformation through Symbolic Modelling*. Available at: www.cleanlanguage.co.uk (accessed 1 March 2020).

LIRIC Journal, December 2020, Volume 1, Number 1. Available at: https://lapidus.org.uk/events-news/liric-journal (accessed 24 February 2021).

Lumley, M, Leisen, J, Partridge, R, Meyer, T, Radcliffe, A, Macklem, D, Naoum, L, Cohen, J, Lasichak, L, Lubetsky, M, Mosley-Williams, A, Granda, J (2011) Does emotional disclosure about stress improve health in rheumatoid arthritis? Randomized, controlled trials of written and spoken disclosure. *Pain* 152(4): 866–877.

Mazza, N (2003) *Poetry Therapy: Theory and Practice*. Hove: Brunner-Routledge.

McGuire, K, Greenberg, M and Gevirtz, R (2005) Autonomic effects of expressive writing in individuals with elevated blood pressure. *Journal of Health Psychology* 10(2): 197–209.

MIND Journal (2020) Available at: www.mindjournals.com (accessed 14 June 2020).

Nyssen, O, Taylor, S, Wong, G, Steed, E, Bourke, L, Lord, J, Ross, C, Hayman, S, Field, V, Higgins, A, Greenhalgh, T, Meads, C (2016) Does therapeutic writing help people with long-term conditions? Systematic review, realist synthesis and economic considerations. *Health Technology Assessment* 20(27): 1–367.

Pennebaker, J (1990) *Opening Up: The Healing Power of Expressing Emotions*. New York: Guilford Press.

Pennebaker, J (1997a) Writing about emotional experiences as a therapeutic process. *Psychological Science* 18(3): 62–166.

Pennebaker, J (1997b) *Opening Up: The Healing Power of Expressing Emotions* (revised edition). New York and London: Guilford Press.

Pennebaker, J and Beall, S (1986) Confronting a traumatic event: toward an understanding of inhibition and disease. *Journal of Abnormal Psychology* 95(3): 274–281.

Pennebaker, J and Chung, C (2007) Expressive writing: emotional upheavals and health, in Friedman, H and Silver, R (eds) *Handbook of Health Psychology*. New York: Oxford University Press, pp. 263–284.

Progoff, I (1975) *At a Journal Workshop, the Basic Text and Guide for Using the Intensive Journal Process*. New York: Dialogue House Library.

Qualley, D (1997) *Turns of Thought, Teaching Composition as Reflexive Inquiry*. Portsmouth, NH: Boynton/Cook.

Reiter, S (2009) *Writing Away the Demons*. St Cloud, MN: North Star Press.

Rosenberg, H, Rosenberg, S, Ernstoff, M, Wolford, G, Amdur, R, Elshamy, M, Bauer-Wu, S, Ahles, T, Pennebaker, J (2002) Expressive disclosure and health outcomes in a prostate cancer population. *International Journal of Psychiatry in Medicine* 32(1): 37–53.

Schön, D (1983) *The Reflective Practitioner: How Professionals Think in Action*. London: Maurice Temple Smith.

Sloan, D, Marx, B, Epstein, E and Dobbs, J (2008) Expressive writing buffers against maladaptive rumination. *Emotion* 8(2): 302–306.

Smyth, J, True, N and Souto, J (2001) Effects of writing about traumatic experiences: the necessity for narrative structuring. *Journal of Social and Clinical Psychology* 20(1): 61–172.

Sullivan, W and Rees, J (2008) *Clean Language, Revealing Metaphors and Opening Minds*. Carmarthen: Crown House Publishing.

Thomas, R (2004) *Collected Later Poems 1988– 2000*. Tarset: Bloodaxe Books.

Thompson, K (2011) *Therapeutic Journal Writing: An Introduction for Professionals*. London: Jessica Kingsley.

UNESCO (2010) *Seoul Agenda: Goals for the Development of Arts Education*. Paris: UNESCO.

Wall, T, Field, V and Sučylaitė, J (2019) Creative writing for health and well-being, in Leal Filho W, Wall T, Azeiteiro U et al. (eds) *Good Health and Well-Being, Encyclopedia of the UN Sustainable Development Goals*. Cham: Springer.

Williamson, C and Wright, J (2018) How creative does writing have to be in order to be therapeutic? A dialogue on the practice and research of writing to recover and survive. *The Journal of Poetry Therapy* 31(2): 113–123.

Measuring Wellbeing in Organizational Contexts

Katharina Näswall, Jennifer Wong, and Sanna Malinen

INTRODUCTION

When telling other researchers and organizational leaders that we study employee wellbeing, often their first reaction is 'How do you measure wellbeing?' This is often followed by 'How do you choose among all the different measures?' And our reply is just as often 'It depends'. Even after decades of research on wellbeing, we still have no consensus on exactly what the best measure of wellbeing at work is. The many approaches that are in use for the measurement of wellbeing are indicative of a lack of agreement on what is to be captured. Adding to the confusion is the fact that the number of measures capturing wellbeing is vast; a review from 2016 counted 42 separate self-report measures (cf. Cooke et al., 2016). Although the list of measures for wellbeing at work is shorter (see, for example, Fisher, 2014, for an overview), there are still many options for someone interested in employee wellbeing,

or wellbeing in organizations, to consider. In addition, the purpose for measuring wellbeing (for example, monitoring wellbeing over time, or evaluating efficiency of work initiatives meant to improve wellbeing) is an important consideration when choosing a measure (Vanderweele et al., 2020), further complicating the selection process. Having a guiding framework, or at least an idea of what different approaches are available, is helpful for making these decisions, and the aim of this chapter is to present a number of different potential considerations that should be taken into account when setting out to measure employee wellbeing. It is our intention that the chapter will assist researchers and practitioners interested in understanding employee wellbeing better.

Our aim is not to provide an exhaustive review of the literature on measuring employee wellbeing; there are already a number of excellent, fairly recent, reviews available on how wellbeing can be conceptualized and measured at work and in general (see, e.g., Cooke et al., 2016; Fisher, 2014; Ilies et al., 2015; Kelloway, 2017; Vanderweele et al., 2020), which we will build on in our exploration. In addition to these reviews, the most recent studies in this area will also be examined to get a sense of how wellbeing is being captured in current research.

The chapter begins with a discussion of what the point of all this is: 'Why measure wellbeing in the first place?' Since any measurement needs to be based on a solid definition, we outline where the literature sits in terms of a unified definition of wellbeing at work (spoiler: it is complicated), before moving on to discussing the different types of measures and how wellbeing can be examined using different study designs. Finally, we propose a way forward by offering a number of key considerations that can be used to guide researchers and organizations in selecting a measure of employee wellbeing that is appropriate to their specific situation.

WHY SHOULD WE MEASURE WELLBEING?

Before exploring what wellbeing is and how it can be measured, it may be helpful to discuss why employee wellbeing should be measured at all. Knowing why employee wellbeing information is being collected is central for selecting the appropriate measures (Vanderweele et al., 2020) and for deciding how the data should be collected and used. One aspect that relates to the reasons for seeking information on wellbeing in the workplace is whether it is being collected for research or for organizational purposes. Although there will often be overlap, organizations tend to focus on practical improvements, sometimes in connection with a certain wellbeing intervention or particular event (e.g., a restructuring or a crisis), while research leans more towards testing

hypotheses regarding causes and correlates of employee wellbeing.

Interest in general wellbeing has been on the rise in the 21st century (Vanderweele et al., 2020). Wellbeing indicators, such as perceived quality of life, are increasingly appearing in government conversations and policies, as a complement to measures of Gross Domestic Product (GDP); traditionally, GDP has been the central indicator of societal wellbeing but has been criticized for not providing a complete picture of citizen wellbeing (Allin, 2014). Simultaneously, there has been an increased interest in employee wellbeing in organizations as the evidence for and awareness of the positive relationship between employee wellbeing and how well employees do their work have increased (Ilies et al., 2015). For example, better employee wellbeing has been linked to better task performance (Kożusznik et al., 2019; Wright and Cropanzano, 2000), better contextual performance (Spence et al., 2014), and lower turnover and turnover intention (Wright and Bonett, 2016), making employee wellbeing a potential productivity-promoting resource for both employees and organizations. Better wellbeing at work has also been found to have a positive impact on individuals' overall sense of quality of life (Ilies et al., 2015). Wellbeing at work can thus be an important factor for a person's life in general.

For organizations, measuring wellbeing over time provides information that can be used for continuing improvements, as, for example, poor wellbeing can serve as an early warning that things are not as good as they should be, and allow organizations to respond. When utilized as part of a long-term approach, wellbeing audits may identify fluctuations in wellbeing that are related to other factors and changes in the organization (Leiter and Cooper, 2017), since data on employee wellbeing can be used to inform the development of initiatives and changes in policy to better support wellbeing (Fisher, 2014; Vanderweele et al., 2020). Measuring wellbeing also provides employees with an outlet for providing feedback to the organization about how they are doing; just by allowing the employees an outlet to express their wellbeing to the organization is itself a signal to them that their wellbeing is something the organization cares about (Leiter and Cooper, 2017). While many organizations may profess that they are wellbeing-oriented, only those that collect information about their employees' wellbeing will be able to properly address wellbeing issues. Increasingly, organizations are investing in wellbeing-promoting initiatives and interventions, many of which come at a significant cost and take up a lot of time for those implementing and participating in them. Follow-up is essential for such efforts: wellbeing audits or surveys, using valid and reliable measures, are needed to find out whether the intended goals of increased wellbeing have been met (cf. Dimoff et al., 2014; Kelloway, 2017). Especially among organizations who take into account the 'return on investment' (ROI) of interventions, knowing whether the intervention has had the expected outcomes should be based on high quality measures and rigorous study design (Kelloway, 2017). Information about ROI can be used to illustrate the benefits of a particular program, and to gain leadership support resources for future initiatives.

Organizations that gather data on employee wellbeing gain the opportunity to address and potentially improve the wellness of their employees, but having such information also places a certain demand on the organization to take greater responsibility regarding wellbeing. Another reason for measuring wellbeing concerns the aspect of employer's social responsibility towards their staff. While workplace health and safety legislation may drive wellbeing initiatives, proactive employers may also gather wellbeing data to ensure their systems and practices are conducive to a healthy workplace. The moral responsibility of employers to focus on employee mental health has been recently noted in the literature (Williams, 2018), and measuring wellbeing is a way to gather information that can assist in fulfilling such responsibilities.

What is done with the information becomes a critical consideration. If the findings indicate, for example, that wellbeing is low, especially compared to previous measures, the organization would likely be expected to address it. Lack of responsiveness to poor employee wellbeing may lead to lack of trust in the organization among employees (cf. Stanley et al., 2005). However, if the organization is responsive, and employees feel supported and valued, they may be more willing to participate in future change initiatives or measurement efforts.

Overall, the case for measuring wellbeing is compelling, both from research and organizational perspectives. However, how to measure wellbeing is a complex issue, particularly given the multitude of measures available, and the different definitions that are currently in use.

WHAT SHOULD WE MEASURE? DEFINING WELLBEING

A very general definition of wellbeing is 'feeling good and functioning well' (Aked et al., 2009; Grant et al., 2007; Huppert, 2009). This definition builds on a conceptualization of wellbeing which spans two perspectives that originate from different world views: the hedonic and eudaimonic views of wellbeing. The hedonic perspective, the 'feeling good' aspect, describes wellbeing as being characterized by high positive affect, low negative affect, and satisfaction with life in general (Diener et al., 1998; Fisher, 2014; Sonnentag, 2015). The eudaimonic perspective characterizes wellbeing as having a sense of purpose and meaning and being able to be one's authentic self (Bartels et al., 2019; Fisher, 2014) – the 'functioning well' aspect. These perspectives are not contradictory; hedonic and eudaimonic wellbeing are highly correlated (Fisher, 2014). Both perspectives are easily applied to the work setting; hedonic work-related wellbeing describes the experiencing of positive affect (and low negative affect) in relation to one's work or the satisfaction derived from it, while eudaimonic work-related wellbeing concerns experiencing a sense of purpose and meaning at work (Sonnentag, 2015). Both perspectives also emphasize that wellbeing is about positive experiences, not just the lack of negative experiences (Dewe and Cooper, 2012), which is in line with the World Health Organization's definition of health that explicitly includes positive experiences and wellbeing (WHO, 2006).

Some of the terminology that has been in use for specifying wellbeing is, unfortunately, not always consistent and is open to ambiguity. Some research, for example, uses 'subjective wellbeing' to refer to hedonic wellbeing (Sonnentag, 2015) and 'psychological wellbeing' to refer to eudaimonic wellbeing (Bartels et al., 2019), while others even use 'subjective' and 'psychological' interchangeably. These terms may lead to potential confusion, as the meaning of 'subjective' could also encompass physical or other non-psychological aspects of wellbeing, and the use of 'psychological' could imply a psychological (clinical) assessment of wellbeing (see, e.g., Vanderweele et al., 2020). Moreover, the two modifiers are not mutually exclusive, as hedonic experiences may be psychological. To avoid potential ambiguity, it is recommended that a more unified approach be adopted. We propose that the term 'wellbeing' can be used for an individual's subjective evaluation of their current emotional state and sense of purpose (i.e., encompassing both hedonic and eudaimonic aspects), while 'work-related wellbeing' or 'employee wellbeing' will refer to this assessment in relation to the individual's work life.

It has also been proposed that wellbeing should encompass further dimensions, additional to hedonic and eudaimonic wellbeing. In a review study from 2014, Fisher suggests that employee wellbeing also has a social component, consisting of satisfaction with social relationships at work and support gained from social connections at work. The incorporation of a social component in the definition of employee wellbeing is still not widespread; however, it has recently been suggested (Bartels et al., 2019) that eudaimonic employee wellbeing is best understood as a combination of intrapersonal and interpersonal components, where intrapersonal perceptions of meaningfulness are achieved through the work that is carried out and through personal development. The interpersonal dimension comprises the social components of wellbeing – acceptance from others and positive interactions at work (Bartels et al., 2019), thus incorporating Fisher's (2014) suggestion that wellbeing has an important social component. Related to the concept of social wellbeing, Vanderweele (2019) proposes that community wellbeing is an important component of wellbeing that can be applied to the workplace. Measured as a subjective evaluation, community wellbeing concerns satisfaction with one's community, but, more specifically, it concerns to what extent the community provides good relationships, opportunities for growth, clear goals, and good leadership (Vanderweele, 2019) – thus combining several aspects of the previously discussed types of wellbeing (hedonic, eudaimonic, and social).

In addition to the dimensions of wellbeing described above, there is an increasing interest in considering spiritual dimensions of wellbeing, as spirituality often plays an important role in people's quality of life (Vanderweele et al., 2020). By paying attention to and supporting spiritual wellbeing as a component of employee wellbeing, organizations have an opportunity to increase perceptions of cultural safety among their employees (Stewart and Gardner, 2015). Efforts to incorporate spiritual wellbeing may be assisted by learning more about indigenous models of wellbeing. One example of such a model of wellbeing comes from Māori, the Indigenous people of New Zealand, and incorporates four pillars on which the health and wellbeing of the individual and community depend (Durie and Kingi, 1997). One of these pillars is the spiritual component of wellbeing and comprises feelings of cultural identity and personal contentment as part of the spiritual. The other components are physical, mental, and social/community wellbeing. All of the pillars need to be present for achieving balance, good health, and overall wellbeing (Durie and Kingi, 1997), and this framework has been extended to employee wellbeing (Stewart and Gardner, 2015). Such non-Western models of wellbeing challenge the domain boundaries of the dominant Western definition of wellbeing, encouraging academics and practitioners to continue searching for wellbeing models that are relatable to increasingly diverse contemporary and global workplaces.

While the exact definition of wellbeing may vary between studies, there is widespread agreement that wellbeing should be conceptualized as a subjective evaluation. This is based on the assumption that individuals are the best judge of their own wellbeing (Chan, 2009; Dewe and Cooper, 2012; Spector, 2006). In studies focusing on, or including, an element of 'objective' wellbeing, it is often measured in terms of 'standard of living' (Vanderweele et al., 2020), based on some pre-set criteria (e.g., income, or socio-economic status) derived from external sources, without any reference to the individual's satisfaction in regard to the criteria. While objective wellbeing ratings may be useful as a contextual description, they are not necessarily in line with individuals' own evaluations of their situation. Since individuals' subjective perceptions, cognitions, and emotions are predictive of their reactions and behaviours (Fishbein and Ajzen, 2010), subjective evaluations of employee wellbeing may thus be more useful than objective wellbeing ratings when investigating the link between employee wellbeing and its potential outcomes. However, there are drawbacks with relying solely on self-report measures of

wellbeing (Kelloway, 2017), and we discuss some alternatives to these in the next section.

Definitions and operationalizations of wellbeing vary in terms of how inclusive they are (i.e., the extent of wellbeing's content domain). For example, Ilies and colleagues (2015) used a very inclusive definition of 'employee wellbeing' which encompassed positive moods originating from work as well as positive evaluations of aspects of work, including job satisfaction as an aspect of hedonic wellbeing. They also considered the quality of experiences employees have while at work (to capture eudaimonic wellbeing) and how these experiences affect life outside work, along with the potential negative effects work can have on employee wellbeing. Relatedly, wellbeing research has focused more specifically on the 'negative' side of employee wellbeing by examining indicators of poor wellbeing, such as burnout, or other stress-related symptoms (Sonnentag, 2015). Such an approach to measuring employee wellbeing may give a one-sided view of wellbeing, especially when considering the definition of hedonic wellbeing, which requires the presence of positive experiences and affect, not just the absence of the negative. Negative aspects, however, may be useful or necessary with other approaches to wellbeing; when measuring physiological wellbeing, for example, somatic indicators of stress, such as heart rate variability or high blood pressure, are clearer indicators than positive readings. We discuss a few examples of wellbeing measures, including physiological measures and their potential to complement self-report measures, in the next section.

HOW DO WE MEASURE WELLBEING?

A large variety of measures have been used to study subjective wellbeing (for reviews, see Cooke et al., 2016; Fisher, 2014; Hone et al., 2014; Vanderweele et al., 2020). One consideration when investigating employee wellbeing is whether it concerns work-specific wellbeing or general wellbeing (Kelloway, 2017; Warr and Nielsen, 2018). While contextualizing wellbeing to the workplace does, on one level, take into account that wellbeing is linked to specific contexts, it could lead to too narrow a view on the phenomenon. If only work-specific variables are used to determine employee wellbeing, other aspects outside of work that may be particularly impactful to the employee's wellbeing and behaviour at work may be overlooked. For example, in the specific case of eudaimonic wellbeing, it has been suggested (Bartels et al., 2019) that *workplace* eudaimonic wellbeing is different from *non-workplace* eudaimonic wellbeing, and that both general and contextualized wellbeing should be included to provide a more complete picture of employee wellbeing. These observations suggest that the decision on whether to use specific or general measures may not be completely straightforward.

A source of guidance for deciding which type of measures to utilize is the purpose for measuring employee wellbeing, including how the results are to be made use of. If working with an organization that would be interested in making practical improvements but that is less able to address deficiencies in wellbeing that are not directly related to work, for example, focusing on work-related measures may be more appropriate. Work-specific wellbeing may also be more suitable to focus on in cases where wellbeing is being measured after an intervention targeting specific organizational factors has taken place. General wellbeing, on the other hand, may be more useful to measure when evaluating interventions that target individual behaviours (Kelloway, 2017), such as healthy eating or stress management, since these may be less directly related to work-specific factors.

The decision on what type of measures to use to capture employee wellbeing, and to what extent measures are specific to the workplace context, can also be guided by a framework that has been established for categorizing interventions into primary, secondary, and tertiary types (Tetrick and Winslow, 2015). Involvement in a primary intervention (e.g., leadership development, training), where the measurement of employee wellbeing and other variables is part of an ongoing organizational approach (Leiter and Cooper, 2017), the scope tends to be broader and proactive, focusing on improving wellbeing in general and preventing wellbeing issues from arising – thus warranting the use of more general measures of employee wellbeing. For secondary interventions (Tetrick and Winslow, 2015), where the focus lies on providing support (e.g., stress coping, mindfulness) during a situation that poses risks to employee wellbeing, such as a restructure or external crisis, it may be that the measures need to be more specific and contextualized to allow for the examination of changes in specific factors. The most specificity in measures would be called for when evaluating tertiary interventions (Tetrick and Winslow, 2015), as such interventions are intended to address particular needs (e.g., related to nutrition, sleep, or stress management) that have arisen after a decline in wellbeing.

Overall, researchers and practitioners need to consider what aspect of employee wellbeing they are most interested in, as well as how the context that wellbeing is framed in (context-specific or general) affects their ability to address their research aims. We will describe some of the most commonly used types of self-report measures as well as other kinds of measures that could complement self-reports.

Hedonic wellbeing is often measured as the combination of positive affect, the absence of negative affect, and a general positive evaluation of, or satisfaction with, one's situation (Fisher, 2014). Positive and negative affect are often captured by the PANAS scale (Watson et al., 1988), which can be contextualized to the workplace. The satisfaction component is often assessed by scales measuring job satisfaction, organizational commitment, or engagement. Job satisfaction has been relied on heavily in previous studies as the primary or only measure of wellbeing, but this has been criticized for being too narrow an approach as it fails to capture a number of other aspects of wellbeing (Inceoglu et al., 2018; Wright and Cropanzano, 2000). Measuring additional aspects of wellbeing is thus recommended.

Increasingly, it has been suggested that both hedonic and eudaimonic aspects of employee wellbeing should be measured to gain a more complete understanding of the phenomenon, especially considering that they are correlated but add different types of information (Bartels et al., 2019) and that it is possible to have high levels of one but not the other (Nix et al., 1999). Measures focusing on the concept of 'flourishing' often include both hedonic and eudaimonic dimensions, as well as measures of social wellbeing and a general evaluation of satisfaction or happiness (see Hone et al., 2014 for an overview). The typical measures of flourishing are not work-specific and quite general, but they could be contextualized to the workplace, as proposed by Fisher (2014).

Eudaimonic wellbeing has received less attention in research on employee wellbeing, and has often been measured with scales capturing meaning or sense of purpose at work (Kożusznik et al., 2019) or, particularly, job involvement or work engagement (Fisher, 2014). Recently, however, there has been a growing interest in examining work-related eudaimonic wellbeing using scales specifically designed for this purpose. One such newly developed scale, by Bartels et al. (2019), captures interpersonal and intrapersonal aspects of eudaimonic wellbeing at work. The scale has been validated and shown to be separate from other wellbeing measures (positive and negative affect, satisfaction, and engagement) and adds incremental validity in predicting lower levels of turnover intentions and higher levels of creativity.

Most wellbeing measures comprise several different scales and approach wellbeing as a multidimensional construct, which results in a large number of items. In some scenarios, a global measure that captures hedonic, eudaimonic, and social aspects of wellbeing using a single dimension may be desirable. A global scale of this type, with a reasonably small number of items, is the Short Warwick-Edinburgh Wellbeing Scale (SWEWBS). It combines hedonic and eudaimonic types of wellbeing as well as an item tapping into social relationships (Stewart-Brown et al., 2009) in one seven-item scale. One potential drawback for those looking for context-specific scales is that the SWEWBS is not specific to the work context, but it may still be relevant if a more general assessment of employee wellbeing is sought.

The variety of self-report measures of employee wellbeing, and wellbeing in general, is large, and the selection of instrument needs to be guided by the purpose of measuring wellbeing. In general, however, an inclusive approach, where several dimensions of wellbeing are captured, is recommended. Such an inclusive approach also allows for the incorporation of measures gathered through methods other than self-report surveys. In the next section we discuss why this may be useful and present a few different options for the types of information that can be gathered and how to do so.

ALTERNATIVES TO SELF-REPORT MEASURES

Research based on self-report measures is often criticized in the research community. The concerns relate to the accuracy of these measures and whether individuals can be trusted to report honestly on how they are feeling. Reasons for not reporting honestly may relate to fears over a lack of anonymity and potentially facing negative consequences for responding truthfully as well as a tendency to portray oneself in a positive light (impression management and social desirability; Spector et al., 2017). Responses may also be less than accurate due to an individual's response style, in that some people tend to provide overly positive answers (leniency bias), while others tend to give more negative answers (severity bias) (Spector et al., 2017). A more technical criticism of self-report measures concerns the risk that associations between self-reported measures of wellbeing and other factors at work may appear stronger ('inflated') than they really are, since some of the association may be due to the source of the ratings being the same, i.e., the same individual, rather than the constructs being correlated (common method variance; Kelloway, 2017). The degree to which this factor may pose a threat to accurately revealing the nature of the relationships under study has been a question of debate (Lance et al., 2010; Spector et al., 2017). Nevertheless, it may be useful to explore other types of measures to complement self-report measures of employee wellbeing; exploring measures that may complement direct self-report measures of wellbeing may be useful. Such alternative measures range from indirectly inferring wellbeing from individuals' open-ended responses about events at work, to using sensors to capture physiological activity interpreted to represent wellbeing levels.

Research measuring wellbeing at work is increasingly adopting techniques from other fields, such as utilizing artificial intelligence and human-computer interaction. One technique, using machine learning, enables sentiment analysis by capturing emotions conveyed in text (Sailunaz et al., 2018). Sentiment analysis using text that the individuals have provided, for example about some phenomenon at work, could be used to assess employee wellbeing without directly posing questions to individuals, thus avoiding some of the potential effects of biases due to response styles discussed earlier. Such an approach would enable a more standardized analysis of qualitative data, which can be collected through interviews and then transcribed, or through open-ended questions in surveys where participants type in their answers. Although the technique is still in development (Sailunaz et al., 2018), it could prove to be a labour-efficient way of analysing data collected in organizations. Sentiment analysis of text can also be done in real time as the text is collected, for example via social media (Rout et al., 2018), which could be monitored to provide an early warning of changes in those wellbeing indicators detectable in text. These types of measures would potentially have high ecological validity since they can be collected outside the potentially artificial setting of a research study.

Other alternatives to self-report measures of wellbeing include those assessing physiological indicators, which have a long history of use in research on stress, but can be applied to research on wellbeing as well. The measures capture physiological activity, which is interpreted to be indicative of psychological states related to poor wellbeing. For example, Wong and Kelloway (2016) used blood pressure monitors that were worn by the participants over the course of a day, including during work and after work. The monitors gathered hourly ratings of systolic and diastolic blood pressure. Increases in blood pressure during the shift indicated the presence of an immediate stress response, and decreases in blood pressure after the shift were indicative of the ability to achieve appropriate cardiovascular recovery (Wong and Kelloway, 2016). Other frequently studied physiological indicators are heart rate and cortisol levels (Kelloway, 2017), where cortisol indicates individuals' reactions to events throughout a particular period. Day-level cortisol measurements require saliva or blood samples to be collected, making it an intrusive method for short-term measures. However, cortisol data can also be collected using hair samples, which would be appropriate for studying the chronic stress response (Russell et al., 2012), representing a less intrusive approach.

Recent developments in 'smart' technology can facilitate the capturing of physiological reactions, such as heart rate, skin conductance, and eye movements, in less intrusive ways, thanks to devices as small as a smart watch (Iakovakis and Hadjileontiadis, 2016) or a ring (Halkola et al., 2019). For example, heart rate can be tracked over time with small wearable devices that are hardly noticeable to the wearer. Skin conductance is indicative of physiological arousal and can be measured by small devices worn on one's finger as a ring (Torniainen et al., 2015). The gathering of information about eye movements and facial recognition can be done using web cameras mounted on computer monitors, and this information can be analysed to detect emotional states (Dzedzickis et al., 2020). The use of various sensors in the workplace can facilitate the capturing of wellbeing-related data without being intrusive (Halkola et al., 2019), thus providing an alternative procurable and broader basis of data with which to better understand employee wellbeing. Studying physiological responses would be even more informative in combination with self-report measures. This would enable the further validation of physiological reactions in relation to specific events and self-reported wellbeing levels (Halkola et al., 2019), and would clarify the relationships between physiological reactions and subjectively rated wellbeing. The use of 'smart technology' to capture employee wellbeing is not yet widespread but offers a potential complement to self-report measures.

STUDY DESIGN

Regardless of the types of measure used, the way the data is gathered also matters and will have a bearing on the choice of measures used. Different study designs (e.g., cross-sectional or longitudinal) can provide differing ranges of information for exploring various questions about employee wellbeing. A one-time measurement focusing on differences between individuals can be useful, for example for investigating which individuals have higher levels of wellbeing, as well as for exploring what other factors may be associated with these differences. Measurements that include more than one timepoint, that is, longitudinal designs, can reveal changes in individual levels of wellbeing, and are more appropriate for investigating what other factors the changes in wellbeing levels are associated with (Ilies et al., 2015). Information about such connections is more useful for those interested in addressing wellbeing deficiencies, since it can assist in examining factors which have contributed to lowered wellbeing as well as the consequences of lower wellbeing (Ilies et al., 2015; Kożusznik et al., 2019).

The longitudinal approach can also allow for the investigation of individuals' 'baseline' levels of employee wellbeing, which shows whether some people are typically always higher in wellbeing than others ('trait wellbeing'), and how the baseline wellbeing levels relate to fluctuations in employee wellbeing over time ('state wellbeing') (Ilies et al., 2015). Study designs which allow for examining trait and state employee wellbeing separately have been recommended, since many of the commonly studied wellbeing constructs are considered to be constituted by within-person and between-person components (Bakker, 2015; Ilies et al., 2015). In studies where intra-individual processes and changes over time are examined, it becomes possible to model fluctuations in individuals' wellbeing over a particular time period (Sonnentag, 2015). This fluctuation may depend on individual characteristics; Bakker (2015) suggests that employee wellbeing is a multilevel phenomenon, where factors such as personality and person-level wellbeing are considered higher-order constructs affecting daily wellbeing levels and daily work experiences. Such a conceptualization of employee wellbeing implies that wellbeing should be examined using study designs and measures that properly allow for analysing different levels of employee wellbeing at different levels (i.e., trait and state components).

When employee wellbeing is to be measured longitudinally, the appropriate measurement interval needs to be determined, based on the particular initiative and intended outcomes, and the temporal aspects of when changes in employee wellbeing may manifest (Spector, 2019). For example, investigating how an individual's wellbeing may vary throughout a day or a week requires a much shorter timeframe between measurements than examining changes in wellbeing after an organizational intervention program, which might not see changes come into effect for several months. Indeed, when the examination of employee wellbeing is in connection with a certain intervention, it is crucial to consider the expected time needed for any of the intended effects of the intervention to come into effect – and to schedule the measurement points so as to have the best opportunity of capturing any effects. In doing so, it can be helpful to use the 'time exposure' model (Zapf et al., 1996) as a guiding framework. Although this model concerns stressor effects, the main principles could extend to the relationships between work factors and employee wellbeing. It suggests, for example, that the relationship between stressors and reactions is not linear and that the stressor-strain relationship may look different depending on how long the stressor has been present (the 'exposure'). Alternatively, if individuals grow accustomed to the stressor ('adjustment model'), measuring a longer time after exposure may show a weak relationship, even if the reaction to the stressor initially was rather strong (Zapf et al., 1996). Application of this model to the measurement of employee wellbeing encourages that the intervals between measurements are based on a clear rationale based on theory or previous empirical studies of how different factors may affect wellbeing differently over time.

The timeframe and frequency of measurements may also affect the type of instrument that is used. Very frequent measurements would call for a scale with fewer items to keep participants motivated, while participants in less frequent surveys tend to be more tolerant of multi-item and multidimensional scales. In regard to time intervals between measures, longitudinal methods comprise a number of different options, including surveys distributed monthly or yearly, diary-type methods that are distributed daily or weekly (Bolger and Laurenceau, 2013), and experience-sampling methods (ESM; also called ecological momentary assessment, or intensive-longitudinal designs), where very short 'pulse' surveys are distributed throughout the day (Hektner et al., 2007; Shiffman et al., 2008). Pulse surveys can be distributed at set or random intervals or in connection with a specific event that the participant identifies (e.g., reporting on wellbeing after a stressful meeting) and can be labour intensive for the participant. The Day Reconstruction Method (DRM; Kahneman et al., 2004) has been developed to provide accurate responses about daily wellbeing levels without being as intrusive as experience sampling methods. This method asks participants to describe not only the activities and situations they experienced during the day but also their feelings about each of those activities or situations. The specificity of reporting is expected to help with recall, and the DRM has been shown to be a viable alternative to more intensive methods (Ilies et al., 2015; Kahneman et al., 2004).

Another aspect worth considering is the possibility that wellbeing is not just an individual phenomenon, but that it also exists in a meaningful way at the work-group or organization level, affecting associations between individual wellbeing and outcomes. This could be investigated by utilizing individual-level measurements of work-group wellbeing by aggregating them to the team or organizational level – thus arriving at a 'wellbeing climate' (similar to psychosocial safety climate, cf. Dollard et al., 2012) that can, in turn, be examined using multilevel analyses. This type of multilevel modelling may require adopting a different approach to the measurement of wellbeing, with work group wellbeing being assessed at the team level, and organizational wellbeing only measured at the organizational level. Assessing work-group wellbeing level may also benefit from types of metrics that are available independently of the work group members' ratings, such as work-group cohesion or climate as rated by a supervisor. This would result in a shift from focusing on direct indicators of employee wellbeing to a more indirect approach, assessing outcomes of employee wellbeing rather than wellbeing itself.

ETHICAL CONSIDERATIONS

Any measurement of employee attitudes or behaviours will require following high ethical standards and ethical principles: respect for persons, beneficence, and justice (Belmont Report, 1979). Following these guidelines may also help prevent attrition (or non-participation), which poses a challenge to collecting high-quality data on employee wellbeing. Concerns about attrition often lead researchers and organizations to explore ways of keeping surveys short. However, one way of reducing attrition and lack of participation is to ensure that the employee perspective is taken into account when collecting information on employee wellbeing, and one way of doing this is to follow ethical guidelines.

Commonly agreed-upon ethical guidelines for collecting information directly from individuals (see, e.g., Belmont Report, 1979) state that all participants (i.e., employees) need to be able to give their informed consent before providing any information (principle of respect for persons). To give such consent, they need to be fully informed about the purpose of the study. Employees should also know how the results will be addressed and how the results may affect them (principle of beneficence). In cases where action plans are involved, it should be clear whether they are to be directed at a particular group and that

employees will be treated fairly (principle of justice). Action plans provide an opportunity for organizations to engage with their staff and to inform employees about what has been done since the last survey, what will happen next, and how their feedback is being incorporated. In conjunction with measuring employee wellbeing, surveys can also explore how well employees feel the organizational action plans have been carried out, providing even more opportunities for employees to have a voice and to provide feedback, which can be incorporated into future action plans.

Common guidelines also state that anyone participating in data collection should be reassured that their responses will be treated confidentially. Measures which gather information about potentially sensitive issues may raise employees' concerns about the confidentiality of the information they are providing, which may influence their willingness to respond honestly (Spector et al., 2017) or to participate at all. One way of increasing participants' willingness to provide sensitive information is to make the surveys anonymous. However, in investigations that utilize individuals' responses from different time-points, it is necessary to link the data by using some sort of identifier to distinguish the unique participants (Saari and Scherbaum, 2011). When collecting identifying information, it is important to inform employees that this is being done and to let them know who will have access to this information and the individual responses. Another possibility is to have an external organization collect and report on the data; this ensures that no identifying information is handled or stored by the home organization. Regardless of who collects the identifying information, participants should also be reassured that when the results are presented, they will be presented in such a way that it will be impossible to trace responses back to any individual. If employees feel that their responses have been treated respectfully and with confidentiality, they will be more likely to participate in future surveys (Saari and Scherbaum, 2011).

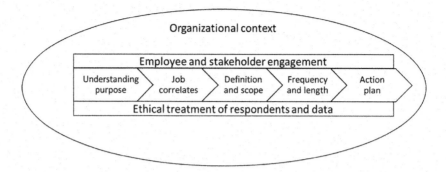

Figure 30.1. Key considerations for the measurement of employee wellbeing.

Anyone collecting information on employee wellbeing thus has to consider how the data collection is presented to the participants, so as to reassure employees that their privacy is protected and the results of the data collection will be used appropriately. Consideration should also be given to the storage of data, including how long data should be kept. Organizations should plan for and have a clear policy in place for data security, rather than relying on individuals for keeping data safe.

CONCLUSION

The aim of this chapter was to present a number of key considerations to guide researchers and practitioners in the decision-making process for selecting a suitable approach when measuring employee wellbeing. Figure 30.1 presents a model of these considerations. First, the reasons for gathering wellbeing data should be thoroughly scrutinized (e.g., be it research, monitoring, evaluation), and there should be engagement with the appropriate stakeholders to explain and discuss these reasons (e.g., informing employees of the purpose for collecting their responses). Second, additional measures of job correlates or precursors of wellbeing should be included in the measurement to provide a better basis for understanding what

contributes to wellbeing. This information can be used to inform organizations on actionable changes that can enhance wellbeing. Third, a consideration of what types of wellbeing to measure (e.g., hedonic, eudaimonic, societal, spiritual, physiological, qualitative, work-specific) and at what level the measurement is meaningful (i.e., individual, group) will further inform the selection of measures. Fourth, a consideration of how often to measure wellbeing will guide how long (in terms of number of items) the measurement instrument can be before employees disengage from the process. Throughout the process, continuous engagement with participants and stakeholders, as well as the adherence to ethical guidelines, will be vital to ensuring that the information collected will be used in a socially responsible manner.

The measurement of employee wellbeing is increasingly common, and while there is no one single measure that fits all situations, the considerations outlined in this chapter may be useful in navigating the different options available.

REFERENCES

Aked J, Marks N, Cordon C and Thompson S. (2009) *Five ways to wellbeing: A report presented to the foresight project on* communicating the evidence base for improving people's well-being. London: Nef.

Allin P. (2014) Measuring wellbeing in modern societies. In: Chen PY and Cooper C (eds) *Wellbeing: A complete reference guide, work and wellbeing.* New York: John Wiley, 409–463.

Bakker AB. (2015) Towards a multilevel approach of employee well-being. *European Journal of Work and Organizational Psychology* 24: 839–843.

Bartels AL, Peterson SJ and Reina CS. (2019) Understanding well-being at work: Development and validation of the Eudaimonic Workplace Well-being Scale. *PLoS ONE* 14: e0215957.

Belmont Report. (1979) *Ethical principles and guidelines for the protection of human subjects of research.* Washington, DC: Government Printing Office.

Bolger N and Laurenceau JP. (2013) *Intensive longitudinal methods: An introduction to diary and experience sampling research.* Cambridge: Guilford Press.

Chan D. (2009) So why ask me? Are self-report data really that bad? In: Lance CE and Vandenberg RJ (eds) *Statistical and methodological myths and urban legends: Doctrine, verity and fable in the organizational and social sciences.* New York: Routledge, 309–336.

Cooke PJ, Melchert TP and Connor K. (2016) Measuring well-being: A review of instruments. *The Counseling Psychologist* 44: 730–757.

Dewe P and Cooper C. (2012) *Well-being and work: Towards a balanced agenda.* Basingstoke: Palgrave MacMillan.

Diener E, Sapyta JJ and Suh E. (1998) Subjective well-being is essential to wellbeing. *Psychological Inquiry* 9: 33–37.

Dimoff JK, Kelloway KE and MacLellan AM. (2014) Health and performance: Science or advocacy? *Journal of Organizational Effectiveness: People and Performance* 1: 316–334.

Dollard MF, Opie T, Lenthall S, Wakerman J, Knight S, Dunn S, Rickard G and MacLeod M. (2012) Psychosocial safety climate as an antecedent of work characteristics and psychological strain: A multilevel model. *Work & Stress* 26: 385–404.

Durie MH and Kingi TKR. (1997) *A Framework for Measuring Maori Mental Health Outcomes: A report prepared for the Ministry of Health.* Massey University, New Zealand: Department of Māori Studies.

Dzedzickis A, Kaklauskas A and Bucinskas V. (2020) Human emotion recognition: Review of sensors and methods. *Sensors* 20: 592.

Fishbein M and Ajzen I. (2010) *Predicting and changing behavior: The reasoned action approach.* New York: Psychology Press.

Fisher CD. (2014) Conceptualizing and measuring wellbeing at work. In: Chen PY and Cooper C (eds) *Wellbeing: A complete reference guide, work and wellbeing.* New York: Wiley, 9–33.

Grant AM, Christianson MK and Price RH. (2007) Happiness, health, or relationships? Managerial practices and employee well-being tradeoffs. *Academy of Management Perspectives* 21: 51–63.

Halkola E, Lovén L, Cortes M, Gilman E and Pirttikangas S. (2019) Towards measuring well-being in smart environments. *Adjunct Proceedings of the 2019 ACM International Joint Conference on Pervasive and Ubiquitous Computing and Proceedings of the 2019 ACM International Symposium on Wearable Computers.* London: Association for Computing Machinery, 1166–1169.

Hektner JM, Schmidt JA and Csikszentmihalyi M. (2007) *Experience sampling method: Measuring the quality of everyday life.* Thousand Oaks, CA: Sage.

Hone LC, Jarden A, Schofield GM and Duncan S. (2014) Measuring flourishing: The impact of operational definitions on the prevalence of high levels of wellbeing. *International Journal of Wellbeing* 4: 62–90.

Huppert FA. (2009) A new approach to reducing disorder and improving well-being. *Perspectives on Psychological Science* 4: 108–111.

Iakovakis D and Hadjileontiadis L. (2016) Standing hypotension prediction based on smartwatch heart rate variability data: A novel approach. *Proceedings of the 18th International Conference on Human-Computer Interaction with Mobile Devices and Services Adjunct.* Florence, Italy: Association for Computing Machinery, 1109–1112.

Ilies R, Aw SSY and Pluut H. (2015) Intraindividual models of employee well-being: What have we learned and where do we go from here? *European Journal of Work and Organizational Psychology* 24: 827–838.

Inceoglu I, Thomas G, Chu C, Plans D and Gerbasi A. (2018) Leadership behavior and employee well-being: An integrated review and a future research agenda. *The Leadership Quarterly* 29: 179–202.

Kahneman D, Krueger AB, Schkade DA, Schwarz N and Stone A. (2004) A survey method for characterizing daily life experience: The day reconstruction method. *Science* 306: 1776–1780.

Kelloway EK. (2017) Toward evidence-based practice in organizational wellbeing: Methods and measures. In: Cooper CL and Leiter MP (eds) *The Routledge companion to wellbeing at work.* New York: Routledge, 70–82.

Kożusznik MW, Peiró JM and Soriano A. (2019) Daily eudaimonic well-being as a predictor of daily performance: A dynamic lens. *PLoS ONE* 14: e0215564.

Lance CE, Dawson B, Birkelbach D and Hoffman BJ. (2010) Method effects, measurement error, and substantive conclusions. *Organizational Research Methods* 13: 435–455.

Leiter MP and Cooper CL. (2017) The state of the art of workplace wellbeing. In: Cooper CL and Leiter MP (eds) *The Routledge companion to wellbeing at work.* New York: Routledge, 1–10.

Nix GA, Ryan RM, Manly JB and Deci EL. (1999) Revitalization through self-regulation: The effects of autonomous and controlled motivation on happiness and vitality. *Journal of Experimental Social Psychology* 35: 266–284.

Rout JK, Choo K-KR, Dash AK, Bakshi S, Jena SK and Williams KL. (2018) A model for sentiment and emotion analysis of unstructured social media text. *Electronic Commerce Research* 18: 181–199.

Russell E, Koren G, Rieder M and Van Uum S. (2012) Hair cortisol as a biological marker of chronic stress: Current status, future directions and unanswered questions. *Psychoneuroendocrinology* 37: 589–601.

Saari LM and Scherbaum CA. (2011) Identified employee surveys: Potential promise, perils, and professional practice guidelines. *Industrial and Organizational Psychology* 4: 435–448.

Sailunaz K, Dhaliwal M, Rokne J and Alhajj R. (2018) Emotion detection from text and speech: A survey. *Social Network Analysis and Mining* 8: 1–26.

Shiffman S, Stone AA and Hufford MR. (2008) Ecological momentary assessment. *Annual Review of Clinical Psychology* 4: 1–32.

Sonnentag S. (2015) Dynamics of well-being. *Annual Review of Organizational Psychology and Organizational Behavior* 2: 261–293.

Spector PE. (2006) Method variance in organizational research: Truth or urban legend? *Organizational Research Methods* 9: 221–232.

Spector PE. (2019) Do not cross me: Optimizing the use of cross-sectional designs. *Journal of Business and Psychology* 34: 125–137.

Spector PE, Rosen CC, Richardson HA, Williams LJ and Johnson RE. (2017) A new perspective on method variance: A measure-centric approach. *Journal of Management* 45: 855–880.

Spence JR, Brown DJ, Keeping LM and Lian H. (2014) Helpful today, but not tomorrow? Feeling grateful as a predictor of daily organizational citizenship behaviors. *Personnel Psychology* 67: 705–738.

Stanley DJ, Meyer JP and Topolnytsky L. (2005) Employee cynicism and resistance to organizational change. *Journal of Business and Psychology* 19: 429–459.

Stewart L and Gardner D. (2015) Developing mahi oranga: A culturally responsive measure of Māori occupational stress and wellbeing. *New Zealand Journal of Psychology* 44: 79–88.

Stewart-Brown S, Tennant A, Tennant R, Platt S, Parkinson J and Weich S. (2009) Internal construct validity of the Warwick-Edinburgh Mental Well-Being Scale (WEMWBS): A Rasch analysis using data from the Scottish Health Education Population Survey. *Health and Quality of Life Outcomes* 7: 15–15.

Tetrick LE and Winslow CJ. (2015) Workplace stress management interventions and health promotion. *Annual Review of Organizational Psychology and Organizational Behavior* 2: 583–603.

Torniainen J, Cowley B, Henelius A, Lukander K and Pakarinen S. (2015) Feasibility of an electrodermal activity ring prototype as a research tool. *2015 37th Annual International Conference of the IEEE Engineering in*

Medicine and Biology Society (EMBC), 6433–6436.

Vanderweele TJ. (2019) Measures of community well-being: A template. *International Journal of Community Well-Being* 2: 253-275.

Vanderweele TJ, Trudel-Fitzgerald C, Allin P, Farrelly C, Fletcher G, Frederick DE, Hall J, Helliwell JF, Kim ES, Lauinger WA, Lee MT, Lyubomirsky S, Margolis S, McNeely E, Messer N, Tay L, Viswanath V, Węziak-Białowolska D and Kubzansky LD. (2020) Current recommendations on the selection of measures for well-being. *Preventive Medicine* 133: 106004.

Warr, P., & Nielsen, K. (2018). Wellbeing and work performance. In E. Diener, S. Oishi, & L. Tay (Eds.), Handbook of well-being. Salt Lake City, UT: DEF Publishers. DOI:nobascholar.com

Watson D, Clark LA and Tellegen A. (1988) Development and validation of brief measures of positive and negative affect: The PANAS Scales. *Journal of Personality and Social Psychology* 54: 1063–1070.

WHO. (2006) *Constitution of the World Health Organization: Basic Documents, 45th edition, Supplement.* Geneva: World Health Organization.

Williams SD. (2018) Social responsibility and potential management interventions to address employees' post traumatic stress. *Review of General Management* 28(2), 22–29.

Wong JHK and Kelloway EK. (2016) What happens at work stays at work? Workplace supervisory social interactions and blood pressure outcomes. *Journal of Occupational Health Psychology* 21: 133–141.

Wright TA and Bonett DG. (2016) Job satisfaction and psychological well-being as nonadditive predictors of workplace turnover. *Journal of Management* 33: 141–160.

Wright TA and Cropanzano R. (2000) Psychological well-being and job satisfaction as predictors of job performance. *Journal of Occupational Health Psychology* 5: 84–94.

Zapf D, Dormann C and Frese M. (1996) Longitudinal studies in organizational stress research: A review of the literature with reference to methodological issues. *Journal of Occupational Health Psychology* 1: 145–169.

31

Evaluating Multicomponent Wellbeing Strategies: Theoretical and Methodological Insights

Jana Patey, Emike Nasamu, Sara Connolly, Kevin Daniels, Rachel Nayani and David Watson

INTRODUCTION

Current evaluation research in organizational health and wellbeing is challenged with comprehensively capturing the nature of complex interventions and assessing their effectiveness. Organizations that value employee health and wellbeing tend to operationalize a coherent programme, comprised of many components, and inclusive of interventions at individual and/or organizational level (Batorsky et al., 2016; Jordan et al., 2003). This complexity presents challenges to evaluators in terms of explaining the effectiveness of interventions, both individually and as part of an overall programme of activities, as well as delineating the underpinning mechanisms that lead to effectiveness or failure in particular settings. The design and implementation of interventions is dynamic and continuous as they tend to go through the process of co-creation by multiple stakeholders and, as such, integrate into the organization (Von Thiele Schwarz et al., 2016).

The design of complex social interventions can also be flexible, as they perform differently in different organizational contexts, thus claims of generalizability need to be approached with caution (Egan et al., 2009).

Whilst the implementation processes should be included in evaluation studies (Egan et al., 2009), it is not straightforward to establish the beginnings of implementation given the continuous nature of organizational change (Bauer and Jenny, 2013) and the length of the actual implementation chain (Pawson, 2014). When it comes to the assessment of intervention effectiveness, evaluators have also been challenged by decision-makers to provide means of assessing the interventions' outcomes in monetary values, so that resource allocation can be more effective. Yet, positive health and wellbeing benefits require a reliable conversion if they are to be reported in monetary terms.

Evaluation methods used to explore health and wellbeing practices (HWPs) and their effectiveness are conventional controlled trials (e.g., randomized controlled trials (RCTs), non-equivalent control groups) and more recent realist approaches. These approaches provide valuable research insights and are attractive to evaluators because of their enhanced internal validity for testing intervention theories along with the ability to explore theoretical mechanisms underpinning health and wellbeing interventions. In this chapter we embrace the need for conventional methods, in particular to provide a better evidence base on the economic effectiveness of health and wellbeing interventions, which has been largely inconsistent (Batorsky et al., 2016). This is despite the long-standing acknowledgement of the need to improve the evaluation of programme outcomes, and to include cost-benefit or cost-effectiveness analysis (Goetzel and Ozminkowski, 2008). However, conventional and realist methods have limited use when it comes to understanding how multicomponent health and wellbeing interventions that evolve over time come to be implemented and take effect. This leads to a gap in our understanding of appropriate methods to investigate fully the effectiveness of multicomponent interventions.

This chapter is split into two parts. Firstly, we advocate the need for a more dynamic and contextually grounded approach to evaluation of complex programmes involving multiple HWPs. We outline the shift of evaluation studies from conventional to realist approaches before examining challenges of realist evaluations. In advocating a more holistic evaluation approach, we explore the value of organizational change and highlight the contribution of processual studies. When discussing guiding principles and appropriate methodologies we focus on longitudinal multiple case study designs. Secondly, we suggest augmenting outcome evaluations by including cost effectiveness approaches. These approaches take into account not only the design, implementation and running costs of interventions but also assess positive health and wellbeing gains by drawing on life satisfaction measures.

FROM CONVENTIONAL TO REALIST EVALUATIONS

When it comes to evaluating health and wellbeing interventions, conventional methods that make use of a control group (randomized or non-equivalent) have traditionally received the highest quality ratings in systematic reviews and methodology guidelines (e.g. Snape et al., 2019). Whilst these methods are valuable and important in assessment of health and wellbeing interventions, their use in organizations to evaluate individual HWPs has been criticized (e.g. Nielsen 2013). One of their main limitations lies in following linear causation logic (i.e. intervention X causes outcome Y), and therefore conventional methods are best suited for the assessment of planned, discrete initiatives. Organizational tendencies to combine HWPs (Batorsky et al., 2016; Jordan et al., 2003) render it more difficult to isolate the unique effects of individual HWPs. As for the complex interventions, evaluation methods need to be able to capture how initiatives are being implemented in different contexts (Egan et al., 2009) whilst being subjected to adaptations, reflecting the continuous nature of change in organizations (Bauer and Jenny, 2013).

These are some of the factors that have led to the shift in evaluation design towards realist approaches, developing the evaluation question from 'does it work?' to 'what works, how, in which conditions and for whom'? Realist designs acknowledge that different HWPs, implemented in differing contexts, may play out in differing ways and potentially with different effects. The premise in realist evaluation is that an intervention may have multiple mechanisms activated in different contexts that have the same or varied outcomes. To accommodate the complexity, the realist evaluation model and methods focus on context-specific causal mechanisms that lead to intervention or programme outcomes (Pawson and Tilley, 1997). This model is expressed as Outcomes equals Context plus Mechanisms (CMO) (Dalkin et al., 2015; Pawson and Manzano-Santaella, 2012).

According to realist evaluation, mechanisms describe what it is about the programme that generates change, whilst context refers to the conditions under which a mechanism is activated. Theoretical explanation is achieved by the method of identifying, testing and refining CMO configurations, i.e. a specific mechanism (or mechanisms) activated in a specific context that causes an intervention to have an effect on some outcome or range of outcomes (Pawson and Manzano-Santaella, 2012). Realist evaluation is also theory-driven and requires researchers to first develop explanatory theories, which are then tested through discussion with organizational stakeholders and data collection leading to collective patterns of outcomes (Pawson, 2014; Pawson and Tilley, 1997). Evaluators engage in theorizing, hypothesizing and refining their CMO configurations alongside data gathering and analysis. Through this refinement a new/refined theory of propositional CMO configurations is generated (Pawson and Manzano-Santaella, 2012).

Despite realist evaluation gaining in popularity as a method for evaluating workplace health and wellbeing interventions, there has been a lack of progress in achieving a cumulative body of evidence (Pawson, 2014). As such, the theory-building goal of realist evaluation has not been achieved (Pawson and Manzano-Santaella, 2012). The contradiction between the popularity of realist evaluation and a lack of a body of evidence in workplace health and wellbeing research lies in application. Although researchers draw on the principles of realist evaluation (e.g. Abildgaard et al., 2019), there are few examples of the realist evaluation methodology. Some argue that this is due to a tendency by researchers to conflate realist evaluation with theory-driven evaluation by developing and testing hypothetical models rather than generating CMO configurations for further

testing and refinement (Chen, 1990; Marchal et al., 2012). Refinement is a key principle of realist evaluation and Pawson and Tilley (1997) argue that a single evaluation is insufficient to produce universally valid findings. Instead the evaluator builds an accumulation of insights to assess whether interventions that are successful in one setting may work in another and how, through a process of specification that often requires prolonged engagement in the organizational setting of the interventions.

The lack of progress in building a cumulative body of evidence may lie in part in practical and methodological challenges of conducting realist evaluation in organizational settings, and in part in the ways the method and model have been interpreted and applied (Pawson and Manzano-Santaella, 2012). In practice, many interventions are adapted over the course of implementation in order to address problems, requiring the evaluator to constantly amend and refine theorizing.

There is a diversity in the application of the principles of realist evaluation, with diverging views as to the nature of mechanisms and in distinguishing between mechanisms and context as well as a lack of substantial methodological guidance (Marchal et al., 2012). Unpacking causal chains and deciding which part to focus on is an additional complexity for realist evaluators. For example, Shaw et al. (2018) found that in complex programmes, CMO configurations may form a causal chain whereby mechanisms may lead to outcomes (e.g. social action) that themselves become contexts for subsequent CMO configurations. These methodological challenges mean that the realist evaluation method can become convoluted when applied to the complex interventions that are more common in organizations. A more dynamic and contextually grounded approach to evaluation is therefore required to complement and support current evaluation methods, thereby enabling examination of multicomponent programmes.

SHIFTING THE UNIT OF ANALYSIS

Although researchers have recognized that health and wellbeing interventions have a reciprocal relationship with the health of the whole organization, the focus of evaluation remains on interventions themselves (Bauer and Jenny, 2012; 2013). In realist evaluations the unit of analysis is wider – the programme theory that describes how the intervention works (e.g. Pawson, 2010). However, even this wider focus can neglect other important processes that can explain how interventions come to have their effects. Often, these factors are relegated to the 'omnibus' context of the intervention (i.e. the organization and its environment; Nielsen and Randall, 2013, after Johns, 2006). In turn, this wider context is seen as static and not affected by the intervention (Russell et al., 2016).

Past studies have viewed everything that is not part of the 'discrete', i.e. immediate delivery context of the intervention, as part of the omnibus context. Elements that are close to but not part of the intervention are treated in the same manner as more distal elements. For example, the competencies of human resources and occupational health practitioners (regarding decisions about what services to purchase, how to implement elements of a programme and its governance) are given the same weight as labour-market factors. This separation of context from the intervention is problematic, because the intervention is part of the context, as this example highlights. There is clearly a need for research to move away from the simply dichotomizing contextual factors into discrete and omnibus, or 'intervention' versus 'not intervention', to a more nuanced and fine-grained analysis.

Such analysis would require choosing methods that should be able to examine how different components of health and wellbeing programmes are decided upon, implemented, adapted and how they interact over time with existing components and components that are introduced at a later date. It is important to consider how the organizational context and context of the programme of health and wellbeing activities shapes and is shaped by the intervention.

Our proposal to use more dynamic and contextually grounded analyses of multiple and interacting interventions entails a shift in the unit of analysis from the intervention (and the intended beneficiaries) to the organization itself (and multiple stakeholders that influence or are affected by the intervention beyond the intended beneficiaries). Researchers have called for a move to using the organization as the unit of analysis (e.g. Herrera-Sánchez et al., 2017) rather than the intervention. However, this move does not lend itself to realist evaluation, which views the organization as a context within which workplace health and wellbeing practices take place (Fridrich et al., 2015; Nielsen and Randall, 2013).

Appreciating the complexity of organizational practice and recognizing that health and wellbeing programmes may have multiple elements also opens up new theoretical accounts of how interventions have effects over and above those mechanisms linked to the specific micro-theories that underpin specific interventions. For example, signalling theory (Bowen and Ostroff, 2004) would suggest that a well-governed and sustained programme of health and wellbeing activities would indicate organizational concern for worker wellbeing, in turn enhancing worker wellbeing through perceived organizational support (Huettermann and Bruch, 2019).

Overall, our argument is not that realist evaluations and the conventional approaches to researching discrete interventions are wrong, but that they are limited. Such research is needed because of enhanced internal validity and an ability to provide an evidence base to inform investment decisions based on (cost) effectiveness. However, such an approach to evaluation cannot reveal the whole story.

ENHANCING EVALUATION FRAMEWORKS OF MULTICOMPONENT STRATEGIES

The organizational change literature has been recognized in the field of evaluation research as valuable in addressing contextual and processual drawbacks of intervention studies (Biron and Karanika-Murray, 2014; Karanika-Murray and Biron, 2013; Von Thiele Schwarz et al., 2016). Biron and Karanika-Murray (2014: 97–99) recommend focusing on a) organizational drivers behind introducing interventions, b) organizational readiness for change, and c) the mechanisms through which positive change is achieved via interventions. These aspects of organizational change shed more light on how some interventions have their effects. However, they do not explain how we should think about analysing the processual and emergent nature of organizational change, and relationships between processes, contexts and outcomes.

When building into evaluation frameworks the awareness of organizational change, we firstly need to acknowledge the debates between organizational stability and fluidity, which are the premise of change theories (Dawson, 2012). For example, punctuated equilibrium theory proposes that organizations oscillate between the longer periods of gradual local adaptations when in equilibrium, and shorter, more radical change periods (Gersick, 1991). Morgan (1997) proposes understanding organizations through eight metaphors, one of which is to imagine the organization as 'flux and transformation'. Organizational phenomena, in this view, become processual and dynamic, rather than static (Schoeneborn et al., 2016). The processual approach re-focuses on 'the how and why of change', capturing the fluidity of processes of changing (a verb) instead of analysing organizational change per se, and situates the processes in the context and as unfolding over time (Dawson, 2012; Pettigrew, 1985: 15) and as emergent and continuous (Burnes, 2012).

Emergent Change, Sense-Making and Change Actors

Whilst recognizing that change has in fact become 'a way of organisational life' (Orlikowski, 1996: 64), the processual approach does not overlook planned, episodic changes. This approach recognizes that change actors (initiators, agents and recipients) interpret planned interventions which are also modified and adapted in practice (Weick, 2000). Such adaptations are not foreseeable at all times, and are also dependent on any other organizational events happening at the same time (Alvesson and Sveningsson, 2016: 31). Taking this realization into intervention research, we advocate accommodating both emergent and planned processes of changing into studies of multicomponent health and wellbeing programmes.

Planned change in organizations is recognized as routine-based and intermittent whereas emergent change is continuous, unfinished and organic (Weick and Quinn, 1999). Traditionally, discrete HWPs have been seen as part of planned change programmes. More recently, complex intervention studies have recognized continuous elements of change in interventions, and have begun to study them through the integration with organizational practices and structures, showing how interventions can evolve in unpredictable ways (Von Thiele Schwarz et al., 2016).

This is important because conventional and realist evaluations have not fully captured unplanned adaptations and outcomes arising from implementation of HWPs, apart from demonstrating new health-conscious preferences of organizational members, alongside improvements on their health and wellbeing. This is despite the acknowledgment of the evaluation literature that implementation processes of HWPs and their outcomes can be both intended and unintended (Bauer and Jenny, 2013: 10). Incorporating an awareness of change as continuous and emergent brings attention to the existence of informal, spontaneous initiatives. It shifts organizational culture and learning processes (Weick, 2000: 225), all of which are important in how health and wellbeing interventions are studied. For example, there is some evidence that interventions which facilitate social activities amongst staff can be seen as important in supporting HWPs (Daniels et al., 2017), but these initiatives and support networks could also arise spontaneously, be staff led and informal. Spontaneous, staff led initiatives would therefore escape those evaluators who focus solely on the use of conventional or realist approaches.

The examination of unanticipated change processes and outcomes means embedding sense-making in the analytical frameworks (Balogun, 2006). Sense-making is first and foremost a process and it focuses on how people come to their interpretations of events and things around them (Weick, 1995). In Weick's (1988) thesis, the action of talking or doing comes before cognition, since 'the clarification often works in reverse' (Weick, 1995: 11). Sense-making therefore refers to studying the continuous development of cognitive frameworks through which organizational members generate their interpretations (Weick, 1995). Studies of change interventions can include not only retrospective but also prospective processes of sense-making and sense-giving, examining mental frameworks of organizational members prior to the implementation of interventions, up to their every-day execution (Konlechner et al., 2019).

When discussing sense-making, we need to take into account its social properties (Weick, 1995). Firstly, because change interventions and subsequent actions are shaped by sense-making during social interactions, shared experiences, stories and gossip (Balogun, 2006), such phenomena should therefore be included in the examination of interventions. Secondly, to understand sense-making as social means paying attention to the roles of, in our case, change actors.

To illustrate, a longitudinal study of McLoughlin et al. (2005) targeted a work redesign intervention as a planned programme and analysed the interplay of change actors' own values and beliefs with the initiative. In this way, the research at first examined ambiguous and ambivalent experiences in response to the initiative. For example, because the opportunity of an intervention working party to voice workers' views was limited, the party members experienced frustrations and confusions when they had to address workers directly through the new organizational values of 'care'. At the same time, this research demonstrated the emergent consequences of this ambiguity over time and the role of the change actors in effecting the initial design and execution of the intervention.

The need to study the role of change agents, in particular, has already been recognized in the change literature, and the distinction has been drawn between studying agents as instigators of planned change programmes and as decision-makers who are making sense of and redirecting change (Weick and Quinn, 1999). Given the ambivalences and ambiguities inherent in organizational change (McLoughlin et al., 2005), evaluators should also give consideration to useful strategies and techniques (but also skills and capabilities) of change agents when navigating through the complex programmes, including facing workforce resistance (Westover, 2010).

So far, we have argued that in order to examine the effectiveness of multicomponent wellbeing strategies, a process approach that recognizes organizational change as emergent, i.e. dynamic, continuous, bi-directional and unfolding alongside planned events, is vital for current evaluation frameworks. There is also a need to consider sense-making processes and different roles of change actors to account for unplanned mechanisms and outcomes of change, as well as ambivalences, conflicts and resistance which accompany organizational change.

Context, Process and Outcome

Amidst different processual ontologies (see Langley, 2007; Langley et al., 2013) there are processual researchers who understand and study contexts, processes and their relationship to outcomes as unfolding over time, such as Pettigrew (1985, 1997, 2012). In this approach, processes as well as the relationship between context, process and outcomes, are shaped by underlying mechanisms (Pettigrew, 2012: 1316).

To explain individual components of the Context-Process-Outcomes (CPO) model, Pettigrew (1997: 338) shares the view of Van de Ven's (1992: 170) theoretical reading of processes as 'a sequence of individual and collective events, actions, and activities unfolding over time in context'. Therefore studying processes means focusing on different sequences within 'the dynamics of changing' (Pettigrew, 1985: 10). Context consists of embedded processes and structures which organizational actors are making sense of and are learning from. In this way, context does not only stimulate or constrain processes of organizing under study (in our case HWPs) but is also influenced and shaped by processes themselves (Pettigrew, 1997). Outcome or the effect that leads the study is considered to be an anchor for processual researchers (Pettigrew, 2012). In taking into account the variability of contexts and processes, processual analysis enables investigation of why and how outcomes differ in different circumstances (Pettigrew, 2012). However, because processes are continuously evolving, processual studies have also considered outcomes to be inputs, and seen them as somewhat artificial points in transit (Langley, 2007).

In the CPO model, processual studies aim to demonstrate the interconnectedness of the individual elements (Pettigrew, 2012). A starting point is to conduct vertical contextual analysis by observing how the inner context of organizational structures, culture and political landscape is shaped by socio-economical, political and sectoral factors of the outer context (Pettigrew, 1985). This interaction of contexts then influences the functioning of the organization and development of organizational processes (Pettigrew, 1992: 9).

To complete contextual analysis, Pettigrew's (1985: 36) processual approach recommends combining vertical analysis with horizontal analysis of processes, referred to as studying 'the sequential interconnectedness' of phenomena as they develop over time.

To combat the complexity of horizontal analysis, Sminia and Van de Ven (2012) propose examining a specific sequence of events from the past, leading to a key event as unfolding in the present and how a group of organizational members make sense of it. With regards to the future, we might ask what opportunities or challenges are envisaged by this group, and also what they believe should be done to navigate these challenges (Sminia and Van de Ven, 2012). The contextual analysis is complete once the variables of the inner and outer context or structure from the vertical analysis are linked with the process tracked in horizontal analysis (Pettigrew, 1985: 35–37). Such holistic analysis differs from the HWP evaluation research which recommends examining the 'fit' of HWPs with the wider organizational context by analysing distal and then omnibus environmental elements (Randall and Nielsen, 2012), suitable for discrete initiatives.

Emphasizing the importance of context, and keeping the principle of 'embeddedness' of processes within their contexts at the forefront of analysis, Pettigrew (1985: 37) underlines the need to change the focus of evaluations. Traditionally, health and wellbeing interventions are presented as one-directional triggers of change and thus the evaluation process starts with the interventions themselves. However, change is a bi-directional process of an unpredictable nature (Burnes, 2004; Lewin, 1943). It is helpful to challenge the evaluation process 'introducing X in order to impart a change in Y, where X is evaluated by comparing pre- and post-Y' (Karanika-Murray and Biron, 2013: 242). Instead the evaluation should re-focus to seeing X as the attempt to change Y in some way. Therefore, the organization and its context (Y) also need to be subjected to continuous evaluation, whilst seeing the processes of change between X and Y as working in both directions and being interconnected.

Through their work on psychological safety climate (PSC), Dollard and colleagues have highlighted the extension of the intervention into its context, demonstrating how and in what ways context shapes and can act as a moderator to the intervention itself (Dollard and Bakker, 2010; Dollard and Karasek, 2010). PSC is defined as policies, procedures and practices that govern psychological health and safety in organizations, and which are driven mainly by senior management (Dollard and Bakker, 2010). The existence of a good PSC as part of the macro-level context in organizations appears to follow from interventions to improve health and wellbeing (Dollard and Karasek, 2010), and also influences the development of work practices that enhance employee engagement and psychological health (Hall et al., 2010: 376).

PSC is assessed through a questionnaire, presently considered as the most advanced climate measure that explicitly evaluates the psychological health of employees (Dollard et al., 2019). However, whilst climate research has focused on attitudes, values, beliefs and behaviours of organizational members (Schneider et al., 2000), it cannot sufficiently capture the dynamics of changing organizational realities (Linstead et al., 2009: 158). Study of PSC analyses an intervention within its context, rather than dichotomizing contextual elements. In doing so it highlights that PSC can function as a mechanism in some instances, or moderate intervention effectiveness in others. Yet only studying climate still takes evaluators half way through the journey. An extension of work on PSC would be to include processual and emergent thinking of organizational change, in order to explore the interplay of the inner context of organizations in terms of their cultures and political landscapes with the outcome of the studied interventions (cf. Pettigrew, 1985).

Methodological Enhancement of Current Evaluation Approaches

So far we have argued for changing the focus of health and wellbeing intervention studies to the organization itself, and to build into current evaluation frameworks processual and emergent thinking about organizational change. In order to examine how and in what way multicomponent HWPs have their effects, we recommend conducting comparative longitudinal case studies.

Case study research has appealed to evaluation studies because it can capture the dynamics of phenomena under study within a single case or across multiple cases (Eisenhardt, 1989), as well as the dynamics of change unfolding over time set in context (Yin, 2014). Comparative longitudinal case studies have the ability to compare not only processes as sequences of events between cases but also patterns within them (Ferlie and McNulty, 1997: 376). Thus critical mechanisms that underpin the dynamic relationship between contexts, processes and outcomes can be explored in depth. When selecting case studies, it is recommended to choose settings where the phenomenon under study and its development is observable, and where opportunities are presented to identify and collect data on critical incidents or extreme events (Pettigrew, 1990). If a relatively small number of case studies is possible, then researchers should aim to select the sites that show relative differences between them over time, rather than aiming for opposites of a spectrum (Pettigrew and Whipp, 1991: 37).

With regards to data collection methods, such case study designs require multiple data sources and triangulation of the empirical data (Yin, 2014), which is processual, comparative, pluralist, historical as well as contextual (Pettigrew, 1990: 277). Processual research uses both quantitative and qualitative methods of data collection (Langley et al., 2013), and for the qualitative methods, the following are favoured – semi-structured interviews, participant and non-participant observation, documentary analysis (Dawson, 2003; Pettigrew and Whipp, 1991). Because researchers in longitudinal case studies are engaged with the case studies and collect data over the long term, being reflexive about involvement of the researchers and management of the data is also a strong feature of processual studies (Langley et al., 2013).

Our second part in arguing for the need to augment current evaluation frameworks involves enhancing outcome evaluations by learning from medical research and health economists, and to consider cost effectiveness analysis.

COST EFFECTIVENESS ANALYSIS (CEA): A WELLBEING APPROACH TO ECONOMIC EVALUATION

In this section we propose a method of economic evaluation which embeds wellbeing as its main measure of outcomes. We argue that this methodology improves upon traditional methods of economic evaluation in two ways. First, by using wellbeing as the benefit measure, the CEA evaluation accounts – albeit indirectly – for important variables which may change but lie outside the discrete intervention. Second, because interventions are targeted towards improving wellbeing, it is essential to consider wellbeing before and after the introduction of an intervention when assessing whether or not it is economically effective.

When decision-makers evaluate different options for interventions and weigh up different types of outcomes, they not only need to know why and how interventions work in different contexts but are mainly looking for reliable measures which are comparable across contexts. The approach favoured by government agencies and policy-makers is to conduct a Cost-Benefit Analysis (CBA). In a CBA, monetary costs and monetary benefits of each intervention are considered, and the intervention which yields the higher monetary benefit relative to monetary cost is selected.

Businesses, on the other hand, tend to favour a Return On Investment (ROI) approach when determining whether an intervention is worth the invested resources. Similar to the CBA, the ROI compares the monetary cost of an intervention to the monetary benefits of the intervention and returns net gain value for every £1 spent. Like CBA, ROI requires that all costs and benefits be successfully reduced to monetary values.

Whilst a case might be made for a wellbeing strategy on the basis of monetary outcomes, the outcome of interest in wellbeing interventions can be wellbeing itself (irrespective of whether there are intended performance gains through enhanced work engagement, for example). In these cases, the CBA and the ROI are not necessarily appropriate methods of evaluation, because there is currently no reliable method of converting wellbeing gains to monetary terms. Therefore, a different kind of approach is needed, one in which the costs are measured in monetary terms but wellbeing benefits are not. A cost effectiveness analysis (CEA) is often appropriate since it evaluates the cost of the intervention in monetary terms and evaluates the benefits of the intervention in terms of the broad objectives and outcomes of the intervention.

For example, in the field of medicine, health economists have adopted a CEA which weighs the cost of a new drug treatment or medical procedure against the health benefits of additional health years of life known as Quality Adjusted Life Years (QALY). In the UK, the National Institute of Clinical Excellence (NICE) set a threshold of £20,000 – £30,000 per QALY when recommending treatments for provision by the National Health Service. Treatments are approved where the cost of a QALY falls below this threshold. In the context of wellbeing, wellbeing benefits can be measured as the gain to life satisfaction over the number of years that the benefits of the intervention are expected to last, referred to simply as the wellbeing-adjusted life years (or WELBY; Layard, 2016; Peasgood and Wright, 2017). A wellbeing CEA provides a relative measure of costs and benefits known as the Cost Effectiveness Ratio; CER = Cost/ Wellbeing change.

Although, there are various ways to measure wellbeing (see Huppert, 2017) in response to the need for a parsimonious measure of wellbeing (Stiglitz et al., 2009), Layard (2016) argues that a measure of wellbeing needs to be meaningful to individuals in terms of providing a summary or an overview measure of their quality of life. It also needs to provide a clear single item metric for decision-makers who monitor wellbeing and thereby compare the wellbeing outcomes of various interventions or activities. Layard (2016: 4) proposed life satisfaction as a general measure on the basis that it meets these criteria and furthermore, 'it has validity and its causes have been widely studied'. Layard recommends life satisfaction to be measured on a 0–10 scale. As such, an extra unit of life satisfaction over a year is equivalent to one-tenth of a QALY. In terms of decision-making, the NICE threshold converts to a wellbeing benefit of between £2,000–£3,000.

Therefore, an intervention which can deliver an extra point in life satisfaction over a year and costs less than £2,000 – £3,000 is considered to be cost effective.

In practice, other metrics such as job satisfaction, mental health, self-esteem and social support may be more relevant to many workplace wellbeing interventions and organizations or researchers may monitor these instead of Life Satisfaction. In such cases, Layard (2016) proposes a set of exchange rates to convert between life satisfaction and wellbeing measures (see Table 31.1). The exchange rates are based on empirical estimates from the analyses of Mukuria et al. (2016) and Powdthavee (2012), where panel data have been used to examine the impact of changes in each of the wellbeing measures upon life satisfaction.

It will be noted that some of the measures considered are either closely related to Life Satisfaction or constitute some form of domain satisfaction which feeds into Life Satisfaction (for example job satisfaction).

Table 31.1 Conversion rates of different measures of wellbeing into life satisfaction.

Wellbeing measure	Range	Exchange rate
Life satisfaction (ONS[1])	0–10	1
Satisfaction with Life Scale[2]	5–35	0.24
Worthwhile (ONS)	0–10	0.75
Happy (ONS)	0–10	0.72
Anxious (ONS)	0–10	0.35
General Health Questionnaire[3]	0–36	−0.21
Short Warwick Edinburgh Mental Wellbeing Scale[4,5]	7–35	0.25
Satisfaction with job (BHPS[6])	1–7	0.49
Satisfaction with income (BHPS)	1–7	0.61
Satisfaction with amount of leisure time (BHPS)	1–7	0.57
Satisfaction with use of leisure time (BHPS)	1–7	0.62
Satisfaction with social life (BHPS)	1–7	0.60
Satisfaction with health (BHPS)	1–7	0.63

Source: Bryce et al., 2020, based on Layard (2016) Tables 1 and 2 and author's own calculations

[1] Office of National Statistics (ONS, 2011)

[2] Pavot and Dienner (2008)

[3] Goldberg and Williams (1988)

[4] Kamman and Flett (1983)

[5] Stewart-Brown et al. (2009)

[6] British Household Panel Survey (Taylor et al., 2018)

Where these types of measures are monitored, they can be translated into Life Satisfaction using these conversion rates. When the reported metrics are less directly related to Life Satisfaction and no conversion rate is available, a standard cost effectiveness analysis is not possible, but the costs can be calculated and assessed separately against the different dimension of measured wellbeing.

Workplace interventions will involve monetary costs with regards to delivery and participation, but can also yield some monetary benefits such as decreases in absence rates, decreases in turnover rates and increases in employee productivity. In order to ensure that benefits have resulted from the wellbeing intervention and not from other economic or workplace factors, these are best estimated by comparing employees who have received the wellbeing intervention (treatment group) to employees who have not received the intervention (control group – preferably with random allocation to treatment and control conditions). This would entail running pilot schemes. In larger organizations, it may even involve running pilots with different interventions to determine which is the most cost effective. However, this is unlikely to be feasible where there are complex multicomponent interventions, as it will be difficult to separate interventions and to have a conventional control group. In this case assessment tools such as CEA might be used alongside broad before and after measures of change informed by qualitative evaluations.[1]

Case Study

The following case study illustrates how health and wellbeing interventions can evolve over time. Graham is a medium-sized family-owned organization with a portfolio of businesses covering construction, asset management and investment projects, operating in the UK and Ireland. In 2017, Graham rolled out a programme, CONNECT, which replaced the traditional appraisal process. CONNECT was a means of integrating wellbeing concerns within day-to-day management processes. 'Standard' appraisals were replaced with formal 'commit' meetings with managers through 'CONNECT' to identify and develop personal goals. It was followed up with informal discussions as a proactive approach to development in the workplace with encouragement to identify and seek out training opportunities, which the company would support.

CONNECT was company-wide, so no comparisons of treatment or control groups were possible, but an economic assessment of the investment could be made. Graham experienced a 20% increase in employee engagement, a 4% decrease in staff turnover and a 50% decrease in sickness absences. The total cost for CONNECT (£220,164 for all 1,500 employees) was more than outweighed by productivity savings as a result of reduced sickness absences and lower staff turnover (£1,906,711). The intervention would clearly satisfy any economic evaluation since the net cost per employee is –£1,124 (i.e. a gain of £1,124 per employee).

Through the CONNECT programme, Graham discovered other avenues for improving employee wellbeing. By 2018, Graham had launched another wellbeing programme, known as CONNECT+, which provided coaching-led, personalized wellbeing plans and resources to their employees. CONNECT+ was rolled out to a group of 400 employees in the first instance, in order to evaluate its cost and wellbeing effectiveness.

Whilst not a formal trial, it is possible to compare the outcomes for the CONNECT+ study group against those for other employees. The productivity savings as a result of reduced sickness absences and reduced turnover rates outweigh the total cost for CONNECT+, yielding a net cost per employee within the study group of –£2,471 (again a monetary gain). Both interventions are not only value for money, they are investments which yield measurable monetary dividends through the significant impact upon productivity. As a consequence, a CEA is not necessary. However, the productivity savings of some interventions may not outweigh the costs and would therefore fail to meet standard economic evaluations. In such cases a CEA should be used because improved wellbeing is the goal of the intervention and as such may outweigh a positive net cost. The CEA thus provides clear guidance to establishing when an intervention is cost effective.

CONCLUSION

Evaluation of health and wellbeing interventions in the workplace have moved from using conventional to realist approaches. The development of realist methodologies reflects an increasing awareness of the importance of context and process. However, this kind of approach can only take us so far in understanding how and why complex multicomponent approaches support wellbeing in organizations, albeit existing methods are notably valuable in the evaluations of outcomes and can be augmented by economic analyses that focus on the ratios of wellbeing benefits to costs, as demonstrated in our chapter.

Understanding the intricacies behind design, implementation and evaluation of HWPs, which often occur in combinations, requires more dynamic and contextually sensitive methodologies. We have proposed to do so by exploring how and why processes of organizing behind HWPs change and how they interact with their contexts. We have also proposed supplementing existing methods of evaluation with longitudinal comparative case studies. This would enable the focus of analysis to shift from intervention/s to the organizational entity and its wider environment, acknowledging the importance and dynamism of organizational context in underpinning effective and sustainable health and wellbeing interventions.

ACKNOWLEDGEMENT

Preparation of this chapter was supported by Economic and Social Research Council grant numbers ES/N003586/1 and ES/S012648/1

Note

1 Bryce et al. (2020) have developed a cost effectiveness calculator which can be used to evaluate workplace interventions. The calculator provides guidance on estimating and interpreting the CER.

REFERENCES

Abildgaard JS, Nielsen K, Wåhlin-Jacobsen CD, Maltesen T, Christensen KB and Holtermann A (2019) Same, but different: A mixed-methods realist evaluation of a cluster-randomised controlled participatory organizational intervention. *Human Relations*. Epub ahead of print 17 October 2019. DOI: 10.1177/0018726719866896.

Alvesson M and Sveningsson S (2016) *Changing organizational culture: Cultural change work in progress*. 2nd edn. London: Routledge.

Balogun J (2006) Managing change: Steering a course between intended strategies and unanticipated outcomes. *Long Range Planning* 39(1): 29–49.

Batorsky B, Van Stolk C and Liu H (2016) Is more always better in designing workplace wellness programs? A comparison of wellness program components versus outcomes. *Journal of Occupational and Environmental Medicine* 58(10): 987–993.

Bauer GF and Jenny GJ (2012) Moving towards positive organizational health: Challenges and a proposal for a research model of organizational health development. In: Houdmont J, Leka S and Sinclair R (eds) *Contemporary occupational health psychology: Global perspectives on research and practice*. Oxford: Wiley-Blackwell, pp. 126–145.

Bauer GF and Jenny GJ (eds) (2013) *Salutogenic organizations and change: The concepts behind organizational health intervention research*. Dordrecht: Springer.

Biron C and Karanika-Murray M (2014) Process evaluation for organizational stress and wellbeing interventions: Implications for theory, method, and practice. *International Journal of Stress Management* 21(1): 85–111.

Bowen DE and Ostroff C (2004) Understanding HRM–firm performance linkages: The role of the 'strength' of the HRM system. *Academy of Management Review* 29(2): 203–221.

Bryce A, Bryan M, Connolly S and Nasamu E (2020) *Workplace Cost Effectiveness Analysis (CEA) calculator: Guidance document.* London: What Works Centre For Wellbeing.

Burnes B (2004) Kurt Lewin and the planned approach to change: A re-appraisal. *Journal of Management Studies* 41(6): 977–1002.

Burnes B (2012) Understanding the emergent approach to change. In: Boje DM, Burnes B and Hassard J (eds) *The Routledge companion to organizational change*. London and New York: Routledge, pp. 133–145.

Chen HT (1990) Issues in constructing program theory. *New Directions for Evaluation* 47: 7–18.

Dalkin SM, Greenhalgh J, Jones D, Cunningham B and Lhussier M (2015) What's in a mechanism? Development of a key concept in realist evaluation. *Implementation Science* 10, article no. 49.

Daniels K, Watson D and Gedikli C (2017) Wellbeing and the social environment of work: A systematic review of intervention studies. *International Journal of Environmental Research and Public Health* 14(8), article no. 918.

Dawson P (2003) *Reshaping change: A processual perspective*. London and New York: Routledge.

Dawson P (2012) The contribution of the processual approach to the theory and practice of organizational change. In: Boje DM, Burnes B and Hassard J (eds) *The Routledge companion to organizational change*. London: Routledge, pp. 119–132.

Dollard MF and Bakker AB (2010) Psychosocial safety climate as a precursor to conducive work environments, psychological health problems, and employee engagement. *Journal of Occupational and Organizational Psychology* 83(3): 579–599.

Dollard MF and Karasek RA (2010) Building psychosocial safety climate: Evaluation of a socially coordinated PAR risk management stress prevention study. In: Houdmont J and Leka S (eds) *Contemporary occupational health psychology: Global perspectives on research and practice, Volume 1*. Hoboken: Wiley-Blackwell, pp. 208–233.

Dollard MF, Dormann C and Awang Idris M (eds) (2019) *Psychosocial safety climate: A new work stress theory*. Cham: Springer.

Egan M, Bambra C, Petticrew M and Whitehead M (2009) Reviewing evidence on complex social interventions: Appraising implementation in systematic reviews of the health effects of organisational-level workplace interventions. *Journal of Epidemiology & Community Health* 63(1): 4–11.

Eisenhardt KM (1989) Building theories from case study research. *Academy of Management Review* 14(4): 532–550.

Ferlie E and McNulty T (1997) Going to market: Changing patterns in the organisation and character of process research. *Scandinavian Journal of Management* 13(4): 367–387.

Fridrich A, Jenny GJ and Bauer GF (2015) The context, process, and outcome evaluation model for organisational health interventions. *BioMed Research International*, article no 414832.

Gersick CTG (1991) Revolutionary change theories: A multilevel exploration of the punctuated equilibrium paradigm. *The Academy of Management Review* 16(1): 10–36.

Goetzel RZ and Ozminkowski RJ (2008) The health and cost benefits of work site health-promotion programs. *Annual Review of Public Health* 29(1): 303–323.

Goldberg DP and Williams P (1988) *A user's guide to the General Health Questionnaire*. Windsor: NFER-Nelson Publications.

Hall GB, Dollard MF and Coward J (2010) Psychosocial safety climate: Development of the PSC-12. *International Journal of Stress Management* 17(4): 353–383.

Herrera-Sánchez IM, León-Pérez JM and León-Rubio JM (2017) Steps to ensure a successful implementation of occupational health and safety interventions at an organizational level. *Frontiers in Psychology* 8, article no. 2135.

Huettermann H and Bruch H (2019) Mutual gains? Health-related HRM, collective wellbeing and organizational performance. *Journal of Management Studies* 56(6): 1045–1072.

Huppert FA (2017) *Measurement really matters*. Discussion Paper 2, Measuring Wellbeing Series, What Works Centre for Wellbeing. Available at: https://whatworkswellbeing.org/resources/measuring-wellbeing-series/ (accessed 20 June 2020).

Johns G (2006) The essential impact of context on organizational behaviour. *Academy of Management Review* 31(2): 386–408.

Jordan J, Gurr E, Tinline G, Giga SI, Faragher B and Cooper CL (2003) *Beacons of excellence in stress prevention: Research Report 133.* London: HSE Books. Available at: www.hse.gov.uk/research/rrhtm/rr133.htm (accessed 2 February 2020).

Kamman R and Flett R (1983) Affectometer 2: A scale to measure current level of general happiness. *Australian Journal of Psychology* 35(2): 259–265.

Karanika-Murray M and Biron C (2013) The nature of change in organizational health interventions: Some observations and propositions. In: Bauer GF and Jenny GJ (eds) *Salutogenic organizations and change: The concepts behind organizational health intervention research.* Dordrecht: Springer, pp. 239–259.

Konlechner S, Latzke M, Güttel WH and Höfferer E (2019) Prospective sensemaking, frames and planned change interventions: A comparison of change trajectories in two hospital units. *Human Relations* 72(4): 706–732.

Langley A (2007) Process thinking in strategic organization. *Strategic Organization* 5(3): 271–282.

Langley A, Smallman C, Tsoukas H and Van de Ven AH (2013) Process studies of change in organization and management: Unveiling temporality, activity, and flow. *Academy of Management Journal* 56(1): 1–13.

Layard R (2016) *Measuring wellbeing and cost-effectiveness analysis using subjective wellbeing.* Discussion Paper 1. Measuring Wellbeing Series, What Works Centre for Wellbeing. Available at: https://whatworkswellbeing.files.wordpress.com/2016/08/common-currency-measuring-wellbeing-series-1-dec-2016.pdf (accessed 20 June 2020).

Lewin K (1943) Psychological ecology. In: Cartwright D (ed.) (1951) *Field theory in social science: Selected theoretical papers.* New York: Harper & Brothers Publishers, pp. 170–187.

Linstead S, Fulop L and Lilley S (2009) *Management and organization: A critical text.* 2nd ed. Basingstoke: Palgrave Macmillan.

Marchal B, Van Belle S, Van Olmen J, Hoerée T and Kegels G (2012) Is realist evaluation keeping its promise? A review of published empirical studies in the field of health systems research. *Evaluation* 18(2): 192–212.

McLoughlin IP, Badham RJ and Palmer G (2005) Cultures of ambiguity: Design, emergence and ambivalence in the introduction of normative control. *Work, Employment and Society* 19(1): 67–89.

Morgan G (1997) *Images of organization.* Thousand Oaks, CA: Sage.

Mukuria C, Rowen D, Peasgood T and Brazier J (2016) *An empirical comparison of wellbeing measures used in UK.* Policy Research Unit in Economic Evaluation of Health and Social Care Interventions. EEPRU Research Interim Report RR 0027: The University of Sheffield and The University of York.

Nielsen K (2013) Review Article: How can we make organizational interventions work? Employees and line managers as actively crafting interventions. *Human Relations* 66(8): 1029–1050.

Nielsen K and Randall R (2013) Opening the black box: Presenting a model for evaluating organizational-level interventions. *European Journal of Work and Organizational Psychology* 22(5): 601–617.

Office for National Statistics (2011) *Initial investigation into subjective well-being from the opinions survey.* Available at: www.ons.gov.uk/ons/rel/wellbeing/measuring-subjective-wellbeing-in-the-uk/investigation-of-subjective-well-being-data-from-the-ons-opinions-survey/index.html (accessed 2 February 2020).

Orlikowski WJ (1996) Improvising organizational transformation over time: A situated change perspective. *Information Systems Research* 7(1): 63–92.

Pavot W and Diener E (2008) The satisfaction with life scale and the emerging construct of life satisfaction. *The Journal of Positive Psychology* 3(2): 137–152.

Pawson R (2010) Middle range theory and program theory evaluation: from provenance to practice 1. In: Vaessen J and Leeuw FL (eds) *Mind the gap: Perspectives on policy evaluation and the social sciences.* New York: Routledge, pp. 171–202.

Pawson R (2014) *The science of evaluation: A realist manifesto.* London: Sage.

Pawson R and Manzano-Santaella A (2012) A realist diagnostic workshop. *Evaluation* 18(2): 176–191.

Pawson R and Tilley N (1997) An introduction to scientific realist evaluation. In: Chelimsky

E and Shadish WR (eds) *Evaluation for the 21st century: A handbook*. Thousand Oaks, CA: Sage, pp. 405–418.

Peasgood T and Wright L (2017) *A guide to wellbeing economic evaluation*. What Works Centre for Wellbeing. Available at: https://whatworkswellbeing.org/product/a-guide-to-wellbeing-economic-evaluation/ (accessed 3 February 2020).

Pettigrew AM (1985) *The awakening giant: Continuity and change in imperial chemical industries*. Oxford: Basil Blackwell Ltd.

Pettigrew AM (1990) Longitudinal field research on change: Theory and practice. *Organization Science* 1(3): 267–292.

Pettigrew AM (1992) The character and significance of strategy process research. *Strategic Management Journal* 13(52): 5–16.

Pettigrew AM (1997) What is a processual analysis? *Scandinavian Journal of Management* 13(4): 337–348.

Pettigrew AM (2012) Context and action in the transformation of the firm: A reprise. *Journal of Management Studies* 49(7): 1304–1328.

Pettigrew AM and Whipp R (1991) *Managing change for competitive success*. Oxford: Blackwell.

Powdthavee N (2012) Jobless, friendless and broke: What happens to different areas of life before and after unemployment? *Economica* 79(315): 557–575.

Randall R and Nielsen K (2012) Does the intervention fit? An explanatory model of intervention success and failure in complex organizational environments. In: Biron C, Kranika-Murray M and Cooper C (eds) *Improving organizational interventions for stress and well-being: Addressing process and context*. London: Routledge, pp. 120–134.

Russell J, Berney L, Stansfeld S, Lanz D, Kerry S, Chandola T and Bhui K (2016) The role of qualitative research in adding value to a randomised controlled trial: Lessons from a pilot study of a guided e-learning intervention for managers to improve employee wellbeing and reduce sickness absence. *Trials* 17(1), article no. 396.

Schneider B, Bowen D, Ehrhart M and Holcombe K (2000) The climate for service: Evolution of a construct. In: Ashkanasy NM, Wilderom CPM and Peterson MF (eds)

Handbook on organizational culture & climate. Thousand Oaks, CA: Sage, pp. 21–36.

Schoeneborn D, Vásquez C and Cornelissen J (2016) Imagining organization through metaphor and metonymy: Unpacking the process-entity paradox. *Human Relations* 69(4): 915–944.

Shaw J, Gray CS, Baker GR, Denis JL, Breton M, Gutberg J, Embuldeniya G, Carswell P, Dunham A, McKillop A and Kenealy T (2018) Mechanisms, contexts and points of contention: Operationalizing realist-informed research for complex health interventions. *BMC Medical Research Methodology* 18, article no. 178.

Sminia H and Van de Ven AH (2012) Aligning process questions, perspectives, and explanations. In: Schultz M, Maguire S, Langley A and Tsoukas H (eds) *Constructing identity in and around organizations*. Oxford: Oxford University Press, pp. 307–319.

Snape D, Meads C, Bagnall A-M, Tregaskis O, Mansfield L, MacLennan S and Brunetti S (2019) *A guide to our evidence review methods*. What Works Centre for Wellbeing. Available at: https://whatworkswellbeing.org/wp-content/uploads/2020/02/WWCW-Methods-Guide-FINAL-APRIL-2019a.pdf (accessed 1 May 2020).

Stewart-Brown S, Tennant A, Tennant R, Platt S, Parkinson J and Weich S (2009) Internal construct validity of the Warwick-Edinburgh mental well-being scale (WEMWBS): A Rasch analysis using data from the Scottish health education population survey. *Health and Quality of Life Outcomes* 7, article no. 15.

Stiglitz JE, Sen A and Fitoussi J-P (2009) *Report by the Commission on the measurement of economic performance and social progress*. Available at: https://ec.europa.eu/eurostat/documents/8131721/8131772/Stiglitz-Sen-Fitoussi-Commission-report.pdf (accessed 20 June 2020).

Taylor MF, Brice J, Buck N, Prentice-Lane E (2018) *British household panel survey user manual Volume A: Introduction, Technical Report and Appendices*. University of Essex, Colchester.

Van de Ven AH (1992) Suggestions for studying strategy process: A research note. *Strategic Management Journal* 13(S1): 169–188.

Von Thiele Schwarz U, Lundmark R and Hasson H (2016) The Dynamic Integrated Evaluation Model (DIEM): Achieving sustainability in organizational intervention through a participatory evaluation approach. *Stress Health* 32(4): 285–293.

Weick KE (1988) Enacted sensemaking in crisis situations. *Journal of Management Studies* 25(4): 305–317.

Weick KE (1995) *Sensemaking in organizations*. Thousand Oaks, CA: Sage.

Weick KE (2000) Emergent change as a universal in organizations. In: Beer M and Nohria N (eds) *Breaking the code of change*. Boston, MA: Harvard Business School Press, pp. 223–241.

Weick KE and Quinn RE (1999) Organizational change and development. *Annual Review of Psychology* 50(1): 361–386.

Westover JH (2010) Managing organizational change: Change agent strategies and techniques to successfully managing the dynamics of stability and change in organizations. *International Journal of Management and Innovation* 2(1): 45–50.

Yin RK (2014) *Case study research: Design and methods*. 5th edn. Thousand Oaks, CA: Sage.

32

Indigenous Peoples' Perspectives and Wellbeing in Organizational Life

Jarrod Haar and Azka Ghafoor

INTRODUCTION

The world is more connected than at any time in its history. The ability to travel, immigrate, and integrate globally means that many workplaces enjoy employees from around the globe. Within western economies, some are dominated by largely white populations, while other societies are more diverse. For example, the UK has a population with over 86% white (Office for National Statistics, 2012), while New Zealand has 70.2% white (Statistics New Zealand, 2019a), and the United States 60.1% white (United States Census Bureau, 2020). Canada has a very broad ethnic spread (Statistics Canada, 2016) with 32.3% Canadians, but with other UK ethnicities equating to 45.7% and French with 13.6%. While these examples reflect growing ethnic minorities in many countries, how indigenous[1] populations function and succeed – especially within the workplace – is much more poorly understood.

The United Nations reports that there are an estimated 370 million indigenous people in the world. There are indigenous people all over the globe, through the Americas (e.g., the Lakota in the United States, the Mayas in Guatemala, and the Aymaras in Bolivia), the circumpolar region (e.g., the Inuit and Aleutians), northern Europe (e.g., the Saami), and the Asia Pacific region (e.g., the Ainu of Japan, Jarai of Vietnam, the Māori of New Zealand, and the Aborigines and Torres Strait Islanders of Australia). Overall, indigenous people live in 90 countries, speak the majority of the world's estimated 7,000 languages and represent 5,000 different cultures (United Nations, 2009). United Nations (2020b) states the following about indigenous people:

Indigenous peoples are inheritors and practitioners of unique cultures and ways of relating to people and the environment. They have retained social, cultural, economic and political characteristics that are distinct from those of the dominant societies in which they live. Despite their cultural differences, indigenous peoples from around the world share common problems related to the protection of their rights as distinct peoples.

In New Zealand, Māori account for 16.5% of the population (Statistics New Zealand, 2019b), making them one of the largest indigenous groups (by proportion) in the world. The indigenous peoples in Vietnam, with 54 recognized ethnic groups, account for 14.6% of the national population of 95 million (IWGIA, 2020). However, many of the indigenous peoples – especially those in western cultures – occupy much smaller proportions of their respective populations. Canada reports 4.9% of their population as indigenous, representing First Nations, Métis, and Inuit peoples. The Australian Bureau of Statistics (2018) puts the Aboriginal and Torres Strait Islander population of Australia at 3.3%, while the United States Census Bureau (2020) reports that the United States has small indigenous populations of American Indian and Alaska Natives (1.3%) and Native Hawaiian and other Pacific Islanders (0.2%).

Despite this modest global proportion, indigenous populations are the focus of the present chapter because they universally report poorer wellbeing. For example, poverty is still high among ethnic minorities. Indeed, despite making up less than 5% of the world's population, indigenous people account for 15% of the poorest (United Nations, 2020a). In a more specific example, within Vietnam, the poverty rate was 23.1% for indigenous peoples, while the national poverty rate was 7% (IWGIA, 2020). Unfortunately, given the small proportions that indigenous people make up in their populations, their minority voice appears to go unheeded – including wellbeing. Overall, the evidence suggests that indigenous people around the world have among the worst rates of wellbeing (Jordan et al., 2010; Prout, 2012).

The present chapter seeks to broadly scope the research around indigenous employee wellbeing, providing details about what is known and can be inferred, and provide key insights into issues for indigenous wellbeing research. Following that, some indigenous approaches to wellbeing are presented, with a focus on Māori wellbeing models, predominantly because they dominate the indigenous wellbeing literature. From these literatures, we identify important gaps in the literature and encourage more research on indigenous employee wellbeing. To complement this research focus, one approach to indigenous research is offered towards helping students and researchers engage appropriately in indigenous employee studies. A future agenda for research is finally presented within the context of indigenous wellbeing in organizational life.

LITERATURE REVIEW

The United Nations (2009: 41) states 'there has been a concerted process to define global indicators for indigenous peoples' wellbeing, which includes, among other factors, health and material wellbeing. This puts the wellbeing of indigenous people as a global issue warranting greater attention. Beyond material wealth, there are also aspects like indigenous peoples using a non-western lens (for example) to view their world and lived experiences (United Nations, 2009). For example, indigenous people hold greater respect and reverence for the land, and therefore indigenous wellbeing is seen as being indistinguishable from their relationship with the land and traditional practices (United Nations, 2006). Doyle (2009) argues that to enhance the wellbeing of indigenous peoples requires new ways of examining their experiences. The present section seeks to draw on such literature to enable insights to be gained.

Fundamentally, when we consider the wellbeing of indigenous peoples in organizational life, there are a number of common issues with most indigenous populations. These include: (1) the challenges to wellbeing through employment, given most indigenous populations have high unemployment – and by this nature, the insecurity around work; (2) a lack of understanding around indigenous models of wellbeing; and (3) how to conduct indigenous research around wellbeing.

UNEMPLOYMENT AND WELLBEING

One of the drivers of the wellbeing inequalities is likely to be job insecurity. Most societies with indigenous populations report significantly higher rates of unemployment. Statistics New Zealand (2020) reports that the unemployment rate for New Zealand Europeans (the ethnic majority) is 3.5% compared to the indigenous population (Māori), which is 8.7% (249% higher for the indigenous peoples). The underutilization rate, which is a proportion of those in the extended labor force (including unemployed and underemployed) is 9.7% for New Zealander Europeans but 18.9% for indigenous Māori (190% higher for the indigenous peoples). The United States Bureau of Labor Statistics (2019) reports that the indigenous population (American Indians and Alaska Natives) unemployment was 6.6%, higher than the rate of 3.9% for the rest of the country (169% higher for the indigenous peoples). However, when indigenous peoples' unemployment is compared to just white Americans (3.5% unemployment), the difference between the majority ethnic group is again higher (189%). Further, we find this indigenous group has a significantly lower labor force participation rate and the United States Bureau of Labor Statistics (2019) notes that this occurred across the entire time of following this data (since the early 2000s).

In Canada, the unemployment rate is 5.5% for non-indigenous employees and 10.1% for the indigenous populations, representing a 184% higher rate of unemployment (Statistics Canada, 2020). However, the labour force participation rate is much closer at 65.7% for non-indigenous and 63.9%

for indigenous groups (Statistics Canada, 2020). Vietnam is an interesting case because unemployment is extremely low, although Demombynes and Testaverde (2018: 5) state 'the profile of employment is complex', and 'the unemployment rate – calculated as per the International Labor Organization definition – is extremely low. Just 1 million people (2% of those in the labor force) are classified as unemployed'. It is noted that farming is the dominant occupation among indigenous workers (Demombynes and Testaverde, 2018) perhaps reflecting subsistence living, although it is noted that indigenous people are 12.3% less likely to be in paid employment. Finally, the Australian Bureau of Statistics (2019) reports stark levels of employment, with Aborigines and Torres Strait Islanders reporting 46.6% employment compared to 71.8% for non-indigenous peoples. It was noted that indigenous Australians (aged 15–64) were unemployed at 190% of non-indigenous Australians (Australian Bureau of Statistics, 2019).

Given the large extent of unemployment, at least compared to others in the country where indigenous people would seek employment, means that indigenous employees are continually faced with issues around job insecurity. Van Vuuren and Klandermans (1990: 133) define job insecurity as an individual's 'concern about the future permanence of the job'. Other definitions include an employee's 'expectations about continuity in a job situation' (Davy et al., 1997: 323) and the 'perception of a potential threat to continuity in his or her current job' (Heaney et al., 1994: 1431). Importantly in the context of indigenous employees and the high statistics around unemployment of indigenous peoples, Greenhalgh and Rosenblatt (1984: 438) define an employee's job insecurity as the 'perceived powerlessness to maintain desired continuity in a threatened job situation'. We suggest that indigenous employees might perceive a 'natural' level of unemployment that is starkly higher than their non-indigenous co-workers and thus feel powerless against job losses. As such, there is likely to be an invidious indigenous premium paid while working, such that they know they are more likely to lose their job when times change, reflecting the perceived powerlessness around employment (Greenhalgh and Rosenblatt, 1984).

Douglas et al. (2017: 25) state that 'job insecurity is increasingly common in a world where businesses' expectations [are] for flexibility, technological innovations and increased just-in-time labour', with this leading to an increase in vulnerable jobs and precarious work (Standing, 2011). However, the above statistics show that indigenous employees have been at the forefront of this precarious movement, becoming ever more vulnerable to work and the potential loss of work (Haar and Brougham, 2013). These trends are not new, with Statistics Canada (2011: 1) reporting that while aboriginal people in Canada 'had a harder time finding work and faced higher unemployment than non-Aboriginal people', after the global financial crisis in 2008–9, the gap widened with aboriginal people experiencing 'sharper declines in employment rates than non-Aboriginal people did'. Globally, it appears that indigenous people are disadvantaged in work.

It is important to understand that job insecurity can have devastating effects on wellbeing. For example, job insecurity is associated with higher job burnout (De Cuyper et al., 2012; Douglas et al., 2017; Lacovides et al., 2003; Piccoli and De Witte, 2015); lower family wellbeing (Mauno et al., 2017); detrimental effects on workplace health and safety (Jiang and Probst, 2014; Probst et al., 2016); lower career satisfaction and higher depression (Brougham and Haar, 2018); and reduced job performance, productivity, and job attitudes (Cotti et al., 2014; Kinnunen et al., 2014). From a wellbeing perspective, Reisel (2003) argues that job insecurity perceptions can activate *compensatory effort*, leading to a high arousal state, which ultimately influences wellbeing. Nakagawa et al. (2013: 1) argue this 'compensatory effort may, when

overexerted, lead to indefinite sick leave for organ dysfunction'. In effect, indigenous people might be focused so hard on trying to stay employed that they ultimately exhaust themselves, and their wellbeing suffers.

The meta-analysis by Sverke et al. (2002) shows strong links between job insecurity and wellbeing, reporting a corrected correlation between job insecurity and mental health of –.23 and –.16 with physical health. Broader work wellbeing outcomes like job satisfaction were highly related (–.41). Importantly in the context of indigenous workers, their results showed the consequences of job insecurity were more detrimental among manual (versus non-manual) workers. For example, manual workers have a relationship between job insecurity and mental health of –.35, but this is a more modest –.20 for non-manual workers. Alas, indigenous workers are typically reported as being in less skilled professions (e.g., Haar and Brougham, 2013) and thus are likely to potentially experience more relative job insecurity.

In a more recent meta-analysis, Cheng and Chan (2008) report a corrected correlation between job insecurity on wellbeing outcomes of –.43 with job satisfaction, –.23 with physical health, and –.28 with psychological health. While that meta-analysis looked at differences (moderators) by age, tenure, and gender, ethnicity is an area that has been neglected in the literature. In the New Zealand context, Gibson and Watane (2001) explore the hypothesis that Māori employees had greater job insecurity because they received less employer training, but this was not supported, indicating endemic and systematic issues driving Māori employee job insecurity. Given the aforementioned statistics, it is imperative that more studies seek to understand the lived experiences of indigenous employees around their job insecurity. Fundamentally, it is likely that indigenous employee wellbeing is massively affected by their perceptions around job threats and unemployment, with such worries leading to lower wellbeing outcomes across a host of different measures. Given some indigenous peoples live in rich western societies (e.g., United States, Canada, Australia, and New Zealand), and Kalleberg (2018) argues wellbeing will be higher in such economies when there is greater job protection (i.e., less precarious work), then these countries have potential policy solutions to enhance the wellbeing of their indigenous populations.

INCOME AND WELLBEING

Overall, being an indigenous person means you are more likely to not get a job. Further, indigenous employees are more likely to be paid less, and in challenging financial times (e.g., the global financial crisis of 2008–9), more likely to lose their job. This is vital because research suggests that income plays a major role in wellbeing (Ferrer-i-Carbonell, 2005; Sacks et al., 2012). A meta-analysis of 54 economically developing countries (111 independent samples) found an average positive effect of economic status to wellbeing that was 'strongest among low-income developing economies (r=.28) and for samples that were least educated (r=.36). The relation was weakest among high-income developing economies (r=.10) and for highly educated samples (r=.13)' (Howell and Howell, 2008: 536). Beyond this, scholars have noted the importance of income as an indicator of indigenous wellbeing, with Yap and Yu (2016: 326) stating for indigenous Australians, 'having a constant stream of income not only ensure[s] stability but [is] … also instrumental in achieving other valued functionings such as autonomy'.

Haar and Brougham (2013) report that Māori employees earn around 18% less than white New Zealanders, and during the global financial crisis had an unemployment rate 337% higher than New Zealand Europeans (whites). Further, 2018 census data shows the disparity is greater with New Zealand Europeans reporting a median income 42%

higher than Māori, and even the rate of change (2013–18) indicates indigenous peoples' income grew more slowly (46% lower growth rate across that time). These trends hold across the United States, where indigenous peoples have a median income 60.2% of that of white Americans (Muhammad et al., 2019), and are at similar levels in Canada (Statistics Canada, 2020). Overall, like unemployment, indigenous peoples receive lower incomes than others in their economies, in particular the dominant ethnic group (usually whites).

STUDYING INDIGENOUS WELLBEING

For indigenous people, wellbeing is understood with a broad, holistic emphasis on the interconnectedness of physical, emotional, spiritual, and intellectual aspects of self, along with the connection to family, community, land, and culture (Adelson, 2005; Graham and Martin, 2016; Mundel and Chapman, 2010; Stewart and Marshall, 2016). The interdependence of these elements is essential to understanding indigenous employee wellbeing, as indigenous people do not separate the individual from society, community, family, and the environment, which are all core to their health and wellbeing (Britten and Borgen, 2010; McCormick, 1997). Haring et al. (2015: 1) state that 'indigenous workforces have existed across the world since the creation of Earth'. One unique aspect of indigenous wellbeing is often around autonomy (Yap and Yu, 2016) and here that specifically relates to being able to conduct, engage, and embrace cultural beliefs and practices, including language. The broad nature of indigenous wellbeing models is captured by Spiller et al. (2011), who note that wellbeing for indigenous groups spans spiritual, cultural, social, environmental, and economic factors. Similarly, Mark and Lyons (2010) propose a model for wellbeing called

Te Whetu (The Star), with five dimensions: mind, body, spirit, family, and land.

Despite the clear evidence around unemployment, income, and underemployment noted earlier, and the unique approaches and challenges facing indigenous employees, there is a remarkable lack of empirical studies into indigenous employee wellbeing. While empirical studies on indigenous employees have looked at traditional work outcomes such as turnover intentions (Haar et al., 2012), there has been more focus on the wellbeing of indigenous employees, although much comes out of New Zealand focusing on Māori employees. This includes studies exploring work–life balance (Haar and Brougham, 2020; Haar et al., 2014), the wellbeing of Māori leaders (Roche et al., 2018), and the wellbeing of Māori employees (Brougham and Haar, 2013; Haar and Cordier, 2020; Sibley et al., 2011).

While some studies have explored Māori employee experiences in combination with other ethnic groups towards work outcomes (Haar et al., 2016), including studies of wellbeing (Hollebeek and Haar, 2012; Sibley et al., 2011), rarely do these studies explore a comparative analysis of indigenous employees versus majority employees. Haar and Brougham (2016) do this with organizational-based self-esteem and find Māori employees had levels equal to New Zealand Europeans, although its influence on work and wellbeing outcomes was significantly higher for Māori employees. This is important in the context of the high unemployment and underemployment of indigenous peoples. Haar and Brougham (2016: 730) state:

> We suggest that the importance and greater strength of OBSE on most outcomes for Māori may relate to the importance of work for Māori. As noted earlier, Māori are over-represented in the unemployment statistics compared with Europeans and, as such, employment and its associated influence on self-esteem may be very different for Māori.

We know that work is important and shapes wellbeing (Boye, 2009; Clark and Oswald,

1994; Wilson and Walker, 1993; Winkelmann, 2009) including for indigenous people (Muriwai et al., 2015). Here we find that self-esteem from work appears to be a key explanatory factor for this important link among indigenous employees. Indeed, Haar and Brougham (2016) argue that given the higher unemployment faced by Māori employees, they likely see extra value in paid work. In their study of work–life balance, Haar et al. (2014) find Māori employees reported the highest levels across seven samples including other New Zealand employees, which is counter to another New Zealand study across employed and unemployed peoples including Māori (New Zealand Ministry of Social Development, 2016). This might illustrate the importance and positivity that paid employment can bring to indigenous people.

There has, at times, been a focus on cultural aspects relating to wellbeing, especially Māori employees (Brougham et al., 2015; Haar and Brougham, 2011, 2013). Kuntz et al. (2014) find Māori working for New Zealand firms that espouse Māori cultural values reported stronger wellbeing via their work attitudes. Brougham and Haar (2013) note the importance of collectivism as a cultural value and find Māori employees with higher workplace collectivism have enhanced wellbeing through lower anxiety and depression. However, Hook et al. (2007) caution working in a non-Māori world for Māori employees, with the complexity around workplace mentoring being potentially fraught with issues. Finally, Houkamau and Sibley (2019) explore different Māori cultural factors and their influence on economic attitudes and values, representing a distinct, but a valuable, form of wellbeing (e.g., respect for Māori values and development in the workplace).

In addition to the empirical body of work around indigenous wellbeing, there are some theoretical models that specifically look to offer models for exploring the wellbeing of indigenous populations. Only a few are presented here to provide insight and direction for researchers. The first model is one of the most popular models of wellbeing in a Māori context and is likely to have many aspects that resonate positively with indigenous peoples, employees, and scholars. It is provided here to highlight the complexity and differences of an indigenous model to wellbeing. Next, we present additional Māori models that are focused on employees and then provide additional models from other indigenous cultures.

Te Whare Tapa Whā Model

Te Whare Tapa Whā is a model of Māori health, wellness, and wellbeing which comprises four essential components of health (Durie, 1998). Durie (1994, 1998, 1999) notes these components are symbolized by the four walls of a house: (1) *taha tinana* (the physical side), (2) *taha whānau* (the extended family side), (3) *taha wairua* (the spiritual side), and (4) *taha hinengaro* (the thoughts and feelings side). All of these quadrants are considered necessary for strength and balance, though for Māori, *taha wairua* is the most essential and of great importance to their health and wellness (Durie, 1998, 1999). *Taha wairua* represents the connection of Māori with their surroundings and also highlights the celebrated kinship with their land that is important to their identity.

Durie (1994: 74) describes his model as 'simple even simplistic, but that was also its appeal'. Due to its comparative simplicity, the *Te Whare Tapa Whā* model has been noted as having broad appeal and is especially applicable within the health field of New Zealand (McNeill, 2009). McNeill (2009: 102) states that the *Te Whare Tapa Whā* model is often used for the holistic perception of health and wellness but also because it is easily 'translated and applied to any cross-cultural analysis of wellbeing'. Thus, this model of indigenous wellbeing seeks to provide a holistic approach to wellbeing that perhaps western scientists tend to shy away from.

Further, the inclusion of spirituality and connections with cultural values and the land can resonate with other indigenous populations and their own value systems.

Te Whare Tapa Whā as a model, provides a holistic understanding of Māori health and wellness in the physical and mental health context (Stewart, 2012). Kingi and Durie (2000) use *Te Whare Tapa Whā* to underpin the *Hua Oranga*, a Māori measure of mental health outcomes and highlight that western models of wellbeing address the physical and psychological wellbeing of individuals at work, but fail to address the spiritual and the family relationship aspects of the individuals' wellbeing. The holistic approach of *Hua Oranga* based on the *Te Whare Tapa Whā* model also ensures that cultural integrity, relevance, specificity, and applicability, as well as intended principles of wellness, are upheld when Māori workers are involved (Stewart, 2012). Similarly, drawing on Te Whare Tapa Whā is a culturally responsive measure of occupational stress and wellbeing for Māori workers called *Mahi Oranga* (Stewart, 2011). This model focuses largely on the workplace and work related stressors, to better understand the experiences of working Māori.

Mahi Oranga notes that Māori experience some aspects of occupational stress at the workplace in the same way as non-Māori, although the impact on Māori may be more acute, due to Māori being under-represented in the workforce (Statistics New Zealand, 2020). Stewart and Gardner (2015) highlight some stressors that Māori and non-Māori workers experience, although these are not only similar but reflect the international literature broadly. However, there are some aspects of occupational stress that are different for Māori workers from non-Māori workers. These include lack of cultural safety, non-Māori workers failing to value the Māori culture properly, and institutional racism (Stewart and Gardner, 2015). Māori workers often also face high demands from their workplace, specifically when they are required to deal with 'Māori' issues because of the lack of cultural competence of their non-Māori colleagues, in addition to the expectations of *whānau* (wider family group), *hapū* (*whānau* grouping connected by a common ancestor), and *iwi* (grouping of many *hapū* and *whānau*), as well as tribalism that contribute Māori-specific issues further adding to the occupational stress of Māori workers (Stewart and Gardner, 2015).

Te Whare Tapa Whā and the associated models highlight how indigenous approaches to wellbeing can be quite different and more complex than western wellbeing approaches. Such models are likely to translate into many indigenous populations and workplace settings, making this a useful starting place for research on indigenous work experiences. These approaches highlight that indigenous workers can experience work differently from their non-indigenous colleagues, and thus experience different drivers of their wellbeing. Finally, some other indigenous models of wellbeing are noted.

Te Wheke Model

Te Wheke (the octopus) is a model focusing on Māori workers' wellbeing and wellness. *Te Wheke* uses the parts of the octopus body to represent components of individual personality within a socio-cultural framework (Love, 2004). As Māori give importance to family and kinship, this model attaches the individual and the family unit to eight aspects symbolizing different configurations of Māori, being similar to an octopus head attached to its tentacles. The aspects are (1) *Taha tinana* (physical aspect), (2) *Whatumanawa* (emotional aspect), (3) *Mauri* (ethos which sustains all life forms including the language), (4) *Hā a kui ma a koro ma* (traditional cultural legacy), (5) *Mana ake* (uniqueness of the individual), (6) *Wairuatanga* (spirituality), (7) *Whānaungatanga* (kinship), and (8) *Hinengaro* (mind). Again, we find an indigenous wellbeing model incorporating a strong affiliation with spiritual, mental, and kinship aspects of Māori culture and values. Each

of these eight components contains different facets attached to an individual's life, and McNeill (2009) notes that the overall model, along with all eight components, represent *Whaiora* (total wellbeing).

Other Indigenous Wellbeing Models

For indigenous Australians, the wellbeing of individuals also represents the wellbeing of the overall community (AHMAC, 2017; Taylor et al., 2012). These indigenous communities pass on their traditions, ceremonies, culture, knowledge, and values from one generation to the next through means of performance, storytelling, language, protection of significant and sacred sites, and the teachings of their elders. According to AHMAC (2017), there are six themes central to indigenous Australians' wellbeing as individuals and community: (1) connection to land, history, culture, and identity; (2) resilience; (3) leadership; (4) feeling of safety; (5) individual role, structure, and routine; and (6) vitality. These themes represent community functioning measures for the Aboriginal and Torres Strait Islander Health Performance Framework (see AHMAC, 2017). Akin with other indigenous peoples (e.g., Māori), the strong connection to land, history, culture, and identity all feature as a measure of health, wellness, and wellbeing, and these themes capture the spiritual element of wellbeing.

Focusing on the indigenous communities of Canada, Overmars (2019) categorizes the wellbeing of indigenous individuals as due to important supporting and hindering elements. Supporting elements include personal perspectives, relationships, holistic health, culture, workplace environments, appreciation, communication, resources, and self-care. Conversely, hindering elements to wellbeing include either non-existence of the supporting elements, lack of resources that influence health, as well as racism and issues concerning identity. Practical implications attached to this research suggest that managers should work towards incorporating indigenous culture in the workplace, building supportive relationships, providing sufficient resources, and challenging racism and stereotypes to improve indigenous wellbeing. Furthermore, wellness programmes that stem from aspects of the self (mind, body, spirit, emotions) are also signalled as a source to build indigenous wellbeing through culture, its safety, and values (Overmars, 2019).

Summary of Indigenous Wellbeing Models

The research around indigenous wellbeing is growing, and more aspects of wellbeing are considered. However, despite there being frameworks that cater to indigenous individuals, their identity, health, wellness, and workplace wellbeing, they appear to have little researcher engagement. Despite the models offering unique insights into indigenous wellbeing, the holistic and broad nature of wellbeing using an indigenous lens, the literature has not sufficiently embraced these models. Almost all empirical studies, whether on life satisfaction (e.g., Sibley et al., 2011), mental health (e.g., Brougham and Haar, 2013), or both (e.g., Haar et al., 2014) simply do not test these more culturally appropriate, but more complex and challenging, models. While some studies have embraced culturally specific approaches (e.g., Haar and Brougham, 2013; Haar and Staniland, 2016; Houkamau and Sibley, 2019; Muriwai et al., 2015; Stewart and Gardner, 2015), there is clearly more work to be done that attempts to understand indigenous wellbeing better. Such research is likely to be complex and holistic but also provide a richer and more complete understanding of indigenous wellbeing.

Jones and Bradshaw (2015) argue that while indigenous wellbeing is complex, there is a greater need by researchers, employers, and government to instigate and make real change. Clearly, the literature highlights that while indigenous wellbeing is different, there is insufficient testing and exploration of these models. As wellbeing becomes more paramount and important, this focus needs to change. Finally, Prout (2012) asserts that to have a greater understanding and to make improvements potentially, greater data is needed on indigenous groups. The next section details one approach to engage with indigenous communities to enable a greater focus on understanding indigenous wellbeing. The current evidence provides us with a backdrop of information on indigenous employee wellbeing, but the future requires a stronger focus on adopting more complex models to fully realize the potential of indigenous wellbeing.

FUTURE DIRECTIONS

There is a need for greater research of indigenous wellbeing and, in particular, embracing the approaches of these alternative models of wellbeing. Clearly, they all share various aspects beyond the physical and mental health of the individual, to their family, community, cultural, and spiritual dimensions. The Perceived Well-being Index (Cummins, 2003) does fundamentally focus on satisfaction but includes various aspects, including family, but also with the option of spirituality. It has been used successfully on general populations (not only employees) including Māori (e.g., Ganglmair-Wooliscroft and Lawson 2008) and Australian aborigines (Tomyn et al., 2013). It is likely this approach – given it has an existing theoretical and empirical body of evidence – might be tailored to meet some of the other holistic aspects of indigenous wellbeing, for example by adding satisfaction with other cultural factors such as cultural identity or being a strong indigenous person (Durie, 1994).

Alternatively, testing of new models of indigenous wellbeing that align with existing theoretical models of indigenous wellbeing, but also existing (western) wellbeing literatures, are encouraged. In the context of conducting indigenous research, it is important to understand how such research can be done safely for researchers and researched. The next section briefly explores one indigenous methodology for researching indigenous communities that might provide a useful framework.

Smith (1999) notes that indigenous populations have historically been the subject of much research that is negative and seeks to blame the indigenous people (e.g., wellbeing). As such, it is suggested that indigenous communities are suspicious of the motives and approaches of typical western scientists. According to Durie (2005), a new research methodology is needed that builds on indigenous research methodologies that seek to create new wisdom merging western or indigenous approaches to research. Smith (1999) offers the *kaupapa Māori research* framework for conducting research not just with Māori but any indigenous population. The goal is to conduct research that is culturally safe (Smith, 1999) – for subjects and researcher. Ideally, such research is driven by the indigenous population (they are the researchers), and in collaboration (with and not 'on'), with a focus on benefitting the indigenous population.

This research approach is expected to consider the worldviews of the indigenous population and engage them not just as stakeholders but, ideally, as the drivers of the research. In the models of indigenous wellbeing exposed here, it might provide the starting point for conversations between the researcher and indigenous communities. Importantly, Mahuika (2008: 4) states that 'unlike the dominant Western paradigms, Kaupapa Māori does not make claims to universal truth or to superiority over other existing paradigms'. Indeed, Smith (2007: 2) states this research methodology is an 'approach developed for and by Māori for the purposes of marrying Māori and Western

theories of research'. While this approach to indigenous research places indigenous people at the centre, there are issues for researchers, specifically those with expertise where there is none among indigenous scholars (e.g., employee wellbeing). However, this does not mean that non-indigenous researchers cannot engage with indigenous communities. Partnering with indigenous community members or mentoring junior indigenous colleagues/scholars and sharing authorship broadly to recognize and embrace a shared and collaborative way to conduct indigenous scholarship, can help transcend these issues.

Finally, this approach to indigenous research also requires effort around the dissemination of research findings, especially beyond traditional academic outlets. Smith (1999) notes that researchers should *manaaki ki te tangata* (share and host people and be generous). Hence, if a community is part of the idea generation and participates in the research, then the findings might be presented back to these communities. If communities are geographically spread, then more modern approaches might be embraced, such as YouTube and other online resources to help the participants understand what the research produced. Further, translating academic research into digestible and understandable findings for everyday employees is encouraged. Few people might understand a structural equation model, so making the findings clear can aid the joining of western and indigenous research. This way, indigenous communities can start to understand the potential benefits of research, especially if exploring a vital topic like indigenous wellbeing.

CONCLUSION

This chapter has highlighted how indigenous populations have a much broader approach to wellbeing, one that often embraces wider cultural and spiritual factors. This is likely due to a colonized history where cultural practices were banned and punished. Thus, for indigenous people to have greater wellbeing at work, they need organizations that can understand and embrace these differences. Indeed, this aligns with inclusion around employees wanting to feel that they belong in their workplace, to feel valued, but also for their unique attributes (Shore et al., 2011). However, there is clearly a need for richer studies of indigenous wellbeing to provide not only greater insights but also enable understanding of organizational and work factors that can shape and enhance indigenous wellbeing. While indigenous mental health might be enhanced with greater teamwork and collaboration (Brougham and Haar, 2013), the workplace factors that shape greater cultural wellbeing (around customs, language, etc.) remain unknown. This provides great research opportunity, although within the context of indigenous scholarship. Hence, non-indigenous scholars are encouraged to seek out collaborations, including mentorship with indigenous communities to offer their expertise.

Note

1   Note the term indigenous is used here as a catch-all phrase to capture any and all indigenous peoples and populations including first nation and aboriginal peoples. It is acknowledged that this term is not used universally around the world (e.g., Vietnam) and is used here to simply capture all these differences. Readers are encouraged to explore the unique terminology used in any indigenous populations they engage with.

REFERENCES

Adelson, N (2005) The embodiment of inequity: Health disparities in Aboriginal Canada. *Canadian Journal of Public Health* 96(s2): 45–61.

Australian Bureau of Statistics (2018) *Estimates of Aboriginal and Torres Strait Islander Australians*. Available at: www.abs.gov.au/ausstats/abs@.nsf/mf/3238.0.55.001 (accessed 10 July 2020).

Australian Bureau of Statistics (2019) *Indigenous Employment*. Available at: www.aihw.gov.au/reports/australias-welfare/indigenous-employment (accessed 10 July 2020).

Australian Health Ministers' Advisory Council (AHMAC) (2017, May 30) *The Aboriginal and Torres Strait Islander Health Performance Framework (HPF)*. Available at: www.niaa.gov.au/indigenous-affairs/evaluations-and-evidence/aboriginal-and-torres-strait-islander-health-performance-framework-hpf (accessed 10 July 2020).

Boye, K (2009) Relatively different? How do gender differences in wellbeing depend on paid and unpaid work in Europe? *Social Indicators Research* 93(3): 509–525.

Britten, L and Borgen, W (2010) Indigenous footprints along the career journey. *Procedia-Social and Behavioral Sciences* 5: 104–115.

Brougham, D and Haar, J (2013) Collectivism, cultural identity and employee mental health: A study of New Zealand Maori. *Social Indicators Research* 114(3): 1143–1160.

Brougham, D and Haar, J (2018) Smart technology, artificial intelligence, robotics, and algorithms (STARA): Employees' perceptions of our future workplace. *Journal of Management & Organization* 24(2): 239–257.

Brougham, D, Haar, J and Roche, M (2015) Work-family enrichment, collectivism, and workplace cultural outcomes: A study of New Zealand Māori. *New Zealand Journal of Employment Relations* 41(1): 19–34.

Cheng, GHL and Chan, DKS (2008) Who suffers more from job insecurity? A meta-analytic review. *Applied Psychology: An International Review* 57(2): 272–303.

Clark, AE and Oswald, A (1994) Unhappiness and unemployment. *Economic Journal* 104: 648–659.

Cotti, C, Haley, MR and Miller, L (2014) Workplace flexibilities, job satisfaction and union membership in the US workforce. *British Journal of Industrial Relations* 54(3): 403–425.

Cummins, RA (2003) Normative life satisfaction: Measurement issues and a homeostatic model. *Social Indicators Research* 64(2): 225–256.

Davy, JA, Kinicki, AJ and Scheck, CL (1997) A test of job insecurity's direct and mediated effects on withdrawal cognitions. *Journal of Organizational Behavior* 18: 323–349.

De Cuyper, N, Mäkikangas, A, Kinnunen, U, Mauno, S and De Witte, H (2012) Cross-lagged associations between perceived external employability, job insecurity, and exhaustion: Testing gain and loss spirals according to the conservation of resources theory. *Journal of Organizational Behavior* 33: 770–788.

Demombynes, G and Testaverde, M (2018) *Employment Structure and Returns to Skill in Vietnam: Estimates using the Labor Force Survey*. Washington, DC: The World Bank.

Douglas, J, Haar, J and Harris, C (2017) Job insecurity and job burnout: Does union membership buffer the detrimental effects? *New Zealand Journal of Human Resources Management* 17(2): 23–40.

Doyle, C (2009) Indigenous peoples and the Millennium Development Goals: 'Sacrificial lambs' or equal beneficiaries? *The International Journal of Human Rights* 13(1): 44–71.

Durie, M (1994) *Whaiora: Maori Health Development*. Oxford: Oxford University Press.

Durie, M (1998) *Whaiora: Maōri Health Development* (2nd ed.). Oxford: Oxford University Press.

Durie, M (1999) Te Pae Māhutonga: A model for Māori health promotion. *Health Promotion Forum of New Zealand Newsletter* 49(2): 5.

Durie, M (2005) Indigenous knowledge within a global knowledge system. *Higher Education Policy* 18(3): 301–312.

Ferrer-i-Carbonell, A (2005) Income and well-being: An empirical analysis of the comparison income effect. *Journal of Public Economics* 89(5–6): 997–1019.

Ganglmair-Wooliscroft, A, and Lawson, R (2008) Applying the international wellbeing index to investigate subjective wellbeing of New Zealanders with European and with Maori heritage. *Kotuitui: New Zealand Journal of Social Sciences Online*, 3(1): 57–72.

Gibson, J and Watane, C (2001) Why is job security lower for Maori and Pacific Island workers? The role of employer-provided training. *New Zealand Economic Papers* 35(1): 1–24.

Graham, H and Martin, S (2016) Narrative descriptions of miyo-mahcihoyān (physical, emotional, mental, and spiritual wellbeing) from a contemporary néhiyawak (Plains Cree) perspective. *International Journal of Mental Health Systems* 10(58): 1–12.

Greenhalgh, L and Rosenblatt, Z (1984) Job insecurity: Toward conceptual clarity. *Academy of Management Review* 9: 438–448.

Haar, J and Brougham, D (2011) Outcomes of cultural satisfaction at work: A study of New Zealand Maori. *Asia Pacific Journal of Human Resources* 49(4): 461–475.

Haar, J and Brougham, D (2013) An indigenous model of career satisfaction: Exploring the role of workplace cultural wellbeing. *Social Indicators Research* 110(3): 873–890.

Haar, J and Brougham, D (2016) Organizational-based self-esteem: A within country comparison of outcomes between Maori and New Zealand Europeans. *Journal of Management & Organization* 22(5): 720–735.

Haar, J and Brougham, D (2020) Work antecedents and consequences of work-life balance: A two sample study within New Zealand. *The International Journal of Human Resource Management*. DOI: 10.1080/09585192.2020.1751238.

Haar, J and Cordier, J (2020) Testing the psychometric properties of the short work-family enrichment scale on under-represented samples. *International Journal of Selection and Assessment* 28: 112–116.

Haar, JM and Staniland, N (2016) The influence of psychological resilience on the career satisfaction of Māori employees: Exploring the moderating effects of collectivism. *New Zealand Journal of Human Resource Management* 16(2): 58–72.

Haar, J, de Fluiter, A and Brougham, D (2016) Abusive supervision and turnover intentions: The mediating role of perceived organizational support. *Journal of Management & Organization* 22(2): 139–153.

Haar, J, Roche, M and Taylor, D (2012) Work-family conflict and turnover intentions amongst indigenous employees: The importance of the whanau/family for Maori. *The International Journal of Human Resource Management* 23(12): 2546–2560.

Haar, JM, Russo, M, Sune, A and Ollier-Malaterre, A (2014) Outcomes of work-life balance on job satisfaction, life satisfaction and mental health: A study across seven cultures. *Journal of Vocational Behavior* 85(3): 361–373.

Haring, RC, Hudson, M, Erickson, L, Taualii, M, and Freeman, B (2015) First nations, Maori, American Indians, and Native Hawaiians as sovereigns: EAP with indigenous nations within nations. *Journal of Workplace Behavioral Health*, 30(1–2): 14–31.

Heaney, CA, Israel, BA and House, JS (1994) Chronic job insecurity among automobile workers: Effects on job satisfaction and health. *Social Science and Medicine* 38: 1431–1437.

Hollebeek, L and Haar, J (2012) Direct and interaction effects of challenge and hindrance stressors towards job outcomes. *New Zealand Journal of Employment Relations* 37(2): 58–76.

Hook, GR, Waaka, T and Raumati, LP (2007) Mentoring Māori within a Pākehā framework. *MAI Review* 1(3): 1–13.

Houkamau, CA and Sibley, CG (2019) The role of culture and identity for economic values: A quantitative study of Māori attitudes. *Journal of the Royal Society of New Zealand* 49(S1): 118–136.

Howell, RT and Howell, CJ (2008) The relation of economic status to subjective wellbeing in developing countries: A meta-analysis. *Psychological Bulletin* 134(4): 536– 560.

IWGIA (2020) *Indigenous Peoples in Vietnam*. Available at: www.iwgia.org/en/vietnam (accessed 10 July 2020).

Jiang, L and Probst, TM (2014) Organizational communication: A buffer in times of job insecurity? *Economic and Industrial Democracy* 35(3): 557–579.

Jones, J and Bradshaw, B (2015) Addressing historical impacts through impact and benefit agreements and health impact assessment: Why it matters for Indigenous wellbeing. *Northern Review* 41: 81–109.

Jordan, K, Bulloch, H and Buchanan, G (2010) Statistical equality and cultural difference in Indigenous wellbeing frameworks: A new expression of an enduring debate. *Australian Journal of Social Issues* 45(3): 333–362.

Kalleberg, AL (2018) *Precarious Lives: Job Insecurity and Well-Being in Rich Democracies*. Medford, MA: Polity Press.

Kingi, TK and Durie, M (2000) *Hua Oranga: A Maori measure of mental health outcomes.* Te Pumanawa Hauora, Palmerston North, New Zealand: School of Maori Studies, Massey University.

Kinnunen, U, Mäkikangas, A, Mauno, S, De Cuyper, N and De Witte, H (2014) Development of perceived job insecurity across two years: Associations with antecedents and employee outcomes. *Journal of Occupational Health Psychology* 19(2): 243–258.

Kuntz, JR, Näswall, K, Beckingsale, A and Macfarlane, AH (2014) Capitalising on diversity: Espousal of Māori values in the workplace. *Journal of Corporate Citizenship* 55: 102–122.

Lacovides, A, Fountoulakis, K, Kaprinis, S and Kaprinis, G (2003) The relationship between job stress, burnout and clinical depression. *Journal of Affective Disorders* 75(3): 209–221.

Love, C (2004) Extensions on Te Wheke. *Working Papers No. 6-04*. Lower Hutt, New Zealand: The Open Polytechnic of New Zealand.

Mahuika, R (2008) Kaupapa Māori theory is critical and anti-colonial. *Mai Review* 3(4): 1–16.

Mark, GT and Lyons, AC (2010) Maori healers' views on wellbeing: The importance of mind, body, spirit, family and land. *Social Science & Medicine* 70(11): 1756–1764.

Mauno, S, Cheng, T and Lim, V (2017) The far-reaching consequences of job insecurity: A review on family-related outcomes. *Marriage & Family Review* 53(8): 717–743.

McCormick, RM (1997) Healing through interdependence: The role of connecting in First Nations healing practices. *Canadian Journal of Counselling* 31(3): 172–84.

McNeill, HN (2009) *Maori Models of Mental Wellness*. Te Kaharoa, 2, ISSN 1178–6035.

Muhammad, DA, Tec, R and Ramirez, K (2019) *Racial Wealth Snapshot: American Indians/ Native Americans*. Available at: https://bridgingtheracialwealthdivide.wordpress.com/2019/11/15/racial-wealth snapshot-american-indians-native-americans/ (accessed 10 July 2020).

Mundel, E and Chapman, GE (2010) A decolonizing approach to health promotion in Canada: The case of the Urban Aboriginal Community Kitchen Garden Project. *Health Promotion International* 25(2): 166–173.

Muriwai, EM, Houkamau, CA and Sibley, CG (2015) Culture as cure? The protective function of Māori cultural efficacy on psychological distress. *The New Zealand Journal of Psychology* 44(2): 14–24.

Nakagawa, S, Sugiura, M, Akitsuki, Y, Hosseini, SH, Kotozaki, Y, Miyauchi, CM, Yomogida, Y, Yokoyama, R, Takeuchi, H and Kawashima, R (2013) Compensatory effort parallels midbrain deactivation during mental fatigue: an fMRI study. *PLoS One* 8(2): e56606.

New Zealand Ministry of Social Development (2016) *The Social Report 2016: Te Pūrongo Oranga Tangata*. Available at: www.social-report.msd.govt.nz/paid-work/satisfaction-with-work-life-balance.html (accessed 13 July 2020).

Office for National Statistics (2012) *Ethnicity and National Identity in England and Wales: 2011*. Available at: www.ons.gov.uk/people-populationandcommunity/culturalidentity/ethnicity/articles/ethnicityandnationalidentityinenglandandwales/2012-12-11 (accessed 10 July 2020).

Overmars, D (2019) *Wellbeing in the workplace among Indigenous people: An enhanced critical incident study*. Doctoral dissertation, University of British Columbia, Canada.

Piccoli, B and De Witte, H (2015) Job insecurity and emotional exhaustion: Testing psychological contract breach versus distributive injustice as indicators of lack of reciprocity. *Work & Stress* 29(3): 246–263.

Probst, TM, Jiang, L and Graso, M (2016) Leader–member exchange: Moderating the health and safety outcomes of job insecurity. *Journal of Safety Research* 56: 47–56.

Prout, S (2012) Indigenous wellbeing frameworks in Australia and the quest for quantification. *Social Indicators Research* 109(2): 317–336.

Reisel, WD (2003) Predicting job insecurity via moderating influence of individual powerlessness. *Psychological Reports* 92: 820–822.

Roche, MA, Haar, J and Brougham, D (2018) Māori leader's wellbeing: A self-determination perspective. *Leadership* 14(1): 25–39.

Sacks, DW, Stevenson, B and Wolfers, J (2012) The new stylized facts about income and subjective wellbeing. *Emotion* 12(6): 1181–1187.

Shore, LM, Randel, AE, Chung, BG, Dean, MA, Ehrhart, KE and Singh, G (2011) Inclusion and diversity in work groups: A review and model for future research. *Journal of Management* 37(4): 1262–1289.

Sibley, CG, Harré, N, Hoverd, WJ and Houkamau, CA (2011) The gap in the subjective wellbeing of Māori and New Zealand Europeans widened between 2005 and 2009. *Social Indicators Research* 104(1): 103–115.

Smith, KT (2007) Supervision and Māori doctoral students: A discussion piece. *MAI Review* 1(3): 1–4.

Smith, LT (1999) *Decolonizing Methodologies: Research and Indigenous Peoples*. London: Zed Books.

Spiller, C, Erakovic, L, Henare, M and Pio, E (2011) Relational wellbeing and wealth: Māori businesses and an ethic of care. *Journal of Business Ethics* 98(1): 153–169.

Standing, G (2011) *The Precariat: The Dangerous New Class*. London: Bloomsbury Academic.

Statistics Canada (2011) *Aboriginal Peoples*. Available at: www150.statcan.gc.ca/n1/pub/11-402-x/2011000/chap/ap-pa/ap-pa-eng.htm (accessed 10 July 2020).

Statistics Canada (2016) *Immigration and Ethnocultural Diversity Highlight Tables*. Available at: www12.statcan.gc.ca/census-recensement/2016/dp-pd/hlt-fst/imm/Table.cfm?Lang=E&T=31&Geo=01&SO=4D (accessed 10 July 2020).

Statistics Canada (2020) *Labour Force Characteristics by Region and Detailed Aboriginal Group*. Available at: www150.statcan.gc.ca/t1/tbl1/en/tv.action?pid=1410036501 (accessed 10 July 2020).

Statistics New Zealand (2019a) *New Zealand's Population Reflects Growing Diversity*. Available at: www.stats.govt.nz/news/new-zealands-population-reflects-growing-diversity (accessed 10 July 2020).

Statistics New Zealand (2019b) *2018 Census of Population and Dwellings*. Census calculation provided directly to first author on 27 November 2019.

Statistics New Zealand (2020) *Household Labour Force Survey Tables for March 2020 Quarter*. Available at: www.stats.govt.nz/assets/Uploads/Household-labour-force-survey-estimated-working-age-population/Household-labour-force-survey-estimated-working-age-population-March-2020-quarter/

Download-data/household-labour-force-survey-estimated-working-age-population-march-2020-quarter.xlsx (accessed 10 July 2020).

Stewart, L (2011) *Developing Mahi Oranga: A culturally responsive measure of Māori occupational stress and wellbeing – A thesis presented in partial fulfilment of the requirements for the degree of Master of Arts in Industrial/Organisational Psychology at Massey University*, Albany, New Zealand. Doctoral dissertation, Massey University, New Zealand.

Stewart, L (2012) Commentary on cultural diversity across the pacific: The dominance of western theories, models, research and practice in psychology. *Journal of Pacific Rim Psychology* 6(1): 27–31.

Stewart, L and Gardner, D (2015) Developing Mahi Oranga: A culturally responsive measure of Māori occupational stress and wellbeing. *New Zealand Journal of Psychology* 44(2): 79–88.

Stewart, SL and Marshall, A (2016) Counselling Indigenous peoples in Canada. In: Stewart, SL, Moodley, R and Hyatt, A (eds) *Indigenous Cultures and Mental Health Counselling*. London: Taylor & Francis, pp. 103–119.

Sverke, M, Hellgren, J and Näswall, K (2002) No security: A meta-analysis and review of job insecurity and its consequences. *Journal of Occupational Health Psychology* 7(3): 242–264.

Taylor, J, Edwards, J, Champion, S, Cheers, S, Chong, A, Cummins, R and Cheers, B (2012) Towards a conceptual understanding of Aboriginal and Torres Strait Islander community and community functioning. *Community Development Journal* 47(1): 94–110.

Tomyn, AJ, Tyszkiewicz, MDF and Cummins, RA (2013) The personal wellbeing index: Psychometric equivalence for adults and school children. *Social Indicators Research* 110(3): 913–924.

United Nations (2006) *SPFII: Report of the Meeting on Indigenous Peoples and Indicators of Well-being*, Canada, March 2006. UN DocE/C.19/2006/CRP.3.

United Nations (2009) *State of the World's Indigenous Peoples* (Vol. 9). Statistical Division. Geneva: United Nations Publications.

United Nations (2020a) *International Day of the World's Indigenous Peoples*. Available at: www.un.org/en/events/indigenousday/ (accessed 10 July 2020).

United Nations (2020b) *Indigenous Peoples at the United Nations*. Available at: www.un.org/development/desa/indigenouspeoples/about-us.html (accessed 10 July 2020).

United States Bureau of Labor Statistics (2019) *American Indians and Alaska Natives in the U.S. labor force*. Available at: www.bls.gov/opub/mlr/2019/article/american-indians-and-alaska-natives-in-the-u-s-labor-force.htm#_edn3 (accessed 10 July 2020).

United States Census Bureau (2020) *QuickFacts United States*. Available at: www.census.gov/quickfacts/fact/table/US/PST045219 (accessed 10 July 2020).

van Vuuren, CV and Klandermans, PG (1990) Individual reactions to job insecurity: An integrated model. In: Drenth, PJD and Sergeant, JA (eds) *European Perspectives in Psychology*. Chichester: Wiley, pp. 133–146.

Wilson, SH and Walker, GM (1993) Unemployment and health: A review. *Public Health* 107: 153–162.

Winkelmann, R (2009) Unemployment, social capital, and subjective wellbeing. *Journal of Happiness Studies* 10(4): 421–430.

Yap, M and Yu, E (2016). Operationalising the capability approach: Developing culturally relevant indicators of indigenous wellbeing–an Australian example. *Oxford Development Studies*, 44(3): 315–331.

33

Play and Wellbeing at Work

Kevin Moore

INTRODUCTION

The rapid rise in research on wellbeing has drawn to itself almost all phenomena within its conceptual neighbourhood. The types of activity we call 'play' have been prime candidates for this conceptual attraction or collision. That is unsurprising. In day-to-day life, being at play is considered emblematic of enjoyable moments and times, for children and adults alike. Remembering a time at play is to relive moments of being lifted out of 'ordinary life' and deposited, if only briefly, in a world without a care – or at least only the passing cares that last only so long as the playing. Most people would hope that a life of wellbeing might be liberally sprinkled with just such moments. Play researchers, however, have discovered that play has many facets and functions, not all positive.

The title of a well-known book on play by psychologist Brian Sutton-Smith (1997) is *The Ambiguity of Play*. In presenting seven 'rhetorics of play', Sutton-Smith argues that play has been ideologically used and deployed to support particular commitments. These commitments (rhetorics) are those of play as *progress* (especially in child development), *fate* (chance, life as beyond human control), *power* (applied to sports and other contests), *identity* (especially community identity), *the imaginary* (usually applied to episodes of improvisation, imagination, creativity and flexibility), the *self* (experiences of players such as fun, relaxation) and *frivolity* (as in the carnivalesque trickster and fool). Play as fate, power, identity and frivolity are 'of ancient hue' (Sutton-Smith, 1997: 10). By contrast, play as progress, the imaginary and the self are of more recent cast. Further, the 'ancient' four are communal and collective rhetorics; the more modern rhetorics (progress, the imaginary and the self) focus on the individual and have been emphasized for the last 200 years. Work has also changed dramatically in the past 200 years and, as is evident in some of the most recent research on play in organizations, the more modern rhetorics of play are now coming to the fore.

The role of play – in general and, specifically, in workplaces – is consequently something of a two-faced Janus. Play has been said to be either entirely non-serious or deadly serious (Gray, 2013; Huizinga, 1955); to scale the heights of enjoyment (Costea et al., 2005, 2007) and be complicit in suffering (Huizinga, 1955); to inspire creativity, innovation and productivity (e.g., Amabile, 1997; Amabile et al., 2005; Deal and Key, 1998; Jacobs and Statler, 2006; Mainemelis and Ronson, 2006; Statler et al., 2011) yet also to undermine performance and productivity (e.g., Abramis, 1990; Sørenson and Spoelstra, 2011); to provide times of passionate immersion and focus (Csikszentmihalyi, 1997); and other times of diversion, dissipation and wastefulness (Sørenson and Soelstra, 2011); to build loyalty, cooperativity, involvement and friendliness (Abramis, 1990; Roy, 1959; Sørenson and Spoelstra, 2011) or cynicism, diversion, disengagement and lack of trust (e.g., Spraggon and Bodolica, 2014, 2018).

Research on play in work settings remains sparse. Play is 'among the least studied and least understood organizational behavior' (Mainemelis and Ronson, 2006: 81). A major review of research on play in organizations spoke of the 'lack of attention given to play at work' and the diffuse and disconnected nature of research on the topic (Petelczyc et al., 2018: 162–163).

Despite the infancy of the research area – or perhaps because of it – there has been a surge in managerial practice based on the belief that the wall between 'play' and 'work' may have finally been breached. There are also claims that this represents the ultimate 'win-win' in which work, play and life can merge to generate both employee and organizational wellbeing (e.g., Berg, 1995, 1998). The importation of play and playfulness, that is, has been seen as a pathway to the development of wellbeing in – and also through – work in organizations.

The aim of this chapter is to review the current state of understanding of the relationships, both theoretical and empirical, between play, wellbeing and work, especially in organizations. This aim raises many questions: 'Does – and can – play develop wellbeing at work?'; 'How has – or might – organizational and management practice influenced play in the workplace?'; 'Is there a 'dark side' to play at work?' (Petelczyc et al., 2018); 'Can 'free' or informal play at work be beneficial for organizations, and in what ways?' (e.g., see Spraggon and Bodolica, 2018).

The relevance of such questions is increasing. The paucity of research on play at work is 'particularly problematic' because of technological, cultural and generational changes (Petelczyz et al., 2018: 163). Employees increasingly work remotely, are concerned about 'work–life balance' and – for millenials and later generations – there are expectations that work should offer not just toil and remuneration but meaning and 'fun'. To attract and retain employees in the future, it is argued, organizations need to refashion themselves as places of freedom, fun, challenge and creativity.

The lack of research on play, work and wellbeing is compounded by the fact that those studies that have been done have concentrated on the benefits of play *for organizations*. Topics such as the potential for play to improve innovation, creativity and performance have drawn most research attention. Occasionally, play has also been investigated in relation to employee-orientated factors such as job satisfaction, morale and engagement. But, again, these employee-related factors have often been studied with an eye on organizational benefits (under the 'a happy worker is a productive worker' hypothesis). There has been little direct research on how play affects wellbeing in work settings or on the variety of ways that workers play (but see Sørenson and Spoelstra, 2011).

Yet, the complex phenomenon of play has deep associations to human wellbeing. It is for this reason (i.e., the complexity of the notion of play) that the first section provides a detailed understanding of the concept of play. Then, the close links between play and wellbeing will be summarized followed by direct discussion of theories and empirical studies of play in work and organizational settings. Once the relationships between play, wellbeing and work have been discussed and relevant literature reviewed, some promising future directions for research will be highlighted.

WHAT IS PLAY?

When Plato (in *The Laws, vii,* 796 cited in Huizinga, 1955: 19) asks 'What, then, is the right way of living?' his answer is emphatic: 'Life must be lived as play, playing certain games, making sacrifices, singing and dancing, and then a [person] will be able to propitiate the gods … and win in the contest'. Humans are 'God's plaything' but 'that is the best part of [them]'. Play (and culture), for Plato, amount to the only activities that are, in this ultimate sense, serious because they enact the reality of our human being. Play – and, again, the culture which manifests play – is in this sense a sacred act.

To the modern ear Plato seems to overstate the nature of play. Today, play is typically thought of as what, in Ancient Greek, was known as *paidia*, 'children's play', with all its connotations of frivolousness and inappropriateness for the responsible and serious adult. But once it is noticed that play is not just one of various activities (such as swimming, writing, thinking, etc.) but is a way of organizing, encountering and engaging in an activity, then the special place Plato reserves for play becomes clearer. Play, as Huizinga (1955) argued, is not said to be *done* (as are most activities) but is said to be 'played'. It is a manner of acting rather than an activity (or set of activities). Psychologists and sociologists of play agree with Huizinga that almost all activities can be played, irrespective of their content (e.g., Bruner, 1972; Caillois,

2001; Sutton-Smith, 1997; Winnicott, 1971). In Plato's sense, play is understood as a particularly noble way to act since, through its fundamental 'non-seriousness', it acknowledges the ultimate uncertainty of outcomes. In this way it becomes, for Plato, among the most serious and sacred of matters.

Irrespective of such an elevated understanding of play, the concept is commonly applied over a vast range of activity and experience (see Sutton-Smith, 1997: 3–5). In the literature many different types of play have been identified. These include physical play (sometimes called locomotor play in animals other than humans) involving physical use of the body (e.g., running games, 'rough and tumble' play); solitary play; social play (involving interactions with others); object play (e.g., playing with a toy); fantasy or pretend play (sometimes called narrative play); unstructured or free play; and organized sports (see Ahloy-Dallaire et al., 2018). This observation alone indicates that the uses made of the word 'play', while hopefully related in some sense, are diverse. Not only are children and adult humans said to play but so also are a range of animals (and not only when young – see Webber and Lee, 2020 on elephant play). In English, even a mechanism might have some 'play' in it (i.e., some degree of looseness) (Huizinga, 1955). The English word 'play' may have, uniquely, brought together a range of variant but related forms of activity that, in other languages, are each referred to with a specific term but have not been brought together beneath an umbrella concept (Huizinga, 1955: 28–45).

Even when attention is limited to children and adults, once more there is a range of uses of the word 'play'. People play games (e.g., board games, card games, games of chance, games of skill), sports and musical instruments or simply play in a spontaneous, open-ended or even idling manner. But, as already emphasized, there is also acknowledgment of a 'playfulness' that can be brought to bear on almost any activity. Therefore, people can be 'at play' or can be playful when they socialize and make conversation (Simmel, 1949), have sex, 'play with words' (for humour or for manipulative purposes, e.g., playing 'mind games'), play with ideas, and so on (Sutton-Smith, 1997: 3–4). Over time, the word 'play' has taken on these numerous meanings and been applied to so many activities that, as the philosopher of play Mihai Spariosu (1989: 1) summarized over thirty years ago in his book *Dionysus Reborn*, 'the play concept remains today as elusive as it was two thousand years ago'.

For practical purposes, what, then, are the essential characteristics of play? In answer, it is worth following the lead of Spariosu (1989: 3–5). He argued that it is probably best to understand the varieties of uses of the concept 'play' by thinking in terms of what philosopher Ludwig Wittgenstein called 'family resemblance'. Using the word 'games' as an example, Wittgenstein (1967: 66–71) argued that such a concept cannot be said to have some strict definitional essence, although – if it was desired for some particular purpose – a strict definition could be imposed to limit the kind of purpose intended. Nevertheless, this lack of a precise definition does not prevent ready use of the concept of 'game' seemingly with little effort as, in everyday life, is also done with the concept of 'play'. What substitutes perfectly adequately for a precise definition, according to Wittgenstein, is the idea of 'family resemblance'. Just as not all family members can be defined by a particular feature (e.g., blonde hair) so, too, the concept 'play' has numerous features associated with it that produce a 'family resemblance' but which, individually, might not occur in any particular instance of what we call 'play'. Definitions proposed by different theorists can usefully be seen as emphasizing one or more of these 'family features' for their own purposes. Approaching play in this open way is also in line with Sutton-Smith's (1997) consideration of the 'seven rhetorics' that make use of the concept (Sutton-Smith also leaned on a Wittgensteinian approach to understanding play).

Most formal definitions of play have this overlapping nature and so can be understood in terms of a family resemblance. A well-used definition from the psychology of play, for example, states that in play activity, 'behaviors must be voluntary, be observed in a "relaxed field," not be functional in the observed context, and have elements that are exaggerated, segmented, and nonsequential in relation to the functional behavior' (Burghardt, 2005 cited in Pellegrini, 2009: 132). Similarly – but not identically – evolutionary psychologist and play researcher Peter Gray (2013: 140) summarized the literature by arguing that there are typically five features involved in play: it is 'self-chosen' (i.e., voluntary); it is an activity where means are more valued than ends (i.e., not functional); the structure and rules of play activity arise from the 'minds of players' not from necessity; play is 'imaginative and non-literal' and removed 'from "real" or "serious" life'; and play is carried out in an 'active, alert, but non-stressed' way (i.e., occurs in a 'relaxed field'). Notably, Gray (2013) includes mention of rules – which Burghardt's definition does not – and emphasizes that these are rules developed by the players.

Beyond psychological definitions, in Johann Huizinga's (1955) landmark work *Homo ludens*, play – or the 'play element' – is investigated in all its diversity and cultural expressions. Given its dominant role in setting the agenda for both theory and empirical research on play, it is worth considering Huizinga's (1955) account in detail. Huizinga (1955: 2) was interested in 'what play is *in itself*' as opposed to its function or goal. Similarly, Csikszentmihalyi (1975) argued that play is 'autotelic' in that it has, and generates, its own *telos* or purpose. This direct focus on play '*in itself*' led Huizinga (1955: 2) to ask, 'what actually is the *fun* in playing?' Why, as he put it, does a baby 'crow with pleasure', a gambler become lost in 'passion' and a football crowd get 'roused to a frenzy'. This feature of play has been identified by other researchers. Berlyne

(1966), for example, understood play as fundamentally a search for arousal and stimulation. Similarly, Henricks (2014: 192) sees human play as an attempt at the Piagetian notion of 'assimilation' of the world and a means 'to experience the pleasure that comes from imposing [one's] own behavioral strategies on the world'.

This intense experiential potential of play Huizinga (1955: 3) called 'the primordial quality of play' and it is this aspect of the experience of 'fun' in playing that 'resists all analysis, all logical interpretation'. That is, despite its supposed 'non-seriousness' and its separation from the material demands of 'serious life', play can nevertheless engulf us in a way that the serious world may not, or perhaps cannot. (As for the supposed 'non-seriousness' of play, Huizinga (1955: 5) simply responds that 'some play can be very serious indeed'.)

It was this human predisposition to become absorbed in play that provided a clue, for Huizinga, of the deep significance that play has for us. This 'primordial quality' led Huizinga to argue not only that much adult (cultural) behaviour could be understood as play, but also that play, in evolutionary times, 'is older than culture', since 'animals play just like men' (Huizinga, 1955: 1). The primacy of play in relation to culture is partly what makes it, for Huizinga (1955), irreducible to other parts of life. Conceptually, play cannot be subsumed within some other category of activity. Play is an end, not a means.

Vitally, to the extent that play does have a function, it is 'a *significant* function', which is to say that it signifies, or means, something to the players themselves (Huizinga, 1955: 1). Play only becomes play if the players go along with the signifiers that indicate that *this* is play. Hence, play 'transcends the immediate needs of life and imparts meaning to the action' and 'all play means something' (Huizinga, 1955: 1). The presence of that inherent meaning ('*significant* function') implies, for Huizinga (1955: 1), that play also has a 'non-materialistic quality in the nature of the thing [play] itself'. By 'non-materialistic' Huizinga is not arguing against a naturalistic view of play – that would be inconsistent with his point about play pre-dating culture in the evolutionary sense. Instead, a focus on the '*significant* function' of play opens up the plethora of human institutions and cultural practices for analysis by the play researcher. All of these practices can be seen, especially in terms of their form, as expressions of the 'play element'. Ritual, poetry, law, the sacred, religion, myth, 'knowing', philosophy, art, war and even contemporary 'Western Civilization' ('*Sub specie ludi*') can all be insightfully understood, according to Huizinga, through the lens of play.

Famously, this insight led Huizinga (1955: 178) to conclude that 'civilization is, in its earliest phases, played' and that 'it does not come *from* play like a baby detaching itself from the womb: it arises *in* and *as* play, and never leaves it'. Simply, cultural activities are played activities and, while the consciousness of their play element may, over historical time, attenuate or even vanish, the play form – and vestiges of the play element – remains. Even a ritual that, today, may seem to have lost its meaning (such as a pro forma farewell for a work colleague) or is deadly serious (as in the formal declaration of a death sentence in court) remains a manifestation of the play element of culture.

There are several components of the notion of play that Huizinga (1955) highlights and are worth briefly reviewing, especially since they relate to wellbeing and work in organizations. The most often cited definition of play that Huizinga (1955: 28 my italics) provides is the following:

> [p]lay is a *voluntary activity* or occupation executed within certain *fixed limits of time and place*, according to *rules freely accepted* but absolutely binding, having its *aim in itself* and accompanied by *a feeling of tension, joy* and the consciousness that it is '*different*' from 'ordinary life'.

Again, Huizinga's definition demonstrates the overlapping nature of definitions of play.

'First and foremost', Huizinga (1955: 7) states, 'all play is a voluntary activity' and 'play to order is no longer play'. As the definitions by Burghardt and Gray (2005 cited in Pellegrini, 2009) demonstrate, freedom and autonomy are widely acknowledged as central to any definition of play. Children and animals may play because of evolutionary and developmental causes, but each instance of play occurs just because 'they enjoy playing' and 'therein lies their freedom'. How best such freedom can be nested within work settings in a way that allows for play remains an interesting and open question.

One of the ways that play is signified is that it is separated, in both space and time, from 'ordinary life'. This is obvious with physical spaces such as playing fields, boards in board games, playgrounds, a children's fort temporarily constructed out of boxes, the performance stage, even the battle 'field' and the courtroom. Within these arenas the rules apply and the play proceeds. To be play, however, the activity must also be limited in time. The starting and final whistles in a sports game signal those limits and, even during the game, 'time out' of play can be signalled or called (children can have special words or signals to declare a pause in play). Even where there is no set time limit the playing ends once the 'goal' is achieved: the first player to 10 points; checkmate in chess; finding the treasure in a treasure hunt; being 'out' in a game. Play that may seem aimless, such as doodling or whittling, lasts only so long as there is time to doodle or wood left to whittle.

Similarly, rules emerge in play as naturally as does joy. Developmental psychologists have often focused on children's play for this reason and noted how central cooperative rule-following is in the social world (e.g., Piaget, 1962; Vygotsky, 1978). The solitary whittler – to continue with that example – transforms a mindless reflex action into playing by aiming to generate the sharpest point or to plane the thinnest sliver of wood and the actions are played out according to tacit rules. The goal and the rules are self-imposed

purely to generate the play element. In social play, children spend a good deal of time establishing, amending and even dispensing with rules that have been constructed to coordinate the playing. Arguments over the rules in more serious sporting events and codes may seem far removed from the play ideal, but it is notable that there is never any argument over whether there should be any rules at all.

Fundamental to Huizinga's (1955) understanding of play is the ancient Greek notion of 'agon' or 'contest' and 'competition'. Associated with any contest is the 'tension' and, potentially, the 'joy' mentioned in Huizinga's definition. Even if the contest is only with oneself, or with the aim of acquiring a skill, or with an environment to be 'conquered' or to 'test' oneself against, the contest presents itself in and through play. Especially for Huizinga (1955), the idea of a contest is vital to the experience of being at play and is connected with the ability of play activity to absorb us so readily. It is no coincidence that Huizinga (1955) makes particular use of the contest aspect of play as a means to detect the play element in so many cultural forms. Contest is not only present in sport and games but also in battle, in the practice of the law, in everyday social performances (epitomized today by much behaviour on social media), in ritual, in artistic performance and production, and in religion. It is also, of course, present in work and business.

Following on from, and in reaction to, Huizinga's account of play, French sociologist Roger Caillois (2001) suggested, like Huizinga, that play is separated off from ordinary space and time, freely undertaken, uncertain in outcome, regulated (rule-based), unproductive and involving pretence in some form. Caillois (2001) was particularly concerned with Huizinga's focus on 'agon' (contest) as an essential feature of play and, in response, formulated a spectrum of play. The spectrum ranged from pure 'paidia' (frivolous, active, exuberant and spontaneous like 'children's play') to the 'ludic' (latin, roughly, for 'game' and involving calculation and rule-bound activity). Caillois' categories along this spectrum included 'agon' (contest); 'alea' (chance – Caillois was particularly interested in gambling and thought it a major omission from Huizinga's account, perhaps unfairly given Huizinga's (1955) extensive discussion of fate and fortune); mimicry (simulation, re-enactment, etc.); and 'ilinx' (vertigo – such as notions of possession and transportation in ritual dances or literal vertigo when a child spins around and around, repetitively).

An important point that Huizinga (1955) and Caillois (2001) agreed upon was the interesting case of cheats versus 'spoil sports' (or what Caillois, 2001: 7 calls 'the nihilist'). While the cheat at least still accepts the rules of play (signified by attempting to break them without notice), the 'spoil sport' questions the playing itself. As Caillois (2001: 7) argued, 'the game is ruined by the nihilist who denounces the rules as absurd and conventional, who refuses to play because the game is meaningless'. This nihilism is the ultimate act of resistance expressed not just *through* play but *against* play, at least in some particular instance. Given both Huizinga's and Caillois' agreement that play can be detected in many cultural spheres – including religion, the law and politics – the harsher treatment of the heretic or revolutionary than the thief becomes understandable. (The same could perhaps be said of the worker who resists an organizational culture of play.)

While Huizinga and Caillois were concerned with play (and games) 'in itself', many other play researchers have been concerned with identifying its *functions*. The assumption that play is 'for' something – that it has a function that goes beyond the playing itself – is widespread. In the 19th century Spencer saw play as using up excess energy; Lazarus, by contrast, saw play as 're-creation' and a means to restore energy; Groos claimed its usefulness for practising instincts (Henricks, 2014: 191). Following in those early functional footsteps, more recent developmental and evolutionary approaches have emphasized both the immediate developmental functions and benefits of play along with the future utility of the behaviours that are practised in play by many young animals (Pellegrini and Bjorklund, 2004; Pellegrini et al., 2007; Piaget, 1962; Vygotsky, 1978). Play has been studied in a remarkable range of species including fish, invertebrates and mammals (Webber and Lee, 2020: 1–19). This is evolutionary evidence for some form of function given its energetic costs. Pelligrini and Bjorklund (2004), for example, point out that the 'non-serious' nature of children's and young animals' play – which accounts for around 10% of energy consumption – is usually explained as involving deferred benefits (that are evolutionarily advantageous). They argue, however, that there are also immediate benefits, especially from fantasy play in children, such as the ability to secure food, sustain social interactions and detect cheaters.

More broadly, the play behaviour observed in young animals involves the exercise and practise of bodily and social skills such as those used for hunting – or evading being hunted – and fighting. Various mammals play versions of the chasing game and, intriguingly, the greatest behavioural expression of excitement (and, in children, laughter) is, in prey species, from the animal being chased rather than the chaser – and vice versa (Gray, 2013). Similarly, in huntergatherer bands children will play at hunting with bows and arrows if that is the means that adults use to hunt and, more generally, will mimic a range of adult behaviours through play (Gray, 2013). Given these functional approaches to play, it is perhaps not surprising that a dominant theme in studies of play at work is an argument for its instrumental value. Nevertheless, one question is 'value for whom?'

WELLBEING AND PLAY

A possibility that follows on from the typical characteristics associated with play is that one of the functions of play might be to contribute to a state of wellbeing in individuals. There is, however, an unanswered question here about the direction of the relationship: play only seems to occur in settings that lack stress or threat. (These settings may well be the original markers for the temporal and spatial separation of play from ordinary life that, as discussed, has been central to many theories of play, e.g., Caillois, 2001; Huizinga, 1955.) Young animals play when the risk from predation, hunger or other threats is least likely. Play happens least often, for example, in young elephants when they are independently foraging (Webber and Lee, 2020). It is also suppressed when animals are poorly nourished or under other threatening situations and has been used, when present, as an indicator of animal welfare (see Ahloy-Dallaire et al., 2018 for a comprehensive review of the links between animal play, including humans, and welfare). Similarly, negative emotional states, especially in children, are well-known to decrease play activity but also are associated with changes in the quality of play. Children under emotional stress and negative states will not only play less but also engage in more solitary than social play and have shorter bouts of play (Ahloy-Dallaire et al., 2018).

What, at least in humans, we might call 'psychological safety' therefore seems essential for play to occur. Interestingly, under conditions of psychological threat, people tend to emphasize extrinsic goals (e.g., money, popularity and appearance) rather than intrinsic goals (e.g., growth, intimacy and community) (Sheldon and Kasser, 2008) despite the former being most often detrimental to wellbeing (Kasser, 2002). In organizational settings, intrinsic goals such as growth and community are arguably as important both for the organization and the employee as extrinsic aspirational goals such as monetary reward and popularity/status.

As Fredrickson and Losada's (2005) 'broaden and build' theory of positive affect

(emotions) posits, only once positive emotional states are achieved is there sufficient opportunity for the development of resources and skills (personal, psychological, social, practical) and the practice of exploratory, open and creative behaviours – all associated with play – to arise. Therefore, one aspect of wellbeing (i.e., positive affective states) may be a *precondition* for the emergence of play in its fullest sense. Yet, play is also frequently – and even fundamentally – defined as the pursuit of enjoyment and fun. Perhaps it is therefore best to consider the relationship between play and wellbeing as mutually constitutive, at least in the ideal and at least in the aspect of enjoyment. Play, for example, has a well-documented ability to generate positive affect. Overall, the argument that animal play – including in humans – can lead to or cause improvements in welfare and positive affect is overwhelming, leading Ahloy-Dallaire et al. (2018: 4) to conclude that 'if animals are motivated to play, then to have a chance of attaining optimal welfare, they should be allowed to play'.

In this spirit, numerous relationships have been found between play and wellbeing. If, broadly, wellbeing can be understood in two traditions – the hedonistic and eudaimonistic (e.g., Diener, 1984; Ryff, 1989) – then both approaches to wellbeing have many connections with play. For example, not only is play fundamentally associated with 'fun' and pleasure but (adult) playfulness has also been found to be closely associated with various so-called character strengths (Proyer and Ruch, 2011). The rules-based nature of play also fits neatly with the conditions for the experience of 'flow' (Csikszentmihalyi, 1975, 1997), a type of activity routinely reported as being highly valued and enjoyable. Flow requires activity that, among other conditions, has clear goals and structure and the provision of fast and accurate feedback. The inherent tendency of play activity to give rise to, and be based upon, structure and rules makes it, like the work setting, a prime site for the experience of flow. Similarly, the depth of engagement that occurs within play activity (Huizinga, 1955) is one of five components in Seligman's (2011) theory of wellbeing known as 'PERMA' (Positive affect, engagement, relationships, meaning, accomplishment). In fact, once features of play already considered are aligned with the PERMA model, the two can appear near identical: 'P'=fun/enjoyment of play; 'E'=absorption and immersion in play; 'R'=interactions of players; 'M'=play's 'significant function' and the way it 'imparts meaning to action' (Huizinga, 1955: 1); 'A'=the aspect of *contest* goals and challenge in play ('agon').

Wellbeing and play have much in common. Considering the definitions of play already discussed, one important feature of play is that it is voluntary, freely undertaken or, simply, autonomous activity. *Auto-nomous* literally means 'self-law' or 'self-governing'. Much play behaviour can therefore be understood as developing, or pre-supposing, autonomy and the skills that enable it. Physical play leads to mastery of the body while social play leads to what psychologists call a 'theory of mind' that helps an individual successfully navigate the social world (Pellegrini and Bjorklund, 2004). Similarly, much play is social in nature and involves cooperative interaction (to the point, according to Huizinga, of developing the full range of cultural practices). Further, the contest aspects of play and the rules that regulate it place a premium on the expression and development of a range of skills, from the physical to the cognitive and even poetic and artistic.

Reflecting on these features of autonomy and social interaction it is worth considering one of the most influential and well-researched theories of both motivation and wellbeing. In their Self-Determination Theory, Ryan and Deci (2000, 2017) argue that three universal needs underpin not only human motivation but also 'wellness'. These needs are (i) the need for autonomy (hence, 'self-determination'); (ii) the need for competence (a sense of effectiveness in the world); and (iii) the need for relatedness (quality connection to others). The alignment between central features of play and this widely used understanding of the basis for human thriving needs little explanation. While play can generate considerable conflict and potentially negative experiences, it is clear that it also has the potential to meet these supposed universal needs and, therefore, to support the experience of wellbeing. Whether wellbeing arises through pleasure, engagement or meaning (or any combination of these), play appears to support the entire package.

PLAY, WORK AND ORGANIZATIONS

For anyone interested in developments in workplace management in the 21st century, it is hard to miss the enthusiasm now being generated for the incorporation of play into work in organizations. The play cultures of the newly dominant digital technology companies like Google, Facebook and LinkedIn (Petelczyc et al., 2018) have been much touted. But there have also been older trends for subsidizing or providing recreational opportunities, exercise facilities, or organized sporting and team-building events in workplaces. Overall, there has been a noticeable increase in acceptance of the idea that play at work can provide opportunities and advantages for organizational performance and employee wellbeing. This insight did not, however, come out of the blue.

Research now supports the assumption that various deliberate or spontaneous attempts to incorporate play, or a 'play culture', into organizational work has its benefits. Play has been found to have a positive effect on job satisfaction, workplace stress and competence (Abramis, 1990; Rood and Meneley, 1991; Sørenson and Spoelstra, 2011), workplace social interactions and bonding (Roy, 1959; Sørenson and Spoelstra, 2011), positive affect (mood) (Webster and Martocchio, 1992), innovation and creativity (Amabile,

1997; Amabile et al., 2005; Deal and Key, 1998; Hunter et al., 2010; Mainemelis and Ronson, 2006; Schrage, 2000; West et al., 2016), problem solving (Jacobs and Statler, 2006) and learning (Spraggon and Bodolica, 2017; Statler et al., 2009; Webster and Martocchio, 1992). (See Mainemelis and Ronson, 2006; Tökkäri, 2015; and Petelczyc et al., 2018 for informative reviews of aspects of play in organizations.) All of these effects are consistent with general findings on play beyond the workplace. Yet, embracing play – and playfulness – in the workplace is a relatively recent phenomenon. The story of the relationship between play, work and wellbeing – both in fact and in the research literature – is a complicated one, in keeping with the ambiguity of the understandings of play discussed previously. It is, though, a story worth telling.

There has been a progression, over time, in views of the relationship between play and work, especially as expressed through the management of work (e.g., Hunter et al., 2010; Petelczyc et al., 2018; Sørenson and Spoelstra, 2011). Costea et al. (2007) provide a detailed account of the development of these understandings of play that generated a variety of management ideologies. In outline, the progression has been from seeing play and work as separate and antithetical spheres of life to the claim that they are almost indistinguishable (or should be). As Costea et al. (2007: 157) summarize: 'Play at work, or play as work?'

This shift in managerial perceptions of the relationship between play and work has, since the 1920s, been dramatic. The fundamental and long-standing separation of work and play is one of the most widely noted cultural and social assumptions of modernity and, in practice, still lingers today. Weber's (1930) seminal work on the *Protestant Ethic and the Spirit of Capitalism* laid bare the rationalist bureaucratic and managerial bases of public and private sector organizations under capitalism. In that light, Huizinga's (1955) characterization of play as inherently

irrational – since it is separate from ordinary life and serves no ends beyond itself despite taking up both time and energy – is therefore set up for an anarchic collision with the very idea of capitalist productivity understood in terms of rational efficiency.

In fact, the roots of this belief in the separation of work and play go down deep into the language. In English, the negation of 'play' is 'earnest' (Huizinga, 1955: 44). The word 'earnest' has a special link to work – to 'earn' a living, perhaps through 'earnest' endeavour. This earnestness is, according to Huizinga (1955: 45), defined simply as a negation of play. The reverse – importantly for the world of work – is not the case. Play is not the negation of earnestness. What a person does in earnest cannot be play; but play can be played in earnest. This asymmetry raises the possibility that modern work can be supplemented and retooled through 'earnest play' (or 'serious play', as soon to be discussed). There is also the possibility that play can be nested within higher-order (serious) organizational goals without losing too much of its fundamental play character. These possibilities have been – and continue to be – explored in both practice and theory.

The notion that work is work and play is play, as Henry Ford believed (Ford and Crowther, 2007), acted for much of the 20th century as a Berlin Wall of managerial belief about the relationship between these two basic human orientations. The scientific management of the workplace under so-called 'Taylorism' institutionalized this belief and is immortalized in the telling expression 'Factory *Hands*'; hands that were in need of strict guidance and direction by the managers of production. Factory hands are not playful hands. Only when this approach became untenable – given worker resistance – did modern Human Resource management arise with the attendant shift to a focus on the 'Sentimental Worker' who had needs to be satisfied, motivation to be ignited and morale to be boosted (Hollway, 1991).

The idea of the 'Sentimental Worker' opened the door to the now familiar concerns with job satisfaction and, latterly, workplace wellbeing. But it also led to the kinds of management innovations that bring – or allow – play into the workplace. As mentioned, initially this was expressed through companies providing 'recreational' facilities on the assumption that engagement in recreational or leisure pursuits, even during the workday, would enable workers to restore their productive capacities. But this initial change was only one of a number of overlapping developments that have taken place.

In a second, later, development, play itself became co-opted into work, initially for specific groups of people – such as managers and strategists – as an aid to achieve work tasks such as developing strategy, learning new management techniques and building team loyalty. The notion of 'Serious Play' (see Schrage, 2000) has been used to indicate these deliberate uses of play as a means to achieve organizational ends. Serious play involves activities that remain distinct from work itself as they 'differ qualitatively from work' but, nevertheless, they are designed to 'purposefully benefit the organization' (Statler et al., 2009: 96). As Sørenson and Spoelstra (2011: 84) pithily phrase it (borrowing from von Clausewitz's famous saying that 'war is politics by other means'): in serious play, play becomes 'a continuation of work by other means'. Serious play has, in turn, generated a commercial opportunity through, for example, the use of specially designed workshops that use the trademarked 'LEGO Serious Play' products. Play has become part of the serious business of business (Butler et al., 2011). It is also worth noting that early work, and many studies since, targeted workplaces in the areas of design, software, and the creative and digital economy (e.g., Sørenson and Spoelstra, 2011; Spraggon and Bodolica, 2017; Sutton and Hargadon, 1996). Indeed, much of the interest in play at work has been confined to these workplaces, which suggests that workplace

developments (e.g., the emergence of new industries) are partly behind the advocacy for play in organizations.

A third, quantitative, shift in the role of play occurred through the 'democratization' of play activity in the workplace. This was a particularly important change as it was the first suggestion that play might be a central feature of work itself and not just confined to particular kinds of work such as designing or strategizing. As Costea et al. (2007: 162) argued, 'the constituency of "players" in organisations expands from training settings and innovative processes confined to those who design, manage, or "think strategically" nowadays all organisational members can and ought to play [sic]'. Play, that is, may be a necessary dimension of organizational culture for all workers so that they can perform their work effectively to a high-performance level and, at the same time, in a manner that enhances job satisfaction, engagement and overall wellbeing. This shift was principally an extension of the functional approach – adopted in the 'serious play' perspective – in seeing play as a tool to be used to enhance organizational performance, but on a more ambitious scale. Consequently, and as already highlighted, research interest on the relationship between work and play remained focused on the organizational functions, strategic purposes or operational needs associated with work that play might influence, for good or ill.

Indeed, underlying this focus on the possibilities of play at work is the same ambiguity found in the idea of play itself. In the workplace, play has either been seen as a wasteful diversion from work or, in the form of 'serious play', as a means to enhance organizational function. That distinction is partly based on who initiates and manages play in the workplace. Employee-initiated, or 'informal' play (Spraggon and Bodolica, 2018), typically has been treated as uncontrolled and therefore potentially threatening to the organization's functioning, while employer-initiated 'formal' or 'serious' play (Schrage,

2000; Statler et al., 2011) has been assumed, ultimately, to serve the 'serious' work of the organization.

By contrast, some research on play in organizational work settings has maintained a position in line with Huizinga's concern with play for its own sake. Roy (1959) found that workplaces could never totally eliminate the 'play instinct'. Workers inevitably find opportunities for playful social interaction that provide for bonding even under the strictest regimes. Such research on the ethnography of play in work and organizations has enjoyed a recent resurgence. Spraggon and Bodolica (2014: 525), for example, introduced the notion of 'Social Ludic Activities' (SLAs), which are 'a specific form of play that is enacted by employees to cope with firm-related events'. SLAs can be efforts of resistance and challenge, but they can also provide valuable contributions to an organization's goals. By understanding the logic of these forms of play and allowing them space to develop, managers, so the authors argue, can save time and effort. A play culture, that is, need not be imposed but, instead, can be cultivated and supported to grow in ways that provide employees with both 'fun' and engagement with their work and organization. Of course, the management skills to turn this possibility into a daily reality in an organization may well be rare.

Interest in the spontaneous, self-initiated play employees engage in has opened up effects and functions of workplace play that are different from those organizational functions and operations that are often considered the most important. In early qualitative work in the design company IDEO, Sutton and Hargadon (1996) gathered evidence that 'brainstorming' – a collective 'playing' with ideas – may not be the failed organizational experiment that, at the time, it seemed. While research till then had shown that brainstorming did not enhance idea generation (because of processes such as evaluation apprehension, 'free-riding' or 'social loafing', and 'production blocking'), Sutton and Hargadon

(1996) found that its efficiency and effectiveness should not be measured purely in the number of ideas generated. Other, unnoticed, benefits included supporting organizational memory for design solutions, supporting an attitude of wisdom, creating skill variety for designers and even impressing clients. In addition, those involved in brainstorming sessions repeatedly mentioned the 'fun' they found through them. In sum, the shift towards an acceptance of the usefulness of play at work – whether 'formal' or 'informal' play – laid the groundwork for a further shift in the potential relationship between the two previously antagonistic notions.

The claim that the boundary between work and play is diminishing is not new, although it is now perhaps asserted more strongly. The equation of life, play and work is now strongly endorsed by some advocates as an exciting and central insight into human existence (e.g., Kane, 2004). As Costea et al. (2007: 161) explain, in Kane's (2004) characterization, a further (large) step has now been taken along the path to seeing play as an inherent component of work: the question 'is no longer whether there can be any suspicion of play being enlisted by business interests to colonise the lifeworlds of employees, but one of extent'. Nevertheless, changes in the degree and intensity with which an idea is put into effect can lead to qualitative change as well as quantitative change. The equation of 'play as work' has not just led to play being seen as 'a proven method for unleashing creative ideas' (Berg, 1998: 54) but also to understanding play as unleashing the self. Play, in this reading, is understood as the ultimate work resource. As the fulfilment of the 'infinite possibilities arising from full engagement of heart, body and soul' the 'Play Ethic' can release today's worker from 'the narrow expectations of a workaday life' (Kane, 2005b, cited in Costea et al., 2007: 161). For Costea et al. (2005, 2007) this development is a natural consequence of the (post)modern focus on the 'subjectivity' of the individual self. This 'Self' is a 'new divinity' in our late-modern times whom they name 'a *Narcissistic-Dionysian Self-Divinity*, the *Me, Me, Me-god*' (Costea et al., 2007: 154). The subjectivity of this 'new divinity' is what allows the formation of a 'new equation between corporate performance and the total involvement of the person in work' (Costea et al., 2007: 153). A few points can be made about this apparent culmination of a 100-year shift from work and play considered as opposites to them practically coinciding.

First, while it is true that the intensity with which play and work are now said, by some, to have fused, Huizinga (1955) – when writing in the 1930s – was already able to observe a two-way morphing of distinct cultural spheres traditionally associated with play and work. While, in the 19th century, 'all Europe donned the boiler suit' (Huizinga, 1955: 192) as the Industrial Revolution progressed, by the first half of the 20th century Huizinga (1955: 200) noted that 'business becomes play' and had already reached the point that 'some of the great business concerns deliberately instil the play-spirit into their workers so as to step up production'. Simultaneously, sport had undergone 'increasing systematization and regimentation' to the point that 'the pure play-quality is inevitably lost' (Huizinga, 1955: 197) or, again, that sport has been 'raised to such a pitch of technical organization and scientific thoroughness that the real play-spirit is threatened with extinction' (Huizinga, 1955: 199). Huizinga (1955) understood that these two spheres could swing from one end of the play-work pendulum to the other largely because of their common element of contest ('agon') and competition. The arrival of business and trade statistics, he argued, fed into this perception that business could be a 'game' that could be won and that the competition was over 'the highest turnover, the biggest tonnage, the fastest crossing' or any other measurable outcome involved in doing business (Huizinga, 1955: 200).

Indeed, the study of leisure and sport confirms the trend that Huizinga (1955) observed and that has now intensified. Duerden et al.

(2018) have noted how postmodern perspectives on leisure and work have blurred the boundary between the two and opened up opportunities to explore what they term 'Leisure at Work' (LAW). Further, in the field of 'serious leisure' (Stebbins, 2007), leisure, like work, can co-opt play. Stebbins (2015) calls this 'augmented play' – play that augments the practice of some leisure activity, especially in its 'core activity'. The core activity of a downhill skier is to ski down a hill but, on the way down or when practising, the skier may 'play' with different movements or switches of centre of gravity perhaps to speed up the descent. Play is a creative engine that serves the core activity. Similarly, Vermeulen et al. (2016: 199) note the 'anomalous character of sport' that results from the 'tension of sport as both play and work'. Further, given that organizations 'are replete with sporting metaphors that give meaning to their practices, such as competition, the notion of the arena, selection, excellence, talent and teamwork' sport in its play aspect 'may be a vantage point to understand organizations and organizing differently' (Vermeulen et al., 2016: 200).

Second, Costea et al.'s (2007) 'Narcissistic-Dionysian' divinity, from a wellbeing perspective, appears to meld the hedonistic and eudaimonic perspectives on wellbeing into a heady brew. Aristotle – from whom we get the term 'eudaimonia' – had already pointed out that the 'good life' would also have a reasonable measure of the 'pleasant life', but he no doubt never envisaged that the assertion of selfhood involved a self that 'has an ultimate entitlement to a "24/7" hedonistic existence' (Costea et al., 2007: 154). But Costea et al.'s (2005, 2007) general point that the incorporation of play into the workplace is today closely linked to cultural understandings of the self is worth considering. In fact, it leads to a third point: consideration of the self, and its wellbeing, in relation to play.

Recall that one of Sutton-Smith's (1997) modern rhetorics of play is the rhetoric of the self. This rhetoric idealizes play through 'attention to the desirable experiences of the players – their fun, their relaxation, their escape' and it is in this rhetoric that 'the central advocacies of the secular and consumerist manner of modern life invade the interpretations of play' (Sutton-Smith, 1997: 11). The idea that one of the functions of play is to express and realize the self has already been mentioned (see Henricks, 2014). For all animals that play, play can be understood as a means to 'make coherent their possibilities for acting in the world' (Henricks, 2014: 190). Simply, it is a process of self-realization. In keeping with educational theorists such as Maria Montessori and John Dewey as well as developmental psychologists such as Jean Piaget and Lev Vygotsky, for Henricks (2014: 193) play is primarily 'something that builds the person'. And, this person-building is achieved particularly through 'make-believe play' that involves engagement with 'complicated forms of cultural imagination and social dialogue' (another of Sutton-Smith's 1997 modern rhetorics – the 'imaginary') (Henricks, 2014: 194). Seen as self-realization, play 'is not a flight from the world: it is inquiry into the challenges and responsibilities of social living' (Henricks, 2014: 194).

In organizational studies there has been research on how identity work is maintained and sustained through work. There has also been the suggestion that people in organizational settings can be thought of as carrying out 'identity play' (Ibarra and Petriglieri, 2010). While 'identity work' involves people 'forming, repairing, maintaining, and strengthening or revising their identities', this omits those situations in which there is uncertainty about what identity should be formed (Ibarra and Petriglieri, 2010: 10). These transitional moments are common in modern workplaces with their repeated changes in roles and responsibilities. That means that today's workers are as often in a process of becoming as they are in a stable process of establishing then maintaining their identities. As Ibarra and Petriglieri (2010: 10

my emphasis) state, 'in organizational life, people work at being certain things but *play* at becoming others'.

Play, that is, can be understood as the medium in which individuals both work out how to be a person in a particular culture and how to sustain personhood within it. To the extent that people today live in what could be termed an 'aspirational culture' (Moore, 2019), with its focus on change, progress and constant improvement, people come to understand their selves in the same way: as projects of unending development of individual potential. Play, with its 'infinite possibilities' may seem like the perfect vehicle for this culturally sanctioned understanding of how best to be a person, given the emphasis on the 'self' and its potential. Indeed, many of the shifts discussed above in research understandings and managerial ideologies concerning the relationship between play, wellbeing and work can be understood as modern work and organizations claiming their position as prime sites for the exercise of such self-realizing play. But a tension remains over whether wellbeing through play is best served by the absorption of play into work – or, indeed, whether or not that absorption is sustainable over time. Understanding how such a tension might be resolved will require more research.

FUTURE DIRECTIONS

As this brief review has shown, exploration of the relationship between play, wellbeing and work is just beginning. Opportunity for further research is therefore vast. The extensive review by Petelczyc et al. (2018: table 2, p. 177) has provided some suggestions for a future research agenda. These suggestions represent a pragmatic approach to advancing empirical and theoretical understanding of play at work. They are also largely in the tradition of emphasizing the functional approach to play – what it is for and, also, what it might be (used) for. Included in their suggestions are four avenues for extending current research and four broad areas for 'breaking new ground'. Petelczyc et al. (2018) propose that current research could be extended through: investigation of the so-called 'dark side' of play at work; investigation of short-term versus long-term outcomes of play and the psychological processes that drive such outcomes; identification of the moderators of the outcomes of play at work at the individual, team and organizational (cultural) levels; and establishing robust methodological means of measuring play from structural, subjective and organizational approaches.

New areas of research identified by Petelczyc et al. (2018) cover various theoretical directions (e.g., understanding the psychological and psychosocial resources that play might generate or help regulate and the different mood effects on employees of structured versus spontaneous play); exploration of what they term 'instrumental motives' (e.g., the motives and underlying needs satisfied by play at work); identification of the various types of play at work and how they are deployed by and between colleagues and supervisors and any differential effects types of play have; and investigating how play interacts across organizational levels from the individual through teams to the organization as a whole (e.g., how does individual-level play – of different types – affect organizational outcomes; how might a 'playful' organizational culture affect team and individual outcomes; etc.)

A particularly important suggestion Petrelczyc et al. (2018) make is their call for more enquiry into the 'dark side' of play at work. As highlighted, much research has focused on the potential benefits of incorporating forms of play into organizational work. Delving deeper into the costs of play at work would have practical use. What happens to those, for example, who are deemed to play inappropriately at work especially if play is valorized in organizational culture? But, more importantly, such research into both

the positive and negative consequences and experiences of play would also do justice to what is almost universally understood as the 'polymorphous' quality of play (Sørenson and Spoelstra, 2011). By its nature, play may well be a prime site for the generation of so-called unintended consequences. That is, the 'ambiguity' of play may not disappear through its incorporation into the management of organizational work.

That ambiguity also suggests that future research could consider how play transforms – and may in the future transform – work and organizational structures. There is always the anarchic and uncertain element in play and there is no reason to think that that element leaves itself behind on the workplace doorstep. If organizational cultures built on the 'play ethic' wish to avoid charges of cynicism, the question of how much freedom and autonomy – how much space – can be provided to support the 'play spirit' will always be difficult to answer in practice. The innovative and creative quality of play has been claimed by play theorists to have propelled and underlain major cultural forms. Presumably that capacity for play has the potential not only to serve the organizational culture that provides space for it but also to usurp and reinvent that culture. Yet little is known about whether or not – or how – this might happen.

Finally, there is an opportunity to see play as an *indicator* of welfare and wellbeing (Ahloy-Dallaire et al., 2018; Winnicott, 1971). In the effort to understand how play has been deployed in workplaces there has been a lack of focus on the play that already occurs and has long been present, perhaps irrepressibly so (e.g., Roy, 1959). Especially in the case of 'informal' play initiated by employees and workers, its presence or absence may say something that, hopefully, may be considered important about the welfare and wellbeing of those who work in different kinds of organizations. Such an approach to play – measuring its occurrence as one might take someone's temperature to check their health – may be one of the most practical relationships that could be established between play and wellbeing at work.

CONCLUSION

Despite its familiarity, play is a complex concept and, more intriguingly, a complex way of being human. Play establishes what appears to be a 'shadow' version of reality but can captivate and motivate people in ways that reality cannot. This captivating feature of play goes a long way to explaining its close association with human wellbeing. But it also provides a basis for understanding what might happen to that wellbeing when play encounters the world of modern work.

Fitting with its complexity, play has undergone a remarkable shift in its relationship to work – from sanctioned outsider to the manifestation of work itself. Current research on play in organizational work settings has provided evidence of many advantages to the deliberate incorporation of play into work, from supporting creativity and innovation to providing employee engagement and loyalty. But – also fitting with its complexity – play has shown itself more than capable of emerging unbidden (at least by managers) in ways that present a challenge to the management of work and to organizational culture. Informal play is summoned not just to complement and continue work tasks and objectives but also to contest them and even to resist and usurp them (Sørenson and Spoelstra, 2011). The fundamental question in both the theory and practice of play at work is the extent to which play can, and should, be left to work itself out.

REFERENCES

Abramis DJ (1990) Play in work: Childish hedonism or adult enthusiasm? *American Behavioral Scientist* 33: 353–373.

Ahloy-Dallaire J, Espinosa J and Mason G (2018) Play and optimal welfare: Does play indicate the presence of positive affective states? *Behavioral Processes* 156: 3–15.

Amabile TM (1997) Motivating creativity in organizations: On doing what you love and loving what you do. *California Management Review* 40(1): 39–58.

Amabile TM, Barsade SG, Mueller JS and Staw BM (2005) Affect and creativity at work. *Administrative Science Quarterly* 50(3): 367–403.

Berg DH (1995) The power of a playful spirit at work. *Journal for Quality & Participation* 18(4): 32–38.

Berg DH (1998) The power of play. *Journal for Quality & Participation* 21(5): 54–55.

Berlyne DE (1966) Curiosity and exploration. *Science* 153: 25–33.

Bruner JS (1972) Nature and sources of immaturity. *American Psychologist* 27: 687–708.

Butler N, Olaison L, Sliwa M, Sørensen BM and Spoelstra S (2011) Work, play and boredom. *Ephemera: Theory and Politics in Organization* 11(4): 329–335.

Caillois R (2001) *Man, Play and Games*. Chicago: University of Illinois Press.

Costea B, Crump N and Holm J (2005) Dionysus at work? The ethos of play and the ethos of management. *Culture and Organization* 11: 139–151.

Costea B, Crump N and Holm J (2007) The spectre of Dionysus: Play, work and managerialism. *Society and Business Review* 2(2): 153–165.

Csikszentmihalyi M (1975) *Beyond Boredom and Anxiety*. San Francisco, CA: Jossey-Bass.

Csikszentmihalyi M (1997) *Creativity: Flow and the Psychology of Discovery and Invention*. New York: HarperPerennial.

Deal T and Key MK (1998) *Corporate Celebration: Play, Purpose, and Profit at Work*. San Francisco: Berrett-Koehler.

Diener E (1984) Subjective well-being. *Psychological Bulletin* 95(3): 542–575.

Duerden MD, Courtright SH and Widmer MA (2018) Why people play at work: A theoretical examination of Leisure-at-Work. *Leisure Sciences* 40(6): 634–648.

Ford H and Crowther S (2007) *My Life and Work*. Sioux Falls, SD: NuVision Publications LLC.

Fredrickson BL and Losada MF (2005) Positive affect and the complex dynamics of human flourishing. *American Psychologist* 60(7): 678–686.

Gray P (2013) *Free to Learn: Why Unleashing the Instinct to Play Will Make Our Children Happier, More Self-Reliant and Better Students for Life*. New York: Basic Books.

Henricks TS (2014) Play as self-realization: Toward a general theory of play. *American Journal of Play* 6(2): 190–213.

Hollway W (1991) *Work Psychology and Organizational Behaviour: Managing the Individual at Work*. London: Sage.

Huizinga J (1955) *Homo Ludens*. Boston, MA: Beacon.

Hunter C, Jemielniak D and Postula A (2010) Temporal and spatial shifts within playful work. *Journal of Organizational Change Management* 23(1): 87–102.

Ibarra H and Petriglieri JL (2010) Identity work and play. *Journal of Organizational Change Management* 23(1): 10–25.

Jacobs CD and Statler M (2006) Toward a technology of foolishness: Developing scenarios through serious play. *International Studies of Management & Organization* 36(3): 77–92.

Kane P (2004) *The Play Ethic: A Manifesto for a Different Way of Living*. London: Macmillan.

Kasser T (2002) *The High Price of Materialism*. Boston, MA: MIT Press.

Mainemelis C and Ronson S (2006) Ideas are born in fields of play: Towards a theory of play and creativity in organizational settings. *Research in Organizational Behavior* 27: 81–131.

Moore K (2019) *Wellbeing and Aspirational Culture*. Cham: Palgrave Macmillan.

Pellegrini AD (2009) *The Role of Play in Human Development*. New York: Oxford University Press.

Pellegrini AD and Bjorklund DF (2004) The ontogeny and phylogeny of children's object and fantasy play. *Human Nature* 15(1): 23–43.

Pellegrini AD, Dupuis D and Smith PK (2007) Play in evolution and development. *Developmental Review* 27(2): 261–276.

Petelczyc CA, Capezio A, Wang L, Restubog SLD and Aquino K (2018) Play at work: An integrative review and agenda for future research. *Journal of Management* 44(1): 161–190.

Piaget J (1962) *Play, Dreams, and Imitation in Childhood* (G Gattegno and FM Hodgson, Trans.). New York: Norton.

Proyer RT and Ruch W (2011) The virtuousness of adult playfulness: The relation of playfulness with strengths of character. *Psychology of Well-Being: Theory, Research and Practice* 1: 1–12.

Rood RP and Meneley BL (1991) Serious play at work. *Personnel Journal* 70(1): 90–97.

Roy DF (1959) 'Banana time': Job satisfaction and informal interaction. *Human Organization* 18: 158–168.

Ryan RM and Deci EL (2000) Self-determination theory and the facilitation of intrinsic motivation, social development, and well-being. *American Psychologist* 55: 68–78.

Ryan RM and Deci EL (2017) *Self-Determination Theory: Basic Psychological Needs in Motivation, Development, and Wellness*. New York: Guilford Press.

Ryff CD (1989) Happiness is everything, or is it? *Journal of Personality and Social Psychology* 57(6): 1069–1081.

Schrage M (2000) *Serious Play*. Boston, MA: Harvard Business School Press.

Seligman MEP (2011) *Flourish: A Visionary New Understanding of Happiness and Well-being*. New York: Free Press.

Sheldon KM and Kasser T (2008) Psychological threat and extrinsic goal striving. *Motivation and Emotion* 32: 37–45.

Simmel G (1949) The sociology of sociability. *American Journal of Sociology* 55: 254–261.

Sørensen BM and Spoelstra S (2011) Play at work: Continuation, intervention and usurpation. *Organization* 19: 81–97.

Spariosu M (1989) *Dionysus Reborn: Play and the Aesthetic Dimension in Modern Philosophical and Scientific Discourse*. Ithaca, NY: Cornell University Press.

Spraggon M and Bodolica V (2014) Social ludic activities: A polymorphous form of organizational play. *Journal of Managerial Psychology* 29(5): 524–540.

Spraggon M and Bodolica V (2017) Collective tacit knowledge generation through play: Integrating socially distributed cognition and transactive memory systems. *Management Decision* 55(1): 119–135.

Spraggon M and Bodolica V (2018) A practice-based framework for understanding (informal) play as practice phenomena in organizations. *Journal of Management and Organization* 24(6): 846–869.

Statler M, Heracleous L and Jacobs CD (2011) Serious play as a practice of paradox. *Journal of Applied Behavioral Science* 47(2): 236–256.

Statler M, Roos J and Victor B (2009) 'Ain't misbehavin'': Taking play seriously in organizations. *Journal of Change Management* 9(1): 87–107.

Stebbins RA (2007) *Serious Leisure: A Perspective for Our Time*. New Brunswick, NJ: Transaction.

Stebbins RA (2015) *The Interrelationship of Leisure and Play: Play as Leisure, Leisure as Play*. Basingstoke: Palgrave Macmillan.

Sutton RI and Hargadon A (1996) Brainstorming groups in context: Effectiveness in a product design firm. *Administrative Science Quarterly* 41(4): 685–718.

Sutton-Smith B (1997) *The Ambiguity of Play*. Cambridge, MA: Harvard University Press.

Tökkäri V (2015) Organizational play: Within and beyond managing. *Qualitative Research in Organizational Management: An International Journal* 10(2): 86–104.

Vermeulen J, Koster M, Loos E and van Slobbe M (2016) Play and work: An introduction to sport and organization. *Culture and Organization* 22: 199–202.

Vygotsky LS (1978) *Mind in Society: The Development of Higher Psychological Processes*. Cambridge, MA: Harvard University Press.

Webber CE, Lee PC (2020) Play in elephants: Wellbeing, welfare or distraction? *Animals* 10, 305. Epub ahead of print; DOI:10.3390/ani10020305.

Weber M (1930) *The Protestant Ethic and the Spirit of Capitalism* (T Parsons, Trans.). London: Unwin University Books.

Webster J and Martocchio JJ (1992) Microcomputer playfulness: Development of a measure with workplace implications. *MIS Quarterly* 16: 201–226.

West SE, Hoff E and Carlsson I (2016) Play and productivity: Enhancing the creative climate at workplace meetings with play cues. *American Journal of Play* 9: 71–86.

Winnicott DW (1971) *Playing and Reality*. London: Routledge.

Wittgenstein L (1967) *Philosophical Investigations*. Oxford: Blackwell.

34

Creative Practices for Wellbeing in Organizations: An Emerging Scholarship of Practice Framework

Tony Wall and Richard Axtell

INTRODUCTION

Early indications of how humans understood the connection between visual and performative practices and the wellbeing of communities are documented in the rock art of indigenous communities over 20,000 years ago (Fleischer and Grehan, 2016). Such creative practices, which promote and prioritize wellbeing, have become increasingly widespread globally, and include a 'constellation of ideas, practices, and approaches which are intentionally engaged for health and wellbeing benefits, ranging from explicitly therapeutic interventions to group-based activity more resonant of cultural activity' (Wall et al., 2019b: 1). This constellation includes the adoption and integration of practices from across the visual, literary, and performing arts traditions for wellbeing outcomes and include, for example, the use of storytelling to re-frame and re-claim an individual's sense of *autonomy* in their life, a group's sense of *belonging*, or an organization's

positive sense of *purpose* (Phillips and Becker, 2019; Wall et al., 2019c).

The growth in the use of creative practices for wellbeing outcomes is driven by two key trends. The first is the use of the arts at the grassroots level to help address social challenges in a wide range of organizations; the arts have been recognized as having a capacity that 'offers an antidote to the mental and emotional pollution of commercialism, which eventually lead to the toxification of air, land, water, and the excessive consumption of carbon' (Shrivastava, 2012: 635). Here, the inclusive and participatory potential of arts practices to engage people with different life circumstances has arguably been part of grassroots wellbeing initiatives within health and social care organizations, community organizations, and social housing organizations (Jensen and Bonde, 2018; Coburn and Gormally, 2020). However, it has also extended to service and manufacturing organizations to support stress management, change management, resilience, and wellbeing development (e.g. Cregan et al., 2019; Evans et al., 2019; Phillips and Becker, 2019; Gordon-Nesbitt and Howarth, 2020).

The second and perhaps more significant driver relates to governmental attraction to the efficacy and efficiency of the arts to deliver health and wellbeing benefits, where arts approaches and practices have been funded to supplement or replace aspects of health and social care provision. Here, such practices have become 'normalized' as an effective way of sustaining and improving the health and wellbeing of a wide range of groups in society to extend contribution and reduce costs of servicing populations (Jensen et al., 2017; Whitelaw et al., 2017). These practices can include, for example, arts on prescription, social prescribing, or cultural commissioning, and have come to replace or supplement medical prescriptions and treatments (Makin and Gask, 2012; Torrissen, 2015; Fleischer and Grehan, 2016; Jensen et al., 2017). Some creative practices for wellbeing have been measured and estimated to generate a strong 'return on investment', between £3 return on every £1 invested (Health Education England, 2016) and £11.55 for every £1 invested (Whelan, 2016). Within a context of governmental austerity and decreasing budgets, such narratives of return cast art as an attractive instrument for wellbeing (Brown, 2011; APPG, 2017).

As such, the use of creative practices for wellbeing has deepened and extended within and across disciplinary and practice boundaries such as art therapy, nursing, psychology, and sociology (Stickley et al., 2017), but also a wide range of fields and organizations, including those specializing in health and social care, community outreach and libraries, but also educational and business organizations (Clift et al., 2016; Nyssen et al., 2016; Clift and Stickley, 2017). However, a critical consequence of such growth means that the organizational arrangements and circumstances in which wellbeing is supported and developed can vary dramatically, from informal, loose collections of people supporting

the personal development or therapeutic applications of the arts across fields (e.g. a creative writing group), to formal hierarchical structures safeguarding the protection of vulnerable adults according to a set of highly specified professional standards or criteria (Wall and Axtell, 2020).

Professional bodies have responded to some of these issues through the development and monitoring of professional and practitioner standards; some of these sit alongside the wider professional caring fields (such as the Health Care and Professionals Council which governs standards for art and dance therapists in the UK), whereas other bodies have emerged to address the specific application of art forms such as in visual arts (e.g. the International Expressive Arts Therapy Association, or the Art Therapy Credentials Board), literary arts (e.g. the National Association for Poetry Therapy or the International Federation for Biblio-Poetry Therapy), and performing arts (e.g. the Association for Dance Movement Psychotherapy). However, such frameworks are designed for practitioners with a shared professional understanding, unambiguously working in a health and social care setting, and as such, do not reflect many of the other organizational settings in which creative practices are currently used (Wall and Axtell, 2020).

This chapter examines the emerging issues from the growing use of creative practices for wellbeing in organizations and draws from a recent international study to explore ways in which these issues might be tackled in the future (ibid.). The next section examines the issues which render existing, international professional frameworks unfit for developments in practice. It then highlights the notion of a *scholarship of practice*, whereby a cluster of ideas – based on codified knowledge – is flexibly deployed by practitioners as reflective guidance prompts. While such prompts provide one dimension of guiding action in practice, the next section then outlines the other governance infrastructures that need to underpin and sustain such prompts in practice. The final section considers future directions of research and practice in relation to the use of creative practices for wellbeing in organizations.

FACILITATING WELLBEING ACROSS DIVERSE ORGANIZATIONAL SETTINGS

In the UK, the All-Party Parliamentary Group Inquiry into Arts, Health and Wellbeing (APPG, 2017) cemented the instrumental nature of the arts as for health and wellbeing as a public narrative. It highlighted the myriad health and wellbeing benefits of engagement in the arts, for example: 'positive physiological and psychological changes in clinical outcomes; reducing drug consumption; shortening length of hospital stay; promoting better doctor–patient relationships; improving mental healthcare' (British Medical Association, 2011: 9). Other evidence more or less consistently reports other wellbeing effects including enhanced quality of life, decreased anxiety, depression, and blood pressure, as well as reduced visits to doctors (British Medical Association, 2011; Stickley and Eades, 2013; Fleischer and Grehan, 2016; Jensen et al., 2017; Zarobe and Bungay, 2017).

The performing arts have been recognized as 'the most integrative of all the arts' (British Medical Association, 2011: 10), and evidence has demonstrated health and wellbeing benefits to youth (Zarobe and Bungay, 2017); older people (Bernard et al., 2015; Organ, 2016); people with dementia and their carers (Harries et al., 2013); prisoners (APPG, 2017); people living within urbanization and climate change (Wang, 2017); people fleeing war (Arts Education Partnership, 2011); across 'homes or through community organizations, hospitals, hospices, day centres or nursing homes' (APPG, 2017: 125).

During 2017–2019, Wall and Axtell (2019, 2020) adopted a collaborative, realist methodology to develop a framework to guide practitioners in the use of creative practices in a diversity of organizational settings (and beyond them; a methodology informed by Nyssen et al., 2016). The framework was developed through three key stages. First, 100 professional frameworks from around the world (e.g. the UK, the United States, Ireland, and Australia) were analysed to identify common themes (e.g. Art Therapy Credentials Board, International Expressive Arts Therapy Association, International Federation for Biblio-Poetry Therapy, Irish Association for Counselling and Psychotherapy, Lapidus International, British Association for Counselling and Psychotherapy, British Psychological Society, New Zealand Speech-Language Therapists Association, General Teaching Council for Northern Ireland, Nursing & Midwifery Council, Health Care and Professionals Council, and Royal College of Occupational Therapists). The selection of frameworks was informed and verified by a range of expert practitioners from existing professional bodies and those using creative practices across a range of contexts.

In the second stage of the process, the themes were summarized into 20 carefully crafted statements, which were then taken into the third stage of study (similar to the statement development stage of the Delphi process). In the final stage of the research, the statements were then used as the basis for 'discussion and development of the statements in participatory face-to-face and online consultation meetings' (Wall and Axtell, 2020: 2), with over 50 different roles from the arts, health, business, charities and third sector organizations, and government (e.g. school and university teachers, a wide range of therapists (e.g. art, dance, music, occupational), community writers, poets, musicians, artists, activists, policy advisors, community development professionals, counsellors, psychologists, nurses, public health professionals, researchers, and business professionals).

The extent of agreement and disagreement with each statement, and dialogue extending beyond the content of the statements generated across the consultations, led to the 20 statements being refined to 10 statements. The themes of discussion which implicated the design of the practice framework are outlined below.

Artistic Independence vs Safety-Accountability

Although practitioners shared a common commitment to caring and facilitating wellbeing, views about how that might be facilitated through creative practices differed across the organizational contexts (reflecting insights in the APPG, 2017 and Daniels et al., 2018). This overarching orientation might be conceptualized as a continuum of two extremes. At one end of the continuum, there was a strong value placed upon, and commitment towards, artistic independence and exploration. Here, wellbeing was often described in relation to the *therapeutic* nature of creative process and product, and in particular, the importance of autonomy to explore these. Such a vision connects with a view that the arts should 'should reject demand and ignore critique … disregard outcomes, and sow discord in the world around it' (Pilikian, 2016), where open and free flowing approaches are supportive in guiding practice and wellbeing. Practitioners here often included artists using various forms, or learning and development professionals who had subsequently turned to using creative practices to facilitate wellbeing, and, reflecting a wider trend in wellbeing practitioners, were often not clinically trained (Coburn and Gormally, 2020).

At the other end of the continuum, there was a shift from *therapeutic* applications, to *therapy*, where there was a strong value placed upon, and commitment towards, ensuring all-encompassing and prescriptive mechanisms to ensure the safety of all engaged in the creative practices. Here, wellbeing was often described in relation to the detailed specification of personal,

environmental, and situational factors which could harm those engaged in the creative practices, including participants and those facilitating it in organizations (Hasan et al., 2019). Such an approach was underpinned by a model of medical accountability, where a body of knowledge is extended over time to then mitigate any risks of harm to those engaged in the creative practices (typically referred to as patients; see British Medical Association, 2011). Practitioners here often included counsellors, psychologists, psychiatrists, nurses, public health professionals, and various forms of arts therapists (e.g. art or music). Though this group shared some similar conceptual underpinnings (e.g. Rogers' 1957 person-centred therapeutics), these were not universally shared.

Scale of the Creative Practice Intervention

The scale of the creative practices used for wellbeing outcomes not only highlighted the diversity of application across organizational contexts but also implicated what might need to be in place for that practice to be delivered effectively and safely (Wall and Axtell, 2019). Again, the notion of a continuum gives a pragmatic way to illustrate the points of difference, e.g. from 1 hour to 13 weeks (Phillips and Baker, 2019). At one end of the continuum, the use of creative practices for wellbeing might be minor and subtle, where it appears as part of a wider set of activity which may or may not be related to wellbeing, but the activity is nonetheless designed to inculcate positive affect (Rossetti and Wall, 2017). For example, the activity might include the writing of a short story within a multi-professional leadership team to capture and then develop leadership values, in a way which amplifies positive appreciation (e.g. Wall et al., 2017b). Here, the activity, which could be 10 minutes, might be positively framed to induce positive emotion, focused on a non-contentious work activity within that organization, and with familiar work colleagues. In this context, the risks of, for example, triggering a traumatic episode, might be considered minimal. The wider practice implications of such a small scale intervention, therefore, were fairly minimal.

Towards the other end of the continuum, the creative practices become the intervention or are a central part of it, perhaps for a larger group of people (Nyssen et al., 2016). For example, the intervention might be a year-long development course involving story work, with the same leadership team working on how they build the wellbeing of their staff, which may increase the possibility of sharing more intimate moments and therefore risks of triggering emotional harm. These risks become greater when those involved in the setting are considered vulnerable in health or medical settings, such as people identifying as having mental health challenges or people living with dementia (Abrams et al., 2019). In these scenarios, there are likely to be more rigorous arrangements to ensure effective and safe practice, for example more detailed 'contracting' with participants where a more precise plan of the 'who, what, where, when, and how' of the creative intervention is discussed and agreed in advance (this is outlined in more detail in the practice framework below).

Organizational Relationships and Roles

The final significant point of diversity relates to the practitioner's relationship with an organization, the location of the facilitator within that organization, and the implications of these for the use of creative practices for wellbeing (e.g. Organ 2016; Bickerdike et al., 2017). In terms of the relationship, practitioners could be employed or could be contracted (or sub-contracted) to undertake a piece of commissioned work (APPG, 2017). Each of these can implicate the arrangements in place when using creative practices for wellbeing and who is responsible for making those

arrangements. For example, a hospital might commission a dance firm to hold dance workshops in a hospital, but that firm may then seek sub-contractors to actually host the workshops. This complexity might create space for ambiguity about (a) the particular mobility needs of the participants, (b) the available space and requirements, and (c) who or what insurance is needed to protect individuals should there be an accident given (a) and (b). Such complexity and opportunity for communication gaps are perhaps less likely in an environment where a practitioner organizes their own space and communicates directly with participants, but the practitioner may need to find ways to identify the prior history of participants (Wall and Axtell, 2019).

When working within organizations, the other point of diversity relates to the role the practitioner occupies within that organization. Here, issues can arise in relation to potential role conflicts between an extant role and the role activated when using creative practices for wellbeing. For example, if a practitioner uses creative practices for wellbeing with their own teams, it can be challenging to reconcile (a) a managerial role which may require giving direct instruction to correct performance and (b) a creative facilitation role which encourages open and honest self-exploration in a non-judgemental environment. This reflects a similar situation to professional coaching (Wall et al., 2017a) where the manager may indeed be a source of stress (Quade et al., 2019). Such role conflicts or ambiguities are important because they might negatively affect a range of wellbeing outcomes in an organization (Bowling et al., 2017), and constrain the use of creative practices for wellbeing.

A SCHOLARSHIP OF PRACTICE THROUGH DELIBERATIVE PROMPTS

A salient implication of this diversity relates to the functionality of a single professional framework to flex to the complex landscapes of practice where creative practices are deployed for wellbeing outcomes. This concern highlights – and perhaps amplifies – a long-standing, wider tension between formal knowledge generated and/or codified by institutions and universities, and that practice knowledge which is enacted in practice settings (Ramsey, 2011, 2014; Lyken-Segosebe, 2017). Here, prescriptive frameworks typically benefit from being able to consistently draw attention to certain aspects of practice, enabling a more targeted learning, development, refinement, and assessment of practice (Stickley et al., 2017).

Yet such formal knowledge structures can also be so removed from the circumstances of practice that they are rendered less authoritative in guiding practice (Banks et al., 2016; Mathieu, 2016; Pettigrew and Starkey, 2016). In some cases, professional frameworks are so prescriptive in directing action, they may even breach local or cultural ethical codes of conduct and risk the wellbeing of participants (Wall et al., 2017a). For example, by *requiring* the formal evaluation of an organizational intervention in an organizational or country context where that intervention is seen as remedial may, counter to the intention of that intervention, induce a sense of shame and additional anxiety or even depression (ibid.). Therefore, rather than a prescriptive framework of using creative practices for wellbeing in organizations, an alternative approach is needed to guide action.

Such discussions highlight how the field of creative practices for wellbeing demonstrates a low level of paradigmatic development, that is, there is little agreement on what is considered as good, best, or poor practice in research or implementation (Lyken-Segosebe, 2017). Previous arts and health practice frameworks have highlighted a range of features relevant to the use of creativity in wellbeing, including the role and activation of intuition, personal commitment to the activity and change, values, space and environment, relationality, and of course creativity (e.g. see Fox, 2013;

Atkinson and Scott, 2015). The way in which these interrelate have been described as 'practice assemblage' (ibid.) to highlight the primacy of practice and the interrelatedness of these aspects to generate outcomes in that practice setting. However, despite this, the role of *the practitioner* in the use of creative practices for wellbeing remains under-represented in this dynamic relationship (Tan, 2020).

An emerging approach is to re-orient practice frameworks as a *scholarship of practice*, centring the way in which *practitioners* imbricate knowledge generation and use into a single enterprise (ibid.), or more precisely, combine formal codified knowledge with their experiential information and longer-standing knowledge of the setting, to guide action and new knowledge. Echoing the conceptualization in arts-health practice frameworks, a scholarship of practice is often understood as a dialogic (e.g. Cunliffe and Scaratti, 2017; MacIntosh et al., 2017) or a relational perspective to arts and health practice, where people, things, and situations 'assemble' (Tan, 2020).

Here, rather than being directed by theory or ideas, within a scholarship of practice, practitioners engage in 'a moment-by-moment dance' with ideas (Ramsey, 2011, 2014), a relationship less motivated by 'the substance of a theory, concept, framework or research finding towards how' and more motivated by how an idea 'stimulates, incites and promotes *changed practice*' (Ramsey, 2011: 470, emphasis added). Here, 'deliberative attention' (Ramsey, 2014: 6) considers the relationships and dynamics of the creative activities, the participants, wellbeing outcomes, and the broader environment (see Tan, 2020). In contrast to the most contemporary relational framework for arts-health practice frameworks (ibid.), however, the framework considered below foregrounds *the practitioner* – and their set of experiences and qualifications – as a core, deliberative, and accountable decision maker within an organizational context which has certain *expectations*. Specifically, the guidance was 'designed to help practitioners across different contexts and settings, and so it is designed to be flexible rather than prescriptive', and is articulated in a way to help practitioners:

> Design your creative activities or programmes, short or long; Decide whether or not to use creative activities in certain contexts or settings; Decide what additional support or arrangements you might organise to ensure effective and safe practice; Reflect on or evaluate your own or others' practices; Decide how to improve what you currently do; Decide how to identify, reward or recognise good and promising practices in your context. (Wall and Axtell, 2020: 3)

The 10 reflective prompts are outlined next (examples of reflective questions and action draw extensively from Wall and Axtell, 2020).

Consider Own Expertise, Experience, and Qualifications in Scoping Work, and Organize Additional Support that Might Be Needed

This prompt encourages the consideration of the past experiences and qualifications in the bidding and scoping of work in organizations, and reflects the view that some groups of people need specialist expertise and experience to effectively and safely facilitate wellbeing (e.g. people identifying as having a mental illness, dementia, autism, or PTSD) (see, for example, Follmer and Jones, 2018). Evidencing experience and qualifications, or organizing work to benefit from the equivalent experience and qualifications, extends beyond current arts-health frameworks (Tan, 2020), and builds confidence (both the practitioner's and others') in the practitioner's current ability to use creative practices for wellbeing effectively and safely. Additional arrangements to secure such confidence might include shadowing or co-delivering creative activities with those who are more experienced and more qualified than the practitioner initiating or designing the intervention (e.g. Wall et al.,

2019a). Examples of reflective questions which explore this area include: *How do I know I have what I need to deliver this activity/work effectively and safely? How can I find out before I agree to deliver the activity/work?* (see Wall and Axtell, 2020 for more examples).

Establish and Maintain Appropriate Relationships

This prompt encourages consideration of the nature of relationships when using creative practices for wellbeing in organizations. Relationships might range from (a) relatively loose, manager–team member relationships which may have some boundaries around when/how people interact at work, through to (b) explicitly articulated relationships in formal settings where the 'what, where, when, how, and who' should be agreed in advance (e.g. with vulnerable staff, customers, or patients). This prompt can be essential for creating the operational trust with various stakeholders needed to engage in creativity for wellbeing activity. Practitioners use a variety of ways to work towards this, such as clearly contextualizing and framing creative activities, and co-creating contracts/agreements to clarify relationship boundaries and expectations (see Torrissen, 2015; Whitelaw et al., 2017). Examples of reflective questions which explore this area include: *What might be helpful forms, channels, or timings of communication? What might be unhelpful forms, channels, or timings of communication? How might I helpfully bring awareness to unhelpful forms, channels, or timings of communication?* (see Wall and Axtell, 2020 for more examples).

Develop a 'Creative Practices' for Wellbeing 'Toolkit' Which Can Be Adapted as Needed

This deliberative prompt highlights the need for an evolving and adaptive set of tools to tackle changing needs over time, including the appropriate adaption of existing tools to reflect subtle differences in settings (Stokes et al., 2019; Wall et al., 2019a). Adaptations might include changes to task structure for different group composition as well as an individual participant's changing circumstances over time. As such, this prompt extends beyond current arts-health frameworks (Tan, 2020) and intends to encourage the evolution of creative practices over time, as part of a wider scheme of improving the effectiveness and safety of creative activity. Deliberative action around this prompt might lead to developing and testing new activities, engaging in supervision (with more experienced practitioners), and attending training courses in specific processes. Examples of reflective questions which might help to explore this area include: *What is currently in my toolkit? When was it last updated?* (see Wall and Axtell, 2020 for more examples).

Facilitate an Environment Conducive to the Wellbeing of All Participants (Including the Practitioner)

This prompt encourages practitioners' attentive sensitivity to the wider environment in which the creativity activity is facilitated, and includes participant perceptions of the physicality of environments as well as the ease of access/exit should participants feel they need to leave the environment (e.g. see Wall et al., 2017b). Importantly, this includes the wellbeing of the practitioner as their own sense of wellbeing can impact participants (e.g. see Nesher Shoshan and Sonnentag, 2020). Deliberative action in this area is critical to the practitioner's ability to respond effectively and safely to the different and unexpected needs of participants, and might include peer-observation, peer support, mentoring, and supervision. Examples of reflective questions to explore this area include: *How can I organize the layout of the physical space [where the activities/work will happen]*

to support the feeling of safety and wellbeing? How can I organize the layout of the physical space [where the activities/work will happen] so people are physically safe, especially if they need to leave quickly? (see Wall and Axtell, 2020 for more examples).

Anticipate and Respond to Risks, Needs, and Presented Challenges to Support the Wellbeing of All Participants (Including the Practitioner)

This deliberative prompt encourages the practitioner to develop their anticipatory capacities to identify a wide range of possible responses and challenges before/during/after an intervention, and consider ways of mitigating risks and their impacts on others (Stokes et al., 2019; Wall et al., 2019a). Again, this capacity was seen as essential to being able to respond effectively and safely to the different and unexpected needs of participants, and could be supported by peer support, mentoring, and supervision before the intervention. Examples of reflective questions which might explore this area include: *What do I know about the participants who will be engaging in the activity/work, and what risks, needs, and challenges might present themselves? What can I practically do to mitigate or manage any significant risks or challenges? Who might I need to inform to help me to do this? What can I do to manage my own wellbeing during any presented challenges?* (see Wall and Axtell, 2020 for more examples).

Develop Mutual Understanding of Collaborative Working When Working with/in Organizations, and Adapt or Challenge Where Appropriate

This prompt highlights the significance of the practitioner's relationality to others when working with others in a wider scheme of work, such as a change programme in a business, or a longer-term scheme of treatment in a helping organization such as a hospice (e.g. see Organ, 2016; Bickerdike et al., 2017). Here, developing a mutual understanding between organizational actors was seen as important to help choose appropriate activities so as not to contradict or conflict with other activities or treatments, and to establish communication protocols across multiple professional roles who may have different expectations related to ways of working. This might include the levels of confidentiality expected between organizations' actors; absolute confidentiality was the norm in some circumstances, whereas in others, facilitators were expected to give regular updates in relation to participant behaviour to enable the tracking of health improvement. Again, this prompt extends beyond current arts-health frameworks (Tan, 2020) to capture a greater diversity of practice setting, and might lead to involving others in the participant contracting stage or briefing others in the participant contracting stage. Examples of reflective questions include: *What relationships do I need to develop in order to deliver an even more effective or safe practice? What organizational practices could be enhanced to benefit collaborators and/or participants? How might I help promote that change?* (see Wall and Axtell, 2020 for more examples).

Arrange Appropriate Insurance When Working Independently, Outside of Employment

This prompt highlights that practitioners using creative practices for wellbeing not only worked within organizations as employees but were often commissioned to undertake interventions through contracting and sub-contracting processes. One of the major implications of this related to the insurance protection that was required, both for the practitioners themselves and the participants

(which is not always a consideration by practitioners across a number of independent or informal fields, see Wall et al., 2017a). This might include arranging personal indemnity and public liability insurance or joining a professional organization that provides such protection as part of membership – but these arrangements differ across the globe. Examples of reflective questions around this area include: *What insurance do I currently have? Does it cover me for my activity/work inside and outside? What insurance cover does the organization have? Does it cover me for my activity/work inside and outside? Is there any ambiguity? How might I resolve or mitigate that ambiguity?* (see Wall and Axtell, 2020 for more examples).

Secure Informed and Valid Consent of Participants Where Appropriate

This prompt not only foregrounds the notion of consent in using creative practices for wellbeing but also what it means to have informed and valid consent. Here, while such ethical and moral considerations are perhaps more overt and common in research, medical, health, and care fields of practice, they are less so in informal settings (Wall et al., 2017a); *informed* consent refers to the notion that participants enter the intervention knowing what will happen and the possible risks, and *valid* consent refers to the extent to which someone is able to agree to those terms and conditions at the time of agreement (see Zürcher et al., 2019). Deliberative action around this prompt might lead to practitioners asking participants to sign information and consent forms before the intervention, or seeking advice about accepted ways of gaining valid consent for those not considered able to give consent. Examples of reflective questions that might explore this area include: *How do I know I have consent to share the work or experiences of participants from my own practice? How might a participant react at some point in the future, under their own different circumstances? How might I inform participants of the possible implications and risks of giving consent?* (see Wall and Axtell, 2020 for more examples).

Respect All Legal Requirements

This prompt unequivocally positions the legal requirements that govern the settings in which creative practices are being deployed as centrally important; this relies on knowing the legalities which apply in a situation and adhering to those. Again, this is not always a concern for those in informal fields or those who work independently (see Wall et al., 2017a). Deliberative action around this prompt might lead to seeking advice from relevant bodies or attending specialist training for particular or vulnerable groups. Examples of reflective questions which explore this area include: *What are the specific legal requirements operating in the range of contexts in which I work? How do I find out? How do I keep up to date? How do I build these checks into my own standard ways of working? How might I learn about my own unconscious biases?* (see Wall and Axtell, 2020 for more examples).

Commit to Developing Own Practice Through Appropriate Means

This prompt foregrounds the importance of the continuous development of practice, as a way of responding to changes in group composition, own expertise and capabilities, and other changes in societal, governance, and legal expectations. This might be driven by participant feedback, reflection, compliance, or may be anticipatory (Stokes et al., 2019), but was seen as being essential for the adaptivity and improvement of own work. However, such development might encapsulate a wide

range of activity including creative, evaluative, and reflective practice, supervision, or keeping up to date through reading the latest articles or books. Examples of reflective questions which might explore this area include: *Which areas of my practice arrest my attention? Why? What can I learn from that? What impact am I creating? How do I know? What might I have missed?* (see Wall and Axtell, 2020 for more examples).

FUTURE DIRECTIONS

The application of creative practices for wellbeing in organizations is expected to diversify across settings as the pursuit for wellbeing across practice settings becomes more widespread (see, for example, the international rise of Mental Health First Aid in workplaces) (APPG, 2017). Such diversity and informality of application will deepen levels of complexity which are already difficult to account for in research and evaluation work. The proposed *scholarship-of-practice* approach above could provide a pragmatic framework for practitioners across the globe, underpinning professional development through formal training programmes, forms of recognition or accreditation, and frameworks for supervision, mentoring, or peer-support. It could also be used to help support practitioners in transitions between and across different context settings, for example from workplace team settings into areas which require additional knowledge sets such as working with people with mental health challenges or dementia. Some of this knowledge may be transferable, but some will need more extensive training (Cregan et al., 2019; Hasan et al., 2019).

However, the ability to achieve a consensus and commitment to a framework across such a diverse and nascent field of practitioners perhaps implies the existence of a wider, overarching body with sufficient resource, credibility, and authority to establish, implement, monitor, and adapt practice over time. In other words, a body which could oversee the establishment of a framework of requisite professional knowledge and skills, and the professional development framework to enable practitioners to coherently acquire and build that knowledge. Such a body might also establish and monitor the expectations about how to acquire independent ethical review to undertake research and evaluation, and how to deal with complaints or disciplinary action when a practitioner breaches such expectations. At the moment, there is no such singular body which applies to all of the creative practices for wellbeing in organizations.

The lack of a singular body for this diverse body of practitioners has also probably hindered the development of agreed standards and processes for research and evaluation (APPG, 2017), or as alluded to earlier, hindered paradigmatic development given the lack of agreement around 'good' research or practice (Lyken-Segosebe, 2017). However, much of the research and evaluation work into creative practices for wellbeing does not adhere to the principles of 'scientific method' (Goulding 2014; APPG, 2017). Specifically, these methodological criticisms include, for example, the proportion of initiatives which lack a 'formal evaluation' methodology (APPG, 2017), the lack of sample sizes which are required to confidently demonstrate statistical significance (Fleischer and Grehan, 2016), the lack of standardized measurement instruments and other comparative controls in experimental designs (Bickerdike et al., 2017), methodological triangulation (Goulding, 2014), researcher independence (Beard, 2012), and longitudinal analyses which aid the pinpointing of the longer-term efficacy or return of such approaches (Carnes et al., 2017).

From one perspective, such methodological criticisms make it difficult to articulate specific recommendations for policy and practice with confidence, but they do provide a basis on which new research and evaluation work might be developed in the future.

Research here will continue to find ways to control for diversity, such as examining specific application groups, the explicit articulation and comparison of interventions, and potentially synthesizing and interpreting empirical work alongside expert practitioners who can identify and codify subtle differences in creative practice (e.g. Nyssen et al., 2016).

Yet from another perspective, such criticisms have not stopped the application of creative practices for wellbeing becoming so widespread across such diverse organizational contexts. This perhaps indicates some level of resistance to measuring creative practices for wellbeing in scientific ways, prioritizing the immeasurable nature of humanity and human-ness of creativity and wellbeing (Johnson, 2019). It might also indicate the resistance of using the arts as 'subservient' to other ideological functions and desires (Bresler, 1995), where the arts should 'close itself off, should make itself useless, should reject demand and ignore critique, should make no excuses, disregard outcomes, and sow discord in the world around it' (Pilikian, 2016) where art should frustrate, baffle, and resist (Johnson, 2019). This reflects the use of arts for wellbeing in an emerging activist space which does not necessarily seek empirical validation (Daykin, 2020). This in turn raises questions about the use of evidence to inform policy and practice (Daykin, 2019).

Future research will continue to grapple with such complex problematics as arts, health, and wellbeing practices continue to grow and reflect wider cultural trends and concerns, one of which will be the use of post-human perspectives practices in art *and* wellbeing to reconfigure and reprioritize human domination in organizational places and spaces towards other beings such as animals or the earth more broadly, and wider interconnections with sustainability and sustainable development (Wall et al., 2019c). As these other concepts become increasingly widespread, the principles which govern what might be safe and effective practice are likely to change, further heightening the need to be sensitive to the contexts and circumstances in which creative practices for wellbeing are deployed – and the need to engage an increasingly sophisticated *scholarship of practice*.

ACKNOWLEDGEMENTS

This International Creative Practices for Wellbeing Framework project was funded by the TS Eliot Foundation and the Old Possum's Trust during 2017 to 2019.

The authors would like to thank Lapidus International and its members across the world for their unwavering support and generosity to be able to undertake this research. Lapidus International is the largest organization in the UK representing creative writing for therapeutic purposes and wellbeing.

REFERENCES

Abrams, R., Vandrevala, T., Samsi, K., & Manthorpe, J. (2019). The need for flexibility when negotiating professional boundaries in the context of home care, dementia and end of life. *Ageing and Society*, 39(9), 1976–1995.

APPG (All-Party Parliamentary Group on Arts, Health and Wellbeing) (2017). *Creative Health: The Arts for Health and Wellbeing*, Available online at: www.artshealthandwellbeing.org.uk/appg-inquiry/. Accessed 24 May 2020.

Arts Education Partnership (2011). *Music Matters: How Music Education Helps Students Learn, Achieve, and Succeed*. Washington DC and National Association of Music Merchants.

Atkinson, S., & Scott, K. (2015). Stable and destabilised states of subjective well-being: Dance and movement as catalysts of transition. *Social & Cultural Geography*, 16(1), 75–94.

Banks, G.C., Pollack, J.M., Bochantin, J.E., Kirkman, B.L., Whelpley, C.E., & O'Boyle, E.H.

(2016). Management's science-practice gap: A grand challenge for all stakeholders, *Academy of Management Journal*, 59(6), 2205–2231.

Beard, R.L. (2012). Art therapies and dementia care: A systematic review, *Dementia: the International Journal of Social Research and Practice*, 11 (5), 633–656.

Bernard, M., Rickett, M., Amigoni, D., Munro, L., Murray, M., et al. (2015). Ages and stages: The place of theatre in the lives of older people. *Ageing and Society*, 35(6), 1119–1145.

Bickerdike, L., Booth, A., Wilson, P.M., Farley, K., & Wright, K. (2017). Social prescribing: Less rhetoric and more reality. A systematic review of the evidence. *BMJ Open*, 7(4), doi:10.1136/bmjopen-2016-013384.

Bowling, N.A., Khazon, S., Alarcon, G.M., Blackmore, C.E., Bragg, C.B., Hoepf, M. R., … & Li, H. (2017). Building better measures of role ambiguity and role conflict: The validation of new role stressor scales. *Work & Stress*, 31(1), 1–23.

Bresler, L. (1995). The subservient, co-equal, affective, and social integration styles and their implications for the arts. *Arts Education Policy Review*, 96(3), 31–37.

British Medical Association (2011). *The Psychological and Social Needs of Patients*. London: British Medical Association Science & Education.

Brown, R. (2011). Performance, culture, industry In Pitches, J. and Popat, S. (eds) *Performance Perspectives: A Critical Introduction*. Basingstoke: Palgrave Macmillan, pp. 180–186.

Carnes, D., Sohanpal, R., Frostick, C., Hull, S., Mathur, R., Netuveli, G., & Tong, J. (2017). The impact of a social prescribing service on patients in primary care: A mixed methods evaluation. *BMC Health Services Research*, 171–179.

Clift, S., & Stickley, T. (eds) (2017). *Arts, Health and Wellbeing: A Theoretical Inquiry for Practice*. Cambridge, Cambridge Scholars.

Clift, S., Camic, P.M., & Royal Society for Public Health (2016). *Oxford Textbook of Creative Arts, Health, and Wellbeing: International Perspectives on Practice, Policy and Research*. Oxford: Oxford University Press.

Coburn, A., & Gormally, S. (2020). Defining well-being in community development from the ground up: A case study of participant and practitioner perspectives. *Community Development Journal*, 55(2), 237–257.

Cregan, K., Rowe, L., & Wall, T. (2019). Resilience education and training. In: Leal Filho, W., Wall, T., Azul, A., Brandli, L., & Özuyar, P. (eds) *Good Health and Well-Being. Encyclopedia of the UN Sustainable Development Goals*. Cham: Springer, pp. 1–12.

Cunliffe, A.L., & Scaratti, G. (2017). Embedding impact in engaged research: Developing socially useful knowledge through dialogical sensemaking. *British Journal of Management*, 28(1), 29–44.

Daniels, K., Connolly, S., Ogbonnaya, C., Tregaskis, O., Bryan, M.L., Robinson-Pant, A., & Street, J. (2018). Democratisation of wellbeing: Stakeholder perspectives on policy priorities for improving national wellbeing through paid employment and adult learning. *British Journal of Guidance & Counselling*, 46(4), 492–511.

Daykin, N. (2019). Social movements and boundary work in arts, health and wellbeing: A research agenda. *Nordic Journal of Arts, Culture and Health*, 1 (1), 1–20.

Daykin, N. (2020). *Arts, Health and Well-being: A Critical Perspective on Research, Policy and Practice*. Abingdon: Routledge.

Evans, V., Cregan, K., & Wall, T. (2019). Organizational resilience and sustainable development. In: Leal Filho, W., Wall, T., Azul, A., Brandli, L., & Özuyar, P. (eds) *Good Health and Well-Being: Encyclopedia of the UN Sustainable Development Goals*. Cham: Springer, pp. 1–12.

Fleischer, S., & Grehan, M. (2016). The arts and health: Moving beyond traditional medicine. *Journal of Applied Arts & Health*, 7(1), 93–105.

Follmer, K.B., & Jones, K.S. (2018). Mental illness in the workplace: An interdisciplinary review and organizational research agenda. *Journal of Management*, 44 (1), 325–351.

Fox, N.J. (2013). Creativity and health: An anti-humanist reflection. *Health*, 17(5), 495–511.

Gordon-Nesbitt, R., & Howarth, A. (2020). The arts and the social determinants of health: Findings from an inquiry conducted by the United Kingdom All-Party Parliamentary Group on Arts, Health and Wellbeing. *Arts & Health: An International Journal for Research, Policy and Practice*, 12(1), 1–22.

Goulding, A. (2014). Arts on prescription for older people: Different stakeholder perspectives on the challenges of providing evidence of impact on health outcomes. *Journal of Applied Arts & Health*, 5(1), 83–107.

Harries, B., Keady, J., & Swarbrick, C. (2013). *The Storybox Project: Examining the Role of a Theatre and Arts-based Intervention for People with Dementia*. Manchester: University of Manchester.

Hasan, I., Hasan, U., Abbasi, S.H., Srinivasan, S., & Rao, B. (2019). Longitudinal curriculum for certified training in evidence-based medicine: Certified evidence-based medicine practitioner. *BMJ Evidence-Based Medicine*, 24 (1), A21.

Health Education England (2016). *More than Heritage: A Museum Directory of Social Prescribing and Wellbeing Activity in North West England*. Manchester: Health Education England.

Jensen, A., & Bonde, L. (2018). The use of arts interventions for mental health and wellbeing in health settings. *Perspectives in Public Health*, 138 (4), 209–214.

Jensen, A., Stickley, T., Torrissen, W., & Stigmar, K. (2017). Arts on prescription in Scandinavia: A review of current practice and future possibilities. *Perspectives in Public Health*, 137(5), 268–274.

Johnson, D. (2019). Those who have suffered understand suffering: Notes on the body (in pain). In: Schmidt, T.U. (ed.) *Agency: A Partial History of Live Art*. Bristol: Intellect, pp. 850–984.

Lyken-Segosebe, D. (2017). The scholarship of practice in applied disciplines. *New Directions for Higher Education*, 178, 21–33.

MacIntosh, R., Beech, N., Bartunek, J., Mason, K., Cooke, B., & Denyer, D. (2017). Impact and management research: Exploring relationships between temporality, dialogue, reflexivity and praxis. *British Journal of Management*, 28(1), 3–13.

Makin, S., & Gask, L. (2012). 'Getting back to normal': The added value of an art-based programme in promoting 'recovery' for common but chronic mental health problems. *Chronic Illness*, 8(1), 64–75.

Mathieu, J.E. (2016). The problem with [in] management theory. *Journal of Organizational Behavior*, 37(8), 1132–1141.

Nesher Shoshan, H., & Sonnentag, S. (2020). The effects of employee burnout on customers: An experimental approach. *Work & Stress*, 34(2), 127–147.

Nyssen, O.P., Taylor, S.J., Wong, G., Steed, E., Bourke, L., Lord, J., Ross, C.A., Hayman, S., Field, V., Higgins, A., Greenhalgh, T., & Meads, C. (2016). Does therapeutic writing help people with long-term conditions? Systematic review, realist synthesis and economic considerations. *Health Technology Assessment*, 20(27), 1–367.

Organ, K. (2016). *A New Form of Theatre: Older People's Involvement in Theatre and Drama*. London: The Baring Foundation.

Pettigrew, A., & Starkey, K. (2016). The legitimacy and impact of business schools: Key issues and a research agenda. *Academy of Management Learning & Education*, 15(4), 649–664.

Phillips, C.S., & Becker, H. (2019). Systematic review: Expressive arts interventions to address psychosocial stress in healthcare workers. *Journal of Advanced Nursing*, 75(11), 2285–2298.

Pilikian, V. (2016). The audience does not exist. In: Curtis, H., Keidan, L., & Wright, A. (eds) *The Live Art Almanac Volume 4*. London: Live Art Development Agency, location 4001–4023.

Quade, M.J., Perry, S.J., & Hunter, E.M. (2019). Boundary conditions of ethical leadership: Exploring supervisor-induced and job hindrance stress as potential inhibitors. *J Bus Ethics*, 158, 1165–1184. https://doi.org/10.1007/s10551-017-3771-4

Ramsey, C. (2011). Provocative theory and a scholarship of practice. *Management Learning*, 42(5), 469–483.

Ramsey, C. (2014). Management learning: A scholarship of practice centred on attention? *Management Learning*, 45(1), 6–20.

Rogers, C. (1957). The necessary and sufficient conditions of therapeutic personality change. *Journal of Counseling Psychology*, 21, 95–103.

Rossetti, L., & Wall, T. (2017). The impact of story: Measuring the impact of story for organisational change. *Journal of Work-Applied Management*, 9(2), 170–184.

Shrivastava, P. (2012). Enterprise sustainability 2.0: Aesthetics of sustainability. In:

Hoffman, A., & Bansal, T. (eds) *The Oxford Handbook of Business and the Natural Environment*. Oxford: Oxford University Press, pp. 630–638.

Stickley, T., & Eades, M. (2013). Arts on prescription: A qualitative outcomes study. *Public Health*, 127(8), 727–734.

Stickley, T., Parr, H., Atkinson, S., Daykin, N., Clift, S., De Nora, T., Hacking, S., Manich, P.M., Jossi, T., White, M., & Hogan, S.J. (2017). Arts, health & wellbeing: Reflections on a national seminar series and building a UK research network. *Arts & Health: An International Journal for Research, Policy and Practice*, 9(1), 14–25.

Stokes, P., Smith, S., Wall, T., Moore, N., Rowland, C., Ward, T., & Cronshaw, S. (2019). Resilience and the (micro-)dynamics of organizational ambidexterity: Implications for strategic HRM. *The International Journal of Human Resource Management*, 30(8), 1287–1322.

Tan, M.K.B. (2020). Towards a caring practice: Reflections on the processes and components of arts-health practice. *Arts & Health: An International Journal for Research, Policy and Practice*, 12(1), 80–97.

Torrissen, W. (2015). 'Better than medicine': Theatre and health in the contemporary Norwegian context. *Journal of Applied Arts and Health*, 6(2), 149–170.

Wall, T., & Axtell, R. (2019). *Creative Practices for Wellbeing Framework Consultation: Final Report December 2019*. Bristol: Lapidus International.

Wall, T., & Axtell, R. (2020). *Creative Practices for Wellbeing: Practice Guidance*. Bristol: Lapidus International. Available at: http://dx.doi.org/10.13140/RG.2.2.11610.90567/1. Accessed 24 May 2020.

Wall, T., Jamieson, M., Csigás, Z., & Kiss, O. (2017a). *Research Policy and Practice Provocations: Coaching Evaluation in Diverse Landscapes of Practice – Towards Enriching Toolkits and Professional Judgement*. Brussels: The European Mentoring and Coaching Council.

Wall, T., Russell, J., & Moore, N. (2017b). Positive emotion in workplace impact: The case of a work-based learning project utilising appreciative inquiry. *Journal of Work-Applied Management*, 9(2), 129–146.

Wall, T., Field, V., & Sučylaitė, J. (2019a). Creative writing for health and well-being. In: Leal Filho, W., Wall, T., Azeiteiro, U., Azul, A., Brandli, L., & Özuyar, P. (eds) *Good Health and Well-Being: Encyclopedia of the UN Sustainable Development Goals*. Cham: Springer, pp. 1–12.

Wall, T., Fries, J., Rowe, N., Malone, N., & Österlind, E. (2019b). Drama and theatre for health and well-being. In: Leal Filho, W., Wall, T., Azeiteiro, U., Azul, A., Brandli, L., & Özuyar, P. (eds) *Good Health and Well-Being: Encyclopedia of the UN Sustainable Development Goals*. Cham: Springer, pp. 1–12.

Wall, T., Österlind, E., & Fries, J. (2019c). Arts-based approaches for sustainability. In: Leal Filho, W. (ed.) *Encyclopedia of Sustainability in Higher Education*. Cham: Springer, pp. 1–12.

Wang, W.-J. (2017). Combating global issues of land reform, urbanisation and climate change with local community theatre devising and praxes in Taiwan. *Research in Drama Education: The Journal of Applied Theatre and Performance*, 22(4), 506–509.

Whelan, G. (2016). *A Social Return on Investment: Evaluation of the St Helens Creative Alternatives Arts on Prescription Programme*. Liverpool: John Moores University.

Whitelaw, S., Thirlwall, C., Morrison, A., Osborne, J., Tattum, L., & Walker, S. (2017). Developing and implementing a social prescribing initiative in primary care: Insights into the possibility of normalisation and sustainability from a UK case study. *Primary Health Care Research and Development*, 18(2), 112–121.

Zarobe, L., & Bungay, H. (2017). The role of arts activities in developing resilience and mental wellbeing in children and young people: A rapid review of the literature. *Perspectives in Public Health*, 137(6), 337–347.

Zürcher, T., Elger, B., & Trachsel, M. (2019). The notion of free will and its ethical relevance for decision-making capacity. *BMC Medical Ethics*, 20(1), 31–10.

35

Micro-activism and Wellbeing: 1,000s of Snowflakes and the Potential Avalanche

The Kintsugi Collective, Tony Wall, Sarah
Robinson, Jamie Callahan, Carole Elliott, Tali
Padan, Annemette Kjærgaard, Maribel Blasco, and
Rasmus Bergmann

INTRODUCTION

Activism, or acts of protest and challenge against wider power structures and injustices, has been emerging (or resurging) as a common and high-profile phenomenon in and around organizations in the 21st century (Mumby et al., 2017). This activism has seemingly emerged as a response to acts and events which stand counter to the positive progress in agendas, such as equality and sustainability in organizations, standing up for the climate emergency, objecting to the intentional cover-up of car emissions and pollution, angered by the way black people are treated in and out of work. They are outraged by systemic sexual harassment of women in Hollywood and beyond. Over this time, evidence has also highlighted that activism can have a positive but variable relationship with wellbeing, in terms of hedonic, eudaimonic, social, and health perspectives. This is not surprising given Aristotle's view that human beings are, by nature, political,

and therefore engaging in political activity is linked to our sense of wellbeing in organizational life (Klar and Kasser, 2009). Activism therefore has the potential to satisfy our basic psychological needs as humans through feeling a sense of *autonomy* to do something (rather than nothing), with a sense of *relatedness* to those with a similar passion, and refining or developing new *competencies* whilst doing so (Vestergren et al., 2017).

However, this evidence tends to focus on forms of activism where there is a public visibility and collective assemblage to the activism, rather than forms which may be relatively hidden and individualistic. There are other forms of activism which intentionally avoid a public visibility or collective character, as doing so might be damaging to the activist in terms of their career or even their life. This 'micro-activism', though contested in terms of its efficacy, is particularly prevalent in contexts where there are salient and insidious power structures infiltrating all aspects of work (and life), and where open resistance can be dramatic and significant. Here, micro-activism therefore becomes a 'weapon of the weak' (Scott, 1990). A contemporary example of this is the hyper-competitive context of academic life in Western universities, where the demands of extreme managerialism are, at their worst, destroying lives.

By drawing on ethnographic accounts from academic life in different cultural contexts, this chapter considers how micro-activism can potentially address positive drivers of wellbeing in organizations. First, the chapter considers the relationships between wellbeing and activism. The extant literature highlights a range of positive relationships, but it is primarily focused on social or public forms of activism, rather than the less conspicuous or hidden forms which may be the only form of activism available to workers in some organizations. Second, this more covert form of activism is considered in more detail, particularly in relation to academic life, and we exemplify how micro-activism can specifically target positive drivers of wellbeing at work in this setting. We then consider three micro-activism case studies in more detail to elucidate the contextualities of the acts. Finally, we draw the analysis of the acts together to highlight important ways in which micro-activism appears to link to wellbeing in organizations, and we conclude by outlining future directions of research. Although the dynamic between micro-activism and wellbeing is an emerging area of study, we highlight the presence of multi-directional relationships underpinned by dialogical dimensions, and pinpoint lines of enquiry for future research.

WELLBEING ASSOCIATED WITH ACTIVISM AND ACTIVISTS

Studies that have explored the relationships between activism and wellbeing in and around organizational life have typically focused on public forms of activism which challenge a form of injustice in society. These studies have, for example, examined the wellbeing of activists who contribute to civil rights or women's liberation movements (Lee, 2004), campus activism (Klar and Kasser, 2009), climate change or environmental action (Vestergren et al., 2017), social justice and democracy in academe (Rhodes et al., 2018), workers' and healthcare rights (Jasko et al., 2019), and civic engagement for democratic rights in communist states (Chan and Mak, 2020). They have involved those identifying as activists as well as those who do not, but who have expressed behavioural indicators or proxies which indicate a level of activism, such as including taking a leadership role, taking on organizational responsibilities, marching or demonstrating, providing financial support, or providing some other form of moral support in relation to political work (e.g. Lee, 2004; Klar and Kasser, 2009).

Activism has been associated with a wide range of biographical changes, from momentary sensations of positive affect through to longer lasting, career and family impacts, or even changes in personality (Boehnke and Wong, 2011), and have been categorized as 'objective' changes (such as marital status and children) or 'subjective' (such as self-reported sense of wellbeing, identity, or empowerment) (Vestergren et al., 2017). Within these studies, wellbeing has been conceptualized through hedonic, eudaimonic, social, and health perspectives. The first of these, *hedonic wellbeing* is the most typical in studies, and examines constructs of life satisfaction, personal satisfaction, positive affect, and negative affect. Such constructs were operationalized through adaptations of the satisfaction with life scale (Diener et al., 1985), a 'state' version of the positive affect/negative affect scale (Watson et al., 1988), and the State Hope Scale (Snyder et al., 1996).

In *eudaimonic wellbeing*, focus moves to the extent to which a human is 'fully functioning', which is conceptualized as a sense of meaning and self-realization (Ryan and Deci, 2001) and vitality, reflecting the energy of the functioning self (Ryan and Deci, 2008). Specifically, scales from a variety of instruments have been used such as: the Short Index of Self-Actualization (Jones and Crandall, 1986), the psychological wellbeing scale which considers autonomy, environmental mastery, and positive relations with others (Ryff, 1989), the Basic Psychological Needs Scale which includes the aspects of autonomy, competence, and relatedness (Deci and Ryan, 2007), the meaning in life questionnaire (Steger et al., 2006), and the 'state' level version of the vitality scale (Ryan and Frederick, 1997).

Social wellbeing, a third perspective examined in the activism and wellbeing literature, focuses on one's own sense of own circumstances and functioning in a society (Keyes, 1998, 2002). This differentiates five distinctive areas: social integration (a sense of having something in common and belonging with others), social acceptance (a sense of feeling at ease with others), social contribution (a sense of value of oneself to a wider society), social actualization (a sense of hope or potential that society will develop and grow), and social coherence (a sense of knowing and meaning in life) (ibid.). Such perspectives join *general health*, *physical health*, and *psychological health* sub-scales to examine wellbeing, the latter of which was informed by the Symptom Checklist (Gurin et al., 1960) (e.g. Vestergren et al., 2018, 2019). And finally, Klar and Kasser (2009) combined a range of these scales to examine *flourishing* (Keyes, 1998, 2002), a state which is operationalized as being a 'high' (upper tertile or quintile) level of life satisfaction or positive affect and in most of the sub-scales used to operationalize wellbeing (e.g. 6 of the 11, see Klar and Kasser, 2009).

Empirical work has typically found positive relationships between behavioural indicators of activism and these different scales for wellbeing, for example across combined hedonic, eudaimonic, social wellbeing scales (Klar and Kasser, 2009), with more specific scales such as psychological and social wellbeing (Chan and Mak, 2020), with personal significance and meaning (Jasko et al., 2019) and with happiness later in life (Boehnke and Wong, 2011). Such findings are consistent with other studies which indicate that activism typically generates a sense of empowerment, self-esteem, and self-confidence (Vestergren et al., 2017). However, evidence also highlights more nuanced dynamics when describing the relationships between activism and wellbeing. For example, Klar and Kasser (2009) found that those who express activism *above the mean* expression of activism were three times more likely to be *flourishing* than those who were *below the mean* expression. As such, this suggests that some expressions of activism may fulfil a wider range of human needs than others, for example feeling a stronger sense of belonging and meaning when engaging in more activity linked to the activism.

Given that causation is still an ongoing criticism of the activism and wellbeing research (Vestergren et al., 2017), the relationship between activism and flourishing may also be explained by a variety of unidirectional dynamics between the various scales of wellbeing. For example, a stronger sense of meaning might simultaneously impact positive affect, sense of social integration, and social acceptance, but a sense of positive affect may not necessarily affect sense of meaning, sense of social integration, or social acceptance. Becker et al.'s (2011) study further problematizes this discussion as it found that engaging in activism can simultaneously generate 'positive' affect (e.g. a self-directed solidarity and unity) *as well as* 'negative' affect (such as anger and contempt directed at those as part of the 'outer group'). Indeed, in some cases, the activism was not so easily understood in these ways, and was more accurately experienced as *coping* (Páez et al., 2007).

This means how activism plays out into wellbeing is not so clear cut and certain, and echoes Lee's (2004) study, which found no significant relationship between wellbeing and activism. In her study, Lee suggested that the Black women activists in her sample were markedly different from prior studies, that is, they had all previously attended a 'historically Black' university, and as such might have had different expectations of their education, life, and their activism (though it was unclear what these were). Nonetheless, other studies have highlighted the importance of expectations and the perceived achievement of them, as well as the identification of activists with the in-group and out-groups to which the activism is targeted, with wellbeing (Becker and Tausch, 2015; Vestergren et al., 2017). For example, evidence suggests there can be negative impacts on wellbeing when activists do not see that their efforts materialize (ibid.), and participation in activism can strain relationships or cause burnout when there are excessive emotional demands (Downton and Wehr, 1998; Einwohner, 2002). The latter can be particularly prevalent when the activist identifies with those within disadvantaged group (e.g. workers) *and* with those at which the activism is targeted (e.g. managers), which ultimately dampens activist action and change work (Becker and Tausch, 2015).

The final aspect which brings nuance to the dynamic between activism and wellbeing relates to the scale or risk of the activist act. In their study, Klar and Kasser (2009: 755) found that those 'who did the *brief* activist behavior reported significantly higher levels of subjective vitality than did the subjects who engaged in the nonactivist behaviour' (emphasis added). As vitality is as an indicator of human needs being met, these findings suggest that smaller-scale activist activity therefore 'fosters the expression of intrinsic motivation' (Klar and Kasser, 2009: 772) and the wellbeing benefits associated with it. However, it is important to recognize that this study, along with the extant literature discussed in this section, predominantly conceptualized activism as a *social* activism,

where activists are engaging with others for a known, wider social purpose. Here, it is possible to conceive of how activity related to social activism maps to basic psychological needs such as autonomy (choosing to protest against an injustice), competence (to deliver a protest, to make the news, maybe to deliver a change), and relatedness (with others who you identify with) (Deci and Ryan, 2007). Yet this social or public form of activism is only one form of activism, and is not always possible. This is where micro-activism can have a role, and has become an emerging phenomenon for wellbeing in and around organizations.

MICRO-ACTIVISM AND WELLBEING: A 'WEAPON OF THE WEAK'

Activism in and around organizations has been conceptualized along two continua which approximate (rather than clearly delineate) extremes: from hidden to public, and individual to collective (Mumby et al., 2017). In relation to the previous discussion, such a conceptualization recognizes forms of activism which are not typically examined, that is, forms of resistance which are typically or for the most part hidden (rather than public or visible to others), and which are typically actioned by individuals (rather than by a collective). This form of activism, which we have referred to here as micro-activism, has been heavily criticized, both in terms of whether 'it counts' as activism and in terms of its efficacy (Mumby et al., 2017). These criticisms, however, are insensitive to the circumstances of such activism; in some contexts, there are salient, asymmetrical, and insidious power structures which render public forms of resistance as highly damaging or even life threatening (Parker, 2018).

Originally in the context of 'peasants', or those without power resources to resist against those with power, Scott (1990) referred to such micro-activism as relatively 'hidden' 'weapons of the weak'. Such notions highlight the behavioural tactics (micro-acts of activism) that people may use or experience as the only possible way to engage in resistance within and around organizational spaces. Yet the relevance of such analyses has been extended to other work contexts where such asymmetries infiltrate and severely constrain the work and life of those who engage in it. This highlights the wider trend towards the precariousness of work in organizations, where even those who are highly skilled and well paid are subject to vulnerabilities. For example, evidence shows that National Football League (NFL) players who have engaged in public protests are more likely to experience pay cuts and are less likely to experience pay growth, compared to those who have not. As Niven (2020: 641) argues:

> If NFL players – who work in the public eye, hold proven track records of accomplishment, and compete in a market that prides itself on analytic efficiency – can be punished by their employers for political activism, it suggests the truly profound vulnerability of everyday workers who labor without those advantages.

A context which is increasingly problematized and documented as an emotionally and physically oppressive and damaging work environment is academe (Sparkes, 2007, 2018; Anderson, 2008; Bristow et al., 2017; Cunliffe, 2018; Rhodes et al., 2018; Smith and Ulus, 2019). Here, managerialist drives have penetrated all aspects of academic work and have even crossed over into home life to propel ever increasing efficiency and outputs. For example, Sparkes (2007) described the ways in which academic work had become deeply entangled with an oppressive audit culture, in terms of teaching, research, and administration, and was ultimately embodied in the increasingly damaged bodies of academics. Consistent with the terrors of the implied and explicit managerialist threats documented in his initial empirical work (Sparkes, 2007), these terrors materialized in Sparkes' own work and life after the publication of this study, documented in a

subsequent study published a decade later (Sparkes, 2018). As Smith and Ulus (2019: 1) describe it, it is a setting where it is a 'taboo' to speak openly about mental health and emotional wellbeing in academic institutions, with masculine structures and encroaching neoliberal discourses that create hostile atmospheres unsupportive of vulnerability and uncertainty. And that:

> The threats to academics' well-being are many: work intensification; job insecurity; expectations to obtain highly competitive grants; Research Excellence Framework (REF) targets and Teaching Excellence and Student Outcomes Framework (TEF) targets in the UK context (ibid.: 5).

Within such contexts, to judge micro-activism within a managerialist regime of efficacy, efficiency, and effectiveness underestimates the contextual constraints (Mumby et al., 2017) and undermines the potential for it to generate other outcomes such as wellbeing. For example, by finding a way to express a micro-act such as foot-dragging (Scott, 1990), a person might be expressing the only modicum of autonomy they feel they have in such a precarious work setting. To bring a more nuanced analysis of the contextual features of academe and how they impact wellbeing at work, we summarize how some of the contextual features undermine the positive drivers of wellbeing at work (Lomas, 2019) (see Table 35.1).

We want to emphasize the contextual nature of resistance (Mumby et al., 2017) to extend Scott's (1990) metaphor, which helps to justify and legitimate micro-activism beyond what some might describe 'petty acts'; what might look like a single 'snowflake' to some, might feel like an avalanche of 1,000 snowflakes for others in terms of the development of their wellbeing. The rest of this chapter takes inspiration from this notion to foreground and document the ways in which micro-activism and wellbeing relate. The following discussion documents three cases of micro-activism and the ways in which they promote, attack, or

Table 35.1 Examples of how academic context undermines positive drivers of wellbeing at work (framework: Lomas, 2019).

Psychological drivers of wellbeing	Physical drivers of wellbeing	Socio-cultural drivers of wellbeing
Strengths: Externally imposed work tasks not necessarily linked to existing strengths, capabilities, skills, or knowledge (e.g. Franco-Santos et al., 2017; Smith and Ulus, 2019).	*Health and safety*: Systemic lack of acknowledgment of mental health risks and harm (e.g. Aubrecht, 2012; Guthrie et al., 2017) or actual emotional or physical damage in the workplace (e.g. Wall et al., 2017).	*Relationships*: Toxic relations related to hyper-competitive, masculine relationships in work teams and culturally prized peer-review systems for project and article selection processes (e.g. Sparkes, 2007; Horn, 2016), and neoliberally enforced pressure to become closer with others (Chory and Offstein, 2016; Wall, et al 2019a).
Emotions: Expectations to self-manage own pain, discomfort, and mental health concerns – often framed and silenced by the 'self-care' agenda (Smith and Ulus, 2019). Fear of the implications of sharing emotions (Askins and Blazek, 2017).	*Workload and scheduling*: Excessive teaching and research workloads (e.g. Sparkes, 2007) and impossibility of prioritizing high priority tasks (e.g. Barnett, 2000).	*Leadership*: Unethical, irresponsible, or threatening leadership behaviours (e.g. Sparkes, 2018; Amis et al., 2018).
Purpose: Lack of opportunity to undertake meaningful work or focus on low-value, repetitive, administrative work (e.g. Sparkes, 2007; Chapman and McClendon, 2018). Sense of alienation (Alakavuklar et al., 2017).	*Control and content*: Limited ability to decide the pattern of teaching and research delivery (e.g. Sparkes, 2007; Wall, 2016). Uncertainty as to how an academic's work will be judged (Griffin et al., 2015; Reinecke, J. 2018).	*Values*: Work which does not align with own personal values, for example dysfunctional conceptions of impact (e.g. Rhodes et al., 2018), or lack of interest in gender or other forms of equality (e.g. Cunliffe, 2018; Wall et al., 2019b) or sustainability (e.g. Wall et al., 2019a).
Personal and professional development: Focus on individual self-care and resilience training leading to cultures of shame and fear rather than wider system change (Smith and Ulus, 2019), expectations that experts should not ask for help (Elraz, 2017), aggressive change programmes (Parker & Parker, 2017).		*Reward-recognition*: Lack of appropriate recognition in the system, for example the strict use of faulty and damaging ranking systems (e.g. Anderson et al., 2020; Tourish, 2020).

have complex relationships with wellbeing in the context of academe. Although a picture has already been painted about the broad contextual features of academe, each case highlights the specific contextual features of the situation which we argue makes the account worthy of being described as (micro)activism in that setting. The three cases are 'Love* & Kisses', 'The Dyslexic Professor Blog', and 'Thank you for revising your manuscript…'.

'LOVE* & KISSES'

Empirical work highlights the ways in which the hyper-masculinized environments of academe frame and position behaviour in particular ways (Smith and Ulus, 2019), and is part of how academic work has become increasingly intensified and pressurized. Within this context, written communication is a pervasive part of academic life, and often exploiting the ubiquity and immediacy of emails with teaching, research and management colleagues, students, and other stakeholders. In academe, email can often be depersonalizing for both writer and recipient, and the humanness of the communicators is annulled by bureaucratic expectations and time pressures. However, how these communications are rendered and received are increasingly associated with anxiety and depression in academic workplaces (Kiriakos and Tienari, 2018). Micro-activism here can be articulated as acts which are counter to the hyper-masculinized and intense pace of academic life, for example attempting to find alternative ways of relating 'with love' *in mind* when interacting (Kiriakos and Tienari, 2018). Although love might be expressed through behaviour, the intention is *in mind* and therefore relatively 'hidden'.

We articulate that an act of activism in this context is a male professor who signed his emails with '*Love from Paul**' (a pseudonym) where the '*' pointed to a short explanation of why he did that; that he wanted to refract a collective 'love' with others, an act which was inspired by his colleague who had spent his life trying to facilitate and mediate collective wellness. It was his standard email 'signature' so it appeared in each email, symbolically repeating and reinforcing the message over time, even when he moved institutions. Within the academic environment, it is important that this act was undertaken by someone identifying as male to others (including other males), in a context where such expression of emotion is not necessary welcomed or valued, especially from males (Askins and Blazek, 2017) given the prevalence of male dominance and sexual harassment in academe as well as high profile cases in the media (Keplinger et al., 2019). The inclusion of the 'explanation' of what was meant by 'love' in the signature indicated, at least in part, an unease in doing so.

In this way, the intentional act of writing out a compassionate closing of emails may be seen as a form of micro-activism that expresses love and compassion as a form of resistance against the 'emptiness' and impersonal character of automated signature blocks and their symbolic resonance to hyper-efficient, masculinized environments. In the tough and often highly impersonal context of academia, such relationality creates a longing for the personal, which is increasingly beleaguered in academics' lives (Cunliffe, 2018). Conscious acts of communication with others reframe us, and reframe others, in often subtle and dialogic ways and, as such, can moderate feelings about one's own communication and the way it is received by the reader (Keplinger et al., 2019).

Such email styles seem to be a simple and quiet form of non-confrontational activism in terms of location, tone, and intent, and seemingly engage the emotional self, and challenge the impersonal banality of email and the 'cold efficiency' of organizational communication. Yet such acts are always contextually located and, indeed, may be so culturally insensitive that they can become problematic for wellbeing. For example, there is a recent case where a woman wrote a letter to their governmental colleague and ended the letter with an 'x' (signifying a kiss). Although the 'x' countered the expectation of formality and therefore expressing a particular way of relation at work, the 'x' was interpreted as unprofessional and unacceptable, breaking an implicit code of practice, and the story spread across social media generating public expressions of disappointment and shame. To emphasize the point, an email from an academic manager which seemingly asserts a caring for employees' wellbeing (against a norm) can generate a variety of wellbeing effects. This semi-fictional example inspired from our collective practice refers to a period of rapid readjustment due to the COVID-19 pandemic:

> Dear colleagues, Just a brief summer note to you all before the holiday. We in management want to express how proud and impressed we are, and how grateful, for your extraordinary efforts, constructive attitude, creativity and innovation in these tremendously challenging times. This enabled us to convert to online teaching at a moment's

notice. We know this has been tough for some of you. Before you go on your well-earned summer break, remember to be good to yourselves and others by taking the time to engage more personally with one another when you meet colleagues online. We really miss seeing you all, we really do. Feel free to email us personally with any concern at all.

The way in which this email is received is entangled with a rich array of contextualities which problematizes how wellbeing can be affected. Indeed, across academe, there have been heterogeneous experiences in relation to the way COVID-19 has impacted academic workloads and the ways in which universities have adjusted workloads, schedules, and compensation for the additional time spent on teaching activity (McKie, 2020). Here, some might read and interpret the email as expressing a genuine and intense, personal caring for colleagues which might generate feelings of *reward and recognition* for the radical adjustment to new ways of works – a driver of wellbeing at work (Lomas, 2019). However, there are many reports in the media about how academics have struggled to work at home and juggle loneliness, children and other caring responsibilities, illness, domestic tasks, and other challenges with a brutal workload, and with no institutional support – leaving them to self-manage their own distress (Smith and Ulus, 2019).

Here, people experiencing such challenges in a *specific* context of the organization and the manager – within a wider trajectory of history and identification (Dwyer et al., 2019) – might read it as a way of normalizing increased *workloads* and rapid response to *scheduling* (another driver of wellbeing). As such, some may feel a sense of (potentially increased) disconnect with an unethical expression of *leadership*, and a heightened sense of disempowerment (*control*) because of the impossibility and illegitimacy of trying to challenge the 'apparent caring' email. Indeed, the 'caring' communication might even act as a silencing mechanism that disarms and deflects protest and therefore a

way for management to strategically displace responsibility for wellbeing (Smith and Ulus, 2019). So although '*Love* & Kisses*' sentiments as a form of micro-activism can be articulated as positively expressing drivers of wellbeing at work (Lomas, 2019), for example to *lead* the reframing of *relationships* within a particular context, the effects on wellbeing are likely to be multifaceted and complex. This echoes Becker et al.'s (2011) notion that activism can generate both positive and negative affect simultaneously.

'THE DYSLEXIC PROFESSOR BLOG'

Empirical work highlights that people with disabilities in academe do not necessarily disclose, share, or discuss their disabilities, partly because of the vulnerabilities of doing so could implicate job or future career prospects (Elraz, 2017). Indeed, academics may actively hide their disabilities and the significant, related struggles that accompany a lack of workplace adjustment, even in the longer term (Smith and Ulus, 2019). Such a response is also linked to an expectation that academics, as expert knowledge workers, should be able to competently manage their workloads (Elraz, 2017). As such, evidence paints a picture of academe as a context where perceived *ability* is normatively foregrounded and valued, and dis-ability, struggle, and vulnerabilities are hidden because they can expose and precaritize the employment prospects of academics.

In the face of such conditions, we position '*The Dyslexic Professor Blog*' as an example of micro-activism from within academe because (1) its speaks directly counter to the wider cultural norms which are omnipresent across academe in relation to disability and revealing vulnerabilities, and (2) whilst the Blog is open access for the academic world to see, it is using a medium which is not (yet) formally recognized as part of the typical academic apparatus for teaching or research, so it is in this sense relatively 'hidden'. The blog enables immediate publication, without a formal review process, and a general absence of controlled content by any governing body. By using this 'outsider' medium and sharing the content inside of academia, the academic is blending the border between academia and other forms of expression, attempting to dissolve at least a portion of this rigid boundary. It is also the case that the author also positions the blog in relation to other 'Dyslexia Activists' and explicitly exposes his own and others' fears of disclosing his 'disability' (The Dyslexic Professor, 2017a). The posts in *The Dyslexic Professor Blog* explain this from the author's own activist perspective in relation to academe where after:

35 years of struggles, achievements and more struggles as I came to realise that dyslexia was not a learning difficulty but a learning difference … *the coping strategies learnt in hostile environments* [could] actually be an advantage? (The Dyslexic Professor, 2016a, emphasis added)

And that:

I am a survivor of dyslexia … as a dyslexic, *I live in a hostile world full of words and with the constant fear of exposure.* So, to survive each day is a big achievement and far from any notion of public recognition or superhero status. (The Dyslexic Professor, 2017a)

So within this context, the professor counters the normative ideas in academe and beyond with a succinct message:

[i]t's time to rethink our view of dyslexia and focus less on what dyslexic people *can't* do and more on what they *can* do. Yes, I am actually suggesting that we consider dyslexia as a superpower! (The Dyslexic Professor, 2016b, original emphasis)

The Dyslexic Professor Blog delivers this intention primarily through foregrounding, valuing and expressing *strengths*, or the skills, knowledge, resources, and capabilities that a person currently possesses (Lomas, 2019). For example, posts highlight the range of strengths that people with dyslexia often demonstrate, such as the 'positive characteristics of my dyslexia: i) environmental scanning, ii) resilience, iii) quick thinking and iv) empathy'

(The Dyslexic Professor, 2017b) or 'i) problem solving, creativity, innovation skills; ii) big picture, visual, spatial thinking; iii) communicating ideas; iv) empathy, teamworking; v) systems thinking; vi) using assistive technologies; vii) selling the superpowered you!' (The Dyslexic Professor, 2017c). Indeed, he highlights how he himself has embodied these strengths and connects them to wider needs; for example in the context of the 'resilience' strength, he says:

Resilience is all about coping with change and new challenges and you simply need buckets of this at the start of a new job. Being a leader sometimes is about making decisions (easy and hard; good and bad!) in a timely manner and, of course, being willing to apologise when you get it wrong! So, quick thinking has been key. (The Dyslexic Professor, 2017b)

The professor also expresses how the disclosure of dyslexia through the blog has impacted his own sense of wellbeing. Primarily, the blog seems to have released what he calls 'the pent-up frustrations and wounds of five decades of learning' (The Dyslexic Professor, 2017d), specifically through this strategic *strengths*-based reframe:

Having survived my school days and emerged with a deep held belief I am 'thick', 'lazy' and 'stupid', I do know I don't actually have a superpower as such but associating this expression with the positive aspects of my dyslexic thinking, does help me let go of some of this ingrained negativity … I do think my dyslexic thinking helps me in all aspects of my work and disclosing I have dyslexia enables me and others to acknowledge the challenges and promote the advantages. In my experience, successful modern academics increasingly work in teams and disclosure provides the opportunity to build neurodiversity into any team from the outset. (The Dyslexic Professor, 2019)

Though he describes 'coming out as a dyslexic has been a truly profound experience' (ibid.), and shares that he feels 'liberated and empowered and connected to fellow Dyslexic Activists' (The Dyslexic Professor, 2017e). So it seems that focusing on strengths through this unrecognized medium has also enabled him to sense control and relationality to others – all drivers of wellbeing at work (Lomas, 2019). Yet at the same time, he also recognizes the negative impacts on his own emotion, in relation to the ruminations and reflections about the wider situation, and through witnessing the experiences of others. He says:

> [i]t would be hard to underestimate the sadness I have observed and the release that acknowledging this can bring ... and acknowledge the personal damage and resulting sadness inflicted by inappropriate and outdated educational systems. (The Dyslexic Professor, 2017e)

In this example, the micro-activism therefore seemingly, and unexpectedly, created a duality. On the one hand, the professor comes head to head with the rigidity of a controlled and 'outdated' system, which both places him as a renegade figure, himself outside of any system, but also a portal for others who share his profound sadness for a system that caters only to a specific and controlled type of intelligence. Although there have been and are still an increasing number of scholars who wish to do things 'differently' (Gilmore et al., 2019), the professor is still in the minority of scholars who uses his own perceived weakness as a way to connect to others and inspire others through his exposure. Yet, on the other hand, he is relating not only to other dyslexic activists but to a larger body of scholars who have felt rejected by the traditional norms of academia and find solace and relief in his expression of vulnerability, regaining a sense of connection and community through this subtle act of activism. So this example seems to both positively support strengths and relatedness drivers of wellbeing, but is also simultaneously a reminder that the wider system attacks such drivers.

'THANK YOU FOR REVISING YOUR MANUSCRIPT...'

Empirical work also suggests that the article peer-review process is entangled with the hyper-masculinized environments of academe, including the ways in which submitted articles are judged and the tone in which feedback is given (Smith and Ulus, 2019). Within this process, journal editors have a powerful role to play in managing the relationship between authors, reviewers, and journals for the purpose of knowledge dissemination. This relationship underpins and shapes the scholarly work that appears in the public domain, although little acknowledgement is given to the personal, political, and relational power dynamics associated with editorial work (Anderson et al., 2020). Editors can make or break individuals' careers, but they can also make mindful and deliberate choices regarding how they practise editorial work, for example by managing editorial relationships with a developmental intent that recognizes the performative context of academic work (Sparkes, 2007; Horn, 2016). Micro-activism in this context is a push-back against individualized performativity (Chory and Offstein, 2016), in order to move away from the toxic relations of hyper-competitive knowledge production processes (Sparkes, 2007; Anderson et al., 2020). Activist editorship in this sense is a practice that is sensitive to the personal, political, and relational dynamics of academic work and value systems that shape academic lives and wellbeing. Yet it is also a largely hidden activity, and little is currently written about the experiences of editors in this sense. The following vignette illustrates a case of micro-activist editorship and how it connects with drivers of wellbeing.

A journal editor was formulating a decision letter for a resubmission that had received mixed reviewer responses (rejection, major revision, minor revision). The authors had made few significant changes since the original submission, despite detailed, constructive feedback. Although the reviewers were enthusiastic about the idea and topic, they pointed out that the paper did not live up to academic standards. The editor was dismayed to read this resubmission and its reviews as she had encouraged the first author, at a conference, to submit the original paper. This author was just out of their PhD and, she suspected, revised the paper with very little support from their very experienced co-author (ex-supervisor).

The editor therefore faced a dilemma of *emotions* versus *control*: should she follow journal conventions and reject a paper not likely to 'make it' in the next round, or should she consider the context and the impact this rejection might have on a young scholar's career trajectory? Were these guidelines effectively not allowing young scholars the space to learn and develop? How would she feel being complicit in this? On the other hand, from a resources perspective, a third review would involve at least six people – already under pressure in a creaking system – spending a lot more time on a risky manuscript. Finally, she decided to follow her own driving *values* around mentoring and supporting community newcomers and offered the authors a second major revision.

How then should she word the decision letter to convey both encouragement but also make the authors cognizant of the paper's shortcomings and satisfy the reviewers? How could she mentor this new writer a little and perhaps indicate to the second author that they needed to do so too? The editor worked on the decision letter for a whole day, calibrating how to be fair to the authors, the reviewers, to her role as steward of the quality mission of the journal, and also to her own sense of collegiality and fair play. She toyed with different formulations to convey the message that 'you've got to play the game a bit more'. She tried to compensate for one review's unkind tone and edited it a bit, yet at the same time she tried to convey her respect for the work put into the process by all concerned. Her effort was first recognized by one reviewer who responded by praising the skilfully woven response and then rewarded when the paper was, after two more rounds, finally published.

As this vignette has illustrated, the peer-review process is fraught with *emotions* that are taxing to authors, reviewers, and editors alike. Yet, when delivering feedback within a performative context, such as writing, the emotions of the recipient are too frequently dismissed (Molloy et al., 2019). Developmental feedback is, thus, a means to manage the emotions of criticism within the hypercompetitive and masculine environment (Smith and Ulus, 2019). Reviewers and editors are nevertheless volunteering their time in service to their fields, whilst performing labour without pay from the publishers (Callahan, 2018), and their goodwill can run thin with the increased pressure for academics to publish.

Because the identities of the reviewers are masked, and there is often very little dialogue in the process, there can be little sense of *control* for the author – a driver for wellbeing at work (Lomas, 2019). The author's fate is in the hands of these anonymous reviewers who may not be empathetic to how their words impact the wellbeing of the recipient. Further, the developmental feedback approach offers editors some level of *control* over the content of their journals in a publishing context in which an editorship increasingly risks becoming little more than a 'traffic controller' (Modarres, 2015).

Authors often have constrained discretion over outlet choices for their publications because of the ubiquity of journal ranking lists as proxies for quality and recognition (Anderson et al., 2020). In such a pressurized, performative system, senior scholars may abuse their positional power to gain authorship credit without providing the substantive guidance that early career researchers need to be successful in the publishing process. This lack of contribution despite the reward of a potential publication shifts the burden of mentorship to the editor and reviewers. Although this can be emotionally wearing for the latter groups, the above case illustrates how activist editorship can model supportive practice to other (senior) members of the community and can also be personally gratifying and deliver positive emotional responses in the longer run.

DISCUSSION AND FUTURE DIRECTIONS

The cases above contribute to an emerging area of study, that is, the ways in which micro-activism and wellbeing relate when the acts are individualistic and are largely – at least in terms of their activist intent – hidden. Yet the cases also demonstrate that although there are aspects of micro-activism which are hidden, they are not expressed in a social or relational vacuum. Indeed, the cases of micro-activism share a common desire by individuals to re-cast and re-position *relationships*, often using some modicum of *control* that is available to the activists at that time – whether that be asserting through an email signature, through using an open technology, or through translating highly emotional reviews of an article submission. Through this process, these activists can also express *leadership* perhaps around certain *values* they hold and, as such, are able to address a range of drivers of wellbeing at work for themselves. Yet at the same time, the expression of such activist work is not always positive, and there may well be negative (or to some extent mixed) *emotions*, or *relationships* may indeed be compromised or damaged; the activist might be saddened to learn how widespread an issue is (cf. The Dyslexic Professor) or they may be met by unappreciative responses which claim their acts are inappropriate or unprofessional and publicly embarrass them (cf. the symbolic Love* & Kisses). So for activists, there seems to be multi-directional relationships between micro-activism and wellbeing at work.

In the same vein, the expression of micro-activism by individuals not only positively and negatively affects the wellbeing of those expressing it but may also impact the wellbeing of those experiencing the acts. In these cases, emails expressing love or kisses, coming out as dyslexic, expressing a care for colleagues without structural recognition, and navigating and negotiating reviewer comments, can potentially evoke positive or negative emotions and relationality for those involved. However, problematically, although expressing care might be done as an act of micro-activism by those with control – such as managers – some might interpret it as an instrument to normalize a wider structural problem of displacing responsibility for wellbeing from the organization to the individual (Smith and Ulus, 2019). In this way, and echoing the above discussion, micro-activism can have multi-directional relationships with wellbeing at work because of the material effects it creates through its expression.

Such multi-directional dynamics do not give a definitive conclusion as to the ways in which micro-activism promotes wellbeing in organizations, but they do initiate a more systematic approach to understanding the relationship. As a nascent area of study, the analysis does highlight that micro-activism is not a 'petty act' in terms of wellbeing despite it being a relatively hidden 'weapon of the weak', and that there is a complex relationship. As such, there are a number of areas of investigation that would be worthy of further exploration: (1) what are the factors or features of micro-activism which seemingly have the most significant effects on wellbeing, (2) what are the temporal dynamics of wellbeing and micro-activism over time (related to the ways in which others experience and interact with the expression of the acts of micro-activism), and (3) how do the drivers of wellbeing which were seemingly hidden in this chapter operate in micro-activism (such as *reward-recognition*)? Underpinning these questions needs to be a recognition that although micro-activism may not be public and social, it can and does shape the way in which we relate to others and so there are dialogical dimensions and dynamics which connect to a material or imagined sense of person-in-context. This is key to understanding why micro-activism can feel like 1,000 snowflakes rather than a single snowflake when it comes to wellbeing in organizations.

REFERENCES

Alakavuklar, O. N., Dickson, A. G., & Stablein, R. (2017). The alienation of scholarship in modern business schools: From Marxist material relations to the Lacanian subject. *Academy of Management Learning & Education*, 16(3), 454–468.

Amis, J. M., Munir, K. A., Lawrence, T. B., Hirsch, P., & McGahan, A. (2018). Inequality, institutions and organizations. *Organization Studies*, 39(9), 1131–1152.

Anderson, G. (2008). Mapping academic resistance in the managerial university. *Organization*, 15(2), 251–270.

Anderson, V., Elliott, C., & Callahan, J. L. (2020). Power, powerlessness, and journal ranking lists: The marginalization of fields of practice. *Academy of Management Learning & Education*, doi:10.5465/amle.2019.0037.

Askins, K., & Blazek, M. (2017). Feeling our way: Academia, emotions and a politics of care. *Social and Cultural Geography*, 18(8): 1086–1105.

Aubrecht, K. (2012). The new vocabulary of resilience and the governance of university student life. *Studies in Social Justice*, 6(1), 67–83.

Barnett, R. (2000). Supercomplexity and the curriculum. *Studies in Higher Education*, 25(3), 255–265.

Becker, J. C., & Tausch, N. (2015). A dynamic model of engagement in normative and non-normative collective action: Psychological antecedents, consequences, and barriers. *European Review of Social Psychology*, 26(1), 43–92.

Becker, J. C., Tausch, N., & Wagner, U. (2011). Emotional consequences of collective action participation: Differentiating self-directed and outgroup-directed emotions. *Personality and Social Psychology Bulletin*, 37(12), 1587–1598.

Boehnke, K., & Wong, B. (2011). Adolescent political activism and long-term happiness: A 21-year longitudinal study on the development of micro- and macrosocial worries. *Personality and Social Psychology Bulletin*, 37, 435–447.

Bristow, A., Robinson, S., & Ratle, O. (2017). Being an early-career CMS academic in the context of insecurity and 'excellence': The dialectics of resistance and compliance. *Organization Studies*, 38(9), 1185–1207.

Callahan, J. L. (2018). The retrospective (im) moralization of self-plagiarism: Power interests in the social construction of new norms for publishing. *Organization*, 25(3), 305–319.

Chan, R. C. H., & Mak, W. W. S. (2020). Empowerment for civic engagement and well-being in emerging adulthood: Evidence from cross-regional and cross-lagged analyses. *Social Science & Medicine*, 244, 112703.

Chapman, J., & McClendon, K. (2018). What's love got to do with higher education? How teaching into the heart of knowing can foster compassionate action. *Human Science Perspectives*, 2(1), 9–16.

Chory, R., & Offstein, E. (2016). "Your professor will know you as a person": Evaluating and rethinking the relational boundaries between faculty and students. *Journal of Management Education* 41(1): 9–38.

Cunliffe, A. (2018). Alterity: The passion, politics, and ethics of self and scholarship. *Management Learning*, 49(1), 8–22.

Deci, E. L., & Ryan, R. M. (2007). *Basic Psychological Needs Scales*. Available at www.psych.rochester.edu/SDT, accessed 8 January 2007.

Diener, E., Emmons, R. A., Larsen, R. J., & Griffin, S. (1985). The satisfaction with life scale. *Journal of Personality Assessment*, 49(1), 71–75.

Downton, J., & Wehr, P. (1998). Persistent pacifism: How activist commitment is developed and sustained. *Journal of Peace Research*, 35, 531–550.

Dwyer, P. C., Chang, Y., Hannay, J., & Algoe, S. B. (2019). When does activism benefit well-being? Evidence from a longitudinal study of Clinton voters in the 2016 U.S. presidential election. *PloS One*, 14(9). doi:10.1371/journal.pone.0221754.

Einwohner, R. (2002). Motivational framing and efficacy maintenance: Animal rights activists' use of four fortifying strategies. *The Sociological Quarterly*, 43, 509–526.

Elraz, H. (2017). Identity, mental health and work: How employees with mental health conditions recount stigma and the pejorative discourse of mental illness. *Human Relations*, 71(5), 722–741.

Franco-Santos, M., Nalick, M., Rivera-Torres, P., & Gomez-Mejia, L. (2017). Governance and well-being in academia: Negative consequences of applying an agency theory logic in higher education. *British Journal of Management*, 28(4), 711–730.

Gilmore, S., Harding, N., Helin, J., & Pullen, A. (2019). Writing differently. *Management Learning*, 50(1), 3–10.

Griffin, M., Learmonth, M., & Elliott, C. (2015). Non-domination, contestation and freedom: The contribution of Philip Pettit to learning and democracy in organisations. *Management Learning*, 46(3), 317–336.

Gurin, G., Veroff, J., & Feld, S. (1960). *Americans View Their Mental Health*. New York: Basic Books.

Guthrie, S., Lichten, C., Van Belle, J., Ball, S., Knack, A., & Hofman, J. (2017). *Understanding Mental Health in the Research Environment: A Rapid Evidence Assessment*. Cambridge: RAND.

Horn, S. (2016). The social and psychological costs of peer review: Stress and coping with manuscript rejection. *Journal of Management Inquiry*, 25(1), 11–26.

Jasko, K., Szastok, M., Grzymala-Moszczynska, J., Maj, M., & Kruglanski, A. W. (2019). Rebel with a cause: Personal significance from political activism predicts willingness to self-sacrifice. *Journal of Social Issues*, 75(1), 314–349.

Jones, A., & Crandall, R. (1986). Validation of a short index of self-actualization. *Personality and Social Psychology Bulletin*, 12(1), 63–73.

Keplinger, K., Johnson, S. K., Kirk, J. F., & Barnes, L. Y. (2019). Women at work: Changes in sexual harassment between September 2016 and September 2018. *PloS One*, 14(7), doi:10.1371/journal.pone.0218313.

Keyes, C. L. M. (1998). Social well-being. *Social Psychology Quarterly*, 61(2), 121–140.

Keyes, C. L. M. (2002). The mental health continuum: From languishing to flourishing in life. *Journal of Health and Social Behavior*, 43(2), 207–222.

Kiriakos, C., & Tienari, J. (2018). Academic writing as love. *Management Learning*, 49(3), 263–277.

Klar, M., & Kasser, T. (2009). Some benefits of being an activist: Measuring activism and its role in psychological well-being. *Political Psychology*, 30(5), 755–777.

Lee, K. S. (2004). The effects of social activism on the occupational experience, locus of control, and well-being of black midlife women. *Journal of Black Psychology*, 30(3), 386–405.

Lomas, T. (2019). Positive work: A multidimensional overview and analysis of work-related drivers of wellbeing. *International Journal of Applied Positive Psychology*, 3, 69–96.

McKie, A. (2020). Covid-19: Universities treating staff in 'vastly different ways'. *The Times Higher Education*. Available at www.timeshighereducation.com/news/covid-19-universities-treating-staff-vastly-different-ways, accessed 1 July 2020.

Modarres, A. (2015). It's not just the author: The reader and the editor are dead, too. *Publications*, 3, 168–173.

Molloy, E., Noble, C., & Ajjawi, R. (2019). Attending to emotion in feedback. In Henderson, M., Ajjawi, R., Boud, D., & Molloy, E. (eds), *The Impact of Feedback in Higher Education: Improving Assessment Outcomes for Learners*. Cham: Palgrave Macmillan, pp. 83–105.

Mumby, D. K., Thomas, R., Martí, I., & Seidl, D. (2017). Resistance redux. *Organization Studies*, 38(9), 1157–1183.

Niven, D. (2020). Stifling workplace activism: The consequences of anthem protests for NFL players. *Social Science Quarterly*, 101(2), 641–655.

Páez, D., Basabe, N., Ubillos, S., & González-Castro, J. (2007). Social sharing, participation in demonstrations, emotional climate, and coping with collective violence after the March 11th Madrid bombings. *Journal of Social Issues*, 63, 323–337.

Parker, M. (2018). *Shut Down the Business School! An Insider's Account of What's Wrong with Management Education*. New York: Pluto Press.

Parker, S. and Parker, M. (2017). Antagonism, accommodation and agonism in Critical Management Studies: Alternative organizations as allies. *Human Relations*, 70(11), 1366–1387.

Reinecke, J. (2018). Social movements and prefigurative organizing: Confronting entrenched inequalities in occupy London. *Organization Studies*, 39(9), 1299–1321.

Rhodes, C., Wright, C., & Pullen, A. (2018). Changing the world? The politics of activism and impact in the neoliberal university. *Organization*, 25(1), 139–147.

Ryan, R. M., & Deci, E. L. (2001). On happiness and human potentials: A review of research on hedonic and eudaimonic well-being. *Annual Review of Psychology*, 52, 141–166.

Ryan, R. M., & Deci, E. L. (2008). From ego depletion to vitality: Theory and findings concerning the facilitation of energy available to the self. *Social and Personality Psychology Compass*, 2, 702–717.

Ryan, R. M., & Frederick, C. M. (1997). On energy, personality and health: Subjective vitality as a dynamic reflection of well-being. *Journal of Personality*, 65, 529–565.

Ryff, C. D. (1989). Happiness is everything, or is it? Explorations on the meaning of psychological well-being. *Journal of Personality and Social Psychology*, 57(6), 1069–1081.

Scott, J. (1990). *Domination and the Arts of Resistance*. New Haven, CT: Yale University Press

Smith, C., & Ulus, E. (2019). Who cares for academics? We need to talk about emotional well-being including what we avoid and intellectualize through macro-discourses. *Organization*, 27(6), 840–857.

Snyder, C. R., Sympson, S. C., Ybasco, F. C., Borders, T. F., Babyak, M. A., & Higgins, R. L. (1996). Development and validation of the State Hope Scale. *Journal of Personality and Social Psychology*, 70(2), 321–335.

Sparkes, A. C. (2007). Embodiment, academics, and the audit culture: A story seeking consideration. *Qualitative Research*, 7(4), 521–550.

Sparkes, A. C. (2018). Autoethnography comes of age. In Beach, D., Bagley, C., & da Silva, S.M. (eds), *The Wiley Handbook of Ethnography of Education*. Hoboken, NJ: John Wiley & Sons, pp. 479–499.

Steger, M. F., Frazier, P., Oishi, S., & Kaler, M. (2006). The meaning in life questionnaire: Assessing the presence of and search for meaning in life. *Journal of Counseling Psychology*, 53(1), 80–93.

The Dyslexic Professor (2016a). *The Dyslexic Professor*. Available at https://nigellockett.com/2016/12/18/thedyslexicprofessor/, accessed 9 July 2020.

The Dyslexic Professor (2016b). *Time to see Dyslexia as a Superpower?* Available at https://nigellockett.com/2016/12/31/dyslexia-superpower/, accessed 9 July 2020.

The Dyslexic Professor (2017a). *Dyslexia: Superpower, Superhero, or Survivor?* Available at https://nigellockett.com/2017/11/26/dyslexia-superpower-superhero-or-survivor/, accessed 9 July 2020.

The Dyslexic Professor (2017b). *The Dyslexic Professor: Can You Teach an Old Dog New Tricks?* Available at https://nigellockett.com/2019/07/17/the-dyslexic-professor-can-you-teach-an-old-dog-new-tricks/, accessed 9 July 2020.

The Dyslexic Professor (2017c). *Dyslexia Superpower: Envisioning a Better Future*. Available at https://nigellockett.com/2017/10/15/dyslexia-superpower-envisioning-a-better-future/, accessed 9 July 2020.

The Dyslexic Professor (2017d). *A Dyslexia Reflection*. Available at https://nigellockett.com/2017/04/02/a-dyslexia-reflection/, accessed 9 July 2020.

The Dyslexic Professor (2017e). *A Year in the Life of The Dyslexic Professor*. Available at https://nigellockett.com/2017/12/17/a-year-in-the-life-of-the-dyslexic-professor/, accessed 9 July 2020.

The Dyslexic Professor (2019). *The Dyslexic Professor: Towards a Dyslexia Superpower – Reflections on the Year in the Life of a Dyslexic Professor of Entrepreneurship*. Available at https://nigellockett.com/2019/03/25/the-dyslexic-professor-towards-a-dyslexia-superpower-reflections-on-the-year-in-the-life-of-a-dyslexic-professor-of-entrepreneurship-march-2019/, accessed 9 July 2020.

Tourish, D. (2020). The triumph of nonsense in management studies. *Academy of Management Learning & Education*, 19(1), 99–109.

Vestergren, S., Drury, J., & Chiriac, E. H. (2017). The biographical consequences of protest and activism: A systematic review and a new typology. *Social Movement Studies*, 16(2), 203–221.

Vestergren, S., Drury, J., & Chiriac, E. H. (2018). How collective action produces psychological change and how that change endures over time: A case study of an environmental campaign. *British Journal of Social Psychology*, 57(4), 855–877.

Vestergren, S., Drury, J., & Hammar Chiriac, E. (2019). How participation in collective action changes relationships, behaviours, and beliefs: An interview study of the role of inter- and intragroup processes. *Journal of Social and Political Psychology*, 7(1), 76–99.

Wall, T. (2016). Author response: Provocative education – From the Dalai Lama's cat to dismal land. *Studies in Philosophy and Education*, 35(6), 649–653.

Wall, T., Clough, D., Österlind, E., & Hindley, A. (2019a). Conjuring a spirit for sustainability: A review of the socio-materialist effects of provocative pedagogies. In Leal Fihlo, W. (ed.), *Sustainability in Higher Education*. Cham: Springer, pp. 313–327.

Wall, T., Giles, D.E., & Stanton, T. (2019b). Service learning and academic activism: A review, prospects and a time for revival. In Billingham, S. (ed.), *Access to Success and Social Mobility through Higher Education: A Curate's Egg?* Bingley: Emerald Publishing, pp. 163–176.

Watson, D., Clark, L. A., & Tellegen, A. (1988). Development and validation of brief measures of positive and negative affect: The PANAS scales. *Journal of Personality and Social Psychology*, 54(6), 1063–1070.

36

Workers' Resistance in Defense of Wellbeing in Contemporary Organizations

Florence Palpacuer

INTRODUCTION

Wellbeing and resistance are rarely associated to each other in organizational studies. To a large extent, they belong to separate research traditions conveying distinct views of the nature of social relations, the work experience and employees' expectations at the workplace. Employees' wellbeing studies build on the founding premises of the human relation school that employees have a strong need for social affiliation, joining in a common cause, and exercising autonomy and creativity at work. Emphasis is put on the convergence of interests and goals within the firm, in support of a central claim that enhancing the wellbeing of employees will positively contribute to the firm's performance, a perspective that tends to evacuate issues of power, domination and conflict at the workplace (Perrow, 2014).

By contrast, critical studies of workplace resistance are endorsing a view of the firm as a site of struggles and domination. Social relations are seen as inextricably linked to the exercise of power, either in the Marxist perspective of labor process theory, for which the very foundation of the firm lies in the antagonism between capital and labor, or in the post-structuralist vein of workplace resistance studies, which adopts a more diffused, fluid and subjectivized conception of power inspired from Foucault and others (Knights and Willmott, 1990). In both cases, conflicts of interest are seen as irreducible and the managerial discourses and techniques that promote shared goals, values and commitment are denounced as new forms of 'concertative control' (Barker, 1999) or 'corporate culturism' (Willmott, 1993), calling for a 'wake up from the nightmare of participation' (Kolowratnik and Miessen, 2012).

Hence the project of exploring resistance movements from the perspective of workers' wellbeing somehow requires a stretch across competing, even conflicting paradigms. The endeavor is worth the effort, however, insofar as it offers an opportunity to overcome some limitations that such mutual rejection may have induced in both perspectives. For organizational wellbeing scholars, acknowledging the dynamics of hegemony and resistance at the workplace might prove useful to account for the growing social tensions that pervade contemporary organizations, as institutions permeable to broader changes in society and the global economy (Fleming, 2014).

A critical political perspective on wellbeing also invites a re-reading of resistance studies that challenges their anthropological closure on struggles conceived as ends in themselves and a worker's impassable horizon. Beyond the inherently exploitative features of capitalism, or the intricate combination of power and resistance at play in the processes of workers' subjectivation, what could a wellbeing perspective tell us about the more humanistic motives and aspirations that may actually be pursued in contemporary workplace struggles?

Such a question is in line with recent initiatives to incorporate elements of ethics (Pullen and Rhodes, 2014) or the moral economy (Hughes et al., 2019) into the study of workers' resistance. Relatedly, this perspective opens the possibility for struggles to be seen as paving the way for broader transformational, emancipatory experiences, at a time of multiple social, ecological and economic crises when the call for alternatives is gaining momentum in management studies (Zanoni et al., 2017).

In this chapter, the wellbeing stakes at play in contemporary resistance struggles will be explored in four steps. The first section draws on critical political readings of wellbeing in order to cast the rise of the concept in the context of broader changes in society and the economy, and to introduce an analytical framework whereby wellbeing is situated in 'a journey of personal and political change', for it can be suppressed, or regained, through processes of domination and resistance operating at personal, relational and collective levels (Prilleltensky

and Nelson, 2002). Equipped with such analytical lens, the second section will revisit core features of contemporary organizational restructuring in order to specify how the corporate foundations of a global neoliberal order may deprive workers of various dimensions of wellbeing, hence casting the 'what' that is being resisted.

The third section will turn to the 'how' of resistance by drawing on a typology recently developed in organization studies (Mumby et al., 2017) to highlight how different forms of resistance might address distinct or combined dimensions of wellbeing. The last section builds on a particularly striking case of workers' resistance (Palpacuer and Seignour, 2019) to highlight the dynamic processes through which a workplace struggle might encompass the three foundational dimensions of wellbeing. All along, our scope of analysis will be centered on large corporations in Western countries, and on new forms of workers' resistance that may involve labor unions but typically fall outside the unions' traditional repertoire of struggles, both because of the type of wellbeing issues being addressed and because of the ways in which these issues are being addressed by resisters.

A CRITICAL POLITICAL READING OF ORGANIZATIONAL WELLBEING

The rise of the notion of wellbeing is a relatively recent phenomenon, situated in the second half of the 20th century, which conveys seemingly contradictory meanings with regards to the ways in which wellbeing needs are being catered for in the workplace and the broader society. This apparent paradox calls for an analytical perspective able to account for the existence of tensions, contradictions and struggles in the processes by which workers might be deprived of, or on the contrary, enabled to regain, the conditions of their wellbeing at the workplace.

Contradictory Wellbeing Trends in the Workplace and Society

The growing attention devoted to wellbeing can be seen as an outcome of social progress and its related shift in emphasis from the material needs that predominated in the early stages of economic development, objectified by indicators such as incomes, wages and working hours, towards more qualitative or subjective needs that gained in importance as societies grew wealthier (Diener and Seligman, 2004). In Western societies, public policies have shown renewed interest in the wellbeing of populations at large, measured by personal satisfaction, emotional comfort and the capacity to exercise meaningful activities in an ethical way, all encompassed in general conceptions of wellbeing (Dalingwater et al., 2019). At the organizational level, policy guidelines and initiatives to stir employees' wellbeing have flourished and received growing attention in business, consulting and human resources management circles.

Paradoxically, wealthier societies and the growing attention devoted to subjective wellbeing have not correlated with widespread improvements in levels of happiness and fulfillment. On the contrary, depression rates, anxiety rates, distrust in others and in institutions have strongly increased since the 1980s, particularly in Anglo-Saxon countries (Diener and Seligman, 2004). Workplace suicides have been on the rise in a broad range of countries such as France, Australia, Japan and the United States – where they reached historical highs in 2018 (Wan, 2020) – in correlation with greater job insecurity, work intensification and declining trade union representation (Danford et al., 2003). In France, research based on workers' testimonies further linked suicides to chaotic restructuring and management bullying, in the context of broader neoliberal economic reforms (Waters, 2017).

The apparent contradiction between better material conditions and rising concerns for subjective wellbeing, on the one hand, and the deterioration of people's mental health both in society at large and at the workplace, on the other, might be understood in light of critical political readings which see the contemporary prominence of wellbeing as embodying a shift in public policy from the collective welfare of 'people' and 'nations' towards individualistic approaches centered on the 'self', following the introduction of neoliberal policies in the 1980s (Dalingwater et al., 2019). These changes in national policies are echoing a firm-level evolution from 'personnel management' geared at the whole workforce and strongly backed by collective bargaining systems, towards increasingly individualized forms of human resources management (HRM), generative of greater inequalities in the workplace and the labor market (Capelli, 1999). In such perspective, the very focus on individuals' wellbeing, to be served by 'enabling' states and corporations, is actually part of a broader process of individualization which undermines established patterns of solidarity and social cohesion in the workplace and society.

Furthermore, wellbeing is casted as being offered to, or withdrawn from, the workers who are seen as passive recipients of the managerial and governmental initiatives. The implicit omission of the workers as agents capable of countering these trends, either individually or collectively, is all the more problematic that it runs counter to some basic premises of the wellbeing concept, such as the capacity to engage oneself in meaningful activities.

Wellbeing, Domination and Emancipation

Wellbeing, domination and emancipation are at the core of the 'critical psychology' promoted by Prilleltensky and Nelson (2002). By seeing power as 'pivotal in attaining wellbeing and in opposing injustice' (ibid.: 5), their approach offers the possibility of integrating core tenets of resistance studies in the analysis of wellbeing, and shares the broader concern of critical management studies for generating knowledge that will serve a process of emancipation by unveiling the forms of domination exercised on deprived people. While resistance studies primarily focus on two uses of power, i.e., the power to oppress and the power to resist, Prilleltensky and Nelson (2002) introduce a third use, the power to thrive for wellbeing. This suggests that the dialectics of oppression and resistance might not be ends in themselves, as often cast in resistance studies, but are rather infused by, or closely intertwined with, a need for thriving and fulfillment.

Prilleltensky and Nelson (2002) further posit that wellbeing should be understood in a dynamic of 'personal and political change', or a process of transformation through which people may emancipate from the situations of domination that deprive them of the conditions needed for their thriving and fulfillment. The question of wellbeing is here approached from the perspective of the people, who are seen as capable of engaging in the active pursuit of their own wellbeing, while being simultaneously constrained or enabled by

their social, economic and political environment. Hence, the authors explicitly reject the 'psycho-centric' definitions of wellbeing that 'concentrate on the cognitive and emotional sources and consequences of suffering and wellbeing, to the exclusion of the social, material and political roots and effects of lack of power' (ibid.: 11).

Wellbeing is here conceptualized in a cross-disciplinary perspective combining psychological, sociological and political elements, as being achieved through the 'simultaneous and balanced satisfaction of personal, relational, and collective needs' (ibid.: 8). These needs, and the conditions that may fulfill or on the contrary repress them, are characterized on all three levels (Table 36.1).

Such framework is particularly well suited for assessing how wellbeing has been affected by changes in corporate forms and practices in the context of diffusion of a neo-liberal regime in Western economies, and how wellbeing is being reclaimed through various forms of workers' resistance. First, it offers an opportunity to encompass personal, relational and collective levels of resistance in an integrative framework, hence overcoming a cleavage in resistance studies between

Table 36.1   Wellbeing, Oppression and Emancipation.

Dimensions	Wellbeing values (and needs)	Oppression	Emancipation
Personal (self)	Self-determination (mastery, voice, choice, skills, growth and autonomy) Health (emotional and physical)	Internalized psychological oppression	Conscientization of personal struggle situated in the context of broader structural political forces
Relational (others)	Respect for human diversity (identity, dignity) Collaboration and democratic participation (involvement, mutual responsibility)	'Power over' Domination of, or by, others	'Power with' Egalitarian relationships Peer mentoring support
Collective (society)	Social justice (fair and equitable allocation of power, obligations and resources) Supportive institutions (cohesion, community)	Oppressive social practices manifested in policies and communities	Empowering social practices manifested in policies and communities provide larger structural context for wellness

Source: adapted from Prilleltensky and Nelson (2002), p.9 and p.18.

the critical materialist scholars concerned with collective struggles, and the pragmatic constructivist promoters of informal, individual forms of resistance (Fournier and Grey, 2000; Contu, 2008; Fleming, 2016).

Second, the framework can be used to highlight some interdependencies, or even trajectories, across the three dimensions involved in the fulfillment of wellbeing needs. For instance, Prilleltensky and Nelson (2002) suggest that personal wellbeing is predicated on the wellbeing of the immediate group (the family, or in organizational contexts, the workplace team), which, in turn, is contingent upon broader corporate and societal conditions. Conversely, the launch of a resistance dynamics to reclaim wellbeing on the collective level would typically start from the conscientization of one's situation of oppression, favoring the connection with others experiencing similar circumstances, which may, in turn, lead to the launch of a broader emancipatory movement.

WELLBEING DEPRIVATION IN THE NEOLIBERAL CORPORATION

Before exploring resistance studies from a wellbeing perspective, a short detour should be made to highlight key features of the transformations undergone by large corporations in Western economies, and to assess their implications from a worker's wellbeing perspective.

Patterns of Corporate Transformation

Although it is beyond the scope of this chapter to engage in the full complexity of the changes to be sketched out in this section, a few lines of direction can be highlighted to signal regularities in the corporate context that workers may be found to be resisting. The evidence stylized here is mainly of a

qualitative nature, allowing us to draw a coherent pattern in the corporate transformations involved by the Western shift to neoliberal economies. Launched in the 1980s in Anglo-Saxon countries, and spreading to Europe during the following decades, these changes run deep into the structure, culture and governance of large corporations and as such, they have unfolded through the years, and even decades, with variable speed and intensity across industries and countries.

In an ideal-typical perspective, the search for scale economies could be identified as a key driver for these transformations. Facilitated by deregulation policies and stirred by flattening growth rates in national economies, scale economies involved shifting from multi-domestic to global or macroregional markets, functions and production organizing (Dicken, 2014). The rise of the global form could not be accomplished without a redeployment of command functions from national to transnational levels, and was sustained by an intense activity of mergers and acquisitions by which large firms also reshuffled their business portfolio, so as to focus on those sectors where global, or at least macro-regional, leadership could be built and sustained.

For the national subsidiaries that had enjoyed substantial autonomy in market, products, production and human resources development policies over decades, the shift came as a severe shock. The local entities found themselves caught between the increasingly standardized operational processes and tight control systems that the newly integrated information technologies have established throughout the multinational (Mohdzain and Ward, 2007), and a new rhetoric of entrepreneurship and competition that continuously benchmarked their local performances against those of other entities in the multinational and beyond (Morgan and Kristensen, 2006; Becker-Ritterspach and Dörrenbächer, 2009). Hence subsidiaries and work sites were to become increasingly disposable and substitutable in the new form of 'market-based management' that also infused HRM policies: the internal labor markets that local subsidiaries had developed in a multi-domestic context were increasingly opened to external competition, and just like local factories could be closed, sold, downsized, and their activities revamped through relocation to other work sites or externalization, so could employees, including managers, be relocated, terminated or externalized through subcontracting and non-standard forms of employment (Palpacuer et al., 2011).

Two other lines of transformation were to have major implications on the work experience of employees. One pertained to the redesign of business models from the manufacturing orientation built in the previous period of 'industrial capitalism' towards a focus on sales, marketing and product development in the new era of 'financial capitalism' (Lazonick and O'Sullivan, 2000; Milberg, 2008). Such redefinition of the firm's core competencies involved not only 'hollowing out' the corporation via externalization but also revamping the firm's culture and identity historically built and embedded in its 'core' workforce. The other concerned corporate governance which became, and still remains, closely tied to financial markets. A variety of tools and discourses were then introduced to diffuse a new injunction to prioritize shareholder returns in the conduct of the firm, all through hierarchical layers and down to the local managers (Froud et al., 2006), with profound implications for the ways in which work was to continue to be done in local settings.

Implications for Workers' Wellbeing

A few effects of the neoliberal transformations on workers' wellbeing can be pinpointed here by returning to Prilleltensky and Nelson (2002)'s analytical grid. Before doing so, it is important to recall that our focus is on the core workforce which enjoyed fairly stable employment, particularly in European countries, and embodied the large firms' backbone in terms of skills, culture, reputation and productive capacities in Western settings. Indeed, such background was pivotal in sustaining the workers' capacity to resist when their work identities, collectives and broader societal status came under attack in the 1980s, 1990s and beyond. Although the point has not been systematically covered in the resistance literature, some of the most significant cases of workers' resistance can be observed in workplace settings where the workers had experienced fairly strong capacities for self-determination and health protection, team solidarity, collective bargaining structures and a recognized contribution and place in the broader society (Courpasson et al., 2012; Contu et al., 2013; Palpacuer and Seignour, 2019).

For the core workforce, then, neoliberal restructuring had important personal, relational and collective implications. On the first level, several of the case studies to be further discussed in the following sections acknowledge how self-determination, personal growth and health could be hampered. The shift in core competencies was a particularly brutal experience for workers who had built professional pride and identity on what came to be seen as non-core, low-value activities (Palpacuer et al., 2011). The threat to identity could also affect a whole work site abruptly destined to close after years of acknowledged technological excellency (for instance, Blyton and Jenkins, 2012). As evidenced by research on workers' suicides, particularly in the widely commented case of the main French telecom company to be discussed later, health was also at stake when the loss of identity was combined with rising stress under intensified work pressures, chaotic restructuring and management bullying (Waters, 2017), together with the loss of social bonding or 'neoliberal anomy' induced by the firm's financialization (Chabrak et al., 2016).

Relational wellbeing has also been affected by individualized HRM policies which, in the context of rising employment insecurity, increasingly pitted workers against each other, and by the loss of trust between workers and the managers in charge of implementing the new corporate policies on the ground (Laaser, 2016). Among sales professionals, relational wellbeing could be affected by changes in the relationship with clients, induced by the shift from a culture valuing proximity, quality and durability in interpersonal relationships, towards a policy of sales' maximization based on the standardization of customer relationships and interchangeability of salespeople (Courpasson et al., 2012; Courpasson, 2016).

Finally, neoliberal restructuring had profound implications for the place and role that workers had gained in the broader society, through supportive bargaining institutions, on the one hand, and the contribution that 'their' firm had made to national economies and societies, all the more so through public services, on the other. First, in subsidiaries and work sites now deprived of any significant managerial autonomy, decision-making appeared as increasingly remote, opaque and de-territorialized. Unless local managers themselves launched active resistance strategies in defense of their work site (Morgan and Kristensen, 2006; Contu et al., 2013), workers no longer had a direct interlocutor in capacity to engage in social dialogue on workplace issues. Second, the social usefulness of workers was deeply unsettled by the prioritization of shareholder value in the firm's governance, which challenged the firm's social contribution by implying that all tasks and decisions should be primarily governed with the objective of maximizing returns on invested capital (Lazonick and O'Sullivan, 2000).[1]

A TYPOLOGY OF RESISTANCE ACCORDING TO WELLBEING NEEDS

The rise of interest in wellbeing which accompanied the neoliberal turn was echoed by a not dissimilar evolution in organizational resistance studies, where the focus moved away from the collective, Marxist-inspired and union-led movements that dominated the field until the 1980s (see, for example, Hyman, 1972; Edwards, 1979), towards more individualized, informal modes of resistance, approached from a post-structuralist perspective which saw power and resistance as inextricably intertwined in the functioning of organizations (Thomas and Davies, 2005; McCabe et al., 2019). Although the dialogue between these two camps of resistance studies has often been tense (Fournier and Grey, 2000), recent developments indicate a renewed interest in more collective forms of resistance (for instance, Courpasson, 2016, 2017), and the adoption of a broader, more inclusive stance on the diversity of forms that resistance may take, as cast in the typology of Mumby et al. (2017) and in the earlier proposition made by Spicer and Böhm (2007). These typologies emphasize that resistance can be overt or hidden, individual or collective, located within the firm or beyond, and point to the existence of interconnections, complementarities or even trajectories between the various types of resistance, as will be further explored in the next section.

Our focus here will be on deciphering what these forms of resistance may tell us from the perspective of the wellbeing needs that workers are attempting to defend, by considering resistance at individual and collective levels, while distinguishing between informal and formal modes within each of these categories.

Individual Resistance

Hidden individual resistance: A focus on personal dimensions of wellbeing

The type of resistance which has attracted major attention among organization scholars since the 2000s has often been cast as 'infrapolitical' (Scott, 1990), for it remains politically invisible, involving a range of mundane, everyday practices by which workers essentially aim at preserving their autonomy and personal beliefs. Cast in a 'discursive turn' of resistance studies, these hidden individual initiatives are often understood as struggles over meaning, by which workers resist the denial of their self-hood and corporate attempts at identity regulation through the assignment of new values and practices. They may involve distancing oneself from corporate discourses (Collinson, 2003), deploying 'alternative meanings' (Mumby et al., 2017: 1166), or engaging in self-reflexive practices whereby employees exploit 'tensions, inconsistencies and contradictions' (Knights and McCabe, 2000: 431) in organizational discourses. In a Foucauldian vein, resistance is here conceived as 'a constant process of adaptation, subversion and re-inscription of dominant discourses' (Thomas and Davies, 2005: 687). For instance, Thomas and Davies (2005) analyze the 'text' of Susan, the head teacher of a small community college, who denounces the marketization of education under New Public Management (NMP) policies, while simultaneously endorsing some of the traits of the new managerial educational leader by praising her own capacity to raise new funds for the college. Susan describes her ambivalent, resisting and complying attitude towards the education authority or government:

> As an intelligent and caring person you make your decision on how far or not you are going to, how much lip service you're going to give to it and whether you're going to go in to it wholeheartedly ... I understand the context within which my school works and therefore I understand the context in which I apply all the things that come down from above. I'm quite a good girl really but I am naughty at times! (Thomas and Davies, 2005: 698)

McCabe et al. (2019) observe similar arbitrations in the ways in which the local staff of a subsidiary implemented a quality improvement program imposed by headquarters. Critical of the highly standardized and bureaucratized format of the procedure, which was deemed inadequate to the nature of the activity at the local worksite, and seen as diverting people away from their 'real work', the staff implemented the program in partial, adapted ways including the gradual abandonment of, and/or fake reporting on, the most cumbersome tasks.

Through such type of resistance, managers and employees are primarily attending to wellbeing needs situated on a personal level, including their capacity for self-determination, which they seek to preserve by maintaining some degree of mastery and control over their work process, as well as their mental health, by being able to continue to engage in meaningful activities at the workplace. Interestingly, while previous generations of workers had resorted to informal individual misbehaviors as a way to resist their exploitation in the labor process, the cases explored in this more recent literature highlight the emergence of an ethical rationale in individual struggles which are also engaged in the defense of broader collective wellbeing needs such as, for instance, the 'standards of care' in social work (Thomas and Davies, 2005) or the principles of 'fairness and equal access' in public services (Harding et al., 2017). By catering primarily to personal needs, however, such approaches lack a broader transformative capacity and may actually accommodate, rather than challenge, the forms of wellbeing deprivation embedded in neoliberal management systems. Such is the point made by critical resistance scholars who cast these initiatives as 'anemic' (Mumby, 1997), 'decaf' (Contu, 2008), or reduced to the 'clever tricks of the weak within the order established by the strong' (De Certeau, 1984: 40).

Public individual resistance: Addressing collective wellbeing at the expense of personal wellbeing

More striking forms of individual resistance have been observed in recent years, which have received surprisingly little attention in organizational resistance studies. They include whistleblowing, hunger strikes and workers' suicides, which are likely to attract media attention due not only to their radicalness, since workers are jeopardizing or even sacrificing their own safety, health and life, but also to the political messages that the resisters' attach to their action.

By threatening explicitly and directly the status quo, whistleblowing introduces what Weiskopf and Tobias-Miersch (2016: 1621) see as a '"critical opening" that harbors the potential for both personal and organizational transformation'. On the personal level, the whistleblower 'reconstitutes himself as a subject' by negating the dominant discourse and counter-identifying with alternative discourses of professional ethics (ibid.: 1632). On the organizational level, shedding light on organizational misconducts may also induce some transformations provided, however, that a spillover effect entails other actors joining and supporting the struggle, as will be discussed in the next section. Indeed, research indicates that whistleblowers quite systematically endure severe retaliation from their employer (Rothschild and Miethe, 1994), underscoring the vulnerability of individuals in the absence of a broader solidarity movement.

Workers have also been found to engage in hunger strikes in defense of wellbeing needs. While hunger strikes have been in the repertoire of Southern labor struggles, they are less usual in the context of skilled work in Western settings, as documented by Courpasson (2016) in the French subsidiary of a large insurance company. Resistance was here mobilized around a managerial initiative that deeply affected the salespeople in their relationships with customers and the principles of their remuneration. Although the struggle had a collective dimension, with 224 salespeople involved who were dismissed for having refused the change in their employment contract, Courpasson (2016) emphasizes the individual dimension of the choice made by 16 of these resisters to engage in a hunger strike that would eventually prompt the firm to enter into negotiations for fear of the media attention, but at the heavy human toll of several strikers suffering permanent health damage.

Finally, the most radical form of individual resistance is found in workers' suicides, themselves the object of discursive struggles between a managerial approach casting these acts as 'personal' and stemming from 'fragile' individuals, and a workers' view that these suicides are 'political' since they sign a critique of neoliberal forms of management (Palpacuer and Seignour, 2019). Along such lines, Waters (2017) analyzed the letters left by 23 workers who committed suicide at three large companies in France between 2005 and 2015, in order to understand the 'profound effect of workplace transformations on subjective, intimate and lived experiences of work' (2017: 24). A common feature of these letters was that they seek to attribute suicide to workplace causes, which entailed, in some cases, the legal liability of the employer. Testimonies point to feelings of being made redundant or useless, overwhelmed by the workload, and left without voice, or rather, without responses to their repeated attempts to voice issues and needs to the management. Here too, as will be further discussed, the 'transformative' capacity of these acts of resistance may crucially depend on the leverage exercised by other resisting actors.

Collective Resistance

Although some resisters may find themselves isolated at the workplace, particularly when they have been displaced from familiar work settings or submitted to ostracizing management practices (Palpacuer et al., 2011), individual resistance is often embedded in broader collective dynamics, either through hidden forms, which could be seen as primarily addressing the relational dimensions of wellbeing, or through more overt forms of struggle tackling broader societal dimensions of wellbeing.

Hidden collective resistance: A focus on relational wellbeing

A distinctive feature of hidden collective resistance in the contemporary neoliberal workplace probably lies in its strong managerial and/or professional dimensions, since this form of struggle involves the mobilization of whole teams in defense of organizational wellbeing. Although research on this type of resistance is less abundant, it has been pointed in several case studies. For instance, Gagnon and Collinson (2017) showed how an international team involved in a firm's leadership program refused to adopt the normalizing practices aiming to put team members in competition with each other, instead promoting group cohesion and valuing diversity among the members' profiles. Interestingly, by nurturing these two central features of relational wellbeing, the resisting team developed more successful projects than did the other – complying – teams, in line with the very objectives of the program.

A similar pattern of hidden collective resistance was observable in the ways in which the managers of an IBM plant in the South of France found ways of ensuring the work site's survival at a time when cost reduction objectives entailed major restructuring and downsizing, thus threatening the capacity of the site to maintain the critical size needed for the continuation of its very existence. There, managers worked 'en perruque' to start redeploying the production site from manufacturing towards marketing services, a clandestine evolution that would later gain approval from headquarters, and even congratulations for being aligned with the new strategic orientations of the firm (Contu et al., 2013). Such resistance was made possible by the strong ties developed within the local managerial team, which persisted through several generations of managers dedicated to ensuring that the site, and the way of life it embodied, would continue to strive within the multinational.

Forsberg and Stockenstrand (2014) similarly emphasize the role of a collective community and its capacity to sustain an alternative culture through 'hidden scripts' (Scott, 1990) in the resistance to financialization observed in two organizations, a chamber orchestra and a shipping company. Their research emphasizes the role of shared spaces, values and know-how among the resisters, here musicians or shipbuilders, which allowed them to sustain resistance in favor of what they considered as 'good music' and 'good ships', against pressures for cost reduction, rationalization and the individualization of control methods. Here, too, managerial support was instrumental in allowing for the persistence of the collective resistance in the face of numerous outside pressures. This was facilitated by the fact that the persons in authority came from the same skilled professional background as the musicians or the shipbuilders, hence sharing their values and quality standards.

As noted by Courpasson (2017), collective infrapolitical resistance may also precede, and need to be leveraged by, more overt forms of resistance, particularly when resisters wish to challenge some broader structural conditions of wellbeing.

New forms of public collective resistance: Tackling the societal dimension of wellbeing

Collective resistance may 'go public' in a variety of ways, which are often intertwined in the unfolding of this kind of struggle. Borrowing from social movement theory, one could say that 'framing' and 'enrolling' (Benford and Snow, 2000) are of central importance in allowing such firm-based resistance to reach out and gain a broader resonance in society. Reaching out is all the more needed in current times when the voice of workers is strongly weakened within the firm, and the balance of power heavily tilted in favor of the managerial and financial elites.

Here, workers' capacity to enroll external allies becomes instrumental, and requires that their struggle be seen not as the defense of categorial or corporatist interests, but rather as an embodiment of broader issues pertaining to the general interest – and wellbeing – of a country, region or community. This has been typically observed in campaigns against plant closures, as documented for instance by Blyton and Jenkins (2012: 38) in the case of a Burberry factory in the UK:

> The arguments that the campaign leaders took to the media were framed in the context of wider social concerns about the decline of British manufacturing, the power of globalizing forces, sweatshop working, and the exploitation of the consumer who would now be required to pay high prices for a garment produced very cheaply in Chinese factories without free trade unions. This 'vocabulary of motive' (Benford and Snow, 2000: 617) had wider social appeal than what might otherwise have been regarded as workers' narrow economistic self-interest in preserving their jobs.

Likewise, the workers' struggle against the closure of a Nestlé plant in the South of France came to embody a broader movement in defense of 'the right to work and live here' for those currently in employment and for future generations; and 'the struggle meant to rehabilitate the sense of work and give voice to those who simply want a stable employment, working in tranquility and building a future' (Contu et al., 2013: 375). In both cases, the workers gained political support, as expressed by two elected officials involved in the Nestlé battle:

> [t]he town will not accept that its struggle for employment of the people in Marseille be affected by the search for profit maximizing ... one needs to see who is in charge here: if it is the French Republic or if it is a multinational. (ibid.)

Such collective resistance typically mobilizes a variety of actors both inside the firm, where leading activists may include not just union representatives but also plain workers, and outside, where politicians, artists, neighbors, customers and fellow workers may come to form a resistance network or 'hybrid space' generative of broader sociopolitical transformations (Palpacuer and Seignour, 2019). The repertoire of actions also goes beyond traditional workplace strikes or union demands, to include artistic events and other initiatives geared at stirring awareness and solidarity in the broader community or society. As will be discussed later, this type of movement actually builds on the three dimensions of wellbeing, involving strong personal and relational commitment from the resisters.

A DYNAMIC VIEW OF WORKERS' RESISTANCE IN FAVOR OF ORGANIZATIONAL WELLBEING

This fourth section draws on a particularly rich case of workers' resistance which brought issues of organizational wellbeing to the fore of the French social and political scene for several months, in relation to a series of employees' suicides at the main French telecom company in the late 2000s.[2] The scandal eventually led to the trial of the firm and its then top managers about ten years later, when the former CEO, COO and HR director were found guilty of 'institutionalized moral harassment at work'. Although the executives appealed on the judgment and the case is still pending at the time of writing, the penal court has accomplished what the business press called a 'legal revolution' by introducing into the French jurisprudence the notion that wellbeing could be hampered in a 'systemic' way, through a managerial policy 'aiming to destabilize the employees, to create an anxiogenic climate and which had the purpose and effect of deteriorating working conditions'.[3]

The society-wide repercussions of the case included heated debates among intellectuals, experts, political parties, labor and business groups, which made the headlines from the summer of 2009 until Spring 2010; the ensuing dismissal of the firm's CEO Didier Lombard; the signing of major collective agreements on stress and violence at work at both national and corporate levels; and the much-awaited decision of the criminal court following the complaint that the firm's labor unions had launched in 2010. Hence the resistance movement is of particular interest since it changed the way in which workers' wellbeing is understood and regulated in France. It also offers a practical illustration of the 'journey of personal and political change' theorized by Prilleltensky and Nelson (2002) by highlighting the critical role of 'conscientization' at the personal level, and building 'power with' at the relational level, in the emancipatory quest towards organizational wellbeing. These two aspects will be further discussed after a quick highlight of the specificities of wellbeing deprivation in the firm's restructuring context.

An Acute Case of Wellbeing Deprivation

The process of wellbeing deprivation entailed by neoliberal restructuring was accentuated in the case of France Telecom (thereafter, FT) by the peculiar conditions of the firm's privatization. At the time of the crisis, FT had become strongly financialized (Chabrak et al., 2016) – ranking in the top three corporations of the CAC 40 index in terms of dividend distribution – while still holding up to 70% of public servants in its workforce, as a concession made to labor unions through what had been a long and hard-fought process of privatization. The top management had set ambitious targets of cash flow delivery to shareholders, implying that 22,000 people should leave under the restructuring plan NExT (New Experience in Telecommunication) in 2006–2008, just before the suicides scandal exploded in the summer of 2009.

Since public servants could not be dismissed, they were submitted to particularly violent attacks on personal and relational wellbeing. Destabilization techniques included a rule of compulsory mobility every three years, compulsory sessions at the 'development space' to stir employee exit through spin off, voluntary retirement or transfer to other services, and training sessions during which people were made to write and then burn their CVs, in a symbolic destruction of their technical skills and identities, so as to make the shift towards the new commercial orientation of the French telecom leader. On a broader societal dimension, workers' wellbeing was also shaken by the abandonment of the firm's public service values to the benefit of sales and profit maximization objectives. A large-scale survey indicated that at the time of the crisis, the percentage of employees who felt proud of belonging to the firm had fallen from 96% to 39%, and 65% felt that their work conditions had deteriorated (Technologia, 2009). Overall, some 35 employee suicides were acknowledged as being linked to work conditions in 2008 and 2009 (De Senneville, 2019), with a broader union estimate of 60 work-related suicides from 2006 to 2010.

'Conscientization' as a First Step Towards Emancipation

Resisters at FT engaged in a struggle which differed from traditional labor union approaches both in its forms of manifestation and in the very object that it chose to address, i.e., the question of work organization and its effect on employees' wellbeing. The movement focused on the issue of mounting stress and suffering within the firm as a consequence of the transformations engaged in since the early stages of the privatization process in the late 1980s, with particular emphasis on the NExT plan and its devastating consequences.

A key player in the resistance was SUD (Solidaires, Unitaires, Démocratiques), a horizontal platform of unaffiliated labor unions which had emerged in the late 1980s in reaction to the waves of privatization in the public sector in France, and grown in importance in the 1990s. A founding member of the French alterglobalization movement, SUD aimed at renewing the labor movement in France and had initiated critical debates and actions on the question of work organization and suffering at work within the firm since the early 2000s. In 2007, the union co-founded the Observatory of Stress and Forced Mobility with another labor union within FT, the CFE-CGC, with the objective of documenting, objectivizing and diffusing knowledge on the restructuring and its effects on workers' wellbeing. The Observatory's slogan *Observe, Understand, Act* expressed the idea that 'conscientization' was needed, or in other words, that work pressures and deteriorating social conditions had to be made visible and recognized in order for wellbeing issues to be acted upon.

The Observatory drew on the expertise of a scientific committee comprising academics from a variety of social sciences in order to produce a large amount of surveys and research. The diffusion of information was simultaneously geared towards FT employees, labor unionists and an outside audience that was reached through the Observatory's website, conferences, meetings and sustained interactions with the media. When an 18th suicide – since early 2008 – attracted major media attention in the summer of 2009, notably because the employee left a letter which was read aloud at his funeral and clearly linked his death to work conditions at FT, the Observatory was suddenly in daily contact with the press, radio and TV channels, playing a key role in feeding the media with information and analyses.

Although the resisters were very cautious on the issue of workers' suicides and devised a collective position, after intense internal debates that suicides should be cast only as extreme manifestations of a broader phenomenon of workers' illbeing within the firm, one could say that these suicides, as individual acts of public resistance, brought a strong resonance to the movement of conscientization launched by the Observatory, and greatly contributed to spreading the concerns for wellbeing deprivation at the workplace into the broader society.

'Power With' as a Lever for Political Changes

The resistance movement was also remarkable in bringing together a broad range of people holding distinct work identities, roles and positions not only within the firm but also in civil society and the state. The seminal alliance between SUD constituents, mostly activist public-sector technicians, and CFE-CGC members, i.e., managers and engineers often under private employment contracts, was forged by the two unions' central delegates who also acted as spokespersons of the Observatory. These key players, like those who supported the Observatory in the media and in academia, and others who extended the resistance movement within the state, were all able to act on the basis of their own mandate and professional position, while simultaneously stretching beyond the established roles and repertoires of action of their institutions, so as to enact genuine political change.

The alliance between SUD and the CFE-CGC within FT had thus required an unusual stretch in terms of valuing diversity ('The top management was amazed that we became allies', in Palpacuer and Seignour, 2019: 8). Such process of building 'power with' was also apparent within the state, where an informal alliance emerged among labor inspectors across the various worksites of FT in order to pool information on the firm's working conditions. This allowed the labor inspector in charge of FT's headquarters to develop a comprehensive report on the pathogenic forms of management and their link to workers' suffering and suicides within the firm. Submitted to the criminal court in February 2010, the report allowed SUD to file a complaint against FT and its top managers, to be joined by other labor unions in the following months.

This building of 'power with' inside the state could be seen as an extension of the resistance movement insofar as key players at the Ministry of Labor had a particular sensitivity to the workers' conditions, which stirred them to leverage the media scandal by launching a counter-offensive against the Ministry of the Economy and Finance, representing the state as a shareholder and active promoter of neoliberal reforms. Such countermovement included pressuring large firms to adopt procedures for the detection and prevention of psychosocial risks at work, and sheltering the solidarity chain formed among the labor inspectors.

To conclude briefly, individual and collective forms of resistance are closely intertwined in the processes by which some broader structural gains might be obtained in favor of workers' wellbeing, spanning the workplace, civil society and the state. The achievements of the resisters should not be overstated, since the root causes of financialization and globalization have been only temporarily challenged through the FT crisis and other cases discussed in this chapter. However, the multiple forms of resistance which have been reviewed may serve to prove that workers and managers have consistently engaged in the defense of organizational wellbeing over the last decades, in reaction to the wellbeing deprivation entailed by neoliberal restructuring. Such overview should open the way for further research to explore the entanglement of power, resistance and humanistic concerns for wellbeing in contemporary organizations, particularly at a time when multiple forms of crisis repeatedly challenge the core tenets of neoliberal organizational management.

Notes

1 The more recent rise of corporate social responsibilities (CSR) has discursively addressed this issue while failing to significantly revamp the governance priorities – on the contrary, the case has often been made that CSR served to secure the firm's financial performance by offering a 'social licence to operate' (Sum, 2010).

2 This section draws mainly from the detailed account of the workers' struggle at France Telecom in Palpacuer and Seignour (2019); also see Doellgast et al. (2020).

3 www.lesechos.fr/tech-medias/hightech/la-revolution-juridique-du-jugement-france-telecom-1158285; www.mdmh-avocats.fr/2020/01/03/harcelement-moral-institutionnel/

REFERENCES

Barker J (1999) *The Discipline of Teamwork: Participation and Concertive Control.* New York: Sage.

Becker-Ritterspach F and Dörrenbächer C (2009) Intrafirm competition in multinational corporations: Towards a political framework. *Competition and Change* 13(3): 199–213.

Benford R and Snow D (2000) Framing processes and social movements: An overview and assessment. *Annual Review of Sociology* 26: 611–639.

Blyton P and Jenkins J (2012) Mobilizing resistance: The Burberry workers' campaign against factory closure. *The Sociological Review* 60(1): 25–45.

Capelli P (1999) *The New Deal at Work: Managing the Market-Based Employment Relationship.* Boston, MA: Harvard Business School Press.

Chabrak N, Craig R and Daidj N (2016) Financialization and the employee suicide crisis at France Telecom. *Journal of Business Ethics* 139(3): 501–515.

Collinson D (2003) Identities and insecurities: Selves at work. *Organization* 10: 527–547.

Contu A (2008) Decaf resistance. *Management Communication Quarterly* 21(3): 364–379.

Contu A, Palpacuer F and Balas N (2013) Multinational corporations' politics and resistance to plant shutdowns: A comparative case study in the south of France. *Human Relations* 66: 363–384.

Courpasson D (2016) Impactful resistance: The persistence of recognition politics in the workplace. *Journal of Management Inquiry* 25: 96–100.

Courpasson D (2017) Beyond the hidden/public resistance divide: How bloggers defeated a big company. *Organization Studies* 38: 1277–1302.

Courpasson D, Dany F and Clegg S (2012) Resisters at work: Generating productive resistance in the workplace. *Organization Science* 23: 801–819.

Dalingwater L, Costantini I and Champroux N (2019) Wellbeing: Political discourse and policy in the anglosphere. *Revue Interventions économiques*. Epub URL: http://journals.openedition.org/interventionseconomiques/6492 (Accessed 24, February 2021).

Danford A, Richardson M and Upchurch M (2003) *New Unions, New Workplaces. A Study of Union Resilience in the Restructured Workplace*. London: Routledge.

De Certeau M (1984) *The Practice of Everyday Life*. Berkeley, CA: University of California Press.

De Senneville (2019) Suicides chez France Télécom: Didier Lombard et l'entreprise condamnés. *Les Echos*. Epub 20 December 2019. www.lesechos.fr/tech-medias/hightech/suicides-chez-france-telecom-didier-lombard-et-lentreprise-condamnes-1158138 (Accessed 24, February 2021).

Dicken P (2014) *Global Shift: Mapping the Changing Contours of the World Economy*. Seventh Edition. London : Sage.

Diener E and Seligman M (2004) *Beyond Money: Toward an Economy of Well-Being*. New Haven, CT: Yale University Press.

Doellgast V, Bellego M and Pannini E (2020) After the social crisis: The transformation of employment relations at France Télécom. *Socio-Economic Review*, Epub ahead of print. DOI: 10.1093/ser/mwaa006.

Edwards R (1979) *Contested Terrain: The Transformation of the Workplace in the Twentieth Century*. New York: Basic Books.

Fleming P (2014) *Resisting Work: The Corporatization of Life and its Discontents*. Philadelphia: Temple University Press.

Fleming P (2016) Resistance and the 'post-recognition' turn in organizations. *Journal of Management Inquiry* 25(1): 106–110.

Forsberg P and Stockenstrand A-K (2014) Resistance to financialization: Insights about collective resistance through distancing and persistence from two ethnographic studies.

Journal of Organizational Ethnography 3(2): 169–187.

Fournier V and Grey C (2000) At the critical moment: Conditions and prospects for Critical Management Studies. *Human Relations* 53(1): 7–32.

Froud J, Johal S, Leaver A and Williams K (2006) *Financialization and Strategy: Narratives and Numbers*. London: Routledge.

Gagnon S and Collinson D (2017) Resistance through difference: The co-constitution of dissent and inclusion. *Organization Studies* 38: 1253–1276.

Harding N, Ford J and Lee H (2017) Towards a performative theory of resistance: Senior managers and revolting subject(ivitie)s. *Organization Studies* 38: 1209–1231.

Hughes E, Dobbins T and Merkl-Davies D (2019) Moral economy, solidarity and labour process struggle in Irish public transport. *Economic and Industrial Democracy*, Epub ahead of print. DOI: 10.1177/0143831X19891235.

Hyman R (1972) *Strikes*. Basingstoke: Macmillan.

Knights D and McCabe D (2000) Ain't misbehavin"? Opportunities for resistance under new forms of 'quality' management. *Sociology* 34(3): 421–436.

Knights D and Willmott H (1990) *Labor Process Theory*. London: Macmillan.

Kolowratnik N and Miessen M (2012) *Waking Up from the Nightmare of Participation*. Utrecht: Expodium.

Laaser K (2016) If you are having a go at me, I am going to have a go at you': The changing nature of social relationships of bank work under Performance Management. *Work, Employment & Society* 30(6): 1000–1016.

Lazonick W and O'Sullivan M (2000) Maximizing shareholder value: A new ideology for corporate governance. *Economy and Society* 29(1): 13–35.

McCabe D, Ciuk S and Gilbert G (2019) 'There is a crack in everything': An ethnographic study of pragmatic resistance in a manufacturing organization. *Human Relations*. Epub ahead of print. DOI: 10.1177/0018726719847268.

Milberg W (2008) Shifting sources and uses of profits: Sustaining U.S. financialization with Global Value Chains. *Economy and Society* 37(3): 420–451.

Mohdzain M and Ward J (2007) A study of subsidiaries views of information systems strategic planning in multinational organisations. *The Journal of Strategic Information Systems* 16(4): 324–352.

Morgan G and Kristensen P (2006) The contested space of multinationals: Varieties of institutionalism, varieties of capitalism. *Human Relations* 59(11): 1467–1490.

Mumby D (1997) The problem of hegemony: Rereading Gramsci for organizational communication studies. *Western Journal of Communication* 61(4): 43–75.

Mumby D, Thomas R, Martí I and Seidl D (2017) Resistance redux. *Organization Studies* 38(9): 1157–1183.

Palpacuer F and Seignour A (2019) Resisting via hybrid spaces: The cascade effect of a workplace struggle against neoliberal hegemony. *Journal of Management Inquiry*, Epub ahead of print. DOI: 105649261984640.

Palpacuer F, Seignour A and Vercher C (2011) Financialization, globalization and the management of skilled employees: Towards a market-based HRM model in large corporations in France. *British Journal of Industrial Relations* 49(3): 560–582.

Perrow C (2014) *Complex Organizations: A Critical Essay*, 4th edn. Brattleboro, VT: Echo Point Books.

Prilleltensky I and Nelson G (2002) *Doing Psychology Critically: Making a Difference in Diverse Settings*. New York: Palgrave McMillan.

Pullen A and Rhodes C (2014) Corporeal ethics and the politics of resistance in organizations. *Organization* 21(6): 782–796.

Rothschild J and Miethe D (1994) Whistleblowing as resistance in modern work organizations. In Jermier JM, Knights D and Nord W (eds) *Resistance and Power in Organizations*. London: Routledge, pp. 252–273.

Scott J C (1990) *Domination and the Arts of Resistance: Hidden Transcripts*. New Haven, CT: Yale University Press.

Spicer A and Böhm S (2007) Moving management: Theorizing struggles against the hegemony of management. *Organization Studies* 28(11): 1667–1698.

Sum NL (2010) Articulation of 'new constitutionalism' with 'new ethicalism': Wal-Martization and CSR-ization in developing countries. In Utting P and Marquez J (eds) *Corporate Social Responsibility and Regulatory Governance: Towards Inclusive Development?* London: Palgrave, pp. 50–76.

Technologia (2009) *France Télécom: Etat des lieux sur le stress et les conditions de travail*. Report prepared for France Telecom.

Thomas R and Davies A (2005) Theorizing the micro-politics of resistance: New public management and managerial identities in the UK public services. *Organization Studies* 26(5): 683–706.

Wan W (2020) More Americans are killing themselves at work. *Washington Post.com*. www.washingtonpost.com/health/2020/01/09/more-americans-are-killing-themselves-work/. (Accessed 24, February 2021)

Waters S (2017) Suicide voices: Testimonies of trauma in the French workplace. *Medical Humanities* 43: 24–29.

Weiskopf R and Tobias-Miersch Y (2016) Whistleblowing, parrhesia and the contestation of truth in the workplace. *Organization Studies* 37: 1621–1640.

Willmott H (1993) Strength is ignorance; slavery is freedom: Managing culture in modern organizations. *Journal of Management Studies* 30(4): 515–552.

Zanoni P, Contu A, Healy S and Mir R (2017) Post-capitalistic politics in the making: The imaginary and praxis of alternative economies. *Organization* 24(5): 575–588.

37

Spiritual Wellbeing in Organizations

Scott Foster, Tony Wall and Anna Foster

INTRODUCTION

Whilst recognizing the increased attention to spirituality in the workplace as being a positive development overall, scholars suggest that the association between spiritual beliefs, management practices and organizational outcomes has been conspicuously ignored in the mainstream management research. This occurs despite there being a large number of people worldwide reporting that spirituality is an important part of their daily lives (Sedikides, 2010; Van den Heuvel, 2018; Karakas et al., 2019). Expression of spirituality within organizations is an opportunity for an individual or organization to grow and to contribute to society in a meaningful way about care, compassion, support of others, integrity, creativity, people being true to themselves and others (Wall et al., 2017). It means individuals and organizations attempting to further integrate their values in the work they do (Panda, 2011; Lee et al., 2014; Houghton et al., 2016).

Spirituality can be understood in a variety of ways with changeable conceptualizations through history and in different cultural contexts, and has included conceptions that place it synonymously with the practice of religious formalities as well as practices which enable people to experience a higher life purpose, separate from a religious belief. However, within the context of organizations its discussion has come to focus upon reorienting or rebalancing the experience of organizational life in developed countries in the West towards a more sustained and meaningful life in the context of workforce diversity and a greater sense of connectedness to others (Wall et al., 2019). Against this backdrop, in the 2010s there has been a steady rise in interest regarding spiritual wellbeing and an increase in the correlation between the expression of one's spirituality and cases that are regarded as discrimination (Krahnke and Hoffman, 2002; Loo, 2017).

Historically, scholars pointed out that a highly committed workplace that embraces spirituality will have benefits to the organization and from a personal level (Ashmos and Duchon, 2000; Fry, 2003). Mitroff et al. (2009) supported these claims by suggesting that employees who view the organization they work for as spiritual, further believe that they become more profitable than their competitors do. Further research has suggested that there is a positive relationship between employee commitment and workplace spirituality and, where evident, spirituality in the workplace has returned a positive impact on job satisfaction and performance (Chawla and Guda, 2010; Marschke et al., 2011; Bodla and Ali, 2012; Foster and Foster, 2019; Garg et al., 2019).

Similarly, Chand and Koul (2012) indicated that employees who feel that they can express their spirituality in the workplace felt that this helped them to manage stress, were generally more hopeful and believed they had a more meaningful working experience. In the same way, spirituality in the workplace has been suggested as an instrument of means to improve an employee's wellbeing. Joelle and Coelho (2019) suggested that encouragement by the organization for spiritual wellbeing can be in the best interests for the longevity of the business. However, Shinde and Fleck (2015) suggested that this could be a response to the troubled environment organizations find themselves in. At the same time, organizations have experienced momentous transformations regarding a wide range of areas related to sustainable development (Wall et al., 2017), for example political and technological advances, and the associated organizational changes such as managerial demands for management to create better efficiencies, and downsizing and employee redundancies (Driver, 2005). The context of workplace spirituality has been advanced as an instrumental remedy for this situation and one that human resource management departments will need to explore (Garg et al., 2019).

The aim of this chapter is to explain the drive for spiritual wellbeing in organizations, which includes a range of strategic and moral factors. In addition, the chapter discusses a range of business driven initiatives, where the focus is the strategic benefits to the organization, and is then followed by a discussion about employee spiritual wellbeing. In recognition of the limits, the next section considers wider interventions and cultural dimensions which can shape the effectiveness of expression of spirituality in the workplace; these wider cultural dimensions are the wider behavioural conditions of what can be counted as legitimate in an organizational context and how this can be measured. The chapter concludes with a review of future directions of research and practice development in relation to creating more space for the expression of spirituality and wellbeing in the workplace.

DEFINING SPIRITUALITY AND RELIGION IN THE WORKPLACE

Despite the amount of key literature on workplace spirituality, less progress has been made towards a clear explanation of a comprehensively acknowledged meaning of the term spirituality and there exists a paucity of broadly accepted workplace spirituality definitions (Afsar and Badir, 2017).

Studies on spirituality have resulted in various terms of emphasis, foci, components and levels of analysis owing to the considerable subjectivity of the topic (Fry, 2003; Mukherjee et al., 2016) and the concept remains under-theorized (Karakas, 2010). One of the key challenges of workplace spirituality and religion is that these concepts are separate but similar. Hodge (2017) has highlighted this in the extensive work on faith and spirituality in the workplace whilst acknowledging the breadth of the field. Miller and Ewest (2013) produced a faith and organizational framework for the spiritual and religious needs of an employee in the workplace. They used the term 'faith' to encompass both spirituality and religion, like both Hodge (2017) and Miller and Ewest (2013).

There is no doubt that workplace spirituality is receiving attention (Young, 2020) with awareness of how an environment that is conducive to self-expressed and inner purpose can enhance capability and raise the consciousness of the organization (Palframan and Lancaster, 2019). However, we also know that self-expression is 'tolerated' (Digh, 1999), that there is tension between the expression of religious identities (Heliot et al., 2019) and that there is limited evidence of impact on management practice in the workplace, with Sedikides (2010) arguing that religion within the workplace is still not given sufficient attention. The rise of interest in the Islamic faith throughout the media (Badrinarayanan and Madhavaram, 2008) has also accelerated debate surrounding spirituality and work, and in particular surrounding the association between religion and management (Cowling, 2013; McNiff, 2013).

Choices of terminology are challenging particularly in a field where there is no universally accepted definition of this complex collection of phenomena (Ali, 2010), and the process of conceptualization has, thus far, produced tentative definitions of the term. However, Kourie (2006) suggests that all individuals express some form of spirituality, whether nihilistic, materialistic, humanistic or religious. Spirituality enables individuals to grow and to contribute to society in a meaningful way with care, compassion, support of others, integrity, creativity; it is about people being true to themselves and others (Wall et al., 2017). Within the workplace, it means individuals and organizations attempting to further integrate their values in the work they do (Panda, 2011; Lee et al., 2014; Houghton et al., 2016). However, the literature is fragmented and dominated by speculative discussion, a US perspective, and a marked lack of empirical data, especially quantitative research (Ali, 2010; Khaled et al., 2012; Palframan and Lancaster, 2019).

SPIRITUALITY AND EMPLOYEE WELLBEING

Research undertaken by scholars suggests as a theory for development within an organizational workplace, spirituality is at an influential stage within the 21st century (Ashmos and Duchon, 2000; Pawar, 2016 Roof, 2015). However, the workplace spirituality concept is not a new idea as it has been grounded in the perspective of organization and management theory previously (Driscoll and Wiebe, 2007). Parboteeah and Cullen (2003) indicated that workplace spirituality, in terms of meaning at work, is related to as far back as Hackman and Oldham's (1980) job characteristics model and this goes beyond the character of interesting and satisfying work to the spiritual view of work, which involves searching for deeper meaning, purpose and feeling good about one's work. Furthermore, the concept of spirituality has also adopted motivation theory, as in Maslow's (1970) hierarchy of needs. Pawinee and McLean (2017) suggest that fulfilling employees' spiritual needs is comparable to accomplishing the highest level of human needs, as in self-actualization (Maslow, 1970; Izak, 2012). Furthermore, according to self-determination theory, nurture of human needs is important for ongoing psychological growth, integrity and wellbeing (Deci and Ryan, 2000).

Spirituality and its association with wellbeing in the workplace is gaining recognition and value amongst researchers and scholars (Wall et al., 2017; Foster and Foster, 2019). The term spirituality is of interest to management, organizations and employees for the reason of good harmony within the workplace. However, predominately two issues challenge it, the first being the struggle to be amongst an effective framework where spirituality is reduced as a means to forward profit-oriented goals, and the second challenge is with spirituality's subjective and multifaceted nature in business management

(Udani and Lorenzo-Molo, 2017). Scholars suggest that when discussing spirituality and employee wellbeing, it is beneficial to clarify the relationship between the two topics (Ashmos and Duchon, 2000; Pawar, 2016).

Employee wellbeing is best described as a significant topic within organizations and, as Ilies et al. (2015) point out, interest in employee wellbeing has risen greatly in recent times. Subsequently, Wright and Huang (2012) indicate that employee wellbeing has emerged as a very important topic within management research. In light of this practical significance of employee wellbeing, it is not surprising that employee wellbeing has recently received intensified research attention (Zhang et al., 2015). Grant et al. (2007) goes on to suggest that employee wellbeing refers to the quality of employees' operational experiences within the organization and is also a demonstration and feature of a healthy organization. The debate includes the importance of employee wellbeing. Thus, whilst organizations implement various actions for enhancing employee wellbeing, Canibano (2013) debates that managerial practices often result in trade-offs, improving only one dimension of employee wellbeing (Joelle and Coelho, 2019; Low and Ayoko, 2020).

Spirituality in the workplace is often seen as a paradox (Richards et al., 2009). Scarce research investigates both the effects and consequences of employees' spiritual wellbeing. To date, little is known about the psychology, dynamics and consequences of expressing and fulfilling spiritual needs. Theories in the area of spirituality have been viewed as existing in their embryonic stage, with a need for further theory development. Wong (2003) pointed out that a healthy dose of spirituality and meaning within the workplace is good for business as it improves morale and productivity. This view is gaining currency amongst management consultants, human resource professionals and mainstream business schools. The movement to bring spirit and soul to business is no passing fad; it

continues to grow, with no signs of abating. Recently it has become even more prevalent when viewed through the lens of the international Black Lives Matter movement and the growing emphasis on organizational need to reflect the diverse nature of their employees and stakeholders in all aspects and levels of organizational structure (Moran, 2017; Opie and Roberts, 2017). Clearly, something significant and enduring is stirring the corporate world (Anderson and Burchell, 2019). The business world is now experiencing an economic downturn and government austerity measures which will be exacerbated further due to the economic impact of Covid-19, whilst research and debate on spirituality is expanding (Richards et al., 2009; Houghton et al., 2016). There remains a growing demand for organizations to enact change to further recognize and meet the needs of the individuals they employ (Carney, 2016; Cole et al., 2019).

It is generally agreed that workplace spirituality encompasses an element of awareness and interconnectedness with one another or a higher existence; it embraces a sense of fulfilment and value, which provides meaning to an individual's vocation (Karakas, 2010; Bodla and Ali, 2012; Brown, 2012; Lundrigan et al., 2012; Wall et al., 2017; Karakas and Sarigollu, 2019). Within the framework factors exist such as ethics, trust and fairness of decisions, respect, honesty and the integrity of actions. It is apparent that, in recent times, spirituality in the workplace has reached greater prominence (Badrinarayanan and Madhavaram, 2008). The reasons for this interest in the spiritual world, however, are less clear, although theories that attempt to account for the rise in awareness are becoming widely acknowledged (Van Tonder and Ramdass, 2009; Bhatia and Arora, 2017). In contrast, Bodla and Ali (2012) suggested that the majority of academics and business leaders are often confused and fail to distinguish the difference between spirituality and religion; this is mainly because spirituality and religion are invariably expressed implicitly and are considered to be a private subjective matter.

In an investigation carried out by Fry and Slocum (2008), it was apparent that one reason for the rise in awareness was that organizations were focusing on the development of models of spirituality leadership, which emphasize spiritual wellbeing, without sacrificing the organization's performance. However, whilst organizations are attempting to take on board the concept of spirituality, it is apparent that there is still some way to go (Glass, 2007; Karakas, 2010; Goyal et al., 2013; Petrucelli, 2017). Lundrigan et al. (2012) argued that for an organization to succeed, management needs to develop their ability to identify conflicts between employees' perception of how spirituality is acknowledged and supported within the workplace and ensure parity in approach to reduce the potential for unpleasant or awkward interactions between individuals when issues associated with spirituality arise within the workplace, thus helping to avert a breakdown of team unity.

As indicated by Anderson and Burchell (2019), due to global competitiveness, economic hardship and government cuts, it is assumed that a clear spirituality workplace policy would secure a competitive advantage for an organization. Indeed, it is argued that engaging the full potential of employees creates a content and successful workforce (Zohar and Marshall, 2004). Javanmard (2012) developed this point further by using Duchon and Plowman's (2005) conceptual model (Figure 37.1) to analyse a number of variables which may impact on spirituality. These variables include: organizational leadership, which seeks to identify the organization's vision; altruism, which refers to an individual's unselfish concern for the welfare of others within the workplace; and faith in the organization, which highlights the belief the employee has in their employers. The variables associated with spirituality at work relate to an employee's rich inner life, meaningful employment and an individual's sense of community. The model suggests that these variables feed into organizational performance.

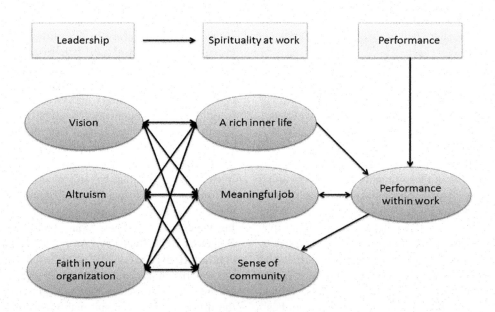

Figure 37.1.   Conceptual framework model created by the author, adapted from Duhon and Plowman (2005: 825).

Sparks and Schenk (2001) contended that workplace spirituality can be examined empirically, by arguing that workplace spirituality acts as a mediator in models of organizational behaviour. However, Pawar (2016) argued that it is necessary to develop specific testable propositions that can address the concerns of academics, before such models are implemented, whilst Marshak (2011) added that organizational development generally embraces a number of theories and, as such, religion tends to represent just one of them.

The potential benefits of workplace spirituality to employees, versus the consequences of a lack of workplace spirituality, have been tested through corresponding research propositions. Badrinarayanan and Madhavaram (2008) investigated specific propositions objectively, by researching the behaviour of supervisors. They reported that behaviour has a significant effect on employees' psychological wellbeing, which included their spiritual wellbeing. This argument was supported by Dent et al. (2005) who suggested that when management inspires and energizes employees' behaviour and attitudes, it provides the workforce with meaning and purpose. However, Singh and Singh (2011) argued that if a business leader chooses to pursue an unethical direction, they may develop a bunker mentality which tends to ignore employee values, deny mistakes made by the organization and break the rules, for the purpose of organizational or personal achievement. Such an approach can adversely impact staff morale and performance. Whilst Singh and Singh's (2011) views may be valid, it is rational for an organization to adopt humanistic values in policies and practices, thereby recognizing the dignity and worth of employees (Badrinarayanan and Madhavaram, 2008; Thakur and Singh, 2016; Gotsis and Grimani, 2017).

Humanistic values in the organization can potentially help the growth and development of employees and their wellbeing, which in turn can sustain greater productivity than organizations with weaker values and beliefs (Jurkiewicz and Giacalone, 2004; Robinson, 2009; Jenkin, 2015). The humanistic approach suggests that all employees need to be treated equally, with this being embedded into the organization's policies and practices. Whilst the humanistic approach perceives that all employees are treated equally, an earlier investigation by Digh (1999) revealed that, depending upon their particular belief system, employees feel their spirituality was observed to differing degrees. A study carried out by Digh (1999) suggested that insensitive and inconsiderate management practices can lead companies into unwanted litigation. Claims of religious discrimination have in fact been increasing. The UK Equal Employment Opportunity Commission reported more than 1,800 religious discrimination cases in 1999 and the number of such cases has increased by 43% within the 2010s. Despite increased legislation to support spiritual beliefs within the workplace (Zohar and Marshall, 2004; Greenwald, 2012; Parris and Peachey, 2013; Low and Ayoko, 2020), there still appears to be a discrepancy in the extent to which differing beliefs are accommodated.

Research conducted by Lips-Wiersma and Mills (2002) provided an example, indicating that Christians have time off over Christmas and Easter, whilst other faith groups are required to use their holiday entitlement to observe significant dates in their own religious calendars. The findings further suggested that 20% of the surveyed population from the United States reported having been a victim of religious bias, such as not being able to take time off to observe particular holidays or for prayer time. The situation is not as straightforward as it may seem, as it may not be feasible for an organization to observe all spiritual practices or occasions.

Due to the individualized nature of spirituality, organizations can experience difficulty in demonstrating fairness and equality within a diverse workforce. However, Benefiel et al. (2014) proposed a model that attempts to create wholesome and rounded workers who are not only knowledgeable, skilful and possess professional skills, but also have strong spiritual beliefs, are ethical and have social awareness in conducting their duties. Consequently, by ensuring potential shortcomings of the organization are identified and acted upon, business leaders can develop strategies that ensure employees' wellbeing and spiritual practices are maximized. Similarly, in Sembuk's model (Biagini et al., 2012), spirituality is at the centre of an organization, because spirituality is potentially central to an individual; an organization which adapts itself to support an employee's spirituality can benefit through increased productivity and motivation (Beheshtifar and Zare, 2013). However, although many organizations approach this through embedding current legislation into their policies and procedures in the belief that this addresses an employee's expression of spirituality, the concept is one which is much more complex than these often acknowledge. Whilst policies may seek to support individuals' right to observe religious practices at work or demonstrate their faith through clothing, etc., they often fail to acknowledge the range of factors which are external to the individual employee but intrinsic to the organizational culture and operations of the business, which can also directly influence the extent to which employees feel their work aligns or conflicts with their spirituality (Figure 37.2).

In a time of public debate about spiritual tolerance and cultural freedom in a multicultural society, it is important to gain a true understanding of how different religions can manifest themselves within an organization (Bello, 2012). In the main, cultural and religious acceptance within the workplace is becoming part of everyday life for the employer and employee (Jones, 2006). Although this acceptance need not be an admission that discrimination is, or was, tolerated in the first place, it does indicate that spirituality in the workplace is a sensitive area which should be treated with caution. Forstenlechner and Al-Waqfi (2010) initially suggested that Muslim workers believe discrimination exists within the workplace. However, their findings indicated that this is to the contrary, whereby employers actually showed a high level of commitment to respecting the traditions and beliefs of the Muslim faith, with little evidence of discrimination against employees being apparent. The view is taken that the conflicting perceptions and expectations regarding spirituality could be associated with limitations such as inclusion and communication within policies and procedures currently being adopted within business.

BUSINESS DRIVEN INITIATIVES: THE STRATEGIC BENEFITS TO THE ORGANIZATION

The development of spiritual awareness across a wider community has produced a series of changes and aroused academic and practitioner interest in management (Baker et al., 2011). However, because of the

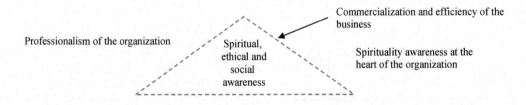

Figure 37.2. Extent to which employees feel their work aligns or conflicts with their spirituality, created by the authors, adapted from Biagini et al. (2012: 32).

dominance and influence of modernization for much of the 20th century, there has been a tendency to show corporations as being preoccupied with a range of performance metrics such as profit, turnover and market dominance.

Throughout management discourse, performance metrics are often termed as the minimum expectation of the organization. These dimensions and their effective management are important in the running of any operation, but it is equally recognized that it is important to pay due diligence to what are called the soft factors in business, which includes human resources management (Stokes, 2011). Therefore, for an organization to continually succeed and prosper in today's harsh economic climate it is important that the moral and ethical strategies promote its foundations. Lips-Wiersma and Nilakant (2008: 61) stipulated that, 'Spirituality at work needs to work with and give meaning to the tensions that arise from acting in accordance with a purpose beyond profit in a neo-liberal business climate'. Soltani et al. (2012) also argued that a successful business requires an outstanding performance in their ethical conduct because the company's ethical conduct strategy should be the foundation for their employees and managers within the business. However, considering the practical approaches to workplace spirituality, a note of caution is offered by Lipps-Wiersma and Mills (2002) advising that thought should be given to the difficulties of getting people to enact spiritual beliefs in the workplace.

In addition, Hans-Ruediger (2007) identified a lack of safety in expressing spirituality in the workplace, and consequently identified several principles that could be utilized to encourage spiritual expression. This lack of safety can arise from a variety of factors, such as fear of expressing views which are seen as outside the norm, for example a Wiccan amongst a heavily Christian organization, or the perception that the organization's ethos differs significantly from the beliefs of the individual. Soltani et al. (2012) agreed with Hans-Ruediger (2007) and pointed out that one of the issues that currently faces organizations is the inability to allow an individual to express their beliefs in the workplace. Therefore, the important issue in the strategic management process should be implementing new strategies to address this.

Failures by employers are often not related to their reluctance in formulating a strategy but instead are due to their failure in strategy implementation barriers, such as lack of employee alignment and a lack of management commitment. This, therefore, indicates that more could be done to facilitate greater engagement with implementation from both the workforce and managers.

Addressing Barriers to Strategic Implementation of Strategies

Identifying and addressing specific barriers towards the implementation of strategies which focus upon spirituality and wellbeing can facilitate greater dialogue about the concepts within the workplace. Hans-Ruediger (2007: 13) stated that:

> It is necessary to recognise that because spirituality is at the heart of many people's sense of identity, its expression is perceived to be risky. Spirituality comprises a sense of personal vulnerability which is magnified for those who perceive themselves to be spiritually different to the majority or norm.

Therefore, providing an open and safe space for discussion can be instrumental in reducing employees' sense of vulnerability whilst maximizing on the opportunities to be gained from allowing them to represent their true selves within the workplace. There does, however, need to be a sense of balance in how this is approached. In reflection of the potential issues, Lips-Wiersma and Nilakant (2008) recommended that it be clear that the dialogue needs to be managed sensibly. Employees should feel that they are represented at strategy level; however, a 'free for all' discussion is likely to stagnate progress within organizational strategy meetings and, instead, a period of consultations with the workforce or discussion with a panel of representatives may prove to be more effective.

Similarly, Wennes and Quinn (2008) argued that workers are concerned with the consequences of making spirituality requests or demands in the workplace and the organization should attempt to support the expression of spirituality. This is in agreement with Lipps-Wiersma and Mills (2002) who stated that any action taken by an organization to enhance trust and relationship development should reduce the potential for spirituality to be a source of marginalization in the workplace. Thus, spirituality is such a personal choice for many individuals, employees sometimes tend to keep their beliefs to themselves for fear of adverse consequences. For those individuals holding beliefs that are different from the majority, the process of encouraging workplace spirituality can appear threatening. Consequently, the introduction of spirituality into an organization needs to be handled with great sensitivity and empathy if successful employee and employer buy-in is to occur (Hans-Ruediger, 2007).

In line with points raised by Lipps-Wiersma and Mills (2002), research by Wong (2003) stated that simply imposing policies relating to spirituality on employees would be counter-productive, as most organizations encourage religious expressions within the workplace and make facilities available such as Halal meals or prayer rooms, to help meet employees' spiritual needs where possible. However, Hans-Ruediger (2007) argued that for an organization to be effective, the spirituality requirements of its employees need to be integrated into the corporate culture and reflected in organizational policies and practices on a daily basis. This can be achieved only when senior management embraces it as part of their vision. Garcia-Zamor (2003) indicated that organizations need to establish themselves as an ethical organization with respect to spirituality and culture. This

then enables the business to create a new organizational culture in which employees feel happier and perform better. Employees find meaning in belonging to a work community that helps when things get tough. At the same time, a culture of sharing and caring will eventually reach all of the organization's stakeholders, suppliers and customers; therefore, in such a humanistic work environment, employees are perceived to be more creative and have higher morale, two factors closely linked to good organizational performance (Garcia-Zamor, 2003).

Howard (2002) concluded that organizations are showing many transformation characteristics when they attempt to use processes that engage people in communication such as instituting real-time strategic change, the use of open space technology and, lastly, encouraging a culture of appreciative enquiry. This is supported by Hans-Ruediger (2007: 25) who stated that these strategies show a move towards 'honouring the core spirit of an enterprise or community'. Howard (2002) stressed, however, that the exploration of spirituality within organizations is still at an early stage and that the benefits or conflicts this might create are, as yet, uncertain. Garcia-Zamor (2003) suggested that continued research is required into how spirituality can underpin transformation at all levels, including the role of leaders in this strategic process. Additionally, scholars echo the same thought and stress that further studies are required to advance and develop spirituality conceptual distinctions (Fry, 2003; Dent et al., 2005).

Spirituality Within the Workplace to Support Wellbeing

The integration of spirituality into effective management and organizations has been regarded as incongruous or, as Goldstein-Gidoni et al. (2009: 600) put it, 'unnatural'. Nonetheless, Ashmos and Duchon (2000: 598) argued that workplace spirituality is a basic right. Workplace spirituality generally includes the recognition that employees have inner lives, a desire to find their work meaningful and a commitment by the company to serve as a context for spiritual growth.

In contrast, organizations aim to concentrate more on outcomes, such as returning a profit and sustaining the longevity of the business, instead of being caught in a competitive struggle to facilitate human activity in the organization (Goldstein-Gidoni et al., 2009). Despite the importance of spiritual beliefs, employers and employees traditionally regard the workplace as off limits for any demonstration of faith (Ali, 2010). However, the separation of spirituality and business, for both the private and public sectors, is becoming blurred and, as such, the workplace is being transformed into an environment where expressions of spirituality and practices are now regarded as more commonplace (Abuznaid, 2006). Consequently, employees' job satisfaction sought through spiritual and cultural facets is a worthwhile endeavour that can enhance an organization's longevity, perceived excellence and their retention of staff Kibui et al. (2014). It has, however, been identified that the beliefs and values of non-Muslim religions are felt to be marginalized within an organization and ignored worldwide because these religions tend not to be as politically supported as Islam (Williams et al., 2010). There is also evidence that ethnic faith groups express spirituality in the workplace differently, which presumes that certain groups are disadvantaged within an organizational setting. For example, in a court case of *Eweida vs British Airways*, Eweida was a member of the check-in staff for British Airways, who was refused permission to wear a cross over her uniform, as this was in breach of the airline's uniform policy. However, British Airways did allow Muslim women to wear the hijab, and Sikh men to wear turbans, on the basis that the items were required by the particular religions, and they could not be concealed under the uniform.

The role of an organization can be seen as crucial to the development of its employees' spiritual needs (Ali, 2010). Doing so will support the employees to clarify community feeling; therefore, it can be anticipated that there will be an increase in productivity for the organization (Garg, 2017). If business leaders want to enhance employee performance, improve the efficiency and effectiveness of their staff, then they may have to seek a leader who is spiritual and who can help reduce uncertainty, ambiguity and insecurity within the organization (Conger, 1995). When the leader exhibits the 'human' qualities of creativity, honesty, truthfulness and trust, employees may feel the power of human bondage and connectedness to the organization (Panda, 2011; Wall et al., 2019).

The spirituality debate is evolving, as an increasing number of organizations seek a greater understanding of spirituality in the workplace. At the same time, employees are practising spirituality in the workplace more frequently. Employers are equally facing situations where employees discuss religious tenets, wear religious symbols or object to employers' decisions based on their faith (Morgan, 2005). Therefore, as Panda (2011: 204) suggested, 'Does it mean that employers will have to be flexible and conform to their policies so that Sikhs will be allowed to wear a turban and carry a "kirpan" to the office and that Muslims should be allowed to go to a Mosque to chant holy Quran on all Fridays at a given time?'

The challenge of integrating spirituality policies and procedures into the organization is now becoming even more complex, due to the wide range of religions being practised. Furthermore, the continued emergence of spirituality movements has led to employers and employees being uncertain of their professional responsibilities, which challenges management decision-making about workplace spirituality. With respect to religious expansion, Sedikides (2010) claimed that Islam is the fastest growing religion worldwide. However, within any population, a number of affiliated subcultural groups exist (Hayward, 2000). The diversity of beliefs provides considerable scope for research to further explore the demographics of employees within the workplace and examine perspectives across the range of groups which exist rather than focusing upon a specific sub-group. In doing so, there is potential to facilitate greater understanding of the breadth of needs and perceptions which exist; information which could be used to further identify strategies to help foster a more inclusive workplace.

The topic of integrating spirituality into the workplace is important, not just to organizations but to society in general, with spiritual wellbeing being viewed as a high level of faith and commitment to a belief that provides a sense of meaning and purpose to an individual's existence (Heintzman and Mannell, 2003). In addition, it is possible that employees who are content in their work will transfer such happiness to outside work and vice versa, thus making the individual more content with life (Jurkiewicz and Giacalone, 2004).

Spirituality plays an important part within an organization and therefore can influence the attitude the workforce shows towards management (Beheshtifar and Zare, 2013). Research suggests that job satisfaction is linked to the extent to which an employer meets the psychological needs of their employees, which embraces spirituality fulfilment within the workplace (Badrinarayanan and Madhavaram, 2008).

Consequently, a key purpose of the research into spirituality is to explore the multifaceted and complex nature of spirituality in the world of work and to evaluate the role and importance of spirituality within business constructs. The outcomes of such an approach could assist businesses to facilitate greater discourse and understanding between employers and employees on spirituality, thereby leading to greater stability, sustainability and competitive advantage (Otaye-Ebede et al., 2019). Shibani and Veena (2016) reported that the correlation between spirituality and wellbeing is evident and researchers are increasingly including positive outcomes for organizations (Foster and Wall, 2019).

CONCLUSION AND FUTURE RESEARCH

In pursuit of the sustainability and general growth of all its stakeholders, organizations have shifted their focus from mere economic progress. Consequently, workplace spirituality and employee wellbeing have been gaining the attention of both researchers and practitioners. For an organization to cope successfully with the complex spirituality challenges ahead, management and business leaders' attitudes still need to make a fundamental shift. Evidence raises several challenges relating to the perception of spirituality and wellbeing within the workplace and how it is accepted within the organization.

The important role spirituality plays in an organization, along with the management benefits of addressing spirituality at work, are key elements that have been raised by numerous researchers (Duchon and Plowman, 2005; Javanmard, 2012; Khaled et al., 2012; Parris and Peachey, 2013; Van den Heuvel, 2018; Low and Ayoko, 2020). As organizations are getting more and more diverse due to different backgrounds, cultures and nationalities, organizational management is faced with the challenge of managing individuals whose values are incongruent with the organizational values. The management who are effective at developing and maintaining working environments and that are characterized by spiritual values such as openness, ethics, accepting diverse viewpoints and differing values, are more likely to engage their employees in extra-role behaviours (Long and Mills 2010; Karakas et al., 2019).

The concept of spirituality and wellbeing is one that requires business leaders to be open-minded towards the range of narratives that express what is understood and intended by the concept of spirituality at work. To respect the practice of organizational spirituality is to respect the diversity of perspectives on what spirituality means. Nonetheless, the subjective nature of spirituality and a lack of common understanding of what spirituality means to an employee presents challenges in implementing such initiatives.

REFERENCES

Abuznaid, S. (2006). Islam and Management: What Can Be Learned? *Thunderbird International Business Review*, 48(1), 77–91.

Afsar, B. and Badir, Y. (2017). Workplace spirituality, perceived organisational support and innovative work behaviour: the mediating effects of person organisation fit. *Journal of Workplace Learning*, 29(2), 95–109.

Ali, A. J. (2010). Islamic challenges to HR in modern organizations. *Personnel Review*, 39(6), 692–711.

Anderson, S. E. and Burchell, J. M. (2019). The effects of spirituality and moral intensity on ethical business decisions: A cross-sectional study. *Journal of Business Ethics*, DOI: https://doi.org/10.1007/s10551-019-04258-w.

Ashmos, D. P and Duchon, D. (2000). Spirituality at work: A conceptualization and measure. *Journal of Management Inquiry*, 9(1), 134–145.

Badrinarayanan, V. and Madhavaram, S. (2008). Workplace spirituality and the selling organization. *Journal of Personal Selling and Sales Management*, 24(4), 421–434.

Baker, C., Stokes, P., Lichy, J., Atherton, J. and Moss, D. (2011), *"Values, beliefs and attitudes in the era of late capitalism: a consideration of the re-emergence and re-positioning of faith and spirituality as spiritual capital in the workplace"*, available at: http://ecoles-idrac.academia.edu/JessicaLichy/Papers/1720140/ Values_Beliefs_and_Attitudes_in_the_Era_of_Late-Capitalism_A_Consideration_of_the_Re- Emergence_and_Re-positioning_of_Faith_and_Spirituality_as_Spiritual (accessed 17 June 2019).

Beheshtifar, M. and Zare, E. (2013). Effect of Spirituality in workplace on Job Performance. *Interdisciplinary Journal of Contemporary Research Business*, 5(2), 248–254.

Bello, S, M. (2012). Impact of ethical leadership on employee job performance. *International Journal of Business and Social Science*, 3 (11), 228–236.

Benefiel, M. Fry, L. W and Geigle, D. (2014) Spirituality and religion in the workplace: history theory and research. *J Psychology of Religion and Spirituality*, 6(3):175–187.

Bhatia, S. and Arora, E. (2017). Workplace spirituality: An employer-employee perspective. *International Journal of Innovate Research and Development*, 6(1), 106–111.

Biagini, A., Carteny, A., Vagnini, A. and Motta, G. (2012). Proceedings of the 2nd International Conference on Human and Social Sciences. *International Scientific Committee ICHSS 2012.*, MCSER Publishing: Italy, 32(6) 1–270.

Bodla, M. A. and Ali, H. (2012). Workplace spirituality: A spiritual audit of banking. *African Journal of Business Management*, 6(11), 1–10.

Brown, M. (2012). Authentic leadership steers firms through unsteady, uncertain times. *Canadian HR Reporter*, 25(3), 22.

Canibano, A. (2013). Implementing innovative HRM: Trade-off effects on employee well-being. *Management Decision*, 51(3), 643–660.

Carney, N. (2016). All lives matter, but so does race: Black lives matter and the evolving role of social media. *Humanity & Society*, 40(2), 180–199.

Chand, P. and Koul, H. (2012). Organizational emotional ownership, workplace spirituality and job satisfaction as moderators of job stress. *International Journal of Humanities and Applied Sciences*, 1(2), 58–64.

Chawla, V and Guda, S. (2010). Individual spirituality at work and its relationship with job satisfaction, propensity to leave and job commitment: An exploratory study among sales professionals. *Journal of Human Values*, 16(2), 157–167.

Cole, C., King, D. D., Morgan Roberts, L. and Robinson, A. (2019). The Black experience: A multi-perspective view of Black employee experiences in the workplace. In *Academy of Management Proceedings* (Vol. 2019, No. 1, p. 15572). Briarcliff Manor, NY: Academy of Management.

Conger, J. (1995). Spirit at Work: Discovering the Spirituality in Leadership. *Journal of Leadership and Organizational Studies*, 2: 158–160.

Cowling, R. (2013). *BBC Sport: Premier League: How Muslims are changing English football culture*. Available at: www.bbc.co.uk/sport/0/football/23159023 (Accessed 28 June 2019).

Deci, E. L. and Ryan, R. M. (2000). The "what" and "why" of goal pursuits: human needs and the self-determination of behavior. *Journal of Psychological inquiry*, 11 (4), 227–268.

Dent, E. B., Higgins, E. and Wharff, D. M. (2005). Spirituality and leadership: An empirical review of definitions, distinctions and embedded assumptions. *Leadership Quarterly*, 16(5), 625–653.

Digh, P. (1999). Religion in the workplace: Make a good-faith effort to accommodate. *HR Magazine*, 43(13), 84–91.

Driver, M. (2005). From empty speech to full speech? Reconceptualizing spirituality in organizations based on a psychoanalytically-grounded understanding of the self. *Human Relations*, 58, 1091–1110.

Driscoll, C. and Wiebe, E. (2007). Technical spirituality at work: Jacques Ellul on workplace spirituality. *Journal of the Academy of Management*. 1–9.

Duchon, D. and Plowman, D. A. (2005). Nurturing the spirit at work: Impact on work unit performance. *Leadership Quarterly*, 16, 807–833.

Forstenlechner, I. and Al-Waqfi, M. (2010). A job interview for Mo, but none for Mohammed. Religious Discrimination Against Immigrants in Austria and Germany. *Personnel Review,* 39(6), 767–784.

Foster, S. and Foster, A. (2019). The impact of workplace spirituality on work-based learners: Individual and organisational level perspectives. *Journal of Work: Applied Management*, 11(1), 63–75.

Foster, S. and Wall, T. (2019). Spirituality and wellbeing in the workplace. Leal Filho, W. Wall, T. Azul, A. Brandli, L. Ozuyar, P. (eds), *Encyclopedia of the United Nations Sustainability Goals: Good Health & Wellbeing*. Cham: Springer.

Fry, L. W. (2003). Toward a theory of spiritual leadership. *The Leadership Quarterly*, 14, 693–727.

Fry, L. W. and Slocum, J. W. (2008). Maximizing the triple bottom line through spiritual leadership. *Organisational Dynamics*, 37(1), 86–96.

Garcia-Zamor, J. (2003) Workplace spirituality and organisational performance. *Public Administration Review,* 63(3), 355–364.

Garg, N. (2017). Workplace spirituality and employee wellbeing: An empirical exploration. *Journal of Human Values*, 23(2), 129–147.

Garg, N., Punia, B. K. and Jain, A. (2019). Workplace spirituality and job satisfaction: Exploring mediating effect of organization citizenship behaviour. *Vision*, 23(3), 287–296.

Glass, A. (2007). Understanding generation differences for competitive success. *Industrial and Commercial Training*, 39(2), 98–103.

Goldstein-Gidoni, G., Nehemya, I. and Zaidman, N. (2009). From temples to organizations: the introduction and packaging of spirituality. *Organizational Articles*, 16(4), 597–621.

Gotsis, G. and Grimani, K. (2017). The role of spiritual leadership in fostering inclusive workplaces. *Journal of Personnel Review*, 46(5), 908–935.

Goyal, M., Singh, S., Sibinga, M. S., Neda, M. H. S. and Gould, F. (2013). Meditation programs for psychological stress and wellbeing: A systematic review and meta-analysis. *Journal of American Medical Association,* 174(3), 357–368.

Grant, A. M., Christianson, M. K. and Price, R. H. (2007). Happiness, health, or relationships? Managerial practices and employee well-being tradeoffs. *Academy of Management Perspectives*, 21(3), 51–63.

Greenwald, J. (2012). Religious discrimination claims rising. *Business Insurance,* 46(7), 3–18.

Hackman, J. R. and Oldham, G. R. (1980). Job Diagnostic Survey (JDS). *Work redesign. Reading, Company. S.* 275–294.

Hans-Ruediger, K. (2007). World research organisation. *World Journal of Managment and Economics,* 7(2):2–52.

Hayward, J. (2000). Growth and Decline of Religious Subcultural Groups. Sustainability in the Third Millennium. *18th International Systems Dynamic Conference* (pp. 1–26). University of Glamorgan: Bergen.

Heintzman, P. and Mannell, R. C. (2003). Spiritual functions of leisure and spiritual well-being. *Leisure Sciences*, 2(3), 207–230.

Heliot, Y., Gleibs, I. H., Coyle, A., Rousseau, D. M. and Rojon, C. (2019). Religious identity in the workplace: A systematic review, research agenda, and practical implications. *Journal of Human Resource Management*, 1(1), 153–173.

Hodge, D. R. (2017). The evolution of spirituality and religion in international social work discourse: Strengths and limitations of the contemporary understanding. *Journal of Religion & Spirituality in Social Work: Social Thought*, 1(1), 1–21.

Houghton, J. D., Neck, C. P. and Krishnakumar, S. (2016). The what, why, and how of spirituality in the workplace revisited: A 14-year update and extension. *Journal of Management, Spirituality and Religion*, 13, 1–29.

Howard, S. (2002). A spiritual perspective on learning in the workplace. *Journal of Management Psychology* 17(3):230–242.

Ilies, R., Plutt, H. and Aw, S. S. Y. (2015). Studying employee well-being: Moving forward. *European. Journal of Work and Organizational Psychology*, 24(6), 848–852.

Izak, M. (2012). Spiritual episteme: sensemaking in the framework of organizational spirituality. *Journal of Organizational Change Management*, 25 (1) 24–47.

Javanmard, H. (2012). Spirituality and work performance. *Indian Journal of Science and Technology*, 5(1), 1–6.

Jenkin, M. (2015). Millennials want to work for employers committed to values and ethics. *The Guardian*. Available at: www.theguardian.com/sustainable-business/2015/may/05/millennials-employment-employers-values-ethics-jobs (Accessed 21 February 2020).

Joelle, M. and Coelho, A. M. (2019). The impact of spirituality at work on workers' attitudes and individual performance. *The International Journal of Human Resource Management*, 30(7), 1101–1135.

Jones, M. D. (2006). Job satisfaction or life satisfaction. *Journal of Behavioural and Applied Management*, 8(1), 20–42.

Jurkiewicz, C. L. and Giacalone, R. A. (2004). A values framework for measuring the impact of workplace spirituality on organizational performance. *Journal of Business Ethics*, 49(2), 129–142.

Karakas, F. (2010). Spirituality and performance in organizations: A literature review. *Journal of Business Ethics*, 94(1), 89–106.

Karakas, F. and Sarigollu, E. (2019). A qualitative study exploring dynamic patterns of spirituality in Turkish organizations. *Journal of Business Ethics*, 156, 799–821.

Khaled, M. T., Banyhamdan, H. H. and Mohi-Adden, Y. A. (2012). Transforming an organization into a spiritual one: A five pathway integrated framework. *International Journal of Business and Management*, 7(11), 74–83.

Kibui, A., Gachunga, H. and Namusonge, G. (2014). Role of talent management on employees retention in Kenya: A survey of state corporations in Kenya – Empirical review. *International Journal of Science and Research*, 3(2), 414–424.

Kourie, C. (2006). The 'turn' to spirituality. *Journal of Acta Theologica Supplementum*, 8(1), 19–38.

Krahnke, K. and Hoffman, L. (2002). The rise of religion and spirituality in the workplace: Employees' rights and employers' accommodations. *Journal for the Institute of Applied and Behavioral Management*, 3(3), 277–285.

Lee, S., Lovelace, K. J. and Manz, C. C. (2014). Serving with spirit: An integrative model of workplace spirituality within service organizations. *Journal of Management, Spirituality and Religion*, 11(1), 45–64.

Lips-Wiersma, M. and Mills, C. (2002) Coming out of the closet: negotiating spiritual expression in the workplace. *Journal of Managerial Psychology*, 17(3), 183–202.

Lips-Wiersma, M., Nilakant, V. (2008). Practical compassion: toward a critical spiritual foundation for corporate responsibility. In: Biberman, J. and Tischler L. (eds) *Spirituality In Business: Theory Practice and Future Directions*. Palgrave Macmillan: New York, pp. 51–72.

Long, B. S. and Mills, J. H. (2010). Workplace spirituality, contested meaning and the culture of organization. *Journal of Organizational Change Management*, 23(3), 325–341.

Loo, M. K. L. (2017). Spirituality in the work-place: Practices, challenges, and recommen-dations. *Journal of Psychology and Theology*, 45(3), 182–204.

Low, J. J. Q. and Ayoko, O. B. (2020). The emergence of spiritual leader and leadership in religion-based organizations. *Journal of Business Ethics*, 161, 513–530.

Lundrigan, M., Mujtaba, B. G., Tangsuvanich, V., Wu, S. and Yu, L. (2012). Coaching a diverse workforce: The impact of changing demographics for modern leaders. *Interna-tional Journal of Humanities and Social Sci-ence*, 2(3), 40–47.

Marschke, E., Preziosi, R. and Harrington, W. J. (2011). How sales personnel view the rela-tionship between job satisfaction and spiritu-ality in the workplace. *Journal of Organisational Culture, Communications and Conflict*, 15(2), 71–110.

Marshak, E. B. (2011). *A Comparative Study: Do Corporations that Embrace Spirituality in the Workplace Encourage Desired Organiza-tional Outcomes?* Charleston, SC: BiblioBa-zaar, 1–116.

Maslow, A. H. (1970). *Religions, Values, and Peak Experiences*. New York: Penguin. (Origi-nal work published 1964)

McNiff, J. (2013). *Action Research: Principles and Practice*. Oxford: Routledge.

Miller, D. and Ewest, T. (2013). The present state of workplace spirituality: A literature review considering context, theory, and measurement/assessment. *Journal of Reli-gious & Theological Information*, 12(1–2), 29–54.

Mitroff, I., Alpasland, C. M. and Denton, E. A. (2009). A spiritual audit of corporate amer-ica. *Journal of Management, Spirituality and Religion*, 6(1), 27–41.

Moran, R. (2017). Workplace spirituality in law enforcement: A content analysis of the liter-ature. *Journal of Management, Spirituality & Religion*, 14(4), 343–364.

Morgan, J. (2005). Religion at work: a legal quagmire. *Managerial Law*, 47(3/4), 247–259.

Mukherjee, S., Bhattacharjee, S. and Singha, S. (2016). Workplace spirituality: A paradigm shift to ethics from business. *IOSR Journal of Business and Management*. Special issue - AETM'16.

Opie, T. and Roberts, L. M. (2017). Do black lives really matter in the workplace? Restora-tive justice as a means to reclaim humanity. *Equality, Diversity and Inclusion*, 36(8), 707–719.

Otaye-Ebede, L., Shaffakat, S. and Foster, S. (2019). A multilevel model examining the relationships between workplace spirituality, ethical climate and outcomes: A social cogni-tive theory perspective. *Journal of Business Ethics*, 166, 611–626.

Palframan, J. and Lancaster, T. (2019). Work-place spirituality and person–organization fit theory: Development of a theoretical model. *Journal of Human Values*, 25(3), 133–149.

Panda, S. A. (2011). India. *International Journal of Business Derivatives*, 1(1), 192–469.

Parboteeah, P. K and Cullen, J. B. (2003). Social institutions and work centrality: explorations beyond national culture. *Journal of Organi-sational science*, 14(2), 107 –225.

Parris, D. L. and Peachey, J. W. (2013). A sys-tematic literature review of servant leader-ship theory in organizational contexts. *Journal of Business Ethics*, 113(2), 377–393.

Pawar, B. S. (2016). Workplace spirituality and employee well-being: An empirical examina-tion. *Employee Relations*, 38(6): 975–994.

Pawinee, P. and McLean, G. (2017). Workplace spirituality, mindfulness meditation, and work engagement. *Journal of Management, Spirituality and Religion*, 14(3), 216–244.

Petrucelli, T. (2017). Winning the 'cat-and-mouse game' of retaining millennial talent. *Strategic HR Review*, 16(1), 42–44.

Richards, P. S., Bartz, J. D. and O'Grady, K. A. (2009). Assessing religion and spirituality in counselling: Some reflections and recommen-dations. *Counselling and Values*, 54(1), 65–79.

Robinson, D. (2009). *Christianity and Islam Do Not Share Values*. Gale. Available at: http://ic.galegroup.com/ic/ovic/Viewpoints DetailsPage/DocumentToolsPortletWindow?d isplayGroupName=Viewpoints&jsid=2f6b337 7e7acca7414e05c44fe97e8e5&action=2&ca tId=&documentId=GALE%7CEJ3010110277 &u=high63991&zid=44157e4e22adcab99fc 3451cc8c07dc4 (Accessed 16 April 2020).

Roof, R. A. (2015). The association of individual spirituality on employee engagement: the spirit at work. *Journal of Business Ethics*, 130(3), 585–599.

Sedikides, C. (2010). Why does religiosity persist? *Personality and Social Psychology Review*, 14(1), 3–6.

Shibani, B. and Veena, V, (2016). Workplace spirituality, job satisfaction and organizational citizenship behaviors: A theoretical model. *International Journal of Business and Management*, 11(8), 256–262.

Shinde, U. and Fleck, E. (2015). What spirituality can bring to leaders and managers: Enabling creativity, empathy and a stress free workplace. *Journal of Organizational Psychology*, 15(1), 101–110.

Singh, R. K. and Singh, A. V. (2011). The interplay of leadership, power and spirituality. *Purushartha*, 4(1), 112–121.

Soltani I., et al (2012) Operational model of cascading values and professional ethics in organization: a context for spiritual development of employees. *Global journal of management and Business Research,* 12(8), 1–13

Sparks, J. R. and Schenk, J. A. (2001). Explaining the effects of transformational leadership. *Journal of Organizational Behavior*, 22(1), 849–869.

Stokes, P. (2011), *Critical Concepts in Management and Organization Studies*. Palgrave Macmillan: Basingstoke.

Thakur, K. and Singh, J. (2016). Spirituality at workplace: A conceptual framework. *Journal of Applied Business*, 14(7), 5181–5189.

Udani, Z. A. S. and Lorenzo-Molo, C. F. (2017). The utility of virtue: Management spirituality and ethics for a secular business world. *Asian Journal of Business Ethics*, 6, 21–39.

Van den Heuvel, S. (2018). *Challenging the New 'One-Dimensional Man': The Protestant Orders of Life as a Critical Nuance to Workplace Spirituality*. Cham: Springer.

Van Tonder, C. L. and Ramdass, P. (2009). A spirited workplace: Employee perspectives on the meaning of workplace spirituality. *Journal of Human Resource Management*, 7(1), 230–242.

Wall, T., Russell, J. and Moore, N. (2017). Positive emotion in workplace impact: The case of a work-based learning project utilising appreciative inquiry. *Journal of Work-Applied Management*, 9(2), 129–146.

Wall, T., Österlind, E. and Fries, J. (2019). Arts-based approaches for sustainability. In: Leal Filho W. (ed.) *Encyclopedia of Sustainability in Higher Education*. Cham: Springer.

Wennes, B. and Quinn, B. (2008). Mind-sets, mirrors and mid-career education. *International Journal of Public Sector Management*, 21(4), 353–367.

Williams, S. Abbott, B. and Heery, E. (2010). Mediating equality at work. *Equality, Diversity and Inclusion: An International Journal*, 29(6), 627–638.

Wong, T. (2003). *Spirituality and Meaning at Work*. Available at: www.meaning.ca/articles/presidentscolumn/printcopy/spirituality-worksept03.htm (Accessed 18 February 2020).

Wright, T. A. and Huang, C. (2012). The many benefits of employee well-being in organizational research. *Journal of Organizational Behavior*, 33(8), 1188–1192.

Young, J. (2020). *That's the Spirit: The Value of Workplace Spirituality*. CIPD. Available at: www.cipd.co.uk/news-views/changing-work-views/future-work/thought-pieces/workplace-spirituality (Accessed 9 July 2020).

Zhang, X., Zhu, W., Zhao, H. and Zhang, C. (2015). Employee well-being in organizations: Theoretical model, scale development, and cross-cultural validation. *Journal of Organizational Behavior*, 36(5), 621–644.

Zohar, D. and Marshall, I. (2004). *Spiritual Capital: Wealth We Can Live By*. London: Bloomsbury.

38

Posthumanism and Wellbeing in the Workplace

Raya A. Jones

INTRODUCTION

At the time of writing, spring 2020, the COVID-19 pandemic is sweeping the world. Under a national lockdown, home has become the workplace for many white-collar workers. For essential workers in sectors involving close proximity to others, the workplace has become a dangerous place requiring extraordinary safety measures. Alongside physical health, mental wellbeing has acquired exceptional poignancy. Tips on how to look after one's wellbeing, including how businesses could promote staff wellbeing during the crisis, abound online. On the one side, workplaces are in flux due to technologies that barely existed a few decades ago and are advancing apace. The pandemic forced many people unexpectedly to work from home, but the transition to remote working was made possible by technologies that have already significantly altered workaday life. Changes in the nature of work environments mean changes in the range of

opportunities and obstacles for wellbeing. Yet, flipping the metaphoric coin, typical advice on wellbeing tacitly perpetuates beliefs about human nature, happiness and wellness that were already articulated in Greco-Roman antiquity though not uniformly agreed. Themes that were debated by the ancients have underpinned humanism in modernity, and are currently queried under the banner of posthumanism.

The phenomenon in focus in this chapter is the discourse of employee wellbeing, specifically mental wellbeing. The term 'discourse' as used here denotes the web of concepts that underlies how we talk, think, investigate, and act with regard to this aspect of life. This discourse exists in the multifaceted interface between organization studies and a variety of other academic disciplines, as well as between the academia and social reality outside it.

In what ways does humanism enter the discourse of employee wellbeing? Could or should posthumanism matter in this context?

The philosophical definition of 'human' is the bone of contention across humanism and posthumanism, but this issue is hardly among the preoccupations or scientific problems defining organization studies. When humanism explicitly enters organization studies, it is often via psychology. Organization-oriented writers import ideas selectively, picking what is relevant for their own research questions. Posthumanism enters organization studies even more sporadically, as will be discussed. Moreover, both humanism and posthumanism elude precise definitions.

Humanism has a long and complex history, with diverse and divergent forms, and consequently different meanings in different contexts. At its broadest definition, humanism denotes any system of thought or ideology that places humans or humanity at its centre (anthropocentrism) and emphasizes the inherent value and potential of human life. Often written with a capital letter, Humanism refers to a major cultural and intellectual tradition that existed in Europe from the 14th to 16th centuries. It also denotes an ethical approach that stresses human rationality and capacity for free thought and moral action. This model of 'Man' has been severely attacked by contemporary thinkers associated with posthumanism.

For present purposes 'posthumanism' serves as an umbrella term for a family of philosophical movements that emerged in the late 20th century and distance themselves from humanism or Humanism. Scholars close to these movements draw fine-grained distinctions between posthumanism, anti-humanism, poststructuralism, postcolonialism, and post-anthropocentrism (Braidotti, 2013) and between posthumanism and transhumanism (Bess and Pasulka, 2018). The definition of 'human' is at stake in all these intellectual communities though with somewhat different emphases. In some disciplinary contexts, the posthumanist gaze looks to the future and to consequences of new technologies, including implications for traditional conceptions of what it means to be human. This challenges us to consider the extent to which current knowledge on wellbeing in workplaces might (or might not) become outmoded. In other contexts, posthumanism signals discontent with traditional Western concepts. Its advocates reiterate claims that were formerly associated with postmodernism, and often politicize the application of humanist ideals and values as a yardstick by which to measure the rest of the world's cultures. The scholarly gaze fixes on sins of the past, so to speak, and ontological remediations are bandied about. This nudges us to consider some taken-for-granted assumptions also within organization studies, notably assumptions about happiness and authenticity of human existence.

The chapter's topic is thus located in a site of tensions, where different agendas 'pull' in different directions. Tensions exist not only between humanism versus posthumanism as worldviews but also between research directions in different contexts of inquiry; the next section expands. The following sections provide a brief overview of humanism and posthumanism before pinpointing the relevance for employee wellbeing. The chapter's second half takes a closer look at concepts of happiness and authenticity, and their relevance for understanding wellbeing in the workplace.

DIRECTIONS OF INQUIRY

The issue of wellbeing in the workplace can be pursued in two opposite directions. One direction comprises inquiries into the effects of employees' wellbeing on the organization employing them. The other direction comprises inquiries into the effects of work on individuals. These options complement each other (somewhat like the proverbial glass that is both half empty and half full) and partially intertwine at several intersections. Person-centred inquiries could be further classed into (a) work-related, typically empiricist research investigating people's workplace experiences and how work impacts on life satisfaction, happiness, family life, and so forth (Caza and Wrzesniewski, 2013); and (b) theory-driven, typically conceptual writings that appraise ideas originating in perspectives that in their indigenous disciplinary contexts are not oriented to the kind of problems that are central in organization studies.

Organization-centred and work-related person-centred inquiries tend to imply a reciprocity between employee wellbeing and the 'health' of the organization, and typically operationalize wellbeing in terms of job satisfaction, job security, motivation, hedonic happiness, and so forth. In contrast, the workplace features peripherally if at all in the clinical discourse of psychiatry, psychotherapy, and affiliated disciplines; and may feature in ways that imply a dichotomy of wellbeing versus work. For example, referring to the tedium of operating machines in a factory, the Swiss psychiatrist Carl Gustav Jung observed that 'for modern man technology is an imbalance that begets dissatisfaction with work' (1949, quoted in Jones, 2019: 299). He advised workers in monotonous jobs to cultivate 'philosophical interests' outside their work so as to compensate for this imbalance. Jung attributed mental health to what he called individuation, and described as a lifelong process towards achieving an inner balance and therefore self-realization. Variations of the theme permeate a variety of humanistic, existentialist, and transpersonal psychologies, which generally associate wellbeing with a state of *eudaimonia*, definable as self-realization.

Despite their divergences, inquiries in all these categories are premised on the existence of empirical regularities and therefore the possibility of theorizing general principles. Within organization studies it is assumed that such principles could inform workplace practices for promoting employee wellbeing. It is believed that psychological correlates of wellbeing apply to all humans and remain constant across all settings. For instance, the 'feel' (*qualia*) of happiness would be the same

for a janitor and a corporate executive who say they are happy. Moreover, it is assumed that certain behaviours, motivations, and attitudes could be desirable qualities in any organizational setting; for instance, qualities of good leadership would be the same irrespective of the nature of the business. Hence the assumption of psychological universals is tacitly yoked with the premise that there are generic characteristics of organizations or of particular types of workplaces.

The dictionary definition of *workplace* as 'the premises of a company, business, etc., such as an office, factory, or shop, at which its employees work' (Oxford English Dictionary Online) may readily conjure the image of a physical site, usually a building, within which employees are grouped. Yet, workplaces differ widely in objective features, including the kind of interpersonal interactions (with co-workers, clients, the general public) associated with each kind of workplace. Offices differ from shops, both differ from factories, and further differ from construction sites or farms, for instance. Workplaces differ also subjectively. An executive is likely to experience different occupational stresses and rewards than would a receptionist working in the same building. Pathways to executives' wellbeing – strength of character, self-awareness, socialized power motivation, self-reliance, and diverse professional supports (Quick and Quick, 2013) – might not equally apply to rank-and-file employees. The lived experience reflects not only one's position in the organizational hierarchy but also aptitude, personality, intelligence, life situation, and demographic factors (gender, ethnicity, social class, and so forth).

Nevertheless, it is reasonable to expect that when most employees are content, their positivity would enhance the organization's productivity and employee retention, and thus contribute to the organization's prosperity. Pragmatic cost-benefit reasoning weighs costs of investing in employee wellbeing against benefits for the employers. In principle, evidence-based models of effective practices could be adopted by organizations towards raising their employees' wellbeing. Managerial decisions, however, might be swayed by popular fads (e.g. Purser, 2019) rather than 'science'. Also, for better or worse, preferences of particular practices – that is, what intuitively feels as the right approach – might reflect the entrenched attitudes and moral claims of humanism.

HUMANISM AND ITS DISCONTENTS

Humanism enters the subfield of wellbeing within organization studies mainly via psychology, as mentioned, but it has a long history. Its roots lie in the Renaissance rediscovery of ancient Greek and Roman philosophy. An educational and political ideal was foundational to Renaissance humanism. Its conceptual cornerstone is trackable to Cicero's concept of *humanitas*, which implies not only qualities such as understanding, benevolence, compassion, and mercy, but also 'fortitude, judgment, prudence, eloquence, and even love of honour' (Grudin, 2020: 1). Fifteenth-century educators advocated the study of grammar, poetry, rhetoric, history, and moral philosophy towards good citizenship: 'Not everyone is called to be a physician, a lawyer, a philosopher, to live in the public eye … but all of us are created for the life of social duty' (Vittorino, quoted in Grudin, 2020: 12). Over the centuries, the earlier emphasis on education towards a virtuous life of social duty became obscured by a shift towards prioritizing self-fulfilment and happiness.

The movement that began in the Italian Renaissance is associated with the emergence of individualism, hence with attitudes that later came to characterize humanism in general, such as an emphasis on personal autonomy or free will. Throughout the 20th century, humanism underscored doctrines and practices premised on the centrality of human experience. This anthropocentrism underlies movements that significantly differ from each other, such as pragmatic humanism, Christian humanism, and secular humanism (Grudin, 2020). Further forms include liberal humanism and, separately, 'technical fix' humanism, which 'advocates efficient management that employs the most technologically advanced equipment to increase productivity and improve the quality of life and general prosperity of each individual (subject) in the workplace and society' (Rosenau, 1992: 48).

In the second half of the 20th century, the humanist model of 'Man' came under severe attack in intellectual circles. The contested concept was first articulated by Protagoras and then revived in the Italian Renaissance: 'an ideal of bodily perfection which doubles up as a set of mental, discursive and spiritual values' (Braidotti, 2013: 2). Championing posthumanism, Braidotti pinpoints 'Faith in the unique, self-regulating and intrinsically moral powers of human reason' as an essential part of humanism, and as foundational for a model of civilization that exalts 'the universalizing powers of self-reflexive reason' (Braidotti, 2013: 2). Political motivations have permeated agendas against this model. Anti-humanism served as the 'rallying cry' of the post-1968 generation. Foucault (1970) famously announced the 'death of Man' in his seminal critique of humanism. Braidotti (2013: 3) reflects, 'The "death of Man" … formalizes an epistemological and moral crisis that … cuts across the different poles of the political spectrum. What is targeted is … the humanistic arrogance of continuing to place Man at the centre of world history'.

It is debatable to what extent this sweeping condemnation of the traditional model of Man might apply also to traditional approaches to wellbeing in general and to employee wellbeing in particular. While traditional perspectives on mental health and wellbeing put the human being at the centre of their concerns by virtue of their *raison d'être*, they differ considerably from each other in terms of endorsing versus disapproving of the privileged place allotted to human rationality (Jung, for instance, regarded this one-sided valuing of rationality as a malaise of modern Western man; Jones, 2007, 2019). A milder critical theme is the question of ethnocentricity or cultural myopia; that is, the extent to which value judgements of what accounts for wellbeing are tacitly based in Western individualism, though are taken as a yardstick for the measure of optimal psychological functioning also in non-Western settings. The query of ethnocentricity has been raised and reiterated within psychology since the 1970s, often under the banner of postmodernism (the term 'posthumanism' has not entered psychology so far).

What exactly is posthumanism? The term in its broad usage covers a variety of late 20th-century intellectual movements, but some writers narrow it to one of these. Making contact with organization studies, Willmott (1998: 100) distanced his position from anti-humanism: anti-humanism 'denies the presence and significance of the subject in the reproduction of social structures' whereas posthumanism decentres the human subject without denying its agentic powers and capacity to transform social structures. Furthermore, posthumanism acknowledges that 'subjects are positioned and constituted within diverse discourses that exist in a relation of tension to each other; and that it is through a process of emotional-rational struggle that a sense of individual and collective self-identity is developed' (Willmott, 1998: 100). Citing Willmott's characterization, Bryant and Cox (2014) suggest that a posthumanist turn has been evident in organization studies since the late 1980s, and 'has shifted attention from the promotion of universal human values and an integrated notion of the human self toward relativism, tension and difference' (2014: 708). Neither Willmott (advising on ethics) nor Bryant and Cox (advising on organizational development) discuss wellbeing. In passing, it may be noted that their characterization of posthumanism parallels what psychologists have

associated with postmodernism (see Jones, 2007).

Outside both psychology and organization studies, some scholars distinguish posthumanism from transhumanism. Introducing their edited volume, Bess and Pasulka (2018) apply the term 'transhuman' to refer to the use of pharmaceutical, bioelectronic, genetic, or other technologies so as to make significant alterations to one's physical, emotional, or cognitive capabilities; and apply the term 'posthuman' to refer to the use of futuristic biotechnological self-modification that would take individuals beyond the range of species-typical performance. Other writers may reverse this transhuman/posthuman designation. Generally defined, transhumanism is a worldview endorsing technologies that will significantly enhance human body and mind, and a future in which human existence will transcend biology. Typically under the rubric of posthumanism, scholars debate whether emerging feasibilities of genetically enhanced humans, humans with machine parts, and machines with humanlike or superior intelligence, will dehumanize or enhance humanity (Wilson and Haslam, 2009). For better or worse, 'the posthuman view configures [the] human being so that it can be seamlessly articulated with intelligent machines' (Hayles, 2008: 3).

Whatever the future may hold, technology alters our lifestyles and the narratives we live by. By the end of the millennium, technology had changed almost every sector of industry and services. Office routines are conducted partially or wholly in the digital world. Automation and collaborative robots are transforming factory floors. Experts foresee 'smart' factories and supply chains in the near future, and herald this development as the Fourth Industrial Revolution (Morgan, 2019). While fears that automation will result in massive unemployment are common, some commentators look forward to a 'world without work' (Thompson, 2015). Others, such as Postelnicu and Câlea (2019: 199), doubt that 'workers will be completely freed from boring and repetitive jobs and, instead, will perform creative activities typical of a smart era in which machines communicate between, and coordinate each other'. Either way, some occupations are likely to become obsolete and new professions will emerge. New hazards for health, safety, and job security might ensue along with new or different sources of anxiety and stress; or, conversely, nascent kinds of employment could be more conducive for wellbeing. Would these require a different 'technology of the self'? At present, any answer would be speculative (and outside this chapter's scope), but the next section explains the meaning and relevance of the phrase.

TECHNOLOGY OF THE SELF

Foucault (1993) admitted to have changed his mind on some issues since the 1970s. Originally he believed that techniques of domination – that is, ways of controlling individuals' conduct and submitting them to certain ends or objectives – were the most important in shaping societies and human subjects. On reflection, he became increasingly aware of another type of techniques that exist in all societies: techniques whereby individuals carry out certain procedures on their bodies, minds, and conduct in order to achieve desired states of perfection, happiness, purity, and so on; 'Let's call this kind of techniques … technology of the self' (Foucault, 1993: 203). This concept is key to evaluating humanism in psychological approaches to mental health and wellbeing. Psychologists disagree regarding the precise qualities that signify the desired state of being. Candidates include: self-identity (Erik Erikson's ego psychology), intrapsychic equilibrium (Jung's analytical psychology), self-actualization (Maslow's humanistic psychology), authenticity and meaning (existential psychologists), transcendence, wholeness, and transformation (transpersonal psychologists). Yet all these perspectives articulate their core constructs in their effort to create an efficient 'technology of the self' whereby persons could achieve and maintain a state of wellbeing.

All the aforementioned perspectives first emerged during the first half of the 20th century. Separately, positive psychology emerged in the late 1990s as the scientific study of human virtue and happiness (Seligman and Csikszentmihalyi, 2000) and is currently the major academic context for theorizing and investigating wellbeing. Positive psychology and humanistic psychology make the most contact with organization studies. Humanistic psychology arose in the mid-20th century in the United States, and is associated with Abraham Maslow and Carl Rogers. Maslow's (1943, 1954) theory of human motivation and its iconic 'hierarchy of needs' pyramid continue to offer insights in organization studies (e.g. Wilson and Madsen, 2008; Acevedo, 2018). Humanistic psychology differs in some fundamental respects from positive psychology (Waterman, 2013; Rich, 2018) but both share individualistic assumptions and rest similarly on eudaimonism – that is, 'an ethical theory that calls people to recognize and to live in accordance with the *daimon* or "true self"' (Waterman, 1993: 678).

The ethical stance of eudaimonism puts the onus on individuals to invest in actualizing their 'true self'. When organizations offer interventions, the provision for techniques of the self might deploy techniques of domination. One large organization known to me once provided a day of workshops on techniques aimed to improve wellbeing, physical and mental (e.g. desktop yoga). While the initiative was meant to educate people in self-care, attendance was compulsory, thus deploying techniques of domination. My informants would have preferred to get on with their work that day. Ironically, by forcing employees away from their desks in order to learn about how to alleviate stress, this initiative increased some people's stress about their heavy workloads.

Some social theorists comment that techniques designed to help individuals become instruments of social control. Focusing on the mindfulness movement, Purser (2019) interrogates the way that corporations appropriate its programmes, contending that 'As a tool of self-discipline, mindfulness is the latest capitalist spirituality, unifying a quest for productivity and corporate profits with individual peace and self-fulfilment'; and further contends that mindfulness training produces docile employees: by directing individuals' attention inwards, these courses deflect from 'questions of power or political economy; external conditions are simply accepted as they are' (Purser, 2019: 134). Whether one agrees or disagrees with it, Purser's claim evinces a tension between notions of the ideal employee (whose happiness is consonant with harmonious organizational life) and the humanistic ideal, where happiness reflects autonomy and authenticity of the self.

CONCEPTUALIZING HAPPINESS

The word *happiness* tends to imply enjoyment, pleasure, or positive affect such as associated with getting the things one wants. However, two rival conceptions – happiness as hedonic enjoyment versus *eudaimonia* – emerged in ancient Greece and have been debated ever since, including within modern psychology (Waterman, 1993; Ryan and Deci, 2001). The word *eudaimonia* in the classics is often translated as 'happiness', though various scholars have suggested terms such as human flourishing, prosperity, the good life (i.e. virtuous), and self-realization as a more accurate translation. Eudaimonism concerns issues of authentic human existence.

Organization-centred research largely bypasses that philosophical debate. Pioneering research in the 1930s explored the relationship between employee happiness and productivity, though later researchers tended to narrowly equate happiness with job satisfaction (Wright, 2013). Outlining directions for investigating employee happiness, Wright (2013: 787) operationalizes happiness as 'both the relative presence of positive emotions and the relative absence of negative emotions'. This empiricist approach accords with the standpoint that Seligman and Csikszentmihalyi (2000: 11) identify as a 'simple hedonic calculus'; namely, the notion that we can get a score that represents overall wellbeing simply by 'adding up a person's positive events in consciousness, subtracting the negatives, and aggregating over time'. Making a case for positive psychology, Seligman and Csikszentmihalyi (2000: 11) point to a fundamental gap in knowledge regarding the relationship between long-lasting wellbeing and momentary experiences of happiness, contending that 'what makes people happy in small doses does not necessarily add satisfaction in larger amounts'.

Equating wellbeing with hedonic pleasure has a millennia-long history. In the 4th century BC, Aristippus of Cyrene held that the goal of life is to optimize pleasure through having proper control over both adversity and prosperity. This outlook has been endorsed by many others throughout the centuries into the present. Proponents of hedonic psychology, such as Kahneman et al. (1999) define wellbeing in terms of pleasure versus pain, and set themselves the task of research and intervention towards maximizing human happiness. Aristotle, however, rejected the hedonistic view of happiness. In *Nicomachean Ethics* he designated the equation of the good life with a life of enjoyment to 'men of the most vulgar type', and contended that those who prefer a life of gratification are opting for a life suitable for cattle (Aristotle, 1941: 938). Aristotle dismissed also the 'good life' of honour, such as pursued by those active in political spheres, as being superficial existence, since achieving honour depends more on others who honour the person than on personal endeavour and virtues. He equated the good life (*eudaimonia*) with inner qualities of virtue and pursuing a life of study.

As mentioned, positive psychology is currently the main disciplinary context for the scientific study of wellbeing. Its influence on organization studies is evident in scholarship that focuses on positive processes, outcomes, and attributes of organizations and their members, and embodies 'the belief that individuals and their organizations … seek goodness for its intrinsic value' (Caza and Cameron, 2013: 672). However, whereas positive psychology arose as a reaction to the focus on negative aspects of human mind and behaviour, which had dominated psychological science, organization studies lack an analogous tradition of bias towards negatives. Although research seldom investigated happiness per se, there is 'a long history of examining closely related phenomena, including job satisfaction, job involvement, organizational commitment, engagement, social concern, collective morale, and intrinsic motivation' (Caza and Cameron, 2013: 672).

However, the role that work-related phenomena such as listed earlier may play towards personal happiness might differ across cultures as well as across gender, social class, or ethnicity within the same culture. For example, research in the United States suggests that men tend to describe themselves in terms of larger group collectives whereas women may define themselves in terms of close relationships, such as relationships with a romantic partner or spouse, close friends, or specific family members (Cross et al., 2011). By implication, having a close friend in work might matter more towards female employees' happiness than factors such as collective morale and organizational engagement, at least in the United States. Cross et al. (2011) also discuss differences across collectivist and individualist societies (see also Markus and Kitayama, 1991, 2010). In individualistic societies, the cultural emphasis is on autonomy, positive self-regard, and personal happiness. In collectivist societies, the cultural emphasis is on belonging and social harmony. A downside of collectivism is that social exclusion can

be particularly harsh. East Asian individuals may develop various cognitive, motivational, behavioural, and affective tendencies that serve to ensure social harmony and yet are detrimental to their own happiness (Suh, 2007).

In sum, seeking to define and operationalize 'happiness' in value-neutral ways – such as an index of overall satisfaction with one's life or high levels of positive emotions – leaves open the question of which norms of happiness are deemed as morally desirable within given societies. Culturally specific values influence how people ordinarily evaluate their life situations, feelings, and aspirations, all of which would contribute to their satisfaction with their lives and therefore sense of wellbeing.

CONCEPTUALIZING AUTHENTICITY

Advocating posthumanism in organization studies, Bryant and Cox (2014: 707) query a concept of authenticity they associate with humanism, namely, 'the notion of an authentic or "real self" … a "unified subject, defined by its autonomy in thought" … and by "an unproblematic universalism which is often associated with the Enlightenment idea of "a core humanity"'" (quoting several scholars). Having interviewed employees on how they managed conflicts arising from organizational change, Bryant and Cox provide two alternative analyses: traditional and posthumanist. The traditional standpoint holds that authenticity has to be 'discovered', that multiplicity has to be overcome, and that negativity has to be downplayed. The posthumanist standpoint regards multiplicity as a source for dialogue and discussion, and therefore authenticity ceases to be of concern, according to these writers. Bryant and Cox make valuable points towards organizational development. Yet, a diametrically opposite stance towards authenticity could be reached from the very standpoint that they highlight as posthumanism. The call to eliminate the epistemological need to theorize about selfhood in terms of some unified, centralized, and constant mental entity – in a word, an ego – has long been made by postmodern psychologists (Jones, 2007). Many contemporary scholars across the humanities and social sciences draw upon Bakhtin's dialogism (Holquist, 2002) towards making their case for 'decentralizing' the human subject and for asserting multivoicedness and dialogicality. In this vein, taking his cue from Bakhtin, Frank (2005) stresses the ethical imperative of reporting participants' real-life accounts as plainly and faithfully as possible, with minimal interpretation, thereby preserving the *authenticity* of human existence. Hence, authenticity becomes of central concern precisely because multivoicedness and dialogicality are affirmed.

The above ambiguity rests on a conflation of two different ways in which the word 'authenticity' is used in relation to the self. One usage emphasizes having one's voice heard by others. It is intrinsically a relational concept, signifying a quality of a social relationship or milieu. The other usage emphasizes a subjective state of being true to one's inner nature, and is intrinsically non-social (a hermit, living in solitude in accordance with some religious creed, could presumably experience this state). While the latter concept is older, its conceptual distinction from the newer concept does not lie in the premise of a 'centralized' versus 'decentralized' human subject. The emphasis on voice underpins writers' calls for an organizational ethos that takes into account employees' views and feelings. Bryant and Cox (2014) make this call through the lens of posthumanism and its assertion of the decentralized subject, but others (e.g. Roberts, 2013) do it by reference to the social-cognitive perspective, which is premised on a traditional notion of a centralized self.

Social cognition refers to how human minds process information about the social world. The self is conceptualized as a mental structure that evolves throughout the life course. Therefore what feels as 'really me' is subject to constant reconstructions in the light of ongoing experiences, influences, opportunities, and barriers encountered in one's life. Roberts (2013) brings this ontology into organization studies in her construct of the Reflected Best Self, defined as 'a changing knowledge structure about who we are when we are at our best' (2013: 769). In social psychology, Harter (1999) and others define authenticity by its contrast to so-called false-self behaviour. Authenticity means acting in ways that express one's genuine feelings, attitudes, and beliefs as opposed to acting in ways that please others or conform to normative expectations. In this vein, Roberts (2013) asserts the importance of an organizational ethos that empowers its employees' voice: 'The authentic experience reflects an individual's gestalt or overall feeling of having sufficiently communicated and acted upon his or her genuine internal experiences in the workplace' (2013: 774).

A dual emphasis on authenticity as an inner state and having a voice is implicit in the social cognitive approach, and by extension enters Roberts' (2013) concept; but humanistic and existentialist psychologies detach their respective concepts of authenticity from the question of 'voice'.

Humanistic psychology links authenticity to self-actualization, and rests on the belief that each of us has a 'true' self awaiting discovery. It does not dictate what this self must be like; one's *daimon* is specific to oneself:

[d]iscontent and restlessness will soon develop, unless the individual is doing what he is fitted for. A musician must make music, an artist must paint, a poet must write, if he is to be ultimately happy. What a man *can* be, he *must* be. This need we may call self-actualisation. (Maslow, 1943: 382)

Maslow originally placed self-actualization at the pinnacle of his pyramid of needs. In the 1960s he added self-transcendence as a motivational factor beyond self-actualization, and introduced the term 'transpersonal' to refer to that which is beyond or above ordinary personality (Koltko-Rivera, 2006). However, it is mostly the original theory that continues to be widely disseminated and to be appraised also within organization studies, although mostly with regard to employees' motivation and training (see, e.g. Wilson and Madsen, 2008; Acevedo, 2018).

A twofold question of sociocultural contextuality can be levelled at humanistic psychology: its ethnocentricity and, separately, its misuse or abuses. Humanistic psychology represents a quest for what makes us human; but, as the Japanese scholar Muramoto (2000: 1) points out, the well-known movement associated with Maslow and Rogers is 'American humanistic psychology'. Muramoto maintains that cultures should each have their unique versions of humanistic psychology. Furthermore, he comments that the discourse of self-actualization (notwithstanding Maslow's original meaning) 'either tends to easily slip into the pursuit of self-interest in the capitalist society or may be abused as a tool for manipulating people and turn over to its opposite, self-annihilation, in the totalitarian state' (Muramoto, 2011: 420).

Existential psychologists generally define authenticity as the state of living fully aware, with compassion and commitment, accepting the inevitability of death, guilt, and anxiety. Inauthenticity therefore means living in denial of one's full humanity. Existential psychology makes little contact with organization studies but is worth including here for its contrast with both the humanistic and social-psychological emphases. It arose as a broad movement that integrated European philosophies and depth psychology, and represented a reaction against the Freudian framework (May, 1958). Its early advocates were psychoanalytically trained clinical practitioners who promoted an understanding of mental illness and personal crisis as disruptions in the integrity of the person's existence, and developed techniques for helping people to move from a state of inauthenticity to authenticity. Suffice

it to cite one of its key figures. Viktor Frankl, a Holocaust survivor and founder of logotherapy, posited the 'will to meaning' as the primary human motivation. Finding meaning in one's adverse circumstances has little or nothing to do with self-actualizing (Maslow) or acting in genuine ways (Harter), and is not necessarily associated with happiness. Frankl (1959/2004) tells of an elderly man who could not overcome his grief after his wife died two years earlier, and consequently suffered severe depression. Prompted by Frankl to consider what would have happened if he had died first, the widower realized that his wife would have suffered if she were to survive him. His own suffering meant that she was spared this fate. Frankl concludes, 'suffering ceases to be suffering at the moment it finds a meaning, such as the meaning of a sacrifice' (1959/2004: 117).

Authenticity as defined by existential psychologists manifests in personal integrity in adversity, accepting negative emotions as well as positive, and the dark side of human nature. As such, it is not necessarily accompanied by happiness. However, it is not fatalistic. Another case told by Frankl (1959/2004: 107) centres on a conflict between someone's job and wellbeing. He tells of a high-ranking US diplomat who had been undergoing psychoanalysis in New York for five years prior to being relocated to Vienna. The diplomat came to Frankl's clinic wishing to continue his treatment. He was discontented with his career and found it difficult to comply with US foreign policy. His New York analyst attributed his discontent to unconscious hatred towards his father since (in that analyst's view) the government and the diplomat's superiors were father images. In Frankl's view, the diplomat's 'will to meaning' was compromised by his vocation and he longed for a different kind of career. Encouraged by Frankl, the man changed his job and was subsequently content.

To round up the comparison of concepts of authenticity in terms of their applicability for organization studies, it could be reflected that having a voice as an employee has little or nothing to do with self-actualizing in Maslow's sense; and conversely, self-actualizing has little or no bearing on having a voice as an employee (which depends on the organization's ethos and one's position within its hierarchy). Similarly, living in an authentic state such as described by existential psychologists could mean stoically accepting working in circumstances that do not permit an outward expression of one's private self, if the sacrifice has a meaning.

PERSONA AT WORK

Many employees find themselves routinely having to act in ways that do not fully reveal their 'real' personality or attitudes. A countryside park ranger once told me how he has different personas when dealing with visitors, with schools, with vandals, with someone with a gun, with co-workers, and so on. His account of stepping in and out of workaday roles evokes Goffman's (1959: 245) metaphor: one's 'body merely provides the peg on which something of collaborative manufacture will be hung for a time. And the means for producing and maintaining selves do not reside in the peg'. The self or selves that employees wear while at work is clearly something of collaborative manufacture. Research by Hochschild, originally published in 1983, describes how flight attendants working for Delta Airlines were expected to act in ways that fitted in with the organization's expectations of the ideal female employee, such as 'being perceived as caring, mildly flirtatious, and impervious to rude customers, as well as dressing in a particularly feminised way that included a certain way of wearing make-up, uniform and hair' (Addison, 2017: 9).

Goffman (1959) rejected notions of a deep, unchanging 'true' self behind the multiplicity of one's situated performances, though his dramaturgical model has been criticized (e.g. Davies and Harré, 1990) for not going far enough in eliminating the idea that the actor playing diverse roles must have a real self off-stage. In contrast with those critics, Hochschild finds Goffman's model lacking an explanation of individuals' sense of self-continuity across stage settings, and she endorses a notion of a 'real' self. Based on her real/false-self dichotomy, Hochschild (2012) delineates three stances that employees may take towards their work:

1 Employees fully identify with their job, and have little or no awareness of a 'false self'. These are at high risk of burnout, which in the short term could be mitigated by emotional numbness (thereby avoiding feelings associated with overwhelming distress) but could have serious long-term costs.
2 Employees make a clear separation of their own self from their job persona – a 'healthy' estrangement, as Hochschild puts it – but they might feel guilty of being hypocritical.
3 Employees develop a 'healthy' estrangement, understand their job persona as an act, and positively regard the job as requiring an acting capacity. There is some risk of becoming cynical about their acting.

Hochschild (2012: 187) summarizes, 'The first stance is potentially more harmful than the other two, but the harm in all three could be reduced, I believe, if workers could feel a greater sense of control over the conditions of their work lives'. Hochschild's distinction of real and false selves is pivotal in her approach to what she regarded as the exploitation and suppression of persons' agency in capitalist organizations (Addison, 2017). Bolton (2005) contests her depiction of employees being coerced to align themselves with organizational rules and consequently losing their sense of self – a depiction that overlooks the possibility of employees becoming active agents. Bolton promotes a view of the modern self-reflexive person, which Giddens (1991) and other sociologists articulated in the 1990s. Carrying the theoretical debate further, Addison (2017) suggests that Bourdieu's concept of habitus and theory of the self as embodied history could be more useful towards explaining individuals' sense of continuity across situations than Hochschild's notion of a real self.

Scholarly debates aside, we may reflect that acting in ways true to oneself does not necessarily correlate with workplace harmony or happiness. Whistleblowing is an extreme case of such conflict: whistleblowers 'talk of the shame and repulsion of being in an organization that does not seem to care about the consequences of its actions', and consequently, 'any personal costs of speaking out are swamped by feelings of righteousness about their concern' (Fineman, 2003: 106). Feeling trapped in one's job is another example of dissonance. Klein (2018) tells of siblings who had worked in the family retail business since they were teenagers. The son eventually left to follow his dream of becoming an engineer. The daughter stayed, and in time bought the business off her father. In less than two years, however, she 'lost her spirit and energy and realized that she had pursued this venture primarily because of her need to prove herself to her father, not because she wanted to be a small-business owner' (Klein, 2018).

Finally, actions that might appear or feel like false-self to persons in individualistic societies might be evaluated differently in collectivist cultures. For instance, Suh (2002) found that Koreans were more likely to regard themselves as flexible across situations and to value flexibility in others whereas Americans were more likely to rate consistent individuals as likeable and socially skilled. Consequently, the correlation between self-consistency and negative affect was weaker in South Korea than in the United States. We may consider also the extent to which cultural attitudes underscore moral stances associated with work ethic, organizational expectations, employees' deference to their superiors, and understanding of their own place.

CONCLUSION

Can there be universally applicable criteria for everyone's wellbeing in all workplaces? As Christopher and Hickinbottom (2008: 565) state, 'There is, quite simply, no such thing as a value-neutral, culture-free psychology'. Focusing on positive psychology, they contend that it embodies dominant Western (especially US) ideologies of individualism. These ideologies are characterized by (a) the Cartesian distinction between an external objective 'real' world of abstract facts and an internal subjective world (values, experiences, beliefs, and meanings); (b) a notion of a fixed essential self that is separate from others and the world; and (c) a moral standpoint stating that people should be free to decide how they want to pursue happiness as long as they don't interfere with others' ability to do the same. This threefold characterization may sum up the general standpoint of modern humanism. It applies not only to most traditions within psychology but also to the standpoint from which criteria for employee wellbeing tend to be considered.

The posthumanist critique goes further than querying the veracity of the Cartesian model. It also politicizes the notion of its cross-cultural applicability, and challenges us to query the universality of beliefs and values that bear on wellbeing-oriented practices. As seen, making a case for her variant of posthumanism, Braidotti contested 'the humanistic arrogance of continuing to place Man at the centre of world history' (2013: 3). Arguably, this charge would be misapplied to 'philosophies of life' such as humanistic, existentialist, transpersonal, and the mindfulness movements. While rooted in Western humanism, these draw also on Far Eastern philosophies and practices. First and foremost, they aim to empower and guide individuals towards a personally meaningful existence through what Foucault called a technology of the self. It remains open to debate – and could be a direction for future scholarship – whether

(a) embracing posthumanist ideology would enhance, undermine, or make little difference to people's actual experience of wellbeing, and (b) what pragmatic insights could be taken towards improving organizational life. This chapter's aim was mainly to set a stage for ongoing explorations of ideas.

REFERENCES

Acevedo A (2018) A personalistic appraisal of Maslow's needs theory of motivation: From 'humanistic' psychology to integral humanism. *Journal of Business Ethics* 148, 741–763.

Addison M (2017) Overcoming Arlie Hochschild's concepts of the 'real' and 'false' self by drawing on Pierre Bourdieu's concept of habitus. *Emotion, Space and Society* 23, 9–15.

Aristotle (1941) *The Basic Works of Aristotle* (trans. R McKeon). New York: Random House.

Bess M and Pasulka DW (eds) (2018) *Posthumanism: The Future of Homo Sapiens.* Farmington Hills, MI: Macmillan.

Bolton SC (2005) *Emotion Management in the Workplace.* Basingstoke: Palgrave.

Braidotti R (2013) Posthuman humanities. *European Educational Research Journal* 12, 1–19.

Bryant M and Cox JW (2014) Beyond authenticity? Humanism, posthumanism and new organization development. *British Journal of Management* 25, 706–723.

Caza A and Cameron KS (2013) An introduction to happiness and organizations. In: Boniwell I, David SA and Ayers AC (eds) *Oxford Handbook of Happiness.* Oxford: Oxford University Press (pp. 672–677).

Caza BB and Wrzesniewski A (2013) How work shapes well-being. In: Boniwell I, David SA and Ayers AC (eds) *Oxford Handbook of Happiness.* Oxford: Oxford University Press (pp. 694–711).

Christopher JC and Hickinbottom S (2008) Positive psychology, ethnocentrism, and the disguised ideology of individualism. *Theory and Psychology*, 18, 563–589.

Cross SE, Hardin EE and Gercek-Swing B (2011) The what, how, why, and where of self-construal. *Personality and Social Psychology Review* 15, 142–179.

Davies B and Harré R (1990) Positioning: The discursive production of selves. *Journal for the Theory of Social Behaviour* 20, 43–64.

Fineman S (2003) *Understanding Emotion at Work.* London: Sage.

Foucault M (1970) *The Order of Things.* New York: Pantheon Books.

Foucault M (1993) About the beginning of the hermeneutics of the self: Two lectures at Dartmouth. *Political Theory* 21, 198–227.

Frank AW (2005) What is dialogical research, and why should we do it? *Qualitative Health Research* 15, 964–974.

Frankl V (1959/2004) *Man's Search for Meaning.* London: Rider.

Giddens A (1991) *Modernity and Self-identity.* Cambridge: Polity.

Goffman E (1959) *The Presentation of Self in Everyday Life.* Harmondsworth: Penguin.

Grudin R (2020) Humanism. In: *Encyclopaedia Britannica.* Available at: www.britannica.com/topic/humanism (accessed 4 March 2020).

Harter S (1999) *The Construction of the Self.* New York: Guilford.

Hayles K (2008) *How We Became Posthuman.* Chicago: University of Chicago Press.

Hochschild AR (2012) *The Managed Heart: Commercialization of Human Feeling.* University of California Press: ProQuest Ebook Central.

Holquist M (2002) *Dialogism* (2nd edition). London: Routledge.

Jones RA (2007) *Jung, Psychology, Postmodernity.* London: Routledge.

Jones RA (2019) Jung, Science and Technology. In: Mills J (ed.) *Jung and Philosophy.* London: Routledge (pp. 289–304).

Kahneman D, Diener E and Schwarz N (eds) (1999) *Well-Being: Foundations of Hedonic Psychology.* New York: Russell Sage Foundation.

Klein M (2018) Thriving or trapped in the family business? *Entrepreneurship and Innovation Exchange.* Available at: https://family-business.org/content/thriving-or-trapped-in-the-family-business (accessed 9 June 2020).

Koltko-Rivera ME (2006) Rediscovering the later version of Maslow's hierarchy of needs: Self-transcendence and opportunities for theory, research, and unification. *Review of General Psychology*, 10, 302–317.

Markus HR and Kitayama S (1991) Culture and the self: Implications for cognition, emotion, and motivation. *Psychological Review* 98, 224–253.

Markus HR and Kitayama S (2010) Cultures and selves: A cycle of mutual constitution. *Perspectives on Psychological Science* 5, 420–430.

Maslow AH (1943) A theory of human motivation. *Psychological Review* 50, 370–396.

Maslow AH (1954) *Motivation and Personality*. New York: Harper and Row.

May R (1958) The origins and significance of the existentialist movement in psychology. In: May R, Angel E and Ellenberger HF (eds) *Existence: A New Dimension in Psychiatry and Psychology*. New York: Basic Books (pp. 3–36).

Morgan J (2019) Will we work in twenty-first century capitalism? A critique of the fourth industrial revolution literature. *Economy and Society* 48, 371–398.

Muramoto S (2000) *Historical reflections for the international development of Japanese humanistic psychology*. Available at: https://cranepsych2.edublogs.org/files/2009/08/Japanese_humanistic_psych.pdf (accessed 25 May 2020).

Muramoto S (2011) Humanistic psychology as the quest for the identity of human being. *Journal of Humanistic Psychology* 51, 419–423.

Postelnicu C and Câlea S (2019) The Fourth Industrial Revolution: Global risks, local challenges for employment. *Montenegrin Journal of Economics* 15, 195–206.

Purser RE (2019) *McMindfulness: How Mindfulness Became the New Capitalist Spirituality*. London: Repeater Books.

Quick JC and Quick JD (2013) Executive wellbeing. In: Boniwell I, David SA and Ayers AC (eds) *Oxford Handbook of Happiness*. Oxford: Oxford University Press (pp. 799–814).

Rich GJ (2018) Positive psychology and humanistic psychology: Evil twins, sibling rivals, distant cousins, or something else? *Journal of Humanistic Psychology* 58, 262–283.

Roberts LM (2013) Reflected best self engagement at work: Positive identity, alignment, and the pursuit of vitality and value creation. In: Boniwell I, David SA and Ayers AC (eds) *Oxford Handbook of Happiness*. Oxford: Oxford University Press (pp. 768–783).

Rosenau P (1992) *Post-modernism and the Social Sciences*. Princeton, NJ: Princeton University Press.

Ryan RM and Deci EL (2001) On happiness and human potentials: A review of research on hedonic and eudaimonic well-being. *Annual Review Psychology* 52, 141–166.

Seligman MEP and Csikszentmihalyi M (2000) Positive psychology: An introduction. *American Psychologist* 55, 5–14.

Suh EM (2002) Culture, identity consistency, and subjective well-being. *Journal of Personality and Social Psychology* 83, 1378–1391.

Suh EM (2007) Downsides of an overly context-sensitive self: Implications from the culture and subjective well-being research. *Journal of Personality* 75, 1321–1343.

Thompson D (2015) A world without work. *The Atlantic Magazine*, July/August 2015. Available at: www.theatlantic.com/magazine/archive/2015/07/world-without-work/395294 (accessed 28 January 2020).

Waterman AS (1993) Two conceptions of happiness: Contrasts of personal expressiveness (eudaimonia) and hedonic enjoyment. *Journal of Personality and Social Psychology* 64, 678–691.

Waterman AS (2013) The humanistic psychology–positive psychology divide: Contrasts in philosophical foundations. *American Psychologist* 68, 124–133.

Willmott H (1998) Towards a new ethics? The contributions of poststructuralism and posthumanism. In: Parker M (ed.) *Ethics and Organizations*. London: Sage (pp. 76–121).

Wilson IW and Madsen SR (2008) The influence of Maslow's humanistic views on an employee's motivation to learn. *Journal of Applied Management and Entrepreneurship* 13, 46–62.

Wilson S and Haslam N (2009) Is the future more or less human? Differing views of humanness in the posthumanism debate. *Journal for the Theory of Social Behaviour* 39, 247–266.

Wright TA (2013) Encouraging employee happiness. In: Boniwell I et al. (eds) *Oxford Handbook of Happiness*. Oxford: Oxford University Press (pp. 783–797).

39

Artificial Intelligence, Big Data, Robots and Wellbeing in Organizational Life

Jarrod Haar and David Brougham

INTRODUCTION

Societies, as we know them, have always evolved and largely grown and improved on the back of technology. Consider the modern-day toilet versus an outhouse. A kerosene lamp versus LED lights. A suite of large books holding all known knowledge (i.e., encyclopedias) versus the Internet and the ability to 'google' anything. Indeed, today we can access this on a device held in our hands (i.e., a smartphone). Further, the processing power of these smartphones is incredible, considering what has come before. On the 50th anniversary of the moon landing, Kendall (2019) compared the technology NASA used to control Apollo 11 versus the latest iPhone. Kendall (2019) showed that the processing speed of an iPhone is 100,000 times stronger, with over a million times more RAM (random-access memory) and 7 million times more ROM (read-only memory). Given the Apollo 11 guidance computer weighed 32kg versus an

iPhone 11 at under 0.2 kg – and the iPhone being able to fit into your pocket – there are fundamental improvements in portability and computing power. Impressively, this technology is now common to many people in developed and developing economies. Smartphone penetration (the percentage of population actively using a smartphone) is highest in the UK with roughly 83%, followed by Germany on 80% and the United States on 79% (Newzoo, 2019). Thus, there is wide use of technology, making such technology ubiquitous to people.

Schwab (2017: 1) states the fourth industrial revolution is being powered by 'artificial intelligence, robotics, the internet of things, autonomous vehicles, 3D printing, nanotechnology, biotechnology, materials science, energy storage and quantum computing'. Brougham and Haar (2018: 239) noted the current everyday incursion of such technology includes 'retail self-checkouts, smartphone applications, automation in accounting'. Brougham et al. (2019) note that STAARA (Smart Technology, Artificial intelligence, Automation, Robotics, and Algorithms) is driving fundamental changes in society, especially within business and employment. Goodwin (2015) summarizes these changes by noting the world's largest taxi company (Uber) largely owns few vehicles, while the world's largest accommodation provider (Airbnb) owns little real estate, and the world's biggest retailers (Amazon and Alibaba) largely hold minimal inventory compared to the traditional business models. This has occurred because technology has allowed for monumental disruption. Instead of firms holding assets, they operate platforms that connect individual asset owners (e.g., houses, vehicles) to those seeking momentary access to such assets (e.g., Airbnb and Uber customers). It is the platform that is ultimately the tool, whether for social interactions (e.g., Facebook and TikTok) or business contacts (e.g., LinkedIn). Interestingly, these 'platforms' have market captializations in the billions of dollars. Indeed, Facebook employs nearly 50,000 employees and had a market valuation of over US$700 billion in mid-2020. But it operates largely as a platform linking people generated content with other people and organizational news.

Such technological disruption has led to important strategic issues, which have been noted for decades. For example, the average life expectancy of a Fortune 500 company changed from averaging 67 years in the 1920s, to averaging 33 years by 1965, and now forecasting the average could drop to less than 15 years by 2026 (Ioannou, 2014; Mochari, 2016). Hence, the speed and rapid change being brought about by technology has created large scale change in societies. The present chapter seeks to broadly capture the examples of STAARA with a specific focus on the workforce. Here, the links tend towards the job insecurity literature, and the relationships between such insecurity and technological disruption. We explore the insecurity literature aligned with STAARA and note that the rapid potential for change

might signal a new era in insecurity perceptions from technological change that is unprecedented. We then focus on these literatures towards wellbeing and detail the largely detrimental effects of these factors towards employee wellbeing. However, we also seek to highlight areas where technology more broadly might play a role in shaping employee wellbeing positively. Following that, we identify important gaps in the literature around the linkages between STAARA and employee wellbeing and outline a future agenda for research. Ultimately, we argue that disruption from STAARA is happening and is likely to impact on how employees perceive their job security and careers. This has important implications for managing employees, which we discuss.

STAARA AND CHANGE

Fundamentally, change in business is increasing at a faster pace (Brougham et al., 2019; Brougham and Haar, 2020) and this has potentially massive implications for employment. For example, Brougham et al. (2019: 21) stated that 'traditional businesses are likely to need to make changes to existing processes and cut costs to remain competitive. The automation of human labour can be a cost-effective way of bringing down overheads within an organisation'. It is here, where technological disruption is likely to be seen in the workplace, that much of the consternation and anxiety arises. Indeed, it has been noted by Heatley (2020: iii) that 'robots, artificial intelligence (AI) and other digital technologies have become very newsworthy', and this 'news coverage is overwhelmingly pessimistic – for individuals and society in general'. The seminal work on the potential for technological disruption to impact jobs was conducted by Frey and Osborne (2013), where they grouped jobs/occupations into risk categories on a spectrum of probabilities. They hypothesized that '47% of total

US employment is at risk' (2013: 1) from being replaced by new technologies. However, they did note that these replacements might occur 'relatively soon, perhaps over the next decade or two' (Frey and Osborne, 2013: 48).

Brougham et al. (2018: 184) stated that job losses can occur because 'automation of a person's job may be considered a raw competition between technology and human labour'. Brougham and Haar (2018) highlight the cost of retail self-checkout systems being relatively low (and falling), and suggest even at current prices, the overall time period for such technology to pay for itself from saved labour costs means they are a financially viable option for retail owners. Another example is Uber, which as a platform might have replaced many taxi drivers, but whereby a driverless vehicle might replace taxi drivers and Uber drivers one day. Indeed, transportation is a major 'flashpoint' for automation specifically, with driverless trucks and other vehicles estimated at replacing potentially millions of drivers in the US economy alone (Solon, 2016). Indeed, driverless trucks have been around for some time (e.g., Bellamy and Pravica, 2011), with Frey and Osborne (2013) calculating the probability of replacement is high at 79%. However, the road testing of driverless trucks has been marred with failures (e.g., Jamasmie, 2019; Krisher, 2019), and a driverless vehicle – with a human driver as backup – suffered a fatal crash (Vlasic and Boudette, 2016). Further, pedestrians have suffered fatal run-ins with driverless cars (e.g., Pavia, 2018).

It has been predicted by Gartner (a global research/advisory firm) that autonomous driving level 4 is still over ten years away (Panetta, 2019). However, driverless technology offers us an example of how often technology may not make a sweeping snap change but evolves slowly over time. Consider a modern car now, with GPS, lane departure warnings, ABS brakes, traction control, stability control, autonomous braking, cruise control, blind-spot detection, heads-up display and alarms that sound when you are over the speed limit, etc. These improvements have occurred incrementally over a long time. Indeed, it is some of these incremental changes that move us towards this driverless future. The same can be said about some office work, where some tasks become automated over time. It is not the entire job that is automated at once, but parts that change over time, as we move towards full automation of some tasks and some jobs.

Ironically, as the driverless technology is widely hyped – and perhaps 'over-hyped' (Eliot, 2019) – in some countries there are a shortage of truck drivers. In New Zealand, it has been noted there is a major skills shortage in the transportation industry (Boot, 2016), mainly truck drivers, with Brougham and Haar (2017) suggesting that attention to automation and the perceived grim future might be partially to blame (as well as long hours and conditions etc.). Brougham and Haar (2017: 14) stated, 'while other reasons for this skills shortage exist, the threat of automation of this job could be a relevant factor preventing new employees from entering this profession, thus adding further to this skills shortage'. Hence, an expectation of replacement might stop employees entering industries where they would expect to be ultimately replaced. For example, on the one hand, Frey and Osborne (2013) noted that it might be one to two decades for these technological disruptions to occur, while alternatively, the popular press asks: 'Will a robot take your job?' (BBC, 2015). Such attention can bring the threat of technological disruptions to the forefront of employees and those seeking training which might create job decisions well in advance of any actual technological disruptions.

The reasons STAARA disruptions might impact the workforce are multiple, but Brougham et al. (2018) argued the low cost was an important factor. They noted robot technology is easy to integrate into organizations and does not require rebuilding a workspace like it used to. Related to the low cost of buying such technology is the important point that a robotic workforce can 'work 24 hours a day, seven days a week without a break' (Brougham et al., 2018: 185). The lack of sick or annual leave, injury compensation and other overheads make such robotics a potential cost saver. Indeed, Foxconn, the makers of iPhones and Samsung hardware, replaced 60,000 workers with factory robots (Wakefield, 2016). These robotic arms move and solder intricate materials (e.g., smartphone motherboards) that might be labour intensive roles for humans. They can also work in cleanrooms limiting the risk of contamination of products. In turn, this cleaner production reduces the cost of rejects and thus increases the efficiency of production.

Such technology has also led to *dark sites*, which are solely an automated workplace, where no lights are needed (Eder, 2018). Eder (2018) conducted a study on managers dealing with robot warehousing and found 'a domino effect in warehousing automation: dark warehouses are smaller, more compact and more efficient, which allows companies to set up shop closer to urban centers, thereby reducing transportation costs' (2018: n.p.). Related to the above comments around the transportation sector, Eder (2018) noted that the ability to place dark warehousing closer to customers also makes drones a potential for firms like Amazon, and this reduced distance to the customer means trucking investments can be lowered, 'which accounts for two million jobs and a $700B industry' (2018: n.p.). Hence, the job losses from STAARA in transportation might also be taken by other STAARA technology. Clearly, the technology provides a wide range of options and outcomes, making all future scenarios hard to predict and account for.

Despite this lack of certainty, recent studies still explore the potential impact of technological disruptions on jobs and careers. In 2015, the Frey and Osborne model was adapted to the New Zealand environment and estimated some 46% of the workforce

in New Zealand faced a high risk of job loss due to automation (Chartered Accountants Australia New Zealand and New Zealand Institute of Economic Research, 2015). This estimate ranged from a low of 12% for professional jobs and a high of 75% for labouring jobs (Chartered Accountants Australia New Zealand and New Zealand Institute of Economic Research, 2015). Further exploration of the Frey and Osborne model was carried out on the OECD, and here the risk of replacement from technology was estimated at 57% of jobs (Citigroup, 2016). In 2017, a study estimated that 40% of New Zealand organizations have considered investing in technology including robotics (Smylie, 2016), highlighting how these themes are starting to shape management decision making. This trend continues to rise year on year (MAIA Financial, 2018) as more organizations explore automation.

Importantly, the effects of technological disruption *may* shape all economies, with The World Bank (2016) arguing technological disruption could potentially impact developing nations as well as developed economies. Despite these troubling statistics, they are just estimating. Arntz et al. (2017) have estimated that technological disruptions leading to job losses might be much lower – below 10%. However, Brougham et al. (2019: 22) remind us that 'even at the lower estimate, 9 per cent of jobs being disrupted within a short amount of time would pose a substantial challenge to many countries'. Whether these changes might occur in a short time is still unknown. We next provide a sample of *potential* workplace changes because of STAARA disruptions and their *potential* impacts in Table 39.1. Here we look to detail some examples of STAARA related replacements, and whether these changes are likely to fully replace the human workforce, or simply remove certain roles (part replacement), or augment them.

In respect to Table 39.1, we urge readers to keep in mind that a large proportion of workforces are employed in retail, fast-food and

Table 39.1   STAARA examples and impacts.

Current job/work	Potential STAARA replacement or augmentation	Full or part replacement
Truckdriver, taxi, Uber driver, courier	Driverless vehicles, drones etc.	Full
Accountant	AI software – extending existing software such as Xero.	Partial
Builder/labourer	Robotic worker, e.g., carrying heavy items. STAARA exists that can 3-D print a house, build a wall, lay a cobblestone pathway, etc.	Partial
Paralegal, basic researcher	AI software – although this will require initial programming.	Partial
Teaching aide, hospital aide	AI software that marks, physical robot overseeing students (e.g., sports etc.).	Full
Checkout operator and retail workers	Self-checkout systems, AI for buying online.	Full
Security guards, police, military	Augmented with robots and AI.	Partial
Warehouse worker	Robots, AI for inventory.	Full
Dangerous jobs, e.g., firefighters, life savers, sea rescues	Robots and AI software for decision making.	Partial
TV and movie actors	AI software (assuming full mimicry of human emotion).	Partial
Customer service	Chat bot and other AI software.	Full
Fast food, short order cooks, chef assistants	Robotic chefs exist.	Partial
Manufacturing jobs	Robotic arms can replicate large portions of jobs.	Full

driving jobs. Despite the arguments around STAARA disruption potentially leading to large scale job losses, other experts are less adamant about STAARA creating job *losses*. Indeed, Brougham et al. (2019: 21) argued that 'automation does not need to do the entire job of one person; it simply needs to do part/s of the job', and this might include the more mundane and 'boring' aspects of work. For example, AI algorithms might aid lawyers seeking out specific case law. Teachers might have their marking done largely through AI. Indeed, this option might also provide detailed feedback and guidance to aid student learning and highlight critical and/or common issues. For another example, imagine a researcher asking the university's AI programme to provide a detailed report on a topic and the next day this is provided, sorted into themes and all associated references provided. The ability to fundamentally make a strong start to work might save researchers considerable time. Brougham et al. (2018) argued that STAARA might lead to role changes rather than job losses. They suggested, for example, that automating repetitive tasks might enable workers to be more focused on customers and generate higher creativity than what is currently achieved in roles.

In the New Zealand context, a forecast of job creation/destruction by McKinsey and Company (2019) provided a balanced view. They forecast in their mid-point scenario that earlier adoption of technologies (e.g., STAARA) would result in higher unemployment, with potentially 21% of work being automated by 2030. However, they also suggested that net employment growth would occur, especially in major cities. Overall, they noted that while workforce reductions would occur in administrative, trade and manual jobs, there would be employment growth in roles associated with managerial, technical and associated professional, service and retail jobs. Similarly, research on almost 1,900 futurists found 52% predicted that STAARA would create more jobs than they displaced in the near future (Bercovici, 2014), highlighting the unknown and divided view of the future. However, futurists predict that new jobs created are likely to be low pay and remain less secure than current levels of job security (Bercovici, 2014). Indeed, McKinsey and Company (2019) forecast that while skilled workers (managers' and professionals') pay is expected to increase due to technological disruption, low-skilled workers' pay is likely to fall.

Despite expectations that new jobs will be created (Deloitte, 2015; Scarpetta, 2016), specific details on what these new jobs will be remains scant. Indeed, using economic analysis, Moretti (2010) argues that for every job lost to technological disruption, there will be roughly five jobs gained. However, the specific details around types of jobs are not provided. Overall, Moretti's (2010) analysis suggest low-skilled jobs lead to a low number of additional low-skilled jobs gained, but with the opposite for high-skilled jobs. Thus, one-way technological disruption that might lead to job *growth* might be through producing new professional and managerial jobs that subsequently lead to more skilled jobs occurring. Similarly, Autor (2015: 5) states that 'automation also complements labor, raises output in ways that lead to higher demand for labor, and interacts with adjustments in labor supply'. These positive linkages with technological disruptions concur with analysis from the UK.

Deloitte (2015) researched employment patterns in the UK over the past 15 years and reported that 'the UK has benefited from a technology-driven shift from low-skill, routine jobs to higher skill, non-routine occupations', and while '800,000 jobs have been lost … nearly 3.5 million new ones have been created' (2015: 2). Hence, this supports Moretti's (2010) argument of more jobs being created than destroyed. Importantly, these new jobs were paid approximately £10,000/annum more than the jobs they replaced. Hence, there are strong benefits from a general growth in higher-skilled occupations. Regarding directions around jobs, the Deloitte (2015: 2) report stated that 'future businesses will need more skills, including: digital know-how, management capability, creativity, entrepreneurship and complex problem solving'.

The lack of specific details around new jobs and careers aligns with the nature of technological disruptions. No one fully understands what new jobs and careers will be created as the fourth industrial revolution begins to play out. Clearly, this will involve new creations: robots, computer programming, AI, but also maintenance related to these new creations. But, as alluded to by Deloitte (2015), a workforce upskilled on problem solving (e.g., managing the mix of humans and STAARA), but also being more creative and entrepreneurial will enable firms to flourish and grow, leading to business success and further employment. Berlin (2017) highlighted that jobs in science, technology, engineering and mathematics (STEM) would be the most difficult to automate. Berlin (2017) argued that humans (versus robots and AI) can provide unique contributions to the workplace including creativity and the 'human touch' and highlighted the importance of emotional intelligence, teaching, character and perseverance. In summary, STAARA is going to cause changes to the global workforce and this might be especially felt among low-skilled workers. However, whether employment changes will be largely detrimental remains open for debate.

STAARA RESEARCH

The unknown associated with the growth of STAARA has led to top business leaders and thought leaders including Elon Musk, Bill Gates and Stephen Hawking issuing warnings and raising concerns (Bort, 2014; Lynch, 2015; Shead, 2020). For example, Bill Gates commented on technology taking over jobs and suggested the need to be careful when there are advances:

Indeed, the attention towards STAARA in the broad media and among researchers is predominantly exploring these employment disruptions – whether real or imagined. However, Autor (2015) noted an important aspect of the attention around STAARA, stating 'a key observation … is that journalists and even expert commentators tend to overstate the extent of machine substitution for human labor and ignore the strong complementarities between automation and labor that increase productivity, raise earnings, and augment demand for labor' (2015: 5). Despite the growth of technology and, indeed, the over-hyped nature of technological disruptions (Eliot, 2019), not a lot of research has been conducted around the impact of STAARA on employee wellbeing. Only recently has such research begun to be conducted, much because of the negative attention noted above (Eliot, 2019). The next section details the theoretical approaches to understanding STAARA and its impact on wellbeing, followed by wellbeing specific research, and then other employee research in general.

Much of the research on the effect of STAARA on employee outcomes relates to job insecurity. Job insecurity has been defined as 'expectations about continuity in a job situation' (Davy et al., 1997: 323), and 'concern about the future permanence of the job' (van Vuuren and Klandermans, 1990: 133). This is clearly highly aligned with STAARA disruptions due to the issue around the future permanence of a job. Having media, for example the BBC (2015) asking 'Will a robot take your job?' and media reporting on an estimation that '47% of total US employment is at risk' (Frey and Osborne, 2013: 1), can shape and frame the context for worker perceptions that robots and technology will take your job – and perhaps, any job! However, seldom does the media report that such changes may take over 20 years to occur! Indeed, Douglas et al. (2017) note the role that technological innovations have played with growing job insecurity, as well as leading to greater job precarity.

Overall, there is strong meta-analytic support for job insecurity impacting wellbeing. The meta-analysis by Sverke et al. (2002) reported a corrected correlation between job insecurity and mental health of $-.23$, and between job insecurity and physical health of $-.16$. In the context of the earlier STAARA discussion, these detrimental effects from job insecurity were more detrimental among manual workers versus high-skilled professionals. Specifically, low-skilled workers links between job insecurity and mental health were $-.35$, highlighting these detrimental pressures are felt more by low-skilled workers. In another meta-analysis, Cheng and Chan (2008) reported a corrected correlation between job insecurity on psychological health of $-.28$ and with physical health of $-.23$. Fundamentally, employees who perceive their job is potentially under threat – even if that is 'just perceived' – are more likely to have their wellbeing detrimentally affected. Hence, there are clear links between worrying about one's job and having poorer wellbeing.

Brougham and Haar (2017, 2018, in press) have conducted empirical research specifically on employee perceptions around whether employees see STAARA as leading to job losses. In their 2018 work, they found these STAARA perceptions around future job insecurity due to technological disruption were only modestly correlated to job insecurity perceptions (at .11). This suggests that employees recognize and perceive job insecurity relating to STAARA as quite distinct from the normal perception of job insecurity. Importantly, aligned with the meta-analyses (Sverke et al., 2002; Cheng and Chan, 2008), Brougham and Haar (2018) found STAARA perceptions were more detrimental towards employee mental health (depression and cynicism) than those of job insecurity. Indeed, their regression analysis showed that their STAARA perception was the dominant predictor, after controlling for job insecurity. Lu (2019) warned that technology like STAARA – especially AI – can lead 'humans … [to] become more and more scared: they will be replaced by machines, their motivation of learning and working will be reduced' (2019: 22). Such opinions are echoed in the literature (e.g., Dasoriya et al., 2018; Tan and Lim, 2018), but empirical evidence relating to these linkages is sparse.

Early work at the turn of the millennium looked at employee perceptions around advanced manufacturing technology leading to unemployment (Vieitez et al., 2001), and this was negatively related to wellbeing, with worse anxiety and depression. Further, Hinks (2020) explored perceptions of almost 20,000 Europeans and found a significant negative relationship between fear of robots and life satisfaction, further highlighting the potential for negative links between STAARA and wellbeing. Beyond mental health, these perceptions around STAARA taking employee jobs have also been found to relate negatively to organizational commitment and career satisfaction and positively towards turnover intentions (Brougham and Haar, 2018). Using the same STAARA construct within a hotel context, Li et al. (2019) found employees who thought STAARA around AI and robotics might replace them were more likely to seek to leave their job.

Lu et al. (2020) acknowledged that technological disruptions and STAARA could potentially lead to negative consequences including psychological outcomes, and how the potential for higher job insecurity is detrimental. However, Lu et al. (2020) are one of the few sources advocating potentially positive outcomes from STAARA. They suggested that potential benefits from STAARA for employees might include a reduction in routine work, which is one of the factors that can shape STAARA insecurity around work (Brougham and Haar, 2017). Lu et al. (2020) advocated that such changes might also enhance job performance and augment employees' cognitive ability and, ultimately, lead to enhanced job satisfaction. They also posited that 'opportunities for human-robot collaboration' (Lu et al., 2020: 375) would exist, perhaps in the health sector. Here the robot (with accompanying AI) might provide initial diagnosis and monitoring, with a human doctor or nurse using this information to provide more timely and accurate services to patients, enhancing the overall health and wellbeing of hospital patients. Imagine a doctor being able to see information through technology that they cannot currently see; This might enhance patient care, make the doctor/surgeon more satisfied in their work, and even lead to positive human–robot relationships. Indeed, future research might seek to understand a unified bond between humans and their technological tools.

Steijn et al. (2016: 25) identified a number of benefits of STAARA technology, including 'opportunities for businesses to achieve greater productivity at lower costs and at a better standard of quality (greater precision). Robots are also capable of taking over physically demanding, repetitive, or dangerous work from people'. For example, Nagatani et al. (2013) discussed mobile rescue robots for use at the Fukushima Daiichi Nuclear Power Plants accident site. For this extreme location, they had to test existing robots to ensure they could operate in such extreme conditions, which ultimately were retrofitted to include wired connections because wireless communication was impossible. So rather than clearing radioactive waste by hand as they did in the Chernobyl disaster, robots were used to clean up the site. In these conditions, humans could not operate safely, and as such, STAARA might provide solutions to dangerous activities and worksites.

Robotic alternatives to humans for firefighting would likely save lives. Imagine fleets of drones in the air or robots on the land with fire repellant in places with major wildfires raging, as we have seen in Australia and California. Thus, technology might enhance the activity (i.e., firefighting) and save the lives of firefighters as well. Zech (2018: n.p.) noted that German scientists are designing 'rescue robots that can act autonomously to a certain extent and perform more complex tasks'. In the Covid-19 pandemic, Murphy et al. (2020: n.p.) highlight that robots have allowed 'health care workers to remotely take temperatures and measure blood pressure and oxygen saturation from patients hooked up to a ventilator'. Other robots disinfect hospital wards with ultraviolet light, bring food to quarantined people, and drones ferry test samples to laboratories. Overall, this has ensured that medical staff and researchers have their personal safety maximized. Here, STAARA disruption has become a potential life saver for human workers.

In summary, the links between technology around STAARA and employee wellbeing are mixed. There are clearly safety issues where robots, in conjunction with AI, do and will provide greater employee safety. Automation may also help with the dirty, dull and dangerous parts of the job. This is clearly positive and beneficial. However, such advances do come at a cost. Workers could lose their jobs and be replaced by STAARA. Importantly, we know that even now, where wholesale job losses through technological disruptions have yet to really occur, it is the perception around these potential job losses that is highly detrimental to wellbeing. Aligned with the general effects on physical and mental health, we find that STAARA perceptions around job losses are detrimental, not only to mental health but also to work attitudes and behaviours, highlighting the broad effect the wide attention to technological disruptions can play.

FUTURE STAARA RESEARCH

Overall, there is a greater need for more research linking STAARA and technological disruptions with employee outcomes including wellbeing. Fundamentally, technology is changing society and organizational life. Ask any truck driver or business owner in the transportation industry what they may think about driverless vehicles and their response is likely to be one of (a) 'doom and gloom', (b) false bravado that everything is fine, or perhaps (c) measured insight by saying 'the future is not here yet, this is miles away!' That said, all these responses might come with anxiety as the future changes are likely to make people worry. Hence, further research around the linkages between STAARA job losses and wellbeing is needed. How do employees cope with this uncertainty? We know from Brougham and Haar (2018) that younger workers are especially affected by these insecurities, probably because they are more attuned to technology and have a much longer career ahead of them to consider this. But are there ways that STAARA is *positively* shaping wellbeing? We need more research specifically on this potentially positive aspect.

During 2020, as we write this chapter, there has been a large global experiment around working from home (due to widespread global lockdowns due to the Covid-19 pandemic), employees because they have been able to work remotely and make social connections via technology (e.g., online or phone/mobile). Exploring the job changes that workers have experienced over time – driven by technology (STAARA) – would be a useful way to examine these changes. This might include the reduction in size, weight and cost of computers until we have laptops and tablets which are extremely common in businesses. The Pew Research Foundation (Smith, 2017) reported that within the United States, 77% of the population have a smartphone, 51% a tablet and 73% broadband at home (Smith, 2017). While smartphones and similar technology have been criticized for bringing work into the home (Diaz et al., 2012), there is little exploration of the potentially positive side to these relationships. Given the hype around STAARA and job losses, acknowledging the potential benefits from technology to job and work options is needed to provide a balanced approach to this literature. While working from home is beneficial (Gajendran and Harrison, 2007) and has become more popular due to technology, we suggest additional fruitful avenues for research might be found by exploring how technology has changed the work employees do, for example acknowledging the removal of routine or mundane aspects due to STAARA advancements. This has the potential to make jobs more enjoyable and positive.

Indeed, research by Brougham et al. (2019: 21) noted, in the context of STAARA, that 'many employees are generally *optimistic* about the future of work and their long-term careers, with them acknowledging potential job changes around automation, but with a strong belief their type of work will remain'. One respondent in that qualitative study commented that while they did not think their construction role could be replaced by STAARA, they did have a sound rationale for their opinion. They stated:

> The amount [of] problem solving and public liaison required in my role makes the idea unrealistic in the next 10 years. I do, however, believe certain parts of my role could be replaced which would allow me to focus on other aspects, reducing potential issues in other areas that may have occurred due to lack of attention. (Brougham et al., 2019: 27)

This shows good understanding by the employee around the soft skills and 'human touch' that makes their job harder for STAARA to replace. Further understanding of this optimism and perhaps how workers see the changing technology – as it relates to their work – might be fruitful for uncovering beneficial (and other detrimental) effects. Also, researching how employees cope with these pressures would be insightful. Are they active and seeking out training opportunities, or do they ignore the situation and hope the 'robots' simply will not come for their job? We do not know, but understanding these distinctions would enrich our understanding of the impact of technology and the future of work on the organizational lives of employees.

CONCLUSION

This chapter has highlighted the growing changes around technology, with the resulting technological disruption. Clearly, many experts and futurists foresee the potential for a detrimental future for society around STAARA's impact on work, especially for low-skilled workers. However, that is clearly not universal, with some research work (Deloitte, 2015) examining historical data and finding that job growth – in higher-paying roles – may well result from STAARA related redundancy. As such, it is rash to suggest that STAARA can only be detrimental. That said, the hyped attention to robots (e.g., driverless vehicles) has likely left employees having concern for their future of work, and this has major implications for their wellbeing. Perhaps governments need to signal more broadly their willingness to facilitate retraining of workforces if STAARA impacts broad professions. Further, perhaps acknowledging these technological disruptions might be 10–20 years out is also one way to more accurately contextualize these potential changes.

Further, employers might seek to operate a business model whereby the employment of humans – and the development of their workforce – is seen as fundamental for good business operations. Perhaps this is viewed as good ethical behaviour within firms? There are clear linkages between technology and employee wellbeing, but the current strong focus on negatives and detrimental effects appears too narrow. We hope this chapter will encourage students, researchers, employers, governments and wider stakeholders to better understand the technology forces driving employee perceptions today and react in a positive and more caring manner around the adoption of technology. Finally, we need to remember that technological disruptions have been occurring for centuries. This is a natural pattern within our world. For example, people moving from farms to factories and then to the service sector over the centuries. Understanding what might occur – and employees being nimble and skilled in the 'human side' of their work – might lead to better employment opportunities for all in the future.

REFERENCES

Arntz, M., Gregory, T., & Zierahn, U. (2017). Revisiting the risk of automation. *Economics Letters*, 159, 157–160.

Autor, D. H. (2015). Why are there still so many jobs? The history and future of workplace automation. *Journal of Economic Perspectives*, 29(3), 7–30.

BBC News (2015). *Will a robot take your job?* 11 September 2015. Retrieved 1 August 2020, from www.bbc.com/news/technology-34066941

Bellamy, D., & Pravica, L. (2011). Assessing the impact of driverless haul trucks in Australian surface mining. *Resources Policy*, 36, 149–158.

Bercovici, J. (2014). Pew finds experts divided on whether robots will be good for society. *Forbes.com*, 12-12.

Berlin, O. (2017). Automation nation: Will advances in technology put people out of work or give them new purpose? *State Legislatures*, 9, 8.

Boot, S. (2016). New Zealand's truck driver shortage. *New Zealand Listener*, 8 April 2016. Retrieved 6 August 2020, from www.noted.co.nz/money/investment/new-zealands-truck-driver-shortage/

Bort, J. (2014). Bill Gates: People don't realise how many jobs will soon be replaced by software bots. *Business Insider*. 14 March 2014. Retrieved 1 August 2020, from https://www.businessinsider.com.au/bill-gates-bots-are-taking-away-jobs-2014-3?r=US&IR=T

Brougham, D., & Haar, J. (2017). Employee assessment of their technological redundancy. *Labour & Industry: A Journal of the Social and Economic Relations of Work*, 27(3), 213–231.

Brougham, D., & Haar, J. (2018). Smart technology, artificial intelligence, robotics, and algorithms (STARA): Employees' perceptions of our future workplace. *Journal of Management & Organization*, 24(2), 239–257.

Brougham, D., & Haar, J. (2020). Technological disruption and employment: The influence on job insecurity and turnover intentions: A multi-country study. *Technological Forecasting and Social Change*, 161, 120276.

Brougham, D., Haar, J., & Olliver-Gray, Y. (2018). Will my job be taken by a robot? In M. Baird & J. Parker (Eds), *The Big Issues in Employment: HR Management and Employment Relations in Australasia*. Wellington, CCH New Zealand.

Brougham, D., Haar, J. M., & Tootell, B. (2019). Service sector employee insights into the future of work and technological disruption. *New Zealand Journal of Employment Relations*, 44(1), 21–36.

Chartered Accountants Australia New Zealand and New Zealand Institute of Economic Research. (2015). *Disruptive technologies: Risks, opportunities – Can New Zealand make the most of them?* 21 December 2016. Retrieved 7 August 2020, from www.charteredaccountantsanz.com//media/19de99aacee74c1dbae36b4d620e94bb.ashx

Cheng, G. H. L., & Chan, D. K. S. (2008). Who suffers more from job insecurity? A meta-analytic review. *Applied Psychology: An International Review*, 57(2), 272–303.

Citigroup. (2016). *Technology at work v2.0: The future is not what it used to be.*

Retrieved 1 August 2020, from www.oxfordmartin.ox.ac.uk/downloads/reports/Citi_GPS_Technology_Work_2.pdf

CNBC-TV18 (2019). AI has huge potential, but its impact on jobs is an issue, says Bill Gates. *CNBC-TV18*, 18 November 2019. Retrieved 1 August 2020, from www.cnbctv18.com/ms/future-of-work/article/ai-has-huge-potential-but-its-impact-on-jobs-is-an-issue-says-bill-gates-4719581.htm

Dasoriya, R., Rajpopat, J., Jamar, R., & Maurya, M. (2018, January). The uncertain future of artificial intelligence. In *2018 8th International Conference On Cloud Computing, Data Science & Engineering* (confluence) (pp. 458–461). Noida: IEEE. DOI:10.1109/CONFLUENCE.2018.8442945

Davy, J. A., Kinicki, A. J., & Scheck, C. L. (1997). A test of job insecurity's direct and mediated effects on withdrawal cognitions. *Journal of Organizational Behavior*, 18, 323–349.

Deloitte. (2015). *From brawn to brains The impact of technology on jobs in the UK.* Online: Deloitte. Retrieved 20 January 2020, from https://www2.deloitte.com/uk/en/pages/growth/articles/from-brawn-to-brains--the-impact-of-technology-on-jobs-in-the-u.html

Diaz, I., Chiaburu, D. S., Zimmerman, R. D., & Boswell, W. R. (2012). Communication technology: Pros and cons of constant connection to work. *Journal of Vocational Behavior*, 80, 500–508.

Douglas, J., Haar, J., & Harris, C. (2017). Job insecurity and job burnout: Does union membership buffer the detrimental effects? *New Zealand Journal of Human Resources Management*, 17(2), 23–40.

Eder, S. (2018). *Dark warehouses pave a bright future for the Internet of Things (IoT).* 12 July 2018. Retrieved 1 August 2020, from www.newtonx.com/insights/2018/07/12/dark-warehouses-pave-bright-future-internet-things-iot/

Eliot, L. (2019). Let's not get too excited by self-driving truck highway stunts. *Forbes*, 16 December 2019. Retrieved 1 August 2020, from www.forbes.com/sites/lanceeliot/2019/12/16/lets-not-butter-up-those-self-driving-truck-highway-stunts/#3791c96d23d5

Frey, C. B., & Osborne, M. A. (2013). *The future of employment: How susceptible are jobs to computerisation?* Retrieved 1 August 2020, from www.oxfordmartin.ox.ac.uk/downloads/academic/future-of-employment.pdf

Gajendran, R. S., & Harrison, D. A. (2007). The good, the bad, and the unknown about telecommuting: Meta-analysis of psychological mediators and individual consequences. *Journal of Applied Psychology*, 92(6), 1524–1541.

Goodwin, T. (2015). *The battle is for the customer interface.* Retrieved 20 January 2020, from https://techcrunch.com/2015/03/03/in-the-age-of-disintermediation-the-battle-is-all-for-the-customer-interface/

Heatley, D. (2020). *New Zealanders' attitudes towards robots and AI.* Research Note 2020/1, New Zealand Productivity Commission. Retrieved 20 April 2020, from https://www.productivity.govt.nz/research/attitudes-towards-robots-and-ai/

Hinks, T. (2020). Fear of robots and life satisfaction. *International Journal of Social Robotics*, 1–14. https://doi.org/10.1007/s12369-020-00640-1

Ioannou, L. (2014). *A decade to mass extinction event in S&P 500.* Retrieved 20 January 2020, from http://www.cnbc.com/2014/06/04/15-years-to-extinction-sp-500-companies.html

Jamasmie, C. (2019). *Not so autonomous: Wifi outage results in driverless truck crash at Fortescue mine.* 15 February 2019. Retrieved 1 August 2020, from www.mining.com/driverless-trucks-not-flawless-two-crash-fortescue-mine-australia/

Kendall, G. (2019). Apollo 11 anniversary: Could an iPhone fly me to the moon? *The Independent*, 9 July 2019. Retrieved 1 August 2020, from www.independent.co.uk/news/science/apollo-11-moon-landing-mobile-phones-smartphone-iphone-a8988351.html

Krisher, T. (2019). Feds: Truck driver likely caused self-driving shuttle crash. *AP News*, 12 July 2019. Retrieved 1 August 2020, from https://apnews.com/d23ec315a3684591bab1f7a04ec2ed4f

Li, J. J., Bonn, M. A., & Ye, B. H. (2019). Hotel employee's artificial intelligence and robotics awareness and its impact on turnover intention: The moderating roles of perceived organizational support and competitive psychological climate. *Tourism Management, 73*, 172–181.

Lu, Y. (2019). Artificial intelligence: a survey on evolution, models, applications and future trends. *Journal of Management Analytics, 6*(1), 1–29.

Lu, V. N., Wirtz, J., Kunz, W. H., Paluch, S., Gruber, T., Martins, A., & Patterson, P. G. (2020). Service robots, customers and service employees: What can we learn from the academic literature and where are the gaps? *Journal of Service Theory and Practice, 30*(3), 361–391.

Lynch, C. (2015). Stephen Hawking on the future of capitalism and inequality. *Counter-Punch*, 15 October 2015. Retrieved 6 August 2020, from www.counterpunch.org/2015/10/15/stephen-hawkings-on-the-tuture-of-capitalism-and-inequality

MAIA Financial. (2018). *Equipment Demand Index, new year, new growth. MAIA Financial*. Retrieved 7 August 2020, from www.maiafinancial.com.au/wp-content/uploads/2018/02/EDI-NZ-Feb-2018-v2.pdf

McKinsey & Company. (2019). *future of work tripartite forum: evidence base on the future of work*. 26 February 2019. Retrieved 1 August 2020, from https://treasury.govt.nz/sites/default/files/2019-04/fowtf-evidence-base-4080406.PDF

Mochari. (2016). *why half of the s&p 500 companies will be replaced in the next decade*. Retrieved January 2020, from https://www.inc.com/ilan-mochari/innosight-sp-500-new-companies.html

Moretti, E. (2010). Local multipliers. *American Economic Review: Papers and Proceedings, 100*, 1–7.

Murphy, R., Adams, J., & Gandudi, V. B. M. (2020). Robots are playing many roles in the coronavirus crisis – and offering lessons for future disasters. *The Conversation*. Retrieved 6 August 2020, from https://theconversation.com/robots-are-playing-many-roles-in-the-coronavirus-crisis-and-offering-lessons-for-future-disasters-135527

Nagatani, Keiji, Seiga Kiribayashi, Yoshito Okada, Kazuki Otake, Kazuya Yoshida, Satoshi Tadokoro, Takeshi Nishimura, Eiji Koyanagi, Mineo Fukushima, Shinji Kawatsuma (2013). Emergency response to the nuclear accident at the Fukushima Daiichi Nuclear Power Plants using mobile rescue robots. *Journal of Field Robotics, 30*, no. 1 (2013): 44–63.

Newzoo. (2019). *Newzoo Global Mobile Market Report 2019: Light Version*. Retrieved 3 August 2020, from https://newzoo.com/insights/trend-reports/newzoo-global-mobile-market-report-2019-light-version/

Panetta, K. (2019). *Gartner 2019 hype cycle for emerging technologies: What's in it for AI leaders?* Retrieved 6 August 2020, from www.gartner.com/smarterwithgartner/5-trends-appear-on-the-gartner-hype-cycle-for-emerging-technologies-2019/

Pavia, W. (2018). Driverless Uber car 'not to blame' for woman's death. *The Times*, 21 March 2018. Retrieved 1 August 2020, from www.thetimes.co.uk/article/driverless-uber-car-not-to-blame-for-woman-s-death-klkbt7vf0

Scarpetta, S. (2016). *What future for work? The future of work policy forum. OECD Policy Forum Ministerial*. Retrieved 6 August 2020, from www.researchgate.net/profile/Stefano_Scarpetta/publication/295083048_What_future_for_work/links/5746c5dd08aea45ee856769a.pdf

Schwab, K. (2017). *The Fourth Industrial Revolution*. London: Penguin Books.

Shead, S. (2020). *Elon Musk has a complex relationship with the A.I. community. CNBC*, 13 May 2020. Retrieved 6 August 2020, from www.cnbc.com/2020/05/13/elon-musk-has-a-complex-relationship-with-the-ai-community.html?&qsearchterm=elonmusk-%20robots-will-take-your-jobs-government-will-have-to-pay-your-wage

Smith, A. (2017). Record shares of Americans now own smartphones, have home broadband. *Pew Research Foundation*. Retrieved 6 August 2020, from www.pewresearch.org/fact-tank/2017/01/12/evolution-of-technology/

Smylie, C. (2016). Kiwi businesses preparing for robot automation, research shows. *National Business Review*, 16 October 2016. Retrieved 6 August 2020, from www.nbr.co.nz/article/kiwi-businesses-preparing-robot-automation-research-shows-cs-p-195591

Solon, O. (2016). Self-driving trucks: What's the future for America's 3.5 million truckers? *Guardian News*. Retrieved 1 August 2020, from www.theguardian.com/technology/

2016/jun/17/self-driving-trucks-impact-on-drivers-jobs-us

Steijn, W., Luiijf, E., & van der Beek, D. (2016). *Emergent Risk to Workplace Safety as a Result of the Use of Robots in the Work Place*. Utrecht: TNO.

Sverke, M., Hellgren, J., & Näswall, K. (2002). No security: A meta-analysis and review of job insecurity and its consequences. *Journal of Occupational Health Psychology*, *7*(3), 242–264.

Tan, K. H., & Lim, B. P. (2018). The artificial intelligence renaissance: Deep learning and the road to human-level machine intelligence. *APSIPA Transactions on Signal and Information Processing*, 7(e6), 1–19.

The World Bank. (2016). *World Development Report 2016: Digital Dividends*. Washington, DC: World Bank. Retrieved 7 August 2020, from www.worldbank.org/en/publication/wdr2016

van Vuuren, C. V., & Klandermans, P. G. (1990). Individual reactions to job insecurity: An integrated model. In P. J. D. Drenth & J. A. Sergeant (Eds), *European Perspectives in Psychology* (pp. 133–146). Chichester: Wiley.

Vieitez, J. C., Carcía, A. D. L. T., & Rodríguez, M. T. V. (2001). Perception of job security in a process of technological change: Its influence on psychological well-being. *Behaviour & Information Technology*, *20*(3), 213–223.

Vlasic, B., & Boudette, N. E. (2016). Self-driving Tesla was involved in fatal crash, U.S. says. *The New York Times*, 30 June 2016. Retrieved 1 August 2020, from www.nytimes.com/2016/07/01/business/self-driving-tesla-fatal-crash-investigation.html

Wakefield, J. (2016). *Foxconn replaces '60,000 factory workers with robots'*. BBC News, 25 May 2016. Retrieved 1 August 2020, from www.bbc.com/news/technology-36376966

Zech, T. (2018). *Intelligent robots save lives. Deutschland.de*. 3 December 2018. Retrieved 6 August 2020, from www.deutschland.de/en/topic/business/artificial-intelligence-robots-will-save-lives

40

International and National Standards in Health, Safety and Wellbeing

Wilson Wong

INTRODUCTION

What Are International and National Standards?

Organizations large or small, and regardless of their sector or field of activity, use voluntary International and National Standards as a basis for consistent, coherent, evidence-based practice in a wide range of domains from technical standards in materials to environmental management, organizational governance, data security, and health and safety. Standards matter to governments as they provide a basis for public policy and amplify regulation. They matter to the standards users because they assure the quality, safety, characteristics and specification of a product or a service.

These standards, as standards do, provide an agreed way of doing something, for example the detailed technical specifications for making something or the quality requirements for management systems. Their aim is to provide a reliable basis for organizations and people to share the same expectations about a product or service. Standards are important to organizations that seek to optimize interoperability, safety and quality of their products and services. This requires the efficient coordination of systems and processes across increasingly complex supply chains, something assured by common standards. Organizations may work with voluntary standards in the form of frameworks, guidance, codes of practice or technical requirements to achieve particular outcomes. The most well-known are the ISO 14000 family on environmental management and the ISO 9000 family on Quality Management. ISO 9001:2015 *Quality management systems: Requirements* sets out the criteria for a quality management system. Over one million companies and organizations in over 170 countries are certified to ISO 9001: usually a prerequisite for their participation in global supply chains.

International and National Standards are developed through the collaboration and consensus of technical experts and interested parties like government agencies, industry, academia, special interest and user groups, and industry and employer bodies. By bringing together all the key stakeholders, an issue can be examined systemically, and a consensus built among the parties who contribute in some way to a successful outcome. For example, standards in ergonomics are likely to be delivered by a range of experts designing and implementing technology and tools which interact with human users. By bringing together technologists, designers, measurement experts, investors, users and customers, the aim is to find an optimal balance of competing priorities and risks, drawing upon best available evidence to guide practice.

In 2020, there are over 160 national standards bodies, of which BSI is one. These standard-setting bodies, and their expert groups, are organized into about 250 Technical Committees (TCs) based on industry domains of knowledge. All standards are usually reviewed at five-yearly intervals to take into account developments in research and practice; more frequently if developments accelerate. These reviews help confirm and mature the consensus around the shared (ethical) principles and values, the underpinning evidence and body of knowledge, and the necessary competencies / skills required to deliver the desired outcomes.

While voluntary, these standards are relied upon by industry in many sectors. During the Covid-19 pandemic in 2020, the BSI made available, freely, the European Standards for medical devices and Personal Protection Equipment (PPE) to support industries retooling to produce, safely, PPE and medical devices during an emergency. The BSI also made available a suite of standards on business continuity and risk management, and developed a rapidly updated *Safe working during the Covid-19 pandemic: General guidelines for organizations* which, while technically not a standard, provides an indication of the trust placed in such standards bodies and their experts by industry users.

National Standards and Their Committees

In the UK, the BSI, as the national standards body, publishes British Standards that are developed entirely within the UK by BSI committees. For example, the Human Capital Standards Committee (HCS / 1) is responsible for the development of people management Standards BS 76000: 2016 *Management system for valuing people in organizations: Requirements and guidance for use*; BS 76005: 2017 *Valuing people through diversity and inclusion (D&I): Code of practice for organizations*; and PD 76006: 2017 *Guide to learning and development.* HCS / 1 sub-committee HCS1 / 2 experts represent the UK at the ISO Technical Committee 260 (TC260) responsible for standards and standardization in human resource management. HCS / 1 / 2 welcomes academics, senior industry experts and adjacent subject matter experts to participate in the development and critique of human capital management (HCM) and Human Resource Management (HRM) Standards.

British Standards are developed using the processes set out in BS 0: 2016 *A standard for standards: Principles of standardization.* This means that the standard is developed by a process that involves a committee made up of key stakeholders and interested parties in the content and application of that particular domain; a transparent consultation of the draft standard enabling public scrutiny; and the principle of consensus, meaning that the content of the standard is decided by general agreement of as many as possible of the committee members, rather than by majority voting.

This process reinforces the authority of the standard and helps to ensure that it will be accepted by a very wide range of people who might be interested in applying it. This is a process widely replicated by many national bodies who develop national standards. The process is like that used by ISO, itself governed rigorously by the ISO / IEC Directives Part 1 (ISO, 2020) and Consolidated ISO Supplement, and ISO / IEC Directives Part 2 (ISO, 2018).

There are also Publicly Available Specifications (PAS). These are developed in response to a commission by an external sponsor who funds a resource-intensive process which allows it to be developed and published quickly to satisfy an immediate business need. PAS 3002: 2018 *Code of practice on improving health and wellbeing within an organization* will be discussed later in this chapter.

Some standards do not need to be backed by the same degree of public consultation and consensus. In many cases they are provisional and subject to further development based on experience gained during the first year or two of their use. These include standard-type documents that do not have the same status as British Standards and come under the catch-all category of Published Documents (PD). These can be developed at speed and an example is *PD 76006 Guide to learning and development*, which is a key source document for an ISO standard.

Categories of Standards

Most standards can also be categorized according to the function they need to perform. The most common is the *Specification*, which is a highly prescriptive standard setting out detailed absolute requirements. It is commonly used for product safety purposes or for other applications where a high degree of certainty and assurance is required by its user community. In ISO TC260, for example, all the people metrics are developed as Technical Specifications, ensuring that the formulae and ratios are consistently applied internationally, facilitating comparability and, in time, benchmarking.

Codes of practice recommend sound good practice as currently undertaken by competent practitioners. They are drafted to reflect the emergent nature of that body of knowledge and incorporate a degree of flexibility in their application, while offering reliable indicative benchmarks. An example of a Code of Practice is BS 76005 *Valuing people through diversity and inclusion*, a British Standard that is contributing to the development of a new ISO on diversity and inclusion (D&I).

Guides are published to give less prescriptive advice than Codes of Practice, which reflect the current thinking and practice among experts in a subject. Most of the Standards being developed by ISO TC260 are guidelines, reflecting the emergent nature of the evidence in people management. As terminology and human capital metrics converge, it is anticipated that there will be growing consensus as to what constitutes good practice. These standards may then evolve into *Management System Standards* (MSS).

A management system is the way in which an organization manages the interrelated parts of its business to achieve its objectives. ISO's MSS are some of the most widely used standards and are recognized by organizations. These include standards such as ISO 9001, ISO 14001 and ISO 50001, which apply to quality management, environmental management and energy management, respectively. In fact, there are more than 80 published MSS. BS 76000 *Management system for valuing people in organizations: Requirements and guidance for use* is a British Standard establishing the principles for how an organization demonstrates to its stakeholders that it values its people; this will be discussed later in the chapter.

A *Vocabulary* standard is a set of terms and definitions to help harmonize the use of language in a subject or discipline. An example is ISO30400: 2016 *Human Resource Management: Vocabulary*, which sets out consistent definitions of HRM terms across all the standards developed by ISO TC260.

The level of complexity of the system will depend on each organization's specific context. For some organizations, especially smaller ones, it may simply mean having decisive leadership from the business owner, providing a clear definition of what is expected from each individual employee and how they contribute to the organization's overall objectives, without the need for extensive documentation. More complex businesses operating in highly regulated sectors may need extensive documentation and controls to fulfil their legal obligations and to meet their organizational objectives.

One of the fundamental principles is that all the standards can work together. Those who already use an MSS in one part of their business, and are considering implementing additional ones in another area, will find that the process has been made simpler due to the common High-Level Structure (HLS). The concept of HLS is that management standards are structured in the same way, regardless of the domain of application.

In addition to being laid out in the same way, there are some parts of a standard where identical text can be used. This improves coherence and recognition, simplifies use and is defined in something called 'Annex SL'. It means that in addition to having the same structure, MSS can contain many of the same terms and definitions. This is particularly useful for those organizations that choose to operate a single (sometimes called 'integrated') management system that can meet the requirements of two or more MSS being used simultaneously. Annex SL plays a key role in the interoperability and user friendliness of MSS. In 2018, a significant new MSS on occupational health and safety ISO 45001 was published.

STANDARDS IN HEALTH, SAFETY AND WELLBEING (HSW)

The duty of care placed on organizations for their workers is of interest to a wide range of stakeholders – policy makers, health professionals, trade unions, workers, managers, contractors, volunteers and even some investors. Traditionally, the focus has been on safety and the minimization of injury. Even in the 21st century, occupational health and safety remains a huge issue. The International Labour Organization (ILO) estimated that in 2018 more than 2.78 million people died because of occupational accidents or work-related diseases. Additionally, there were some 374 million non-fatal work-related injuries each year. (ILO, n.d. -b). There is therefore considerable pressure to manage the area of Occupational Health and Safety (OH&S) and its outcomes through regulation.

However, given the breadth of interested parties to OH&S (or its equivalent term Occupational Safety and Health, OSH), it is not surprising that the issue is addressed not just at the national regulatory and legal level. OH&S is addressed at international, national, regional, sectoral and organizational levels deploying a range of levers from guidance to practice tools, policies and procedures, levers which have matured over time with research and evidence (Jain et al., 2018). The understanding of interventions and the evidence linking the quality of the employment relationship and wellbeing is also considerable (see Guest et al., 2010).

The International standard ISO 45001: 2018 *Occupational health and safety management systems: Requirements with guidance for use* is the principal document in HSW. This will be discussed together with several national standards preceding ISO 45001's publication in 2018.

For many not involved in the world of OH&S, this new management system standard ISO 45001 may seem late to the game, especially when you consider that quality management (ISO 9001) was first published in 1987. This was, in part, due to the substantive health and safety regulations at national level with each (developed) country evolving frameworks to reflect their local socio-economic development experiences;

a focus by OH&S specialists on technical interventions to reduce the risks of injury and ill health and pressures to assure organizational compliance with legislation; and scepticism in many quarters of the value a management systems approach (with its independent conformity assessments for certification) would bring over and above legislative compliance.

The first pan-sector guide in the UK was HSG65, followed by a British Standard in 1996 which provided guidance in the form of two alternative structures. The first was based on the HSG65 management system model and the alternative, a plan-do-check-act (PDCA) model based on the environmental management system standard ISO 14001.

By the late 1990s. there was growing interest in voluntary third-party certification of OH&S systems which was served by a mix of proprietary certification schemes. Opinion was divided as many felt such certification exercises were of uncertain veracity, would encourage a 'tick-box' culture and / or pose yet another burden on small and medium-sized enterprises (SMEs).

The need to address the question of a proper national reference standard for OH&S management brought several interested parties in the UK together, and BS OHSAS 18001: 1999 *Occupational health and safety management systems: Specification* and BS OHSAS 18002: 2000 *Occupational health and safety management systems: Guidelines for the implementation of OHSAS 18001* were published. In time BS OHSAS 18001 and BS OHSAS 18002 replaced the proprietary schemes, and several national accreditation bodies including the UK Accreditation Service (UKAS) began to offer accreditation for BS OHSAS 18001.

The success of such a certification regime in the UK prompted the BSI, yet again in 2013, to propose the development of an international standard providing the requirements specifications for an OH&S management system. This garnered the requisite support and the journey towards ISO 45001 started later that year. BS OHSAS 18001 and BS OHSAS 18002, both key inputs into ISO 45001, were withdrawn following the successful publication of ISO 45001 in 2018, and organizations will have until March 2021 to migrate their certification to ISO 45001 should they wish to maintain their OH&S certification.

The key distinctions between BS OHSAS 18001 and BS OHSAS 18002, and the new ISO 45001 are the adoption of the ISO MSS enabling integration of OS&H management into other global management systems, the requirements for an analysis of an organization's 'context' and its 'risks and opportunities', the engagement and involvement of workers, and the use of common MSS terminology (Cottam, 2019).

ISO 45001 provides a framework for managing OH&S risks and opportunities. The aims of the OH&S management system are to prevent work-related injury and ill health to workers and to provide safe and healthy workplaces. An organization's context (e.g. number of workers, size, locations, culture, nature of business activities and so on) will determine the level of detail, the extent of documented information and the resources needed to ensure the success of an organization's OH&S management system. Successful implementation of ISO 45001 can be evidenced, and this gives assurance to workers and other interested parties that an effective OH&S management system is in place and functioning.

A measure of the success of the OH&S management system is how the leadership behaves, and a high level of commitment and participation from all levels and functions of the organization. Antecedents to the successful deployment of an OH&S management system include:

a. the leadership, commitment, and accountability of an organization's top management.
b. the development, leadership, and promotion of an organizational culture by the senior management that supports the outcomes stated in their OH&S management system.

c. effective communication throughout.

d. the consultation and participation of workers, and, where applicable, their representatives.

e. the allocation of the requisite resources to maintain the OH&S management system.

f. OH&S policies that are compatible with the overall strategic objectives and direction of the organization.

g. effective process(es) for identifying hazards, controlling OH&S risks, and evidence of seizing opportunities to reduce or otherwise mitigate OH&S risks / dangers.

h. the continual evaluation and monitoring of the OH&S management system to improve OH&S performance.

i. the integration of the OH&S management system into the organization's business processes.

j. OH&S objectives that align with the OH&S policy and to give due consideration to the organization's hazards, OH&S risks and mitigation opportunities.

k. compliance with its legal and other requirements.

Consistent with other ISO management system standards, ISO 45001 uses the ISO high-level structure. The concept of the PDCA cycle, as illustrated in Figure 40.1, is integral to this standard. This is an iterative process used by organizations to achieve continual improvement.

For OH&S professionals, it is important to note that ISO 45001 does not state specific criteria for OH&S performance and does not provide a prescriptive list for the design of an OH&S management system. An organization must assess its context and circumstances and design a system that addresses its risks and hazards, and the opportunities for mitigation. The standard also does not specifically address product safety, property damage or environmental impacts, and an organization is not required to take account of these issues unless these form part of the assessed risks to its workers. It is probably helpful to add that

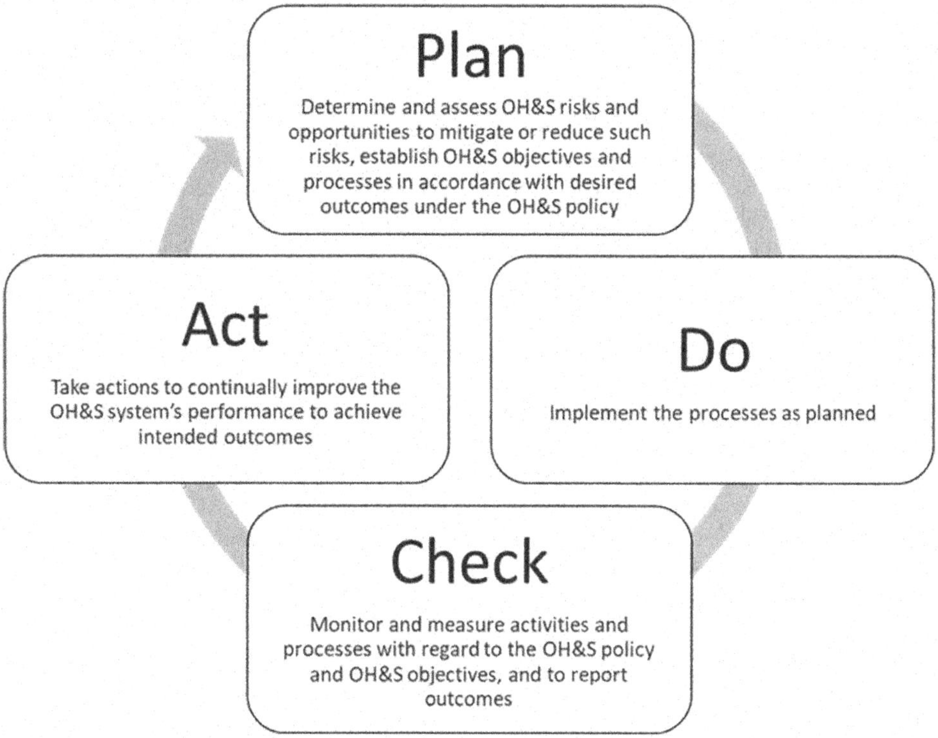

Plan
Determine and assess OH&S risks and opportunities to mitigate or reduce such risks, establish OH&S objectives and processes in accordance with desired outcomes under the OH&S policy

Act
Take actions to continually improve the OH&S system's performance to achieve intended outcomes

Do
Implement the processes as planned

Check
Monitor and measure activities and processes with regard to the OH&S policy and OH&S objectives, and to report outcomes

Figure 40.1. The plan-do-check-act approach in ISO 45001.

in drawing together key interested parties, ISO 45001 is broadly aligned to a number of ILO conventions and standards concerning OH&S, as adopted, in part or whole, by many countries around the world (ILO, 2009, ILO, n.d.-a).

In addition to the benefits of having a well-designed and functioning OS&H management system with reduced downtime / operations disruption and enhanced reputation as a safe place to work, the integration into the ISO MSS means that organizations already using another MSS, like ISO 9001 or ISO 14001, can integrate the performance metrics and documented evidence required for various business aims, while submitting the same documentation for recertification of both ISO MSS.

There are two standards in development that complement ISO 45001. ISO / AWI 45002 *Occupational health and safety management: General guidelines for the implementation of ISO 45001*, and ISO / DIS 45003 *Occupational health and safety management: Psychological health and safety at work – Managing psychosocial risks: Guidelines*. The latter is designed to focus on the management of psychosocial risks within the ISO 45001 framework.

The journey of ISO 45001 reflects shifts in the perspectives about management. Hale and Hovden (1998) provide a helpful frame of reference. They argue that there are three ages in the way OH&S has evolved – the technical age, the age of human factors and that of management and culture. The first age focused on technical measures to protect machinery, prevent explosions and accidents, and to prevent structures failing. Accidents were deemed to have a technical cause. This paradigm formed during the industrial revolution and lasted well into the mid 20th century.

The second age on human factors reflected the growth in studies in personnel management after WWI. It was at this time that the Welfare Workers Association, the forerunner of today's HRM professional body, the Chartered Institute of Personnel and Development (CIPD), was founded. The focus was on personnel selection, training and motivation. The idea was that accidents and their incidents could be reduced with the proper induction and training of the personnel, requiring both prescriptive protections and hands-on management. In the 1960s and 1970s, the rise of the use of ergonomics and probabilistic risk analysis contributed to a re-evaluation of OH&S as a primarily technical issue. There was more research into the contribution of human error and prevention of incidents by human action.

The third age, approximately from the 1990s, emerged from a dissatisfaction that OH&S could be achieved simply by matching humans to the technology. It was felt that over-reliance on OH&S management systems in ignorance of workplace culture could lead to failure (Reason, 2000). Drawing on seminal works like the social organizational theory of Lewin (1951), there was more emphasis on competencies, worker engagement / involvement and how these interact with the redesign of processes, policies and interfaces to achieve OH&S goals.

In the 1990s, two drivers also shaped the way OH&S was framed – risk management and positive psychology. In approaching risk management, hazards were identified, assessed and mitigated before any intervention. The risk of harm from hazards was to be reduced to an acceptable level, insofar as that was possible, recognizing that elimination may not be feasible, nor always possible.

Then there was the shift from the prevention of the pathology to the maintenance of the positive, the optimal where individuals are in the 'flow' (Czikszentmihalyi, 1990) where a confluence of organizational support, competence and full engagement with a well-designed task brings individual fulfilment and optimal productivity.

These shaped the ISO MSS, which not only incorporates the industrial paradigm of the management system but also the contribution worker voice, participation and engagement, leadership and organizational culture play in achieving desired organizational outcomes, not least the management of OS&H. The ISO MSS high-level structure, published in 2012, is itself undergoing a review. A new high-level MSS structure is expected in 2021.

PAS 3002: 2018 *Code of practice on improving health and wellbeing within an organization* is a UK document that provides recommendations to the leadership of any organization to establish, promote, maintain and review the health and wellbeing of their workforce, with a focus on organizational culture and the role of line managers. Sponsored by Hitachi Europe, both HCS / 1 and the CIPD were part of the steering committee. This standard, a Publicly Available Specification (PAS), drew inter alia on the evidence contained in the National Institute for Health and Care Excellence (NICE) guidance (NICE, 2016).

PAS 3002: 2018 (2018) provides five key principles to guide an organization's approach:

a. capitalize on diversity and inclusion as an organizational strength;
b. proactively support the physical and psychological health and wellbeing of workers;
c. foster a work culture that offers strong, ethical relationships, a collaborative and communicative management style, and an organizational culture in which learning and development are encouraged;
d. ensure jobs are designed so that they offer meaningful work (see 3.5); and
e. support good people management policies and practices, including procurement design and risk management.

The PAS covers issues around workforce support, culture, work and job design and provides a systematic way for organizations to understand their context, develop a strategy and then effect policies. In the implementation, it looks at role clarity for the leadership, line managers, the workers, human resource management and occupational health and safety specialists; monitoring; appropriate analysis of the data; and then review for lapses or for improvement.

Another national standard is PAS 1010 *Guidance on the management of psychosocial risks*, or the management of risks associated with work organization and the social context of work which have the potential for causing psychological or physical ill health in the workplace. This was the first recognized standard in the UK for psychosocial risk assessment and management, and in part a response to the European Council Directive 89 / 391 / EEC which stipulates the assessment and management of all types of risks to workers' health as an employer responsibility.

PAS 1010 sought to minimize the risks to personnel and other parties who could be exposed to the risk of psychosocial harm through their work activities by implementing, reviewing and continually improving the psychosocial risk management processes and practices. It was also designed to provide assurance that the organization would be compliant with its stated OH&S and psychosocial health policy. The PAS was aimed at human resources managers and specialists, occupational health and safety managers and specialists, managers, and owners of SMEs, as well as employee representatives. The significance of this initiative was reflected in the steering committee which included the World Health Organization (WHO), the European Trade Union Confederation (ETUC), the European Agency for Safety and Health at Work (EU-OSHA), Health and Safety Executive UK (HSE) and the Finnish Institute of Occupational Health (FIOH).

Another influential national standard is the Canadian CSA-Z1003: 2013 *Psychological health and safety in the workplace: Prevention, promotion, and guidance to staged implementation*. The standard sets out the requirements for a documented and systematic approach for a psychologically healthy and safe workplace. This involved:

a. The identification and elimination of hazards in the workplace that pose a risk of psychological harm to workers.

b. The assessment and control of the risks in the workplace associated with hazards that cannot be eliminated (for example, stressors due to organizational change or reasonable job demands).
c. Implementing structures and practices that support and promote psychological health and safety in the workplace.
d. Fostering a culture that promotes psychological health and safety in the workplace.

Very similar in scope to PAS 1010, the CSA-Z1003 organizational framework establishes, documents, implements and maintains a psychological health and safety management system (PHSMS) in the workplace. The elements of this PHSMS include facets of organizational commitment, the role of leadership and the importance of stakeholder participation. It then outlines the planning process and the implementation, before looking at the evaluation data for corrective action and improvements.

Both PAS 1010 and CSA-Z1003 were key inputs into the soon to be published ISO 45003 *Occupational health and safety management: Psychological health and safety at work – Managing psychosocial risks*. At the time of writing this is at the Draft International Standard stage, the final drafting stage before publication. Wellbeing of workers is a core part of this new international standard.

HUMAN CAPITAL MANAGEMENT (HCM) AND HUMAN RESOURCE MANAGEMENT AND DEVELOPMENT (HRMD) STANDARDS SUPPORTING HSW

One of the key domains affecting the management of HSW is the professional and ethical management of the workforce. The core intent of standardization in the domain of HCM and HRM is the improvement of workforce effectiveness, improved workforce productivity, satisfaction, worker engagement, measurement and focus on desired outcomes.

Managers in organizations by choosing to adopt and implement these Standards are also expected to further their professional skills in the principled management of people by learning and adopting new skills. Regardless of whether there is a dedicated HR function, managers in organizations of any size or maturity can also enhance their knowledge, skills and measurement of organizational performance through the introduction and review of these HCM and HRMD standards.

National HCM and HRMD Standards

In the UK, standards in this domain are developed by the Human Capital Standards Committee (HCS / 1) at the BSI directly or in collaboration with other UK parties, to support the development of evidence-based people-management practices in the UK. These may, in time, become European or International Standards as the practices become more widespread.

The standards developed under HCS / 1 are guided by the following principles and inform all the contributions we make to other committees, subject to consensus. These principles are enshrined in the MSS, BS 76000 *Human resource: Valuing people – Management system: Requirements and guidance*:

- People working on behalf of the organization have intrinsic value, in addition to their protections under the law or in regulation, which needs to be respected.
- Stakeholders and their interests are integral to the best interests of the organization.
- Every organization is part of wider society and has a responsibility to respect its social contract as a corporate citizen and operate in a manner that is sustainable.
- A commitment to valuing people who work on behalf of the organization and to meeting the requirements of the standard is made and supported at the highest level.
- Each principle is of equal importance.

BS 76000 establishes the principles that underpin a thoughtful and structured approach of any organization that appreciates it workforce and the relationships that brings. It takes a human rights approach such that 'valuing people' is not predicated on monetary value, their performance and the short-term returns on investment. BS 76000 places the valuing of the workforce centrally as a key asset of an organization, and provides the framework for an organization to establish strategic, sustainable, long-term foci on the value people bring to the table and to develop an environment where the workers are able to give their best.

Supporting the UK family of principles-based people-management standards are BS 76005 *Valuing people through diversity and inclusion: Code of practice for organizations*; PD 76006 *Guide to learning and development*, and PAS 3002: 2018 *Code of practice on improving health and wellbeing within an organization*, in conjunction with ISO 45001 *Occupational health and safety management systems: Requirements with guidance for use*. These mutually reinforcing standards may have different foci but provide a system of management that pays attention to factors that affect the HSW of an organization's workforce.

In the UK, citizens enjoy the protection of the Equality Act 2010. Under the Act, there are nine 'Protected Characteristics' – age, disability, gender reassignment, race, religion or belief, sex, sexual orientation, marriage and civil partnership, and pregnancy and maternity. The focus of BS 76005 *Valuing people through diversity and inclusion: Code of practice for organizations* is on improving the inclusion of individual difference at the organizational level.

Based on the principles in BS 76000, BS 76005 takes a holistic approach to inclusion by valuing each person's individual difference, life experience and historical, socio-economic and cultural exclusion. The standard, in keeping with this focus on inclusion, takes a very broad approach to the stakeholders

(or interested parties) and encourages dialogue and encouragement of D&I by valuing and embedding D&I not only within the organization but also furthering D&I via its relationships with customers / clients, its supply chain and related communities.

BS 76005 requires organizations to regard D&I not as an issue of compliance with the 'protected characteristics' of the Equality Act 2010 (the 'equal opportunities' approach), neither is it to encourage managers to pursue D&I as a competitive advantage to attract better talent and improve brand reputation (the 'business case' paradigm, or don't do it if there's no commercial advantage approach), but to consciously pursue a policy of increased D&I. As we can see, while the equal opportunities and business-case approaches have had their moment in the maturation of the D&I agenda, statistics show neither has been entirely successful. Where organizations are seeking to pursue greater D&I into practical interventions that are inclusive and go beyond compliance, there is the option of a more mature approach in BS 76005.

There are four key considerations for management to begin the D&I journey under BS 76005 (see McBride and Hoel, 2019):

a. Who is responsible for leading change? Here the focus is establishing the accountability of an organization's leadership to value their workforce and their commitment to actively supporting a culture that values D&I by putting in objectives, policies, practices, behaviours, mechanisms and measures to enable the organization to be more diverse and inclusive.

b. Where do we start? Here the organization needs to understand its context in relation to D&I and establish where the risks and opportunities are for increasing D&I in relation to their workforce and other relevant stakeholders (e.g. customers). With the assessment of the context complete, objectives, planning and metrics can be set and implemented.

c. Which stakeholders? Linked with the organization's context and its ambitions, this addresses the multiple stakeholders with whom an organization must build relationships to engage a more diverse and inclusive workforce.

d. What activities? The activities with each stakeholder group should include communications, consultation, jointly exploring areas of potential for furthering or deepening D&I and a transparent commitment to improve.

The standard, in trying to ensure a holistic worker experience that engenders inclusion and welcomes diversity, has adopted a lifecycle approach suggesting issues and recommendations around a worker's life with an organization from 'getting in' and 'staying in' to 'moving on' (McBride and Hoel, 2019). This has implications for selection approaches, job design, learning and development, pay and reward, promotion, performance assessments, job autonomy, voice and HSW (McBride and Hoel, 2019), of which any of the HRM functions could impact.

The importance of standards in learning and development (L&D) in HSW, over and above that of ensuring the requisite level of skill and competence for the tasks required, is well established (see Short and Anderson, 2020). In fact, ISO 9001 Quality Management has a supporting standard ISO 10015: 2019 *Quality management: Guidelines for competence management and people development* (first published in 1999). PD 76006: 2017 *Guide to learning and development* supports the development of a learning culture within an organization. PD 76006 is a Published Document, a rapidly developed guide which can be later developed into a National or an International Standard. HCS / 1 chose this type of document to ensure speed to market for building the family of standards under BS 76000. As mentioned, an ISO L&D standard in development, ISO 30415, draws on PD 76006 as a key source document.

In establishing each organization's context, PD 76006 sets out some questions for organizations to consider (Anderson and Garad, 2019):

What proportion of your workforce are operating at an acceptable level of competence?

How quickly do your workers acquire new skills and assimilate new information to meet changes that mean fresh challenges and opportunities?
How successful are knowledge sharing processes among the workforce (including interns, volunteers, and casual workers)?
How effective is organizational cross-functional collaboration?
How successful is the organization in retaining those in 'critical' roles?

PD 76006 sets out the distinctions between individual, team and organization-wide and organizational learning. At each unit of analysis, there are distinct structures, processes, resources deployed, roles and relationships. These levels are mutually reinforcing of the dynamics of learner-learning process-learning outcomes each with their foci and outcomes. The standard draws the distinction between training and learning, the former on acquiring specific technical or behavioural skills, the latter being experiential, involving activity, reflection, 'sense-making' and knowledge application to a variety of situations. PD 76006 offers recommendations and interventions at each level, always careful to emphasize that the whole L&D system is greater than the sum of its parts.

There is also a dedicated section on the role of learning technologies and how these have enriched the learning environment beyond formal directed learning to self-directed learning and development. The role of social capital as part of a learning environment is also highlighted in the PD. For a more detailed discussion of PD 76006, see Anderson and Garad (2019).

International Standards in HRMD

ISO formed a Technical Committee, TC260, in 2011, to develop international standards in HRMD. These standards aimed to assist organizations to assess and measure, recruit, retain, develop, deploy, engage and otherwise manage their workforce via guiding standards in HRMD for sustainable value creation for relevant internal and external stakeholders.

The following are general objectives of ISO TC260:

- Create standards that recognize the needs of organizations throughout the world, remaining sensitive to their applicability given business scope, size, maturity or culture.
- Develop a common terminology of HR terms and definitions to establish consistency of functions and processes and to enable international comparison.
- Provide clear guidance to organizations to improve HR practice and increase confidence that HR practice is consistent, transparent and fair.
- Provide clear guidance on workforce metrics to support evidence-based people management practices and sustainable organizational success.

There are published standards and standards in development in ISO TC260 in the areas of recruitment, human capital reporting, workforce planning, sustainable employability, D&I, L&D, employee engagement and so on. Here, a selection of the ISO TS260 standards is introduced. A comprehensive overview of the published standards in this area may be explored in Wong et al. (2019).

The following published standards from ISO TC260 are outlined:

ISO 30408: 2016 *HRM: Guidelines on human governance.*
ISO 30401: 2018 *Knowledge management systems: Requirements.*
ISO 30409: 2016 *HRM: Workforce planning.*
ISO 30414: 2018 *HRM: Guidelines for internal and external human capital reporting, and requisite metrics.*

ISO 30408 Human governance
The purpose of ISO 30408 is to provide organizations with guidelines to structure a human governance system covering relationships, roles and responsibilities and align these to meet the needs of the organization.

Human governance refers specifically to the system or systems by which people within an organization are directed and held accountable. The governance of people is as important as the governance of physical assets or financial capital, and how this is done is instrumental in promoting appropriate behaviour within an organization. By considering human and social factors in the decision-making process, the human governance system should lead to positive outcomes for all stakeholders.

ISO 30408 aims to focus on the proper governance of workers and the systems and processes within an organization that affect their experience at work. This was heavily influenced by BS 76000, which focuses on the principles which organizations should adopt in valuing their people while ISO 30408 examines the touchpoints with the workers that provide leverage for better governance of the human capital.

ISO 30401 Knowledge management systems (KMS)
ISO 30401, unlike the other ISO TC260 standards published, is an MSS. This was, in part, because it was deemed that knowledge management, as a domain and practice area, had matured sufficiently. It also reflects the shift in management thinking from human factors to that of management and culture (Hale and Hovden, 1998). The standard, instead of focusing on affecting human factors to fit the technology paradigm, sought to build a knowledge management system that was cognisant of the role played by good management, social capital and the learning derived from searching, curating, classifying, reviewing and sharing knowledge.

The ISO 30401 KMS enablers for success included clear roles, responsibilities and accountabilities for your workforce; clear internal processes involving procedures, instructions, methods and measures, for example how you detect and learn from failures and successes; technology and infrastructure for knowledge exchange, sharing and transformation which may be digital or physical spaces and facilities; appropriate governance of the knowledge shared and created; the organization's culture for learning and sharing and the quality of leadership. As with ISO 45001, the KMS follows the PDCA framework and therefore has evaluation built into the learning cycle to encourage learning from previous application for subsequent improvements to the MSS.

ISO 30409 Workforce planning

ISO 30409 represents a core competence of an HRM function. Workforce planning identifies current, transitional and future workforce needs and the labour supply. Through this discipline, the organization can make explicit the workforce requirements and to plan the 'talent pipeline'. Workforce planning enables management to anticipate and respond to identified needs to strengthen organizational performance outcomes.

Strategic workforce planning is relevant because we live and work in an ever-changing environment. Major disruptions like warfare, systemic crises, disease and pestilence are all risks that can dramatically alter the viability of workforce assumptions for many businesses. We also live in a highly connected and inter-dependent global economy with large flows of financial, intellectual, natural and human capital and points of failure. Technologies like machine learning and automation also impact the quality and quantity of an organization's future workforce. To operate effectively in these environments, organizational leaders and their organizations are required to plan and prepare alternatives for future success (Sloan, 2019). This requires foresight, flexibility, adaptability and resilience (Wong, 2019).

Organizations may change radically over time through changed business models, mergers and acquisitions, divestments and closures. The value of strategic workforce planning is that it supports organizational change, growth and success by connecting your people strategy and practices to business strategy and financial plans.

The discipline of workforce planning in this standard is divided into strategic workforce planning and operational workforce planning, each requiring a different time horizon and different skills from the respective teams. When done in concert, workforce planning strengthens the capacity, among others, to:

retain high-performing staff, skillsets, and attract good staff;

manage the workforce to minimise skill shortages or oversupply despite economic cycles, sub-optimal labour market, introduction of new business models and new technology;

maintain the optimal skill mix and manage workforce risk to remain competitive in your sector; and

plan the human resource function's capability to analyse people data to support dynamic and strategic workforce planning. (Sloan, 2019)

ISO 30414 Human capital reporting (HCR)

There have been many attempts to encourage and improve HCR following the Kingsmill's (2003) *Accounting for People* report and the publication of a variety of reporting frameworks (see FRC, 2018; Hartley and Robey, 2005; Hesketh, 2014; IIRC, 2013; SASB, 2018; UKCES, 2013). More recently, following the publication of ISO 30414, the US Securities and Exchange Commission (SEC) Investor Advisory Committee made recommendations on HCR in corporate disclosures (SEC, 2019a). The SEC proposed inter alia that companies be required to report on their human capital to the extent that the disclosure would be material to understanding the business (SEC, 2019b).

On August 26, 2020, the SEC (2020b) approved the proposed changes to Reg S-K, making it a requirement 30 days after publication on the US Federal Register that member organizations disclose and comment on areas of human capital deemed material to business performance. The SEC did not prescribe a set of metrics for organizational reporting or disclosure, but the Chair highlighted the contribution of 'attracting, developing and enhancing (an organization's) people' as drivers of performance and of interest to investors (SEC, 2020a).

These new disclosure requirements, while prescriptive in some respects, are rooted in materiality, and are designed to facilitate an understanding of each registrant's business, financial condition and prospects. The rules are designed for this information to be presented on a basis consistent with the lens that management and the board of directors use to manage and assess the registrant's performance. The modernization of Items 101, 103 and 105 is intended to elicit improved disclosures, tailored to reflect registrants' circumstances, which are designed to improve disclosures for investors and add efficiencies to the compliance efforts of registrants. The amendments are also intended to improve the readability of disclosure documents, as well as discourage repetition and reduce the disclosure of information that is not material.

Measuring the value in a manner that is conceptually sound, evidence-based, consistent and material to a broad range of potential users of this people-data is problematic (see Charlwood et al., 2017). Human capital, defined as the value your workforce may bring via 'knowledge, skills, abilities, and other capabilities which describe individual capacities' (Ployhart et al., 2014) means different things to different users. The paradox is that in seeking stability in measurement, HCR projects have exposed measurement as a value-laden process. Measurement raises questions of intent, power and sustainability. There are dangers of the commodification of labour, which is at odds with the history of personnel management, as well as a harsher gaze on the effectiveness of people processes and practices, and performance. And then there is the question of interpretation.

Huus' (2015) focus is HC measures related to worker attitudes and behaviour: measures of leadership effectiveness, worker engagement / behaviours / competencies / performance and indicators of organizational

culture. These measures are used to explain variations in operational and customer metrics. She makes the case that measures of efficiency are conceptually different from measures of effectiveness. She conceptualizes efficiency measures as 'HR statistics' and argues that they belong in the same class of measures as basic descriptive data on the workforce, providing measures of how efficiently the HR function services the organization. Huus sees effectiveness measures as human capital metrics, more broadly focused on all people-related decisions and results.

In ISO 30414 the desire was to quantify the human capital contribution with internationally agreed standardized metrics to support sound sustainable people management practices and decisions, and to signal, unequivocally, notwithstanding prior reservation from many HRM professionals, the normalization of data-driven HRM. The metrics contained in ISO 30414 are, in the main, efficiency measures or as Huus would classify 'HR statistics'.

The reporting areas under ISO 30414 are:

compliance and ethics;
costs (e.g. workforce costs, recruitment costs);
diversity (e.g. age, gender and so on with workforce segmentation);
leadership (e.g. trust in leadership);
organizational culture (e.g. engagement and retention);
organizational health, safety and wellbeing (e.g. deaths and injuries during work);
productivity (e.g. revenue per employee, human capital return on investment);
recruitment, mobility and turnover (e.g. quality of hire, time to hire, turnover);
skills and capabilities (e.g. workforce competency rate);
succession planning;
workforce availability.

There are altogether 60 metrics in the ISO 30414 guidance standard system to be published as ISO Technical Specifications (TS). Most of these metrics are for internal reporting, with aggregated headline metrics for external stakeholders. By the end of 2021, the ISO 30414 metrics will probably be the most comprehensive non-proprietary regime published on HCR. ISO TS24179: 2020 *Human resource management: Occupational health and safety metrics* is already published. The TS covers classification, formulae, contextual factors in the interpretation and analysis for future action, in relation to worker deaths, injury and disease. The promise is clear – a standardized formula with guidance on interpretation, enabling international comparisons or comparisons across different business units. By default, a number of the ISO 30414 human capital metrics may be adopted by US organizations to fulfil the new SEC reporting requirements.

Relevant HCM / HRMD Standards in Development

Other international standards in development under ISO TC260 impacting HSW include ISO DIS 30415 *HRM: Diversity and inclusion*; ISO CD 233263 *HRM: Employee engagement – Guidelines* (see also ISO 10018: 2020 *Quality management: Guidance for people engagement*). There is also ISO CD 30422 *HRM: Learning and development.* Both *Employee engagement* and *Learning and development* are led by experts on the UK committee HCS / 1 / 2.

OTHER INTERNATIONAL STANDARDS IMPACTING WORKER HEALTH, SAFETY AND WELLBEING

The integration of HSW into ISO standards is increasingly common as this is a prerequisite for the safe, consistent delivery of any number of organizational outcomes. In this section, in addition to the health and safety and people management standards discussed earlier, brief introductions to five additional domains that have a strong focus on HSW are

included for completeness: ergonomics / human factors, social responsibility, risk management, the ageing society and human data management.

Ergonomics / Human Factors

In the area of ergonomics or human factors, there is a family of mutually reinforcing standards that put the people at the centre of any system design from conception through development, and implementation, use, maintenance, to its decommissioning. ISO 6385 *Ergonomic principles in the design of work systems* provides core ergonomic principles to improve, (re)design and modify working systems and situations to make the workplace safer, more conducive for the worker and more productive. These principles cover a wide range of occupations including machine operators, assembly line workers, car / lorry drivers, airport personnel, healthcare professionals, teaching staff as well as office workers and mobile workers.

The ISO 10075 family of standards on ergonomic principles related to mental workload provides system-design guidelines specifically intended to prevent mental strain. Mental stress can result from many different and interacting factors including the requirements of the task, the physical conditions of the job, social and organizational factors or societal factors. The idea behind this family of standards is to help design systems that prevent mental strain. You can immediately see the overlaps and connections with the soon to be published ISO 45003 on psychosocial risks.

Another standard, ISO 27500: 2016 *The human-centred organization: Rationale and general principles*, describes the values and beliefs that make an organization human-centred, the significant business benefits that can be achieved, and explains the risks for the organization of not being human-centred. It provides recommendations for the policies that executive board members need to implement to achieve this. It sets out high-level human-centred principles, addressed to executive board members to appreciate and endorse, to optimize performance, minimize risks to organizations and individuals, maximize wellbeing in their organization and enhance their stakeholder relationships.

The science of ergonomics / human factors is ultimately designing optimal working conditions in relation to human HSW, including the development of existing skills and the acquisition of new ones, while considering technological and economic effectiveness and efficiency. Within the context of a work system, issues like work stress, work strain and work fatigue are central concerns as people interact with equipment within a work environment.

Other related standards in this domain include ISO 9241 *Ergonomics of human-system interaction*; ISO 26800 *Ergonomics: General approach, principles and concepts*; *ISO 28803 Ergonomics of the physical environment: Application of International Standards to people with special requirements*; and ISO / TR 7250 *Basic human body measurements for technological design.*

Risk Management and Business Continuity

ISO 31000 was first published in 2010. The 2018 edition is substantially revised reflecting the shift from systems to a greater understanding of the dynamics of external factors (their context) interacting with the organization's needs and objectives, what happens within the organization in strategy development and planning, organizational resilience, IT, corporate governance, HRM, compliance, quality, health and safety, business continuity, crisis management and security. The revised standards are ISO 31000: 2018 *Risk management: Principles and guidelines* and the ISO 31000 family of standards ISO / TS

22330: 2018 *Security and resilience: Business continuity management systems – Guidelines for people aspects of business continuity.* Risk is now defined as the 'effect of uncertainty on objectives', which focuses on the effect of incomplete knowledge of events or circumstances on an organization's decision making.

ISO 31000 provides guidance on a risk management framework that supports all activities, including decision making across all levels of the organization. The ISO 31000 framework and its processes, while not a certifiable MSS, could be integrated with management systems to ensure consistency and the effectiveness of management control across all areas of the organization in order to address risks like damage to reputation or brand, cyber-crime, political risk and terrorism.

The 2018 edition of ISO 31000 has:

Reviewed the principles of risk management.
Increased focus on leadership by top management who should ensure that risk management is integrated into all organizational activities, starting with the governance of the organization.
Greater emphasis on the iterative nature of risk management, drawing on new experiences, knowledge and analysis for the revision of process elements, actions and controls at each stage of the process.
Streamlined the content so the focus is on sustaining an open systems model able to scan and gain insights from its external environment to meet the organization's varied needs and contexts.

While ISO 31000 provides guidance on developing the capability and processes for managing risk in general, there is a standard that looks specifically at the risk to people following a crisis / incident – ISO 22330 *Security and resilience: Business continuity management systems – Guidelines for people aspects of business continuity.* This standard and ISO 31000 were included in the suite of standards made available to support organizations during the 2020 pandemic. This open-access initiative led by the BSI was a collaboration with other international standards organizations and the UK Cabinet Office Civil Contingencies Secretariat.

ISO 22330 provides guidelines for the planning and development of policies, strategies and procedures for the preparation and management of people affected by an incident. This includes:

preparation through awareness, analysis of needs, and learning and development.
coping with the immediate effects of the incident (respond).
managing people during the period of disruption (recover).
continuing to support the workforce after returning to business as usual (restore).

Where organizations want to do the right thing by their workforce but have no idea what that could be apart from shifting the responsibility to HR, Occupational Health or an Employee Assistance Scheme, ISO 22330 provides clear-eyed, practical and evidence-based actions to assess the situation including internal resources and external support services; a comprehensive and structured plan which respects worker needs and voice; and a picture of what effective implementation entails. The document encourages shared ownership and collaboration among professionals working in business continuity, risk management, crisis response, human resources, health and welfare, and leadership roles.

There is additional guidance in the annexes to ISO 22330:

a. On working out a response that considers the resources and impact on society.
b. Designing an incident management structure with a more resilient chain of command having sight of the key HSW risks and interventions.
c. Examples of incident management tasks to help build and resource the incident command team.
d. A suggested list of considerations to aid planning.

For organizations responding to a crisis or a critical incident, this standard provides a clear, balanced approach to HSW risks not only to workers but also to those with whom the organization interacts, like visitors and workers from other organizations.

Social Responsibility

An organization's commitment to the welfare of society and the environment has become a central criterion in measuring its overall performance and its ability to continue operating effectively. The impetus behind this standard is its commitment to sustainable development: the recognition that we need to ensure healthy ecosystems, social equity and good organizational governance for the wellbeing of people, their communities and societies. It is probably superfluous to add that all International and National Standards must actively support one or more of the UN Sustainable Development Goals (SDG). ISO 26000 supports SDGs 1 to 16. Organizations are also interested in this standard because they are subject to ever greater scrutiny by their various stakeholders and a recognition that legal compliance is no longer deemed adequate by many of their key stakeholders.

Ageing Societies

The *World Population Ageing Report 2019* (UN, 2020) identifies population ageing as a global phenomenon with countries experiencing growth in both the size and the proportion of older persons in the population. In 2019, globally, there were 703 million persons aged 65 years and over (9% of the world's population). This number is projected to double to 1.5 billion in 2050 (about 16% of the world population).

This reflects successes in public health, medicine, and economic and social development, and their contribution to the control of disease, prevention of injury and reduction in the risk of premature death. However, this extension of human longevity and the shift in the population age distribution from younger to older ages requires a concerted rethinking of assumptions by governments, policy makers and organizations.

BSI convened experts from government, public health, product manufacturers and health research in a workshop to discuss and develop a framework of the fundamental principles when providing community-based, integrated health and care services for societies with a growing ageing population. This resulted in the successful publication of International Workshop Agreement (IWA) IWA 18: 2016, *Framework for integrated community-based life-long health and care services in aged societies*, which covered areas such as the medical needs of the elderly, personal care, daily living tasks, maintaining relationships and community involvement, and keeping safe. An IWA is not a standard but a (promising precursor) document produced in an 'open workshop' for interested market players to negotiate an area of common understanding.

Following publication, an ISO Strategic Advisory Group (SAG) on Ageing Societies was formed, which led to the creation of ISO Technical Committee ISO TC 314, Ageing societies. It comprised experts from 30 countries, including those involved in the SAG and the development of IWA 18. Its mandate is to develop standards and solutions to tackle the challenges posed by an ageing society, as well as harness the opportunities that ageing populations bring. Dementia, preventative care, ageing workforces, technologies and accessibility are just some of the areas of standardization that TC314 intends to focus. Standards currently in development under ISO TC 314 are ISO CD 23617 *Ageing societies: Guidelines for an age inclusive work force*; ISO CD 23623 *Ageing societies: Framework for dementia-inclusive communities*; and ISO CD 23889 *Ageing societies: Carer-inclusive and accommodating organizations*.

Health Data and Information Governance

In managing HSW whether at a national, sector or organizational level, the design, collection, analysis and interpretation, and ethical governance of health data are essential. As we rely on digital collection and management of health records, there is the work of ISO TC 215 *Health informatics*. Its focus is standardization in the field of health informatics − to facilitate capture, interchange, interoperability and use of health-related data, information and knowledge to support and enable all aspects of the health system − without which an HSW management system cannot function effectively.

Health informatics standards developed by ISO TC 215 are aimed at supporting the growing use of ICT in the health system ('eHealth'). These standards have a vital role in enabling health information systems to collect information, exchange it seamlessly and protect its security and privacy, while making it widely available for authorized access by many potential users including health service provider organizations, individual practitioners, regulators, consumers of health services and those that support or care for them.

There are nearly 200 published standards under ISO TC 215, with over 60 more in development. While these may not be directly relevant to organizations managing the HSW of their workforce, it is helpful to realize the extent to which standards govern the health data infrastructure and ecosystem with which any organization's HSW management system must operate. These consensus standards provide some stability to the proliferation of new, competing eHealth standards for different standards development organizations (SDOs) globally. It is impossible to cover adequately the breadth of the work in ISO TC 215, but the Work Groups (WG) in this TC provide a useful indication of this breadth. These WGs cover eHealth data structure (e.g. terminology, health summary records and eHealth system architecture); messaging and communication; health concepts and their representation; privacy and security; specific work on pharmacy and medicines business (e.g. identification of medicines); devices (e.g. how these are used / communicated and interoperate); business requirements for Electronic Health Records; and Service, Delivery and Organization (SDO) harmonization.

An example of a standard that influences the operation of HSW management in organizations is ISO 21667: 2010 *Health informatics: Health indicators conceptual framework*. The term *health indicator* refers to a single summary measure, most often expressed in quantitative terms, that represents a key dimension of health status, the health care system or related factors. Indicators can flag issues that require more in-depth examination to determine causes for variation, and to identify opportunities for improvement, as well as establishing the most effective use of research resources. They may also be used as a rapid means to evaluate the effects of interventions or to make comparisons as health systems evolve. Determining and monitoring health indicators using enhanced ICT infrastructure makes more explicit the health of populations and influences organizational HSW management systems.

This standard provides the explicit criteria to be applied to choosing and defining health indicators. This framework is intended to inform the selection of health indicators internationally that can be used to monitor and manage the health care system and overall performance improvements. Working towards a standard health indicators framework will undoubtedly foster a common language for communication between countries and ultimately lead to greater commonalities for indicator development. This, and the complementary work at the Organization for Economic Cooperation and Development (OECD), should lead to greater potential for generating internationally comparable health data in the long term, and so permit consistent reporting, dissemination and analysis.

CONCLUSION

The significance and import of voluntary International and National Standards in HSW in influencing regulation, maturing practice and in advancing general understanding of HSW in management, and the HSW management interconnections with other systems, is probably under-reported and consequently less understood, other than to those involved in the development, implementation and evaluation of such standards. By the very nature of standards, they provide the building blocks for the development and maturation of the HSW ecosystem and infrastructure. Much of the inputs and benefits of standards are embedded in systems and remain invisible. Foundational work on typologies, common terminology and principles often have far-reaching implications in the design of HSW management systems while making comparability and interoperability the norm for the benefit of industry and users alike. This chapter aims to raise awareness of the role of such International and National Standards and to encourage wider participation in shaping the HSW agenda in standardization for the future.

ACKNOWLEDGEMENTS

Permission to reproduce extracts from British Standards is granted by BSI Standards Limited (BSI). No other use of this material is permitted. British Standards can be obtained in PDF or hard copy formats from the BSI online shop: https://shop.bsigroup.com/

REFERENCES

Anderson V and Garad A (2019) Learning and development. In: Wong W, Anderson V and Bond H (eds) *Human Capital Management*

Standards: A Complete Guide. London: Kogan Page, pp. 111–137.

BS 0: 2016 (2016) *A standard for standards. Principles of standardization.*

BS76000: 2016 (2016) *Human resource. Valuing people. Management system. Requirements and guidance.*

BS76005: 2017 (2017) *Valuing people through diversity and inclusion. Code of practice for organizations.*

BS OHSAS 18001: 2007 (2007) *Requirements for occupational health and safety management systems: Requirements.* [Withdrawn].

BS OHSAS 18002: 2008 (2008) *Occupational health and safety management systems: Guidelines for the implementation of OHSAS 18001: 2007.* [Withdrawn].

BSI (2020) *Safe Working during the Covid-19 Pandemic: General Guidelines for Organizations.* Available at: www.bsigroup.com/en-GB/topics/novel-coronavirus-covid-19/covid-19-guidelines/ (accessed 1 August 2020).

Charlwood A, Stuart M and Trusson C (2017) *Technical Report: Human Capital Metrics and Analytics – Assessing the Evidence of the Value and Impact of People Data.* London: CIPD.

Cottam M (2019) Occupational health and safety management. In: Wong W, Anderson V and Bond H (eds) *Human Capital Management Standards: A Complete Guide.* London: Kogan Page, pp. 160–184.

CSA-Z1003-13/BNQ 9700-803: 2013 (2013) *Psychological health and safety in the workplace: Prevention, promotion, and guidance to staged implementation.*

Czikszentmihalyi M (1990) *Flow: The Psychology of Optimal Experience.* New York: Harper and Row.

Financial Reporting Council (FRC) (2018) *Guidance on the Strategic Report.* Available at: www.frc.org.uk/getattachment/fb05dd7b-c76c-424e-9daf-4293c9fa2d6a/Guidance-on-the-Strategic-Report-31-7-18.pdf (accessed 1 August 2020).

Guest DE, Isaksson K and De Witte H (eds) (2010) *Employment Contracts, Psychological Contracts, and Employee Well-Being.* Oxford: Oxford University Press.

Hale AR and Hovden J (1998) Management and culture: The third age of safety – A review of approaches to organizational aspects of safety, health and environment. In: Freyer AM and Williamson A (eds) *Occupational Injury: Risk Prevention and Intervention.* London: Taylor and Francis, pp. 129–158.

Hartley V and Robey D (2005) *Reporting on Human Capital Management.* Institute of Employment Studies. Available at: www.employment-studies.co.uk/system/files/resources/files/423.pdf (accessed 1 August 2020).

Hesketh A (2014) *Managing the Value of Your Talent: A New Framework for Human Capital Measurement.* CIPD. Available at: www.cipd.co.uk/Images/managing-the-value-of-your-talent-a-new-framework-for-human-capital-measurement_2014_tcm18-9266.pdf (accessed 1 August 2020).

Huus T (2015) *People Data: How to Use and Apply Human Capital Metrics in Your Company.* Basingstoke: Palgrave Macmillan.

International Integrated Reporting Council (IIRC) (2013) *The international <IR> framework.* Available at: www.theiirc.org/wp-content/uploads/2013/12/13-12-08-THE-INTERNATIONAL-IRFRAMEWORK-2-1.pdf (accessed 30 July 2020).

International Labour Organization (ILO) (2009) *Guidelines on Occupational Safety and Health Management Systems, ILO-OSH 2001.* 2nd ed. Available at: www.ilo.org/safework/info/standards-and-instruments/WCMS_107727/lang–en/index.htm (accessed 1 August 2020).

International Labour Organization (ILO) (n.d.-a) *International Labour Standards.* Available under 'Instruments' and 'Conventions and Recommendations'. Available at: www.ilo.org/normlex (accessed 30 July 2020).

International Labour Organization (ILO) (n.d. -b) *Statistics on Safety and Health at Work.* Available at: https:// ilostat.ilo.org/topics/safety-and-health-at-work/ (accessed 30 July 2020).

International Organization for Standardization ISO (2020) ISO/IEC Directives Part 1 and Consolidated ISO Supplement 11th edition. Available at: https://www.iso.org/sites/directives/current/consolidated/index.xhtml (accessed 1 March 2021)

International Organization for Standardization ISO (2018) ISO/IEC Directives Part 2 - Principles and Rules for the Structure and

Drafting of ISO and IEC Documents 8th edition. Available at: https://www.iso.org/sites/directives/current/part2/index.xhtml (accessed 1 March 2021)

ISO AWI 45002 (forthcoming) *Occupational Health and Safety Management: General Guidelines for the Implementation of ISO 45001: 2018.*

ISO AWI 45003 (forthcoming) *Occupational Health and Safety Management: Psychological Health and Safety at Work – Managing Psychosocial Risks: Guidelines.*

ISO CD 233263 (forthcoming) *HRM: Employee Engagement – Guidelines.*

ISO CD 30422 (forthcoming) *Human Resource Management: Learning and Development.*

ISO DIS 30415 (forthcoming) *Human Resource Management: Diversity and Inclusion.*

ISO/IWA 18: 2016 (2016) *Framework for Integrated Community-based Life-long Health and Care Services in Aged Societies.*

ISO 6385: 2016 (2016) *Ergonomics Principles in the Design of Work Systems.*

ISO 7250-1: 2017 (2017) *Basic Human Body Measurements for Technological Design, Part 1: Body Measurement Definitions and Landmarks.*

ISO/TR 7250-2: 2010 (2017) *Basic Human Body Measurements for Technological Design, Part 2: Statistical Summaries of Body Measurements from National Populations.*

ISO 7250-3: 2015 (2015) *Basic Human Body Measurements for Technological Design, Part 3: Worldwide and Regional Design Ranges for Use in Product Standards.*

ISO 9000: 2015 (2015) *Quality Management Systems: Fundamentals and Vocabulary.*

ISO 9001: 2015 (2015) *Quality Management Systems: Requirements.*

ISO 9241-210: 2019 (2019) *Ergonomics of Human-System Interaction – Part 210: Human-centred Design for Interactive Systems.*

ISO 10015: 2019 (2019) *Quality Management: Guidelines for Competence Management and People Development.*

ISO 10018: 2020 (2020) *Quality Management: Guidance for People Engagement.*

ISO 10075-1: 2017 (2017) *Ergonomics Principles Related to Mental Workload, Part 1: General Issues and Concepts, Terms and Definitions.*

ISO 10075-2: 1996 (1996) *Ergonomic Principles Related to Mental Workload, Part 2: Design Principles.*

ISO 10075-3: 2004 (2004) *Ergonomic Principles Related to Mental Workload, Part 3: Principles and Requirements Concerning Methods for Measuring and Assessing Mental Workload.*

ISO 14001: 2015 (2015) *Environmental Management Systems: Requirements with Guidance for Use.*

ISO 21667: 2010 (2010) *Health Informatics: Health Indicators Conceptual Framework.*

ISO 22330: 2018 (2018) *Security and Resilience: Business Continuity Management Systems – Guidelines for People Aspects of Business Continuity.*

ISO 26000: 2010 (2010) *Guidance on Social Responsibility (Confirmed 2017).*

ISO 26800: 2011 (2011) *Ergonomics: General Approach, Principles and Concepts.*

ISO 27500: 2016 (2016) *The Human-centred Organization: Rationale and General Principles.*

ISO 28803: 2012 (2012) *Ergonomics of the Physical Environment: Application of International Standards to People with Special Requirements.*

ISO 30400: 2016 (2016) *Human Resource Management: Vocabulary.*

ISO 30401: 2018 (2018) *Knowledge Management Systems: Requirements.*

ISO 30408: 2016 (2016) *Human Resource Management: Human Governance.*

ISO 30409: 2016 (2016) *Human Resource Management: Workforce Planning.*

ISO 30414: 2018 (2018) *Human Resource Management: Guidelines for Internal and External Human Capital Reporting.*

ISO 31000: 2018 (2018) *Risk Management: Principles and Guidelines.*

ISO 45001: 2018 (2018) *Occupational Health and Safety Management Systems: Requirements with Guidance for Use.*

ISO 50001: 2018 (2018) *Energy Management.*

ISO TS 24179: 2020 (2020) *Human Resource Management: Occupational Health and Safety Metrics.*

Jain A, Leka S and Zwetsloot GJM (2018) *Managing Health, Safety and Well-being: Ethics, Responsibility and Sustainability.* Dordrecht: Springer.

Kingsmill D (2003) *Accounting for People: Report of the Task Force on Human Capital Management*. London: UK Department of Trade and Industry.

Lewin K (1951) *Field Theory in Social Science: Selected Theoretical Papers*. New York: Harper and Row.

McBride A and Hoel H (2019) Diversity and inclusion. In Wong W, Anderson V and Bond H (eds) *Human Capital Management Standards: A Complete Guide*. London: Kogan Page, pp. 138–159.

National Institute of Clinical Excellence (NICE) (2016) *Workplace Health: Management Practices. NICE Guideline [NG13]*. Available at: www.nice.org.uk/guidance/ng13 (accessed 20 July 2020).

PAS 1010: 2011 (2011) *Guidance on the Management of Psychosocial Risks in the Workplace*.

PAS 3002: 2018 (2018) *Code of Practice on Improving Health and Wellbeing Within an Organization*.

PD 76006: 2017 (2017) *Guide to Learning and Development*.

Ployhart RE, Nyberg AJ and Maltarich MA (2014) Human Capital is Dead; Long Live Human Capital Resources! *Journal of Management*, 40(2), 371–398.

Reason J (2000) *Beyond the Limitations of Safety Systems*. Company Director. 1 April. Available at: www.companydirectors.com.au/director-resource-centre/publications/company-director-magazine/2000-to-2009-back-editions/2000/april/beyond-the-limitations-of-safety-systems (accessed 1 August 2020).

Securities and Exchange Commission (2019a) *Recommendation of the Investor Advisory Committee: Human Capital Management Disclosure*. Available at: www.sec.gov/spotlight/investor-advisory-committee-2012/human-capital-disclosure-recommendation.pdf (accessed 1 August 2020).

Securities and Exchange Commission (2019b) *Modernization of Regulation S-K Items 101, 103, and 105*. SEC. Available at: www.sec.gov/rules/proposed/2019/33-10668.pdf (accessed 1 August 2020).

Securities and Exchange Commission (2020a) *Modernizing the Framework for Business, Legal Proceedings and Risk Factor Disclosures*. Available at: www.sec.gov/news/public-statement/clayton-regulation-s-k-2020-08-26 (accessed 28 August 2020).

Securities and Exchange Commission (2020b) *SEC Adopts Rule Amendments to Modernize Disclosures of Business, Legal Proceedings, and Risk Factors under Regulation S-K*. Available at: www.sec.gov/news/press-release/2020-192 (accessed 28 August 2020).

Short H and Anderson VA (2020) Standards formation and the implications for HRD. *European Journal of Training and Development*. DOI: 10.1108/EJTD-02-2020-0019.

Sloan J (2019) Workforce planning. In: Wong W, Anderson V and Bond H (eds) *Human Capital Management Standards: A Complete Guide*. London: Kogan Page, pp. 66–85.

Sustainability Accounting Standards Board (SASB) (2018) *SASB Materiality Map*. Available at: https:// materiality.sasb.org/ (accessed 3 August 2020).

UK Commission for Employment and Skills (UKCES) (2013) *Encouraging Employers to Use Human Capital Reporting: A Literature Review of Implementation Options*. Available at: https:// dera.ioe.ac.uk/17367/1/encouraging-employers-to-use-human-capital.pdf (accessed 1 August 2020).

United Nations (2020) *World Population Ageing 2019 (ST/ESA/SER.A/444)*. Available at: www.un.org/development/desa/pd/sites/www.un.org.development.desa.pd/files/files/documents/2020/Jan/un_2019_world-populationageing_report.pdf (accessed 30 July 2020).

Wong W (2019) The future of standards affecting human capital management and development. In: Wong W, Anderson V and Bond H (eds) *Human Capital Management Standards: A Complete Guide*. London: Kogan Page, pp. 254–290.

Wong W, Anderson V and Bond H (eds) (2019) *Human Capital Management Standards: A Complete Guide*. London: Kogan Page.

Index

Note: Page numbers followed by "*f*" indicate figure and "n" indicate endnote in the text.